MFC Programming with Visual C++® 6

Eugene Olafsen

Kenn Scribner

K. David White

SAMS

Unleashed

MFC Programming with Visual C++® 6 Unleashed

Copyright © 1999 by Sams Publishing

International Standard Book Number: 0-672-31557-2

Library of Congress Catalog Card Number: 98-88891

Printed in the United States of America

First Printing: June 1999

02   01   00   99   4   3   2   1

Trademarks

Warning and Disclaimer

EXECUTIVE EDITOR
Bradley L. Jones

ACQUISITIONS EDITOR
Chris Webb

DEVELOPMENT EDITORS
Keith Davenport
Matt Purcell

MANAGING EDITOR
Jodi Jensen

PROJECT EDITOR
Dana Rhodes Lesh

COPY EDITOR
Margaret Berson

INDEXER
Erika Millen

PROOFREADERS
Linda Morris
Eddie Lushbaugh

TECHNICAL EDITOR
Greg Guntle

SOFTWARE DEVELOPMENT SPECIALIST
Craig Atkins

INTERIOR DESIGNER
Gary Adair

COVER DESIGNER
Aren Howell

COPY WRITER
Eric Borgert

LAYOUT TECHNICIANS
Brian Borders
Susan Geiselman
Mark Walchle

Overview

Contents

PART III   MFC AND COM PROGRAMMING   371

10   COM   373

PART VII   MFC AND GRAPHICS PROGRAMMING   1021

29   MFC AND OpenGL   1023

Foreword

The Microsoft Foundation Classes are a excellent example of how an object-oriented approach to packaging software functionality can lead to code reuse, reduced application complexity, and in the end, a more efficient software development environment.

MFC has been around for about seven years now. The first version of MFC was released with version 7 of Microsoft's 16-bit C/C++ compiler, and it represented little more than a wrapper around the Window GDI calls. (Visual C++ version 1 followed Microsoft C/C++ version 7.)

For those who had been developing applications using the Windows API, MFC promised an immense gain in programming productivity. Rather than write Petzold-style `WinMain` procedures, message loops, and `switch` statements to dispatch messages, you could create an instance of a class that would take care of much of the drudgery. Rather than create GDI objects, write many lines of code to initialize and use the objects, carefully track their lifetimes, and be sure to release them properly, you could instantiate an MFC class, often simply use the default values, and then let the destructor worry about cleaning up system resources.

Indeed, to truly comprehend the advantages of using MFC, you should write a significant graphics application first using MFC and then using strictly the Windows API. Then compare war stories.

But although MFC made the programmer's life easier, early versions were not without cost. MFC applications were much larger than a non-MFC equivalent. They tended to run slower as well (probably because they were so much larger...). And whenever it was necessary to stretch the MFC envelope a bit, a working knowledge of the Windows API was still a prerequisite.

MFC has gone through many iterations since version 1 was released. The current revision of MFC is version 6. MFC added the Document/View architecture in version 2, ODBC and drag-and-drop support in version 2.5, and multithreading and Unicode support in version 3. Subsequent releases have added support for socket classes, Internet classes, OLE automation, and thread synchronization. MFC has constantly evolved in its support of new graphic interface features and now offers a rich collection of support classes such as arrays, lists, and strings, to name a few.

Over the years, I've used MFC on many projects. One of the most rewarding of those endeavors was being part of the software development team for Qualcomm's Eudora versions 3 and 4. We used MFC extensively in the creation of the Windows version of that product.

The real world still holds challenges for programmers! MFC has not changed that; MFC is still supplied with source code for good reason. But without MFC, I believe developing Eudora would have been a much more difficult and time-consuming task. MFC allowed us to build a product that conformed to Windows GUI standards, incorporated new and improved user interface metaphors, and ran with a high degree of independence on many versions of operating systems and hardware platforms. MFC also saved time when constructing non-GUI data structures and objects used by the internals of Eudora.

This book is an authoritative reference document that describes MFC: what it is and how to get the most out of it. This book is written by programmers for programmers. It is filled with sample applications and code snippets to clarify and demonstrate the use of MFC 6. If you are new to MFC, this book will get you up to speed quickly. If you are familiar with MFC but need to drill down into the details of a specific MFC class, this book will be quite valuable as well. This book can also be used as a companion to the Microsoft documentation, which is typically quite good but perhaps a bit terse in spots.

I hope you find this book both educational and enjoyable.

Keith McIntyre
Vice President—Engineering
Internet Systems Division
Stellcom, Inc.

About the Authors

Eugene Olafsen has been working with Microsoft Windows since the 3.0 release. At that time, he was attempting to build a product using Digital Research's GEM (Graphics Environment Manager), decided to port to Windows, and has never looked back. He has worked with MFC/OLE since its humble beginnings. Gene has worked to develop applications ranging from engine test simulators for Boeing to search and publishing systems for Reuters. He is an independent consultant and a principal partner in Stratton & Associates, Ltd. (`www.strattonassociates.com`), a software-engineering firm. His current projects include application development that leverages COM and Web technologies.

Kenn Scribner actually began his career in computers in 1980 as a pizzeria manager. After he realized he didn't want to make pizzas for a living, he joined the Air Force as a computer operator. Two degrees and a commission later, he found himself designing silicon-based Fast Fourier Transform processors and running a research flight simulation facility. As the Air Force downsized, he retired and began writing Windows applications. (He's delighted to earn a living with his previous hobby!) Kenn has written several commercial Windows applications, and he now finds himself writing all the client user interface code and major ATL-based COM components for a large-scale n-tier client/server application. Kenn also started his own company, the EnduraSoft Corporation (`http://www.endurasoft.com`), writes the "Windows Programming" column for "TechTalk"—the newsletter of the Small Computer Book Club (`http://www.booksonline.com`)—and acts as a Windows programming technical reviewer for several publishers. In his dwindling spare time, Kenn enjoys the company of his lovely wife and two wonderful children, works with his horse, remodels parts of his house, and generally acts as EnduraSoft's chief groundskeeper. Kenn can be reached at `kenn@endurasoft.com`.

K. David White has been developing software since 1981, using a wide variety of products, platforms, and languages. During this time, Dave implemented several systems, ranging from a facilities security system based on DEC MACRO-32 to several large supervisory control systems in the oil industry on DEC VMS. Seeing the handwriting on the wall in 1993, Dave started developing Windows-based software using Microsoft C and C++. Since that time, Dave has produced several MFC-based products and is currently developing ATL COM objects. Dave also contributed to the Sams book *Sams Teach Yourself Database Programming with Visual C++ in 21 Days*. In what little spare time that Dave has, he thoroughly enjoys woodworking, golf, singing, and spending time with his wife and three kids. Dave can be reached through email at `kdwhite@donet.com`.

Contributing Authors

Michael Morrison is a writer, developer, toy inventor, and author of a variety of books including *Sams Teach Yourself MFC in 24 Hours* (Sams Publishing, 1999), *Windows 95 Game Developer's Guide Using the Game SDK* (Sams Publishing, 1997), *Complete Idiot's Guide to Java 1.2* (Que Corporation, 1998), and *Java 1.1 Unleashed* (Sams Publishing, 1997). Michael is also the instructor of several Web-based courses, including DigitalThink's Win32 Programming series, the Introduction to Java 2 series, and the JavaBeans for Programmers series. Michael cut his teeth on Windows programming by codeveloping one of the first action games for Windows, Combat Tanks. When not glued to his computer, risking life and limb on his skateboard, or watching movies with his wife, Mahsheed, Michael enjoys hanging out by his koi pond.

Davis Chapman first began programming computers while working on his master's degree in music composition. Writing applications for computer music, he discovered that he enjoyed designing and developing computer software. It wasn't long before he came to the realization that he stood a much better chance of eating if he stuck with his new-found skill and demoted his hard-earned status as a "starving artist" to a part-time hobby. Since that time, Davis has focused on the art of software design and development, with a strong emphasis on the practical application of client/server technology. Davis is the lead author of *Sams Teach Yourself Visual C++ 6 in 21 Days*, *Web Development with Visual Basic 5*, and *Building Internet Applications with Delphi 2*. Davis is also a contributing author on *Special Edition Using Active Server Pages* and *Running a Perfect Web Site, Second Edition*. He has been a consultant working and living in Dallas, Texas, for the past ten years and can be reached at davischa@onramp.net.

David Lowndes is a senior software developer at Boldon James Ltd. A Microsoft MVP since 1996, Davis is a frequent contributor to the microsoft.public.vc newsgroups, helping with Visual C++ and general Win32 issues. When not programming, he can be found playing guitar and trying to muscle in on his son's band. David can be contacted at davidl@mvps.org.

Bill Heyman is an independent software consultant who specializes in systems and applications software development using Microsoft Visual C++ and MFC Windows platforms. As a ten-year software development veteran who has provided software engineering services for IBM and Andersen Consulting, Bill has experience in DOS, OS/2, Windows, UNIX, and PalmOS. For more information, including consultation for your own project, visit Bill at his Web site, http://www.heymansoftware.com/~heyman/. His email address is heyman@heymansoftware.com.

Ed Harris is the lead engineer for tools and components development at NetPro Computing, Inc. His group designs reusable frameworks for distributed network and directory service monitoring on both Win32 and NetWare networks. Previous to that, Ed spent eight years as a Visual C, Windows, and MFC consultant, specializing in the unlikely combination of custom control development and mouse drivers. When not developing software, Ed enjoys spending time with his fiancée, Angela, flying airplanes, and playing basketball. Ed can be contacted at edh@netpro.com.

Keith McIntyre has been developing software since the days of 4-bit processors. He has watched and participated in the personal computer, local area network, client/server, and Internet evolutions. During his years as a consultant/contract engineer, Keith has worked on a myriad of technologies, including turbine engineer control systems, satellite communication systems, tape drive firmware, UNIX and Windows device drivers, imaging and document management software, and custom application development. Keith has contributed to many shrink-wrap software products including those published by Optigraphics, Emerald Systems, Compton's New Media, and Qualcomm. Keith is currently vice president of engineering for Stellcom's Internet Systems division. Keith McIntyre holds a B.S. in Computer Science.

Rob McGregor began exploring computer programming in BASIC as a teenager in 1978. Since then, Rob has worked as a programmer, software consultant, and 3D computer artist; he has written a variety of programs for Microsoft and numerous other companies. Rob lives in Rockledge, Florida, and in his free time, enjoys ray tracing, reading, writing, and playing guitar. You can contact Rob via email at rob_mcgregor@compuserve.com.

Dedication

To my wife, Donna, for her love, encouragement, and understanding—and to my children, Ashley and Eric, for the insight and wisdom they offer, beyond their years.

—Gene Olafsen

This, my first book, is lovingly dedicated to my wife, Judi, and to my children, Aaron and Katie.

—Kenn Scribner

Acknowledgments

I would like to thank Chris Webb at Macmillan for his advice and support throughout my involvement with this book. Additionally, I cannot praise the various editors and individuals involved in production enough for their input and the value they add to this project. I would like to thank Hub and Simon at TSCentral for their flexible working arrangements during the final push to complete this text. Thanks to John Penrose of Progressive Technologies for his late-night calls, reminding me that I'm not the only one up working. Thanks to my brother Stephen for getting my network running and answering my NT Server administration questions. Thanks also to my friends at Reuters, especially Steve, Dave, Ray, Joe, and Ed. Finally, I must acknowledge Gina for her tireless code reviews throughout the years.

—Gene Olafsen

If there was a time *not* to write a book, it was while I was writing this one. My wife was studying for medical school entrance, my current project at work wanted to consume all my time and then some, and my children were very, very young (miss a day and you miss a *lot*). I couldn't forget to thank them for their sacrifice so that I could make this effort. I would also like to thank the terrific team at MCP, especially Chris Webb, who put up with this cranky author. (I was, too; just ask him.) I would like to extend most heartfelt thanks to Keith Davenport, Dana Lesh, and Margaret Berson, all at MCP. It was they who had to read my raw material and fire it in the crucible of experience to produce the fine product you hold in your hands. And thanks to the nameless (to me) crew, who tirelessly set the type, adjusted the margins, and actually put my words to paper. From experience, I know it's not a small task. Finally, thanks to you for taking the time to look over my work and find it worthy of your hard-earned dollar. I hope you enjoy reading it and find it tremendously useful in your daily work.

—Kenn Scribner

There are so many people that have been supportive through the writing of this book. I want to thank Chris Webb of Macmillan Publishing for being extremely patient during this ordeal. Writing a book about a topic that has a plethora of coverage already is no easy task. Coupling that with the demands of a job and family leads to very long nights and extended schedules. Even though the publishing deadlines loomed large in the rear-view mirror, Chris remained supportive during the entire effort. He was also responsible for tracking down contributing authors. Another person that needs recognition is my mother. I would like to thank her for helping me through school all those years ago. Her sacrifices to her family have paid off in dividends that cannot be described by mere words. Thanks, Mom! I would also like to thank Kenn Scribner for his contribution to this effort and his insight into helping me put together the table of contents. His daily support and encouragement helped me cope with the daily pressures. If you need an ActiveX guru, Kenn is your man! But, most of all, I want to thank the love of my life, my wife, for allowing me to put myself into this work. The late nights and missed opportunities can never be regained, and I just want to tell my family how much I love them!

—K. David White

Tell Us What You Think!

As the reader of this book, *you* are our most important critic and commentator. We value your opinion and want to know what we're doing right, what we could do better, what areas you'd like to see us publish in, and any other words of wisdom you're willing to pass our way.

As an associate publisher for Sams Publishing, I welcome your comments. You can fax, email, or write me directly to let me know what you did or didn't like about this book— as well as what we can do to make our books stronger.

Please note that I cannot help you with technical problems related to the topic of this book, and that due to the high volume of mail I receive, I might not be able to reply to every message.

When you write, please be sure to include this book's title and author as well as your name and phone or fax number. I will carefully review your comments and share them with the author and editors who worked on the book.

Fax: (317)581-4770

Email: adv_prog@mcp.com

Mail: Bradley L. Jones
            Associate Publisher
            Sams Publishing
            201 West 103rd Street
            Indianapolis, IN 46290 USA

Introduction

If you shop like I do, you've just noticed this book on the shelf and picked it up to see what interesting topics it covers. You've read the table of contents. Aggressive. There is obviously a lot of detailed MFC information, but there is also a lot of ATL and COM information. Interesting.

So you turn to the introduction to see what it has to say about the wealth of information and hard-won experience contained in this (very large) volume. Will it convince you this book is the best MFC programming book on the market today?

Absolutely not. If by now you aren't convinced that this is the best MFC programming book on the market, this introduction won't sway you. However, this *is* the best MFC programming book on the market today. Why? Simply because the information contained within these pages represents decades of collective MFC programming experience—not the hobby-shop kind of programming, but rather the hard-core, schedule-pressure, "we need it now" kind of programming. From the basic to the intricate, every page contains more experience per page than any other MFC book out there today.

Programmers of all levels will benefit from the information you find here. You don't understand the Document/View architecture? It's explained here. You want to extend and go beyond the Document/View architecture? That's here too, as well as all other aspects of MFC programming. In a nutshell, here is what you'll find:

- MFC's architecture and class layout
- MFC as C++
- MFC as a Windows application programming tool
- How to create compelling MFC applications
- Using Developer Studio to create more compelling MFC applications
- Using the Windows Common Controls from MFC applications
- Implementing your own custom controls using MFC
- MFC and the GDI
- All about MFC's message routing scheme
- Documents and views, and how to supercharge their use
- MFC application user interface programming
- MFC and printing
- MFC as a COM server programming platform, including ActiveX programming

- MFC as a COM client programming platform
- Adding scripting to your MFC applications
- MFC and databases
- MFC's utility classes, including exception processing
- MFC and the Web, including DHTML, WinInet, and ISAPI programming
- MFC and hot graphics programming using both OpenGL and DirectX
- How to add help access to your MFC applications

It is true that many of these topics can be found in some of the other books you see sitting on the shelf alongside this book. But none of them cover this much information in one place, and each topic here is covered in the deepest detail. After all, that is why the book is titled *MFC Programming with Visual C++ 6 Unleashed*.

How This Book Is Organized

This book is designed to be the most comprehensive MFC programming resource available anywhere today. As you work from chapter to chapter, you'll not only learn what makes MFC tick, but you'll also learn how to supercharge MFC, customize it, and take the architecture and make it work the way you want it to work. You'll go way beyond the wizard-generated code and see how experienced MFC programmers do *their* magic. Soon, it'll be *your* magic, too:

- Part I, "Core MFC," covers the core MFC concepts. Here, you see how MFC was crafted to be a tremendous general-purpose application framework. When you understand the basic mechanics, you'll see how to tailor MFC to better fit your programming requirements. Chapter 1 shows you the MFC architecture and introduces you to the major MFC classes you need to understand to get the most from the tool. Chapter 2 initiates your journey through MFC application development by showing you how MFC interacts with data and windows through the use of dialog boxes. Chapter 3 provides the details you need to get the most from the Windows common controls, especially the useful list and tree controls. Chapter 4 shows you how to manage GDI resources using MFC, as well as how you work with fonts, brushes, and so on. After you know how to deal with standard controls and paint screen items, you have what you need to tackle Chapter 5, which shows you how to create custom controls specific to your application. Finally, Chapter 6 dispels the myths surrounding MFC's idle processing, allowing you to use seemingly idle application processing time to your advantage.

- Part II, "Documents, Views, and Applications That Use Them," details the MFC architecture and how you can both optimize it and modify it to suit your personal needs. Chapter 7 describes the Document/View architecture. Chapter 8 shows you how to extend your application's user interface. Finally, Chapter 9 blows the cover off using the printer from your MFC application, allowing you to move past the basic wizard-based code to *really* use the printer.

- Part III, "MFC and COM Programming," describes MFC and COM programming, as most of today's Windows applications use COM to provide at least some of their functionality. Chapter 10 introduces you to COM, and Chapter 11 provides an explanation of MFC's implementation of COM. Chapters 12 and 13 discuss OLE servers and clients, and Chapter 14 shows you how to write feature-packed ActiveX controls that the containers you'll develop in Chapter 15 can use to their advantage. Chapter 16 gives you the facts about mixing MFC and ATL, a templated COM framework. Chapter 17 shows you how to add scripting capabilities to your MFC applications.

- Part IV, "MFC Database Programming," shows you how MFC and databases work together. Chapter 18 looks at MFC and various database programming concepts and technologies. Chapter 19 moves past the basics and shows you the current technologies in MFC (and COM) database processing.

- Part V, "MFC Utility Classes," nails down the details regarding the MFC utility classes. Chapter 20 covers MFC string and collection management. Chapter 21 shows you how to work with files using MFC. Chapter 22 provides the critical details you need to process exceptional runtime conditions.

- Part VI, "MFC and the Web," marries MFC and the Web. Chapter 23 introduces you to Dynamic HTML (DHTML) and how you can access DHTML from your MFC application. Chapter 24 shows you the basics of MFC network programming. Chapter 25 moves to advanced MFC network programming. Chapter 26 describes MFC ISAPI programming. Need to add telephonic or electronic mail support to your MFC application? Then Chapters 27 and 28 are here for you.

- Part VII, "MFC and Graphics Programming," introduces you to the fascinating area of MFC graphics programming. Chapter 29 describes OpenGL and how you can exploit that technology in your MFC applications. Chapter 30 similarly describes MFC and DirectX. Chapter 31 goes a step further by adding full-fledged multimedia support to your MFC applications.

- Part VIII, "Advanced MFC," gives you a wealth of insight born of experience. Chapter 32 shows you how to work with the Windows Registry database. Chapter 33 describes using MFC from within DLLs. And the final chapter, Chapter 34, breaks open the secrets of Developer Studio AppWizard programming.

Who Should Read This Book?

Actually, this book is perfect for just about anyone interested in programming Windows applications using MFC. Whether you are just beginning or have weathered MFC programming from its inception, there are valuable nuggets for you here:

> Beginners—The basic concepts are clearly and concisely covered. More important than that, however, is the valuable coverage you'll find regarding pitfalls and potential optimizations. You'll learn the basics, but you'll also learn how to avoid common beginning MFC programmer mistakes.

> Casual and accomplished MFC programmers—Use this book as a reference to delve into topics of specific interest. You will be able to reuse much of the code you find here to enhance your ongoing Windows programming tasks. You'll also find detailed coverage of the latest Microsoft technologies with specific use from within MFC-based applications.

> Experts—For you, this book provides the detailed programmer-to-programmer information you won't find elsewhere. Our goal was to provide you with the deepest details and provide alternative methods of accomplishing intricate programming tasks. If you need it, it's here for you.

We have worked exceptionally hard to provide you with *the* definitive work to date regarding MFC programming. Enjoy!

Core MFC

PART

I

The MFC Architecture

by Bill Heyman

IN THIS CHAPTER

CHAPTER 1

The Microsoft Foundation Classes (MFC) allow you to develop C++ GUI applications for Windows using its rich set of classes. This chapter discusses the evolution of MFC and the fundamental classes used in almost every MFC-based application.

A Brief History of MFC

Since its beginnings in 1987, Windows has introduced legions of traditional DOS programmers to a new way of programming: a device-independent, event-driven model. Although the Windows API has grown to add much new functionality, it still retains the basic functions that existed in the early versions of Windows (such as Windows/286 and Windows/386).

In the late 1980s, BASIC, 8088 assembler, and Pascal were the *lingua francae* for DOS software development. At this time, the C language was starting to grow beyond its UNIX roots and become a high-performance, systems development language on other platforms. Microsoft's choice of using C (combined with 8088 assembler) for the development of Windows allowed C to gain a foothold among the PC developers.

The original Windows API (now sometimes called Win16) catered to using a C development environment. The American National Standards Institute (ANSI) standardized the C language in 1989, thus solidifying C as a language for application and systems development. Armed with the Windows Software Development Kit (SDK) and the Microsoft C compiler, developers started developing GUI applications that took advantage of the Windows API.

The C language was procedural—it had no built-in support for the object-oriented features that are commonly used today: encapsulation, inheritance, and polymorphism. The Windows API was designed and delivered as a procedure-based interface and, hence, was perfect for the development technology of the time. However, as object-oriented extensions to C were developed and more widely accepted in a new language called C++, an object-oriented wrapper interface to the Windows API seemed a natural next step. Microsoft developed this interface as its Application Frameworks (AFX) product in 1992. This evolved into the Microsoft Foundation Classes (MFC) product that exists today.

> **NOTE**
>
> The Windows API is *object-based*. This means that you can programmatically interact with the system objects (such as windows, semaphores, and pens) through a handle and a defined interface. The actual implementation and data

used by the implementation is hidden from the view of the program. This "data hiding" is called *encapsulation*.

The MFC Class Libraries are *object-oriented*. This means that in addition to the encapsulation, the interfaces (packaged in a set of C++ classes) also provide inheritance and polymorphism. *Inheritance* is the capability to share and extend the functionality of an existing class. *Polymorphism* is the capability of objects to support the same interface, but provide different implementations.

> **NOTE**
>
> Although the Windows API is procedural and designed to be called from procedural languages (like C), you can (and will) use the Windows API directly from your MFC applications written in C++.

The concept of device independence was a boon for both software developers and hardware manufacturers (well, at least the manufacturers that didn't have a great amount of market share at the time). Unlike the traditional DOS programs that required specific routines for different video and print devices, programs coded for Windows could be written to a common interface and work across a wide variety of video and print devices. The result is that developers could focus more on the problem on hand, rather than the hardware used to solve the problem; and manufacturers could focus more on creating device drivers for Windows and allow a much wider variety of software that can use their devices.

Concomitant with the move to device independence, Windows GUI development forced a paradigm shift on the traditional DOS programmers. At that time, most software was written in a procedural manner: one function calling another, with the main program always being in control. The event-driven model forced programs to give up their total control and, instead, wait and respond to external events to provide their functionality to the end users.

The structure of Win16 (and now Win32) GUI programs remains the same today as it was in 1987. Figure 1.1 shows the basic structure of a Windows GUI application. Observe that each program consists of an entry point, the creation of a main window, a message loop, and the destruction of the main window. In addition, there is a function associated with the main window, called a *window procedure*, which contains the code that handles the system and application events (such as keyboard entry, mouse movement and clicks, timer alarms, menu selections, and pushbutton clicks).

FIGURE 1.1

Structure of a Windows GUI application.

```
WinMain() ───────────────── Entry Point
{
    RegisterClass();        ┐
    CreateWindowEx();       ├─ Create Main Window

    while (GetMessage())  { ┐
        TranslateMessage(); ├─ Message Loop
        DispatchMessage();  ┘
    }

    DestroyWindow(); ─────────── Destroy Main Window
}
```

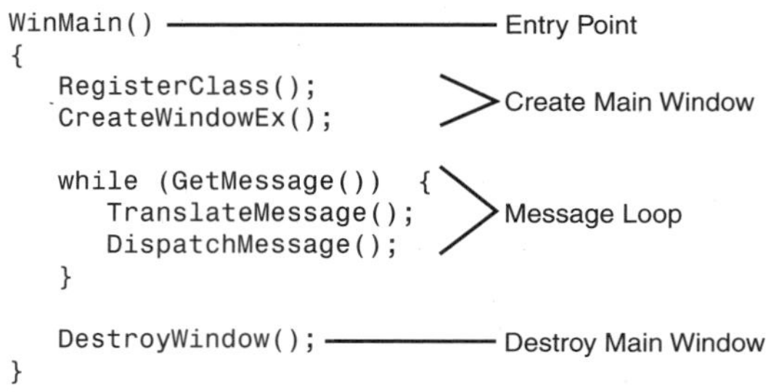

The entry point of a Windows GUI program is called WinMain. Named similarly to the entry point of C programs, main, every Windows GUI application must provide a WinMain function. Unlike main, it is passed different parameters and is declared as follows in Win32 programs:

```
int CALLBACK WinMain(HINSTANCE hInstance, HINSTANCE hPrevInstance,
                     LPSTR lpCmdLine, int nShowCmd);
```

The four parameters to the WinMain function include two handles (HINSTANCE), a pointer to a string (LPSTR), and an integer (int). The instance handle represents a unique application identifier for the program's main executable file in memory. The previous instance handle is no longer used in Win32 and is always equal to zero. The pointer to a string contains the command-line arguments passed to the program at start time. Finally, the integer contains an integer value that the program is supposed to pass to the ShowWindow function that indicates whether the main window is to appear minimized, maximized, or normal.

NOTE

A handle is simply a 16- or 32-bit value that uniquely identifies a system object to an application. By exposing only the handle of a system object, Windows can hide (encapsulate) that object's implementation and data and provide a controllable interface to that system object. This allows Microsoft to add more functionality to existing system objects, yet still support old applications—as long as they do not change the behavior of the existing interfaces. (Occasionally some interface's behavior does change between releases. This often is the exception rather than the rule.)

The most basic C++ classes in MFC wrap the handles to the Windows system objects: windows, device contexts, pens, and brushes, to name a few.

Because it needs to perform a great deal of initialization at program startup and it provides an object-oriented interface to the Windows API, MFC provides a WinMain function for your application. The MFC-provided WinMain calls another function, AfxWinMain, which creates and manages your CWinApp-derived application object. If you need to perform application-specific initialization, run handling, and/or termination, refer to the more detailed discussion of the CWinApp class and CWinApp::InitInstance, CWinApp::Run, and CWinApp::ExitInstance methods later in this chapter.

Without a main window, an application wouldn't have a graphical user interface and would find it hard to respond to window-related events. Consequently, almost all Windows GUI applications create a main window as their first order of business when starting.

Using direct calls to the Win32 API, your application calls RegisterClass to register a window class (basically associating a name with a window event callback function), followed by CreateWindowEx, to create a main window (which is an instance of the registered window class). In MFC, this work is done "automagically" when Visual Studio generates the code for you. Generally, in generated code, your main frame's application window is created in the CWinApp::InitInstance code.

The next basic feature required for every Windows application is the message loop. Typically in programs that call the Windows API directly, this is accomplished as shown following:

```
MSG msg;
while (GetMessage(&msg, 0, 0, 0)) {
    TranslateMessage(&msg);
    DispatchMessage(&msg);
}
```

This loop allows the current application thread to get system events that are queued up for windows created by that thread. The GetMessage function returns a Boolean value TRUE for all messages, except the WM_QUIT message, which allows the while loop to end, due to application termination. After the call to GetMessage returns with a message (event) for one of the thread's windows, that thread calls TranslateMessage, to process any accelerator keys and menu hot keys, followed by DispatchMessage, to send the message to the window to which it belongs by calling that window's registered window procedure.

WHAT IS A *THREAD*?

You are probably intimately familiar with the concept of a process. In many operating systems, a *process* corresponds to an instance of executing code in the computer's memory. Processes contain memory (usually some for code and some for data) and open resources, such as files, pipes, and other system objects. Traditionally, many operating systems had the current execution state (current machine registers, including the instruction pointer, and a stack) associated with the process. As a result, each process was treated as a single unit of execution when the operating system shared the CPU via multitasking.

Windows and many other modern operating systems allow multiple units of execution within the same process. Each unit of execution is called a *thread*. Each thread within a process has the same access to all the memory and resources owned by the process. However, each thread maintains its own copy of the machine registers and call stack.

Threads are often used to perform some operation "concurrently" within the process and provide a simpler and more efficient mechanism as compared to creating or "forking" a new process. (Actually, on a uniprocessor system, threads cannot literally run at the same time; however, on a multiprocessor system they actually could run simultaneously.)

Another advantage of threads is that they enable you to separate logical units of code and maximize throughput in your programs. For example, if one thread is waiting for (blocking) a file I/O request, another thread could perform some mathematical calculation, and yet another thread can handle user interface events. The end result is that the program's overall performance can be improved because its utilization of the CPU(s) is maximized for a given amount of time.

For MFC applications, once again the message loop is automatically included as part of your application. In the case of Single Document Interface (SDI) and Multiple Document Interface (MDI) applications, this message loop is put into control through the `CWinApp::Run` method. (More specifically, `CWinApp::Run` calls the `CWinThread::Run` method, which is in its base class.) For dialog-based applications, the message loop is instantiated during the `CWinApp::initInstance` through a call to `CDialog::doModal`. In addition, when messages are dispatched from the thread's message loop, they are routed through the standard MFC-owned window procedures (`AfxWndProcBase` and `AfxWndProc`) and finally mapped to a function within your window or dialog class. (This process will be explained in more detail later in this chapter.)

The final phase of a typical Windows program's `WinMain` function is the destruction of the main window via a call to the `DestroyWindow` function. Of course, this is also part of the MFC code that your application uses. If you need to do termination processing in your application, you would override the `CWinApp::ExitInstance` method in your application's `CWinApp`-derived class.

At this point you should have a basic understanding of how some of the more basic features of a standard Windows API application correlate to an MFC application. From this point forward, the discussions will leave the Windows API behind and deal with the features of MFC. Of course, specific Windows APIs might be mentioned from time to time, but not as a major part of any section in this book.

The MFC Class Hierarchy

So far several MFC classes have been mentioned. This section covers some of the more important classes that make up the MFC architecture.

Figure 1.2 shows the inheritance hierarchy of some of the most important application architectural classes within MFC. You might immediately observe that these classes all ultimately derive from a class named `CObject`.

FIGURE 1.2

*MFC architecture
class hierarchy.*

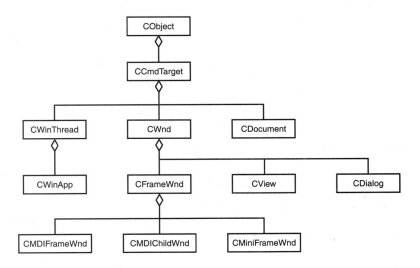

CObject

The CObject class is the "mother of all MFC classes." Well, actually not quite *all* MFC classes, but quite a few of them. Its primary responsibilities are to support handle runtime type information and object persistence (or *serialization* in MFC-speak), and to perform diagnostic output for derived objects.

Classes that are derived from the CObject class can support its features in one of four ways:

1. (Most basic) General diagnostic support.
2. (Dynamic) All features described thus far plus runtime type identification.
3. (DynCreate) All features thus far plus the capability of unbound dynamic object creation. That is, the class can be constructed by code that does not know the class's name at the time it was compiled and linked.
4. (Serial) All features thus far plus the capability of storing and restoring instances of the object to and from a byte stream.

Diagnostic Support (All CObject-Derived Classes)

The diagnostic support within the CObject class is limited to two methods: AssertValid and Dump. Each of these methods can be called at any time from your derived class.

AssertValid

The AssertValid method allows a class to perform a sanity check on itself before continuing. It is declared as a public method in the CObject class as follows:

```
virtual void AssertValid() const;
```

If you choose to override this method, you will typically use the ASSERT macro to perform sanity checks on your object's data. In addition, you should call your base class's implementation of this method so it can also validate its data. Because this method is const, you cannot change your object's state from within this method.

> **CAUTION**
>
> Do not depend on AssertValid working in release code. This is because the ASSERT macro is only defined when _DEBUG is defined at compilation time.

Because it is a public method, you can call it either from inside your class or from outside your class at any time.

Dump

The `Dump` method allows a class to put diagnostic information in the human-readable form of text and/or numbers to a stream, typically through the `OutputDebugString` API, which displays it in the debugger's output window (or any other program that traps debug strings). It is declared as a public method in the `CObject` class as follows:

```
virtual void Dump(CDumpContext& dc) const;
```

If you override this method, first call your base class's dump method. Next, call the insertion operator (`<<`) on the `CDumpContext` object to output information about your object. As a C++ programmer, this is no different from how you would use the `cerr` or `cout` object to output diagnostic information about your object. Finally, make sure that you do not output a trailing newline (`\n`) on your final line of output.

> **NOTE**
>
> If your `CObject`-derived class does not include runtime type information, `CObject::dump` displays only `CObject` as the class name. Otherwise, it properly displays the name of your derived class.

Runtime Type Information (`Dynamic` and `DynCreate` Classes)

When a class supports MFC's Runtime Type Information (RTTI), it can respond to a request for its name and its base class. To support the `Dynamic` form of RTTI, simply include a `DECLARE_DYNAMIC` macro invocation within your class declaration and an `IMPLEMENT_DYNAMIC` macro invocation near your class definition.

> **CAUTION**
>
> Do not confuse MFC's RTTI with the RTTI support built into the newer C++ compilers (and activated using Visual C++'s `/GR` switch). As of MFC 4.2, MFC's RTTI support does not use C++'s RTTI support in any way, shape, or form.

If you have a class named `CMyClass` that is derived from `CObject` and you want your class to support RTTI, add the following to your header file:

```
class CMyClass : public CObject {
   DECLARE_DYNAMIC(CMyClass)
   // other class information
};
```

In your source file, add the following at file scope:

```
IMPLEMENT_DYNAMIC(CMyClass, CObject)
```

When your class is Dynamic, it has a static CRuntimeClass object associated within it that contains the runtime type information for the object. You can obtain a pointer to the runtime class object using the RUNTIME_CLASS macro, invoking it using the name of the class that you'd like. So, to obtain a pointer to the CRuntimeClass object associated with CMyClass (a Dynamic class), simply use the following code:

```
RUNTIME_CLASS(CMyClass)
```

An extension of the Dynamic class is a DynCreate class. When a class is DynCreate, a program can construct an object of that class simply by knowing its name at runtime as opposed to compilation time.

To support dynamic creation, your class must have a default constructor (that is, a constructor with no parameters) that creates a stable object, and you must add macro invocations for DECLARE_DYNCREATE and IMPLEMENT_DYNCREATE, as you did for dynamic objects previously.

> **NOTE**
>
> Because dynamic creation is a superset of the dynamic support, do not add invocations of the DECLARE_DYNAMIC/IMPLEMENT_DYNAMIC macros to your class files.

The DynCreate macros add a method named CreateObject to your class. The implementation of this method simply calls new on your specific object and returns it as a pointer to a CObject. If you have a class named CMyClass that supports dynamic creation, you can instantiate one of these objects by using the RUNTIME_CLASS macro to get the RTTI information and call the CreateObject method on it as follows:

```
CMyClass *myObj = DYNAMIC_DOWNCAST(CMyClass,
                RUNTIME_CLASS(CMyClass)->CreateObject());
```

> **NOTE**
>
> The DYNAMIC_DOWNCAST and STATIC_DOWNCAST macros improve the type safety for casting operations on MFC CObject-derived types. By using MFC's RTTI, they can check if the cast is valid at runtime.

You can use the C++ dynamic_cast and static_cast keywords to perform type-safe casts on MFC objects as long as you compile your application with C++ RTTI turned on (Visual C++'s /GR compiler switch). MFC is already built with this switch on; however, the Visual Studio default is off.

Serialization (Serial Classes)

Serialization is the capability of an object to save its state to a byte stream and rebuild itself from that stream. If an object supports serialization, it can be saved to a file, transmitted over a socket or pipe, and later reconstituted either from that file or on the other end of the socket or pipe.

To create a CObject-derived class that supports serialization, you must add the DECLARE_SERIAL macro inside its class declaration in the header file and the IMPLEMENT_SERIAL macro in the source file containing the class's method and data definitions, in the same manner as was demonstrated for a Dynamic class.

> **NOTE**
>
> Because serialization is a superset of the dynamic and dynamic creation support, do not add invocations of the DECLARE_DYNAMIC/IMPLEMENT_DYNAMIC or the DECLARE_DYNCREATE/IMPLEMENT_DYNCREATE macros to your class files.

When a CObject-derived class supports serialization, there are two methods that are used: IsSerializable and Serialize.

IsSerializable

The IsSerializable method allows another object to determine whether this CObject-derived class supports serialization. It is declared as a public method in the CObject class as follows:

```
BOOL IsSerializable() const;
```

Because this function is not virtual, you cannot override it in any meaningful way. The MFC CRuntimeClass object determines whether serialization is supported from its m_wSchema field. The only valid values supported within this field are 0xffff (meaning not serializable) and VERSIONABLE_SCHEMA (meaning supports standard MFC serialization).

Serialize

The `Serialize` method is called to actually perform the saving and restoring of the object from a serialization stream (within a `CArchive` object). It is declared as a public method in the `CObject` class as follows:

```
virtual void Serialize(CArchive& ar);
```

If your class needs to save or restore its state when being serialized, you must override this method.

Of course, if you're implementing this method so your class can support serialization, you first need to know whether or not you need to save your object's data to or restore your object's data from the `CArchive` stream. You can use either the `CArchive::IsLoading` or `CArchive::IsStoring` methods to determine which direction you need to go.

> **NOTE**
>
> You are guaranteed that if `CArchive::IsLoading` returns `TRUE`, `CArchive::IsStoring` returns `FALSE` and vice versa.

Next, if the archive object is in loading mode, you can use the `CArchive` class's extraction operators (`>>`) to retrieve data from the data stream. Likewise, if it is in storing mode, you can use its insertion operators (`<<`) to add data to the data stream.

> **SERIALIZATION "GOTCHAS"**
>
> The serialization protocol requires that you call your base class's `Serialize` method before performing your own serialization support.
>
> If you detect an error while handling your `Serialize` method, you can safely throw one of the following exceptions: `CMemoryException`, `CFileException`, or `CArchiveException`.
>
> You must store your data in exactly the same order that you load it.
>
> All MFC lists support serialization. Be very careful when serializing lists of objects. If your list contains a pointer to an object being serialized, it will attempt to "reserialize" the object and get trapped in a recursive loop. This will cause a hang followed by a stack overflow in your application.

A typical implementation of the `Serialize` method for the fictitious `CMyClass` class is shown here:

```
void CMyClass::Serialize(CArchive& ar)
{
    CObject::Serialize(ar);

    if (ar.IsStoring()) {
        ar << m_myData;
    } else {
        ar >> m_myData;
    }
}
```

Serialization can be done either explicitly or implicitly by your application through the MFC framework. When your MFC application is generated by Visual Studio, it implicitly creates a `CArchive` object, associates it with a `CFile` object, and calls the `CArchive::ReadObject` or `CArchive::WriteObject` methods in response to the File menu bar, Open, Save, and Save As commands. These methods call the `Serialize` method on the appropriate objects.

Likewise, you can perform your own serialization explicitly within your application. First, create a `CFile` or `CFile`-derived object (such as `CSocketFile`). Next, construct a `CArchive` object passing a pointer to your `CFile` object to its constructor. Finally, call either the `CArchive::WriteObject` or `CArchive::ReadObject` method to save or restore your object, respectively.

CCmdTarget

The `CCmdTarget` class, derived from `CObject`, is responsible for managing the routing of system and window events to the objects that can respond to these events. So, any class that expects to receive one of these events derives from this class and overrides the `CCmdTarget::OnCmdMsg` method.

Examples of classes that expect to receive system and window events are `CWnd` (the window class), `CView` (the view class), `CDocument` (the document class), `CWinThread` (the user interface thread class), and `CWinApp` (the application class). These classes are described in more detail later in this chapter.

The methods within the `CCmdTarget` class can be organized into three categories: message routing, wait cursor, and automation support.

Message Routing

In all Windows GUI applications, the application thread's message loop processes all system and window events for that thread's windows. MFC is no exception. However, unlike the procedural window procedure with a large `switch` statement, the MFC architecture maps these events to object methods for each object.

In fact, a C++ programmer would immediately think that C++ does provide a mechanism for doing just this: virtual functions. Continuing on this logic, that programmer would think that to process and dispatch the window messages, simply create a base Window object and add virtual functions for each of the possible events that could arrive. Furthermore, you would derive from the base Window object and simply override those events to which your window needs to respond.

Ah, if it were only that simple. MFC does not use the C++ virtual function mechanism for handling the various Windows events. Instead, it creates a static data structure for each `CCmdTarget` class called a *message map*. In essence, this structure maps an event to its corresponding handler in the object.

WHY DOESN'T MFC USE THE C++ VIRTUAL FUNCTION MECHANISM?

One explanation suggests that there is a large amount of performance overhead carrying around the virtual tables (vtables) for all the possible objects.

In analyzing this explanation, a few issues need to be considered: What does "carry" mean and how large are these vtables anyway? Certainly most MFC objects do, in fact, have vtables and, certainly, each object has an extra four bytes to store a pointer to the table. These four bytes have to be "carried" around anyway.

However, for each class of object, there is only one vtable; that is, all `CWnd` objects share the same vtable in memory. Also, each abstract class has a vtable that won't ever be used. (Actually MFC now uses the `_declspec(novtable)` keyword to prevent these from being linked into the application.) So, the number of static vtables is less than or equal to the number of classes that exist within the executable.

In addition, each vtable has one four-byte entry for each possible event that can occur. Assuming that there are 256 events, each vtable would be approximately 1KB in size. So, if you have 100 different concrete `CCmdTarget`-derived classes in your application, this would add about 100KB to your application size. Certainly on a system that has only 16MB of RAM, it could eat up 2% of your physical RAM if you were running three of these programs (and all the vtables were not paged out to disk).

In the context of 16MB machines, this might be unreasonable. Today, with 128MB to 256MB standard on some machines, it might not be that bad. However, if the number of events is increased, the cost increases linearly, of course. Overall, the explanation seems plausible, but still not totally satisfying. (The term *carry* still seems off base, however, unless used in the context of the actual executable image.)

Another rarely espoused explanation, however, seems to indicate another possibility. C++'s virtual table mechanism does not provide any sort of forward compatibility. As a result, as Windows evolves and more events are possible, either reserved space would have to be allocated in each object's vtable beforehand or the application would have to be recompiled for each release.

So, it would require early versions of MFC to determine up front what virtual table size is required going forward. That would be a very difficult task, except perhaps for an oracle of some sorts (no pun intended).

When MFC was originally developed, it did not have the advantage of the Component Object Model (COM) to provide a more flexible, maintainable vtable mechanism. Consequently, the designers created the message map as a slightly slower, but more memory-efficient and maintainable custom "vtable" mechanism.

The method that MFC uses for mapping system and window events to objects is called *message mapping*. Each class that is derived ultimately from `CCmdTarget` contains a message map that allows it to specify the events that it can handle and map those events to a method within the class.

To add a message map to your class, you must add an invocation of the `DECLARE_MESSAGE_MAP` macro within your object. For the fictitious `CMyView` class, this code is as follows:

```
class CMyView : public CView { // CView is a subclass of CCmdTarget
   DECLARE_MESSAGE_MAP()
   // other class information
};
```

The `DECLARE_MESSAGE_MAP` macro expands to declare two static members in your class, the combination of which comprises your message mappings. In addition, two methods are added; one internal (`_GetBaseMessageMap`), which returns the message map in the base class, and one external (`GetMessageMap`), which returns a pointer to the message map mappings for this class.

Next, you need to add macro invocations within your source code at file scope to actually define the message map for your class. An example of such code for the `CMyView` class is as follows:

```
BEGIN_MESSAGE_MAP(CMyView, CView)
    ON_COMMAND(ID_FILE_OPEN, OnFileOpen)
    ON_WM_SIZE()
END_MESSAGE_MAP()
```

The key elements are the macro invocations for BEGIN_MESSAGE_MAP and END_MESSAGE_MAP that provide the appropriate delimiting code. In between these macros, there are macros that describe the exact events that can be handled by this class. In this case, using the ON_COMMAND macro, CMyView maps the menu item command identifier ID_FILE_OPEN to the OnFileOpen method. In addition, using the ON_WM_SIZE macro maps the WM_SIZE window event to a method named OnSize (which is actually defined in that specific macro). Because there are a large number of actual events, there are a large number of macros that you can use in a message map. For more information, please refer to header file AFXMSG_.H.

OnCmdMsg

There is one method that supports the dispatching of system and window events, OnCmdMsg. Typically, you do not need to modify the handling of this method and, hence, you can just let the event dispatching occur automatically. However, if you need to provide custom and/or dynamic routing of events, you can override this virtual function in your CCmdTarget-derived class. The declaration of this method is as follows:

```
virtual BOOL OnCmdMsg(UINT nID, int nCode, void *pExtra,
                      AFX_CMDHANDLERINFO *pHandlerInfo);
```

Your override method must return TRUE if it handles the event, and FALSE otherwise.

Wait Cursor

The CCmdTarget class defines three methods that applications can use to change the state of the mouse pointer. These methods are BeginWaitCursor, EndWaitCursor, and RestoreWaitCursor.

BeginWaitCursor, EndWaitCursor, and RestoreWaitCursor

Use the BeginWaitCursor method to change the mouse pointer to an hourglass, thus notifying the user that the current operation might take some time. When your operation is complete, call EndWaitCursor to change the pointer back to what it was at the BeginWaitCursor call.

Use RestoreWaitCursor to change the pointer back to its original state after the pointer had been changed by some external operation, such as displaying a message box.

These methods are declared as follows in the public access section of the CCmdTarget class:

```
void BeginWaitCursor();
void EndWaitCursor();
void RestoreWaitCursor();
```

Automation Support

If your MFC application allows interaction through an `IDispatch` COM interface, it supports automation. The `CCmdTarget` class not only can dispatch system and window events to objects of its derived classes, but also it can translate automation interface methods in a similar way.

The methods within `CCmdTarget` that support automation are: `EnableAutomation`, `FromIDispatch`, `GetIDispatch`, `IsResultExpected`, and `OnFinalRelease`.

EnableAutomation

The `EnableAutomation` method is called from your `CCmdTarget`-derived class's constructor to indicate that it contains both a dispatch and an interface map. It is declared in the public section of the `CCmdTarget` class as follows:

```
void EnableAutomation();
```

The dispatch and interface maps are very similar in layout to the message map that was described previously in this chapter. Like the message map, they require macro invocations in the class declaration using the `DECLARE_DISPATCH_MAP` and `DECLARE_INTERFACE_MAP` macros, respectively. The following code demonstrates these macros for the sample `CMyDocument` class:

```
class CMyDocument : public CDocument {
   DECLARE_DISPATCH_MAP()
   DECLARE_INTERFACE_MAP()
   // other class member declarations...
};
```

When declared in the class declaration, the dispatch map and interface maps must be defined in the source file for the class. In the case of the `CMyDocument` class (located in the MyApp application), these maps look as follows:

```
// {6C9C4209-9D58-11D2-8FAF-00400566CE21}
static const IID IID_IMyApp =
➥{ 0x6c9c4209, 0x9d58, 0x11d2,
➥{ 0x8f, 0xaf, 0x0, 0x40, 0x5, 0x66, 0xce, 0x21 } };

BEGIN_INTERFACE_MAP(CMyDocument, CDocument)
   INTERFACE_PART(CMyDocument, IID_IMyApp, Dispatch)
END_INTERFACE_MAP()

BEGIN_DISPATCH_MAP(CMyDocument, CDocument)
   DISP_FUNCTION(CMyDocument, "OpenFile", OpenFile, VT_EMPTY, VTS_BSTR)
END_DISPATCH_MAP()
```

In this example, the COM automation interface for the MyApp application is mapped to be a dispatch interface. Additionally, one automation (dispatch) function, `OpenFile`, is mapped to a method of the same name.

`FromIDispatch` and `GetIDispatch`

The `FromIDispatch` and `GetIDispatch` methods allow an application to get the `CCmdTarget` object given an `IDispatch` interface pointer and vice versa. Of course, not all `CCmdTarget` objects contain `IDispatch` interfaces and, hence, might return a `NULL` pointer. These methods are declared in the public section of the `CCmdTarget` class as follows:

```
static CCmdTarget * FromIDispatch(LPDISPATCH lpDispatch);
LPDISPATCH GetIDispatch(BOOL bAddRef);
```

`IsResultExpected`

The `IsResultExpected` method returns `TRUE` if the automation client is waiting for a return value from the function. Otherwise, if a result is not expected, the application can ignore calculating it (particularly if it might take time to do so) and improve automation performance. This function is declared as follows in the public section of the `CCmdTarget` class:

```
BOOL IsResultExpected();
```

`OnFinalRelease`

The `OnFinalRelease` method is a virtual method that the `CCmdTarget`-derived class can choose to override to perform any sort of special processing when the last COM interface reference to or from the object is released. Otherwise, the `CCmdTarget`-derived object is simply deleted. This method is declared in the public section of the `CCmdTarget` class as shown here:

```
virtual void OnFinalRelease();
```

CWinThread

The `CWinThread` class is derived from the `CCmdTarget` class and represents a thread of execution within the MFC application. All MFC applications have at least one `CWinThread` object—the main application's `CWinApp` object (which is derived from `CWinThread`). If you want to provide additional asynchronous processing within your application, you can construct and run additional `CWinThread` objects, as needed.

You can obtain a pointer to the current `CWinThread` object by calling `AfxGetThread`.

Within MFC, there are two different types of threads: worker threads and user interface threads.

Worker Threads

Worker threads are threads that are created to do some additional processing, but do not require any sort of system or window event processing. A worker thread would be useful to perform a time-consuming calculation or to read data from a file. By creating a worker thread, you can do additional work without interfering with the operation of the application's user interface.

A worker thread is created using the AfxBeginThread function. In its simplest form, you simply need a callback function and a user-defined data pointer. After it has been created, a CWinThread object is returned to the calling thread, and the new worker thread starts execution. This form of AfxBeginThread is declared as follows:

```
CWinThread *AfxBeginThread(AFX_THREADPROC pfnThreadProc, LPVOID pParam,
                    int nPriority = THREAD_PRIORITY_NORMAL,
                    UINT nStackSize = 0, DWORD dwCreateFlags = 0,
                    LPSECURITY_ATTRIBUTES lpSecurityAttrs = NULL );
```

In addition, your callback function, AFX_THREADPROC, must be declared as shown here:

```
typedef UINT (AFX_CDECL *AFX_THREADPROC)(LPVOID);
```

When the thread function is complete and wants to end itself, it simply returns or calls AFXEndThread. If you want to end the created thread from another thread, you must set up your own signaling mechanism, probably via the use of system event semaphores.

User Interface Threads

User interface threads are threads that have their own message loop and can create, interact with, and destroy user interface objects, such as modeless dialog windows that operate separately from the main application thread's user interface.

To use user interface threads, you must first derive a class from the CWinThread class that creates a user interface element for which to handle events. You can choose to use the InitInstance and ExitInstance methods to show and hide your user interface elements. When that is done, you can choose one of two approaches to create and start the thread.

The first approach is to construct your derived CWinThread function and then call the CreateThread method to start it. This method is declared as follows in the CWinThread class:

```
BOOL CreateThread(DWORD dwCreateFlags = 0, UINT nStackSize = 0,
                LPSECURITY_ATTRIBUTES lpSecurityAttrs = NULL);
```

Using the CreateThread method is a fairly clean coding approach to creating and starting a new user interface thread.

The second approach to creating a user interface thread is very similar to the technique for creating a worker thread, except for using a different overload of the AfxBeginThread function. This overload is declared as follows:

```
CWinThread *AfxBeginThread(CRuntimeClass* pThreadClass,
                           int nPriority = THREAD_PRIORITY_NORMAL,
                           UINT nStackSize = 0, DWORD dwCreateFlags = 0,
                           LPSECURITY_ATTRIBUTES lpSecurityAttrs = NULL);
```

You might note that the primary difference between the two overloads is in the initial parameter. Instead of requiring a callback function and a user-defined pointer, the user interface AFXBeginThread overload requires a pointer to the runtime class of the CWinThread-derived object that you want to instantiate. Remember to use the RUNTIME_CLASS macro to obtain a pointer to this object for a specific class.

When creating CWinThread objects, you might find it necessary to initialize some members of the CWinThread object *before* the thread starts executing. To do this, pass CREATE_SUSPENDED to the dwCreateFlags parameter, which creates the thread in suspended mode. After the thread has been created, set the members that you require and call the CWinThread::ResumeThread method to allow the thread to start executing.

When the thread needs to terminate, it can simply call AfxPostQuitMessage to end its message loop and set an exit code for the thread. This function is declared thus:

```
void AFXAPI AfxPostQuitMessage(int nExitCode);
```

CWinThread Methods

The methods described in the following sections are contained in the CWinThread class. Remember that because your CWinApp-derived application object has CWinThread as a base class, you can use these methods on that object.

InitInstance and ExitInstance

The InitInstance and ExitInstance virtual functions can be overridden by your application to provide pre-message loop and post-message loop initialization and termination. If you override the Run method, as you can do to create a worker thread, these virtual functions do not get called, unless you call them directly. These public methods are declared as follows:

```
virtual BOOL InitInstance();
virtual int ExitInstance();
```

The CWinThread::ExitInstance implementation automatically deletes the CWinThread object if the m_bAutoDelete member is set to TRUE. Therefore, if you override ExitInstance, call your base class's ExitInstance to maintain this behavior. Additionally, if the call to InitInstance fails, ExitInstance is called.

Run

The Run method is where the actual thread operation occurs. The default implementation provides a message loop for the thread and continues until a WM_QUIT message is encountered. You can create a CWinThread-derived worker thread if you override the Run method to perform your worker thread processing. This method is declared as a public method as follows:

```
virtual int Run();
```

The return value from this function becomes the exit code from the thread. This value can be obtained by calling the GetExitCodeThread function in the Windows API.

SuspendThread and ResumeThread

Use the SuspendThread and ResumeThread methods to control the execution of a thread. A suspend count is maintained with each thread; thus, for each call that you make to SuspendThread, you must make an equal number of calls to ResumeThread before the thread resumes execution. These public methods are declared as shown here:

```
DWORD SuspendThread();
DWORD ResumeThread();
```

The return value from each of these methods is the suspend count for the thread upon completion of the call.

GetThreadPriority and SetThreadPriority

If you want control over the priority of a thread owned by a CWinThread object, use the GetThreadPriority and SetThreadPriority methods. The Windows thread scheduler, of course, prefers higher priority threads to lower priority ones. The priority values can be one of the following (or an integer between any two levels): THREAD_PRIORITY_IDLE, THREAD_PRIORITY_LOWEST, THREAD_PRIORITY_BELOW_NORMAL, THREAD_PRIORITY_NORMAL, THREAD_PRIORITY_ABOVE_NORMAL, THREAD_PRIORITY_HIGHEST, and THREAD_PRIORITY_TIME_CRITICAL.

The thread priority methods are declared as follows:

```
int GetThreadPriority();
void SetThreadPriority(int nPriority);
```

> **CAUTION**
>
> Do not assume that priority is an absolute value in Windows. The thread scheduler, by default and design, can randomly and temporarily boost a thread's priority. If you need to disable this behavior, use the SetThreadPriorityBoost API.

IsIdleMessage and OnIdle

You can use the `IsIdleMessage` and `OnIdle` methods to control processing that occurs when no messages exist in the thread's message queue.

If you think that idle message processing might be required for your application, first consider using either worker or user interface threads to do the work. If you do not want the overhead and synchronization required for threading, use the age-old technique of Windows idle message processing.

The `OnIdle` method is called when the thread's message queue is empty. In your override implementation, it is suggested that you call `PeekMessage` with the `PM_NOREMOVE` flag to check for the arrival of new messages in the queue. If a message arrives, return from this function to allow the thread's message processing to continue. The `OnIdle` method is declared as follows:

```
virtual BOOL OnIdle(LONG userCount);
```

By overriding the `IsIdleMessage` method when you also override the `OnIdle` method, you can prevent `OnIdle` from being repeatedly called in response to recurring messages. This public method is declared as shown here:

```
virtual BOOL IsIdleMessage(MSG *pMsg);
```

PreTranslateMessage

You can override the `PreTranslateMessage` virtual function to handle a message before it is translated from an accelerator to a command and dispatched to a window. Return `TRUE` from this method if you do not want the message to be processed any more. This public method is declared as follows:

```
virtual BOOL PreTranslateMessage(MSG *pMsg);
```

ProcessMessageFilter

The `ProcessMessageFilter` virtual function allows your application to catch messages that are trapped by the MFC message hooks. Return `TRUE` if you process a message passed to your implementation. In addition, call your class's base class implementation to ensure that the message hook processing continues as designed. This method is declared as follows:

```
virtual BOOL ProcessMessageFilter(int hookCode, LPMSG lpMsg);
```

ProcessWndProcException

Override the `ProcessWndProcException` method to handle any MFC exceptions that have been trapped from within the Windows message processing. This method is declared as shown here:

```
virtual LRESULT ProcessWndProcException(CException *xcp,
➥const MSG *pMsg);
```

CWinApp

The `CWinApp` class, derived from the `CWinThread` class, represents not only the program's main thread of execution, but also the application itself. As a result, there is only one `CWinApp` object in any MFC application.

Typically, you derive your application class from `CWinApp`. In addition, you would override the `InitInstance` and `ExitInstance` virtual functions to provide your own initialization and termination support (like creating and destroying your application's main window). If you do override these functions, remember to call your base class's implementations, too.

Functions

There are several functions that you can call to obtain global application information. They are `AfxGetApp`, `AfxGetInstanceHandle`, `AfxGetResourceHandle`, and `AfxGetAppName`.

AfxGetApp and AfxGetAppName

Use the `AfxGetApp` function to obtain the pointer to the executable's `CWinApp` object. Similarly, you can use `AfxGetAppName` to get the name of your MFC program. These functions are declared as shown here:

```
CWinApp * AFXAPI AfxGetApp();
LPCTSTR AFXAPI AfxGetAppName();
```

> **NOTE**
>
> The MFC application name is determined first by finding a string resource with an ID equal to `AFX_IDS_APP_TITLE`. If a matching string resource does not exist, the fully qualified executable filename is returned.

AfxGetInstanceHandle, AfxGetResourceHandle, and AfxSetResourceHandle

Use the `AfxGetInstanceHandle` to obtain a handle to the loaded executable file (EXE or DLL) within which the current code is located. Use the `AfxGetResourceHandle` and `AfxSetResourceHandle` functions to find and specify the location of the executable file that contains your bound resources. With these functions, your strings and dialogs are not required to be located in the same executable file as your code. By default, the resource handle for each module is set to be the handle of the executable file that contains that code. These functions are declared as follows:

```
HINSTANCE AFXAPI AfxGetInstanceHandle();
HINSTANCE AFXAPI AfxGetResourceHandle();
void AFXAPI AfxSetResourceHandle(HINSTANCE hInstResource);
```

If you need to determine whether or not your code is in an EXE or a DLL, use the Boolean value from the `afxContextIsDLL` macro.

Registry Support

Applications often use the registry to store custom parameters that assist in the usability of the software. For example, applications store items such as window positions, path names, and so on, to allow them to be customized to the user's preferences. If your application needs to store large amounts of data, you are strongly encouraged to store this data in your own custom file, rather than the registry.

For more information about using the registry, refer to Chapter 32, "Inside the Registry."

SetRegistryKey

Use the `SetRegistryKey` method to inform MFC of the location (under `HKEY_CURRENT_USER\Software`) at which to store all application profile data. You should use a key value that is unique and is unlikely to conflict with other applications. For example, the trademarked name of your company is an excellent choice. If you do not specify a registry key, all registry method calls will refer to a text-based .INI file.

This public method is declared as follows in the `CWinApp` class:

```
void SetRegistryKey(LPCTSTR lpszRegistryKey);
void SetRegistryKey(UINT nIDRegistryKey);
```

> **NOTE**
>
> The second form of the `SetRegistryKey` method takes the ID of a string resource as a parameter.

> **TIP**
>
> After you've called `SetRegistryKey`, you can use the `GetAppRegistryKey` and `GetSectionKey` methods to get the `HKEY` registry handle directly. When finished with the handle, you must call `RegCloseKey` to release it.

GetProfile*DataType* and WriteProfile*DataType*

Use the GetProfileInt, WriteProfileInt, GetProfileString, WriteProfileString, GetProfileBinary, and WriteProfileBinary methods to store or retrieve key and value pairs in or from the registry (or an .INI file, if no registry has been set via SetRegistryKey). When using these functions, use a unique name (within your specified registry key) for your application as the "section" name.

These public methods are declared as follows:

```
UINT GetProfileInt(LPCTSTR lpszSection, LPCTSTR lpszEntry, int nDefault);
BOOL WriteProfileInt(LPCTSTR lpszSection, LPCTSTR lpszEntry, int nValue);
CString GetProfileString(LPCTSTR lpszSection, LPCTSTR lpszEntry,
        LPCTSTR lpszDefault = NULL);
BOOL WriteProfileString(LPCTSTR lpszSection, LPCTSTR lpszEntry,
        LPCTSTR lpszValue);
BOOL GetProfileBinary(LPCTSTR lpszSection, LPCTSTR lpszEntry,
        LPBYTE* ppData, UINT* pBytes);
BOOL WriteProfileBinary(LPCTSTR lpszSection, LPCTSTR lpszEntry,
        LPBYTE pData, UINT nBytes);
```

Document Support

For more information about MFC document and view support, refer to Chapter 7, "The Document/View Architecture."

AddDocTemplate

The AddDocTemplate method adds a document template to the list of document templates available to the application. You would typically call this method in your override of the InitInstance method. This method is declared as follows:

```
void AddDocTemplate(CDocTemplate *pTemplate);
```

GetFirstDocTemplatePosition and GetNextDocTemplate

The GetFirstDocTemplatePosition and GetNextDocTemplate methods allow you to iterate through all the document template objects (CDocTemplate) that currently are added to the application. If no document templates are available, GetFirstDocTemplatePosition returns NULL.

These public methods are declared as follows:

```
POSITION GetfirstDocTemplatePosition() const;
CDocTemplate *GetNextDocTemplate(POSITION& pos) const;
```

NOTE

Because `GetNextDocTemplate` updates the position value, always check that the current position is not `NULL` before calling `GetNextDocTemplate`.

OpenDocumentFile

The `OpenDocumentFile` method opens a file representing a document. It creates a frame and view for that document, based on matching the file extension to a registered document template. If the document is already loaded, this method activates that frame and view. This public method is declared as shown here:

```
virtual CDocument *OpenDocumentFile(LPCTSTR lpszFileName);
```

LoadStdProfileSettings and AddToRecentFileList

Use the `LoadStdProfileSettings` and `AddToRecentFileList` methods to initialize and manage your application's recent file list. Call `LoadStdProfileSettings` in your `InitInstance` override to add the list of most recently used files to your application. Call `AddToRecentFileList` when you want to add another file to the recent file list. These methods are declared thus:

```
void LoadStdProifleSettings(UNIT nMaxMRU = _AFX_MRU_COUNT);
virtual void AddToRecentFileList(LPCTSTR lpszPathName);
```

EnableShellOpen, RegisterShellFileTypes, and UnregisterShellFileTypes

Call the `EnableShellOpen` and `RegisterShellFileTypes` methods in sequence to register your document templates in the system registry. By default, the `RegisterShellFileTypes` method iterates through your document templates and adds support for printing from the desktop shell (though the Print and PrintTo keys) and associates an icon for each template type (via the DefaultIcon key). If `EnableShellOpen` is called first, the `RegisterShellFileTypes` method will add support for opening the document from the desktop shell. Call `UnregisterShellFileTypes` to remove all the registered associations.

These methods are declared as follows:

```
void EnableShellOpen();
void RegisterShellFileTypes(BOOL bCompat=FALSE);
void UnregisterShellFileTypes();
```

TIP

Make sure that you add all your application's document templates (via `AddDocTemplate`) before calling `RegisterShellFileTypes`.

Command-Line Parsing

Sometimes you'll find it necessary to handle the command line passed to your application in a standard Windows application way. Use the `RunEmbedded`, `RunAutomated`, `ParseCommandLine`, and `ParseShellCommand` methods to help your application respond properly to command-line options passed to it.

RunEmbedded and RunAutomated

The `RunEmbedded` and `RunAutomated` methods search for /Embedding or /Automated (or the dash forms) in the passed command line. If found, the appropriate option is removed from the command line and `TRUE` is returned. Your program will receive these options if it is being launched as a server to an automation client application. Refer to Chapter 12, "MFC OLE Servers," for more information.

These public methods are declared as follows:

```
BOOL RunEmbedded();
BOOL RunAutomated();
```

ParseCommandLine and ProcessShellCommand

The `ParseCommandLine` and `ProcessShellCommand` methods parse the command-line parameters and perform the standard application actions (such as printing, DDE, and automation) for your application. Use these methods in sequence in your application's `InitInstance` override. These public methods are declared as follows:

```
void ParseCommandLine(CComandLineInfo& rCmdInfo);
BOOL ProcessShellCommand(CCommandLineInfo& rCmdInfo);
```

TIP

If you need to handle additional options that could be passed from the command line, derive a class from the `CCommandLineInfo` object and override its `ParseParam` method.

CWnd

The CWnd class, derived from CCmdTarget, is the most fundamental GUI object class in MFC. Instances of this class and derived classes are windows and have a system window handle (HWND) associated with them.

From the Windows point of view, a window is an object that has a registered window procedure, and consequently, can receive and handle system and window events. Most windows have a graphical representation and many respond to user input. Examples of windows include main application windows, dialogs, and controls (such as list boxes, pushbuttons, and static text fields).

NOTES ON MFC CLASSES THAT WRAP SYSTEM HANDLES

Several classes in MFC (such as CWnd, CDC, CPen, and CBrush, to name a few) provide wrappers to their respective system handles (HWND, HDC, HPEN, and HBRUSH, respectively).

When using these classes, you must understand the relationship of the lifetime of objects of that class and the lifetime of the associated system handles.

First, you can create the system handle for some classes, like CPen, in either a one- or two-step process. To create this object in one step, simply use one of its nondefault constructors that takes a style, width, and color parameter. To create a CPen object in two steps, use its default constructor and then call one of the CreatePen or CreatePenIndirect methods.

Classes typically have a Create method. However, some classes can have completely different names. For example, CFrameWnd has both a Create and a LoadFrame method to accomplish this.

Likewise, some system handle wrapper classes require a two-step process to fully construct the object. For example, if you construct a CWnd class, no system handle is created until you call the Create (or similar) method on the class. Therefore, there is a two-step process for constructing system handle wrapper objects.

First, when the MFC object has the system handle, that remains valid until the object is destroyed—at which time the handle is returned to the system.

Second, if you happen to have a system handle for which you'd like an object constructed, use the object's Attach method to assign handle ownership to the object.

If you'd like to take ownership of the system handle from an MFC object, call its Detach method. When this call is made, the handle is disconnected completely from the object and you are responsible for releasing the handle back to the system.

Finally, if you have a system handle, you can look up and/or create a temporary instance of a wrapper class. Most system handle wrapper classes provide a `FromHandle` function that returns an instance of a class given a handle. If the handle does not have an object associated with it, a temporary object is created.

The `CWnd` class and `CImageList` classes also provide a `FromHandlePermanent` function that returns an object only if one exists for the handle. This function does not create a temporary object.

Registering New Window Classes

You can use either `AfxRegisterClass` or `AfxRegisterWndClass` to register a new window class. In either case, you can pass the registered window class's name in a subsequent call to `CWnd::Create` to create an instance of that window.

`AfxRegisterClass` is very similar to the Win32 `RegisterClass` API, except that if the class is registered from within a DLL, that class is automatically unregistered when the DLL is unloaded.

The preferred window class registration function, `AfxRegisterWndClass`, returns a string containing the generated class name.

These functions are prototyped as follows:

```
BOOL AFXAPI AfxRegisterClass(WNDCLASS *lpWndClass);
LPCTSTR AFXAPI AfxRegisterWndClass(UINT nClassStyle, HCURSOR hCursor = 0,
            HBRUSH hbrBackground = 0, HICON hIcon = 0);
```

Obtaining an Application's Main Window

The `AfxGetMainWnd` function to get the pointer to the `CWnd` object that represents the main window for your thread. Typically, it simply returns the `m_pMainWnd` member of the active `CWinThread` object. It is prototyped as follows:

```
CWnd * AFXAPI AfxGetMainWnd();
```

> **NOTE**
>
> Don't assume that every `CWinThread` object in an application has the same `m_pMainWnd` object. When a new `CWinThread` object is constructed, it "inherits" the `m_pMainWnd` pointer from the thread that created it. However, each thread can change this pointer at any time.

Creation and Use

Like other system handle wrapper classes, CWnd provides many of the standard mechanisms for creating system handles or attaching existing ones. The methods supported are Create, CreateEx, CreateControl, FromHandle, FromHandlePermanent, Attach, and Detach.

Create and CreateEx

The Create and CreateEx methods map very closely to the Win32 APIs CreateWindow and CreateWindowEx. Like the Win32 APIs, the difference between the two is the ability to specify extended window styles in the extended version. These methods are declared as follows:

```
virtual BOOL Create(LPCTSTR lpszClassName, LPCTSTR lpszWindowName,
            DWORD dwStyle, const RECT& rect, CWnd *pParentWnd,
            UINT nID, CCreateContext* pContext = NULL);
BOOL CreateEx(DWORD dwExStyle, LPCTSTR lpszClassName,
➡LPCTSTR lpszWindowName,
            DWORD dwStyle, int x, int y, int nWidth, int nHeight,
            HWND hWndParent, HMENU nIDorHMenu, LPVOID lpParam = NULL);
BOOL CreateEx(DWORD dwExStyle, LPCTSTR lpszClassName,
➡LPCTSTR lpszWindowName,
            DWORD dwStyle, const RECT& rect, CWnd *pParentWnd,
            ➡UINT nID,
            LPVOID lpParam = NULL);
```

CreateControl

Use the CreateControl method to instantiate an ActiveX control and associate it with the CWnd object. Specify either the control's ProgID or CLSID for the class name. The various forms of this method are declared as follows:

```
BOOL CreateControl(REFCLSID clsid, LPCTSTR pszWindowName, DWORD dwStyle,
    const RECT& rect, CWnd* pParentWnd, UINT nID, CFile* pPersist=NULL,
    BOOL bStorage=FALSE, BSTR bstrLicKey=NULL);
BOOL CreateControl(LPCTSTR pszClass, LPCTSTR pszWindowName, DWORD dwStyle,
    const RECT& rect, CWnd* pParentWnd, UINT nID, CFile* pPersist=NULL,
    BOOL bStorage=FALSE, BSTR bstrLicKey=NULL);
BOOL CreateControl( REFCLSID clsid, LPCTSTR pszWindowName, DWORD dwStyle,
    const POINT* ppt, const SIZE* psize, CWnd* pParentWnd, UINT nID,
    CFile* pPersist = NULL, BOOL bStorage = FALSE, BSTR bstrLicKey = NULL );
```

FromHandle and FromHandlePermanent

The FromHandle and FromHandlePermanent static functions look up and return an existing CWnd object based upon a passed system window handle (HWND). If a matching CWnd object does not exist, the FromHandle function creates a temporary CWnd object and attaches the specified handle to it. These functions are prototyped as shown here:

```
static CWND * PASCAL FromHandle(HWND hWnd);
static CWND * PASCAL FromHandlePermanent(HWND hWnd);
```

Attach and Detach

You can associate and unassociate a system window handle (HWND) with a CWnd object using the Attach and Detach methods. After you've attached the handle to the object, the object is responsible for releasing the handle back to the system, unless you detach the handle. These methods are declared as follows:

```
BOOL Attach(HWND hWndNew);
HWND Detach();
```

ExecuteDlgInit

The ExecuteDlgInit method creates a dialog window based upon the specified dialog resource. Use this function if you need to load a window from a dialog resource. It is recommended that you try to use the CDialog class first, however. This method is declared as shown here:

```
BOOL ExecuteDlgInit(LPCTSTR lpszResourceName);
BOOL ExecuteDlgInit(LPVOID lpResource);
```

PreCreateWindow

The PreCreateWindow virtual function is called before a window gets created. You can override this function if you need to modify the CREATESTRUCT of a window before it gets created. If you need to terminate the construction of a window, return FALSE. This function is declared as follows:

```
virtual BOOL PreCreateWindow(CREATESTRUCT& cs);
```

Subclassing Windows

Briefly, subclassing a window is the process of hooking its window procedure to change how that window receives and responds to specific window events. You can subclass a window to give that control a different look and feel. Subclassing windows is described in detail in Chapter 5, "Custom Control Development." The methods that support subclassing are SubclassWindow, SubclassDlgItem, UnsubclassWindow, and PreSubclassWindow.

SubclassWindow, SubclassDlgItem, and UnsubclassWindow

The SubclassWindow and SubclassDlgItem methods provide an easy mechanism to hook into the window procedure of another window. After the window has been subclassed, you can respond to system and window messages passed to that control's window procedure via the MFC message map mechanism. The UnsubclassWindow method returns the subclassed window to its original state.

These methods are declared as follows:

```
BOOL SubclassWindow(HWND hWnd);
BOOL SubclassDlgItem(UINT nID, CWnd *pParent);
HWND UnsubclassWindow();
```

PreSubclassWindow

Your CWnd-derived object receives the PreSubclassWindow notification prior to being subclassed. If you choose to override this virtual function, your object can perform whatever operations it needs to do prior to being subclassed. This function is declared as follows:

```
virtual void PreSubclassWindow();
```

GetSafeHwnd

Use the GetSafeHwnd method to obtain the window handle attached to the window object. It is called "safe" because it returns NULL if the this pointer of the CWnd object is equal to NULL. Additionally, this method returns NULL if the CWnd object is not attached to a window, or is attached to a NULL window handle (usually meaning the desktop window). This public method is declared as follows:

```
HWND GetSafeHwnd() const;
```

GetStyle, GetExStyle, ModifyStyle, and ModifyStyleEx

Use the GetStyle, GetExStyle, ModifyStyle, and ModifyStyleEx methods to obtain and change the style and extended style flags for a window. These public methods are declared thus:

```
DWORD GetStyle() const;
DWORD GetExStyle() const;
BOOL ModifyStyle(DWORD dwRemove, DWORD dwAdd, UINT nFlags = 0);
BOOL ModifyStyleEx(DWORD dwRemove, DWORD dwAdd, UINT nFlags = 0);
```

GetOwner and SetOwner

Use the GetOwner and SetOwner methods to obtain and modify the owner of the current window. Some controls, such as CToolBar, send notification messages to their owner windows. If the window has no owner, the parent becomes its owner. Unlike the parent/child relationships, owner/ownee relationships between windows do not limit the drawing area for the owned window. These public methods are declared as follows:

```
CWnd *GetOwner() const;
(e)void SetOwner(CWnd *pOwnerWnd);
```

ToolTip Support

ToolTips are the small yellow textual pop-ups that appear when the mouse pointer is positioned over user interface elements. You can control their appearance using the methods described in the following sections.

EnableToolTips and OnToolHitTest

Use the `EnableToolTips` method to turn on or off the display of ToolTips for the current window. You can override the `OnToolHitTest` virtual function to control the location and positioning of the ToolTip message. These methods are declared as shown here:

```
BOOL EnableToolTips(BOOL bEnable);
virtual int OnToolHitTest(CPoint point, TOOLINFO *pTI) const;
```

UpdateData

You can override the `UpdateData` virtual function to either initialize data into the window's child controls or validate and save the data. If the `bSaveAndValidate` parameter is equal to `TRUE`, your function must validate and save the child controls' data. Otherwise, you must initialize the child controls from their appropriate data source.

This public virtual function is declared as follows:

```
BOOL UpdateData(BOOL bSaveAndValidate = TRUE);
```

This method is the primary mechanism for Dialog Data Validation (DDV) and Dialog Data Exchange (DDX). For more information, refer to the section "Dialog Data Exchange" section in Chapter 2, "MFC Dialogs, Controls, and Data Interaction."

UpdateDialogControls

Use the `UpdateDialogControls` method to disable child controls, menu items, and toolbar buttons if no handler exists for them. This method is declared as follows:

```
void UpdateDialogControls(CCmdTarget *pTarget, BOOL bDisableIfNoHandler);
```

CenterWindow

The `CenterWindow` method centers a window relative to another window. By default, it centers the window relative to its parent. If the window is owned, it centers the window relative to its owner. This public method is declared as follows:

```
void CenterWindow(CWnd *relativeTo = NULL);
```

RunModalLoop, ContinueModal, and EndModalLoop

Use the `RunModalLoop`, `ContinueModal`, and `EndModalLoop` methods to make the specified window modal. `RunModalLoop` places the window into a modal mode. The window remains modal until your application calls `EndModalLoop`, which causes `ContinueModal` to return `FALSE` and the modal loop to be ended. These methods are declared as follows:

```
int RunModalLoop(DWORD dwFlags = 0);
virtual BOOL ContinueModal();
virtual void EndModalLoop(int nResult);
```

Win32 Methods

As an experienced Win32 programmer, you are probably familiar with many of the functions and windows messages. Many of the methods in the `CWnd` class map (more or less) directly to the Win32 API functions of the same name (but without the `HWND` parameter, of course). Others map to some of the standard notification messages. Please consult documentation on each of these Win32 API functions and messages for more information.

Arranged by functional category, these methods are as follows:

Message Handling

`SendMessage`, `PostMessage`, `IsDialogMessage`, `SendNotifyMessage`

Window Text

`SetWindowText`, `GetWindowText`, `GetWindowTextLength`, `SetFont`, `GetFont`

Menu Support

`GetMenu`, `SetMenu`, `DrawMenuBar`, `GetSystemMenu`, `HiliteMenuItem`

Window Size and Positioning

`IsIconic`, `IsZoomed`, `MoveWindow`, `SetWindowRgn`, `GetWindowRgn`, `SetWindowPos`, `ArrangeIconicWindows`, `BringWindowToTop`, `GetWindowRect`, `GetClientRect`, `GetWindowPlacement`, `SetWindowPlacement`

Coordinate Mapping

`ClientToScreen`, `ScreenToClient`, `MapWindowPoints`

Painting

`BeginPaint`, `EndPaint`, `GetDC`, `GetWindowDC`, `ReleaseDC`, `UpdateWindow`, `SetRedraw`, `GetUpdateRect`, `GetUpdateRgn`, `Invalidate`, `InvalidateRect`, `InvalidateRgn`, `ValidateRect`, `ValidateRgn`, `ShowWindow`, `IsWindowVisible`, `ShowOwnedPopups`, `GetDCEx`, `LockWindowUpdate`, `UnlockWindowUpdate`, `RedrawWindow`, `Print`, `PrintClient`

Timer

`SetTimer`, `KillTimer`

Window Styles

IsWindowEnabled, EnableWindow, GetActiveWindow, SetActiveWindow,
SetForegroundWindow, GetForegroundWindow, GetCapture, SetCapture,
GetFocus, SetFocus, GetDesktopWindow

Child Window

GetDlgCtrlID, SetDlgCtrlID, GetDlgItem, CheckDlgButton, CheckRadioButton,
GetCheckedRadioButton, DlgDirList, DlgDirListComboBox, DlgDirSelect,
DlgDirSelectComboBox, GetDlgItemInt, GetDlgItemText, GetNextDlgGroupItem,
GetNextDlgTabItem, IsDlgButtonChecked, SendDlgItemMessage, SetDlgItemInt,
SetDlgItemText

Scrolling

GetScrollPos, GetScrollRange, ScrollWindow, SetScrollPos, SetScrollRange,
ScrollWindowEx, GetScrollInfo, SetScrollInfo, GetScrollLimit,
ShowScrollBar, EnableScrollBarCtrl, GetScrollBarCtrl

Z-order and Location

ChildWindowFromPoint, FindWindow, GetNextWindow, GetTopWindow, GetWindow,
GetLastActivePopup, IsChild, GetParent, SetParent, WindowFromPoint,
DestroyWindow

Alert

FlashWindow, MessageBox

Clipboard

ChangeClipboardChain, SetClipboardViewer, OpenClipboard,
GetClipboardOwner, GetClipboardViewer, GetOpenClipboardWindow

Caret

CreateCaret, CreateSolidCaret, CreateGrayCaret, GetCaretPos, SetCaretPos,
HideCaret, ShowCaret

Shell Interaction

DragAcceptFiles

Icon

SetIcon, GetIcon

Help

GetWindowContextHelpId, SetWindowContextHelpId

CFrameWnd

The CFrameWnd class, derived from CWnd, is a window that contains the title bar, system menu, border, minimize/maximize buttons, and an active view window. The CFrameWnd class supports the single document interface (SDI).

For multiple document interface (MDI) frame windows, use CMDIFrameWnd for the work-space frame and CMDIChildWnd for the MDI child windows. Both of the aforementioned classes are derived from CFrameWnd.

For the thinner, toolbox-style frame window, use the CMiniFrameWnd class. To support in-place editing, use the COleIPFrameWnd class.

Functions

The CFrameWnd class provides several functions that allow you to obtain the active document, view, and frame. In addition, there are functions to interact with the title bar and status bar text. These functions are described in this section.

GetActiveDocument, GetActiveView, SetActiveView, and GetActiveFrame

The GetActiveDocument, GetActiveView, and GetActiveFrame methods return a pointer to the current document, view, or frame, respectively. The SetActiveView method activates a view window. These methods are declared as follows:

```
virtual CDocument *GetActiveDocument();
virtual CFrameWnd *GetActiveFrame();
CView *GetActiveView() const;
void SetActiveView(CView *pViewNew, BOOL bNotify = TRUE);
```

GetTitle and SetTitle

The GetTitle and SetTitle methods obtain and set the text in the frame window's title bar. These methods are declared as shown here:

```
CString GetTitle() const;
void SetTitle(LPCTSTR lpszTitle);
```

SetMessageText

The SetMessageText method sets the status bar text (in pane zero of the status bar). You can specify either a string or a string resource identifier. The variations of this method are declared as follows:

```
void SetMessageText(LPCTSTR lpszText);
void SetMessageText(UINT nID);
```

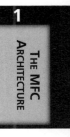

BeginModalState, EndModalState, and InModalState

The `BeginModalState`, `EndModalState`, and `InModalState` methods control the modality of the frame window. Use `BeginModalState` to enter the modal state, `ExitModalState` to end the modal state, and `InModalState` to determine your current state. These methods are declared as follows:

```
virtual void BeginModalState();
virtual void EndModalState();
BOOL InModalState() const;
```

CView

The `CView` class, derived from `CWnd`, is responsible for displaying/printing and handling all user interactions for the document attached to it. You need to derive classes from `CView` to present your document's data to the user in the required ways.

When you create a `CView`-derived class, at the minimum, you need to override the `OnDraw` and `OnUpdate` methods.

Methods

The `CView` class provides methods that you can override to allow your application to respond to external events (such as redraw requests, window activation, and document changes). Additionally, there is a method to return a pointer to the document associated with the view.

OnDraw

Override the `OnDraw` method to draw your document view to the passed device context. This method handles drawing both to the display and a printer. If you need to have printer versus screen drawing logic within this method, call `CDC::IsPrinting` to determine the current state. The `OnDraw` method is declared as shown here:

```
virtual void OnDraw(CDC *pDC) = 0;
```

OnUpdate

Override the `OnUpdate` method to allow your view class to be notified when the document has changed. This method is invoked when `CDocument::UpdateAllViews` is called or when the view is initially attached to the document, but before it is displayed.

When you receive this notification, do not redraw the changes directly. You can cause the changes to be redrawn by calling `CWnd::InvalidateRect`.

The OnUpdate method is declared as follows:

```
virtual void OnUpdate(CView *pSender, LPARAM lHint, CObject *pHint);
```

GetDocument

The GetDocument method returns the document to which this view is attached. It is declared as follows:

```
CDocument *GetDocument() const;
```

OnActivateView and OnActivateFrame

Override the OnActivateView and OnActivateFrame if your view needs to respond in some way to its activation or deactivation. These virtual functions are declared as follows:

```
virtual void OnActivateView(BOOL bActivate, CView *pActivateView,
                            CView *pDeactivateView);
virtual void OnActivateFrame(UINT nState, CFrameWnd *pFrameWnd);
```

CDocument

HOW ARE DOCUMENTS RELATED TO VIEWS?

With MFC, you can partition your application into a document and one or more views of that document. A *document* contains the data that your application works with. A *view* is a graphical representation of that data. Hence, all the views reference the same document. If a change is made to the document from one view, all the other views get updated with that change.

An example of a document could be a set of data that correlates the names of cities with a value representing each city's population.

You could have several types of views of this same data. One view could be a text list that allows the user to sort itself by either city name or by population. Another view could display a map that puts the population value next to the appropriate city name. Yet another view could be the same as the first view text list, except scrolled down to a different location in the list. So, in this case, you have three total view instances of two view types.

To create a document, derive a class that represents your data from the CDocument class. To create a view type, derive a class from the CView or a CView-derived class.

For more information about MFC document and view support, refer to Chapter 7.

GetTitle and SetTitle

The `GetTitle` and `SetTitle` methods obtain and set the text in the frame window's title bar for all the views attached to this document. These methods are declared as shown here:

```
const CString& GetTitle() const;
virtual void SetTitle(LPCTSTR lpszTitle);
```

GetPathName and SetPathName

The `GetPathName` and `SetPathName` methods obtain and set the fully qualified path associated with the document. You only need to call these methods if you are also overriding `OnOpenDocument` and `OnSaveDocument`. The `GetPathName` and `SetPathName` methods are declared as shown here:

```
const CString& GetPathName() const;
virtual void SetPathname(LPCTSTR lpszPathname, BOOL bAddToMRU = TRUE);
```

GetDocTemplate

The `GetDocTemplate` method returns the `CDocTemplate` object upon which this document is based. If this document does not have a document template associated with it, `NULL` is returned. This method is declared as follows:

```
CDocTemplate *GetDocTemplate() const;
```

IsModified, SetModifiedFlag, and SaveModified

The `IsModified`, `SetModifiedFlag`, and `SaveModified` methods are used to control the modification state within the document object. Call `SetModifiedFlag` whenever you make a change to your document. To determine the current modification state, call `IsModified`. If you want to prompt the user about saving the document modification in a way different from the default implementation, override the `SaveModified` method.

These methods are declared as shown here:

```
virtual BOOL IsModified();
virtual void SetModifiedFlag(BOOL bModified = TRUE);
virtual BOOL SaveModified();
```

AddView, RemoveView, and OnChangedViewList

Call the `AddView` and `RemoveView` methods to attach and detach a `CView`-derived object to and from this document. Each successful call to `AddView` and `RemoveView` results in a call to `OnChangedViewList`. The default implementation of `OnChangedViewList` deletes the document when the last view is detached. These public methods are declared as shown here:

```
void AddView(CView *pView);
void RemoveView(CView *pView);
virtual void OnChangedViewList();
```

GetFirstViewPosition and GetNextView

The `GetFirstViewPosition` and `GetNextView` methods enable you to iterate through all the view objects (`CView`) that currently are associated with the document. If no views are available, `GetFirstViewPosition` returns `NULL`.

These public methods are declared as follows:

```
virtual POSITION GetFirstViewPosition() const;
virtual CView *GetNextView(POSITION& pos) const;
```

> **NOTE**
>
> Because `GetNextView` updates the position value, always check that the current position is not `NULL` before calling `GetNextView` again.

UpdateAllViews

Use the `UpdateAllViews` method to have the `CView::OnUpdate` method to be called on one or all views associated with this document. If the `pSender` parameter is equal to `NULL`, the update is broadcast to all views associated with this document. This method is declared as shown here:

```
void UpdateAllViews(CView *pSender, LPARAM lHint = 0, CObject
➡*pHint = NULL);
```

DeleteContents

Override the `DeleteContents` method to delete your document's data before the document is destroyed or reused. Because SDI applications have only one document, it is reused. Consequently, it is important to delete your document's data in this method. This method is declared as follows:

```
virtual void DeleteContents();
```

OnNewDocument, OnOpenDocument, OnSaveDocument, and OnCloseDocument

Override the OnNewDocument, OnOpenDocument, OnSaveDocument, and OnCloseDocument virtual functions to respond to each of the new, open, save, and close events for the document.

> **TIP**
>
> Because a single document object is used in SDI applications, you must initialize it by overriding the OnNewDocument method.

These functions are declared as follows:

```
virtual BOOL OnNewDocument();
virtual BOOL OnOpenDocument(LPCTSTR lpszPathName);
virtual BOOL OnSaveDocument(LPCTSTR lpszPathName);
virtual void OnCloseDocument();
```

ReportSaveLoadException

Override the ReportSaveLoadException virtual function if you need to provide custom error reporting when an exception is caught while saving or loading the document. This virtual function is declared as shown here:

```
virtual void ReportSaveLoadException(LPCTSTR lpszPathName,
                                     CException *e, BOOL bSaving,
                                     UINT nIDPDefault);
```

GetFile and ReleaseFile

Override the GetFile and ReleaseFile methods to provide a custom mechanism for opening and closing the document data file. These methods are declared as follows:

```
virtual CFile *GetFile(LPCTSTR lpszFileName, UINT nOpenFlags,
                       CFileException *pError);
virtual void ReleaseFile(CFile *pFile, BOOL bAbort);
```

CanCloseFrame and PreCloseFrame

The CanCloseFrame and PreCloseFrame methods give you an opportunity to handle the closing of document views contained in frame windows. Override the CanCloseFrame virtual function if you need to provide special handling when frame windows are closed. The default implementation prompts the user to save the document upon closing the last frame. Override the `PreCloseFrame` virtual function to provide custom handling when a frame window containing views associated with a document is closed. These methods are declared as shown here:

```
virtual void CanCloseFrame(CFrameWnd *pFrame);
virtual void PreCloseFrame(CFrameWnd *pFrame);
```

Summary

This chapter covers the fundamental architectural classes involved in almost every MFC-based application. You will incorporate all these classes either directly or indirectly in every MFC GUI application that you write.

The `CObject` class is the root of all other MFC classes and provides general methods that are useful to classes derived from it. The runtime type information allows each class to identify its type. The serialization support provides a mechanism for persisting the object to any byte stream. Finally, the diagnostic support provides a standard way of dumping the contents of an object and ensuring that the object is in a valid state.

The `CCmdTarget`, `CWinThread`, and `CWinApp` classes are a line of related classes in the MFC class hierarchy that form the basis of your GUI application. These classes allow your application to receive and process GUI events. Additionally, these classes provide the general framework for the controller part of the object-oriented model/view/controller (MVC) paradigm.

The object-oriented model and view classes are supported via MFC's document/view architecture and the `CDocument` and `CView` classes, respectively. When you derive from each of these classes, you can separate your application's business logic from its display logic.

Finally, the document views are displayed in GUI windows that are represented by the `CFrameWnd` and `CWnd` classes. The windowing classes are the fundamental objects that manage your GUI application and present its data to the user.

MFC Dialogs, Controls, and Data Interaction

by Bill Heyman

IN THIS CHAPTER

CHAPTER **2**

This chapter describes the general techniques for creating dialog-based MFC applications using Microsoft Visual Studio. If you have already created MFC applications using AppWizard, you are probably already familiar with this material and might want to move to the more in-depth topics in later chapters.

Creating an Application

This section describes the MFC AppWizard supplied by Visual Studio. It leads you through the process of generating a new dialog-based MFC application and describes the basic features of the generated code.

Starting and Using MFC AppWizard

If you want, you can certainly derive your own classes from CWinApp and create your own MFC application from scratch. However, you can save yourself much effort by using the AppWizard, which automatically creates a lot of the common application code for you. The AppWizard gives you a jump start on getting into the actual coding of the business logic necessary for your application—without having to worry about the MFC infrastructure issues initially.

Starting the AppWizard is easy. In Microsoft Visual Studio, simply choose File, New from the menu. This displays the dialog shown in Figure 2.1, which gives you a choice of new projects to create.

FIGURE 2.1

The Projects tab of the New dialog displaying a list of the types of projects that you can create.

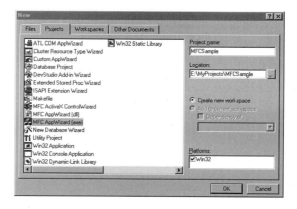

Because you want to create an MFC application, choose the project type entry named MFC AppWizard (exe). In the Location entry field, type the parent directory to contain this project (in Figure 2.1, e:\MyProjects was typed). Finally, in the Project Name, type the name of your project (in the Figure 2.1, `MFCSample` was typed). When you type the project name, the project location is automatically extended to have a subdirectory with the name of the project (in the Figure 2.1, this is how `E:\MyProjects\MFCSample` was created).

NOTE

Among the project types, you could also choose MFC AppWizard (dll). Choose this AppWizard if you want to package your MFC application in a dynamic link library to be used by other applications.

You might also note that the Create New Workspace radio button is automatically selected for you. A *project* contains all of the file references and compile and link options to allow you to create a single executable (EXE) or dynamic link library (DLL). When you have a more sophisticated application that has multiple DLLs and EXEs, you can associate all of your projects in an entity called a *workspace*. In the case of MFCSample, you are only creating a single executable—so a single workspace is appropriate. Choose OK to move to the start of the MFC AppWizard.

NOTE

You can add a project to an existing workspace at a later time, by opening that workspace. From the FileView tab, select the Workspace entry (on the top line), and right-click to display the context menu. Choose Insert Project into Workspace to display a dialog that allows you to select the project to add to the workspace.

Also, if you need to logically associate your EXE and DLL projects in multiple groupings, you can add your projects to more than one workspace.

The MFC AppWizard generates the initial code for your application, so you don't have to code it by hand. Consequently, it guides you through the process of defining the general characteristics of your application, so it can generate code suited to your application's needs. Figure 2.2 shows the MFC AppWizard - Step 1 dialog box.

The MFC AppWizard - Step 1 dialog box enables you to select whether your application uses the Single Document Interface (SDI), Multiple Document Interface (MDI), or is dialog-based. In addition, you choose whether or not your application uses the MFC document/view architecture, which separates the logic that displays your data to the user from logic that interacts with your data. Refer to Chapter 7, "The Document/View Architecture," for more specific information on using the MFC document/view architecture. Because the document/view architecture is described later (and to keep things simple), the MFC Sample application is a dialog-based application. The document/view architecture is not available to dialog-based applications; hence, that check box is disabled. Click Next to proceed to the next MFC AppWizard step.

FIGURE 2.2

The first MFC AppWizard dialog box enables you to specify whether your application is a single document, multiple documents, or dialog-based.

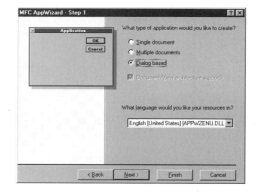

SDI, MDI, AND DIALOG-BASED APPLICATIONS

A Single Document Interface (SDI) application is like the Paint accessory shipped with Windows. It has a single client area and often has a pull-down menu and toolbar. Use an SDI application when each instance of an application interacts with a single file or data and it displays data within a client area.

A Multiple Document Interface (MDI) application is like Microsoft Word. It has multiple client areas, but often has a single pull-down menu and toolbar. Use an MDI application when you want the user to have multiple documents open within the same application.

A dialog-based application is similar to the AppWizard within Visual Studio. It consists of a single form-based window with any of the various Windows controls, such as pushbuttons, list boxes, and entry fields. Use a dialog-based application when you do not need a client area in which to draw in your application or when your application is form-based and needs only the various Windows controls to interact with the user.

The MFC AppWizard - Step 2 of 4 dialog enables you to specify some of the features of the generated code. These include whether or not your application has an About box,

WinSock capabilities, and ActiveX controls, and whether it supports automation. In addition, you can specify text that appears in your dialog's title bar. This dialog is shown in Figure 2.3. Click Next to move to the next AppWizard step.

FIGURE 2.3

The Step 2 MFC AppWizard dialog enables you to add an About box and specify title bar text for your application.

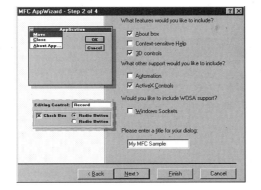

Figure 2.4 shows the MFC AppWizard - Step 3 of 4 dialog. Using this dialog, you can specify whether you'd like your application to appear as an MFC Standard application or as a Windows Explorer-like application, with a tree view in one child window and a list view in another. In addition, you can indicate whether you'd like to link the MFC class library statically as part of your application—or have your application use the MFC dynamic link library. Click Next to move to the final step.

FIGURE 2.4

The Step 3 MFC AppWizard dialog allows you to choose to make your application appear like Windows Explorer.

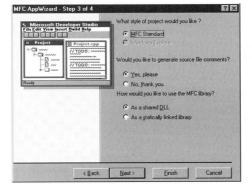

The MFC AppWizard - Step 4 of 4 dialog is informational and requires no input from you. It lists the classes and source files that will be generated for your application. For the MFCSample project, Figure 2.5 shows the classes and files that are generated. Click Finish to complete the AppWizard process.

FIGURE 2.5

The Step 4 MFC AppWizard dialog shows you the classes and source files that AppWizard will generate for your application.

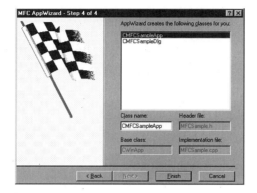

The AppWizard-Generated Code

After AppWizard has generated code for your MFC application, your current project will be loaded into the Visual Studio environment. You might be interested to know that, without any modification, you can compile and run this application. Of course, without the logic that you need to add, this application won't do anything specific.

On the left side of the Visual Studio environment, there are three tabs containing different views of your application: FileView, ClassView, and ResourceView.

The FileView Tab

The rightmost tab, FileView, is shown in Figure 2.6 for the MFCSample application. There are five source files that are used to contain the definitions for the primary application classes. These files are MFCSample.cpp and MFCSampleDlg.cpp. The description of these files' contents is discussed with the ClassView tab later in this section.

FIGURE 2.6

The FileView tab in Visual Studio for MFCSample.

Other files of interest include MFCSample.rc and Resource.h. The MFCSample.rc file contains the binary resource definitions of the icons, string table, version information, and dialogs for the application. Additionally, a file named Resource.h accompanies this file to define the numeric ids for each of the resources. The actual resources are discussed with the ResourceView tab later in this section.

Some of the more intriguing files that AppWizard generates for every MFC application are StdAfx.cpp and StdAfx.h. These are common files that are used to improve compile-time performance for MFC applications. Specifically, StdAfx.h is included by every source file first and contains the #include lines for each of the MFC class library headers. If you do this, this header file (and all of the MFC headers) can be parsed and pre-compiled into a binary form. Consequently, when subsequent source files are compiled, the compiler does not have to read in and parse all of the system header files. Thus, each of the source files can be compiled much faster.

> **CAUTION**
>
> Although each project can contain files of the same name (StdAfx.h and Resource.h), these files are likely to have different contents, particularly if the AppWizard options are different between projects.

The ClassView Tab

The leftmost tab, ClassView, for the MFCSample application is shown in Figure 2.7. The class view of your application lists all of the classes in it, as well as all of the methods and data members contained within each class. For the MFCSample application, three classes are generated: CAboutDlg, CMFCSampleApp, and CMFCSampleDlg.

FIGURE 2.7
The ClassView tab for MFCSample in Visual Studio.

The primary application class that AppWizard generated is named CMFCSampleApp. Declared in MFCSample.h and defined in MFCSample.cpp, this class is derived from CWinApp and represents the main class for your MFC application. See Chapter 1, "The MFC Architecture," for more information on the CWinApp class.

The `CMFCSampleDlg` class represents the main window of the dialog-based MFCSample application. The `CMFCSampleDlg` class is derived from the `CDialog` class, and you can modify it to add the data and logic required for your application. This class is associated with a generated dialog resource, named `IDD_MFCSAMPLE_DIALOG`, which you can edit via the ResourceView tab. The `CMFCSample` class is declared in MFCSampleDlg.h and defined in MFCSampleDlg.cpp.

Likewise, the `CAboutDlg` class represents the About box in your application. You can add methods and data to this class if you need to modify the look and feel of the modal window that is displayed when Help, About is selected from your application's pull-down menu. The `CAboutDlg` class is derived from `CDialog` and is associated with a generated dialog resource, named `IDD_ABOUTBOX`. The `CAboutDlg` class declaration is located in MFCSampleDlg.h and its definition is located in MFCSampleDlg.cpp.

The ResourceView Tab

The final tab available for browsing your application in the Visual Studio environment is the ResourceView tab. Shown in Figure 2.8, this tab enables you to browse and edit the binary resources associated with your application. The actual resources are contained in the file MFCSample.rc, and the numeric identifiers for the resources are stored in a file named Resources.h.

FIGURE 2.8

*The ResourceView
tab for
MFCSample in
Visual Studio.*

The MFC AppWizard generated four different types of resources for your application: dialog, icon, string table, and version. Each of these types has one or more instances of that type of resource.

The dialog resource contains the layout and controls contained on your application's dialog windows. MFC AppWizard generated two dialog resources for the MFC Sample application, named `IDD_ABOUTBOX` and `IDD_MFCSAMPLE_DIALOG`, representing the About box and the main window, respectively. By double-clicking on the dialog's name (such as `IDD_ABOUTBOX`), you can edit and make changes to the layout of and controls within that dialog. By default, the About box dialog contains a generic icon, application name, and copyright string, and the main window dialog contains an OK and a Cancel pushbutton. You will certainly need to edit both of these dialogs before shipping your application.

MFCAppWizard also generated a graphical icon resource named `IDR_MAINFRAME` for the MFCSample application. The `IDR_MAINFRAME` icon is the image that appears in your application's upper-left hand corner of the main frame, in its About box, and is associated with your executable.

The next resource type is the string table resource, which maps numeric identifiers to language-dependent strings. If you double-click on the string table resource, you can see that the MFC AppWizard generated a single string that can be used in a menu resource within the application for displaying the About box.

> **NOTE**
>
> It is a good idea to isolate all of your language-dependent strings into a string resource table. In this way, your application code refers only to numeric identifiers, rather than literal strings. If you use string resources, when you need to translate your application to another language, the string tables can be translated to that language without change to your source code.

Finally, the MFC AppWizard generated a version resource named `VS_VERSION_INFO` for the MFCSample application. The version information contains both standard numeric information (such as a four-part version number, like 1.0.0.1, and an operating system flag on which the application can run, such as `VOS__WINDOWS32`) and standard and user-definable string information (such as an application description and copyright string). Utilities such as installation programs can use this information to compare one executable file to another to decide whether they need to replace an older version with a new one, for example.

Modifying the Application

At this point, you have a shell MFC dialog-based application called MFCSample. Of course, it contains no business logic, and the dialog is pretty boring with the lonely OK and Cancel buttons. If you want, you can run and debug it from the Visual Studio environment. Next, you can starting doing something interesting—like adding more controls and actually having the application do something.

Adding Dialog Controls

Certainly the first thing that you need to do is to add controls to your dialog. Otherwise, you cannot add code to handle and trigger events for the controls. Consequently, you'll add a few basic controls to the MFCSample application to demonstrate some of the features of dialog-based MFC applications.

This chapter glosses over the actual functionality of the controls it describes and defers the in-depth analysis of control events and behavior to Chapter 3, "The Windows Common Controls." However, this chapter does introduce you to the look and feel of the controls that you can add to your application.

In the MFCSample application, there are simply some pushbuttons that demonstrate some of the standard dialogs available to you as well as some entry fields and static text fields to demonstrate Dialog Data Exchange (DDX). The MFCSample main window is shown in Figure 2.9.

FIGURE 2.9

The MFCSample main window containing pushbuttons and other controls.

Dialog Control Types

A *control* is a specialized GUI object that can allow passive or active user interaction with the application. Controls usually serve a limited number of purposes and provide an intuitive means of the user interacting with those purposes. Controls can be sorted in three basic categories: information presentation, information request, and information modifiers. Some controls can be classified in only one category, whereas others could be classified in more than one category.

An information presentation type of control simply displays data to the user. Perhaps the most basic information presentation controls are the static text and the picture controls. Other controls such as the tree control and the list box can be classified in the other two categories—but, in any case, still present information to the end user.

The second type of control is the information request control, which enables the user to obtain more information from the application. The most basic control serving this purpose is the button control. However, depending on how the application is written, a tree control and list box could be in this category also; namely, where an application adds more data to the tree control when a node is expanded and a list box item is double-clicked.

Finally, the last type of control is the information modifier, which enables the user to change the application's data. The edit box, radio button, and check box are the most basic controls that serve this purpose. Alternatively, the list control can be used to serve this purpose if it allows data to be edited within its cells.

Furthermore, three classifications of Windows controls are available to you through the Visual Studio resource editor palette. These are the standard controls, the common controls, and the custom controls.

Standard Controls

The standard controls are the classic controls that have been a part of Windows since its earliest days. These are the most basic controls that all Windows users know and love. These include buttons, list boxes, check boxes, radio buttons, and scrollbars. In the subsequent sections, the behavior and use of each of these controls is discussed briefly. Again, refer to Chapter 3 for a more in-depth discussion of the methods and events for each of these controls that are programmatically available to your application.

Picture

The picture control represents a set of information presentation controls available to your application. This control can contain an icon, a bitmap, a metafile, a rectangular outline (called a frame), or a filled rectangle, depending on the style flag set at design time. Use this control to display an image or draw a filled or outlined rectangle in your dialog. Figure 2.10 shows an example of a picture control with the default MFC icon in it.

FIGURE 2.10

A picture control with the default MFC icon in it.

Static Text

The static text control is another information presentation control. It simply displays a line of text to the user—however, the user typically does not directly interact with this text in any way. This control simply displays text to the user. Figure 2.11 shows an example of a static text control.

FIGURE 2.11

A static text control with an output-only message in it.

Edit Box

The edit box control is very similar to the static text control, except that the user can actually edit the textual data contained within it. Use this type of control when you want the user to edit a single line or multiple lines of textual data. It is considered to be both an information presentation and an information modifier type of control. Figure 2.12 shows an example of an edit box control.

FIGURE 2.12

An edit box control just waiting for its text to be modified.

Group Box

The group box control is an information presentation control that provides simply a way of grouping other controls. Group boxes are often used to contain a set of radio buttons that provide a mutually exclusive choice. Figure 2.13 demonstrates this case.

FIGURE 2.13

A group box control with a set of mutually exclusive radio button choices within it.

Button

The button control (also known as a pushbutton) is an information request control. Use this control to enable your application to respond to a user-triggered event. Perhaps the most common control on dialogs is a button named Cancel that typically dismisses the dialog without saving its data. Figure 2.14 shows a Cancel button.

FIGURE 2.14

A button control named Cancel.

Check Box

The check box control is often used as an information modifier. It can represent either two or three states; two states are true and false and three states are true, false, and indeterminate. Use this control when you'd like the user to choose a Boolean state. Figure 2.15 shows a check box.

FIGURE 2.15

A check box control enables the user to specify his or her preferences.

Radio Button

The radio button control is another information modifier. Rarely used in isolation, this control is often part of a group of mutually exclusive choices. Use a group of these controls when you'd like the user to choose one of a finite number of selections that are known at application design time. Figure 2.13, earlier in the chapter, shows such a group of radio buttons.v

Combo Box

Like the radio button, the combo box control is another information modifier. It provides a similar purpose to a group of radio buttons, except the finite number of selections can be specified at runtime. Using the combo box, the user can choose one of its entries. There are three types of combo box available to you: simple, drop-down, and drop-list. The simple and drop-list combo boxes are different only in visual appearance. The drop-down combo box allows the user to enter a new entry in the edit box portion of the control. Figures 2.16 and 2.17 demonstrate each of these types.

FIGURE 2.16

A simple combo box control.

FIGURE 2.17

A drop-down or drop-list combo box control.

List Box

The list box control is another information modifier. It displays a list of choices to the user—and, depending on its actual style, the user can choose either none, one, or many of its items. With a single selection list box, only one entry can be selected, which makes its behavior similar to that of a simple combo box. Figure 2.18 shows a list box.

FIGURE **2.18**

A list box control.

Horizontal and Vertical Scrollbars

The scrollbar control is often used to enable the user to move a graphical image or text within the current view. Additionally, it can enable the user to select a contiguous range within a finite set, similar to the Slider control (described following). Figures 2.19 and 2.20 show a horizontal and a vertical scrollbar, respectively.

FIGURE **2.19**

*A horizontal
scrollbar control.*

FIGURE **2.20**

*A vertical
scrollbar control.*

Common Controls

As Windows matured and the user-interaction needs of applications increased, Microsoft introduced a set of advanced controls for dialogs. Called the "common" controls, they were shipped as a separate, redistributable DLL and were not part of any standard Windows installation until Windows 95 and Windows NT 4. These controls include the spin control, progress indicator, slider, hot key, list control, tree control, tab control, animation control, rich text edit, date/time picker, month calendar, and IP address control.

Spin

The spin control (sometimes called a spin button or an up-down control) allows the user to increment or decrement a value in an associated control. Consequently, it is an information modifier. This control allows the user to fine-tune the data in another control and is often used to allow the user to scroll through a list of numeric values. The spin control is shown in Figure 2.21.

Progress

The progress indicator control is an information presentation control that displays a graphical representation of the percent progress. Use this control when you'd like your application to indicate graphically the current amount of progress. Figure 2.22 demonstrates this control.

FIGURE 2.21
A spin control.

FIGURE 2.22
*A progress indica-
tor control.*

Slider

The slider control allows the user to select one of a range of values. It is similar to a level control on a stereo's equalizer. You can choose to have either horizontal or vertical sliders. This control is shown in Figure 2.23.

FIGURE 2.23
*A horizontal slider
control with a
point and tick
marks.*

Hot Key

The hot key control enables the user to enter a combination keystroke that includes Alt, Shift, or Ctrl, and another key to define a hot key to the application. Use this control when you let the user define a keystroke combination for the application. Figure 2.24 demonstrates this control.

FIGURE 2.24
A hot key control.

List Control

The list control is essentially the classic list box on steroids. It allows one of four views: large icon (single column with text), small icon (single column with text), list (multi-column, small icon with text), and report (single column, small icon with text and other textual details in columns). Figure 2.25 shows a list control in report view.

FIGURE 2.25
*A list control in
report view.*

Tree Control

The tree control provides a means of displaying a hierarchy of data within your application. The standard Windows Explorer window is a tree control, showing a hierarchy of drives, folders, and files. The tree control is shown in Figure 2.26.

FIGURE 2.26

A tree control showing a hierarchy of data.

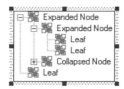

Tab Control

The tab control provides a means of logically organizing your application's data in your user interface. If you use this control, your GUI needs to display only the controls in which the user is interested—rather than overwhelming him with a large number of controls at once. Figure 2.27 shows a tab control.

FIGURE 2.27

A tab control.

Animation

The animation control enables you to display an AVI file within the control's area when clicked. Use this control when you have multimedia graphics that you'd like displayed within your dialog.

Rich Edit

The rich edit control enables you to embed more sophisticated text processing in your application, so you can provide the user a means of formatting text and paragraphs, as well as loading and saving the text in RTF format. This control is shown in Figure 2.28.

> **NOTE**
>
> You must call `AfxInitRichEdit` in your application class's `InitInstance` method to use the rich edit control.

FIGURE 2.28

A rich edit control.

Date/Time Picker

The date/time picker control provides a means of allowing the user to select a date or time through your user interface. Its visual appearance can be similar to a combo box or an edit text/spin control combination. The latter combination is shown in Figure 2.29.

FIGURE 2.29

A date/time picker control using a spin control.

Month Calendar

The month calendar control allows your application to display an entire calendar month to the end user. It provides an intuitive way for the user to interact with dates in your application. The month calendar control is shown in Figure 2.30.

FIGURE 2.30

The month calendar control.

IP Address

The IP address control provides a straightforward means of displaying and allowing the user to modify an Internet network address in a way consistent with the rest of the system. This control is shown in Figure 2.31.

FIGURE 2.31

An IP address control.

Extended Combo Box

The extended combo box control has the same behavior and types as the standard combo box control. However, unlike the standard control, it supports the use of images—without requiring an owner draw routine to draw them. Use this control if you need to allow the user to select one of a set of items with images.

Custom Controls

Another type of control that you can add to your dialog is called a *custom* control. You can create your own controls to satisfy specific requirements for your application. Refer to Chapter 5, "Custom Control Development," for information on how to create and use custom controls.

Adding Initialization

There are two locations where dialog initialization is typically performed: in the constructor and in the `OnInitDialog` method for your dialog class. The actual location for your particular initialization code depends on what is required at the time of initialization.

Use the dialog class constructor to initialize member variables that have no dependence on any controls on the dialog. For example, the constructor is an excellent place to initialize any class pointers to zero. Listing 2.1 demonstrates how the constructor is used in the MFCSample application to initialize the *m_currentColor* member variables.

LISTING 2.1 INITIALIZATION OF CLASS MEMBERS IN THE CONSTRUCTOR

```
CMFCSampleDlg::CMFCSampleDlg(CWnd* pParent /*=NULL*/)
    : CDialog(CMFCSampleDlg::IDD, pParent)
    , m_currentColor(RGB(0,0,255))
{
    //{{AFX_DATA_INIT(CMFCSampleDlg)
    m_fileName = _T("");
    //}}AFX_DATA_INIT

    // [omitted code]
}
```

Listing 2.1 also shows the initialization of a member variable, *m_fileName*, used in DDX. This variable represents the filename that is displayed in the MFCSample application's main window, as shown earlier in Figure 2.9.

> **NOTE**
>
> The initialization of *m_fileName* is contained within a set of comments that are tagged with AFX_DATA_INIT. These comments are flags that indicate to the Visual Studio environment that the code between the comments was generated. As a general rule, you typically leave this code alone and do not put your own code within these comments, for fear of losing it at a later date.

The second (and perhaps most common) location of initialization code for your dialog is in the OnInitDialog method. MFC calls OnInitDialog after the dialog window and all of its controls have been created. Consequently, feel free to interact with any of the controls in your dialog window in your dialog class's OnInitDialog method. Listing 2.2 shows the calls to EnableToolTips and DrawBitmapWithColor in initialization section for the MFCSample application.

LISTING 2.2   DIALOG INITIALIZATION IN THE OnInitDialog METHOD

```
BOOL CMFCSampleDlg::OnInitDialog()
{
    CDialog::OnInitDialog();

    // [omitted code]

    // TODO: Add extra initialization here
    EnableToolTips();
    DrawBitmapWithColor();

    return TRUE;  // return TRUE  unless you set the focus to a control
}
```

> **NOTE**
>
> In general, insert your application's initialization code after the Visual Studio-generated comment, "TODO: Add extra initialization here."

Using Dialog Controls

After you've created your dialog class, you'll most certainly need to programmatically interact with and receive events from the controls in your dialog. The next section describes exactly how to do just that.

Interacting with Controls

To interact with your dialog's controls, you'll need instances of classes for each of your dialog's controls that you need to manipulate. There are two basic ways of creating an instance of an object class. The first way is by using the Visual Studio ClassWizard to define a member variable that is associated with your dialog's control. The second way is to create an MFC control class object on-the-fly.

To create an instance of an object class using Class Wizard, you must first open the ClassWizard dialog by selecting View, ClassWizard from the Visual Studio pull-down menu. When the ClassWizard dialog appears, choose the tab named Member Variables. The ClassWizard open to this tab is shown in Figure 2.32.

FIGURE 2.32

Using the ClassWizard to view the current member variables associated with dialog controls.

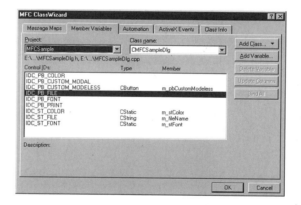

Next, select the control for which you need a member variable defined and click Add Variable. At this point, the Add Member Variable dialog appears as shown in Figure 2.33. Enter a name for your variable, choose the Control category, and select the type for your variable. When you click OK, this member variable is added automatically to your class.

NOTE

Some controls might have additional categories beyond Control—usually types such as CString and int. These types of member variables are used with Dialog Data Exchange, which is explained later in this chapter.

Now that the member variable is defined, you can manipulate the control as required. Hence, to disable a button named *m_pbOK*, code the following:

```
m_pbOK.EnableWindow(FALSE);
```

FIGURE 2.33

Using the ClassWizard to define a member variable for a dialog control.

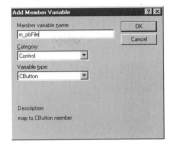

The methods that you use are limited to the methods available to you for the control type that you specified when you created the member variable.

The second way of interacting with a dialog control is by creating an automatic variable directly within your code. To do this, you must first create an automatic instance of the class appropriate for your control. Next, you must obtain a pointer to a CWnd object for your dialog's control using the GetDlgItem method. Listing 2.3 demonstrates the creation of an automatic variable named *pbOK* that is associated with the IDOK control in your dialog.

LISTING 2.3   ON-THE-FLY CONTROL VARIABLE CREATION

```
CButton *pbOK = DYNAMIC_DOWNCAST(CButton, GetDlgItem(IDOK))
```

CAUTION

Because the pointer returned from GetDlgItem is temporary and is not owned by your application, do not store or delete it.

Receiving Events from Controls

Each type of control (CButton, CListCtrl, and so on) has its own set of events that you can handle in your application. With the Visual Studio environment, it is straightforward to add event handlers to your application.

The MFCSample application sets up several event handlers to perform different actions. For example, each button on its dialog has an event handler to perform an action when the user pushes it. To create an event handler for a button click, you can use ClassWizard to help you quickly add it to your class.

First, from the Visual Studio pull-down menu, select View, ClassWizard. When the ClassWizard window opens, select the Message Maps tab, if that tab is not already on top. Figure 2.34 shows this tab for the MFCSample application.

FIGURE 2.34

Using the ClassWizard to view the current message maps associated with dialog controls.

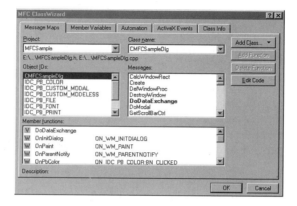

Next, select the class owning a control for which you'd like to set up a message map in the Class Name combo box. After you choose the class, a list of the objects for which you can set up a message map is shown in the Object IDs list box. By selecting the various Object IDs, you can see which events can be handled for that object. Additionally, the events that are in bold in the Messages list box already have a handler defined.

To add a new event handler, choose the appropriate message in the Messages list box and click the Add Function button. At this point, you are prompted for the name of the function to add, as shown in Figure 2.35. When you click OK to name the function, Visual Studio generates code within your application to handle that event.

FIGURE 2.35

Using the ClassWizard to name a member function to handle a dialog control event.

Finally, when you click Edit Code, Visual Studio displays the handler method for that event and allows you to edit it. Listing 2.4 shows the handler method for the File button in the MFCSample application.

LISTING 2.4 HANDLING A FILE PUSHBUTTON CLICK IN MFCSAMPLE

```
void CMFCSampleDlg::OnPbFile()
{
    // TODO: Add your message handler code here and/or call default
}
```

ToolTips

ToolTips are small, yellow text windows that appear over certain dialog controls after the mouse pointer stops for a moment. They provide a mechanism for you to give the user more detailed information about how that control is used. By adding ToolTips to your application, you can make it more user-friendly and usable.

Enabling ToolTips

To use ToolTips, you must first enable them for your dialog window by calling `EnableToolTips`. An ideal place for doing this is in your `OnInitDialog` method, as shown earlier in Listing 2.2. After you've done this, your application receives `TTN_NEEDTEXT` notification messages when a ToolTip window is about to be displayed by Windows.

> **NOTE**
>
> If you need to disable ToolTips in your application, call `CancelToolTips`.

Displaying Text

The ToolTip notification message, `TTN_NEEDTEXT`, gives your application the opportunity to provide the text that needs to appear in the ToolTip window. Follow these steps to add a handler for this message:

1. Add the following line to your message map declaration for your class in its declaration in the header file:
   ```
   afx_msg BOOL OnNeedToolTipText(UINT id, NMHDR * pTTTStruct,
                                  LRESULT * pResult);
   ```

2. Add the following line to your class's message map definition in the source file between `BEGIN_MESSAGE_MAP` and `END_MESSAGE_MAP`:
   ```
   ON_NOTIFY_EX(TTN_NEEDTEXT, 0, OnNeedToolTipText)
   ```

3. Add a definition of the `OnNeedToolTipText` method that you just declared in your class's header file and message map. Listing 2.5 shows the definition of this method for MFCSample.

LISTING 2.5   HANDLING OF TOOLTIPS IN MFCSAMPLE

```
BOOL CMFCSampleDlg::OnNeedToolTipText(UINT id, NMHDR * pNMHdr,
                                     LRESULT * pResult)
{
   TOOLTIPTEXT *pTTT = (TOOLTIPTEXT *) pNMHdr;

   if (pTTT->uFlags & TTF_IDISHWND) {
       UINT idCtrl = ::GetDlgCtrlID(HWND(pTTT->hdr.idFrom));

       if (idCtrl == IDC_PB_CUSTOM_MODELESS && m_custDlg.m_hWnd) {
           pTTT->lpszText = MAKEINTRESOURCE(IDS_TT_PB_CUSTOM_MODELESS2);
       }
       else {
           pTTT->lpszText = MAKEINTRESOURCE(idCtrl);
       }

       pTTT->hinst    = AfxGetResourceHandle();

       return TRUE;
   }

   return FALSE;
}
```

Listing 2.5 demonstrates how to add custom logic to dynamically change the actual ToolTip text according to the current state of the application. In MFCSample, generally all ToolTips are loaded from string resources where the string resource identifier is equal to the control identifier. However, if a modeless dialog is currently displayed, the ToolTip for the custom modeless pushbutton changes accordingly.

Dialog Data Exchange

Dialog Data Exchange is a powerful means of associating non-control datatypes with controls. When DDX is used, your application logic can deal with the data itself, rather than the controls to get and set the data.

The "Interacting with Controls" section discussed associating a control-type member variable with a control. With DDX, you can associate a data member variable with a control. For example, rather than having an m_edMyText CEditBox member variable, you can have an m_myText CString member variable. Furthermore, using a DDX method named

UpdateData, your application can always ensure that the data member variable and actual control remain in sync.

Standard DDX

When you create a non-control member variable that is associated with a control, Visual Studio generates code to initialize and associate the data member and the control. The MFCSample application has one member variable, *m_fileName*, which is associated with a static text control to display its data.

Upon creating the member variable (as discussed in "Interacting with Controls"), Visual Studio creates initialization code for those data members in the class's constructor, as shown earlier in Listing 2.1.

Additionally, it creates a method named DoDataExchange that exchanges the data between the control and the data member (and vice versa). For the MFCSample application, this method is shown in Listing 2.6.

LISTING 2.6   DDX METHOD DoDataExchange IN MFCSAMPLE

```
void CMFCSampleDlg::DoDataExchange(CDataExchange* pDX)
{
    CDialog::DoDataExchange(pDX);
    //{{AFX_DATA_MAP(CMFCSampleDlg)
    DDX_Control(pDX, IDC_ST_COLOR, m_stColor);
    DDX_Control(pDX, IDC_PB_CUSTOM_MODELESS, m_pbCustomModeless);
    DDX_Control(pDX, IDC_ST_FONT, m_stFont);
    DDX_Text(pDX, IDC_ST_FILE, m_fileName);
    //}}AFX_DATA_MAP
}
```

In the DoDataExchange method for the CMFCSampleDlg class, four DDX associations are implemented. The first three associate the dialog control with the control-type member variable that references it. In this way, IDC_ST_COLOR is associated with *m_stColor*, IDC_PB_CUSTOM_MODELESS is associated with *m_pbCustomModeless*, and IDC_ST_FONT is associated with *m_stFont*. The fourth association is between a control and a data member variable: IDC_ST_FILE and *m_fileName*.

UpdateData

The UpdateData method is what keeps all of the DDX associations in sync. Using this method, you can force the data to go either from the control to the member variable or vice versa, based upon the passed parameter.

This `UpdateData` method is declared as follows in the `CWnd` class:

```
BOOL UpdateData(BOOL bSaveAndValidate = TRUE);
```

If you pass `TRUE` as the parameter to `UpdateData`, the data moves from the controls to their associated data members. Passing `FALSE` does the reverse. If an error occurs due to a data validation error, `FALSE` is returned from this method.

Using Standard Dialog Boxes

MFC provides four standard dialog boxes that allow your application to get information from the user in a way consistent with other applications. These dialogs are the file open/save dialog, the color selector, the font selector, and the print configuration dialog.

File Open/Save

The MFC `CFileDialog` class represents the File Open/Save dialog. By instantiating an object from this class, your application can prompt the user for a filename to open or save. The File Open dialog is shown in Figure 2.36.

FIGURE 2.36

The Windows standard File Open dialog.

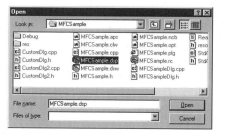

The MFCSample application displays the File Open dialog when the user clicks the File button. If the user selects a file and clicks OK, that file is displayed in the main dialog. The code to support this use is shown in Listing 2.7.

LISTING 2.7   SIMPLE CODE TO DISPLAY THE FILE OPEN DIALOG

```
void CMFCSampleDlg::OnPbFile()
{
   CFileDialog fileDlg(TRUE);

   if (fileDlg.DoModal() == IDOK) {
      m_fileName = fileDlg.GetFileName();
      UpdateData(FALSE);
   }
}
```

Color Selector

The MFC `CColorDialog` class represents the Color selection dialog. By instantiating an object from this class, your application can prompt the user for a color. The Color selection dialog is shown in Figure 2.37.

FIGURE 2.37
The Windows standard Color selection dialog.

The MFCSample application displays the Color Selection dialog when the user clicks the Color button. If the user selects a color and clicks OK, that color is displayed in the main dialog. The code to support this use is shown in Listing 2.8.

LISTING 2.8   SIMPLE CODE TO DISPLAY THE COLOR SELECTION DIALOG

```
void CMFCSampleDlg::OnPbColor()
{
   CColorDialog colorDlg(m_currentColor);

   if (colorDlg.DoModal() == IDOK) {
     m_currentColor = colorDlg.GetColor();
     DrawBitmapWithColor();
   }
}
```

Font Selector

The MFC `CFontDialog` class represents the Font selection dialog. By instantiating an object from this class, your application can prompt the user for a font face, size, and style. The Font selection dialog is shown in Figure 2.38.

The MFCSample application displays the Font Selection dialog when the user clicks the Font button. If the user selects a font face, size, and style and clicks OK, that font is used to draw some sample text that is displayed in the main dialog. The code to support this use is shown in Listing 2.9.

FIGURE 2.38

*The Windows
standard Font
selection dialog.*

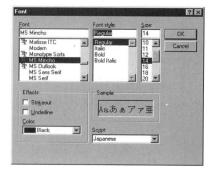

LISTING 2.9   SIMPLE CODE TO DISPLAY THE FONT SELECTION DIALOG

```
void CMFCSampleDlg::OnPbFont()
{
   CFontDialog fontDlg;

   if (fontDlg.DoModal() == IDOK) {
      CFont   font;
      LOGFONT logFont;

      fontDlg.GetCurrentFont(&logFont);
      font.CreateFontIndirect(&logFont);

      m_stFont.SetFont(&font);
   }
}
```

Print Dialog

The MFC CPrintDialog class represents the Print selection dialog. By instantiating an
object from this class, your application can prompt the user for a printer. The Print selection dialog is shown in Figure 2.39.

The MFCSample application displays the Printer Selection dialog when the user clicks
the Print button. If the user selects a printer and clicks OK, a sample page is printed on
that printer. The code to support this use is shown in Listing 2.10.

LISTING 2.10   SIMPLE CODE TO DISPLAY THE PRINTER SELECTION DIALOG

```
void CMFCSampleDlg::OnPbPrint()
{
   CPrintDialog printDlg(FALSE);

   if (printDlg.DoModal() == IDOK) {
      CDC printerDC;
```

```
printerDC.Attach(printDlg.GetPrinterDC());

int cx = printerDC.GetDeviceCaps(PHYSICALWIDTH);
int cy = printerDC.GetDeviceCaps(PHYSICALHEIGHT);

// add printing logic here...
printerDC.StartDoc("MFCSample Document");
printerDC.StartPage();

DrawClock(printerDC, __min(cx, cy));

printerDC.EndPage();
printerDC.EndDoc();

CString msg = "Printed to: ";
msg += printDlg.GetDeviceName();
MessageBox(msg);
    }
}
```

2

MFC DIALOGS AND CONTROLS

FIGURE 2.39

The Windows standard Print selection dialog.

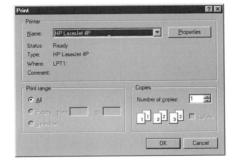

Summary

Microsoft Visual Studio's AppWizard makes creating a simple dialog-based MFC application easy. After you have followed the AppWizard through its steps and have generated an application shell, you can add your application's functionality in a relatively straightforward manner.

Additionally, the Visual Studio resource editor enables you to add standard controls to your application—from basic controls such as pushbuttons and list boxes to the newer, more specialized controls such as the hot key control and IP address control. You can use one of standard selection dialogs to prompt the user for a file, printer, color, and font at the appropriate places within your application.

The MFC architecture provides a standard mechanism, Dynamic Data Exchange, for interchanging data between variables and your dialog's controls. When equipped with DDX support, your application's dialogs can validate and transfer user input to your dialog in a well-designed manner.

For more information on programming the dialog controls, see Chapter 3.

The Windows Common Controls

by Rob McGregor

IN THIS CHAPTER

Windows controls, those doodads and widgets that make the Windows GUI so appealing, include both the Windows standard controls and the Windows common controls. The Windows standard controls include list boxes, edit boxes, combo boxes, scrollbars, and various types of buttons. The Windows common controls were introduced with Windows 95, and they add a lot of additional GUI power to the Windows programmer's toolkit.

Because the common controls are specific to Win32, the MFC common control classes are available only to programs running under Windows 95 or later, Windows NT version 3.51 or later, and Windows 3.1x with Win32s 1.3 or later.

Initializing and Using the Common Controls

Before you can use any of the Windows common controls in your applications, you must initialize the common control DLLs with a Win32 API function call. Windows 95 applications use the `InitCommonControls()` function to register and initialize *all* the common control window classes. Its use is easy, as you can see by its function prototype:

```
void InitCommonControls(VOID);
```

The `InitCommonControls()` function is now obsolete; it has been replaced with the more intelligent `InitCommonControlsEx()` function, which loads only the specific control classes that you specify. Its function prototype looks like this:

```
BOOL InitCommonControlsEx(LPINITCOMMONCONTROLSEX lpInitCtrls);
```

`InitCommonControlsEx()` registers specific common control classes, specified by the parameter `lpInitCtrls`, from the common control dynamic-link library (DLL). The `lpInitCtrls` parameter is of type `LPINITCOMMONCONTROLSEX`, which is a structure containing information about which control classes to load from the common control DLL.

The `INITCOMMONCONTROLSEX` structure looks like this:

```
typedef struct tagINITCOMMONCONTROLSEX
{
    DWORD dwSize;
    DWORD dwICC;
}
INITCOMMONCONTROLSEX, *LPINITCOMMONCONTROLSEX;
```

The parameters are as follows:

- `dwSize` The size of the structure, in bytes.
- `dwICC` The set of bit flags that specifies which common control classes to load from the common control DLL. This parameter can be any combination of the values in Table 3.1.

TABLE 3.1 THE BIT FLAGS USED BY THE INITCOMMONCONTROLSEX STRUCTURE

Bit Flags Name	Meaning
ICC_ANIMATE_CLASS	Loads the animate control class.
ICC_BAR_CLASSES	Loads the toolbar, status bar, trackbar, and tooltip control classes.
ICC_COOL_CLASSES	Loads the rebar control class.
ICC_DATE_CLASSES	Loads the date and time picker control class.
ICC_HOTKEY_CLASS	Loads the hot key control class.
ICC_INTERNET_CLASSES	Loads the IP address class.
ICC_LISTVIEW_CLASSES	Loads the list view and header control classes.
ICC_PAGESCROLLER_CLASS	Loads the pager control class.
ICC_PROGRESS_CLASS	Loads the progress bar control class.
ICC_TAB_CLASSES	Loads the tab and tooltip control classes.
ICC_TREEVIEW_CLASSES	Loads the tree view and tooltip control classes.
ICC_UPDOWN_CLASS	Loads the up-down control class.
ICC_USEREX_CLASSES	Load the ComboBoxEx class.
ICC_WIN95_CLASSES	Loads the animate control, header, hot key, list view, progress bar, status bar, tab, tooltip, toolbar, trackbar, tree view, and up-down control classes.

3

THE WINDOWS
COMMON
CONTROLS

Notifications for Windows Common Controls

Windows common controls use a different messaging system than do standard Windows controls. This section takes a look at just what's going on in the new messaging system and demonstrates how to tap into common control communications.

Each of the Win32 common controls has a corresponding set of notification codes defined for its control type. In addition to these codes, there is a set of codes shared by all the common controls. These notifications all pass a pointer to an NMHDR structure (described in the following section), and are shown in Table 3.2.

TABLE 3.2 NOTIFICATION CODES USED BY ALL THE WIN32 COMMON CONTROLS

Notification Code	Meaning
NM_CLICK	Sent when a user clicks the left mouse button within the control.
NM_DBLCLK	Sent when a user double-clicks the left mouse button within the control.
NM_KILLFOCUS	Sent when the control loses the input focus.
NM_OUTOFMEMORY	Sent when the control can't finish an operation because of insufficient free memory.
NM_RCLICK	Sent when a user clicks the right mouse button within the control.
NM_RDBLCLK	Sent when a user double-clicks the right mouse button within the control.
NM_RETURN	Sent when a user presses the Enter key and the control has the input focus.
NM_SETFOCUS	Sent when the control receives the input focus.

The Notification Message Structure

Win32 common controls use a special structure to send notification messages: the NMHDR structure. This structure contains the window handle of the sender, the control ID of the sender, and the notification code being sent. The NMHDR structure looks like this:

```
typedef struct tagNMHDR
{
    HWND hwndFrom;   // Window handle of the sender
    UINT idFrom;     // Control ID
    UINT code;       // Notification code
} NMHDR;
```

Overview of the Notification Process

Win32 common controls send most notification messages as WM_NOTIFY messages; Windows standard controls (also used by 16-bit Windows) send most notification messages as WM_COMMAND messages.

NOTE

The WM_NOTIFY message isn't used for 16-bit Windows because the message was designed specifically for 32-bit Windows.

WM_NOTIFY provides a standard way for the Win32 common controls to communicate information about control activities to Windows and to your applications (as opposed to creating a huge number of new WM_* macros for each new control).

A Win32 common control sends WM_NOTIFY notification messages to its parent window, which is usually a CDialog-derived class; in response, MFC calls the CWnd::OnNotify() method to process these messages. To intercept and handle these messages for a common control, you can override the CWnd::OnNotify() method for the control's owner class. The prototype for CWnd::OnNotify() looks like this:

BOOL CWnd::OnNotify(WPARAM wParam, LPARAM lParam, LRESULT* pResult)

To discover the reason for the occurrence of the WM_NOTIFY message (or, "What's the user doing with this control?"), you must look closely at the parameters of the CWnd::OnNotify() method:

- The wParam parameter is the control ID of the control that sent the message or is NULL if the message didn't come from a control.
- The lParam parameter is a pointer to a notification message structure (NMHDR) that contains the current notification code along with some additional information.
- The pResult parameter is a pointer to an LRESULT variable that stores the result code if the message is handled.

If the NMHDR structure is actually a member of a larger structure (as it is for most Win32 common controls), you must cast it to an NMHDR when you use it; only a few common controls actually use the simple NMHDR structure.

The lParam parameter can be a pointer to either an NMHDR structure or some other structure that has an NMHDR structure embedded as its first data member and has been typecast to an NMHDR structure.

Usually, the pointer *is* to a larger structure containing an NMHDR structure and not to the NMHDR structure itself. In these cases, because the NMHDR structure is the first member of the larger structure, it can be successfully typecast to an NMHDR structure.

A Better Notification Handling Scheme

As stated earlier in this chapter, the CWnd::OnNotify() method handles notification messages. Although you *can* do it, you really *shouldn't* override the CWnd::OnNotify() method to receive notifications from controls—there's no need to do so in most cases. Instead, you should provide a message handler method to trap the notification and add a corresponding message map entry in a control's parent class.

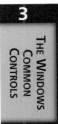

The `ON_NOTIFY` message map macro uses this syntax:

```
ON_NOTIFY(NotifyCode, ControlID, ClassMethod)
```

In this syntax, `NotifyCode` represents the notification code being sent, `ControlID` represents the control identifier the parent window uses to communicate with the control that sent notification, and `ClassMethod` represents the message handler method called in response to the notification.

Your message handler method must be declared using this prototype format:

```
afx_msg void ClassMethod(NMHDR* pNotifyStruct, LRESULT* result);
```

In this syntax `pNotifyStruct` is a pointer to an `NMHDR` structure, and `result` is a pointer to the result code your message handler method sets.

Specifying Notification Ranges with `ON_NOTIFY_RANGE`

To allow several controls to process a notification using the same message handler method, you can use the `ON_NOTIFY_RANGE` macro in the message map instead of using the `ON_NOTIFY` macro. When you use `ON_NOTIFY_RANGE`, you must specify the beginning and ending control IDs for the controls that will have access to the notification message.

CAUTION

The control IDs used for the `ON_NOTIFY_RANGE` macro must be numerically contiguous. For example, if three `CHeader` controls are to use the same notification message handler, these control IDs would work:

```
// Contiguous
#define IDC_HEADER1  100
#define IDC_HEADER2  101
#define IDC_HEADER3  102
```

These control IDs wouldn't work:

```
// Non-contiguous
#define IDC_HEADER1  100
#define IDC_HEADER2  103
#define IDC_HEADER3  108
```

The `ON_NOTIFY_RANGE` message map macro uses this format:

```
ON_NOTIFY_RANGE(NotifyCode, FirstCtrlID, LastCtrlID, ClassMethod)
```

In this syntax, `NotifyCode` represents the notification code being sent, `ControlIDFirst` represents the control identifier of the first control in the contiguous range, `ControlIDFirst` represents the control identifier of the last control in the contiguous range, and `ClassMethod` represents the message handler method called in response to the notification.

The message handler method prototype in the owner's class declaration is as follows:

```
afx_msg void ClassMethod(UINT ControlID, NMHDR* pNotifyStruct,
    LRESULT* result);
```

In this syntax, `ControlID` is the identifier of the control that sent the notification, `pNotifyStruct` is a pointer to an `NMHDR` structure, and `result` is a pointer to the result code your message handler method sets when it processes the notification.

The new common controls provide a more structured method of notification messaging that takes some getting used to, but makes MFC programs more readable and easier to maintain in the long run. Now let's take a look at Windows common controls and see how MFC makes using them fairly easy.

Hot Key Controls: Class CHotKeyCtrl

A *hot key* is a key combination used to perform some action quickly. A *hot key control* is a window that stores the virtual key code and shift state flags that represent a hot key. The window displays the key combination as a text string (for example, Alt+X). The control doesn't actually set the hot key, however; your code must do this explicitly. To enable a hot key, your application must get the hot key's values and associate these values with either a window or a thread.

MFC provides the services of a Windows hot key common control in the class `CHotKeyCtrl`, which is derived directly from `CWnd` (and therefore inherits all the functionality of `CWnd`). The `CHotKeyCtrl` class is defined in AFXCMN.H. A hot key control can be created as a child control of any window by writing code; it can also be defined in a dialog resource template. MFC automatically attaches a Windows hot key common control to a `CHotKeyCtrl` object when the object is created.

CHotKeyCtrl Class Methods

The `CHotKeyCtrl` class offers a minimal set of methods for manipulating the control and its data. The constructor, `CHotKeyCtrl::CHotKeyCtrl()`, allocates a `CHotKeyCtrl` object that is initialized with the `CHotKeyCtrl::Create()` method. Table 3.3 describes the class's methods.

TABLE 3.3   CHotKeyCtrl CLASS METHODS

Method	Description
GetHotKey()	Gets the virtual-key code and modifier flags of a hot key from a hot key control.
SetHotKey()	Sets the hot key combination for a hot key control.
SetRules()	Defines invalid key combinations and the default modifier combination for a hot key control.

Creating and Initializing a CHotKeyCtrl Object

To create a CHotKeyCtrl object, you use the two-step construction process typical of MFC:

1. Call the class constructor CHotKeyCtrl::CHotKeyCtrl() to allocate the object.

2. Initialize the CHotKeyCtrl object and attach an actual Windows hot key common control to it with a call to the CHotKeyCtrl::Create() method.

The prototype for the CHotKeyCtrl::Create() method is shown here:

```
BOOL Create(DWORD dwStyle, const RECT& rect,
            CWnd* pParentWnd, UINT nID);
```

In this syntax, the parameters are defined as follows:

- dwStyle   Specifies the window style for the control.
- rect   The rectangle specifying the size and position of the control.
- pParentWnd   A pointer to the owner of the control.
- nID   The control ID used by the parent to communicate with the control.

Using a Hot Key Control

After a hot key control is created, a default hot key value can be set by calling the SetHotKey() method. To prevent specific shift states, call the SetRules() method. A user can choose a hot key combination when the control has the focus, and an application uses the GetHotKey() method to get the virtual key and shift state values from the hot key control.

Armed with the details of the selected key combination, you can set the actual hot key by doing one of the following:

- Set up a *global hot key* for activating a top-level window by using the CWnd::SendMessage() method, sending a WM_SETHOTKEY message to the window to be activated.

- Set up a *thread-specific hot key* by calling the Win32 API function `RegisterHotKey()`.

Global Hot Keys

A *global hot key* enables a user to activate a top-level window from any part of the system. To set a global hot key for a specific window, you must send the `WM_SETHOTKEY` message to that window. Assume that `m_pHotKey` is a pointer to a `CHotKeyCtrl` object and that `pWnd` is a pointer to the target window. When the hot key is activated, you can associate `m_pHotKey` with `pWnd` like this:

```
WORD wKeyShift = m_pHotKey->GetHotKey();
pWnd->SendMessage(WM_SETHOTKEY, wKeyShift);
```

Thread-Specific Hot Keys

A *thread-specific hot key* enables a user to activate a top-level window that was created by the current thread. To set a thread-specific hot key for a particular window, you must call the Win32 API function `RegisterHotKey()`. This function has the following prototype:

```
BOOL RegisterHotKey(HWND hWnd, int id, UINT fsModifiers, UINT vk);
```

In this syntax, `hWnd` identifies the window to receive the `WM_HOTKEY` messages generated by the hot key. The `id` parameter is the control ID of the hot key, which must be in the range of `0x0000` through `0xBFFF` for an application, or `0xC000` through `0xFFFF` for a shared DLL. The `fsModifiers` parameter is the modifier keys that must be pressed in combination with the key specified by the `vk` parameter to generate the `WM_HOTKEY` message. This can be a combination of the values shown in Table 3.4. The `vk` parameter is the virtual-key code of the hot key.

TABLE 3.4   THE MODIFIER FLAGS USED WITH `RegisterHotKey()`

Value	Meaning
MOD_ALT	The Alt key must be held down.
MOD_CONTROL	The Ctrl key must be held down.
MOD_SHIFT	The Shift key must be held down.

NOTE

If the key combination specified for a hot key has already been registered by another hot key, the call to `RegisterHotKey()` fails.

3

THE WINDOWS
COMMON
CONTROLS

Spin Controls: Class CSpinButtonCtrl

A *spin control* (or up-down control) is a friendly little control sporting a matching set of two linked arrow buttons. These controls are often found hanging around with their buddies, trying to get information from a user. Seriously, spin controls *do* usually interact intimately with another Windows control, and the spin control's arrow buttons increment or decrement an internal spin control value (called the *current position*) when clicked. This value can be displayed as a number in a *buddy window*, which is most often an edit control used to get numeric input from a user.

A spin control and its buddy window (if used) often look and act like a single control. The spin control can align itself with its buddy window automatically, and it can send its current scroll position to the buddy, changing the buddy's window text accordingly. The current position is limited to an application-defined minimum and maximum range of values. Figure 3.1 shows the typical use of a spin control: getting a value from the user.

FIGURE 3.1

Typical spin controls with their buddies, conspiring to get values from a user.

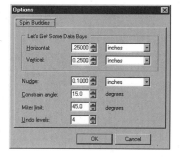

A spin control doesn't *need* a buddy control; it can be used for many things all by itself, very much like a minimalist scroll bar. MFC provides the services of a Windows spin common control in the class CSpinButtonCtrl. Like other MFC controls, CSpinButtonCtrl is derived directly from CWnd and inherits all the functionality of CWnd.

A spin control can be created as a child control of any window by writing code, or it can be defined for use in a dialog resource template. A spin control sends Windows notification messages to its owner (usually a CDialog-derived class), and these messages can be trapped and handled by writing message map entries and message-handler methods for each message. These message map entries and methods are implemented in the spin control's parent class.

Spin Control Styles

Like all windows, spin controls can use the general window styles available to CWnd. In addition, they use the spin styles shown in Table 3.5 (as defined in AFXCMN.H). A spin control's styles determine its appearance and operations. Style bits are typically set when the control is initialized with the `CSpinButtonCtrl::Create()` method.

TABLE 3.5   THE WINDOW STYLES DEFINED FOR A SPIN CONTROL

Style Macro	Meaning
UDS_ALIGNLEFT	Aligns a spin control to the left edge of the buddy window.
UDS_ALIGNRIGHT	Aligns a spin control to the right edge of the buddy window.
UDS_ARROWKEYS	Allows the control to increment and decrement the current position when the up-arrow and down-arrow keys are pressed on the keyboard.
UDS_AUTOBUDDY	Automatically selects a buddy window by choosing the previous window in the Z-order.
UDS_HORZ	Makes the control's arrows point left and right instead of up and down.
UDS_NOTHOUSANDS	Prevents the thousands separator between every three decimal digits.
UDS_SETBUDDYINT	Tells the control to set the text of the buddy window when the current position changes. The text represents the current position formatted as a decimal or hexadecimal string.
UDS_WRAP	Allows the current position to wrap around. Values above the maximum wrap around to start back at the minimum of the scroll range, and vice versa.

3

THE WINDOWS COMMON CONTROLS

NOTE

The spin button styles all have the UDS_* prefix. This is an indication of the SDK name for this control (and the name many people use): the *up-down control* (Up-Down Styles—UDS). But because the MFC team at Microsoft wrapped this control into a class called a *spin button control*, that's what I'll call it, too.

CSpinButtonCtrl Messages

Because MFC wraps the Windows spin control messages (such as UDM_GETRANGE or UDM_SETBUDDY) into CSpinButtonCtrl class methods, an MFC program usually only has to handle notification messages. These messages can be trapped and handled by writing message map entries and message-handler methods for each message. You map the spin control messages to class methods by creating message map entries in the control's parent class. Table 3.6 shows the message map entries for spin control messages.

TABLE 3.6   MESSAGE MAP ENTRIES FOR SPIN BUTTON CONTROL MESSAGES

Message Map Entry	*Meaning*
ON_WM_HSCROLL	Sent by a spin control with the UDS_HORZ style when the arrow buttons are clicked.
ON_WM_VSCROLL	Sent by a spin control with the UDS_VERT style (the default) when the arrow buttons are clicked.
ON_EN_UPDATE	Sent by a buddy edit control when the text is changed.

CSpinButtonCtrl Class Methods

The CSpinButtonCtrl class offers a concise set of methods for manipulating the control and its data. Because the MFC help files shipped with your compiler contain all the CSpinButtonCtrl class method declarations and detailed descriptions of their parameters, you won't find detailed descriptions here, but I *will* provide an overview of each method so that you know what to look for when you need it.

The CSpinButtonCtrl constructor, CSpinButtonCtrl::CSpinButtonCtrl(), allocates a spin control object that is initialized with the CSpinButtonCtrl::Create() method to set attributes and ownership. The methods listed in Table 3.7 describe the methods used to get and set control attributes.

TABLE 3.7   CSpinButtonCtrl CLASS METHODS

Method	*Description*
GetAccel()	Retrieves acceleration information for a spin control.
GetBase()	Retrieves the current base for a spin control.
GetBuddy()	Retrieves a pointer to the current buddy window.
GetPos()	Retrieves the current position of a spin control.
GetRange()	Retrieves the upper and lower limits (range) for a spin control.

SetAccel()	Sets the acceleration for a spin control.
SetBase()	Sets the base for a spin control.
SetBuddy()	Sets the buddy window for a spin control.
SetPos()	Sets the current position for the control.
SetRange()	Sets the upper and lower limits (range) for a spin control.

Creating and Initializing a Spin Control

A CSpinButtonCtrl object, like most MFC objects, uses a two-step construction process. To create a spin control, perform the following steps:

1. Allocate an instance of a CSpinButtonCtrl object by calling the constructor CSpinButtonCtrl::CSpinButtonCtrl() using the C++ keyword new.
2. Initialize the CSpinButtonCtrl object and attach a Windows spin button common control to it with the CSpinButtonCtrl::Create() method to set the spin control's parameters and styles.

For example, a CSpinButtonCtrl object is allocated and a pointer to that object is returned with this code:

```
CSpinButtonCtrl* pMySpinner = new CSpinButtonCtrl ;
```

The pointer pMySpinner is then initialized with a call to the CSpinButtonCtrl::Create() method. This method is declared as follows:

```
BOOL Create(DWORD dwStyle, const RECT& rect,
            CWnd* pParentWnd, UINT nID);
```

The first parameter, dwStyle, specifies the window style for the spin control. The window style can be any combination of the general window styles and the special spin control styles listed in Table 3.5, earlier in this chapter. The second parameter, rect, is the rectangle specifying the size and position of the control. The parameter pParentWnd is a pointer to the owner of the control, and nID is the control ID used by the parent to communicate with the spin control.

Sample Program: SPIN1

Now let's take a look at a basic MFC program (SPIN1.EXE on the CD-ROM) that creates and displays several spin controls and buddy windows in a frame window (see Figure 3.2).

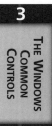

3

THE WINDOWS
COMMON
CONTROLS

FIGURE 3.2

The SPIN1 frame window with three child spin controls and their buddy controls.

The SPIN1 program uses three spin controls to set the RGB color components of the client area window color, and uses both left-aligned and right-aligned buddy windows.

Examining the SPIN1 Application Header (SPIN1.H)

The header file for the SPIN1 program begins by defining window styles for the frame window's child controls:

```
// Define some spin window styles
#define SBS_LEFT  (WS_VISCHILD | UDS_ALIGNLEFT | UDS_SETBUDDYINT)
#define SBS_RIGHT (WS_VISCHILD | UDS_ALIGNRIGHT | UDS_SETBUDDYINT)

// Buddy control style
#define ES_SINGLE (WS_VISCHILD | ES_LEFT | WS_BORDER)
```

Then the control IDs for the child window controls in this program are defined, as are the two classes used in this application: CSpinApp and CMainWnd.

The first class is the application class CSpinApp, which is a descendant of CWinApp and simply overrides the inherited InitInstance() method to provide custom application initialization.

The second class is CMainWnd, derived from CMainFrame. This class contains pointers to the child windows as class data members. These child windows consist of three spin controls and three edit controls. The class also provides the UpdateClientColor() helper method for changing the frame window's client area color as well as these two message-handler methods:

```
// Message handlers
afx_msg void OnSize(UINT nType, int cx, int cy);
afx_msg void OnBuddyUpdate();
```

Finally, the DECLARE_MESSAGE_MAP() macro is used to set up message handling for the class.

Implementing the SPIN1 Program (SPIN1.CPP)

The first order of business is setting up the message map for the CMainWnd class. This message map contains four entries that correspond to the four message-handler method prototypes given in the class definition:

```
// Message map for CMainWnd
BEGIN_MESSAGE_MAP(CMainWnd, CMainFrame)
    ON_WM_SIZE()
    ON_EN_UPDATE(IDC_BUDDY1, OnBuddyUpdate)
    ON_EN_UPDATE(IDC_BUDDY2, OnBuddyUpdate)
    ON_EN_UPDATE(IDC_BUDDY3, OnBuddyUpdate)
END_MESSAGE_MAP()
```

Notice that the CEdit buddy windows all use the same message handler to process update messages. The class constructor initializes all child control pointers to NULL, and the class destructor destroys any allocated child objects.

CMainWnd::CreateChildControls() allocates and initializes the child controls. After this, the spin controls are each assigned a buddy edit window that displays their current position value:

```
// Set buddies
m_pSpin1->SetBuddy(m_pBuddy1);
m_pSpin2->SetBuddy(m_pBuddy2);
m_pSpin3->SetBuddy(m_pBuddy3);
```

The spin buttons then receive a scroll range of 0 to 255, the possible range of byte values used by the RGB macro (that macro is used to change the frame window's client area color later):

```
// Set scroll ranges
m_pSpin1->SetRange(0, 255);
m_pSpin2->SetRange(0, 255);
m_pSpin3->SetRange(0, 255);
```

As a final step in initializing the spin controls, their individual current positions are set to the halfway position, at 128:

```
// Set current position
m_pSpin1->SetPos(128);
m_pSpin2->SetPos(128);
m_pSpin3->SetPos(128);
```

The `CMainWnd::OnSize()` message handler is quite simple, consisting of a call to the inherited method that it overrides, and another call to `CMainWnd::UpdateClientColor()` to repaint the client area in the color specified by the spin button positions:

```
void CMainWnd::OnSize(UINT nType, int cx, int cy)
{
    // Call inherited method
    CWnd::OnSize(nType, cx, cy);

    // Repaint the window at the new size
    UpdateClientColor();
}
```

The `CMainWnd::UpdateClientColor()` method is the heart of the program, reading the values from the buddy windows and converting them to the byte values needed for the color components of the RGB macro. Three `CString` local variables are declared to hold these values: szBuddy1Text, szBuddy2Text, and szBuddy3Text. The values are retrieved with a call to the `CWnd::GetWindowText()` method, returning the text from the edit controls:

```
m_pBuddy1->GetWindowText(szBuddy1Text);
m_pBuddy2->GetWindowText(szBuddy2Text);
m_pBuddy3->GetWindowText(szBuddy3Text);
```

These strings are converted to integers by calling the `CMainFrame::StringToInt()` method; the result is stored in three local integer variables:

```
INT nBuddy1 = StringToInt(szBuddy1Text);
INT nBuddy2 = StringToInt(szBuddy2Text);
INT nBuddy3 = StringToInt(szBuddy3Text);
```

A `CBrush` object is declared and initialized using these integers in an RGB macro to create a new brush of the desired color:

```
CBrush br(RGB(nBuddy1, nBuddy2, nBuddy3));
```

To finish off the method (and the SPIN1 program), the frame window's client area is retrieved into a `CRect` object and passed to the `CWnd::FillRect()` method, along with the new brush, to specify the fill color:

```
CRect rcClient;
GetClientRect(&rcClient);

CBrush br(RGB(nBuddy1, nBuddy2, nBuddy3));
GetDC()->FillRect(&rcClient, &br);
```

> **NOTE**
>
> For more information about brushes, rectangles, and device contexts such as those used in the SPIN1 program, read Chapter 4, "Painting, Device Contexts, Bitmaps, and Fonts."

Slider Controls: Class `CSliderCtrl`

Similar to a scroll bar, a *slider control* (or *trackbar*) is an interactive, highly visual control consisting of a slider box that runs along the length of the control, and optional tick marks that delineate range values. The slider control also has a built-in keyboard interface that allows movement of the slider with the arrow keys on the keyboard. Figure 3.3 shows a typical use of slider controls in the Windows Volume Control applet.

FIGURE 3.3
Slider controls provide instant visual feedback as the main user-interface component in this applet.

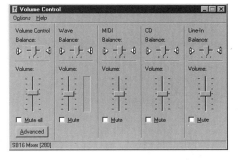

MFC provides the services of a Windows slider common control in the class `CSliderCtrl`. Like other MFC controls, `CSliderCtrl` is derived directly from `CWnd` and inherits all the functionality of `CWnd`. A slider control can be created as a window's child control by writing code; alternatively, it can be defined for use in a dialog resource template.

A slider control sends Windows notification messages to its owner (usually a `CDialog`-derived class), and these messages can be trapped and handled by writing message map entries and message-handler methods for each message. These message map entries and methods are implemented in the slider control's parent class.

Slider Control Styles

Like all windows, slider controls can use the general window styles available to `CWnd`. In addition, they use the slider control styles shown in Table 3.8 (as defined in

3

THE WINDOWS COMMON CONTROLS

AFXWIN.H). A slider control's styles determine its appearance and operations. Style bits are typically set when the control is initialized with the `CSliderCtrl::Create()` method. Slider controls can be oriented either horizontally or vertically and can have tick marks on one side, both sides, or no tick marks at all (depending on the following styles).

TABLE 3.8   THE WINDOW STYLES DEFINED FOR A SLIDER CONTROL

Style Macro	Meaning
TBS_AUTOTICKS	Gives a slider tick marks for each increment in its range of values. Tick marks are automatically created with a call to the `SetRange()` method.
TBS_BOTH	Puts tick marks on both sides of a slider control, no matter what its orientation.
TBS_BOTTOM	Puts tick marks on the bottom of a horizontal slider control.
TBS_ENABLESELRANGE	Gives a slider tick marks in the shape of triangles that indicate the starting and ending positions of a selected range.
TBS_HORZ	Orients a slider horizontally (the default).
TBS_LEFT	Puts tick marks on the left side of a vertical slider control.
TBS_NOTICKS	A slider won't have tick marks.
TBS_RIGHT	Puts tick marks on the right side of a vertical slider control.
TBS_TOP	Puts tick marks on the top of a horizontal slider control.
TBS_VERT	Orients a slider vertically.

NOTE

These styles all have the `TBS_*` prefix. Like the spin button control's `UDS_*` prefix, the `TBS_*` prefix is an indication of the SDK name of the slider control (and the name many people use): the *Track Bar control* (Track Bar Styles—TBS). But because the MFC team at Microsoft has wrapped this control into a class called a *slider control*, I refer to it as a slider, too.

`CSliderCtrl` Messages

An MFC program usually has to handle only two notification messages from slider controls. A slider control sends its parent window notifications of user actions in the form of scroll messages (`WM_HSCROLL` and `WM_VSCROLL`), just like a scroll bar control. These messages can be trapped and handled by writing message map entries and message-handler methods for each message. You map the slider control messages to class methods by creating message map entries in the control's parent class. Table 3.9 shows the message map entries for slider control messages.

TABLE 3.9   THE TWO MESSAGE MAP ENTRIES FOR SLIDER CONTROL MESSAGES

Message Map Entry	Meaning
ON_WM_HSCROLL	Sent by a slider control with the TBS_HORZ style when the arrow buttons are clicked.
ON_WM_VSCROLL	Sent by a slider control with the TBS_VERT style (the default) when the arrow buttons are clicked.

But there is more to the messaging than a few simple WM_* messages. The ON_WM_HSCROLL and ON_WM_VSCROLL messages have some interesting information hidden away inside them. MFC gives you access to this information through the OnHScroll() and OnVScroll() methods, which are called by MFC when a user clicks a slider's tick marks, drags the slider box, or uses the keyboard arrows to otherwise control slider movement. These scroll methods are typically used to give the user some interactive feedback while a slider control is scrolling or while the scroll box is dragging across a slider control's range of possible values. Here's the prototype for the OnVScroll() method (the OnHScroll() method is exactly the same):

```
afx_msg void OnVScroll(UINT nSBCode, UINT nPos,
   CSliderCtrl* pScrollBar);
```

The first parameter, nSBCode, specifies one of 10 possible scrolling codes that tell your application what the user is doing with the slider control. The slider control has its own set of notification codes (which are just like the scroll bar codes), as listed in Table 3.10.

TABLE 3.10   THE NOTIFICATION CODES USED BY THE SLIDER CONTROL IN THE OnHScroll() AND OnVScroll() METHODS

Code	Meaning
TB_BOTTOM	A user pressed the End key on the keyboard.
TB_ENDTRACK	A user released a key, causing some virtual key code to be sent (WM_KEYUP).
TB_LINEDOWN	A user pressed the down-arrow or right-arrow key on the keyboard.
TB_LINEUP	A user pressed the up-arrow or left-arrow key on the keyboard.
TB_PAGEDOWN	A user clicked the channel below or to the right of the slider or pressed the PageDown key.

continues

3

THE WINDOWS
COMMON
CONTROLS

TABLE 3.10   CONTINUED

Code	Meaning
TB_PAGEUP	A user clicked the channel above or to the left of the slider or pressed the PageUp key.
TB_THUMBPOSITION	A user released the left mouse button (WM_LBUTTONUP) after dragging the slider (TB_THUMBTRACK).
TB_THUMBTRACK	A user dragged the slider.
TB_TOP	A user pressed the Home key on the keyboard.

NOTE

When a user interacts with a slider control through the keyboard interface (and only then), the TB_BOTTOM, TB_LINEDOWN, TB_LINEUP, and TB_TOP codes are sent. Likewise, the TB_THUMBPOSITION and TB_THUMBTRACK codes are sent only when a user uses the mouse to drag the slider box. The other notification codes are sent no matter how a user interacts with the control.

The second parameter in the OnVScroll() or OnHScroll() method, nPos, reveals the current slider position when the notification code is either SB_THUMBPOSITION or SB_THUMB-TRACK. If the nSBCode parameter is anything other than these two codes, nPos isn't used.

The third and final parameter, pScrollBar, is a pointer to the slider control that sent the message. Even though a slider control isn't a scroll bar, this pointer does refer to a slider control. When overriding the OnHScroll() or OnVScroll() method, simply typecast the point to a CSliderCtrl pointer, like this:

```
void OnVScroll(UINT nSBCode, UINT nPos, CSliderCtrl* pScrollBar)
{
    CSliderCtrl* pSlider = (CSliderCtrl*) pScrollBar;

//
// use the pointer...
//
}
```

CSliderCtrl Class Methods

The CSliderCtrl class offers a nice set of methods for manipulating the control and its data. Because the MFC help files shipped with your compiler contain all the

CSliderCtrl class method declarations and detailed descriptions of their parameters, detailed descriptions aren't given here, but I *do* provide an overview of each method so that you know what to look for when you need it.

The CSliderCtrl constructor, CSliderCtrl::CSliderCtrl(), allocates a slider control object that is initialized with the CSliderCtrl::Create() method to set attributes and ownership. The methods listed in Table 3.11 describe the methods used to get and set slider control attributes.

TABLE 3.11 CSliderCtrl CLASS METHODS THAT DEAL WITH ATTRIBUTES

Method	Description
GetChannelRect()	Gets the size of the slider control's channel.
GetLineSize()	Gets the line size of a slider control.
GetNumTics()	Gets the number of tick marks in a slider control.
GetPageSize()	Gets the page size of a slider control.
GetPos()	Gets the current position of the slider.
GetRange()	Gets the minimum and maximum positions for a slider.
GetRangeMax()	Gets the maximum position for a slider.
GetRangeMin()	Gets the minimum position for a slider.
GetSelection()	Gets the range of the current selection.
GetThumbRect()	Gets the size of the slider control's thumb.
GetTic()	Gets the position of the specified tick mark.
GetTicArray()	Gets the array of tick mark positions for a slider control.
GetTicPos()	Gets the position of the specified tick mark, in client coordinates.
SetLineSize()	Sets the line size of a slider control.
SetPageSize()	Sets the page size of a slider control.
SetPos()	Sets the current position of the slider.
SetRange()	Sets the minimum and maximum positions for a slider.
SetRangeMax()	Sets the maximum position for a slider.
SetRangeMin()	Sets the minimum position for a slider.
SetSelection()	Sets the selection range for a slider.
SetTic()	Sets the position of the specified tick mark.
SetTicFreq()	Sets the frequency of tick marks per slider control increment.

3

THE WINDOWS COMMON CONTROLS

Table 3.12 shows the three operational methods a slider control can perform.

TABLE 3.12   CSliderCtrl CLASS METHODS THAT DEAL WITH OPERATIONS

Method	Description
ClearSel()	Clears the current selection from a slider control.
ClearTics()	Removes the current tick marks from a slider control.
VerifyPos()	Verifies that the position of a slider control is zero.

Creating and Initializing a Slider Control

A CSliderCtrl object, like most MFC objects, uses a two-step construction process. To create a slider control, perform the following steps:

1. Allocate an instance of a CSliderCtrl object by calling the constructor CSliderCtrl::CSliderCtrl() using the C++ keyword new.

2. Initialize the CSliderCtrl object and attach a Windows slider common control to it with the CSliderCtrl::Create() method to set slider parameters and styles.

For example, a CSliderCtrl object is allocated, and a pointer to the CSliderCtrl object is returned with this code:

```
CSliderCtrl* pMySlider = new CSliderCtrl;
```

The pointer pMySlider must then be initialized with a call to the CSliderCtrl::Create() method. This method is declared as follows:

```
BOOL Create(DWORD dwStyle, const RECT& rect,
            CWnd* pParentWnd, UINT nID);
```

The first parameter, dwStyle, specifies the window style for the slider control. This can be any combination of the general SDK window styles and the special slider control styles listed in Table 3.8, earlier in this chapter. The second parameter, rect, is the rectangle specifying the size and position of the control. The parameter pParentWnd is a pointer to the owner of the control, and nID is the control ID used by the parent to communicate with the slider control.

Sample Program: Slider Controls (SLIDER1)

The sample program SLIDER1 is just like sample program SPIN1 except that it uses sliders instead of spin controls, and it creates and displays three slider controls in a frame window (see Figure 3.4).

FIGURE 3.4

The SLIDER1 frame window with three child slider controls.

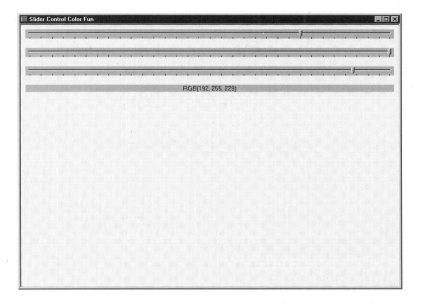

Sliders don't respond to the system-wide scroll bar size change messages like scroll bars and spin controls do. Also, slider controls are much more independent than their scroll bar cousins. They update their own current positions and are smart enough to know how much to move for page change and line change notifications. To tell the sliders how much you want them to change for the notifications, use the following code in the `CMainWnd::CreateChildControls()` method (which includes the tick frequency):

```
// Set tick frequency
m_pSlider1->SetTicFreq(8);
m_pSlider2->SetTicFreq(8);
m_pSlider3->SetTicFreq(8);

// Set page size
m_pSlider1->SetPageSize(8);
m_pSlider2->SetPageSize(8);
m_pSlider3->SetPageSize(8);

// Set line size
m_pSlider1->SetLineSize(1);
m_pSlider2->SetLineSize(1);
m_pSlider3->SetLineSize(1);
```

3

THE WINDOWS COMMON CONTROLS

This makes a big difference between the code for a scroll bar and the code for a slider in the SLIDER1 program's `CMainWnd::OnHScroll()` method, thanks to the automatic tracking of the slider control. Here is the entire function that handles scrolling code:

```
void CMainWnd::OnHScroll(UINT nSBCode, UINT nPos,
                         CScrollBar* pScrollBar)
{
    // *Much* simpler than a scroll bar!

    // Change to the new color
    UpdateClientColor();

    // call inherited handler
    CMainFrame::OnHScroll(nSBCode, nPos, pScrollBar);
}
```

If you've ever written scrollbar code, you'll see instantly that the slider control is a lot more user-friendly than a scroll bar—and makes for much easier coding!

Sample Program: SLIDER1

Next let's take a look at the sample program SLIDER1. This simple program creates and displays three slider controls in a frame window (refer to Figure 3.4), and it's very similar in design to the sample program SPIN1 that you saw earlier in this chapter. The SLIDER1 program uses three slider controls to set the RGB color components of the client area window color.

Examining the SLIDER1 Application Header (SLIDER1.H)

The header file for the SLIDER1 program begins by defining window styles for the frame window and its child controls:

```
// Main window style
#define WS_VISCHILD (WS_VISIBLE | WS_CHILD)

// Define a slider control window style
#define TBS_COLOR  \
    (TBS_HORZ | TBS_AUTOTICKS | WS_VISCHILD | WS_TABSTOP)

// Static control style
#define SS_STATIC (WS_VISCHILD | SS_CENTER)
```

Then the control IDs for the child window controls in this program are defined, as are the two classes used in this application: CSliderApp and CMainWnd.

The application class CSliderApp is almost exactly like class CspinApp, which you saw earlier. The CMainWnd class, derived from CMainFrame, contains pointers to the child windows as class data members. These child windows consist of three slider controls and three static controls. The class also provides the `UpdateClientColor()` helper method for changing the frame window's client area color as well as these two message-handler methods:

```
// Message handlers
afx_msg BOOL OnEraseBkgnd(CDC* pDC);
afx_msg void OnHScroll(UINT nSBCode, UINT nPos,
   CScrollBar* pScrollBar);
afx_msg void OnSize(UINT nType, int cx, int cy);
```

Finally, the `DECLARE_MESSAGE_MAP()` macro is used to set up message handling for the class.

Implementing the SLIDER1 Program (SLIDER1.CPP)

The first order of business is setting up the message map for the `CMainWnd` class. This message map contains four entries that correspond to the four message-handler method prototypes given in the class definition:

```
// Message map for CMainWnd
BEGIN_MESSAGE_MAP(CMainWnd, CMainFrame)
   ON_WM_ERASEBKGND()
   ON_WM_HSCROLL()
   ON_WM_SIZE()
END_MESSAGE_MAP()
```

`CMainWnd::CreateChildControls()` allocates and initializes the child controls. The sliders then receive a scroll range of 0 to 255, the possible range of byte values used by the RGB macro (that macro is used to change the frame window's client area color later):

```
// Set slider ranges
m_pSlider1->SetRange(0, 255);
m_pSlider2->SetRange(0, 255);
m_pSlider3->SetRange(0, 255);
```

As a final step in initializing the spin controls, their individual current positions are set to the halfway position, at 128:

```
// Set current positions
m_pSlider1->SetPos(128);
m_pSlider1->SetPos(128);
m_pSlider1->SetPos(128);
```

The `CMainWnd::OnSize()` message handler first calls the inherited method that it overrides, then resizes each of the sliders by calling the `CSliderCtrl::SetWindowPos()` method, and finally calls `CMainWnd::UpdateClientColor()` to repaint the client area in the color specified by the current slider positions. Listing 3.1 shows how it's done.

3

THE WINDOWS
COMMON
CONTROLS

LISTING 3.1   RESIZING THE SLIDER CONTROLS ALONG WITH THE WINDOW

```cpp
////////////////////////////////////////////////////////////////////
// CMainWnd::OnSize()

void CMainWnd::OnSize(UINT nType, int cx, int cy)
{
   // Call inherited method
   CWnd::OnSize(nType, cx, cy);

   // set some initial positions
   int nHeight = 20;
   int cyTop   = 10;

   // Resize the color sliders
   m_pSlider1->SetWindowPos(0, 10, cyTop, cx - 20, nHeight,
      SWP_SHOWWINDOW);
   cyTop += nHeight * 2;

   m_pSlider2->SetWindowPos(0, 10, cyTop, cx - 20, nHeight,
      SWP_SHOWWINDOW);
   cyTop += nHeight * 2;

   m_pSlider3->SetWindowPos(0, 10, cyTop, cx - 20, nHeight,
      SWP_SHOWWINDOW);
   cyTop += nHeight * 2;

   // Resize the static control
   m_pStatic1->SetWindowPos(0, 10, cyTop, cx - 20,
      m_nTextHeight, SWP_SHOWWINDOW);

   // Repaint the window at the new size
   UpdateClientColor();
}
```

To get the current position of the sliders, the UpdateClientColor() method calls CSlider::GetPos() for each, like this:

```cpp
// Get the current scroll position
nRed   = m_pSlider1->GetPos();
nGreen = m_pSlider2->GetPos();
nBlue  = m_pSlider3->GetPos();
```

This is followed by some informative text that I set into each static child window. The CString::Format() method takes care of the dirty work for formatting the string:

```cpp
// Display current RGB color as a text string
CString szText;
szText.Format(_T("RGB(%d, %d, %d)"), nRed, nGreen, nBlue);
m_pStatic1->SetWindowText(szText);
```

Progress Bar Controls: Class CProgressCtrl

A *progress bar control* is a window that provides visual feedback to a user during a lengthy application operation. Because a progress bar control simply keeps a user apprised of an operation's progress, the progress bar is typically for output only.

Like a slider control, a progress bar control has a *range* and a *current position*. The range specifies the length of some operation, and the current position represents how far along the operation has come at that time. Using these two values, the percentage of fill for the control is determined automatically.

A typical use of the progress bar control is for relaying information about the progress of file operations on a disk (see Figure 3.5).

FIGURE 3.5

Relaying information about the progress of a disk operation with a progress bar.

MFC provides the services of a Windows progress bar common control in the class CProgressCtrl, which is derived directly from CWnd and inherits all the functionality of CWnd. A progress bar control can be created as a child control of any window by writing code; it can also be defined in a dialog resource template.

CProgressCtrl Class Methods

The CProgressCtrl class offers a minimal set of methods for manipulating the control and its data. The constructor, CProgressCtrl::CProgressCtrl(), allocates a CProgressCtrl object that is initialized with the CProgressCtrl::Create() method. Table 3.13 describes the class's methods.

TABLE 3.13   CProgressCtrl CLASS METHODS

Method	Description
OffsetPos()	Advances the current position of a progress bar control by a specified increment and redraws the bar to show the new position.

continues

TABLE 3.13 CONTINUED

Method	Description
SetPos()	Sets the current position for a progress bar control and redraws the bar to show the new position.
SetRange()	Sets the minimum and maximum ranges for a progress bar control and redraws the bar to show the new ranges.
SetStep()	Specifies the step increment for a progress bar control.
StepIt()	Advances the current position for a progress bar control by the step increment and redraws the bar to show the new position.

Creating and Initializing a `CProgressCtrl` Object

To create a `CProgressCtrl` object, you use the two-step construction process typical of MFC:

1. Call the class constructor `CProgressCtrl::CProgressCtrl()` to allocate the object.
2. Initialize the `CProgressCtrl` object and attach an actual Windows progress common control to it with a call to the `CProgressCtrl::Create()` method.

The prototype for the `CProgressCtrl::Create()` method is shown here:

```
BOOL Create(DWORD dwStyle, const RECT& rect,
            CWnd* pParentWnd, UINT nID);
```

In this syntax, the parameters are defined as follows:

- `dwStyle`   Specifies the window style for the control. This can be any combination of the general window styles.
- `rect`   The rectangle specifying the size and position of the control.
- `pParentWnd`   A pointer to the owner of the control.
- `nID`   The control ID used by the parent to communicate with the control.

Using a Progress Control

The only necessary settings for a progress control are the range and current position. The *range* represents the entire duration of the operation. The *current position* represents the progress that your application has made toward completing the operation. Any changes to the range or position cause the progress control to redraw itself.

The default range for a progress control is from 0 to 100, with the default initial position set to zero. Use the `SetRange()` method to change the range of the progress control; use the `SetPos()` method to set the current position. Alternatively, you can change the position by a preset amount by calling the `SetStep()` method to set an increment amount for the control (10 by default) and then calling the `StepIt()` method to change the position.

> **NOTE**
>
> The `StepIt()` method wraps around to the minimum range if the maximum is exceeded. The `OffsetPos()` method, however, doesn't wrap back around to the minimum value—instead, the new position is adjusted to remain within the control's specified range.

In the TAB1 program I demonstrate a progress bar control on the third tab, creating the progress bar like this:

```
// Create the progress bar control
if (!m_ctlProgress.Create(
     WS_CHILD | WS_VISIBLE | WS_BORDER,
     CRect(0,0,0,0), &m_ctlTab, IDC_PROGRESSCTRL))
{
   TRACE0(_T("Problem creating progress bar control!"));
   return FALSE;
}
```

Next, set the lower and upper limits of the progress range with a call to `CProgressCtrl::SetRange()`:

```
m_ctlProgress.SetRange(0, 100);
```

To force the visual aspect of progress occurring, I simply call the `CProgressCtrl::SetPos()` method, like this:

```
// Make some progress...
for (int i = 0; i < 100; i++)
{
   m_ctlProgress.SetPos(i);
   this->Wait(20);
}
```

Image Lists: Class `CImageList`

An *image list* maintains an array of images. Each image is the same size, and each element in the list is referred to by its zero-based index. To efficiently handle large numbers of icons or bitmaps, all images in an image list are placed into a single memory bitmap stored in DDB format. This bitmap has the same height as the images in the list; all the list's images are contained side by side horizontally, usually making a very short, wide bitmap.

An image list can also include a monochrome bitmap mask used to draw images transparently. Win32 API image list functions give you the ability to draw images, replace images, merge images, add and remove images, drag images, and create and destroy image lists. This functionality is used by other common controls that make internal use of image lists, including list view, tree view, and tab controls. MFC provides the services of a Windows image list common control in the class `CImageList`, which is derived directly from `CObject`.

`CImageList` Class Methods

The `CImageList` class offers a complete set of methods for manipulating the images stored in a control. The `CImageList` constructor, `CImageList::CImageList()`, allocates a `CImageList` object that's initialized with the `CImageList::Create()` method. Table 3.14 describes the methods provided by `CImageList`.

TABLE 3.14 `CImageList` CLASS METHODS

Method	*Description*
`Add()`	Adds an image (or multiple images) to an image list.
`Attach()`	Attaches an image list to a `CImageList` object.
`BeginDrag()`	Begins dragging an image.
`DeleteImageList()`	Deletes an image list.
`Detach()`	Detaches an image list object from a `CImageList` object and returns a handle to an image list.
`DragEnter()`	Locks the window to prevent updates during a drag operation and displays a drag image at the specified location.
`DragLeave()`	Unlocks the window and hides the drag image so that the window can be updated.
`DragMove()`	Moves the image being dragged during a drag-and-drop operation.
`DragShowNolock()`	Shows or hides the drag image during a drag operation without locking the window.
`Draw()`	Draws the image being dragged during a drag-and-drop operation.
`EndDrag()`	Ends a drag operation.
`ExtractIcon()`	Creates an icon based on an image and mask in an image list.

GetBkColor()	Gets the current background color for an image list.
GetDragImage()	Gets the temporary image list used for dragging.
GetImageCount()	Gets the number of images in an image list.
GetImageInfo()	Gets information about an image.
GetSafeHandle()	Gets the underlying Windows image list stored in m_hImageList.
Read()	Reads an image list from an archive.
Remove()	Removes an image from an image list.
Replace()	Replaces an image in an image list with a new image.
SetBkColor()	Sets the background color for an image list.
SetDragCursorImage()	Creates a new drag image.
SetOverlayImage()	Adds the zero-based index of an image to the list of images to be used as overlay masks.
Write()	Writes an image list to an archive.

Creating and Initializing a `CImageList` Control

To create a CImageList object, you use the two-step construction process typical of MFC:

1. Call the class constructor CImageList::CImageList() to allocate the object.
2. Initialize the CImageList object and attach an actual Windows image list common control to it with a call to the CImageList::Create() method.

There are four overloaded prototypes for the CImageList::Create() method:

```
// 1
BOOL Create(int cx, int cy, BOOL bMask, int nInitial, int nGrow);

// 2
BOOL Create(UINT nBitmapID, int cx, int nGrow, COLORREF crMask);

// 3
BOOL Create(LPCTSTR lpszBitmapID, int cx, int nGrow,
   COLORREF crMask);

// 4
BOOL Create(CImageList& imagelist1, int nImage1,
   CImageList& imagelist2, int nImage2, int dx, int dy);
```

The parameters used by these prototypes are listed in Table 3.15.

3

THE WINDOWS
COMMON
CONTROLS

TABLE 3.15 The Parameters Used by the `CImageList` Control

Parameter	Description
cx, cy	Width and height of each image, in pixels.
dx, dy	Width and height of each image, in pixels (same as `cx` and `cy`).
bMask	A Boolean flag that specifies whether an image contains a monochrome mask.
nInitial	The number of images initially contained in an image list.
nGrow	The number of new images a resized image list can contain.
nBitmapID	The resource ID of a bitmap to be associated with an image list.
crMask	The color used to generate an image mask. Each pixel of this color in the specified bitmap is changed to black.
lpszBitmapID	A string that contains the resource IDs of all images stored in an image list.
imagelist1	A pointer to another `CImageList` object.
nImage1	The number of images contained in `imagelist1`.
imagelist2	A pointer to another `CImageList` object.
nImage2	The number of images contained in `imagelist2`.

List View Controls: Class `CListCtrl`

A *list view control* is a window that provides several ways of arranging and displaying a list of items. Each item is made up of an icon and a label. Unlike the list box control, a list view control can display list items using four different views, and the current view is specified by the control's current window style. Table 3.16 describes the four view styles provided by the list view control.

TABLE 3.16 The Four Types of Views Supported by the List View Common Control

View	Description
Icon view	In this view, list items are displayed as full-sized icons with labels below them, as specified by the `LVS_ICON` window style. In this view, a user can drag list items to any location in the list view window.

View	Description
Small icon view	In this view, list items are displayed as small icons with the labels to their right, as specified by the LVS_SMALLICON window style. In this view, a user can drag list items to any location in the list view window.
List view	In this view, list items are displayed as small icons with labels to their right, as specified by the LVS_LIST window style. In this view, items are arranged and fixed in columns; they can't be dragged to any other list view location.
Report view	In this view, list items are displayed each on its own line, with information arranged in columns as specified by the LVS_REPORT window style. The left column displays a small icon and a label; the columns that follow contain application-specific subitems. Each column uses a Win32 header common control unless the LVS_NOCOLUMNHEADER window style is also specified.

As you'll see later in this chapter, other window styles enable you to manage a list view control's visual and functional aspects. Figure 3.6 shows four instances of Explorer, using the four view styles.

FIGURE 3.6

Four instances of Explorer, showing the four view styles.

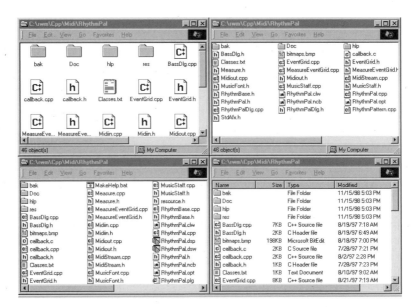

MFC provides the services of a Windows list view common control in the class CListCtrl, which is derived directly from CWnd and inherits all the functionality of CWnd.

A list view control can be created as a child control of any window by writing code; it can also be defined in a dialog resource template. A list view control sends Windows notification messages to its owner (usually a `CDialog`-derived class), and these messages can be trapped and handled by writing message map entries and message-handler methods for each message. These message map entries and methods are implemented in the list view control's parent class.

List View Control Styles

Like all windows, list view controls can use the general window styles available to `CWnd`. In addition, list view controls use the list view styles listed in Table 3.17 (as defined in AFXCMN.H). A list view control's styles determine its appearance and operations. Style bits are typically set when the control is initialized with the `CListCtrl::Create()` method.

> **TIP**
>
> To retrieve the style bits present in a control, use the Windows API function `GetWindowLong()`. To change the style bits after the control has been initialized, use the corresponding Windows API function `SetWindowLong()`.

TABLE 3.17 THE WINDOW STYLES DEFINED FOR A LIST VIEW COMMON CONTROL

Style Macro	*Meaning*
LVS_ALIGNLEFT	Items are left-aligned in icon and small icon view.
LVS_ALIGNTOP	Items are aligned with the top of the control in icon and small icon view.
LVS_AUTOARRANGE	Icons are automatically arranged in icon view and small icon view.
LVS_EDITLABELS	Allows item text to be edited in place.
LVS_ICON	Icon view.
LVS_LIST	List view.
LVS_NOCOLUMNHEADER	No column header is displayed in report view.
LVS_NOLABELWRAP	Item text is displayed on a single line in icon view.
LVS_NOSCROLL	Disables scrolling.
LVS_NOSORTHEADER	Column headers don't function as buttons.
LVS_OWNERDRAWFIXED	Enables the owner window to paint items as desired while in report view.

Style Macro	Meaning
LVS_REPORT	Report view.
LVS_SHAREIMAGELISTS	Enables image lists to be used by multiple list view controls.
LVS_SINGLESEL	Allows only one item at a time to be selected.
LVS_SMALLICON	Small icon view.
LVS_SORTASCENDING	Sorts items in ascending order based on item text.
LVS_SORTDESCENDING	Sorts items in descending order based on item text.

In addition, many styles defined for the new Windows common controls can be used (see Table 3.18). These styles determine how a common control positions and resizes itself.

TABLE 3.18 WINDOWS COMMON CONTROL WINDOW STYLES USED BY A LIST VIEW CONTROL

Style Macro	Meaning
CCS_BOTTOM	The control aligns itself at the bottom of the parent window's client area and sizes itself to the width of its parent window's client area.
CCS_NODIVIDER	Prevents a two-pixel highlight from being drawn at the top of the control.
CCS_NOHILITE	Prevents a one-pixel highlight from being drawn at the top of the control.
CCS_NOMOVEY	Causes the control to resize and move itself horizontally (but not vertically) in response to a WM_SIZE message (default).
CCS_NOPARENTALIGN	Prevents the control from automatically aligning to the top or bottom of the parent window.
CCS_NORESIZE	Forces a control to use the width and height specified when created or resized.
CCS_TOP	The control aligns itself at the top of the parent window's client area and sizes itself to the width of its parent window's client area.

Image Lists and the List View Control

The icons used by list view items are stored as image lists; there are three image lists available to a list view control:

- Large image list   An image list that contains images of the full-sized icons used by the LVS_ICON list view style.

- Small image list   An image list that contains the images of the small icons used by views that don't have the LVS_ICON list view style.
- State image list   An image list that can contain state images that can appear next to an item's icon. These images are typically used to denote some application-specific state.

The large and small icon image lists should contain an icon for each type of item in the list. These lists are created individually as needed, and each uses the same index values. This arrangement means that images in the large icon list, for example, should correspond one to one with the images in the small icon list and the state icon list.

If you use a state image list for a list view control, the control reserves space for the state image just to the left of the icon for each list item.

> **NOTE**
>
> The large and small icon image lists can also contain overlay images that can be superimposed on list item icons. Because of a 4-bit indexing scheme for overlay images, overlay images must be stored within the first 15 images in a list.

List View Items and Subitems

A list view control contains a list of items; each item consists of four parts:

- An icon
- A label
- A current state
- An application-defined value

Each item can also contain strings called *subitems*. These subitems are used in the report view, and each subitem is displayed in its own column. You can use the CListCtrl methods to add, modify, retrieve, find, and delete list view items.

> **NOTE**
>
> Every item in a list view control must have the same number of subitems, even if the items represent different types of data.

A list view item or subitem is defined with a Windows LV_ITEM structure, which looks like this:

```
typedef struct _LV_ITEM
{
    UINT    mask;
    int     iItem;
    int     iSubItem;
    UINT    state;
    UINT    stateMask;
    LPSTR   pszText;
    int     cchTextMax;
    int     iImage;
    LPARAM  lParam;
}
LV_ITEM;
```

The data members of this structure are as follows:

- mask   A set of bit flags specifying the members of the LV_ITEM structure that contain valid data or that need to be filled in (see Table 3.19).
- iItem   The zero-based index of an item.
- iSubItem   The one-based index of a subitem.
- state   The current state of an item.
- stateMask   Specifies the bits of the state member that are valid.
- pszText   A pointer to a string that contains the item text if the structure specifies item attributes.
- cchTextMax   The size of the buffer pointed to by the pszText member.
- iImage   The index of an item's icon in the icon and small icon image lists.
- lParam   An application-defined 32-bit value to associate with the item.

TABLE 3.19   THE BIT FLAGS USED FOR THE LV_ITEM mask MEMBER

Value	Meaning
LVIF_TEXT	The pszText member is valid.
LVIF_IMAGE	The iImage member is valid.
LVIF_PARAM	The lParam member is valid.
LVIF_STATE	The state member is valid.
LVIF_DI_SETITEM	Windows should store the requested list item information.

List View Notification Messages

Like most Windows common controls, a list view control sends WM_NOTIFY notification messages to its parent window. These messages can be trapped and handled by writing message handlers in the list view control's parent class. Table 3.20 shows the notifications used by list view controls, as defined in COMMCTRL.H.

TABLE 3.20   NOTIFICATION MESSAGES DEFINED FOR LIST VIEW CONTROLS

Message Map Entry	Meaning
LVN_BEGINDRAG	A drag-and-drop operation involving the left mouse button is beginning.
LVN_BEGINLABELEDIT	A label-editing operation is beginning.
LVN_BEGINRDRAG	A drag-and-drop operation involving the right mouse button is beginning.
LVN_COLUMNCLICK	A column was clicked.
LVN_DELETEALLITEMS	A user has deleted all items from the control.
LVN_DELETEITEM	A user has deleted a single item from the control.
LVN_ENDLABELEDIT	A label-editing operation is ending.
LVN_GETDISPINFO	A request for the parent window to provide information needed to display or sort a list view item.
LVN_INSERTITEM	A new item was inserted.
LVN_ITEMCHANGED	An item was changed.
LVN_ITEMCHANGING	An item is changing.
LVN_KEYDOWN	A key was pressed.
LVN_PEN	Used for pen Windows (for systems with a pen and digitizer tablet).
LVN_SETDISPINFO	Forces the parent to update display information for an item.

Creating and Initializing a CListCtrl Object

To create a CListCtrl object, you use the two-step construction process typical of MFC:

1. Call the class constructor CListCtrl::CListCtrl() to allocate the object.
2. Initialize the CListCtrl object and attach an actual Windows list view common control to it with a call to the CListCtrl::Create() method.

The prototype for the `CListCtrl::Create()` method is shown here:

```
BOOL Create(DWORD dwStyle, const RECT& rect,
            CWnd* pParentWnd, UINT nID);
```

In this syntax, the parameters are as follows:

- `dwStyle`   Specifies the combination of styles used by a list control.
- `rect`   Specifies a list control's size and position.
- `pParentWnd`   Specifies the list control's parent window.
- `nID`   Specifies the control identifier for a list control.

The `dwStyle` parameter specifies the styles used by a list control, which can be any of the values listed in Table 3.17 (earlier in this chapter).

> **NOTE**
>
> MFC encapsulates the list control in the view class `CListView`, allowing you to take advantage of the benefits of an integrated list view control by allowing you to typecast a `CListView` object to a `CListCtrl` object at runtime.

Using the List View Control

Using the list view control generally requires several steps, including these:

1. Attaching the image list(s).
2. Adding columns for report view.
3. Adding items to a `CListCtrl` object.
4. Overriding the inherited `OnChildNotify()` method to handle `WM_NOTIFY` messages.

The following sections look at each of these items a little more closely.

Attaching the Image List(s)

If the list view control you're creating uses the `LVS_ICON` style, you'll need image lists for the list view items. Use the `CImageList` class to create an image list (or lists) for the list view to display. Next, call the `CListCtrl::SetImageList()` for all image lists used by the control.

Adding Columns for Report View

Columns can be used only with the `LVS_REPORT` style, which is the report view. The report view typically uses the header common control (`CHeaderCtrl`) to allow users to resize the column. Adding columns is easy: Simply initialize an LV_COLUMN structure and call the InsertColumn() method to create each desired column. An LV_COLUMN structure is defined as follows:

```
typedef struct _LV_COLUMN
{
    UINT    mask;        // Specifies valid data members
    int     fmt;         // Column alignment specifier
    int     cx;          // Width of column, in pixels
    LPTSTR  pszText;     // Column heading
    int     cchTextMax;  // Character size of pszText
    int     iSubItem;    // Index of a subitem
}
LV_COLUMN;
```

The members for this structure are described following:

- mask   Specifies which members of this structure contain valid information. This member can be zero, or one or more of the values listed in Table 3.21.

- fmt   Specifies the alignment of the column heading and the subitem text in the column. This can be one of the following values: LVCFMT_CENTER (centered text), LVCFMT_LEFT (flush-left text), or LVCFMT_RIGHT (flush-right text).

- cx   Specifies the pixel width of a column.

- pszText   A pointer to a column's heading text string.

- cchTextMax   Specifies the number of characters in the buffer pointed to by the pszText member.

- iSubItem   Specifies the index of subitem associated with the column.

Table 3.21   The Possible Values for the LV_COLUMN mask Member

Value	*Meaning*
LVCF_FMT	The fmt member is valid.
LVCF_SUBITEM	The iSubItem member is valid.
LVCF_TEXT	The pszText member is valid.
LVCF_WIDTH	The cx member is valid.

Note

The LV_COLUMN structure is used with the LVM_GETCOLUMN, LVM_SETCOLUMN, LVM_INSERTCOLUMN, and LVM_DELETECOLUMN list view control messages. The CListCtrl class wraps these messages with the default handler methods GetColumn(), SetColumn(), InsertColumn(), and DeleteColumn().

Adding Items to a `CListCtrl` Object

Depending on the type of data that's going into a list view control, you can call one of the overloaded `InsertItem()` methods. Each version of this method takes a different type of data, and the list view control manages the storage for list items. For example, Listing 3.2 shows a code fragment from the TREELIST program that adds the names of items found in the tree control (`m_ctlTree`) to a list control (`m_ctlList`).

LISTING 3.2 ADDING ITEMS TO A LIST CONTROL

```
///////////////////////////////////////////////////////////////
// CMainWnd::ShowChildren()

void CMainWnd::ShowChildren(HTREEITEM hti)
{
   m_ctlList.DeleteAllItems();

   HTREEITEM htiNext  = 0;
   HTREEITEM htiChild = m_ctlTree.GetChildItem(hti);

   if (htiChild)
   {
      // Add the child's tree text to the list
      int i = 0;
      CString str = m_ctlTree.GetItemText(htiChild);

      m_ctlList.InsertItem(i, (LPCTSTR) str);
      htiNext = htiChild;

      // Add sibling tree text to the list
      while (TRUE)
      {
         htiNext = m_ctlTree.GetNextSiblingItem(htiNext);
         if (!htiNext) return;

         CString str = m_ctlTree.GetItemText(htiNext);
         i++;
         m_ctlList.InsertItem(i, (LPCTSTR) str);
      }
   }
}
```

Tree View Controls: Class CTreeCtrl

A *tree view control* is a window that provides a hierarchical view of some set of data, such as a directory structure on a disk. Each item in the tree is made up of a label and an optional bitmap. Each item can own a list of subitems; by clicking an item, a user can expand or collapse the tree to reveal or hide subitems. MFC provides the services of a Windows tree view common control in the class CTreeCtrl, which is derived directly from CWnd and inherits all the functionality of CWnd.

A tree view control can be created as a child control of any window by writing code, or it can be defined in a dialog resource template. A tree view control sends Windows notification messages to its owner (usually a CDialog-derived class), and these messages can be trapped and handled by writing message map entries and message-handler methods for each message. These message map entries and methods are implemented in the list view control's parent class.

Tree View Control Styles

Like all windows, tree view controls can use the general window styles available to CWnd. In addition, tree view controls use the tree view styles listed in Table 3.22 (as defined in COMMCTRL.H). A list view control's styles determine its appearance and operation. Style bits are typically set when the control is initialized with the CTreeCtrl::Create() method.

TABLE 3.22   THE WINDOW STYLES DEFINED FOR A TREE VIEW CONTROL

Style Macro	*Meaning*
TVS_HASLINES	Child items have lines linking them to corresponding parent items.
TVS_LINESATROOT	Child items have lines linking them to the root of the tree.
TVS_HASBUTTONS	The tree has a button to the left of each parent item.
TVS_EDITLABELS	Tree view item labels can be edited.
TVS_SHOWSELALWAYS	A selected item will remain selected, even if the tree view control loses the input focus.
TVS_DISABLEDRAGDROP	Prevents the tree view control from sending TVN_BEGINDRAG notification messages.

Tree View Notification Messages

Like most of the Windows common controls, a tree view control sends `WM_NOTIFY` notification messages to its parent window, which is usually a `CDialog`-derived class. These messages can be trapped and handled by writing message handlers in the list view control's parent class. Table 3.23 shows the notification messages defined in COMMC-TRL.H.

TABLE 3.23 NOTIFICATION MESSAGES USED BY `CTreeCtrl` OBJECTS

Notification	Meaning
TVN_BEGINDRAG	A drag-and-drop operation has begun.
TVN_BEGINLABELEDIT	In-place label editing has begun.
TVN_BEGINRDRAG	A drag-and-drop operation, using the right mouse button, has begun.
TVN_DELETEITEM	A specific item has been deleted.
TVN_ENDLABELEDIT	In-place label editing has ended.
TVN_GETDISPINFO	Gets information that the tree control requires to display an item.
TVN_ITEMEXPANDED	A parent item's list of child items was expanded or collapsed.
TVN_ITEMEXPANDING	A parent item's list of child items is about to be expanded or collapsed.
TVN_KEYDOWN	A key was pressed down.
TVN_SELCHANGED	The current selection has changed from one item to another.
TVN_SELCHANGING	The selection is about to change from one item to another.
TVN_SETDISPINFO	Updates the information maintained for an item.

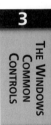

`CTreeCtrl` Class Methods

The `CTreeCtrl` class offers a full set of methods for manipulating the control and its data. The `CTreeCtrl` constructor, `CTreeCtrl::CTreeCtrl()`, allocates a `CTreeCtrl` object that is initialized with the `CTreeCtrl::Create()` method to set attributes and ownership. Table 3.24 describes the methods used to get and set button control attributes, as well as methods that perform operations on the control and its data.

TABLE 3.24 CTreeCtrl CLASS METHODS

Method	Description
CreateDragImage()	Creates a dragging bitmap for the specified tree view item.
DeleteAllItems()	Deletes all items in a tree view control.
DeleteItem()	Deletes a new item in a tree view control.
EditLabel()	Edits a specified tree view item in place.
EnsureVisible()	Ensures that a tree view item is visible in its tree view control.
Expand()	Expands or collapses the child items of the specified tree view item.
GetChildItem()	Gets the child of a specified tree view item.
GetCount()	Gets the number of tree items associated with a tree view control.
GetDropHilightItem()	Gets the target of a drag-and-drop operation.
GetEditControl()	Gets the handle of the edit control used to edit the specified tree view item.
GetFirstVisibleItem()	Gets the first visible item of the specified tree view item.
GetImageList()	Gets the handle of the image list associated with a tree view control.
GetIndent()	Gets the offset (in pixels) of a tree view item from its parent.
GetItem()	Gets the attributes of a specified tree view item.
GetItemData()	Gets the 32-bit application-specific value associated with an item.
GetItemImage()	Gets the images associated with an item.
GetItemRect()	Gets the bounding rectangle of a tree view item.
GetItemState()	Gets the state of an item.
GetItemText()	Gets the text of an item.
GetNextItem()	Gets the next tree view item that matches a specified relationship.
GetNextSiblingItem()	Gets the next sibling of the specified tree view item.
GetNextVisibleItem()	Gets the next visible item of the specified tree view item.
GetParentItem()	Gets the parent of the specified tree view item.
GetPrevSiblingItem()	Gets the previous sibling of the specified tree view item.
GetPrevVisibleItem()	Gets the previous visible item of the specified tree view item.
GetRootItem()	Gets the root of the specified tree view item.
GetSelectedItem()	Gets the currently selected tree view item.
GetVisibleCount()	Gets the number of visible tree items associated with a tree view control.
HitTest()	Gets the current position of the cursor related to the CTreeCtrl object.

Method	Description
InsertItem()	Inserts a new item in a tree view control.
ItemHasChildren()	Determines whether an item has child items.
Select()	Selects, scrolls into view, or redraws a specified tree view item.
SelectDropTarget()	Redraws the tree item as the target of a drag-and-drop operation.
SelectItem()	Selects a specified tree view item.
SetImageList()	Sets the handle of the image list associated with a tree view control.
SetIndent()	Sets the offset (in pixels) of a tree view item from its parent.
SetItem()	Sets the attributes of a specified tree view item.
SetItemData()	Sets the 32-bit application-specific value associated with an item.
SetItemImage()	Associates images with an item.
SetItemState()	Sets the state of an item.
SetItemText()	Sets the text of an item.
SortChildren()	Sorts the children of a given parent item.
SortChildrenCB()	Sorts the children of a given parent item using an application-defined sort function.

Creating and Initializing a Tree View Control

To create a CTreeCtrl object, you use the two-step construction process typical of MFC:

1. Call the class constructor CTreeCtrl::CTreeCtrl() to allocate the object.

2. Initialize the CTreeCtrl object and attach an actual Windows tree view common control to it with a call to the CTreeCtrl::Create() method.

The prototype for the CTreeCtrl::Create() method is shown here:

```
BOOL Create(DWORD dwStyle, const RECT& rect,
            CWnd* pParentWnd, UINT nID);
```

In this syntax, the parameters are as follows:

- dwStyle   Specifies the window style for the control. This can be any combination of the general window styles and the special tree view styles listed in Table 3.22.

- rect   The rectangle specifying the size and position of the control.

- pParentWnd   A pointer to the owner of the control.

- nID   The control ID used by the parent to communicate with the tree view control.

Using a `CTreeCtrl` Object

If a tree control is to use images, create and set an image list by calling `SetImageList()`. You can further initialize the control by calling `SetIndent()` to change the indentation. Changing the indentation is usually done once, when the control is first initialized, typically in `OnInitDialog()` for a dialog box or in `OnInitialUpdate()` for a view.

Use the `InsertItem()` method to add data items to the control. Each call to `InsertItem()` results in an item handle being returned for each item added to the tree. These handles should be saved for later use.

Use an `ON_NOTIFY` macro in the message map entry for control notifications in the parent class, or make the class more reusable by placing an `ON_NOTIFY_REFLECT` macro in the control window's message map to let it handle its own notifications. The tree control's notification messages are listed in Table 3.23, earlier in this chapter.

Sample Program: TREELIST.EXE

On the companion CD-ROM, you'll find the program TREELIST.EXE. This program uses the tree view and list view control classes (see Figure 3.7).

FIGURE 3.7
The TREELIST program.

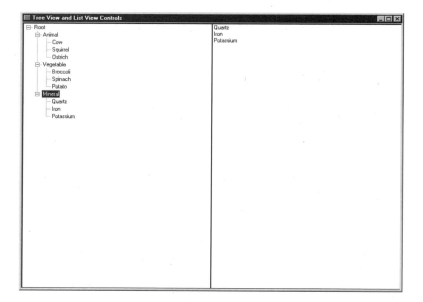

The TREELIST program uses a `CTreeCtrl` object and a `CListCtrl` object; the list displays the children (if any) of the currently selected tree item. Tree item labels can also be edited in place.

Tab Controls: Class `CTabCtrl`

A *tab control* is a GUI metaphor for the tabs found on file folders. A tab control is a window that can be divided into several pages, each of which typically has a set of controls. Each tab page provides a tab that, when clicked, displays its corresponding page. Figure 3.8 shows a typical tab window used for displaying various controls.

FIGURE 3.8

A typical tab control window.

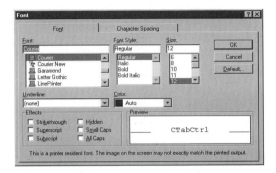

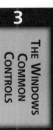

> **NOTE**
>
> A tab control can also display buttons in place of tabs. Clicking a button should immediately perform a command instead of displaying a page.

MFC provides the services of a Windows tab common control in the class `CTabCtrl`, which is derived directly from `CWnd` and inherits all the functionality of `CWnd`. A tab control can be created as a child control of any window by writing code; it can also be defined in a dialog resource template.

A tab control sends Windows notification messages to its owner (usually a `CDialog`-derived class), and these messages can be trapped and handled by writing message map entries and message-handler methods for each message. These message map entries and methods are implemented in the tab control's parent class.

Tab Control Styles

Like all windows, tab controls can use the general window styles available to `CWnd`. They can also use the additional styles listed in Table 3.25. A tab control's styles determine its appearance and operations; style bits are typically set when the control is initialized with the `CTabCtrl::Create()` method.

> **TIP**
>
> To retrieve the style bits present in a control, use the Windows API function `GetWindowLong()`. To change the style bits after the control has been initialized, use the corresponding Windows API function `SetWindowLong()`.

TABLE 3.25   THE WINDOW STYLES DESIGNED FOR USE WITH TAB CONTROLS

Style Macro	*Meaning*
TCS_BUTTONS	Makes tabs appear as standard pushbuttons.
TCS_FIXEDWIDTH	Makes all tabs the same width.
TCS_FOCUSNEVER	Specifies that a tab never receives the input focus.
TCS_FOCUSONBUTTONDOWN	A tab will receive the input focus when clicked (typically used only with the TCS_BUTTONS style).
TCS_FORCEICONLEFT	Forces a tab's icon to the left but leaves the tab label centered.
TCS_FORCELABELLEFT	Left-aligns both the icon and label.
TCS_MULTILINE	A tab control displays multiple rows of tabs to ensure that all tabs can be displayed at once.
TCS_OWNERDRAWFIXED	The parent window draws the tabs for the control.
TCS_RAGGEDRIGHT	A default style that doesn't force each row of tabs to fill the width of the control.
TCS_RIGHTJUSTIFY	Right-justifies tabs.
TCS_SHAREIMAGELISTS	A tab control's image lists aren't destroyed with the control. This allows multiple controls to use the same image lists.
TCS_SINGLELINE	Displays all tabs in a single row.
TCS_TABS	The standard tab style; specifies that tabs appear as tabs (as opposed to buttons) and that a border is drawn around the display area.
TCS_TOOLTIPS	The tab control uses a ToolTip control.

Tab Control Notification Messages

Like most Windows common controls, a tab control sends WM_NOTIFY notification messages to its parent window, which is usually a CDialog-derived class. Table 3.26 shows the notification messages used by the tab control, as defined in COMMCTRL.H.

TABLE 3.26   NOTIFICATION MESSAGES USED BY THE TAB CONTROL

Notification	Meaning
TCN_KEYDOWN	A key was pressed.
TCN_SELCHANGE	The currently selected tab has changed.
TCN_SELCHANGING	The currently selected tab is about to change. By returning TRUE in response to this notification, you can prevent the selection from changing.

TIP

Use the GetCurSel() method to determine the currently selected tab.

CTabCtrl Class Methods

The CTabCtrl class offers a complete set of methods for manipulating the control and its data. The CTabCtrl constructor, CTabCtrl::CTabCtrl(), allocates a CTabCtrl object that is initialized with the CTabCtrl::Create() method to set attributes and ownership. The CTabCtrl class methods are described in Table 3.27.

TABLE 3.27   CTabCtrl CLASS METHODS

Method	Description
AdjustRect()	Calculates a tab control's display area given a window rectangle; alternatively, calculates the window rectangle that corresponds to a given display area.
DeleteAllItems()	Removes all items from a tab control.
DeleteItem()	Removes an item from a tab control.
DrawItem()	Draws a specified tab control item.
GetCurFocus()	Gets the tab control tab that has the input focus.
GetCurSel()	Gets the currently selected tab control tab.
GetImageList()	Gets the image list associated with a tab control.
GetItem()	Gets information about a tab in a tab control.
GetItemCount()	Gets the number of tabs in the tab control.
GetItemRect()	Gets the bounding rectangle for a tab in a tab control.
GetRowCount()	Gets the current number of rows of tabs in a tab control.

TABLE 3.27 CONTINUED

Method	Description
GetTooltips()	Gets the handle of the ToolTip control associated with a tab control.
HitTest()	Determines which tab (if any) is located at a specified screen position.
InsertItem()	Inserts a new tab into a tab control.
RemoveImage()	Removes an image from a tab control's image list.
SetCurSel()	Selects one of a tab control's tabs.
SetImageList()	Assigns an image list to a tab control.
SetItem()	Sets some or all of a tab's attributes.
SetItemSize()	Sets the width and height of an item.
SetPadding()	Sets the amount of padding around each tab's icon and label in a tab control.
SetTooltips()	Assigns a ToolTip control to a tab control.

The Tab Item Structure (TC_ITEM)

The GetItem(), SetItem(), and InsertItem() methods all take a parameter of type TC_ITEM. This is a new datatype for Win32 that specifies or receives the attributes of a tab. The TC_ITEM structure has the following form:

```
typedef struct _TC_ITEM
{
    UINT    mask;
    UINT    lpReserved1;  // reserved; do not use
    UINT    lpReserved2;  // reserved; do not use
    LPSTR   pszText;
    int     cchTextMax;
    int     iImage;
    LPARAM  lParam;
}
TC_ITEM;
```

The members of this structure are as follows:

- mask   A value specifying which members to retrieve or set. This member can be all members (TCIF_ALL), zero (0), or one or more of the values listed in Table 3.28.
- pszText   A pointer to a string containing the tab text.
- cchTextMax   The size of the buffer pointed to by the pszText member.
- iImage   The index into the tab control's image list, or –1 if the tab has no image.
- lParam   Application-defined data associated with the tab.

TABLE 3.28 TAB ITEM STRUCTURE mask VALUES

Value	Description
TCIF_IMAGE	The iImage member is valid.
TCIF_PARAM	The lParam member is valid.
TCIF_RTLREADING	Displays the text pointed to by pszText using right-to-left reading order when running on Hebrew or Arabic systems.
TCIF_TEXT	The pszText member is valid.

Creating and Initializing a Tab Control

To create a CTabCtrl object, you use the two-step construction process typical of MFC:

1. Call the class constructor CTabCtrl::CTabCtrl() to allocate the object.
2. Initialize the CTabCtrl object and attach an actual Windows tab common control to it with a call to the CTabCtrl::Create() method.

The prototype for the CTabCtrl::Create() method is shown here:

```
BOOL Create(DWORD dwStyle, const RECT& rect,
            CWnd* pParentWnd, UINT nID);
```

In this syntax, the parameters are as follows:

- dwStyle   Specifies the combination of styles used by the control.
- rect   Specifies a control's size and position.
- pParentWnd   Specifies a control's parent window.
- nID   Specifies the control identifier for a control.

> **NOTE**
>
> As with other Windows controls, a tab control is created implicitly when used in a dialog box; a tab control is created explicitly when created in a nondialog window.

Using a Tab Control

After the CTabCtrl object is constructed, you add tabs to the tab control to complete its initialization. You are responsible for handling any tab notification messages that apply to your application.

Adding Tabs to a Tab Control

After constructing the `CTabCtrl` object, add tabs as needed by preparing a `TC_ITEM` structure and calling the `CTabCtrl::InsertItem()` method. Pass the `TC_ITEM` structure as a parameter as shown in this simple example:

```
// Initialize the TC_ITEM structures
TC_ITEM tci;

CString str = "Tab 1";

tci.mask       = TCIF_TEXT;
tci.pszText    = (LPSTR)(LPCTSTR)str;
tci.cchTextMax = str.GetLength();

// Add this tab to the tab control
m_ctlTab.InsertItem(0, &tci);
```

Note this line of code in the preceding example:

```
tci.pszText = (LPSTR)(LPCTSTR)str;
```

The `CString` variable `str` uses the `LPCTSTR` operator to get a `const` pointer to the character string contained in the string object. The `const` is then cast away to the `LPSTR` expected by `tci.pszText`.

Trapping Tab Notification Messages

The final step in dealing with tab controls is handling any tab notifications for your application. A simple notification handler that fires when a user clicks the control is given in Listing 3.3. In this case, the hypothetical tab control (`m_ctlTab`) is assumed to be a class data member; this control is assumed to contain two tab items.

LISTING 3.3 A SIMPLE TAB NOTIFICATION MESSAGE HANDLER

```
//////////////////////////////////////////////////////////////////
// CMainWnd::OnClickTabCtrl()

void  CMainWnd::OnClickTabCtrl(NMHDR* pNotifyStruct,
                                LRESULT* pResult)
{
    // Set the return code
    *pResult = 0;

    // Get the currently active tab
    int nCurTab = m_ctlTab.GetCurSel();
```

```
    // Perform some action in response to the tab becoming active
    switch (nCurTab)
    {
        case 0:
            MessageBeep(MB_ICONASTERISK);
            AfxMessageBox("You activated Tab 1!",
                MB_OK | MB_ICONINFORMATION);
            break;

        case 1:
            MessageBeep(MB_ICONASTERISK);
            AfxMessageBox("You activated Tab 2!",
                MB_OK | MB_ICONINFORMATION);
    }
}
```

The corresponding handler in the class's message map looks something like this (where `IDC_TABCTRL` is assumed to be a valid control identifier for the tab control in question):

```
BEGIN_MESSAGE_MAP(CMainWnd, CMainFrame)
    // ...Other possible entries...
    ON_NOTIFY(NM_CLICK, IDC_TABCTRL, OnClickTabCtrl)
END_MESSAGE_MAP()
```

Animate Controls: Class `CAnimateCtrl`

An *animation control* is a rectangular window that displays an animation in Audio Video Interleaved (AVI) format, which is the standard video for Windows file format. Viewed simplistically, an AVI file is composed of a series of animation frames; each frame is a bitmap image. Figure 3.9 shows three frames from the AVI clip SPINTORI.AVI, which shows a spinning red object (run the program TAB1.EXE on the companion CD-ROM to see this in action).

NOTE

Nine bitmaps were used to create the SPINTORI.AVI file, and all were generated using the Persistence of Vision ray tracing tool kit (POVRAY). The POVRAY source files for the spinning tori animation are also included on the CD-ROM.

FIGURE 3.9

Three bitmaps from the SPIN-TORI.AVI animation file.

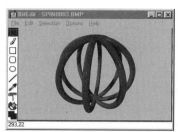 

Animation controls can play only simple AVI clips, and they don't support sound. In fact, the types of AVIs an animate control can play are quite limited, and must meet the following specifications:

- There must be only one video stream containing at least one frame.

- In addition to a single video stream, an AVI can also have a single audio stream, although audio is ignored by an animate control.

- The only type of data compression allowed for use with animate controls is Microsoft's RLE8 compression. Uncompressed AVIs work well with the animate control, but can be quite large.

- A single palette must be used throughout the video stream.

The animate control allows full multithreading in your applications, which makes the control useful for keeping users entertained during lengthy operations—or at least to assure them that their system hasn't locked up. In this capacity, the animation acts as a reassuring "don't worry, we're still working on it" element for the user. The animate control is a nice alternative to the progress bar control, especially when the remaining duration of an operation is unknown.

MFC provides the services of a Windows animate common control in the class CAnimateCtrl, which is derived directly from CWnd and inherits all the functionality of CWnd. An animate control can be created as a child control of any window by writing code; it can also be defined in a dialog resource template.

Animate Control Styles

Like all windows, animate controls can use the general window styles available to CWnd. In addition, they can use the animate control styles listed in Table 3.29 (as defined in COMMCTRL.H). An animate control's styles determine its appearance and operations. Style bits are typically set when the control is initialized with the CAnimateCtrl::Create() method.

TABLE 3.29 THE WINDOW STYLES SPECIFIC TO AN ANIMATE CONTROL

Style	*Description*
ACS_AUTOPLAY	Tells the control to play an AVI clip when it's opened and to automatically loop the video playback indefinitely.
ACS_CENTER	Centers the AVI clip in the control window.
ACS_TRANSPARENT	The background color specified in the AVI clip is drawn as transparent.

NOTE

If the ACS_CENTER style isn't specified, the animate control is resized to the size of the images in the video clip when the file is opened for reading.

Animate Control Notification Messages

Like most Windows common controls, an animate control sends WM_NOTIFY notification messages to its parent window. These messages can be trapped and handled by writing message map entries and message-handler methods implemented in the animate control's owner class for each message. Table 3.30 shows the notification messages used by an animate control.

TABLE 3.30 MESSAGE MAP ENTRIES FOR ANIMATE CONTROL NOTIFICATION MESSAGES

Notification	*Meaning*
ACN_START	An animation control has started playing an AVI clip.
ACN_STOP	An animation control has either finished playing or stopped playing an AVI clip.

3

THE WINDOWS COMMON CONTROLS

CAnimateCtrl Class Methods

The CAnimateCtrl class offers a minimal set of methods. These methods are described in Table 3.31.

TABLE 3.31   CAnimate CLASS METHODS

Method	Description
Close	Closes an open AVI clip.
Open	Opens an AVI clip from a file or resource and displays the first frame.
Play	Plays an AVI clip, leaving out any audio tracks that might be present (audio is ignored).
Seek	Displays a selected single frame of an AVI clip.
Stop	Stops playing an AVI clip.

Creating and Initializing an Animate Control

To create a CAnimateCtrl object, you use the two-step construction process typical of MFC:

1. Call the class constructor CAnimateCtrl::CAnimateCtrl() to allocate the object.
2. Initialize the CAnimateCtrl object and attach an actual Windows animate common control to it with a call to the CAnimateCtrl::Create() method.

The prototype for the CAnimateCtrl::Create() method is shown here:

```
BOOL Create(DWORD dwStyle, const RECT& rect,
            CWnd* pParentWnd, UINT nID);
```

In this syntax, the parameters are defined as follows:

- dwStyle   Specifies the combination of styles used by a control.
- rect   Specifies a control's size and position.
- pParentWnd   Specifies the control's parent window.
- nID   Specifies the control identifier for a control.

Using an Animate Control

After the `CAnimateCtrl` object is constructed, you open and play an AVI clip by performing the following steps:

- Open the AVI clip by calling the `CAnimateCtrl::Open()` method.
- Play the AVI by calling the `CAnimateCtrl::Play()` method.

For example, the TAB1 program plays an AVI clip like this, where `m_ctlAnim` is a `CAnimateCtrl` object:

```
// Open and play the AVI
if (m_ctlAnim.Open((LPCTSTR)"spintori.avi"))
{
   m_ctlAnim.ShowWindow(SW_SHOWNORMAL);
   m_ctlAnim.Play(0, (UINT)-1, (UINT)-1);
}
```

The following section looks at the big brother of the hearty edit control: the rich edit control.

Rich Edit Controls: Class CRichEditCtrl

A *rich edit control* is a window that, at first glance, looks very similar to a standard edit control. But a rich edit control has the additional benefits of letting users perform character and paragraph formatting, as well as embed OLE objects. Although the rich edit control provides the functionality, your application must implement the user interface components that allow users to perform formatting operations on the text.

The MFC classes `CRichEditDoc`, `CRichEditView`, and `CRichEditCntrItem` encapsulate the functionality of a rich edit control into full-featured classes for use in your document/view programs. Figure 3.10 shows the WordPad application that ships with Windows 95. Note that this application is mainly just a rich edit control with some GUI trappings (toolbar, status bar, and so on) wrapped in a nice document/view framework.

A rich edit control provides support for changing the character attributes of selected text, such as whether a character is displayed as bold, italicized, or with a certain font family and point size. A rich edit control also provides support for setting paragraph attributes, such as justification, margin size, and tab-stop values.

FIGURE 3.10

A typical rich edit control makes the WordPad application possible.

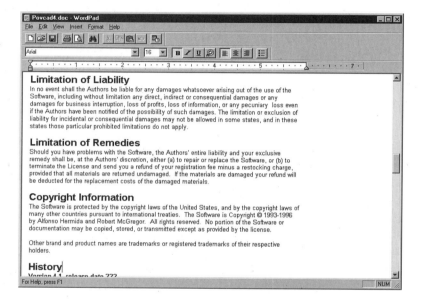

MFC provides the services of a Windows rich edit common control in the class `CRichEditCtrl`, which is derived directly from `CWnd` and inherits all the functionality of `CWnd`.

Although the `CRichEditCtrl` class isn't derived from `CEdit`, a `CRichEditCtrl` object supports most of the operations and notification messages used for multiple-line edit controls. In fact, the default style for a rich edit control is single line, just as it is for an edit control; you *must* set the `ES_MULTILINE` window style to create a multiple-line rich edit control. This style makes it easy for applications that already make use of edit controls to be easily modified to use rich edit controls. Figure 3.11 shows the TAB1 program displaying rich text on the second tab.

Figure 3.11

Displaying rich text in the TAB1 program.

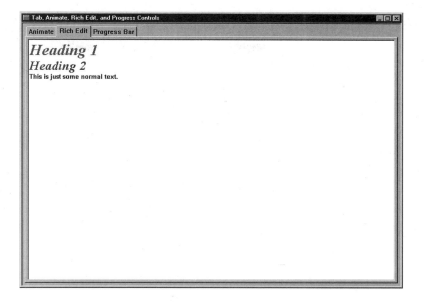

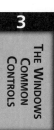

> **Note**
>
> Because the rich edit control is specific to Win32, the `CRichEditCtrl` class is available only to programs running under Windows 95, Windows NT version 3.51 or later, and Windows 3.1x with Win32s 1.3 or later.

A rich edit control can be created as a child control of any window by writing code; it can also be defined in a dialog resource template. A rich edit control sends Windows notification messages to its owner (usually a `CDialog`-derived class), and these messages can be trapped and handled by writing message map entries and message-handler methods for each message. These message map entries and methods are implemented in the rich edit control's parent class.

Rich Edit Control Window Styles

Like all windows, rich edit controls can use the general window styles available to `CWnd`. Unlike other controls, the rich edit control defines no additional window styles.

The Character Format Structure (CHARFORMAT)

The `CRichEditCtrl` class's `GetDefaultCharFormat()`, `GetSelectionCharFormat()`, `SetDefaultCharFormat()`, `SetSelectionCharFormat()`, and `SetWordCharFormat()` methods all take a parameter of type `CHARFORMAT`. This is a Win32 datatype (see Listing 3.4) that contains information about character formatting in a rich edit control.

LISTING 3.4   THE CHARFORMAT STRUCTURE

```
typedef struct _charformat
{
    UINT      cbSize;
    _WPAD     _wPad1;
    DWORD     dwMask;
    DWORD     dwEffects;
    LONG      yHeight;
    LONG      yOffset;
    COLORREF  crTextColor;
    BYTE      bCharSet;
    BYTE      bPitchAndFamily;
    TCHAR     szFaceName[LF_FACESIZE];
    _WPAD     _wPad2;
}
CHARFORMAT;
```

The data members for this structure are as follows:

- `cbSize`   Size in bytes of this structure. Must be set before passing the structure to the rich edit control.

- `dwMask`   Members containing valid information or attributes to set. This member can be zero or one or more of the values listed in Table 3.32.

- `dwEffects`   Character effects. This member can be a combination of the values listed in Table 3.33.

- `yHeight`   Character height.

- `yOffset`   Character offset from the baseline. If this member is positive, the character is a superscript; if it is negative, the character is a subscript.

- `crTextColor`   Text color. This member is ignored if the `CFE_AUTOCOLOR` character effect is specified.

- `bCharSet`   Character set value. Can be one of the values specified for the `lfCharSet` member of the `LOGFONT` structure.

- `bPitchAndFamily`   Font family and pitch. This member is the same as the `lfPitchAndFamily` member of the `LOGFONT` structure.

- `szFaceName`   NULL-terminated character array specifying the font face name.

TABLE 3.32   POSSIBLE CHARFORMAT dwMask VALUES

Value	*Meaning*
CFM_BOLD	The CFE_BOLD value of the dwEffects member is valid.
CFM_COLOR	The crTextColor member and the CFE_AUTOCOLOR value of the dwEffects member are valid.
CFM_FACE	The szFaceName member is valid.
CFM_ITALIC	The CFE_ITALIC value of the dwEffects member is valid.
CFM_OFFSET	The yOffset member is valid.
CFM_PROTECTED	The CFE_PROTECTED value of the dwEffects member is valid.
CFM_SIZE	The yHeight member is valid.
CFM_STRIKEOUT	The CFE_STRIKEOUT value of the dwEffects member is valid.
CFM_UNDERLINE.	The CFE_UNDERLINE value of the dwEffects member is valid.

TABLE 3.33   POSSIBLE RICH EDIT CONTROL CHARACTER EFFECTS VALUES

Value	*Meaning*
CFE_AUTOCOLOR	The text color is the return value of GetSysColor (COLOR_WINDOWTEXT).
CFE_BOLD	Characters are **bold**.
CFE_ITALIC	Characters are *italic*.
CFE_STRIKEOUT	Characters are ~~struck out~~.
CFE_UNDERLINE	Characters are underlined.
CFE_PROTECTED	Characters are protected; an attempt to modify them causes an EN_PROTECTED notification message.

3

THE WINDOWS
COMMON
CONTROLS

The Paragraph Format Structure (PARAFORMAT)

Another Win32 structure, called PARAFORMAT, is used as a parameter with the GetParaFormat() and SetParaFormat() methods. The PARAFORMAT structure contains information about formatting attributes in a rich edit control and is shown in Listing 3.5.

LISTING 3.5   THE PARAFORMAT STRUCTURE

```
typedef struct _paráformat
{
   UINT cbSize;
   _WPAD _wPad1;
```

continues

LISTING 3.5   CONTINUED

```
    DWORD dwMask;
    WORD  wNumbering;
    WORD  wReserved;
    LONG  dxStartIndent;
    LONG  dxRightIndent;
    LONG  dxOffset;
    WORD  wAlignment;
    SHORT cTabCount;
    LONG  rgxTabs[MAX_TAB_STOPS];
}
PARAFORMAT;
```

The data members for this structure are as follows:

- cbSize   Size in bytes of this structure. Must be filled before passing to the rich edit control.

- dwMask   Members containing valid information or attributes to set. This parameter can be zero or one or more of the values shown in Table 3.34.

- wNumbering   Value specifying numbering options. This member can be zero or PFN_BULLET.

- dxStartIndent   Indentation of the first line in the paragraph. If the paragraph formatting is being set and PFM_OFFSETINDENT is specified, this member is treated as a relative value that is added to the starting indentation of each affected paragraph.

- dxRightIndent   Size of the right indentation, relative to the right margin.

- dxOffset   Indentation of the second and subsequent lines, relative to the starting indentation. The first line is indented if this member is negative; it is outdented if this member is positive.

- wAlignment   Value specifying the paragraph alignment. This member can be one of the values listed in Table 3.35.

- cTabCount   Number of tab stops.

- rgxTabs   Array of absolute tab-stop positions.

TABLE 3.34   RICH EDIT CONTROL PARAGRAPH dwMask VALUES

Value	*Meaning*
PFM_ALIGNMENT	The wAlignment member is valid.
PFM_NUMBERING	The wNumbering member is valid.

Value	Meaning
PFM_OFFSET	The dxOffset member is valid.
PFM_OFFSETINDENT	The dxStartIndent member is valid and specifies a relative value.
PFM_RIGHTINDENT	The dxRightIndent member is valid.
PFM_STARTINDENT	The dxStartIndent member is valid.
PFM_TABSTOPS	The cTabStobs and rgxTabStops members are valid.

TABLE 3.35   POSSIBLE RICH EDIT CONTROL PARAGRAPH ALIGNMENT VALUES

Value	Meaning
PFA_LEFT	Paragraphs are aligned with the left margin.
PFA_RIGHT	Paragraphs are aligned with the right margin.
PFA_CENTER	Paragraphs are centered.

CRichEditCtrl Class Methods

The CRichEditCtrl class offers a full set of methods for manipulating the control and its data. The CRichEditCtrl class is complex, and its methods can be broken out into several categories:

- Line-related methods
- Text-selection methods
- Text-formatting methods
- Editing methods
- Clipboard methods
- General-purpose methods

The following sections look at descriptions for all these CRichEditCtrl methods.

CRichEditCtrl Line-Related Methods

The CRichEditCtrl methods related to manipulating lines of text are described in Table 3.36.

3

THE WINDOWS
COMMON
CONTROLS

TABLE 3.36   CRichEditCtrl LINE-RELATED METHODS

Method	Description
GetLineCount()	Retrieves the number of lines in this CRichEditCtrl object.
GetLine()	Retrieves a line of text from this CRichEditCtrl object.
GetFirstVisibleLine()	Determines the topmost visible line in this CRichEditCtrl object.
LineIndex()	Retrieves the character index of a given line in this CRichEditCtrl object.
LineFromChar()	Determines which line contains the given character.
LineLength()	Retrieves the length of a given line in this CRichEditCtrl object.
LineScroll()	Scrolls the text in this CRichEditCtrl object.

CRichEditCtrl Text-Selection Methods

The CRichEditCtrl methods related to selecting text, clearing or getting selected text, and so on, are described in Table 3.37.

TABLE 3.37   CRichEditCtrl TEXT-SELECTION METHODS

Method	Description
Clear()	Clears the current selection.
GetSel()	Gets the starting and ending positions of the current selection.
GetSelectionType()	Retrieves the type of contents in the current selection.
GetSelText()	Gets the text of the current selection.
HideSelection()	Shows or hides the current selection.
ReplaceSel()	Replaces the current selection with specified text.
SetSel()	Sets the selection.

CRichEditCtrl Formatting Methods

The CRichEditCtrl methods related to formatting text are described in Table 3.38.

TABLE 3.38 CRichEditCtrl FORMATTING METHODS

Method	Description
GetDefaultCharFormat()	Gets the current default character formatting attributes.
GetParaFormat()	Gets the paragraph formatting attributes in the current selection.
GetSelectionCharFormat()	Gets the character formatting attributes in the current selection.
SetDefaultCharFormat()	Sets the current default character formatting attributes.
SetParaFormat()	the paragraph formatting attributes in the current selection.
SetSelectionCharFormat()	Sets the character formatting attributes in the current selection.
SetWordCharFormat()	Sets the character formatting attributes in the current word.

CRichEditCtrl Editing Methods

The CRichEditCtrl methods related to editing text are described in Table 3.39.

TABLE 3.39 CRichEditCtrl EDITING METHODS

Method	Description
CanUndo()	Determines whether an editing operation can be undone.
EmptyUndoBuffer()	Resets a CRichEditCtrl object's undo flag.
StreamIn()	Inserts text from an input stream.
StreamOut()	Stores text from a CRichEditCtrl object in an output stream.
Undo()	Undoes the last editing operation.

CRichEditCtrl Clipboard Methods

The CRichEditCtrl methods that allow a rich edit control to interact with the Windows Clipboard are described in Table 3.40.

TABLE 3.40 CRichEditCtrl CLIPBOARD METHODS

Method	Description
CanPaste()	Checks to see whether the contents of the Clipboard can be pasted into a rich edit control.
Copy()	Copies the current selection to the Clipboard.
Cut()	Cuts the current selection to the Clipboard.
Paste()	Inserts the contents of the Clipboard into a rich edit control.
PasteSpecial()	Inserts the contents of the Clipboard into a rich edit control using the specified data format.

CRichEditCtrl General-Purpose Methods

General-purpose CRichEditCtrl methods are described in Table 3.41.

TABLE 3.41 GENERAL-PURPOSE METHODS

Method	Description
DisplayBand()	Displays a portion of the contents of a CRichEditCtrl object.
FindText()	Locates text within a CRichEditCtrl object.
FormatRange()	Formats a range of text for the target output device.
GetCharPos()	Gets the location of a given character within this CRichEditCtrl object.
GetEventMask()	Gets the event mask for a CRichEditCtrl object.
GetLimitText()	Gets the limit on the amount of text a user can enter into a CRichEditCtrl object.
GetModify()	Determines whether the contents of a CRichEditCtrl object have been modified since last saved.
GetRect()	Gets the formatting rectangle for a CRichEditCtrl object.
GetTextLength()	Gets the length of the text in a CRichEditCtrl object.
LimitText()	Limits the amount of text a user can enter into the CRichEditCtrl object.
RequestResize()	Forces a CRichEditCtrl object to send notifications to its parent window requesting that it be resized.
SetBackgroundColor()	Sets the background color in a CRichEditCtrl object.
SetEventMask()	Sets the event mask for a CRichEditCtrl object.
SetModify()	Sets or clears the modification flag for a CRichEditCtrl object.

Method	Description
SetOptions()	Sets the options for a CRichEditCtrl object.
SetReadOnly()	Sets the read-only option for a CRichEditCtrl object.
SetRect()	Sets the formatting rectangle for a CRichEditCtrl object.
SetTargetDevice()	Sets the target output device for a CRichEditCtrl object.

Creating and Initializing a Rich Edit Control

To create a CRichEditCtrl object, you use the two-step construction process typical of MFC:

1. Call the class constructor CRichEditCtrl::CRichEditCtrl() to allocate the object.

2. Initialize the CRichEditCtrl object and attach an actual Windows rich edit common control to it with a call to the CRichEditCtrl::Create() method.

The prototype for the CRichEditCtrl::Create() method is shown here:

```
BOOL Create(DWORD dwStyle, const RECT& rect,
            CWnd* pParentWnd, UINT nID);
```

In this syntax, the parameters are defined as follows:

- dwStyle   Specifies the combination of styles used by a control.
- rect   Specifies a control's size and position.
- pParentWnd   Specifies the control's parent window.
- nID   Specifies the control identifier for a control.

Using a Rich Edit Control

After constructing the CRichEditCtrl object, you add text and format it as desired by doing the following:

1. Prepare PARAFORMAT and CHARFORMAT structures to define paragraph and character formatting specifics.

2. Call on the CRichEditCtrl methods that use these structures to perform their magic.

For example, the sample program TAB1 (located on the companion CD-ROM) uses the code shown in Listing 3.6 to set the character formatting specifics for a given CHARFORMAT structure.

LISTING 3.6 INITIALIZING A CHARFORMAT STRUCTURE

```
////////////////////////////////////////////////////////////////
// CMainWnd::SetStyleHeading1()

void CMainWnd::SetStyleHeading1(CHARFORMAT& cf)
{
    cf.cbSize           = sizeof(CHARFORMAT);
    cf.dwMask           = CFM_COLOR | CFM_FACE | CFM_SIZE |
                          CFM_ITALIC | CFM_BOLD;
    cf.dwEffects        = CFE_BOLD | CFE_ITALIC;
    cf.yHeight          = 500;
    cf.crTextColor      = crRed;                // from colors.h
    cf.bCharSet         = ANSI_CHARSET;
    cf.bPitchAndFamily  = FF_ROMAN;

    lstrcpy(cf.szFaceName, "Times New Roman");
}
```

As you can see, you can easily control the characteristics of a display font with the CHARFORMAT structure. With a little extra work you can make various formatting changes an interactive experience for the user—try creating various functions and attaching them to user-interface elements such as buttons on a toolbar.

Summary

In this chapter you've examined several MFC classes that encapsulate the Win32 common controls. You've explored the messages and methods of these classes, and seen how to use them in an application context. Next, you'll take a closer look at graphics programming in MFC.

Painting, Device Contexts, Bitmaps, and Fonts

by Rob McGregor

IN THIS CHAPTER

Graphics are extremely important in today's GUI OS world, and Windows is certainly no exception. Because Windows provides a graphical user interface (GUI) to the underlying operating system (OS) and hardware, graphics are the mainstay of Windows programs. This chapter explains how MFC packages and exposes device contexts and graphics objects. This chapter also introduces the basic concepts of creating, drawing, and using graphics in Windows.

> **NOTE**
>
> Four sample programs (VECTEXT1, RASTER1, BEZIER1, and BITMAP1) included on this book's accompanying CD-ROM demonstrate all of the techniques described in this chapter, and more, with fully commented source code.

Everything—even text—paints to the screen as graphics under Windows. The logical representation of a physical device's drawing surface is packaged into a complex data structure called a *device context* (DC). Windows provides several special datatypes and structures to represent and describe each of the fundamental Windows *graphic objects* (including pens, brushes, fonts, and bitmaps).

Device Contexts

When a Windows program (including Windows itself) draws text and graphics to a display or some other device (such as a printer), it usually doesn't draw directly to the hardware as DOS programs do. In fact, applications that write directly to hardware are considered taboo in the world of Windows. Applications use a device context (DC) to represent a logical version of the physical device, be it a monitor, a printer, a plotter, or some other physical device. A DC contains information about the pen, brush, font, and bitmap currently selected for use on a device. MFC provides classes for several different types of DCs, and an application must explicitly ask for a DC before drawing anything to a device, even simply writing some text on the video display.

Device contexts aren't limited to physical devices, however; DCs can refer to logical devices as well. An example of a logical device is a *metafile*, which is a collection of structures that stores a picture in a device-independent format. Another example is a *bitmap*, a collection of pixels that represents some graphic image. You can draw on a bitmap or a metafile as easily as you can draw on a display or a printer.

Four types of device contexts are supplied by the Win32 API:

- Display contexts—Support graphics operations on a video display.

- Information contexts—Provide for the retrieval of device data.
- Memory contexts—Support graphics operations on a bitmap.
- Printer contexts—Support graphics operations on a printer or plotter.

The Graphics Device Interface

Device contexts are used extensively by the Graphics Device Interface (GDI), a main component of the Windows architecture. Non-MFC Windows programs written in Standard C/C++ use a device context to give Windows the specifics of the device it should draw on. This device context is sent as a parameter to any of several GDI function calls provided by the Windows API. The GDI provides all the basic drawing functionality for Windows; the DC represents the device, providing a layer of abstraction that insulates your applications from the nastiness of drawing directly to hardware. (Figure 4.1 shows this hardware abstraction.) The GDI provides this insulation by calling the appropriate device driver in response to Windows graphics function calls. This abstraction frees you from having to write low-level driver code to support each device you'll draw to—Windows includes drivers for and already knows how to draw hundreds of devices.

Figure 4.1

The layers of insulation between the hardware and an MFC application.

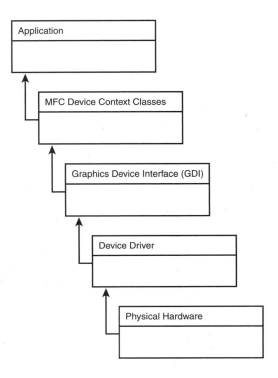

MFC Wrapping

When writing MFC programs, you get an added benefit when using DCs and the GDI functions: The GDI functions are built right into the MFC DC classes as DC methods. This makes using the GDI functions very convenient, especially with the Intellisense pop-up lists provided by Microsoft Visual C++ 6.0 (see Figure 4.2).

FIGURE 4.2

Visual C++ Intellisense pop-up lists make using device context methods easier than ever.

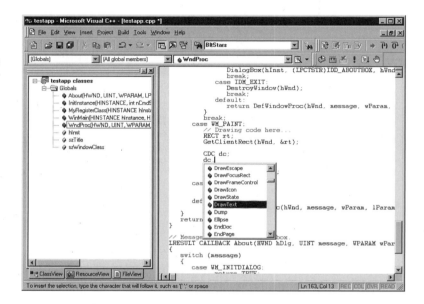

MFC Device Context Classes

MFC encapsulates the various types of device contexts provided by Windows into distinct DC classes that wrap a handle to a device context (HDC) within a C++ class. The class effectively contains information about the drawing attributes of a device. All drawing done in Windows is done on a device context, and all drawing methods are nicely wrapped into a DC object.

The following DC classes are the predefined MFC base classes for device contexts; they provide drawing and painting capabilities to MFC applications:

- CDC
- CPaintDC
- CClientDC
- CWindowDC
- CMetaFileDC

Figure 4.3 shows the relation of these classes in the MFC class hierarchy.

FIGURE 4.3

The hierarchy of MFC device context classes.

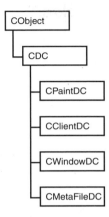

The Base Class: CDC

As you can see in Figure 4.3, the CDC class is the base class for the other DC classes. The CDC base class defines device context objects and provides methods for drawing on a display, a printer, or a window's client area.

All graphic output should be rendered using the class methods provided by CDC. These class methods provide services for using drawing tools, manipulating device contexts, type-safe GDI object selection, manipulating color and palettes, coordinate mapping and conversion, working with polygons and regions, drawing shapes, drawing text, working with fonts, handling metafiles, and more. The CDC class is a monster that encapsulates the GDI functions that use device contexts.

It might surprise you to know that a CDC object actually contains not one, but two device contexts. These DCs are stored as the class members described in Table 4.1; they allow a CDC object to point to two different devices simultaneously. It is this very useful property of an extra DC within a CDC object that makes advanced MFC features such as print preview so easy to achieve.

TABLE 4.1 CLASS MEMBERS OF A CDC OBJECT

Class Member	Description
m_hDC	The output device context for a CDC object. Most CDC GDI calls that create output go to this member DC.
m_hAttribDC	The attribute device context for this CDC object. Most CDC GDI calls requesting information from a CDC object are directed to this member DC.

> **NOTE**
>
> The two class member DCs initially refer to the same device, but they can be manipulated to refer to different devices at any time. Setting and releasing these DCs is accomplished through the CDC methods SetAttribDC(), SetOutputDC(), ReleaseAttribDC(), and ReleaseOutputDC().
>
> The CDC::SetAttribDC() method sets m_hAttribDC (the attribute device context); SetOutputDC sets m_hDC (the output device context). Likewise, the CDC::ReleaseAttribDC() method releases m_hAttribDC, and the CDC::ReleaseOutputDC() method releases m_hDC.

The CDC methods are broken into several categories of functionality; these categories are reflected in other MFC device context classes, as described later in this chapter. The main categories of functionality are listed in Table 4.2.

TABLE 4.2   FUNCTIONAL CATEGORIES OF CDC METHODS

Category	*Purpose*
Bitmap methods	Methods for manipulating bitmaps and pixels.
Clipping methods	Functions that define and manipulate clipping bounds for a device.
Color and color palette methods	Methods for dealing with palette selection and realization and mapping logical colors.
Coordinate methods	Methods for converting between device and logical units.
Device context methods	Methods that retrieve information about a DC and its attributes.
Drawing attribute methods	Methods for getting and setting colors and modes for a DC.
Drawing tool methods	Methods for manipulating brush origins and enumerating the pens and brushes available in a DC.
Ellipse and polygon methods	Methods for drawing ellipses and polygons.
Font methods	Methods for retrieving font attributes.
Initialization methods	Methods for creating and setting DC properties and retrieving information about the graphic objects within the DC.
Line output methods	Methods for drawing lines on a DC.
Mapping methods	Methods to set, retrieve, and manipulate origins and extents for windows and viewports, and to get and set mapping modes for a DC.
Metafile methods	Methods to record and play metafiles.

Category	Purpose
Path methods	Methods for manipulating paths in a DC. (Paths are created using GDI functions that generate curves and polygons.)
Printer escape methods	Methods that access and manipulate printers and print jobs.
Region methods	Methods for filling regions and manipulating region colors.
Simple drawing methods	Methods that provide simple rectangle and icon drawing features.
Text methods	Methods that output text and retrieve information about the font currently selected for the DC.
Type-safe selection methods	Methods for selecting graphic objects or Windows stock objects.

The CDC class is very large, containing over 170 methods and data members. The following sections look at the basics of creating and using a DC.

Painting with Class CPaintDC

A CPaintDC object represents a drawing surface for a window. To fully understand the purpose of CPaintDC, let's go back to the API level and see how things are done in SDK-land. Traditional C programs, as described in the Microsoft Win32 Software Development Kit (SDK), get a device context by using the Win32 API functions BeginPaint() and EndPaint() within the message handler for the Windows message WM_PAINT. The BeginPaint() function prepares a specified window for painting, fills a special PAINTSTRUCT structure with painting information, and returns a handle to a display device context (or painting DC). The EndPaint() function is always paired with a call to BeginPaint() to signify the end of painting in the specified window. The C code looks like this within the window procedure:

```c
HDC            hDC;
PAINTSTRUCT    paintstruct;

switch (msg)
   case WM_PAINT:
   {
      hDC = BeginPaint(hwnd, &paintstruct);
      //
      // Perform graphics operations using hDC
      //
      EndPaint(hwnd, &paintstruct);
      return 0;
   }
```

A CPaintDC object performs these same steps—it just wraps them in an MFC class, and this makes your job considerably easier. The basic steps to follow when using a CPaintDC object are given here:

1. Create a `CPaintDC` object.
2. Draw on the `CPaintDC` object.
3. Destroy the `CPaintDC` object.

The `CPaintDC` constructor automatically calls `BeginPaint()` and returns the paint DC to use for painting. Likewise, the destructor automatically calls `EndPaint()`. If you use the automatic storage class for your DC objects, you can forget about step 3 from the preceding list, making your job easier still.

> **NOTE**
>
> MFC removes much of the tedium involved in using `CPaintDC` by providing `View` classes that automate the process. A `View` class receives a `CPaintDC` object as a parameter of the `CView::OnDraw()` method. This `CPaintDC` is used for graphics methods and is destroyed by MFC when `OnDraw()` returns (the device contexts wrapped within the `CPaintDC` are released to Windows at this time).

Listing 4.1 gives a simple example of using a `CPaintDC` to draw graphics in a window—in this case, an ellipse. The result is shown in Figure 4.4. The window receives `WM_PAINT` messages from the MFC-provided window procedure in the window's `OnPaint()` message handler. This member function must be added to the window's message map to enable `WM_PAINT` message reception, like this:

```
// Message map for CMainWnd
BEGIN_MESSAGE_MAP(CMainWnd, CFrameWnd)
   ON_WM_ PAINT()
END_MESSAGE_MAP()
```

LISTING 4.1   USING A `CPaintDC` OBJECT TO DRAW AN ELLIPSE IN RESPONSE TO `WM_PAINT` MESSAGES IN THE WINDOW'S `OnPaint()` MESSAGE HANDLER

```
/////////////////////////////////////////////////////////////////////
// CMainWnd::OnPaint()

void CMainWnd::OnPaint()
{
   // Create a paint DC
   CPaintDC dc(this);

   // Draw an ellipse on the DC
   CRect rc;
   GetClientRect(&rc);
   dc.Ellipse(rc);
}
```

FIGURE **4.4**

The ellipse resulting from the call to a CPaintDC *object's* Ellipse() *method.*

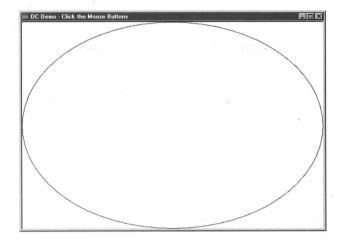

Managing Client Areas with Class **CClientDC**

MFC supplies the CClientDC class (which is directly derived from CDC) to automate the process of calling and releasing a device context representing the client area of a window. The Win32 API function GetDC() is called in the CClientDC constructor; the corresponding API function ReleaseDC() is called in the destructor. Listing 4.2 gives a simple example of using a CClientDC to draw graphics in a window—in this case, a diamond (see Figure 4.5).

FIGURE **4.5**

The diamond resulting from four successive calls to a CClientDC *object's* CDC::LineTo() *method.*

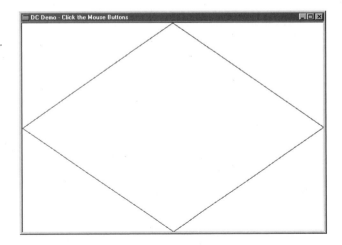

4

PAINTING, DEVICE
CONTEXTS,
BITMAPS, AND
FONTS

LISTING 4.2 USING A `CClientDC` OBJECT TO DRAW A DIAMOND IN RESPONSE TO `WM_LMBUTTONDOWN` MESSAGES IN THE WINDOW'S `OnLButtonDown()` MESSAGE HANDLER

```
//////////////////////////////////////////////////////////////////////
// CMainWnd::OnLButtonDown()

void CMainWnd::OnLButtonDown(UINT nFlags, CPoint point)
{
    // Create a client DC to draw on
    CClientDC dc(this);

    // Draw a diamond on the DC
    CRect rc;
    GetClientRect(&rc);

    dc.MoveTo(0, (rc.bottom + rc.top) / 2);
    dc.LineTo((rc.right + rc.left) / 2, 0);
    dc.LineTo(rc.right, (rc.bottom + rc.top) / 2);
    dc.LineTo((rc.right + rc.left) / 2, rc.bottom);
    dc.LineTo(0, (rc.bottom + rc.top) / 2);
}
```

Managing Frame Windows with Class `CWindowDC`

MFC supplies the `CWindowDC` class (which is directly derived from `CDC`) to automate the process of calling and releasing a device context representing the entire surface of a window, including both the client and nonclient areas. The Win32 API function `GetDC()` is called in the `CWindowDC` constructor; the corresponding API function `ReleaseDC()` is called in the destructor.

Listing 4.3 gives a simple example of using a `CWindowDC` to draw graphics in a window—in this case, a series of ellipses in the title bar (see Figure 4.6). The ellipses clip everything in their path as they draw, obliterating all nonclient area components (System menu, window caption, minimize, maximize, and close buttons).

FIGURE 4.6

The series of circles across the main nonclient area results from successive calls to a CWindowDC *object's* Ellipse() *method.*

LISTING 4.3 USING A CWindowDC OBJECT TO DRAW A SERIES OF CIRCLES IN RESPONSE TO WM_RBUTTONDOWN MESSAGES IN THE WINDOW'S OnRButtonDown() MESSAGE HANDLER

```
/////////////////////////////////////////////////////////////////////
// CMainWnd::OnRButtonDown()

void CMainWnd::OnRButtonDown(UINT nFlags, CPoint point)
{
    // Create a window DC to draw on
    CWindowDC dc(this);

    // Draw a series of ellipses on the DC,
    // in the window's NC title bar area
    CRect rc;
    GetWindowRect(&rc);

    // Get the title bar height
    int cyCaption = GetSystemMetrics(SM_CYCAPTION);

    // Define the ellipse's bounding rect
    CRect rcEllipse(0, 0, cyCaption, cyCaption);

    // Draw the ellipses
    while (rcEllipse.right < rc.right)
    {
        dc.Ellipse(rcEllipse);
        rcEllipse.left  += cyCaption;
        rcEllipse.right += cyCaption;
    }
}
```

Windows Graphic Objects

The display device contexts provided by Windows define logical display surfaces; the GDI provides drawing tools used to draw on the DC. MFC defines several types of graphic objects that correspond to the Windows drawing tools, including the following:

- Pens
- Brushes
- Fonts
- Bitmaps
- Palettes
- Regions

These Windows drawing tools are encapsulated by MFC graphic object classes. These classes are all derived from a common base class called `CGdiObject` (see Figure 4.7).

FIGURE 4.7

The location of graphic objects in the MFC class hierarchy.

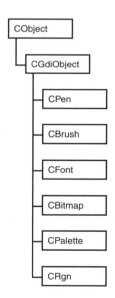

The relation of the standard SDK drawing tool datatypes to the MFC graphic object classes is shown in Table 4.3.

TABLE 4.3   THE RELATION OF THE STANDARD SDK DRAWING TOOL DATATYPES TO MFC GRAPHIC OBJECT CLASSES

SDK Drawing Tool	MFC Class	Windows Datatype
Pen	CPen	HPEN
Brush	CBrush	HBRUSH
Font	CFont	HFONT
Bitmap	CBitmap	HBITMAP
Palette	CPalette	HPALETTE
Region	CRgn	HRGN

To use a graphic object in an MFC program, you'll usually follow these three steps:

1. Define a graphic object within a code block and initialize the object with a corresponding Create*() method. For example, to create a CPalette object, use CreatePalette().

2. Select the new object into the current device context, typically by using the CDC::SelectObject() method. This method returns a pointer to the object being replaced (a pointer to a CGdiObject-derived object).

3. When the graphic object has finished its task, use the CDC::SelectObject() method again to select the replaced graphic object back into the device context, leaving things as they were originally.

> **NOTE**
>
> A graphic object declared on the stack is automatically deleted when the object goes out of scope. Graphic objects declared as pointers and allocated with the new operator must be explicitly deleted after restoring the DC's previous state.

The following sections look at each of these tools and how they're used.

> **NOTE**
>
> Class CGdiObject provides the interface to the raw Win32 API in terms of graphics object handles and so on. You never create a CGdiObject object directly; you create an object from one of its derived classes (for example, CPen or CBrush).

Pens: Class `CPen`

A `CPen` object encapsulates a Windows GDI pen and provides several methods for working with `CPen` objects (see Table 4.4).

TABLE 4.4   METHODS FOR CREATING AND USING `CPen` OBJECTS

Method	Description
`CreatePen()`	Creates a logical pen with the specified style, width, and brush attributes and attaches it to a `CPen` object.
`CreatePenIndirect()`	Creates a pen with the style, width, and color defined in a `LOGPEN` structure and attaches it to a `CPen` object.
`FromHandle()`	Returns a pointer to a `CPen` object from a Windows `HPEN`.
`GetExtLogPen()`	Gets a pen's underlying `EXTLOGPEN` structure.
`GetLogPen()`	Gets a pen's underlying `LOGPEN` structure.
operator `HPEN`	Returns the handle of the Windows pen currently attached to the `CPen` object.

You create a pen to use when drawing in a device context. Pens come in several styles and a rainbow of colors. A Windows pen is typically created and attached to a `CPen` object with the `CPen::CreatePen()` method, which uses this prototype:

```
BOOL CreatePen(int nPenStyle, int nWidth, COLORREF crColor);
```

The `nPenStyle` parameter can be any of the values shown in Table 4.5; the `nWidth` parameter is the width of the pen; the `crColor` parameter specifies the color of the pen.

TABLE 4.5   THESE PEN STYLES DEFINED BY THE GDI ARE USED FOR `CPen` OBJECT CLASSES

Pen Style	Description
`PS_SOLID`	Creates a solid pen.
`PS_DASH`	When the pen width is 1, creates a dashed pen.
`PS_DOT`	When the pen width is 1, creates a dotted pen.
`PS_DASHDOT`	When the pen width is 1, creates a pen with alternating dashes and dots.
`PS_DASHDOTDOT`	When the pen width is 1, creates a pen with alternating dashes and double dots.
`PS_NULL`	Creates a `NULL` (invisible) pen.
`PS_INSIDEFRAME`	Creates a pen that draws inside the bounding rectangle of a Windows GDI shape such as an ellipse or a rectangle.

For example, to create and use a red, dashed pen, you would do this:

```
// Create a new red-dashed pen
CPen penRed;
penRed.CreatePen(PS_DASH, 1, RGB(255, 0, 0));
```

To select it into a device context, you would use the `SelectObject()` method of the DC, like this:

```
// Select the new pen into the device context, and save
// the old pen to restore on clean up...
CPen* ppenOld;
ppenOld = dc.SelectObject(&penRed);
```

Now any lines drawn in the window will have the red dashed style you just put into the DC. When you're done drawing, restore the original pen by selecting it back into the DC, like this:

```
dc.SelectObject(ppenOld);
```

Brushes: Class `CBrush`

A `CBrush` object encapsulates a Windows GDI brush and provides several methods for working with `CBrush` objects (see Table 4.6).

TABLE 4.6   THE METHODS PROVIDED BY MFC FOR `CBrush` OBJECTS

Method	Description
CreateBrushIndirect()	Creates a brush with the style, color, and pattern specified in a LOGBRUSH structure and attaches it to a CBrush object.
CreateDIBPatternBrush()	Creates a brush with a pattern specified by a device-independent bitmap (DIB) and attaches it to a CBrush object.
CreateHatchBrush()	Creates a brush with the specified hatched pattern and color and attaches it to a CBrush object.
CreatePatternBrush()	Creates a brush with a pattern specified by a bitmap and attaches it to a CBrush object.
CreateSolidBrush()	Creates a brush with the specified solid color and attaches it to a CBrush object.
CreateSysColorBrush()	Creates a brush that is the default system color and attaches it to a CBrush object.
FromHandle()	Returns a pointer to a CBrush object from a Windows HBRUSH object.
GetLogBrush()	Gets the underlying LOGBRUSH structure from a CBrush object.
operator HBRUSH	Returns the Windows handle attached to a CBrush object.

4

PAINTING, DEVICE
CONTEXTS,
BITMAPS, AND
FONTS

You create a brush to use when painting in a device context. Like pens, brushes come in several styles and a rainbow of colors. A Windows brush is most conveniently created and attached to a CBrush object with the constructor, CBrush::CBrush(), which uses these overloaded prototypes:

```
CBrush();
CBrush(COLORREF crColor);
CBrush(int nIndex, COLORREF crColor);
CBrush(CBitmap* pBitmap);
```

The crColor parameter specifies the color of the brush. The nIndex parameter specifies the pattern of the brush, which can be any of the values shown in Table 4.7. The pBitmap parameter is a pointer to a CBitmap object that contains a bitmap to use as a brush pattern.

TABLE 4.7   HATCH STYLES DEFINED FOR GDI BRUSHES ARE USED FOR CBrush OBJECTS

Brush Style	Description
HS_BDIAGONAL	Downward hatch (left to right) at 45 degrees
HS_CROSS	Horizontal and vertical crosshatch
HS_DIAGCROSS	Crosshatch at 45 degrees
HS_FDIAGONAL	Upward hatch (left to right) at 45 degrees
HS_HORIZONTAL	Horizontal hatch
HS_VERTICAL	Vertical hatch

Fonts: Class CFont

A CFont object encapsulates a Windows GDI font and provides several methods for working with CFont objects (see Table 4.8).

TABLE 4.8   CFont CLASS METHODS FOR CREATING AND MANIPULATING FONTS

Method	Description
CreateFontIndirect()	Creates a CFont object with the characteristics given in a LOGFONT structure.
CreateFont()	Creates a CFont object with the specified characteristics.
CreatePointFont()	Creates a CFont object with the specified height (measured in tenths of a point) and typeface.
CreatePointFontIndirect()	Creates a CFont object with the characteristics given in a LOGFONT structure; the font height is measured in tenths of a point instead of logical units.
FromHandle()	Returns a pointer to a CFont object from a Windows HFONT.

Method	Description
operator HFONT()	Returns the underlying Windows GDI font handle attached to a CFont object.
GetLogFont()	Fills a LOGFONT with information about the logical font attached to a CFont object.

You create a font to use when drawing text in a device context. Fonts come in thousands of typefaces and styles. A Windows GDI font is typically created and attached to a CFont object with one of the first four methods listed in Table 4.8.

Bitmaps: Class **CBitmap**

A *bitmap* is an array of pixels that defines a graphic image—a picture or a pattern. The colors of the pixels are described by the data in the bitmap bits. The MFC class CBitmap encapsulates a handle to a Windows bitmap and provides some 14 methods and operators to create and manipulate bitmap objects.

Palettes: Class **CPalette**

A *palette* is a Windows GDI object that stores color information. A GDI palette object is basically a color lookup table used by the system to determine which colors to display on a 256-color palette display device. Windows defines 20 palette colors for the system, leaving 236 for applications to use for their own purposes. MFC encapsulates a Windows color palette within the CPalette class. Windows uses both logical palettes (which are lists of desired colors) and the system palette (which defines color slots currently available in the hardware palette). The CPalette class provides nine methods and one operator for creating and manipulating CPalette objects.

> **NOTE**
>
> The terms *hardware palette* and *system palette* are used interchangeably even though, technically, the system palette is really a copy of the values found in the hardware palette. The Windows Palette Manager uses the system palette values.

Regions: Class **CRgn**

A region is a Windows GDI object that stores polygonal or elliptical information about regions on a display device. The CRgn class encapsulates a GDI region object and provides several methods for creating and working with regions. These methods are described in Table 4.9.

TABLE 4.9 CLASS CRgn METHODS FOR CREATING AND USING REGIONS

Method	Description
CombineRgn()	Creates a union of two specified CRgn objects.
CopyRgn()	Copies one CRgn object into another.
CreateEllipticRgn()	Creates a CRgn object with an elliptical region.
CreateEllipticRgnIndirect()	Creates a CRgn object with an elliptical region defined by a RECT structure as its bounding box.
CreateFromData()	Creates a region based on a given region and geometrical transformation data.
CreateFromPath()	Creates a region based on a path that's selected into a given device context.
CreatePolygonRgn()	Creates a CRgn object with a polygonal region. Polygon regions are automatically closed, if necessary, by connecting the last vertex of the polygon to the first.
CreatePolyPolygonRgn()	Creates a CRgn object with a region made up of a series of closed polygons.
CreateRectRgn()	Creates a CRgn object with a rectangular region.
CreateRectRgnIndirect()	Creates a CRgn object with a rectangular region defined by a RECT structure.
CreateRoundRectRgn()	Creates a CRgn object with a rounded corner rectangular region.
EqualRgn()	Creates two CRgn objects to determine whether they are equivalent.
FromHandle()	Returns a pointer to a CRgn object from a handle to a Windows region.
GetRegionData()	Fills a buffer with data that describes a given region.
GetRgnBox()	Gets the coordinates of a CRgn object's bounding rectangle.
OffsetRgn()	Moves a CRgn object by the specified offsets.
PtInRegion()	Determines whether a specified point lies within a region.
RectInRegion()	Determines whether any part of a specified rectangle lies within the boundaries of a region.
SetRectRgn()	Sets an existing CRgn object to a specified rectangular region.
operator HRGN	Returns the Windows handle wrapped in the CRgn object.

GDI Coordinate Systems

The GDI supports two types of coordinate systems: physical and logical. The physical coordinate system is that of the physical device, such as a video display. A window on the display starts at the origin—location (0,0)—at the upper-left corner of the display, with the x-axis increasing going to the right and the y-axis increasing going down. The lower-right corner of the window corresponds with the lower-right corner of the display (see Figure 4.8), but the actual numbers for a video display depend on the current video resolution. Typical locations are (640, 480), (800, 600), or (1024, 768).

FIGURE 4.8
The physical (device) coordinate system.

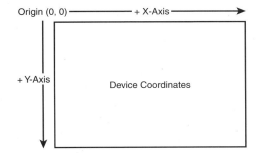

> **TIP**
>
> Use the Win32 API function `GetSystemMetrics()` to find the actual display size in pixels.
>
> Use `GetSystemMetrics(SM_CXSCREEN)` to get the screen width; use `GetSystemMetrics(SM_CYSCREEN)` to get the screen height.

There are several logical coordinate systems, and Windows maps coordinates on the current logical display to the physical device before displaying any graphical output. Each of the GDI functions—and therefore the MFC wrapper methods in class `CDC`—use logical coordinates. The resulting output can vary depending on a device context's current *mapping mode*. Mapping modes allow an application to send GDI graphics output to a logical window. The GDI then maps the output to the physical window or some other device (such as a printer).

4

PAINTING, DEVICE CONTEXTS, BITMAPS, AND FONTS

Logical Mapping Modes

Windows uses mapping modes to project a logical coordinate system into the physical coordinate system. The *origin* of a logical window defines the upper-left corner of the window. All other points are referenced from the origin. The mapping mode defines the length of a logical unit of measure used when converting logical units to physical device units. The mapping mode also determines the orientation of the device's x and y axes. The GDI uses a DC's current mapping mode to convert logical coordinates into the corresponding device coordinates. Table 4.10 lists the logical mapping modes supported by Windows.

TABLE 4.10 THE LOGICAL MAPPING MODES SUPPORTED BY WINDOWS

Mapping Mode	Description
MM_ANISOTROPIC	The mapping between logical and physical coordinates uses variably scaled axes; images in the logical window can be stretched in any direction when redrawn. This mode doesn't change the current window or viewport settings. Use the CDC::SetWindowExt() and CDC::SetViewportExt() methods to change units, orientation, and scaling. The positive x-axis is to the right and the positive y-axis goes up.
MM_HIENGLISH	Each unit in the logical window is 0.001 inch long. The positive x-axis is to the right and the positive y-axis goes up.
MM_HIMETRIC	Each unit in the logical window is 0.01 millimeter long. The positive x-axis is to the right and the positive y-axis goes up.
MM_ISOTROPIC	The mapping between logical and physical coordinates uses equally scaled axes; images in the logical window can be resized in any direction but retain the same *aspect ratio* when redrawn. To make sure that both x and y units remain the same size, the GDI adjusts sizes as necessary. Setting the mapping mode to MM_ISOTROPIC doesn't change the current window or viewport settings. Use the SetWindowExt() and SetViewportExt() methods to change units, orientation, and scaling. The positive x-axis is to the right and the positive y-axis goes up.
MM_LOENGLISH	Each logical unit represents 0.01 millimeters. The positive x-axis is to the right and the positive y-axis goes up.
MM_LOMETRIC	Each logical unit represents 0.1 millimeter. The positive x-axis is to the right and the positive y-axis goes up.
MM_TEXT	Each logical unit represents 1 device pixel. The positive x-axis is to the right and the positive y-axis goes down.

Mapping Mode	Description
MM_TWIPS	Each logical unit represents 1/20 of a point. Because a point is 1/72 inch, that makes a *twip* 1/1440 inch. The positive x-axis is to the right and the positive y-axis goes up.

> **TIP**
>
> It's a good idea to clearly distinguish between logical and physical devices when using Win32 API functions and their MFC wrapper methods. In general, logical coordinates are used for most drawing functions; physical coordinates are used in window management functions (such as SetWindowPos()).

Vector Graphics

Many types of vector graphic output functions are available for your applications from the Win32 GDI. These functions fall into two basic categories:

- Lines and curves
- Closed figures

These categories can further be broken into the following, more detailed, categories of Win32 GDI functions, which are reflected in CDC class methods:

- Lines
- Ellipses
- Rectangles and regions
- Polygons
- Bézier curves
- Metafiles
- Fonts and text output

4

PAINTING, DEVICE
CONTEXTS,
BITMAPS, AND
FONTS

Drawing Modes

Windows provides several drawing modes. A *drawing mode* specifies how the colors combine between the current pen and objects already present on the display surface. The drawing modes represent all possible Boolean combinations of two variables. They use the binary operators AND, OR, and XOR, and the unary operation NOT in the binary raster-operation codes listed in Table 4.11.

The drawing mode is set using the `CDC::SetRop2()` method, which has the following prototype:

```
int SetROP2( int nDrawMode );
```

The nDrawMode parameter specifies the new drawing mode, which can be any of the values in Table 4.11. This method returns the previous drawing mode.

TABLE 4.11 THE DRAWING MODES DEFINED BY WIN32 REPRESENT ALL POSSIBLE BOOLEAN COMBINATIONS OF TWO VARIABLES

Mode Identifier	Description
R2_BLACK	The pixel color is always black.
R2_COPYPEN	The pixel is the color of the pen.
R2_MASKNOTPEN	The pixel color is a combination of the colors common to both the screen and the inverse of the pen (final pixel = [NOT pen] AND screen pixel).
R2_MASKPEN	The pixel color is a combination of the colors common to both the pen and the screen (final pixel = pen AND screen pixel).
R2_MASKPENNOT	The pixel color is a combination of the colors common to both the pen and the inverse of the screen (final pixel = [NOT screen pixel] AND pen).
R2_MERGENOTPEN	The pixel color is a combination of the screen color and the inverse of the pen color (final pixel = [NOT pen] OR screen pixel).
R2_MERGEPEN	The pixel color is a combination of the pen color and the screen color (final pixel = pen OR screen pixel).
R2_MERGEPENNOT	The pixel color is a combination of the pen color and the inverse of the screen color (final pixel = [NOT screen pixel] OR pen).
R2_NOP	The pixel color stays the same.
R2_NOT	The pixel color is the inverse of the screen color.
R2_NOTCOPYPEN	The pixel color is the inverse of the pen color.
R2_NOTMASKPEN	The pixel color is the inverse of the R2_MASKPEN color (final pixel = NOT[pen AND screen pixel]).
R2_NOTMERGEPEN	The pixel color is the inverse of the R2_MERGEPEN color (final pixel = NOT[pen OR screen pixel]).
R2_NOTXORPEN	The pixel color is the inverse of the R2_XORPEN color (final pixel = NOT[pen XOR screen pixel]).
R2_WHITE	The pixel color is always white.
R2_XORPEN	The pixel color is a combination of the colors that are in the pen or in the screen, but not in both (final pixel = pen XOR screen pixel).

Figure 4.9 shows the results of using each of the named raster operations in the sample program RASTER1.EXE.

FIGURE 4.9

The results of using each of the named raster operations to combine two ellipses into a single image.

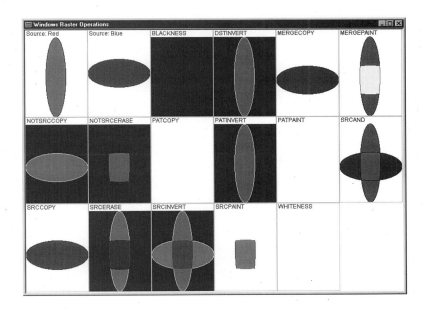

Points

Windows drawing functions typically take location parameters as x and y coordinates defining a point. Windows defines a point in the POINT structure (see windef.h) that looks like this:

```
typedef struct tagPOINT
{
  LONG x;
  LONG y;
} POINT, *PPOINT, NEAR *NPPOINT, FAR *LPPOINT;
```

MFC wraps the POINT structure with the CPoint class structure that provides the methods shown in Table 4.12. Note that the CPoint class isn't derived from CObject like most other MFC classes, but from the tagPOINT typedef structure just shown.

4

PAINTING, DEVICE
CONTEXTS,
BITMAPS, AND
FONTS

TABLE 4.12 CPoint CLASS METHODS AND OPERATORS

Method	Description
Offset()	Adds values to the x and y members of the CPoint object.
operator ==	Checks two points for equality.
operator !=	Checks two points for inequality.
operator +=	Offsets a CPoint object by adding a size or point.
operator =	Offsets a CPoint object by subtracting a size or point.
operator +	Returns the sum of a CPoint object and a size or point, or returns a CRect offset by a size.
operator -	Returns the difference of a CPoint object and a size (or the negation of a point), or returns a CRect offset by a negative size, or returns the size difference between two points.

As you can see, the CPoint class offers numerous operators to make point calculations easier.

Drawing Points

To draw a single point on a device context, call the CDC::SetPixel() method using this prototype:

```
COLORREF SetPixel(POINT point, COLORREF crColor);
```

In this syntax, point specifies the raster display pixel to set, and crColor specifies the color of pixel.

Lines and Polylines

Lines are drawn on a DC using the CDC methods MoveTo(), LineTo(), and PolyLine(). These methods all use the pen currently selected into the DC for their drawing.

> **NOTE**
>
> In MFC, the CPen object currently selected into a device context is the one that controls line styles, colors, and thickness. Windows defines the following six pen styles in WINGDI.H:
>
> ```
> #define PS_SOLID       0    // _____
> #define PS_DASH        1    // -- -- -- -
> #define PS_DOT         2    // .......
> #define PS_DASHDOT     3    // _._._._
> #define PS_DASHDOTDOT  4    // _.._.._
> #define PS_NULL        5
> ```

Setting the Current Drawing Position

The `CDC::MoveTo()` method sets the current drawing position (*current position*). CDC provides two overloaded prototypes for this method to make setting the current position easy:

```
CPoint MoveTo(int x, int y);
CPoint MoveTo(POINT point);
```

This means that you can pass the x and y coordinates for the new current position separately or in a `POINT` structure (or in a `CPoint` object).

Drawing a Single Line

The `CDC::LineTo()` method draws a line from the current position up to, but not including, the point specified by either x and y, or by a point. For each case, CDC again provides overloaded methods:

```
BOOL LineTo(int x, int y);
BOOL LineTo(POINT point);
```

The code fragment in Listing 4.4 shows how the VECTEXT1 program displays all six pen line-styles (pDC is assumed to be a valid pointer to a `CClientDC`). Figure 4.10 shows the result of this code; note that the sixth style is `PS_NULL`, the invisible pen, and doesn't appear at all.

FIGURE 4.10

Drawing all six line-styles in the VECTEXT1 program.

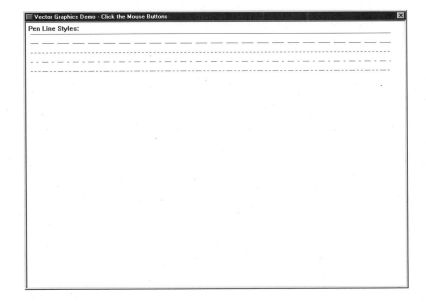

4

PAINTING, DEVICE
CONTEXTS,
BITMAPS, AND
FONTS

LISTING 4.4 DRAWING LINES USING ALL SIX PEN LINE-STYLES

```cpp
// Six different pen styles
int cy = 25;
for (int nLineStyle = 0; nLineStyle < 6; nLineStyle++)
{
   // Create a new pen
   CPen penBlue;

   // Pick the current pen style
   penBlue.CreatePen(nLineStyle, 1, crBlue);

   // Select the new pen into the device context, and save
   // the old pen to restore on clean up...
   CPen* ppenOld;
   ppenOld = pDC->SelectObject(&penBlue);

   // Draw on the DC
   pDC->MoveTo(10, cy);
   pDC->LineTo(10 + nLineLength, cy);
   cy += 20;

   // Leave things as you found them (clean up)
   pDC->SelectObject(ppenOld);
}
```

Drawing a Polyline

The CDC::PolyLine() method draws a set of line segments connecting the points specified in an array of points. The lines use the current pen, but unlike the CDC::LineTo() method, the CDC::PolyLine() method doesn't use or update the current position. The prototype for CDC::PolyLine() is shown here:

```cpp
BOOL Polyline(LPPOINT lpPoints, int nCount);
```

In this syntax, lpPoints is a pointer to an array of points, and nCount is the number of points in the array.

In the VECTEXT1 program, class CMainWnd defines an array of CPoint objects as the member array variable m_apt. This array is initialized to the following values:

```cpp
// Define an array of points
m_apt[0].x = 200; m_apt[0].y = 420;
m_apt[1].x = 200; m_apt[1].y = 200;
m_apt[2].x = 375; m_apt[2].y = 300;
m_apt[3].x = 480; m_apt[3].y = 310;
m_apt[4].x = 590; m_apt[4].y = 350;
m_apt[5].x = 465; m_apt[5].y = 200;
m_apt[6].x = 320; m_apt[6].y = 150;
```

```
m_apt[7].x = 205; m_apt[7].y = 100;
m_apt[8].x = 115; m_apt[8].y = 150;
m_apt[9].x = 100; m_apt[9].y = 175;
```

The `DoPolyLine()` method in Listing 4.5 shows how the VECTEXT1 program draws a polyline using the `CMainWnd` class member array of points: `m_apt[10]` (`pDC` is assumed to be a valid pointer to a `CClientDC`). This code produces the result shown in Figure 4.11.

FIGURE 4.11

A polyline from 10 points in the VECTEXT1 program.

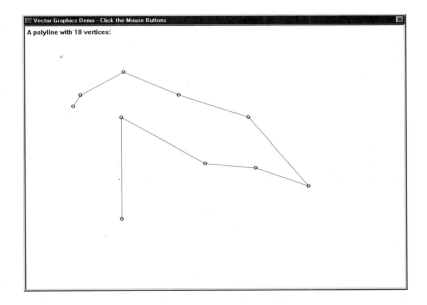

LISTING 4.5   DRAWING A POLYLINE WITH VISIBLE VERTICES: THE VECTEXT1
`CMainWnd::DoPolyLine()` METHOD

```
void CMainWnd::DoPolyLine(CClientDC* pDC)
{
    // Create a label
    CString str = "A polyline with 10 vertices:";
    pDC->TextOut(5, 5, str);

    // Draw points
    for (int i = 0; i < 10; i++)
        pDC->Ellipse(m_apt[i].x - 4, m_apt[i].y - 4,
                     m_apt[i].x + 4, m_apt[i].y + 4);

    // Create a new pen
    CPen penRed;
    penRed.CreatePen(PS_SOLID, 1, crRed);
```

continues

LISTING 4.5 CONTINUED

```
    // Select a new pen into the device context, and save
    // the old pen to restore on clean up...
    CPen* ppenOld;
    ppenOld = pDC->SelectObject(&penRed);

    // Draw lines with red pen to connect vertex points
    pDC->Polyline(m_apt, 10);

    // Leave things as you found them (clean up)
    pDC->SelectObject(ppenOld);
}
```

Rectangles

Like the POINT structure, the rectangle structure (RECT) is one of the most important in Windows. RECT structures are used to store window coordinates and sizes, and as parameters for many MFC methods and Win32 API functions. The following RECT structure defines the position and size of a logical rectangle:

```
typedef struct tagRECT
{
    LONG     left;
    LONG     top;
    LONG     right;
    LONG     bottom;
} RECT, *PRECT, NEAR *NPRECT, FAR *LPRECT;
```

MFC wraps the RECT structure within the CRect class that provides the methods and operators listed in Table 4.13.

TABLE 4.13 CRect CLASS METHODS AND OPERATORS

Method	Description
BottomRight()	Returns the bottom-right point of a CRect object.
CenterPoint()	Returns the center point of a CRect object.
CopyRect()	Copies the dimensions of a source rectangle to a CRect object.
DeflateRect()	Decreases the width and height of a CRect object.
EqualRect()	Compares the coordinates of a CRect object and a given rectangle for equality.
Height()	Returns the height of a CRect object.
InflateRect()	Increases the width and height of a CRect object.

Method	Description
IntersectRect()	Returns a CRect object defined by the area of intersection between two rectangles.
IsRectEmpty()	Determines whether a CRect object is empty (if width or height are zero).
IsRectNull()	Determines whether the top, bottom, left, and right member variables all equal zero (NULL).
NormalizeRect()	Normalizes the height and width of a CRect object.
OffsetRect()	Moves a CRect object by the specified offset values.
PtInRect()	Tests whether a specified point lies within a CRect object.
SetRect()	Sets the size of a CRect object.
SetRectEmpty()	Sets all coordinates of a CRect object to zero, making an empty rectangle.
Size()	Returns the size of a CRect object.
SubtractRect()	Subtracts one rectangle from another.
TopLeft()	Returns the top-left point of a CRect object.
UnionRect()	Returns a CRect object defined by the area of union of two rectangles.
Width()	Calculates the width of a CRect object.
operator LPCRECT	Converts a CRect object to an LPCRECT.
operator LPRECT	Converts a CRect object to an LPRECT.
operator =	Copies the size and position of a rectangle to a CRect object.
operator ==	Tests the bounding coordinates of two CRect objects to see whether they are the same.
operator !=	Tests the bounding coordinates of two CRect objects to see whether they are *not* the same.
operator +=	Adds the specified offset values to a CRect object or inflates the object.
operator =	Subtracts the specified offset values from a CRect object or deflates the object.
operator &=	Sets a CRect object equal to the intersection of the object and a rectangle.
operator |=	Sets a CRect object equal to the union of the object and a rectangle.

4

PAINTING, DEVICE
CONTEXTS,
BITMAPS, AND
FONTS

continues

TABLE 4.13 CONTINUED

Method	Description
operator +	Adds the given offset values to a CRect object or inflates the object and returns the resulting CRect.
operator –	Subtracts the given offset values from a CRect object or deflates the object and returns the resulting CRect.
operator &	Creates the intersection of a CRect object and a rectangle and returns the resulting CRect.
operator ¦	Creates the union of a CRect object and a rectangle and returns the resulting CRect.

As you can see, the CRect class offers many useful methods that return the length, width, and coordinates of a rectangle and that allow you to move, resize, intersect, and combine rectangles. There are also many operators for working with CRect objects.

Drawing Rectangles

Regular rectangles (those with square corners) are typically drawn on a DC using the CDC methods Rectangle() and FillRect(). The CDC::Rectangle() method uses overloaded prototypes to specify the rectangle to draw in two ways:

```
BOOL Rectangle(int x1, int y1, int x2, int y2);
BOOL Rectangle(LPCRECT lpRect);
```

In this syntax, x1, y1, x2, and y2 are the coordinates of a rectangle, and lpRect is a pointer to a rectangle. This method draws the outline of a rectangle with the current pen and fills it with the current brush.

The CDC::FillRect() method doesn't draw a rectangle border, it just fills the rectangle with the current brush. This brush can be of any type (bitmap, dithered, and so on). The prototype for this method is shown here:

```
void FillRect(LPCRECT lpRect, CBrush* pBrush);
```

In this syntax, lpRect is a pointer to a rectangle, and pBrush is a pointer to a brush. To fill a rectangle with a solid COLORREF color, call the CDC::FillSolidRect() method using this prototype:

```
void FillSolidRect(LPCRECT lpRect, COLORREF clr);
```

In addition to the regular square-cornered rectangles, Windows provides the *rounded rectangle*—a rectangle with rounded corners. To draw a rectangle with rounded corners, call the CDC::RoundRect() method using this prototype:

```
BOOL RoundRect(LPCRECT lpRect, POINT point);
```

In this syntax, `lpRect` is a pointer to a rectangle, and `point` is the offset from the upper-left corner that defines the amount of fillet (rounding) applied to the rounded corners. Figure 4.12 shows the result of using a point offset of `CPoint(50, 50)`.

```
// Draw a rounded rect on the DC
pDC->RoundRect(arcSection[x][y], CPoint(50, 50));
```

FIGURE 4.12

Rounded rectangles created with `CDC::RoundRect()` *in the* `VECTEXT1` *program.*

Regions

A *region* is a Windows graphic object that represents an area of the device context's work space. This area can be composed of rectangles, ellipses, and polygons. Regions can be filled with the current brush or used to determine the *clipping region* of the DC (the area where drawing takes place). The clipping region can be any shape derived from the union, difference, or intersection of rectangles, ellipses, and polygons.

A region is created with one of the CDC region-creation methods such as `CDC::CreateRectRgn()` or `CDC::CreatePolygonRgn()`. A region can be displayed using the methods `CDC::FillRgn()`, `CDC::FrameRgn()`, `CDC::InvertRgn()`, and `CDC::PaintRgn()` and must be destroyed using the `CDC::DeleteObject()` method after you're done using it. The CDC methods for creating regions are listed in Table 4.14.

4

PAINTING, DEVICE
CONTEXTS,
BITMAPS, AND
FONTS

TABLE 4.14 THE METHODS PROVIDED BY CLASS CDC FOR CREATING REGIONS

Method	Description
CombineRgn()	Creates a union of two specified CRgn objects and assigns the result of the union to a third CRgn object.
CopyRgn()	Copies a CRgn object and assigns the result to a second CRgn object.
CreateEllipticRgn()	Creates an elliptical region and attaches it to a CRgn object.
CreateEllipticRgnIndirect()	Creates an elliptical region defined by a RECT structure and attaches it to a CRgn object.
CreateFromData()	Creates a region from the given region and transformation data.
CreateFromPath()	Creates a region from the path that is selected into the given device context.
CreatePolygonRgn()	Creates a polygonal region and attaches it to a CRgn object. If needed, Windows automatically closes the polygon by drawing a line from the last vertex to the first.
CreatePolyPolygonRgn()	Creates a region consisting of a series of closed polygons and attaches it to a CRgn object. The polygons can be disjointed, or they can overlap.
CreateRectRgn()	Creates a rectangular region and attaches it to a CRgn object.
CreateRectRgnIndirect()	Creates a rectangular region defined by a RECT structure and attaches it to a CRgn object.
CreateRoundRectRgn()	Creates a rectangular region with rounded corners and attaches it to a CRgn object.

The CDC methods for working with regions are listed in Table 4.15.

TABLE 4.15 THE METHODS PROVIDED BY CLASS CDC FOR WORKING WITH REGIONS

Method	Description
EqualRgn()	Tests two CRgn objects for equivalency.
FromHandle()	Returns a pointer to a CRgn object from a handle to an existing Windows region.
GetRegionData()	Fills a buffer with data describing the given region.
GetRgnBox()	Gets the coordinates of the bounding rectangle of a CRgn object.

Method	Description
OffsetRgn()	Moves a CRgn object according to the specified offsets.
PtInRegion()	Determines whether a specified point lies within the region.
RectInRegion()	Determines whether any part of a specified rectangle lies within the bounding rectangle of a CRgn object.
SetRectRgn()	Sets an existing CRgn object to a specified rectangular region.

The CRgn::CombineRgn() method uses Boolean operations to create a new region. The prototype for this method is as follows:

```
int CombineRgn(CRgn* pRgn1, CRgn* pRgn2, int nCombineMode);
```

In this syntax, the parameters pRgn1 and pRgn2 are pointers to existing CRgn objects, and the nCombineMode parameter is one of the Boolean operations listed in Table 4.16. These operation values are defined by the Win32 API for combining regions.

TABLE 4.16 THE BOOLEAN OPERATIONS PROVIDED BY THE WIN32 API AND THE MFC CLASS CRgn

Boolean Value	Description
RGN_AND	Uses overlapping areas of both regions (intersection).
RGN_COPY	Creates a copy of the first region.
RGN_DIFF	Creates a region consisting of the areas of region 1 (identified by pRgn1) that are *not* part of region 2 (identified by pRgn2).
RGN_OR	Combines both regions in their entirety (union).
RGN_XOR	Combines both regions but removes overlapping areas.

These operations are explored a bit in the VECTEXT1 program.

Polygons

The CDC::Polygon() method draws a closed polygon with the current pen, filled by the current brush. The points specified in an array of points are connected to create the polygon, and the last vertex is connected to the first if necessary. The prototype for CDC::Polygon() is as follows:

```
BOOL Polygon(LPPOINT lpPoints, int nCount);
```

In this syntax, lpPoints is a pointer to an array of points, and nCount is the number of points in the array.

4

PAINTING, DEVICE CONTEXTS, BITMAPS, AND FONTS

The `DoPolygon()` method in the VECTEXT1 program is very similar to the `DoPolyLine()` method; the difference is a call to `CDC::Polygon()` instead of `CDC::Polyline()`. Figure 4.13 shows the result of using the array of points in the class member m_apt[10] to draw the polygon with 10 vertices.

Figure 4.13

Drawing a closed polygon in the VECTEXT1 program.

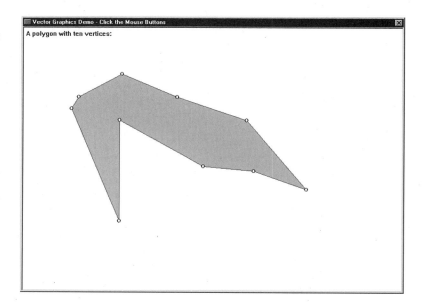

Ellipses

Ellipses use rectangles as bounding boxes, and the `CDC::Ellipse()` method takes a rectangle as a parameter. The `CMainWnd::DoEllipses()` method from the VECTEXT1 program (shown in Listing 4.6) divides the client area into six equal logical rectangles and uses them as bounding boxes for six ellipses. Each ellipse has one of the six different hatch brush styles. The result of this code is shown in Figure 4.14.

The `CDC::Ellipse()` method draws an ellipse with the current pen, filled by the current brush. There are two overloaded prototypes for `CDC::Ellipse()`:

```
BOOL Ellipse(int x1, int y1, int x2, int y2);
BOOL Ellipse(LPCRECT lpRect);
```

In this syntax, x1, y1, x2, and y2 are the corners of a bounding rectangle for the ellipse. The lpRect parameter is a pointer to a bounding rectangle for the ellipse.

The `DoEllipses()` method in the VECTEXT1 program uses various hatch brush styles to fill ellipses in the client area. Figure 4.14 shows the result of using these hatch brushes.

FIGURE 4.14

Drawing ellipses with various hatch brush styles in the VECTEXT1 program.

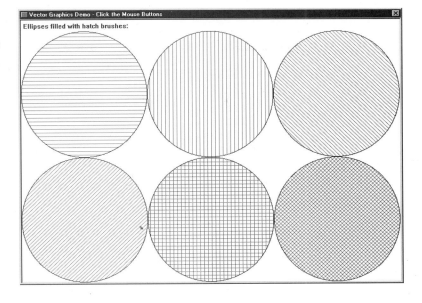

LISTING 4.6 THE CODE TO DRAW SIX ELLIPSES WITH THE SIX DIFFERENT HATCH BRUSH STYLES

```
/////////////////////////////////////////////////////////////////
// CMainWnd::DoEllipses()

void CMainWnd::DoEllipses(CClientDC* pDC)
{
    // Create a label
    CString str = "Ellipses filled with hatch brushes:";
    pDC->TextOut(5, 5, str);

    // Subdivide the display into 6 sections
    CRect   rc;
    CRect   arcSection[4][3];

    GetClientRect(&rc);
    int cx = rc.right / 3;
    int cy = (rc.bottom - 25) / 2;

    int nHeight = cy;

    for (int x = 0; x < 2; x++)
    {
        int nWidth = cx;
        for (int y = 0; y < 3; y++)
        {
```

continues

LISTING 4.6 CONTINUED

```cpp
        arcSection[x][y].left   = nWidth - cx;
        arcSection[x][y].top    = nHeight - cy + 25;
        arcSection[x][y].right  = arcSection[x][y].left + cx;
        arcSection[x][y].bottom = arcSection[x][y].top + cy;

        nWidth += cx;
    }
    nHeight += cy;
}

// Six different hatch brush styles
cy = 25;
int nHatchStyle = 0;

for (x = 0; x < 2; x++)
{
    for (int y = 0; y < 3; y++)
    {
        /*====================================================
            From WINGDI.H:

            // Hatch Styles
            #define HS_HORIZONTAL    0    // -- -- -
            #define HS_VERTICAL      1    // |||||
            #define HS_FDIAGONAL     2    // \\\\\
            #define HS_BDIAGONAL     3    // /////
            #define HS_CROSS         4    // +++++
            #define HS_DIAGCROSS     5    // xxxxx
        ====================================================*/

        // Create a hatch brush
        CBrush br(nHatchStyle, crRed);

        // Select the new brush into the device context, and save
        // the old brush to restore on clean up...
        CBrush* pbrOld;
        pbrOld = pDC->SelectObject(&br);

        // Draw an ellipse on the DC
        pDC->Ellipse(arcSection[x][y]);
        nHatchStyle++;

        // Leave things as you found them (clean up)
        pDC->SelectObject(pbrOld);
    }
}
}
```

Bézier Curves

A *Bézier curve* is a parametric curve (or *spline curve*) defined by a set of control points. Blending functions are applied to groups of control points to calculate the curve. MFC provides a third-order Bézier blending function in the form of the `CDC::PolyBezier()` and `CDC::PolyBezierTo()` methods. The prototype for the `CDC::PolyBezier()` method is as follows:

```
BOOL PolyBezier(const POINT* lpPoints, int nCount);
```

In this syntax, `lpPoints` is a pointer to an array of `POINT` data structures (or `CPoint` objects) that contains the endpoints and control points of the splines, and `nCount` specifies the number of points in the `lpPoints` array.

> **NOTE**
>
> The value must be one more than three times the number of splines to be drawn, because each Bézier spline requires two control points and an endpoint, and the initial spline requires an additional starting point.

The code in Listing 4.7 shows how the VECTEXT1 program uses the array of points in the `m_apt[10]` class member to draw a static Bézier curve composed of three splines. The result of the `DoBezier()` method can be seen in Figure 4.15.

FIGURE 4.15
Drawing a static Bézier curve in the VECTEXT1 program.

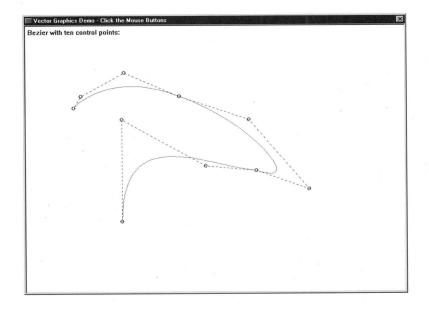

4

PAINTING, DEVICE CONTEXTS, BITMAPS, AND FONTS

LISTING 4.7 THE DoBezier() METHOD FROM VECTEXT1 DRAWS A SERIES OF BÉZIER CURVES AND CONTROL POINTS

```cpp
void CMainWnd::DoBezier(CClientDC* pDC)
{
    // Create a label
    CString str = "Bezier with ten control points:";
    pDC->TextOut(5, 5, str);

    // Draw points
    for (int i = 0; i < 10; i++)
        pDC->Ellipse(m_apt[i].x - 4, m_apt[i].y - 4,
                     m_apt[i].x + 4, m_apt[i].y + 4);

    // Create new pens
    CPen penBlue;
    CPen penRed;

    penBlue.CreatePen(PS_DOT, 1, crBlue);
    penRed.CreatePen(PS_SOLID, 1, crRed);

    // Select a new pen into the device context, and save
    // the old pen to restore on clean up...
    CPen* ppenOld;
    ppenOld = pDC->SelectObject(&penBlue);

    // Draw lines with blue pen to connect control points
    pDC->Polyline(m_apt, 10);

    // Draw Bezier curve with red pen
    pDC->SelectObject(&penRed);
    pDC->PolyBezier(m_apt, 10);

    // Leave things as you found them (clean up)
    pDC->SelectObject(ppenOld);

}
```

Fonts and Text

Text is very important to users of computer programs, even users of programs created for a GUI OS like Windows. In fact, text output is one of the most important features of the operating system. Since the days of Windows 3.1, Windows programs have been able to access a wonderful technology called the TrueType font (TTF). TrueType fonts are vector fonts scaleable to virtually any size with no degradation of image quality.

> **NOTE**
>
> To get you started working with fonts, some font terminology should be explained. The term *typeface* refers to the style of lettering and the visual appearance of the text. The term *font* refers to a set of characters in a given typeface (for example, *Arial*). In font terminology, a *point* is 1/72 of an inch and is used to measure the height of font characters.

Font Characteristics

Two main categories of fonts are used in Windows: *fixed width* (or monospace) and *variable width*. Monospace font characters are all the same width; variable-width font characters each take up as much space as they need. Windows defines three different types of fonts: raster fonts (bitmapped fonts), vector fonts (fonts composed of a series of line segments), and TrueType (fonts that use lines and spline curves to define character outlines).

Font Families

All typefaces are grouped into font families that represent the style (or mood) of the font. Identifiers for the default families are found in the header file WINGDI.H; these font family (FF_*) identifiers are listed in Table 4.17.

TABLE 4.17 FONT FAMILIES PROVIDED BY WINDOWS

Family Name	Description
FF_DECORATIVE	This is a novelty font family. One example is Viking Runes.
FF_DONTCARE	This is a generic family name used when no information about a font is needed.
FF_MODERN	This is a monospace font with or without serifs. Monospace fonts are usually modern; examples include Pica, Elite, and Courier New.
FF_ROMAN	Specifies a proportional font with serifs. An example is Times New Roman.
FF_SCRIPT	Specifies a font designed to look like handwriting; examples include Script and Cursive.
FF_SWISS	Specifies a proportional font without serifs; an example is Arial.

These IDs are used when creating, selecting, or getting information about a font. Fonts can have various point sizes and styles (like bold or italics). This book is concerned mainly with the TrueType variety because it's the most versatile and is relatively easy to use (even if it is somewhat complex).

The TEXTMETRIC Structure

To output text, Windows uses a bounding rectangle and paints a representation of the current character to the display pixels as a bitmap. There are Win32 API functions and MFC methods that use a Windows TEXTMETRIC structure to get information about text characters on the display.

The TEXTMETRIC structure contains information about a display font and gives size information in logical units that depend on the current mapping mode. The TEXTMETRIC structure is shown in Listing 4.8.

LISTING 4.8   THE WINDOWS TEXTMETRIC STRUCTURE

```
typedef struct tagTEXTMETRIC
{
    LONG tmHeight;             // Character height (ascent + descent)
    LONG tmAscent;             // Character ascent above base line
    LONG tmDescent;            // Character descent below base line
    LONG tmInternalLeading;    // Extra space inside tmHeight
    LONG tmExternalLeading;    // Extra space between text rows
    LONG tmAveCharWidth;       // Average width of font characters
    LONG tmMaxCharWidth;       // Width of the widest font character
    LONG tmWeight;             // The weight of the font
    LONG tmOverhang;           // Extra width padding
    LONG tmDigitizedAspectX;   // Horizontal aspect of target device
    LONG tmDigitizedAspectY;   // Vertical aspect of target device
    BCHAR tmFirstChar;         // Char value of first font character
    BCHAR tmLastChar;          // Char value of last font character
    BCHAR tmDefaultChar;       // Default substitution character
    BCHAR tmBreakChar;         // Char value for word break formats
    BYTE tmItalic;             // An italic font if it's nonzero
    BYTE tmUnderlined;         // An underlined font if it's nonzero
    BYTE tmStruckOut;          // A strikeout font if it's nonzero
    BYTE tmPitchAndFamily;     // Font pitch and family information
    BYTE tmCharSet;            // Character set of the font
} TEXTMETRIC;
```

> **NOTE**
>
> In addition to the TEXTMETRIC structure, there is a NEWTEXTMETRIC structure defined to hold additional information about TrueType fonts.

To get basic information about the font currently selected into a device context, you can use the CDC::GetTextMetrics() method. The prototype for this method is shown following:

```
BOOL GetTextMetrics(LPTEXTMETRIC lpMetrics) const;
```

In this syntax, lpMetrics is a pointer to a TEXTMETRIC structure that receives the text metrics. For example, to find the average width of the font currently in a given device context, simply call GetTextMetrics(), as in this code fragment:

```
TEXTMETRIC tm;
if (dc.GetTextMetrics(&tm))
    int nAveCharWidth = tm.tmAveCharWidth;
```

The VECTEXT1 program displays complete TEXTMETRIC information about the Windows default system font by calling the CMainWnd::DoTextSystem() method (see Listing 4.9). Figure 4.16 shows the result of this method.

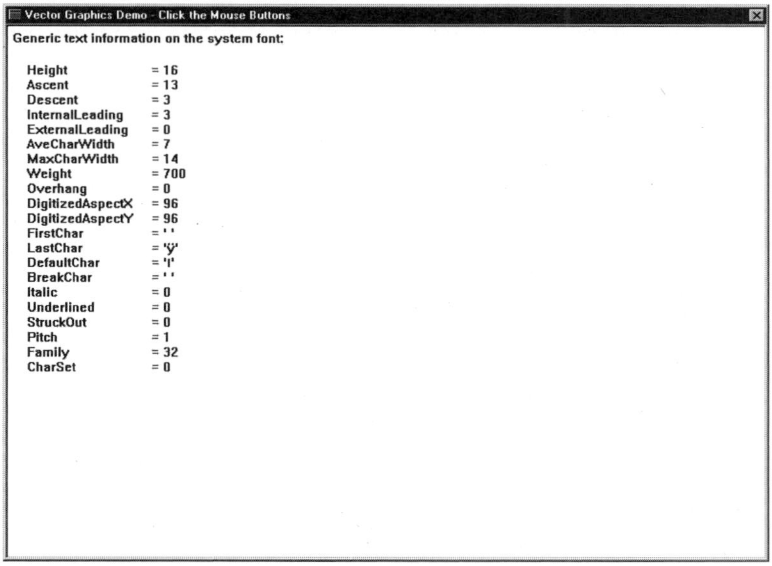

FIGURE 4.16

Displaying complete TEXTMETRIC information about the Windows default system font.

LISTING 4.9   DISPLAYING SYSTEM FONT TEXTMETRIC INFORMATION IN THE VECTEXT1 PROGRAM'S CMainWnd::DoTextSystem() METHOD

```
void CMainWnd::DoTextSystem(CClientDC* pDC)
{
    // Create a label
    CString strLbl = "Generic text information on the system font:";
    pDC->TextOut(5, 5, strLbl);
```

continues

LISTING 4.9   CONTINUED

```
// Select the system font into the DC
HFONT hFont = (HFONT)::GetStockObject(SYSTEM_FONT);
CFont fnt;
CFont* pFont = fnt.FromHandle(hFont);
CFont* pfntOld = pDC->SelectObject(pFont);

// Get some info about the current font
TEXTMETRIC tm;
pDC->GetTextMetrics(&tm);

UINT nCurLineHeight = 40;

// Create an array of strings to display the TEXTMETRIC data
CString str[42];

// Label strings
str[0] = "Height";
//
// etc. for all label strings
//
str[20] = "CharSet";

// Data strings
str[21].Format(" = %d", tm.tmHeight);
//
// etc. for all data strings
//
str[41].Format(" = %d", tm.tmCharSet);

// Display strings 0-20
for (int i = 0; i < 21; i++)
{
   pDC->TextOut(20, nCurLineHeight, str[i]);
   nCurLineHeight += tm.tmHeight;
}

// Reset line height
nCurLineHeight = 40;

//
// Now you need to determine the distance that the data strings
// should move to the right to align the data evenly.
//
// str[9] is the longest string, so you calculate the width + 2
// to space the = signs nicely.
//

UINT nLeft = 20 + tm.tmAveCharWidth * (str[9].GetLength() + 2);

// Display strings 21-41
```

```
    for (i = 21; i < 42; i++)
    {
        pDC->TextOut(nLeft, nCurLineHeight, str[i]);
        nCurLineHeight += tm.tmHeight;
    }
    if (pfntOld)
        pDC->SelectObject(pfntOld);
}
```

The LOGFONT Structure

If you need more information about a font or want to create a custom font, you have to understand *logical fonts*, which are defined with the Windows LOGFONT structure (see Listing 4.10). A *logical font* is an abstract font description that defines the font's characteristics (bold, italic, size, and so on). A logical font must be selected into a device context before it can be used. After being selected into a device context, the logical font becomes a *physical font*.

LISTING 4.10   THE LOGFONT STRUCTURE DEFINES A LOGICAL FONT

```
typedef struct tagLOGFONT
{
    LONG lfHeight;
    LONG lfWidth;
    LONG lfEscapement;
    LONG lfOrientation;
    LONG lfWeight;
    BYTE lfItalic;
    BYTE lfUnderline;
    BYTE lfStrikeOut;
    BYTE lfCharSet;
    BYTE lfOutPrecision;
    BYTE lfClipPrecision;
    BYTE lfQuality;
    BYTE lfPitchAndFamily;
    TCHAR lfFaceName[LF_FACESIZE];
} LOGFONT;
```

4

PAINTING, DEVICE
CONTEXTS,
BITMAPS, AND
FONTS

The members of this structure are described in Table 4.18.

TABLE 4.18   THE MEMBERS OF THE LOGFONT STRUCTURE

Member	Description
lfHeight	The logical height of a character cell or character.
lfWidth	The average logical width of characters in the font.

continues

TABLE 4.18 CONTINUED

Member	Description
lfEscapement	The angle, in tenths of degrees, between the escapement vector (parallel to the base line of a row of text) and the x-axis of the device.
lfOrientation	The angle, in tenths of degrees, between each character's base line and the x-axis of the device.
lfWeight	The weight of the font (ranging from 0 to 1000).
lfItalic	An italic font if TRUE.
lfUnderline	An underlined font if TRUE.
lfStrikeOut	A strikeout font if TRUE.
lfCharSet	The font's character set.
lfOutPrecision	The output precision, which defines how closely the output must match a requested font's height, width, character orientation, escapement, pitch, and font type.
lfClipPrecision	The clipping precision, defining how to clip characters that lie on clipping boundaries.
lfQuality	The output quality, defining how well the GDI must match logical-font attributes to physical font attributes.
lfPitchAndFamily	The pitch and family of a font.
lfFaceName	A string, limited to 32 characters, that denotes the typeface name of the font.

The LOGFONT structure is used when creating a logical font for use in a device context; the following section explains how.

Font Creation

MFC wraps logical fonts and methods into the CFont class. To create a logical font for use in your applications, you can use any of the initialization methods provided by the CFont class. Table 4.19 lists the creation methods class CFont provides.

TABLE 4.19 CLASS CFont CREATION METHODS

Method	Description
CreateFontIndirect()	Initializes a CFont object as defined by a LOGFONT structure.
CreateFont()	Initializes a CFont object with the specified characteristics.

Method	Description
CreatePointFont()	Initializes a CFont object with the specified height and typeface.
CreatePointFontIndirect()	Initializes a CFont object as defined by a LOGFONT structure. Font height is measured in tenths of a point instead of logical units.

As you do with most MFC objects, you use two-step construction when creating a CFont object. The VECTEXT1 program's CMainWnd::DisplayLogFont() method in Listing 4.11 shows how to create a logical font. This method also uses text metrics and logical font members to display the font in various locations and sizes. Calling the method like this produces the image in Figure 4.17:

```
DisplayLogFont(pDC, "Arial");
```

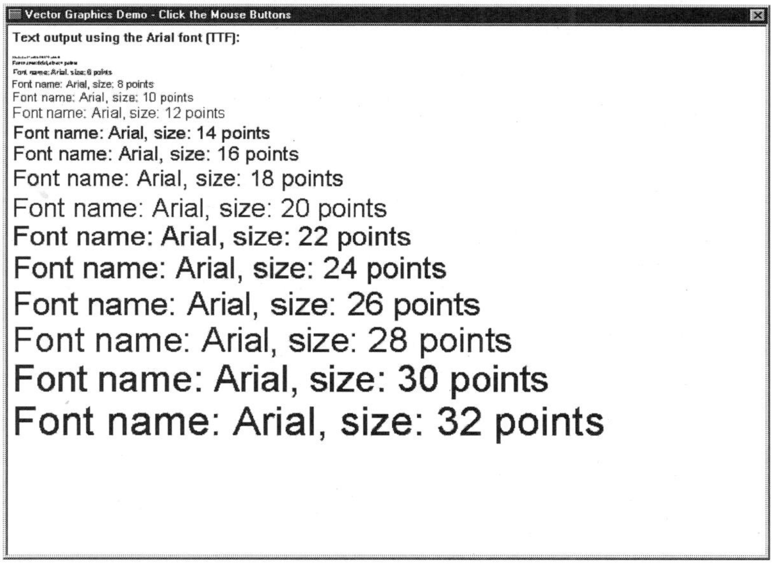

FIGURE 4.17

The result of using
CMainWnd::
DisplayLogFont()
to display various sizes of text.

4

PAINTING, DEVICE
CONTEXTS,
BITMAPS, AND
FONTS

LISTING 4.11   CREATING A LOGICAL FONT AND DISPLAYING 16 SIZES FROM 2 POINTS TO 32 POINTS

```
//////////////////////////////////////////////////////////////////
// CMainWnd::DisplayLogFont()

void CMainWnd::DisplayLogFont(CClientDC* pDC, CString sFont)
{
```

continues

LISTING 4.11   CONTINUED

```
// Draw various sizes of fonts
UINT uSize      = 2;   // Starting point size
int  cyDrawHere = 30;  // Start vertical drawing text here
CFont* pfntOld  = 0;

// 16 lines of text, font sizes from 2 to 32 points
for (int i = 0; i < 16; i++)
{
    // Create a new font and init a LOGFONT structure
    CFont      fnt;
    LOGFONT    lf;
    TEXTMETRIC tm;

    memset(&lf, 0, sizeof(LOGFONT));

    // Set initial font typeface name and font size
    lstrcpy(lf.lfFaceName, sFont);

    int cyPixels = pDC->GetDeviceCaps(LOGPIXELSY);
    lf.lfHeight  = -MulDiv(uSize, cyPixels, 72);

    // Create the new font
    fnt.CreateFontIndirect(&lf);

    // Get the text metrics
    pDC->GetTextMetrics(&tm);
    cyDrawHere += abs(lf.lfHeight) + tm.tmExternalLeading;

    // Make the new font current in the DC
    pfntOld = pDC->SelectObject(&fnt);

    // Draw a line of text
    CString str;
    str.Format("Font name: %s, size: %d points",
               lf.lfFaceName, uSize);
    pDC->TextOut(5, cyDrawHere, str);

    uSize += 2;
}
// Restore the previous font to the DC
pDC->SelectObject(pfntOld);
}
```

The CDC::TextOut() method used in Listing 4.11 is only one of class CDC's text output methods—text can be drawn in several ways.

Drawing Text

Text is drawn using a device context's selected font, text color, and background color. You can set the text color by calling the `CDC::SetTextColor()` method; you can set the background color by calling the `CDC::SetBkColor()` and `CDC::SetBkMode()` methods.

To change the text in a DC to blue and make the text background transparent (so that what's behind the text shows through), simply use this code (assuming that `pDC` is a pointer to `CDC`-derived object):

```
#define crBlue RGB(0, 0, 255)     // macro for naming a color

pDC->SetTextColor(crBlue);
pDC->SetBkMode(TRANSPARENT);
```

MFC provides several text output methods in class `CDC`. The most often used of these are `DrawText()`, `TextOut()`, and `TabbedTextOut()`.

The `DrawText()` Method

The `DrawText()` method formats text within a given rectangle using many advanced formatting features, including expanding tabs into spaces; justifying text to the left, right, or center of the rectangle; and automatically breaking text into lines to fit within the rectangle. When using the `CDC::DrawText()` method, you usually use this overloaded prototype:

```
int DrawText(const CString& str, LPRECT lpRect, UINT nFormat);
```

The `str` parameter is a `CString` object that contains the text to draw; the `lpRect` parameter points to a `RECT` or `CRect` object that forms the bounding box in which the text is to be formatted; the `nFormat` parameter specifies how the text is formatted.

The `TextOut()` Method

The `TextOut()` method draws a text string at a specified location using the currently selected font and colors. The overloaded prototype you most often use is shown here:

```
BOOL TextOut(int x, int y, const CString& str);
```

In this syntax, `x` and `y` specify the logical coordinate where the text begins drawing, and `str` is a `CString` object that contains the text to draw.

4

PAINTING, DEVICE
CONTEXTS,
BITMAPS, AND
FONTS

The `TabbedTextOut()` Method

The `TabbedTextOut()` method draws a text string at the specified location and expands tabs to values specified in an array of tab-stop positions. The overloaded prototype you most often use is as follows:

```
CSize TabbedTextOut(int x, int y, const CString& str,
    int nTabPositions, LPINT lpnTabStopPositions,
    int nTabOrigin );
```

The parameters for this method are listed in Table 4.20.

TABLE 4.20   THE PARAMETERS OF THE CDC::`TabbedTextOut()` METHOD

Parameter	Meaning
x, y	The logical x and y coordinates of the starting point of the string.
str	A CString object that contains the specified characters.
nTabPositions	The number of values in the array of tab-stop positions.
lpnTabStopPositions	A pointer to an array containing the tab-stop positions in logical units.
nTabOrigin	Specifies the logical x coordinate of the tab expansion starting position.

Sample Program: Vector Graphics and Text Methods (VECTEXT1.EXE)

The VECTEXT1 program on the companion CD-ROM provides examples of many CDC graphics and text methods. The program creates a frame window with a non-sizable, dialog-style window border that handles mouse clicks (left and right) in its client area. The functionality for the program is mostly in the frame window class (CMainWnd). Many protected methods are provided as examples of many common graphics needs. These methods are listed and described in Table 4.21.

NOTE

 The VECTEXT1 program is much too long to list in this book, but the full source code is on the CD-ROM.

TABLE 4.21   THE GRAPHICS AND HELPER METHODS FOUND IN THE VECTEXT1
PROGRAM'S CMainWnd CLASS

Method	*Description*
DoBezier()	Displays three Bézier curves defined by ten control points.
DoEllipses()	Displays six ellipses with various hatch brush styles.
DoLines()	Displays randomly generated lines.
DoMetafile()	Creates an enhanced metafile, records lines with random colors and thicknesses at random locations, and plays back the finished metafile on the CMainWnd client area.
DoPixels()	Displays a random number of pixels with random locations and colors.
DoPoints()	Displays 4×4-pixel-bounded ellipses with random locations and colors (just like DoPixels(), but with small 4×4 ellipses).
DoPolygon()	Displays a filled polygon using the CMainWnd class array of points: m_apt[10].
DoPolyLine()	Displays a polyline and its vertices using the CMainWnd class array of points: m_apt[10].
DoRects()	Displays six rectangles with various hatch brush styles.
DoRegions()	Displays two overlapping regions, one an elliptical region, the other a rectangular region.
DoRegionsUnion()	Displays the result of the union of two overlapping regions, one an elliptical region, the other a rectangular region.
DoRegionsDifference()	Displays the result of the difference of two overlapping regions, one an elliptical region, the other a rectangular region.
DoRegionsIntersect()	Displays the result of the intersection of two overlapping regions, one an elliptical region, the other a rectangular region.
DoRoundRects()	Displays six rounded rectangles filled with randomly colored solid brushes.
DoTextArial()	Specifies, creates, and displays the standard Arial TrueType font in sizes from 2 points to 32 points.
DoTextRoman()	Specifies, creates, and displays the standard Times New Roman TrueType font in sizes from 2 points to 32 points.
DoTextSystem()	Displays complete TEXTMETRIC information about the standard system font.

The VECTEXT1 program uses the concept of *graphics pages* that change with each mouse click in the client area. The current "page" is determined by the CMainWnd member variable m_CurPage; each click triggers a call to one of the methods listed in Table 4.21 (within the CMainWnd::ProcessMouseClick() method), changing the "page." When all the "pages" have been displayed, they start over from the beginning. The source code for this program should be enough to get you well on your way to mastering GDI graphics, MFC-style!

Raster Graphics

Vector graphics use mathematical formulas to describe images on a device context. *Raster graphics* differ from vector graphics in that they are based on information displayed in an array of pixels. Vector graphics are size-independent; they can be stretched to virtually any size without losing clarity or becoming distorted. Raster graphics, on the other hand, are constrained by the pixels that represent them. Resizing raster images most often results in distortion of the image, with a jagged, pixelized, staircase effect.

Named Raster Operations (ROPs)

Windows supports 256 ternary raster operations for use with the GDI bit block transfer operations (BitBlt() and related functions). These raster operations (ROPs) provide logical operations that combine the source, destination, and current brush pattern. Although there are 256 of these operations, in practice only a small number of them are used; only 15 are important enough to have earned *common names* for themselves. These 15 named ternary ROPs are described in Table 4.22.

TABLE 4.22 THE 15 NAMED TERNARY RASTER OPERATIONS (ROPs) USED BY GDI BIT BLOCK TRANSFER FUNCTIONS

ROP	*Description*
BLACKNESS	Creates black output in the destination bitmap.
DSTINVERT	Inverts the destination bitmap.
MERGECOPY	Combines a pattern bitmap with a source bitmap using the Boolean AND operator.
MERGEPAINT	Inverts the source bitmap and combines it with the destination bitmap using the Boolean OR operator.
NOTSRCCOPY	Inverts the source bitmap and copies it to the destination.
NOTSRCERASE	Combines the destination and source bitmaps using the Boolean OR operator and then inverts the result.
PATCOPY	Copies a pattern to the destination bitmap.

ROP	Description
PATINVERT	Combines the destination bitmap with a pattern using the Boolean XOR operator.
PATPAINT	Inverts the source bitmap, combines it with a pattern using the Boolean OR operator, and combines the result with the destination bitmap using the Boolean OR operator.
SRCAND	Combines the destination and source bitmaps using the Boolean AND operator.
SRCCOPY	Copies the source bitmap to the destination bitmap.
SRCERASE	Combines the inverted destination bitmap with the source bitmap using the Boolean AND operator.
SRCINVERT	Combines the destination and source bitmaps using the Boolean XOR operator.
SRCPAINT	Combines the destination and source bitmaps using the Boolean OR operator.
WHITENESS	Creates white output in the destination bitmap.

Raster operation codes define how GDI combines the bits from a source bitmap with the bits in a destination bitmap. The ROP codes used for bit block transfer operations are called *ternary ROPs* because they use three operands:

- A source bitmap
- A brush
- A destination bitmap

Bitmaps

A *bitmap* is an array of bits that form an image of some kind. All raster devices, including video displays, use bitmaps to display images. The video display uses pixels to show the bitmap bits onscreen. Bitmaps come in various bit depths (or color depths) and flavors. The two types of bitmaps used by Windows are device-dependent bitmaps (DDBs) and device-independent bitmaps (DIBs). Both of these bitmap types can have different color depths.

The *color depth* of an image is directly related to the number of bits used to store the color data in a bitmapped image. A 1-bit image is called *monochrome* and can display two colors (black and white by default). A 4-bit image can display 16 colors (this is the standard for VGA video adapters). An 8-bit image can display up to 256 colors (the minimum for super VGA video adapters). A 16-bit image (also called a *hicolor image*) doesn't need a palette to describe its colors; it can display 32,768 colors. A 24-bit image (also called a *true color image*) doesn't use palettes because it can display the full spectrum of 16.8 million colors visible to the human eye.

4

PAINTING, DEVICE
CONTEXTS,
BITMAPS, AND
FONTS

> **NOTE**
>
> Bitmaps with color-depths ranging from 1 bit to 8 bits use palette information to specify the color table of the bitmapped image. Images with higher bit depths don't need palettes.

Device-Dependent Bitmaps

Bitmaps that rely on the hardware palette are called *device-dependent bitmaps* (DDBs). DDBs were the only bitmap format available to Windows programmers before the release of Windows 3.0. DDBs are currently supported mainly for compatibility with older applications written for those early Windows versions. A developer writing a new application, or porting an application written for a previous version of Windows to the Win32 platform, should use DIBs. A DDB is defined by a Windows BITMAP structure and comes in two types:

- Discardable bitmaps—Windows can discard these from memory if the bitmap isn't selected into a device context and system memory is running low.

- Nondiscardable bitmaps—Windows must retain these bitmaps in memory.

The BITMAP Structure

A DDB is defined by a BITMAP structure that holds the data for a bitmap. The BITMAP structure is defined as follows:

```
typedef struct tagBITMAP
{
    LONG    bmType;
    LONG    bmWidth;
    LONG    bmHeight;
    LONG    bmWidthBytes;
    WORD    bmPlanes;
    WORD    bmBitsPixel;
    LPVOID  bmBits;
}
BITMAP;
```

The data members of this structure are described in Table 4.23.

TABLE 4.23 THE DATA MEMBERS OF THE BITMAP STRUCTURE

Member	Description
bmType	Specifies the bitmap type. Always set this member to zero.
bmWidth	The width, in pixels, of the bitmap.
bmHeight	The height, in pixels, of the bitmap.
bmWidthBytes	The number of bytes per scan line. Because Windows expects the bit values of a bitmap to form a word-aligned array, this value must be divisible by 2.
bmPlanes	The number of color planes in the bitmap.
bmBitsPixel	The number of bits needed to describe the color of a pixel.
bmBits	A pointer to the array of character values that make up the image data.

Device-Independent Bitmaps (DIBs)

Windows 3.0 introduced the *device-independent bitmap* (DIB), which was designed to solve some of the device dependency inherent in DDBs. DIBs are much more useful than DDBs for storing bitmap data in disk files because they contain more useful information about the image. Here are the main features of a DIB:

- Contains information about the color format of the device on which the DIB image was created.

- Contains information about the resolution of the device on which the DIB image was created.

- Contains information about the palette for the device on which the image was created.

- Contains an array of bits used to map the red, green, blue (RGB) color components of the palette to pixels in the DIB image.

- Contains a data-compression identifier that indicates which data compression scheme (if any) is used to compact the size of the file on disk.

The `CBitmap` Class

The `CBitmap` class encapsulates GDI bitmaps into a convenient MFC object wrapper that makes it easier to work with bitmaps in MFC than it is in the SDK. Figure 4.18 shows the location of `CBitmap` in the MFC class hierarchy.

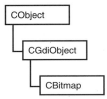

FIGURE 4.18
The location of the CBitmap *class in the MFC class hierarchy.*

CBitmap Class Methods

The CBitmap class provides several class methods that wrap GDI bitmap-related functions. Table 4.24 describes these CBitmap methods.

TABLE 4.24   CBitmap CLASS METHODS

Method	Description
CreateBitmap()	Creates a device-dependent memory bitmap with the specified width, height, and bit pattern.
CreateBitmapIndirect()	Creates a bitmap with the width, height, and bit pattern defined in a BITMAP structure.
CreateCompatibleBitmap()	Creates a bitmap compatible with a specified device context.
CreateDiscardableBitmap()	Creates a discardable bitmap compatible with a specified device context.
FromHandle()	Gets a pointer to a CBitmap object from a specified Windows bitmap handle (HBITMAP).
GetBitmap()	Gets a pointer to a specified CBitmap object.
GetBitmapBits()	Copies a bitmap's bits into a specified buffer.
GetBitmapDimension()	Gets the width and height of a bitmap that have been set previously by the SetBitmapDimension() method.
LoadBitmap()	Loads a bitmap from resource data and attaches it to a CBitmap object.
LoadMappedBitmap()	Loads a bitmap from resource data and maps colors to current system colors.
LoadOEMBitmap()	Loads a predefined Windows bitmap and attaches it to a CBitmap object.
SetBitmapBits()	Sets the bits of a bitmap to the specified bit values.
SetBitmapDimension()	Designates a width and height to a bitmap using 0.1-millimeter units.

Class CBitmap also provides the operator HBITMAP, which returns the underlying Windows handle attached to the CBitmap object.

Transferring and Contorting Bitmaps

To transfer bitmap data from one place to another—that is, from one DC to another—you must transfer blocks of bits from one DC to another. This activity is commonly referred to as a *bit block transfer (BBT)*, or BitBlt (pronounced *bit-blit*). When transferring bit blocks, you must use a memory DC as a buffer—you can't "blit" directly to the display.

Transferring Bits with BitBlt()

The CDC class provides methods to blast bits from one DC to another; the most useful of these is CDC::BitBlt(). The prototype for this method is complex, taking eight parameters as shown here:

```
BOOL BitBlt(
    int x, int y,               // upper left corner of destination DC
    int nWidth, int nHeight,    // width and height of destination DC
    CDC* pSrcDC,                // the source DC
    int xSrc, int ySrc,         // upper left corner of source DC
    DWORD dwRop);               // the ternary raster operation code
```

The parameters for this method are described following:

- x and y—These values specify the logical coordinates of the upper-left corner of the destination rectangle.

- nWidth and nHeight—These values specify the logical height of the destination rectangle and source bitmap.

- pSrcDC—Pointer to a CDC object that identifies the device context from which the bitmap will be copied. It must be NULL if dwRop specifies a raster operation that does not include a source.

- xSrc and ySrc—These values specify the logical coordinates of the upper-left corner of the source bitmap.

- dwRop—This value specifies the ternary raster operation to be performed (refer to Table 4.22, earlier in this chapter).

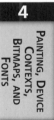

> **NOTE**
>
> Not all device contexts support bit block transfers. You can test to see whether
> a DC conforms by calling the `CDC::GetDeviceCaps()` method, specifying the
> RASTERCAPS index as the sole parameter, and checking for the presence of the
> RC_BITBLT bit in the return value. Consider this example:
>
> ```
> if ((dc.GetDeviceCaps(RASTERCAPS) & RC_BITBLT) == 0)
> {
>     // device doesn't support BitBlt
>     ;
> }
> else
> {
>     // device does support BitBlt
>     ;
> }
> ```
>
> For more information about `CDC::GetDeviceCaps()` and the index values and
> bits used, see the MFC documentation for the Win32 API function of the same
> name.

Stretching Bits to Fit with `StretchBlt()`

The `CDC` class provides a method similar to `BitBlt()`, but one that stretches or compresses bits to fit a specified destination rectangle: `CDC::StretchBlt()`. The prototype for this method is even more complex than the one for `BitBlt()`—`StretchBlt()` takes ten parameters as shown following:

```
BOOL StretchBlt(
    int x, int y,              // upper left corner of destination DC
    int nWidth, int nHeight,   // width and height of destination DC
    CDC* pSrcDC,               // the source DC
    int xSrc, int ySrc,        // upper left corner of source DC
    int nSrcWidth,             // width of the source bitmap
    int nSrcHeight,            // height of the source bitmap
    DWORD dwRop);              // the ternary raster operation code
```

The parameters for this method are the same as those used for `BitBlt()` with the exception of the two additional `nSrcWidth` and `nSrcHeight` values. These two values define the width and height of the source bitmap.

> **NOTE**
>
> To determine how to stretch or compress the bitmap, `StretchBlt()` uses the current stretching mode of the destination device context. This mode is set using the `CDC::SetStretchBltMode()` method.
>
> Again, not all device contexts support `StretchBlt()` bit block transfers. You can test to see whether a DC conforms by calling the `CDC::GetDeviceCaps()` method, specifying the `RASTERCAPS` index as the sole parameter. As the final step, check the return value for the presence of the `RC_STRETCHBLT` flag. Consider this example:
>
> ```
> if ((dc.GetDeviceCaps(RASTERCAPS) & RC_STRETCHBLT) == 0)
> {
>     // device doesn't support StretchBlt
>     ;
> }
> else
> {
>     // device does support StretchBlt
>     ;
> }
> ```

Bitmap Resources

Windows applications make use of several different kinds of resources. Icons, menus, and bitmaps are some examples of resources. *Resources* are clusters of binary data tacked on to the end of an application's executable file during the linking process. When Windows fires up a program, it loads into memory only what it needs at that time. Resources typically stay on disk (floppy, hard, or compact) until Windows calls for them.

Most resources are discardable read-only data Windows can load or unload from memory at any time as current system memory requirements change. Even Windows itself uses resources to display its message boxes, file copy animations, toolbar bitmaps, and more. Next you'll see how to create and use embedded bitmap resources in MFC programs, retrieving them on-the-fly at runtime with the relevant MFC methods.

Tacking Resources onto an Executable File

So how do you go about putting resources into a Windows executable file? After creating a resource, you must compile it, using a resource compiler, into a special *resource file* (a binary file with a `.RES` file extension). The resource file is then linked into your compiled

executable to attach the resource data to your program. To tell the resource compiler what to include in the resource file, you must create a *resource script*: a text file with an `.RC` file extension that describes the resource. If external files are used (as they are with image resources), these files are named in the script.

After you create a bitmap file for the image resource, you must add a statement to your application's resource script to identify it. For resources that reference external files, the syntax generally looks like this:

```
ImageName    IMAGETYPE   DISCARDABLE    FileName
```

For example, a resource statement for an icon with the resource identifier `IDR_BMP` (some integer value) and stored on disk in a bitmap file named MYIMAGE.BMP would look like this:

```
IDR_BMP    BITMAP    DISCARDABLE    "myimage.bmp"
```

Visual C++ does all of this for you automatically when you insert a bitmap resource using the Insert, Resource menu commands.

Getting Image Resources out of an Executable File

After a resource is embedded into an executable, the real trick is to successfully get it back out and use it. To retrieve resource data for use in your application at runtime, you can use a variety of functions provided by MFC and the Win32 API. The functions you use depend on the type of resource data. For image resources (icons, cursors, and bitmaps), you typically use the `LoadImage()` Win32 API function. The `LoadImage()` function prototype is as follows:

```
HANDLE LoadImage(
    HINSTANCE   hinst,      // instance handle containing the image
    LPCTSTR     lpszName,   // name or identifier of image
    UINT        uType,      // type of image
    int         cxDesired,  // desired width
    int         cyDesired,  // desired height
    UINT        fuLoad      // load flags
);
```

This function is used in all the sample programs in this chapter to load image resources. As you can see, the function returns a generic handle to your icon, cursor, or bitmap resource. Most of the parameters should look familiar, but some of them need a little explanation:

- The utype parameter can be any of three macros that specify the type of image to load: IMAGE_BITMAP loads a bitmap, IMAGE_CURSOR loads a cursor, and IMAGE_ICON loads an icon.

- The fuLoad parameter is any combination of the flags in Table 4.25.

TABLE 4.25 THE LoadImage() LOAD FLAGS

Value	Meaning
LR_DEFAULTCOLOR	A default flag that just means "not LR_MONOCHROME".
LR_CREATEDIBSECTION	If the uType parameter specifies IMAGE_BITMAP, the function returns a DIB section bitmap instead of a DC-compatible bitmap (the default). This flag is useful for loading a bitmap without mapping its colors to a display device and gives you access to its palette information.
LR_DEFAULTSIZE	Uses the width or height specified by the system metric values for cursors and icons if cxDesired or cyDesired are zero. If this flag isn't specified and cxDesired and cyDesired are zero, the resource is loaded at its actual size. If the resource contains multiple images, the size of the first image is used.
LR_LOADFROMFILE	Loads an image from the file specified by the lpszName parameter. If this flag isn't specified, lpszName is the name of the resource.
LR_LOADMAP3DCOLORS	Searches the image's color table and replaces the various shades of gray with a corresponding Windows or Windows NT 4.0 3D system color.
LR_LOADTRANSPARENT	Causes all pixels with the same color as the first pixel in the image to become the default window color (COLOR_WINDOW).
LR_MONOCHROME	Loads an image in black and white.
LR_SHARED	Shares the image handle if the image is loaded multiple times. If LR_SHARED is not set, each call to LoadImage() for the same resource loads the image again and returns a different handle each time.

Almost all the bitmaps you see attached to various Windows dialog boxes, animations, and image lists are bitmap resources. In the BITMAP1 program, the bitmap resources are loaded using the more convenient CBitmap::LoadBitmap() method.

Sample Program: Exploring Bitmap Resources (BITMAP1)

Now let's look at a program that performs the remarkable feat of lighting up a bitmapped icon area when the mouse passes over it. The BITMAP1 program makes use of five bitmap resources: one ray-traced image for the background bitmap, two for the "unlit" versions of the icon bitmaps, and two for the "lit" versions of the icon bitmaps (see Figure 4.19). The BITMAP1 program is shown in Figure 4.20 at runtime with the BTN1LIT.BMP displayed.

FIGURE 4.19

The BITMAP1 program uses these four bitmap resources to simulate light-up bitmap areas.

 BTN1.BMP

 BTN2.BMP

 BTN1LIT.BMP

 BTN2LIT.BMP

FIGURE 4.20

The BITMAP1 program at runtime with the BTN1LIT.BMP displayed as the cursor passes over it.

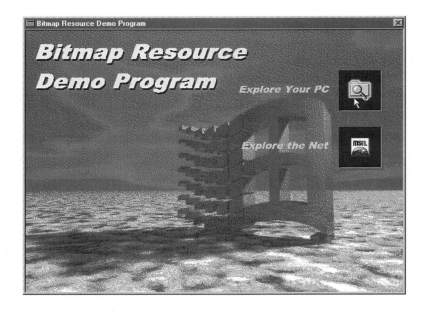

The five bitmaps are compiled into a resource file (BITMAP1.RES) by telling the resource compiler about them. This is done in the resource script (BITMAP1.RC) for the program. The bitmap resource IDs are given in the header file RESOURCE.H, which is used by both the resource script (BITMAP1.RC) and the program's sole source file (BITMAP1.CPP). The resulting resource file is linked into the BITMAP1 executable to provide access to the five bitmaps.

Examining the BITMAP1 Program

Let's take a look at the important sections of code that perform the magic for the program. Listing 4.12 shows the CMainWnd class declaration for the BITMAP1 program. All the important goings-on within the program happen here.

LISTING 4.12   THE DECLARATION OF CLASS CMainWnd IN THE BITMAP1 PROGRAM

```
/////////////////////////////////////////////////////////////////
// Class CMainWnd - derived from MFC's CFrameWnd

class CMainWnd : public CFrameWnd
{
protected:
    CBitmap    m_bmpBack;      // resource IDR_BMPBACKGROUND
    CBitmap    m_bmpBtn1;      // resource IDR_BMPBTN1
    CBitmap    m_bmpBtn1Lit;   // resource IDR_BMPBTN1LIT
    CBitmap    m_bmpBtn2;      // resource IDR_BMPBTN2
    CBitmap    m_bmpBtn2Lit;   // resource IDR_BMPBTN2LIT

    CRect m_rcTop;      // rect for drawing
    CRect m_rcBtm;      // rect for drawing
    CRect m_rcClient;   // rect for drawing

    void BlitBitmap(CRect& rc, CBitmap& bm);
    void ShowBitmaps();

public:
    // Helper method called by MFC
    virtual BOOL PreCreateWindow(CREATESTRUCT& cs);

    void PositionRects();

    // Message handler
    afx_msg BOOL OnEraseBkgnd(CDC* pDC);
    afx_msg void OnMouseMove(UINT nFlags, CPoint point);

    DECLARE_MESSAGE_MAP();
};
```

The message map for CMainWnd is as follows:

```
BEGIN_MESSAGE_MAP(CMainWnd, CFrameWnd)
    ON_WM_ERASEBKGND()
    ON_WM_MOUSEMOVE()
END_MESSAGE_MAP()
```

As you can see from the message map macros and the class declaration, the
`CMainWnd::OnEraseBkGnd()` and `CMainWnd::OnMouseMove()` methods have some special
importance.

In the `CMainWnd::PreCreateWindow()` method, the bitmap resources are loaded with
several calls to `CBitmap::LoadBitmap()`, one for each bitmap resource:

```
// Get the bitmaps from the resource data
//
m_bmpBack.LoadBitmap(IDR_BMPBACKGROUND);
m_bmpBtn1.LoadBitmap(IDR_BMPBTN1);
m_bmpBtn1Lit.LoadBitmap(IDR_BMPBTN1LIT);
m_bmpBtn2.LoadBitmap(IDR_BMPBTN2);
m_bmpBtn2Lit.LoadBitmap(IDR_BMPBTN2LIT);
```

Now that the bitmap handles are safely stored in the member variables, the
`CMainWnd::OnEraseBkgnd()` method makes use of them to draw the bitmaps on the
client area of the window with the `CMainWnd::BlitBitmap()` method:

```
PositionRects();

// draw the background bitmap
BlitBitmap(m_rcClient, m_bmpBack);

// "Blit" the unlit versions to the screen
BlitBitmap(m_rcTop, m_bmpBtn1);
BlitBitmap(m_rcBtm, m_bmpBtn2);
```

The `PositionRects()` method does just that—positions the two rectangles in which the
four small bitmaps are drawn:

```
m_rcTop.left  = 523; m_rcTop.top    = 70;
m_rcTop.right = 598; m_rcTop.bottom = 145;

m_rcBtm.left  = 523; m_rcBtm.top    = 168;
m_rcBtm.right = 598; m_rcBtm.bottom = 243;
```

The `CMainWnd::BlitBitmap()` method is the most important part of the program. It performs the actual work of drawing the bitmaps on the client area and is worth a closer
look. The entire method is shown in Listing 4.13.

LISTING 4.13 THE `BlitBitmap()` METHOD HANDLES THE BITMAP DRAWING CHORES FOR
THE BITMAP1 PROGRAM

```
/////////////////////////////////////////////////////////////////
// CMainWnd::BlitBitmap()

void CMainWnd::BlitBitmap(CRect& rc, CBitmap& bm)
{
    CClientDC dc(this);
```

```
CDC         dcMem;
HBITMAP     hbmpOld;

// Get compatible memory DCs
dcMem.CreateCompatibleDC(&dc);

// Select bitmaps into the DCs
hbmpOld = (HBITMAP)dcMem.SelectObject(bm);

// "Blit" the bitmap to the screen
//
GetDC()->BitBlt(rc.left, rc.top, rc.right, rc.bottom,
                &dcMem, 0, 0, SRCCOPY);

// Clean up
dcMem.SelectObject(hbmpOld);
}
```

The goal here is to put the bitmap data into a memory device context, and then do a bit block transfer (bit blit) to move the bitmap image to the display.

> **NOTE**
>
> The positions of the rectangles used for image "blitting" were determined during the creation of the large bitmap file used for the background bitmap resource.

A client device context (DC) is obtained for the frame window, and another device context is created for the memory DC (dcMem). The memory DC creates a memory device context compatible with the display surface by calling CDC::CreateCompatibleDC(). Then the handle to the bitmap you want to draw (the hbm method parameter) is passed to the Win32 API function SelectObject() along with dcMem. This copies the bitmap into the memory device context (which is compatible with the device), displacing the object currently in the DC. A handle to this object (which you store for later cleanup duties) is returned from SelectObject(). You then blast the bitmap bits to the display with a call to the CDC::BitBlt() method.

CDC::BitBlt() must know the destination rectangle for the image blit; you use the rc parameter sent to BlitBitmap() to define the destination drawing area. When the new bitmap is safely on the display, you select the original object back into the client DC, to leave things as you found them before the swap.

4

PAINTING, DEVICE
CONTEXTS,
BITMAPS, AND
FONTS

The final piece of the puzzle is to make the icon areas on the window appear to glow when the mouse passes over one of them. The mechanism for displaying the bitmaps has been explained, but the events leading up to the blitting frenzy haven't. The controlling factor in all this is the position of the cursor on the display. The `CMainWnd::OnMouseMove()` method tracks the cursor position at all times. To determine whether to swap bitmaps or not, use the `CPoint::PtInRect()` method you've seen before. The following code snippet should make it all clear:

```
void CMainWnd::OnMouseMove(UINT nFlags, CPoint point)
{
    // check to see if the pointer is over a bitmap area
    //
    if (m_rcTop.PtInRect(point))
        BlitBitmap(m_rcTop, m_hbmpBtn1Lit); // "light" the top image

    else if (m_rcBtm.PtInRect(point))
        BlitBitmap(m_rcBtm, m_hbmpBtn2Lit); // "light" the bottom image

    else  // turn the lights off
    {
        // "Blit" the unlit versions to the screen
        BlitBitmap(m_rcTop, m_hbmpBtn1);
        BlitBitmap(m_rcBtm, m_hbmpBtn2);
    }
    // Call the inherited method
    CMainFrame::OnMouseMove(nFlags, point);
}
```

There you have it—how to light up bitmaps using embedded bitmap resources!

Summary

Windows provides a Graphical User Interface (GUI) to the underlying operating system and hardware, and provides hardware information to applications via device contexts: data structures that are logical representations of physical devices or virtual devices.

MFC provides device context classes for general devices (CDC), window client areas (CClientDC), total window area (CWindowDC), and for Windows metafiles (CMetaFileDC). MFC also provides graphic objects that are used to draw on these device contexts. These graphic objects are pens (CPen), brushes (CBrush), fonts (CFont), bitmaps (CBitmap), and regions (CRgn).

Vector graphics are mathematical descriptions of graphical imagery, and in this chapter you've looked at the vector graphics methods of the MFC device context classes. Vector images typically consist of lines, polygons, rectangles, regions, polygons, metafiles, fonts, and curves.

You've looked at the TEXTMETRIC structure that holds basic text information as it applies to the display. You've also seen that fonts are generally defined by a LOGFONT structure that holds information about font construction. Text output methods were presented, as was sample code from the sample program VECTEXT1 located on the companion CD-ROM. Working with the GDI graphics functions and CDC font and text methods does take some getting used to.

This chapter has also provided a look at the usage of bitmaps as resources stored as data within executable files, and along the way you've learned how to retrieve the image data using the Win32 API, and how display and manipulate them. All of this may seem complex at first, but with time, experimentation, and experience, you'll be an old hand with graphics and text manipulation in no time!

Custom Control Development

by Ed Harris

CHAPTER 5

Custom controls, or widgets, are useful when the standard input and display controls cannot provide the user with the most optimal input mechanism. Not too long ago, Windows featured a bare-minimum control palette—static text control, button, edit box, and list box. The combo box, now considered a basic staple of user interface, was a welcome addition to Windows 3.

Now, of course, there are dozens of built-in controls, and hundreds of third-party add-ons. This chapter focuses on the whens, whys, and hows of extending stock controls and developing brand new controls of your own.

> **NOTE**
>
> This chapter covers the development techniques needed to create new window behavior. What it doesn't cover is the wisdom—and the usability testing—required to determine whether new window behavior is warranted. Sure, your new widget may display editable information to the user in a highly efficient manner. However, if the user can't understand how to manipulate the control without breaking out the documentation, your application becomes unusable. Make sure that the user has the proper affordances to use your new widget. (*Affordance* is GUI usability-speak for intuitive understanding.) Generally, it's a good idea not to stray too far from the beaten path.

Window Classes Versus C++ Classes

One of the confusing aspects of custom control development is the overloaded use of the word *class*. When Windows was introduced, class was an underused term, and C++ was merely a toy used by AT&T labs. The Windows architects chose to use the term class to represent the collective behavior of a set of windows. Window class attributes include the class name (such as `Edit`), icon, background color, cursor, and window procedure.

Object-oriented languages use the term class in a similar way, to identify the set of behavior that a family of code (the class) provides. These two uses overlap in the area of custom control development because the programmatic class is used to implement the behavior of the window class.

The term *subclass*, in object parlance, means a new class (a child) derived from one or more existing classes. In this naming scheme, the parent class is called the *superclass*.

In the Windows world, subclassing is the action of modifying the behavior of an existing window. Subclassing is done on a window-by-window basis. Superclassing is the act of creating a new breed of window based on the behavior of an existing type (class) of window. As you will see, subclassing is done extensively by MFC. Although superclassing is possible with MFC, it has some significant drawbacks.

In pure Windows-API based development, window class behavior is provided by the message procedure (message proc). Each message destined for a particular window is sent to a single function, where it is routed to code specific to that message. In the early days of Windows development, message procedures sometimes grew to be thousands of lines long.

MFC replaced the message procedure with the concept of a message map. When an MFC-owned window receives a message, the framework looks up the message map for that window, and routes it to the most-derived handler for that message. MFC uses a single window procedure (`AfxWndProc`) to receive all messages and route them to the appropriate code. When you call `CreateWindow`, `CreateDialog`, or any other API that causes a window to be instantiated, you are subclassing that window procedure with `AfxWndProc`. From that point on, all messages from the system to that window are routed through the message map for processing. This simplifies subclassing enormously and removes the most tedious and error-prone parts of the process.

When creating a custom class, consider whether an existing class provides any of the functionality you need. For example, if the class requires textual input, subclassing the standard `edit` class might be appropriate. Extending an existing class is generally much easier than creating a new one from scratch.

A Validating Edit Control

Perhaps the seminal subclass example is an edit control that validates or reformats its contents. This control, `CZipEdit`, will format zip codes into ZIP+4 format when focus leaves the control. The control contains one message map handler, for the `WM_KILLFOCUS` (`OnKillFocus`) method.

```
class CZipEdit : public CEdit
{
    // Implementation
    public:
        virtual void    FormatContents  (const TCHAR* pszText);

    // Message Map
    public:
        //{{AFX_MSG(CZipEdit)
```

5

CUSTOM CONTROL
DEVELOPMENT

```
    afx_msg void    OnKillFocus    (CWnd* pwndNew);
    //}}AFX_MSG
    DECLARE_MESSAGE_MAP()
};

void CZipEdit::OnKillFocus (CWnd* pwndNew)
{
    CString strText;
    GetWindowText (strText);

    FormatContents (strText);

    CEdit::OnKillFocus (pwndNew);
}
```

The kill focus message handler retrieves the window text, passes it to the
FormatContents method, and then invokes the default CEdit kill focus handler. The processing is done prior to the default code so that the new edit control contents (if any) are
available to the application when the EN_KILLFOCUS notification is received.

The function FormatContents is responsible for taking a character string, doing any necessary transformations, and then setting the resulting text into the edit control. It has public scope; this allows it to be used as a formatting replacement for SetWindowText.

The implementation for the zip code is rather trivial. It verifies that the first five characters of the zip code are digits, and then inserts a single dash at the fifth character.

```
void CZipEdit::FormatContents (const TCHAR* pszText)
{
    CString strOutput (pszText);

    if (strOutput.GetLength() >= 9)
    {
        BOOL bValidZip = TRUE;
        for (int nDigit = 0; nDigit < 5; nDigit++)
        {
            if (!isdigit (strOutput[nDigit]))
                bValidZip = FALSE;
        }

        if (bValidZip && strOutput[5] != _T('-'))
        {
            if (!ispunct (strOutput[5]) && !isspace (strOutput[5]))
                strOutput = strOutput.Left (5) + _T('-') +
                ➡strOutput.Mid (5);
            else
                strOutput.SetAt (5, _T('-'));
        }
    }

    SetWindowText (strOutput);
}
```

To convert a dialog box edit control into a formatting edit control, use ClassWizard to bind a CEdit object to an edit control. Then, in your dialog box header file, replace the CEdit object with a CZipEdit object. When MFC binds the control to the window, it subclasses the control and the formatting behavior is enabled.

The Clock Static Control

The second custom control, CClockCtrl, displays an analog clock or stopwatch face (see Figure 5.1). Because it is a display-only control, accepting neither keyboard nor mouse input, it is derived from CStatic. Patterned on the analog face of the Windows clock accessory application, this control has the following features:

- The control will shrink or grow to fill the entire window area.
- The window will contain colored studs at each of the 12 face points. If the control is large enough, each minute mark will have a smaller stud as well. The control will dynamically determine whether the client area is large enough to contain the minute marks.
- The control will display up to three hands: an hour hand, a minute hand, and a second hand. The hands will be drawn in such a way that there is no discernible flicker if the control is used to display real time.
- The control will not have any timing built in. The user of the clock will need to set the time as appropriate. Thus, the control can be used as a countdown timer, count-up timer, clock, or static display.

FIGURE 5.1

An analog clock face created with the CClockCtrl class.

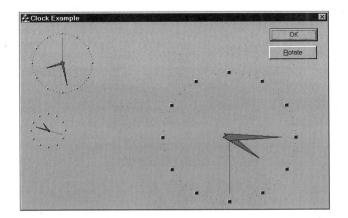

Here is the class definition for the complete clock control:

```cpp
class CClockCtrl : public CStatic
{
    // Internal constants
    enum HANDTYPE { HOUR_HAND, MINUTE_HAND, SECOND_HAND };

    // Ctor / dtor
public:
    CClockCtrl();

    // Members
protected:
    COLORREF    m_rgbHands;         // Hand color
    COLORREF    m_rgbPoints;        // Point color
    CPoint      m_ptMiddle;         // Center point of window
    int         m_nPointWidth;      // Width of face point
    int         m_nRadius;          // Radius of circular portion
                                    // of window
    int         m_nHour;            // Hour hand value
    int         m_nMinute;          // Minute hand value
    int         m_nSecond;          // Second hand value

    // API
public:
    BOOL CreateFromStatic   (CWnd* pwndParent, UINT wID);
    void SetTime            (int nHour, int nMinute, int nSecond);

    // Members
protected:
    void    RecalcLayout        (void);
    CPoint  ComputeFacePoint    (int nMinute,
                                    int nFaceLength) const;
    void    GetHandPoints       (int nFaceValue, HANDTYPE typeHand,
                                    CPoint* pptHand);
    void    DrawFacePoint       (CDC& dc, const CPoint& ptFace,
                                    BOOL bMajor);
    void    DrawHand            (CDC& dc, int nFaceValue,
                                    HANDTYPE typeHand, BOOL bDraw);
    // Message Map
public:
    //{{AFX_MSG(CClockCtrl)
    afx_msg void    OnSize  (UINT nType, int cx, int cy);
    afx_msg void    OnPaint (void);
    //}}AFX_MSG
    DECLARE_MESSAGE_MAP()
};
```

Control Metrics

One of the stated requirements for the clock control is that it grow to fill its window area. Because my trigonometry isn't that good, and because I don't enjoy lopsided clocks, the control "squares" itself up within the window. All of the metrics are set in a single function, RecalcLayout. For the clock control, you track three items: the center of the clock face, the maximum radius that can be inscribed in the circle, and the face point width. The need for the center point and radius should be reasonably apparent; the point width is the width of one of the hash marks on the outside of the clock.

```
void CClockCtrl::RecalcLayout (void)
{
    CRect rectClient;
    GetClientRect (&rectClient);

    // Square off the control and determine radius
    m_ptMiddle.x = rectClient.Width() / 2;
    m_ptMiddle.y = rectClient.Height() / 2;
    m_nRadius = min (m_ptMiddle.x, m_ptMiddle.y);

    // Point width is used to determine hash-mark widths
    m_nPointWidth = (int) m_nRadius / 20;
    if (m_nPointWidth < 2)
        m_nPointWidth = 2;

    Invalidate (TRUE);

    return;
}
```

To limit the proliferation of math throughout the control, the trigonometric calculations have been contained in a single routine. This routine, ComputeFacePoint, takes a minute value and a face length (generally a fraction of the radius). It returns a CPoint, in client window coordinates, of the specified point. Because the control is being used for time display, it was easier to accept a minute value than an angle in degrees.

```
CPoint CClockCtrl::ComputeFacePoint (int nMinute, int nFaceLength) const
{
    CPoint ptCalc;

    // Convert minutes to degrees
    double fDegrees = 180 + ((15 + nMinute) % 60) * 6;

    // Begin conversion to radians
    double fAngle = fDegrees / 180;
```

5

CUSTOM CONTROL
DEVELOPMENT

```
    ptCalc.x = m_ptMiddle.x + (int) (cos (fAngle * pi) * nFaceLength);
    ptCalc.y = m_ptMiddle.y + (int) (sin (fAngle * pi) * nFaceLength);

    return (ptCalc);
}
```

Painting the Face

With the basic control math out of the way, you can go ahead and draw the surface of the clock. This is done in the `OnPaint` handler. The painting routine is pretty straightforward: You allocate a device context and brush for the face points, and then inscribe each face point from 12 o'clock clockwise through 11 o'clock. Each face point is located 90 percent out from the midpoint, using a function `DrawFacePoint`. `DrawFacePoint` accepts a device context (DC), the face-point location, and a Boolean indicating whether the point should be drawn in large format (the o'clock points) or small format (the minute hashes).

```
void CClockCtrl::OnPaint (void)
{
    // Force initialized
    if (m_nRadius == -1)
        RecalcLayout ();

    CPoint      ptFace;
    CPaintDC    dc (this);

    CBrush brPoint (m_rgbPoints);
    CBrush* pbrOld = dc.SelectObject (&brPoint);

    // The face points go 90% out from the radius
    int nFaceLength = MulDiv (m_nRadius, 9, 10);

    // Inscribe a circle from 12 O'clock clockwise in radians
    for (int nMinute = 0; nMinute < 60; nMinute++)
    {
        ptFace = ComputeFacePoint (nMinute, nFaceLength);

        DrawFacePoint (dc, ptFace, ((nMinute % 5) == 0) ? TRUE : FALSE);
    }

    DrawHand (dc, m_nHour, HOUR_HAND, TRUE);
    DrawHand (dc, m_nMinute, MINUTE_HAND, TRUE);
    DrawHand (dc, m_nSecond, SECOND_HAND, TRUE);

    (void) dc.SelectObject (pbrOld);

    return;
}
```

```
void CClockCtrl::DrawFacePoint (CDC& dc, const CPoint& ptFace,
➥BOOL bMajor)
{
    CRect rectPoint (ptFace.x, ptFace.y, ptFace.x, ptFace.y);

    if (bMajor)
    {
        rectPoint.InflateRect ((m_nPointWidth / 2) + 1,
                                (m_nPointWidth / 2) + 1);

        dc.Rectangle (&rectPoint);
        dc.Draw3dRect (&rectPoint, GetSysColor (COLOR_BTNHIGHLIGHT),
                                    GetSysColor (COLOR_BTNSHADOW));
    }
    else
    {
        if (m_nPointWidth > 2)
        {
            rectPoint.InflateRect (1, 1);
            dc.Draw3dRect (&rectPoint, GetSysColor (COLOR_BTNHIGHLIGHT),
                                        GetSysColor (COLOR_BTNSHADOW));
        }
    }

    return;
}
```

DrawFacePoint uses the previously calculated point width value to determine the width of the hashmarks. The function CDC::Draw3dRect is used to draw a bevel around the hashpoint: a highlight on the upper-left side of the hash and a shadow on the lower-right side. This single function saves dozens of lines of code allocating pens and computing start and stop points for the beveling.

Locating the Hands

The final drawing-related code for the clock control is the hand-painting scheme. After looking at several clocks, I decided that the hands should be a simple polygon extending from either side of the midpoint. Because the control needs to scale to different sizes, the entire math is done as a multiple of the radius and the point width. The hour hand extends to 50 percent of the radius, the minute hand extends to 70 percent, and the second hand 80 percent.

The approach I took in drawing the hour and minute hands leverages the face point location math. Each of the four vertices of the hand is calculated as the hand angle plus a constant. Consider a hand pointing at the 12 o'clock position. To draw the hand, you start from the 6 o'clock position, a little behind the midpoint. From there, you draw a line to the 3 o'clock position, parallel to the midpoint. After that, you go to the 12 o'clock position (the actual point of the hand). The last point is at the 9 o'clock position (again, parallel to the midpoint). This strategy simplified the hand drawing tremendously.

Not to be left out, the second (or sweep) hand is drawn as a thin (single-pixel) line extending out from the midpoint.

```
void CClockCtrl::GetHandPoints (int nValue, HANDTYPE typeHand,
➥CPoint* pptHand)
{
    int       nLength = 0;

    switch (typeHand)
    {
        case HOUR_HAND:
            nLength = MulDiv (m_nRadius, 50, 100);   // 50% of radius
            // Convert the hour value (0-11) to a minute value (0-59)
            // for drawing, then adjust for a gradual transition from
            // hour to hour.
            nValue *= 5;
            nValue += (m_nMinute / 12);
            break;
        case MINUTE_HAND:
            nLength = MulDiv (m_nRadius, 70, 100);   // 70% of radius
            break;
        case SECOND_HAND:
            nLength = MulDiv (m_nRadius, 80, 100);   // 80% of radius
            break;
        default:
            ASSERT (FALSE);
    }

    if (typeHand == HOUR_HAND || typeHand == MINUTE_HAND)
    {
        // Compute the hand points.  First point is the back side,
        // second point is the right, third point is the tip,
        // and fourth is left.
        pptHand[0] = ComputeFacePoint (nValue + 30, m_nPointWidth * 2);
        pptHand[1] = ComputeFacePoint (nValue + 15, m_nPointWidth);
        pptHand[2] = ComputeFacePoint (nValue,        nLength);
        pptHand[3] = ComputeFacePoint (nValue - 15, m_nPointWidth);
    }
    else
    {
        pptHand[0] = m_ptMiddle;
        pptHand[1] = ComputeFacePoint (nValue, nLength);
    }
}
```

Painting the Hands

The first attempt at painting the hands was pretty simplistic. I invalidated the area underneath the hands, and then waited for a WM_PAINT to be generated to update the window. Unfortunately, this caused far too many flickers in the window, as each paint message caused the middle of the face to be filled with the background, and then painted.

To remove the flicker, the control needed to take care of both the erasing and redrawing of the hands. For draw operations, the hand color (currently a light blue) is used to fill the hand polygon; for erase operations, the hands are drawn in the background color.

The sweep hand is drawn using a NOT XOR raster operation (ROP) code. The NOT XOR ROP causes the hand to be visible as a combination of the line and the existing background. An additional call with this ropcode erases the line. This was key to being able to update the control quickly, as the sweep hand generally moves every second.

```
void CClockCtrl::DrawHand (CDC& dc, int nValue,
➥HANDTYPE typeHand, BOOL bDraw)
{
    COLORREF rgbBrush;
    COLORREF rgbPen;
    CPoint ptHand[4];

    if (nValue == HIDE_HAND)
        return;

    GetHandPoints (nValue, typeHand, ptHand);
    if (typeHand == HOUR_HAND || typeHand == MINUTE_HAND)
    {
        DrawHand (dc, m_nSecond, SECOND_HAND, FALSE);

        rgbBrush = (bDraw) ? m_rgbHands : GetSysColor (COLOR_BTNFACE);
        rgbPen   = (bDraw) ? RGB (0, 0, 0) : GetSysColor (COLOR_BTNFACE);

        CBrush  brHand (rgbBrush);
        CPen    penHand (PS_SOLID, 1, rgbPen);

        CBrush* pbrOld  = dc.SelectObject (&brHand);
        CPen*   ppenOld = dc.SelectObject (&penHand);

        dc.Polygon (ptHand, 4);

        (void) dc.SelectObject (pbrOld);
        (void) dc.SelectObject (ppenOld);

        DrawHand (dc, m_nSecond, SECOND_HAND, TRUE);
    }
    else
    {
```

```
        int noldROP = dc.SetROP2 (R2_NOTXORPEN);

        dc.MoveTo (ptHand[0]);
        dc.LineTo (ptHand[1]);

        (void) dc.SetROP2 (noldROP);
    }

    return;
}
```

Setting the Time

The last function in the clock control is used to set the time displayed by the hands. The hour, minute, and second values are set independently of each other—either as a numeric value or as the constant HIDE_HAND. To avoid flicker, remove the old hands, and then redraw the new ones.

```
void CClockCtrl::SetTime (int nHour, int nMinute, int nSecond)
{
    CClientDC dc (this);

    // Hour or minute is changing.  Erase both
    if (m_nHour != nHour || m_nMinute != nMinute)
    {
        DrawHand (dc, m_nSecond, SECOND_HAND, FALSE);

        m_nSecond = -1; // Inhibit second hand drawing
        DrawHand (dc, m_nMinute, MINUTE_HAND, FALSE);
        DrawHand (dc, m_nHour,   HOUR_HAND,   FALSE);

        // Update the internals
        m_nHour   = nHour % 12;
        m_nMinute = nMinute % 60;

        DrawHand (dc, m_nHour,   HOUR_HAND,   TRUE);
        DrawHand (dc, m_nMinute, MINUTE_HAND, TRUE);

        m_nSecond = nSecond % 60;
        DrawHand (dc, m_nSecond, SECOND_HAND, TRUE);
    }
    else
    {
        DrawHand (dc, m_nSecond, SECOND_HAND, TRUE);
        m_nSecond = nSecond % 60;
        DrawHand (dc, m_nSecond, SECOND_HAND, TRUE);
    }

    ValidateRect (NULL);
}
```

Pitfalls of Subclassing Standard Controls

One of the problems of subclassing existing controls is that you must understand the default behavior *very* thoroughly. In some cases, you might need to intercept messages prior to the default processing. In others, you might need to do additional processing after default processing. Finally, in some cases you might need to eat messages entirely, substitute additional ones, or both. The best tool for understanding existing behavior is Spy++. Spy++ displays the messages a window receives and even provides user decodes to common messages.

If no close match exists, subclass CWnd instead. When you subclass CWnd, you inherit no behaviors other than those provided by Windows. It's like starting with a blank sheet of paper.

The Hyperlink Control

The second custom control is the CHyperlink control. The CHyperlink appears like a static window with underlined text, as shown in Figure 5.2. Unlike a static window, however, the hyperlink control accepts keyboard and mouse input. If the user clicks on the hyperlink or hits Enter while the hyperlink has focus, the text of the link is launched via the shell. The hyperlink control derives directly from CWnd.

FIGURE 5.2

An example of the CHyperLink control with three fonts.

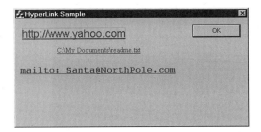

The first step of the custom control process is defining the observable behavior of the control:

- All text in the control will be displayed with an underlined version of the current font. If the user passes a font to the control through the SetFont() API, the control creates an underlined version. This simplifies using the class because you won't have to make your own underlined copies of fonts.

- By default, the link is displayed in light blue. The color is not changed if the user clicks on the link (link tracking is left as an exercise for the reader). The user can control the display color programmatically.

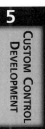

- When the mouse is over the textual part of the control, a hand cursor is displayed. At this point, clicking on the underlined text causes the appropriate registered application to be launched via the shell. If the mouse is not over the textual portion, the arrow cursor is displayed.

- Because the control accepts mouse input, the Enter key will trigger the hyperlink as well. This implies that the control accepts focus.

- The parent window of the control will receive a notification after the link is launched.

- The control will obey left, right, and center justify styles (SS_LEFT, SS_RIGHT, and SS_CENTER).

For the hyperlink control, you'll need to modify stock window behavior for fonts, painting, cursor display, keyboard input, and mouse clicks:

```
class CHyperlink: public CWnd
{
    public:
        CHyperlink();
        ~CHyperlink();

    // Attributes
        public:
        COLORREF    m_rgbURLColor; // link display color
        CFont       m_fontControl; // link display font
        CRect       m_rectText;    // Text position
        HCURSOR     m_hcHand;      // Cursor for selecting

    // User API
    public:
        HINSTANCE ExecuteLink (void);
        inline COLORREF GetURLColor (void) const
            { return (m_rgbURLColor); }
        inline void SetURLColor (COLORREF rgb)
            { m_rgbURLColor = rgb; RecalcLayout(); }

    // Implementation
    protected:
        CFont* GetCorrectFont (void);
        void RecalcLayout (BOOL bRedraw = TRUE);
        void SendParentNotify(WORD wID, WORD wNotify) const;

    // Message Map
    public:
    //{{AFX_MSG(CHyperlink)
    afx_msg LRESULT OnSetFont (WPARAM wParam, LPARAM lParam);
    afx_msg LRESULT OnSetText (WPARAM wParam, LPARAM lParam);
    afx_msg void OnSize (UINT nType, int cx, int cy);
```

```
    afx_msg UINT OnGetDlgCode(void);
    afx_msg void OnPaint (void);
    afx_msg UINT OnNcHitTest (CPoint ptScreen);
    afx_msg BOOL OnSetCursor (CWnd* pWnd, UINT nHitTest, UINT message);
    afx_msg void OnSetFocus (CWnd* pwndOld);
    afx_msg void OnKillFocus (CWnd* pwndNew);
    afx_msg void OnLButtonDown(UINT /* nFlags */, CPoint ptMouse);
    afx_msg void OnLButtonUp    (UINT /* nFlags */, CPoint ptMouse);
    afx_msg void OnCancelMode (void);
    afx_msg void OnKeyDown (UINT nChar, UINT nRepCnt, UINT nFlags);
    //}}AFX_MSG
    DECLARE_MESSAGE_MAP()
};
```

Implementation Strategy

Before diving into the messages to process, take a look at the internal design of the class. The overall implementation strategy is to leave as much data and processing as possible to Windows default behavior. For this reason, you do not cache the text of the window, but rather use the GetWindowText API wherever needed.

You'll monitor for specific messages that change the control's display: text changes (WM_SETTEXT), font changes (WM_SETFONT), and sizing (WM_SIZE). If any of these messages are received, you use a catchall function, RecalcLayout, to recompute display metrics and optionally force the control to repaint. RecalcLayout (re)sets the text bounding rectangle (m_rectText) to the region of the control that contains the text. Note how this example handles the static styles (SS_LEFT, SS_RIGHT, and SS_CENTER) during rectangle calculation.

```
void CHyperlink::RecalcLayout (BOOL bRedraw)
{
    CString     strText;
    CRect       rectClient;
    CWindowDC   dc (this);
    DWORD       dwWindowStyle = GetStyle();

    // Compute the size of the text using the current font
    CFont* pfontControl = GetCorrectFont();
    CFont* pfontOld = dc.SelectObject (pfontControl);
    CSize sizeText = dc.GetTextExtent (strText);
    dc.SelectObject (pfontOld);

    GetClientRect (&rectClient);
    GetWindowText (strText);

if (dwWindowStyle & SS_CENTER)
    {
        m_rectText.SetRect (rectClient.Width()/2 - sizeText.cx / 2, 0,
```

```
                              rectClient.Width()/2 + sizeText.cx / 2,
                              sizeText.cy);
    }
    else if (dwWindowStyle & SS_RIGHT)
    {
        m_rectText.SetRect (rectClient.right - sizeText.cx, 0,
                            rectClient.right, sizeText.cy);
    }
    else // SS_LEFT is equal to zero
    {
        m_rectText.SetRect (0, 0, sizeText.cx, sizeText.cy);
    }

    if (bRedraw)
        Invalidate (TRUE);
}
```

Font Processing

The hyperlink control should fit into the overall layout of its containing dialog box as
gracefully as possible. To do this, the control captures the message WM_SETFONT. Note
that MFC does not provide a message-map entry for this message, so the raw-form
ON_MESSAGE (WM_SETFONT, OnSetFont) syntax is used. Upon receipt of WM_SETFONT, the
control retrieves the font characteristics, adds the underline style, and creates a new font.
If the WM_SETFONT message is not received by the control, the control synthesizes a font
from the font of its parent window.

```
CFont* CHyperlink::GetCorrectFont (void)
{
    // If the internal font is valid, skip processing
    if (m_fontControl.GetSafeHandle() == 0)
    {
        // Get parent window font for modification
        CWnd* pwndParent = GetParent();
        if (pwndParent)
        {
            LOGFONT logFont;
            CFont* pfontParent = pwndParent->GetFont();

            pfontParent->GetObject (sizeof (logFont),&logFont);
            logFont.lfWidth  = 0;
            logFont.lfQuality = PROOF_QUALITY;
            logFont.lfUnderline = TRUE;

            m_fontControl.CreateFontIndirect (&logFont);
        }
    }
```

```
        return (&m_fontControl);
}

LRESULT CHyperlink::OnSetFont (WPARAM wParam, LPARAM lParam)
{
    LOGFONT logFont;
    HFONT   hFont = (HFONT) wParam;

    Default(); // Pass message to default handler

    CFont* pfontDisplay = CFont::FromHandle (hFont);
    pfontDisplay->GetObject (sizeof (logFont), &logFont);
    logFont.lfUnderline = TRUE;
    logFont.lfWidth  = 0;
    logFont.lfQuality = PROOF_QUALITY;

    m_fontControl.DeleteObject();
    VERIFY (m_fontControl.CreateFontIndirect (&logFont));

    RecalcLayout();

    return (0L);
}
```

Notice how the `RecalcLayout` function is used to reset control metrics prior to exiting the `WM_SETFONT` message handler.

Painting the Window

Given the bounding rectangle for the text and the font, painting the control is rather trivial. The control allocates a paint DC, sets the font and text color, paints the text with a single `DrawText` call, and then resets the DC settings. When the control has the focus, `DrawFocusRect` is used to display a dotted rectangle around the text:

```
void CHyperlink::OnPaint()
{
    CString  strText;
    CPaintDC dc (this);

    // If we presently have the focus, remove it prior to painting
    if (GetFocus() == this)
        dc.DrawFocusRect (m_rectText);

    if (m_rectText.IsRectNull())
        RecalcLayout (FALSE);

    GetWindowText (strText);
```

```
        CFont* pfontControl = GetCorrectFont();
        CFont* pfontOld = dc.SelectObject (pfontControl);
        COLORREF rgbOldBk   = dc.SetBkColor (GetSysColor (COLOR_BTNFACE));
        COLORREF rgbOldText = dc.SetTextColor (m_rgbURLColor);

        CRect   rectClient;
        GetClientRect (rectClient);
        CBrush brushBack (GetSysColor (COLOR_BTNFACE));
        dc.FillRect (&rectClient, &brushBack);

        // Draw the text using the bounding rectangle from DrawText
        dc.DrawText (strText, m_rectText, DT_NOPREFIX¦DT_SINGLELINE);

        dc.SetBkColor    (rgbOldBk);
        dc.SetTextColor (rgbOldText);
        dc.SelectObject (pfontOld);

        // If we have the focus, draw the standard focus rectangle
        // around the text
        if (GetFocus() == this)
            dc.DrawFocusRect (m_rectText);

        return;
}
void CHyperlink::OnSetFocus (CWnd* pwndOld)
{
    CWindowDC dc(this);
    dc.DrawFocusRect (m_rectText);
}

void CHyperlink::OnKillFocus (CWnd* pwndOld)
{
    CWindowDC dc(this);
    dc.DrawFocusRect (m_rectText);
}
```

To complete focus processing, catch the WM_SETFOCUS (OnSetFocus) and WM_KILLFOCUS
(OnKillFocus) messages. As in the OnPaint handler, these message handlers invoke the
DrawFocusRect to paint a highlight around the hyperlink text. The DrawFocusRect API
uses an XOR drawing scheme, so the second call erases the rectangle drawn by the
first one.

Be careful if your subclass relies on the default paint handler (that is, your class lets the
control draw itself, and then overlays on top of the existing control). CPaintDC uses the
Win32 BeginPaint and EndPaint APIs to allocate and release the device context. The
EndPaint API has the normally beneficial side effect of revalidating the paint area. When
your control allocates another CPaintDC, the drawing (clipping) area will be empty, and

none of your output will appear. To overlay on top of an existing control's output, use a CWindowDC instead. By default, the clipping area of a CWindowDC is the complete area of the window.

Controlling the Cursor

In most cases, the text of the hyperlink does not occupy the entire area of the window. When the cursor is over the text, you would like to display the traditional hand cursor that users associate with a hyperlink. When the cursor is over a whitespace area of the control, you display the arrow. To control the cursor, you catch and respond to the WM_SETCURSOR (OnSetCursor) message.

WM_SETCURSOR is passed to a window whenever a mouse event (move, click, and so on) happens over the client area of the window, or when the window has set input capture. The WM_SETCURSOR message includes the window under the cursor, the mouse location in screen coordinates, and the mouse message being processed. The handler converts the mouse coordinates from screen to client coordinates and compares it to the bounding rectangle of the hyperlink text. If the point is inside the text rectangle, the hand cursor is set; otherwise, the default (arrow) cursor is displayed.

```
BOOL CHyperlink::OnSetCursor (CWnd* pWnd, UINT nHitTest, UINT message)
{
    CPoint ptMouse;

    GetCursorPos (&ptMouse);
    ScreenToClient (&ptMouse);

    if (pWnd == this && m_rectText.PtInRect (ptMouse))
    {
        // If cursor has been loaded, don't re-load.
        if (m_hcHand == (HCURSOR) 0)
        {
            m_hcHand = LoadCursor (AfxGetInstanceHandle(),
                                   MAKEINTRESOURCE (IDC_HANDCURSOR));

            // If you get this assert, you forgot to include
            // IDC_HANDCURSOR in your resources.
            ASSERT (m_hcHand);
        }

        ::SetCursor (m_hcHand);

        return (TRUE);
    }

    return (CWnd::OnSetCursor (pWnd, nHitTest, message));
}
```

After the `WM_SETCURSOR` handler was added, the initial version of the hyperlink control did not display the hand cursor. Some investigation with Spy++ revealed that the default window handler for `WM_NCHITTEST` does not specify that the window has a client area.

Windows sends a message, `WM_NCHITTEST` (non-client hit test), whenever the mouse is over any area of a window. The purpose of the message is to allow the window to identify the specific region under the mouse. In other words, the window can return that the mouse is over a border, menu or title bar, close or size box, and so on. Windows handles the cursor display (and suppresses `WM_SETCURSOR` messages) unless the return from `WM_NCHITTEST` indicates that the mouse is over the client area of the window.

To solve the problem, the control catches the `WM_NCHITTEST` message. If the mouse cursor is over the hyperlink text, `HTCLIENT` is returned. This informs Windows of the boundaries of the client area and causes the mouse cursor to display properly.

```
UINT CHyperlink::OnNcHitTest (CPoint ptScreen)
{
    CRect   rectClient;
    CPoint  ptClient (ptScreen);

    GetClientRect (rectClient);
    ScreenToClient (&ptClient);

    if (rectClient.PtInRect (ptClient))
        return (HTCLIENT);
    else
        return (CWnd::OnNcHitTest (ptScreen));
}
```

Mouse Input

Mouse handling for the hyperlink control follows the pushbutton model. When the mouse goes down in a pushbutton, the face of the button is depressed; however, if the mouse is moved outside of the button, the face returns to its normal position. The button action isn't taken unless the mouse is released over the button face. Although the appearance of the hyperlink isn't altered when the mouse is clicked, the program does wait until receiving a mouse-up before launching the hyperlink.

To accomplish this, you need to ensure that you receive a mouse-up event (`WM_LBUTTONUP`) to match the mouse-down event (`WM_LBUTTONDOWN`). This is done through the `SetCapture()` API. Normally, input goes to the window under the cursor (for mouse), or the window with focus (keyboard). After `SetCapture` is invoked, *all* mouse and keyboard inputs for the process are routed directly to the capturing window. Only one window in a process can have "capture" at any given time.

Setting capture on the mouse-down event ensures that the control will receive the mouse-up event, regardless of where it occurs. If the user clicks down on another window and clicks up in yours, the hyperlink will not launch.

```
void CHyperlink::OnLButtonDown(UINT /* nFlags */, CPoint ptMouse)
{
    if (m_rectText.PtInRect (ptMouse))
    {
        // Make us the focus window.
if (GetFocus() != this && (GetStyle() & WS_TABSTOP))
            SetFocus();

        SetCapture();
    }

    return;
}

void CHyperlink::OnLButtonUp(UINT /* nFlags */, CPoint ptMouse)
{
    // If capture is set to us, then the mouse went down
    // over our window
    if (GetCapture() == this)
    {
        ReleaseCapture();

        // Verify that the user didn't mouse up over another window
        if (m_rectText.PtInRect (ptMouse))
        {
            ExecuteLink ();

            SendParentNotify ((WORD) ::GetWindowLong (GetSafeHwnd(),
                              GWL_ID), HL_LINKCLICKED);
        }
    }

    return;
}

void CHyperlink::SendParentNotify (WORD wID, WORD wNotify) const
{
    HWND hwParent = GetParent()->GetSafeHwnd();

    ::SendMessage (hwParent, WM_COMMAND,
                   MAKEWPARAM (wID, wNotify), (LPARAM) GetSafeHwnd());
}

void CHyperlink::OnCancelMode (void)
{
    if (GetCapture() == this)
```

```
    ReleaseCapture();

CWnd::OnCancelMode();

return;
}
```

Besides the mouse-down and mouse-up events, you also catch and process `OnCancelMode` (`WM_CANCELMODE`). Windows sends this message to any window that captured input through `SetCapture` when a new window must be displayed. For example, if another application is becoming active due to a system keypress or a message box that is being displayed, the Window manager sends the window capturing input a `WM_CANCELMODE`. This allows the window to cancel capture and release any other allocated resources (such as timers).

Keyboard Input

One of the original requirements for the hyperlink control was that it accept keyboard input. This enables the user to tab to and from the hyperlink, much as he would with any other editable control in a dialog box. Several actions are necessary to accomplish this feat.

Normal keyboard input is processed by catching the `WM_KEYDOWN` (`OnKeyDown`), `WM_KEYUP` (`OnKeyUp`), and `WM_CHAR` (`OnChar`) messages. Windows sends a key-down message when a key is pressed on the keyboard, and sends a key-up message when a key is released. Key-up and key-down messages are sent for all keystrokes—not only alphanumeric characters, but also Shift keys, Control keys, Caps Lock, and so on.

If your control is interested only in the resulting keypress, use the `WM_CHAR` message. `WM_CHAR` messages are generated from multiple `WM_KEYDOWN` messages. For example, to type a capital *A*, you hold down the Shift key and press the A key. Your application will receive a `WM_KEYDOWN` for both the Shift key (`VK_SHIFT`) and the A key. Finally, a `WM_CHAR` message is generated specifying the resulting A keypress. After the `WM_CHAR`, `WM_KEYUP` messages are generated for both the A and Shift keys.

In general, custom controls that accept input, like edit controls, need a mixture of key-down/key-up messages and `WM_CHAR` messages. The hyperlink control needs only the Enter key. When this key is pressed, the hyperlink will launch.

Unfortunately, the Enter key is a very special key to Windows. By default, this keypress is intercepted by the dialog manager and routed to the default button in a dialog box. Other keys intercepted include the Tab key (changes focus through the controls of a dialog box), the arrow keys (change the current control within a group), and mnemonics (used with the Alt key to jump to a specific control). To receive the Enter key (or any of the other special keys), you need to jump through some hoops.

The dialog manager is willing to concede these keys on an as-needed basis. To determine which keys a control requires, the dialog manager sends a WM_GETDLGCODE (OnGetDlgCode) message prior to sending a keyboard message. The return from the recipient window controls whether a specific keypress is intercepted or not.

Besides values for stock controls (buttons, edit controls, or static text controls), the following return values can be combined to make a valid WM_GETDLGCODE response:

WM_GETDLGCODE *Constant*	*Description*
DLGC_WANTALLKEYS	Window receives all WM_KEYDOWN/WM_KEYUP messages.
DLGC_WANTARROWS	Window receives non-intercepted messages plus arrow keys.
DLGC_WANTCHARS	Window receives all WM_CHAR messages.
DLGC_WANTMESSAGE	Window receives each keyboard message to decide on a message-by-message basis.
DLGC_WANTTAB	Window receives non-intercepted messages plus Tab messages.

Conspicuously absent from the list is a code to receive just the Enter key. Experimenting with the dialog code for default pushbuttons yielded no results, so the window is stuck with the catchall DLGC_WANTALLKEYS.

If your control receives *all* keyboard messages, you are on your own to handle navigation commands. That is, instead of relying on the dialog manager to process tabs, arrow keys, and Esc, you must handle them yourselves. This is reasonably simple to do.

When the hyperlink control receives the Enter key (VK_RETURN), the link is launched, and a notification is sent to the parent window. In response to the Esc key, the control masquerades as the Cancel button (IDCANCEL) and sends a button-clicked message to its parent window. Finally, if the Tab key is pressed, focus is moved forward or backward through any sibling windows to find the next one with the tabstop style set. This mimics the standard behavior of the dialog manager.

```
UINT CHyperlink::OnGetDlgCode(void)
{
    return (DLGC_WANTALLKEYS);
}

void CHyperlink::OnKeyDown (UINT nChar, UINT nRepCnt, UINT nFlags)
{
    if (nChar == VK_RETURN)
```

```
        {
            ExecuteLink ();

            SendParentNotify ((WORD) ::GetWindowLong (GetSafeHwnd(),
                            GWL_ID), HL_LINKCLICKED);
        }
        else if (nChar == VK_ESCAPE)
        {
            SendParentNotify (IDCANCEL, BN_CLICKED);
        }
        else if (nChar == VK_TAB)
        {
            CWnd*   pwndFocus = this;
            BOOL    bForwardTab = (GetKeyState (VK_SHIFT) & 0x8000) ?
            ➥FALSE : TRUE;

            // Find the next or previous window which has the
            // tabstop bit set.
            do
            {
                pwndFocus = pwndFocus->GetWindow (((bForwardTab)
                                            ? GW_HWNDNEXT :
                                            GW_HWNDPREV));

                if (!pwndFocus)
                    pwndFocus = GetWindow (((bForwardTab)
                                        ? GW_HWNDFIRST : GW_HWNDLAST));

            } while (pwndFocus != this &&
                    (!pwndFocus->IsWindowEnabled() &&
                    !(::GetWindowLong (pwndFocus->GetSafeHwnd(),
                                    GWL_STYLE) & WS_TABSTOP)));

            if (pwndFocus)
                pwndFocus->SetFocus ();
        }
        else
            CWnd::OnKeyDown (nChar, nRepCnt, nFlags);
}
```

Launching the Link

To launch the hyperlink, the hyperlink control retrieves the current window text and passes it to the Windows shell for execution, with the "open" opcode. So far, I've tested the hyperlink with http and ftp links, the mailto: command, and local document files (C:\My Documents\Readme.wri, for example). Any filename registered as a shell extension will work. A logical improvement would be to display one set of text, while executing another—this would hide ugly or complex URLs and present the user with a comprehensible interface.

```
HINSTANCE CHyperlink::ExecuteLink (void)
{
    HINSTANCE hInstReturn;
    CString strText;

    GetWindowText (strText);

    hInstReturn = ShellExecute(GetSafeHwnd(),
                               _T("open"),
                               strText,
                               NULL,
                               NULL,
                               SW_SHOWNORMAL);

    return (hInstReturn);
}
```

It's quite a bit of code for a seemingly simple class.<

Advanced Custom Control Topics

Although the clock and hyperlink static controls demonstrate the basics of custom control design, there are some additional techniques that can be useful. One is a technique for accessing Windows messages during the creation of a custom control. I also present various methods for sending notifications from a custom control to its parent window in this section. This section also includes a discussion of how to use a custom control with the Visual Studio Resource Editor.

Subclassing Limitations

Choosing an existing window class has the advantage of overcoming some significant MFC problems dealing with Window creation and initialization.

The MFC message-map paradigm has some severe limitations in creating custom controls. The biggest problem is initialization. Normally, newly created windows are initialized by catching the WM_CREATE message. At this point, the window has text, size, and positioning information. When embedded in dialog boxes, however, MFC window classes do not always get a chance to process WM_CREATE messages.

When a dialog box is created, the dialog manager creates the new dialog window, and then creates any child windows in the dialog template. MFC can subclass the dialog box during its creation; however, the child windows are created without subclassing. The soonest the child windows can be subclassed is during the WM_INITDIALOG (OnInitDialog) message. However, by that time, the new child windows have all received their WM_CREATE, WM_SIZE, and several other important messages.

5

CUSTOM CONTROL
DEVELOPMENT

Of course, if you create your window directly, rather than from a dialog template, you will get WM_CREATE and the other "early" messages. A common technique for controls that require the early messages is to use a placeholder window, typically a static. The static is placed on the dialog template with the same position, size, style, and ID as the target window. Then, a member function in the target window class is called to gather the information from the static, destroy it, and create the actual window.

```
BOOL CHyperlink::CreateFromStatic(CWnd* pwndParent, UINT wID)
{
    BOOL bSuccess = FALSE;
    CWnd* pwndStatic = pwndParent->GetDlgItem (wID);

    if (pwndStatic != (CWnd*) 0)
    {
        DWORD dwStyle = pwnd->GetStyle();
        CString strText;
        CRect rect;

        // Get the window text
        pwndStatic->GetWindowText (strText);

        // Get the window position and convert from screen -> client
        pwndStatic->GetWindowRect (rect);
        pwndParent->ScreenToClient(rect);

        pwndStatic->DestroyWindow();

        bSuccess = CWnd::Create (NULL,
                        strText,
                        dwStyle,
                        rect,
                        pwndParent,
                        wID,
                        NULL);
    }

    return (bSuccess);
}
```

This is a point that causes outrage among Windows API developers. The non-MFC mechanism for creating a class is to register a window class (with a window procedure), and then create windows of that class by embedding them on a dialog box. Why doesn't MFC support registering window classes and doing the same thing?

MFC does in fact support window class registration; however, after you've registered the class, it's difficult to do anything with it. If you register a custom window procedure, you can handle early messages, but you lose the ability to use message maps and to associate instance-specific data (such as the members of a class object in memory) with a window handle. That negates most of the advantages of using MFC for window class development in the first place.

If you use AfxWndProc, you get the message mapping, but no messages until the window is subclassed. This isn't an obvious point. In fact, each message sent to the window is received by AfxWndProc, but no message mapping can exist until somebody associates a class with the window. After the class is attached, messages are routed to the proper handlers. But you can't really attach to the window until your dialog gains control (generally WM_INITDIALOG), and at that point the "early" messages have been received and discarded.

Notifications

Controls that accept input need to be able to communicate with their parent windows when the user acts. Well-known examples of this include the EN_CHANGE notification, sent by edit controls when the contents change, and the BN_CLICKED message sent by pushbuttons when activated.

Most built-in window classes use notifications of this ilk; they send a WM_COMMAND message to their parent, along with the control ID, the message code, and their window handle. The WPARAM contains the control ID and message code in the low and high words, respectively. The LPARAM contains the window handle (HWND, not CWnd) of the sending control.

Of course, this use of message parameters leaves no mechanism to send details. It is incumbent on the parent window to query for details if needed. The SendParentNotify function of the CHyperlink control automates sending these kinds of notifications.

If you need to send back detailed parameters, consider sending a message in the WM_USER range to the parent. That way, you have the WPARAM and LPARAM parameters available for data (or to act as pointers). Better still, use the WM_NOTIFY message. The more recent common controls (property sheet, tree control, and so on) use WM_NOTIFY to send data to their parent windows. WM_NOTIFY messages contain the window handle of the sending control in the WPARAM, and a pointer to a structure in the LPARAM. The structure varies from control to control, but all start with an NMHDR.

For the ultimate in notification, use a callback interface. Allow the parent window (or delegate) to register itself with the control via an interface class; when the control needs to send details back to the parent, it invokes one or more functions in the callback interface. Of course, using this mechanism makes your control unusable by non-C++ applications.

5

CUSTOM CONTROL
DEVELOPMENT

Using the Resource Editor with Custom Classes

The Visual Studio Resource Editor gives you the ability to place unknown window classes into a dialog template. To do this, you must know the registered class name and the style bits appropriate for the class. The style bits are set as a 32-bit hexadecimal number (no constants)—so be prepared to do some math.

Reevaluating the style bits causes no end of grief during maintenance. There isn't a place to put any comments into the dialog template, and who can remember that 0x10830000 is equivalent to WS_TABSTOP, WS_GROUP, WS_BORDER, and WS_VISIBLE? It's far easier to create the controls during OnInitDialog processing, using CWnd::Create and symbolic constants.

Summary

Creating a custom control can be a very simple process or an extremely complex one. Start by documenting the observable behavior of the control: response to input, output formats, and the effect of any style flags. If you can, base it off an existing control, such as an edit control or combo box. These controls have years of testing and improvement behind them.

If you must start from scratch, map from observable behavior to Windows messages. Which messages do you need to capture, and what does each signal to your control? What are the different states (such as capture) that the control supports?

Be sure to test your control in a variety of scenarios. For example, make sure that the control works both in a dialog box and on a standalone basis. Change the Windows color scheme to some absurd setting to ensure that the control paints properly. Check that the control resizes properly under very high and very low display resolutions.

Ensure that the control creation strategy is valid. Does the control require a ::CreateFromStatic member (or similar), or can it be subclassed from an existing dialog control?

The MFC Application Object, Message Routing, and Idle Processing

by David Lowndes

IN THIS CHAPTER

In this chapter, you will learn about the CWinApp object. In doing so, I hope to encourage you to examine the MFC source code and discover what happens beneath the surface of your MFC application.

The MFC Application Object

The CWinApp class is the starting point of your MFC application. It controls the initialization and startup operations, runs the main message loop, and handles shutdown. CWinApp can handle command messages in the same way as your view and document classes, and it contains several important public member variables that set the help file, the root registry key, and other system-wide settings for your application.

A CWinApp object never appears directly in your application; instead, it is the base class of your application object. This is a global object named theApp, created by AppWizard in your main application source file. If you use AppWizard to create a project named MyProject, your application class is named CMyProjectApp and the theApp object is declared in MyProject.cpp.

Because it is a global variable, this object is instantiated along with any other global C++ objects as part of the runtime startup code. You can access it from anywhere in your source code using the AfxGetApp function like this:

```
CMyApp * pApp = static_cast<CMyApp*>( AfxGetApp() );
```

Because the object is a global variable, you might wonder why MFC exposes it this way rather than providing an extern definition in a header file. In the context of your executable, you could just as well access the object directly, but in the context of an MFC DLL, it is significant. Listing 6.1, a code snippet of an exported function in an MFC DLL, illustrates the point.

LISTING 6.1   AfxGetApp AND APPLICATION MODULE STATE

```
BOOL PASCAL ExportedFunction1( )
{
    CWinApp * pApp = AfxGetApp();
    AFX_MANAGE_STATE(AfxGetStaticModuleState( ));
    pApp = AfxGetApp();
```

The returned pApp object pointer from the first call to AfxGetApp is the calling application's CWinApp object. The result of the second call to AfxGetApp is the DLL's CWinApp object. This apparent switch is accomplished by the AFX_MANAGE_STATE macro. It constructs an object that chains a module state to the calling application's module data, so that in this example, the DLL module state (returned by the call to

AfxGetStaticModuleState) is linked to the application. There's no need to remember to reset these state variables; it's done automatically by the object's destructor when the function exits.

It's common to use AFX_MANAGE_STATE in any exported MFC DLL functions where you want the program to use a resource from the DLL.

If you are writing an EXE application, you can add the following extern definition to your application object's header file and access the global theApp object directly in any source file that includes the header file:

```
extern CMyProjectApp theApp;
```

CWinApp and Application Lifetime

As mentioned previously, the CWinApp-derived object is a global variable, and therefore exists for the lifetime of your program.

The class member variables are initialized by the class's constructor code. Because the object is global, the constructor is called by the compiler's runtime startup code, and therefore all the default values are set before the main part of your program code executes.

After global variables and other aspects of the C runtime support are initialized, your program code executes and is essentially as straightforward as the pseudocode in Listing 6.2.

LISTING 6.2 PROGRAM EXECUTION SEQUENCE

```
if ( InitInstance() )
{
    Run;
}
else
{
    Destroy the main window if there is one;
}
ExitInstance;
```

In practice, if you examine the MFC source code in WinMain.cpp, you'll find that it's a little more involved, but this simple representation expresses the general idea.

It's rare that you'll need to know about or override the default implementations of Run or ExitInstance, but it's almost mandatory for you to modify the boilerplate code for your application's InitInstance.

InitInstance

InitInstance performs all the application-specific initialization. I'll cover this in depth later in the chapter (see "InitInstance—Application-Specific Initialization").

Run

Run is the heart of your application and is where your application spends the vast majority of its processing life. This function is a loop that retrieves and processes messages from your application's message queue. If there are no messages in the queue, it calls the OnIdle function. If there is a message, and it's not WM_QUIT, it is dispatched into the MFC message processing code. If the message is WM_QUIT, the loop ends and the function returns. You can think of the Run function as something like the pseudocode in Listing 6.3.

LISTING 6.3 Run() PSEUDOCODE

```
for (;;)
{
    MSG msg;
    while ( !PeekMessage( &msg, ...) )
    {
        OnIdle();
    }

    if ( msg.message == WM_QUIT )
    {
        return ExitInstance();
    }
    else
    {
        DispatchMessage( &msg );
    }
}
```

I'll discuss the path that dispatched messages take later on in this chapter under the "Message Routing" topic.

ExitInstance

You're only likely to need to override the ExitInstance member function if you need to free some special allocated resource that your application used. The return value from ExitInstance is the exit code value that your application returns on termination. The normal convention is to return zero if the application shuts down normally, and any other value to indicate an error.

> **TIP**
>
> If you override `ExitInstance`, be sure to call the base class function because it saves your application Registry settings and performs necessary cleanup of resources used by MFC.

OnIdle

Override the `OnIdle` function if you need to perform background processing in your application. `OnIdle` is covered in more depth under "Idle Processing" later in the chapter.

The `CWinApp` Data Members

The `CWinApp` data members are documented in the Visual C++ help, but the help doesn't give any examples of typical values that these variables take. I've included a few examples of those public member variables that you might find useful in your own programs.

> **NOTE**
>
> Some of these members are actually declared in `CWinThread` (which is the base class of `CWinApp`), but for now, you can regard them as being part of `CWinApp`.

m_pszAppName

The `m_pszAppName` variable contains the name of the application as a string, for example, "MyProject". MFC displays this string for the caption bar text if you use `AfxMessageBox`.

If you look at the help for the `CWinApp` constructor, you'll find that it accepts a string parameter. In the boilerplate code generated by AppWizard, this is `NULL`. This `NULL` value instructs MFC to use the `AFX_IDS_APP_TITLE` string resource to initialize the m_pszAppName member. However, if you want to, you can modify the line of code that constructs this object to set this variable this way:

```
CMyProjectApp::CMyProjectApp() : CWinApp("I want to set this string as the
➡application name")
{
}
```

m_hInstance

Although the Visual C++ help describes m_hInstance as the current instance of the application, the concept of an instance handle is a relic from 16-bit Windows, and it doesn't exist as such under Win32. It is better described as a module handle because it's actually the load address of the module in the process's address space.

For a default Visual C++ project, an EXE module will have the value 0x00400000, whereas a DLL would have 0x10000000. The linker assigns these values. You can override them from your project's Link settings.

> **NOTE**
>
> The EXE module values can be different at runtime because the Win32 loader can relocate a module if the default address space is already in use by another module.

m_hPrevInstance

m_hPrevInstance is a relic from 16-bit Windows applications, where it is used to indicate the previous instance handle of a running application. Under Win32, it is always NULL.

Under 16-bit Windows, you could use this variable to restrict an application to a single instance. Under Win32, you can achieve the same result using a mutex, as illustrated in Listing 6.4.

LISTING 6.4   USING A MUTEX TO LIMIT AN APPLICATION TO A SINGLE INSTANCE

```
BOOL CDlgApp::InitInstance()
{
    bool bAlreadyRunning;

    HANDLE hMutexOneInstance = CreateMutex( NULL, TRUE,
                        "18A5330D_9DCA_11D2_9847_006052028C2E" );
    bAlreadyRunning = ( GetLastError() == ERROR_ALREADY_EXISTS );
    if ( hMutexOneInstance )
    {
        ReleaseMutex( hMutexOneInstance );
    }
    if ( bAlreadyRunning )
    {
        AfxMessageBox( "Already running" );
```

```
        return FALSE;
    }
    ...
```

The `CreateMutex` call is an atomic operation and guarantees that this operation is fail-safe.

> **NOTE**
>
> The string I've used in `CreateMutex` is a GUID generated by the MFC AppWizard in the header file for my project. If you use this technique, be sure to use your own guaranteed unique string from your own project's header file.

m_lpCmdLine

`m_lpCmdLine` is a pointer to the null-terminated command-line string. This string is the portion of the command line *after* the executable name. There is no additional processing of the command line, so all white space characters between parameters are intact.

For example, if you ran the program from the following command line

```
>C:\Tests\MyApp -a -b   c:\Tests\filename.ext
```

this member would be "-a -b   c:\Tests\filename.ext".

> **TIP**
>
> You might find the `m_lpCmdLine` member difficult to use, but don't forget that you can always make use of the global C runtime `__argc` and `__argv` facilities to handle command-line parameters in the same easy way that you could if you were writing a console application. The `__argc` and `__argv` variables are global and can be accessed anywhere in your program.

m_nCmdShow

When the shell or another application starts your program, it passes a parameter to suggest the initial show state of the main frame window. This value is eventually passed to the ShowWindow API by way of the `m_nCmdShow` member variable.

The m_nCmdShow variable takes on different values depending on how you invoked your application. For example, if you start your application by double-clicking the executable in Explorer, the value in m_nCmdShow will instruct ShowWindow to display the window in its visible, nonmaximized state. However, if you invoke the application through a shortcut, you can use the shortcut's property page to specify the initial window state as Normal, Maximized, or Minimized.

m_bHelpMode

m_bHelpMode indicates whether the application is in help context mode (typically invoked when you press Shift+F1).

m_pActiveWnd

m_pActiveWnd is used as a pointer to the main window of the container application when an OLE server is in-place active. It is NULL if the application is not in-place activated.

m_pMainWnd

m_pMainWnd is used to store a pointer to the application's top-level window. MFC terminates the application when this window is closed. A consequence of this is discussed under the topic "Dialog Application" later in this chapter.

m_pszExeName

m_pszExeName is the module name of the application, for example, "MYPROJECTAPP".

m_pszHelpFilePath

m_pszHelpFilePath is the full path to the application's Help file, for example, "C:\SAMPLES\MYPROJECT\MYPROJECTAPP.HLP".

m_pszProfileName

m_pszProfileName is the application's INI filename or Registry key name.

Initially, this is an INI filename, such as "MYPROJECTAPP.INI". If your application calls SetRegistryKey, this variable becomes a duplicate of the m_pszAppName variable (MyProjectApp). If you prefer your application to store its settings in an INI file rather than the Registry, remove the call to SetRegistryKey in your application's InitInstance.

m_pszRegistryKey

The m_pszRegistryKey variable is the name of the Registry key for your application's settings. It is set up in the SetRegistryKey function.

The MFC Application Object, Message Routing, and Idle Processing

CHAPTER 6

249

6

THE MFC
APPLICATION
OBJECT

If you examine your application's `InitInstance` function, you'll see that it includes a call to `SetRegistryKey` with a fixed string. The code comment inserted by AppWizard rightly suggests that you should set this string to your company name.

Internally, MFC concatenates this string with the `m_pszProfileName` variable to form the Registry key for your application. For example, if you set this value to "MyCompanyName", your application's Registry key is "Software\MyCompanyName\MyProjectApp".

This is used by the `CWinApp` registry routines such as `GetAppRegistryKey`, `GetProfileInt`, `GetProfileString`, `GetProfileBinary`, `WriteProfileInt`, `WriteProfileString`, and `WriteProfileBinary`.

> **NOTE**
>
> There's an alternative form of the `SetRegistryKey` function that loads this string from a resource:
>
> ```
> void SetRegistryKey(UINT nIDRegistryKey);
> ```
>
> You might find this form useful if you produce a program that is resold to OEMs who need to rebadge the program with their own application name. Placing the string in the resource file means that you won't have to modify the source code to accommodate this requirement.

The `CWinApp` Member Functions

`CWinApp` includes many member functions that are small wrappers, such as the `LoadCursor` and `LoadIcon` routines. These are not of any great interest except to note that they make use of `AfxFindResourceHandle`, which enables your program to access resources from within the EXE or MFC extension DLLs.

`Run`, `InitInstance`, and `ExitInstance`, are actually members of `CWinThread`, but for this discussion, you can assume they belong to `CWinApp`.

Perhaps the most significant member function of `CWinApp` is the one that performs the application-specific initialization—`InitInstance`. Unlike most other functions in `CWinApp`, the AppWizard generates different code for this function depending on the type of application and the options you chose. I will now cover the `InitInstance` code for the three most common types of MFC applications generated with the default AppWizard options.

InitInstance—Application-Specific Initialization

The code examples in the following sections show the boilerplate code generated by the AppWizard for three types of MFC applications: Listing 6.5 shows a dialog application, Listing 6.6 an SDI doc/view application, and Listing 6.7 an MDI doc/view application.

For clarity, and to emphasize the important aspects, I've removed the comments and the less significant lines of code.

LISTING 6.5 A DIALOG APPLICATION'S InitInstance CODE

```
BOOL CDlgApp::InitInstance()
{
    AfxEnableControlContainer();
    CDlgDlg dlg;
    m_pMainWnd = &dlg;
    int nResponse = dlg.DoModal();
    if (nResponse == IDOK)
    {
    }
    else if (nResponse == IDCANCEL)
    {
    }
    return FALSE;
}
```

The dialog application is quite straightforward. After calling AfxEnableControlContainer to enable ActiveX container support, the application consists of a modal dialog box.

> **NOTE**
>
> One point to note in the dialog application is that it returns FALSE from InitInstance. If you refer back to the Program Execution Sequence shown earlier in Listing 6.2, you'll see that this bypasses the Run message-processing loop and terminates the application.

Note also that the m_pMainWnd variable is assigned to the modal dialog. This has the side effect of causing MFC to generate a WM_QUIT message when the dialog closes. This in turn gives rise to a common problem. If you want to use another dialog or a message box after the main dialog has closed, these subsequent windows might briefly appear and

The MFC Application Object, Message Routing, and Idle Processing

CHAPTER 6

251

6

THE MFC
APPLICATION
OBJECT

promptly close. Microsoft's Knowledge Base article Q138681 gives the answer and suggests either removing the line of code that assigns m_pMainWnd in InitInstance, or setting the m_pMainWnd member to NULL in the dialog's WM_NCDESTROY (OnNcDestroy) message handler. Because other aspects of a program might need the m_pMainWnd variable, I'd recommend the latter action. If you want to show another modal dialog after the first, duplicate the assignment of m_pMainWnd to this new dialog.

SDI/MDI Document/View Applications

The SDI and MDI application startup code is remarkably similar, so I'll discuss them together.

LISTING 6.6   AN SDI APPLICATION'S InitInstance CODE

```
BOOL CSdiApp::InitInstance()
{
    AfxEnableControlContainer();
    SetRegistryKey(_T("Local AppWizard-Generated Applications"));
    LoadStdProfileSettings();
    CSingleDocTemplate* pDocTemplate;
    pDocTemplate = new CSingleDocTemplate(
        IDR_MAINFRAME,
        RUNTIME_CLASS(CSdiDoc),
        RUNTIME_CLASS(CMainFrame),
        RUNTIME_CLASS(CSdiView));
    AddDocTemplate(pDocTemplate);
    CCommandLineInfo cmdInfo;
    ParseCommandLine(cmdInfo);
    if (!ProcessShellCommand(cmdInfo))
        return FALSE;
    m_pMainWnd->ShowWindow(SW_SHOW);
    m_pMainWnd->UpdateWindow();
    return TRUE;
}
```

LISTING 6.7   AN MDI APPLICATION'S InitInstance CODE

```
BOOL CMdiApp::InitInstance()
{
    AfxEnableControlContainer();
    SetRegistryKey(_T("Local AppWizard-Generated Applications"));
    LoadStdProfileSettings();
    CMultiDocTemplate* pDocTemplate;
    pDocTemplate = new CMultiDocTemplate(
        IDR_MDITYPE,
        RUNTIME_CLASS(CMdiDoc),
```

continues

LISTING 6.7   CONTINUED

```
        RUNTIME_CLASS(CChildFrame),
        RUNTIME_CLASS(CMdiView));
    AddDocTemplate(pDocTemplate);
    CMainFrame* pMainFrame = new CMainFrame;
    if (!pMainFrame->LoadFrame(IDR_MAINFRAME))
        return FALSE;
    m_pMainWnd = pMainFrame;
    CCommandLineInfo cmdInfo;
    ParseCommandLine(cmdInfo);
    if (!ProcessShellCommand(cmdInfo))
        return FALSE;
    pMainFrame->ShowWindow(m_nCmdShow);
    pMainFrame->UpdateWindow();
    return TRUE;
}
```

The InitInstance function of the doc/view applications is quite different from that of the dialog application. They add Registry support, SDI/MDI document/view, and MFC command-line handling.

The differences between an MDI and SDI application are as follows:

1. MDI and SDI each have their own specific document template classes.

2. The MDI application explicitly creates its main frame window.

3. MDI and SDI have a subtly different usage of ShowWindow.

The latter two differences come about because an MDI application has an extra layer of window hierarchy, as shown in Figure 6.1.

FIGURE 6.1

SDI and MDI window hierarchy.

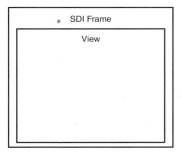 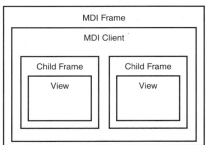

In the SDI, the document view window has a single-frame window that is the main application window. In the MDI, the main frame window holds the MDI client window that in turn holds the child frame windows. These child frame windows in turn contain the document's view windows.

Automation Doc/View Application

Adding Automation support to an application incorporates a fair amount of extra boiler-plate code to InitInstance. Listing 6.8 shows the `InitInstance` function for an MDI application with automation support.

LISTING 6.8   InitInstance FOR AN MDI APPLICATION WITH OLE AUTOMATION SUPPORT

```
BOOL CMdiAutoApp::InitInstance()
{
    if (!AfxOleInit())
    {
        AfxMessageBox(IDP_OLE_INIT_FAILED);
        return FALSE;
    }
    AfxEnableControlContainer();
    SetRegistryKey(_T("Local AppWizard-Generated Applications"));
    LoadStdProfileSettings();  // Load standard INI file options
➥(including MRU)
    CMultiDocTemplate* pDocTemplate;
    pDocTemplate = new CMultiDocTemplate(
        IDR_MDIAU1TYPE,
        RUNTIME_CLASS(CMdiAutoDoc),
        RUNTIME_CLASS(CChildFrame), // custom MDI child frame
        RUNTIME_CLASS(CMdiAutoView));
    AddDocTemplate(pDocTemplate);
    m_server.ConnectTemplate(clsid, pDocTemplate, FALSE);
    COleTemplateServer::RegisterAll();
    CMainFrame* pMainFrame = new CMainFrame;
    if (!pMainFrame->LoadFrame(IDR_MAINFRAME))
        return FALSE;
    m_pMainWnd = pMainFrame;
    m_pMainWnd->DragAcceptFiles();
    EnableShellOpen();
    RegisterShellFileTypes(TRUE);
    CCommandLineInfo cmdInfo;
    ParseCommandLine(cmdInfo);
    if (cmdInfo.m_bRunEmbedded || cmdInfo.m_bRunAutomated)
    {
        return TRUE;
    }
    m_server.UpdateRegistry(OAT_DISPATCH_OBJECT);
    COleObjectFactory::UpdateRegistryAll();
    if (!ProcessShellCommand(cmdInfo))
        return FALSE;
    pMainFrame->ShowWindow(m_nCmdShow);
    pMainFrame->UpdateWindow();
    return TRUE;
}
```

If you compare the preceding listing with Listing 6.7, you can see that there's quite a lot more code to this one.

Functionality in `InitInstance`

To help you understand the functions in `InitInstance`, I've grouped them into their functional areas, as described in the following sections.

OLE Container Support

If you set the ActiveX Controls check box on step 3 of the AppWizard, the AppWizard adds a call to `AfxEnableControlContainer` in `InitInstance`, as illustrated in Listing 6.8. This allows your application to host ActiveX controls.

3D Look for Windows NT 3.5x

Prior to Windows 95, the 3D dialog look was implemented in an additional DLL. It was quite easy to make use of this in an application, and MFC wrapped this up behind the scenes, which made it even easier. Windows 95 and subsequent operating systems have implemented this 3D look natively, and you no longer need this extra DLL or the support in MFC.

Because Visual C++ still supports developing applications for versions of Windows earlier than Windows 95, AppWizard defaults to including the code found in Listing 6.9 in `InitInstance`.

LISTING 6.9   3D-LOOK SUPPORT CODE

```
#ifdef _AFXDLL
    Enable3dControls();
#else
    Enable3dControlsStatic();
#endif
```

If you don't need to run your application under earlier versions of Windows, you can safely uncheck the 3D Controls check box on the AppWizard or delete these lines of code afterwards. Leaving this code in under Windows 9x and NT 4 has no detrimental effect because the MFC code checks which operating system the program is running under and ignores the facility if it is not needed.

Registry Usage

You can choose to have your application use private INI files or the registry by using the `SetRegistryKey` function.

The MFC Application Object, Message Routing, and Idle Processing

CHAPTER 6

255

6

THE MFC
APPLICATION
OBJECT

Calling `SetRegistryKey` causes your application to use the Registry rather than a private INI file. If you call this function, the `CWinApp` profile functions (such as `GetProfileString` and `WriteProfileString`) and the application's most recently used (MRU) filenames are stored in the Registry.

Most Recently Used Files List

When you open documents in your application, the `CWinApp` object keeps a note of the last documents you used. These are stored in the Registry or your application's private INI file.

The `LoadStdProfileSettings` function loads the most recently used filename information and the print preview's number of pages setting.

SDI and MDI Document/View

The most significant (if not immediately visible) difference between the code in `InitInstance` for SDI and MDI applications is that they use different document template classes, which are described in the following sections.

CSingleDocTemplate and CMultiDocTemplate

The `CSingleDocTemplate` and `CMultiDocTemplate` classes handle the differences between SDI and MDI document management. `CSingleDocTemplate` can handle a single document of a single type, whereas `CMultiDocTemplate` can handle many documents of a single type.

AppWizard adds code to `InitInstance` to create a single document template type for both SDI and MDI applications. In an MDI application, it's common to need to support several types of documents and views. It's quite easy to add additional document/views to your application. Using the `ClassView`, right-click the project and choose New Form. This lets you create a document/view based on a new form. If you don't want a form view, you can do it yourself by replicating the few lines of code that create and add a new document template to `CWinApp` (see Listing 6.10).

LISTING 6.10 CREATING ADDITIONAL DOCUMENT TYPES

```
pDocTemplate = new CMultiDocTemplate(
    IDR_MDITYPE1,
    RUNTIME_CLASS(CMdiDoc1),
    RUNTIME_CLASS(CChildFrame),
    RUNTIME_CLASS(CMdiView1));
AddDocTemplate(pDocTemplate);
```

Because you will presumably want to differentiate your document types from one another, you'll need to use a new resource ID. In the preceding code, I've used IDR_MDITYPE1. MFC uses this ID in three places:

1. As a multisection resource string. See Knowledge Base article Q129095 in your Visual C++ help for the details of the format of this string.

2. As the menu ID for your document type.

3. As the document icon ID.

The easiest way to identify the usage of this resource is to use the Resource Symbols dialog which is accessed from the View, Resource Symbols menu. Select the existing document resource ID, view its usage, and then duplicate and change the three resources to create the resources for your new type.

Although I've cited this as something you might want to do for an MDI application, in fact the same technique also works for SDI.

In addition to the resources, you'll probably want to create new document and view classes to support your alternative document. To do this, right-click your project in the Class View, choose New Class, and select the appropriate MFC Classes.

DragAcceptFiles

DragAcceptFiles tells Windows that your application window supports drag-and-drop file opening.

EnableShellOpen

EnableShellOpen enables your application to support activation by DDE commands.

If your MDI application is already running, and you activate one of your application's supported documents from the shell, the shell uses a DDE command to open the document in the instance of your application that is currently running, rather than start a new instance of your program.

RegisterShellFileTypes

RegisterShellFileTypes sets all the Registry command strings that let the Windows shell automatically invoke your application to open and print your supported documents.

Main Frame Window Creation

In the SDI, the frame window is created when the initial document is created, that is, when ProcessShellCommand is called. An MDI application creates its main frame

The MFC Application Object, Message Routing, and Idle Processing

CHAPTER 6

257

6

THE MFC
APPLICATION
OBJECT

window explicitly in `InitInstance` and sets the `CWinApp m_pMainWnd` member to this window.

Automation Support

If you create an application with (OLE) Automation support, you'll have an application that can be instantiated by other applications through Automation facilities. See Chapter 11, "COM and MFC," for more information on Automation.

AfxOleInit

The `AfxOleInit` call initializes COM support in your application.

ConnectTemplate

`ConnectTemplate` creates a class factory and links it to the document template.

RegisterAll

`RegisterAll` performs the registration of the application's class factory objects.

UpdateRegistry

`UpdateRegistry` puts information in the Registry that identifies your application document types.

UpdateRegistryAll

`UpdateRegistryAll` registers all the application's class factory objects in the Registry.

Rich Edit Control Support

If you use the rich edit control in your application, you need to call `AfxInitRichEdit` to ensure that the rich edit DLL is loaded for your application.

Command-Line Handling

MFC handles a predefined set of standard command-line parameters by the lines of code shown in Listing 6.11, which are common to doc/view architecture applications.

LISTING 6.11 COMMAND-LINE HANDLING CODE

```
CCommandLineInfo cmdInfo;
ParseCommandLine(cmdInfo);
if (!ProcessShellCommand(cmdInfo))
    return FALSE;
```

As you can see, there's not much to it. The key is really in the `CCommandLineInfo` class. It's parsed by `ParseCommandLine` (surprisingly), and then "executed" by `ProcessShellCommand`.

MFC supports the command-line options shown in Table 6.1.

TABLE 6.1   MFC COMMAND-LINE OPTIONS

Command	Operation
AppName	Creates a new file
AppName filename	Opens the file
AppName /p filename	Prints the file to the default printer
AppName /pt filename printer driver port	Prints the file to the specified printer
AppName /dde	Starts up and executes the DDE command
AppName /Automation	Starts up as an OLE Automation server
AppName /Embedding	Starts up to edit an embedded OLE item
AppName /unregister	Removes the application's standard registry settings from the Registry

The following sections examine the data members of this class to clarify how the class works:

- **m_bShowSplash**   Setting m_bShowSplash to TRUE indicates that a splash screen should be shown. This value defaults to TRUE unless the command line has the /Embedding or /Automation parameters, which invoke the application without a main window. In a plain AppWizard-generated application, m_bShowSplash is useless because nothing ever uses it. To see it in action, you can add the splash screen component to your application. This is covered a little later in the chapter; see "The Splash Screen Component."

- **m_bRunEmbedded**   The m_bRunEmbedded value is TRUE if the application was started with the /Embedding switch.

- **m_bRunAutomated**   The m_bRunAutomated value is TRUE if the application was started with the /Automation switch.

- **m_nShellCommand**   The m_nShellCommand value is one of the enumerated values—FileNew, FileOpen, FilePrint, FilePrintTo, FileDDE, or AppUnregister—that correspond to the options available in Table 6.1. This value is used to determine the operation of the ProcessShellCommand function.

The MFC Application Object, Message Routing, and Idle Processing

CHAPTER 6

259

6

THE MFC
APPLICATION
OBJECT

- m_strFileName   m_strFileName is the command-line filename parameter. If there isn't a command-line filename, this string is empty.

- m_strPrinterName   If the command is FilePrintTo, m_strPrinterName is the printer name.

- m_strDriverName   If the command is FilePrintTo, m_strDriverName is the printer driver name.

- m_strPortName   If the command is FilePrintTo, m_strPortName is the printer port name.

Message Routing, Message Maps, and Message Categories

Windows is a message-driven environment that communicates with an application through messages placed in a queue. An application retrieves these queued messages and dispatches them to functions that correspond to the type of destination window. In traditional non-MFC Windows applications, these messages are handled in a large switch statement.The MFC architecture refines this mechanism and handles these messages in a more elegant manner.

Message Routing

Earlier in this chapter, I mentioned that the Run function is the "heart" of your application. Run retrieves messages from your application's message queue and pumps them into the MFC framework. Run is essentially a traditional message loop, as shown in Listing 6.12.

LISTING 6.12   TRADITIONAL MESSAGE LOOP PSEUDOCODE

```
MSG msg;
while ( GetMessage( &msg, NULL, 0, 0 ) )
{
    DispatchMessage( &msg );
}
```

When your application calls GetMessage, it relinquishes control to Windows and never returns until Windows has a message for it. If the message returned in the MSG structure isn't WM_QUIT, the message is then passed to DispatchMessage. DispatchMessage examines the MSG hwnd member and calls the registered window function for that class of window.

MFC can't alter this fundamental aspect of how Windows works, but it does refine the mechanism so that you might never need to know about registered window procedures. Instead, you write specific functions for those messages that your application classes handle.

If you examine the Run function in the MFC source code, you'll find this traditional message loop in the CWinThread::PumpMessage function. One key point to note in this function is that MFC calls a PreTranslateMessage function to try to handle the message before calling DispatchMessage. I cover PreTranslateMessage separately because it's a useful function to know.

If the message isn't fully handled by the PreTranslateMessage handlers, the message is finally passed to DispatchMessage and on to the target window's message-handling procedure. The pseudocode in Listing 6.13 illustrates the operation.

LISTING 6.13   MESSAGE PROCESSING CALLS PSEUDOCODE SHOWING PreTranslateMessage USAGE

```
MSG msg;
while ( GetMessage( &msg, NULL, 0, 0 ) )
{
    if ( !PreTranslateMessage( &msg ) )
    {
        DispatchMessage( &msg );
    }
}
```

MFC hides raw window message-handling procedures from you, but they're still there, lurking in the depths. MFC provides its own window procedure in the guise of AfxWndProc. This eventually calls CWnd::OnWndMsg, and it is this function that processes the messages and deals with the next stage of processing: message maps. If you have a look at the source for OnWndMsg, you'll see that it treats some messages, such as WM_COMMAND and WM_NOTIFY, as special cases before it gets down to working with the message maps.

What Does the Message Routing?

You can't see the full picture of the command routing from a casual inspection of the MFC source code in your project. From the BEGIN_MESSAGE_MAP, you can see that a derived class defers messages to its base class, but the relationship between a view and its document class isn't visible. These relationships are embedded in the MFC source code—in a specific class's implementations of OnCmdMsg, to be precise. For example, if you examine CView::OnCmdMsg, you'll see that if the view itself doesn't handle the message, it tries the attached CDocument class.

The MFC Application Object, Message Routing, and Idle Processing

CHAPTER 6

261

6

THE MFC
APPLICATION
OBJECT

Following are a few of the embedded relationships. Note that in each of these, the message proceeds to the next stage only if the current class doesn't handle the message.

CFrameWnd

CFrameWnd first passes the message to the active view, tries to handle the message itself, and finally passes the message to the CWinApp-derived object.

CView

CView first handles the message itself and then passes the message to the document class.

CDocument

CDocument first handles the message itself and then passes the message to its document template class.

CDialog and CPropertySheet

CDialog and CPropertySheet handle the message themselves, pass the message to their parent window, and finally pass the message to their CWinThread object.

For a command message in a doc/view arrangement, the message flow is therefore as follows:

View->Document->Document Template->Frame->Application

PreTranslateMessage

I'll not delve into the nitty-gritty depths of MFC here, but the gist is that MFC first lets the child-parent window hierarchy try to process the message through their own PreTranslateMessage handlers.

First, the window that the message is intended for has its PreTranslateMessage handler called. If that doesn't handle the message, the message is then passed to its parent window's PreTranslateMessage handlers. Each parent window, up to the top-level frame window, gets its chance to handle the message. This makes PreTranslateMessage a key function to remember if you need to handle messages in a slightly unorthodox manner.

For example, in a dialog box, keystroke messages are intended for the child window that has focus, but you might want to do something slightly out of the ordinary—such as have the Enter key function as the Tab key normally does. PreTranslateMessage is a great place to do these sorts of things because you can handle the message before it is dispatched to its default handler. I don't recommend the example in Listing 6.14 because it goes against the consistency of Windows applications, but it does illustrate the point. Please don't use this as anything other than an illustration—unless your boss makes you use it.

LISTING 6.14 USING `PreTranslateMessage` TO HANDLE KEYSTROKES IN A DIALOG BOX

```
BOOL CMyDlg::PreTranslateMessage(MSG* pMsg)
{
    if ( ( pMsg->message == WM_KEYDOWN ) &&
         ( pMsg->wParam == VK_RETURN ) )
    {
        // Simulate the normal TAB operation
        PostMessage( WM_NEXTDLGCTL, 0, false );
        // Return TRUE as we don't want anyone else to handle this message
        return TRUE;
    }
    else
        // Let the base class try to handle the message
        return CDialog::PreTranslateMessage(pMsg);
}
```

Message Maps

Message maps are essentially a lookup table that links a message number to a member function of a class. The message map is implemented as an array of message numbers and pointers to functions that handle that message. Each derived message map is chained to its base class map, so that if the derived class doesn't handle the message, the base class can have a chance at it.

MFC handles groups of messages differently. Generally, you can assume the categories that are described in the following sections.

Windows Messages

The Windows Messages category forms the bulk of the WM_* messages, with the notable exception of those in the following categories.

Control Notification Messages

The Control Notification Messages are traditionally passed as WM_COMMAND messages from a child window to its parent window. Newer common controls use a WM_NOTIFY message, rather than the much-abused WM_COMMAND message.

These first two message classifications are handled by classes derived from CWnd. In other words, these messages are handled by classes that represent real windows.

Command Messages

Command messages are WM_COMMAND messages from menus, accelerator keys, and toolbar buttons. MFC makes special provision for these messages, by enabling them to be handled not only by window classes, but also by any class derived from `CCmdTarget`. This includes `CDocument`, `CDocTemplate`, and the `CWinApp` object as well. Most of these messages are targeted to the frame window only—there is no other window that has context information to send the message elsewhere. For example, the menu is attached only to the main frame window; there is no data attached to menu items that would enable a message to be sent to a particular type of view window. This is why MFC provides an enhanced routing mechanism; it lets you decide where a message is most appropriately handled.

The first two classifications, Windows and Control Notification Messages, are dispatched directly to their destination window, where the message map is searched for a match with the appropriate parameters of the MSG structure.

MFC routes command messages first to the active top-level child window and then back down through the MFC window/class hierarchy. Thus, for example, in the case of a view window, the view class tries to handle the message and then passes it down to the document class. If the document class can't handle the message, it passes it down to the document template, which in turn passes it to the main frame window and lastly to the application object.

To summarize this, you can assume that MFC routes messages first to the most specific class object. If that doesn't handle the message, it is then passed to the next less specific object.

Which Is the Best Class to Handle Command Messages?

You might wonder why you'd want to handle Windows messages by classes that don't have a window. I hope to explain why I think you'll find it's actually very useful to do so.

Although the traditional MDI model is apparently losing favor, I find its facility of having multiple views on a document is a good model to remember when deciding where a message should be handled—even if your application won't have multiple views or multiple documents. Let me illustrate.

In an SDI application, it often doesn't matter if a message is handled in the view or document class because there's a one-to-one correspondence between the two, and from either class you can access the other. Let's say you have a command in a word processor application that implements a Select All facility. In a simple SDI application, you could handle this command in the document class and keep the state variables that determine the selection in the `CDocument`-derived class. Because the view reflects the document, it will display the entire document as selected. However, if you consider that your application could have multiple views simultaneously displaying the document, you'll realize that you'd probably want to have different selections for both views. Therefore, your decision of where to store the selection variables, as well as how to handle the selection commands, would immediately place them as the responsibility of the view class.

On the other hand, if you had a command that changed the font of the selected text, because you'd want all views to reflect the change in the font, you would probably choose to handle the command in the document class.

These contrived examples don't present any situation that you couldn't achieve in either case. However, in real-world situations, things can get rather messy if you get the design wrong by handling a command in an inappropriate class. Therefore, I find it's best to always consider the MDI multiple-document, multiple-view situation.

What's Behind the Message Map Macros

You can think of an MFC Message Map as the equivalent of a traditional non-MFC application's message switch logic. In order to understand a little more about Message Maps, I'll explain how they are constructed.

Listing 6.15 provides an example of a message map.

LISTING 6.15   MESSAGE MAP EXAMPLE

```
BEGIN_MESSAGE_MAP(CMainFrame, CFrameWnd)
    //{{AFX_MSG_MAP(CMainFrame)
    ON_WM_CREATE()
    //}}AFX_MSG_MAP
    ON_WM_NCLBUTTONDOWN()
END_MESSAGE_MAP()
```

The map begins with the BEGIN_MESSAGE_MAP macro. If you decipher the macro, this expands to give your class the following items:

- An array named _messageEntries.
- A messageMap structure that points to this array and also the base class's messageMap structure.
- A function named GetMessageMap that returns a pointer to the messageMap structure.

`END_MESSAGE_MAP` creates a predefined end for the message map array.

In your class's header file, there's also a corresponding `DECLARE_MESSAGE_MAP` macro that declares these variables and functions.

In the main body of the message map, you can see the comment block lines shown in Listing 6.16.

LISTING 6.16 MFC COMMENT BLOCKS

```
//{{AFX_MSG_MAP(CMainFrame)
...
//}}AFX_MSG_MAP
```

These delimit the area that the Visual C++ Wizards use. You should not edit anything between these comments. If you do, you'll probably prevent ClassWizard from working.

The Visual C++ wizards are a great help most of the time, but they don't handle every eventuality. ClassWizard is there to handle the most common messages that you're likely to come across, but it doesn't know about all messages. At some point, you will likely have to add a handler that the wizard doesn't cater to. In these circumstances, you can add the appropriate entry to the message map outside the comment blocks as shown by the `ON_WM_NCLBUTTONDOWN` line in Listing 6.15.

You'll probably need to cross-check with the Visual C++ help, but there's usually a direct macro equivalent to most messages. In Listing 6.15, the `WM_NCLBUTTONDOWN` message has an `ON_WM_NCLBUTTONDOWN` macro. Where there isn't a direct macro, such as with a user-defined message number, you can use the general `ON_MESSAGE` macro—see your Visual C++ help for details.

Message Map Efficiency

In traditional Windows applications, the window procedure consisted of a large switch statement that checked each message against all the messages that the window needed to handle, and finally, if the message wasn't handled, it was passed to the `DefWindowProc` routine.

MFC does away with these protracted switch statements and introduces its more refined message-routing mechanisms. You might assume that the extra code added by MFC to do this would result in slower operation. In some circumstances, such as a trivial Windows program, that may well be the case, but in real-world complex applications, the old switch statement method is grossly inefficient because the compiler generates code that performs an `if-then-else` operation for every case statement. For an unhandled message (which is probably most messages), every test is performed every time.

In MFC's message maps, the message tests are performed in an efficient tight loop of code (which is better for processor caches). MFC also caches recent hits on the message maps so that frequent messages are routed more efficiently. This performance boost is probably most significant for the vast majority of unhandled messages.

Idle Processing

When your application has no messages to process, the `Run` function calls the `OnIdle` function. You can override this to have your application perform any background tasks.

OnIdle

`Run` passes a single value to `OnIdle`, which counts the number of times `OnIdle` has been successively called, and has little reflection on the real time your application has been idle. Each time your application processes a message, this count is reset to zero. If you need to determine the real idle time, the code example in Listing 6.17 shows how you can do this yourself.

Because `OnIdle` is intended for background task operation, you need to prevent your application from making Windows unresponsive. Therefore, you should only perform short processing tasks there. If you need to do a long operation, you should break up the task into a set of short states and do one operation on each call to `OnIdle`.

If your application needs further calls to `OnIdle`, return `TRUE` to have `OnIdle` called again (providing there are no messages pending). If your application has completed all its background tasks, return `FALSE` to relinquish processing and wait for the next message.

> **NOTE**
>
> Returning `FALSE` will not permanently stop `OnIdle` being called. As soon as your application processes all the messages in its queue, `OnIdle` will once again be called with a count of zero.

The MFC Application Object, Message Routing, and Idle Processing

CHAPTER 6

267

6

THE MFC
APPLICATION
OBJECT

The documented place to override the OnIdle function is in your CWinApp-derived class. The example in Listing 6.17 determines the real idle time in seconds and displays it along with the count value on the status bar.

LISTING 6.17   OnIdle EXAMPLE

```
BOOL CSdiApp::OnIdle(LONG lCount)
{
    static CTime StartTime;
    CTimeSpan Span;
    /* If this is the first call to OnIdle, initialize the start time
     * Otherwise, calculate the idle time
     */
    if ( lCount == 0 )
    {
        StartTime = CTime::GetCurrentTime();
    Span = 0;
    }
    else
    {
        Span = CTime::GetCurrentTime() - StartTime;
    }
    char szMsg[100];
    wsprintf( szMsg, "Idle for %d seconds,
            lCount %d", Span.GetTotalSeconds(), lCount );
    static_cast<CFrameWnd*>( AfxGetMainWnd() )->SetMessageText( szMsg );
    /* Call the default handler to run MFC debugging
     * facilities and temporary object cleanup
     */
    CWinApp::OnIdle(lCount);
    return true;
}
```

> **NOTE**
>
> It's important to call the default OnIdle handler in your OnIdle routine, as it performs debug checks (in a DEBUG build) and garbage collection of temporary MFC objects. See "About Temporary Objects" in TN003 in your Visual C++ help for details.

An interesting, largely undocumented aspect is that the default implementation of CWinApp::OnIdle calls an OnIdle function for any document templates and their documents. Although these functions aren't documented in the Visual C++ help, they are public functions and I would expect them to remain in later versions of Visual C++. You can therefore handle OnIdle not only in CWinApp, but also in your derived CDocument class.

This is a useful facility to remember if your `OnIdle` requirements are related to your document data rather than application-wide. For example, if your application is a word processor, it might be appropriate to perform background spelling and grammar checking in the `CDocument::OnIdle` handler.

In Visual C++ 6, the default `CDocument::OnIdle` does nothing, but you should still call it on the off chance that any future version of MFC could use the default behavior.

Idle Processing for Dialogs

If you look at the sample `InitInstance` for a dialog application (in Listing 6.5), you'll see that the application has effectively ended when `InitInstance` returns. This is unlike other MFC applications that normally return `TRUE` from `InitInstance` and enter the `Run` function to process messages.

Because the dialog application doesn't call `Run`, it also never benefits from the normal `OnIdle` handling. So how do you perform idle processing in a dialog application? The answer is the MFC `WM_KICKIDLE` message.

When you call a dialog's `DoModal` function, MFC no longer creates a real modal dialog box. Instead, it fakes it by disabling any main frame window, and performs its own message loop to handle the "modal" dialog box. You can find the code in the MFC source code `RunModalLoop` function. When you know about `WM_KICKIDLE`, it's easy to perform background tasks in a dialog application. All you have to do is add a handler for `WM_KICKIDLE`. You'll need to add this manually, as illustrated in Listing 6.18, because the wizards don't know about this message.

LISTING 6.18   MESSAGE MAP FOR WM_KICKIDLE

```
BEGIN_MESSAGE_MAP(CDlgAppDlg, CDialog)
    //{{AFX_MSG_MAP(CDlgAppDlg)
    ...
    //}}AFX_MSG_MAP
    ON_MESSAGE(WM_KICKIDLE, OnKickIdle)
END_MESSAGE_MAP()
```

NOTE

The `WM_KICKIDLE` message map entry is added outside of the commented wizard block code so as not to confuse ClassWizard.

6

In your dialog class's header file, add the following definition,

```
afx_msg LRESULT OnKickIdle(WPARAM, LPARAM lCount);
```

and in the source module, add the function

```
LRESULT CDlgAppDlg::OnKickIdle(WPARAM, LPARAM lCount)
{
    // Add your idle code and return TRUE or FALSE in the same way as
    ➥OnIdle
}
```

Dialog Command Updating

In a dialog application, the normal MFC command update mechanism that enables and disables menu items and toolbar buttons doesn't work—you need to add a few lines of code to make it happen.

You can do this quite easily by calling UpdateDialogControls from the WM_KICKIDLE handler:

```
LRESULT CDlgAppDlg::OnKickIdle(WPARAM, LPARAM lCount)
{
    UpdateDialogControls( this, TRUE );
    return 0;
}
```

The only other additions you need to make are to write the command handlers and add entries to the message map. The following code shows the function:

```
void CDlgAppDlg::OnUpdateCommandX(CCmdUI* pCmdUI)
{
    pCmdUI->Enable( your_expression_logic_to_enable_the_control );
}
```

To add the update command handler, modify the message map like this:

```
BEGIN_MESSAGE_MAP(CDlgAppDlg, CDialog)
    //{{AFX_MSG_MAP(CDlgAppDlg)
    ...
    //}}AFX_MSG_MAP
    ON_MESSAGE(WM_KICKIDLE, OnKickIdle)
    ON_UPDATE_COMMAND_UI( IDM_COMMANDX, OnUpdateCommandX )
END_MESSAGE_MAP()
```

If you use UpdateDialogControls with its second parameter set to TRUE, most controls on your dialog that don't have a handler routine are automatically disabled. I say "most" because MFC explicitly skips disabling controls with the following button styles:

BS_AUTOCHECKBOX

BS_AUTO3STATE

BS_AUTORADIOBUTTON

BS_GROUPBOX

I'm not aware of the reason behind this, but it seems reasonable to assume that auto check boxes and radio buttons may well be used to selectively enable and disable some of the controls on a dialog. Consequently, it's unlikely that you'd want to disable the control that enables you to select other options on your dialog.

The Splash Screen Component

If you feel the urge to express your artistic talents in the form of a splash screen, it's easy to add the code for one in your MFC application.

Although the default applications generated by AppWizard don't give you a splash screen, you can add one using the additional component and controls with Visual C++. Click Project, Add to Project, Components and Controls. Double-click the Visual C++ Components and insert the Splash Screen component.

This adds a new class module (CSplashWnd) to your project and the following lines of code. This line is added to the CMainFrame::OnCreate handler to create the splash window:

```
CSplashWnd::ShowSplashScreen(this);
```

These are added to InitInstance:

```
        CCommandLineInfo cmdInfo;
        ParseCommandLine(cmdInfo);
```

```
CSplashWnd::EnableSplashScreen(cmdInfo.m_bShowSplash);
```

This last line enables the splash screen if there are no command-line parameters that dictate otherwise.

The MFC Application Object, Message Routing, and Idle Processing

CHAPTER 6

271

6

THE MFC
APPLICATION
OBJECT

In the application's `PreTranslateMessage` handler, this code handles messages for the splash screen window so that any keyboard or mouse messages destroy the splash window.

```
if (CSplashWnd::PreTranslateAppMessage(pMsg))
    return TRUE;
```

In order to remove the splash screen window automatically, the splash window starts a timer for itself. When the timer expires, the splash window self-destructs.

That's the easy bit—now you need to create your artwork. Have fun!

Summary

In this chapter, I've tried to cover the most common aspects of the CWinApp class, application lifetime, and the message routing architecture. In doing so, I've touched on other areas, such as the document/view architecture, and passed on a few tips learned from my own experiences with MFC. When you come across problems in your own development, it's always worth remembering that the MFC source code is provided with Visual C++ so that you can delve deeper and gain a better understanding. I hope that you find this information helpful in your own MFC applications, and I encourage you to investigate the inner workings of MFC.

Documents, Views, and Applications That Use Them

PART

II

The Document/View Architecture

by K. David White

In This Chapter

CHAPTER 7

In most books on MFC and Visual C++, the document/view architecture is usually given top billing. There are reasons for this. Microsoft, in developing MFC, decided that a consistent framework was needed to encapsulate the Windows functionality. Although some might argue that the document/view architecture is really all you need to understand in order to create robust MFC applications, it is apparent to the experienced MFC developer that this is not the case. The document/view architecture is a consistent framework and provides the necessary control over MFC applications; however, it lends itself to expansion and flexibility. There are also many situations in which the doc/view architecture should be abandoned entirely. This chapter tries to unlock the doc/view framework and concentrate on using it to the best advantage.

The first section covers all the components and provides an overview of the doc/view architecture. The "Creating New Documents" section explores the means necessary to utilize the framework to create new documents. Next, the chapter explores views and how the views interact with the document and frames. After you gain an understanding of views, you'll take a look at the base of this framework, the document. With this knowledge of all the pieces, you'll look to ways to manage it above and beyond the framework. The last section of this chapter takes a quick look at other frameworks to consider.

Documents, Frames, and Views

Most senior-level developers understand how data should be managed and how it should be presented. In object-oriented presentation, a class contains member variables that are accessed through member functions. This encapsulation ensures that the class is basically responsible for itself. How then does an application that contains many classes manage the data contained within those classes in a controlled and structured manner? If you look at the problem of presenting data versus managing data, you can quickly see where the document/view architecture solves this dilemma. Let's take a closer look.

As you can easily see from Figure 7.1, the document contains the data store, and the view is a window into a certain location of that data. This store can be ultimately a database connection, a disk storage file, or some other mechanism. Later sections look at the problem of where to store data needed by a view. Simply put, however, the view is a window into the data that is stored within the document. Within this architecture, the document is responsible for exposing the necessary interfaces for the view to display the data.

7

THE DOCUMENT/VIEW ARCHITECTURE

FIGURE 7.1

A simple represen-tation of the document/view architecture.

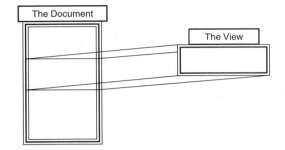

The doc/view architecture comes in two primary flavors: the Single Document Interface (SDI) and the Multiple Document Interface (MDI). An SDI application contains one and only one document class with which to control the data. The MDI application can contain any number of documents. You will notice from Figure 7.2 that the documents are created through a document template class.

FIGURE 7.2

Document types within the doc/view architecture.

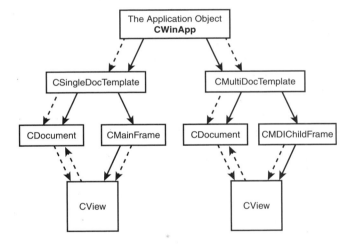

The solid dark lines in Figure 7.2 represent the instantiation path for creating views, and the dotted lines represent the pointer direction. Now that you've seen how this picture is painted, let's start looking at each individual piece of the puzzle.

NOTE

There are many different document classes, which are usually derived from the base class CDocument. For instance, if you are using COM and want compound document support, you might want to choose the COleDocument class.

NOTE

As Chapter 27, "MAPI and MFC," points out, the CDocument class also provides the necessary structure to support the Microsoft Messaging Application Program Interface (MAPI). This is done through the two CDocument member functions: OnFileSendMail and OnUpdateFileSendMail.

Document Templates

Imagine, if you will, trying to manage all the necessary information about data without the different classes to define the structure of the data. But what about relating the data contained within the document with the necessary display constraints defined by a view? Some overhead mechanism is needed to keep track of the document and its relation to the views that it owns. Enter the document template.

The document template class defines all the menus, accelerators, and other important resources that a view requires. This template mechanism loosely ties the document class with the view class.

As Figure 7.2 shows, the CWinApp class creates and contains a pointer to one or more document templates, depending on whether the application is an SDI or MDI application. CSingleDocTemplate is responsible for managing one and only one CDocument class. CMultiDocTemplate maintains a list of CDocument classes that are currently opened from that template. MFC breaks the object-oriented paradigm (only a little bit) here by allowing the CDocument class and the CDocTemplate classes to be *friends*. The CDocument contains a back pointer to its owning CDocTemplate class. This allows an application to traverse the CWinApp/CDocument/CView hierarchy in either direction.

Whenever the CWinApp class creates a document template, it does so in a two-step process. It first instantiates the DocTemplate class and then performs an AddDocument to add the document to the template's list and sets the back pointer. Listing 7.1 shows the CSingleDocTemplate constructor, and Listing 7.2 shows the AddDocument method.

Notice that the back pointer is set during the `AddDocument` method. One reason that it is done this way is to enable the user to create templates and specify document types outside what the framework automatically provides. Listing 7.3 is from the SDI sample UNL_Single.

LISTING 7.1 THE `CSingleDocTemplate` CONSTRUCTOR

```
CSingleDocTemplate::CSingleDocTemplate(UINT nIDResource,
    CRuntimeClass* pDocClass, CRuntimeClass* pFrameClass,
    CRuntimeClass* pViewClass)
    : CDocTemplate(nIDResource, pDocClass, pFrameClass, pViewClass)
{
    m_pOnlyDoc = NULL;
}
```

LISTING 7.2 THE `CSingleDocTemplate` `AddDocument` METHOD

```
void CSingleDocTemplate::AddDocument(CDocument* pDoc)
{
    ASSERT(m_pOnlyDoc == NULL);       // one at a time, please
    ASSERT_VALID(pDoc);

    CDocTemplate::AddDocument(pDoc);
    m_pOnlyDoc = pDoc;
}
```

LISTING 7.3 THE UNL_SINGLE.CPP `InitInstance` ROUTINE

```
CSingleDocTemplate* pDocTemplate;
pDocTemplate = new CSingleDocTemplate(
    IDR_MAINFRAME,
    RUNTIME_CLASS(CUNL_SingleDoc),
    RUNTIME_CLASS(CMainFrame),          // main SDI frame window
        RUNTIME_CLASS(CUNL_SingleView));
    AddDocTemplate(pDocTemplate);
```

The sample application, UNL_Single, is a fairly simple application that is used to represent the doc/view framework. Notice the creation of a single document template and the use of the `AddDocTemplate` method. In this snippet of code, you see that the framework is adding a single template that is defined by a document class, a view class, and something I haven't discussed yet.

> **NOTE**
>
> The RUNTIME_CLASS macro returns a pointer to the CRuntimeClass class. The CRuntimeClass class defines runtime attributes for the class, allowing certain information to be obtained by the owning application. Information such as object size, name, base class, and other pertinent details is stored in the CRuntimeClass class.

I have discussed the view and that the view is a way to visualize the data stored in the document, but in the Windows environment, the view must sit inside a Windows container. The CMainFrame class is that container. The menus, sidebars, and window control mechanisms are all part of the frame. As discussed earlier, the DocTemplate sets up the information that applies to the views, and it does so through the frame.

The separation of the frame components and view into two different mechanisms makes the application framework flexible. This framework puts the code functionality into three distinct areas, which allows each area to be expanded to meet the need of the application. If the view had to worry about the frame specifics, for example, each view would carry around its own framework, which would make it quite cumbersome to understand and maintain.

> **NOTE**
>
> Be sure to refer to the Developer Studio online help for additional information regarding other document template classes, methods, and attributes. The online help is quite good in this area.

Creating New Documents

Let's take a closer look at what really happens when new documents are created.

I discussed the fact that the DocTemplates do a lot of work in creating and managing the doc/view architecture, but what manages the DocTemplates? Every application contains a derivative of the CWinApp class. Listing 7.3 illustrates the creation of the DocTemplate for this application, and it resides in the InitInstance method of CUNL_SingleApp, which is derived from CWinApp.

Every MFC application generated by the AppWizard will create the CWinApp class for the user. In most MFC applications, the derived CWinApp class will handle the File, Open and the File, New commands from the menu. The framework doesn't have to worry about opening and managing files. Rather, file management is now carried out through the DocTemplates. Remember, CWinApp is derived from CCmdTarget, which allows it to process messages and events such as those presented through an applications menu. Therefore, it passes the event messages from File, Open and File, New through to the DocTemplates.

If you were to peruse AFXWIN.H, you would notice that CWinApp does not really contain the list of document templates, or does it? Look closely! It contains a pointer to the CDocManager, which is an undocumented feature that creates the binding between the CWinApp and the document templates. Check out Listing 7.4.

LISTING 7.4   THE CDocManager DECLARATION (FROM **AFXWIN.H**)

```
/////////////////////////////////////////////////////////////////
// CDocManager

class CDocManager : public CObject
{
    DECLARE_DYNAMIC(CDocManager)
public:

// Constructor
    CDocManager();

    //Document functions
    virtual void AddDocTemplate(CDocTemplate* pTemplate);
    virtual POSITION GetFirstDocTemplatePosition() const;
    virtual CDocTemplate* GetNextDocTemplate(POSITION& pos) const;
    virtual void RegisterShellFileTypes(BOOL bCompat);
    void UnregisterShellFileTypes();
    virtual CDocument* OpenDocumentFile(LPCTSTR lpszFileName);
    // open named file
    virtual BOOL SaveAllModified(); // save before exit
    virtual void CloseAllDocuments(BOOL bEndSession);
    // close documents before exiting
    virtual int GetOpenDocumentCount();

    // helper for standard commdlg dialogs
    virtual BOOL DoPromptFileName(CString& fileName, UINT nIDSTitle,
            DWORD lFlags, BOOL bOpenFileDialog,
            ➥CDocTemplate* pTemplate);

//Commands
    // Advanced: process async DDE request
    virtual BOOL OnDDECommand(LPTSTR lpszCommand);
    virtual void OnFileNew();
    virtual void OnFileOpen();
```

continues

LISTING 7.4 CONTINUED

```
// Implementation
protected:
    CPtrList m_templateList;
    int GetDocumentCount(); // helper to count number
                            // of total documents

public:
    static CPtrList* pStaticList; // for static CDocTemplate objects
    static BOOL bStaticInit;      // TRUE during static initialization
    static CDocManager* pStaticDocManager;  // for static
                                            // CDocTemplate objects

public:
    virtual ~CDocManager();
#ifdef _DEBUG
    virtual void AssertValid() const;
    virtual void Dump(CDumpContext& dc) const;
#endif
};
```

The line CPtrList m_templateList; contains a declaration of a CPtrList that defines the list of document templates. If you look closely, you will notice that the implementation declarations for the DocManager contain many of the same routines that the CWinApp does. These functions used to reside in CWinApp, but CWinApp now calls these functions through its pointer to the DocManager. In the MDI sample app, you'll take a look at what the DocManager provides.

Opening New Files

The OnFileNew that CWinApp contains is actually passed through to the DocManager's OnFileNew. OnFileNew creates a new document template. It does so through the CDocTemplate->OpenDocumentFile() routine.

> **NOTE**
>
> If more than one document template exists in CDocManager's m_templateList member variable, a system dialog is presented to the user to select the appropriate template. This dialog, the CNewTypeDlg, is a simple list box that shows the available templates from which to choose. Later in this chapter, you will see how to override this feature and provide your own File, New or File, Open dialog. This will also be discussed in Chapter 21, "File I/O and MFC."

So how do the CDocTemplate classes go about creating new documents, frames, and views? If you look closely at CDocTemplate, you see that there are two functions that do this: CreateNewDocument() and CreateNewFrame(). But what about the views? And what do these functions actually do? Listing 7.5 is from DOCTEMPL.CPP, which is part of the MFC source code. The line

```
CDocument* pDocument = (CDocument*)m_pDocClass->CreateObject();
```

does a CreateObject from the RUNTIME_CLASS CDocument. What this is doing is creating an object at runtime defined by the CDocument class. The line AddDocument(pDocument); is the AddDocument call that will add the document to the list. The CreateNewFrame is similar in what it does, by creating an object based on the CFrameWnd class defined by the application.

LISTING 7.5 DOCUMENT AND FRAME CREATION (FROM **DOCTEMPL.CPP**)

```
CDocument* CDocTemplate::CreateNewDocument()
{
    // default implementation constructs one from CRuntimeClass
    if (m_pDocClass == NULL)
    {
        TRACE0("Error: you must override
        ➥CDocTemplate::CreateNewDocument.\n");
        ASSERT(FALSE);
        return NULL;
    }
    CDocument* pDocument = (CDocument*)m_pDocClass->CreateObject();
    if (pDocument == NULL)
    {
        TRACE1("Warning: Dynamic create of document type %hs failed.\n",
            m_pDocClass->m_lpszClassName);
        return NULL;
    }
    ASSERT_KINDOF(CDocument, pDocument);
    AddDocument(pDocument);
    return pDocument;
}

/////////////////////////////////////////////////////////////////////
// Default frame creation

CFrameWnd* CDocTemplate::CreateNewFrame(CDocument* pDoc,
➥CFrameWnd* pOther)
{
    if (pDoc != NULL)
        ASSERT_VALID(pDoc);
    // create a frame wired to the specified document

    ASSERT(m_nIDResource != 0); // must have a resource ID
                                // to load from
```

continues

LISTING 7.5   CONTINUED

```
    CCreateContext context;
    context.m_pCurrentFrame = pOther;
    context.m_pCurrentDoc = pDoc;
    context.m_pNewViewClass = m_pViewClass;
    context.m_pNewDocTemplate = this;

    if (m_pFrameClass == NULL)
    {
        TRACE0("Error: you must override
        ➥CDocTemplate::CreateNewFrame.\n");
        ASSERT(FALSE);
        return NULL;
    }
    CFrameWnd* pFrame = (CFrameWnd*)m_pFrameClass->CreateObject();
    if (pFrame == NULL)
    {
        TRACE1("Warning: Dynamic create of frame %hs failed.\n",
            m_pFrameClass->m_lpszClassName);
        return NULL;
    }
    ASSERT_KINDOF(CFrameWnd, pFrame);

    if (context.m_pNewViewClass == NULL)
        TRACE0("Warning: creating frame with no default view.\n");

    // create new from resource
    if (!pFrame->LoadFrame(m_nIDResource,
        WS_OVERLAPPEDWINDOW | FWS_ADDTOTITLE,
        // default frame styles
            NULL, &context))
    {
        TRACE0("Warning: CDocTemplate couldn't create a frame.\n");
        // frame will be deleted in PostNcDestroy cleanup
        return NULL;
    }

    // it worked !
    return pFrame;
}
```

Single Versus Multiple Document Templates

You've looked at the CDocManager and its relationship to the Document class and the document templates. You've also taken a look at some internals to get an idea of how things start fitting together. Now let's look on the practical side of things. I've talked a little about document templates, but I really haven't looked at the differences between single and multiple document template interfaces.

You know that a CSingleDocTemplate basically defines the application as having one document, which can have more than one view associated with it. Switching views in an SDI requires a little bit of work. The next section takes a look at what takes place when you switch views in an SDI.

You also know that the CMultiDocTemplate contains many document types for the application, each having one or more views associated with it. But what does that really do for you? Well, if you have multiple documents, even if the individual documents possibly represent the same data, you have the ability to have multiple views active at the same time. The SDI interface doesn't give you that ability.

Also, the last section takes a quick look at why you might want to have an MDI application with the same document type and why you might have to control it a little differently.

Views

By now you should have an understanding of what a document is and how the CWinApp and DocTemplates interact with the CFrameWnd classes to create a framework for working with views. I haven't talked about any specifics with views up to this point. I would like to take the next few subsections and discuss the different view types and what sets them apart. When you have that, you will see what it takes to move around the views inside an SDI application and what really happens when a new view is pulled up in an MDI application.

The CView Class

Because all MFC classes somehow derive from CObject, all view classes are derived from the CView class. The CView class provides the necessary functional elements that each view must use to function properly. Most importantly, any view class derived from CView must implement an OnDraw function to render itself.

> **TIP**
>
> The CView class is defined in AFXWIN.H. If you have the time, take a quick look at what it provides. Understanding CView will take you a long way toward understanding all the view classes.

The `CScrollView` Class

One `CView`-derived view that MFC provides is the `CScrollView` class. This class allows a view to scroll the data provided by the document automatically, or what appears to be automatically. If the data or object to be rendered is somewhat bigger than a normal viewport, a `CScrollView` should be used. This view adds scrolling regions, controllable by scrollbars on the frame, to the view area.

This view implementation solves a multitude of problems. There is, however, work that has to be done. The view must know where the scrollbars are in relation to the viewing region, and the scroll mechanism must know the size of the complete view.

`SetScrollSizes()` is the method used to define the size of the document to render. `SetScrollSizes()` requires a mapping mode, which is defined in Table 7.1. The second argument is the total size of the scroll view. The third argument is the horizontal and vertical amounts to scroll in each direction in response to a mouse click on the scrollbar. The fourth argument is the horizontal and vertical amounts to scroll in each direction in response to a mouse click on the scroll arrow. The horizontal and vertical sizes, or amounts, are defined by a `SIZE` structure.

TABLE 7.1   `CScrollView` MAPPING MODES

Mapping Mode	Logical Unit
MM_TEXT	1 pixel
MM_HIMETRIC	0.01 mm
MM_TWIPS	1/1440 in
MM_HIENGLISH	0.001 in
MM_LOMETRIC	0.1 mm
MM_LOENGLISH	0.01 in

The `CScrollView` responds automatically to not only the scrollbar actions, but also those of the keyboard, such as word wrap, paging, and other functions that would cause the focus to extend past the current viewing port.

To scale the viewport to the current window size, use the `SetScaleToFitSize()` method. This will appear to pop off the scrollbars, but what actually is happening is that the entire document is being scaled to fit inside the present window. This zoom capability allows documents that are only a fraction bigger than a view window to be viewed inside the window without the hindrances of scrollbars.

The `CFormView` Class

I'm sure that you are probably aware of some form-based application or dialog that contained data entry boxes to enter data into a database or spreadsheet. MFC provides a view, derived from `CView`, that provides the basic functional elements to enable the developer to create a view based on dialog resources. Essentially, the developer will create a dialog similarly to creating one for a dialog-based application. The DDX mechanisms are then tied to the `CFormView` class, and the framework takes care of rendering the dialog within the view's framework.

The Database View Classes

I've covered the `CFormView` just briefly and indicated that it can be used to create a data entry application for a database. There are views that encapsulate the database-document framework for ODBC and DAO.

A `CDaoRecordView` object is a view that displays database records in controls similar to the `CFormView`. In fact, the view is a form view! It is directly connected to a `CDaoRecordset` object. The `CDaoRecordView` automates the implementation for moving to the first, next, previous, or last record and provides an interface for updating the record currently in view. Wow! This makes short work of having to create form views and manually code the data exchange mechanisms for moving around the database.

The `CRecordView` is essentially the same mechanism, but uses the ODBC layer instead of the DAO layer.

> **NOTE**
>
> The DAO layer is the MFC classes that encapsulate the Jet database engine. The other database classes are referred through the ODBC layer. Refer to Chapter 18, "MFC Database Processing," for a discussion on DAO and ODBC.

The Control Views

There is a group of views that are essentially control containers. The views, although derived from `CView`, are nothing more than a single control contained within the frame of a single view. These are as follows:

- `CTreeView`—This view encapsulates the `CTreeCtrl` class inside the doc/view architecture.

- CEditView—This view encapsulates the CEditCtrl class inside the doc/view architecture.

- CRichEditView—This view encapsulates the CRichEditCtrl class inside the doc/view architecture.

- CListView—This view encapsulates the CListCtrl class inside the doc/view architecture.

All these classes are derived from CCtrlView, which is derived from CView. Each of these view types has a member function that will return the appropriate control for manipulation. This method of exposing the control makes life easy for developing useful applications.

Let's expand the CEditView because UNL_SingleApp contains an edit view. The CEditView breaks the framework a little here. The data that is contained within the CEditCtrl is actually contained in the control and not the document. Is that okay? Although the document is normally the place to hold data, this exception is acceptable. The control contained within the view is entirely self-contained. This makes it easy to work with as well. There is a function in CEditView called GetEditCtrl() that will return the edit control. Functions such as saving data and copying data are performed on the edit control directly.

Listing 7.6 is the header file for the UNL_Single application. Listing 7.7 is the implementation of that class. Notice that this doesn't appear much different than other view definitions. The encapsulation of the control within the view is implemented at a lower level (CCtrlView).

CAUTION

You have to be careful when working with a control view. Because the control is contained by a view, that view must be aware of the state of the control at all times! Changing certain characteristics might create unwanted results.

LISTING 7.6 THE UNL_EdView CLASS DEFINITION

```
#if !defined(AFX_UNL_EDVIEW_H__5C9EF3D1_D28B_11D2_9116
➥_00C04FBEDB74__INCLUDED_)
#define AFX_UNL_EDVIEW_H__5C9EF3D1_D28B_11D2_9116_00C04FBEDB74__INCLUDED_

#if _MSC_VER > 1000
#pragma once
#endif // _MSC_VER > 1000
// UNL_EdView.h : header file
//
```

```
//////////////////////////////////////////////////////////////////
// CUNL_EdView view

class CUNL_EdView : public CEditView
{
//  protected: // create from serialization only
public: // change from protected to public for view switching

    CUNL_EdView(); // protected constructor used by dynamic creation
    DECLARE_DYNCREATE(CUNL_EdView)

// Attributes
public:

// Operations
public:

// Overrides
    // ClassWizard generated virtual function overrides
    //{{AFX_VIRTUAL(CUNL_EdView)
    protected:
    virtual void OnDraw(CDC* pDC); // overridden to draw this view
    //}}AFX_VIRTUAL

// Implementation
protected:
    virtual ~CUNL_EdView();
#ifdef _DEBUG
    virtual void AssertValid() const;
    virtual void Dump(CDumpContext& dc) const;
#endif

    // Generated message map functions
protected:
    //{{AFX_MSG(CUNL_EdView)
        // NOTE - the ClassWizard will add and remove member
        // functions here.
    //}}AFX_MSG
    DECLARE_MESSAGE_MAP()
};

//////////////////////////////////////////////////////////////////

//{{AFX_INSERT_LOCATION}}
// Microsoft Visual C++ will insert additional declarations
// immediately before the previous line.

#endif // !defined(AFX_UNL_EDVIEW_H__5C9EF3D1_D28B_11D2_9116
➥_00C04FBEDB74__INCLUDED_)
```

LISTING 7.7   THE UNL_EdView CLASS IMPLEMENTATION

```cpp
// UNL_EdView.cpp : implementation file
//

#include "stdafx.h"

#include "UNL_SingleDoc.h"

#include "UNL_Single.h"
#include "UNL_EdView.h"

#ifdef _DEBUG
#define new DEBUG_NEW
#undef THIS_FILE
static char THIS_FILE[] = __FILE__;
#endif

/////////////////////////////////////////////////////////////
// CUNL_EdView

IMPLEMENT_DYNCREATE(CUNL_EdView, CEditView)

CUNL_EdView::CUNL_EdView()
{
}

CUNL_EdView::~CUNL_EdView()
{
}


BEGIN_MESSAGE_MAP(CUNL_EdView, CEditView)
    //{{AFX_MSG_MAP(CUNL_EdView)
        // NOTE - the ClassWizard will add and remove
        // mapping macros here.
    //}}AFX_MSG_MAP
END_MESSAGE_MAP()

/////////////////////////////////////////////////////////////
// CUNL_EdView drawing

void CUNL_EdView::OnDraw(CDC* pDC)
{
}

/////////////////////////////////////////////////////////////
// CUNL_EdView diagnostics

#ifdef _DEBUG
void CUNL_EdView::AssertValid() const
```

```
{
    CEditView::AssertValid();
}

void CUNL_EdView::Dump(CDumpContext& dc) const
{
    CEditView::Dump(dc);
}
#endif //_DEBUG

/////////////////////////////////////////////////////////////
// CUNL_EdView message handlers
```

Changing Views in an SDI

If you are familiar with the MDI interface, you are probably painfully aware of the complications that you can get into managing multiple documents. The framework goes a long way in solving this dilemma, but let's face it—the MDI framework is not the prettiest to look at or the easiest to use (from a user's perspective). Most users prefer a single view to work in, and if they want to change views, they can do so through a menu or accelerator keys.

Suppose that you have a text editor or a view that represents ASCII data. In addition, though, imagine you also need another view that allows the user to enter information via a form. The sample program represented by the MDI has a CFormView-based view that enables users to enter strings in a list. The Format button will take the list of strings and write them to a comma-delimited file. Although this is a functional element of many database utility programs, it is somewhat overrepresented by the MDI. There are other situations in which you might want to consider implementing an SDI.

Let's take a close look at what you have to do to enable view switching within your SDI. The following numbered subsections outline the functional steps that need to be performed to do the view switching:

- Adding a second (or other) view class—The first step is obviously to define another view to switch to. Remember that this view is essentially owned by a single document.

- Modifying the frame class—Now you need to insert the switching code to either the frame class or the view class. Remember that you have only one frame class and more than one view. For the sake of simplifying the code, you will do this from the frame class.

- Implementing the switching code—Now that you've modified the header to add the new function, it's time to write the code to switch the views.

- Telling the document about its new view—After you have switched your views, you need to set the appropriate pointers into the document class.

- Defining the resources to allow the switching messages—Without a way to exercise your switching code, the application is not useful to the user.

Step 1: Adding Another View

The first step in expanding the restraints of an SDI application is to add a desired view. This view can be a control-based view, a form view, or a simple view for drawing purposes. You can let your mind go wild with the expansion possibilities. To add this view, you can use the ClassWizard to create the view. If it's a form view that you are adding, you would use the resource editor to define the view's dialog.

Step 2: Modifying the Frame Class

Because you know that the frame class does most of the work in drawing views and managing view characteristics, it makes perfect sense to manage the view switching inside the frame class. Take a look at Listing 7.8.

LISTING 7.8   THE MainFrm CLASS DEFINITION

```
// MainFrm.h : interface of the CMainFrame class
//
/////////////////////////////////////////////////////////////////////

#if !defined(AFX_MAINFRM_H__9442E449_C853_11D2_9113
➥ _00C04FBEDB74__INCLUDED_)
#define AFX_MAINFRM_H__9442E449_C853_11D2_9113_00C04FBEDB74__INCLUDED_

#if _MSC_VER > 1000
#pragma once
#endif // _MSC_VER > 1000

class CMainFrame : public CFrameWnd
{

protected: // create from serialization only
    CMainFrame();
    DECLARE_DYNCREATE(CMainFrame)

// Attributes
public:

// Operations
public:

// Overrides
```

```
    // ClassWizard generated virtual function overrides
    //{{AFX_VIRTUAL(CMainFrame)
    virtual BOOL PreCreateWindow(CREATESTRUCT& cs);
    //}}AFX_VIRTUAL

// Implementation
public:
    virtual ~CMainFrame();
#ifdef _DEBUG
    virtual void AssertValid() const;
    virtual void Dump(CDumpContext& dc) const;
#endif

protected:   // control bar embedded members
    CStatusBar   m_wndStatusBar;
    CToolBar     m_wndToolBar;

// Generated message map functions
protected:
    //{{AFX_MSG(CMainFrame)
    afx_msg int OnCreate(LPCREATESTRUCT lpCreateStruct);
    afx_msg void SwitchViews();
    //}}AFX_MSG
    DECLARE_MESSAGE_MAP()

public:

    int      m_nCurrentView;
};

//////////////////////////////////////////////////////////////////////

//{{AFX_INSERT_LOCATION}}
// Microsoft Visual C++ will insert additional declarations
// immediately before the previous line.

#endif // !defined(AFX_MAINFRM_H__9442E449_C853_11D2_9113
       // _00C04FBEDB74__INCLUDED_)
```

Notice the declaration of the SwitchViews method and the m_nCurrentView member
variable. (More about these later.) This is basically all you have to do to modify the Main
Frame declaration. These are discussed in the next section.

Step 3: Implementing the View-Switching Code

Now that you've defined the functions that need to be implemented, take a look at the
implementation shown in Listing 7.9.

7

**THE
DOCUMENT/VIEW
ARCHITECTURE**

LISTING 7.9   THE SwitchViews METHOD

```
BEGIN_MESSAGE_MAP(CMainFrame, CFrameWnd)
    //{{AFX_MSG_MAP(CMainFrame)
    ON_WM_CREATE()
    ON_COMMAND(ID_VIEW_SWITCHVIEWS, SwitchViews)
    //}}AFX_MSG_MAP
END_MESSAGE_MAP()
```

```
01:    /////////////////////////////////////////////////////////////
02:    // CMainFrame message handlers
03:
04:    void CMainFrame::SwitchViews()
05:    {
06:        CDocument*    pDoc = GetActiveDocument();
07:
08:        CView* pCurrView = GetActiveView(); // save old view
09:        CView* pNewView;
10:
11:        if (m_nCurrentView == 0)
12:          {
13:              pNewView = (CView*)new CUNL_SingleView;
14:              m_nCurrentView = 1;
15:          }
16:        else
17:          {
18:              pNewView = (CView*)new CUNL_EdView;
19:              m_nCurrentView = 0;
20:          }
21:
22:
23:        pNewView->Create(    NULL,
24:                             NULL,
25:                             AFX_WS_DEFAULT_VIEW,
26:                             rectDefault,
27:                             this,
28:                             AFX_IDW_PANE_FIRST,
29:                             NULL    );
30:
31:
32:
33:        pNewView->OnInitialUpdate();
34:
35:        pNewView->ShowWindow(SW_SHOW); // show it..
36:        pCurrView->ShowWindow(SW_HIDE); // don't forget to hide
           ➥our current (old) view
37:
38:        pDoc->AddView(pNewView);
39:        pDoc->RemoveView(pCurrView);
```

```
40:
41:            SetActiveView(pNewView); // let's go with it..
42:
43:        RecalcLayout();
44:
45:    }
```

Notice line 6. To enable step 4 to be successful, you have to have a pointer to an owning document. To switch views, you have to maintain a pointer to your current view and also one to the new one you are switching to. The m_nCurrentView member variable keeps track of which view you are using. There are other methods for maintaining this count, but you are interested in the view-switching steps themselves. Depending on which view you have active, you have to create the other view by using the Create method. After the Create is performed, you do an OnInitialUpdate on the view to perform any initialization that might be specific to the view's first rendering. You then have to show your new view and hide your old view.

Step 4: Updating the Document

Lines 38–41 perform the update to the necessary pointers to the document. You first Add the new view to the document and then Remove the old view. You then activate the new view. See how simple this is!

Step 5: Defining the Resources You Need

When you are done with the code, you are almost there. You now have to figure a way to activate the switching code. This is most often done through the menu resource, as in the UNL_Single application. Notice the Switch Views menu command on the View menu. Notice the message map declared in Listing 7.9 before the line-numbered section. This map defines the DDX/DDV command map. Notice the ON_COMMAND for the SwitchViews method. Whenever the menu command is selected, the SwitchViews method is activated. Congratulations—you now have a switching-view SDI application!

Using the MDI

I've been discussing primarily the SDI, but a truly robust application would have to manipulate many forms of data to be productive. One way to do this would be to create an MDI application. With the advancing popularity of COM, many functions that were performed by single MDI applications are now being handled through a variety of functions. Indeed, you might have already noticed the decreasing popularity of some midsize applications. However, if you are saddled with creating a large desktop application, you will need to understand the MDI.

With an MDI, the framework essentially creates a list of document templates. Every time the `AddDocTemplate` function is called, a template is added to a linked list of templates. (You should be seeing the flexibility here!) With a linked list of templates, each having the possibility of having multiple views, you can quickly see that data can be represented in a multitude of ways.

An SDI application creates a `CFrameWnd` instance, usually in `MainFrm.cpp`. An MDI application, on the other hand, creates a `CMDIFrameWnd` instance. As part of this construct, the `CMDIFrameWnd` contains a child window frame for each document template. This is defined by deriving from `CMDIChildWnd`. This allows the application to have multiple viewing frames contained within the main frame window.

Take a look at the UNL_MultiEd sample application. Notice the frame windows that are associated with each document template type. To handle command messages, these frame windows contain overridden message handlers that are applied for each menu or toolbar command.

> **NOTE**
>
> I normally make it a point to create a menu for each document type (child frame) and then override all possible commands. This saves confusion in the long run and makes the application easier to maintain. This, however, is just one way to handle messages for the application. You can choose to have the main frame window process the messages and maintain a single menu for all child frames. If you do this, don't forget that you need to keep track of which document/view component is active.

Finding a Document Template

Some applications require that you override the framework's automatic creation of a view at startup. The framework creates an `InitInstance` method of the derived `CWinApp` class that will automatically display the child frame window that was created as part of the initial framework. This arrangement is depicted in Listing 7.10.

LISTING 7.10 THE STANDARD `CWinApp::InitInstance`

```
// Parse command line for standard shell commands, DDE, file open
CCommandLineInfo cmdInfo;
ParseCommandLine(cmdInfo);

// Dispatch commands specified on the command line
if (!ProcessShellCommand(cmdInfo))
    return FALSE;
```

```
// The main window has been initialized, so show and update it.
pMainFrame->ShowWindow(m_nCmdShow);
pMainFrame->UpdateWindow();

return TRUE;
```

However, if you define multiple documents, and you want to control how these are created (or opened), Listing 7.11 is a portion of what you need to do.

LISTING 7.11   REMOVING THE AUTOMATIC FRAME STARTUP

```
// Parse command line for standard shell commands, DDE, file open
CCommandLineInfo cmdInfo;
ParseCommandLine(cmdInfo);

if (CCommandLineInfo::FileNew == cmdInfo.m_nShellCommand)
    cmdInfo.m_nShellCommand = CCommandLineInfo::FileNothing;

if (!ProcessShellCommand(cmdInfo)) return FALSE;

// Dispatch commands specified on the command line
if (!ProcessShellCommand(cmdInfo))
    return FALSE;

// The main window has been initialized, so show and update it.
pMainFrame->ShowWindow(m_nCmdShow);
pMainFrame->UpdateWindow();

return TRUE;
```

Essentially, you are telling the framework, through `CCommandLineInfo::FileNothing`,
that you will be handling the frame opening through `FileNew` and `FileOpen` methods in
the main frame.

When you have this portion of code in, you need to create a `FileNew` command message
handler to open the document you want. MFC provides a default `FileNew` dialog that will
display the registered templates and provide a selection list to the user. The user can then
select the document type with which to open. This is fine if you think your user will be
able to understand what document types are and how they are applied to what he or she
is doing. In most cases, the application developer wants to develop the application in
such a manner as to control what the user sees and how he or she works. The MDI
framework is so flexible that a myriad of options is available to the developer. In some
cases, the developer might want only one document type to be opened, and that document type is essentially the controlling document for all other documents. In some cases,

the developer might want to create a unique `OnFileNew` dialog that displays the document type in a more "readable" fashion. Either way, it is imperative that the developer understand how to find a document template.

Listing 7.12 is the `OnFileNew` handler for the UNL_MultiEd sample application. Notice the line `POSITION curTemplatePos = pApp->GetFirstDocTemplatePosition();`. This is essentially positioning to the front of the linked list of document templates. The application object maintains this list. From that point, you iterate the list to find the document template you need. Notice the line `if(str == _T("StringForm"))`. The document template maintains a "describing" string you can use to search for templates that meet your criteria.

LISTING 7.12   THE `OnFileNew` HANDLER (TYPICAL)

```
void CMainFrame::OnFileNew()
{
    //
    // First get our app, and then position to the first
    // template.  Iterate your templates, until you find
    // the desired one.
    //
        CUNL_MultiEdApp* pApp = (CUNL_MultiEdApp*)AfxGetApp();

    POSITION curTemplatePos = pApp->GetFirstDocTemplatePosition();

    while(curTemplatePos != NULL)
    {
        CDocTemplate* curTemplate =
            pApp->GetNextDocTemplate(curTemplatePos);
        CString str;
        curTemplate->GetDocString(str, CDocTemplate::docName);
        if(str == _T("StringForm"))
        {
                CStringDoc* pCSDoc;
            pCSDoc = (CStringDoc*)curTemplate->OpenDocumentFile(NULL);
            return;
        }
    }
    AfxMessageBox("Why are we here ??");
}
```

Managing Data in MDI Applications

Although most developers start out by managing the applications data inside the document, this shouldn't be a limiting factor. There is no constraint inside MFC that dictates that the developer must represent all application data inside a `CDocument` class. In fact, in the case of the UNL_MultiEd application, I broke with tradition and created a global `StringKeeper` class mechanism to manage the application's data. If you maintain a pointer to the class instance inside the application object, the data is only an `AfxGetApp` call away.

In some cases, this example might need to be expanded, depending on the application's requirements. For example, on one project that I worked on a few years back, the application represented a design process in which one phase relied on information from a previous phase. The phases were uniquely different from one another, thus requiring an MDI architecture. To manage the data, a global keeper class was created to manage the context of the data that was shared between phases. Because the data was maintained in a database, this keeper class managed the transition and context between phases. The point here is that a developer should not be limited to the framework. Make it work for you!

Summary

You've just taken a whirlwind tour of a fairly robust architecture. You know that not all applications are created equal. Some applications maintain a fairly simple user interface and can be represented by a single document. Other applications require a more flexible approach in being able to represent many forms of different data in the same application. MFC, by providing the document/view architecture, gives the developer a starting point for creating truly robust applications. The application developer can choose to stay within the framework and create solid applications with a minimal level of difficulty. He or she might also choose to create a truly flexible application by expanding the framework. At this point, the developer is armed with enough information to actively consider many possible choices when designing user interface applications.

Extending the User Interface

by Michael Morrison

IN THIS CHAPTER

You've learned a fair amount about user interfaces up to this point in the book. However, you haven't really looked into how to extend user interfaces and support modern features such as floating pop-up menus, control bars, and wizards. Users have come to expect flexible and intuitive user interfaces, and it's your job to give them what they want. Fortunately, MFC includes plenty of support for building rich user interfaces without too much suffering on the part of the MFC programmer.

Indeed, supporting modern user interface features in your own applications is very straightforward thanks to MFC. This chapter shows you how to extend user interfaces and examines the MFC classes that make it possible to support these types of features.

Responding to the User

Before you get into the different ways to extend user interfaces with GUI elements, let's take a moment to examine user input and how it is handled with MFC. This is important because you can greatly improve the feel of an application simply through the handling of the keyboard and mouse. Keyboard and mouse handling begins with a special set of messages that are sent when the user presses or releases a key on the keyboard, moves the mouse, or clicks a mouse button.

Handling keyboard and mouse messages is as simple as determining the specific messages you want to handle and then creating the appropriate message handlers for them. Win32 supports a variety of different keyboard and mouse messages, so it's important to make sure you are handling the proper messages to achieve your desired functionality.

Keyboard Messaging

When you press a key in a Windows application, Windows generates a keyboard message. This message is sent to the application whose main frame window has keyboard focus. The application then handles the message and does whatever it needs to do with the keystroke information. In the case of a word processor, the application might store away a character based on the key press and draw the character on the screen.

Because internationalized applications must be capable of handling multiple languages, keyboard messages aren't directly associated with specific characters on the keyboard. Instead, the Win32 API defines virtual key codes that are mapped to each key on the keyboard. Virtual key codes serve as device-independent identifiers for keys on the keyboard. Applications always interpret keystrokes as virtual key codes instead of raw characters. Following are some examples of virtual key codes defined in the Win32 API:

- VK_A
- VK_B

- VK_C
- VK_F1
- VK_F2
- VK_RETURN
- VK_DELETE

The routing of keyboard messages is based on which window has keyboard focus, which is a specific type of input focus. Input focus is a temporary property that only one window at a time is capable of having. Input focus is associated with the currently active window, which is often identifiable by a highlighted caption bar, dialog frame, or caption text, depending on the type of window. Although input focus plays an important role in determining where keyboard messages are sent, it doesn't tell the whole story.

Keyboard focus determines when a window actually receives keyboard messages. Keyboard focus is a more specific type of input focus that requires that a window not be minimized. For example, a minimized word processor shouldn't accept keyboard input because you can't see what you're typing. Minimized applications don't receive keyboard messages because they don't have keyboard focus.

Each time you press and release a key in Windows, a keyboard message is generated. In fact, an individual message is generated both for the key press and the key release. Table 8.1 lists the Win32 messages associated with keystrokes, along with the MFC message handlers for each.

TABLE 8.1   WIN32 KEYSTROKE MESSAGES AND THEIR MFC MESSAGE HANDLERS

Message	Message Handler
WM_KEYDOWN	OnKeyDown()
WM_KEYUP	OnKeyUp()
WM_CHAR	OnChar()
WM_SYSKEYDOWN	OnSysKeyDown()
WM_SYSKEYUP	OnSysKeyUp()

The WM_KEYDOWN and WM_KEYUP messages are used to process the vast majority of keystrokes. The WM_CHAR message is similar to the WM_KEYDOWN message, except it contains a translated character associated with the key press. The WM_CHAR message is sent after a WM_KEYDOWN and WM_KEYUP message combination. The WM_SYSKEYDOWN and WM_SYSKEYUP messages are sent in response to system keystrokes such as key combinations involving the Alt key. All the keyboard messages except WM_CHAR are sent in "key down"/"key up" pairs. However, when a key is held down and the typematic repeat for the keyboard kicks in, Windows sends a series of "key down" messages followed by a single "key up" message when the key is released.

> **NOTE**
>
> Windows automatically handles system keystrokes such as using the Alt key to access menus. It is rare that you would want to handle system keystrokes in an application. Windows also automatically handles keyboard accelerators, which are used as shortcuts to invoke some menu commands.

The `OnKeyDown()` message handler is relatively straightforward—it accepts a few parameters that contain information about the key press. Its declaration follows:

```
afx_msg void OnKeyDown(UINT nChar, UINT nRepCnt, UINT nFlags);
```

All the keyboard message handlers accept these same parameters. The `nChar` parameter specifies the virtual-key code of the key being pressed. The `nRepCnt` parameter specifies the repeat count, which applies if a key is being held down and the typematic repeat function of the keyboard is invoked. Finally, the `nFlags` parameter specifies additional information such as whether the Alt key was down when the key was pressed.

Handling Keyboard Messages

To handle keyboard messages, you must add a message map entry for each message handler you want to use. For example, the following message map entry is required to handle the `WM_KEYDOWN` message using the `OnKeyDown()` message handler:

```
ON_WM_KEYDOWN()
```

One interesting way to experiment with handling keyboard messages is to move the mouse cursor in response to the user pressing the arrow keys on the keyboard. The `OnKeyDown()` message handler is the only one you need to implement to carry out this functionality. Listing 8.1 contains the source code for an `OnKeyDown()` message handler that moves the mouse cursor in response to the user pressing the arrow keys.

LISTING 8.1   AN `OnKeyDown()` MESSAGE HANDLER THAT MOVES THE MOUSE CURSOR IN RESPONSE TO THE ARROW KEYS

```
void CMainFrame::OnKeyDown(UINT nChar, UINT nRepCnt, UINT nFlags) {
  CPoint  ptCurPos;
```

```
  // Calculate new cursor position based on key press
  if (::GetCursorPos(&ptCurPos))
  {
    // Get the client area rect and convert to screen coordinates
    CRect rcClient;
    GetClientRect(&rcClient);
    ClientToScreen(&rcClient);

    switch (nChar) {
      case VK_LEFT:
        ptCurPos.x -= 5;
        if (rcClient.PtInRect(ptCurPos))
          ::SetCursorPos(ptCurPos.x, ptCurPos.y);
        break;

      case VK_RIGHT:
        ptCurPos.x += 5;
        if (rcClient.PtInRect(ptCurPos))
          ::SetCursorPos(ptCurPos.x, ptCurPos.y);
        break;

      case VK_UP:
        ptCurPos.y -= 5;
        if (rcClient.PtInRect(ptCurPos))
          ::SetCursorPos(ptCurPos.x, ptCurPos.y);
        break;

      case VK_DOWN:
        ptCurPos.y += 5;
        if (rcClient.PtInRect(ptCurPos))
          ::SetCursorPos(ptCurPos.x, ptCurPos.y);
        break;
    }
  }
}
```

The `OnKeyDown()` message handler gets the current mouse cursor position and modifies it based on the key pressed. The `nChar` parameter is used as the basis for determining which key was pressed. The four arrow keys are used to control the cursor, which explains the virtual key codes `VK_LEFT`, `VK_RIGHT`, `VK_UP`, and `VK_DOWN`. The cursor is actually moved by calling the Win32 API function `SetCursorPos()` and providing the new cursor position.

Mouse Messaging

Similar to keyboard messages, mouse messages are generated when you move the mouse or press a mouse button. Unlike keyboard messages, however, mouse messages are sent to any window that the mouse cursor passes over or that the mouse is clicked over, regardless of input focus. Every window is responsible for responding to mouse messages according to its own particular needs.

> **NOTE**
>
> Windows automatically handles many mouse functions, such as displaying menus that are clicked and altering the state of pushbuttons and check boxes that are clicked.

The mouse is represented on the screen by a mouse cursor, which typically takes the shape of an arrow. The mouse cursor has a single-pixel hotspot that pinpoints an exact location on the screen. The hotspot of the mouse cursor is significant because the position of all mouse operations is based on the hotspot. Figure 8.1 shows the hotspot location on the standard arrow mouse cursor.

FIGURE 8.1

The hotspot location on the standard arrow mouse cursor.

Mouse Cursor

Hot Spot

As an aspiring MFC guru, I'm sure you know the different ways a mouse can be used in Windows. However, it's worth clarifying exactly what constitutes each different mouse operation because different mouse messages are generated based on how the mouse is used. Following are the different operations that can be performed with a mouse in Windows:

- Clicking—Pressing and releasing a mouse button
- Double-clicking—Pressing and releasing a mouse button twice in quick succession
- Moving—Moving the mouse around without pressing any buttons
- Dragging—Moving the mouse around while holding down a button

These operations determine the kinds of mouse messages generated by Windows. Mouse messages are divided into two types: client area messages and nonclient area messages. Client area messages are by far the more commonly used of the two types, and are therefore the ones you're going to focus on. Table 8.2 lists the Win32 messages associated with the mouse, along with the MFC message handlers for each.

> **NOTE**
>
> The *client area* is the part of a window where an application displays output such as text in a word processor or graphics in a paint program. The *nonclient area*, on the other hand, includes the border, Maximize button, Minimize button, menu bar, scrollbar, title bar, and System menu.

TABLE 8.2   WIN32 MOUSE MESSAGES AND THEIR MFC MESSAGE HANDLERS

Message	Message Handler
WM_MOUSEMOVE	OnMouseMove()
WM_MOUSEACTIVATE	OnMouseActivate()
WM_MOUSEHOVER	OnMouseHover()
WM_MOUSELEAVE	OnMouseLeave()
WM_MOUSEWHEEL	OnMouseWheel()
WM_LBUTTONDOWN	OnLButtonDown()
WM_MBUTTONDOWN	OnMButtonDown()
WM_RBUTTONDOWN	OnRButtonDown()
WM_LBUTTONUP	OnLButtonUp()
WM_MBUTTONUP	OnMButtonUp()
WM_RBUTTONUP	OnRButtonUp()
WM_LBUTTONDBLCLK	OnLButtonDblClk()
WM_MBUTTONDBLCLK	OnMButtonDblClk()
WM_RBUTTONDBLCLK	OnRButtonDblClk()

8

EXTENDING THE
USER INTERFACE

The WM_MOUSEMOVE message is sent when the mouse moves over the client area of a window. The WM_MOUSEACTIVATE message is sent when the mouse is clicked over a previously inactive window, thereby activating the window. The WM_MOUSEHOVER and WM_MOUSE-LEAVE messages are sent in response to the mouse being tracked through a call to TrackMouseEvent(). The WM_MOUSEHOVER message is sent if the mouse has not moved outside of a given rectangle in a specified period of time while being tracked; you might display a ToolTip in response to this message. The WM_MOUSELEAVE message is sent when the mouse leaves the client area of a window while being tracked.

The remaining mouse messages have to do with rotating the wheel of a mouse or clicking mouse buttons. The mouse wheel is a relatively new enhancement that appears on the

Microsoft Intellimouse. Rotating the wheel of a mouse generates WM_MOUSEWHEEL messages, which contain information about how far the wheel was rotated. Most applications use the mouse wheel as an alternate means of scrolling. In other words, rotating the mouse wheel is equivalent to clicking the arrows on a scroll bar.

The WM_XBUTTONDOWN messages are sent when a mouse button is pressed within the client area of a window, whereas the WM_XBUTTONUP messages are sent when a mouse button is released. The WM_XBUTTONDBLCLK messages are sent when a mouse button is double-clicked in the client area of a window. All the button messages come in three versions that correspond to the left, right, and middle mouse buttons. Many mice don't have a middle button, in which case they aren't capable of generating middle mouse button messages.

Following is the declaration for the OnMouseMove() message handler, which indicates the parameters accepted by most of the mouse message handlers:

```
afx_msg void OnMouseMove(UINT nFlags, CPoint point);
```

The nFlags parameter indicates whether various virtual keys are down. This parameter can be any combination of the following values:

- MK_LBUTTON—Set if the left mouse button is down
- MK_MBUTTON—Set if the middle mouse button is down
- MK_RBUTTON—Set if the right mouse button is down
- MK_CONTROL—Set if the Ctrl key is down
- MK_SHIFT—Set if the Shift key is down

The other parameter, point, specifies the x and y coordinates of the mouse cursor. These coordinates indicate the specific position of the mouse cursor's hotspot, and are relative to the upper-left corner of the window the mouse is over.

Handling Mouse Messages

It is common in many graphical drawing applications to use the mouse as a drawing tool; the user moves the mouse around and clicks to draw various shapes. As a simple example of how you might use the mouse in this type of application, consider the situation where clicking the left mouse button draws an image at the current mouse cursor position. This involves handling the WM_LBUTTONDOWN message, which requires implementing the OnLButton() message handler:

```
afx_msg void  OnLButtonDown(UINT nFlags, CPoint point);
```

Following is the message map entry required to use this message handler:

```
ON_WM_LBUTTONDOWN()
```

Listing 8.2 contains the source code for an OnLButtonDown() message handler that displays an image at the current mouse cursor position.is common in many graphical drawing applications to use the mouse

LISTING 8.2 AN OnLButtonDown() MESSAGE HANDLER THAT DRAWS AN IMAGE AT THE CURRENT MOUSE CURSOR POSITION

```
void CMainFrame::OnLButtonDown(UINT nFlags, CPoint point) {
  CDC       dcMem;
  CBitmap   bm;
  CBitmap*  pbmOld;
  BITMAP    bmInfo;
  CSize     bmSize;

  // Load the bitmap
  VERIFY(bm.LoadBitmap(IDB_BITMAP));

  // Get the size of the bitmap
  bm.GetObject(sizeof(BITMAP), &bmInfo);
  bmSize.cx = bmInfo.bmWidth;
  bmSize.cy = bmInfo.bmHeight;

  // Setup the DCs
  CClientDC dc(this);
  dcMem.CreateCompatibleDC(&dc);
  VERIFY(pbmOld = dcMem.SelectObject(&bm));

  // Draw the image
  dc.BitBlt(point.x, point.y - bmInfo.bmHeight, bmSize.cx,
    bmSize.cy, &dcMem, 0, 0, SRCAND);
}
```

The OnLButtonDown() message handler first loads the bitmap using the resource identifier IDB_BITMAP, and then determines its size. The bitmap is then drawn to a device context at the position determined by the point parameter to the message handler. If you recall, this point specifies the position of the mouse cursor.is common in many graphical drawing applications to use the mouse

User Interfaces and AppWizard

Now that you have an understanding of how the keyboard and mouse are handled using MFC, you're ready to move on to some more interesting user interface topics. Perhaps the best place to start is to assess the user interface features that are included in an application generated by AppWizard. As you know, AppWizard leads you through a series of questions that determine the type of application it generates. Following are application properties that directly correspond to user interface features prompted by AppWizard questions:

- SDI, MDI, or dialog-based application window
- Toolbar
- Status bar
- Printing and print preview
- 3D controls
- Normal toolbars or Internet Explorer rebars

By simply checking the appropriate check boxes in AppWizard, you can gain these user interface features with very little work. Additionally, AppWizard provides a standard menu regardless of what options you select. This standard menu includes File, Edit, View, and Help pop-up menus, along with menu items in each that are associated with commonly used commands. For example, the View menu includes Toolbar and Status Bar menu items for showing and hiding an application's toolbar and status bar. Also, the Edit menu includes menu items for the familiar Undo, Cut, Copy, and Paste commands.

If you've used Internet Explorer, you're probably familiar with its toolbar, which is known as a *rebar*. A rebar is a control containing multiple bands that can each contain a toolbar or other control. Each band has a gripper bar that can be used to resize or reposition the band. A rebar ultimately functions in a manner similar to a traditional toolbar in that it contains buttons that act as shortcuts to menu commands. However, rebars are much more flexible and make it easier to create feature-rich toolbars.

You'll learn how the menu, toolbar, and status bar AppWizard user interface features are implemented throughout the remainder of the chapter.

Extending Menus

You typically define an application menu using a menu resource that is placed in the application's resource script. Although this approach certainly works well for defining the initial structure of a menu, in some situations you might want to alter a menu programmatically. You might even want to swap out a menu with an entirely different menu.

MFC's `CMenu` class gives you complete control over dynamically modifying menus. Following are the member functions that make this possible:

- `GetSubMenu()`—Gets a pop-up menu (submenu) within a menu
- `GetMenuItemCount()`—Gets the number of items in a menu
- `AppendMenu()`—Adds an item to the end of a menu
- `InsertMenu()`—Inserts an item at some point within a menu
- `DeleteMenu()`—Deletes a menu item
- `ModifyMenu()`—Modifies a menu item

These member functions enable you to dynamically alter a menu in just about any way you want. Before you move on to modifying a menu, however, let's take a quick look at how menus and pop-up menus are retrieved.

Obtaining Menus and Pop-up Menus

Before you can modify a menu or pop-up menu, you must create a `CMenu` object that represents an application menu. Because most applications typically already have a menu, you can obtain a `CMenu` object pointer from an application frame window instead of creating a `CMenu` object yourself. You obtain a `CMenu` object pointer from an application frame window by calling the `GetMenu()` member function on the window object, like this:

```
CMenu* pMenu = GetMenu();
```

The menu pointer obtained with `GetMenu()` is associated with the top-level menu bar, and doesn't enable direct access to pop-up menu items. Generally speaking, the majority of menu modification takes place in pop-up menus. So it is necessary to use a member function of `CMenu` to obtain a pop-up menu pointer. To get a menu pointer for a pop-up menu, you must call the `GetSubMenu()` function on the top-level menu object, like this:

```
CMenu* pFileMenu = GetMenu()->GetSubMenu(0);
```

This code gets a menu pointer to the first pop-up menu in the application menu, which is typically the File pop-up menu.

Adding Menu Items

After you obtain a `CMenu` object pointer, you are ready to use menu modification functions to dynamically alter the application menu. One of the most useful functions is `InsertMenu()`, which inserts a new menu item at a specific location within a menu. If you use the `InsertMenu()` function on a top-level menu, it will insert a new pop-up

menu. To insert a menu item to the top of a pop-up menu, you must call the
InsertMenu() member function on a submenu object:

```
pFileMenu->InsertMenu(0, MF_BYPOSITION | MF_STRING | MF_ENABLED,
  ID_FILE_CLOSE, "&Close");
```

The first parameter is an integer that has different meanings based on the flags specified
in the second parameter (see Table 8.3).

TABLE 8.3   FLAGS USED BY THE CMenu::InsertMenu() MEMBER FUNCTION

Flag	Description
MF_BYCOMMAND	Indicates that the first parameter to InsertMenu() is the menu command identifier of an existing menu item; the new menu item is inserted at this position.
MF_BYPOSITION	Indicates that the first parameter to InsertMenu() is a zero-based integer index for the menu position; the new menu item is inserted at this position.
MF_CHECKED	The menu item is initially checked.
MF_UNCHECKED	The menu item is initially unchecked.
MF_HILITE	The menu item is initially highlighted.
MF_UNHILITE	The menu item is initially unhighlighted.
MF_ENABLED	The menu item is initially enabled.
MF_DISABLED	The menu item is initially disabled.
MF_GRAYED	The menu item is initially grayed.
MF_STRING	The menu item is a normal menu item.
MF_POPUP	The menu item is a new pop-up menu.

Based on the InsertMenu() flags shown in the table, you might be able to guess that the
previous sample code adds a menu item named Close as the first item under the File pop-
up menu. The integer identifier ID_FILE_CLOSE identifies the menu item and its associated command.

If you just want to add a menu item to the end of a pop-up menu, you can use the
AppendMenu() member function, like this:

```
pHelpMenu->AppendMenu(MF_STRING | MF_ENABLED, ID_APP_ABOUT,
  "&About...");
```

Using Floating Pop-up Menus

You've no doubt used floating pop-up menus in Windows applications such as Windows Explorer. These pop-up menus are typically context-sensitive, and are invoked with the right mouse button. For this reason, floating pop-up menus are sometimes referred to as context menus. Floating pop-up menus are very easy to implement in MFC applications thanks to a member function defined in the CMenu class.

The TrackPopupMenu() member function of CMenu is the key to using floating pop-up menus. TrackPopupMenu() displays a floating pop-up menu representing the CMenu object on which it is called. Following is an example of displaying a floating pop-up menu using the TrackPopupMenu() function:

```
pFileMenu->TrackPopupMenu(TPM_CENTERALIGN ¦ TPM_LEFTBUTTON,
  x, y, this);
```

The first parameter to TrackPopupMenu() is a flag indicating the alignment and mouse button used to select menu items from the pop-up menu. Table 8.4 shows the flags used by TrackPopupMenu().

TABLE 8.4   FLAGS USED BY THE CMenu::TrackPopupMenu() MEMBER FUNCTION

Flag	*Description*
TPM_CENTERALIGN	The menu is centered horizontally on the x position of the menu.
TPM_LEFTALIGN	The left edge of the menu is aligned with the x position of the menu.
TPM_RIGHTALIGN	The right edge of the menu is aligned with the x position of the menu.
TPM_LEFTBUTTON	The left mouse button is used to make menu selections.
TPM_RIGHTBUTTON	The right mouse button is used to make menu selections.

The x position referenced in the table is the second parameter to TrackPopupMenu(), which indicates the horizontal position of the menu relative to the screen. The third parameter is the y position of the menu. The last parameter is a pointer to the parent window of the menu; it is sufficient to pass this if you call TrackPopupMenu() from your main application window object.

Let's take a look at how you might use TrackPopupMenu() in an application. Listing 8.3 contains an OnRButtonUp() message handler that displays a floating pop-up menu containing the menu commands for an application's File menu.

LISTING 8.3   AN `OnRButtonUp()` MESSAGE HANDLER THAT DISPLAYS A FLOATING POP-UP MENU

```
void CMainFrame::OnRButtonUp(UINT nFlags, CPoint point) {
  // Display the File menu as a floating pop-up menu
  CMenu* pFileMenu = GetMenu()->GetSubMenu(0);
  ClientToScreen(&point);
  pFileMenu->TrackPopupMenu(TPM_CENTERALIGN ¦ TPM_LEFTBUTTON,
    point.x, point.y, this);
}
```

The `OnRButtonUp()` message handler first obtains a menu pointer for the File pop-up menu using the `GetSubMenu()` member function of `CMenu`. Before displaying the floating pop-up menu, `OnRButtonUp()` calls the `ClientToScreen()` member function of `CWnd` to convert the client window position in the `point` parameter to screen coordinates. This call is necessary because the `TrackPopupMenu()` function expects the pop-up menu position in screen coordinates, not client window coordinates. The `OnRButtonUp()` message handler finishes up by calling `TrackPopupMenu()` to display a pop-up menu containing the File menu commands.

> **NOTE**
>
> Although most floating pop-up menus are based on a submenu of a main application menu, you can also create custom pop-up menus as resources that aren't necessarily used elsewhere in the application. To do this, you must first create a menu resource in the application's resource file. You then create a `CMenu` object and call the `LoadMenu()` member function to load a menu from a resource. This menu object can then be used with the `TrackPopupMenu()` member function to display the menu as a floating pop-up menu.

Putting Control Bars to Use

Control bars are prevalent in most Windows applications and include toolbars, status bars, and dialog bars. The primary purpose of control bars is to enhance the user interface of applications and provide an alternative means of issuing commands and altering application settings. Toolbars and dialog bars are similar in that they both can contain buttons. However, dialog bars are more flexible in that they can contain any control. On the other hand, toolbars are easier to use and more efficient if you only need buttons.

Not surprisingly, MFC provides a set of classes that model each type of control bar, as well as a general base class from which each control bar class is derived. Following are the MFC classes that support control bars:

- CControlBar
- CToolBar
- CReBar
- CStatusBar
- CDialogBar

The CControlBar class provides the basic support required of all control bars, and serves as the base class for the other control bar classes. The CControlBar class supports a control bar window that can be aligned to the left or right edge of a frame window. Control bars can be docked, which allows a floating control bar to be attached to the edge of a frame window. Most control bars are docked by default; you initially make a control bar float by dragging it away from the edge of a frame window. Generally speaking, control bar windows are children of an application's frame window, and siblings of the client window.

The CToolBar class implements a control bar with a row of bitmap buttons and optional separators. Each button in a toolbar contains a bitmap image, and can act like a pushbutton, a check box, or a radio button. In the latter two cases, a button remains depressed to indicate that it is checked. Toolbars are typically placed at the top of an application's frame window in between the menu and the client area.

The CReBar class supports a rebar control that functions somewhat like an array of control bars. A rebar control contains multiple bands that can each contain a toolbar or other control. Each band in a rebar control has a gripper bar that can be used to resize or reposition the band. After creating a rebar control, you can add other control bars as bands of the rebar. For example, you could have three different toolbars that occupy different bands of a rebar control. You can also combine different types of control bars within a rebar, meaning that one band can be a toolbar while another is a dialog bar.

The CStatusBar class implements a control bar with a row of text panes that display information about the state of an application. These panes are commonly used to show help messages and keyboard status indicators such as the state of the CapsLock, NumLock, and ScrollLock keys. The most important usage of status bars is the display of help messages for menu commands. When the user highlights a command on a menu, a help message is displayed in the status bar containing information about the command.

8

EXTENDING THE
USER INTERFACE

Status bars are typically placed at the bottom of an application's frame window just below the client area.

The `CDialogBar` class implements a control bar that is much like a dialog box in that it can contain different types of controls. You typically create a dialog bar from a dialog box resource. Dialog bars are often placed at the top of an application's frame window like a toolbar, but depending on the needs of a particular application, they might appear on the left or right side of the frame window, or even at the bottom.

Using Toolbars and Rebars

Toolbars consist of a row of bitmap buttons that are typically used as an alternative means of issuing menu commands. The majority of toolbar functionality is encapsulated in the `CToolBar` class, and is automatically enabled after you create and initialize a `CToolBar` object. Following are the steps required to create a toolbar:

1. Create a toolbar bitmap and include it in the application as a bitmap resource.
2. Create a toolbar resource.
3. Create a `CToolBar` object.
4. Call the `Create()` member function to create the toolbar.
5. Call the `LoadToolBar()` member function to load the toolbar resource and bitmap.

Each button in a toolbar has a bitmap image associated with it that is displayed on the button. To make toolbar button images a little easier to manage, the images are specified in a single toolbar bitmap. You can think of this bitmap as an array of button images. Figure 8.2 shows a zoomed view of the default toolbar bitmap image generated by AppWizard.

FIGURE 8.2

A zoomed view of the default toolbar bitmap image generated by AppWizard.

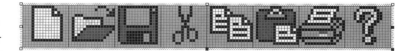

As Figure 8.2 shows, individual button images are tiled from left to right across the toolbar bitmap. Each button image is 16×15 pixels, which is the standard size for most Windows applications. This image must be included as a bitmap resource in the resource script for the application to which you are adding the toolbar. After you've created a toolbar bitmap and included it as a bitmap resource, you need to create a toolbar resource. Listing 8.4 contains the toolbar resource generated by AppWizard for use with the toolbar bitmap you just saw.

LISTING 8.4   THE DEFAULT TOOLBAR RESOURCE DEFINITION GENERATED BY APPWIZARD

```
IDR_MAINFRAME TOOLBAR DISCARDABLE  16, 15
BEGIN
  BUTTON      ID_FILE_NEW
  BUTTON      ID_FILE_OPEN
  BUTTON      ID_FILE_SAVE
  SEPARATOR
  BUTTON      ID_EDIT_CUT
  BUTTON      ID_EDIT_COPY
  BUTTON      ID_EDIT_PASTE
  SEPARATOR
  BUTTON      ID_FILE_PRINT
  SEPARATOR
  BUTTON      ID_APP_ABOUT
END
```

A toolbar resource is similar to a menu resource in that each button is defined by assigning it a menu command identifier. Keep in mind that the number of buttons in the toolbar resource must match the number of tiled button bitmaps in the toolbar bitmap. Also notice that the size of the button images (16×15) is specified at the start of the toolbar resource. Spaces between buttons are created using the SEPARATOR identifier.

After creating a toolbar resource, you need to create a CToolBar object. The first step in doing this is to declare a CToolBar member variable in the frame window of your application:

```
CToolBar m_wndToolBar;
```

The best place to create and initialize a toolbar is in the OnCreate() message handler for an application's main frame window, which is associated with the WM_CREATE message. Listing 8.5 contains the code for an OnCreate() message handler that creates and initializes a toolbar.

LISTING 8.5   AN OnCreate() MESSAGE HANDLER THAT CREATES A TOOLBAR

```
int CMainFrame::OnCreate(LPCREATESTRUCT lpCreateStruct) {
  if (CFrameWnd::OnCreate(lpCreateStruct) == -1)
    return -1;

  // Create and load the toolbar
  if (!m_wndToolBar.Create(this) ||
  !m_wndToolBar.LoadToolBar(IDR_MAINFRAME))
    return -1;

  return 0;
}
```

The Create() member function is first called on the CToolBar object to create the tool-bar. However, at this stage the toolbar resource hasn't been associated with the toolbar, so the toolbar really isn't of much use. The toolbar is properly initialized by calling the LoadToolBar() member function, which loads the toolbar resource and bitmap.

Creating a toolbar as a band of a rebar control is also very straightforward. You must first declare a CReBar member variable in the frame window of your application:

CReBar m_wndReBar;

Then you create the CReBar object in the OnCreate() member function and call the AddBar() member function on it to add the toolbar. Listing 8.6 demonstrates how this is done.

LISTING 8.6   AN OnCreate() MESSAGE HANDLER THAT CREATES A TOOLBAR AS A BAND OF A REBAR

```
int CMainFrame::OnCreate(LPCREATESTRUCT lpCreateStruct) {
  if (CFrameWnd::OnCreate(lpCreateStruct) == -1)
    return -1;

  // Create and load the toolbar
  if (!m_wndToolBar.Create(this) ||
  !m_wndToolBar.LoadToolBar(IDR_MAINFRAME))
    return -1;

  // Create the rebar and add the toolbar band
  if (!m_wndReBar.Create(this) || !m_wndReBar.AddBar(&m_wndToolBar))
    return -1;

  return 0;
}
```

Of course, you would typically want to create multiple control bars and add them to a rebar because the whole point of a rebar is to allow multiple bands.

You can modify an application's toolbar using member functions defined in the CToolBar class. For example, the SetBitmap() member function allows you to change the tiled bitmap containing the individual button images. Also, the SetButtons() member function allows you to change the command identifiers associated with toolbar buttons. Following is an example of changing a toolbar to support only the commands on the File menu:

```
UINT[] cmds = { ID_FILE_NEW, ID_FILE_OPEN, ID_FILE_SAVE };
m_wndToolBar.SetBitmap(hbmFile);
m_wndToolBar.SetButtons(cmds, 3);
```

This code assumes that you've already loaded a suitable toolbar bitmap image into the `hbmFile` bitmap handle. The `SetButtons()` member function accepts an array of command identifiers that are associated with the button images. The second parameter to `SetButtons()` indicates how many buttons are on the toolbar.

Although the user will typically take on the responsibility of docking a floating toolbar, you can also do so programmatically. The `DockControlBar()` member function of the `CFrameWnd` class performs exactly this task:

```
void DockControlBar(CControlBar* pBar, UINT nDockBarID = 0,
  LPCRECT lpRect = NULL);
```

Its first parameter is a pointer to the control bar you want to dock, and the second parameter is a constant identifying the side of the frame window to which the control is to dock. Table 8.5 lists the valid constants for the second parameter to `DockControlBar()`.

TABLE 8.5 CONSTANTS THAT IDENTIFY THE SIDE OF THE FRAME WINDOW FOR A DOCKED CONTROL BAR

Constant	Docks Control Bar to
`AFX_IDW_DOCKBAR_TOP`	The top of the frame window
`AFX_IDW_DOCKBAR_BOTTOM`	The bottom of the frame window
`AFX_IDW_DOCKBAR_LEFT`	The left of the frame window
`AFX_IDW_DOCKBAR_RIGHT`	The right of the frame window

The third parameter to `DockControlBar()` allows you to specify a rectangle in which the control bar is docked. This rectangle is specified in screen coordinates and indicates a location in the nonclient area of the frame window. You can accept the default value of `NULL` if you don't want to specify a rectangle.

Using Status Bars

Status bars are used to convey information to the user such as help messages and keyboard status indicators. Help messages are displayed in the main section of a status bar, and other information is displayed in panes that appear inset on the status bar. In addition to keyboard status indicators, status bar panes can be used to display application-specific information.

Like toolbars, the functionality of status bars is largely automatic after you create and initialize a status bar object. Following are the steps required to create a status bar:

1. Create string resources for the status bar help messages and keyboard status indicators.

2. Create a `CStatusBar` object.

3. Create a static `UINT` array specifying the panes for the status bar.

4. Call the `Create()` member function to create the status bar.

5. Call the `SetIndicators()` member function to set the panes for the status bar.

A status bar requires two different sets of string resources: a set identifying the help messages for menu commands and a set identifying the panes. Listing 8.7 contains string resources for status bar help messages.

LISTING 8.7   HELP MESSAGE STRING RESOURCE DEFINITIONS FOR A STATUS BAR

```
STRINGTABLE
BEGIN
    ID_FILE_NEW         "Create a new document"
    ID_FILE_OPEN        "Open an existing document"
    ID_FILE_SAVE        "Save the document"
    ID_FILE_SAVE_AS     "Save the document with a new name"
    ID_FILE_PRINT       "Print the document"
    ID_EDIT_CUT         "Cuts the selection to the Clipboard"
    ID_EDIT_COPY        "Copies the selection to the Clipboard"
    ID_EDIT_PASTE       "Inserts Clipboard contents"
    ID_APP_ABOUT        "Displays program information"
    ID_APP_EXIT         "Quit the application; prompts to save document"
END
```

Associating status bar help messages with menu commands involves identifying the menu command identifier and the text message associated with it. Listing 8.8 is a little more interesting in that it specifies the keyboard status indicators used in the status bar panes.

LISTING 8.8   KEYBOARD STATUS INDICATOR STRING RESOURCE DEFINITIONS FOR A STATUS BAR

```
STRINGTABLE
BEGIN
    ID_INDICATOR_CAPS       "CAP"
    ID_INDICATOR_NUM        "NUM"
    ID_INDICATOR_SCRL       "SCRL"
END
```

The identifiers used in the keyboard status indicators are standard identifiers defined in MFC. They represent the CapsLock, NumLock, and ScrollLock keys, respectively. The purpose of these string resources is simply to determine the size of each keyboard status indicator pane within the status bar. More specifically, each pane is automatically sized so that it will fit the string resource. The creation of the panes is handled in a moment after you create the status bar object.

The creation of the CStatusBar object is handled by simply declaring a CMainFrame member variable of type CStatusBar:

```
CStatusBar m_wndStatusBar;
```

The panes for this status bar are specified using a static array of UINT pane identifiers:

```
static UINT indicators[] = { ID_SEPARATOR, ID_INDICATOR_CAPS,
  ID_INDICATOR_NUM, ID_INDICATOR_SCRL };
```

The ID_SEPARATOR identifier is used to place the panes on the right side of the status bar, which leaves room for help messages to be displayed on the left side. This array of identifiers is used to establish the status bar panes in the OnCreate() message handler, which is shown in Listing 8.9.

LISTING 8.9 AN OnCreate() MESSAGE HANDLER THAT CREATES A TOOLBAR AND A STATUS BAR

```
int CMainFrame::OnCreate(LPCREATESTRUCT lpCreateStruct) {
  if (CFrameWnd::OnCreate(lpCreateStruct) == -1)
    return -1;

  // Create toolbar
  if (!m_wndToolBar.Create(this) ||
    !m_wndToolBar.LoadToolBar(IDR_TOOLBAR))
    return -1;

  // Create status bar
  if (!m_wndStatusBar.Create(this) ||
    !m_wndStatusBar.SetIndicators(indicators,
    sizeof(indicators)/sizeof(UINT)))
    return -1;

  return 0;
}
```

The status bar is created with a call to Create(), and the panes are set with a call to SetIndicators().

Showing and Hiding Control Bars

Control bars are typically considered an enhancement to an application's graphical user interface, which means that they aren't essential to using an application. Knowing this, there might be situations where a user would prefer not having them around. Therefore, it is nice to enable the user to hide control bars if desired. This gives users some flexibility in customizing an application to their own tastes, which is very important. Fortunately for you, it is easy to add this functionality to MFC applications.

The first step is to add menu commands that can be used to show and hide the toolbar and status bar of an application. Listing 8.10 shows a menu resource definition that includes a View pop-up menu containing the commands Toolbar and Status Bar.

LISTING 8.10   A MENU RESOURCE DEFINITION THAT INCLUDES A VIEW POP-UP MENU

```
IDR_MENU
BEGIN
  POPUP "&File"
    BEGIN
      MENUITEM "&New\tCtrl+N",          ID_FILE_NEW
      MENUITEM "&Open...\tCtrl+O",       ID_FILE_OPEN
      MENUITEM "&Save\tCtrl+S",          ID_FILE_SAVE
      MENUITEM "Save &As...",            ID_FILE_SAVE_AS
      MENUITEM SEPARATOR
      MENUITEM "E&xit",                  ID_APP_EXIT
    END
  POPUP "&Edit"
    BEGIN
      MENUITEM "&Undo\tCtrl+Z",          ID_EDIT_UNDO
      MENUITEM SEPARATOR
      MENUITEM "Cu&t\tCtrl+X",           ID_EDIT_CUT
      MENUITEM "&Copy\tCtrl+C",          ID_EDIT_COPY
      MENUITEM "&Paste\tCtrl+V",         ID_EDIT_PASTE
    END
  POPUP "&View"
    BEGIN
      MENUITEM "&Toolbar",               ID_VIEW_TOOLBAR
      MENUITEM "&Status Bar",            ID_VIEW_STATUS_BAR
    END
  POPUP "&Help"
    BEGIN
      MENUITEM "&About...",              ID_APP_ABOUT
    END
END
```

The View menu commands use standard menu command identifiers (ID_VIEW_TOOLBAR and ID_VIEW_STATUS_BAR) that automatically invoke the show/hide functionality for control bars. In other words, an application gains the capability to show and hide its toolbar and status bar by simply supporting two menu commands.

Supporting ToolTips

The last control bar topic you're going to learn about is ToolTips. If you recall, ToolTips are shorthand help messages that are displayed when you pause the mouse cursor over a toolbar button. Support for ToolTips is actually a toolbar style, which means that you can alter the style of a toolbar to enable ToolTips. You alter the style of a toolbar using the SetBarStyle() member function. The toolbar style for supporting ToolTips is CBRS_TOOLTIPS, which should be added to the toolbar styles when calling SetBarStyle(). Listing 8.11 contains an OnCreate() message handler that supports ToolTips.

LISTING 8.11   AN OnCreate() MESSAGE HANDLER THAT SUPPORTS TOOLTIPS

```
int CMainFrame::OnCreate(LPCREATESTRUCT lpCreateStruct) {
  if (CFrameWnd::OnCreate(lpCreateStruct) == -1)
    return -1;

  // Create toolbar
  if (!m_wndToolBar.Create(this) ||
    !m_wndToolBar.LoadToolBar(IDR_TOOLBAR))
    return -1;

  // Create status bar
  if (!m_wndStatusBar.Create(this) ||
    !m_wndStatusBar.SetIndicators(indicators,
    sizeof(indicators)/sizeof(UINT)))
    return -1;

  // Enable tooltips
  m_wndToolBar.SetBarStyle(m_wndToolBar.GetBarStyle() |
    CBRS_TOOLTIPS | CBRS_FLYBY | CBRS_SIZE_DYNAMIC);

  // Set tool bar as dockable
  m_wndToolBar.EnableDocking(CBRS_ALIGN_ANY);
  EnableDocking(CBRS_ALIGN_ANY);
  DockControlBar(&m_wndToolBar);
  return 0;
}
```

This code creates a toolbar and status bar, and also sets up the toolbar to support ToolTips and docking. The SetBarStyle() member function is used to set the CBRS_TOOLTIPS style for the toolbar. Two other styles, CBRS_FLYBY and CBRS_SIZE_DYNAMIC, are also specified. These styles are used to jazz up the toolbar a little. The CBRS_FLYBY style results in the display of status bar help messages for toolbar buttons any time a ToolTip is activated. Without this style, a help message is only displayed when the user clicks a button. The CBRS_SIZE_DYNAMIC style allows the user to resize the toolbar window when it is detached from the application's frame window and used as a floating toolbar.

At this point the toolbar is ready to use ToolTips, but you've yet to actually provide any of them. The actual text for ToolTips is provided as part of the status bar help messages for each menu command. You accomplish this by inserting a newline (\n) character at the end of each help message, followed by the ToolTip text. Listing 8.12 shows the new help message string resources with ToolTip text added.

LISTING 8.12 A HELP MESSAGE STRING RESOURCE DEFINITION FOR A STATUS BAR THAT SUPPORTS TOOLTIPS

```
STRINGTABLE
BEGIN
  ID_FILE_NEW        "Create a new document\nNew"
  ID_FILE_OPEN       "Open an existing document\nOpen"
  ID_FILE_SAVE       "Save the document\nSave"
  ID_FILE_SAVE_AS    "Save the document with a new name\nSave As"
  ID_FILE_PRINT      "Print the document\nPrint"
  ID_EDIT_CUT        "Cuts the selection to the Clipboard\nCut"
  ID_EDIT_COPY       "Copies the selection to the Clipboard\nCopy"
  ID_EDIT_PASTE      "Inserts Clipboard contents\nPaste"
  ID_APP_ABOUT       "Displays program information\nAbout"
  ID_APP_EXIT        "Quit the application; prompts to save\nExit"
END
```

Updating the User Interface

Most commercial Windows applications intelligently enable and disable menu items based on the state of the application. Without MFC, injecting this type of menu state intelligence into an application is very tricky. MFC provides an elegant solution for managing the state of user interface elements including menu items, toolbar buttons, and status bar text. MFC's solution to user interface state management comes in the form of command update message handlers. A command update message handler is associated with an individual user interface element such as a menu item or a toolbar button, and is called to refresh the state of the user interface element. For example, the command update message handler for a pop-up menu item is called just before the pop-up menu is displayed.

Each command update message handler requires a message map entry that ties the handler to a user interface element. The `ON_UPDATE_COMMAND_UI` macro is used to carry out this connection. Following is an example of wiring a command update message handler to a menu item:

```
ON_UPDATE_COMMAND_UI(ID_EDIT_UNDO, OnUpdateEditUndo)
```

This code wires the `OnUpdateEditUndo()` command update message handler to the menu item identified by `ID_EDIT_UNDO`. This handler is called just before the Edit menu item is displayed to the user. Following is the prototype of the `OnUpdateEditUndo()` command update message handler:

```
afx_msg void  OnUpdateEditUndo(CCmdUI* pCmdUI);
```

The parameter to `OnUpdateEditUndo()`, `pCmdUI`, is sent to all update command message handlers, and provides a means of modifying the state of the user interface element. Following are the primary member functions used in conjunction with the `CCmdUI` class:

- `Enable()`—Enables or disables the user interface element
- `SetCheck()`—Checks or unchecks the user interface element
- `SetRadio()`—Checks or unchecks the radio state of the user interface element
- `SetText()`—Sets the text of the user interface element

Following is an example of enabling a user interface element using the `Enable()` member function:

```
pCmdUI->Enable(TRUE);
```

You can disable a user interface element by calling the same member function and passing `FALSE`:

```
pCmdUI->Enable(FALSE);
```

The other member functions of the `CCmdUI` class work in roughly the same way. For example, the following code checks a user interface element:

```
pCmdUI->SetCheck(TRUE);
```

You might notice that menu items and toolbar buttons are disabled automatically if they don't have command message handlers associated with them. This default behavior is carried out by MFC because a menu item or toolbar button is typically useless without a command message handler. When you implement a command message handler for a menu item or toolbar button, MFC automatically enables the item or button. You then control the state of the item or button using a command update message handler.

Property Sheets and Wizards

Property sheets have become an important part of the Windows user interface. A property sheet is a user interface component that presents multiple dialog boxes as pages within a single window; each page is accessed through a tab. The pages in a property sheet are called property pages and provide a solution to the problem of trying to gather lots of information within a single dialog box. Property pages enable you to use multiple dialog boxes within the same context, the property sheet. Wizards are very close relatives of property sheets and represent another user interface feature that has enjoyed widespread use in Windows.

Each property page in a property sheet is logically equivalent to an individual dialog box. In fact, you can think of the property sheet tabs as the names of the different dialog boxes (pages) contained within the property sheet. It isn't just a coincidence that property pages appear to be so similar to dialog boxes; property pages are actually implemented as dialog boxes. In fact, you define the layout of individual property pages using dialog box resources.

Property sheets are different from wizards in that property sheets enable the user to click a tab and go to any page at will. Wizards are more restrictive and enforce an ordered approach to navigating the pages. To enforce this page order, wizards don't provide tabs for page navigation. Also, property sheets don't provide Back or Next buttons to navigate between pages because the user can just use the tabs.

Other than navigational differences, property sheets and wizards are actually very much alike. Following are some of the similarities between them:

- They serve as a container for multiple pages.
- Their pages are laid out as dialog box resources.
- They provide a means of navigating through the pages.
- They automatically provide buttons for performing standard tasks such as OK, Finish, Cancel, and so on.

Although wizards and property sheets differ slightly in their approaches to some of these things, such as navigating through pages, they are still very similar. In fact, creating a property page is little different than creating a wizard; the same MFC class is used as the basis for creating both property pages and wizards.

MFC's Support for Property Sheets and Wizards

There are two MFC classes that encapsulate the functionality of both property pages and wizards:

- CPropertySheet—Represents both property sheets and wizards
- CPropertyPage—Represents pages within a property sheet or wizard

The CPropertySheet Class

Property sheets and wizards are implemented in the CPropertySheet class, which is derived from CWnd. The CPropertySheet class serves as a container for property pages, which themselves represent dialog boxes. Within an application, a property sheet consists of a CPropertySheet object and multiple CPropertyPage objects. You can communicate with the individual pages in a property sheet by calling member functions of the CPropertySheet class.

Although the CPropertySheet class is derived from CWnd, interacting with a property sheet or wizard is a lot like interacting with a dialog box through a CDialog object. To invoke a property sheet, you use the familiar two-step process required of dialog boxes:

1. Create a CPropertySheet object.
2. Call the DoModal() member function to display the property sheet or wizard as a modal dialog box.

> **NOTE**
>
> The CPropertySheet class also supports modeless property sheets, in which case you use the Create() member function instead of DoModal(). Modeless property sheets are generally more complex to implement than their modal counterparts. Technically speaking, you could also create a modeless wizard, but it probably wouldn't make much sense.

Following is an example of creating a property sheet that is implemented in a CPropertySheet-derived class named CMyPropSheet:

```
CMyPropSheet propSheet;
propSheet.DoModal();
```

Creating and displaying a wizard requires an additional member function call to indicate that the property sheet is in fact a wizard:

```
CMyWizard wiz;
wiz.SetWizardMode();
wiz.DoModal();
```

The `SetWizardMode()` member function establishes that a property sheet is to operate as a wizard. The result is that Back and Next buttons are used to navigate the pages instead of tabs. The Finish button is also typically used on the last page to indicate that the user is finished with the wizard. When you call the `DoModal()` member function on a wizard, it will return `ID_WIZFINISH` or `IDCANCEL`, depending on whether the user clicked the Finish button or the Cancel button to exit the wizard.

Getting back to the `CPropertySheet` class, Table 8.6 lists some of the member functions commonly used with wizards.

TABLE 8.6 THE MOST COMMONLY USED `CPropertySheet` MEMBER FUNCTIONS

Member Function	Description
DoModal()	Displays the wizard as a modal dialog box
SetWizardMode()	Forces the property sheet to operate as a wizard
SetWizardButtons()	Determines which wizard buttons are displayed/enabled
AddPage()	Adds a page to the wizard
RemovePage()	Removes a page from the wizard

The `SetWizardButtons()` member function is called to specify which buttons are displayed in the wizard. You will typically call this function within a property page to set the wizard buttons when the page becomes active. `SetWizardButtons()` accepts a flag that can be a combination of the following button identifiers:

- `PSWIZB_BACK`—Back button
- `PSWIZB_NEXT`—Next button
- `PSWIZB_FINISH`—Finish button
- `PSWIZB_DISABLEDFINISH`—Disabled Finish button

The `AddPage()` and `RemovePage()` member functions of `CProperySheet` are used to add and remove pages in a wizard. Following is an example of how the `AddPage()` function is used:

```
CWizPage1 page1;
page1.Construct(IDD_WIZPAGE1, 0);
AddPage(&page1);
```

This creates a property page and adds it to a property sheet. The property page is based on the dialog box resource identified by IDD_WIZPAGE1. This identifier is passed into the Construct() member function of the property page.

The CPropertyPage Class

The CPropertyPage class provides the functionality required of a dialog-based property page. Table 8.7 lists the most commonly used member functions defined in the CPropertyPage class.

TABLE 8.7 THE MOST COMMONLY USED CPropertyPage MEMBER FUNCTIONS

Member Function	Description
Contruct()	Constructs the property page
OnSetActive()	Called when the page becomes active
OnKillActive()	Called when the page is no longer active
OnWizardBack()	Called when the user clicks the Back button
OnWizardNext()	Called when the user clicks the Next button
OnWizardFinish()	Called when the user clicks the Finish button

In the previous section, you saw how to use the Construct() member function. The remaining member functions in Table 8.7 are called in response to different events. The last three member functions apply only to wizards.

Because the CPropertyPage class is derived from CDialog, you use it much as you would use the CDialog class. A property page class derived from CPropertyPage can override the OnInitDialog() member function to perform any one-time initialization chores. Property page classes also have message maps that enable them to respond to messages just like dialog boxes.

Creating a Simple Wizard

Let's pull together what you've learned about property sheets and wizards to create a functioning example. The next few sections lead you through the development of a wizard named Investment that calculates interest on an investment. You could feasibly use this wizard as part of a financial application. The Investment Wizard consists of three pages that gather information about an investment and display the results. Figures 8.3 through 8.5 show the finished Investment Wizard as it appears in an application. This should give you a good idea about what you are creating as you work through the code for the wizard.

FIGURE 8.3

The first page of the Investment Wizard.

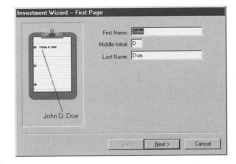

FIGURE 8.4

The second page of the Investment Wizard.

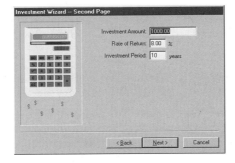

FIGURE 8.5

The third page of the Investment Wizard.

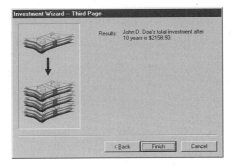

The best place to start when building a wizard is to assemble the dialog box resources for each wizard page. Because the Investment Wizard is ultimately part of an application, its resources must be defined along with the application's resources. Listing 8.13 contains resource identifiers for the Investment Wizard's dialog boxes, controls, and bitmaps.

LISTING 8.13 RESOURCE IDENTIFIERS FOR THE INVESTMENT WIZARD

```
// Dialog Boxes
#define IDD_INVESTWIZPAGE1    1000
#define IDD_INVESTWIZPAGE2    1001
```

```
#define IDD_INVESTWIZPAGE3      1002

// Controls
#define IDC_FNAME               2000
#define IDC_MINITIAL            2001
#define IDC_LNAME               2002
#define IDC_AMOUNT              2003
#define IDC_RETURNRATE          2004
#define IDC_PERIOD              2005
#define IDC_RESULT              2006

// Bitmaps
#define IDB_INVESTWIZPAGE1      3000
#define IDB_INVESTWIZPAGE2      3001
#define IDB_INVESTWIZPAGE3      3002
```

The dialog box resources for each page in the Investment Wizard are identified by the constants IDD_INVESTWIZPAGE1, IDD_INVESTWIZPAGE2, and IDD_INVESTWIZPAGE3. The control identifiers are associated with controls in each of the dialog boxes. As you might have noticed in Figures 8.3–8.5, which show the completed Investment Wizard, each page of the wizard displays a bitmap. These bitmaps are identified by the constants IDB_INVESTWIZPAGE1, IDB_INVESTWIZPAGE2, and IDB_INVESTWIZPAGE3. The resources required of the wizard, including the bitmaps and dialog boxes, are shown in Listing 8.14. These resources should be included in the resource script for the application that uses the wizard.

LISTING 8.14 RESOURCES FOR THE INVESTMENT WIZARD

```
// Bitmaps
IDB_INVESTWIZPAGE1 BITMAP "IWPage1.bmp"
IDB_INVESTWIZPAGE2 BITMAP "IWPage2.bmp"
IDB_INVESTWIZPAGE3 BITMAP "IWPage3.bmp"

// Dialog Boxes
IDD_INVESTWIZPAGE1 DIALOGEX 0, 0, WIZ_CXDLG, WIZ_CYDLG
CAPTION "Investment Wizard -- First Page"
STYLE WS_POPUP | WS_CAPTION | WS_SYSMENU | WS_VISIBLE
FONT 8, "MS Sans Serif"
BEGIN
  RTEXT         "First Name:", IDC_STATIC, 106, 10, 42, 8, 0
  EDITTEXT      IDC_FNAME, 152, 7, 99, 12
  RTEXT         "Middle Initial:", IDC_STATIC, 106, 25, 42, 8, 0
  EDITTEXT      IDC_MINITIAL, 152, 22, 16, 12
  RTEXT         "Last Name:", IDC_STATIC, 106, 42, 42, 8, 0
  EDITTEXT      IDC_LNAME, 152, 38, 99, 12
END
```

continues

8

EXTENDING THE USER INTERFACE

LISTING 8.14   CONTINUED

```
IDD_INVESTWIZPAGE2 DIALOGEX 0, 0, WIZ_CXDLG, WIZ_CYDLG
CAPTION "Investment Wizard -- Second Page"
STYLE WS_POPUP ¦ WS_CAPTION ¦ WS_SYSMENU ¦ WS_VISIBLE
FONT 8, "MS Sans Serif"
BEGIN
  RTEXT        "Investment Amount:", IDC_STATIC, 112, 10, 64, 8, 0
  RTEXT        "Rate of Return:", IDC_STATIC, 112, 26, 64, 8, 0
  EDITTEXT     IDC_AMOUNT, 180, 8, 66, 12, ES_NUMBER
  EDITTEXT     IDC_RETURNRATE, 180, 24, 23, 12, ES_NUMBER
  LTEXT        "%", IDC_STATIC, 206, 27, 8, 8
  RTEXT        "Investment Period:", IDC_STATIC, 112, 42, 64, 8, 0
  EDITTEXT     IDC_PERIOD, 180, 40, 23, 12, ES_NUMBER
  LTEXT        "years", IDC_STATIC, 207, 43, 17, 8
END

IDD_INVESTWIZPAGE3 DIALOGEX 0, 0, WIZ_CXDLG, WIZ_CYDLG
CAPTION "Investment Wizard -- Third Page"
STYLE WS_POPUP ¦ WS_CAPTION ¦ WS_SYSMENU ¦ WS_VISIBLE
FONT 8, "MS Sans Serif"
BEGIN
  LTEXT        "Results:", IDC_STATIC, 112, 10, 30, 8, 0
  LTEXT        "", IDC_RESULT, 146, 8, 120, 60, 0
END
```

Perhaps the most important thing to notice about the dialog box resources for the Investment Wizard is their width and height. The dialog boxes are set to the standard wizard page dimensions defined by the WIZ_CXDLG and WIZ_CYDLG constants. These constants are defined in the standard PrSht.h header file, which must be included in the resource script containing the wizard resources.

Although you can't tell it by looking at the resource code, the controls in the wizard page dialog boxes are intentionally placed to the right of the boxes to make room for the bitmaps. The bitmaps are drawn in the source code for the property pages, which you'll learn about in a moment.

Wizard Data

Before moving on to the page classes and wizard class for the Investment Wizard, it is helpful to define a couple of global variables used by them:

```
CInvestmentWiz* pInvestmentWiz;
CInvestWizData  wizData;
```

These global variables are defined in the InvestmentWiz.cpp source code file along with the page classes and wizard class. The pInvestmentWiz pointer keeps track of the wizard object for the sake of the page objects. This is necessary so that the pages can call `SetWizardButtons()` on the wizard to display and enable the appropriate wizard buttons.

The `wizData` global variable is of type `CInvestWizData`, which is a custom data class used to hold the information edited by the user in the wizard. Listing 8.15 contains the declaration of the `CInvestWizData` class.

LISTING 8.15 THE `CInvestWizData` CLASS DECLARATION

```
class CInvestWizData : public CObject {
  // Public Member Data
public:
  CString m_sFName;
  CString m_sMInitial;
  CString m_sLName;
  float   m_fAmount;
  float   m_fReturnRate;
  int     m_nPeriod;

  // Public Constructor(s)/Destructor
public:
  CInvestWizData();
};
```

The `CInvestWizData` class provides member variables that keep track of the state of the wizard. Sometimes you will want to include member data directly in the property pages, but in this case you need to share the information across the entire wizard. So it makes sense to place the data in a global object. Listing 8.16 contains the code for the `CInvestWizData` constructor, which provides initial values for the member data.

LISTING 8.16 THE `CInvestWizData:: CInvestWizData()` CONSTRUCTOR

```
// CInvestWizData Public Constructor(s)/Destructor
CInvestWizData::CInvestWizData() {
  // Initialize the wizard data
  m_sFName = "John";
  m_sMInitial = "D";
  m_sLName = "Doe";
  m_fAmount = 1000.0;
  m_fReturnRate = 8.0;
  m_nPeriod = 10;
}
```

8

**EXTENDING THE
USER INTERFACE**

Wizard Pages

The Investment Wizard page classes closely resemble dialog box classes. Listing 8.17 contains the class declaration for the `CInvestWizPage1` wizard page class.

LISTING 8.17 THE `CInvestWizPage1` CLASS DECLARATION

```
class CInvestWizPage1 : public CPropertyPage {
  // Private Member Data
private:
  CBitmap m_bitmap;

  // Public Member Functions
public:
  BOOL          OnInitDialog();
  BOOL          OnSetActive();
  void          DoDataExchange(CDataExchange* pDX);

  // Message Handlers
public:
  afx_msg void  OnPaint();

  // Message Map & Runtime Support
protected:
  DECLARE_MESSAGE_MAP()
};
```

The `OnPaint()` message handler is used to paint the bitmap on the page. Painting on a dialog box isn't all that common, but in the case of wizards it makes perfect sense. Listing 8.18 contains the implementation of the `CInvestWizPage1` wizard page class.

LISTING 8.18 THE `CInvestWizPage1` CLASS IMPLEMENTATION

```
// CInvestWizPage1 Message Map & Runtime Support
BEGIN_MESSAGE_MAP(CInvestWizPage1, CPropertyPage)
  ON_WM_PAINT()
END_MESSAGE_MAP()

// CInvestWizPage1 Public Member Functions
BOOL CInvestWizPage1::OnInitDialog() {
  // Load the bitmap
  m_bitmap.LoadBitmap(IDB_INVESTWIZPAGE1);

  return TRUE;
}
```

```
BOOL CInvestWizPage1::OnSetActive() {
  // Show only the Next button
  pInvestmentWiz->SetWizardButtons(PSWIZB_NEXT);

  // Set the control values
  SetDlgItemText(IDC_FNAME, wizData.m_sFName);
  SetDlgItemText(IDC_MINITIAL, wizData.m_sMInitial);
  SetDlgItemText(IDC_LNAME, wizData.m_sLName);

  return TRUE;
}

void CInvestWizPage1::DoDataExchange(CDataExchange* pDX) {
  CDialog::DoDataExchange(pDX);

  // Exchange the dialog data
  DDX_Text(pDX, IDC_FNAME, wizData.m_sFName);
  DDX_Text(pDX, IDC_MINITIAL, wizData.m_sMInitial);
  DDX_Text(pDX, IDC_LNAME, wizData.m_sLName);
}

// CInvestWizPage1 Message Handlers
void CInvestWizPage1::OnPaint() {
  CPaintDC dc(this);

  // Select the bitmap into a memory DC
  CDC dcMem;
  dcMem.CreateCompatibleDC(&dc);
  dcMem.SelectObject(&m_bitmap);

  // Copy the bitmap to the dialog DC
  dc.BitBlt(0, 0, 129, 226, &dcMem, 0, 0, SRCCOPY);
}
```

8

EXTENDING THE
USER INTERFACE

The bitmap for the page is loaded in the OnInitDialog() member function. The
OnSetActive() member function is then used to set the wizard buttons for the page,
which in this case consist only of the Next button. OnSetActive() also takes on the task
of initializing the dialog controls with the global wizard data that applies to this page.
This global data is updated in the DoDataExchange() member function, which wires
variables to dialog controls. Finally, the OnPaint() message handler handles drawing the
page's bitmap on the left side of the page.

The remaining two wizard page classes, CInvestWizPage2 and CInvestWizPage3, are
implemented very similarly to CInvestWizPage1. Listings 8.19 through 8.22 contain the
code for these classes.

LISTING 8.19   THE CInvestWizPage2 CLASS DECLARATION

```
class CInvestWizPage2 : public CPropertyPage {
  // Private Member Data
private:
  CBitmap m_bitmap;

  // Public Member Functions
public:
  BOOL          OnInitDialog();
  BOOL          OnSetActive();
  void          DoDataExchange(CDataExchange* pDX);

  // Message Handlers
public:
  afx_msg void  OnPaint();

  // Message Map & Runtime Support
protected:
  DECLARE_MESSAGE_MAP()
};
```

LISTING 8.20   THE CInvestWizPage2 CLASS IMPLEMENTATION

```
// CInvestWizPage2 Message Map & Runtime Support
BEGIN_MESSAGE_MAP(CInvestWizPage2, CPropertyPage)
  ON_WM_PAINT()
END_MESSAGE_MAP()

// CInvestWizPage2 Public Member Functions
BOOL CInvestWizPage2::OnInitDialog() {
  // Load the bitmap
  m_bitmap.LoadBitmap(IDB_INVESTWIZPAGE2);

  return TRUE;
}

BOOL CInvestWizPage2::OnSetActive() {
  // Show the Back and Next buttons
  pInvestmentWiz->SetWizardButtons(PSWIZB_BACK | PSWIZB_NEXT);

  // Set the control values
  CString sVal;
  sVal.Format("%.2f", wizData.m_fAmount);
  SetDlgItemText(IDC_AMOUNT, sVal);
  sVal.Format("%.2f", wizData.m_fReturnRate);
  SetDlgItemText(IDC_RETURNRATE, sVal);
```

```
  sVal.Format("%d", wizData.m_nPeriod);
  SetDlgItemText(IDC_PERIOD, sVal);

  return TRUE;
}

void CInvestWizPage2::DoDataExchange(CDataExchange* pDX) {
  CDialog::DoDataExchange(pDX);

  // Exchange the dialog data
  DDX_Text(pDX, IDC_AMOUNT, wizData.m_fAmount);
  DDX_Text(pDX, IDC_RETURNRATE, wizData.m_fReturnRate);
  DDX_Text(pDX, IDC_PERIOD, wizData.m_nPeriod);
}

// CInvestWizPage2 Message Handlers
void CInvestWizPage2::OnPaint() {
  CPaintDC dc(this);

  // Select the bitmap into a memory DC
  CDC dcMem;
  dcMem.CreateCompatibleDC(&dc);
  dcMem.SelectObject(&m_bitmap);

  // Copy the bitmap to the dialog DC
  dc.BitBlt(0, 0, 129, 226, &dcMem, 0, 0, SRCCOPY);
}
```

LISTING 8.21   THE CInvestWizPage3 CLASS DECLARATION

```
class CInvestWizPage3 : public CPropertyPage {
  // Private Member Data
private:
  CBitmap m_bitmap;

  // Public Member Functions
public:
  BOOL         OnInitDialog();
  BOOL         OnSetActive();

  // Message Handlers
public:
  afx_msg void  OnPaint();

  // Message Map & Runtime Support
protected:
  DECLARE_MESSAGE_MAP()
};
```

LISTING 8.22   THE `CInvestWizPage3` CLASS IMPLEMENTATION

```
// CInvestWizPage3 Message Map & Runtime Support
BEGIN_MESSAGE_MAP(CInvestWizPage3, CPropertyPage)
  ON_WM_PAINT()
END_MESSAGE_MAP()

// CInvestWizPage3 Public Member Functions
BOOL CInvestWizPage3::OnInitDialog() {
  // Load the bitmap
  m_bitmap.LoadBitmap(IDB_INVESTWIZPAGE3);

  return TRUE;
}

BOOL CInvestWizPage3::OnSetActive() {
  // Show the Back and Finish buttons
  pInvestmentWiz->SetWizardButtons(PSWIZB_BACK | PSWIZB_FINISH);

  // Calculate the investment
  float fTotal = wizData.m_fAmount;
  for (int i = 0; i < wizData.m_nPeriod; i++)
    fTotal += (fTotal * (wizData.m_fReturnRate / 100));

  // Display the result
  CString sResult;
  sResult.Format("%s %s. %s's total investment "
    "after %d years is $%.2f.",
    wizData.m_sFName, wizData.m_sMInitial, wizData.m_sLName,
    wizData.m_nPeriod, fTotal);
  SetDlgItemText(IDC_RESULT, sResult);

  return TRUE;
}

// CInvestWizPage3 Message Handlers
void CInvestWizPage3::OnPaint() {
  CPaintDC dc(this);

  // Select the bitmap into a memory DC
  CDC dcMem;
  dcMem.CreateCompatibleDC(&dc);
  dcMem.SelectObject(&m_bitmap);

  // Copy the bitmap to the dialog DC
  dc.BitBlt(0, 0, 129, 226, &dcMem, 0, 0, SRCCOPY);
}
```

The most important difference to note between all the wizard page classes is the wizard buttons that each of them displays. Also, note that the third page doesn't provide a

`DoDataExchange()` member function because it is an output-only page and doesn't need to store user input.

The Wizard

The majority of the work in a wizard is in creating the wizard pages. This means that an actual wizard class requires relatively little code. Listing 8.23 contains the class declaration for the `CInvestmentWiz` wizard class.

LISTING 8.23 THE `CInvestmentWiz` CLASS DECLARATION

```
class CInvestmentWiz : public CPropertySheet {
  // Private Member Data
private:
  CInvestWizPage1 m_page1;
  CInvestWizPage2 m_page2;
  CInvestWizPage3 m_page3;

  // Public Constructor(s)/Destructor
public:
                CInvestmentWiz();

  // Message Map & Runtime Support
protected:
  DECLARE_MESSAGE_MAP()
};
```

The `CInvestmentWiz` wizard class contains the individual wizard pages as member objects. This handles their initial creation, but it is still necessary to call the `Construct()` member function on each page to properly construct the pages. This is carried out in the constructor for `CInvestmentWiz`, which is shown in Listing 8.24.

LISTING 8.24 THE `CInvestmentWiz` CLASS IMPLEMENTATION

```
// CInvestmentWiz Message Map & Runtime Support
BEGIN_MESSAGE_MAP(CInvestmentWiz, CPropertySheet)
END_MESSAGE_MAP()

// CInvestmentWiz Public Constructor(s)/Destructor
CInvestmentWiz::CInvestmentWiz() : CPropertySheet() {
  // Create the investment wizard
  Construct("Investment Wizard", this);

  // Add the wizard pages
  m_page1.Construct(IDD_INVESTWIZPAGE1, 0);
```

continues

8

EXTENDING THE
USER INTERFACE

LISTING 8.24   CONTINUED

```
m_page2.Construct(IDD_INVESTWIZPAGE2, 0);
m_page3.Construct(IDD_INVESTWIZPAGE3, 0);
AddPage(&m_page1);
AddPage(&m_page2);
AddPage(&m_page3);

// Set the wizard global variable for page access
pInvestmentWiz = this;
}
```

The CInvestmentWiz class implementation consists solely of a message map and a constructor. The constructor constructs each wizard page and then adds them to the wizard through the AddPage() member function. It then sets the global wizard pointer variable, pInvestmentWiz. As the code demonstrates, the wizard class intelligently delegates most of its functionality to the wizard pages.

Using the Investment Wizard is very straightforward. Following is the code necessary to invoke the wizard from an application:

```
CInvestmentWiz wiz;
wiz.SetWizardMode();
wiz.DoModal();
```

Of course, the application containing this code would also need to include the wizard's resources in its resource script.

Splitting a View

It is sometimes useful to support multiple views in order to provide an alternative means of viewing or modifying document data. A good way to manage multiple views is to use a splitter window, which divides the client area of an application into separate panes. Each pane of a splitter window contains a view. You can use the splitter window to adjust the sizes of the views. Figure 8.6 should give you an idea of how a splitter window supports multiple views.

It's relatively easy to add a splitter window to an MFC application. The first step is to declare a member variable of type CSplitterWnd:

```
CSplitterWnd  m_wndSplitter;
```

The CSplitterWnd class is defined in the AfxCView.h header file, which should be added to the application's StdAfx.h header file. The splitter window should be created in the OnCreateClient() member function of CMainFrame because the splitter window resides in the client area of CMainFrame. Following is the prototype for the OnCreateClient() member function:

```
virtual BOOL OnCreateClient(LPCREATESTRUCT lpcs,
  CCreateContext* pContext);
```

FIGURE 8.6

A splitter window used to support multiple views.

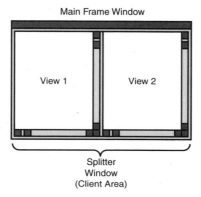

Main Frame Window

View 1   View 2

Splitter
Window
(Client Area)

Listing 8.25 contains the source code for an OnCreateClient() member function that creates the splitter window as well as the two views residing in each splitter pane.

LISTING 8.25   AN OnCreateClient() MEMBER FUNCTION THAT CREATES A SPLITTER WINDOW

```
BOOL CMainFrame::OnCreateClient(LPCREATESTRUCT lpcs, CCreateContext*
  pContext) {
  // Create the splitter window and views
  m_wndSplitter.CreateStatic(this, 1, 2);
  m_wndSplitter.CreateView(0, 0, RUNTIME_CLASS(CMyView),
    CSize(400, 400), pContext);
  m_wndSplitter.CreateView(0, 1, RUNTIME_CLASS(CYourView),
    CSize(400, 400), pContext);
  return TRUE;
}
```

The CreateStatic() member function is used to create the splitter window. The second and third parameters to this function indicate the number of rows and columns of panes in the splitter window. A 1×2 splitter window consists of two panes separated by a vertical splitter bar. The two calls to CreateView() create the views associated with each pane. The left pane (0, 0) is of type CMyView, which is a hypothetical view class. The right pane (0, 1) is of type CYourView, another hypothetical view class. Both views are given a size of 400×400 upon creation, which is arbitrary.

> **NOTE**
>
> The `CSplitterWnd` class also supports a `Create()` member function that is used to create dynamic splitter windows. Dynamic splitter windows are limited to supporting views of the same class. The `CreateStatic()` member function must be used to create a static splitter window if you want to use views of differing types.

You might have reason to want to keep the user from being able to resize the panes managed by a splitter window. In this case, you don't want the user to be able to move the divider separating the panes of the splitter window. To carry out this functionality, you have to understand that the functionality of the divider is handled automatically by the `CSplitterWnd` class. So, to alter this functionality, you must derive a class from `CSplitterWnd` and override the appropriate message handlers that control the divider. Following are the three message handlers that you must override in your derived class, which you might call `CFixedSplitterWnd`:

- `OnLButtonDown()`
- `OnMouseMove()`
- `OnSetCursor()`

The key to dodging the default functionality provided by `CSplitterWnd` is to not allow these message handlers to call up to the parent versions in `CSplitterWnd`. Rather, you should call the generic versions of these handlers in the `CWnd` class. Following is a suitable implementation for the `OnLButtonDown()` message handler, which demonstrates how this is accomplished:

```
void CFixedSplitterWnd::OnLButtonDown(UINT nFlags, CPoint point) {
  CWnd::OnLButtonDown(nFlags, point);
}
```

Similar implementations for the `OnMouseMove()` and `OnSetCursor()` message handlers will finish up the `CFixedSplitterWnd` class.

Summary

This chapter tackles a wide range of topics dealing with user interfaces and how to extend them. In the beginning of the chapter, you learned how to respond to user input from the keyboard and mouse. You then learned about the standard user interface features included in applications generated by AppWizard. From there, you explored menus and how to modify them programmatically. Control bars were next on the agenda; you learned how to use toolbars, status bars, and ToolTips.

In the next part of the chapter, you shifted gears a little when you were introduced to MFC's command update mechanism. However, things quickly turned graphical again when you learned how to design and implement property sheets and wizards. In the last part of the chapter, you were introduced to splitter windows and how they allow you to present multiple views.

Printing

by Michael Morrison

Printing is a significant part of most document-centric applications because most users require a hard copy of their work at some point. Although the "paperless office" has received a lot of hype, in reality it isn't as easy giving up paper as many people would like to believe. So, for the foreseeable future at least, printing is still something programmers have to support in most applications. Fortunately, MFC provides solid support for printing within the document/view architecture that removes a lot of the burden of printing from the programmer.

This chapter tackles printing in MFC and how it affects the design and construction of MFC applications. You'll learn about the MFC classes used to support printing and how to use them to build WYSIWYG (what you see is what you get) applications.

Printing Fundamentals

In Chapter 4, "Painting, Device Contexts, Bitmaps, and Fonts," you learned how MFC employs a device context to provide an abstraction for a drawing surface. This abstraction enables you to draw graphics to virtually any graphical output device with a suitable Windows graphics driver. Printing using MFC is handled in a similar manner. Printing to a printer is little different from drawing to the screen—in both cases a device context is used to abstract the drawing process. From the perspective of Windows, a printer is considered just another graphical output device, and therefore requires a graphics driver in order to be used in Windows.

It isn't just coincidental that printers are handled no differently than monitors. It is a very beneficial part of the design of Windows to enable developers to draw graphics to a printer using the same code that they use to draw graphics to the screen. As an example, consider a graphical application such as the Paint application that ships with Windows 98. This application could use practically the same code to render a drawing to the printer as it does to render a drawing to the screen. On the other hand, adding printing support to form-based applications isn't so simple, because they rely on child controls as the basis for their user interface. In this case, it is up to the programmer to implement a custom printing solution. Even so, you can still use familiar Windows GDI operations and an MFC device context object to carry out the printing.

Speaking of supporting printing in an application, you're probably aware of the fact that print preview has become a standard feature in many applications. Print preview is a visualization of a document on the screen as it will appear on the printed page. You can think of print preview as a simulated print to a special preview window. In fact, it is common to use the same code in print preview as in the actual printing. MFC provides specific support for print preview in addition to its printing support.

Printing with MFC

Before the days of MFC, you had to use Win32 functions to carry out the arduous task of printing. Trust me—adding printing support to an application using straight Win32 functions was a hassle at best, and in many cases could turn into a nightmare. The problem wasn't that drawing graphics to the printer is difficult but that it required myriad Win32 function calls to move the process along. There were also complex data structures that you had to initialize and use properly. And last but not least, you were responsible for implementing a special modeless dialog box that allowed the user to cancel out of printing a lengthy document.

MFC has simplified the process of printing significantly, thanks primarily to its document/view architecture. As a matter of fact, MFC's document/view architecture provides you with default support for printing without your having to do any additional work. By default, MFC will use the OnDraw() member function in your view class to print a document. If you recall, OnDraw() accepts a pointer to a CDC object as its only parameter. During the printing process, this CDC object represents a printer device context instead of a screen device context.

Of course, in most cases you will want to expand on MFC's default printing support and add print features such as headers and footers, along with pagination of documents. MFC provides a printing framework of virtual member functions that makes it easy to add exactly the functionality you need. You can add full-featured printing support to an application, including print preview, by simply overriding appropriate member functions in a view class.

Printing in the View

The majority of MFC's printing support is encapsulated in the CView class, which means that all document/view applications have some form of default printing. There is also a set of special printing member functions in CView that you can use to alter the way in which documents are printed. For example, you must alter the default CView printing functionality if you want to print multiple pages or if you want to print a header or footer on a page.

Table 9.1 lists the most important CView member functions used for printing.

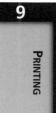

TABLE 9.1 THE MOST IMPORTANT CView MEMBER FUNCTIONS USED FOR PRINTING

Member Function	Description
OnPreparePrinting()	Called before a document is printed or previewed
DoPreparePrinting()	Displays the Print dialog box and creates a printer device context (DC); called from OnPreparePrinting()
OnBeginPrinting()	Called when a print job begins; allocates print-related GDI resources
OnPrepareDC()	Called before OnDraw() to prepare a DC for drawing
OnPrint()	Called to print or preview a document page
OnEndPrintPreview()	Called when the user exits preview mode
OnEndPrinting()	Called when a print job ends; frees print-related GDI resources

The member functions listed in the table represent a printing sequence that is common across all document/view applications. Figure 9.1 shows how this process works.

FIGURE 9.1

The CView member functions called in the standard MFC printing sequence.

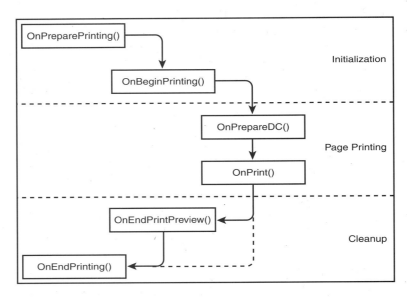

The printing process begins when the user requests to print a document. The framework calls the OnPreparePrinting() member function to display the Print dialog box and get things started. OnPreparePrinting() carries out this request by delegating the work to the DoPreparePrinting() function, which actually handles displaying the Print dialog box and creating a printer DC. You can alter the default values displayed in the Print dialog box by overriding the `OnPreparePrinting()` function and altering the `CPrintInfo` object that is passed into `DoPreparePrinting()`. You learn more about the `CPrintInfo` object in a moment.

Getting back to the print sequence, the framework calls the `OnBeginPrinting()` member function at the beginning of a print or print preview job, after `OnPreparePrinting()` has been called. The main purpose of `OnBeginPrinting()` is to provide a convenient place to allocate any GDI resources specifically required for printing, such as fonts. After the `OnBeginPrinting()` function returns, printing commences one page at a time.

The `OnPrepareDC()` and `OnPrint()` member functions are called for each page that is printed. `OnPrepareDC()` is responsible for making any modifications to the device context required to print the current page. It is also used to analyze attributes of the `CPrintInfo` object, such as the number of pages in the document. If a document length isn't specified, `OnPrepareDC()` assumes the document is one page long and stops the printing sequence after one page.

The `OnPrint()` member function is called just after `OnPrepareDC()`, and is used to perform any graphical output specific to printing. Many applications call the `OnDraw()` function from `OnPrint()` to print the document as it appears in the view. These applications typically use `OnPrint()` to print page elements such as headers and footers. Other applications might use `OnPrint()` to print a document completely independent of the `OnDraw()` function. These applications typically have a view whose `OnDraw()` function isn't helpful for printing. An example of such an application would be one that uses `CFormView`, which is a view containing controls based on a dialog resource.

The `OnEndPrinting()` member function is called at the end of a print job or print preview to free any GDI resources allocated for printing. These resources are typically allocated in the `OnBeginPrinting()` function. If the print sequence was issued for a print preview instead of an actual print job, the `OnEndPrintPreview()` function is called just before `OnEndPrinting()`. The default `OnEndPrintPreview()` function actually calls `OnEndPrinting()` after destroying the view window and restoring the application window to its original state.

Now that you have an idea how a view fits into the print sequence, let's clarify exactly what an application's view is responsible for in terms of printing. An application's view class must take on the following responsibilities to support printing:

- Inform the framework of how many pages are in the document (or accept the default of one page).
- Allocate and free any GDI resources required for printing.
- When asked to print a specific page, draw that portion of the document.

9

PRINTING

This might seem like relatively little work to support printing in an application's view class. That's because MFC does a lot of the work for you. More specifically, the MFC framework must take on the following responsibilities to support printing:

- Display the Print dialog box
- Create a suitable CDC object for the printer
- Inform the view class of which page to print
- Call CView printing member functions at the appropriate times

The PrintInfo Object

You've encountered the CPrintInfo object a few times in the previous discussion on the CView member functions associated with printing. The CPrintInfo object maintains information about a print or print preview job. You don't ever need to create a CPrintInfo object yourself—the framework automatically creates it when the print sequence begins.

The CPrintInfo object contains information such as the range of pages to be printed and the current page being printed. This information is accessible through public data members of the CPrintInfo class. Following are the most commonly used public data members in the CPrintInfo class:

- m_nCurPage—Identifies the page currently being printed
- m_nNumPreviewPages—Identifies the number of pages displayed in the print preview (1 or 2)
- m_bPreview—Indicates whether the document is being previewed
- m_bDirect—Indicates whether the document is being printed directly (bypassing the Print dialog box)
- m_rectDraw—Specifies the usable page area for printing

The first two members, m_nCurPage and m_nNumPreviewPages, are useful for controlling the printing of a multiple-page document. The m_bPreview member is used to determine whether the document is being printed to the printer or displayed in a print preview window. Finally, the m_rectDraw member contains a rectangle that represents the usable page area for printing. You will typically shrink this rectangle to reduce the page area available for printing, which makes room for headers and footers on the page.

The CPrintInfo object serves as a means of exchanging information between an application's view and MFC's built-in printing functionality. A CPrintInfo object is passed between the framework and your view class during the printing process. As an example, your view class knows which page to print because the framework sets the m_nCurPage member of CPrintInfo.

Printing Menu Commands

MFC provides a set of standard identifiers that represent menu commands associated with printing. These command identifiers are extremely useful when creating a user interface for printing from an application. Following are the standard print command identifiers defined by MFC:

- ID_FILE_PRINT_SETUP
- ID_FILE_PRINT
- ID_FILE_PRINT_DIRECT
- ID_FILE_PRINT_PREVIEW

MFC provides default message handler implementations for each of these commands. The CWinApp::OnFilePrintSetup() message handler for the ID_FILE_PRINT_SETUP command invokes the standard print setup dialog that allows the user to alter the printer settings. All you must do to include this functionality in an application is provide the following message map entry in your application class:

```
ON_COMMAND(ID_FILE_PRINT_SETUP, CWinApp::OnFilePrintSetup)
```

The CView::OnFilePrint() message handler for the ID_FILE_PRINT command calls the OnPreparePrinting() function to display the standard Print dialog and create the printer DC. For each page, it calls OnPrepareDC() followed by a call to OnPrint() for that page. When the print job finishes, the OnEndPrinting() function is called, and the printing progress dialog is closed. The ID_FILE_PRINT_DIRECT command uses the OnFilePrint() message handler to print without first displaying the Print dialog box; the default printer and related settings are used. The ID_FILE_PRINT_DIRECT command is typically reserved for use with a toolbar Print button.

The CView::OnFilePrintPreview() message handler for the ID_FILE_PRINT_PREVIEW command initiates the print preview of a document. You don't have to do anything but provide a message map entry for this command to support a default print preview. Following are the view class message map entries required to include the functionality of the ID_FILE_PRINT, ID_FILE_PRINT_DIRECT, and ID_FILE_PRINT_PREVIEW commands in an application:

```
ON_COMMAND(ID_FILE_PRINT, CView::OnFilePrint)
ON_COMMAND(ID_FILE_PRINT_DIRECT, CView::OnFilePrint)
ON_COMMAND(ID_FILE_PRINT_PREVIEW, CView::OnFilePrintPreview)
```

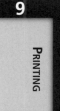

Printing and GDI Mapping Modes

Because printers are inherently different graphical output devices than monitors, you must make sure that GDI operations performed on a printer device context yield consistent results as if they were performed on a screen device context. What I'm getting at is that printers have different resolutions than monitors, which means that you must use a GDI mapping mode that doesn't depend on physical device coordinates.

By default, GDI operations use the MM_TEXT mapping mode, which performs a one-to-one mapping of physical device units to logical units. In other words, logical and physical units are equivalent in the MM_TEXT mapping mode. Furthermore, the coordinate system in this mapping mode increases down and to the right from the upper-left origin in a window.

Consider the ramifications of this mapping mode on the resolutions of monitors and printers. You probably are using a monitor with the resolution set at 800×600, 1024×768, 1152×864, or 1280×1024. These numbers reflect the number of individual pixels in the x and y directions, respectively. Now consider the resolution of a laser printer. Laser printers all have resolutions of 300dpi or greater. That means that there are 300 printer pixels for every inch of page. That means that an 8 1/2×11 inch page has a resolution of 2550×3300 pixels. If you were to print graphics on a 300dpi laser printer using the MM_TEXT mapping mode, they would be displayed at around 45% of their screen size. Figure 9.2 illustrates the problem with the MM_TEXT mapping mode.

FIGURE 9.2

Graphics printed using the MM_TEXT *mapping mode will appear smaller on the printed page than they do on the screen.*

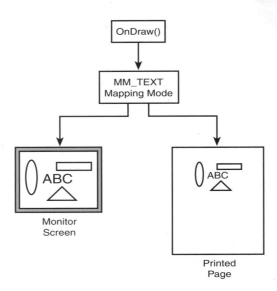

The source of the problem is the MM_TEXT mapping mode, which doesn't take into account the differences in hardware device resolutions. As long as you're mapping logical units on a one-to-one basis with hardware pixels, you're guaranteed to get inconsistent results on different types of hardware. The solution is to use a mapping mode that doesn't think in terms of pixels.

Win32 supports a few different mapping modes that are suitable for printing. One of these is MM_LOENGLISH, which maps a logical unit to a 0.01-inch physical unit. In other words, 100 logical units would appear as 1 inch regardless of the physical device. This functionality is expected in modern applications and is sometimes referred to as WYSIWYG. Figure 9.3 illustrates how the MM_LOENGLISH mapping mode solves the WYSIWYG problem.

FIGURE 9.3

The MM_LOENGLISH *mapping mode results in graphics appearing the same in print as they do on the screen.*

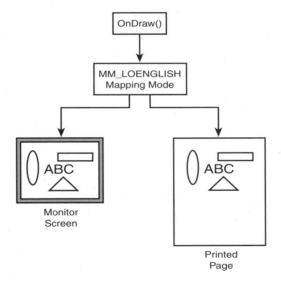

NOTE

The y-axis of the MM_LOENGLISH coordinate system increases in the opposite direction of MM_TEXT. This means that y values decrease down from the origin in the upper-left corner of a window, which results in negative y coordinate values. This sometimes requires special handling because most applications aren't accustomed to dealing with negative graphics coordinates.

WYSIWYG Printing

Now that you have an idea as to how printing works in MFC, let's take a look at a practical example. I built an application called Shaper that allows you to draw primitive graphic shapes including lines, rectangles, triangles, and ellipses. All of these shapes are drawn using standard GDI operations invoked through the CDC class. This is a good sample application for printing because it is necessary to print the shapes accurately so that they appear the same on the printer as they do on the screen. If you recall, this is known as WYSIWYG, and is an important requirement of most graphical applications that support printing.

In addition to the code that specifically supports WYSIWYG printing, there are also some other areas of the Shaper application that affect its printing capability. This chapter touches on all of these areas in order to show you how a real application supports printing. Let's begin with the application's resources.

Application Resources

It isn't possible to print from an application if the user interface doesn't provide print-related menu commands. So it is necessary to include print menu commands in the Shaper application's menu. Listing 9.1 contains the menu resource for Shaper.

LISTING 9.1   THE MENU RESOURCE DEFINITION FOR SHAPER

```
IDR_SHAPER MENU
BEGIN
  POPUP "&File"
    BEGIN
      MENUITEM "&New\tCtrl+N",          ID_FILE_NEW
      MENUITEM "&Open...\tCtrl+O",       ID_FILE_OPEN
      MENUITEM "&Save\tCtrl+S",          ID_FILE_SAVE
      MENUITEM "Save &As...",            ID_FILE_SAVE_AS
      MENUITEM SEPARATOR
      MENUITEM "&Print...\tCtrl+P",      ID_FILE_PRINT
      MENUITEM "Print Pre&view",         ID_FILE_PRINT_PREVIEW
      MENUITEM "P&rint Setup...",        ID_FILE_PRINT_SETUP
      MENUITEM SEPARATOR
      MENUITEM "Recent File",            ID_FILE_MRU_FILE1,GRAYED
      MENUITEM SEPARATOR
      MENUITEM "E&xit",                  ID_APP_EXIT
    END
  POPUP "&Edit"
    BEGIN
      MENUITEM "Clear &All",             ID_EDIT_CLEAR_ALL
    END
  POPUP "&Draw"
```

```
      BEGIN
        MENUITEM "&Line",                ID_DRAW_LINE
        MENUITEM "&Rectangle",           ID_DRAW_RECTANGLE
        MENUITEM "&Triangle",            ID_DRAW_TRIANGLE
        MENUITEM "&Ellipse",             ID_DRAW_ELLIPSE
        MENUITEM SEPARATOR
        MENUITEM "Change C&olor..."      ID_DRAW_CHANGECOLOR
      END
    POPUP "&View"
      BEGIN
        MENUITEM "&Toolbar",             ID_VIEW_TOOLBAR
        MENUITEM "&Status Bar",          ID_VIEW_STATUS_BAR
      END
END
```

The `IDR_SHAPER` menu defines the following important print menu commands, along with their associated standard command identifiers:

- File, Print—`ID_FILE_PRINT`
- File, Print Preview—`ID_FILE_PRINT_PREVIEW`
- File, Print Setup—`ID_FILE_PRINT_SETUP`

To provide a more complete user interface for the Shaper application, it is good to include a toolbar that provides access to commonly used menu commands. A single Print button is sufficient for allowing the user to print using the toolbar. Figure 9.4 shows a zoomed view of the toolbar bitmap image for the Shaper application, which includes a Print button.

FIGURE 9.4

A zoomed view of the toolbar bitmap image for Shaper.

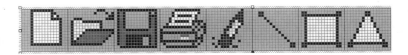

Listing 9.2 contains the toolbar resource for the Shaper application, which associates a print command identifier with the Print toolbar button.

LISTING 9.2 THE TOOLBAR RESOURCE DEFINITION FOR SHAPER

```
IDR_SHAPER TOOLBAR  16, 15
BEGIN
  BUTTON     ID_FILE_NEW
  BUTTON     ID_FILE_OPEN
  BUTTON     ID_FILE_SAVE
  BUTTON     ID_FILE_PRINT_DIRECT
```

continues

9

PRINTING

LISTING 9.2   CONTINUED

```
  SEPARATOR
  BUTTON          ID_EDIT_CLEAR_ALL
  SEPARATOR
  BUTTON          ID_DRAW_LINE
  BUTTON          ID_DRAW_RECTANGLE
  BUTTON          ID_DRAW_TRIANGLE
  BUTTON          ID_DRAW_ELLIPSE
  BUTTON          ID_DRAW_CHANGECOLOR
END
```

Notice that the command `ID_FILE_PRINT_DIRECT` is used for the Print button instead of `ID_FILE_PRINT`. This is done so that the button will print a document without displaying the Print dialog box, which is a little quicker for the user. This also happens to be the standard approach taken by most Windows applications.

Another way to make things quicker for the user is to support a print accelerator. Listing 9.3 contains the keyboard accelerator resources for the Shaper application, which defines a print accelerator.

LISTING 9.3   THE KEYBOARD ACCELERATOR RESOURCE DEFINITIONS FOR SHAPER

```
IDR_SHAPER ACCELERATORS
BEGIN
  "N",             ID_FILE_NEW,          VIRTKEY,CONTROL
  "O",             ID_FILE_OPEN,         VIRTKEY,CONTROL
  "S",             ID_FILE_SAVE,         VIRTKEY,CONTROL
  "P",             ID_FILE_PRINT,        VIRTKEY,CONTROL
END
```

That wraps up the print-related resources required for the Shaper application. Let's move on to the application code.

The Application Class

You might not expect the application class to have anything to do with printing. In truth, it doesn't play much of a role, but there is a small piece of code in the application class that is required to support printing in the Shaper application. More specifically, the default `OnFilePrintSetup()` message handler is implemented in the `CWinApp` class, which makes it necessary to place the `ID_FILE_PRINT_SETUP` menu command message handler in the `CShaperApp` application class. Following is the message map entry for this command:

```
ON_COMMAND(ID_FILE_PRINT_SETUP, CWinApp::OnFilePrintSetup)
```

The default implementation of `OnFilePrintSetup()` handles all of the details of displaying the Print Setup dialog box and interpreting the user responses. Thus, supporting the print setup feature in an MFC application requires only the `ID_FILE_PRINT_SETUP` message map entry.

The View Class

Most of the printing support in an application takes place in the view. In the case of the Shaper application, the `CShaperView` class takes on much of the work of printing Shaper documents. Perhaps the best place to start in analyzing the `CShaperView` class is its message map, which includes entries for print-related menu commands. Listing 9.4 contains the `CShaperView` message map.

LISTING 9.4   THE `CShaperView` MESSAGE MAP FOR SHAPER

```
BEGIN_MESSAGE_MAP(CShaperView, CScrollView)
  ON_WM_LBUTTONDOWN()
  ON_COMMAND(ID_FILE_PRINT, CView::OnFilePrint)
  ON_COMMAND(ID_FILE_PRINT_DIRECT, CView::OnFilePrint)
  ON_COMMAND(ID_FILE_PRINT_PREVIEW, CView::OnFilePrintPreview)
  ON_COMMAND(ID_DRAW_LINE, OnDrawLine)
  ON_COMMAND(ID_DRAW_RECTANGLE, OnDrawRectangle)
  ON_COMMAND(ID_DRAW_TRIANGLE, OnDrawTriangle)
  ON_COMMAND(ID_DRAW_ELLIPSE, OnDrawEllipse)
  ON_COMMAND(ID_DRAW_CHANGECOLOR, OnDrawChangeColor)
  ON_UPDATE_COMMAND_UI(ID_DRAW_LINE, OnUpdateDrawLine)
  ON_UPDATE_COMMAND_UI(ID_DRAW_RECTANGLE, OnUpdateDrawRectangle)
  ON_UPDATE_COMMAND_UI(ID_DRAW_TRIANGLE, OnUpdateDrawTriangle)
  ON_UPDATE_COMMAND_UI(ID_DRAW_ELLIPSE, OnUpdateDrawEllipse)
END_MESSAGE_MAP()
```

Three of these message map entries are associated with printing: `ID_FILE_PRINT`, `ID_FILE_PRINT_DIRECT`, and `ID_FILE_PRINT_PREVIEW`. As you can see, all three of these message map entries route messages to existing `CView` message handlers.

MFC's printing architecture doesn't require you to provide application-specific message handlers for any printing commands. Instead, you are expected to override other `CView` member functions that perform specific printing operations. You learned about these member functions earlier in the chapter. Following is the declaration of one of them in the `CShaperView` class:

```
virtual BOOL  OnPreparePrinting(CPrintInfo* pInfo);
```

If you recall, the `OnPreparePrinting()` member function is called by the `CView::OnFilePrint()` message handler to initiate the printing process. Following is the

9

PRINTING

implementation of the `OnPreparePrinting()` member function in `CShaperView`, which simply calls `DoPreparePrinting()` to delegate the work of starting the printing process:

```
BOOL CShaperView::OnPreparePrinting(CPrintInfo* pInfo) {
  return DoPreparePrinting(pInfo);
}
```

You learned earlier in the chapter that the `MM_TEXT` mapping mode is problematic for printing because physical device coordinates differ between the monitors and printers. For this reason, the Shaper application uses the `MM_LOENGLISH` mapping mode, which results in graphics being drawn consistently across all graphical output devices. The mapping mode is set in the call to `SetScrollSizes()` in the `OnInitialUpdate()` member function, which follows:

```
void CShaperView::OnInitialUpdate() {
  // Set the scroll sizes
  CShaperDoc* pDoc = GetDocument();
  ASSERT_VALID(pDoc);
  SetScrollSizes(MM_LOENGLISH, pDoc()->GetDocSize());
}
```

The other place in the view where the `SetScrollSizes()` member function is called is in the `OnUpdate()` member function. Listing 9.5 contains the source code for the `OnUpdate()` member function.

LISTING 9.5 THE `CShaperView::OnUpdate()` MEMBER FUNCTION FOR SHAPER

```
void CShaperView::OnUpdate(CView* pSender, LPARAM lHint,
  CObject* pHint) {
  // Make sure the hint is valid
  if (pHint != NULL) {
    if (pHint->IsKindOf(RUNTIME_CLASS(CShape))) {
      // Update the scroll sizes
      CShaperDoc* pDoc = GetDocument();
      ASSERT_VALID(pDoc);
      SetScrollSizes(MM_LOENGLISH, pDoc->GetDocSize());

      // Invalidate only the rectangular position of the new shape
      CShape* pShape = DYNAMIC_DOWNCAST(CShape, pHint);
      CClientDC dc(this);
      OnPrepareDC(&dc);
      CRect rc = pShape->GetPosition();
      dc.LPtoDP(&rc);
      rc.InflateRect(1, 1);
      InvalidateRect(&rc);
      return;
    }
  }
}
```

```
  // Invalidate the entire view
  Invalidate();
}r
```

The `OnDraw()` member function is called to draw both to the screen and the printer and must draw graphics properly using the `MM_LOENGLISH` mapping mode. More specifically, `OnDraw()` has to deal with the issue of the `MM_LOENGLISH` mapping mode's y-axis increasing in the negative direction. Listing 9.6 contains the source code for the `OnDraw()` member function.

LISTING 9.6 THE `CShaperView::OnDraw()` MEMBER FUNCTION FOR SHAPERR

```
void CShaperView::OnDraw(CDC* pDC) {
  // Get a pointer to the document
  CShaperDoc* pDoc = GetDocument();
  ASSERT_VALID(pDoc);

  // Get the clipping rect for the DC
  CRect rcClip, rcShape;
  pDC->GetClipBox(&rcClip);
  rcClip.top = -rcClip.top;
  rcClip.bottom = -rcClip.bottom;

  // Draw the view (paint the shapes)
  POSITION pos = pDoc->m_shapeList.GetHeadPosition();
  while (pos != NULL) {
    // Get the next shape
    CShape* pShape = pDoc->m_shapeList.GetNext(pos);

    // Only draw if the shape rect intersects the clipping rect
    rcShape = pShape->GetPosition();
    rcShape.top = -rcShape.top;
    rcShape.bottom = -rcShape.bottom;
    if (rcShape.IntersectRect(&rcShape, &rcClip))
      pShape->Draw(pDC);
  }
}
```

The solution to the negative y-axis problem in `OnDraw()` is to negate the y components of each rectangle in the code. Notice that the top and bottom members of the `rcClip` and `rcShape` rectangles are both negated before the rectangles are used. This results in positive values for the y components of the rectangles. Unless you make this change, the `IntersectRect()` function would have trouble interpreting the negative rectangle components, and would never detect a rectangle intersection.

9

PRINTING

By the way, the CShape class represents a simple shape and includes the constant shape identifiers LINE, RECTANGLE, TRIANGLE, and ELLIPSE. The document maintains a list of CShape objects in the m_shapeList member variable. When drawing shapes from the list, the OnDraw() member function checks to see if the bounding rectangles for each shape intersect the clipping rectangle, and draws only shapes that intersect it. This makes the drawing of shapes much more efficient.

You might feel that I'm straying a bit from the topic of printing with all this shape talk. However, I'm trying to show you how printing isn't just about margins and page counts; printing affects many parts of an application. Let's take a look now at how the view specifically supports printing.

If you recall from earlier in the chapter, the OnPrint() member function is responsible for performing any additional drawing when a document is being printed. Following is the declaration of OnPrint() in the CShaperView class:

```
virtual void  OnPrint(CDC* pDC, CPrintInfo* pInfo);
```

Listing 9.7 contains the source code for the OnPrint() member function.

LISTING 9.7   THE CShaperView::OnPrint() MEMBER FUNCTION FOR SHAPER

```
void CShaperView::OnPrint(CDC* pDC, CPrintInfo* pInfo) {
  // Get a pointer to the document
  CShaperDoc* pDoc = GetDocument();
  ASSERT_VALID(pDoc);

  // Print the page header and adjust the DC window origin
  CString sDocTitle = pDoc->GetTitle();
  PrintPageHeader(pDC, pInfo, sDocTitle);
  pDC->SetWindowOrg(pInfo->m_rectDraw.left, -pInfo->m_rectDraw.top);

  // Print the document data
  OnDraw(pDC);
}
```

The OnPrint() member function takes on the task of printing the header on the page before allowing OnDraw() to draw the actual document data. Notice how the window origin of the device context is altered to reflect the drawing rectangle maintained by the CPrintInfo object. This is necessary so that the OnDraw() function can't draw in the header; in fact, OnDraw() doesn't even know about the header thanks to the shrunken drawing rectangle.r

One member function that definitely does know about the header is PrintPageHeader(), which is called by OnPrint(). The PrintPageHeader() member function is responsible for printing the document header. Following is the declaration of the `PrintPageHeader()` member function:

```
void PrintPageHeader(CDC* pDC, CPrintInfo* pInfo, CString& sHeader);
```

The `PrintPageHeader()` member function accepts a string as its third parameter and prints it, along with a horizontal line below the string that goes across the page. Listing 9.8 contains the source code for the `PrintPageHeader()` member function.

LISTING 9.8   THE `CShaperView::PrintPageHeader()` MEMBER FUNCTION FOR SHAPERR

```
void CShaperView::PrintPageHeader(CDC* pDC, CPrintInfo* pInfo,
  CString& sHeader) {
  // Draw the header text aligned left
  pDC->SetTextAlign(TA_LEFT);
  pDC->TextOut(0, -25, sHeader);

  // Draw a line across the page just below the header text
  TEXTMETRIC tm;
  pDC->GetTextMetrics(&tm);
  int y = -35 - tm.tmHeight;
  pDC->MoveTo(0, y);
  pDC->LineTo(pInfo->m_rectDraw.right, y);

  // Adjust the drawing rect to not include the header
  y -= 25;
  pInfo->m_rectDraw.top += y;
}
```

The header text is drawn in `PrintPageHeader()` using a negative y coordinate, which is necessary when working within the `MM_LOENGLISH` mapping mode. The value of `-25` equates to 1/4 inch in this mapping mode because each logical unit is equivalent to 0.01 inch ($25 \times 0.01 = 0.25$). A line is drawn across the page just below the text, after which the `PrintPageHeader()` function adjusts the drawing rectangle to exclude the header.

Figure 9.5 shows the completed Shaper application. I encourage you to try out the application and print a few documents to see how closely the printed page matches the screen. You should also try out the print preview feature, which is shown in Figure 9.6.

Pagination

The default printing functionality built into MFC is designed to support single-page printing. MFC certainly doesn't prevent you from printing multiple pages, but you can't rely solely on its default functionality if you are printing a multiple-page document. Even

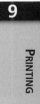

so, printing multiple pages isn't too difficult, and MFC definitely makes the task easier than the old Win32 API approach.

FIGURE 9.5

The completed Shaper application.

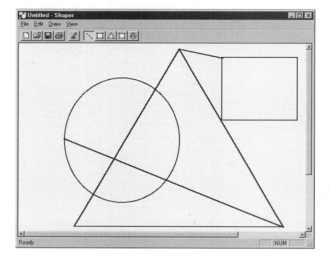

FIGURE 9.6

The Print Preview window in the Shaper application.

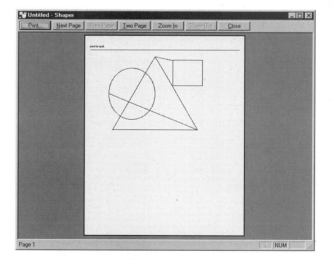

When it comes to printing multiple-page documents, it is very important whether the number of pages can be determined prior to printing. If the page count can be determined in advance, you can use a simpler approach to establish a print loop that iterates through the pages. If it isn't possible to calculate the page count in advance, you can still print multiple pages, but it requires a little more work.

Printing with a Known Page Count

If you know the page count in advance, establishing the print loop is as simple as calling the SetMaxPage() member function on the CPrintInfo object passed into the OnPreparePrinting() function. This sets the number of pages in the print job, which directly affects the number of pages printed in the print loop. Listing 9.9 contains an example of an OnPreparePrinting() function that sets the number of pages for a print job using SetMaxPage().

LISTING 9.9   AN OnPreparePrinting() MEMBER FUNCTION THAT SETS THE PAGE COUNT

```
BOOL CMyView::OnPreparePrinting(CPrintInfo* pInfo) {
  // Set the number of pages in the print job
  CMyDoc* pDoc = GetDocument();
  ASSERT_VALID(pDoc);
  int nPages = pDoc->CalcNumPages();
  pInfo->SetMaxPage(nPages);

  return DoPreparePrinting(pInfo);
}
```

This code assumes that the document class, CMyDoc, defines a member function named CalcNumPages() that calculates the number of print pages based on the document data. You could also implement a similar function in the view class because the number of pages is arguably an attribute of the view and not the document. However, a document such as a word processor document would maintain its own page breaks and would therefore probably have knowledge of the page count directly in the document class.

Regardless of where the page count is calculated, it enters the printing picture when the SetMaxPage() member function is called in OnPreparePrinting(). Keep in mind that the OnPrint() function takes on the responsibility of printing the appropriate information based on the page being printed. It is passed a CPrintInfo object that it can use to obtain information about the current page. For example, the m_nCurPage member variable contains the page number of the page currently being printed. You can also determine the first and last pages in the range of pages being printed by calling the GetFromPage() and GetToPage() member functions.

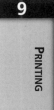

9

PRINTING

Printing with an Unknown Page Count

It's easy enough to support pagination when you know the page count in advance. However, pagination is a little trickier when the page count is an unknown. You might be wondering how it could be possible that you wouldn't know the page count prior to invoking a print job in an application. However, consider as an example a database application that must perform a query in order to print a series of records. This type of application would typically retrieve and print records obtained from a database query during the print process, which makes it impossible to know in advance how many pages there are to be printed.

Printing a document with an unknown page count is referred to as on-the-fly pagination, because you are effectively calculating the page count on-the-fly as the print job proceeds. Instead of setting the page count using the SetMaxPage() member function, you inform MFC that you aren't finished printing as long as there is more data to be printed. This is taken care of in the OnPrepareDC() function, which is called before each page is printed.

To inform MFC that there is more to be printed, you set the m_bContinuePrinting member variable in the CPrintInfo object that is passed into OnPrepareDC(). Setting this member variable to TRUE tells MFC that it should go ahead and continue printing the next page. Listing 9.10 contains a sample OnPrepareDC() function that shows how to set this member variable in order to continue printing a document of unknown size.

LISTING 9.10 AN OnPrepareDC() MEMBER FUNCTION THAT PRINTS A DOCUMENT OF UNKNOWN PAGE COUNT

```
BOOL CMyView::OnPrepareDC(CDC* pDC, CPrintInfo* pInfo) {
  CView::OnPrepareDC(pDC, pInfo);

  // Set the mapping mode
  pDC->SetMapMode(MM_LOENGLISH);

  // Continue printing until the query finishes
  CMyDoc* pDoc = GetDocument();
  ASSERT_VALID(pDoc);
  if (pInfo != NULL)
    pInfo->m_bContinuePrinting = !pDoc->QueryFinished();
}
```

This example shows how to dynamically control the print loop in a hypothetical database application. A function called QueryFinished() is called on the document object to determine whether the database query that controls the printing has finished. The m_bContinuePrinting member variable is set based on the return value of the QueryFinished() function.

Earlier I mentioned that MFC's default printing functionality was geared toward printing single-page documents. This is apparent when you take a look at the source code for the default CView::OnPrepareDC() member function, which is shown in Listing 9.11.

LISTING 9.11 THE DEFAULT CView::OnPrepareDC() MEMBER FUNCTION THAT PRINTS A SINGLE PAGE

```
void CView::OnPrepareDC(CDC* pDC, CPrintInfo* pInfo) {
  ASSERT_VALID(pDC);
  UNUSED(pDC); // unused in release builds

  // Default to one page printing if doc length not known
  if (pInfo != NULL)
    pInfo->m_bContinuePrinting = (pInfo->GetMaxPage() != 0xffff ||
      (pInfo->m_nCurPage == 1));
}
```

In the default implementation of OnPrepareDC(), the m_bContinuePrinting member variable is set to TRUE only if the current page is the first page. In other words, m_bContinuePrinting is set to FALSE after the first page of a document is printed. This results in only a single page being printed regardless of the page count. Of course, explicitly setting the page count through a call to SetMaxPage() in the OnPreparePrinting() function bypasses this functionality, which is evident in the code for CView::OnPrepareDC().

Printing Page Numbers

Regardless of how you establish the page count for a multiple-page print job, you will probably want to print the current page number on each printed page. The most logical place to print page numbers is in the footer of the page, which appears just below the body of the page.

The CPrintInfo object that is passed into the OnPrint() function provides information about the current page being printed, along with the range of pages being printed in the print job. You can use this information to print the current page number and its relationship to other pages in the print job. More specifically, the m_nCurPage member variable of CPrintInfo contains the current page number. You can determine the number of pages being printed by calling the `GetToPage()` and `GetFromPage()` member functions. Following is an example of how this number can be calculated:

```
int nPageCount = pInfo->GetToPage() - pInfo->GetFromPage() + 1;
```

As an example, consider the situation where you are printing pages 7 through 15 of a document. Because the page range is inclusive, the print job in this example consists of a total of 9 pages. The previous calculation would correctly calculate this total. Listing 9.12 contains a more complete example that shows how to print an entire page footer including the current page and the page range.

LISTING 9.12   A `PrintPageFooter()` MEMBER FUNCTION FOR PRINTING PAGE FOOTERS

```cpp
void CMyView::PrintPageFooter(CDC* pDC, CPrintInfo* pInfo) {
  // Assemble the footer string and calculate its size
  CString sFooter;
  int nPageCount = pInfo->GetToPage() - pInfo->GetFromPage() + 1;
  sFooter.Format("Page %d of %d", pInfo->m_nCurPage, nPageCount);
  CSize sizFooter = pDC->GetTextExtent(sFooter);

  // Draw a line separating the footer from the document body
  CRect& rcPage = pInfo->m_rectDraw;
  int nYBottom = rcPage.bottom + sizFooter.cy * 2 + 100);
  int nYCur = nYBottom;
  pDC->MoveTo(0, nYCur);
  pDC->LineTo(rcPage.right, nYCur);
  nYCur -= sizFooter.cy;

  // Draw the footer
  pDC->TextOut(rcPage.left + (rcPage.Width() - sizFooter.cx) / 2,
    nYCur,
    sFooter);

  // Adjust printable area
  rcPage.bottom = nYBottom;
}
```

You would call this function from the `OnPrint()` function just before printing the body of the document. It's very important to print both the header and footer of a page before printing the document body because printing the header and footer requires adjustments to the drawing rectangle. Printing the header and footer before the body ensures that the body won't be printed over them. Listing 9.13 contains an example of an `OnPrint()` function that prints a header, footer, and document body in the proper order.

```
void CMyView::OnPrint(CDC* pDC, CPrintInfo* pInfo) {
  // Print the page header and footer
  PrintPageHeader(pDC, pInfo);
  PrintPageFooter(pDC, pInfo);

  // Print the document body
  PrintPageBody(pDC, pInfo);
}
```

This example assumes that you aren't printing a WYSIWYG document, which means that the `OnDraw()` function isn't used for printing. That's why the `PrintPageBody()` function is called instead of `OnDraw()`. For a WYSIWYG document, you should call `OnDraw()` instead of creating a `PrintPageBody()` function.

Stopping and Aborting Print Jobs

Although the user can stop or abort the printing process by selecting a printer from the Windows Printers folder and using the Print Manager, it is sometimes useful to halt a print job programmatically. You have two options for programmatically halting a print job:

- Stopping the print job, which stops the print job but allows pages that have already been rendered to be printed
- Aborting the print job, which stops the print job and stops all pages from being printed

Along with these two choices of how to halt a print job, you also have the option of performing the halt either in the `OnPrepareDC()` function or the `OnPrint()` function.

Halting a Print Job in `OnPrepareDC()`

To stop a print job from within the `OnPrepareDC()` function, you simply set the `m_bContinuePrinting` member variable to `FALSE`. This results in the print loop exiting, but any pages already rendered to the print spooler will continue to print. To stop all pages from printing, you must call the `AbortDoc()` member function on the printer device context after setting the `m_bContinuePrinting` member variable to `FALSE`. The `AbortDoc()` function terminates the print job and clears out any rendered pages that have yet to be printed. Listing 9.14 contains a sample `OnPrepareDC()` function that is capable of stopping and aborting the print job.

9

PRINTING

LISTING 9.14 AN `OnPrepareDC()` MEMBER FUNCTION THAT IS CAPABLE OF STOPPING AND ABORTING A PRINT JOB

```
BOOL CMyView::OnPrepareDC(CDC* pDC, CPrintInfo* pInfo) {
  CView::OnPrepareDC(pDC, pInfo);

  // Set the mapping mode
  pDC->SetMapMode(MM_LOENGLISH);

  // Stop the print job if necessary
  if (bStopPrinting || bAbortPrinting)
    if (pInfo != NULL)
      pInfo->m_bContinuePrinting = FALSE;

  // Abort the print job if necessary
  if (bAbortPrinting)
    pDC->AbortDoc();
}
```

This example uses two Boolean member variables named `bStopPrinting` and `bAbortPrinting` to determine whether the print job should be stopped or aborted. Presumably, you would set these member variables elsewhere in an application in response to the user canceling the print job.

Halting a Print Job in `OnPrint()`

The other approach to halting a print job involves the `OnPrint()` function. In this case, you call the `EndDoc()` member function on the printer device context to stop the print job, or call the `AbortDoc()` member function to abort the print job. Listing 9.15 contains a sample `OnPrint()` function that is capable of stopping and aborting a print job using `EndDoc()` and `AbortDoc()`, respectively.

LISTING 9.15 AN `OnPrint()` MEMBER FUNCTION THAT IS CAPABLE OF STOPPING AND ABORTING A PRINT JOB

```
void CMyView::OnPrint(CDC* pDC, CPrintInfo* pInfo) {
  // Stop the print job if necessary
  if (bStopPrinting)
    pDC->EndDoc();

  // Abort the print job if necessary
  if (bAbortPrinting)
    pDC->AbortDoc();

  // Print the page header and footer
  PrintPageHeader(pDC, pInfo);
  PrintPageFooter(pDC, pInfo);
```

```
   // Print the document body
   PrintPageBody(pDC, pInfo);
}
```

This sample code uses the same bStopPrinting and bAbortPrinting member variables to determine whether the print job should be stopped or aborted. The code is very straightforward in that a call to EndDoc() or AbortDoc() is all that is required to stop or abort the print job.

Summary

This chapter introduces you to printing and how it fits into the MFC framework. You started off the chapter by learning some basics about printing, along with the main MFC classes that facilitate printing in applications based upon MFC's document/view architecture. You then learned about the significance of mapping modes when it comes to printing, and how some mapping modes are more suited to printing than others. From there, you examined how to add printing support to a graphics application.

You then shifted gears a little and took a look at pagination and how to manage the printing of multiple-page documents. Finally, I wrapped up by explaining how to stop and abort print jobs programmatically using MFC.

9

PRINTING

MFC and COM Programming

PART
III

COM

CHAPTER 10

by K. David White

ActiveX and OLE seem to be in the forefront of application development news these days. These technologies, however, are driven from a base specification referred to as Component Object Model (COM). COM, COM, everywhere COM! It appears that everything is becoming *active*. From desktop applications working with compound documents to the current desktop, you find this technology as a major focus of Microsoft's direction. Object-oriented programming has been around for some time now, but COM still can't simply be defined as another implementation. It is much more than that.

The COM specification describes a methodology for implementing compon ents: reusable objects that can be attached in different ways to create different applications. Obviously, if you are reading this book, you are familiar with the C++ representation of object-oriented programming. In the interest of "doing it better," you are always looking for better and more efficient ways to solve software development problems. One such approach is reuse.

Reuse has been a hot topic for some time. Think of a manufacturing process that simply takes parts out of inventory, moves them to stations along the manufacturing line, and then assembles them in order, making a usable product. The software industry's desire for a similar manufacturing paradigm also provides the thrust behind a reusable solution to software development. As hardware technology has progressed, so has the process of developing software. I could ramble on and on about the benefits and disadvantages of object reuse, but let's take an inside look at this amazingly simple yet paradoxically complex method of reusability.

A Little History

Long ago and far away (okay, so it's Redmond and was only a few years ago), there was OLE 1. *Object linking and embedding* was developed primarily to support compound documents. OLE provides an application with the capability to contain and manipulate a document that was produced by another application as if it were its own. Thus a *compound document* could give the appearance of a single entity. This integration provided a large boost to the productivity of the users of these applications. No longer did a user have to use two applications to work with a single set of information; to the user it appeared as if only one application was performing the work.

Then along came OLE 2, which was a marked improvement not only in functionality, but also in performance. OLE 1 was simply a methodology to solve a unique problem, but it didn't go far enough in solving the bigger problem of reusable objects. OLE 2 was aimed at creating a way for objects to communicate with each other in a consistent and reliable manner.

Microsoft decided to drop OLE as an abbreviation, as well as any future version numbers, and to simply call the technology OLE. No longer was OLE to represent object linking and embedding and compound documents, but was used to represent any application that was COM-based. Well, Microsoft wasn't finished with its marketing terminology "switcharoo." In 1996, ActiveX was born, or was it? Was this another name for OLE/COM, or was this something entirely different? It appeared that ActiveX was used to refer to Internet technologies, although in fact ActiveX replaced the former VBX components. 16-bit Visual Basic had a mechanism for incorporating extension "controls," which was well-known but not formally specified. ActiveX changed that while at the same time providing Microsoft with a portable Internet control methodology. ActiveX was, in fact, a derivative technology based on a central core—COM. Today, other technologies have followed a similar development theme, such as DirectX (see Chapter 30, "MFC and DirectX").

Because COM terminology was so interchangeable, OLE now refers only to object linking and embedding. ActiveX refers mainly to visual components used in developing user-interface extensions to applications or Web pages. But the underlying technology that binds all this terminology is COM.

Interfaces, Objects, and Methods

COM provides the capability for one subset of an application to communicate not only with another subset of the same application, but also with a subset of a different application. This interchangeability is the goal of object-oriented application development: Creating reusable components that can not only be "plugged in" by applications to perform work, but that can also communicate with other components is exactly what COM has accomplished. COM does this by supporting one or more *interfaces* that other applications and objects can use to access the component's internal methods.

Some Terminology

If you're new to COM, some of the terminology might be a little confusing. Hopefully, you are not new to object-oriented terminology. In the following sections, I will explain some of the terms I will be using to define this technology.

10

COM

Interfaces

An *interface* is defined as an exposed connection for a controlling application to access a COM object. Here's what a COM interface is not:

- Interfaces are not classes. It is common to assume that an interface is a class definition. This mistake is commonly made because of interface inheritance. The interface has no implementation—it is simply a window into the COM object, which is defined by a class. (If you are totally confused, I can clear it up in a minute.)

- An interface is not a COM object. When I first started working with COM, I was confusing an interface with the COM object itself. An interface is a collection of functions and is the exposing mechanism of the object itself.

There can be multiple interfaces for one COM object. In fact, COM objects normally do support more than one interface.

Interfaces are immutable. The COM specification dictates that COM interfaces cannot be versioned. Interface version conflicts are avoided by creating entirely new interfaces for even the most minor modification to the original interface.

Objects

A COM object, also commonly referred to as a COM component, is a particular instance of a COM class. It can contain many functions accessible through its interfaces. A COM object must have at least the IUnknown interface, which I will discuss later in this chapter.

Classes

A COM component is a specific instance of a COM class, which defines the component's interfaces and methods. Whenever a COM component is instantiated, its *class object* or *class factory* is called to do the initialization. When this takes place, the component's interfaces are exposed to the client application.

> **NOTE**
>
> If you are developing your COM objects in C++, your class factory might indeed ultimately call a C++ class constructor to actually create the COM object. In general, though, COM objects are created using a static class object (C++ terminology) whose singular purpose is to create instances of a given COM object. How this is accomplished is encapsulated within the class object itself. You probably don't know how any given COM object is created, nor should you be concerned. COM will handle the details for you.

A Real-World View

Imagine that you are creating a checkbook application. Looking at this application simplistically, you might need a method that would deposit funds, one to withdraw funds, and probably another one to calculate the balance. To implement this as a COM object that could be reused in a banking application, you would need to define an interface for the checkbook that would *expose* your three methods. Figure 10.1 provides a representation of how this might be shown in a design methodology.

FIGURE 10.1

A design representation of the checkbook COM object.

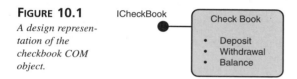

If you are new to COM, you might be wondering how one object might know about another's interfaces, or how to invoke the methods that the object contains. Let's find out a little more about how COM really works.

> **NOTE**
>
> COM objects exporting interfaces for another's use are called *servers*. Those objects that use another's interfaces are referred to as *clients*. The interfaces themselves are typically named according to their function, although they are usually preceded with a capital I, as in ISomeCOMInterface.

The IUnknown Interface

COM's architects knew there must be some mechanism for querying an interface to determine its capabilities and to provide for the interface's *reference count*, which determines how long the interface remains available for use before destruction. They designed a very special interface, which they called IUnknown. This interface is so important that a basic tenet in the COM specification requires that all COM interfaces support the IUnknown interface in addition to their specialized interfaces.

> **NOTE**
>
> As I mentioned, the COM specification dictates that every COM component must support the IUnknown interface. Every interface defined for the component must be derived from IUnknown or from another interface that is itself derived from IUnknown. This is referred to as *interface inheritance.*

For the longest time, I was confusing interfaces and methods and their relationships. It wasn't apparent to me that the interface was nothing more than a directing mechanism to get to the method that I needed. A COM interface provides access to a table that contains pointers to the object's methods. This table is referred to as the *vtable*, and it serves the same function as the C++ vtable, which is a table of virtual pointers to constituent object methods. Figure 10.2 depicts this relationship. When a client application obtains an interface pointer, it can invoke any method that is exposed by the interface. The interface pointer is essentially a redirected memory pointer to the vtable. The pointers in the vtable are offset from this internal pointer as defined by the Interface Definition Language (IDL). Listing 10.1 is an IDL listing for this chapter's example, a CheckBook application.

FIGURE 10.2

The representation between an interface and its methods.

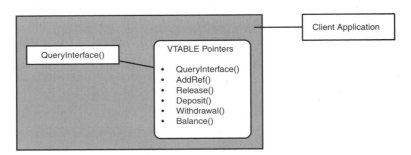

Notice from Figure 10.2 that this interface contains not only the three methods (Deposit(), Withdrawal(), and Balance()), but also three additional methods. If you are following this discussion or have previously learned a little bit about COM, you probably already know the answer to the question "Where do the other three methods come from?"

Back to IUnknown. IUnknown has three methods. These are QueryInterface(), AddRef(), and Release(). Look familiar? COM specifies that the ICheckBook interface must be derived from IUnknown, and therefore the interface will contain not only the checking-related methods but also the IUnknown methods.

LISTING 10.1   THE IDL LISTING FOR THE ICheckBook INTERFACE COM OBJECT

```
// CheckBook.idl : IDL source for CheckBook.dll
//

// This file will be processed by the MIDL tool to
// produce the type library (CheckBook.tlb) and marshalling code.

import "oaidl.idl";
import "ocidl.idl";
    [
        object,
        uuid(6EC5AB0E-A254-11D2-9D87-000000000000),

        helpstring("ICCheckBook Interface"),
        pointer_default(unique)
    ]
    interface ICCheckBook : IUnknown
    {
        [helpstring("method Deposit")] HRESULT Deposit(long lAmount);
        [helpstring("method Withdrawal")] HRESULT Withdrawal(long lAmount);
        [helpstring("method Balance")] HRESULT Balance();
    };

[
    uuid(6EC5AB01-A254-11D2-9D87-000000000000),
    version(1.0),
    helpstring("CheckBook 1.0 Type Library")
]
library CHECKBOOKLib
{
    importlib("stdole32.tlb");
    importlib("stdole2.tlb");

    [
        uuid(6EC5AB0F-A254-11D2-9D87-000000000000),
        helpstring("CCheckBook Class")
    ]
    coclass CCheckBook
    {
        [default] interface ICCheckBook;
    };
};
```

The QueryInterface() method, as its name implies, will answer the question "Is this interface the same as the interface I am looking for?" The AddRef() and Release() methods are used for reference counting. More about that later.

> **NOTE**
>
> The vtable is a redirecting mechanism to allow the client to execute a method exposed by the interface. Whenever a COM client obtains an interface pointer, it has a pointer to the vtable. By using pointer dereferencing, the client can invoke any method exposed by the interface—a simple, yet extremely powerful technique!

The `QueryInterface` Method

Whenever an application creates an instance of a COM object, it receives a handle to an interface exposed by the object. To find other interfaces on the object, the client application must invoke `IUnknown`'s `QueryInterface()` method. At this point you might be asking how an interface is really defined.

How do you use `QueryInterface()` to find another interface? Suppose that the name for the `Deposit` interface is not unique. It is not beyond the realm of possibility that the interface name `Deposit` might be used by another COM object. You need to pass `QueryInterface()` a unique *interface identifier*, or IID.

Now back to the IDL listing. Notice the line above the interface definition. Enclosed in square brackets is the interface's Universally Unique Identifier (UUID) definition. The RPC-defined UUID is uniquely defined in time and space. In COM parlance, it is typically referred to as a Globally Unique Identifier (GUID). This particular GUID denotes an interface, so it is yet again renamed to IID. How can you be certain that these interfaces are indeed unique, and that some other machine doesn't create an identifier that is identical to yours? First, the identifier is unique in time, but that still doesn't guarantee that they will be unique. Applying a unique machine identifier to the GUID will guarantee that you have created a unique identifier for the interface. Given these unique IIDs, `QueryInterface()` can locate the requested interface.

> **NOTE**
>
> A GUID that defines an interface is referred to as an Interface Identifier (IID). A GUID that defines a class is referred to as a Class Identifier (CLSID). The term *GUID* is essentially interchangeable with either.

If you are following me to this point, you might also be wondering how all this applies if the COM object is updated, or one of the interfaces has changed. Uh-oh! The COM specification dictates that interfaces can*not* change. And that includes the methods that it supports. If you change one of the methods that it supports, you change the interface definition itself. So how do you deal with this dilemma? Whenever a COM object is updated, a new interface must be created.

At first, this might seem like overkill, but to maintain the portable nature of COM objects, their interfaces must remain unique. If you need to add functionality to a method, or add more methods to a COM object, it is necessary to follow the rules. This ensures that users of your previous COM object aren't adversely affected whenever they attempt to use a new version of your COM object.

> **NOTE**
>
> The COM specification dictates that an interface definition cannot change. If you need to make changes to your existing interface, you have effectively defined a *new* interface.

If you go back to this chapter's CheckBook application, you might want to add a `CalculateInterest()` method. Because the COM specification doesn't allow you to do this, you must create another interface for your object. Let's take a closer look at this.

In this case, you have an `ICheckBook` interface with three methods. Assuming that you want to add another method, you can either add a completely new interface with just the one (new) method, or you can add another interface that has your new method yet also inherits the existing methods from your old interface. Because the first method will add only your new method, the client using your COM object would have to know about the existing interface in addition to your new interface. This is not always practical or prudent, although there might be times when this is an effective alternative. On the other hand, by inheriting a new interface from your old interface, your new clients only have to know about (or query for) the new interface. This happens often in real-world situations. (`ISomeCOMInterface` becomes an enhanced `ISomeCOMInterface2`.)

Suppose that you want to modify or enhance your existing methods. This problem is a little more difficult in the COM world. Because you can't change an interface, you can't update your existing methods. You would have to provide a new interface that contains new versions of these methods. In this situation, you cannot inherit from your old interface, because you would probably name the methods identically to the pre-existing ones. Figure 10.3 is a representation of the new COM object with the new interface derived from the old interface. `ICheckBook2` is derived from `ICheckBook` and contains the new method that you need.

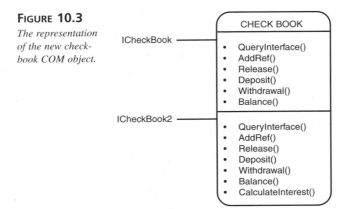

FIGURE 10.3

The representation of the new check-book COM object.

Reference Counting

Remember that a COM object is a specific instance of a class. It is not uncommon to need to use a COM object more than once. When a client starts an object, it might not be the only one that wants to use it. If other clients use the object, they do so by acquiring a pointer, either from the originating client or by invoking CoCreateInstance(). Whenever an object passes out one of its pointers, it increments the reference count for that interface. Whenever the client is done with the interface, the reference count is decremented. When the reference counts for all interfaces on an object are zero, the object can be unloaded. The AddRef() method is called by the CoCreateInstance method when an instance is created for a client. The client calls Release() to decrement the usage count. When a client passes an object's pointer to another client, the new client must call AddRef() to tell the object that it is using the interface.

> **NOTE**
>
> It is very important that clients follow the rules of reference counting. It could be problematic for an instance of an object to remain in memory when not used anymore.

Servers, Clients, and Classes

COM is commonly viewed as a client/server model, and for good reason. As I mentioned previously, an application that uses the services of a COM component is commonly called a client. A COM component that exposes methods and provides services is referred to as a server. This approach simplifies the problem solving solution and lends itself to the definition of reusability. Whenever a COM component crashes, or the server that encapsulates the COM components develops a problem, the client can deal with the situation gracefully. If the client/server relationship were not implemented in this fashion, clients would have to know implementation details to handle these situations gracefully.

COM is unique in allowing clients to also be servers. By having components share pointers with each other, you can develop truly robust peer-to-peer applications. This flexibility leads to obvious advantages over other component models available today.

A COM object is implemented in a server. This server can be in the form of a Dynamic Linked Library (DLL) or can be implemented as a separate executable. A DLL is loaded at runtime, and can be unloaded when no longer in use. Servers take on three forms:

- In-process server—The object is implemented in a DLL and resides in the same memory space as the client.

- Local server—The object is implemented in a separate process on the same machine.

- Remote server—Objects are executed on a separate machine. I will discuss this topic in the section that covers DCOM.

> **NOTE**
>
> Each object is an instance of a class. The unique identifier for a class is commonly referred to as a CLSID. A client uses this CLSID to create an instance of the COM object. A server can have more than one object of a specific class, and can also support multiple classes.

To a client, the implementation remains the same regardless of which type of server the object resides in. Without this transparency a client would not only have to know about the interfaces on a component, but the implementation details as well. This defeats the purpose of the COM standard.

As you are undoubtedly realizing, the COM specification has dictated a standard by which clients written in any language can access components implemented in any language. This solves a multitude of problems when developing applications, as developers can now concentrate on the "building-block" approach to defining workable solutions to common everyday problems. Let's expand what you know to further define COM.

The COM Runtime Environment

The COM runtime environment is a suite of system components that enables COM to work. Using the COM runtime, clients can make IUnknown calls across processes or over a network. It is the mechanism that provides the ability to establish connections between components. It also contains system calls necessary to instantiate components. An application creates a COM component by passing the CLSID of the component to the COM runtime. The CLSID is a key stored in the registration database (the *Registry*) that identifies the component, some other specific component features (in-process and so on), and where it resides on disk for later instantiation.

As I mentioned earlier, a COM component can either reside on an executable server or a DLL server. There is a difference in the way that COM starts the components. For an executable, COM will start the executable and then wait for it to register its class factory through CoRegisterClassFactory. For a DLL, COM loads the DLL into the client's address space and calls DllGetClassFactory(), a mandatory DLL exported function.

When a client instantiates a component and requests an interface pointer, COM will create the component and then pass back the requested interface pointer to the client if the COM object supports that interface. Object creation is accomplished using the IClassFactory interface. The client worries only about communicating with the component through the returned interface pointer. It doesn't care about the object's specific implementation details, or even where the component resides (local, remote, and so on).

Figure 10.4 defines a simple startup relationship between a client, a COM object, and the COM runtime environment.

FIGURE 10.4

The COM runtime environment.

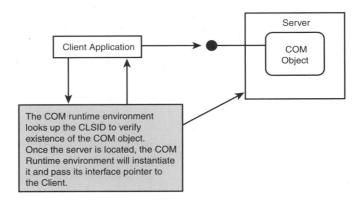

Server

Client Application

COM Object

The COM runtime environment looks up the CLSID to verify existence of the COM object. Once the server is located, the COM Runtime environment will instantiate it and pass its interface pointer to the Client.

Defining the Class Factory

A well-designed application would use an instance of a component as many times as possible to gain the benefits not only of reusability, but also of performance. If a client were concerned only about creating one instance of a component, the CoCreateInstance() call would be used to create it. However, if the client wants to create multiple components, it could do it directly through the server's class factory. Class factories expose IUnknown like other COM components, but like most interfaces of interest, they go a little further in what they are able to do.

Even when only one instance of a COM class is created, the COM runtime calls the object's class factory to instantiate it. It makes sense to provide for object creation using one and only one mechanism.

The IClassFactory interface defines the methods needed to create the instances of its COM object for the client. The IClassFactory interface defines the two following methods:

- CreateInstance—The CreateInstance does exactly what its name implies; it creates an instance of the specific object that the factory is designed to create. Because the class factory is concerned only with a specific COM object, the client does not need to pass in the CLSID. However, the client does need to specify which interface it requires. It does this by passing in the IID.

- LockServer—Forces the newly created COM object to remain in memory. This is in addition to the standard COM reference counting capability. By locking the factory's server in memory, COM guarantees that individual object's reference counts will not inadvertently remove the (static) class factory from memory until all the objects that it creates have been removed.

Some class factories also support the IClassFactory2 interface, which inherits from IClassFactory. This interface enhances the basic IClassFactory interface by dealing with licensing issues. I will cover this a little later in the chapter.

To directly access a class factory, a client would invoke the CoGetClassObject() method instead of the normal CoCreateInstance() COM API call. CoGetClassObject() requires a CLSID and an IID, as well as other parameters, just as CoCreateInstance() does. However, when you use CoGetClassObject(), you are given a pointer to an object's class factory instead of a pointer to an instance of the object. Given this pointer, you can create as many specific instances of the object as you want (using IClassFactory::CreateInstance()). If you will require many instances of a given COM object, this is by far the most efficient approach.

10

COM

How Are COM Objects Reused?

Suppose that an object were to change. I've talked about this scenario, and have determined that there are ways to make it happen. I discussed creating a new COM object that supported old interfaces. Here are some other ways:

- Containment—The term delegation is sometimes used to refer to containment. In COM, containment signifies that the outer object acts as a client to the inner (older) object. With containment, the outer object does not expose the inner object's interfaces.

- Aggregation—Aggregation exposes an inner object's interfaces as its own interface.

Containment is by far the most common form of COM object reuse. It is also easy to implement, although you must be aware of situations where the delegation goes several layers deep. If layer upon layer of COM objects contains other objects, error-reporting can sometimes be watered down or even masked when lower-level COM objects have a problem.

Aggregation is not without its problems either. Reference counting on an inner object can be cumbersome. Implementing aggregation requires the inner object to do work to support reference counting on the outer object. To solve this problem, the inner object must redirect all calls made on its IUnknown method to the outer object's IUnknown method. To do this, however, requires the inner object to know about the outer object. This is done through the creation of the inner object. When the client invokes CoCreateInstance (or the object's class factory), it passes its IUnknown to the inner object. This is sometimes referred to as the controlling unknown. If the controlling unknown parameter is NULL in these calls, the inner object knows that it is not being aggregated. Note also there is no requirement that any given COM object must support aggregation.

Marshaling and Threading

I mentioned earlier that a COM object could possibly be active inside the client's address space, or it could be active somewhere else (to include over a network on another computer). Whenever you invoke a COM object's methods, the parameters you pass into the method and the return information you receive from the COM object could require some manipulation. For example, the data might need to be converted to network order for transmission over the network to another computer. Or imagine you are passing in an interface pointer—your pointer is *completely* invalid on a remote machine!

COM handles these data transmission situations by a process known as *marshaling*. Marshaling is no more than a data conversion to safely, and sanely, transmit data from one process or address space to another. In addition, marshaling is used to transfer data from one *thread of execution* to another, so there is no requirement that any given COM object reside in the same thread as the client (although this is often the case, and as an optimization, you can force this to be the case). Let's look at this in more detail.

Marshaling

You've just taken a "nickel" tour of COM. You know that the methods that you need to invoke can reside in the same process, a different process, or even on a different machine. One of the nice things you can derive from this is that COM provides a transparent mechanism for the client to invoke the desired COM methods. I really haven't discussed what unknown entity makes all this possible.

You know that if the COM object is implemented as an in-process server, you are simply provided pointers in memory to the object's methods. What happens if the COM object actually resides in another process? You can't simply be handed a pointer to memory to another application. To give you the illusion that you are communicating with an object in process, COM provides a mechanism known as a *proxy*. The proxy is a COM object that presents the same interface for the real COM object.

When a client invokes a method on an interface, the proxy will pick it up, package it, and send it to the real COM object through some sort of interprocess communication mechanism. There is another step in this process. When the proxy sends the package, it sends it to a *stub* object, which will unpack the information for the real COM object. This packing of information is referred to as *marshaling*, while the unpacking is referred to as *;*. If the real COM object resides on the same machine, an optimized form of the Remote Procedure Call (RPC) mechanism called Local Procedure Call (LPC) is used. On the other hand, if the real COM object resides on another machine, the interprocess communication mechanism is actually performed as a true RPC call. Figure 10.5 depicts this relationship.

Figure 10.5
The proxy/stub relationship.

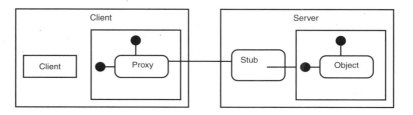

10

COM

Marshaling is structured for each interface. Essentially, the marshaling code for the interface knows how to pack and unpack the information for the methods on the interface. The client marshaling code must know how to pack information and unpack results, and the server marshaling code must know how to unpack information and pack results. At this point, you might be asking how to create the marshaling code. The best way to accomplish this is to use the IDL language to create what you need automatically. Creating the marshaling code through the IDL also makes it easy to create the proxy and stub code. The Microsoft Interface Definition Language (MIDL) compiler will generate the necessary code for you.

In many cases, the *standard marshaler* handles the data packaging for you. If you pass integers, doubles, certain types of strings, and even interface pointers as parameters to a COM method, the standard marshaler takes care of things for you.

If you are really feeling brave, you might want to sit down and write your own marshaling code. I have yet to do that, as the MIDL has met all my needs to this date. That option, however, is available. The process of developing your own marshaling is simply referred to as custom marshaling (as if it would be named anything else). The question that is probably floating around in your mind now might be, "Why should I do custom marshaling?" One reason would be to improve performance. If you know the object that you are writing the marshaling code for, you can create better-performing code. Limiting the information packaged and unpacked can also improve performance.

Automation Interfaces and Early Versus Late Binding

COM also supports *automation*, such that scripting languages can access a COM object's capabilities. If you use a given COM object using a special automation interface, IDispatch, you can use the standard marshaler and some special invocation mechanisms to access the COM object's functionality with no foreknowledge of the other interfaces the COM object supports. This is critical for scripting languages because they are typically *interpreted* rather than *compiled*. The scripting engine has no idea what COM object support will be required until the COM object is actually needed. (Chapter 17, "Scripting Your MFC Application," has more information.)

This is accomplished through the use of a *type library*, which is a tokenized form of the original IDL used to create the COM object's interface(s). The MIDL compiler not only can build proxy/stub code, as you saw previously, but it can also build the type library. The type library includes all the information that a client needs in order to determine the object's interface information.

If you access the COM object's methods directly, you are using *early binding*. That is, you determine what functionality you will use when you compile your client code.

However, as I mentioned, scripts do not work in this fashion. They access the object's type library to see if the required functionality they need (coded into the script) is in fact supported by the COM object at runtime. This is known as *late binding*. If the script author claimed some COM object would support given functionality at runtime, but the script found no such capability when actually executing, the scripting engine will terminate the script with an error.

Most automation clients use IDispatch, coupled with late binding, to invoke the COM object's methods. However, if you want to access the type library directly, there are two interfaces you can use to do so. These are the ITypeLib interface, which enables a client access to the library as a whole, and the ITypeInfo interface, which provides the client the necessary informational structure to work with the object in question. On the surface, this might appear trivial, but it is anything but! A client must first ask the ITypeLib interface some information to get information on the ITypeInfo interface, and then in turn use the ITypeInfo interface to get information regarding the objects that the type library contains.

Here is a list of some methods that are exposed by the ITypeLib interface:

- FindName—This method will return a pointer to any number of ITypeInfo interfaces found that contains the name.
- IsName—Determines whether an object exists in the type library.
- GetTypeInfoOfGuid—Finds the ITypeInfo interface based on a GUID.
- GetTypeInfoCount—Returns the number of accessible objects in the type library.

When the client has the information about the ITypeInfo interfaces in the library, it can then use that interface to find information about the object in question. Here is a small list of ITypeInfo methods.

- GetTypeAttr—Returns information about the TypeInfo object.
- GetFuncDesc—This is the workhorse for dynamic binding. This method will return the information about a method on the interface desired.
- GetVarDesc—Returns parameter information.

The COM API call LoadRegTypeLib() can be used to acquire the pointer to the type library for an object. Simply pass in the CLSID for the object in question.

Threading

In today's computing industry, most processes are multithreaded, which enables a single application to perform a multitude of tasks almost simultaneously. There are enormous

10

COM

advantages to making a process multithreaded, but there are also drawbacks. Record-locking scenarios in database applications would be one.

COM provides support for multithreading in different ways. Early on, when threading became an issue, the *apartment model*, or *single-threaded apartment* (STA) was coined. The STA model implies that Windows itself manages the object's data access using a standard message pump. Two clients cannot access a single COM object simultaneously because the COM object uses a message pump. COM itself forces calls to the COM object to be transformed into Windows messages, sent to the object's message queue, and acted on in order (first in, first out).

Free threading appeared with Windows NT version 4. Free threading is essentially the multithreading of the COM object, which will be active in the *multithreaded apartment* (MTA). The essential difference between COM objects in the STA versus objects in the MTA is objects in the MTA must now coordinate their data access using traditional multithreaded techniques, such as semaphores and mutexes. Windows relinquishes the data access responsibility to you, so you gain performance benefits at the cost of additional data access code.

COM, OLE, and Automation

Now you are getting to the point where you need to see benefit from all this really cool technology. I briefly discussed OLE, and then jumped right into the COM architecture. Now it's time to see COM work.

As I write this, I am using a word processing application that supports compound documents. If I needed to, I could insert a spreadsheet, or pull up the help window to show me how to format my margins. Let's say that I wanted to use the spreadsheet to calculate the number of times that I've used the word "mechanism" in this chapter. Suppose that I wanted to provide the output in bar chart form and somehow place that back into the help file information regarding proper grammatical structure. Okay, I think I'm going a little overboard, but you can see where I am going! In the old days, if I wanted to use a spreadsheet to calculate information that I wanted to incorporate into my word processing program, I would need to move back and forth between the two applications. It would mean copying (cutting and pasting) the information that I needed. Another method would be to write macros if the spreadsheet and word processor supported them. Now, however, I can run the functions of the spreadsheet right from my word processor, and automatically format its output.

This amazing capability is brought to you by COM (and OLE) and the capability for applications to expose their programmability through the COM paradigm. The capability to program this functionality is referred to as *automation*.

Suppose that a shipping clerk needed to verify an end-of-day report that would be run against an inventory spreadsheet and then create a new inventory spreadsheet. By developing an application, or a scripting file that used information in a shipping spreadsheet to remove items from an inventory spreadsheet, the developer would simplify the shipping clerk's life. This is the beauty of automation.

The goal of automation is to let an application expose the services that it contains. COM is the logical choice for enabling applications to relay their information. If every application or scripting program could support pointers and pointer traversal, the problem would be solved. However, some languages still have a tough time traversing the vtable. Some languages don't directly support pointers, such as Visual Basic. To get around this problem, a universal interface was developed that would allow languages such as Visual Basic access to a COM component's methods.

IDispatch

Any application that exposes its functionality can do so through the IDispatch interface, as I mentioned previously. Listing 10.2 is the actual definition (OAIDL.H) of the IDispatch interface. Notice that it is derived from IUnknown. Also notice the type information methods that allow marshaling (late binding) to take place.

LISTING 10.2   THE DEFINITION (OAIDL.H) FOR IDispatch

```
interface IDispatch : public IUnknown
    {
    public:
        virtual HRESULT STDMETHODCALLTYPE GetTypeInfoCount(
            /* [out] */ UINT __RPC_FAR *pctinfo) = 0;

        virtual HRESULT STDMETHODCALLTYPE GetTypeInfo(
            /* [in] */ UINT iTInfo,
            /* [in] */ LCID lcid,
            /* [out] */ ITypeInfo __RPC_FAR *__RPC_FAR *ppTInfo) = 0;

        virtual HRESULT STDMETHODCALLTYPE GetIDsOfNames(
            /* [in] */ REFIID riid,
            /* [size_is][in] */ LPOLESTR __RPC_FAR *rgszNames,
            /* [in] */ UINT cNames,
            /* [in] */ LCID lcid,
            /* [size_is][out] */ DISPID __RPC_FAR *rgDispId) = 0;

        virtual /* [local] */ HRESULT STDMETHODCALLTYPE Invoke(
            /* [in] */ DISPID dispIdMember,
            /* [in] */ REFIID riid,
            /* [in] */ LCID lcid,
            /* [in] */ WORD wFlags,
```

10

COM

continues

LISTING 10.2 CONTINUED

```
        /* [out][in] */ DISPPARAMS __RPC_FAR *pDispParams,
        /* [out] */ VARIANT __RPC_FAR *pVarResult,
        /* [out] */ EXCEPINFO __RPC_FAR *pExcepInfo,
        /* [out] */ UINT __RPC_FAR *puArgErr) = 0;

    };
```

So what makes it so different from other COM interfaces? How can a program that doesn't support pointers interface with IDispatch? Unlike other COM interfaces, it provides a method called Invoke that can be used to actually invoke the methods that the COM object supports. A client can invoke any method in the COM object by calling the IDispatch Invoke method. But how does this work?

This is done through a *dispinterface*, which is also known as dispatch interface. The dispinterface specifies the methods that are available through the IDispatch Invoke method. If you think this sounds a little like a vtable, you're right; a dispinterface is similar to the vtable in that it contains a list of methods. But, unlike the vtable, the methods defined in a dispinterface are uniquely identified with a DISPID (an integer). This DISPID uniquely identifies the method to be invoked.

Whenever a program such as Visual Basic creates an instance of a COM object, the IDispatch interface is returned as a handle. Visual Basic, for example, has a function called CreateObject that accepts the CLSID of the object/application to instantiate. Because these programs don't really support pointers, they use the value (handle) of the created instance to call the Invoke method, passing in the desired dispinterface for processing. Listing 10.3 shows a simple Visual Basic example that doesn't do anything but show the calling structure.

LISTING 10.3 A VISUAL BASIC EXAMPLE OF CREATING A COM OBJECT

```
Sub DoSomething()
    Dim OurObject As Object
    Set OurObject = CreateObject("Excel.Application")
    Order = OurObject.Sort()
End Sub
```

The IDispatch::Invoke method is nothing more than a conceptual switch statement that will find the method identified by the DISPID and invoke it. This "behind the scenes" mechanization gives the appearance of a vtable, which allows programming languages that don't support true pointers to still support COM.

Automation Servers, Objects, and Controllers

Any application that exposes its services using automation does so by providing these services as COM objects. Applications that do this are referred to as *automation servers*. However, the term ActiveX comes into play here. Automation servers are now referred to as ActiveX components acting as a server.

The objects that an automation server creates, on the other hand, are referred to as *automation objects*. In keeping with the "name game," they are now simply referred to as objects or ActiveX components.

Applications that used applications through their IDispatch interfaces where commonly referred to as *automation controllers*. Now, however, they are referred to as *COM clients*. This naming convention actually makes sense. When you pull off all the names, you are strictly talking about COM.

Supporting Both IDispatch and IUnknown

Dispinterfaces make it easy for some programming languages to implement COM objects. Using a dispinterface, however, is slower than using the vtable method. There is a way to provide support for both interfaces. This is referred to as a *dual interface.* Dual interfaces inherit from IDispatch. If you look closely, IDispatch's vtable contains the IUnknown interfaces as well as its own methods. By having both the QueryInterface method and the Invoke method, a COM object supports dual access—directly using the interface pointer or indirectly using the dispinterface. This allows a programming language such as C++ to use the IUnknown methods (for better performance), yet also allows script-based languages to use the dispinterface methods. The COM object now can be used by a wider variety of clients.

Persisting COM Data

As an application developer you understand the importance of persisting data. An application that can close and then be reopened to continue where it left off is a definite production boost. COM objects, if you think about it, need to do this. Take, for example, the checkbook COM object. When the Balance method runs, it calculates the running balance in the checking account. When the server for the checkbook closes, that balance needs to be persisted, or the entire application is worthless.

There are many ways to store data permanently—file systems, databases, or the Registry, just to name a few. These are referred to as *persistence servers*.

10

COM

In most cases, the client application must be able to tell the COM object to persist its data. A COM object's capability to persist its data is normally provided by defining two sets of interfaces. The first is defined as a storage mechanism known as structured storage. The second is the IPersist interfaces.

Structured Storage

Data comes in many forms, and it can also be stored in many forms. Flat files are commonly used for simple objects, but these don't always solve the problem. In many cases, several COM objects can use the same file, storing data in different parts of the file. But what about storing data on a different machine? Structured storage comes into play when several objects need to access the same file. If the objects storing data to the file were created by the same developer, the structured storage mechanism would really be needed. In the real world, however, COM objects are developed by many different sources, which made it necessary to develop a mechanism to provide consistent storage for a wide range of object data requirements.

Structured storage allows many objects to access and maintain a single file. But how does it do this? How to provide some mechanism inside a file that allows different objects to consistently store information is not readily apparent. You know that COM objects provide consistent interfaces for allowing clients to communicate not only with them, but also with other COM objects. Why not implement a system inside a file similar to that of COM? To do this, a single file is made up of any number of *storages*, which function in a similar manner as directories do for a file system. Files that contain multiple *storages* are referred to as *compound files*.

Each file supporting structured storage contains a root storage, as depicted in Figure 10.6. Each storage for the file is connected back through the root storage. Notice the other element inside the structured storage. This is the stream, which supports the actual data in the file. The storage represents a directory, and the stream represents a file. The storages inside the structured storage file basically keep track of the streams below them. The streams are simple mechanisms that store streams of bytes. These streams are very basic, with no indexing or complex storage overhead associated with the data.

Each component that accesses a compound file can be attached to its own stream in which to store its own data. It can also create its own hierarchy, adding additional storages and streams for compartmentalizing its data. Each component, having its own storage area, doesn't have to rely on maintaining a separate file, or where other components might be storing their data. This is an obvious performance advantage!

FIGURE 10.6

*The structured
storage paradigm.*

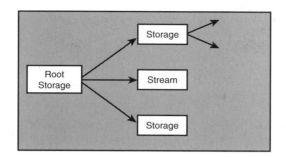

Although there are obvious advantages to persisting data by this method, there are also disadvantages. The structured storage file must contain the overhead to manage the storage hierarchy. These files can become quite large, which adds unnecessary overhead for the operating system, not to mention the disk space requirements. Let's return to my earlier statement, "Why not implement a system inside a file similar to that of COM?" By viewing storages and streams as COM objects, you open up the architecture of the structured file. Let's take a closer look.

Storages have an interface called IStorage, and streams have an interface called IStream. COM objects interact with their storages and streams through these interfaces, thereby keeping the COM paradigm intact for structured storage. Each of these interfaces contains many methods similar to working with a file system.

> **NOTE**
>
> Structured storage also supports transactions. As it relates to the structured storage file, a transaction is a group of data reads and/or writes where all must succeed in order to save any of the data.

Although structured storage gives the COM object the capability to persist important data, it is actually the client that tells the COM object when to store the data. COM doesn't dictate what interfaces must be used—clients and objects are free to define their own. As with any good specification, however, there are some defaults that clients and objects are free to use.

- IPersistStream—This is probably the most used interface. It allows a client to tell the COM object when to store or retrieve stream data.

- IPersistStreamInit—This interface, which is inherited from IPersistStream, adds another method to signify to the COM object that its persistence is being initialized.

- `IPersistStorage`—This interface tells the COM object that the client is requesting it to save its data using a storage. (Remember, the storage controls all streams and storages below it.) A COM object that would implement this interface probably controls many data items that would be maintained in separate streams.

- `IPersistFile`—This interface tells the COM object to use a flat file for its storage mechanism.

- `IPersistMemory`—This interface is similar in many respects to `IPersistStreamInit`. However, it references specific memory regardless of initialization.

- `IPersistPropertyBag`—This interface tells the COM object that the client wants to use its data as property sets.

- `IPersistMoniker`—This interface tells the COM object that the client wants to load and save data remotely through a moniker. (I'll talk about that in the next subsection.)

Identifying COM Data (Monikers)

I've talked about specific naming conventions for interfaces and uniquely identifying the COM object in time and space. But what about a specific instance of an object? In fact, the COM specification doesn't indicate any way for you to identify the instance. How then is this important if COM doesn't specify how you are to do this, and why would you want to do it? Suppose that your checkbook COM object is being controlled by a savings and loan application that is Web-aware. It controls many accounts, each managed by a checkbook COM object. The savings application must keep track of each specific instance, but how do you do this?

To adequately name a particular instance of a COM object, you need to know about its interfaces, methods, and most importantly its properties and data. Your savings and loan application must identify not only a specific COM object, but also the balance data that the object maintains. There are many ways to make this identification. One method is to create the object through `CoCreateInstance` and pass it the object's CLSID. The client can then use one of the persistence interfaces that I discussed previously to load the data that it needs. Of course, the client would need to know the object's CLSID to do this, which is not always practical or available.

A moniker is a name for a specific instance. You are probably asking how the client would come to know about a moniker when no easy method of knowing the COM object itself is available. In fact, the moniker is a combination of the CLSID and the specific data for the object. But a moniker is more than a name—it is a COM object! If you are not confused now, you probably will be, but let's dig a little deeper. As stated, the moniker is a COM object, and exposes this capability through an interface known as IMoniker. Each moniker has everything that it needs to create an instance of the object that it represents. It does this through the BindToObject method of the IMoniker interface. The client will invoke this method, passing it an IID of the interface it requires on the target object. The moniker can then instantiate the object and pass back the desired interface to the client. When the client has this information, it can then start using the object. This appears similar to what the COM library does, but the moniker maintains the necessary initialization data for a specific instance of the object.

Transferring Data

Transferring data between applications, systems, and even objects is the most common function that software undertakes. It makes sense that COM provides a unique mechanism to perform data transfer. Uniform Data Transfer (UDT) contains an interface, IDataObject, which provides an identifiable way of transferring data between clients and objects.

Requiring a client to continually request data from an object implies bad performance. If the object were smarter, it would automatically update the data that the client is expecting from it. Uniform Data Transfer does just this, but is fairly limited. Another method, referred to as *connectable objects*, is commonly used for this purpose.

Uniform Data Transfer

A plethora of options are available when it comes to transferring data between software applications. Windows provides the clipboard, Dynamic Data Exchange (DDE), and recently—with the advent of Microsoft Message Queue (MSMQ)—an application can even take advantage of a full message processing system to transfer data.

An object that supports the IDataObject interface is commonly referred to as a data object. Data objects can make many forms of data available to their client through the IDataObject interface. A client can access data in many different objects, in files, and in memory through one object's IDataObject interface. But how does a client know how to handle data transfer with objects it knows nothing about? What about learning how the data might be represented?

Because UDT is a standard, it must define certain characteristics and mechanisms that all participants must know about and implement. Data objects use the FORMATETC data structure, which is a subset of the Clipboard. It contains information regarding the data formats, device information, data instance information, and role information. Data objects also support and use the STGMEDIUM structure, which describes the medium to store the data.

Drag and Drop

One of the most common productivity tools in use today is the Clipboard model, which provides the ability to drag and drop and cut and paste data between applications. The application that contains the data from which the copy is made is referred to as the *drop source,* and the target is referred to as a *drop target.* The application or object that is the drop source must support the IDataObject interface (that is, it must be a data object). The target must support and implement the IDropTarget application. But how is the data actually transferred?

Notice in Figure 10.7 that the target actually receives a pointer to the drop source's IDataObject interface, and in turn invokes the methods on that interface.

FIGURE 10.7

The IDropTarget actually gets a pointer to the IDataObject interface.

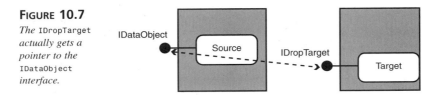

Event Notification

To take advantage of UDT, you need a way to enable an object to update a client whenever an important piece of data changes. This greatly improves performance. The object needs a way to inform the client that data has changed, and then must be able to get the data to the client. The IAdviseSink interface provides just this capability. The object must support the IDataObject interface and provide an interface that will define what data requires notification. There is no standard interface for this, so the object must define one that the client knows about. The client must implement an interface by which the source notifies it of data change.

Connectable Objects

Another method by which an object can communicate with its client is that of connectable objects. Connectable objects provide a method by which logical connections between an object and its client can be made. To do this, the object must support an interface commonly referred to as an *outgoing interface.* An *incoming interface* is one that receives, or sinks, the connection information. An outgoing interface is one that is commonly referred to as a source interface. Figure 10.8 depicts this relationship.

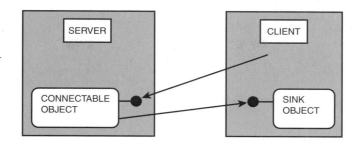

FIGURE 10.8
Connectable object topology: incoming and outgoing interfaces.

In Figure 10.8, the connectable object contains an incoming interface to receive a request from the client. The Sink object in the client contains an incoming sink interface for communicating with the connectable object. There is no rocket science going on here. These interfaces define a standard mechanism for defining connections, and are not too different from any other interfaces that can be defined.

An object must support IConnectionPointContainer to fully support connection points. This interface basically informs the object and its client which interfaces are outgoing interfaces for the data object. In Figure 10.8, the client will implement its sink interface, query for the IConnectionPointContainer interface, and then ask for a specific connectable point object for the sink interface. The client will then pass its sink interface to the connection object to make the connect for communicating between the objects.

Whenever the connectable object contains an outgoing interface, the object has to implement a connectable point. This is also a small object that is responsible for maintaining the list of sink interfaces with which it needs to communicate. To do this, the client that implements the sink must register itself with the connection point object. The IConnectionPoint interface is the interface that the connection point must expose. The Advise method and Unadvise methods are used by the client to register its sink interface.

DCOM

COM is a very extensive technology, and I've only covered the basics at a very high level. I've done so primarily at the local server level, with all clients and objects running on the same system. But what about applying this technology to a distributed network with objects running on different machines? Distributed COM (DCOM) is the implementation of COM at the networking level. And amazingly, DCOM introduces very little deviation for the client for implementing COM. Objects on a local server or a distributed network are instantiated and communicated with in a similar manner, giving the appearance that the client is working with standard COM objects. There are, however, things going on under the covers that give this appearance.

Beyond the capability to start and manage remote objects, DCOM has to take into consideration all the communication and security aspects that come into play when working with networks. DCOM provides security services in such a way that clients don't need to implement specific security code. Applications or objects that *are* familiar with the security services Windows networking provides can have the capability to implement specific security services via the DCOM infrastructure.

DCOM provides three extensions to standard COM for working in the distributed environments:

- Object creation—DCOM provides some details that enable object creation for distributed computing.
- Invoking methods—DCOM provides a protocol for invoking methods on a remote object.
- Security—DCOM provides several mechanisms to handle network security issues, probably the biggest addition to COM.

Object Creation

COM provides a simple and effective standard for creating objects. Objects are created through the COM runtime environment or by using monikers. DCOM allows object creation in a similar manner, but several things must be taken into consideration.

CoCreateInstance

Normally, one calls CoCreateInstance to create the object, and then QueryInterface to get interface pointers for the object's interfaces. The client can use the same method to create a remote object. Passing both a CLSID and an IID, the client can call CoCreateInstance to create the remote object. With this method, the client doesn't have to know or be concerned with where the object resides. But how does the system know where the object is? You might be thinking that the COM runtime might store this in some form. The logical place, however, is the Registry.

You know that the only real difference in the object creation is where the object is stored. This machine information is stored in the Registry! The COM runtime will go to the Registry to look up the object and instead finds a machine name. It will then go to the Registry on that machine and locate the object. Figure 10.9 shows this process.

Figure 10.9

CoCreateInstance
for remote objects.

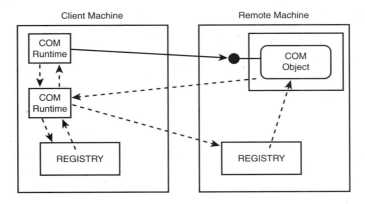

You can tell from Figure 10.9 that this is a lot of work, but you also see that to the client, it appears the same as if the object were created locally. The COM runtime will look into the Registry in order to map the CLSID to the file of the object to activate. If COM finds that the COM object in question is a remote object, COM will then search the Registry of the remote machine (as indicated in the local machine's Registry). COM will then create the object by running the executable (out-of-process server) or loading the DLL into a surrogate executable (in-process server) on the remote machine. When the server for the object is active on the remote end, COM will return the (marshaled) interface pointer back to the local client.

CoCreateInstanceEx

As you can see from what's just been discussed, using CoCreateInstance to create your remote objects is cumbersome if more than one interface is desired. It is also fairly slow, because it is dependent on network and machine speeds as well as communications traffic. If only one interface *is* desired, CoCreateInstance is still sufficient. If, however, the client needs more than one or isn't sure, a better way is to use CoCreateInstanceEx(). CoCreateInstanceEx() provides a way for the client to request a list of IIDs. CoCreateInstanceEx() will query the object for all the interfaces in the list and then return the entire list of pointers when it has them. This prevents the client from having to make multiple QueryInterface() calls on the remote object.

CoCreateInstanceEx() goes a step further and allows the client to specify where the remote object should be created. This allows the client to be dynamic and not rely on the local Registry. This also adds to the portability of a client implementing objects in a distributed system.

10

COM

Object Initialization

DCOM allows for the creation of a remote object; the next step is to initialize it. This can involve loading persistent data, defining runtime variables, and so on in the typical COM fashion. This is usually done with either the `IPersistFile::Load` or the `IPersistStorage::Load` methods. If you think about it, however, doing this over a remote network might be inordinately slow. DCOM provides two ways to create and initialize an object in one step.

The first method is through `CoGetInstanceFromFile()`, which will create the object and initialize it from a file on the remote system. This is similar to the `IPersistFile::Load` method, but requires less overhead. The second method is `CoGetInstanceFromIStorage()`, except it loads and initializes the object from a structured storage file on the remote system.

Creation Through Monikers

Monikers can also be used to create remote objects, which is, in fact, sometimes the preferred method. Whenever a client calls the `BindToObject` method on the `IMoniker` interface, the moniker will call `CoCreateInstance()` with a CLSID from persistent data. Using the persistent data, the moniker will then initialize the object. It does this through information in the Registry. If a remote machine is allocated in the Registry, and it specifies a DCOM object, the object is created on the remote machine in much the same manner as mentioned previously.

Invoking Methods

After you've created your object, you have to be able to use it. You know that to a client the creation is basically hidden. What about being able to invoke methods on the interfaces given to you? For the client, there is no difference in the way that you invoke methods of a local object to that of a remote object. When the object has been created, and the client has an interface pointer, it can then invoke the methods on that interface just as it would for locally created objects.

You learned that for in-process servers, you are essentially calling vtable methods within memory of your process. When you invoke methods for an object instantiated in a local server, you use a proxy and a stub. I also briefly stated that the same is true for the remote object. You need a proxy and a stub, but you also need the communication layer that transfers your data request to the remote machine, and receives back your responses from the remote machine. This layer, or protocol, is referred to as a Remote Procedure Call (RPC). I don't have enough space in this book to discuss all the existing RPC protocols available, but I will briefly look at what is available in DCOM.

MS RPC, which Microsoft based on the Open Software Foundation's Distributed Computing Environment (DCE), is what DCOM implements to carry out the communications between client and remote object.

> **NOTE**
>
> DCOM's usage of MS DCE is sometimes referred to as Object RPC, or ORPC.

MS DCE and ORPC actually use two protocols. One is a connection protocol and the other is a connectionless protocol. The connection protocol, sometimes referred to as CN or CO, assumes that the underlying transfer protocol will transfer data reliably, whereas the connectionless protocol, referred to as DG or CL, assumes the exact opposite. To a client, however, these protocols appear similar.

A client must use some sort of binding information for the remote machine prior to making any ORPC calls. Binding information basically consists of the remote machine identifiers (such as an IP address) and what protocol combination to use. Other important binding information includes the port that identifies the process on the remote machine that will handle the request.

When a machine name is passed to `CoCreateInstanceEx()`, that name can be used to load some of the *binding information*. It is possible, and sometimes mandatory, for an object to pass binding information to another object. For the client to access or invoke methods on a remote object, it must first acquire the OXID for the server. When it has this ID, the object can rely on an *OXID resolver*. Every system that supports DCOM includes some sort of OXID resolver, which contains an interface called `IObjectExporter`. At first glance, it appears that the resolver is another COM object. It is not a COM interface, but an RPC interface.

> **NOTE**
>
> A server application that implements one or more COM objects for a remote client is referred to as an *object exporter*. An OXID identifies the object exporter.

The `IObjectExporter` interface contains three methods. These are `ResolveOxid`, `SimplePing`, and `ComplexPing`. Each OXID resolver has a table of OXIDs and their corresponding string bindings. It can also include string bindings for objects running on other machines. One thing that you might notice here is an apparent likeness of this RPC mechanism to a vtable or an IDispatch table. But when working with networks, you must also consider that some objects might be running on different systems with different operating systems. Although most systems utilize an ASCII string protocol, others use EBCDIC. The same is true as to how integers and consequently interface pointer definitions are stored.

RPC handles this mismatch of datatypes with a network format called Network Data Representation (NDR). NDR provides a common way of moving parameters across a network to machines of different environments. One thing that is not handled very well with NDR is that of interface pointers. Ouch!

DCOM to the rescue! Whenever an interface pointer needs to be transferred to another machine, DCOM uses *object references* (OBJREFS), which include the following elements:

- An OXID—An unsigned hyper (64-bit integer) value representing an RPC connection identifier for the server.
- Object Identifier (OID)—A unique identifier for the object itself
- Interface Pointer Identifier (IPID)—A unique identifier for the interface
- Binding String—String binding for the OXID Resolver on the remote machine

If the resolved binding information is not present in the local resolver table, the object must get the information from the resolver table on the remote machine and then store it locally. When this is done, the client or local object can then communicate with the remote object. All this communications layer is hidden through DCOM.

Security Issues

With any open network, there are security risks. DCOM also provides mechanisms that provide security layers to be applied to the communications. One such method, commonly referred to as *activation security*, is concerned with controlling who is allowed to create remote objects. Activation security uses the Registry for defining who is allowed to launch servers on its machine. Activation security also uses the Access Control List (ACL) to define who has privileges on a class basis.

Another mechanism is that of *call security*. Call security involves the following:

- Authentication—Authentication enables the object to determine the client's identity.
- Authorization—Authorization provides a set of permissions for the client.
- Data integrity—Basically, data integrity uses a CRC or some other method to verify that the data was transmitted intact.

- Data privacy—Data privacy usually requires some sort of encryption to verify that the data is protected during the transmission.

Although I have only briefly discussed DCOM, you can see the benefit to the client application invoking remote objects. DCOM provides a broadening of possibilities without sacrificing the interface specification of COM.

> **TIP**
>
> I strongly recommend reading *Inside Distributed COM* by Guy Eddon and Henry Eddon (Microsoft Press, ISBN-1-57231-849-X). This book provides insight into all of the communications layers of DCOM. I would be hard pressed to give this technology adequate coverage in this short chapter.

Some Important Information

When you start working with COM, you will notice that there are several related items—items that are covered in the following sections.

BSTR

A BSTR is a type of string that is used by COM. Because there are no defined lengths or sizes for a string, as there are for other datatypes (`int`, `long`, and so on), it is wise to use the BSTR. If the COM object is to be used and deployed by Visual Basic or Java programs, BSTRs must be used extensively. The BSTR contains a length prefix that indicates the number of bytes for the string.

> **TIP**
>
> I would recommend using the CComBSTR ATL class for managing BSTRs. This class handles dynamic pointer allocation and deallocation, as well as pointer reference counting. See Chapter 16, "Using MFC and ATL," for more information.

SAFEARRAY

If you've ever had to handle variable size arrays, you will understand the difficulty of trying to do so in Visual Basic. The SAFEARRAY is a mechanism that COM provides gives Visual Basic that capability. The array itself is a fairly complex structure. Take a look at Listing 10.4.

LISTING 10.4   THE DEFINITION FOR A SAFEARRAY(oaidl.h)

```
 1:    typedef struct  tagSAFEARRAYBOUND
 2:       {
 3:         ULONG cElements;
 4:            LONG lLbound;
 5:       }    SAFEARRAYBOUND;
 6:
 7:    typedef struct tagSAFEARRAYBOUND __RPC_FAR *LPSAFEARRAYBOUND;
 8:
 9:    typedef struct  tagSAFEARRAY
10:      {
11:        USHORT cDims;
12:        USHORT fFeatures;
13:        ULONG cbElements;
14:        ULONG cLocks;
15:        PVOID pvData;
16:        SAFEARRAYBOUND rgsabound[ 1 ];
17:      }    SAFEARRAY;
18:
19:    typedef /* [wire_marshal] */ SAFEARRAY __RPC_FAR *LPSAFEARRAY;
```

Lines 1 through 5 defines the SAFEARRAYBOUND structure, which defines the number of elements that will be defined in the array structure. At first glance, this appears to be somewhat confusing. Line 15 contains a definition of the actual data. Everything else is essentially metadata. The SAFEARRAYBOUND array is a bounding array (hence the name) that encapsulates the actual data in the array. The cDims field (line 11) indicates the number of dimensions applied to the array, and not the number of elements. Hopefully, you are beginning to see how this array makes it easy to define multidimension arrays in COM by using a standard passing mechanism. The cbElements field defines the size of each element in the array, and not the actual number of elements.

> **NOTE**
>
> The cDims field is also used for memory allocation of the array. Given the size of a single dimension of the array (SAFEARRAYBOUND), the number of dimensions is applied to determine the memory allocation size.

If you are developing ActiveX components or COM objects that will be used by Visual Basic applications, get to know the SAFEARRAY mechanism. Even though it is a little difficult to pick up and understand, there are plenty of examples out there to get you started.

HRESULT

There is no magic to the HRESULT. It is nothing more than a 32-bit integer that is used exclusively in COM to help define result types. These integers contain important information about errors that can occur in the COM environment. HRESULTs contain three sections:

- Severity—Basically a bit indicating success or failure
- Facility code—Details where a particular error occurred
- Information code—Information as to the specific error within the specified facility

COM provides two macros for working with HRESULTS. The SUCCEEDED(hresult) and the FAILED(hresult) are Boolean values that allow a COM developer to check error codes prior to proceeding.

> **TIP**
>
> Because of the very nature of COM, always use error checking with the SUC-CEEDED and FAILED macros. Not verifying error conditions prior to continuing to use the object could yield indeterminate results.

VARIANT

The VARIANT is basically a very large union of datatypes. But more than that, the VARIANT denotes the datatypes the COM standard marshaler is able to automatically marshal for you. The VARIANT is covered in some detail in both Chapters 16 and 17.

Further Reading

Many books on the shelves provide a wealth of information in a very informative manner, and many others are nothing more than a waste of money and shelf space. To keep the peace, I won't list the books that I think are a waste of time, and I won't list all the books that I think have merit.

You might be wondering why I would promote other books in this fashion. I am a firm believer in learning, and I am always on the lookout for good teachers. Kenn Scribner, who contributed to this book, is one of those few who can articulate a complex subject in a simple and elegant manner. If you have never been exposed to COM, I would hope that I have imparted some small nugget of information, and presented it in such a manner that only serves to pique your interest. Remember, you learn by doing!

I used to develop MFC database applications, and now mainly develop COM objects. I thoroughly enjoy developing with COM, and have found two amazing authors that have opened up this technology to me. One is David Chappell, who authored *Understanding ActiveX and OLE* (Microsoft Press, ISBN-1-57231-216-5). The other, referred to in some circles as "Mr. COM," is Don Box. Don authored *Essential COM* (Addison-Wesley, ISBN-0-201-63446-5), which goes beyond David Chappell's book. Both of these books convey the complex subject of COM in a simple and effective manner. My hat is off to both of these gentlemen! Any serious COM developer should have both of these books on his or her shelf.

Summary

So you want to do COM. What you will find after reading this chapter is that you have only a cursory knowledge of a very deep subject. I've covered COM in only an introductory fashion, and COM is a technology that is amazingly simple, yet infinitely difficult! (Arnold Palmer once used this statement to define the game of golf. Fitting, don't you think?)

Start by creating a simple COM application with one interface and a few methods. When you've conquered this, move on to more demanding exercises such as containers and servers, and then into DCOM. Pretty soon, you will be developing ActiveX components, and wondering why you hadn't done it sooner. Good luck—and COM rules!

COM and MFC

by Gene Olafsen

IN THIS CHAPTER

MFC provides a powerful set of classes, macros, and global functions to provide access to a sizeable portion of the vast OLE empire.

Understanding the Afx Global Functions

The MFC framework prefixes global public functions with the letters *Afx*. These functions are available to you whether you develop an EXE-based (CWinApp-derived) application or a DLL-based (COleControlModule-derived) object server. There are little more than two dozen Afx functions, and they basically all either perform initialization operations or offer some kind of object lifetime support.

Application Lifetime Control

A number of functions are globally available to an MFC-based application or DLL that enable you to control the circumstances under which the program will terminate or the DLL will unload.

AfxOleCanExitApp

The AfxOleCanExitApp function returns a Boolean value indicating whether or not the application can terminate. The AfxOleLockApp and AfxOleUnlockApp functions increment and decrement, respectively, the m_nObjectCount variable. This function simply returns a value based on the state of that counter.

```
BOOL AFXAPI AfxOleCanExitApp()
{
    AFX_MODULE_STATE* pModuleState = AfxGetModuleState();
    return pModuleState->m_nObjectCount == 0;
}
```

In addition, this method is called internally by the MFC framework to determine whether an application can terminate or an OLE-server DLL can unload.

```
SCODE AFXAPI AfxDllCanUnloadNow(void)
{
    // return S_OK only if no outstanding objects active
    if (!AfxOleCanExitApp())
        return S_FALSE;

    // check if any class factories with >1 reference count
    AFX_MODULE_STATE* pModuleState = AfxGetModuleState();
}
```

AfxOleGetMessageFilter

The `AFxOleGetMessageFilter` retrieves the application object's current message filter. The message filter object that this function returns derives from the `COleMessageFilter` class.

```
_AFXWIN_INLINE COleMessageFilter* AFXAPI AfxOleGetMessageFilter()
{
ASSERT_VALID(AfxGetThread());
return AfxGetThread()->m_pMessageFilter;
}
```

AfxOleGetUserCtrl

The `AfxOleGetUserCtrl` function retrieves the current state of the user-control flag. When the application was launched by the OLE system DLLs, the user is not considered "in control"; thus this function returns a `FALSE` value. Such a condition exists when the application is launched with command-line arguments that indicate the conditions under which the application was started. The companion set function (`AfxOleSetUserCtrl`) is seen setting the variable retrieved by this function to `FALSE` under those conditions where the application is launched with such arguments.

```
void CCommandLineInfo::ParseParamFlag(const char* pszParam)
{
    // OLE command switches are case insensitive, while
    // shell command switches are case sensitive

    if (lstrcmpA(pszParam, "pt") == 0)
        m_nShellCommand = FilePrintTo;
    else if (lstrcmpA(pszParam, "p") == 0)
        m_nShellCommand = FilePrint;
    else if (lstrcmpiA(pszParam, "Unregister") == 0 ¦¦
            lstrcmpiA(pszParam, "Unregserver") == 0)
        m_nShellCommand = AppUnregister;
    else if (lstrcmpA(pszParam, "dde") == 0)
    {
        AfxOleSetUserCtrl(FALSE);
        m_nShellCommand = FileDDE;
    }
    else if (lstrcmpiA(pszParam, "Embedding") == 0)
    {
        AfxOleSetUserCtrl(FALSE);
        m_bRunEmbedded = TRUE;
        m_bShowSplash = FALSE;
    }
    else if (lstrcmpiA(pszParam, "Automation") == 0)
    {
        AfxOleSetUserCtrl(FALSE);
        m_bRunAutomated = TRUE;
```

```
        m_bShowSplash = FALSE;
    }
}
```

Otherwise, the code for the `AfxOleGetUserCtrl` function is very straightforward, return-ing the value of a global variable.

```
BOOL AFXAPI AfxOleGetUserCtrl()
{
    AFX_MODULE_STATE* pModuleState = AfxGetModuleState();
    return pModuleState->m_bUserCtrl;
}
```

AfxOleSetUserCtrl

The `AfxOleSetUserCtrl` function accepts a Boolean argument, and you can use it to set or clear the user-control flag. The conditions under which this flag is called are described in more detail in the previous section.

It is interesting to note, however, the framework code that implements this function. In the debug build of the libraries, the application does not shut down if you have obtained control of the application.

```
void AFXAPI AfxOleSetUserCtrl(BOOL bUserCtrl)
{
    AFX_MODULE_STATE* pModuleState = AfxGetModuleState();
#ifdef _DEBUG
    CWinApp* pApp = AfxGetApp();
    if (bUserCtrl && !pModuleState->m_bUserCtrl &&
        (pApp == NULL || pApp->m_pMainWnd == NULL ||
        !pApp->m_pMainWnd->IsWindowVisible()))
    {
// If the user gets control while the application window is
//  not visible, the application may not shut down when the object
        //  count reaches zero.
        TRACE0("Warning: AfxOleSetUserCtrl(TRUE) called \
                with application window hidden.\n");
    }
#endif
    pModuleState->m_bUserCtrl = bUserCtrl;
}
```

AfxOleLockApp

The `AfxOleLockApp` function increments a global lock count variable. MFC keeps track of the number of OLE objects that are active and calls this function accordingly. The framework uses the `InterlockedIncrement` function to adjust the value of the pModuleState->m_nObjectCount variable. This function synchronizes access to a variable and prevents more than one thread from accessing that variable simultaneously.

```
void AFXAPI AfxOleLockApp()
{
    AFX_MODULE_STATE* pModuleState = AfxGetModuleState();
    InterlockedIncrement(&pModuleState->m_nObjectCount);
}
```

AfxOleUnlockApp

The AfxOleUnlockApp function is the counter-function to AfxOleLockApp. This function decrements the framework's object counter variable in a thread-safe manner.

```
void AFXAPI AfxOleUnlockApp()
{
    AFX_MODULE_STATE* pModuleState = AfxGetModuleState();
    ASSERT(pModuleState->m_nObjectCount != 0);
    if (InterlockedDecrement(&pModuleState->m_nObjectCount) == 0)
    {
        // allow application to shut down when all the objects have
        //  been released
        ::AfxOleOnReleaseAllObjects();
    }
}
```

AfxOleRegisterServerClass

The AfxOleRegisterServerClass function provides a mechanism for you to register your server in the system Registry. The function takes a large number of parameters, but the gist of this function's purpose is to provide more control over the registration process than the Register function in COleTemplateServer offers.

The type of OLE application that this function registers is specified by the OLE_APPTYPE enumeration. Valid application types include the following:

- Full in-place document server (OAT_INPLACE_SERVER)
- Server that supports only embedding (OAT_SERVER)
- Container that supports links to embeddings (OAT_CONTAINER)
- Automation-capable object (OAT_DISPATCH_OBJECT)

AfxOleSetEditMenu

The AfxOleSetEditMenu function offers additional flexibility in determining the manner in which OLE-server verbs are displayed in menus, above and beyond the way the default COleDocument implements this feature.

COleDocument uses the command ID range, ID_OLE_VERB_FIRST through
ID_OLE_VERB_LAST, for the verbs that the selected OLE server supports. At runtime, the
text description of the verb updates the appropriate menu. The AfxOleSetEditMenu function allows many of the default values for these operations to be changed.

Client Control Management

There are three global functions supporting control containment and creation:
AfxEnableControlContainer, AfxOleLockControl, and AfxOleUnlockControl.

AfxEnableControlContainer

The AfxEnableControlContainer function enables support for OLE-control containment
by an application. This function is automatically inserted into your application's
InitInstance function if you specified ActiveX control support when creating your
application with AppWizard.

AfxOleLockControl

The AfxOleLockControl function locks the class factory for the specified control in
memory. Locking a control's class factory significantly speeds up the creation of controls. This function has the additional advantage by keeping controls of this type in memory between display occurrences of a dialog box containing such controls.

This function is overloaded and has two different argument lists. The first takes the
CLSID (class ID) of the control, and the other accepts the control's ProgID (program
ID).

AfxOleUnlockControl

The AfxOleUnlockControl function unlocks the class factory for the specified control.
As with the lock function, this unlock function is overloaded to accept either the class
factory's CLSID or ProgID. Turning the class factory locking feature off adversely
affects ActiveX control creation and dialog box display response.

Connection Point Management

Connection points offer an implementation-independent mechanism for managing outgoing COM interfaces.

AfxConnectionAdvise

The AfxConnectionAdvise function establishes a connection between a COM server
connection source (the caller) and a connection sink (the callee). The concept of

connection points is a very powerful one. It is, however, somewhat confusing, so I will take a bit more time to explain its use. `AfxConnectionAdvise` accepts five parameters:

- A pointer to the object calling the interface (an OLE server)
- The interface ID of the object that calls the interface
- A pointer to the object that implements the interface (an OLE container)
- A flag that indicates whether or not creating the connection increments the reference count on the object that implements the interface
- A pointer to a connection identifier (a cookie)

You commonly use this function to configure `CCmdTarget`-derived classes as sinks for OLE-server object events. By examining the MFC framework code, you will be able to understand the purpose of the function's arguments and the mechanics that involve setting up a connection.

First, a pointer to the connection point container is obtained. Then an interface pointer to the connection point for the specified IID is obtained. Finally, the advise method is called, establishing a connection between source and sink.

```
BOOL AFXAPI AfxConnectionAdvise(LPUNKNOWN pUnkSrc, REFIID iid,
    LPUNKNOWN pUnkSink, BOOL bRefCount, DWORD* pdwCookie)
{
    ASSERT_POINTER(pUnkSrc, IUnknown);
    ASSERT_POINTER(pUnkSink, IUnknown);
    ASSERT_POINTER(pdwCookie, DWORD);
    BOOL bSuccess = FALSE;
    LPCONNECTIONPOINTCONTAINER pCPC;
    if (SUCCEEDED(pUnkSrc->QueryInterface(
                    IID_IConnectionPointContainer,
                    (LPVOID*)&pCPC)))
    {
        ASSERT_POINTER(pCPC, IConnectionPointContainer);
        LPCONNECTIONPOINT pCP;
        if (SUCCEEDED(pCPC->FindConnectionPoint(iid, &pCP)))
        {
            ASSERT_POINTER(pCP, IConnectionPoint);
            if (SUCCEEDED(pCP->Advise(pUnkSink, pdwCookie)))
                bSuccess = TRUE;
            pCP->Release();
            if (bSuccess && !bRefCount)
                pUnkSink->Release();
        }
        pCPC->Release();
    }
    return bSuccess;
}
```

Only three steps are required to use the `AfxConnectionAdvise` function:

1. Derive a class from `CCmdTarget`, `CMyClass`, and create a dispatch map entry that matches the signature of the event you want to receive. In this case, the event's name is `MyEvent` and it has no return value. It does, however, require a `BSTR` argument. You must implement the `OnMyEvent` function as a member function of `CMyClass`.

   ```
   BEGIN_DISPATCH_MAP(CMyClass, CCmdTarget)
   DISP_FUNCTION_ID(CMyClass,"MyEvent",1, \
   OnMyEvent,VT_EMPTY,VTS_BSTR)
   END_DISPATCH_MAP()
   ```

2. Create an instance of the sink class:

   ```
   pSink = new CMyClass();
   ```

3. Before you can hook up the sink interface with the server so that you can start to receive events, you must obtain a pointer to the dispinterface of `CMyClass`. By deriving your class from `CCmdTarget`, you have an object that supports the `IDispatch` interface.

   ```
   LPUNKNOWN pUnkSink = pSink->GetIDispatch(FALSE);
   ```

4. Now you can establish a connection between the source and your sink—`MyClass`. The function returns a cookie to identify the connection.

   ```
   AfxConnectionAdvise(m_pUnkSrc, IID_MYEVENT,
   pUnkSink, FALSE, &m_dwCookie);
   ```

AfxConnectionUnadvise

The `AfxConnectionUnadvise` function disconnects a connection previously established with `AfxConnectionAdvise`. This function accepts the same arguments as its advise counterpart.

```
BOOL AFXAPI AfxConnectionUnadvise(LPUNKNOWN pUnkSrc, REFIID iid,
    LPUNKNOWN pUnkSink, BOOL bRefCount, DWORD dwCookie)
{
    ASSERT_POINTER(pUnkSrc, IUnknown);
    ASSERT_POINTER(pUnkSink, IUnknown);
    if (!bRefCount)
        pUnkSink->AddRef();
    BOOL bSuccess = FALSE;
    LPCONNECTIONPOINTCONTAINER pCPC;
    if (SUCCEEDED(pUnkSrc->QueryInterface(
                    IID_IConnectionPointContainer,
                    (LPVOID*)&pCPC)))
    {
        ASSERT_POINTER(pCPC, IConnectionPointContainer);
        LPCONNECTIONPOINT pCP;
        if (SUCCEEDED(pCPC->FindConnectionPoint(iid, &pCP)))
```

```
        {
            ASSERT_POINTER(pCP, IConnectionPoint);
            if (SUCCEEDED(pCP->Unadvise(dwCookie)))
                bSuccess = TRUE;
            pCP->Release();
        }
        pCPC->Release();
    }
    // If we failed, undo the earlier AddRef.
    if (!bRefCount && !bSuccess)
        pUnkSink->Release();
    return bSuccess;
}
```

Control Registration

One of the two requirements a component must fulfill to be considered an ActiveX control is control registration. (The other requirement is that the component must support the IUnknown interface.) The methods in this section identify control registration and unregistration.

AfxOleRegisterControlClass

The AfxOleRegisterControlClass function registers a control class with the Windows operating system. This function accepts ten parameters, updating the Registry with a number of control attributes including the threading model the control supports.

AfxOleRegisterPropertyPageClass

The AfxOleRegisterPropertyPageClass function registers a property page class with the Windows operating system. It is necessary to register all the custom property pages you create for your control or other COM object.

AfxOleRegisterTypeLib

The AfxOleRegisterTypeLib function updates the Windows Registry with information about the location and identity of a type library. This function requires the HINSTANCE of the application, the file path to the type library (.TLB) file, and the GUID of the type library.

AfxOleUnregisterClass

The AfxOleUnregisterClass function removes a property page or ActiveX control's registration from the Windows Registry. This function requires both the object's GUID and ProgID.

AfxOleUnregisterTypeLib

The `AfxOleRegisterClass` function requires only the type library's GUID and removes its entry from the Windows Registry.

Exceptions

You are probably already familiar with the MFC exception-handling functions and classes. Two additional functions have been added to throw exceptions that relate to OLE activity: `AfxThrowOleDispatchException` and `AfxThrowOleException`.

AfxThrowOleDispatchException

Use the `AfxThrowOleDispatchException` function to indicate a problem with an automation server. This function is overloaded to either accept descriptive text for the user as a string of characters in your code, or to accept a resource ID, from which the system obtains the necessary text.

AfxThrowOleException

The `AfxThrowOleException` function is overloaded and provides a version that accepts an `SCODE` and another that accepts an `HRESULT`. Both functions create the necessary `COleException` object for you. Your exception handling code (you did provide exception handling in your code—right?) receives the `COleException` object and can take the appropriate action.

Initialization

Before you can issue any calls that involve COM, you must initialize the OLE system libraries.

AfxOleInit

The `AfxOleInit` function initializes the OLE DLLs. The AppWizard will automatically include this call at the beginning (yes, it is *that* important) of your application's `InitInstance` function.

Here's a quick review of what the initialization steps include:

- Send a call to initialize the COM library as a single-thread apartment (STA).
- Issue any nonsuccess initialization messages.
- Obtain the current thread, and then create and attach a `COleMessageFilter` object.
- Register the message filter with the OLE system DLLs.

The preceding steps are performed in the MFC code for OLE initialization, shown in the following:

```
BOOL AFXAPI AfxOleInit()
{
    _AFX_THREAD_STATE* pState = AfxGetThreadState();
    ASSERT(!pState->m_bNeedTerm);     // calling it twice?
    // during a DLL_PROCESS_DETACH.
    if (afxContextIsDLL)
    {
        pState->m_bNeedTerm = -1;   // -1 is a special flag
        return TRUE;
    }
    // first, initialize OLE
    SCODE sc = ::OleInitialize(NULL);
    if (FAILED(sc))
    {
        // warn about non-NULL success codes
        TRACE1("Warning: OleInitialize returned scode = %s.\n",
            AfxGetFullScodeString(sc));
        goto InitFailed;
    }
    // termination required when OleInitialize does not fail
    pState->m_bNeedTerm = TRUE;
    // hook idle time and exit time for required OLE cleanup
    CWinThread* pThread; pThread = AfxGetThread();
    pThread->m_lpfnOleTermOrFreeLib = AfxOleTermOrFreeLib;
    // allocate and initialize default message filter
    if (pThread->m_pMessageFilter == NULL)
    {
        pThread->m_pMessageFilter = new COleMessageFilter;
        ASSERT(AfxOleGetMessageFilter() != NULL);
        AfxOleGetMessageFilter()->Register();
    }
    return TRUE;
InitFailed:
    AfxOleTerm();
    return FALSE;
}
```

AfxOleInitModule

The `AfxOleInitModule` is for DLLs what `AfxOleInit` is for MFC applications. `AfxOleInitModule` initializes the OLE DLLs.

If you are using the ControlWizard to create the skeleton for your control application, you will not find a call directly to `AfxOleInitModule`. The reason is that your `InitInstance` function calls `COleControlModule::InitInstance`, and that function makes the appropriate calls to initialize the OLE DLLs for you.

Licensing

More recent additions to the OLE specification include COM object licensing support. With licensing, you can control the number of components a class factory creates. So if you are building a source control management system based on COM, each user's connection to the server component might require connection by a licensed client object.

AfxVerifyLicFile

The AfxVerifyLicFile function verifies the existence of a license file for a control.

Type Information

Type information describes a COM object's interfaces. Such information allows a program requiring services provided by the component to be identified at runtime. In addition, a design tool can use this information to display editing dialogs for properties and methods.

AfxOleTypeMatchGuid

The AfxOleTypeMatchGuid function determines if the given type descriptor describes a particular interface. You can easily obtain type information that an object provides using the ITypeInfo interface. This function allows you to work backwards in a sense: You already have type information, and you want to verify the object which it describes.

Reviewing the OLE Macros

MFC's support for OLE requires the use of a substantial number of macros. The purpose of these macros spans the range of functionality that OLE offers. The common theme running through these macro categories is that most offer some kind of map construct. MFC programmers have long been familiar with the message map architecture prevalent through the framework, especially with regard to the document-view architecture.

Class Factories

When you think of the word *factory,* you might conjure up images of car parts moving down an assembly line, one after the other, while various welding and stamping machines take their turn bending and shaping these pieces. The concept of a factory isn't much different when describing the operation of an OLE class factory. A class factory's purpose is to create multiple objects of the same type. The rationale behind having class factories is to define a generic model for an action that you will need to use in countless situations in the COM universe. Factory classes implement either the IClassFactory or

IClassFactory2 interface, where the latter interface offers object creation through a license.

DECLARE_OLECREATE

The DECLARE_OLECREATE macro enables CCmdTarget-derived classes to be created through OLE automation. This macro requires one argument—the name of the class to create. This macro must appear in the class definition.

DECLARE_OLECREATE_EX

The DECLARE_OLECREATE_EX macro declares the class factory of a control that does not require licensing.

IMPLEMENT_OLECREATE_EX

The IMPLEMENT_OLECREATE_EX macro implements the class factory for a control. The macro requires 13 arguments (*class_name*, *external_name*, *l*, *w1*, *w2*, *b1*, *b2*, *b3*, *b4*, *b5*, *b6*, *b7*, and *b8*), which identify the name of the class, the object's exposed name, and the CLSID for the class.

BEGIN_OLEFACTORY

The BEGIN_OLEFACTORY macro identifies the beginning of the class factory definition. The macro requires the name of the class that is constructed by this factory.

END_OLEFACTORY

The END_OLEFACTORY macro identifies the end of the class factory definition. The macro accepts the same name of the class that appears as an argument to the associated begin macro.

Client/Container Common Commands

Communication between the OLE document server and container, especially with regard to menu command execution, has been cumbersome in previous releases of MFC. The recent addition of Active document support allows the invocation of common menu commands in a standard manner.

ON_OLECMD

The ON_OLECMD macro routes commands through the IOleCommandTarget interface, which enables bidirectional communication between a container application and any DocObjects. Thus, common document-oriented commands, such as Open, Save, and Print, can be exchanged between a container and an object it contains. This macro requires three arguments: a command group identifier (or NULL for standard group designation), the OLE command identifier, and the menu (or other dispatch command) ID. See Table 11.1 for a description of the macros in which the IOleCommandTarget standard menu commands are implemented.

TABLE 11.1   THE MACROS THAT IMPLEMENT THE IOleCommandTarget MENU COMMANDS

Macro	Description
ON_OLECMD_CLEARSELECTION( )	Initiates the Edit Clear command
ON_OLECMD_COPY( )	Initiates the Edit Copy command
ON_OLECMD_CUT( )	Initiates the Edit Cut command
ON_OLECMD_NEW( )	Initiates the File New command
ON_OLECMD_OPEN( )	Initiates the File Open command
ON_OLECMD_PAGESETUP( )	Initiates the File Page Setup command
ON_OLECMD_PASTE( )	Initiates the Edit Paste command
ON_OLECMD_PASTESPECIAL( )	Initiates the Edit Paste Special command
ON_OLECMD_PRINT( )	Initiates the File Print command
ON_OLECMD_PRINTPREVIEW( )	Initiates the File Print Preview command
ON_OLECMD_REDO( )	Initiates the Edit Redo command
ON_OLECMD_SAVE( )	Initiates the File Save command
ON_OLECMD_SAVE_AS( )	Initiates the File Save As command
ON_OLECMD_SAVE_COPY_AS( )	Initiates the File Save Copy As command
ON_OLECMD_SELECTALL( )	Initiates the Edit Select All command
ON_OLECMD_UNDO( )	Initiates the Edit Undo command

Control Property Persistence

A control allows the storing of its properties between activations. This is known as *persistence.* The mechanism that allows this storage and retrieval to take place is known as *serialization.* In serializing properties, a stream of property information is written to a storage device. At a later time, the contents of this stream is read back in the order in which it was written, and defines the control's property settings. Aside from the order, which must remain the same between read and write operations, the size of each property value must also remain the same—or the stream is meaningless.

The MFC framework supports a number of functions and macros to support control persistence. The `DoPropExchange` member function of the `COleControl` class offers you a convenient way to support the property persistence model. The function requires one parameter, a `CPropExchange` object pointer, establishing the property exchange context. `DoPropExchange` works in conjunction with a number of `PX_` prefix functions that aid in the storage and retrieval of common property datatypes.

```
void CMyCtrl::DoPropExchange(CPropExchange* pPX)
{
    COleControl::DoPropExchange(pPX);
    PX_Bool(pPX, _T("BoolProp"), m_boolProp, TRUE);
    PX_Short(pPX, _T("ShortProp"), m_shortProp, 0);
    PX_Color(pPX, _T("ColorProp"), m_colorProp, RGB(0xFF,0x00,0x00));
    PX_String(pPX, _T("StringProp"), m_stringProp, _T(""));
}
```

An issue that you must address when implementing control persistence is version support. As a control evolves, it will acquire more properties that it must manage (generally speaking). Because the control's properties are written to a stream, the control must be able to determine the version of the control that wrote the stream and read back only those properties that were present when that version of the control created the stream.

```
void CMyCtrl::DoPropExchange(CPropExchange* pPX)
{
    ExchangeVersion(pPX, MAKELONG(_wVerMinor, _wVerMajor));
    COleControl::DoPropExchange(pPX);
...
}
```

Call this function within your control's `DoPropExchange` member function to serialize or initialize a property of type `BOOL`. The property's value will be read from or written to the variable referenced by `bValue`, as appropriate. If `bDefault` is specified, it will be used as the property's default value. This value is used if, for any reason, the control's serialization process fails. Table 11.2 lists the functions you can call within `DoPropExchange` and describes their use.

TABLE 11.2 FUNCTIONS CALLED WITHIN YOUR CONTROL'S `DoPropExchange` MEMBER FUNCTION

Function	*Description*
`PX_Blob`	The `PX_Blob` function serializes or initializes a property that stores Binary Large OBject (BLOB) data.
`PX_Bool`	The `PX_Bool` function serializes or initializes a Boolean property.

continues

TABLE 11.2 CONTINUED

Function	Description
PX_Color	The PX_Color function serializes or initializes an OLE_COLOR type property. The property window will automatically display a color-picker dialog box that allows you to click the color you want, rather than entering the numeric values for the color. Internally, an OLE_COLOR type is a Long.
PX_Currency	The PX_Currency function serializes or initializes a currency type property.
PX_DataPath	The PX_DataPath function serializes or initializes.
PX_Double	The PX_Double function serializes or initializes.
PX_Font	The PX_Font function serializes or initializes.
PX_Float	The PX_Float function serializes or initializes.
PX_IUnknown	The PX_IUnkown function serializes or initializes.
PX_Long	The PX_Long function serializes or initializes.
PX_Picture	The PX_Picture function serializes or initializes.
PX_Short	The PX_Short function serializes or initializes.
PX_ULong	The PX_ULong function serializes or initializes.
PX_UShort	The PX_UShort function serializes or initializes.
PX_String	The PX_String function serializes or initializes.
PX_VBXFontConvert	The PX_VBXFontConvert function serializes or initializes.

Dialog Data Exchange

The MFC framework supports a standard mechanism for initializing and validating controls in a dialog box. You are certainly familiar with a number of the Dialog Data Exchange (DDX) functions and dialog data validation (DDV) functions that ClassWizard generates for you when you are laying out dialog boxes. MFC supplies a number of DDX and DDV functions to aid in the exchange and validation of data with OLE controls.

The general case for these functions includes the following parameters:

- A pointer to a CDataExchange object. The framework supplies this object to establish the context of the data exchange, including its direction.
- The ID of an OLE control in the dialog box.

- The control's dispatch ID.
- A reference to a member variable of the dialog box, with which data is exchanged.

The specific exchange and validation macros appear in Table 11.3.

TABLE 11.3 THE EXCHANGE AND VALIDATION MACROS

Function	Description
DDX_OCBool	Manages the transfer of a BOOL datatype property between a control and its container.
DDX_OCBoolRO	Manages the transfer of a read-only BOOL datatype property, between a control and its container.
DDS_OCColor	Manages the transfer of an OLE_COLOR datatype property between a control and its container.
DDX_OCColorRO	Manages the transfer of a read-only OLE_COLOR datatype property between a control and its container.
DDX_OCFloat	Manages the transfer of a double datatype property between a control and its container.
DDX_OCFloatRO	Manages the transfer of a read-only double datatype property between a control and its container.
DDX_OCInt	Manages the transfer of an int datatype property between a control and its container.
DDX_OCIntRO	Manages the transfer of a read-only int datatype property between a control and its container.
DDX_OCShort	Manages the transfer of a short datatype property between a control and its container.
DDX_OCShortRO	Manages the transfer of a read-only short datatype property between a control and its container.
DDX_OCText	Manages the transfer of a CString datatype property between a control and its container.
DDC_OCTextRO	Manages the transfer of a read-only CString datatype property between a control and its container.
DDX_MonthCalCtrl	Manages the transfer of a CTime or COleDateTime datatype property between a control and its container.
DDX_DateTimeCtrl	Manages the transfer of a CTime or COleDateTime datatype property between a control and its container.
DDV_MinMaxDateTime	Verifies the date or time value in the date-time control.

Dispatch Maps

Dispatch maps offer a way to call automation methods and get or set automation properties. Interfacing with OLE automation in this manner requires the map constructs you are already familiar with, including map declaration, begin and end map designators, and map entry macros.

BEGIN_DISPATCH_MAP

The BEGIN_DISPATCH_MAP macro designates the beginning of a block of one or more dispatch macros that identify an object's OLE automation methods and properties. This macro requires two arguments: theClass and baseClass. The first argument, theClass, identifies the class in which the map is declared. The second argument, baseClass, (not surprisingly) identifies the base class of theClass. The purpose of supplying both the base class and its superclass is to enable the chaining of maps—a mechanism that is common throughout the MFC framework and not special to the OLE class hierarchy.

END_DISPATCH_MAP

The END_DISPATCH_MAP macro indicates the end of a dispatch map definition. This macro requires no arguments and generates an entry that flags the end of the dispatch map.

DECLARE_DISPATCH_MAP

The DECLARE_DISPATCH_MAP macro declares the dispatch map by defining the variables, structures, and functions that support the dispatch map's functionality. This macro appears in your class declaration. The macro requires no arguments.

DISP_DEFVALUE

The DISP_DEFVALUE macro defines a special use case of automation properties for Visual Basic. This macro identifies an existing property as the default value for the object. The macro requires two arguments, the name of the automation class, and the external name of a property whose definition occurs elsewhere in the map. The concept behind the default value property is to allow easier programming of the object. Thus the value of the object is modified as the result of an assignment to the object itself.

DISP_FUNCTION

The DISP_FUNCTION macro can appear in a dispatch map, between the BEGIN_DISPATCH_MAP and END_DISPATCH_MAP macros, and identifies an OLE automation method. This macro requires five arguments, describing the name of the method, the return type, and the argument list.

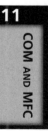

DISP_PROPERTY

The DISP_PROPERTY macro can appear in a dispatch map and identifies an automation property. This macro requires four arguments, describing the name of the property and the property's datatype. Automation properties differ from automation methods in that they can result in the generation of two interface methods: one to set the property and the other to get the property. Read-only properties only define a get property method.

DISP_PROPERTY_EX

The DISP_PROPERTY_EX macro can appear in a dispatch map and also identifies an automation property. This macro differs from DISP_PROPERTY in that it enables you to define the name of both the set method and the get method exposed by the interface.

DISP_PROPERTY_NOTIFY

The DISP_PROPERTY_NOTIFY macro can appear in a dispatch map and identifies an automation property that automatically calls a function when the value of the property changes. This macro requires five arguments:

- *theClass*—The name of the class
- *szExternalName*—The property's external name
- *memberName*—The member variable where the property is stored
- *pfnAfterSet*—The name of the notification function for the external name
- *vtPropType*—The property's type

DISP_PROPERTY_PARAM

The DISP_PROPERTY_PARAM macro can appear in a dispatch map and identifies an automation property. This macro accepts, in a sense, a variable number of parameters that can be appended to the end of the required six arguments. The purpose of this property macro variation is to support indexing of the property.

Event Maps

Event maps are an MFC convention that simplify the programming of both control and container applications. ActiveX controls use events to notify their containers that something important has occurred. Examples of such events are a user pressing a key or a clicking a mouse. The word *fire* is used when describing the act of a control that issues event; hence, the control fires events to the container. The container then responds to the event appropriately.

Map Definition

A control's event map requires at minimum, the begin and end macros in the definition (.CPP) file of the COleControl-derived class and the declare macro in the class declaration (.H) file. If you begin your project using AppWizard or ControlWizard, these macros will already be in place, in the proper files.

DECLARE_EVENT_MAP

The DECLARE_EVENT_MAP macro resides in a COleControl-derived class declaration and provides a map of the events that the control can fire. The macro requires no arguments.

BEGIN_EVENT_MAP

The BEGIN_EVENT_MAP macro identifies the beginning of the event map. The macro requires two arguments, the name of the control class on which the map is being defined and the name of the base class.

END_EVENT_MAP

The END_EVENT_MAP macro identifies the end of the control's event map and requires no arguments.

Event Mapping Entries

The event entry mapping macros identify the control functions that fire each event. You can use ClassWizard to add event entries to the control's event map.

EVENT_CUSTOM

The EVENT_CUSTOM macro can reside in the event map, between the BEGIN_EVENT_MAP and END_EVENT_MAP macros, and identifies a custom event. The macro requires three arguments: the name of the event, the callback function, and a parameter list. The last argument allows a variable number of event parameters, in that multiple parameter datatypes can be supplied, separated by spaces.

EVENT_CUSTOM_ID

The EVENT_CUSTOM_ID macro defines a custom event and specifying a dispatch ID.

Message Mapping Verbs

In grade school you were taught that a verb is an action word. In OLE, verbs are a way for one object, generally a container object, to tell another object, commonly a server object, to perform an action. In fact, although you can define your own verbs, the standard verbs that OLE provides will cover most of your needs. Such standard verbs include open, edit, and print.

ON_OLEVERB

The ON_OLEVERB macro defines a message map entry that associates a custom verb to a specific member function on a control. The macro requires two arguments: the resource string ID containing the verb's text and the function to call when invoking the verb.

The function to invoke argument must adhere to the following prototype:

```
BOOL memeberFxn(LPMSG lpMsg, HWND hWndParent, LPCRECT lpRect);
```

In this prototype, the values for the parameter list are taken from the corresponding IOleObject::DoVerb method.

ON_STDOLEVERB

The purpose of ON_STDOLEVERB is to enable you to override the default behavior for a standard verb. The macro requires two arguments: the standard verb's index, and the function to call on verb invocation.

Sink Maps

Sink maps are an MFC construct that manages ActiveX control events in a container application. These sink maps offer a mechanism to deal with ActiveX controls that is similar to the way normal Windows controls are managed by message maps. The entries in a sink map associate event handlers with ActiveX controls.

BEGIN_EVENTSINK_MAP

The BEGIN_EVENTSINK_MAP macro identifies the beginning of a container's event sink map. As with all macros that begin a map definition, this macro requires two arguments: the name of the class on which implementation is occurring, and the name of the base class.

DECLARE_EVENTSINK_MAP

The DECLARE_EVENTSINK_MAP macro resides in the container classes' declaration and specifies the events for which the container receives notification.

END_EVENTSINK_MAP

The END_EVENTSINK_MAP macro accepts no arguments and indicates the end of the container class's sink map.

Sink Mapping

ClassWizard generates a number of sink map entry macros that allow a container to respond to events from a control.

ON_EVENT

The ON_EVENT macro can be an entry in a container's event sink map, and defines an event handler function that responds to an event fired from a control. The macro requires five arguments, among which are a pointer to the container function that responds to the event and the argument datatypes for the method.

ON_EVENT_RANGE

The ON_EVENT_RANGE macro identifies an event handler for an OLE control event that maps to a contiguous range of ids. This macro is a map entry that can appear between the BEGIN_EVENTSINK_MAP macro and the END_EVENTSINK_MAP macro.

ON_EVENT_REFLECT

The ON_EVENT_REFLECT macro offers message reflection that is analogous to the message reflection that MFC supports for a number of common controls. In this case, the macro allows the control to receive events before they are handed off to the control's container. This macro requires four arguments, and it must appear as an entry between the begin and end macros of the sink map.

ON_PROPNOTIFY

The ON_PROPNOTIFY macro defines a sink map entry that handles property notifications of an OLE control.

ON_PROPNOTIFY_RANGE

The ON_PROPNOTIFY_RANGE macro is another event sink map entry that enables you to define a single handler function for a range of OLE control IDs.

ON_PROPNOTIFY_REFLECT

The ON_PROPNOTIFY_REFLECT macro enables you to assign a function that receives an OLE control's property notification prior to the container receiving the event. The handler function returns a Boolean state of true or false, thus either allowing the property to change or disallowing such an action.

Connection Maps

The connection map macros work in conjunction with the CConnectionPoint class. Connection maps are MFC's implementation of OLE automation's outgoing interfaces. This mechanism allows server objects to make calls on a client object.

BEGIN_CONNECTION_PART

The BEGIN_CONNECTION_PART macro identifies the beginning of a list of CONNECTION_IID entries, where each entry identifies the sink's interface identifier (IID).

END_CONNECTION_PART

The END_CONNECTION_PART macro designates the end of the CONNECTION_IID entries.

CONNECTION_IID

The CONNECTION_IID macro is a connection map entry and always appears between the BEGIN_CONNECTION_PART and END_CONNECTION_PART macros. The macro requires a single argument, which identifies the IID of the sink interface.

DECLARE_CONNECTION_MAP

The DECLARE_CONNECTION_MAP macro associates a connection map with a COleControl-derived class. This macro accepts no arguments and resides in the class declaration.

BEGIN_CONNECTION_MAP

The BEGIN_CONNECTION_MAP macro identifies the beginning of the connection point map for your control. This macro requires a single argument, which is the name of the class that contains the connection points.

END_CONNECTION_MAP

The END_CONNECTION_MAP macro identifies the end of the connection point map for the control. The macro accepts no arguments.

CONNECTION_PART

The CONNECTION_PART macro is a connection map entry that can reside between the BEGIN_CONNECTION_MAP macro and the END_CONNECTION_MAP macro.

Property Page Data Mapping

The DDP_ functions synchronize property page dialog member variables with an ActiveX control's properties. The DDP_ functions are similar to their DDX_ counterparts, with the addition of a single string argument at the end of the function that accepts the name of the control property. The argument list for a DDP_ function follows:

- Pointer to a CDataExchange object. The framework supplies this object to establish the context of the data exchange, including its direction.

- The resource ID of the combo box control associated with the control property specified by pszPropName.

- The member variable associated with the property page control specified by ID and the property specified by pszPropName.

- The property name of the control property to be exchanged with the combo box control specified by ID.

MFC offers a number of functions to exchange data with the most common dialog controls:

DDP_CBIndex	Use the DDP_CBIndex function to map a combo box's selected string's index with a control property.
DDP_CBString	Use the DDP_CBString function to map a partial string match with the string that is selected in a combo box with a control property.
DDP_CBStringExact	Use the DDP_CBStringExact function to map an exact string match.
DDP_Check	Use the DDP_Check function to map the property's value with the property page check box control.
DDP_LBIndex	Use the DDP_LBIndex function to map an integer property's value with the index of the current selection in a list box on the property page.
DDP_LBString	Use the DDP_LBString function to map a string property's value with the current selection in a list box on the property page.
DDP_LBStringExact	Use the DDP_LBStringExact function to map a string property's value when it is an exact match of the current selection in a list box on the property page.
DDP_PostProcessing	Use the DDP_PostProcessing function to complete the transfer of property values from the property page to your control when property values are being preserved.
DDP_Radio	Use the DDP_Radio function to map a property's value with the associated property page radio button control.
DDP_Text	Use the DDP_Text function to map a property's value with the associated property page control.

Property Pages

Property pages offer a standard mechanism for displaying and allowing user modification of an object's properties. A tabbed dialog box offers your object's users a familiar Windows standard for interacting with (that is, getting and setting) property values.

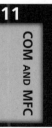

PROPPAGEID

The PROPPAGEID macro adds a property page to an ActiveX control. This macro requires a single argument, which is the CLSID of the property page. This macro is an entry in the property page map and must be declared between the BEGIN_PROPPAGEIDS and END_PROPPAGEIDS macros in the control's class implementation file.

DECLARE_PROPPAGEIDS

The DECLARE_PROPPAGEIDS macro resides in your control's class declaration file and identifies the property pages that belong to the control.

BEGIN_PROPPAGEIDS

The BEGIN_PROPPAGEIDS macro identifies the beginning of an ActiveX control's property page map. The macro requires two arguments, the name of the control's class and the number of property pages the class uses.

END_PROPPAGEIDS

The END_PROPPAGEIDS macro identifies the end of your control's property page map.

Type Library Access

Type libraries describe the interfaces implemented by an object server. Such a description includes the number of parameters, the datatype for each parameter, the direction each parameter is passed, and the return value. In addition, type library information includes the names of the methods and properties, as well as the location of help files describing their use.

DECLARE_OLETYPELIB

The DECLARE_OLETYPELIB macro defines the GetTypeLib member function for a control's class. This macro accepts a single argument—the name of the control's class. This macro must appear in the class declaration.

IMPLEMENT_OLETYPELIB

The IMPLEMENT_OLETYPELIB macro implements the control's GetTypeLib member function. The macro requires four parameters, including the major and minor version numbers of the control's type library.

MFC and the OLE Class Categories

MFC's COM support focuses on the technologies that rely heavily on visual integration with other components and applications.

Active Document

An active document is what old-timers will remember as OLE document servers. Essentially an *active document* is a complex COM server object that, when activated in a container application, takes over the entire client workspace and hijacks all the user interface components, including the toolbars, menus, and so on. Figure 11.1 shows an active document server in an active state in a container. In this case, the server is Microsoft Word and the container is Internet Explorer.

FIGURE 11.1

An active document in a container.

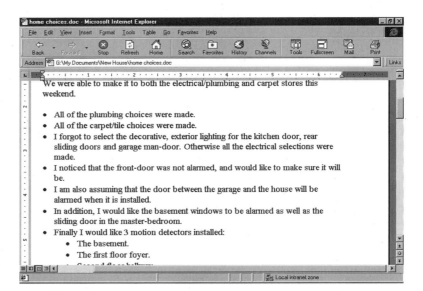

CDocObjectServer

The CDocObjectServer class inherits directly from the CCmdTarget class, and you use it when building applications that implement OLE server documents. This class implements the following interfaces: IOleCommandTarget, IOleDocument, IOleDocumentView, and IPrint. This class is necessary in making a normal COleDocument server, which is only a simple OLE container, into a full DocObject server.

A `DocObject` server, also referred to as an active document, allows in-place activation in the container application. Common container applications include Microsoft Office Binder and Microsoft Internet Explorer.

CDocObjectServerItem

The `CDocObjectServerItem` class inherits directly from the `COleServerItem` class and is necessary in the construction of `DocObject` servers. The `CDocObjectServerItem` constructor requires a pointer to a `COleServerDoc` object, which will contain the new `DocObject` item that `CDocObjectServerItem` represents. The class also provides three overridable functions: `OnHide`, `OnOpen`, and `OnShow`. These functions enable you to perform custom operations at various times of the `DocObject`'s lifecycle.

COleDocObjectItem

The `COleDocObjectItem` class inherits from the `COleClientItem` class. A `COleDocObjectItem` is managed by an OLE container application, and it implements the interfaces necessary for active document containment. An active document differs from a normal container object in that it occupies the entire client area during in-place activation and it assumes full control of the container application's Help menu.

Automation

The origin of OLE lies in some pretty obscure documentation that speaks of variant datatypes, type library information spelunking, and the ever-cryptic MkTypLib utility. Well, automation has come a long way since those times and is almost the undisputed king of the COM-enabling technologies. Automation provides the lingua franca for applications, ActiveX controls, COM object servers, and scripting languages to speak to one another. Although automation's `IDispatch` interface isn't the fastest way for COM-aware objects to communicate, the capability of a program to discover the methods, properties, and associated argument datatypes and return value at runtime is a very powerful feature.

CCmdTarget

The `CCmdTarget` class is one of the MFC framework's most familiar classes. It seems as if you can't do anything without deriving from, or making calls to, this most common base class. Although not strictly an OLE class, because `CCmdTarget` forms the heart of MFC's message routing architecture by supporting message maps, it also enables automation by exposing `IDispatch` functionality with dispatch maps. You can create an automation server by deriving a class from `CCmdTarget` and using ClassWizard to create the necessary dispatch map entries and ODL text.

CConnectionPoint

The CConnectionPoint class derives from CCmdTarget and implements the IConnectionPoint interface. Connection points are commonly referred to as *outgoing interfaces*. The most common use of outgoing interfaces is ActiveX control events. In this case, the ActiveX control container responds to events, whose source is the control. Connection point management requires support of the CONNECTION_MAP macros.

> **NOTE**
>
> The COleControl class implements two connection points by default: one for property change notification and the other for property change events.

COleDispatchDriver

The COleDispatchDriver class is the heart of client-side automation for MFC applications. This class provides the necessary member functions for invoking automation server methods as well as obtaining and manipulating automation properties. The most common deployment of this object involves the use of ClassWizard where you add a class to your project whose source is a type library. ClassWizard then constructs the appropriate wrapper class, deriving it from COledispatchDriver. The properties and methods of the automation server are then exposed to your program as functions on this class.

COleDispatchException

The COleDispatchException class derives from CException and is thrown as the result of trying to complete an OLE automation operation. You can issue an exception of this type by calling AfxThrowOleDispatchException.

Common Dialogs for OLE

Microsoft provides a familiar set of common dialogs for the Windows operating system, including File Open, Print, File Save, and File Save As. There probably isn't a Windows program on the planet that doesn't present one or more of this dialog boxes. Likewise, Microsoft offers a number of common dialog boxes for those operations that are OLE-centric. You will notice, however, that with the exception of the COleBusyDialog and COlePropertiesDialog, these dialogs offer support for active document containment and management.

COleBusyDialog

The COleBusyDialog class offers a standard user interface component to the user that indicates whether an OLE document or automation server is either not responding or unavailable. This class offers OLEUIBUSY.

This class requires the support of the OLEUIBUSY structure for purposes of initialization and format of the dialog. In addition, this structure offers a field to identify the user's response to the display of this dialog. Finally, this structure offers access to hook the message loop that is active during the modal display of this dialog for purposes of intercepting messages that are intended for the dialog box.

COleChangeIconDialog

The COleChangeIconDialog class displays a dialog box, which enables the user to identify the icon that is displayed for an embedded or linked OLE-document item. Although this class offers you (a programmer) the ability to display this dialog under program control, it is commonly displayed as the result of user actions taken from many of the other standard OLE-document management dialog boxes, which include Insert Object, Paste Special, and Convert.

The use of this class requires the OLEUICHANGEICON structure, which contains fields to manage initialization of the Change Icon dialog box and offers a field that accepts the return information when user interaction with the dialog completes. This structure offers fields to support a hook to the message loop that is active during the modal display of this dialog for purposes of intercepting messages that are intended for the dialog box.

COleChangeSourceDialog

The COleChangeSourceDialog class displays an OLE standard dialog box that enables a user to modify an OLE document item's link. Construction of an object of this class requires a pointer to the COleClientItem-derived class object whose source attributes are being modified. This class provides a number of member functions to obtain the name of the object and its moniker. Use of this class requires an instance of the OLEUICHANGE-SOURCE structure.

ColeConvertDialog

The COleConvertDialog class derives from COleDialog and enables you to change the document server object that is associated with an embedded or linked item. As with most of the OLE common dialogs, this dialog also requires a structure to define properties on initialization and provide a place for return information. In this case, the COleConvertDialog class requires a OLEUICONVERT structure.

COleDialog

The COleDialog class is the base class for all standard OLE dialogs. This class derives from CCommonDialog and offers only a single member function—GetLastError. GetLastError returns an error code that is specific to deriving dialog class.

COleInsertDialog

The COleInsertDialog class aids in the creation of one of the most common standard OLE dialogs—the Insert Object dialog. This dialog is certainly familiar to anyone who is a Windows user and is present in any OLE-compatible document container. COleInsertDialog offers a member function, CreateItem, which creates an object of the type identified by the dialog on exit. The OLEUIINSERTOBJECT structure supports this class.

COleLinksDialog

The COleLinksDialog class can display the OLE Edit Links dialog box. The OLEUIEDITLINKS structure supports this class.

COlePasteSpecialDialog

The COlePasteSpecialDialog class enables you to display an OLE common dialog that aids a user in the process of linking or embedding data in your application's compound document. The user can also select to render the data in its native format or simply represent the data with an icon.

COlePropertiesDialog

The COlePropertiesDialog class offers a user interface component, which is common to the Windows operating system and supports modification of an OLE object's properties. This is the same properties dialog that is displayed when a user right-clicks any desktop icon and selects the Properties menu. Figure 11.2 shows the COM and MFC Properties dialog.

The OLE Object Properties dialog contains three property pages by default: General, View, and Link. Unlike the other OLE common dialogs, this dialog makes use of the following five structures:

- OLEUIGNRLPROPS—Supports the General page of the dialog box.
- OLEUILINKPROPS—Supports the Link page of the dialog box.
- OLEUIOBJECTPROPS—Initializes the Object Properties dialog box, containing pointers to all the page structures.

- `OLEUIVIEWPROPS`—Supports the View page of the dialog box
- `PROPSHEETHEADER`—Supports custom property sheets

FIGURE 11.2
The COM and MFC Properties dialog.

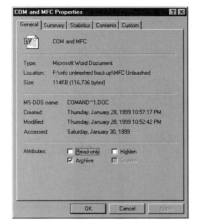

`COleUpdateDialog`

The `COleUpdateDialog` class provides an OLE standard dialog allowing a user to update existing linked or embedded objects in an OLE document. This class derives directly from the `COleLinksDialog` and offers no additional functions or data members—the user interface is simply tailored to this specific case of the `COleLinksDialog`.

Container

The MFC framework provides the document/view architecture as a model for separating the management of a program's data from the visual presentation of such data. The framework offers the base class `CView`, from which specific user interface views are derived, and the `CDocument` class, which offers a base for data management. This model has been extended to offer support for OLE documents with the `COleDocument` class. OLE documents must manage data whose format is defined by external applications. These data sources can either be *embedded* or *linked* to the document. Embedded data is stored inside the file along with the data that is native to your application, whereas linked data is stored outside your application's data file and referenced by a *moniker*. A moniker uniquely identifies a COM object. Until recently this moniker was almost certainly a file-moniker, thus providing path information to the data file. However, today it would not be uncommon for this link to exist as a url-moniker. Figure 11.3 contains a decision tree that might help you identify the OLE document class that you require.

FIGURE **11.3**
OLE ServerDoc
decision tree.

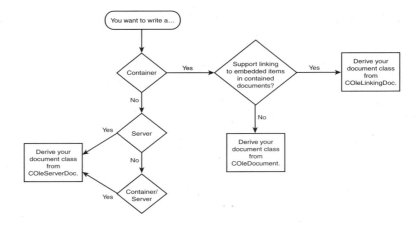

CDocItem

The CDocItem class derives from CCmdTarget and is the base class for COleClientItem, COleServerItem, and CDocObjectServer. The class offers a single method, GetDocument, and one overridable method, IsBlank.

COleClientItem

The COleClientItem class can be used in conjunction with the COleDocument, ColeLinkingDoc, or COleServerDoc classes (see Figure 11.4). Each OLE item that is managed by the document is wrapped in this class.

FIGURE **11.4**
How documents
manage items.

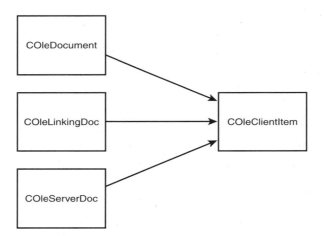

COleDocument

The CDocument base class offers methods that manage the views to the data. Storing and retrieving data, as well as managing the dirty or change state information for the document, falls under the list of responsibilities for this class.

COleLinkingDoc

The COleLinkingDoc class derives from the COleDocument class and offers the additional functionality of linking support to your application's data management model.

CRichEditCntrItem

A common OLE-enabled document type is an edit control. Microsoft provides access to the edit control that is used by the WordPad utility with the CRichEditCtrl class. In addition, the CRichEditCntrItem class provides container-side access to the COleClientItems that are stored in the control.

The CRichEditCntrItem class works in conjunction with the CRichEditView and CRichEditDoc classes in providing rich edit container support for OLE server objects that jives with MFC's document view architecture. The CRichEditView performs those functions in displaying text and embedded object placeholders, whereas CRichEditDoc maintains a list of COleClientItems. CRichEditCntrlItem derives directly from COleClientItem and offers a single additional member function, which creates a CRichEditCntrlItem object and adds it to the container document.

CRichEditDoc

The CRichEditDoc class derives from COleServerDoc and manages OLE client items for a CRichEditView.

Control

What do controls, OLE Controls, ActiveX controls, and even OCXs have in common? Everything. Leave marketing people to their own devices long enough and before long, they'll get bored with the name—and change it. The fact of the matter is though, that the widespread popularity of the Internet forced Microsoft's hand to redefine an OLE control. Initially, these components were designed to replace the VBX architecture, but soon they were needed to shore up Microsoft's defense against Java and the JavaBean component model.

CAsyncMonikerFile

The CAsyncMonikerFile class derives from CMonikerFile and offers asynchronous monikers to ActiveX controls. The purpose of asynchronous monikers is to allow ActiveX controls to appear more responsive during activation. This class offers a number of member functions that allow control over a callback and transfer progress.

CCachedDataPathProperty

The CCachedDataPathProperty inherits from CDataPathProperty and is a variation on the base class's theme. The CCachedDataPathProperty also allows the asynchronous loading of an OLE control property; however, this class stores the contents in RAM.

CDataPathProperty

The CDataPathProperty inherits from CAsyncMonikerFile and allows the asynchronous loading of an OLE control property. This class enables you to download large control properties, such as image files, in the background without blocking initialization of the control.

CFontHolder

The CFontHolder class wraps the IFont interface. This class helps you manage ActiveX control font properties.

CMonikerFile

The CMonikerFile class derives from COleStreamFile. COleStreamFile wraps the IStream interface, whereas CMonikerFile identifies the stream with a moniker.

COleCmdUI

The COleCmdUI class offers a mechanism for a DocObject and a container application to exchange commands. Thus, a container can receive and process commands that originate from a DocObject's user interface and vice versa.

COleControl

The COleControl class is the class you base your ActiveX controls on when developing such controls with MFC. This class provides you with a huge toolkit of functions, attributes, and overridable methods. This class alone requires an entire chapter to describe (and in fact this book includes such a discussion in Chapter 14, "MFC ActiveX Controls") the flexibility that the COleControl provides you in constructing ActiveX controls. Although MFC is very capable in developing such controls, you must remember that for these controls to work, the target machine must have the correct MFC DLLs installed. Also, the controls that you develop with this framework can result in some sizeable code, which might be an issue for users downloading such controls from a slow Internet connection. Microsoft of course comes to the rescue, or saw this deficiency, and provides another technology for building lightweight COM objects, including ActiveX controls, with ATL.

COleControlModule

The `COleControlModule` class derives from `CWinApp` and is to MFC-based ActiveX controls what the `CWinApp` class is to MFC applications. The `COleControlModule` provides only two virtual functions, `InitInstance` and `ExitInstance`, and as with `CWinApp`, these are the places that you put your initialization and termination code, respectively. The `InitInstance` function calls `AfxOleInitModule` for you and also calls `COleObjectFactory`'s `RegisterAll` function, thus initializing the OLE DLLs and registering your control's class factories. The `ExitInstance` function revokes class factory registration.

COlePropertyPage

The `COlePropertyPage` class derives from `CDialog` and displays an ActiveX control's property pages. If you use ControlWizard to build your control, it will automatically generate a single property page that derives from this class. If you want to add additional property pages to your control, you must create your own classes that also derive from `COlePropertyPage`. Getting your control to recognize these additional pages requires editing the `PROPPAGEID` map. You must add the additional `PROPPAGEID` entry macros, supplying the GUID that you generate for each page.

CPictureHolder

The `CPictureHolder` class helps you manage picture properties in your ActiveX control. This class helps you display images in your control that originate as bitmap, icon, or metafile sources. You can also get and set the `IPictureDisp` interface with a pair of member functions. You can obtain various picture attributes through the `IPictureDisp` interface, such as the height and width of the image.

CPropExchange

The `CPropExchange` class aids in the serialization of an ActiveX control's properties. Your control's `DoPropExchange` function receives a pointer to a `CPropExchange` object where it provides context for all the PX_ methods that you call to serialize or initialize a property.

Drag and Drop (Universal Data Transfer)

The OLE drag-and-drop functions involve a data transfer protocol that involves exchanging an IDataObject pointer between a source and a destination.

COleDataObject

The COleDataObject class is central to MFC's uniform data transfer (UDT) implementation. This class enables you to easily access the IDataObject interface, which enumerates data formats, enables data transfer, and advises of data change. COleDataObjects are created on the receiving side of a data transfer—for example, the paste operation of a clipboard transfer or the drop operation of a drag-and-drop transfer.

COleDataSource

The COleDataSource class derives from CCmdTarget and offers a source for data transfer. Unlike ColeDataObjects, which come into play at the receiving end of a UDT operation, COleDataSource objects are created at the initiating side of such a transfer. The act of copying to a clipboard or selecting data for a drag-and-drop operation results in the creation of a COleDataSource object.

COleDropSource

The COleDropSource class offers a convenient mechanism for initiating uniform data transfer in an interactive manner, observing standard OLE user interface conventions. The class offers three overridable functions that are called during the appropriate times of the drop-target selection process.

COleDropTarget

The OLE classes that support drag-and-drop operations rely heavily upon the interaction between the OLE uniform data transfer mechanism and various user interface elements that are identified as data sources and drop targets. In addition, a number of overridable methods allow customization of user feedback when the mouse cursor, engaged in a drag-and-drop operation, hovers over a window registered as a drop target.

Document Servers

The classes that fall within the Document Server heading include those classes that manage the workspace or client area of the container application.

CDocItem

The CDocItem is useful to both container applications and document server applications. If you are building an OLE container or control, you will not instantiate the CDocItem class directly—you will use one of its derived classes instead. Figure 11.5 shows the CDocItem base class.

FIGURE 11.5

The CDocItem *base class.*

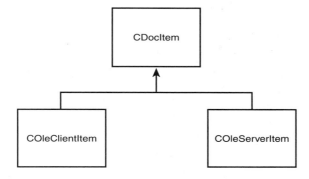

There might be times, however, when you are building an OLE-aware container and have reason to manage non-OLE document items. The COleDocument class treats a document as a collection of CDocItem objects (see Figure 11.6).

FIGURE 11.6

Components of a document.

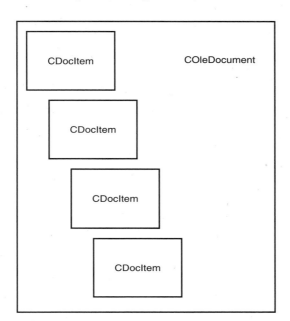

When you select compound document support for a container and check Active Document Container, you get code that displays the Insert Object dialog as part of the framework that AppWizard builds for you. You might also want to support document components that are not OLE document servers. In this case, you derive your own class from CDocItem and implement the necessary functions.

COleIPFrameWnd

The COleIPFrameWnd class provides the necessary functionality for an application's window that supports in-place activation of OLE document server objects. This class aids in the management of client area screen real estate and control bar positioning.

COleResizeBar

The COleResizeBar class derives from the MFC CControlBar class and supports the resizing of in-place OLE items.

COleServerDoc

The COleServerDoc class is the base class for OLE document servers.

COleServerItem

The COleServerItem class, derived from CDocItem, manages interaction between a server document and its container application.

COleTemplateServer

The COleTemplateServer class offers support to applications that implement OLE servers—both automation servers and document servers. The COleTemplateServer class derives from the COleObjectFactory class and adds two additional methods.

Support

The classes that this section describes do not fall under any particular category. They are, however, vital to the implementation of one or more of the OLE class categories.

COleMessageFilter

The COleMessageFilter class is useful in managing the concurrency that is necessary for OLE automation and document server tasks. This class is derived from CCmdTarget, and an instance of this object is automatically created for the MFC framework as a result of a call to initialize the OLE libraries with AfxOleInit(). Among the methods this class supports are those to set and reset an application's busy state, and those that register and revoke the message filter with the OLE system libraries. An MFC-based application's message filter object can be retrieved with a call to AfxOleGetMessageFilter.

COleObjectFactory

The COleObjectFactory class offers flexible support for OLE object creation, registration, and licensing. A class factory object creates objects of a type that you specify. This class wraps much of the functionality that the IClassFactory and IClassFactory2 interfaces offer.

COleStreamFile

The COleStreamFile class wraps the IStream interface. A *stream* is the structured storage equivalent of a file in a traditional file system. This class is derived from the standard MFC CFile class, thus aiding you in the migration from standard file I/O to compound file support.

CRectTracker

The CRectTracker class does not have a base class and is useful not only in enabling OLE applications: The CRectTracker class draws a rectangular item outline on a screen device context and allows you to interact with it by pulling on its handles. Thus you can move and resize the rectangle in any direction. The CRectTracker object is commonly found in OLE container applications, allowing a user to arrange server objects.

COleException

The COleException class is derived from MFC's CException class and contains a status code that identifies the condition that caused the exception. Objects of this class are generated as a result to calls to AfxThrowOleException.

COleCurrency

The COleCurreny class wraps the currency datatype. This class overloads the constructor and assignment operator, providing you much flexibility in exchanging currency values with any automation-compatible VARIANT, whose value is of the VT_CY type. Additionally, this class provides methods to access the units and fractional units that constitute the currency value.

COleDateTime

The COleDateTime class wraps the DATE datatype. As with the COleCurrency class, COleDateTime also overloads the constructor and assignment operator, extending the class's capability to exchange date values with any automation compatible VARIANT, whose value is of the VT_DATE type. In addition, this class simplifies date time information with other common formats, including SYSTEMTIME and FILETIME structures. Other member functions enable you to get and set individual components of the time and date, as well as parse date/time strings.

COleDateTimeSpan

The `COleDateTimeSpan` class is useful in determining and manipulating a time span value. Various constructors are available, and you can specify a value of time in several ways, including the day, hour, and minute values or as a single floating-point value (a value of 1.5, for example, yields 1 day and 12 hours).

COleDBRecordView

The `COleDBRecordView` class inherits from `CFormView` and is useful for displaying the fields that constitute a row in a database table. This class works in conjunction with a `CRowSet` object, using DDX function to populate dialog controls with record data.

Summary

This chapter offers a quick overview of the classes, structures, and functions that compose the OLE support of MFC. This support is broad and deep, allowing you to build applications that exploit almost every COM category. The MFC classes place an emphasis on the visual COM technologies, such as those that require in-place activation. Server objects that require this support must provide complex activation code in order to achieve proper integration with their containers. The Microsoft Foundation Classes are a perfect way to achieve this level of compatibility, leveraging a large body of reliable code.

MFC OLE Servers

by Gene Olafsen

CHAPTER 12

There are essentially two types of OLE server objects: automation servers and document servers. Likewise, the document server category can be further divided into in-place servers and active document servers. In-place editing server applications are those OLE server applications that MFC has supported for a number of releases and are compatible with the container applications that AppWizard creates. There are a few differences between in-place servers and active documents, which I will explore later in this chapter.

Active documents, from a framework perspective, use classes that derive from the in-place object server classes. This derivation offers a set of classes that tailor the more general OLE server base classes into a new breed of base classes for active document support. Specifically, this change involves using a new in-place frame class and a different server item class.

Document Servers

Document servers are applications that you probably use every day. Both Microsoft Word and Excel are perfect examples of OLE document servers. In Figure 12.1, an Excel spreadsheet is shown in-place active in a Word document. You can see how convenient it is to edit a document's data using the application in which it was created.

FIGURE 12.1

Excel in-place active inside Word.

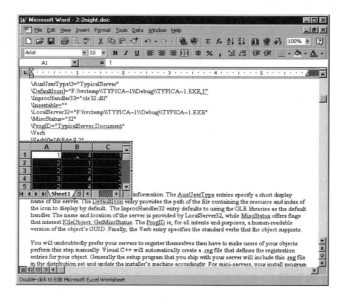

12

Server Types

You have a number of options when using AppWizard to create your document server application, as shown in Figure 12.2.

FIGURE 12.2

*AppWizard docu-
ment server
options (step 3).*

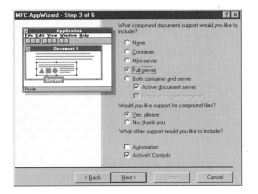

Full Server

A full server is the real deal. You can execute a full server either as a standalone application or from within a container. Because the server can act as a standalone application, it can load, store, and create data files. A container application can then either instantiate full server objects to create embedded data items, or activate the server by linking to external data files.

Active Document

An active document server derives from OLE server technology. From an MFC coding view, there is little that differentiates an active document from a more traditional OLE server object other than a couple of classes and the addition of some command message routing.

The differences between active documents and OLE server objects are purported to be *advantages*. The following is a list of differences (read advantages) of active documents over embedding servers:

- Active documents always display in the entire client area of the container application. They are always in-place active. They cannot display themselves in a small rectangular region of the document, whose border is identified by a hatched border rectangle—as is a familiar representation by common embedding servers.

- The container may route menu commands to the active document server. Thus, from a user interface perspective, this seamless integration of container and server application defines an inextricable joining.

- You can view active documents in a Web browser, part of the Internet-everywhere approach. Essentially, this point means that the Web browser is not just for viewing pages on the Internet but is a viewer (and editor) of all file types, regardless of origin.

AppWizard offers options to implement any server as an active document server and any container as an active document container.

Container/Server

A container-server application is one that can function either as a standalone container program, in which case you can link or embed other document servers, or embedded as a document server in a different container. In fact, your server can continue to act as a container while it is performing server functions for a container. It sounds a bit more complex than it really is. Both Microsoft Excel and Word are container-server applications. As container applications, either can embed the other performing in its document server role. In the most extreme scenario, a document server retains its container functionality; thus, it can offer document viewing and activation facilities.

Mini-Server

A mini-server offers a subset of full server functionality. The most differentiating aspect of a mini-server is that it cannot run as a standalone application. Because the server can never execute in the same sense as a normal application, it can load only as store data through the container application. Mini-servers can only be embedded in a server, as linking requires the document data to exist outside the container's document—something that you have already seen is not permitted.

Document Server Design

When creating a document server, there is no better place to start than with AppWizard (see Figure 12.3). The project name for the application is *activedocserv*. You will see how to create a simple active document server and then host it in Internet Explorer.

FIGURE 12.3
*Starting the
activedocserv
project.*

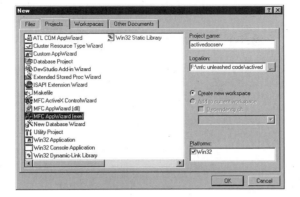

OLE Documents

The concept of OLE Documents can be found in the initial release of OLE. After all, the words "Object Linking and Embedding" describe a document-centric technology. The early implementation of OLE documents was very crude, generally requiring an object packager utility to combine the elements of the document. Today, OLE document construction occurs seamlessly in word processors and spreadsheets, while viewing such documents can even occur in Web browsers.

Servers and the Document/View Architecture

MFC's implementation of embedding servers leverages the document/view architecture to manage multiple container support. Servers are very complicated animals, requiring operation under a number of circumstances. One of the most taxing of all situations is a document server object simultaneously supporting two containers. Your server will handle this situation differently depending on the options that you select in AppWizard when constructing the server application, as shown in Figure 12.4. An OLE server that is an MDI application simply "opens" a new window for each document that the server requires to support. Hence, a single instance of the executable can handle multiple container requests or multiple document instantiations in a single container. An SDI server or mini-server doesn't contain the necessary framework *wiring* for a single application instance to share across multiple containers. The solution to this problem is multiple application instances.

FIGURE **12.4**

*Document archi-
tecture selection.*

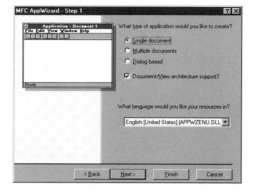

The activedocserv application will only be an SDI application. As part of navigating through the wizard, you should also do the following:

- Take the default for step 2, No Database Support.
- For step 3, select Full-Server and Active Document Server.

Registration

The Windows operating systems, and more specifically the OLE DLLs, make extensive use of the Registry as a directory of file locations, service mappings, preference settings, and object registration. All OLE servers must perform a registration process that places the filespec location, among other properties, in the Registry for access by container applications. The following lines illustrate the Registry entries for a typical OLE server object:

```
[HKEY_CLASSES_ROOT\CLSID\{723B4D4D-B8AA-11D2-8FAF-00105A5D8D6C}]
"Typical Document"
\AuxUserType
\AuxUserType\2="Typical"
\AuxUserType\3="TypicalServer"
\DefaultIcon]="F:\\vctemp\\TYPICA~1\\Debug\\TYPICA~1.EXE,1"
\InprocHandler32="ole32.dll"
\Insertable=""
\LocalServer32="F:\\vctemp\\TYPICA~1\\Debug\\TYPICA~1.EXE"
\MiscStatus="32"
\ProgID="TypicalServer.Document"
\Verb
\Verb\0="&Edit,0,2"
\Verb\1="&Open,0,2"
```

The entries identify the following basic information. The AuxUserType entries specify a short display name of the server. The DefaultIcon entry provides the path of the file containing the resource and index of the icon to display by default. The

InprocHandler32 entry defaults to using the OLE libraries as the default handler. The name and location of the server is provided by LocalServer32, whereas MiscStatus offers flags that interest IOleObject::GetMiscStatus. The ProgID is, for all intents and purposes, a human-readable version of the object's GUID. Finally, the Verb entry specifies the standard verbs that the object supports.

You will undoubtedly prefer your servers to register themselves than have to make users of your objects perform this step manually. Visual C++ will automatically create a .REG file that defines the registration entries for your object. Generally the setup program that you ship with your server will include this .REG file in the distribution set and update the installer's machine accordingly. For mini-servers, either your install program must insert these Registry entries or the user must import the .REG file with RegEdit. Mini-servers cannot perform self-registration simply because they cannot be run in a stand-alone fashion. MFC supports self-registration of OLE servers with a call to the static member function COleTemplateServer::RegisterAll() in your server's InitInstance function.

The fourth step of the AppWizard enables you to select miscellaneous options including whether you want to support a status bar, printing, and so on. You will not be able to progress past this step without defining a file extension for your active document server. Selecting the Advanced button displays the Advanced Options dialog, as shown in Figure 12.5.

FIGURE 12.5

The Advanced Options dialog.

Many of the strings that you can define in this dialog box are stored in the Registry. You can also use the second tab in this dialog to customize various frame window attributes.

Accept the default settings for the last AppWizard steps and return to the Visual C++ editor.

Command-Line Arguments

A full server can execute both under the context of a container application and as a standalone Windows application. Your program identifies the circumstances under which it is executing by examining the command-line arguments that are passed to it on initialization.

The following lines will appear in your `InitInstance` function, courtesy of AppWizard:

```
// Parse command line for standard shell commands, DDE, file open
CCommandLineInfo cmdInfo;
ParseCommandLine(cmdInfo);

// Check to see if launched as OLE server
if (cmdInfo.m_bRunEmbedded || cmdInfo.m_bRunAutomated)
{
    // Register all OLE server (factories) as running.
    //This enables the
    //  OLE libraries to create objects from other applications.
    COleTemplateServer::RegisterAll();

    // Application was run with /Embedding or /Automation.
    // Don't show the main window in this case.

    return TRUE;
}
```

A `CCommandLineInfo` object is passed to your application object's `ParseCommandLine` function, which handles the command-line arguments and flags. A check is performed to see if your application is running as a request from an embedding container or as an automation server for an automation controller. Your server will register all of its class factories and return without creating a main window.

Server Item/Client Item

The relationship between container and server is a complex one. It should not be difficult for you to believe that in order for this relationship to function, a container must manage a list of servers that it *links* or *embeds*, whereas a server must manage a list of containers that it is serving. The `CDocItem` class offers a bridge between MFC-based containers and document servers. The classes `COleClientItem` and `COleServerItem` both derive from `CDocItem`, whose only methods are `GetDocument` and a virtual overridable `IsBlank` method. The `COleClientItem` class represents a server object, and the container maintains a collection of these objects—one for each object it embeds or links. `COleServerItem` class objects are maintained by document servers and either represent a whole document, in the case of embedded items, or part of a document, for linked items.

In-Place Frames

The in-place frame window contains the client area that your server "draws on" when it is active. For traditional embedding servers, a hatched border is drawn around your in-place frame when the server is in-place active in a container. The additional effect added to the border helps you to more easily identify the boundary of your server with respect to the rest of the container's document. Active document servers differ both by the class that they derive from offering in-place frame window support, and by the fact that active documents take over the total client area of a container when they are active.

A major function of the in-place frame class is to manage toolbar creation. From a user interface perspective, your server's toolbars will be active in the container's space, outside your in-place frame, and will appear and function as if they are part of the container. AppWizard will create a toolbar that includes buttons for cut, paste, copy, and help by default. The `OnCreateControlBars` method will be overridden, and the following code is generated:

```
BOOL CInPlaceFrame::OnCreateControlBars(CFrameWnd* pWndFrame, \
                                        CFrameWnd* pWndDoc)
{
    // Remove this if you use pWndDoc
    UNREFERENCED_PARAMETER(pWndDoc);

    // Set owner to this window, so messages
    // are delivered to correct app
    m_wndToolBar.SetOwner(this);

    // Create toolbar on client's frame window
    if (!m_wndToolBar.CreateEx(pWndFrame, \
        TBSTYLE_FLAT,WS_CHILD | WS_VISIBLE | CBRS_TOP
        | CBRS_GRIPPER | CBRS_TOOLTIPS | CBRS_FLYBY | \
        CBRS_SIZE_DYNAMIC) ||
        !m_wndToolBar.LoadToolBar(IDR_TYPICATYPE_SRVR_IP))
    {
        TRACE0("Failed to create toolbar\n");
        return FALSE;
    }

    // TODO: Delete these three lines if you don't want the toolbar to
    //   be dockable
    m_wndToolBar.EnableDocking(CBRS_ALIGN_ANY);
    pWndFrame->EnableDocking(CBRS_ALIGN_ANY);
    pWndFrame->DockControlBar(&m_wndToolBar);

    return TRUE;
}
```

Adding additional toolbars requires you to perform the following steps:

1. Create a new toolbar resource.

2. Define a CToolBar member variable in your in-place frame declaration.

3. Call the SetOwner method on the CToolBar class with the in-place frame as its parent window.

4. Create the toolbar with the CreateEx method and load the toolbar specifying the resource ID.

5. Finally, decide if you want your toolbar to be dockable. If you want the toolbar to dock in the container application, call the EnableDocking method specifying the sides of the container to which the toolbar can dock.

Active Documents

There are a number of differences between the traditional OLE embedding document server and active document servers. These differences mostly involve the server's presentation to the user.

CDocObjectServerItem

The CDocObjectServerItem class derives from COleServerItem and is the class that active document servers use to help manage document state. CDocObjectServerItem does not add additional methods to its base class; however, it modifies the behavior of three virtual functions: OnHide, OnOpen, and OnShow.

OnOpen and OnShow behave similarly, defaulting to the base-class implementation if the server item is not a DocObject.

```
void CDocObjectServerItem::OnOpen()        // or OnShow
{
   COleServerDoc* pDoc = GetDocument();
   ASSERT_VALID(pDoc);

   if (pDoc->IsDocObject())
      pDoc->ActivateDocObject();
   else
      COleServerItem::OnOpen();    // or OnShow
}
```

OnHide behaves differently, throwing an exception if an attempt is made to hide the object. Because active documents reside in the full client area of a container, it does not make sense to hide the server's view.

```
void CDocObjectServerItem::OnHide()
{
   COleServerDoc* pDoc = GetDocument();
```

```
    ASSERT_VALID(pDoc);

    if (pDoc->IsDocObject())
        AfxThrowOleException(OLEOBJ_E_INVALIDVERB);
    else
        COleServerItem::OnHide();
}
```

COleDocIPFrameWnd

No reference material is available from Microsoft for one of the base classes enabling
active document servers. The COleDocIPFrameWnd class is used in place of the
COleIPFrameWnd for active document servers and, not surprisingly, derives from
COleIPFrameWnd. Here is the class declaration:

```
class COleDocIPFrameWnd : public COleIPFrameWnd
{
    DECLARE_DYNCREATE(COleDocIPFrameWnd)
// Constructors
public:
    COleDocIPFrameWnd();
// Attributes
public:
// Operations
public:
// Overridables
protected:
// Implementation
public:
    virtual ~COleDocIPFrameWnd();
#ifdef _DEBUG
    virtual void AssertValid() const;
    virtual void Dump(CDumpContext& dc) const;
#endif
    // Overrides
    // ClassWizard generated virtual function overrides
    //{{AFX_VIRTUAL(COleDocIPFrameWnd)
    //}}AFX_VIRTUAL
protected:
    virtual void OnRequestPositionChange(LPCRECT lpRect);
    virtual void RecalcLayout(BOOL bNotify = TRUE);
    // Menu Merging support
    HMENU m_hMenuHelpPopup;
    virtual BOOL BuildSharedMenu();
    virtual void DestroySharedMenu();
    // Generated message map functions
    //{{AFX_MSG(COleDocIPFrameWnd)
        // NOTE - the ClassWizard will add and remove
        //        member functions here.
    //}}AFX_MSG
    DECLARE_MESSAGE_MAP()
};
```

Although this class doesn't appear in any Microsoft documentation, some of the functions that it implements are themselves undocumented virtual functions of COleIPFrameWnd. These functions can be found in the class declaration and are commented with an "Advanced:" prefix, as shown following:

```
// Advanced: in-place activation virtual implementation
// virtual BOOL BuildSharedMenu();
    virtual void DestroySharedMenu();
    virtual HMENU GetInPlaceMenu();

    // Advanced: possible override to change in-place sizing behavior
    virtual void OnRequestPositionChange(LPCRECT lpRect);
```

If you are interested in what separates active document in-place frame behavior from traditional document servers, you have to look no further than the code that the MFC framework offers as implementation.

GetInPlaceMenu

The GetInPlaceMenu function simply returns the in-place menu associated with the active document's document template:

```
HMENU COleIPFrameWnd::GetInPlaceMenu()
{
    // get active document associated with this frame window
    CDocument* pDoc = GetActiveDocument();
    ASSERT_VALID(pDoc);

    // get in-place menu from the doc template
    CDocTemplate* pTemplate = pDoc->GetDocTemplate();
    ASSERT_VALID(pTemplate);
    return pTemplate->m_hMenuInPlaceServer;
}
```

OnRequestPositionChange

Server objects that want to change their size issue IOleInPlaceSite::OnPosRectChange calls. The container application responds with IOleInPlaceObject::SetObjectRects to position the in-place window. The following MFC code returns immediately if it identifies the server object as one that is an active document; otherwise, the request is passed to the server document. The IsDocObject() function determines whether the server object is an active document with the presence of a DocObject key under the server's CLSID entry.

```
void COleDocIPFrameWnd::OnRequestPositionChange(LPCRECT lpRect)
{
    COleServerDoc* pDoc = (COleServerDoc*) GetActiveDocument();
    ASSERT_VALID(pDoc);
    ASSERT_KINDOF(COleServerDoc, pDoc);
```

```
    // DocObjects don't need to generate OnPosRectChange calls, so you
    // just return if this is a DocObject.
    if (pDoc->IsDocObject())
        return;
    // The default behavior is to not affect the extent during the
    //   call to RequestPositionChange.  This results in consistent
    //   scaling behavior.
    pDoc->RequestPositionChange(lpRect);
}
```

BuildSharedMenu

The BuildSharedMenu function acquires the in-place menu and merges it with the container's menu. A menu descriptor is then stored, which is used when dispatching menu messages and commands by OLE:

```
BOOL COleDocIPFrameWnd::BuildSharedMenu()
{
    HMENU hMenu = GetInPlaceMenu();

    // create shared menu
    ASSERT(m_hSharedMenu == NULL);
    if ((m_hSharedMenu = ::CreateMenu()) == NULL)
        return FALSE;

    // start out by getting menu from container
    memset(&m_menuWidths, 0, sizeof m_menuWidths);
    if (m_lpFrame->InsertMenus(m_hSharedMenu, &m_menuWidths) \
        != NOERROR)
    {
        ::DestroyMenu(m_hSharedMenu);
        m_hSharedMenu = NULL;
        return FALSE;
    }

#ifdef _DEBUG
    // container shouldn't touch these
    ASSERT(m_menuWidths.width[1] == 0);
    ASSERT(m_menuWidths.width[3] == 0);

    // container shouldn't touch this unless you're
    // working with a DocObject
    COleServerDoc* pDoc = (COleServerDoc*) GetActiveDocument();
    ASSERT_VALID(pDoc);
    ASSERT_KINDOF(COleServerDoc, pDoc);
    if (!pDoc->IsDocObject())
        ASSERT(m_menuWidths.width[5] == 0);
#endif

    // only copy the popups if there is a menu loaded
    if (hMenu == NULL)
```

```
        return TRUE;

    // insert our menu popups amongst the container menus
    m_hMenuHelpPopup = AfxMergeMenus(m_hSharedMenu, hMenu,
        &m_menuWidths.width[0], 1, TRUE);

    // finally create the special OLE menu descriptor
    m_hOleMenu = ::OleCreateMenuDescriptor(m_hSharedMenu, \
                                            &m_menuWidths);

    return m_hOleMenu != NULL;
}
```

DestroySharedMenu()

The `DestroySharedMenu` function behaves in no particularly interesting manner and simply deletes any objects created in `BuildSharedMenu` and returns the menu to its original state.

Registration

There are a few registration differences that you should be aware of between active document servers and traditional OLE document servers. AppWizard will place the following lines in your program's `InitInstance` function:

```
// When a server application is launched standalone,
// it is a good idea
//  to update the system registry in case it has been damaged.
    m_server.UpdateRegistry(OAT_DOC_OBJECT_SERVER);
```

If you are building an active document server, the `UpdateRegistry` function will appear as shown previously; otherwise, the constant will be `OAT_INPLACE_SERVER`. Active document servers also require an `#include <afxdocob.h>` definition in your stdafx.h file.

Building an Active Document Server

You can create an active document server with a minimum of work using the Visual Studio AppWizard. The wizard will lead you through a number of steps from which you select the type of server support you require, and it generates skeletal code into which you "plug" your server-specific functionality.

Persistence

Document servers can support file operations in the same manner as traditional Windows applications. You can override the `Serialize` function and perform the appropriate read and write operations. In the case of this sample document server, a single character is written to and read from a file.

```
void CActivedocservDoc::Serialize(CArchive& ar)
{
    CString sData;

    if (ar.IsStoring())
    {
        char buf[10];
        itoa(dwData, buf, 10);
        sData = buf;
        ar << sData;
    }
    else
    {
        ar >> sData;
        dwData = -atoi(sData);
    }
}
```

The member variable dwData is converted to a string and stored in a CString variable whose name is sData. The numeric value is written and read from the stream using CString because it derives from CObject and thus implements serialization. Notice that when the data value is read from the file, the member variable is set to a negative value. In this manner, the server knows that the value was read from a file and should not be changed.

The document also contains two member functions for member data access. SetData is the mutator function, setting the dwData value, and GetData is the accessor function for dwData.

```
void CActivedocservDoc::SetData(int dw)
{
    dwData = dw;
}

int CActivedocservDoc::GetData()
{
    return dwData;
}
```

Rendering the View

You draw in the client area of your server's view as you would in any other application. In this case, the system's tick-count value is obtained and the remainder after a division operation is used to obtain a small number. Using this number as the bounds for a loop, a number of lines are drawn out from each corner of the client window (see Figure 12.6).

FIGURE **12.6**
*The activedocserv
application
executing
standalone.*

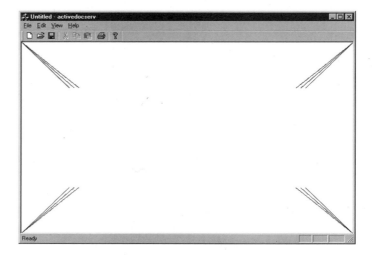

Changing the size of the view, by dragging a corner or side of the window, will cause a repaint and a different number of lines to appear.

```cpp
void CActivedocservView::OnDraw(CDC* pDC)
{
    CActivedocservDoc* pDoc = GetDocument();
    ASSERT_VALID(pDoc);
    pDC->SelectObject(::GetStockObject(BLACK_PEN));
    RECT rect;
    GetClientRect(&rect);
    int dw = 0;
    dw = GetDocument()->GetData();
    if (dw >= 0) {
        dw = (int)(::GetTickCount() % 3);
        GetDocument()->SetData(dw);
    }
    else
        dw = -dw;
    for (int i=0; i< (dw+1); ++i)
    {
        pDC->MoveTo(0,0);
        pDC->LineTo(100+(10*i),100);
        pDC->MoveTo(rect.right,0);
        pDC->LineTo(rect.right-100-(10*i), 100);
        pDC->MoveTo(0,rect.bottom);
        pDC->LineTo(100+(10*i), rect.bottom-100);
        pDC->MoveTo(rect.right,rect.bottom);
        pDC->LineTo(rect.right-100-(10*i), rect.bottom-100);
    }
}
```

Running this program as a standalone application, you can choose to save your document with the number of lines that it displays. Of course, this is an almost totally useless server and can never be considered important for any purpose but this demonstration. If you display the document you saved, either in Internet Explorer or Microsoft Office Binder, your view will redisplay with the number of lines that you saved, as shown in Figure 12.7.

FIGURE 12.7

The activedocserv application as an active document server inside Internet Explorer container.

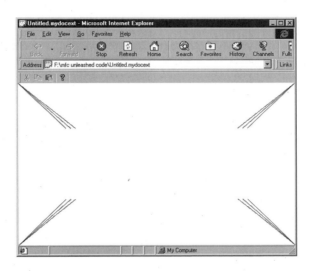

You will see that if the document's member variable dwData contains a negative value, the view code ignores calculating a line count and uses the absolute value of this variable as the bounds for a counter.

Automation Servers

OLE automation (or as it is now simply referred to, automation) has been one of the best-exploited technologies of the early COM/OLE offerings. The idea behind automation is to expose an application's functionality through a standard, language-independent, programmable interface. Microsoft has continued to embrace automation by exposing functionality through programmable interfaces for almost every program it offers. Additionally, it has extended its new Web technology languages (J++ and VBScript) the capability to easily program automation servers.

Automation can be summed up as offering the following features:

- Provides a programming language-independent model for exposing application functionality.

- Defines standard datatypes and provides the necessary marshaling for parameters.

- Defines a standard mechanism for a controller to explore and identify interface methods and properties. This information is available from the automation server's type library.

Automation defines objects that expose the IDispatch interface as servers, more specifically, *automation servers*. However, clients are referred to as *automation controllers*. The word "controller" is used because these clients are generally languages, such as Visual Basic, Java, VBScript, or even C++. In fact, Microsoft Office provides a language called VBScript that is an automation controller and can "program" any automation server.

Defining interfaces for automation servers is not much different from defining interfaces for ordinary COM interfaces. The primary difference between the interfaces you have dealt with in COM servers to this point have been derived from IUnknown. Automation server interfaces must derive from IDispatch. These interfaces are commonly referred to as *dispinterfaces*.

You define interfaces with either Interface Definition Language (IDL) or Object Definition Language (ODL). Actually there is some history to explain, because it doesn't seem necessary to have two languages that perform the same operation. Actually, IDL is a language whose roots are in Remote Procedure Call (RPC) technology. COM and Distributed COM (DCOM) have their roots in the interface-modeling scheme and Globally Unique Identifier (GUID) concept that are part of RPC definition. Microsoft made its changes to this standard definition, changing the file extension to .ODL and providing a utility MkTypLib to create type library information. Over the past few years, the IDL specification has come to include the ODL extensions, and now the MIDL utility can perform the functions that MkTypeLib does. For historical purposes only, MFC and Visual C++'s ClassWizard still generates .ODL files.

The results of ODL/IDL compilation are proxy and stub files, which aid in marshaling parameters, and a type library. For a COM client to "call" methods on an interface that resides on a COM server, it must make calls through a proxy. Information contained in header files provides the client developer with strict compile-time checking of method names and argument datatype and ordering. If the checking is successfully implemented, the client can then proceed to interact with the server.

At issue are those languages that don't support header file definitions of interfaces, thus ruling out almost every language on the planet except C/C++. Automation solves this problem with the capability to discover at runtime the methods, parameters, and return values that an interface exposes. Runtime identification has become a hot topic with the advent of Java. Java's *reflection* API allows a programmer to identify similar attributes as exposed by Java objects. This mechanism, along with a standard method and property naming convention, forms the heart of the Javabean specification.

IDispatch

The IDispatch interface, as every COM interface must, derives from IUnknown. In addition to the three IUnknown methods (QueryInterface, AddRef, and Release), IDispatch defines four additional methods, which are summarized in the following sections.

GetIDsOfNames

The GetIDsOfNames method is used to retrieve the DISPID value of a dispinterface method given its name. The name is provided in the form of a "human readable" string.

This function can translate more than one method name to its associated DISPID at a single time because it accepts an array of names and returns an array of dispatch IDs. It is always advisable to use functions such as this to their fullest extent because OLE calls (round trips) are very "expensive" in terms of processor time and network time. So you would be wise to process method names in groups wherever possible instead of calling this function for each name separately.

GetTypeInfo

The GetTypeInfo method returns a pointer to an ITypeInfo object. The methods of the ITypeInfo interface describe the methods, properties, and arguments of the dispinterface on which it is called.

GetTypeInfoCount

The GetTypeInfoCount method returns the number of type information interfaces that are provided by the dispinterface on which it is called. Simply put, this method returns either a one or a zero. If a one is returned, GetTypeInfo will return a useful interface; otherwise, a value of zero indicates that type information is not available.

Invoke

The Invoke method is used to call the methods of the dispinterface. This method is the heart of an automation object with arguments that identify the DISP of the method being called, the associated argument list, and space for return values.

IDispatch-Derived Interface in ODL

Automation servers derive from the IDispatch interface. Thus in addition to the properties and methods that you define on your object, the interface must also support the three

methods of IUnknown and the four methods of IDispatch. The interface definition for
IDispatch follows. You can see that as with custom interface methods, this definition
provides argument direction and HRESULT return value information.

```
[
    object,
    uuid(00020400-0000-0000-C000-000000000046),
    pointer_default(unique)
]
interface IDispatch : IUnknown
{
    typedef [unique] IDispatch * LPDISPATCH;

    HRESULT GetTypeInfoCount(
                [out] UINT * pctinfo
            );

    HRESULT GetTypeInfo(
                [in] UINT iTInfo,
                [in] LCID lcid,
                [out] ITypeInfo ** ppTInfo
            );

    HRESULT GetIDsOfNames(
                [in] REFIID riid,
                [in, size_is(cNames)] LPOLESTR * rgszNames,
                [in] UINT cNames,
                [in] LCID lcid,
                [out, size_is(cNames)] DISPID * rgDispId
            );

    [local]
    HRESULT Invoke(
                [in] DISPID dispIdMember,
                [in] REFIID riid,
                [in] LCID lcid,
                [in] WORD wFlags,
                [in, out] DISPPARAMS * pDispParams,
                [out] VARIANT * pVarResult,
                [out] EXCEPINFO * pExcepInfo,
                [out] UINT * puArgErr
            );

    [call_as(Invoke)]
    HRESULT RemoteInvoke(
                [in] DISPID dispIdMember,
                [in] REFIID riid,
                [in] LCID lcid,
                [in] DWORD dwFlags,
                [in] DISPPARAMS * pDispParams,
```

```
            [out] VARIANT * pVarResult,
            [out] EXCEPINFO * pExcepInfo,
            [out] UINT * pArgErr,
            [in] UINT cVarRef,
            [in, size_is(cVarRef)] UINT * rgVarRefIdx,
            [in, out, size_is(cVarRef)] VARIANTARG * rgVarRef
        );
}
```

The Visual C++ compiler's AppWizard and ClassWizard mask the interface derivation in ODL behind a dispinterface statement, but you shouldn't forget that it is there.

Calling Methods Through `IDispatch`

The `IDispatch` interface offers all of the methods necessary for an automation controller to identify and initiate methods on the server and get/set properties.

`GetIDsOfNames`

You might already know, or be shocked to learn, that the `IDispatch` method `GetIDsOfNames` returns a `DISPID` given a method's name. Okay, maybe "shocked" is a bit of a strong word, but the fact is that the `Invoke` method doesn't accept the name of the method to call—instead it relies on `DISPID`s to identify methods and properties. `DISPID` is short for *dispatch id*, and it is essentially boils down to the fact that each method and property is assigned a unique integer identifier. Think of it as a handle to a method:

```
HRESULT GetIDsOfNames(REFIID riid, LPOLESTR*, UINT cNames, \
                LCID lcid, DISPID* rgdispid)
```

The `GetIDsOfNames` function requires five arguments. The first four parameters are used to specify the method or property of interest, and the `DISPID` is returned as the fifth.

`REFIID riid`	A reserved parameter and must always be `IID_NULL`.
`LPOLESTR*`	Identifies an array of names that are to be mapped.
`UINT cNames`	The number of entries in the name array.
`LCID lcid`	The locale context identifier, normally `LOCALE_SYSTEM_DEFAULT`.
`DISPID* rgdispid`	Storage space for the IDs of the method names when the function returns.

An automation client can use `GetIDsOfNames` to acquire the `DISPID`s of each method and property and keep these values cached for subsequent calls to `Invoke`. It is important to remember that each call to a COM object can be expensive if the server resides on a different machine. Therefore it is important to carefully consider the performance penalty for each call you must make. One of the tenets of COM interface design is that an interface is "immutable." That is, the interface should never change after it is "published" (made available by a server). If this "rule" is followed, there is no reason that an automation client could not query a server for the DISPIDs of each method and property it intends to use the first time the application is started and store the values away in a file or database for subsequent use. Additional invocations of the client could retrieve the values from this permanent store, instead of making a number of GetIDsOfNames calls.

Type Information Methods

Before I move on to describing the Invoke method, arguably the most important of the IDispatch methods, I should discuss GetTypeInfo and GetTypeInfoCount. A little history is in order to understand their names and their purpose. When OLE2 was introduced, developers had only one book to turn to for help with the seemingly mind-boggling technology. The book was *Inside OLE* and its author, Kraig Brockschmidt, eclipsed Petzold in the hearts and minds of any readers wanting to "do COM." Brockschmidt goes through an extensive discussion and presents a number of examples that describe the process of creating a type library, without the use of MkTypeLib. Because the OLE technology was so new, it wasn't apparent where type libraries would be used—except for automation. Today it is common to generate type information for almost every server that you create.

Invoke

The final method of IDispatch to discuss is Invoke:

```
HRESULT Invoke( DISPID dispidMember, REFIID riid, LCID lcid, \
WORD wFlags, DISPPARMS* pdispparams, VARIANT* pvarResult, \
EXCEPINFO* pexcepinfo, UINT* puArgErr )
```

Invoke takes a number of arguments, and its purpose is to call automation methods and get or set automation properties.

TABLE 12.1 ARGUMENTS FOR THE Invoke METHOD

Argument	Description
DISPID dispidMember	Identifies the method or property to invoke.
REFIID riid	The *riid* argument must be IID_NULL.
LCID lcid	Specifies the locale context. Unless you are supporting multiple objects, this can be LOCALE_SYSTEM_DEFAULT.

WORD wFlags	Identifies the action to take by Invoke.
DISPATCH_PROPERTYGET	Retrieve a property value.
DISPATCH_PROPERTYPUT	Put a property value.
DISPATCH_PROPERTYPUTREF	Put a property value by reference.
DISPATCH_METHOD	Method invocation.
DISPPARMS* pdispparams	A pointer to a DISPPARAMS structures containing the arguments.
VARIANT* pvarResult	A pointer to a variant that will store the result.
EXCEPINFO* pexcepinfo	If the function returns DISP_E_EXCEPTION, this structure will contain the exception information.
UINT* puArgErr	If the function returns DISP_E_TYPEMISMATCH or DISP_E_PARAMNOTFOUND, this is the index of the first argument whose format is in question.

Dispinterfaces Differ from Interfaces

The dispinterface certainly broadens the number of languages that can take advantage of COM object servers; however, there are differences with non–IDispatch-derived interfaces that should be noted:

- Methods can use only OLE automation-compliant datatypes when specifying parameters in IDL.
- The keyword dispinterface supports the concept of methods and properties in its definition block.

Accessing Automation Servers in C++ Through IDispatch

This is probably a good time to show how an automation server is exercised by a C++ controller application. The steps taken in this example illustrate many of the concepts that were introduced in the previous section. These steps do not use the MFC framework; they are just a quick review to show you how a client uses the IDispatch methods to exercise a server.

The IDispatch pointer must be obtained from the server, as follows:

```
hresult = punk->QueryInterface(IID_IDispatch,\
(void FAR * FAR *)&pIDispatch);
    if (FAILED(hresult)){
        MessageBox(NULL,"Could not get IDispatch","Client",MB_OK);
        return FALSE;
        }
    punk->Release();
```

Next the `DispID` of the method which you want to invoke must be obtained:

```
char    FAR* szDispName = "MyProperty";
hresult = pIDispatch->GetIDsOfNames(IID_NULL, &szDispName,1,\
 LOCALE_SYSTEM_DEFAULT,&dispid);
```

The variant argument values must be configured:

```
VARIANTARG   vargResult;
VariantInit(&vargResult);
hresult = pIDispatch->Invoke(dispid,IID_NULL,
     LOCALE_SYSTEM_DEFAULT,DISPATCH_PROPERTYGET,&disp,&vargResult,\
NULL,NULL);
```

The property returned is a string value and the result is displayed in a message box:

```
LPSTR    lpszRetString;

    VariantChangeType(lpv,lpv,0,VT_BSTR);
    lpszRetString = (LPSTR)V_BSTR(lpv);
    MessageBox(NULL,lpszRetString,"String Returned",MB_OK);
```

Dual Interfaces

Although dispinterfaces can be ideal for languages that make it difficult, if not impossible, to deal with the pointers of a vtable of an ordinary interface, the overhead involved with accessing automation servers in C++ might be unacceptable. Thankfully there is quite a simple solution to this problem, and it is called *dual interfaces*.

Dual interfaces are derived from `IDispatch`, just like dispinterfaces; however, they also expose their vtable. This is really quite convenient because it allows a single server to provide both implementations in the same physical DLL or EXE package (if an automation can be envisioned as residing in the physical universe) and allows the client to select the method with which it is most comfortable accessing the component. After an automation server is installed on a machine, a VBScript program can access the server's methods through the `Invoke` method of the `IDispatch` interface, whereas a C++ program can access methods directly through the server's vtable.

Fortunately Microsoft strongly recommends that anytime you build a COM server component and expose its interfaces, you do so as a dual interface. In fact, the MFC AppWizard and ClassWizard create components with dual interfaces by default.

A further development of common development languages such as Visual Basic and Java is that they both bind to an automation server's vtable, thus eliminating much of the overhead involved in calling through automation interfaces. Today it is mainly scripting languages or scripting interpreters that interface with automation servers through the slower IDispatch interface (see Figure 12.8).

FIGURE 12.8

Dispatch interface and Invoke *with methods and properties.*

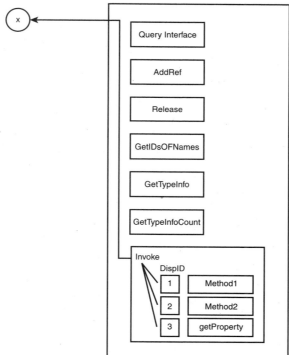

The Variant

One of the challenges that automation must deal with is the fact that, as with most COM object servers, there is no guarantee that the client and server reside either in the same process space or on the same machine. For that matter, both objects might reside on different machines with differing architectures. For example, an automation client (commonly referred to as a *controller*) can exist on an Intel-based computer, and the automation server can reside on an Alpha processor-based machine. The differences between these architectures can extend to native data lengths and byte ordering. An *int* on an Intel machine can be 32 bits long, whereas the corresponding Alpha representation can default to 64 bits. Also the high-byte/low-byte ordering can be opposite. Moving further away from such primitive types as these to more complex ones, such as strings and time/date representations, involves more processor time and data manipulation. The act of exchanging data and correctly reconstituting the data to a format native to the machine that is acting on it, is known as *marshaling*.

Automation employs a datatype known as the `Variant` to help exchange data values between client and server objects. The variant can be thought of as a *union* structure in C or C++. In fact, even better than thinking of it as being a union, it is actually represented internally as a union.

```
/* VARIANT STRUCTURE */
    VARTYPE vt;
    WORD wReserved1;
    WORD wReserved2;
    WORD wReserved3;
    union {
        LONG               VT_I4
        BYTE               VT_UI1
        SHORT              VT_I2
        FLOAT              VT_R4
        DOUBLE             VT_R8
        VARIANT_BOOL       VT_BOOL
        SCODE              VT_ERROR
        CY                 VT_CY
        DATE               VT_DATE
        BSTR               VT_BSTR
        IUnknown *         VT_UNKNOWN
        IDispatch *        VT_DISPATCH
        SAFEARRAY *        VT_ARRAY
        BYTE *             VT_BYREF¦VT_UI1
        SHORT *            VT_BYREF¦VT_I2
        LONG *             VT_BYREF¦VT_I4
        FLOAT *            VT_BYREF¦VT_R4
        DOUBLE *           VT_BYREF¦VT_R8
        VARIANT_BOOL *     VT_BYREF¦VT_BOOL
        SCODE *            VT_BYREF¦VT_ERROR
        CY *               VT_BYREF¦VT_CY
        DATE *             VT_BYREF¦VT_DATE
        BSTR *             VT_BYREF¦VT_BSTR
        IUnknown **        VT_BYREF¦VT_UNKNOWN
        IDispatch **       VT_BYREF¦VT_DISPATCH
        SAFEARRAY **       VT_BYREF¦VT_ARRAY
        VARIANT *          VT_BYREF¦VT_VARIANT
        PVOID              VT_BYREF (Generic ByRef)
        CHAR               VT_I1
        USHORT             VT_UI2
        ULONG              VT_UI4
        INT                VT_INT
```

```
  UINT              VT_UINT
  DECIMAL *         VT_BYREF|VT_DECIMAL
  CHAR *            VT_BYREF|VT_I1
  USHORT *          VT_BYREF|VT_UI2
  ULONG *           VT_BYREF|VT_UI4
  INT *             VT_BYREF|VT_INT
  UINT *            VT_BYREF|VT_UINT
}
```

The OLE system DLLs provide all the code necessary to move the variant datatypes back and forth between controller and server. MFC offers a wrapper class for this structure, the COleVariant class, helping you to construct and interpret automation method arguments. Also, this class offers helper methods to convert between common datatypes.

As you work with unions, you will recognize the fact that you will sooner or later have to determine the data that the union actually stores. After all, a union doesn't actually allocate the space for each of the datatypes; the compiler simply allocates space for the largest of the types, thus creating enough room for any of the smaller types as well. Identifying the data that the union contains is the job of the VARTYPE variable. Looking at the structure in the preceding code listing, you will notice a variable whose declaration is vt. You use (or your wrapper class uses) this variable to determine the data in the union. Table 12.2 gives the possible values of the vt variables.

TABLE 12.2   VALUES OF vt VARIABLES

Constant	Value	Description
VT_EMPTY	0	Not specified
VT_NULL	1	Null
VT_I2	2	2-byte signed int
VT_I4	3	4-byte signed int
VT_R4	4	4-byte real
VT_R8	5	8-byte real
VT_CY	6	Currency
VT_DATE	7	Date
VT_BSTR	8	Binary string
VT_DISPATCH	9	IDispatch
VT_ERROR	10	SCODES
VT_BOOL	11	Boolean TRUE=-1, FALSE=0
VT_VARIANT	12	VARIANT FAR*
VT_UNKNOWN	13	IUnknown FAR*
VT_UI1	17	Unsigned char

In addition to moving common datatypes back and forth, the standard OLE marshaler can exchange IUnknown interface pointers as well as IDispatch-derived interface pointers.

String representation is the BSTR datatype. Such a string is not NULL-terminated as is common in C or C++. Instead, the length of the string is prefixed to the beginning of the byte array.

An Automation Server Using MFC

Developing an automation server in MFC is not difficult—various wizards perform much of the work. Time to thank the wizards, again. Before you begin, here is a quick review of the steps necessary to produce an automation server:

- Select the automation object's deliver vehicle—EXE or DLL.
- Define a dispinterface (an interface that derives from IDispatch).
- Add methods and properties to perform actions necessary by the server.
- Register the server and automation classes.

Server Type

As with ATL-based automation servers, MFC supports both executable (EXE) and dynamic link library (DLL) delivery vehicles for automation servers. When starting a new project, there are wizards named MFC AppWizard (dll) and MFC AppWizard (exe), which can be selected to house automation objects (see Figure 12.9). You will select an EXE server application for this example. The name of the project is *autoserv*.

FIGURE 12.9

Beginning the autoserv project.

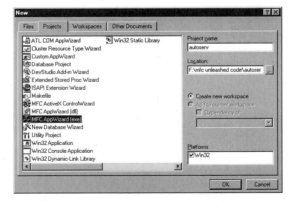

The next step is to enable automation in the wizard-generated code. The steps that enable automation are different for the different server types. For DLLs (see Figure 12.10), it is step 1, and for EXEs (see Figure 12.11), it is step 3.

FIGURE 12.10

DLL automation option.

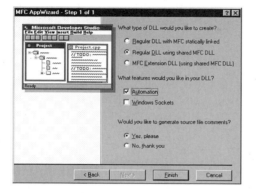

FIGURE 12.11

EXE automation option.

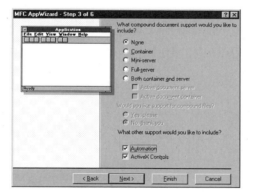

Upon completion of the AppWizard steps, both code and an .ODL will be generated. Your interface definition file will contain a single dispinterface definition and ClassWizard placeholders for properties and methods.

```
// autoserv.odl : type library source for autoserv.exe

// This file will be processed by the MIDL compiler to produce the
// type library (autoserv.tlb).

[ uuid(723B4DA4-B8AA-11D2-8FAF-00105A5D8D6C), version(1.0) ]
library Autoserv
{
    importlib("stdole32.tlb");
    importlib("stdole2.tlb");
```

```
//  Primary dispatch interface for CAutoservDoc

[ uuid(723B4DA5-B8AA-11D2-8FAF-00105A5D8D6C) ]
dispinterface IAutoserv
{
    properties:
    // NOTE - ClassWizard will maintain property information here.
        //     Use extreme caution when editing this section.
        //{{AFX_ODL_PROP(CAutoservDoc)
        //}}AFX_ODL_PROP

    methods:
     // NOTE - ClassWizard will maintain method information here.
        //     Use extreme caution when editing this section.
        //{{AFX_ODL_METHOD(CAutoservDoc)
        //}}AFX_ODL_METHOD

};

//  Class information for CAutoservDoc

[ uuid(723B4DA3-B8AA-11D2-8FAF-00105A5D8D6C) ]
coclass Document
{
    [default] dispinterface IAutoserv;
};

//{{AFX_APPEND_ODL}}
//}}AFX_APPEND_ODL}}
};
```

Adding methods and properties to your interface is simple using ClassWizard. In the ClassView tab of the project management pane in Visual C++, right-click the interface icon to display the context-sensitive menu for interface objects, as shown in Figure 12.12.

FIGURE 12.12

Context menu for interface definition.

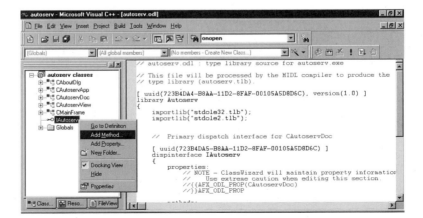

Selecting the Add Method menu (refer to Figure 12.12) displays a dialog that you fill out to identify the parameters and return type for the method (see Figure 12.13). The name of the method is `TrackInfo`. It returns an `SCODE`, which is common for OLE calls, and it takes two arguments, a `short` named `Index` and a `BSTR` value named `Title`.

FIGURE 12.13

Adding a method.

Defining a property is just as easy. Select the Add Property menu (see Figure 12.12) on the interface object and complete the dialog. Figure 12.14 shows an `AlbumLength` property defined as a `short` value with a `get` and `set` function.

FIGURE 12.14

Adding a property.

ClassWizard inserts the following definitions into your .ODL file:

```
    properties:
// NOTE - ClassWizard will maintain property information here.
        //     Use extreme caution when editing this section.
        //{{AFX_ODL_PROP(CAutoservDoc)
        [id(1)] short AlbumLength;
        //}}AFX_ODL_PROP

    methods:
     // NOTE - ClassWizard will maintain method information here.
```

```
//    Use extreme caution when editing this section.
//{{AFX_ODL_METHOD(CAutoservDoc)
[id(2)] SCODE TrackInfo(short Index, BSTR* Title);
//}}AFX_ODL_METHOD
```

The methods and properties are added to your project's document object. Thus three methods appear on CAutoServDoc as a result of these operations: SetAlbumLength, GetAlbumLength, and TrackInfo.

Declaring and Defining Additional Dispinterfaces

MFC, as with ATL, allows a server to provide multiple automation class objects. EXE-based servers differ from DLL-based servers in that the AppWizard defines the first coclass. The preceding section describes how the ProgID is established in the Advanced dialog. In MFC, Automation classes must derive from CCmdTarget. If you look at an EXE-based server, you will find that the CDocument-derived class contains the automation property and method definitions. This is acceptable because CDocument derives from CCmdTarget.

To add automation class objects to a DLL, or add additional class objects to an EXE, you must use the New Class dialog. This dialog is invoked from the Insert, New Class menus. The dialog appears in Figure 12.15.

FIGURE 12.15

The New Class dialog.

The following review summarizes the steps or conditions that must be met to add another automation interface to a server:

- The class type must be MFC class.
- The class must be given a name.

- The base class must be `CCmdTarget`.
- An automation option must be selected.

By default the `ProgID` for the dispinterface is the name of the DLL or EXE project, followed by a period, followed by the name of the class. If you select automation, this is the `ProgID` that your interface receives. You can, however, select Createable by Type ID and supply a different `ProgID`.

In this case, the name of the class is `SecondInterface`, it correctly derives from `CCmdTarget`, and it can be created by the type ID, which is `autoserv.SecondInterface`.

Adding Methods and Properties

You might think that defining the interface for this new class is the same as defining the original interface: You right-click an interface in the ClassView pane of the Workspace window and select Add Method or Add Property. This is not entirely correct. If you view the ClassView tab, you will not find another interface with the name you expect; you do, however, find `SecondInterface` as a class.

To add properties and methods to your new class, you must display ClassWizard, select the Automation tab (see Figure 12.16), select the `SecondInterface` class in the Class Name combo box, and use the Add Method or Add Property functions.

FIGURE 12.16

The Automation tab of ClassWizard.

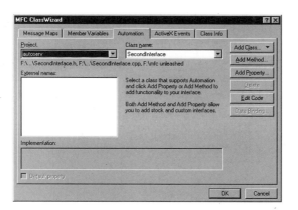

These buttons display the same methods and property editors that are discussed earlier.

It is interesting to note the OLE support code that ClassWizard adds to your new class to support the automation functionality, as follows:

```
///////////////////////////////////////////////////////////////////////////
// SecondInterface
```

```
IMPLEMENT_DYNCREATE(SecondInterface, CCmdTarget)

SecondInterface::SecondInterface()
{
    EnableAutomation();

    // To keep the application running as long as an OLE automation
    //     object is active, the constructor calls AfxOleLockApp.

    AfxOleLockApp();
}

SecondInterface::~SecondInterface()
{
    // To terminate the application when all objects created with
    //      with OLE automation, the destructor calls AfxOleUnlockApp.

    AfxOleUnlockApp();
}

void SecondInterface::OnFinalRelease()
{
    // When the last reference for an automation object is released
    // OnFinalRelease is called.  The base class will automatically
    // deletes the object.  Add additional cleanup required for your
    // object before calling the base class.

    CCmdTarget::OnFinalRelease();
}


BEGIN_MESSAGE_MAP(SecondInterface, CCmdTarget)
    //{{AFX_MSG_MAP(SecondInterface)
    // NOTE - the ClassWizard will add and remove mapping macros here.
    //}}AFX_MSG_MAP
END_MESSAGE_MAP()

BEGIN_DISPATCH_MAP(SecondInterface, CCmdTarget)
    //{{AFX_DISPATCH_MAP(SecondInterface)
    // NOTE - the ClassWizard will add and remove mapping macros here.
    //}}AFX_DISPATCH_MAP
END_DISPATCH_MAP()

// Note: you add support for IID_ISecondInterface to support
// typesafe binding
//   from VBA.  This IID must match the GUID that is attached to the
//   dispinterface in the .ODL file.

// {723B4DBA-B8AA-11D2-8FAF-00105A5D8D6C}
static const IID IID_ISecondInterface =
{ 0x723b4dba, 0xb8aa, 0x11d2, { 0x8f, 0xaf, 0x0, 0x10, 0x5a, 0x5d,\
```

```
0x8d, 0x6c } };

BEGIN_INTERFACE_MAP(SecondInterface, CCmdTarget)
    INTERFACE_PART(SecondInterface, IID_ISecondInterface, Dispatch)
END_INTERFACE_MAP()

// {723B4DBB-B8AA-11D2-8FAF-00105A5D8D6C}
IMPLEMENT_OLECREATE(SecondInterface, "autoserv.SecondInterface", \
 0x723b4dbb, 0xb8aa, 0x11d2, 0x8f, 0xaf, 0x0, 0x10, 0x5a, 0x5d, \
0x8d, 0x6c)

/////////////////////////////////////////////////////////////////////
// SecondInterface message handlers
```

The constructor for SecondInterface calls AfxOleLockApp, keeping this server in memory during use, and calls AfxOleUnlockApp in the destructor, allowing the server to release as necessary. The constructor also makes a call to EnableAutomation. This call is also made in InitInstance for this application, but if an automation-enabled class was added to a project that didn't currently support such operations, this call would cover your bases. Additionally, a template copy of OnFinalRelease is offered, calling the CCmdTarget base class. Prior to releasing the server, this method is called, allowing you to perform additional cleanup.

Summary

In this chapter you have explored the server technologies that the MFC OLE libraries support. While the problems that are solved by document servers and automation servers differ vastly, you have seen that the concept of interface programming by COM is easily leveraged by both.

You will exercise the automation server interfaces in the next chapter, "MFC OLE Clients." You will see that there are a number of ways to access dispinterfaces from an MFC client application.

MFC OLE Clients

by Gene Olafsen

IN THIS CHAPTER

This chapter teaches you a number of ways to implement automation clients—often called *controllers*. This discussion includes details about the IDispatch interface, as well as the various ways you can put automation servers to work in your application.

IDispatch and Its Place in Automation

Any discussion regarding automation usually begins with a description of the IDispatch interface because it is the most recognizable aspect of automation development and its methods form a framework for presentation of automation topics. This is certainly the case for this chapter. However, back in the days when the only material available on the subject was *Inside OLE* by Kraig Brockschmidt, it sometimes became confusing whether the discussion centered on material that was implemented by the server or the controller. There is a relatively simple set of rules to remember when tackling IDispatch and its place in automation:

- IDispatch identifies four methods whose implementation is provided by the OLE runtime library.
- Automation servers expose interfaces that derive from IDispatch. This differs from nonautomation servers whose interfaces derive directly from IUnknown.
- A controller calls methods on an automation interface through the interface's Invoke method. That is to say that an interface pointer to the automation-enabled interface is acquired, except that the actual method invocation is performed indirectly through a helper method.

You can understand IDispatch's place in an automation server/controller system by knowing that the IDispatch methods are implemented by the OLE runtime and exposed by the server object's custom interface. Notice, too, that the base IUnknown methods are also available to an automation controller; however, the implementation of such methods falls under the jurisdiction of the server object developer and not the OLE runtime. Automation servers differ from other COM object server configurations in which the server exposes the interface methods directly to the client.

Interface Definition for Automation Servers

Normal or nonautomation COM server interfaces derive directly from the IUnknown interface. Automation servers, however, derive from the IDispatch interface. Automation has been around a while, and, as such, both MFC and ATL support it—this is the good news. The bad news is that automation has been around for a while. The earliest definitions of automation interfaces are grounded in a format known as *Object Definition Language* (ODL). Just as C was the predecessor to C++, so too does ODL predate IDL. Before Visual Studio's wizards came along to generate a sizeable portion of an interface's definition, the files were generated by hand and compiled with a command-line utility named MkTypLib. This program is notorious for outputting error messages that are cryptic at best. It turns out that although Visual Studio's AppWizard and ClassWizard still generate ODL code, a command-line compatibility switch allows the more common MIDL compiler to process the syntax.

A review of IDL and ODL yields the following differences:

- ATL-based projects define interface definitions in IDL syntax.
- MFC-based projects still define interface definitions using an ODL-compatible syntax.

To illustrate the similarities and differences between the languages, I will define an interface with the following characteristics.

The interface whose name is Slang contains two methods and two properties. The first method, Pass2Short, passes two shorts to the server, whereas the second method, Retrieve2Long, retrieves two longs from the server. The property methods, PropShort and PropLong, put and get a single short and long respectively.

It might seem odd that I have decided to define interfaces with such primitive types, but as you will soon find out, automation is very specific regarding the datatypes it marshals between components. That is not to say that there is no way of passing Boolean and string arguments; it is just that there is a specific manner in which to declare such datatypes.

IDL and ATL

The IDL definition of the interface description appears in Listing 13.1 and is the result of an interface definition using the various helper dialogs that Microsoft provides for ATL object creation.

LISTING 13.1 THE IDL DEFINITION OF THE INTERFACE DESCRIPTION

```
import "oaidl.idl";
import "ocidl.idl";
    [
        object,
```

continues

LISTING **13.1**   CONTINUED

```
        uuid(D5F6CF73-615F-11D2-B10B-0000861D2934),
        dual,
        helpstring("ISlang Interface"),
        pointer_default(unique)
    ]
    interface ISlang : IDispatch
    {
        [id(1), helpstring("method Pass2Short")]
         HRESULT Pass2Short(short nS1, short nS2);
        [id(2), helpstring("method Retrieve2Long")]
         HRESULT Retrieve2Long(long* nL1, long* nL2);
        [propget, id(3), helpstring("property PropShort")]
         HRESULT PropShort([out, retval] long *pVal);
        [propput, id(3), helpstring("property PropShort")]
         HRESULT PropShort([in] long newVal);
        [propget, id(4), helpstring("property PropLong")]
         HRESULT PropLong([out, retval] long *pVal);
        [propput, id(4), helpstring("property PropLong")]
         HRESULT PropLong([in] long newVal);
    };

[
    uuid(D5F6CF66-615F-11D2-B10B-0000861D2934),
    version(1.0),
    helpstring("IDLandATL 1.0 Type Library")
]
library IDLANDATLLib
{
    importlib("stdole32.tlb");
    importlib("stdole2.tlb");

    [
        uuid(D5F6CF74-615F-11D2-B10B-0000861D2934),
        helpstring("Slang Class")
    ]
    coclass Slang
    {
        [default] interface ISlang;
    };
};
```

The first entries of any IDL file that is generated by ATL include import statements for oaidl.idl and ocidl.idl. The import statement is similar in function to the #include statement in C/C++, instructing the compiler to include datatypes that are defined in the imported IDL files. In this case, the interface definition relies upon an IDL definition for the IDispatch interface. This definition appears in the \include\OAIDL.IDL file of your

Visual Studio installation. The interface derives from IUnknown, as all interfaces ultimately must.

A quick summary of the remaining IDL elements for this file follows:

- Automation methods are assigned a unique id integer in their attribute definition block.
- Each automation property's get/put combination is assigned the same id integer in its attribute definition block.
- The propput and propget attributes specify property mutator and accessor functions, respectively.
- The retval attribute indicates that an out parameter is to be used as the return value of the method. This attribute is required to be on the last parameter of a propget method.

ODL and MFC

The ODL syntax, which Visual Studio's AppWizard and ClassWizard generate, differs slightly from the more common IDL file format. Here is the same interface implementation for an MFC-based automation server:

LISTING 13.2 THE ODL DEFINITION OF THE INTERFACE DESCRIPTION

```
[ uuid(D5F6CF78-615F-11D2-B10B-0000861D2934), version(1.0) ]
library ODLandMFC
{
    importlib("stdole32.tlb");
    importlib("stdole2.tlb");


    //  Primary dispatch interface for Slang

    [ uuid(D5F6CF79-615F-11D2-B10B-0000861D2934) ]
    dispinterface ISlang
    {
        properties:
        // NOTE - ClassWizard will maintain property information here.
            //      Use extreme caution when editing this section.
            //{{AFX_ODL_PROP(Slang)
            [id(1)] short PropShort;
            [id(2)] long PropLong;
            //}}AFX_ODL_PROP

        methods:
```

continues

13

MFC OLE
CLIENTS

LISTING 13.2   CONTINUED

```
            // NOTE - ClassWizard will maintain method information here.
            //     Use extreme caution when editing this section.
            //{{AFX_ODL_METHOD(Slang)
            [id(3)] void Pass2Short(short nS1, short nS2);
            [id(4)] void Retrieve2Long(long* nL1, long* nL2);
            //}}AFX_ODL_METHOD

    };

    //  Class information for Slang

    [ uuid(D5F6CF77-615F-11D2-B10B-0000861D2934) ]
    coclass Slang
    {
        [default] dispinterface ISlang;
    };

    //{{AFX_APPEND_ODL}}
    //}}AFX_APPEND_ODL}}
};
```

The ODL representation of the interface should not be a shock to your system. In fact, ODL shares all the syntax elements of IDL. You will notice that an attribute block precedes every definition block, as in IDL. There are a few differences worth noting, though.

Unlike an IDL, which commonly imports additional interface definitions outside the scope of any library or interface, ODL files access external library definitions with the importlib statement. An importlib must appear in the scope of the library that requires such definition. Unlike IDL, which imports the source of other .IDL files, ODL's importlib accesses compiled type library information.

The next difference you will notice is that dispinterface precedes the ISlang definition. Instead of indicating IDispatch inheritance, as in the IDL example, the definition, which Visual Studio generates, exposes the automation interface without a vtable.

Dispinterfaces (Dispatch Interfaces)

The dispinterface certainly increases the number of languages that can take advantage of COM object servers. However, there are differences with non–IDispatch-derived interfaces that should be noted:

- Methods can only use automation-compliant datatypes when specifying parameters in IDL.

- The IDL keyword `dispinterface` supports the concept of methods and properties in its definition block.

- `Dispinterface` defines an interface that does not expose a vtable. ODL-style syntax does, however, provide a mechanism for exposing dual interfaces.

Dual Interfaces

Although dispinterfaces might be ideal for languages that make it difficult, if not impossible, to deal with the pointers of a vtable of an ordinary interface, the overhead involved with accessing automation servers in C++ might be unacceptable. Thankfully, there is quite a simple solution to this problem, and it is called *dual interfaces*.

Dual interfaces are derived from `IDispatch`, just like dispinterfaces; however, they also expose their vtable. This is really quite convenient because it allows a single server to provide both implementations in the same physical DLL or EXE package (if an automation can be envisioned as residing in the physical universe) and allows the client to select the method with which it is most comfortable accessing the component. After an automation server is installed on a machine, a Visual Basic or VBScript program can access the server's methods via the `Invoke` method of the `IDispatch` interface, whereas a C++ program can access methods directly through the server's vtable.

Fortunately, Microsoft strongly recommends that whenever you build a COM server component and expose its interfaces, you do so as a dual interface. In fact, the ATL Object Wizard creates components with dual interfaces by default. For developers using MFC, you can support dual interfaces by changing the `dispinterface` keyword in your .ODL file to `dual`.

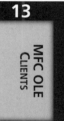

MFC and Automation

Automation is one of the COM technologies that is supported by the Microsoft Foundation Classes for both client-side and server-side development. Under the MFC implementation, the COM basics remain the same. Automation is based upon the `IDispatch` interface, and `Invoke` still plays the part of "calling" methods and properties on servers—so far, so good.

Controller

MFC provides a class that aids in the development of automation controllers. An automation controller must be able to connect to an automation server and call the `Invoke` method on an interface that derives from `IDispatch`, with a properly defined array of arguments. The beginning of this chapter contains a listing that shows a primitive OLE-SDK level application, performing the functions just described. The COleDispatchDriver shields the developer somewhat from these details. The good news is that although this section demonstrates low-level client-side automation development, the next section illustrates MFC's capability to exploit type libraries in a manner similar to ATL.

The steps necessary to produce an automation controller are not much different from building a standard COM client:

1. Identify the CLSID or ProgID of the automation server with which to connect.
2. Acquire the DISPIDs of the method(s) to invoke.
3. Configure an argument list for a method.
4. Call Invoke with the argument list.

The first place to explore when building an automation controller is the COleDispatchDriver class. This class stands alone in the MFC hierarchy—it has no base class. Here is the class definition for ColeDispatchDriver:

```
class COleDispatchDriver
{
// Constructors
public:
    COleDispatchDriver();
    COleDispatchDriver(LPDISPATCH lpDispatch,
                       BOOL bAutoRelease = TRUE);
    COleDispatchDriver(const COleDispatchDriver& dispatchSrc);

// Attributes
    LPDISPATCH m_lpDispatch;
    BOOL m_bAutoRelease;

// Operations
    BOOL CreateDispatch(REFCLSID clsid, COleException* pError = NULL);
    BOOL CreateDispatch(LPCTSTR lpszProgID,
                        COleException* pError = NULL);

    void AttachDispatch(LPDISPATCH lpDispatch,
                        BOOL bAutoRelease = TRUE);
    LPDISPATCH DetachDispatch();
        // detach and get ownership of m_lpDispatch
    void ReleaseDispatch();

    // helpers for IDispatch::Invoke
```

```
    void AFX_CDECL InvokeHelper(DISPID dwDispID, WORD wFlags,
        VARTYPE vtRet, void* pvRet, const BYTE* pbParamInfo, ...);
    void AFX_CDECL SetProperty(DISPID dwDispID, VARTYPE vtProp, ...);
    void GetProperty(DISPID dwDispID, VARTYPE vtProp, void* pvProp) \
        const;

    // special operators
    operator LPDISPATCH();
    const COleDispatchDriver& operator=(const COleDispatchDriver&
                                    dispatchSrc);

// Implementation
public:
    ~COleDispatchDriver();
    void InvokeHelperV(DISPID dwDispID, WORD wFlags, VARTYPE vtRet,
        void* pvRet, const BYTE* pbParamInfo, va_list argList);
};
```

The function `InvokeHelperV` is not documented in MFC programmer guides. It differs from `InvokeHelper` in that it defines the last argument as a variable-argument list (`va_list`) datatype. This variation on `InvokeHelper` is used internally by MFC in both control (ActiveX) operation and containment.

Connecting to a Server

Identifying the automation server to which `COleDispatchDriver` is to connect can occur in three ways. Two of the ways require that you have already acquired an `IDispatch` pointer, whereas the third retrieves an `IDispatch` pointer by `CLSID` or `ProgID`.

Acquiring an `IDispatch` Connection

The `CreateDispatch` function comes in two flavors: one that accepts the `CLSID` of an object that implements the `IDispatch` interfaces and one that accepts a `ProgID`. Both functions can also return error state information in an optional `COleException` structure. The `CreateDispatch` function loads the object's server if it is not already loaded and running, performs a `QueryInterface` for the interface whose identification has been provided, and then performs the necessary initialization for `COleDispatchDriver` to access the interface methods through `InvokeHelper`.

Using either of these functions is simply a matter of instantiating a `COleDispatchDriver` class and calling the appropriate `CreateDispatch` function:

```
COleDispatchDriver dispatcher;
dispatcher.CreateDispatch(clsid);
dispatcher.CreateDispatch(progid);
```

Connecting to an Existing `IDispatch` Pointer

If your automation controller program already has a pointer to an `IDispatch` interface, there are two ways to exploit `COleDispatchDriver`. The first involves passing the pointer to a `COleDispatchDriver` declared variable during construction:

```
LPDISPATCH pValidDispatchInterface(__uuid(DispatchObject));
COleDispatchDriver dispatcher(pValidDispatchInterface);
```

An instance of `COleDispatchDriver` is created whose name is `dispatcher`. It is constructed with a pointer to a valid `IDispatch` interface pointer `pValidDispatchInterface`.

The second way that `COleDispatchDriver` can be used with an existing `IDispatch` pointer involves connecting to an instance of the class:

```
COleDispatchDriver dispatcher;
LPDISPATCH pValidDispatchInterface(__uuid(DispatchObject));
dispatcher.AttachDispatch(pValidDispatchInterface);
```

An instance of `COleDispatchDriver` is instantiated, this time through the default constructor. At some point later, the `dispatcher` object is associated with an `IDispatch` interface pointer: `pValidDispatchInterface`. The second argument of `AttachDispatch` is `bAutoRelease`, and it defaults to a `TRUE` value. This instructs the `dispatcher` object to call the `Release` method on `pValidDispatchInterface` when it goes out of scope. Two other `COleDispatchDriver` methods allow a single instance of the class to be used with one or more `IDispatch` pointers. These functions include `DetachDispatch` and `ReleaseDispatch` and are exercised in the following example:

```
COleDispatchDriver dispatcher;
LPDISPATCH pValidDispatchInterface1(__uuid(Dispatch1Object));
LPDISPATCH pValidDispatchInterface2(__uuid(Dispatch2Object));
dispatcher.AttachDispatch(pValidDispatchInterface1);
dispatcherDetachDispatch();
dispatcher.AttachDispatch(pValidDispatchInterface2);
dispatcherDetachDispatch();
dispatcher.AttachDispatch(pValidDispatchInterface1);
dispatcher.ReleaseDispatch();
dispatcher.AttachDispatch(pValidDispatchInterface2);
dispatcher.ReleaseDispatch();
```

As a final note, `COleDispatchDriver` exposes the `LPDISPATCH` member variable, named `m_Dispatch`. This enables you to bypass the "helper" functions that deal with `IDispatch` pointer management and allow classes that derive from `COleDispatchDriver` to directly manipulate its instance data. The following definition for LPDISPATCH appears in the Oleauto.h file:

```
typedef IDispatch * LPDISPATCH;
```

Acquiring DISPIDs

Invoking methods on an IDispatch interface requires knowing the DISPID (dispatch ID) for each method or property to be called. The InvokeHelper function in the COleDispatchDriver class is no different; the first parameter requires a valid DISPID. The IDispatch interface defines a method whose name is GetIDsOfNames and whose purpose is to return a DISPID given a method name.

The GetIDsOfNames is called on a valid IDispatch pointer to obtain the dispatch ID of MyMethod:

```
LPDISPATCH pValidDispatchInterface(__uuid(DispatchObject));
OLECHAR FAR* szName = "MyMethod";
HRESULT hResult;
DISPID dispid;
hResult = pValidDispatchInterface->GetIDsOfNames(IID_NULL,
1,
LOCALE_SYSTEM_DEFAULT,
&dispid);
```

Invoking Methods

The heart of method invocation with COleDispatchDriver is named InvokeHelper. This function is defined with a variable argument list that allows it to be invoked (if you will) with a parameter list that matches the method it is calling. The dispatch ID, dispid, was acquired in the GetIDsOfNames method called previously.

```
long result = 0L;
pValidDispatchInterface->InvokeHelper(dispid, DISPATCH_METHOD,
VT_I4, (void*)&result, VTS_I4, nData);
```

Server Review

Developing an automation server in MFC is not difficult, with various wizards performing much of the work. The following steps offer a review of the operations you must take in creating a server:

1. Select the automation object's deliver vehicle, EXE or DLL.
2. Define a dispinterface (an interface that derives from IDispatch).
3. Add methods and properties as required.
4. Register the server and automation classes.

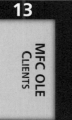

13

MFC OLE
CLIENTS

Building a Controller

An automation controller is the client side of the OLE automation equation. The controller you will construct in this section is designed to exercise the automation server presented in the preceding chapter.

Using `COleDispatchDriver`

MFC offers the `COleDispatchDriver` class to help you develop automation controller applications. The `COleDispatchDriver` class is somewhat orphaned in the MFC framework, as it does not inherit from any other MFC class, nor does any other MFC class derive from it. The class is rather small, consisting of just three constructor variations and seven class methods. The easiest way to use this class is to have ClassWizard do all the work for you. Using `ClassWizard`'s Add Class option, you can select a file containing a type library and have a `COleDispatchDriver` class built for you. This option will be explained in the next section. First, let's explore this class.

Create a project, `MFCDispatchDriver`, using AppWizard (see Figure 13.1). Select automation and a single document interface; all the other options are taken as default.

FIGURE 13.1

Creating the `MFCDispatchDrive` *r project.*

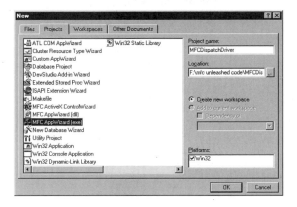

The next step is to add a class to the project that derives from `COleDispatchDriver`. At first this would seem rather trivial, and it is not that bad, but the New Class dialog is not as helpful as it could be. The New Class dialog is available under the Insert menu. This dialog creates a header and implementation file for the class you specify and adds them to the current project. The dialog allows you to select a base class from a combo box control. Unfortunately, this combo box does not contain an entry for the `COleDispatchDriver` class. The steps necessary to derive a class from this base class require you to change your Class Type combo box at the top of the dialog to Generic Class. This causes a change in options in the lower section of the dialog box.

Enter the name of the class you want to create; in this case it can be IDrive (see Figure 13.2). In the lower portion of the dialog, derive your class publicly from COleDispatchDriver. This generates the following header file and constructor and destructor stubs in the implementation file:

```
#if !defined
(AFX_IDRIVE_H__9ECED411_C6A5_11D2_B17B_0000861D2934__INCLUDED_)
#define AFX_IDRIVE_H__9ECED411_C6A5_11D2_B17B_0000861D2934__INCLUDED_

#if _MSC_VER > 1000
#pragma once
#endif // _MSC_VER > 1000

class IDrive : public COleDispatchDriver
{
public:
    IDrive();
    virtual ~IDrive();

};

#endif //
!defined(AFX_IDRIVE_H__9ECED411_C6A5_11D2_B17B_0000861D2934__INCLUDED_)
```

FIGURE 13.2

Creating a dispatch driver class.

Before the dialog is dismissed that indicates the base class definition might not be available and might have to be manually added as an #include file, the warning message box shown in Figure 13.3 might appear. You can safely ignore this warning.

FIGURE 13.3

Header file warning dialog.

The COleDispatchDriver class contains two member variables, m_bAutoRelease and m_lpDispatch. The first variable determines whether or not Release is called on the IDispatch interface when the ReleaseDispatch method is called, or when the object goes out of scope and is destroyed. The second variable contains the IDispatch interface that you operate on when calling member functions of this class. IDispatch interface attachment might occur using one of the classes' constructors, calling AttachDispatch or indirectly with a CreateDispatch method call. Before attaching a dispatch interface to this class, you must define implementation methods.

Interface Definition

The *Autoserv* project developed in the OLE Servers directory is the perfect object to exercise with a home-brew controller. The first step is to decide the interface methods that you want to call and create a header definition and a function body. In this case, three methods will be created. These methods will access the single interface method on the server, and the other two will offer accessor and mutator operations on a single property.

```
class IDrive : public COleDispatchDriver
{
public:
    IDrive();
    virtual ~IDrive();

    // interface method
    void TrackInformation(short nIndex, BSTR * Title);

    // property methods
    short GetAlbumLength();
    void  PutAlbumLength(short nLength);
}
```

The next step is to put some flesh on the bones of these functions and actually call the automation server. You can easily accomplish this task with a helper function; in fact, the function you need is part of the IDrive base case, InvokeHelper. This function performs a lot of the grunt work for you in calling the IDispatch::Invoke method. InvokeHelper throws COleException and COleDispatchException as a result of any error in processing your request.

InvokeHelper supports a variable argument list, but there are only five arguments that you must supply. Table 13.1 summarizes the InvokeHelper arguments.

TABLE 13.1   A SUMMARY OF InvokeHelper's ARGUMENTS

Parameter	Description
DispID	Identifies the dispatch ID of the property or method to invoke.
dwFlags	Can be any of the following four self-explanatory values: DIS-PATCH_METHOD DISPATCH_PROPERTYGET DISPATCH_PROPERTYPUT DISPATCH_PROPERTYPUTREF
vtRet	Identifies the variant type of the return variable. This argument requires one of the VT_ constants that VARENUM defines.
pvRet	Address of a variable to contain the return value. This variable must match the datatype that *vtRet* defines.
pbParamInfo	This parameter requires rather strange formatting. You pass the function a null-terminated string and specify the argument types as a space-delimited list of variant identifiers. These identifiers exist as *VTS_* constants. This value may be NULL if there is no argument list.
(variable argument list)	The last argument or arguments that are to be passed by Invoke to the automation server. These datatypes must match the *VTS_* constants, which you give in *pbParamInfo*.

Using this function is very straightforward. The following sample definition passes a string and three long values to an automation interface method and returns a long value:

```
long ISample::VerifyRequest(LPCTSTR strConfig, long Context,
                            long bNewRequest, long Flags)
{
    long result;
    static BYTE parms[] = VTS_BSTR VTS_I4 VTS_I4 VTS_I4;
    InvokeHelper(0x6, DISPATCH_METHOD, VT_I4, (void*)&result,
                 parms, strConfig, Context, bNewRequest, Flags);
    return result;
}
```

Notice that the params variable contains a space-delimited list of *VTS_* types and the function accepts arguments, of these types, in the defined order.

Method Implementation

The method bodies for the *Autoserv* interface are much simpler. These three methods call the single method, TrackInfo, and the single property, AlbumLength, in the primary Autoserv automation interface.

13

MFC OLE CLIENTS

```
void IDrive::TrackInformation(short nIndex, BSTR * bstrTitle)
{
    DISPID dispid;
    unsigned short* szName = L"TrackInfo";
    SCODE scodeReturnError = 0L;
    HRESULT hresult = m_lpDispatch->GetIDsOfNames(IID_NULL,
                &szName, 1, LOCALE_USER_DEFAULT, &dispid);
    static BYTE params[] = VTS_I2 "\x48";
                            // \x48 = VTS_BSTR and VT_MFCBYREF;
    InvokeHelper(dispid, DISPATCH_METHOD, VT_ERROR,
            (void*) &scodeReturnError, params, nIndex, bstrTitle);
}

short IDrive::GetAlbumLength()
{
    DISPID dispid;
    unsigned short* szName = L"AlbumLength";
    short nReturnLength = 0L;
    HRESULT hresult = m_lpDispatch->GetIDsOfNames(IID_NULL,
                &szName, 1, LOCALE_USER_DEFAULT, &dispid);
    InvokeHelper(dispid, DISPATCH_PROPERTYGET, VT_I2,
                (void*) &nReturnLength, NULL);
    return nReturnLength;
}

void  IDrive::PutAlbumLength(short nLength)
{
    DISPID dispid;
    unsigned short* szName = L"AlbumLength";
    HRESULT hresult = m_lpDispatch->GetIDsOfNames(IID_NULL,
                &szName, 1, LOCALE_USER_DEFAULT, &dispid);
    static BYTE params[] = VTS_I2 ;
    InvokeHelper(dispid, DISPATCH_PROPERTYPUT, VT_EMPTY,
                (void*) NULL, params, nLength);
}
```

The only strange part of the code is that I failed to identify how to use the VTS_ constants in a way that could identify a BSTR passed by reference. You can step through the InvokeHelper code and see that there appears to be no way of identifying this relationship except to use bit-masks.

Before making calls on your IDrive interface, you must associate the class instance with a dispatch interface. You can accomplish this by calling CreateDispatch with the ProgID of the automation interface in the constructor.

```
IDrive::IDrive()
{
    CreateDispatch(_T("Autoserv.Document"));
}
```

The final step in constructing the controller application is to instantiate an IDrive object, connect the server's IDispatch interface, and make calls to the methods and properties. Although it presents a user interface that is lacking, the easiest way to perform these functions is in the OnNewDocument function of the application in the CMFCDispatchDriverDoc class.

```
BOOL CMFCDispatchDriverDoc::OnNewDocument()
{
    if (!CDocument::OnNewDocument())
        return FALSE;

    IDrive driver;
    _bstr_t b("Call through InvokeHelper");
    wchar_t* pBstr = (wchar_t*)b;
    driver.TrackInformation(23, &pBstr);
    driver.PutAlbumLength(45);
    short nOut = driver.GetAlbumLength();

    // Indicate success if we get back what we sent
    // using direct access of the property
    if (nOut == 45)
        AfxMessageBox("Property access a success!");

    return TRUE;
}
```

Exercising the Server

That's all there is to it. Compile and link the code. Executing this program will result in a dialog box that indicates that you successfully set the server's property, and read back the same value (see Figure 13.4).

FIGURE 13.4
COLEDispatchDriver *success.*

Using #import

Visual C++ offers a preprocessor directive to help you work with automation servers in a manner that makes them almost as easy to work with as in Visual Basic or Visual J++. This directive is the #import statement, and it instructs Visual C++ to use type library information in generating wrapper classes for COM interfaces. This command operates on the type library and generates two header files containing C++ source. These files are

13

MFC OLE
CLIENTS

output to the directory that your /Fo compiler option specifies. Generally this is either the Debug or Release directory under your project. The name of the type library provides the base name for the header files with extensions of .TLH and .TLI. The first file, with the .TLH extension, is known as the Primary Type Library header file. This file consists of seven sections and contains the second file with the .TLI extension. The .TLI file is known as the *implementation* file. The magic that makes this directive work is that the compiler reads and produces object code for the header file, and then the preprocessor makes the #import appear as a #include of the primary header file.

As a preprocess directive, the #import directive syntax is similar to that of other directives, such as #include. The command can appear in either of the following formats:

```
#import <filename> [attributes]
```

```
#import "filename" [attributes]
```

In the first *angle-bracket* form, the preprocessor is instructed to search directories in the *path* environment variable, followed by the *lib* environment variable path list and finally any additional include directories that the /I compiler option specifies. This search ordering is common among other preprocessor directives and is familiar to most using these tools.

The *filename* argument is the name of any file containing the type library information. Path information may precede the filename. The following file types commonly contain type information:

Extension	Description
.TLB or .ODL	Type library
.DLL	Dynamic link library file
.EXE	Executable
.OCX	ActiveX or OLE control

Additionally, there are two more categories of files that may contain type information that do not have standard file extensions. A compound document may hold a type library, as well as any other file that the LoadTypeLib function can load.

The #import directive supports a number of attributes. Table 13.2 gives the names and uses of each attribute.

TABLE 13.2 ATTRIBUTES FOR THE #import DIRECTIVE

Attribute	*Description*
exclude	Excludes the specified items or type libraries from code that is generated in the header files.
high_method_prefix	Specifies a prefix to precede the naming of high-level methods and properties.
high_property_prefixes	Allows you to substitute prefixes for the standard Get, Put, and PutRef text that appears before property method names.
implementation_only	Suppresses generation of the primary header file.
include(...)	Forcibly includes definitions of other type libraries or items whose definition occurs in other system files.
inject_statement	Places a line of "text" at the beginning of the namespace definition of the type-library header file.
named_guids	Instructs the compiler to define and initialize old-style GUID variables.
no_auto_exclude	Disables automatic exclusion of item definitions.
no_implementation	Suppresses generation of the .TLI file.
no_namespace	The namespace, whose specification resides in the library statement, is not used.
raw_dispinterfaces	Instructs the compiler to generate all method and property calls through Invoke with HRESULT error code return. High-level wrappers are not generated.
raw_interfaces_only	Allows you to expose only the low-level contents of the type library, suppressing the generation of higher-level wrapper functions.
raw_method_prefix	The compiler substitutes the name you provide here for the *raw_* prefix that it normally attaches to low-level member functions.
raw_native_types	Forces the use of low-level datatypes, such as BSTR and VARIANT instead of "_bstr_t" and "_variant_t".
raw_property_prefixes	Allows you to specify the low-level prefix for property put, get, and putref methods.
rename	Allows you to rename the type library. This is useful in resolving namespace collisions.
rename_namespace	Allows you to define the namespace that contains the type library contents.

13

MFC OLE
CLIENTS

It is now time to use the `#import` directive. You will see how easy it is to build an automation controller using this Visual C++ feature, importing the *Autoserv* project from the last chapter.

Creating a Project

Create a new project with the name *controllerimport* using the MFC AppWizard for executables, and select an SDI document model. The `#import` command will appear in the document file, so add the following line to your controllerimportDoc.cpp file:

```
#import "..\autoserv\Debug\autoserv.tlb"
```

The type library file may reside in your Release directory if you only built the example with this option. Compiling the project will result in the creation of two additional files in your Debug directory. Again, this may be your Release directory, depending on your project settings. An autoserv.tlh file is your primary type library and autoserv.tli is the implementation file.

TLH File

The primary type library file for the Autoserv type library appears below. This file can consist of the seven sections. Only six sections follow. The seventh section is optional, containing old-style GUID definitions. The option to generate these statements is not necessary.

Header Boilerplate

The first section identifies the source from which the compiler generated this code. In this case, the path to the Autoserv type library is also included. Two `pragma` directives appear, which specify that this file is only included once by the compiler with the second defining packing alignment for structures. Next is the `#include` directive for *<comdef.h>*. This header file contains definitions for classes and templates that are used by this header source code. Specifically, this file contains definitions for `_bstr_t`, `_variant_t`, `_com_error`, and `_com_ptr`. Finally, a namespace of Autoserv is declared for a region that defines the rest of this file.

```
// Created by Microsoft (R) C/C++ Compiler Version 12.00.8168.0
//
// f:\mfc unleashed code\controllerimport\debug\autoserv.tlh
//
// C++ source equivalent of Win32 type library
//      ..\autoserv\Debug\autoserv.tlb
// compiler-generated file created 02/15/99 at 20:22:23 - DO NOT EDIT!

#pragma once
```

```
#pragma pack(push, 8)

#include <comdef.h>

namespace Autoserv {
```

Forward References and Typedefs

This second section, as its name implies, contains forward references to structures and typedefs that are used prior to definition later in the file:

```
struct __declspec(uuid("723b4da5-b8aa-11d2-8faf-00105a5d8d6c"))
/* dispinterface */ IAutoserv;
struct /* coclass */ Document;
struct __declspec(uuid("723b4dba-b8aa-11d2-8faf-00105a5d8d6c"))
/* dispinterface */ ISecondInterface;
struct /* coclass */ SecondInterface;
```

Smart Pointer Declarations

The smart pointer section of this file goes a long way in making automation servers as simple to work with in C++ as they are in languages such as Visual Basic or Visual J++. Smart pointers encapsulate COM interface pointers. Visual C++ supports this both with a template class, _com_ptr_t, and a typedef, _COM_SMARTPTR_TYPEDEF. Smart pointers help solve one of the biggest problems in working with COM-reference counting.

The template class manages all resource allocation and deallocation for you. This template makes the appropriate calls to the IUnknown methods QueryInterface, AddRef, and Release. The "smart" in smart pointers especially comes into play when using the template's assignment operator and destructor. The template code is smart enough to perform the necessary AddRef and Release calls based on the object assignment, and Release will be called for you when the object goes out of scope. The template eliminates the need for calling AddRef and Release directly.

Smart pointers, however, are usually referenced by the _COM_SMARTPTR_TYPEDEF macro. This macro requires an interface name and the IID of the interface for which you want to acquire a smart pointer. The first argument is simple to provide—this is simply the text for the name of the template specialization with a Ptr appended to the end. Thus, the following code contains IAutoserv as the first macro argument. The resulting parameterized template will have the name IAutoservPtr. The second macro argument requires the IID of an interface. IIDs are obscure structures that contain the unique hexadecimal value for the interface; fortunately, the Visual C++ compiler includes the reserve word __uuid, which retrieves this value for a given type name, reference, variable, or pointer. In the cases that follow, this value is retrieved for the IDispatch interface definition.

13

MFC OLE
CLIENTS

A final advantage to using smart pointers that are based upon the _com_ptr_t template is that error conditions are returned as exceptions. The _com_error class encapsulates the HRESULT error code, thus saving you the trouble of having to inspect this value for every call. You can use smart pointers for COM interface manipulation outside of automation and specifically these header files; just remember to include *<comdef.h>*. In addition, this header file contains smart pointer classes for almost every documented interface. Thus, if you want to use the smart pointer for the IShellIcon interface, you simply declare an object of type IshellIconPtr:

```
_COM_SMARTPTR_TYPEDEF(IAutoserv, __uuidof(IDispatch));
_COM_SMARTPTR_TYPEDEF(ISecondInterface, __uuidof(IDispatch));
```

Typeinfo Declarations

This section consists primarily of class definitions. Two definitions appear in this section: IAutoserv and ISecondInterface. The most obscure of the actions that are taken in this section revolves around the definition of properties. The __declspec keyword is a Microsoft extension allowing COM properties to be accessed as member functions. The command accepts a number of attributes; among them is the property statement. This attribute creates "virtual data members" in a class or structure definition.

The virtual data members have the effect of enabling you to manipulate property values directly without the need for calling a member function. When the compiler sees a data member of this type being accessed as a member selection operator (such as "." or "->"), a corresponding put or get function is substituted. This substitution depends on the side of the expression on which the property exists. That is, an l-value position will result in a put operation and an r-value position results in a get operation. The compiler is even smart enough to handle such complex statements as a -= condition, performing both a get and a put.

```
//
// Type library items
//

struct __declspec(uuid("723b4da5-b8aa-11d2-8faf-00105a5d8d6c"))
IAutoserv : IDispatch
{
    //
    // Property data
    //

    __declspec(property(get=GetAlbumLength,put=PutAlbumLength))
    short AlbumLength;
```

```
    //
    // Wrapper methods for error-handling
    //

    // Methods:
    SCODE TrackInfo (
        short Index,
        BSTR * Title );

    // Properties:
    short GetAlbumLength ( );
    void PutAlbumLength ( short _val );
};

struct __declspec(uuid("723b4da3-b8aa-11d2-8faf-00105a5d8d6c"))
Document;
    // [ default ] dispinterface IAutoserv

struct __declspec(uuid("723b4dba-b8aa-11d2-8faf-00105a5d8d6c"))
ISecondInterface : IDispatch
{
    //
    // Property data
    //

    __declspec(property(get=GetInspect,put=PutInspect))
    _bstr_t Inspect;

    //
    // Wrapper methods for error-handling
    //

    // Methods:
    SCODE SetCounter (
        short Count );

    // Properties:
    _bstr_t GetInspect ( );
    void PutInspect ( _bstr_t _val );
};

struct __declspec(uuid("723b4dbb-b8aa-11d2-8faf-00105a5d8d6c"))
SecondInterface;
    // [ default ] dispinterface ISecondInterface

//
// Wrapper method implementations
//
```

Implementation

The implementation section simply includes the .TLI header file and closes the name-space definition block:

```
#include "f:\mfc unleashed code\controllerimport\debug\autoserv.tli"
} // namespace Autoserv
```

Footer Boilerplate

The last section returns the structure alignment setting to its previous state:

```
#pragma pack(pop)
```

TLI FILE

The .TLI file contains the implementation code for the method declarations that appear in the Typeinfo Declaration section of the .TLH file. This file can be thought of as the equivalent of a .CPP file. For each method, the appropriate `Invoke` call is made on the `IDispatch` interface. This invoke operation requires identification of the method or property's `DispID` value and an argument list whose datatypes are automation-compatible:

```
//
// dispinterface IAutoserv wrapper method implementations
//

inline SCODE IAutoserv::TrackInfo ( short Index, BSTR * Title ) {
    SCODE _result;
    _com_dispatch_method(this, 0x2, DISPATCH_METHOD, VT_ERROR,
                         (void*)&_result,
        L"\x0002\x4008", Index, Title);
    return _result;
}

inline short IAutoserv::GetAlbumLength ( ) {
    short _result;
    _com_dispatch_propget(this, 0x1, VT_I2, (void*)&_result);
    return _result;
}

inline void IAutoserv::PutAlbumLength ( short _val ) {
    _com_dispatch_propput(this, 0x1, VT_I2, _val);
}

//
// dispinterface ISecondInterface wrapper method implementations
//
```

```
inline SCODE ISecondInterface::SetCounter ( short Count ) {
    SCODE _result;
    _com_dispatch_method(this, 0x2, DISPATCH_METHOD, VT_ERROR,
                         (void*)&_result,
        L"\x0002", Count);
    return _result;
}

inline _bstr_t ISecondInterface::GetInspect ( ) {
    BSTR _result;
    _com_dispatch_propget(this, 0x1, VT_BSTR, (void*)&_result);
    return _bstr_t(_result, false);
}

inline void ISecondInterface::PutInspect ( _bstr_t _val ) {
    _com_dispatch_propput(this, 0x1, VT_BSTR, (BSTR)_val);
}
```

Building this project should not result in any compiler errors or warnings. However, it is not uncommon to have namespace collisions when using the #import directive.

Putting the Server to Work

Now it is time to put your server through its paces. The last thing to do is actually write code that uses the wrapper classes. The code to exercise the server will be put in the OnNewDocument method of the CControllerimportDoc class. In this way the controller will immediately make calls to the server, and you can rerun the code to perform these functions by selecting New from the File menu.

The wrapper classes raise exceptions, whose information is contained in _com_error classes; therefore, the controller code must appear in a try block. The catch block of this exception handler will report the error in a message box.

```
try {
    // automation controller code goes here
}
catch(const _com_error& e){
    TCHAR buf[255]={0};
    wsprintf(buf,_T("0x%0"),e.Error());
    ::MessageBox(NULL,buf,_T("Automation Error"),MB_OK);
}
```

The first statement in the try block creates the automation controller. Accomplishing this is as easy as instantiating a class whose definition appears in the header files that the #import statement generates. An object ptr is created for the interface that was defined in the document object of the *Autoserv* automation server. In creating that server, the default name for the File Type ID was used. This value is Document. You can verify that this is true by looking at the struct definition in your .TLH file.

```
struct __declspec(uuid("723b4da3-b8aa-11d2-8faf-00105a5d8d6c"))
Document;
```

```
struct __declspec(uuid("723b4dbb-b8aa-11d2-8faf-00105a5d8d6c"))
SecondInterface;
```

The constructor acquires the CLSID for the server using the __uuidof keyword and any of the valid expression arguments, including a type name, pointer, reference, template specialization, and so on. In this case you will use the Autoserve::Document definition. Thus, here's the line of code that returns a smart pointer to this interface on the automation server:

```
Autoserve::IAutoservPtr ptr(__uuidof(Autoserve::Document));
```

Exercising the server is now just a matter of making method calls on the ptr object. Visual C++'s smart tooltip identifies the methods and properties that are available to this object as you type (just as it does for every other object you reference). Add the following lines to call a method and set a property:

```
// Manipulate the interface through method calls
_bstr_t b("test");
wchar_t* p2 = (wchar_t*)b;
ptr->PutAlbumLength(10);
ptr->TrackInfo(3, &p2);
```

Now you can prove that your server is actually performing these functions by retrieving the property value that you set.

```
short nReturnValue = ptr->GetAlbumLength();
```

Finally, you can exploit the advanced compiler options that Microsoft provides by directly manipulating properties without calling mutator or accessor methods:

```
// Access the properties directly
ptr->AlbumLength = 5;
short nReturnLength = ptr->AlbumLength;
```

When you have finished, your code looks like this:

```
try {
    // Create an automation server and access IAutoserv
    Autoserv::IAutoservPtr ptr(__uuidof(Autoserv::Document));

    // Manipulate the interface through method calls
    _bstr_t b("test");
    wchar_t* p2 = (wchar_t*)b;
    ptr->PutAlbumLength(10);
```

```
        ptr->TrackInfo(3, &p2);
        short nReturnValue = ptr->GetAlbumLength();

        // Indicate success if we get back what we sent
        // using method calls on a property
        if (nReturnValue == 10)
            AfxMessageBox("Server method access a success!");

        // Access the properties directly
        ptr->AlbumLength = 5;
        short nReturnLength = ptr->AlbumLength;

        // Indicate success if we get back what we sent
        // using direct access of the property
        if (nReturnLength == 5)
            AfxMessageBox("Direct property access a success!");

        // Create an automation server and access ISecondInterface
        Autoserv::ISecondInterfacePtr ptr2(__\
        uuidof(Autoserv::SecondInterface));
        ptr2->SetCounter(15);
    }
    catch(const _com_error& e){
        TCHAR buf[255]={0};
        wsprintf(buf,_T("0x%0"),e.Error());
        ::MessageBox(NULL,buf,_T("Automation Error"),MB_OK);
    }
```

It is now time to put your automation server to work. Compile and link the *controllerim-port* project. When you run the program, you will see dialog boxes appear indicating that you successfully set a property value and read the same value back (see Figure 13.5). Success!

FIGURE 13.5
Controller success dialog.

Selecting New from the File menu will create a new document and rerun the automation code. What you might be asking yourself at this point is, "Where is the automation serv-er program? I don't see the window and its statistics information." Well, you are right, the Autoserv application window never appeared. There is code in that project to present some well-formatted output of the internal server state. This effort shouldn't go to waste. Let's look at the code from that project:

```
// Check to see if launched as OLE server
if (cmdInfo.m_bRunEmbedded || cmdInfo.m_bRunAutomated)
```

```
    {
        // Register all OLE server (factories) as running.
        // This enables the
        //  OLE libraries to create objects from other applications.
        COleTemplateServer::RegisterAll();

        // Application was run with /Embedding or /Automation.
        // Don't show the
        //  main window in this case.
        return TRUE;
    }
```

Looking at the InitInstance code, you will see that AppWizard wires in some code that automatically keeps the application frame hidden when starting under automation control. You can remove this line or comment it out and the server will be visible:

```
//        return TRUE;
```

Rebuild the server and rerun the controller application. This time the Autoserv application appears when your controller program executes (see Figure 13.6). The server will also display information in its view as the controller changes the server's state.

FIGURE 13.6

The Autoserv automation server's application frame and view.

Remote Automation

One of the strengths of COM, and more specifically automation, is the concept of *location transparency*. This term identifies the fact that it isn't important where an object resides for it to be put to use by another object or client. For many cases, this transparency refers to the fact that the object server need not exist in the process space of the client, that is, the server may be running as a separate program. Such a configuration is referred to as out-of-proc, meaning out of process. The server may also reside in the process space of the caller in the form of a DLL; this is referred to as in-proc, or in-process. The transparency issue comes into play in the fact that the client need not concern itself with the details of whether the server object is in-proc or out-of-proc. The OLE system DLLs manage these details.

NT version 4.0 and Windows 98 extend the notion of location transparency to include activation and use of servers residing on different machines. A set of utilities and DLLs are also available for remote automation on Windows 95 as well. Hence it is now possible for a server, either written by you or not, to reside on a remote machine and be used by a client or controller process on a different machine.

Remote automation allows programs to invoke implementations of IDispatch across a network on different machines. There is complete transparency on the part of both the object server and client, and complete marshaling support is offered for supported automation datatypes. The amazing part of remote automation is the fact that all this happens without the need to change a line of code!

You must follow a number of steps to enable remote automation both on the client application machine and on the server object's machine.

The first thing you should do is to test the automation server and client on a single machine. Actually, this is a bit more than a suggestion. The purpose of loading and executing the server application on your client machine is to allow the programs to perform the necessary registration.

Registration of the server application can occur by a number of means. If the server is a full server, that is it can run in a standalone fashion, simply executing it will cause the Registry to update. If the server is a DLL, you have two options. You can use the REGSVR32.EXE program, providing it the name and path of the DLL. Otherwise, if your server has a .REG file, you can merge the contents with your Registry. Visual C++ generates .REG file contents for your projects; this file is generally used by your installation program. If you don't have an installation program, you must edit this file to provide the specific path location for your server—by default this file is created without such information. Finally, if the server is one you built, and it doesn't perform automatic registration, add the code yourself.

The second step involves using one of the two remote automation utilities. Microsoft provides two utilities, the Remote Automation Connection (RACMGR32.EXE) Manager and the Automation Manager (AUTMGR32.EXE). You will run the first utility, RACMGR32.EXE, on the client machine (see Figure 13.7), that is, the machine running the program that requires the services of a remote automation server.

13

MFC OLE
CLIENTS

FIGURE 13.7

*The Remote
Automation
Connection
Manager.*

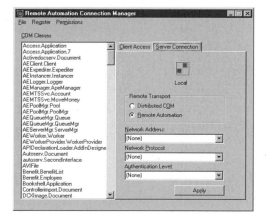

The purpose of running RACMGR32 on the client machine is to instruct the computer
where to go to resolve the automation server load request. You want to identify the serving computer from the Server Connection tab. A list box to the left of the dialog contains
the COM classes. Locate the server you want to address remotely and select it. In the
Network Address combo box, enter the name of the machine that will serve the automation object (see Figure 13.8). (You can see how it was important for you to register the
automation server application or DLL on this machine in the first step, or this utility
would not be able to add the server object to the list box as it scans the Registry.)

FIGURE 13.8

*Configuration of
Autoserv automa-
tion server object.*

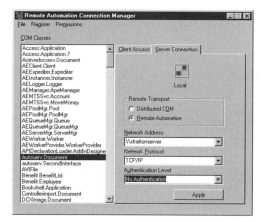

In this case, the `Autoserv` server object's network address is being set to \\strattonserver. The Network Protocol combo box contains the following choices:

- none
- TCP/IP
- SPX
- Named Pipes
- NetBIOS over NetBEUI
- NetBIOS over TCP
- NetBIOS over SPX
- Datagrams - IPX
- Datagrams - UDP

The selection is set to TCP/IP. You might have to speak to your network administrator in determining the protocol appropriate for your network. The machines you intend to connect may not support some protocols, or there may be security or routing issues involved in your selection. The last combo box on this tab, Authentication Level, offers the following choices:

- None
- Default
- No Authentication
- Connect
- Call
- Packet
- Packet Integrity
- Packet Privacy

The final client-side step in configuration using this utility is selecting local or remote operation for the server. You accomplish this by switching to the Client Access tab of the utility. You are given four System Security Policy options (see Figure 13.9).

For demonstration purposes, the Allow All Remote Creates option is selected. It is now time to move over to the machine on which the automation server will execute.

FIGURE **13.9**
*Client Access
options.*

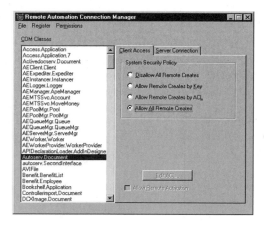

On the machine that is to host the automation object, install and register the application
or DLL as appropriate. If the application is a standalone program, executing it will generally cause self-registration. Otherwise, the .REG file may have to be merged with the
Registry or the REGSVR32.EXE may have to be used. When you are significantly convinced that you have been successful in your registration endeavors, you are ready to
configure remote activation.

Run the RACMGR32.EXE program again, this time on the server machine. Select the
Client Access tab pane to choose the activation model. There are four choices, just as
there were when this utility was executed on the client machine. The default for this
option is Remote Creates by Key. This is the option that you will continue with. You
must also select the Allow Remote Activation check box at the bottom of the dialog as
well.

Selecting the Allow Remote Creates (ACL) option under the Windows NT Operating
System requires you to edit the ACL list. The Edit ACL button will be enabled under
these conditions, from which you make the appropriate assignment (see Figure 13.10).

Now it is time to use the second automation utility—AUTMGR32.EXE. For remote activation of automation servers, you must have the Automation Manager utility installed
and running on the server computer. Generally this program is copied either to the
Windows system directory or somewhere on the machine's path. Executing the AUTM-
GR32.EXE utility displays a small dialog window. After a few seconds and a couple of
initialization messages, the window will automatically minimize itself. If you activate
this task, you will see the number of connections and the number of objects in use on
your machine (see Figure 13.11).

FIGURE 13.10
The Remote Class Permissions dialog.

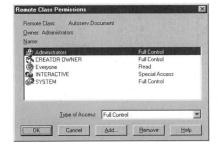

FIGURE 13.11
The Automation Manager dialog.

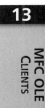

It is now time to test remote automation. This is relatively simple: Run the *controllerimport* program on your client machine. After a brief period of time the success dialog boxes should appear.

Summary

You have seen a number of ways to use MFC to construct automation servers. Between the MFC classes and the Visual Studio wizards, you shouldn't have any trouble putting automation to use in your applications. A final note of thanks should go to the Microsoft C++ preprocessor, which offers the powerful #import command.

13

**MFC OLE
CLIENTS**

CHAPTER 14

MFC ActiveX Controls

by Gene Olafsen

IN THIS CHAPTER

One of the most visible incarnations of COM is ActiveX controls. Visual C++ 6.0 generally refers to ActiveX controls as simply controls. The control component group encompasses a wide range of component offerings from familiar image buttons to network communication libraries.

Controls built with COM are, to a certain degree, descendents of an earlier initiative by Microsoft to plug a third-party interface into a language. The language was Visual Basic and the plug-in standard was the VBX. It didn't take long for developers to embrace VBX's, and soon there were literally hundreds on the market, which enabled developers to implement everything from modem communication protocols to animated picture buttons. The problem with VBX's was that as Visual Basic grew in sophistication, the VBX specification left little room for the scope Microsoft had in mind. Also, VBX's were firmly grounded in the Visual Basic language. It would be great if a programming-language-neutral third-party interface could be defined. Here comes COM to the rescue.

A plug-in or control based on the original COM control specification required implementing a fairly hefty number of interfaces. These interfaces included those that implement property sheets, display a user interface, and manage container-control communication. For most controls, this specification was overkill. The tools and documentation that were available to aid in the development in such "compliant" controls were not up to the job. The resulting controls occupied a sizeable memory footprint, and activation was lethargic. To combat these problems, Microsoft introduced incremental improvements, including a number of control-container extensions that sped up activation and reduced UI requirements.

As the browser wars started to heat up, and Java and the JavaBean specification (a Java-based component architecture) started to take shape, Microsoft's browser became a control container. A sticking issue was the fact that the controls were still pretty big, and took a relatively long time to download to the browser—remember that most modems were cranking along at 2400 to 9600 baud. The control specification was changed one last time, where it remains today.

The control requirements are as follows:

- Implement IUnknown
- Support self-registration

The specification of a control is thus so broad that it encompasses just about any COM server. This is exactly the point—in this manner, Microsoft defines a requirement set that has minimal overhead and allows the developer to produce components that are tailored for an exact purpose.

Development Strategy

Both MFC and ATL support control development. In fact, both make it relatively painless to develop controls through the support of various wizards and powerful helper classes or templates. There are certain advantages to creating your control using either framework, and it is important to understand the major issues with each before beginning development.

MFC

The Microsoft Foundation Classes have been around for a long time, and you are certainly familiar with the object hierarchy, even if you haven't explored control development. Because there can be a lot more to control development than simply generating the skeleton code and pointing to the control's device context, your familiarity with the MFC collection classes, runtime identification, and creation and serialization mechanisms can be a big advantage in writing the code for the control.

There are, however, some disadvantages to creating a control with MFC. One of the easiest ways to determine whether it is appropriate for you to build a control using MFC is to identify the context in which you will use the control. If you are building the control as part of the process of *componentizing* an installable application, or you intend the control for use as part of a toolkit for another developer's application, basing the control on MFC is appropriate. If, however, you expect control deployment to occur on an HTML page, you might have to consider several points.

Controls built using MFC require the presence of the appropriate MFC DLLs for the control to execute. This might not be an issue for controls in use as part of an installable application, because the libraries can be included on the distribution media, but it can be an issue with use in a browser. The end user can navigate to a page on the Internet with an ActiveX control that is built with MFC, and the appropriate libraries might not be present on the user's system. In addition, controls built using MFC can become quite large, and downloading the control can be frustrating to the end user. The DLLs weigh in at over one megabyte in size, so download is tedious at best. This is not to say that you cannot build a lightweight control using MFC, but if size is an issue, there is an alternative: the Active Template Library (ATL).

ATL

The Active Template Library offers you a lightweight alternative to controls built using MFC. The term *lightweight* doesn't necessarily refer to the fact that controls built with

ATL are less powerful than their MFC counterparts; rather, it refers to the fact that this new framework carries around less baggage than its older sibling.

ATL utilizes templates (no surprise there) in the creation of COM components. A template, at the most basic level of understanding, offers you a way to specify a generic representation of a class and a template and then create parameterized instances of the class. The ATL framework offers a large number of templates for many of the standard COM interfaces. In use, templates differ from a class hierarchy in that there is no additional complexity as the result of inheritance. The resulting class doesn't depend on overriding virtual functions, thus there is no overhead in terms of execution penalty or object size because the functionality is not dependent on vtables. In summary, the footprint for ATL-based components is smaller than for the equivalent MFC-based control.

MFC and ATL

The previous section might make you believe that there is an impenetrable barrier between framework approaches. You select one approach, stick with it, and ignore the other option. In fact, this relationship isn't as antagonistic as you might think. It is quite possible to use MFC classes within an ATL project, as well as create ATL-based COM objects in an MFC application.

The ATL COM AppWizard (see Figure 14.1) allows you to specify that you want MFC support during project creation.

FIGURE **14.1**

ATL COM AppWizard, step 1.

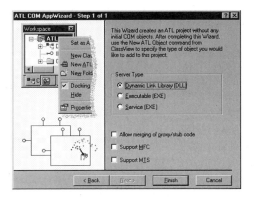

The Support MFC option is available to DLL projects only, and it links the MFC library to your code. This allows you to access any MFC classes or functions. Selecting this option will not necessarily add a significant amount of code to your base project, but it will establish a dependency with the MFC library. This approach contains your project in an MFC application object, which initializes and frees an ATL module. In essence, it is the same as creating an MFC DLL project and inserting ATL components.

The class declaration for the project identifies an object that derives from CWinApp:

```
class CATL_COMApp : public CWinApp
{
    public:
    virtual BOOL InitInstance();
    virtual int ExitInstance();
};
```

The implementation in InitInstance associates an application instance handle with a managed list of ATL objects:

```
CATL_COMApp theApp;

BOOL CATL_COMApp::InitInstance()
{
    _Module.Init(ObjectMap, m_hInstance, &LIBID_ATL_COMLib);
    return CWinApp::InitInstance();
}

int CATL_COMApp::ExitInstance()
{
    _Module.Term();
    return CWinApp::ExitInstance();
}
```

Supporting ATL in an MFC project is possible for both EXE- and DLL-based applications. The Insert menu offers access to the New ATL Object dialog (see Figure 14.2).

FIGURE 14.2

The ATL Object Wizard dialog.

This dialog allows you to insert all the ATL components that are available to an ATL-based project. There is one issue with this approach, however. Visual C++ supports insertion only as it applies to simple COM objects. Adding more complex objects, which includes ActiveX controls, can result in unexpected behavior.

Control Development

Part of selecting a control's foundation may include considering the extent of support that the wizard provides in generating skeleton code. Each of the control implementations makes it simpler to perform different objectives. Table 14.1 lists these functions.

TABLE 14.1 CONTROL IMPLEMENTATIONS AND THEIR FUNCTIONS

Category	Feature	MFC	ATL (Full Control)
General Wizard Options	Support for multiple controls in a project	X	X
	Runtime licensing	X	
	Comments in code	X	X
	Help files	X	
	Threading: single/apartment		X
Interfaces	Dual/custom		X
	Aggregation: Yes/No/Only		X
	ISupportErrorInfo		X
	Connection Points	X	X
	Free-threaded marshaler		X
Control Subclassing	button	X	X
	combobox	X	X
	edit	X	X
	listbox	X	X
	richedit		X
	msctls_hotkey32	X	
	msctls_progress32	X	
	msctls_statusbar32	X	
	msctls_trackbar32	X	
	msctls_updown32	X	
	scrollbar	X	X
	static	X	X
	SysAnimate32	X	X
	SysHeader32	X	X
	SysListView32	X	X
	SysTabControl32	X	X
	SysTreeView32	X	X

Category	Feature	MFC	ATL (Full Control)
Features	Active when visible	X	
	Invisible at runtime	X	X
	Available in Insert Object dialog	X	X
	Has an About box	X	
	Acts as a simple frame control	X	
	Acts like a label		X
	Acts like a button		X
	Opaque background		X
	Solid background		X
Enhanced Features	Windowless activation	X	
	Unclipped device context	X	
	Flicker-free activation	X	
	Mouse pointer notifications when inactive	X	
	Optimized drawing code	X	
	Load properties asynchronously	X	
	Normalize DC		X
	Windowed only		X
	Stock property selection		X

This comparison is of the ATL full control to an MFC Active ControlWizard component. ATL supports the following control types:

- Full control
- HTML control
- Composite control
- Lite control
- Lite HTML control
- Lite composite control

Controls other than the full control offer subsets of the functionality that the full control wizard implements (see Figure 14.3).

14

MFC ACTIVEX CONTROLS

There are two primary control categories, those that are specified as *lite* and their regular implementations. The lite controls support only those interfaces needed by Internet Explorer, including support for a user interface. The HTML control includes a DHTML resource and displays an HTML Web page as its user interface. The composite control can host multiple controls within itself.

Two Faces of a Control

Suppose you are developing a control that provides a graphic representation of a person's vital signs—pulse, respiration, and so on. Such a control is certainly a candidate for implementing user interface extensions, such as screen invalidation, focus management, and keyboard traversal. However, if you are building a control whose purpose is to control frequency hopping for a spread spectrum radio modem, you might not need a user interface at runtime, but what about at design time? Controls can implement separate user interfaces for runtime and design time.

Runtime

The runtime UI is the one that you commonly associate with a control (see Figure 14.4). If the control provides image button functionality, you think of the arrangement of buttons that are selected either by the click of the mouse or by keyboard hot keys/accelerators. You can also envision the button's color changing as a mouse passes over or the image changing as the button is clicked.

FIGURE **14.4**
The Date time picker control at runtime.

Design Time

The design-time UI is usually displayed only to the developer. Consider the frequency hopping control discussed earlier. The control may not have a graphical runtime component because it is not preferable for the user to know anything about the control's operation. However, the designer might want to configure or tailor the control for operation in the product under development (see Figure 14.5). A design-time user interface can offer the developer a range of frequencies to hop between, perhaps in a multiselect list box. A combo box can offer a choice of algorithms that are applied to filter background noise.

FIGURE 14.5

Date time picker control properties.

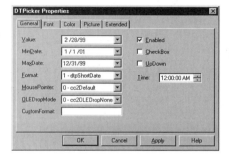

Subclassing a Control

Creating a control can be a tedious process; that is why both ATL and MFC provide the ability to subclass an existing control.

MFC

Selection of the control to subclass is made from the wizard during project creation. The class name of the control to subclass is wired into the `COleControl` class during the window precreate function.

```
//////////////////////////////////////////////////////////////////////
// CSublistboxCtrl::PreCreateWindow - Modify parameters
//                                    for CreateWindowEx

BOOL CSublistboxCtrl::PreCreateWindow(CREATESTRUCT& cs)
{
    cs.lpszClass = _T("LISTBOX");
    return COleControl::PreCreateWindow(cs);
}
```

The wizard automatically overrides the `IsSubClassedControl` function to return `TRUE` for a control that subclasses a well-known control.

```
//////////////////////////////////////////////////////////////////////
// CSublistboxCtrl::IsSubclassedControl - This is a subclassed control

BOOL CSublistboxCtrl::IsSubclassedControl()
{
    return TRUE;
}
```

Access to control messages is available in the handler that the wizard provides for you.

```
//////////////////////////////////////////////////////////////////////
// CSublistboxCtrl::OnOcmCommand - Handle command messages

LRESULT CSublistboxCtrl::OnOcmCommand(WPARAM wParam, LPARAM lParam)
{
#ifdef _WIN32
    WORD wNotifyCode = HIWORD(wParam);
#else
    WORD wNotifyCode = HIWORD(lParam);
#endif

    // TODO: Switch on wNotifyCode here.

    return 0;
}
```

ATL

The ATL approach provides the framework with the class name of the control that you subclass in the constructor:

```
Csublistbox()  : m_ctlListBox(_T("ListBox"), this, 1)
{
    m_bWindowOnly = TRUE;
}
```

You add event handlers to the control by right-clicking the control's class in the Class View tab of the project window and selecting the Add Windows Message Handler menu.

Component Categories

The first COM-based controls implemented a large number of interfaces. Through various calls to these interfaces, a container application could go through a discovery process to identify various characteristics of a control and display it accordingly. The most recent control specification literally identifies any COM component as a control—a different means of identifying and categorizing controls was needed. The concept of component categories offers an extensible solution to classifying control characteristics.

As with any system that provides an extensible mechanism for creating new entries in a namespace that is not centrally managed, there is the possibility, if not certainty, that a collision will occur. Allowing developers to use character strings to establish new component categories can result in one or more programmers using the same value to mean two different things. Fortunately, this problem is inherent to COM and has already been solved.

Remember that every COM server and every interface is uniquely identified by a Globally Unique IDentifier (GUID). The term GUID also has a number of manifestations that are specific to the object or element that it describes. A CLSID (CLass IDentifier) is a GUID that describes a class, whereas an IID (Interface IDentifier) describes an interface. Component categories also employ GUID technology to avoid collision as well. A CATID or category identifier is a GUID that is associated with control category identification.

COM defines a number of interfaces that make identifying component categories an easier task.

ICatRegister

The `ICatRegister` interface offers functions for registration and unregistration of component category information.

ICatInformation

The `ICatInformation` interface offers functions that obtain information about categories that a class implements. Additionally, this interface can return information about categories that a machine registers.

Registered component categories appear under the `HKEY_CLASSES_ROOT\Component Categories` key. The categories on a system can be reviewed either by firing up RegEdit or RegEdt32 and viewing the path given in the last sentence or by looking at Object Classes\Grouped by Component Category in the OLEVIEW utility. In this case the Bitmap Transition category contains two entries: Alpha Transition and Reveal Transition (see Figure 14.6).

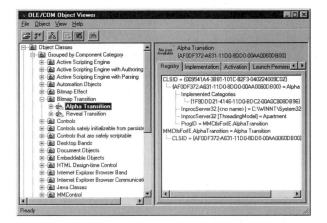

Methods, Properties, and Events

The control guidelines specify that a control expose its methods, properties, and events through an IDispatch-derived or dual interface.

Properties

Properties represent a control's internal state. A common naming convention for property methods is prepending the words get or set to the beginning of the attribute you are defining. In fact, the concept of object properties is not unique to COM controls. Java offers a component architecture named JavaBeans. Part of this specification is a *design pattern* (naming convention) that requires property methods to begin with either the word get or set. The Java container for these components identifies properties by evaluating the actual name of the method. COM identifies property methods using an IDL construct named *property*.

Property Types

The flexibility that COM offers should never cease to amaze you. It would be simple if COM offered a single type of property, but no, that would be much too restricting. So COM provides three kinds of properties: Custom, Stock, and Ambient. As you will see, it only makes sense that all of these property types exist.

Custom Properties

The term "custom" might seem at first to be the most involved type of property to add to a control. In fact, custom properties are probably the easiest property type to understand and the easiest to add and implement. Custom properties are simply a pair of get/set methods that are added to a control. These methods can be as simple as setting a Boolean state (set) and returning a Boolean value (get), or they can expose and manage an array of objects.

A developer can define properties as *read-only* or *write-only*. Read-only properties can only be *set*. This is accomplished by not exposing a get method. Write-only properties can only be *set*—their get method is not defined.

As with methods and events, you can create custom properties in one of two ways: either edit the component's IDL or use a wizard to do the dirty work. There are helpful wizards for creating your own control properties for both ATL and MFC controls.

Stock Properties

The next property type to discuss is stock properties. A stock property is a property whose purpose is defined by OLE/COM. Stock properties can be exposed by a control and identify specific characteristics that Microsoft deems are important for a container application to be interested in. Such characteristics generally concern themselves with the control's visual representation. Unlike custom properties, which have a positive integer DISPID, stock properties are identified by a negative integer DISPID. The following table contains each property's DISPID constant, the constant's value, and a description of the property:

Stock Property	*Dispatch Entry Macro*
Appearance	DISP_STOCKPROP_APPEARANCE
BackColor	DISP_STOCKPROP_BACKCOLOR
BorderStyle	DISP_STOCKPROP_BORDERSTYLE
Caption	DISP_STOCKPROP_CAPTION
Enabled	DISP_STOCKPROP_ENABLED
Font	DISP_STOCKPROP_FONT
ForeColor	DISP_STOCKPROP_FORECOLOR
hWnd	DISP_STOCKPROP_HWND
Text	DISP_STOCKPROP_TEXT

14

MFC ACTIVEX CONTROLS

The datatypes for each stock property are specific to the value or values that the property is identified with. For instance, the MousePointer property exposes methods that get and set an HCURSOR value, while the FillColor property can be translated to a COLORREF.

Ambient Properties

The final type of property to explore is ambient properties. Ambient properties are a way for the container to "give back" to the control a meager offering in appreciation of all the properties the control has exposed. More to the point, ambient properties are read-only values that represent characteristics of a control's container. As with stock properties, ambient properties generally reflect visual states of the container, including foreground/background colors and text alignment information. The following table summarizes the ambient property names and constants:

Ambient Property	DispID Constant
LocaleID	-705
UserMode	-709
UIDead	-710
ShowGrabHandles	-711
ShowHatching	-712
DisplayAsDefault	-713

Accessing Ambient Properties

Ambient properties are exposed by the container through its default IDispatch interface. Controls are required to implement the IOleObject interface. This interface is the principal means by which a control provides functionality to, and communicates with, its container. The default IDispatch interface, by which ambient properties are accessed, is passed to the control with a call by the container on the client's IOleObject::SetClientSite method.

ATL

The ambient properties exposed by a container can be accessed through the GetAmbientX methods, where X is the property name (as defined in the preceding table), provided by the CComControl class.

MFC

Accessing ambient properties in an MFC-implemented control is painless. The COleControl base class provides two ways to acquire ambient property information. The easiest way is to call any one of the number of functions of the form Ambient<*property-name*>. Such functions include AmbientBackColor, AmbientUserMode, and so on.

A second way to acquire ambient property information is to use a more generic call named GetAmbientProperty. This call is useful when responding to ambient property changes because of the returned dispid value.

Responding to Change

A control usually queries its container for ambient property values during initialization. Many of these values are then used to configure the control so that its appearance reflects the look and feel of the container. An important aspect to consider when dealing with ambient properties is that they can change at any time. Although chances are slim that the `LocaleID` or `MessageReflect` properties will modify during a control's lifetime, it is not a stretch to say that container colors or the control's activation state will remain the same.

MFC- and ATL-based controls are implementations of the `IOleControl` interface. This interface provides a method that amounts to a callback, which returns the `DISPID` of an ambient property when the container changes the value.

```
HRESULT OnAmbientPropertyChange(DISPID dispid);
```

Methods

The methods that your control exposes are little more than a variation on the OLE automation method theme. Because the methods that your control exposes exist in a dispinterface, argument datatypes must be compatible with the `VARIANT` datatype.

Visual C++ provides wizards to help construct methods for the controls you build with either ATL or MFC. Chapter 12 contains further details on the creation of methods and the available helper dialogs.

Events

Events are a further variation on the automation method theme. As a Windows programmer, you are undoubtedly familiar with the events that window messages represent. You program in a manner that is different from procedural programs. As a general rule, instead of guiding a user through your program, your program responds to actions taken by the user, hence the term *event-driven* programming. The concept of events in OLE controls extends this notion that allows the control to inform the container that something happened. When the control wants to notify the container of a change, it is said to fire an event.

Adding events to a control is not much different from adding standard methods. The difference is that you must add the event definitions to an *outgoing* interface. Methods and properties exist in *incoming* interfaces.

The following ODL describes a control's coclass with an interface for methods and properties and an outgoing (denoted by *source*) interface for events: _DMFCActiveXEvents.

```
[ uuid(D33E5F36-CC5B-11D2-8FBA-00105A5D8D6C),
  helpstring("MFCActiveX Control"), control ]
coclass MFCActiveX
{
```

```
    [default] dispinterface _DMFCActiveX;
    [default, source] dispinterface _DMFCActiveXEvents;
};
```

Although the specifics differ between MFC and ATL with regard to implementation of
the event methods, wizards generally perform all the work for you in creating the event
functions that you call in your control code to issue notification to the container. For
MFC, an *event map* manages event methods on your outgoing interface.

```
// Event maps
//{{AFX_EVENT(CMFCActiveXCtrl)
void FireDataStream(BSTR Control)
    {FireEvent(eventidDataStream,EVENT_PARAM(VTS_BSTR), Control);}
void FireThermalValue(short Indicator)
    {FireEvent(eventidThermalValue,EVENT_PARAM(VTS_I2), Indicator);}
//}}AFX_EVENT
DECLARE_EVENT_MAP()
```

Whenever you want to notify the container of a thermal condition change, you simply
call `FireThermalValue` with a `short` argument.

ATL generates a class from the `IConnectionPointImpl` template and defines the necessary event methods.

```
template <class T>
class CProxy_IATLActiveXCtlEvents : public IConnectionPointImpl<T, \
 &DIID__IATLActiveXCtlEvents, CComDynamicUnkArray>
{
    //Warning this class may be recreated by the wizard.
public:
    HRESULT Fire_ThermalValue(SHORT nIndicator)
    {
        CComVariant varResult;
        T* pT = static_cast<T*>(this);
        int nConnectionIndex;
        CComVariant* pvars = new CComVariant[1];
        int nConnections = m_vec.GetSize();

        for (nConnectionIndex = 0; nConnectionIndex < nConnections;
            nConnectionIndex++)
        {
            pT->Lock();
            CComPtr<IUnknown> sp = m_vec.GetAt(nConnectionIndex);
            pT->Unlock();
            IDispatch* pDispatch = reinterpret_cast<IDispatch*>(sp.p);
            if (pDispatch != NULL)
            {
                VariantClear(&varResult);
                pvars[0] = nIndicator;
                DISPPARAMS disp = { pvars, NULL, 1, 0 };
```

```
        pDispatch->Invoke(0x1, IID_NULL, LOCALE_USER_DEFAULT,
            DISPATCH_METHOD, &disp, &varResult, NULL, NULL);
    }
}
delete[] pvars;
return varResult.scode;

    }
};
```

In this case, an ATL control programmer calls `Fire_ThermalValue`, again with a `short` value, to notify the container application of a change in "temperature."

Property Pages

The ability to view and/or modify an object's properties can be programmed in a number of ways. Many development environments provide property inspectors that identify an object's property methods, datatypes, and, if possible, a collection of appropriate values. Visual Basic and Visual J++ are examples of development systems that display a property editor window that displays and allows modification of a selected object's attributes at design time.

There are times, however, when either such generic property editors do not suffice, because of property interdependencies, or the property values are a datatype that is not easily configurable without a more complex interface (see Figure 14.7). In fact, a property sheet may not be confined to design-time only availability. Property sheets may be available at runtime as well, although some functionality might be gated by disabling controls or by presenting read-only access to an object's internal state. Other times, property sheets can offer much more dynamic runtime configuration.

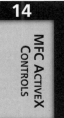

FIGURE 14.7

A generic property editor window.

Finally, property sheets are not confined to controls. Windows shortcuts offer a perfect example of property sheets that allow a user to display and interact with property settings at runtime (see Figure 14.8).

FIGURE 14.8

An OLE control property sheet.

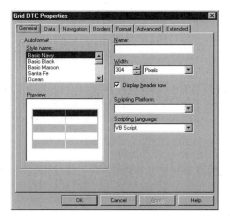

A wizard is available to develop property page objects using ATL. This wizard automates much of the grunge work that such page construction requires. If you want to construct property page objects for MFC-based controls, you must do a little more work; however, MFC is kind enough to provide a few "helper" classes.

The implementation definition for property pages exists as the IPropertyPage COM interface. This interface manages a single page within a property sheet collection. Each property page is a COM component. A property page object must create and manage the UI components that reside on the page. The collection of pages or sheets is an implementation of the IPropertyPageSite COM interface. An object that implements IPropertyPageSite is responsible for managing the pages that appear within the dialog. Property page changes are communicated back to the control through its default IDispatch interface.

Property Pages in ATL

Creating a property page object in ATL is as simple as adding another COM object to your existing project. Using the Insert, New ATL Object menu, the ATL Object Wizard allows the selection of a Property Page object from the Controls category selection.

Selecting the Next> step displays a dialog with three tabs. The first two, Names and Attributes, are identical to those found in the Simple Object wizard that has been discussed in detail in earlier chapters. The third tab, Strings, is specific to the property page object.

The Strings page offers three edit fields: Title, Doc String, and Helpfile (see Figure 14.9). It isn't too difficult to discern the meaning and acceptable values for each of these fields. An important thing to remember is that inserting this object into your project inserts a single property page. If you want to have more than one property page associated with your project, simply add another Property Page object.

FIGURE 14.9

Configuring an ATL property page.

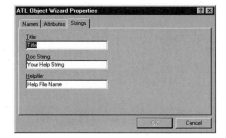

Property Pages in MFC

If you are developing a new control in MFC using ControlWizard, a single property page is created by the wizard's code generation facilities. If you are adding additional pages to the control, you must use ClassWizard. In either case, MFC-based controls rely on COlePropertyPage as the base class for your own property pages.

Adding property pages to an MFC control is not difficult—if you know where to look. Switch your project workspace window to the ResourceView tab. Right-click any of the resource objects and select the Insert menu option to display the Insert Resource dialog (see Figure 14.10). You will not find a property page resource type to insert, but the Dialog resource object can expand the tree. Clicking this object reveals a number of resource templates.

FIGURE 14.10

Dialog resource templates for OLE property sheets.

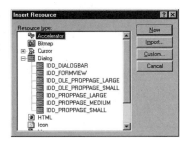

The IDD_OLE_PROPPAGE_LARGE and IDD_OLE_PROPPAGE_SMALL templates should interest you. These templates are the proper size and exhibit the correct style settings for OLE property sheets.

To add the necessary code behind a property sheet, insert a new class that derives from `COlePropertyPage` (see Figure 14.11).

FIGURE **14.11**

*Creating a class
that derives from*
`COlePropertyPage`.

The New Class dialog doesn't perform all the necessary work for you, though. You need to manually add the `PROPPAGEID` macro entry to the MFC property page map construct. Make sure that the macro entry you provide includes the proper GUID for the page. In addition, you must increment the property page count argument in the `BEGIN_PROP-PAGEIDS` macro. The application wizard kindly generates a reminder in the comment block that precedes the map:

```
// TODO: Add more property pages as needed.
// Remember to increase the count!
BEGIN_PROPPAGEIDS(CMFCActiveXCtrl, 1)
    PROPPAGEID(CMFCActiveXPropPage::guid)
END_PROPPAGEIDS(CMFCActiveXCtrl)
```

Component Registration

This section provides an overview of the registration process for MFC-based and ATL-based servers and their contained objects: classes and type libraries. Registration is the process of making information about a component, such as its location and function, known to the operating system and other installed applications. The Windows Registry is a database that stores COM server, object, and type library information.

Registering a control adds the following information to the registration database:

- The text name of the control
- The class name of the control

- An indicator stating that the control conforms to the MFC ActiveX control protocols
- The path of the control's executable
- The path and resource ID of the control palette bitmap
- An indication of whether the control is insertable
- The IDispatch IDs of the control's properties and events interfaces

Registration Scripts

Component registration (and unregistration) is performed by registration scripts. Registration scripts generally exist in a file with an .RGS extension. ATL supports registration scripts with a COM component, deriving from IDispatch and whose name is IComponentRegistrar.

Registration scripts can either be stored inside the COM server file they register or appear in standalone files. A registration script is stored in a server as part of the component's resource file.

Registration and Controls

The second requirement for a COM object to identify itself as a legal control is self-registration. A number of keys are important in identifying a component as a control.

Because the definition of a control is broad enough to encompass any COM object, the location of control registration in the registry is no different than any other component. Controls are located under \HKEY_CLASSES_ROOT\CLSID\<clsid>. The subkeys described in the following sections, however, are commonly present as part of a control's definition.

COM Object Subkeys

Unless otherwise defined, it is assumed that the default value for each key is undefined (""):

- \Programmable—The presence of the Programmable key indicates that the object supports automation.
- \Insertable—This key identifies the object as one that should appear in the Insert Object dialog box's list of possible selections.
- \Control—Indicates that the object that possesses this key is to be included in a list of registered controls for applications that display a list of controls.

- \ToolboxBitmap32—This key's default value specifies the name of the file and the index of the resource (icon) to display for the component. This icon is a 16×16 pixel resource and is generally displayed in the tool palette of an application that exploits the control's design-time interface.

- \MiscStatus—This key aids in the construction and presentation of the object, including aspect ratio values.

- \Verb—This key is instrumental in registering OLE-compatible verbs and associated menu flags. Common verbs include Open, Hide, and Edit.

- \TypeLib—This key contains the CLSID of the type library for the object.

- \InprocServer32—Use this key to register a 32-bit in-process server object. Additionally, this key identifies the server's threading model: Single, Apartment, Free, or Both (Apartment or Free).

- \InprocHandler32—This key specifies a custom handler used by an application. Generally, this entry should be COM32.DLL.

- \LocalServer—This key specifies a path to a 16-bit server object.

- \LocalServer32—This key specifies a path to a 32-bit server object.

- \ProgID—The ProgID key associates a human-readable tag with a CLSID.

- \Implemented Categories—Identifies the category functions that this server object implements.

- \DefaultIcon—The DefaultIcon key allows you to specify the icon to display for OLE servers. Thus, this is the icon that displays when a control is minimized or an OLE document server object is inserted as an icon.

- \DataFormats—This key identifies an object's data formats. Such data formats can be enumerated using EnumFormatEtc.

- \AuxUserType—This key provides an object's short name, which is usually recommended to be no longer than 15 characters.

- \TreatAs—This key enables an OLE server to work in place of another server object. This key provides a way for your object to offer emulation for a different object—perhaps one you didn't even write.

- \Version—This key identifies the version of the OLE server and should match the type library associated with the server.

Building an MFC Control

The control that is going to be built using both MFC and ATL performs the radar-mapping functions for a space probe that is scheduled to enter orbit around Mars later this year. Okay, I'm lying. The control simulates a component that performs such mapping functions. As such, it exposes a number of methods and properties and fires events, which identify the data stream and any error conditions. The control also offers a very primitive user interface. The following table identifies the methods, properties, and events for this control:

Type	Name	Datatype	Description
Method	SetAntenna	Short	Identifies the antenna to use for collection/ transmission.
Property	m_AcquireData	Boolean	Turns on and off the event firing that passes the data buffer.
Property	m_BufferSize	Short	Identifies the size of the data buffer.
Event	DataStream	BSTR	The data buffer is sent to the container when the buffer is full.
Event	ThermalValue	Short	Identifies thermal changes.

Creating a control using the MFC ActiveX ControlWizard results in the creation of a DLL (in-proc server) with an .OCX extension. Unlike its ATL counterpart, which uses IDL, the interface from this control resides in an .ODL file, and its definition employs the Object Definition Language. The name of this project is MFCActiveX (see Figure 14.12). Accept all the default values for the steps of the wizard.

FIGURE 14.12

Starting an ActiveX control using MFC ActiveX ControlWizard.

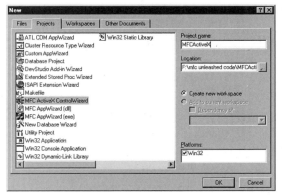

There are two classes that perform the bulk of the work for the control, COleControlModule and COleControl. The COleControlModule class performs a function similar to that of CWinApp in a standard MFC application. COleControlModule provides both the InitInstance and ExitInstance virtual functions.

```
/////////////////////////////////////////////////////////////////////
// CMFCActiveXApp::InitInstance - DLL initialization

BOOL CMFCActiveXApp::InitInstance()
{
    BOOL bInit = COleControlModule::InitInstance();

    if (bInit)
    {
        // TODO: Add your own module initialization code here.
    }

    return bInit;
}


/////////////////////////////////////////////////////////////////////
// CMFCActiveXApp::ExitInstance - DLL termination

int CMFCActiveXApp::ExitInstance()
{
    // TODO: Add your own module termination code here.

    return COleControlModule::ExitInstance();
}
```

The file that contains these definitions also contains two functions that every in-proc server must export: DllRegisterServer and DllUnregisterServer. These functions offer known entry points into the DLL for applications that perform control registration. The Regsvr32.exe is one such program that exercises a control in this manner. Your Visual C++ Tools menu contains a Register Control entry, which uses the Regsvr32 utility to register the control or controls in your current project. This utility also supports a number of command-line arguments. Among the most useful is the /u option, which unregisters a control—calling DllUnregisterServer.

```
/////////////////////////////////////////////////////////////////////
// DllRegisterServer - Adds entries to the system registry

STDAPI DllRegisterServer(void)
{
    AFX_MANAGE_STATE(_afxModuleAddrThis);

    if (!AfxOleRegisterTypeLib(AfxGetInstanceHandle(), _tlid))
        return ResultFromScode(SELFREG_E_TYPELIB);

    if (!COleObjectFactoryEx::UpdateRegistryAll(TRUE))
        return ResultFromScode(SELFREG_E_CLASS);

    return NOERROR;
```

```
}

/////////////////////////////////////////////////////////////////
// DllUnregisterServer - Removes entries from the system registry

STDAPI DllUnregisterServer(void)
{
    AFX_MANAGE_STATE(_afxModuleAddrThis);

    if (!AfxOleUnregisterTypeLib(_tlid, _wVerMajor, _wVerMinor))
        return ResultFromScode(SELFREG_E_TYPELIB);

    if (!COleObjectFactoryEx::UpdateRegistryAll(FALSE))
        return ResultFromScode(SELFREG_E_CLASS);

    return NOERROR;
}
```

Registration of a control usually takes place when you install a control. It is important to remember to reregister your control whenever you make changes that affect the type library. Such changes include supporting or removing support for properties and events.

The `COleControl` class is the base class from which you derive your control. A project can contain more than one control, each deriving from this class. In fact, the MFC ActiveX ControlWizard allows you to specify the number of controls in the project, and it allows you to identify the properties and options that you want to support on an individual control basis.

Interface Definition

Now it is time to add the methods, properties, and events to the control. The first thing to do is switch the workspace pane to display the Class View (see Figure 14.13). You will notice that there are two interfaces: `_DMFCActiveX` and `_DMFCActiveXEvents`. The first interface, `_DMFCActiveX`, is a *standard* incoming interface. Such an interface identifies methods and properties that are called from a container application. This type of interface was explored in Chapter 12, "MFC OLE Servers." The second interface, `_DMFCActiveXEvents`, is an outgoing interface. An outgoing interface is one that calls the container, usually as the result of an event inside the control. A common use of an outgoing event is one in which the control mimics the behavior of a button control and a mouse click on the ActiveX control issues a click event.

Going in order from methods to properties and finally events, you will start by adding methods to the control. There is only a single method, `SetAntenna`, that takes a short datatype representing the antenna to use for data collection. Add the method by selecting the Add Method menu selection from the context menu that you display with a right-click on the `_DMFCActiveX` interface.

14

MFC ACTIVEX
CONTROLS

FIGURE 14.13

Classes and inter-faces as seen in the Class View pane.

The method dialog is identical to the Add Method dialog that you use when creating automation servers (see Figure 14.14). In this case the method will return an SCODE and accepts a single short parameter whose name is Antenna.

FIGURE 14.14

The Add Method context menu.

The control also contains two properties, one to turn data acquisition on and off and another to set and retrieve the data buffer size. The data buffer is actually a variable-length BSTR, so this value is more of a *high-water* marker, rather than for use in allocating a predefined buffer. You create properties using a context menu to select Add Property and populate the Add Property dialog.

The first property's definition includes a name of AcquireData of type BOOL. The second property's name is BufferSize and its datatype is short.

The next step is to define the two control events. This time you will make modifications to the _DMFCActiveXEvents interface. Clicking the right mouse button on this interface in Class View results in a context menu that offers an Add Event menu (see Figure 14.15).

FIGURE 14.15

*The Add Event
context menu.*

The Add Event dialog box offers a combo box into which you enter the External Name of the event or select from a list of predefined events. These event types include the following:

- `Click`
- `Double-Click`
- `Error`
- `KeyDown`
- `KeyUp`
- `KeyPress`
- `MouseDown`
- `MouseMove`
- `MouseUp`
- `ReadyStateChange`

Provide the name `DataStream` with a single argument control whose datatype is a `BSTR*`. The dialog will automatically generate an internal name of `FireDataStream`, which you can edit if necessary (see Figure 14.16).

FIGURE 14.16

*The Add Event
dialog for the*
`DataStream` *event.*

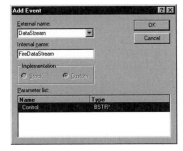

14

**MFC ACTIVEX
CONTROLS**

The next event reports thermal conditions inside the scanning unit. The name you give to this event is ThermalValue, and it defines a single short argument whose name is indicator. Upon defining all the methods, properties, and events for the control, your interface looks like Listing 14.1.

LISTING 14.1   THE COMPLETED INTERFACE

```
// MFCActiveX.odl : type library source for ActiveX Control project.

// This file will be processed by the
// Make Type Library (mktyplib) tool to
// produce the type library (MFCActiveX.tlb)
// that will become a resource in
// MFCActiveX.ocx.

#include <olectl.h>
#include <idispids.h>

[ uuid(D33E5F33-CC5B-11D2-8FBA-00105A5D8D6C), version(1.0),
  helpfile("MFCActiveX.hlp"),
  helpstring("MFCActiveX ActiveX Control module"),
  control ]
library MFCACTIVEXLib
{
    importlib(STDOLE_TLB);
    importlib(STDTYPE_TLB);

    //   Primary dispatch interface for CMFCActiveXCtrl

    [ uuid(D33E5F34-CC5B-11D2-8FBA-00105A5D8D6C),
    helpstring("Dispatch interface for MFCActiveX Control"), hidden ]
    dispinterface _DMFCActiveX
    {
        properties:
        // NOTE - ClassWizard will maintain property information here.
            //     Use extreme caution when editing this section.
            //{{AFX_ODL_PROP(CMFCActiveXCtrl)
            [id(1)] boolean AcquireData;
            [id(2)] short BufferSize;
            //}}AFX_ODL_PROP

        methods:
        // NOTE - ClassWizard will maintain method information here.
            //     Use extreme caution when editing this section.
            //{{AFX_ODL_METHOD(CMFCActiveXCtrl)
            [id(3)] SCODE SetAntenna(short Antenna);
            //}}AFX_ODL_METHOD
```

```
            [id(DISPID_ABOUTBOX)] void AboutBox();
};

// Event dispatch interface for CMFCActiveXCtrl

[ uuid(D33E5F35-CC5B-11D2-8FBA-00105A5D8D6C),
  helpstring("Event interface for MFCActiveX Control") ]
dispinterface _DMFCActiveXEvents
{
    properties:
        // Event interface has no properties

    methods:
        // NOTE - ClassWizard will maintain event information here.
        //     Use extreme caution when editing this section.
        //{{AFX_ODL_EVENT(CMFCActiveXCtrl)
        [id(1)] void DataStream(BSTR Control);
        [id(2)] void ThermalValue(short Indicator);
        //}}AFX_ODL_EVENT
};

// Class information for CMFCActiveXCtrl

[ uuid(D33E5F36-CC5B-11D2-8FBA-00105A5D8D6C),
  helpstring("MFCActiveX Control"), control ]
coclass MFCActiveX
{
    [default] dispinterface _DMFCActiveX;
    [default, source] dispinterface _DMFCActiveXEvents;
};


//{{AFX_APPEND_ODL}}
//}}AFX_APPEND_ODL}}
};
```

The last step is to supply code and flesh out the skeleton framework. Contriving the operations for this component is almost more difficult than pulling down menus and filling out dialog boxes. The gist of this control's operation is that the control asynchronously notifies its container of data. The antenna that the container selects determines the interval at which the control notifies its container. The control also asynchronously notifies its container of various thermal conditions. If the control sends too much data in a short amount of time, it overheats and stops the data collection operation.

The SetAntenna method allows you to select one of three antennas, whose values are, oddly enough, one, two, and three.

```
SCODE CMFCActiveXCtrl::SetAntenna(short Antenna)
{
    // the antenna selection identifies the supported data rate
    m_nAntenna = Antenna;
    switch(Antenna)
    {
    case 1:
        m_nDataRate = 100;
        break;
    case 2:
        m_nDataRate = 10;
        break;
    default:
        m_nDataRate = 5;
        break;
    }

    InvalidateControl();
    SetModifiedFlag();

    return S_OK;
}
```

The antenna setting directly affects the data rate of the component. A setting of one yields the highest data rate, three the lowest.

The m_AcquireData Boolean property turns data collection on and off. Setting this variable to a TRUE state establishes a timer that results in data generation as a function of the current data rate selection.

```
void CMFCActiveXCtrl::OnAcquireDataChanged()
{
    if (m_acquireData)
    {
        SetTimer(3442, (1000/m_nDataRate)*500, NULL);
    }
    else
    {
        KillTimer(3442);
    }
    SetModifiedFlag();
    InvalidateControl();
}
```

The m_BufferSize property specifies the limit of data that is collected before it is returned to the container. The DataStream event returns data to your container, and the ThermalValue reports a temperature condition as a short between the values of one and three.

```
void CMFCActiveXCtrl::OnTimer(UINT nIDEvent)
{
    if (nIDEvent == 3442)
    {
        CString sData;

        // create data stream
        if ((m_nDataCount % 2))
            sData = "1";
        else
            sData = "0";
        ++m_nDataCount;

        // convert data stream to BSTR
        BSTR bstrData = sData.AllocSysString();

        // issue event
        FireDataStream(bstrData);

        // thermal values based on how much "work" is being performed
        DWORD dwCurrentTick = ::GetTickCount();
        if ((dwCurrentTick - dwLastTick) < 3000)
        {
            FireThermalValue(1);
            m_nDataCount = 501;
            m_nThermal = 3;
        }
        else if ((dwCurrentTick - dwLastTick) < 6000)
        {
            FireThermalValue(2);
            m_nThermal = 2;
        }
        else if ((dwCurrentTick - dwLastTick) < 10000)
        {
            FireThermalValue(3);
            m_nThermal = 1;
        }

        // store tick count
        dwLastTick = dwCurrentTick;

        // check maximum transmission
        if (m_nDataCount > 500)
        {
            m_acquireData = false;
            m_nDataCount = 0;
            OnAcquireDataChanged();
        }

        SetModifiedFlag();
```

```
        InvalidateControl();
        COleControl::OnTimer(nIDEvent);
    }
}
```

Finally, you override the OnDraw function to provide visual feedback of your control's state. The background of the control is green, yellow, or red, indicating the thermal state of the control. When the control reaches the red state, the data collection is shut down. The control displays two labels: Power and Antenna. A green or red rectangle follows the Power label. Green indicates the control is collecting data, and red indicates data collection is off. Blue rectangles follow the Antenna label. Three blue rectangles indicate that antenna three is in use, two blue rectangles indicate antenna two is in use, and so on.

```
void CMFCActiveXCtrl::OnDraw(
            CDC* pdc, const CRect& rcBounds, const CRect& rcInvalid)
{
    // the background of the control represents the thermal indication
    switch (m_nThermal)
    {
    case 1:
        pdc->FillSolidRect((LPCRECT)rcBounds, COLORREF(0x000000ff));
        break;
    case 2:
        pdc->FillSolidRect((LPCRECT)rcBounds, COLORREF(0x0000ffff));
        break;
    case 3:
        pdc->FillSolidRect((LPCRECT)rcBounds, COLORREF(0x0000ff00));
        break;
    }

    // provide a white area for the indicators
    CRect rcEmpty(rcBounds);
    rcEmpty.top = 9;
    rcEmpty.bottom = 25;
    rcEmpty.left = 9;
    rcEmpty.right = 92;
    pdc->FillSolidRect((LPCRECT)rcEmpty,COLORREF(0x000ffffff));
    rcEmpty.top = 29;
    rcEmpty.bottom = 45;
    rcEmpty.left = 9;
    rcEmpty.right = 136;
    pdc->FillSolidRect((LPCRECT)rcEmpty,COLORREF(0x000ffffff));

    // indicator labels
    pdc->SelectObject(::GetStockObject(ANSI_VAR_FONT));
    pdc->TextOut(rcBounds.left+10, rcBounds.top+10,"Power", 5);
    pdc->TextOut(rcBounds.left+10, rcBounds.top+30,"Antenna", 7);

    // draw power indicator
```

```
CRect rcPower(rcBounds);
rcPower.top += 12;
rcPower.bottom = rcPower.top + 10;
rcPower.left = 70;
rcPower.right = rcPower.left + 10;
if (m_acquireData)
    pdc->FillSolidRect((LPCRECT)rcPower,COLORREF(0x0000ff00));
else
    pdc->FillSolidRect((LPCRECT)rcPower,COLORREF(0x000000ff));

// draw antenna indicator
CRect rcTemp(rcBounds);
rcTemp.top += 32;
rcTemp.bottom = rcTemp.top+10;
rcTemp.left +=70;
for (int i=0; i<m_nAntenna; ++i)
{
    rcTemp.right = rcTemp.left + 10;
    pdc->FillSolidRect((LPCRECT)rcTemp,COLORREF(0x00ee0000));
    rcTemp.left += 25;
}
}
```

The constructor initializes the default values for various data members of the control.

```
CMFCActiveXCtrl::CMFCActiveXCtrl()
{
    InitializeIIDs(&IID_DMFCActiveX, &IID_DMFCActiveXEvents);

    // Initialize your control's instance data here.
    m_nDataRate = 100;
    m_nAntenna = 1;
    m_nDataCount = 0;
    m_bufferSize = 5;
    m_nThermal = 3;
}
```

You can exercise the control using the ActiveX Control Test Container. This utility is available from the Tools menu. Insert the control using the Insert New Control option from the Edit menu (see Figure 14.17).

FIGURE 14.17

Inserting the MFCActiveX control.

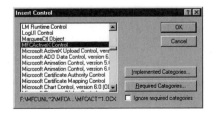

14

MFC ACTIVEX CONTROLS

Locate the MFCActiveX Control and click OK. The control will appear in the application's view window (see Figure 14.18).

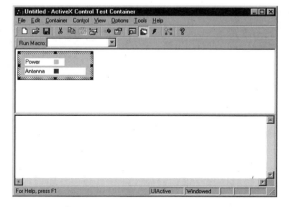

If the control is not active, select it and select the Invoke Methods dialog from the Control menu. Changing the antenna causes the corresponding number of blue indicators to appear next to the antenna label. Select the SetAntenna method, and enter a number between one and three in the Parameter Value field. Press Set Value and Invoke (see Figure 14.19).

Figure 14.19
Invoking the
SetAntenna
method.

You will see the control update itself (see Figure 14.20).

To start the radar-mapping functions, select AcquireData (PropPut). Set the Parameter Value to one or any positive number. Click Invoke, and the bottom window of the test container application will begin reporting events that the control fires (see Figure 14.21).

FIGURE 14.20

An updated MFCActiveX control view.

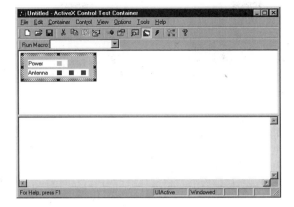

FIGURE 14.21

The MFCActiveX control is firing events.

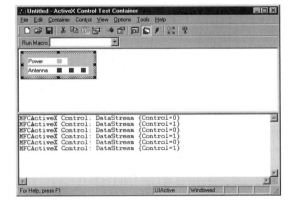

A Quick ATL Port

Now you will build the same control using ATL. The steps you take are similar to those in constructing an MFC control. ATL supports an application builder wizard and offers helper dialogs for defining methods, properties, and events. This project's name is ATLActiveX (see Figure 14.22).

Accept the default wizard values, allow AppWizard to generate the code, and switch the workspace window to the Class View pane. Clicking the right mouse button on ATLActiveX classes displays a context menu with the New ATL Object option (see Figure 14.23).

FIGURE 14.22

*Creating the
ATLActiveX
project.*

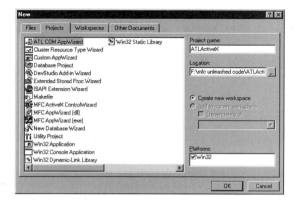

FIGURE 14.23

*Creating a new
ATL object from
the context menu.*

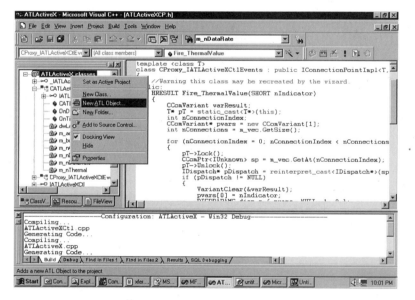

The ATL Object Wizard offers a category list on the left and an object list on the right. Select the Controls category and the Full Control object. The name for the class is ATLActiveXCtl. Switching to the Attributes tab, you select Support Connection Points (see Figure 14.24). This allows you to define control events in an outgoing interface. You can take the defaults for all other values and select OK to generate code.

The wizard creates a new class, CATLActiveXCtl, and a new interface, _IATLActiveXCtlEvents. You add the method and properties in a manner that is similar to the procedures you follow when creating an MFC control. Right-clicking the

IATLActiveXCtl interface entry in the Class View pane of the project window displays a context menu, allowing you to add methods and properties. Follow the steps for adding the methods and properties to the MFCActiveX project.

FIGURE 14.24

The Attributes tab in the ATL Object Wizard.

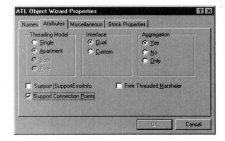

Now it is time to add events to the control. Identifying events in an ATL control is where things differ significantly from the steps you follow for an MFC control. A quick check of the context menu reveals that there is no Add Event menu. Instead you add events using the Add Method menu on an outgoing interface, in this case _IATLActiveXCtlEvents. Add two events with the same signatures as in the MFCActiveX project. The resulting .IDL file will appear as follows:

```
// ATLActiveX.idl : IDL source for ATLActiveX.dll
//

// This file will be processed by the MIDL tool to
// produce the type library (ATLActiveX.tlb) and marshalling code.

import "oaidl.idl";
import "ocidl.idl";
#include "olectl.h"


    [
        object,
        uuid(D33E5F63-CC5B-11D2-8FBA-00105A5D8D6C),
        dual,
        helpstring("IATLActiveXCtl Interface"),
        pointer_default(unique)
    ]
    interface IATLActiveXCtl : IDispatch
    {
        [propget, id(1), helpstring("property AcquireData")]
         HRESULT AcquireData([out, retval] BOOL *pVal);
        [propput, id(1), helpstring("property AcquireData")]
         HRESULT AcquireData([in] BOOL newVal);
        [propget, id(2), helpstring("property BufferSize")]
         HRESULT BufferSize([out, retval] short *pVal);
```

```
            [propput, id(2), helpstring("property BufferSize")]
             HRESULT BufferSize([in] short newVal);
            [id(3), helpstring("method SetAntenna")]
             HRESULT SetAntenna(short Antenna);
        };

    [
        uuid(D33E5F57-CC5B-11D2-8FBA-00105A5D8D6C),
        version(1.0),
        helpstring("ATLActiveX 1.0 Type Library")
    ]
    library ATLACTIVEXLib
    {
        importlib("stdole32.tlb");
        importlib("stdole2.tlb");

        [
            uuid(D33E5F64-CC5B-11D2-8FBA-00105A5D8D6C),
            helpstring("_IATLActiveXCtlEvents Interface")
        ]
        dispinterface _IATLActiveXCtlEvents
        {
            properties:
            methods:
            [id(1), helpstring("method DataStream")]
             HRESULT DataStream(BSTR Control);
            [id(2), helpstring("method ThermalValue")]
             HRESULT ThermalValue(short Indicator);
        };

        [
            uuid(D33E5F55-CC5B-11D2-8FBA-00105A5D8D6C),
            helpstring("ATLActiveXCtl Class")
        ]
        coclass ATLActiveXCtl
        {
            [default] interface IATLActiveXCtl;
            [default, source] dispinterface _IATLActiveXCtlEvents;
        };
    };
```

Build the project. This ensures that the .IDL is compiled, which is necessary before proceeding.

The second step is to implement the connection point, which results in the creation of a proxy class. Right-click on the CATLActiveXCtl class and select the Implement Connection Point menu option. This displays the dialog shown in Figure 14.25.

FIGURE 14.25

The Implement Connection Point dialog.

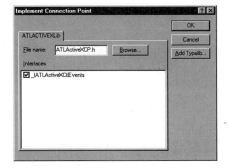

The dialog contains an entry for the _IATLActiveXCtlEvents interface. Select the interface and click OK. The wizard will create a new class, CProxy_IATLActiveXCtlEvents, deriving from the IConnectionPointImpl template.

```cpp
template <class T>
class CProxy_IATLActiveXCtlEvents : public IConnectionPointImpl<T, \
&DIID__IATLActiveXCtlEvents, CComDynamicUnkArray>
{
    //Warning this class may be recreated by the wizard.
public:
    HRESULT Fire_DataStream(BSTR Control)
    {
        CComVariant varResult;
        T* pT = static_cast<T*>(this);
        int nConnectionIndex;
        CComVariant* pvars = new CComVariant[1];
        int nConnections = m_vec.GetSize();

        for (nConnectionIndex = 0; nConnectionIndex < nConnections; \
             nConnectionIndex++)
        {
            pT->Lock();
            CComPtr<IUnknown> sp = m_vec.GetAt(nConnectionIndex);
            pT->Unlock();
            IDispatch* pDispatch = reinterpret_cast<IDispatch*>(sp.p);
            if (pDispatch != NULL)
            {
                VariantClear(&varResult);
                pvars[0] = Control;
                DISPPARAMS disp = { pvars, NULL, 1, 0 };
                pDispatch->Invoke(0x1, IID_NULL, LOCALE_USER_DEFAULT, \
                        DISPATCH_METHOD, &disp, &varResult, NULL, NULL);
            }
        }
        delete[] pvars;
        return varResult.scode;
```

14

MFC ACTIVEX
CONTROLS

```
    }
    HRESULT Fire_ThermalValue(SHORT Indicator)
    {
        CComVariant varResult;
        T* pT = static_cast<T*>(this);
        int nConnectionIndex;
        CComVariant* pvars = new CComVariant[1];
        int nConnections = m_vec.GetSize();

        for (nConnectionIndex = 0; nConnectionIndex < nConnections; \
            nConnectionIndex++)
        {
            pT->Lock();
            CComPtr<IUnknown> sp = m_vec.GetAt(nConnectionIndex);
            pT->Unlock();
            IDispatch* pDispatch = reinterpret_cast<IDispatch*>(sp.p);
            if (pDispatch != NULL)
            {
                VariantClear(&varResult);
                pvars[0] = Indicator;
                DISPPARAMS disp = { pvars, NULL, 1, 0 };
                pDispatch->Invoke(0x2, IID_NULL, LOCALE_USER_DEFAULT,
                    DISPATCH_METHOD, &disp, &varResult, NULL, NULL);
            }
        }
        delete[] pvars;
        return varResult.scode;

    }
};
```

The final steps involve cutting and pasting the application code from the MFC control to the appropriate places in the ATL control. You add the timer callback function by selecting the Add Windows Message Handler option from the CATLActiveXCtl class object (see Figure 14.26).

FIGURE 14.26

Adding an event handler for the timer message.

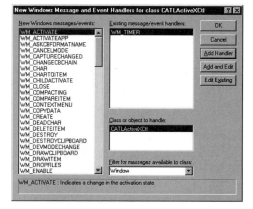

Select the `WM_TIMER` message and proceed to edit the handler. There are a few porting issues in moving the code from MFC to ATL. Here is a summary of these issues:

- Replace `InvalidateControl()` calls with `FireViewChange();`.

- The device context is not a CDC object. Replace `pdc->` references with GDI-level calls that accept `di.hdcDraw` as the first parameter.

- Replace `FillSolidRect` with `FillRect`, and create your own solid brushes with `CreateSolidBrush`. Delete the brush with a `DeleteObject` call.

- Replace `FireThermalValue` with `Fire_ThermalValue`.

You can exercise the control using the ActiveX Control Test Container.

Summary

In this chapter, you were made aware of the different "faces" a control has to offer: run-time and design time. You have seen how OLE control technology leverages automation to expose methods and properties. Finally, you have experimented with control creation using both MFC and ATL.

14

MFC ACTIVEX CONTROLS

MFC ActiveX Control Containers

by Gene Olafsen

IN THIS CHAPTER

This chapter describes the function and implementation of OLE containers. In previous chapters, you built various COM servers: active document, automation, and controls. With the exception of automation servers, there is still a need to explore client-side issues for active documents and ActiveX control containment.

Active Document Container

An *active document container* is an application that supports the in-place activation of an active document server. The two most popular active document containers are the Microsoft Office Binder and Internet Explorer. Although the Office Binder application has been shipping for a number of years, unless your line of business calls for its use, you probably ignore this application when it is installed with Office. The purpose of the binder program is to organize "documents" of various types: Word, Excel, and PowerPoint, by project. Thus, when you want to work on the "TideWater" account, you simply open the binder project, and the associated files appear in a pane that anchors to the left of the application while Word, Excel, and so on, activate in the remaining client area.

Likewise, Internet Explorer is an active document container. You can demonstrate this for yourself by entering the path and name of a file in the Address field, and Explorer will activate the appropriate application in the space usually reserved for the HTML content. Notice as well that IE's help menu merges with Word, producing a composite menu of both applications. See Figure 15.1 for an illustration of this document containment and menu merging.

FIGURE 15.1

An active document container.

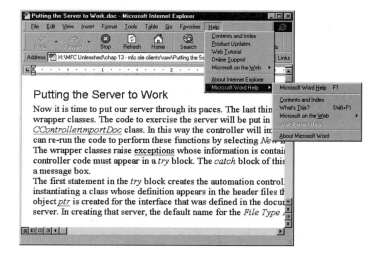

The active document container specification is a variation on the original OLE document container specification. The major difference is that active document server objects must populate the client area of the container application when they become in-place active. Thus, your container adopts the menus and toolbars of the document server and presents them as its own. The details of merging menus and toolbars are not a trivial operation. However, MFC provides a number of classes that make this behavior nearly painless.

Applications that claim active document containment must implement a number of interfaces. These interfaces represent the contract guaranteeing that the necessary functionality is available at such time as the document server requires it.

Storage

A container is responsible for providing a document server with a place, usually a file, to store its contents. In the world of COM, the concept of a container *providing* a server with a file into which it stores its contents indicates that the container provides an IStorage interface.

The IStorage interface is central to the concept of COM's *structured storage*. Structured storage manages data in a hierarchical format within a single physical file. The components of structured storage are *storages* and *streams*. Storages can be thought of as directories in a traditional file system. Storages can contain other storages and/or can contain streams. This is akin to a directory containing other directories and/or files. Thus, streams can be thought of as files within a traditional file system. Streams contain an object's data (see Figure 15.2).

FIGURE 15.2
Storage and stream relationship.

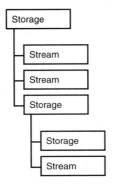

It should not surprise you that the IStorage interface provides the methods and properties for creating and modifying storage objects. See Table 15.1 for a list and description of the IStorage interface's member functions.

TABLE 15.1   THE METHODS OF THE `IStorage` INTERFACE AND THEIR DESCRIPTIONS

Method	Description
CreateStream	Creates and opens a stream object in this storage object
OpenStream	Opens an existing stream object within this storage object
CreateStorage	Creates and opens a new storage object within this storage object
OpenStorage	Opens an existing storage object
CopyTo	Copies the contents of an open storage object into another storage object
MoveElementTo	Copies or moves a storage or stream from this storage object to another storage object
Commit	Completes an operation on a transacted storage object
Revert	Discards an operation on a transacted storage object
EnumElements	Returns an enumerator object of storages and streams in this object
DestroyElement	Removes the specified storage or stream from this storage object
RenameElement	Renames the specified storage or stream in this storage object
SetElementTimes	Sets the various time properties of this storage object
SetClass	Allows you to assign a specific CLSID to this storage object
SetStateBits	Stores up to 32 bits of state information in this storage object
Stat	Retrieves STATSTG for this storage object

You can glean a lot of understanding of this interface by reviewing the methods. There are methods to create, rename, enumerate, and delete objects. These operations correspond nicely to those operations you perform using either a command-line interface or graphical shell of a traditional file system.

The `Stat` method enables you to retrieve information that is similar to that which you retrieve using the `_stat` runtime function. The properties that `_stat` returns reside in the STATSTG structure, which is defined as follows:

```
typedef struct tagSTATSTG
{
    LPWSTR          pwcsName;
    DWORD           type;
    ULARGE_INTEGER  cbSize;
    FILETIME        mtime;
    FILETIME        ctime;
```

```
    FILETIME          atime;
    DWORD             grfMode;
    DWORD             grfLocksSupported;
    CLSID             clsid;
    DWORD             grfStateBits;
    DWORD             reserved;
} STATSTG;
```

Objects that implement the IStream interface support operations that are similar to those you perform on files. Such operations include reading and writing data, as well as the file pointer type operations you perform with seek. See Table 15.2 for a list and description of the IStream interface's member functions.

TABLE 15.2   THE METHODS OF THE IStream INTERFACE AND THEIR DESCRIPTIONS

Method	Description
Read	Reads the specified number of bytes
Write	Writes the specified number of bytes
Seek	Changes the seek pointer to a new location relative to the beginning of the stream, the end of the stream, or the current seek pointer
SetSize	Changes the size of the stream object
CopyTo	Copies a specified number of bytes to another stream
Commit	Completes a transaction operation
Revert	Cancels a transaction operation
LockRegion	Restricts access to a specified range of bytes in the stream
UnlockRegion	Removes any access restrictions to a specified range of bytes
Stat	Retrieves the STATSTG structure for this stream
Clone	Creates a new stream object that references the same bytes as this stream

You must implement the IPersistStorage interface in your container application. This interface allows you to pass an object that derives from IStorage to an active document server. In this manner, a container application can offer persistence to the document servers it contains, without actually knowing anything about the file format or contents. This interface is one of the cornerstones of OLE structured storage. See Table 15.3 for a list and description of the IPersistStorage interface's member functions.

15

**MFC ACTIVEX
CONTROL
CONTAINERS**

TABLE 15.3 THE METHODS OF THE `IPersistStorage` INTERFACE AND THEIR DESCRIPTIONS

Method	Description
IsDirty	Indicates whether the object has changed
InitNew	Initializes a new storage object
Load	Initializes an object from its existing storage
Save	Saves an object and any nested objects
SaveCompleted	Notifies the object that it can enter a state to accept changes
HandsOffStorage	Instructs the object to release all storage objects that have been passed to it by its container

You see that by the interface for `IPersistStorage` there are vanilla `Load` and `Save` methods that are content-independent. As a general rule, a container application does not call these methods directly; instead, it calls `OleLoad` and `OleSave`. These functions create uninitialized object instances and call the `Commit` function where appropriate.

Site Objects

It should not come as a surprise to you that it is important for a document server to be able to obtain information about its container. The `IOleClientSite` interface defines methods that offer a server just such information. Your container application must create an object of `IOleClientSite` for each server that it contains. For active document containers, there is only a single instance because the container allows only a single active server at a time. This interface must also be present in ActiveX containers, and an object based on this interface must be available to each control that the container embeds. See Table 15.4 for a list and description of the `IOleClientSite` interface's member functions.

TABLE 15.4 THE METHODS OF THE `IOleClientSite` INTERFACE AND THEIR DESCRIPTIONS

Method	Description
SaveObject	Saves embedded object
GetMoniker	Requests object's moniker
GetContainer	Requests pointer to object's container
ShowObject	Asks container to display object
OnShowWindow	Notifies container when object becomes visible or invisible
RequestNewObjectLayout	Asks container to resize display site

Communication between the container and the objects it contains is possible by method invocation on an interface. Responding to asynchronous events requires a different approach. Therefore, the container application must implement IAdviseSink to receive data change notifications, presentation changes, and so on, from document and control server objects. See Table 15.5 for a list and description of the IAdviseSink interface's member functions.

TABLE 15.5 THE METHODS OF THE IAdviseSink INTERFACE AND THEIR DESCRIPTIONS

Method	Description
OnDataChange	Advises that data has changed
OnViewChange	Advises that view of object has changed
OnRename	Advises that name of object has changed
OnSave	Advises that object has been saved to disk
OnClose	Advises that object has been closed

In-Place Activation

When it comes to in-place activation, the container must give up a lot of control in order to belong to the active document container club. Activation of server objects leads to an extensive series of user interface changes; your application toolbars and menus will augment with the document server's menus and toolbars. Implement this interface in the site objects that the container provides for each document server.

TABLE 15.6 THE METHODS OF THE IOleInPlaceSite INTERFACE AND THEIR DESCRIPTIONS

Method	Description
CanInPlaceActivate	This function allows the container to process an activation request, returning TRUE if the server can activate.
OnInPlaceActivate	Notification to the container that an embedded object is activating.
OnUIActivate	Notification to the container that its menu is about to be replaced with a composite menu.
GetWindowContext	Enables an in-place object to retrieve window interfaces that form at the window object hierarchy, and the position in the parent window to locate the object's in-place activation window.

continues

15

TABLE 15.6   CONTINUED

Method	Description
Scroll	Specifies the number of pixels the container will scroll the server.
OnUIDeactivate	The container can now reinstate the interface it had before the in-place server went active.
OnInPlaceDeactivate	The container receives this notification that the in-place object is no longer active.
DiscardUndoState	Instructs the container to discard its undo state.
DeactivateAndUndo	Deactivate the object and revert to undo state.
OnPosRectChange	Object's width and/or height have changed.

You already know that each document server requires a site object to help manage interaction with the container. There is, however, an integration issue with the container application's frame window. The frame is responsible for managing menus, keyboard accelerators, the status bar, and so on. For in-place activation to succeed in a visual sense, it must be able to wrest some control over these resources from the container. The IOleInPlaceFrame interface provides methods to achieve these activation objectives. See Table 15.7 for a list and description of the IOleInPlaceFrame interface's member functions.

TABLE 15.7   THE METHODS OF THE IOleInPlaceFrame INTERFACE AND THEIR DESCRIPTIONS

Method	Description
InsertMenus	Allows a container to insert menus into the in-place composite menu
SetMenu	Activates the composite menu in the container's frame
RemoveMenus	Allows a container to remove menus from the in-place composite menu
SetStatusText	Sets and displays status text
EnableModeless	Enables or disables modeless dialog boxes
TranslateAccelerator	Translates container-frame accelerator keystrokes

Document Extensions

There are a few differences between traditional OLE document servers and the newer breed of active document servers. You can broadly define these extensions as a means to establish better lines of communication between container and server.

The IOleDocumentSite interface instructs the container to bypass the normal activation sequence and requests activation directly from the document site. See Table 15.8 for a list and description of the IOleDocumentSite interface's member functions.

TABLE 15.8 THE IOleDocumentSite INTERFACE METHOD AND ITS DESCRIPTION

Method	Description
ActivateMe	Activates the server as a document object as opposed to an in-place active object

The IOleCommandTarget interface is extremely helpful because it allows the container and the document server to dispatch commands to each other. With this interface, a container can leave in place its Print, Save, New, and so on, toolbar buttons and menus, allowing the server to respond appropriately. See Table 15.9 for a list and description of the IOleCommandTarget interface's member functions.

TABLE 15.9 THE METHODS OF THE IOleCommandTarget INTERFACE AND THEIR DESCRIPTIONS

Method	Description
QueryStatus	Use this command to identify the supported commands.
Exec	Execute the specified command.

The last interface to consider with active document containment is IContinueCallback. Generally, asynchronous event processing is the domain of outgoing interfaces and connection points. Active document containers are given a break with this lightweight callback mechanism for interruptible processes. See Table 15.10 for a list and description of the IContinueCallback interface's member functions.

TABLE 15.10 THE METHODS OF THE IContinueCallback INTERFACE AND THEIR DESCRIPTIONS

Method	Description
FContinue	Identifies whether an operation should continue
FContinuePrinting	Identifies whether a printing operation should continue

15

MFC ACTIVEX CONTROL CONTAINERS

Building the Simplest Active Document Container

Constructing an active document container is straightforward, and AppWizard offers much help with the generation of skeleton code. The project name is ActiveDocContainer (see Figure 15.3).

FIGURE 15.3

The ActiveDoc-Container project.

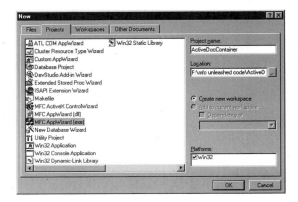

This application uses the single document interface (SDI), and it is important to specify Active Document Container support on the third wizard step page (see Figure 15.4).

FIGURE 15.4

Project options.

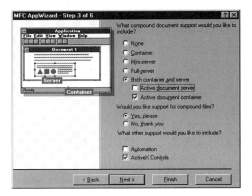

Accepting the defaults for the remaining options, AppWizard will proceed to generate code for you, which results in the creation of almost two dozen files.

You end up with the standard application, frame, document, and view files: ActiveDocContainer.cpp, MainFrm.cpp, ActiveDocContainerDoc, and ActiveDocContainerView. In addition, the wizard generates files for an in-place frame and OLE document support: IpFrame.cpp, CntrlItem.cpp, and SrvrItem.cpp.

Compiling this code yields a simple application that supports the embedding of any registered document server. Run the application and insert the active document that you built in Chapter 12, "MFC OLE Servers" (see Figure 15.5).

FIGURE 15.5

Active document server in container.

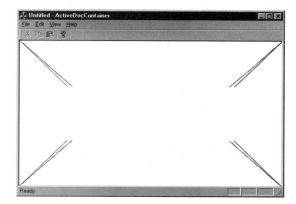

OLE Controls

ActiveX controls are probably among the most recognizable COM objects. In introducing the OLE control architecture (the original name for ActiveX controls), Microsoft offers Visual C++ developers a taste of the component good life, which Visual Basic developers had enjoyed for a while with VBXs. Although the VBX architecture was not COM-based, it offered Visual Basic developers to leverage third-party components in a visual development environment. Unfortunately, VBXs were not available to the Visual C++ development environment. This probably turned out for the best, because in developing a COM strategy, Microsoft came up with a platform-independent, language-neutral replacement—OLE controls.

Visual C++ is quite adept at helping you build applications that host ActiveX controls. The development environment provides you almost the same level of graphical application development that you find in Visual Basic. The term *control* is somewhat misleading, though. When you think of Windows controls, you probably envision list boxes and combo boxes. Although ActiveX controls can have visual representation and behave in a manner similar to these dialog controls, they don't have to. In fact, many controls forego a runtime visual interface and offer services that you do not have to write otherwise. Such services can include compression algorithms or communication protocols.

There is an AppWizard option for supporting ActiveX controls at project creation time, but adding ActiveX control support to an existing project is not difficult.

Adding Containment to an Existing Project

The AppWizard provides an ever-increasing number of options that influence the initial skeleton code generation. In many cases, ignoring an option, or selecting the wrong option, results in code that is difficult at best to massage into a state that offers a compatible solution. If you didn't select ActiveX containment during project creation, you are not far from where you want to be. Essentially, you just add a single function call and include the appropriate header file:

```
#include <Afxdisp.h>

BOOL CContainerApp::InitInstance()
{
    AfxEnableControlContainer();
}
```

ActiveX Container

This section focuses on static containment of ActiveX controls. Different from the active document container that allows you to select the document server to embed at runtime, the containers you develop for ActiveX controls are "wired" for specific controls. There are many similarities between automation controllers and ActiveX control containers. ActiveX controls employ `IDispatch` communication for properties and methods, in a manner identical to automation. Additionally, you use the same MFC functions (`SetProperty`, `GetProperty`, `InvokeHelper`) to control the ActiveX component.

The similarities end with the actual class that wraps the automation server of active control. Whereas in an automation controller the `COleDispatchDriver` class is the base class, control containers use the `CWnd` class.

```
class IDrive : public COleDispatchDriver
{
public:
    IDrive();
    virtual ~IDrive();

    // interface method
    void TrackInformation(short nIndex, BSTR * bstrTitle);
```

```
    // property methods
    short GetAlbumLength();
        void  PutAlbumLength(short nLength);
};

class CMFCActiveX : public CWnd
{
protected:
    DECLARE_DYNCREATE(CMFCActiveX)
public:
// Constructors

// Attributes (properties)
public:
    BOOL GetAcquireData();
    void SetAcquireData(BOOL);

// Operations (methods)
public:
    SCODE SetAntenna(short Antenna);
    void AboutBox();
};
```

You might have a hard time believing that the lowly CWnd class has anything to do with OLE. However, it supports a number of control containment functions that you never took notice of.

Method	Description
SetProperty	Sets an OLE control property
OnAmbientProperty	Implements ambient property values
GetControlUnknown	Retrieves a pointer to an unknown OLE control
GetProperty	Retrieves an OLE control property
InvokeHelper	Invokes an OLE control method or property

Two methods that are not found in COleDispatchDriver are GetControlUnknown and OnAmbientProperty.

Just as a number of wizards and helper dialogs are available to you for automation controller construction, so too are a number of tools that make it easy to incorporate ActiveX controls into your application. There are a number of ways to use ActiveX controls in a project. The first approach that you will see involves constructing a proxy based on the CWnd class. You then instantiate an object of this type and add it manually to a window or dialog. The second approach is more interactive, where you add the control directly to a dialog, in the same manner that you add edit controls and list boxes.

15

MFC ACTIVEX
CONTROL
CONTAINERS

Create a project whose name is `ControlProxy` and which implements a Single Document Interface (SDI) (see Figure 15.6). Accept all the other defaults that AppWizard supplies. Step 3 of this process includes ActiveX support.

FIGURE 15.6

The ControlProxy project.

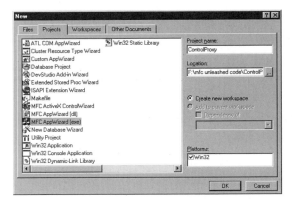

The next step is to identify the control you want to incorporate into your project. Visual C++ provides a tool to select an ActiveX component and construct a proxy class. The tool that supports this operation has gone through changes with almost each release of Visual C++ because support for ActiveX controls was introduced. Open the Components and Controls Gallery by selecting Add To Project from the Project menu (see Figure 15.7). This will produce a submenu with a Components and Controls selection.

FIGURE 15.7

The Add To Project menu command.

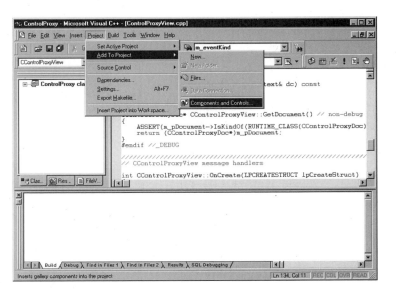

The dialog, which is really just a glorified File Open dialog, contains two subdirectories: Registered ActiveX Controls and Visual C++ Components. These directories reside below your Visual Studio install directory and contain shortcuts to the appropriate items (see Figure 15.8).

FIGURE 15.8

The Components and Controls Gallery dialog.

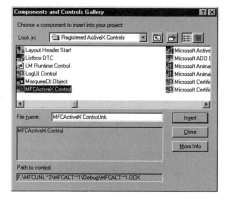

Select the MFCActiveX control that you developed in the previous chapter and click Insert. A dialog box will appear with a list of incoming interfaces from which you select the ones for which the tool will generate proxy code (see Figure 15.9).

FIGURE 15.9

The Confirm Classes dialog.

Incoming interfaces are those that expose methods and properties. The incoming interface for the MFCActiveX component offers two properties and a single method.

```
[ uuid(D33E5F34-CC5B-11D2-8FBA-00105A5D8D6C),
helpstring("Dispatch interface for MFCActiveX Control"), hidden ]
dispinterface _DMFCActiveX
{
    properties:
        // NOTE - ClassWizard will maintain property information here.
```

```
        //    Use extreme caution when editing this section.
        //{{AFX_ODL_PROP(CMFCActiveXCtrl)
        [id(1)] boolean AcquireData;
        [id(2)] short BufferSize;
        //}}AFX_ODL_PROP

    methods:
     // NOTE - ClassWizard will maintain method information here.
        //    Use extreme caution when editing this section.
        //{{AFX_ODL_METHOD(CMFCActiveXCtrl)
        [id(3)] SCODE SetAntenna(short Antenna);
        //}}AFX_ODL_METHOD

        [id(DISPID_ABOUTBOX)] void AboutBox();
    }
```

The properties, which you are familiar with, are `AcquireData` and `BufferSize`. The single method is `SetAntenna`. This interface appears in the `coclass` definition as an incoming interface whose name is `_DMFCActiveX`.

```
[ uuid(D33E5F36-CC5B-11D2-8FBA-00105A5D8D6C),
  helpstring("MFCActiveX Control"), control ]
coclass MFCActiveX
{
    [default] dispinterface _DMFCActiveX;
    [default, source] dispinterface _DMFCActiveXEvents;
};
```

In addition, the Confirm Classes dialog allows you to override the default declaration and implementation file names. Dismissing the dialog causes Visual C++ to generate the following class definition:

```
/////////////////////////////////////////////////////////////////
// CMFCActiveX wrapper class

class CMFCActiveX : public CWnd
{
protected:
    DECLARE_DYNCREATE(CMFCActiveX)
public:
    CLSID const& GetClsid()
    {
        static CLSID const clsid
            = { 0xd33e5f36, 0xcc5b, 0x11d2,
                { 0x8f, 0xba, 0x0, 0x10, 0x5a, 0x5d, 0x8d, 0x6c } };
        return clsid;
    }
    virtual BOOL Create(LPCTSTR lpszClassName,
        LPCTSTR lpszWindowName, DWORD dwStyle,
        const RECT& rect,
```

```
                CWnd* pParentWnd, UINT nID,
                CCreateContext* pContext = NULL)
        { return CreateControl(GetClsid(), lpszWindowName,
                                dwStyle, rect, pParentWnd, nID); }

        BOOL Create(LPCTSTR lpszWindowName, DWORD dwStyle,
            const RECT& rect, CWnd* pParentWnd, UINT nID,
            CFile* pPersist = NULL, BOOL bStorage = FALSE,
            BSTR bstrLicKey = NULL)
        { return CreateControl(GetClsid(), lpszWindowName,
                                dwStyle, rect, pParentWnd, nID,
            pPersist, bStorage, bstrLicKey); }

// Attributes
public:
    BOOL GetAcquireData();
    void SetAcquireData(BOOL);
    short GetBufferSize();
    void SetBufferSize(short);

// Operations
public:
    SCODE SetAntenna(short Antenna);
    void AboutBox();
};
```

The class contains sections that define the methods and properties as well as generating
the code necessary to construct a control. The CWnd class defines a virtual Create function. The wrapper overrides this function and calls CreateControl with the appropriate
CLSID. Thus, all you have to do to display the control is create an instance of the object
and then call the Create function.

The implementation code for each of the properties uses the CWnd GetProperty and
SetProperty functions. These functions simply require a DispID of the property to
access, the variant type identifier constant, and either the value to set or a variable of the
proper datatype to hold the value from an accessor.

```
//////////////////////////////////////////////////////////////////
// CMFCActiveX properties

BOOL CMFCActiveX::GetAcquireData()
{
    BOOL result;
    GetProperty(0x1, VT_BOOL, (void*)&result);
    return result;
}

void CMFCActiveX::SetAcquireData(BOOL propVal)
{
```

```
    SetProperty(0x1, VT_BOOL, propVal);
}

short CMFCActiveX::GetBufferSize()
{
    short result;
    GetProperty(0x2, VT_I2, (void*)&result);
    return result;
}

void CMFCActiveX::SetBufferSize(short propVal)
{
    SetProperty(0x2, VT_I2, propVal);
}
```

The single method relies on `InvokeHelper` to call a method on the ActiveX control. The `InvokeHelper` function is identical to the one that you use when invoking methods on an automation server.

```
///////////////////////////////////////////////////////////////////
// CMFCActiveX operations

SCODE CMFCActiveX::SetAntenna(short Antenna)
{
    SCODE result;
    static BYTE parms[] =
        VTS_I2;
    InvokeHelper(0x3, DISPATCH_METHOD, VT_ERROR,
                 (void*)&result, parms,
        Antenna);
    return result;
}
```

Now it is time to put the control to use. You will add code to the `Create` function of the `CControlProxyView` object. The class does not provide a handler for the `WM_CREATE` message by default so you must add one. Display the context menu for the `CControlProxyView` class in the ClassView pane of the Workspace window and select Add Windows Message Handler (see Figure 15.10).

Locate the `WM_CREATE` message and select Add and Edit (see Figure 15.11).

FIGURE 15.10
The ClassView context menu.

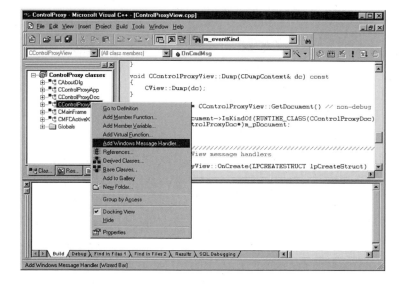

FIGURE 15.11
Windows message handler for `WM_CREATE`.

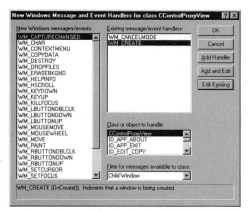

This operation generates code that calls the `CView` base class, returning a –1 value if there is a problem creating the window.

```
int CControlProxyView::OnCreate(LPCREATESTRUCT lpCreateStruct)
{
    if (CView::OnCreate(lpCreateStruct) == -1)
        return -1;
```

```
    // TODO: Add your specialized creation code here

    return 0;
}
```

Before you add code to create the ActiveX control, you will add a member variable to the CControlProxyView header file to contain the object. Display the context menu for this class again and select Add Member Variable. The variable type is CMFCActiveX; give it the name mycontrol and allow public access (see Figure 15.12).

FIGURE 15.12

The Add Member Variable dialog.

Now you must include the CControlProxy header before the ControlProxyView header or there will be no class definition for the compiler.

```
#include "stdafx.h"
#include "ControlProxy.h"

#include "ControlProxyDoc.h"
#include "MFCActiveX.h"
#include "ControlProxyView.h"
```

The final steps are to create the control and add it to the view window.

```
int CControlProxyView::OnCreate(LPCREATESTRUCT lpCreateStruct)
{
    if (CView::OnCreate(lpCreateStruct) == -1)
        return -1;

    CRect rect(10,10,150,70);
    mycontrol.Create(NULL, WS_VISIBLE, rect, this, 123);

    return 0;
}
```

You create the ActiveX control, oddly enough, using the Create function. The arguments to this function include the text appearing in the control (or NULL), various window style bits, the encompassing rectangle, the parent window, and a control ID.

You can run the program and see that it is indeed attached to the view window (see Figure 15.13). You can make additional method and property calls on the mycontrol class; however, you are missing event support. You can build the event map manually, but there is an easier way, as you will see in the next example. It is possible to put a wizard to work and have the event handlers stubbed for you.

FIGURE 15.13

The `MFCActiveX` *control in ControlProxy view.*

Control Containment and Events

In this next example, you will see how easy it is to add an ActiveX control to a dialog and use Visual C++ to aid in the creation of event handlers. This project's name is ControlDialog, and it is a dialog-based application (see Figure 15.14). The ActiveX Controls option is selected by default, so you can select the Finish option after you make the application type selection in step 2.

FIGURE 15.14

The ControlDialog project.

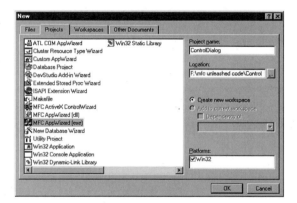

As soon as AppWizard is done generating code, it will display a dialog on which you begin placing controls. You can delete the static text control that says "TODO: Place dialog controls here." The first thing you will want to do is place the ActiveX control in the dialog. You can easily accomplish this by right-clicking over the dialog to display the context menu and selecting the Insert ActiveX Control menu command (see Figure 15.15).

FIGURE 15.15

The dialog context menu.

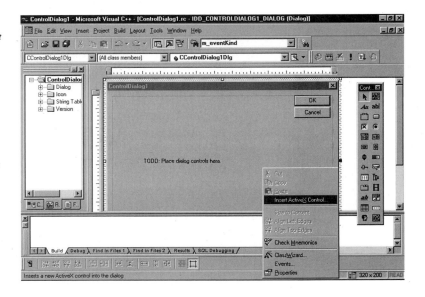

Locate the MFCActiveX Control entry in the list box and select OK (see Figure 15.16).

FIGURE 15.16

Inserting an ActiveX control.

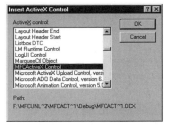

You can proceed to add additional controls for the purpose of activating the radar mapping component and selecting an antenna. Upon completion, your dialog might look like Figure 15.17.

FIGURE 15.17

The final dialog layout.

A check box will turn the system on and off. There are three possible antennas to select from. Three radio buttons represent these settings. The control fires events that represent the data feed and the onboard thermal conditions. The data feed values are added to a list box, and the thermal reading appears in a non-editable edit control.

The next step is to "wire" the dialog components together. Before you can make calls to and accept events from the MFCActiveX control, you must add it to your project. You can accomplish this by displaying ClassWizard and adding a member variable for the control (see Figure 15.18).

FIGURE 15.18

The ClassWizard Member Variables tab.

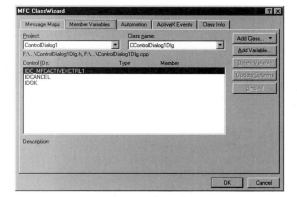

Select the control ID of the ActiveX control IDC_MFCACTIVEXCTRL1 and select Add Variable. Visual C++ responds with a dialog box indicating that the control is not in the project and it will generate a wrapper class for you. Selecting OK will cause the Confirm Classes dialog to appear (see Figure 15.19).

FIGURE 15.19

The Confirm Classes dialog.

This is the same dialog that you used in the previous project. Accept the defaults and select OK. The Add Member Variable dialog will appear (see Figure 15.20).

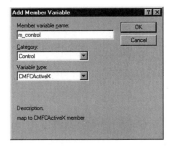

FIGURE 15.20

The Add Member Variable dialog.

You can name the variable m_control and select OK. Dismissing the ClassWizard dialog, you will see that a CMFCActiveX class is now part of the project. This class is a wrapper for the control, whose base class is CWnd and is identical to the class you used in the previous example.

```cpp
class CMFCActiveX : public CWnd
{
protected:
    DECLARE_DYNCREATE(CMFCActiveX)
public:
    CLSID const& GetClsid()
    {
        static CLSID const clsid
            = { 0xd33e5f36, 0xcc5b, 0x11d2,
{ 0x8f, 0xba, 0x0, 0x10, 0x5a, 0x5d, 0x8d, 0x6c } };
        return clsid;
    }
    virtual BOOL Create(LPCTSTR lpszClassName,
        LPCTSTR lpszWindowName, DWORD dwStyle,
        const RECT& rect,
        CWnd* pParentWnd, UINT nID,
        CCreateContext* pContext = NULL)
    { return CreateControl(GetClsid(), lpszWindowName,
                    dwStyle, rect, pParentWnd, nID); }

    BOOL Create(LPCTSTR lpszWindowName, DWORD dwStyle,
        const RECT& rect, CWnd* pParentWnd, UINT nID,
        CFile* pPersist = NULL, BOOL bStorage = FALSE,
        BSTR bstrLicKey = NULL)
    { return CreateControl(GetClsid(), lpszWindowName,
                    dwStyle, rect, pParentWnd, nID,
        pPersist, bStorage, bstrLicKey); }

// Attributes
public:
```

```
    BOOL GetAcquireData();
    void SetAcquireData(BOOL);
    short GetBufferSize();
    void SetBufferSize(short);

// Operations
public:
    SCODE SetAntenna(short Antenna);
    void AboutBox();
};
```

The final step is to respond to events from the ActiveX control. This control provides two events: `DataStream` and `ThermalValue`. You can establish handlers for these events by displaying the context menu for the ControlDialog in the resource editor and selecting the Events menu (see Figure 15.21).

FIGURE 15.21

The ClassView context menu with events.

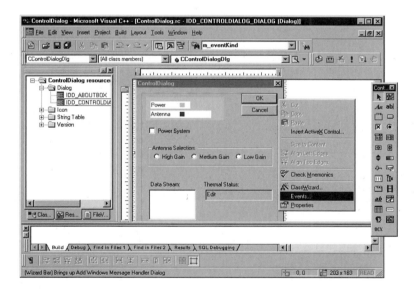

You are familiar with this dialog; it is the one you use to create handlers for window messages. You will notice, however, that the Class or Object to Handle list box contains the control ID for the ActiveX control (see Figure 15.22). Selecting this entry displays the two events this control supports in the list box to the left.

FIGURE 15.22

The event handler for the MFCActiveX control.

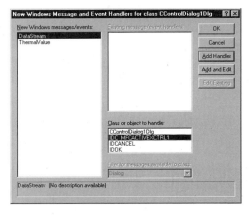

Adding handlers for both of these events results in code that generates a sink map and defines the appropriate entries.

```
BEGIN_EVENTSINK_MAP(CControlDialogDlg, CDialog)
    //{{AFX_EVENTSINK_MAP(CControlDialogDlg)
    ON_EVENT(CControlDialogDlg, IDC_MFCACTIVEXCTRL1,
1 /* DataStream */, OnDataStreamMfcactivexctrl1, VTS_BSTR)
    ON_EVENT(CControlDialogDlg, IDC_MFCACTIVEXCTRL1,
2 /* ThermalValue */, OnThermalValueMfcactivexctrl1, VTS_I2)
    //}}AFX_EVENTSINK_MAP
END_EVENTSINK_MAP()

void CControlDialogDlg::OnDataStreamMfcactivexctrl1(LPCTSTR Control)
{
    // TODO: Add your control notification handler code here

}

void CControlDialogDlg::OnThermalValueMfcactivexctrl1(short Indicator)
{
    // TODO: Add your control notification handler code here

}
```

All you have to do now is add code to update the dialog box as a result of calls made to these functions by the ActiveX control. You can use the Power System check box to interface with the AcquireData property and identify the SetAntenna value by the contents of the radio buttons.

```
void CControlDialogDlg::OnPower()
{
    if (m_checkPower.GetCheck())
        m_control.SetAcquireData(true);
    else
```

```
        m_control.SetAcquireData(false);
}

void CControlDialogDlg::OnHiRadio1()
{
    m_control.SetAntenna(1);
}

void CControlDialogDlg::OnMedRadio2()
{
    m_control.SetAntenna(2);
}

void CControlDialogDlg::OnLoRadio3()
{
    m_control.SetAntenna(3);
}
```

The MFCActiveX control's background will change color to identify the thermal condition inside the module. The control also supports an event that identifies changes to temperature changes. Status text is placed in an edit control, indicating the comfort level of this subsystem. Notice that when the system gets too hot, the component stops acquiring data. A call is made to the check box UI component to remove the check from the box, keeping the dialog in-sync with the control.

```
void CControlDialogDlg::OnThermalValueMfcactivexctrl1(short Indicator)
{
    switch(Indicator)
    {
    case 1:
        m_editThermal.SetWindowText("Overload");
        m_checkPower.SetCheck(false);
        break;
    case 2:
        m_editThermal.SetWindowText("Uncomfortable");
        break;
    case 3:
        m_editThermal.SetWindowText("Normal");
        break;
    }
}
```

Finally, you respond to the data stream event of the control by adding a string to the list box. One thing you might want to double-check is that you do not have the LBS_SORT bit set, or the data will not be added to the control in chronological order.

```
void CControlDialogDlg::OnDataStreamMfcactivexctrl1(LPCTSTR Control)
{
    m_listData.AddString(Control);
}
```

15

MFC ACTIVEX
CONTROL
CONTAINERS

When you run the program, you will have a simple control panel that allows you to switch the radar mapping subsystem on and off and select the gain of the antenna (see Figure 15.23).

FIGURE 15.23

The radar map-ping component in use.

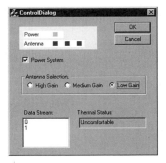

Summary

Containers are a powerful concept in OLE. In this chapter, you created applications that demonstrate both active document containers and ActiveX control containers. Although the purpose for creating a container of one type or the other is a function of the job you are trying to accomplish, many of the concepts you learn for one can easily be applied to your understanding of another.

Using MFC and ATL

by Kenn Scribner

IN THIS CHAPTER

CHAPTER 16

What Is ATL and Why Is It Important for Programming in MFC?

If you've never developed COM components in plain C++, there are many reasons why using the Active Template Library (ATL) from within an MFC application makes sense. Before you learn about the specifics of COM, however, step back in time a moment and remember how programmers used to develop Windows applications.

Imagine yourself writing a large-scale Windows program, but in 1990. "What, no MFC?" No, you cannot use MFC—the MFC framework hadn't been written yet. (Or at least MFC hadn't been released to the general development community.) You must write code to handle each and every Windows message you want to process. You crack every WM_COMMAND, read every lParam, and generally write a ton of grungy support code. For your efforts, you have total control over the flow and operation of your application. On the other hand, those same efforts cost you time to market, time to reach "code complete," and more bugs (or "features") than anyone should have to face.

This is the thrust behind MFC, or at least one of the main goals. You fire up Developer Studio, click a few buttons, and *whammo!* you have a working Windows application. The application initially lacks many of the features your low-level design would have you incorporate, but you didn't spend a lot of time creating the basic framework to support those same features. You get right to the meat of the application much more quickly, and you can feel quite confident the basic framework code is relatively bug-free.

Well, this is the same argument I would make regarding the history of ATL and COM. "Pure" COM, written in C++ (or C, if you've really been doing it a long time), is just as detail-oriented and bug-prone as Windows code using the old Software Development Kit. In fact, you could easily find COM programmers who would tell you it's *more* detailed-oriented and bug-prone. And they'd be correct—COM programming can be far more challenging (and that's "challenging" in the "difficult" sense). The simple stuff isn't so bad, but the truly brilliant code takes work.

Microsoft took hundreds of man-years of COM development experience and wrapped it up in ATL. What's even more intriguing is the *T* in ATL: *template*. We're literally talking C++ templates here, which are recent and exciting additions to the C++ specification. Not only will you save time coding your application, but you'll also gain those hundreds of man-years of Microsoft coding experience and be at the forefront of C++ development and code reuse technology.

Helpful ATL COM Support for MFC Applications

You will begin your examination of ATL within an MFC application by looking at ways ATL might help you manage a few of the details COM requires you to handle. First, you will examine the COM object's pointer itself and how you might better tackle the object's reference count. Then, you will look more deeply into both COM binary strings, or BSTRs, and converting textual information from Unicode (wide characters) to something more easily handled programmatically. Finally, you will unlock some of the secrets behind the VARIANT and see how ATL can help you there as well. Let's begin with COM pointers.

COM Pointers the Smart Way

When you work with COM, and in particular some specific COM object, all you are really doing is accessing the given object's member functions through a pointer. Sure, the "plumbing" is a bit more extravagant with COM, as your pointer could actually access an object outside of your current address space, or even on a different computer over a network connection. But it's still just a pointer, and you call functions using the pointer just as you always have in the past. To you, the object's consumer, this code is equivalent:

```
pObject1->Foo(); // a C++ object
```

and:

```
pObject2->Bar(); // a COM object
```

Yes, the objects are of different types (a C++ object versus a COM object), but you're accessing the member function in the same manner—through a pointer.

But when using COM objects, you must be cognizant of the object's reference count (as you saw in Chapter 10, "COM"). In C++, you would delete the object. When using COM, you *release* it by using the object's Release() method (which is guaranteed by the rules of COM to exist). To handle the situations where you don't want to forget to delete the object (or release it), smart pointers were created. A *smart pointer* is a C++ class that encapsulates the actual memory pointer. The true beauty of a smart pointer is that it can handle the object deletion for you when the smart pointer goes out of scope. At that time its destructor is called, and it may then delete or release the constituent object for you. This relieves you of the burden of doing it yourself. By definition, you can't "forget" to delete or release the object. The C++ language handles the details for you.

Memory leaks are bad enough. But rogue COM objects can be truly nasty (your COM object becomes "rogue" when your pointer variable leaves its scope without releasing the object). These COM objects might be dynamic link libraries (DLLs) loaded into your address space, munching your valuable virtual and resource memory, or they might be actual processes, consuming CPU cycles and system resources you should be using. They can even hang the system. Therefore, it's usually desirable to use a smart pointer when dealing with COM objects. Why invite disaster?

ATL has the ideal solution—a smart pointer template. Actually, there are two major varieties of ATL smart COM pointer templates, and you select the most appropriate based on the mechanics of obtaining the COM pointer. If you create the object from dust, so to speak, you'll use the CComPtr template class:

```
template< class T > class CComPtr
```

On the other hand, if you're calling IUnknown::QueryInterface() (see Chapter 10) though a COM object pointer you have already obtained, you'll use ATL's CComQIPtr template:

```
template< class T, const IID* piid > class CComQIPtr
```

To make more sense of these odd-looking definitions, let's look at some code. In Chapter 23, "MFC and DHTML," I describe the use of Dynamic HTML, or DHTML, from within an MFC application. There you will request an IDispatch pointer from the Internet Explorer Web browser control using code much like the following:

```
CComPtr<IDispatch> pDocDispatch;
HRESULT hr = m_pBrowser->get_Document(&pDocDispatch);
if ( FAILED(hr) || pDocDispatch.p == NULL ) {
TRACE("No active document...load failed.\n");
return;
} // if
```

Here you see an example of a CComPtr-based smart COM pointer. The Web browser ActiveX control will provide you with its current document (a COM object), which you access through its base interface, IDispatch.

Given that you were able to obtain the document interface pointer—that is, the pDocDispatch pointer is valid—you probably want to access its IHTMLDocument2 pointer, which is where you start burrowing into the DHTML aspects of the HTML document. To do that, you must call the object's QueryInterface() method for its HTML document pointer:

```
CComQIPtr<IHTMLDocument2,&IID_IHTMLDocument2>
➥pHTMLDocument2(pDocDispatch);
if ( pHTMLDocument2.p == NULL ) {
```

```
TRACE("IHTMLDocument2 interface not supported.\n");
ASSERT(FALSE);
return;
} // if
```

You should note two things in particular with this example. First, the code to perform the
`QueryInterface()` is encapsulated in the `CComQIPtr` template, making the code more
concise (and bug-free). Second, if for some reason you were unable to obtain the
`IHTMLDocument2` pointer from the Web control's document pointer, you needn't worry
about calling `pDocDispatch`'s `Release()` method. `CComPtr` handles this detail for you.
When `pDocDispatch` goes out of scope, the COM object is released for you
automatically.

> **TIP**
>
> At certain times, you probably do not want to use a smart pointer for your
> COM work, such as during a tight loop of some kind (you probably won't want
> to sustain the overhead of construction and destruction). If it makes sense to
> use such a tool, use the smart pointer. Otherwise, forgo it and keep track of the
> COM object's reference count yourself. In real-world applications you'll usually
> find a mixture of both.

> **NOTE**
>
> If you use the smart pointer templates, you won't be required to link with
> ATL.LIB (which provides, among other things, self-registration support). You
> will, however, need to include atlbase.h, preferably in your stdafx.h file:
>
> ```
> #include <atlbase.h>
> ```

One place where the smart COM pointer makes a lot of sense to use is when using C++
exception handling (see Chapter 22, "Exceptions"). If you declare the COM smart pointer within a `try` block, and an exception is somehow thrown, the smart pointer handles
the object's release for you. You don't need to worry about the COM object's reference
count yourself. This naturally leads to more exception-aware code and alleviates your
need to code even more defensively.

Other ATL COM Support

You've just examined two of the most important ATL templates—after all, if you don't have a pointer to a COM object, you don't have a COM object. But there are at least several other useful areas where ATL can be of benefit. The first is when dealing with the BSTR ("B-stir"), which is a specialized COM string you'll look at more closely in a moment. A second area is when dealing with Unicode (wide-character) strings and their conversions, as COM is completely Unicode-aware (even on Windows 95 and 98 systems). These useful conversion functions are there to use when COM hands you a Unicode string. And a third area is ATL assistance with VARIANTs, which are data structures used as parameters in COM method calls (especially for scripting purposes).

The BSTR

Before you see what a BSTR is composed of, first examine a generic wide-character string. Unicode (wide-character) strings are essentially just strings that require more than a single byte to encode their constituent character data. That is, when you deal with the ANSI character set, all characters, printable or not, range from 0-127. Although in some cases you also include the upper characters from 128-255, the point is the same. The character can be encoded in a single 8-bit byte.

Some languages, especially those with more idiomatic character sets, require more than 256 characters to comprise their alphabets (such as Kanji, a Japanese alphabet). Naturally, 8 bits won't do to describe a single character in such an alphabet. To solve this, Unicode was invented. Essentially, Unicode uses two bytes for encoding instead of one (there is more to it than that, but now you understand the basic data storage requirements).

> **Note**
>
> As with almost any rule, there are exceptions. On the Apple PowerMac, Unicode strings are based on single-byte characters.

A BSTR, then, is a binary data storage medium that consists of three main parts: the length (4 bytes), the Unicode string, and a final NULL terminator (a single byte). This is depicted in Figure 16.1. It is perfectly legal for the Unicode string to contain NULL characters, so don't simply examine memory for zero-value bytes expecting to find the end of the string.

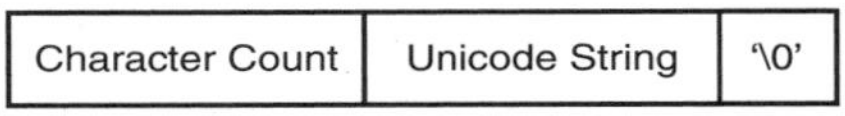

FIGURE 16.1

BSTR *memory layout.*

Character Count	Unicode String	'\0'

The conversion implications alone might make you stop and think a moment—what do you do in Windows 95/98, where you don't have Unicode? Outside of COM you also have to deal with the Win32 API calls to allocate and deallocate BSTR variable memory. This can be painful at times.

ATL provides one mechanism for a more programmer-friendly use of the BSTR. It provides the CComBSTR class, which you'll find defined in atlbase.h but implemented in atlimpl.cpp.

> **NOTE**
>
> As with the smart pointer templates, you won't be required to link with ATL.LIB to use CComBSTR, but you will need to include atlimpl.cpp once somewhere in your source files, preferably in stdafx.cpp:
>
> ```
> #include <atlimpl.cpp>
> ```

To see how you might use CComBSTR, and why it's so useful, consider this COM method from this chapter's first sample, ATLServer, shown in Interface Description Language (IDL) in Chapter 10:

```
[helpstring("method Encrypt")] HRESULT Encrypt(
➡[in] BSTR bstrClearText, [out] BSTR* pbstrMunged);
```

This function accepts a BSTR and a pointer to a BSTR. The first BSTR is encrypted and stored into the second. Without CComBSTR support, you might use the Encrypt function like this from the MFC application as seen in Listing 16.1.

LISTING 16.1   MANUAL BSTR ALLOCATION AND DEALLOCATION

```
// Now that you have your COM object, you create some BSTRs and call it
BSTR bstrClearText = ::SysAllocString(L"123abc");
BSTR bstrMunged; // will be filled by COM object
hr = pEncrypt->Encrypt(bstrClearText,&bstrMunged);
if ( FAILED(hr) ) {
// Problem encrypting the string...
AfxMessageBox("Error encrypting string!",MB_OK ¦ MB_ICONERROR);
::SysFreeString(bstrClearText);
```

continues

LISTING 16.1 CONTINUED

```
::SysFreeString(bstrMunged);
return;
} // if
... // do something
::SysFreeString(bstrClearText);
::SysFreeString(bstrMunged);
```

Doesn't look that scary? Let's look a bit more closely. First, you can't simply do a new to allocate the memory for the BSTR. You must use the Win32 API SysAllocString, which has this prototype:

```
BSTR SysAllocString( OLECHAR FAR* sz );
```

So not only can't you use new to allocate the memory for the BSTR, but you also can't even pass in to SysAllocString a simple char*-based string! You have to pass in some nasty thing known as an OLECHAR (which is, in reality, a Unicode string, hence the *L* positioned before the literal).

Given that you've properly created your BSTR, you pass it to the COM object. When the Encrypt method has completed its task, you're done, right? Nope. Just as you used a special function to create the BSTR in the first place, you must also use a special Win32 API function to deallocate the BSTR memory, SysFreeString:

```
HRESULT SysFreeString( BSTR bstr );
```

It's messy because you have to place the same code in two (or more) locations to perform the deallocation—upon successful completion *and* upon failure. The problem you face if you do this incorrectly is the potential memory leak from improper deallocation of the BSTR. Consider what would happen if, for some reason, the intervening code between the allocation and deallocation of the BSTR threw an exception (see Chapter 22 for details regarding exception handling). The BSTR would be left in memory until the computer was shut down.

A similar example using CComBSTR would look like this (taken from this chapter's MFCClient sample):

```
// Now that you have your COM object, you create some BSTRs and call it
CComBSTR bstrClearText(m_strOriginal); // a CString...
CComBSTR bstrMunged; // will be filled by COM object
hr = pEncrypt->Encrypt(bstrClearText,&bstrMunged);
if ( FAILED(hr) ) {
// Problem encrypting the string...
AfxMessageBox("Error encrypting string!",MB_OK | MB_ICONERROR);
return;
} // if
```

This looks much better. In this case, you use a simple CString variable to contain your programmer-friendly text. You pass that, as a LPCTSTR value, to CComBSTR, which automatically performs the SysAllocString for you (after converting the TCHAR-based string to an OLECHAR-based string). What's even better is that the CComBSTR destructor performs the SysFreeString for you too. Now, when the CComBSTR variable goes out of scope, for whatever reason, the BSTR itself (contained within the CComBSTR class) is deallocated. Exceptions are no longer problematic.

> **NOTE**
>
> CComBSTR is not the only class available to you for friendly BSTR programming. You can also use the _bstr_t class found in comutil.h. I'm using CComBSTR here simply because it's part of the ATL.

If smart pointers and BSTR assistance were all ATL provided, it would probably suffice. However, how do you convert an OLECHAR to something you can actually use? ATL helps here too.

Wide-Character Conversions

CComBSTR had to have some mechanism for converting the LPCTSTR to an OLECHAR string. By using the ATL conversion macros, you can convert just about any string type to just about any other string type. They follow this basic pattern:

```
MACRONAME(string_address)
```

The macro itself is named according to this convention:

```
{from type}2{to type}
```

So, converting from a TCHAR (LPTSTR) string to an OLECHAR string would use the T2OLE macro:

```
USES_CONVERSION; // only required once per MFC member function
TCHAR strTString[] = _T("My TCHAR string.");
OLECHAR* lpOleString = T2OLE(strTString);
```

The USES_CONVERSION macro defines a private function that actually performs some of the conversions. To avoid compiler errors, it's best to put it at the beginning of each and every function that uses the conversion macros.

> **NOTE**
>
> Interestingly, neither atlbase.h nor atlimpl.cpp are required to use the conversion macros. Instead, you may simply include atlconv.h in the specific MFC source file where the macros will be used, if the conversion macros are all that interests you.

The conversion macros take their direction from the current compiler settings. That is, if both the from and to types are the same, no conversion is required (a value is simply returned). How would you know if a conversion would take place, or that the from and to string types were the same? Table 16.1 shows how the T and OLE types are converted based upon the current compiler settings.

TABLE 16.1 CONVERSION MACRO COMPILER TYPE ASSIGNMENTS

Compiler Directive	T *Becomes*	OLE *Becomes*
None	ANSI	WIDE
OLE2ANSI	ANSI	ANSI
_UNICODE	WIDE	WIDE
OLE2ANSI and _UNICODE	WIDE	ANSI

Essentially, all you really need to do is select the starting type, the ending type, and decide if the ending type is const (in which case you add a C to the macro name, such as A2COLE for converting an ANSI string to a const OLESTR). The compiler directives in place will resolve the correct starting and ending types for you. Table 16.2 gives you the complete set of conversion macros. Here A indicates ANSI (or a standard char*-based sting), T indicates a TCHAR-based string, W is a wide-character string, OLE is an OLESTR-based string, and BSTR is self-explanatory.

TABLE 16.2 ATL CONVERSION MACROS

Macro	*Conversion*
A2BSTR	(LPSTR to BSTR)
OLE2A	(LPOLESTR to LPSTR)
T2A	(LPSTR/LPOLESTR to LPSTR)
W2A	(LPWSTR to LPSTR)
A2COLE	(LPSTR to LPCOLESTR)

Macro	*Conversion*
OLE2BSTR	(LPOLESTR to BSTR)
T2BSTR	(LPSTR/LPOLESTR to BSTR)
W2BSTR	(LPWSTR to BSTR)
A2CT	(LPSTR to LPCTSTR/LPCOLESTR)
OLE2CA	(LPOLESTR to LPCSTR)
T2CA	(LPSTR/LPOLESTR to LPCSTR)
W2CA	(LPWSTR to LPCSTR)
A2CW	(LPSTR to LPCWSTR)
OLE2CT	(LPOLESTR to LPCSTR/LPCOLESTR)
T2COLE	(LPSTR/LPOLESTR to LPCOLESTR)
W2COLE	(LPWSTR to LPCOLESTR)
A2OLE	(LPSTR to LPOLESTR)
OLE2CW	(LPOLESTR to LPCWSTR)
T2CW	(LPSTR/LPOLESTR to LPCWSTR)
W2CT	(LPWSTR to LPCSTR/LPCOLESTR)
A2T	(LPSTR to LPSTR/LPOLESTR)
OLE2T	(LPOLESTR to LPSTR/LPOLESTR)
T2OLE	(LPSTR/LPOLESTR to LPOLESTR)
W2OLE	(LPWSTR to LPOLESTR)
A2W	(LPSTR to LPWSTR)
OLE2W	(LPOLESTR to LPWSTR)
T2W	(LPSTR/LPOLESTR to LPWSTR)
W2T	(LPWSTR to LPSTR/LPOLESTR)

Now that you've seen that ATL provides string conversion assistance, you can see how useful it is, especially when dealing with COM or general-purpose internationalization issues. There is also another area in which ATL can help your COM programming task. ATL simplifies working with VARIANT data.

VARIANTs

VARIANT is a somewhat mysterious datatype to many strictly MFC programmers. The reason is easy to see: A VARIANT is a purely COM-based datatype. It's also specific to the COM scripting architecture. But if you program in COM at all, you'll run across the

VARIANT. So, to clear up the mystery, step back a minute and think about COM and the COM architecture. Then I'll describe the VARIANT and how ATL can help you work with VARIANT data.

Ultimately, COM provides a data-sharing mechanism. COM is more than that, but at the lowest level, COM simply provides a conduit for sharing data. If you're using an in-process COM server (a DLL), you have no worries. All the data passed between your main application and the COM DLL is created and used within the same virtual address space.

But have you ever tried to send data from one executable (process) to another? How did you do it? Named pipes? Memory-mapped files? Perhaps simple data embedded in a WPARAM or LPARAM of a custom message? All of these work and have their place. COM, on the other hand, acts as a facilitator to provide you with a highly optimized and relatively automatic data transfer mechanism. Clearly COM does much more than that, but the underlying data-passing mechanisms are critical to COM's functionality.

When COM takes data from one address space and sends it to another (same machine or networked), the process of converting the data is called *marshaling*. Nearly all types of data can be marshaled without too much trouble, though some datatypes are more difficult to marshal than others are. For example, think about a pointer. A pointer, after all, is just another number. But it represents an address of some particular piece of information, and that address is only valid in a specific address space. If you create a memory-mapped file, the (virtual address) pointers used to access the data in the two application's address spaces will be different, even though the physical address of the data is the same.

What does this have to do with VARIANTs? Everything, as it happens. COM's architects, or possibly the Visual Basic team (it's unclear to me which), sat down and compiled a list of "standard" datatypes COM would automatically "know" how to marshal. With no further work on your part, if you declare your interface member parameters to be of datatypes from this list, you are relieved from writing the marshaling code yourselves (an arduous process for most people). For example, you don't need to concern yourselves with how a DATE structure is passed from address space to address space—you simply send the DATE information on its merry way, allowing COM to handle the gritty details for you.

Listing 16.2 and the individual items it contains collectively make up the VARIANT datatype list. The VARIANT itself is simply a discriminated union that contains an integer denoting the type (the discriminator) and a union containing all of the possible datatypes. You assign the integer an enumerated value that indicates what data is stored in the union, and then assign the data itself.

LISTING 16.2 THE VARIANT DISCRIMINATED UNION

```
typedef struct tagVARIANT{
VARTYPE vt;
WORD wReserved1;
WORD wReserved2;
WORD wReserved3;
union {
        long          lVal;          /* VT_I4                    */
        unsigned char bVal;          /* VT_UI1                   */
        short         iVal;          /* VT_I2                    */
        float         fltVal;        /* VT_R4                    */
        double        dblVal;        /* VT_R8                    */
        VARIANT_BOOL  boolVal;       /* VT_BOOL                  */
        SCODE         scode;         /* VT_ERROR                 */
        CY            cyVal;         /* VT_CY                    */
        DATE          date;          /* VT_DATE                  */
        BSTR          bstrVal;       /* VT_BSTR                  */
        IUnknown      punkVal;       / VT_UNKNOWN                */
        IDispatch     pdispVal;      / VT_DISPATCH               */
        SAFEARRAY     parray;        / VT_ARRAY|*                */
        unsigned char pbVal;         / VT_BYREF|VT_UI1           */
        short         piVal;         / VT_BYREF|VT_I2            */
        long          plVal;         / VT_BYREF|VT_I4            */
        float         pfltVal;       / VT_BYREF|VT_R4            */
        double        pdblVal;       / VT_BYREF|VT_R8            */
        VARIANT_BOOL  pbool;         / VT_BYREF|VT_BOOL          */
        SCODE         pscode;        / VT_BYREF|VT_ERROR         */
        CY            pcyVal;        / VT_BYREF|VT_CY            */
        DATE          pdate;         / VT_BYREF|VT_DATE          */
        BSTR          pbstrVal;      / VT_BYREF|VT_BSTR          */
        IUnknown      **ppunkVal;    /* VT_BYREF|VT_UNKNOWN      */
        IDispatch     **ppdispVal;   /* VT_BYREF|VT_DISPATCH     */
        SAFEARRAY     **pparray;     /* VT_BYREF|VT_ARRAY|*      */
        VARIANT       pvarVal;       / VT_BYREF|VT_VARIANT       */
        void          * byref;       /* Generic ByRef            */  };
} VARIANT, VARIANTARG;
```

The discriminator, VARTYPE, is defined in this manner:

```
typedef unsigned short VARTYPE;
```

If used properly, it will contain an enumeration from VARENUM as seen in Listing 16.3.

LISTING 16.3 THE VARENUM DISCRIMINATORS

```
enum VARENUM
{   VT_EMPTY              = 0,
    VT_NULL               = 1,
```

continues

LISTING 16.3 CONTINUED

```
    VT_I2                = 2,
    VT_I4                = 3,
    VT_R4                = 4,
    VT_R8                = 5,
    VT_CY                = 6,
    VT_DATE              = 7,
    VT_BSTR              = 8,
    VT_DISPATCH          = 9,
    VT_ERROR             = 10,
    VT_BOOL              = 11,
    VT_VARIANT           = 12,
    VT_UNKNOWN           = 13,
    VT_DECIMAL           = 14,
    VT_I1                = 16,
    VT_UI1               = 17,
    VT_UI2               = 18,
    VT_UI4               = 19,
    VT_I8                = 20,
    VT_UI8               = 21,
    VT_INT               = 22,
    VT_UINT              = 23,
    VT_VOID              = 24,
    VT_HRESULT           = 25,
    VT_PTR               = 26,
    VT_SAFEARRAY         = 27,
    VT_CARRAY            = 28,
    VT_USERDEFINED       = 29,
    VT_LPSTR             = 30,
    VT_LPWSTR            = 31,
    VT_RECORD            = 36,
    VT_FILETIME          = 64,
    VT_BLOB              = 65,
    VT_STREAM            = 66,
    VT_STORAGE           = 67,
    VT_STREAMED_OBJECT   = 68,
    VT_STORED_OBJECT     = 69,
    VT_BLOB_OBJECT       = 70,
    VT_CF                = 71,
    VT_CLSID             = 72,
    VT_BSTR_BLOB         = 0xfff,
    VT_VECTOR            = 0x1000,
    VT_ARRAY             = 0x2000,
    VT_BYREF             = 0x4000,
    VT_RESERVED          = 0x8000,
    VT_ILLEGAL           = 0xffff,
    VT_ILLEGALMASKED     = 0xfff,
    VT_TYPEMASK          = 0xfff
};.
```

As you know, a union is always allocated enough memory to contain the largest datatype within its scope. Therefore, a VARIANT always has the same memory footprint. The "universal marshaler," then, merely has to treat the VARIANT as a chunk of memory, of known size, and be able to interpret the various VARENUM types. You leave this to COM. If you select parameter types from the VARENUM list, you have no marshaling problems. However, if you select something else for your parameter type, such as a Win32 POINT structure, you have to handle the marshaling yourselves.

> **TIP**
>
> Strive to select your parameter types from the VARENUM list if you are writing an in-process server. If you do, you won't need to compile a separate "proxy/stub" DLL to perform the custom marshaling, which reduces the number of files you'll need to ship and install. (Local servers will require a proxy/stub DLL in any case, as you'll see shortly.)

The CComVariant template handles the details for you. Without such help, you need to allocate (and deallocate) memory for the discriminated union, assign the discriminator, and handle setting the union value. Granted, it's bread and butter for highly skilled C++ programmers such as yourself, but why write all of that redundant code? Save your typing skills for the really cool algorithms.

With CComVariant, you simply declare a variable and pass in the VARIANT type:

```
CComVariant varError(VT_ERROR);
```

You've written much less code, and the code is less error-prone than dealing with the VARIANT discriminated union directly.

> **NOTE**
>
> *Dual interfaces*, which are COM interfaces that inherit from IDispatch rather than directly from IUnknown, by definition use VARIANTs to pass method parameters. Many of the newer COM technologies use dual interfaces, like ActiveX and OLE DB. VARIANTs are then unavoidable, which makes VARIANT support code that much more valuable. You don't have to use ATL, as you could use MFC's COleVariant, but if you're already using ATL for other reasons, it may make sense to stick with it, depending upon your application.

All of these ATL support templates and conversion macros are exceptionally helpful, and you'll probably find if you're working with MFC and COM objects they're invaluable. But what about the case where your MFC application needs to expose an interface or two itself? ATL can help there, too.

Advanced ATL Support for MFC Applications

Ignoring the potentially networked COM object, there are essentially two types of COM servers, in-process (DLLs) and local (EXEs). If your requirements dictate a simple in-process server, by all means choose your favorite COM implementation methodology (like ATL) and code away. Sometimes, however, a local server fills the requirement(s) more elegantly. In this case, you might still choose to use ATL to implement your COM server, but there are strong arguments in favor of using MFC, too. For one, MFC has a rich and robust architecture with plenty of support classes. But MFC's implementation of COM is limited because of this basic MFC tenet—no multiple inheritance. Sure, you can do just about anything COM-wise with MFC, but the MFC architecture isn't quite as natural as ATL's is to a COM programmer.

Why would I claim this? Well, MFC implements COM interfaces as nested classes. The MFC architects decided this was the easiest and most straightforward way to implement COM, and it works. But COM interfaces usually have an "is-a" relationship, not a "has-a" relationship. For illustration purposes, the (imaginary) IMyInterface interface "is-a" IDispatch interface, whereas IDispatch "is-a" IUnknown interface, and so on. Therefore, multiple inheritance, from a COM-based architectural standpoint, makes more sense than a nested class, which is a class contained within some enclosing class. The enclosing class "has-a" nested class.

Perhaps, then, you could write most of your basic local server code in MFC, yet expose your COM interface(s) using ATL. As it happens, this is not only possible, but it is also a great way to use the best features of both tools.

Begin with Your MFC Application

Perhaps the best way to get started is to concentrate on your MFC application first, and then add the requisite ATL COM support later (as you'll see). This example simply increments a counter in the COM object when called by a client application. True, it's not a tremendously exciting example, but this way, the example isn't cluttered with code that's not germane to mixing ATL with MFC.

The MFCServer example is a very basic MFC SDI application that has the addition of a single static attribute in the CWinApp-derived class (CMFCServerApp). This long-valued attribute will hold the number of "hits" the server sustained through its COM interface. The basic MFC framework was created in the usual fashion; nothing special, in this case.

> **TIP**
>
> Be sure that when you create the MFC application using the MFC AppWizard, you accept the default setting for automation (which is unchecked, for "no automation support"). The automation aspects of your program are precisely what you're about to add using ATL, so you don't want old MFC automation code causing problems further down the road.

Assuming you have your MFC application running and debugged, or at least nearly so, let's see how to actually add the COM interface.

Add the Required ATL Support

Stepping back for a moment, you now have an MFC application to which you intend to add ATL code. Do you want to write this ATL code yourselves, or is there some other way to produce it for you automatically? As it happens, there is. The ATL Object Wizard naturally provides you with robust ATL code. Visual C++ 6 has a new feature you can use to automatically add the ATL support required. In a moment, you'll go through the process step by step. Before you start, here's a quick road map. When you get bogged down in the details, you'll at least have some idea where you are in the process and how much more remains to be done.

Here are the steps you will follow to add full-fledged ATL support:

- Create (and examine) the ATL COM support code using the ATL Object Wizard.
- Manually add/edit the files you require that the Object Wizard didn't produce for you.
- Modify your project settings to automatically create and register your proxy/stub DLL.
- Write a client (test) application to check out your COM object.

After you've added the ATL COM support, you will examine the code the wizard inserted. After all, it's not usually a good idea to accept wizard-based code without some understanding of its functionality.

Creating the ATL COM Support Code Automatically

MFC programmers are quite used to running the MFC ClassWizard to add methods to their C++ classes. Invoking the ClassWizard couldn't be easier: Select it from Developer Studio's View menu or right-click the mouse in an edit window. But the ATL Object Wizard doesn't share such an obvious user-interface mechanism. To invoke it, you right-click the project name from the project's Workspace window (see Figure 16.2). The associated context menu will have a menu option for New ATL Object, and it's this menu item you select to actually bring up the wizard.

FIGURE 16.2

Developer Studio's Workspace window.

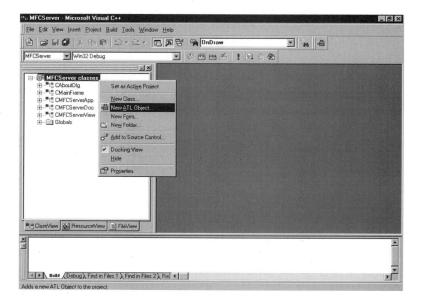

> **NOTE**
>
> Developer Studio may inform you that the ATL code insertion failed after you first invoke the ATL Object Wizard. Don't believe it! It's a bug Microsoft is examining (at the time of this writing). Go ahead and invoke it a second time and add your new ATL object just as if you hadn't seen the error dialog.

When you invoke the ATL Object Wizard, your MFC application (CWinApp-derived) class will be modified and ATL-specific files will be added to your project (assuming you click Yes when asked for confirmation). This is enough of a framework to actually get ATL up and running within your application. When the wizard has finished processing

your existing MFC files, it will ask you for the type of COM object you want to insert (see Figure 16.3). You can select from a wide variety of COM object types; in this case, you will select the simple COM object and click Next.

FIGURE 16.3

The ATL Object Wizard.

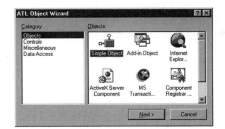

After you have decided what type of COM object you want, the wizard will ask you for the specific COM interface information it requires to build the ATL-specific files. It displays the object properties property sheet, as shown in Figure 16.4.

FIGURE 16.4

The ATL Object Wizard's Names property sheet.

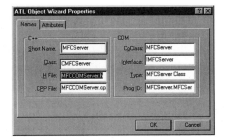

Because this is an MFC book, this particular ATL wizard won't be described in tremendous detail—there is a lot there for such a simple-looking dialog box. Essentially, though, you will name the interface and source files in the first property sheet and establish the object's operating parameters in the second.

The first property sheet is the Names sheet, as you see in Figure 16.4. On this sheet you provide a basic name string in the Short Name edit control. The text you type is propagated to the other seven edit controls as default values. Feel free to change this text if you want. Here you provide such basic information as the name of your interface, the ProgID, the name of your CoClass, and the ever-present C++ filenames (declaration and implementation).

The second property sheet might at first seem to be fairly simple, but you're about to make decisions with huge implications when you select each option (see Figure 16.5), so choose carefully.

FIGURE 16.5

The ATL Object Wizard's Attributes property sheet.

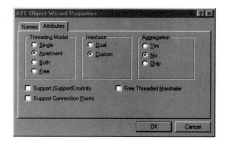

All these implications cannot be adequately described here. It'll have to suffice to say you want an apartment-threaded object with a custom interface that does not support aggregation. What that basically says is you want a COM object that uses a regular Windows message queue for thread synchronization (apartment threading), is not an automation object (the custom versus dual interface), and is not willing to have its interfaces "consumed" by another COM object (aggregation). The deeper meaning is that you want a COM object that

- Does not require you to use multithreaded synchronization mechanisms, like critical sections and/or mutexes
- Does not have an interface that inherits from `IDispatch` (dual) versus simply `IUnknown` (custom)
- Won't allow another COM object to control access to your interfaces

After you've selected these attributes and clicked OK, the wizard will actually add code to your basic ATL framework. At this time you have a simple COM object with a single custom interface. But the interface has no methods. You now need to add those, just as you add message handlers to your MFC classes. For this, you again ignore MFC's ClassWizard (which can't help you with ATL code) in lieu of the context menu in the Workspace window. Just as you right-clicked to invoke the ATL Object Wizard, you will right-click to add methods and properties.

Here, it makes a difference where you right-click. In Figure 16.6, you see both C++ classes and COM interfaces in the tree control, where before (in Figure 16.2) there were only C++ classes. If you right-click on a C++ class, you can add member functions and variables, virtual functions, and message handlers. On the other hand, if you right-click on a COM interface (denoted by a leading *I* in the name), you can add properties and methods. It's a method you want to add to your interface, so select that menu option to activate the dialog depicted in Figure 16.7.

FIGURE 16.6
*The Developer
Studio Workspace
window revisited.*

FIGURE 16.7
*The ATL Add
Method to
Interface dialog.*

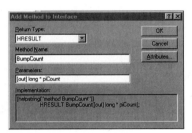

You are essentially designing the interface, or API, for your COM object. The interface you design—its methods and parameters—determines the functionality your object provides to other objects and applications. For this simple example, you want a method to increment a counter and somehow provide the new value to you. You can do this by adding a method called BumpCount that returns something known as an HRESULT. The HRESULT is a 32-bit COM return code comprised of several component fields that together serve to indicate the success or failure of the COM method call from a COM perspective (refer to any good COM text for the specific field meanings and values). If your object was successfully called with valid parameters, it will return a successful result code. From a COM perspective, the method call was a success.

In this case, it makes sense to pass into the method a pointer to the client's integer variable used to accept the new counter value. The client will create your object, call BumpCount(), and then typically check the HRESULT to see if COM was happy. If the HRESULT was successful, the client will then do something with the count value it received.

Based on these design ideas, your interface method would look something like this:

```
BumpCount(long * piCount)
```

This is what you would type into the Add Method to Interface dialog's Parameters edit control, with the addition of the IDL directional tags [in] and [out]. With the IDL tags, your parameter list would look like this:

```
BumpCount([out] long * piCount)
```

> **NOTE**
>
> The IDL parameter tags add semantics to the parameter list. They tell the COM marshaling functions the direction of data flow. The marshaling functions require this information, as these functions are responsible for actually passing data between processes. This "data passing" is quite a trick: How do you represent a pointer to the same thing in two different address spaces? A good COM book will tell you why this is necessary and how it is done.

in parameter data is something akin to read-only, or const. The data comes into your address space and is dropped off at the secretary's desk for further processing, so to speak. You grab it, you use it. (This does not relieve you from your responsibility to deallocate any BSTRs you are passed, however.) The out parameters, however, are far more interesting. They're always pointers. You fill whatever they are pointing to with outgoing data, which in this case is simply a long result. To be somewhat more complete, there is also "in-out" data, which I'll leave to a good COM textbook for further explanation.

After you've clicked OK, the wizard will add the necessary code to the many places within your framework it is required to declare and implement the BumpCounter method. If you were continuing on in ATL, you would now add the code to actually handle the counter.

In this case, though, all you really wanted was to have as much code automatically generated for you as was possible, so you will stop with your ATL wizard work and turn again to your MFC project. You'll be visiting many of the various ATL source code files, however, for editing and revising as you more fully integrate ATL into your MFC project.

Examining the ATL Code Added to Your MFC Application

Now that you have the basic ATL code inserted, it's time to tweak and modify what you were given. Turning to your example, from Developer Studio open the file MFCServer.cpp. As you can see from Listing 16.4, the wizard added quite a bit of code automatically (shown in italics). This code is required to initialize COM (and ATL) and provides the basic plumbing your COM server will require.

LISTING 16.4   MFCSERVER.CPP WITH ATL SUPPORT

```cpp
// MFCServer.cpp : Defines the class behaviors for the application.
//

#include "stdafx.h"
#include "MFCServer.h"

#include "MainFrm.h"
#include "MFCServerDoc.h"
#include "MFCServerView.h"
#include <initguid.h>
#include "MFCServer_i.c"
#include "MFCCOMServer.h"

#ifdef _DEBUG
#define new DEBUG_NEW
#undef THIS_FILE
static char THIS_FILE[] = __FILE__;
#endif


/////////////////////////////////////////////////////////////////////
// CMFCServerApp
(Message mapping removed for clarity...)

/////////////////////////////////////////////////////////////////////
// CMFCServerApp construction
long CMFCServerApp::m_lnNumHits = 0;
CMFCServerApp::CMFCServerApp()
{
// TODO: add construction code here,
// Place all significant initialization in InitInstance
}


/////////////////////////////////////////////////////////////////////
// The one and only CMFCServerApp object
CMFCServerApp theApp;

/////////////////////////////////////////////////////////////////////
// CMFCServerApp initialization
BOOL CMFCServerApp::InitInstance()
{
if (!InitATL())
return FALSE;
AfxEnableControlContainer();
// Standard initialization
// If you are not using these features and wish to reduce the size
//   of your final executable, you should remove from the following
//   the specific initialization routines you do not need.
```

continues

LISTING 16.4   CONTINUED

```
#ifdef _AFXDLL
Enable3dControls();            // Call this when using MFC in
                              // a shared DLL
#else
Enable3dControlsStatic();     // Call this when linking to
                              // MFC statically
#endif
// Change the registry key under which your settings are stored.
// TODO: You should modify this string to be something appropriate
// such as the name of your company or organization.
SetRegistryKey(_T("Local AppWizard-Generated Applications"));
LoadStdProfileSettings();  // Load standard INI file options
                              // (including MRU)
// Register the application's document templates.  Document
// templates serve as the connection between documents,
// frame windows and views.
CSingleDocTemplate* pDocTemplate;
pDocTemplate = new CSingleDocTemplate(
IDR_MAINFRAME,
RUNTIME_CLASS(CMFCServerDoc),
RUNTIME_CLASS(CMainFrame),          // main SDI frame window
RUNTIME_CLASS(CMFCServerView));
AddDocTemplate(pDocTemplate);
// Parse command line for standard shell commands, DDE, file open
CCommandLineInfo cmdInfo;
ParseCommandLine(cmdInfo);
// Dispatch commands specified on the command line
if (!ProcessShellCommand(cmdInfo))
return FALSE;
// The one and only window has been initialized, so show and
// update it.
m_pMainWnd->ShowWindow(SW_SHOW);
m_pMainWnd->UpdateWindow();

return TRUE;
}


/////////////////////////////////////////////////////////////////
// CAboutDlg dialog used for App About
("About" code removed for clarity...)

/////////////////////////////////////////////////////////////////
// CMFCServerApp message handlers
CMFCServerModule _Module;
BEGIN_OBJECT_MAP(ObjectMap)
OBJECT_ENTRY(CLSID_MFCServer, CMFCServer)
END_OBJECT_MAP()
LONG CMFCServerModule::Unlock()
```

```
{
AfxOleUnlockApp();
return 0;
}

LONG CMFCServerModule::Lock()
{
AfxOleLockApp();
return 1;
}
LPCTSTR CMFCServerModule::FindOneOf(LPCTSTR p1, LPCTSTR p2)
{
while (*p1 != NULL)
    {
LPCTSTR p = p2;
while (*p != NULL)
        {
if (*p1 == *p)
return CharNext(p1);
p = CharNext(p);
        }
p1++;
    }
return NULL;
}


int CMFCServerApp::ExitInstance()
{
if (m_bATLInited)
    {
_Module.RevokeClassObjects();
_Module.Term();
CoUninitialize();
    }

return CWinApp::ExitInstance();

}

BOOL CMFCServerApp::InitATL()
{
m_bATLInited = TRUE;
#if _WIN32_WINNT >= 0x0400
HRESULT hRes = CoInitializeEx(NULL, COINIT_MULTITHREADED);
#else
HRESULT hRes = CoInitialize(NULL);
#endif
if (FAILED(hRes))
```

continues

LISTING **16.4**   CONTINUED

```
    {
m_bATLInited = FALSE;
return FALSE;
    }


_Module.Init(ObjectMap, AfxGetInstanceHandle());
_Module.dwThreadID = GetCurrentThreadId();

LPTSTR lpCmdLine = GetCommandLine(); //this line necessary for
                                     // _ATL_MIN_CRT
TCHAR szTokens[] = _T("-/");
BOOL bRun = TRUE;
LPCTSTR lpszToken = _Module.FindOneOf(lpCmdLine, szTokens);
while (lpszToken != NULL)
    {
if (lstrcmpi(lpszToken, _T("UnregServer"))==0)
    {
_Module.UpdateRegistryFromResource(IDR_MFCSERVER, FALSE);
_Module.UnregisterServer(TRUE); //TRUE means typelib is
                                // unreg'd
bRun = FALSE;
break;
    }
if (lstrcmpi(lpszToken, _T("RegServer"))==0)
    {
_Module.UpdateRegistryFromResource(IDR_MFCSERVER, TRUE);
_Module.RegisterServer(TRUE);
bRun = FALSE;
break;
    }
lpszToken = _Module.FindOneOf(lpszToken, szTokens);
    }

if (!bRun)
    {
m_bATLInited = FALSE;
_Module.Term();
CoUninitialize();
return FALSE;
    }

hRes = _Module.RegisterClassObjects(CLSCTX_LOCAL_SERVER,
REGCLS_MULTIPLEUSE);
if (FAILED(hRes))
    {
```

```
m_bATLInited = FALSE;
CoUninitialize();
return FALSE;
    }

return TRUE;

}
```

From the top, after inserting some required header files, the wizard added these lines to InitInstance():

```
if (!InitATL())
return FALSE;
```

If the InitATL() member fails, the application itself will terminate.

InitATL() begins its work by initializing the COM library, the specific mechanism for which depends upon the system you're compiling on (Windows NT 4 or better, or something else, like Windows 98). Assuming that the libraries activated properly, the ATL module is initialized with its object map and thread ID. The ATL object map is similar in concept to MFC's message map, in that the object map identifies the COM interfaces the module is responsible for servicing. From there, the command line is parsed to determine whether the server is being called to register or unregister. If this is the case, the Registry is updated appropriately and the application terminates (as it should). If the object is being created for use, the module registers its class objects, which are used to create the individual objects the module services (in this case you have only one). In COM terms, it is taking care of the objects' Class Factories. If this went well, ATL is initialized and the application continues its MFC initialization.

The remainder of InitInstance() is standard MFC application initialization code, with the exception of these lines (added by the wizard):

```
if (cmdInfo.m_bRunEmbedded ¦¦ cmdInfo.m_bRunAutomated)
    {
return TRUE;
    }
```

When the MFC application is invoked by COM, the command line passed to the application will indicate it is embedded. In this case, InitInstance() will return (with a successful result). At this point, the MFC code required to create a new document and to show the window has been skipped.

> **CAUTION**
>
> At this point, you have no document, no view, and no frame window, so do not make calls to these C++ objects from within your COM methods. To do this, you must either modify the default wizard-based code to allow the window to be displayed or you handle things otherwise in your COM method(s), such as creating a particular MFC object yourself.

`InitInstance()` is completed for you whenever you run the MFC AppWizard. However, in this case you not only need `InitInstance()`, but you also require `ExitInstance()`. You must undo what you have done:

```
int CMFCServerApp::ExitInstance()
{
if (m_bATLInited)
    {
_Module.RevokeClassObjects();
_Module.Term();
CoUninitialize();
    }

return CWinApp::ExitInstance();

}
```

When the application exits, `ExitInstance()` will handle the details of revoking the class objects (the Class Factories mentioned previously) and terminating the ATL module. Then, of course, COM itself is shut down.

The wizard also added several other helper functions that are used when initializing and terminating the application. The `lock` and `unlock` helper functions serve to increment and decrement the application's active object count. When the count reaches zero, the application exits:

```
LONG CMFCServerModule::Unlock()
{
AfxOleUnlockApp();
return 0;
}

LONG CMFCServerModule::Lock()
{
AfxOleLockApp();
return 1;
}
```

To determine whether the application requires registration or unregistration, the wizard added a helper function used to scan the command line for the specific COM command-line parameters `RegServer` and `UnregServer`:

```
LPCTSTR CMFCServerModule::FindOneOf(LPCTSTR p1, LPCTSTR p2)
{
while (*p1 != NULL)
    {
LPCTSTR p = p2;
while (*p != NULL)
        {
if (*p1 == *p)
return CharNext(p1);
p = CharNext(p);
        }
p1++;
    }
return NULL;
}
```

The final changes the wizard made were to add the actual ATL module and object map. The ATL module is the piece that actually serves as the COM server. The module uses the array of objects, listed in the object map, to maintain the set of Class Factories for each object in the list. This enables the module to handle such important details as individual object registration and unregistration, reference counting, establishing the communications between the client and the individual object, and, of course, object creation through its Class Factory:

```
CMFCServerModule _Module;
BEGIN_OBJECT_MAP(ObjectMap)
OBJECT_ENTRY(CLSID_MFCServer, CMFCServer)
END_OBJECT_MAP()
```

To compile the ATL code you have just examined, the wizard had to add information to the MFC application's main precompiled header files, stdafx.h and stdafx.cpp. In the case of stdafx.h, it adds a definition to compile the COM code as apartment-threaded (remember your selection when you ran the wizard?), adds the requisite ATL base header files, and declares your ATL module, `CMFCServerModule`:

```
#define _ATL_APARTMENT_THREADED
#include <atlbase.h>
//You may derive a class from CComModule and use it if you want
//to override something, but do not change the name of _Module
class CMFCServerModule : public CComModule
{
public:
LONG Unlock();
LONG Lock();
```

```
LPCTSTR FindOneOf(LPCTSTR p1, LPCTSTR p2);
DWORD dwThreadID;
};
extern CMFCServerModule _Module;
#include <atlcom.h>
```

The wizard then added code to stdafx.cpp to add static Registry support (don't use ATL.DLL) and the usual atlimpl.cpp file you've seen before:

```
#ifdef _ATL_STATIC_REGISTRY
#include <statreg.h>
#endif
#include <atlimpl.cpp>
```

Finally, the wizard created several new files for you, modified your resource file, and changed your project settings. The files added include your COM interface definition file, MFCServer.idl, the COM interface files themselves, MFCCOMServer.h and MFCCOMServer.cpp, and the Registry script file MFCServer.rgs. The IDL file defines your interface(s) and will be compiled by a special compiler to produce several output files, which will be discussed shortly. The interface files are where you'll add the true COM functionality for each of your interface member functions. The Registry script file is compiled into a binary form and used by ATL to register and unregister your application as a whole as well as the individual interfaces themselves. (This alone is a handy benefit when using ATL.)

The resource file was modified in two ways: the binary form of the Registry script was added, and a COM type library was inserted. The type library is a compiled, tokenized form of your IDL source file that allows COM clients to scan your object to determine, at runtime, what your COM interfaces do. This is used, in most cases, for scripting purposes.

Your project settings were modified to include a custom build step for the MFCServer.idl file (using Visual C++ 6's new MIDL settings tab). IDL files are compiled by a special compiler, which in this case is the Microsoft IDL compiler, or MIDL for short. MIDL produces, as output, several files you'll be required to compile and execute for the COM application. First, the basic C++ files declaring the COM object are generated— MFCServer_i.cpp and MFCServer_i.h. These files define and declare the COM class identifier (CLSID) and interface identifier (IID) values, which you will require when compiling code that uses your COM object(s). MIDL then produces the type library, MFCServer.tlb, which is compiled into your application resources. And finally, MIDL produces source files you will need to generate a proxy/stub DLL.

Interestingly, the ATL Object Wizard did all of this for you, yet it didn't go far enough. If you were to compile this COM application, and then develop an application that used this COM server, the `CoCreateInstance()` would fail with the `HRESULT E_NOINTERFACE`. Why?

Adding the Additional ATL COM Support Files

To understand this, go back to the basic COM principle that COM, among other things, serves as a data conduit between address spaces. You have the two applications you require, the COM server and your client application, but how will they actually communicate? The mechanism the COM marshaling code uses is the proxy/stub DLL, which you can imagine as a "modem" between the two address spaces. The ATL Object Wizard inserted the project settings to build the source code for creating the proxy/stub DLL, but it didn't add any support for actually building the DLL. To me, this is a huge oversight and a bug.

However, you can recover relatively easily. You need to create two files from scratch and then modify your project settings to actually compile the proxy/stub source code into the DLL itself. The two files you need are a makefile and the DLL definition (DEF) file.

> **TIP**
>
> In practice, you would typically find another COM-based project and copy its files for editing rather than actually type the source code from scratch.

For this example, I created the proxy/stub makefile, MFCServerps.mk and inserted the code in Listing 16.5.

LISTING 16.5 MFCSERVERPS.MK PROXY/STUB MAKEFILE

```
MFCServerps.dll: dlldata.obj MFCServer_p.obj MFCServer_i.obj
link /dll /out:MFCServerps.dll /def:MFCServerps.def /entry:DllMain
➥ dlldata.obj MFCServer_p.obj MFCServer_i.obj kernel32.lib
➥ rpcndr.lib rpcns4.lib rpcrt4.lib oleaut32.lib uuid.lib
.c.obj:
cl /c /Ox /DWIN32 /D_WIN32_WINNT=0x0400 /DREGISTER_PROXY_DLL $<
clean:
@del MFCServerps.dll
@del MFCServerps.lib
@del MFCServerps.exp
@del dlldata.obj
@del MFCServer_p.obj
@del MFCServer_i.obj
```

Then, because you're compiling a DLL, you need to create the DEF file to indicate what DLL functions are to be visible to external clients (see Listing 16.6).

LISTING 16.6 MFCSERVERPS.DEF PROXY/STUB DLL EXPORT DEFINITION FILE

```
LIBRARY        "MFCServerps"
DESCRIPTION    'Proxy/Stub DLL'
EXPORTS
    DllGetClassObject      @1  PRIVATE
    DllCanUnloadNow        @2  PRIVATE
    GetProxyDllInfo        @3  PRIVATE
    DllRegisterServer      @4  PRIVATE
    DllUnregisterServer    @5  PRIVATE
```

The proxy/stub DLL exports the standard COM methods.

Modifying Your Project Settings

Now that you have all of the proxy/stub files you require, you need to add a project setting to actually compile and register the proxy/stub DLL. To do this, you right-click on the project name in the Workspace window, or select Project, Settings from the Developer Studio menu, and add a post-build step, as shown in Figure 16.8.

FIGURE 16.8

Proxy/stub post-build step.

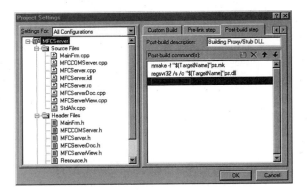

Essentially what you're doing is running the nmake command-line compiler against your proxy/stub makefile. Because the typical proxy/stub makefile uses the extension mk rather than the standard mak, you have to use the nmake -f option. You also handle the DLL registration by calling regsvr32.exe. Nothing atypical here.

With this final step, assuming your project source files have no syntax errors, you can compile the source code and build your application executable and proxy/stub DLL.

NOTE

Don't forget that the application must be registered by running it with the -RegServer command-line option. If you forget to do this, you'll receive the error HRESULT REGDB_E_CLASSNOTREG (0x80040154).

Building a Client Application

Having compiled and registered your COM server, it's time to actually use it to do something useful. In this case, create your MFC application as you normally would, by using the MFC AppWizard. After you have a basic framework established, you then add any of the ATL support files (such as for smart pointers). After this is done, you have to decide when and where to create the COM object and insert the CoCreateInstance() call, as well as individual interface member calls where appropriate.

For demonstration purposes, I created a test application MFCServerTest, which is a simple dialog-based test driver (see Figure 16.9).

FIGURE 16.9

The MFCServerTest application.

The MFCServer object is created in OnInitDialog(). I decided to create it here because this would keep the COM server around throughout the lifetime of the test application. In this manner, when you increment the counter (using the BumpCount member you created previously), you see the count increase. Had you created the object when you clicked the Test button, you would always see a count value of one. The server would be created, increment its count from zero to one, return that value, and then be released. The count you would see displayed would never increase past one. Listing 16.7 is the code to create the MFCServer object.

LISTING 16.7 MFCSERVERTEST'S OnInitDialog() MEMBER

```
/////////////////////////////////////////////////////////////////////
// CMFCServerTestDlg message handlers
BOOL CMFCServerTestDlg::OnInitDialog()
{
CDialog::OnInitDialog();
// Add "About..." menu item to system menu.
```

continues

LISTING 16.7   CONTINUED

```
// IDM_ABOUTBOX must be in the system command range.
ASSERT((IDM_ABOUTBOX & 0xFFF0) == IDM_ABOUTBOX);
ASSERT(IDM_ABOUTBOX < 0xF000);
CMenu* pSysMenu = GetSystemMenu(FALSE);
if (pSysMenu != NULL)
    {
CString strAboutMenu;
strAboutMenu.LoadString(IDS_ABOUTBOX);
if (!strAboutMenu.IsEmpty())
    {
pSysMenu->AppendMenu(MF_SEPARATOR);
pSysMenu->AppendMenu(MF_STRING, IDM_ABOUTBOX, strAboutMenu);
    }
    }

// Set the icon for this dialog.  The framework does this
// automatically when the application's main window is not a dialog
    SetIcon(m_hIcon, TRUE);      // Set big icon
    SetIcon(m_hIcon, FALSE);     // Set small icon

// Create your COM object
HRESULT hr = CoCreateInstance(CLSID_MFCServer,
NULL, // no aggregation
CLSCTX_LOCAL_SERVER,
IID_IMFCServer,
reinterpret_cast<void**>(&m_pIMFCServer));
if ( FAILED(hr) ) {
// Problem creating the COM object...
AfxMessageBox("Error creating MFCServer object",
              MB_OK|MB_ICONERROR);
EndDialog(IDCANCEL);
return TRUE;
} // if
return TRUE;  // return TRUE  unless you set the focus to a control
}
```

If you failed to create the object, you'll display an error message and terminate the dialog box. Otherwise, dialog initialization continues, and you can actually call the COM server by clicking the Test button. The values `CLSID_MFCServer` and `IID_IMFCServer` came from the files MIDL created when you compiled your COM server. You must include those same files in this project. I elected to include the definition file in stdafx.h:

```
// Your COM object interface definitions
#include "..\MFCServer\MFCServer_i.h"
```

Similarly, I included the interface declarations in stdafx.cpp:

```
// COM Object GUID definitions
#include "..\MFCServer\MFCServer_i.c"
```

Feel free to include them anywhere it makes the most sense. My decision to include them in the precompiled header files was simply to allow them to be visible to all of the source files in the project, but your project's needs may not require (or desire) this.

When you've successfully compiled and debugged your test application, you're done. Well, you're done with the initial testing, anyway. Now you can get to the real work at hand, which is to integrate the COM server functionality into your main application.

Summary

In this chapter you examined techniques for adding ATL COM support to an MFC application. As you'll see, this will prove useful to you when you examine other Microsoft technologies such as adding scripting capabilities to your applications (Chapter 17, "Scripting Your MFC Application"); using COM-based technologies, such as Dynamic HTML (Chapter 23); DirectX (Chapter 30, "MFC and DirectX"); and, in some cases, shell programming.

CHAPTER 17

Scripting Your MFC Application

by Kenn Scribner

IN THIS CHAPTER

If there is one area where mixing MFC and COM is truly exciting (there are many), it has to be in adding scripting capability to your MFC application. Many MFC applications exist, as do many COM objects. Many MFC applications use COM objects. But few applications you find, except those coming from Microsoft, truly give you the ability to customize and automate their use through scripting. Frankly, many people I've talked with find this topic very mysterious. Yet it is one of the more interesting.

What is so exciting about scripting is the manner in which the application (MFC) and the COM objects work together in more than just a simple client/server relationship. To be truly useful, the COM object needs to be a part of the application yet still satisfy the requirements of COM. This can be challenging to implement.

In this chapter, I show you how to add scripting capabilities to your application. My techniques are not the only way this can be done, but I have found these techniques to be as faithful to COM as is possible yet still allow the COM objects to expose information private to the application. I'll start with some basic concepts.

Scripting Basics

When I use the term *scripting*, I truly mean anointing your application with the capability to parse and execute VBScript or JScript code designed to access portions of your application. Perhaps your script will change the size of the application's window. Or just as likely, your script might be designed to take some action after the application's document has been modified (I refer to this state as *dirty*). You might also want a script available to quit the application when a predetermined set of criteria is met.

Your goal, as the application designer, is to think like your users and provide them with the best possible automation tools your application can provide. By this I mean that you begin your scripting architectural design process by laying out an *object model* for your application (I'll cover this in more detail later in the chapter). When your users write a script for your application, they will be accessing *objects* your application *exposes*. The trick is to understand your application's problem domain well and design an object model that best fits that problem domain.

Any objects your application exposes will have certain requirements levied upon them due to the nature of the Microsoft scripting architecture, which inherits its needs from Visual Basic. After all, VBScript is a language subset of Visual Basic. Microsoft used the same technology when it implemented Visual J++ and its scripting language subset JScript. To be sure you have an understanding of these architectural requirements, I'll detail them later in this section.

> **NOTE**
>
> Throughout the remainder of this chapter, I will refer primarily to VBScript. This isn't to neglect JScript, but rather to simplify the conceptual descriptions by referring solely to a single scripting language. When it comes to ActiveX scripting, either language is interchangeable from a scripting engine perspective.

Adding scripting capability to your MFC application requires you to provide scripting functionality in three major areas:

- The application itself and its object model
- The objects that fit into the application's object model
- The script engine plumbing (such as parsing, execution, and so on)

Fortunately, you need only concentrate on the first two areas. Microsoft has provided the third free of charge, although you do have to license the technology and acknowledge Microsoft in your application. As an MFC programmer you already manage the first task, so the only added work on your part is to design the application's object model and write the code to support the objects themselves. I'll begin my detailed description of the scripting process by describing the piece Microsoft provides.

Scripting Interfaces

When you add scripting capability to your MFC application, you have several alternatives. First, you might design a completely proprietary scripting language and the tools that go with it (runtime environment, parsing, execution, and so on). Second, you might fake a scripting environment by providing some customization and pseudo-executable commands that might appear to be script-like. Of course, you could purchase a third-party package that provides most of the tools you need. But the alternative I find most attractive is using freely available scripting technology. I'm referring to the ActiveX Scripting engine provided by Microsoft.

Microsoft makes scripting available to you, the application programmer, by providing several COM objects and interfaces. If you know something about the scripting libraries and the COM interfaces, and if you have the compiler tools to support it (header files and such things), you can add scripting functionality to your application by invoking COM and using the scripting objects already available. And best of all, they're free. Therefore, incorporating the ActiveX Scripting engine into your application is what this chapter really explores.

Microsoft ActiveX Scripting

The scripting technology you'll use in this chapter is called *Microsoft ActiveX Scripting*. This technology provides you with the scripting runtime environment, a small set of development files, and a brief text file describing what is included in the download you will receive when you agree to the online licensing agreement (more on this later). The primary language files are VBScript.dll and JScript.dll, and the scripting runtime is provided by scrrun.dll. Each of these files is a COM in-process server DLL.

These DLLs collectively expose many COM interfaces, and describing them all is well beyond the scope of this chapter. However, the good news is that there are only a few you need to understand to provide basic scripting services. Microsoft has provided what I consider the four main scripting engine interfaces: `IActiveScript`, `IActiveScriptParse`, `IActiveScriptSite`, and `IActiveScriptSiteWindow`, and these are the four scripting interfaces I'll deal with in this chapter. There are additional ActiveX scripting interfaces you might find interesting, so be sure to refer to the online documentation for more details.

The `IActiveScript` interface is used to initialize and control the scripting engine. For example, you add scripted objects from your object model using `IActiveScript::AddNmedItem()`. Or you terminate the engine and any running script using `IActiveScript::Close()`.

`IActiveScriptParse` provides the methods you need to parse and execute a script. This interface is necessary because VBScript itself has no prescribed editing environment (unlike Visual Basic). Therefore, a simple VBScript file has no mechanism for loading itself from a file—this is something you provide in your application. Because of this, there has to be a mechanism in place to accept VBScript text and provide it to the scripting engine for parsing and execution. This role is shared by your application and `IActiveScriptParse::ParseScriptText()`, which is the main method you use for executing scripts.

Your application, as the host for scripted elements, must provide some basic plumbing to enable the scripting engine to do its work. You provide this by supplying implementations for the `IActiveScriptSite` interface. The most critical method in this interface is `IActiveScriptSite::GetItemInfo()`, which the engine calls to retrieve *type information* from your scripted objects. I'll cover type information and type libraries in more detail later in this chapter.

The final of the four primary scripting interfaces is `IActiveScriptSiteWindow`. This interface has only two methods and is relatively simple, but it's required because the scripting engine must have a way to retrieve a window handle if the engine has to display information to the user (as with an error, for example). The `IActiveScriptSiteWindow::GetWindow()` method provides for just this. As you might expect, applications with no user interface don't support `IActiveScriptSiteWindow`. In this chapter, though, where your MFC application is hosting the scripting environment, its implementation is mandatory.

Now that you've been introduced to the COM interfaces your application will deal with, it's time to actually retrieve the files you'll need to incorporate scripting into your application. As always, there is much more interface-specific information contained within the online files.

Licensing

For you to integrate the Microsoft ActiveX Scripting engine into your application, you must agree to a licensing arrangement and acknowledge Microsoft's scripting engine in your application. The licensing agreement and scripting runtime components are available at the Microsoft Internet site, `http://msdn.microsoft.com/scripting/default.htm?/scripting/vbscript`. This site works for both VBScript and JScript, as the scripting runtime engine handles both languages.

After you've provided some basic information, such as your name and that of your company, you'll download the scripting engine and some necessary development tools (header files and such). Save these! You'll need some portions of this download to compile your code, and other portions are used on your user's systems to upgrade (or install for the first time) the files the scripting engine will require to execute.

You'll also be asked to acknowledge Microsoft as the provider for the scripting engine on your About dialog box. Microsoft doesn't specify precisely what you must say, only that you acknowledge Microsoft's contribution to your application. For this chapter's sample application, I created the dialog you see in Figure 17.1.

FIGURE 17.1

Sample application About dialog box.

Scripting Engine Implementation Details

When you have the requisite header files, msscript.h and activscp.h (from the download in the previous section), you have what you need to develop your basic scripting functionality. Of the four interfaces I mentioned previously, two are interfaces you call

(IActiveScript and IActiveScriptParse), and two are interfaces you must provide for the scripting engine to call (IActiveScriptSite and IActiveScriptSiteWindow). As it happens, the implementations are relatively simple to implement, and in many cases you can use your code in many other scripted applications with little to no change.

The sample program provided with this chapter contains a COM object I named ScriptObject, as it is the COM object I use to marry the MFC application to the scripting engine. ScriptObject uses as its source a file named ScriptImpl.h, the code for which you see in Listing 17.1. This code provides the majority of the implementation of the IActiveScriptSite and IActiveScriptSiteWindow interfaces (the IActiveScriptSite::GetItemInfo() method is implemented elsewhere due to the nature of ATL).

LISTING 17.1 IActiveScriptSite AND IActiveScriptSiteWindow IMPLEMENTATION USING ATL TEMPLATES

```
// ScriptImpl.h : Implementation of IActiveScript* interfaces

#ifndef __SCRIPTIMPL_H_
#define __SCRIPTIMPL_H_

// IActiveScript* definitions
#include <activscp.h>

// swprintf definition
#include <stdio.h>

class ATL_NO_VTABLE IActiveScriptSiteImpl : public IActiveScriptSite
{
    STDMETHOD(QueryInterface)(REFIID riid, LPVOID* ppvObject) = 0;
    ATL_DEBUG_ADDREF_RELEASE_IMPL(IActiveScriptSiteImpl)

    // This method *must* be overridden in your implementation
    // (hence the E_FAIL).
    STDMETHOD(GetItemInfo)(LPCOLESTR pstrName, DWORD dwReturnMask,
        IUnknown** ppiunkItem, ITypeInfo** ppti)
    {
        // You must override this and provide your own implementation.
        return E_NOTIMPL;
    }

    STDMETHOD(OnScriptError)(IActiveScriptError *pscripterror)
    {
        // Set up the exception record
        EXCEPINFO ei;
        ::ZeroMemory(&ei,sizeof(ei));
```

```
    // Determine from where the error came
    DWORD dwCookie;
    LONG nChar;
    ULONG nLine;
    pscripterror->GetSourcePosition(&dwCookie, &nLine, &nChar);

    // Retrieve the source line
    BSTR bstrSourceLine = NULL;
    pscripterror->GetSourceLineText(&bstrSourceLine);

    // Fill the exception record
    pscripterror->GetExceptionInfo(&ei);

    // Create an output string
    OLECHAR wszMsg[2048];
    swprintf(wszMsg, OLESTR("%s\n[Line: %d] %s\n%s"),
            ei.bstrSource, nLine, ei.bstrDescription,
            bstrSourceLine ? bstrSourceLine : OLESTR(""));

    // Display the error string
    ::MessageBoxW(GetDesktopWindow(),
                  wszMsg,
                  L"Script Error",
                  MB_SETFOREGROUND);

    // Free your BSTRs
    ::SysFreeString(bstrSourceLine);
    ::SysFreeString(ei.bstrSource);
    ::SysFreeString(ei.bstrDescription);
    ::SysFreeString(ei.bstrHelpFile);

    return S_OK;
}

STDMETHOD(GetLCID)(LCID *plcid)
{
    // Change the LCID value to meet your internationalization
    // requirements...
    *plcid = MAKELCID(LANG_USER_DEFAULT,SORT_DEFAULT);
    return S_OK;
}

STDMETHOD(GetDocVersionString)(BSTR *pbstrVersion)
{
    *pbstrVersion = SysAllocString(L"");
    return S_OK;
}

STDMETHOD(OnScriptTerminate)(const VARIANT *pvr,
➥const EXCEPINFO *pei)
```

continues

LISTING 17.1   CONTINUED

```
    {
    return S_OK;
    }

    STDMETHOD(OnStateChange)(SCRIPTSTATE ssScriptState)
    {
        return S_OK;
    }

    STDMETHOD(OnEnterScript)(void)
    {
        return S_OK;
    }

    STDMETHODIMP OnLeaveScript(void)
    {
        return S_OK;
    }
};

class IActiveScriptSiteWindowImpl : public IActiveScriptSiteWindow
{
    STDMETHOD(QueryInterface)(REFIID riid, void ** ppvObject) = 0;
    _ATL_DEBUG_ADDREF_RELEASE_IMPL(IActiveScriptSiteImpl)

    STDMETHODIMP GetWindow(HWND *phwnd)
    {
        *phwnd = GetDesktopWindow();
        return S_OK;
    }

    STDMETHODIMP EnableModeless(BOOL)
    {
        return S_OK;
    }
};

#endif // __SCRIPTIMPL_H_
```

You will also need to instantiate the scripting engine itself to retrieve the IActiveScript and IActiveScriptParse interfaces. In the sample program, I activate the scripting engine in CScriptObject::FinalConstruct(), as shown in Listing 17.2. If you look at the actual CoCreateInstance(), you'll see I use a class identifier of CLSID_VBScript. This activates the VBScript.dll COM in-process server and allows me to provide

VBScript services to my application's users. However, I could have instead (or in addition to) requested the JScript version by using `CLSID_JScript`. The choice is yours. I used VBScript because it's the scripting language of Developer Studio and many other Microsoft products, so I know my application's users will be somewhat familiar with that language.

LISTING 17.2   `IActiveScript` AND `IActiveScriptParse` INSTANTIATION

```
HRESULT CScriptObject::FinalConstruct()
{
    // CoCreate the scripting engine
    HRESULT hr = CoCreateInstance(CLSID_VBScript,
                                  NULL,
                                  CLSCTX_ALL,
                                  IID_IActiveScriptParse,
                                  reinterpret_cast<LPVOID*>
                                  ➥(&m_pScriptParser));
    if ( SUCCEEDED(hr) ) {
        // Query for the script interface
        CComQIPtr<IActiveScript,&IID_IActiveScript>
        ➥pScript(m_pScriptParser);
        if ( pScript.p != NULL ) {
            // Assign our attribute
            m_pScript = pScript;

            // Initialize the script engine
            hr = m_pScriptParser->InitNew();
            if ( SUCCEEDED(hr) ) hr = m_pScript->SetScriptSite(this);
            if ( SUCCEEDED(hr) ) hr =
            ➥m_pScript->SetScriptState(SCRIPTSTATE_STARTED);
        } // if
        else {
            // Failed...
            hr = E_FAIL;
        } // else
    } // if

    return hr;
}
```

The mechanics you've seen so far are aimed at bringing the scripting engine into your application. I'll provide much more detail later in the chapter when I analyze the sample program. Before I do that, though, you should have some idea what your application must provide the scripting engine to make things work as they should. Therefore, a little COM background is in order.

17

SCRIPTING YOUR MFC APPLICATION

Dual Interfaces

When you have the scripting engine and the scripting plumbing your application will use in place, you can turn to developing your application's objects. Before I discuss that topic, which is the topic of the next section, I will introduce some key concepts and terms you must be aware of when developing these objects.

The first concept you must understand is the nature of the COM *dual interface*. This is a COM interface like many others, but the major difference is that it inherits directly from the IDispatch interface rather than from the more common IUnknown interface. The significance of this is that the interfaces you develop for your scripted objects have a split personality. On the one hand, they have a *custom interface*, which is the type of COM interface C++ programmers traditionally deal with. This is the traditional IUnknown interface. On the other hand, though, they have this other IDispatch nature. As it happens, it's the IDispatch side of their behavior that is required for scripting, and the key lies in the concept of *late binding*.

Late Binding

To me, the easiest way to describe early versus late binding is to think in terms of compilation and execution timelines. That is, if you are writing a traditional C++ program, you undoubtedly are linking in static libraries (the C runtime library, for example). Because the executable will have access to the functionality of the libraries (they're compiled into the executable), they are bound to the executable before it actually runs. This is *early binding*. Traditional linking (versus dynamic linking) places the library code in your executable's image for when the executable runs.

On the other hand, when you run a script, what you are really doing is submitting your script text to a script engine (otherwise known as an *interpreter*). The script engine cannot be given prior knowledge regarding the precise needs of your script because it is a general purpose engine—it knows only which methods you call and in what objects you call them when it encounters the code in the script. The script is *interpreted*. This is very much like reading a book. You only know how the story goes when you actually read the pages.

Therefore, the script engine has to have some other mechanism for querying the objects it has access to when it encounters them while interpreting the script. This query process is known as *late binding* because the script is already executing before the script engine knows what libraries to access.

Microsoft provides for late binding with something known as a *type library*. If you've read Chapter 16, "Using MFC and ATL," you were introduced to the Interface

Description Language, or IDL. The IDL file describes the COM interface by codifying the methods and properties the interface supports as well as the parameter lists each function requires. A type library is a tokenized form of IDL (some information is removed, unfortunately). When the script engine parses a script that accesses a given object's method, the script engine retrieves the type library for that object and compares what it finds there to what the script actually requested. If there is a match in function signatures, the script engine executes the object's method on behalf of the script. On the other hand, if the function signatures don't match (or there is some other error), the scripting engine halts the script with an error message to the user.

Dispinterfaces

Given the preceding discussion, assuming the script requested a particular object's method and the script engine found a matching function signature in the object's type library, the scripting engine will execute the method. But in this case the script engine cannot simply execute compiled code. After all, the script engine in all likelihood wasn't compiled with your particular object in mind. It was compiled, however, with a generic means of executing object methods. How it executes those methods is through the use of the `IDispatch::Invoke()` method. When the script engine calls `IDispatch::Invoke()`, it is using a *dispinterface* (short for *dispatch interface*).

In this case, the object's methods are enumerated. That is, each object method is assigned a number at compilation time (in both the IDL and C++ source files). The script engine passes the associated number to the object for execution through `Invoke()`. In this fashion, the script engine merely needs to support `IDispatch`. It can handle an infinite number of different interfaces, so long as each interface is callable through `Invoke()`. The object's type library informs the script engine which method number is associated with what method, and then the script engine passes that number to the object through `Invoke()`. The object receives the number, through the mechanics of `Invoke()`, and then executes the associated method on behalf of the script and script engine. This pseudo-interface is the dispinterface.

> **NOTE**
>
> I mentioned that an infinite number of interfaces could be supported through `IDispatch::Invoke()`. That is not to say, however, that a single interface could have an infinite number of methods. On the contrary, the current limits are 512 methods for Windows 95 and Windows 98, and 1024 for Windows NT 4, SP3.

Properties

Scriptable objects also typically support *properties*. A property is akin to a C++ attribute. Say, for example, that an object in your application's object model draws text. That object might logically have a font property that tells the object what typeface to use. Related properties might include font size, face, and color.

Objects implemented with a dual interface, however, treat properties in one of two ways, depending upon your point of view. To your script, the property is simply an attribute of an object. You set and retrieve the property value based upon the context of the script text. Using an imaginary font object as an example, this VBScript code would retrieve the text color:

```
color = FontObject.color
```

It would similarly set a new text color by placing the object and property on the left-hand side of the assignment:

```
FontObject.color = 255
```

However, to the COM object the script is accessing, the property is an attribute with access limited by get and put accessor functions. That is, the object actually implements a property as an attribute and a method pair. One method *puts* the new attribute value, and the other *gets* it. For example, to the COM object itself, the property is a combination of the following:

```
protected:
   COLORREF m_clrFont;

public:
   HRESULT get_Color(VARIANT* newVal);
   HRESULT put_Color(VARIANT newVal
```

The object *encapsulates* the actual property. The script is allowed a shorthand notation for property access, but the COM object always implements data hiding. The property itself is never actually exposed to the script.

> **NOTE**
>
> What this means is this: the object's developers provide for scripted properties by adding methods to their object. This is completely hidden from the script itself. To the script, the property appears to be a single, public value.

You will see these concepts in action later. The objects to which I've been referring collectively work together to provide the script access to your application's infrastructure. This collection of objects is called an *object model*, and this topic merits some discussion. Proper object model design is critical to your application's ease of use and logical architectural design.

Object Models

Before I get started, I must confess that the sample program's object model isn't an ideal model for a text editor. My goal with the sample program was to demonstrate one technique for introducing scripting into an MFC application, not to demonstrate some arbitrarily limited object architecture. The final form of my object model isn't what is important here. How I derived it is, however.

There are probably as many definitions of object model as there are programmers. But in this case, I loosely define the term *object model* to mean scripting architecture. Your application's object model is the view your users see of your architecture when they look at it from a scripting perspective. Each of these objects will have *properties*, *methods*, and exposed *events*. Through a script, your user will be able to manipulate the properties, methods, and events to combine functionality from one or many objects into a single action (the running script).

For example, if your application were a paint program, you might design an object model something like that shown in Figure 17.2. Then again, you might add objects, or remove some of the objects I've added.

FIGURE 17.2

One possible paint program object model.

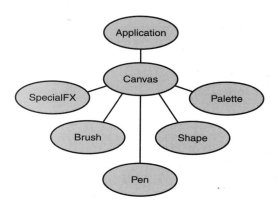

In this object model, the application object would manage the MFC application itself. Perhaps you could manipulate the frame window (or add a window object for that purpose). Or you could quit the application.

The canvas object would contain the actual bitmap. It would do such things as load and save a bitmap, manage cut-and-paste operations, and it would have subordinate objects that could manipulate important aspects of the bitmap, such as detailed color management (palette object), bitmap flipping and rotation (special effects), and pen, brush, and shape management.

When this application's user writes a script, she would (presumably) be able to clear the canvas, create a shape, draw the shape, apply a color to the shape, and draw lines over the shape. She then might be able to save the bitmap (contained by the canvas) to disk and print a copy.

This particular architecture tells me many things. For one, for any application object, there is a single canvas object. This is a single document (SDI) application. If it had multiple canvas objects, or if it indicated there was a canvas object collection from which you retrieved a particular canvas object, it would be a multiple document (MDI) application. I also see that for this canvas object, there is a single object for special effects, pen, and so on. At any one time, then, you can apply only a single special effect or place one shape. This isn't necessarily bad—it's a design decision you make when you lay out the object model.

Some objects are notably missing, which could have been by omission or by design (it's sometimes hard to tell). For example, there is no obvious mechanism for writing text onto the canvas. Granted, Figure 17.2 doesn't provide tremendous detail. You don't see the properties, methods, and events each object implements. The application's user is the person best qualified to tell you whether the omission of a text and font object is a good or poor design decision.

The point of this exercise is this: Design an object model. And when you design your application's object model, think like your users and ask yourself, "What would I want to automate using this application?" This should naturally lead you to design some basic objects. Then, as you imagine scripting scenarios, add to and modify your design as necessary to provide the means to adequately automate your application from your user's perspective.

There is no hard and fast rule to guide you through this process, though a software engineering background will be helpful. But just as you can tell a good job from a poor job, generally you will know a good object model from a poor one, even if the programmer in the next office has a different opinion. In any case, when you have your application's object model designed, it's time to implement the objects in code.

Implementing a Scripted Application

In this section I'll describe the practical aspects of adding scripting to your application. This chapter's sample program consists of the simple text editor you see in Figure 17.3. In fact, it uses a CEditView view class, so actually creating the application couldn't have been easier. I simply created a new SDI application and selected CEditView as its view class. After the AppWizard had generated the code and I compiled what it gave me, I had a fully functional text editor.

FIGURE 17.3

The scripted text editor.

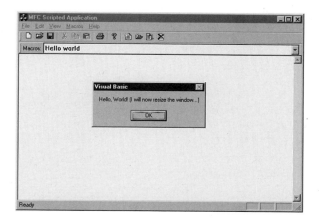

For demonstration purposes, I designed a very simple object model for the text editor. This object model consists of three objects: the application object, the document object, and a selected text object. Their descriptions follow.

The following are the specifications of the application object:

- Properties

  Document—Retrieves the document object

  Height—Frame window height

  Width—Frame window width

  Top—Frame window top coordinate

  Left—Frame window left coordinate

  WindowState—Frame window state (minimized, and so on)

  Caption—Frame window caption

- Method

  Quit—Terminate the application
- Events

  DocumentNew—A new document was created

  DocumentOpen—A document was opened

  DocumentSave—The document was saved

  DocumentSaveAs—The document was saved with a new name

These are the specifications of the document object:

- Properties

  Application—Retrieves the application object

  TextSelection—Retrieves the text selection object

  Dirty—Indicates the document has been modified
- Methods

  Save—Saves the document to disk

  SaveAs—Saves the document to disk with a new name

  Open—Opens a document from disk

  New—Creates a new document

  Print—Prints the document

  Clear—Clears (deletes) all document text
- Event

  IsDirty—Fired when document becomes dirty

The following are the specifications of the text selection object:

- Properties

  Application—Retrieves the application object

  Document—Retrieves the document object

  UpperSelBound—Upper selection character index

  LowerSelBound—Lower selection character index
- Methods

  GetCursorPos—Retrieves the cursor position

  SetCursorPos—Moves the cursor to a specific position

  Cut—Cuts the selection to the clipboard

`Copy`—Copies selection to the clipboard

`Paste`—Pastes from clipboard

`SelectAll`—Selects all document text

`SelectRange`—Selects a text range

`ClearAll`—Clears all document text

`ClearSelection`—Clears selected text

`InsertText`—Inserts text at cursor

- Event

`KeyPressed`—Fired when a character is entered into the edit control

Given this object model, it is time to examine how the objects were developed.

Object Implementation

I chose to implement the objects in ATL using the following recipe. Unfortunately, it's beyond the scope of this chapter to examine each object in detail. The basic thought behind each is the same, though. I created a simple ATL COM object with a dual interface and added methods and properties to give it the proper functionality. You need not use ATL, however. Any COM programming paradigm that enables you to implement a dual interface will work just fine, to include MFC. In this case, though, I followed the steps outlined in the next section.

ATL Object Creation

Creating an ATL COM DLL is very much like creating the local server object you saw in Chapter 16. The main difference is that you create an ATL project from scratch rather than add ATL support to an existing MFC project. In any case, here are the basic steps:

- Create the basic ATL (DLL) project.
- Add an ATL simple object.
- Name the object and assign the attributes (be sure it has a dual interface and supports connection points and error information).
- In the source code, add support for object safety (this assists with security so warning dialogs don't appear each time the user runs a script).
- Add all the methods and properties required, including those methods for events (added to the event interface).
- Compile the code to create a type library.
- Add the connection point table using the Connection Point Wizard (this step requires the type library you just created).

- Add the required attributes (pointers to parent objects, and so on).
- Add (iteratively) the meat to each of the methods.

If you're unsure how to create the ATL COM objects, please refer to a good ATL COM programming book. Using the text selection object as an example, Listing 17.3 shows you the IDL file I created. When you examine Listing 17.3, look especially at the IDL you see versus the methods and properties I described previously. They should match up quite well.

LISTING 17.3 THE TEXT SELECTION OBJECT'S IDL DEFINITIONS

```
// TextObject.idl : IDL source for TextObject.dll
//

// This file will be processed by the MIDL tool to
// produce the type library (TextObject.tlb) and marshaling code.

import "oaidl.idl";
import "ocidl.idl";
    [
        object,
        uuid(1E1B8551-B15D-11D2-B235-00C04FBEDB8F),
        dual,
        helpstring("ITextSelObject Interface"),
        pointer_default(unique)
    ]
    interface ITextSelObject : IDispatch
    {
        [propget, id(1), helpstring("property Application")]
        ➥HRESULT Application([out, retval] VARIANT *pVal);
        [propget, id(2), helpstring("property Document")]
        ➥HRESULT Document([out, retval] VARIANT *pVal);
        [propget, id(3), helpstring("property UpperSelBound")]
        ➥HRESULT UpperSelBound([out, retval] VARIANT *pVal);
        [propput, id(3), helpstring("property UpperSelBound")]
        ➥HRESULT UpperSelBound([in] VARIANT newVal);
        [propget, id(4), helpstring("property LowerSelBound")]
        ➥HRESULT LowerSelBound([out, retval] VARIANT *pVal);
        [propput, id(4), helpstring("property LowerSelBound")]
        ➥HRESULT LowerSelBound([in] VARIANT newVal);
        [id(5), helpstring("method SetApplication"), hidden]
        ➥HRESULT SetApplication([in] LPDISPATCH newVal);
        [id(6), helpstring("method SetDocument"), hidden]
        ➥HRESULT SetDocument([in] LPDISPATCH newVal);
        [id(7), helpstring("method GetCursorPos")]
        ➥HRESULT GetCursorPos([out] VARIANT *pLineVal,
        ➥[out] VARIANT *pIndexVal);
        [id(8), helpstring("method SetCursorPos")]
```

```
      ➥HRESULT SetCursorPos([in] VARIANT lineVal,
      ➥[in] VARIANT indexVal);
      [id(9), helpstring("method Cut")] HRESULT Cut();
      [id(10), helpstring("method Copy")] HRESULT Copy();
      [id(11), helpstring("method Paste")] HRESULT Paste();
      [id(12), helpstring("method SelectAll")] HRESULT SelectAll();
      [id(13), helpstring("method SelectRange")]
      ➥HRESULT SelectRange([in] VARIANT lowerVal,
      ➥[in] VARIANT upperVal);
      [id(14), helpstring("method ClearAll")] HRESULT ClearAll();
      [id(15), helpstring("method ClearSelection")]
      ➥HRESULT ClearSelection();
      [id(16), helpstring("method InsertText")]
      ➥HRESULT InsertText([in] VARIANT newVal);
      [id(17), helpstring("method InitHwnd"), hidden]
      ➥HRESULT InitHwnd([in] OLE_HANDLE hWnd);
   };


[
   uuid(1E1B8545-B15D-11D2-B235-00C04FBEDB8F),
   version(1.0),
   helpstring("TextObject 1.0 Type Library")
]
library TEXTOBJECTLib
{
   importlib("stdole32.tlb");
   importlib("stdole2.tlb");

   [
      uuid(1E1B8553-B15D-11D2-B235-00C04FBEDB8F),
      helpstring("_ITextSelObjectEvents Interface")
   ]
   dispinterface _ITextSelObjectEvents
   {
      properties:
      methods:
      [id(1), helpstring("event BeforeTextChange")]
      ➥BOOL BeforeTextChange();
      [id(2), helpstring("event TextChange")] HRESULT TextChange();
   };

   [
      uuid(1E1B8552-B15D-11D2-B235-00C04FBEDB8F),
      helpstring("TextSelObject Class")
   ]
   coclass TextSelObject
   {
      [default] interface ITextSelObject;
      [default, source] dispinterface _ITextSelObjectEvents;
   };
};
```

There are several things to note when examining Listing 17.3, and most of these revolve around the requirements of scriptable interfaces you saw earlier in the chapter. The next section outlines the code required to meet the basic requirements I mentioned.

Meeting Scriptable Object Requirements

To briefly review, COM interfaces designed to work with a scripting environment must be dual interfaces (derived from `IDispatch`), must support late binding through type libraries, must expose events as dispinterfaces, and must pass parameters as `VARIANT`s. Let's see how all of this is done in code.

Referring back to Listing 17.3, this code tells you the object implements a dual interface:

```
[
    object,
    uuid(1E1B8551-B15D-11D2-B235-00C04FBEDB8F),
    dual,
    helpstring("ITextSelObject Interface"),
    pointer_default(unique)
]
interface ITextSelObject : IDispatch
{
    (properties and methods described here...)
}
```

The object has the `dual` attribute set as well as clearly inheriting the `IDispatch` interface.

You also see the use of `VARIANT` datatypes for parameter values. Scripts use `VARIANT` datatypes because they are a discriminated union and therefore might contain any of a number of data values. Chapter 16 provides more information in this area.

Also note the differences in how properties are declared as compared to methods. The `Document` property, for example, is a particularly interesting property as it is a *read-only* property (there is no corresponding `propput` attribute):

```
[propget, id(2), helpstring("property Document")]
➥HRESULT Document([out, retval] VARIANT *pVal);
```

I removed the corresponding property method to assign the document object pointer and replaced it with a hidden method:

```
[id(6), helpstring("method SetDocument"), hidden]
➥ HRESULT SetDocument([in] LPDISPATCH newVal);
```

I did this because the script has no reason to set the document object pointer. To do so could cause horrific results, and none of the possible outcomes are good. The hidden attribute, by the way, makes the method unavailable to type library viewers such as

Visual Basic. In effect, this method is private to the object, though there is no enforcement of that privacy (as there is with private C++ class attributes and methods).

The actual implementations for these two methods are also interesting to see, as there is some work involved with accessing the VARIANT. Listing 17.4 shows the code I use to return the document object pointer back to the script.

LISTING 17.4   THE TEXT SELECTION OBJECT'S get_Document() METHOD

```
STDMETHODIMP CTextSelObject::get_Document(VARIANT *pVal)
{
   HRESULT hr = S_OK;
   try {
      // Check their pointer
      if ( pVal != NULL ) {
         // Clear their variant
         ::VariantClear(pVal);

         // Copy in our document's IDispatch pointer
         VARIANT var;
         var.vt = VT_DISPATCH;
         var.pdispVal = m_pDocObject.p;
         ::VariantCopy(pVal,&var);
      } // if
      else {
         // Wasn't a valid pointer
         hr = E_POINTER;
      } // if
   } // try
   catch (...) {
      // Some error...
      hr = E_FAIL;
   } // catch

   return S_OK;
}
```

Note that the IDL *property* Document was translated to be a method declared as STD-METHODIMP CTextSelObject::get_Document(VARIANT *pVal) when implemented in the C++ source file. As I mentioned, properties to the script are really methods to the COM object. In any case, when the script requests the document object's pointer, I check for a valid return pointer, and if it is valid, I create a new VARIANT that I fill with the pointer this object contains. Then, after that has been completed, I copy the local VARIANT to the remote VARIANT for the script to interpret. Most of the remaining object properties and methods follow this vein. After the objects have been implemented, it is time to integrate them into the MFC application.

Adding the Scriptable Objects to Your MFC Application

At this point you have a basic text editor and a handful of COM objects. A good question you might be asking yourself is how do I intend to marry the COM objects to the application? This is the tricky part, in many cases. After all, what you're asking is how to retrieve information from an executable and pass it to a DLL when the DLL requires the information. It's easy to go the other way. When an application wants information from a DLL, it simply asks the DLL, through a function pointer, for the data. COM DLLs (in-process servers) are more than mere DLLs, however. Moreover, your objects will be reacting to directives from a running script and might require information or call methods that are otherwise private to the application.

There are several ways to attack this problem. I personally try to use the least intrusive method possible, and if that doesn't work, move to a more intrusive approach. The mechanisms I see available are these, though undoubtedly there are additional ways to solve this problem:

1. Pass an HWND to the COM object and use that HWND for SendMessage() calls for information and/or subclass the HWND (especially useful for event processing).

2. Implement connection points in the application, so that when the COM object requires information it fires an event to retrieve the data.

3. Expose methods and attributes in the MFC C++ classes and somehow pass a pointer to them to the COM object.

I use the first mechanism almost exclusively, even though it involves something COM normally would advise against—you have to somehow pass an HWND down to the COM object. This is typically discouraged in COM programming, as HWNDs are system-specific. If for some reason someone were to create your object and expect it to work in a distributed environment, they would be in for a shock. HWNDs cannot be passed over a network! However, this is the least distasteful alternative, as you'll see.

> **TIP**
>
> Using this mechanism, there is no reason why you could not use RegsterWindowMessage() to create application-specific Windows messages. This would allow your COM objects to retrieve information private to your application easily. Simply send the message from your COM object, and add a handler to your MFC class.

The second alternative, implementing connection points, is not necessarily a bad alternative. It simply involves a lot more code and wiring to properly implement the connection point mappings in the MFC application. Depending upon your point of view, however, it might be easier than subclassing the application's HWND.

The last alternative should rarely (if ever) be considered. For one thing, the C++ method you call will have to be static. Nonstatic methods have an implied this pointer, which you do not have when running in your COM object. Static methods themselves introduce other (typically) undesirable artifacts, such as a single static method/attribute for all instantiations of the class. It's also difficult to access nonstatic class data. But the worst problem, by far, with this last mechanism is the fact you would be passing a local process pointer from the application to the COM object. Remember, COM will want to marshal everything (see Chapter 16), and your normal, everyday function/data pointer's marshaling will be tenuous at best. The reasons for this are complex and steeped in COM lore. It's best to avoid any temptations you might entertain with this mechanism. Don't do it.

Now let's examine how you set the document pointer in the first place. To reiterate, remember that the text selection COM object contains pointers to both the application and document objects. These pointers are IDispatch pointers, and you obtain them when you create the objects in the first place. After their creation, you must somehow provide to each object the other relevant pointers. I'll discuss that process a bit further in the chapter. For now, Listing 17.5 shows you the code you would use to store a local IDispatch pointer.

LISTING 17.5   STORING A RELATED OBJECT'S *IDispatch* POINTER

```
STDMETHODIMP CTextSelObject::SetDocument(LPDISPATCH newVal)
{
   HRESULT hr = S_OK;
   try {
      // Accept new value
      if ( newVal == NULL ) {
         // Invalid pointer
         _ATLASSERT(newVal != NULL);
         hr = E_POINTER;
      } // if
      else {
         // Set the pointer
         m_pDocObject = newVal;
      } // else
   } // try
```

continues

LISTING 17.5 CONTINUED

```
catch (...) {
    // Some error...
    hr = E_FAIL;
} // catch

return hr;
}
```

The attribute m_pDocObject is declared using CComPtr, so the incoming object is automatically AddRef()'d (which is according to the rules of COM when passing in object pointers). If you're not using CComPtr or some other smart pointer, don't forget that AddRef(). You might find yourself at some time calling an object that was terminated without your knowledge or consent.

The code I use to perform this wiring feat is found in the application's view class, in a helper function I called InitializeObjects(). You see this helper function in Listing 17.6.

LISTING 17.6 INITIALIZING THE OBJECT MODEL OBJECTS

```
void CScriptView::InitializeObjects()
{
    try {
        // Create your scripting objects
        HRESULT hr = m_pDocObject.CreateInstance(CLSID_DocObject);
        if ( SUCCEEDED(hr) ) {
            // Initialize the document object
            CMainFrame* pFrame = (CMainFrame*)AfxGetMainWnd();
            ASSERT(pFrame != NULL);
            pFrame->AddDocObject(bstr_t("document"),m_pDocObject);
            m_pDocObject->InitViewHwnd(reinterpret_cast<long>(m_hWnd));
            m_pDocObject->InitEditHwnd(reinterpret_cast<long>
            ➥(GetEditCtrl().m_hWnd));

            // Text selection object...
            hr = m_pTextSelObject.CreateInstance(CLSID_TextSelObject);
            if ( SUCCEEDED(hr) ) {
                // Initialize the document object
                pFrame->AddTextSelObject(bstr_t("textselection"),
                                         m_pTextSelObject);
                m_pTextSelObject->InitHwnd(reinterpret_cast<long>
                ➥(GetEditCtrl().m_hWnd));

                // Wire up the objects
                m_pDocObject->SetApplication(pFrame->GetAppObject());
                m_pDocObject->SetTextSelection(m_pTextSelObject);
```

```
            m_pTextSelObject->SetApplication(pFrame->GetAppObject());
            m_pTextSelObject->SetDocument(m_pDocObject);
        } // if
        else {
            // Some error...
            AfxMessageBox("Unable to create the text selection
            ➥object",MB_OK¦MB_ICONERROR);
        } // else
    } // if
    else {
        // Some error...
        AfxMessageBox("Unable to create the document object",
                    MB_OK¦MB_ICONERROR);
    } // else
} // try
catch (...) {
    // Some error...
    AfxMessageBox("Unable to create scripted objects",
                MB_OK¦MB_ICONERROR);
} // catch
}
```

This method is called by the frame window class (`CMainFrame`) when the frame is initially shown by `CMainFrame::ActivateFrame()`. The frame window class helper functions `CMainFrame::AddDocumentObject()` and `CMainFrame::AddTextSelObject()` are similar, though much more brief. Those functions have the added chore of adding the names of the scripted objects to the scriptable object name vector `m_vScriptElements` in the script object by using `IScriptObject::AddObject()`.

Events

Another interesting topic is event generation. Scripts certainly can alter an object's state by changing the object properties and calling object methods. But in many cases a script might like asynchronous information from the object. These are events. An example of an event could be when the user initially types something into the edit control. Before this time, the edit control has no text and is not dirty. After the keypress, the control contains modified text and is now dirty. If a script were to look for some sort of dirty event, the script could take action when notified the document was now dirty.

I manage this behavior in the objects by implementing connection points and subclassing the windows of interest. For example, I know when the edit control has dirty text because I subclass the edit control and intercept `WM_CHAR` messages, as well as several other messages that indicate a dirty status. The code shown in Listing 17.7, found in the document object, shows how such an event would be generated (*fired*).

LISTING 17.7   FIRING A DOCUMENT-IS-DIRTY EVENT

```
LRESULT OnChar(UINT, WPARAM wParam, LPARAM lParam, BOOL& bHandled)
{
   if ( !m_bIsDirty ) {
      // If we haven't already fired the event, do so
      // now...
      m_bIsDirty = TRUE;
      Fire_IsDirty();
   } // if

   // Allow the control to handle the character
   return m_CEditCtrl.DefWindowProc(WM_CHAR,wParam,lParam);
}
```

The function Fire_IsDirty() is part of the ATL connection point architecture. How it is created and how it works are beyond the scope of this chapter. (Refer again to a good COM book for more information, such as Sams Publishing's *COM/DCOM Unleashed*.) However, it is nothing more than a method assigned to the document object event interface. It merely looks for all of the objects connected to its interface (through an internally kept list) and notifies each of the change in document status. The main concept to take from this is that events are fired based upon Windows messages you intercept when you subclass a given HWND.

> **TIP**
>
> Window subclassing is also beyond the scope of this chapter, though you'll find MFC window subclassing discussed in Chapter 5, "Custom Control Development." In ATL, however, you easily subclass windows using CContainedWindow. Simply create a variable of type CContainedWindow and use its SubclassWindow() method (passing in an HWND).

When you intercept a message of note, you fire the particular event that corresponds to the message. For example, had I wanted to fire an event each time the user pressed a key, this handler would intercept the WM_CHAR message and I'd fire my keypress event at that time.

Any Windows message you intercept is a candidate. I use this technique to determine when the user opened a new text file, for example. I subclass the MFC view window and intercept the WM_COMMAND message with the command identifier of ID_FILE_OPEN (defined in afxres.h). When I receive this message, from the subclassed window (the

MFC view), I fire an event to signal a document has been opened. A script can then do with that information whatever it will.

> **TIP**
>
> For those interested in the ATL connection point code, if your events don't fire as expected even after you've inserted the connection point proxy using the Connection Point Wizard, you probably need to include `IProvideClassInfo2Impl` in your object's inheritance list. The scripting engine retrieves information from your object using `IProvideClassInfo2`. Don't forget to add entries to your COM map for `IProvideClassInfo` and `IProvideClassInfo2`.

Script Management

This final section discusses what I call *script management*. By this, I mean your application is responsible for not only providing the objects that implement your object model, activating and using the scripting engine, and performing the tasks it was designed to perform: It also must have a mechanism for storing and accessing script text.

The sample application you've been examining takes a fairly common approach. The scripts themselves are stored as text files with a custom file extension. They must be located in the current working directory to be available to the application. I provide fairly robust code to locate the files and bring them from disk into memory, from where they can be used by either the script engine or my simple script editor.

The bottom line is that your application must also host the scripts as well as the conduit to the script engine. Helping your users manage their scripts helps them use your application more effectively, and ultimately that's the best reason for adding scripting capability in the first place.

Summary

Hopefully, this brief look at MFC and scripting has whet your appetite, and you'll give scripting a try when you implement your next MFC application. The programming challenges are intriguing—even fun. Be sure to begin your work by thinking like your users and designing an object model accordingly. The challenges, and the rewards, will be well worth your efforts.

MFC Database Programming

PART

IV

IN THIS PART

MFC Database Processing

by Bill Heyman

IN THIS CHAPTER

Using MFC's `CFile` class to handle normal file I/O operations is the most common way to store your application data. In many applications, however, simple file I/O operations are not enough. For example, if your application needs fast access to data elements matching specific criteria, you can use a relational database to access your organized data. MFC supports relational databases via a number of interfaces: ODBC (open database connectivity), DAO (Data Access Objects), OLE DB, and ADO (ActiveX Data Objects). Each interface represents an evolutionary stage in Microsoft's development of programmatic database support: ODBC is the tried-and-true and ADO is the up-and-coming.

This chapter and Chapter 19, "Advanced Database Support," show you how to access relational databases from your MFC application. This chapter starts with an introduction to relational database concepts (with an MFC accent) and finishes with a description of ODBC and DAO interfaces. If you are already familiar with relational database concepts, feel free to skim ahead to the MFC specifics in the later part of the chapter.

Relational Database Concepts

A *database* provides a way to group and organize your data logically. In general, a database is nothing more than a structured file. To access the information in this structured file, you use an interface that understands how to manipulate the data within the structured file.

Although there are different types of databases (Indexed Sequential Access Method (ISAM), relational, and object-oriented, to name a few), the majority of the world's data that is stored in databases is in relational databases. A *relational database* provides a means of storing data in logical groupings of similar data items. In addition, these data items can reference other logical groupings of other similar data items, which are the actual relations.

A relational database contains tables, columns, and records. In addition, it can support cursors and transactions. Furthermore, most relational databases support a language for interacting with the information contained within them—a language called SQL (Structured Query Language).

> **NOTE**
>
> Most people spell out "S-Q-L" when they speak in reference to the SQL language. However, you might run into some folks who say "sequel," as in Sybase (and Microsoft's) SQL ("sequel") Server. Both pronunciations are referencing the same language, so feel free to treat both pronunciations as referring to the same thing.

Tables

The key entity within a relational database is a table. Use tables to group your data logically. For example, in the TechBooks sample database provided with this chapter, there are several tables: Books, Authors, Publishers, Topics, Categories, and BookAuthors, as shown in Figure 18.1. Each table is designed to store data of a specific type. Thus, the Books table contains all the book information, the Authors table contains all the author information, and the BookAuthors table matches (relates) each entry in the Books table to one or more entries in the Authors table.

FIGURE 18.1

The tables in the TechBooks database.

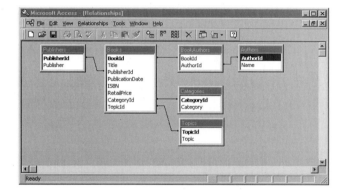

Columns

The database contains "fields" for each logical grouping of data within your table. These fields are called *columns*. Figure 18.2 demonstrates the columns within the Books table in the TechBooks database. Observe that the Books table contains columns for each data element that you would expect to be associated with a book, including title, ISBN, and retail price. Each column has a datatype and size associated with it. For example, the title column is text type and limited to 150 characters, whereas the retail price column is currency type and supports two digits past the decimal point.

Records

So far, I've discussed only the *meta* information about the data—that is, the tables and columns provide a general description of the data, but not the data itself. The data itself, as stored in each table, is called that table's *records*. For example, each book in the Books database has its own record. The set of all books in the TechBooks database is called the records in the Books table. Figure 18.3 shows the records in the TechBooks database.

18

GETTING STARTED WITH JAVASCRIPT

FIGURE 18.2

The columns in the Books table.

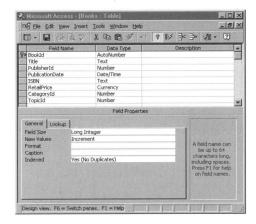

FIGURE 18.3

The data records in the Books table.

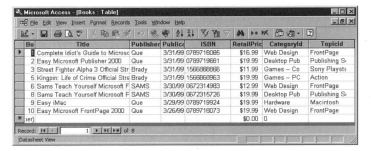

> **NOTE**
>
> Records are also called *rows*. In relational database terminology, records and rows are equivalent.

HOW DO YOU DEFINE THE STRUCTURE OF YOUR DATA INTO RELATIONAL DATABASE TABLES AND COLUMNS?

Depending on the data itself, this question can be answered simply or with much difficulty. Indeed, some software engineers have dedicated their careers to the science and art of relational database design. (Therefore, don't expect anything near a complete answer in this book.)

In particular, one goal is to eliminate redundancy in your database. In the TechBooks database, for example, you might have noticed that authors were not included in the Books table, even though an author appears to be a logical element associated with a book. Instead, a new table called BookAuthors was created to store these relationships. The primary reason for this was to eliminate redundancy—specifically, the Books table does not need duplicate records for a single book when it has multiple authors. Nor does the Books table need a fixed number of columns to support multiple authors.

Likewise, the Authors table maps the author's name as a text string to a unique number, the AuthorId. This number is stored in the BookAuthors Author column, rather than the string itself. This approach saves disk space and provides rapid lookup.

The science of squeezing the redundancy out of relational databases is called *normalization*.

Cursors

When you have tables, columns, and records, the next logical step is to look at and modify the data in your table's columns. MFC defines database interfaces around the concept of a cursor.

A *cursor* represents a current record in a table. If you are programmatically scanning the records in your table, your program can look at each record, one at a time. The cursor contains an internal reference to the row that your program is visiting. The MFC CRecordSet and CDaoRecordSet classes provide interfaces for your application to move forward and backward through table records.

Transactions

A *transaction* is a way of packaging a set of changes to a group of relational database tables together, allowing you to specify whether all or none of the changes are made to the database. Transactions enable you to maintain data consistency within your database. Thus, if you're adding information about a new book to the TechBooks database and you have to update the Books, Authors, BookAuthors, and Publishers tables, when an update to one of the tables fails, you can handle the case in a straightforward manner.

Transactions have three actions: begin, commit, and rollback.

The begin action starts a transaction. Any insertions, updates, and deletions to the database after the begin are temporarily stored by the database, but not integrated into it. After the transaction is started, your application can perform any insertions, updates, or deletions to the database records in multiple tables.

If your application detects an error condition where one of its insertions, updates, or deletions fails, it can choose to roll back. When a rollback occurs, all insertions, updates, and deletions since the last begin are "forgotten."

However, if your application has successfully completed all insertions, updates, and deletions, it can commit the transaction. The commit action causes the database to record permanently all the changes that had occurred since the transaction was started.

Transactions solve data integrity problems, but they are not without cost in terms of database performance. The actual performance of a particular transaction depends on the structure of the database tables and the specific relational database (such as Oracle or SQL Server) that you are using. Keep in mind, however, that when a transaction is open and locks a particular database table, other users of that table might not be able to modify it until the transaction is complete. Consequently, transactions can slow down your overall throughput dramatically.

Storing and Retrieving Data

When you have to store and retrieve data from a relational database, SQL is often preferred. Fortunately, most relational databases support some implementation of the SQL language. Although SQL is standardized, each database may speak a slightly different dialect of it to support features that are native to its implementation. Fortunately, the basics of SQL remain much the same between the databases.

SQL is an action-oriented language. You start out by specifying the action that you want to perform by using one of its standard verbs: INSERT (for inserting records), SELECT (for querying records), UPDATE (for updating records), and DELETE (for deleting records). Each SQL verb then has additional syntax to enable you to describe which table(s) and column-based criteria to use for performing the requested action. For example, you can use SQL to ask the TechBooks database for all books that reference a particular topic.

TIP

Use the TrySQL sample program included in this chapter to try SQL syntax on Microsoft Access databases.

The syntax for TrySQL is

```
TrySQL "<mdb name>" "<SQL statement>"
```

> **NOTE**
>
> SQL commands can be executed on a database by using the `ExecuteSQL` method of the `CDatabase` or `CDaoDatabase` class.

SELECT

The SQL `SELECT` statement enables you to retrieve data from one or more database tables flexibly. There are four parts to the `SELECT` statement: the columns to display, the table that owns the columns, the record selection criteria, and the returned sort order. Its format is as follows:

```
SELECT list of columns
FROM list of tables
WHERE Boolean criteria for selection
ORDER BY list of columns
```

> **NOTE**
>
> In the `SELECT` statement, the `WHERE` and `ORDER BY` clauses are optional. If no `WHERE` clause is specified, all rows are returned. If no `ORDER BY` clause is specified, no row ordering is guaranteed.

The best way to give you a feel for SQL is by modeling it. In the following examples, all these SQL statements apply to the sample TechBooks database.

If you'd like to obtain the titles and ISBN numbers for all the books, use this:

```
SELECT [Title], [ISBN] FROM [Books]
```

To obtain the titles and ISBN numbers for only books with a retail price greater than $25, use this:

```
SELECT [Title], [ISBN] FROM [Books] WHERE [RetailPrice] > 25.0
```

If you want to obtain the titles and ISBN numbers for all the books sorted by ISBN number, use this:

```
SELECT [Title], [ISBN] FROM [Books] ORDER BY [ISBN]
```

Finally, if you'd like to obtain only the titles and ISBN numbers for books with a retail price greater than $25 with the output sorted by ISBN number, use this:

```
SELECT [Title], [ISBN]
FROM [Books]
WHERE [RetailPrice] > 25.0
ORDER BY [ISBN]
```

> **NOTE**
>
> Strictly speaking, the brackets around the table and column names are required only when your table or column name contains spaces. Some dialects of SQL do not support spaces in table and column names and hence may not support the bracket notation.

INSERT

The SQL INSERT statement enables you to add another row of data to a table. The INSERT statement has two formats. The first format enables you to specify the values to place in each column for the inserted row. Its format is as follows:

```
INSERT INTO table (list of columns)
VALUES (list of comma-delimited values)
```

The alternative format enables you to synthesize a row of data for the table using a SELECT statement. This format is as follows:

```
INSERT INTO table
SELECT list of columns
FROM list of tables
WHERE Boolean criteria for selection
ORDER BY list of columns
```

> **NOTE**
>
> As in the SELECT statement, the WHERE and ORDER BY clauses are optional.

For example, if you'd like to add a new topic to the TechBooks Topics table, you can use the following SQL command:

```
INSERT INTO [Topics] (TopicId, Topic)
VALUES(11, 'MFC')
```

DELETE

The SQL DELETE statement removes rows from a table based on the criteria specified in its optional WHERE clause. The format of the DELETE statement is as follows:

```
DELETE FROM table
WHERE Boolean criteria for deletion
```

> **NOTE**
>
> If no WHERE clause is specified, all the rows in the table are deleted.

For example, in the TechBooks database, to delete all books whose price is greater than $20, use the following form of the DELETE statement:

```
DELETE FROM [Books]
WHERE [RetailPrice] > 20.00
```

UPDATE

The SQL UPDATE statement changes column data that is present in a table. The format of the UPDATE statement is as follows:

```
UPDATE table
SET column = value
WHERE Boolean criteria for updating
```

For example in the TechBooks database, if you need to change the name of the "Publisher" topic to "Publishing Software" in the Topics table, use the following UPDATE statement:

```
UPDATE [Topics]
SET [Topic] = 'Publishing Software'
WHERE [Topic] = 'Publisher'
```

Database Communication Mechanisms

The standard database communication mechanisms encapsulated by MFC are ODBC and DAO. Originally, the ODBC interface was created. Later, DAO was built upon the ODBC interface and added more functionality and better support for the capabilities of Microsoft Access databases.

ODBC

In the early 1990s, there were several database providers, each with its own proprietary interface. If applications had to interact with multiple datasources, each application needed custom code to interact with each database.

To solve this problem, Microsoft and some other companies created a standard interface for obtaining data from and sending data to datasources of different types. This interface was called open database connectivity, or ODBC in its shortened form.

With ODBC, programmers could write applications to use a single data access interface without worrying about the details of interacting with multiple datasources. Although this is possible, be aware that each ODBC provider may support different capabilities and may not be fully compliant.

MFC improves ODBC for application developers. The native ODBC interface is a simple functional API. Rather than provide a simple wrapper of the functional API, the MFC developers created a set of abstract classes that represent logical entities with the database. Specifically, the key classes in MFC's ODBC implementation support databases (`CDatabase`), recordsets (`CRecordset`), and record views (`CRecordView`). (Refer to the "ODBC/MFC" section later in this chapter for more information on each of these classes.)

DAO

Although ODBC became an industry standard, Microsoft engineered a means of exposing much richer database functionality for the users of Microsoft Jet databases (as created by Microsoft Access). The new functionality includes Database Definition Language (DDL) support that allows programs to interact with the structure of the tables and columns in a database. In addition, by creating a new, direct interface to the Jet engine, Microsoft improved its data access speed as compared to the same access via the Jet database's ODBC driver.

Thus, a new set of classes (`Cdao…`), modeled on the MFC's original ODBC classes, was developed and released. Like the ODBC/MFC classes, DAO supports databases (`CDaoDatabase`), recordsets (`CDaoRecordset`), and record views (`CDaoRecordView`). However, in addition, DAO supports table definitions (`CDaoDatabases`), query definitions (`CDaoQueryDef`), and greatly improved transactions through the introduction of a workspace (`CDaoWorkspace`). (See the "DAO" section later in this chapter for more information on each of these classes.)

Which Methodology Should I Use?

Like most technologies, each database communication mechanism has its advantages and disadvantages. Although Microsoft is attempting to steer new database development toward using ADO, you might have valid technical reasons to stick with the tried-and-true ODBC and DAO support. Of course, ultimately, the answer depends upon the current and anticipated requirements for your application.

The advantages of using ODBC remain true today. First, it is well supported—most database providers provide ODBC interfaces. Next, you will get better performance from accessing the ODBC driver directly as opposed to interfacing with it through the DAO layer. In addition, MFC provides a nice object-based interface for programming to the ODBC layer.

With DAO, you often get better performance in accessing Microsoft Jet databases, such as those created using Microsoft Access. In addition, the MFC object-based implementation maintains much of its ODBC counterpart's implementation, but with more functionality (such as more access to the actual structure of the database tables and columns.) Finally, each application can have multiple transactions to the same database in progress simultaneously.

The next chapter describes using a COM approach to interacting with databases using OLE DB and ADO. If you need to use a language-neutral way of accessing your data or to get all the latest and greatest features of Microsoft's data access implementation, consider using OLE DB and ADO. Refer to Chapter 19 for more information.

ODBC/MFC

The ODBC standard defines an application programming interface (API) that is functional and centered on the C language. Through this interface, applications simply pass SQL statements to the database engine. When creating a C++ interface for ODBC, Microsoft chose to create more of an abstraction of a general database as compared to a simple C++ wrapper.

As a result, the MFC C++ ODBC interface has databases (CDatabase) and recordsets (CRecordset). Using these classes, applications do not necessarily have to concern themselves with SQL at all—a lot of that dirty work is done "automagically."

CDatabase

The CDatabase class provides an abstraction for an ODBC database connection. You must have an open CDatabase object (using OpenEx) before you can use most of the other database classes and methods. When you are finished with your connection to the database, use Close to release all the associated resources.

OpenEx and Close

The OpenEx method allows your application to create a connection to a database. The Close method releases this connection. These public methods are declared in CDatabase as follows:

```
virtual BOOL OpenEx(LPCTSTR lpszConnectString, DWORD dwOptions = 0);
virtual void Close();
```

The connection string, *lpszConnectionString*, represents the semicolon-delimited list of standard ODBC options needed to open your database. Some of the more common options are shown in Table 18.1. If you pass a 0 as the connection string parameter, the user receives a dialog that enables him or her to select the appropriate datasource to open.

TABLE 18.1   COMMON ODBC CONNECTION STRING OPTIONS

Option	Description
DSN=	Datasource name, as defined in the ODBC Control Panel applet
UID=	User id
PWD=	Password
DBQ=	Database filename
Driver=	ODBC driver name, such as {Microsoft Access Driver (*.mdb)}

The options parameter, *dwOptions*, is a set of flags that you can logically OR together to set the behavior of the OpenEx method. You can specify that the database is to be opened in read-only mode (CDatabase::openReadOnly) and whether the ODBC database dialog is displayed (CDatabase::forceOdbcDialog, and CDatabase::noOdbcDialog, respectively).

Listing 18.1 shows the use of OpenEx and Close in the TrySQL sample application in this chapter.

LISTING 18.1 THE USE OF THE OpenEx, ExecuteSQL, AND Close METHODS OF THE
CDatabase CLASS IN THE TRYODBC SAMPLE APPLICATION

```
try {
    CDatabase db;

    CString connect;

    connect += "UID=Admin;";
    connect += "DRIVER={Microsoft Access Driver (*.mdb)};";
    connect += "DBQ=";
    connect += argv[1];

    db.OpenEx(connect);
    db.ExecuteSQL(argv[2]);
    db.Close();
}
catch (CDBException *xcp) {
    cerr << _T("Database exception: ")
         << (const TCHAR *) xcp->m_strError << endl;
    xcp->Delete();
}
```

ExecuteSQL

The ExecuteSQL method enables you to send a SQL command to the open database
object. As you would expect, this public method simply takes a single string parameter
that represents the SQL command to execute. It is declared as follows:

```
void ExecuteSQL(LPCSTR lpszSQL);
```

Listing 18.1 demonstrates the use of the ExecuteSQL method of the CDatabase class.

> **NOTE**
>
> You cannot obtain the data results of a SELECT call using ExecuteSQL. If you
> need to receive the data, use a CRecordset class object.

CanTransact, BeginTrans, CommitTrans, and Rollback

The CanTransact, BeginTrans, CommitTrans, and Rollback methods of the CDatabase
class allow your application to use and manage database transactions. These public methods are declared as follows:

```
BOOL CanTransact() const;
BOOL BeginTrans();
BOOL CommitTrans();
BOOL Rollback();
```

Before invoking any of the other transaction calls, call `CanTransact` to ensure that the current datasource supports transactions. To start a new transaction, call `BeginTrans` before inserting, updating, or deleting data in the database. If you need to abandon your changes, call `Rollback`. If you want to update the database with your changes, call `CommitTrans`.

> **NOTE**
>
> The ODBC interface supports a single transaction for the open database object. If you need more transactions to the same database, consider using the DAO data access classes and the `CDaoWorkspace` class.

CRecordset

The `CRecordset` class encapsulates a group of similar records, usually the records within a database table or returned from a query. Using this class, you can isolate your programming logic from the actual SQL required to SELECT, INSERT, DELETE, or UPDATE rows in a database. Although you can use the `CRecordset` class directly, it is much easier to derive a new class from it and associate class member variables with the database columns.

Deriving from CRecordset

You can easily create a `CRecordset`-derived class and generate code to support dynamic field exchange via the Visual Studio ClassWizard. The following process demonstrates how to create a recordset class for the Books table in the TechBooks sample database:

1. Display the MFC ClassWizard either by selecting View, ClassWizard from the pull-down menu or by pressing Ctrl+W.

2. Choose the Class Info tab from the MFC ClassWizard window. This should look like Figure 18.4.

3. Click the Add Class push button and choose New.

4. In the New Class dialog, name your class. For this example, name it `CBooksRecordset`. Choose `CRecordset` as the base class as shown in Figure 18.5. Choose OK.

FIGURE 18.4

The MFC ClassWizard Class Info tab.

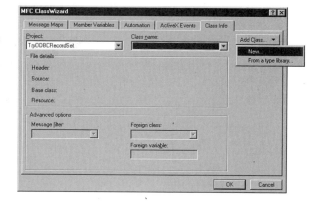

FIGURE 18.5

Creating a CRecordset-derived class.

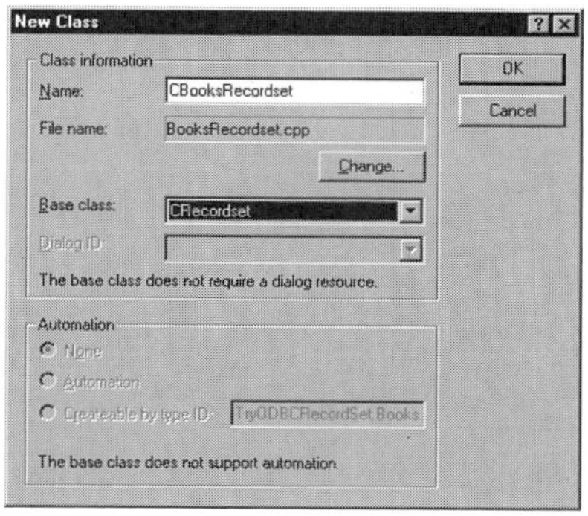

5. In Database Options, choose your ODBC datasource for this class. In this example, because the TechBooks database is a Microsoft Access database, Figure 18.6 shows MS Access 97 Database as the ODBC datasource. Choose whether you want the recordset to be by default a snapshot or a dynaset. Click OK.

FIGURE 18.6

Choosing an ODBC data-source.

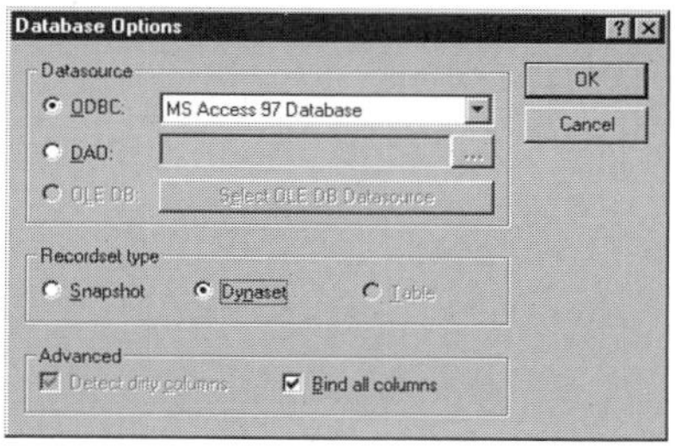

6. As shown in Figure 18.7, select your Microsoft Access database file. In the example, select the TechBooks.mdb database file. Click OK.

7. Next, choose the table or query to mirror with this recordset. Figure 18.8 shows selecting the Books table for the sample recordset.

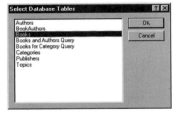

8. Finally, from the ClassWizard window, click OK to generate the recordset class.

DYNASET VERSUS SNAPSHOT RECORDSET TYPES

A *snapshot* represents the state of the database at the time the recordset is opened. The data contained within the recordset can be different from what is actually contained in the database if updates have occurred while the recordset is open.

A *dynaset* represents a dynamic view of the recordset's records. If updates occur to any of the records, those changes are reflected in the recordset.

The Components of a `CRecordset`-Derived Class

A `CRecordset`-derived class must override several virtual functions and add several class member variables to support deriving from a `CRecordset` class. Take a look at the code that the ClassWizard generated for the `CBooksRecordset` class you created in the last section. Note that all the code for the code listings here can be found in the TryODBCRecordset sample application for this chapter.

The CBooksRecordset class is defined as shown in Listing 18.2. This code can be found in the BooksRecordset.cpp source file or quickly located by using the ClassView tab in Visual Studio.

LISTING 18.2 THE GENERATED CBooksRecordset CLASS DEFINITION

```
class CBooksRecordset : public CRecordset
{
public:
    CBooksRecordset(CDatabase* pDatabase = NULL);
    DECLARE_DYNAMIC(CBooksRecordset)

// Field/Param Data
    //{{AFX_FIELD(CBooksRecordset, CRecordset)
    long      m_BookId;
    CString   m_Title;
    long      m_PublisherId;
    CTime     m_PublicationDate;
    CString   m_ISBN;
    CString   m_RetailPrice;
    long      m_CategoryId;
    long      m_TopicId;
    //}}AFX_FIELD

// Overrides
    // ClassWizard generated virtual function overrides
    //{{AFX_VIRTUAL(CBooksRecordset)
    public:
    virtual CString GetDefaultConnect();// Default connection string
    virtual CString GetDefaultSQL();     // Default SQL for Recordset
    virtual void DoFieldExchange(CFieldExchange* pFX);  // RFX support
    //}}AFX_VIRTUAL

// Implementation
#ifdef _DEBUG
    virtual void AssertValid() const;
    virtual void Dump(CDumpContext& dc) const;
#endif
};
```

Of interest are the class's constructor, the class members representing the field and parameter data, and the virtual function overrides. Let's take a look in detail at each of these features of this class.

CBooksRecordset Constructor

The constructor for the `CBooksRecordset` class simply takes a single parameter, a pointer to the `CDatabase` object owning this record. The constructor initializes each of the class member variables that correspond to the columns in the Books database table and sets the default type for the recordset to whatever was chosen in the ClassWizard when this class was generated. Listing 18.3 shows the `CBooksRecordset` constructor.

LISTING 18.3   THE `CBooksRecordset` CONSTRUCTOR

```
CBooksRecordset::CBooksRecordset(CDatabase* pdb)
    : CRecordset(pdb)
{
    //{{AFX_FIELD_INIT(CBooksRecordset)
    m_BookId = 0;
    m_Title = _T("");
    m_PublisherId = 0;
    m_ISBN = _T("");
    m_RetailPrice = _T("");
    m_CategoryId = 0;
    m_TopicId = 0;
    m_nFields = 8;
    //}}AFX_FIELD_INIT
    m_nDefaultType = snapshot;
}
```

When you construct the `CBooksRecordset` class, if you pass a pointer to a `CDatabase` object, the recordset is automatically associated with the specified database. Otherwise, if you pass `NULL`, a default database object is constructed for you using the default data-source attributes returned by the `GetDefaultConnect` and `GetDefaultSQL` virtual function overrides.

Listing 18.4 shows the generated `GetDefaultConnect` and `GetDefaultSQL` methods in the `CBooksRecordset` class. The `GetDefaultConnect` method returns the connection string used to locate the database file to open. The `GetDefaultSQL` method returns the name of the table or query with which this recordset is associated.

LISTING 18.4   THE `GetDefaultConnect` AND `GetDefaultSQL` METHODS IN THE `CBooksRecordset` CLASS

```
CString CBooksRecordset::GetDefaultConnect()
{
    return _T("ODBC;DSN=MS Access 97 Database");
}

CString CBooksRecordset::GetDefaultSQL()
{
    return _T("[Books]");
}
```

> **NOTE**
>
> You must call the `CRecordset::Open` method before the recordset is connected to the data in the database.

Field Data and `DoFieldExchange`

Listing 18.2 shows the definition of all the columns that are available within this recordset. Each member variable corresponds to a column in the Books table. For example, *m_BookId* corresponds to the BookId column and *m_ISBN* corresponds to the ISBN column.

The `DoFieldExchange` method behaves similarly to the `CWnd::DoDataExchange` method for graphical dialogs. This method is used to associate the column name with the class member variable so that data can be transferred in each direction, as required. The `DoFieldExchange` for the `CBooksRecordset` class is shown in Listing 18.5.

LISTING 18.5 THE CBooksRecordset DoFieldExchange METHOD

```
void CBooksRecordset::DoFieldExchange(CFieldExchange* pFX)
{
    //{{AFX_FIELD_MAP(CBooksRecordset)
    pFX->SetFieldType(CFieldExchange::outputColumn);
    RFX_Long(pFX, _T("[BookId]"), m_BookId);
    RFX_Text(pFX, _T("[Title]"), m_Title);
    RFX_Long(pFX, _T("[PublisherId]"), m_PublisherId);
    RFX_Date(pFX, _T("[PublicationDate]"), m_PublicationDate);
    RFX_Text(pFX, _T("[ISBN]"), m_ISBN);
    RFX_Text(pFX, _T("[RetailPrice]"), m_RetailPrice);
    RFX_Long(pFX, _T("[CategoryId]"), m_CategoryId);
    RFX_Long(pFX, _T("[TopicId]"), m_TopicId);
    //}}AFX_FIELD_MAP
}
```

One of the key differences between the `DoFieldExchange` and the `CWnd::DoDataExchange` methods is its usage of `RFX_` macros to do the association. The Record Field Exchange (RFX) macros bind the column name to the appropriate member variable.

Basic Recordset Functionality

Recordset classes hide some of the intricacies of SQL programming through the use of a higher abstraction. When using recordsets, you no longer need to worry about the syntax of the SQL `INSERT`, `SELECT`, `UPDATE`, and `DELETE`. Instead, you can focus on using the `AddNew`, `MoveFirst`/`MoveNext`, `Edit`, and `Delete` methods.

AddNew

The AddNew method creates a new empty database record in the open recordset. After you've called this method, you can set the data member variables to the values that you'd like to insert in the database. The public AddNew method is declared as shown here:

```
virtual void AddNew();
```

After setting all the data class members, call Update to cause this record to be inserted into the table associated with the recordset. If you need the new row to be reflected in the currently open recordset, call the Requery method.

Listing 18.6 demonstrates the use of the AddNew method to insert a new Book record into the Books table in the TechBooks sample database.

LISTING 18.6 USING AddNew TO INSERT A NEW DATABASE RECORD

```
CBooksRecordset rst(db);

rst.Open(CRecordset::dynaset);

rst.AddNew();

rst.m_BookId       = 123;
rst.m_ISBN         = "1234567890";
rst.m_Title        = "MFC Unleashed";
rst.m_RetailPrice  = "49.99";

rst.Update();

cout << _T("added record") << endl;

rst.Close();
```

MoveFirst, MoveNext, MovePrev, MoveLast, IsBOF, and IsEOF

The MoveFirst, MoveNext, MovePrev, and MoveLast methods are used to scan through a recordset from first record to last record (or vice versa). Additionally, you use the IsBOF and IsEOF methods to determine whether the recordset is currently at the beginning or end. These public methods are declared as follows:

```
void MoveFirst();
void MoveNext();
void MovePrev();
void MoveLast();
BOOL IsBOF() const;
BOOL IsEOF() const;
```

To use these methods to scan and list a set of database records, call these methods as shown in Listing 18.7. This code simply creates a `while` loop that checks `IsEOF` and calls `MoveNext` to advance to the next record. The data class members contain the data associated with the current record.

> **NOTE**
>
> If you make changes to the recordset's data class members while scanning the table, your changes will be lost. Use the `Edit`, `Update`, and `Requery` methods to change the record's data and reflect the data in the recordset.

LISTING 18.7   DOING A FORWARD SCAN OF A TABLE'S RECORDS

```
CBooksRecordset rst(db);

    rst.Open();

    while (!rst.IsEOF()) {
        cout << (const TCHAR *) rst.m_ISBN  << _T("\t")
             << (const TCHAR *) rst.m_Title << endl;
        rst.MoveNext();
    }

    rst.Close();
```

Edit

The `Edit` method permits you to modify the current database record associated with the recordset. You can modify the fields within the recordset after calling `Edit`. When you need to force the update of your changes in the database, call `Update`. If you would like your changes reflected in the current recordset, call `Requery`. The public `Edit` method is declared as follows:

```
virtual void Edit();
```

Listing 18.8 demonstrates how to update records in a recordset. If you need to make a common change among all records matching a particular criteria, you might want to use a SQL `UPDATE` statement and the `CDatabase::ExecuteSQL` method for much better performance.

LISTING 18.8   UPDATING A TABLE'S RECORDS

```
CBooksRecordset rst(db);

rst.Open(CRecordset::dynaset);

while (!rst.IsEOF()) {
    if (_tcscmp(rst.m_ISBN, _T("1234567890")) == 0) {
        rst.Edit();
        rst.m_ISBN = "0987654321";
        rst.Update();

        cout << _T("edited record") << endl;
    }
    rst.MoveNext();
}

    rst.Close();
```

Delete

The Delete method deletes the current record pointed to by the recordset. After you've called this method, the current record is no longer valid; you must call one of the move methods (MoveNext, MovePrev, MoveFirst, or MoveLast) to force the recordset to point to a valid record in the recordset.

> **NOTE**
>
> Unlike Edit and AddNew, you do not call Update to force the database to be updated with the changes. The Delete method makes the changes directly.

Listing 18.9 shows how to delete books that match specific ISBNs from the TechBooks sample database. If you need to delete all records matching a particular criteria, you might want to use a SQL DELETE statement and the CDatabase::ExecuteSQL method for much better performance.

LISTING 18.9   DELETING A TABLE'S RECORDS

```
CBooksRecordset rst(db);

rst.Open(CRecordset::dynaset);

while (!rst.IsEOF()) {
    if ((_tcscmp(rst.m_ISBN, _T("1234567890")) == 0)
        || (_tcscmp(rst.m_ISBN, _T("0987654321")) == 0)) {
```

```
        rst.Delete();

        cout << _T("deleted record") << endl;
    }
    rst.MoveNext();
}

rst.Close();
```

Update and `CancelUpdate`

The `Update` method updates the database file with the recordset's current record. Use `Update` after a call to `AddNew` (to insert a new record) or `Edit` (to change the current record). Use `CancelUpdate` to cancel an open `AddNew` or `Edit` on the current recordset. These public methods are declared as follows:

```
virtual BOOL Update();
void CancelUpdate();
```

Listing 18.6 demonstrates the use of `Update` to insert a database record. Listing 18.8 demonstrates its use to edit a record.

Requery

The `Requery` method ensures that the current recordset contains the most recent data in the database. This public method is declared as follows:

```
virtual BOOL Requery();
```

Use the `Requery` method to obtain the latest data if your recordset is not a dynaset or if other users might be updating the records that exist in your recordset.

DAO

The Data Access Object support within MFC has much in common with its original ODBC class support. Specifically, the general model of database development (using database and recordset classes) remains the same. However, additional functionality is included to provide better support for Microsoft Jet databases.

> **NOTE**
>
> The Microsoft Access product uses the Microsoft Jet engine to access its database files. Consequently, any references to Microsoft Access databases can be mapped to Microsoft Jet databases (and vice versa). These database files typically have an .mdb file extension.

18

GETTING STARTED
WITH JAVASCRIPT

This section describes some of the most salient new features and classes of the MFC DAO interface. It also attempts to highlight the basic differences between the classes that are similar between the ODBC and DAO class interfaces.

CDaoWorkspace

Microsoft created the CDaoWorkspace class to enhance the ways in which you can do transactions. Using this class, you can have a single transaction across a set of databases. In addition, that transaction can be independent of a concurrent transaction to the same database.

When you use the DAO interface and create a database object, that database object is created as part of the default workspace by default. However, by specifying a specific workspace when you construct the CDaoDatabase object, you can associate it with a non-default workspace.

> **TIP**
>
> Unless you need better control over your database transaction logic, you don't have to create a workspace. You can use the default workspace by constructing your CDaoDatabase object without parameters.

You can open and close a workspace using its Create, Open, and Close methods. To manage a transaction, you can use the BeginTrans, CommitTrans, and Rollback methods.

Create, Open, and Close

Call the Create and Open methods to associate your CDaoWorkspace object with a workspace. After your object is associated, you can create and manage transactions and call many of the other methods within this class. When you are finished with the workspace, call Close to release its resources back to the system. These public methods are declared as follows:

```
virtual void Create(LPCTSTR lpszName, LPCTSTR lpszUserName,
                    LPCTSTR lpszPassword);
virtual void Open(LPCTSTR lpszName = NULL);
virtual void Close();
```

When you Create a workspace, you must give it a name (of no more than 14 characters) that is used to identify it, particularly from a call to Open. Additionally, the *lpszUserName* and *lpszPassword* parameters enable you to specify the security information to use when opening databases in this workspace.

Call Open with no parameters (or NULL) to open the default workspace.

BeginTrans, CommitTrans, and Rollback

The BeginTrans, CommitTrans, and Rollback methods of the CDaoWorkspace class allow your application to use and manage database transactions across all databases that are included in the workspace. These public methods are declared as follows:

```
void BeginTrans();
void CommitTrans();
void Rollback();
```

To start a new transaction, call BeginTrans before inserting, updating, or deleting data in any of the databases contained in the workspace. If you need to abandon your changes, call Rollback. If you want to update the database with your changes, call CommitTrans.

CDaoDatabase

Like the MFC ODBC CDatabase, the CDaoDatabase class represents a single open connection to a database. However, with the introduction of workspaces (CDaoWorkspace), the methods to control and manage database transactions are not a part of the CDaoDatabase class.

The constructor for the CDaoDatabase object enables you to specify which workspace to associate this database connection with. If you do not specify a parameter or pass NULL, this database object becomes part of the default workspace. The CDaoDatabase class constructor is declared as follows:

```
CDaoDatabase(CDaoWorkspace* pWorkspace = NULL);
```

After you've constructed a CDaoDatabase object, it still is not connected to a database. To manage its connects, use its Open and Close methods. To execute a SQL command against this database, use the Execute method.

One of the major enhancements to DAO support includes the capability to actually create a new database; add and delete tables, relations, and queries from it; and obtain information describing the fields of the tables. These methods are used in specialized database administration applications and are beyond the scope of this book. Some of this information is discussed, however, in the section on the CDaoTableDef class later in this chapter.

Open and Close

The Open method allows your application to create a connection to a database. The Close method releases this connection. These public methods are declared in CDaoDatabase as follows:

```
virtual void Open(LPCTSTR lpszName, BOOL bExclusive = FALSE,
                  BOOL bReadOnly = FALSE,
                  LPCTSTR lpszConnect = _T("") );
virtual void Close();
```

You might note that unlike the CDatabase class's OpenEx method, the CDaoDatabase's Open method does not use the ODBC connection string as its primary parameter. With Open, the *lpszName* parameter is the name of the actual Microsoft Jet database to open. If you'd like to open an ODBC datasource through the DAO interfaces, specify the ODBC connection string using the *lpszConnect* parameter and pass NULL for the *lpszName* parameter.

Execute

The Execute method enables you to send a SQL command to the open database object. This method is declared as follows:

```
void Execute(LPCTSTR lpszSQL, int nOptions = 0);
```

Except for the addition of the *nOptions* parameter, this method's use is identical to the CDatabase::ExecuteSQL method. Using the *nOptions* parameter, you can logically OR one or more of the flags listed in Table 18.2.

TABLE 18.2   CDaoDatabase::Execute METHOD FLAGS

Flag	Description
dbInconsistent	Inconsistent updates (default).
dbConsistent	Consistent updates.
dbDenyWrite	Denies database write access to other users.
dbSQLPassThrough	DAO passes the SQL statement directly without processing first.
dbFailOnError	Updates occur within a transaction.
dbSeeChanges	Notifies the user that another user is editing the data.

CDaoRecordset

The CDaoRecordset provides functionality similar to the ODBC CRecordset class. Encapsulating a list of database records of a similar type, this class enables you to insert, update, delete, and peruse records in a database table or returned from a query. Please refer to the ODBC CRecordset class for more information on creating a derived class and using the basic functionality.

CDaoTableDef

The CDaoTableDef class allows your application to view and change the actual internal structure of your database. Specifically, it enables you to obtain a list of columns (fields) in particular tables, along with each column's type and size.

Use Open and Close to access the structure of a table and release your use of that structure, respectively. In addition, you can use GetFieldCount and GetFieldInfo to obtain the structural information about each field in a particular table.

Open and Close

The Open method allows your application to access the structure of a table. Call the Close method when you are finished with it. These public methods are declared as follows:

```
virtual void Open(LPCTSTR lpszName);
virtual void Close();
```

Listing 18.10 demonstrates the use of each of these methods to open and close the table definition within a database. This example is located in the TryDAOTableDef sample application and can be used with any DAO-accessible database.

LISTING 18.10   VIEWING A TABLE'S LAYOUT USING CDaoTableDef

```
CDaoTableDef tableDef(db);

tableDef.Open(tableName);

cout << _T("Table: ") << tableName << endl;

CDaoFieldInfo fieldInfo;

short numFields = tableDef.GetFieldCount();

for (short i=0; i<numFields; i++) {
    tableDef.GetFieldInfo(i, fieldInfo);

    cout << _T("\t") << getFieldType(fieldInfo.m_nType)
         << _T("\t") << fieldInfo.m_lSize
         << _T("\t") << (const TCHAR *) fieldInfo.m_strName << endl;

}

tableDef.Close();
```

18

GETTING STARTED WITH JAVASCRIPT

GetFieldCount and GetFieldInfo

You can enumerate the columns and obtain information about each column using the GetFieldCount and GetFieldInfo methods. The GetFieldCount method returns the number of columns within the current table definition. The GetFieldInfo method enables you to get specific information about each column either by ordinal or by name. These public methods are declared as follows:

```
short GetFieldCount();
void GetFieldInfo(int nIndex, CDaoFieldInfo& fieldinfo,
DWORD dwInfoOptions = AFX_DAO_PRIMARY_INFO);
void GetFieldInfo(LPCTSTR lpszName, CDaoFieldInfo& fieldinfo,
                DWORD dwInfoOptions = AFX_DAO_PRIMARY_INFO);
```

The GetFieldInfo method uses a CDaoFieldInfo structure that is shown in Listing 18.11. The *dwInfoOptions* parameter enables you to control the amount of information that is entered in this structure; you can specify one of AFX_DAO_PRIMARY_INFO, AFX_DAO_SECONDARY_INFO, or AFX_DAO_ALL_INFO. The comments associated with the structure indicate which fields are filled in for each level.

LISTING **18.11**   THE CDaoFieldInfo STRUCTURE

```
struct CDaoFieldInfo
{
// Attributes
    CString m_strName;                  // Primary
    short m_nType;                      // Primary
    long m_lSize;                       // Primary
    long m_lAttributes;                 // Primary
    short m_nOrdinalPosition;           // Secondary
    BOOL m_bRequired;                   // Secondary
    BOOL m_bAllowZeroLength;            // Secondary
    long m_lCollatingOrder;             // Secondary
    CString m_strForeignName;           // Secondary
    CString m_strSourceField;           // Secondary
    CString m_strSourceTable;           // Secondary
    CString m_strValidationRule;        // All
    CString m_strValidationText;        // All
    CString m_strDefaultValue;          // All
};
```

Listing 18.10 demonstrates how to use these methods with each other to obtain information about the structure of a table.

CDaoQueryDef

The CDaoQueryDef class encapsulates a query that either is stored in the database or is in memory. Applications typically use queries to store common SQL statements and provide a way of reusing this functionality by specifying a name of the query, compared to respecifying the SQL statement itself. Additionally, queries can improve application performance because the database does not have to reparse the actual SQL statement on each invocation.

> **NOTE**
>
> You do not need to use the CDaoQueryDef class to use queries. In fact, for those queries that return data, you cannot. Instead, use CDaoRecordset to obtain the data returned from a query.

Use the Open and Close methods to use a query stored either in the physical database or in the CDaoDatabase's query definitions collection. The Create method creates a new in-memory query. The Append adds that in-memory query to the physical database. The GetSQL and SetSQL methods allow your application to obtain and modify the SQL statement associated with the query. Finally, the Execute method executes the SQL statement associated with the query.

Open and Close

The Open method opens an existing in-memory or stored database query. The Close method releases all resources associated with a query. These public methods are declared as follows:

```
virtual void Open(LPCTSTR lpszName = NULL);
virtual void Close();
```

The query must exist before opening it. If you need to Create an in-memory query, call the Create method.

Create and Append

The Create method creates an in-memory query that is added to the CDaoDatabase object's collection of queries. The Append method adds this query to the physical database. These public methods are declared as shown here:

```
virtual void Create(LPCTSTR lpszName = NULL, LPCTSTR lpszSQL = NULL);
virtual void Append();
```

When creating the query, you can specify the SQL statement associated with it using the *lpszSQL* parameter. Otherwise, you can specify or change it at a later time using the SetSQL method.

GetSQL and SetSQL

Use the GetSQL and SetSQL methods to view and modify the SQL statement associated with the current query. These methods are declared as follows:

```
CString GetSQL();
void SetSQL(LPCTSTR lpszSQL);
```

These methods enable you to modify the meaning of a query on-the-fly, if required by your application. As a general rule, most applications do not need to do this, however.

Execute

The Execute method runs the current query on the data in the database. Except for a possible speed improvement, it is equivalent to executing the SQL statement via the CDaoDatabase::Execute method. The CDaoQueryDef::Execute statement is declared as follows:

```
virtual void Execute(int nOptions = dbFailOnError);
```

The *nOptions* parameter is the same as in the CDaoDatabase::Execute method and is shown in Table 18.2.

Summary

This chapter introduces you to basic relational database topics and the use of the SQL language to interact with data in a relational database. You can apply this information to a variety of programming environments; it is not limited to MFC.

Also, this chapter discusses how to use the two MFC-based class interfaces, MFC/ODBC and Data Access Objects (DAO), to add relational database support to your application. Although MFC/ODBC is the tried-and-true interface for accessing data in a relational database, DAO gives you more information and a finer degree of control.

The next chapter discusses Microsoft's newest means of obtaining data: OLE DB and ADO.

CHAPTER 19

Advanced Database Support

by Bill Heyman

IN THIS CHAPTER

The COM Approach

Beyond ODBC and ADO, the next step in the evolution of data access requires that the focus be less on databases and more on general datasources. At the same time, the general software development approach requires the packaging of reusable software parts in components. The convergence of these requirements resulted in the development of Microsoft's strategic software direction, called Universal Data Access (UDA).

A key component of UDA is OLE DB. Based on COM, OLE DB defines a set of interfaces for interacting with general datasources from both the client (consumer) side and the server (provider) side. In addition, Microsoft created a language-independent, higher-level data consumer interface called ActiveX Data Objects (ADO), which is built upon the OLE DB infrastructure. This chapter discusses these new interfaces for data access for Windows-based applications: OLE DB and ADO.

OLE DB

OLE DB is a datasource-independent, COM-based interface for providing and consuming data. It is generic enough to support any datasource that can provide tabular data, yet still powerful enough to enable specific interaction with each datasource to enable it to perform at its optimum.

In the standard client/server world, there are sources of data (commonly called *servers*) and there are users of data (commonly called *clients*). In OLE DB, these are called *providers* and *consumers*, respectively.

This chapter discusses the development of OLE DB consumers using the ATL template interface provided by Microsoft Visual C++. Please refer to the OLE DB documentation from Microsoft for more information on the creation of OLE DB providers.

ADO

By itself, OLE DB is extremely powerful and very general purpose. However, its interface is not always the easiest way of interacting with datasources in a straightforward, standard manner. Furthermore, OLE DB is not well suited for interfacing to Visual Basic, Java, and other languages.

To meet the requirements for "everyday" datasource development and to be a logical extension of MFC/ODBC and DAO, Microsoft created ActiveX Data Objects (ADO). ADO is implemented using OLE DB provider interfaces. However, its interface allows programmers to interact with data at a higher level than OLE DB provides.

Which One Should I Use?

Certainly, you can use both OLE DB and ADO from Visual C++ code. In fact, because both are COM-based components, there is a variety of mechanisms for interfacing them, from using #import to using the Microsoft-defined C++ interfaces.

If you are looking for a high-performance and more functional interface, select OLE DB. The ATL class wrappers for OLE DB enhance and extend its base functionality, without sacrificing its performance.

If you are looking for a set of high-level objects that can easily be used from a variety of languages and retains some of the look-and-feel of MFC/ODBC and DAO, select ADO.

OLE DB Consumers Using the ATL Wrapper Classes

Although you can access the OLE DB COM objects directly, there is an Active Template Library (ATL) set of classes that encapsulate the COM objects for you. This makes using OLE DB much easier from the C++ environment. To use the ATL OLE DB consumer classes, you must add the following file inclusion line to your program, usually in the stdafx.h file in your project:

```
#include <atldbcli.h>
```

Visual Studio provides an ATL Object Wizard that can greatly assist you in creating programs that act as OLE DB consumers. The following steps demonstrate how to generate classes for the Books table in the TechBooks sample database. To add this support to your application, follow these steps:

1. Load the project to which you would like to add data access using OLE DB into Visual Studio.

2. From the menu bar, choose Insert, New ATL Object.

3. If prompted to add ATL support to your MFC project, click Yes. Otherwise, proceed to the next step.

4. From the ATL Object Wizard dialog, choose the category Data Access and the object Consumer, as shown in Figure 19.1. Click Next.

FIGURE **19.1**

The ATL Object Wizard dialog.

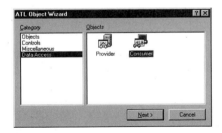

5. Figure 19.2 shows the ATL Object Wizard Properties dialog. In this dialog, click Select Datasource. This displays the Data Link Properties dialog shown in Figure 19.3.

FIGURE **19.2**

The ATL Object Wizard Properties dialog.

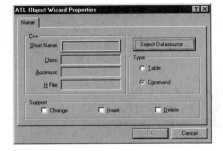

FIGURE **19.3**

The Data Link Properties dialog's Provider tab.

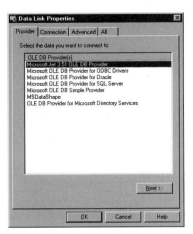

6. From the Data Link Properties dialog's Provider tab, select the datasource provider that is appropriate to your datasource. Because the TechBooks database is an Access database, Microsoft Jet 3.51 OLE DB Provider is selected.

7. Figure 19.4 shows the Data Link Properties dialog's Connection tab. Depending on the type of provider selected in the preceding step, the controls on this tab can vary. In the example for a Microsoft Jet OLE DB Provider, you can enter a filename for the database. Click OK.

FIGURE 19.4

The Data Link Properties dialog's Connection tab.

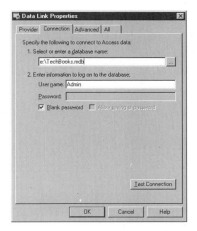

8. Next, the Select Database Table dialog is shown, which allows you to choose one of the datasource's available tables, queries, or procedures (depending on your datasource). Figure 19.5 shows the selection of the Books table. Click OK.

FIGURE 19.5

The Select Database Table dialog.

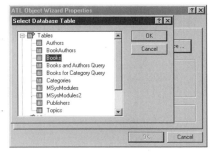

9. Figure 19.6 shows the updated ATL Object Wizard Properties dialog. Note that in the example, the ATL Object Wizard will generate a data class (`CBooks`) and an accessor class (`CBooksAccessor`). If you plan on inserting, updating, and deleting records from this table, check the appropriate check boxes. Next, choose whether you want your generated class to be derived from `CCommand` (Command) or `CTable` (Table). Click OK.

FIGURE **19.6**

The ATL Object Wizard Properties dialog with class information.

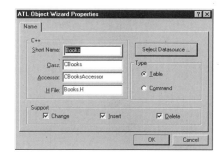

10. At this point, your project will contain two new classes: The first is the CAccessor-derived class for your table, and the second is the CCommand- or CTable-derived class for your table. Listing 19.1 shows the CBooksAccessor class and Listing 19.2 shows the CBooks class.

LISTING 19.1   THE GENERATED CBooksAccessor CLASS

```cpp
class CBooksAccessor
{
public:
    LONG m_BookId;
    LONG m_CategoryId;
    TCHAR m_ISBN[13];
    DATE m_PublicationDate;
    LONG m_PublisherId;
    CURRENCY m_RetailPrice;
    TCHAR m_Title[251];
    LONG m_TopicId;

BEGIN_COLUMN_MAP(CBooksAccessor)
    COLUMN_ENTRY(1, m_BookId)
    COLUMN_ENTRY(2, m_Title)
    COLUMN_ENTRY(3, m_PublisherId)
    COLUMN_ENTRY_TYPE(4, DBTYPE_DATE, m_PublicationDate)
    COLUMN_ENTRY(5, m_ISBN)
    COLUMN_ENTRY_TYPE(6, DBTYPE_CY, m_RetailPrice)
    COLUMN_ENTRY(7, m_CategoryId)
    COLUMN_ENTRY(8, m_TopicId)
END_COLUMN_MAP()

    // You may wish to call this function if you are inserting a
    // record and wish to initialize all the fields, if you are
    // not going to explicitly set all of them.
    void ClearRecord()
    {
        memset(this, 0, sizeof(*this));
    }
};
```

LISTING 19.2   THE GENERATED CBOOKS CLASS

```
class CBooks : public CTable<CAccessor<CBooksAccessor> >
{
public:
    HRESULT Open()
    {
        HRESULT    hr;
        hr = OpenDataSource();
        if (FAILED(hr))
            return hr;

        return OpenRowset();
    }
    HRESULT OpenDataSource()
    {
        HRESULT      hr;
        CDataSource db;
        CDBPropSet   dbinit(DBPROPSET_DBINIT);

        dbinit.AddProperty(DBPROP_AUTH_CACHE_AUTHINFO, true);
        dbinit.AddProperty(DBPROP_AUTH_ENCRYPT_PASSWORD, false);
        dbinit.AddProperty(DBPROP_AUTH_MASK_PASSWORD, false);
        dbinit.AddProperty(DBPROP_AUTH_PASSWORD, OLESTR(""));
        dbinit.AddProperty(DBPROP_AUTH_PERSIST_ENCRYPTED, false);
        dbinit.AddProperty(DBPROP_AUTH_PERSIST_SENSITIVE_AUTHINFO,
                                                          false);
        dbinit.AddProperty(DBPROP_AUTH_USERID, OLESTR("Admin"));
        dbinit.AddProperty(DBPROP_INIT_DATASOURCE,
                           OLESTR("e:\\samples\\TechBooks.mdb"));
        dbinit.AddProperty(DBPROP_INIT_MODE, (long)16);
        dbinit.AddProperty(DBPROP_INIT_PROMPT, (short)4);
        dbinit.AddProperty(DBPROP_INIT_PROVIDERSTRING,
                           OLESTR(";COUNTRY=0;CP=1252;LANGID=0x0409"));
        dbinit.AddProperty(DBPROP_INIT_LCID, (long)1033);
        hr = db.Open(_T("Microsoft.Jet.OLEDB.3.51"), &dbinit);
        if (FAILED(hr))
            return hr;

        return m_session.Open(db);
    }
    HRESULT OpenRowset()
    {
        // Set properties for open
        CDBPropSet    propset(DBPROPSET_ROWSET);
        propset.AddProperty(DBPROP_IRowsetChange, true);
        propset.AddProperty(DBPROP_UPDATABILITY, DBPROPVAL_UP_CHANGE |
                            DBPROPVAL_UP_INSERT | DBPROPVAL_UP_DELETE);
```

19

continues

LISTING 19.2   CONTINUED

```
      return CTable<CAccessor<CBooksAccessor> >::Open(m_session,
_T("Books"), &propset);
   }
   CSession   m_session;
};
```

CDataSource

The CDataSource class contains the information required to open sessions for a data-source. You must create an instance of the CDataSource class before you can open a session (CSession) with that datasource.

Open and Close

The Open method specifies the connection information to the data provider. The Close method releases all the system resources associated with this connection information. These methods are declared as follows:

```
HRESULT Open(const CLSID& clsid, DBPROPSET* pPropSet = NULL);
HRESULT Open(const CLSID& clsid, LPCTSTR pName = NULL,
             LPCTSTR pUserName = NULL, LPCTSTR pPassword = NULL,
             long nInitMode = 0 );
HRESULT Open(LPCTSTR szProgID, DBPROPSET* pPropSet);
HRESULT Open(LPCTSTR szProgID, LPCTSTR pName = NULL,
             LPCTSTR pUserName = NULL, LPCTSTR pPassword = NULL,
             long nInitMode = 0 );
HRESULT Open(const CEnumerator& enumerator,
             DBPROPSET* pPropSet = NULL);
HRESULT Open(const CEnumerator& enumerator,
             LPCTSTR pName = NULL, LPCTSTR pUserName = NULL,
             LPCTSTR pPassword = NULL, long nInitMode = 0);
HRESULT Open(HWND hWnd = GetActiveWindow(),
             DBPROMPTOPTIONS dwPromptOptions =
                               DBPROMPTOPTIONS_WIZARDSHEET );
void Close();
```

You can specify the datasource provider that you need to access by using either its class identifier (CLSID) or program identifier string. Alternatively, you can specify a CEnumerator object that has been initialized to point to the datasource to open. The final alternative form (which has HWND and DBPROMPTOPTIONS parameters) allows the users to select a datasource provider from those available on the system.

In addition to the more basic Open method, several other methods allow you to open a datasource. These methods are declared as follows:

```
HRESULT OpenWithPromptFileName(HWND hWnd = GetActiveWindow(),
             DBPROMPTOPTIONS dwPromptOptions = DBPROMPTOPTIONS_NONE,
             LPCOLESTR szInitialDirectory = NULL);
```

```
HRESULT OpenFromFileName(LPCOLESTR szFileName);
HRESULT OpenFromInitializationString(LPCOLESTR szInitializationString);
```

The OpenWithPromptFileName opens a dialog that allows the user to select a data link file (with .MDL extension) for the data connection to open. If you don't need to prompt the user for the location of the data link file, call the OpenFromFileName method and specify the filename directly. Finally, the OpenFromInitializationString method allows you to specify the connection string for the datasource to open.

CONNECTION STRINGS

Like the ODBC connection string described in Chapter 18, the OLE DB connection string is used to specify the exact nature and location of the datasource connection to open. However, the OLE DB connection string has a slightly different syntax and slightly different keywords than its ODBC counterpart.

In general, an OLE DB connection string is a set of semicolon-delimited keyword/value pairs that is of the following form:

```
keyword1=value1;keyword2=value2
```

The keywords are often datasource provider–specific, except for the standard Provider keyword. You can use Provider=MSDASQL to specify an ODBC connection string or Provider=Microsoft.Jet.OLEDB.3.5.1 to specify a Microsoft Access database. Note that if no provider keyword is specified, the connection string is assumed to be equal to MSDASQL (ODBC datasource), and the string is equal to the ODBC connection string.

CSession

The CSession class encapsulates an active connection to the datasource. All interactions with the datasource are done through the open session. Additionally, use the CSession class to manage transactions to your datasource via its StartTransaction, Commit, and Abort methods.

Open and Close

Like many of the other Open and Close methods available to Microsoft's data access classes, the CSession class's Open and Close methods follow the same paradigm. The Open method allows you to put the CSession object in a usable state and associate it with an active database connection. The Close method releases the resources opened by its Open counterpart. These methods are declared as follows:

```
HRESULT Open(const CDataSource& ds);
void Close();
```

> **NOTE**
>
> The datasource object (`CDataSource`) that you specify to the `CSession::Open` method must be in an `Open` state or an error will occur.

When your datasource session object is open, you can interact with it using the `CTable`, `CCommand`, and `CRowset` classes.

StartTransaction, Commit, and Abort

You can manage database transactions through the `StartTransaction`, `Commit`, and `Abort` methods. Call `StartTransaction` to initiate a datasource transaction; when initiated, all database changes are included in the transaction. When you want the changes to be saved to the datasource, call `Commit`. If you need to roll back the changes, call `Abort`. These methods are declared as follows:

```
HRESULT StartTransaction(ISOLEVEL isoLevel =
            ISOLATIONLEVEL_READCOMMITTED, ULONG isoFlags = 0,
            ITransactionOptions* pOtherOptions = NULL,
            ULONG* pulTransactionLevel = NULL ) const;
HRESULT Commit(BOOL bRetaining = FALSE, DWORD grfTC = XACTTC_SYNC,
            DWORD grfRM = 0) const;
HRESULT Abort(BOID* pboidReason = NULL, BOOL bRetaining = FALSE,
            BOOL bAsync = FALSE );
```

The parameters to `StartTransaction` allow you to modify the behavior of the transaction that you're starting. The first parameter, *isoLevel*, allows you to specify the transaction isolation level. The datasource uses the isolation level to manage the transaction to handle some specific database actions that could occur in the transaction (dirty reads, nonrepeatable reads, and phantoms), a discussion of which is beyond the scope of this book. The second parameter, *isoFlags*, is reserved and must be equal to zero. The third parameter, *pOtherOptions*, is typically equal to NULL, but can be the object returned by `CSession::GetOptionsObject`. Finally, the last parameter, *pulTransactionLevel*, returns the nesting level of the current transaction; the top-level transaction returns 1. Fortunately, your application can call `StartTransaction` without parameters and use its default behavior.

The parameters to `Commit` allow you to specify the behavior of the datasource commit operation. The first parameter, *bRetaining*, allows you to specify whether a new transaction is immediately started after the data is committed. The second parameter, *grfTC*, indicates how quickly the `Commit` method should return to the caller: immediately (`XATTC_ASYNC_PHASEONE`), upon completion of phase one (`XATTC_SYNC_PHASEONE`), or upon completion of a full two-phase commit (`XATTC_SYNC_PHASETWO`/`XATTC_SYNC`). The third parameter, *qrfRM*, must be equal to zero. In the future, it may be used to specify a resource manager for the transaction. Because all the parameters are optional, you can simply call Commit with no parameters to get the most commonly needed behavior.

The parameters to Abort allow you to modify the behavior or the rollback action. The first parameter, *pboidReason*, is used to specify the unit of work that has been aborted. The second parameter, *bRetaining*, allows you to specify whether a new transaction is immediately started when the data has been rolled back. Finally, the third parameter, *bAsync*, allows you to specify whether the call should return immediately or wait until the rollback has occurred. As with the Commit method, all the parameters are optional, and you can simply call Abort with no parameters to get the most likely behavior that your application requires.

> **NOTE**
>
> Some datasource providers allow you to nest transactions. When your data-source supports nested transactions, you can call StartTransaction more than once for an open datasource session. When a nested transaction is opened, the database changes are committed or rolled back for the most recently started transaction. In addition, the transaction is not complete until the number of calls to Abort and Commit equals the number of calls to StartTransaction.

Accessors

Accessors are the glue that binds variables within your application to columns in your datasource. Using accessors, you can obtain and change the data in a datasource. Refer to the section "OLE DB Consumers Using the ATL Wrapper Classes" earlier in this chapter for information on using Visual Studio to associate your classes with a datasource.

All accessors derive from an abstract base class named CAccessorBase. There are four CAccessorBase-derived classes that OLE DB consumers can use to do data binding: CAccessor, CDynamicAccessor, CDynamicParameterAccessor, and CManualAccessor.

CAccessor

The CAccessor template class statically connects data elements within your application to the data values returned from the CRowset class. This template is declared as follows:

```
template < class T >
class CAccessor : public T, CAccessorBase
```

The template parameter class, *T*, is the user-defined class that contains the data elements to which you need to bind the datasource columns. Listing 19.2 shows an example of a generated `CBooks` class that is bound to the Books table in the sample TechBooks database.

CDynamicAccessor

Use the `CDynamicAccessor` class when your application does not know the actual structure of the data returned from a rowset. The `CDynamicAccessor` class allows your application to retrieve the metadata for the rowset, including the number of columns and each column's type, length, and value.

GetColumnCount

The `GetColumnCount` returns the number of columns of data available in the current rowset. This method is declared as follows:

```
ULONG GetColumnCount() const;
```

Use `GetColumnCount` to obtain the total number of available columns to iterate through each of the columns in the rowset. Most of the other methods in this class (including `GetColumnName`, `GetColumnType`, and `GetLength`) allow you to specify a zero-based ordinal value to indicate which specific column to interact with.

GetColumnName, GetColumnType, and GetLength

The `GetColumnName`, `GetColumnType`, and `GetLength` methods return metadata about a specific column, specifically its name, type, and size, respectively. These methods are declared as follows:

```
LPOLESTR GetColumnName(ULONG nColumn) const;
bool GetColumnType(ULONG nColumn, DBTYPE* pType) const;
bool GetLength(ULONG nColumn, ULONG* pLength) const;
bool GetLength(TCHAR* pColumnName, ULONG* pLength) const;
```

The most common column types that are returned by `GetColumnType` are shown in Table 19.1. Note that the return type includes one of the flags shown in Table 19.1 to indicate that the data is an array, vector, or pointer to the base column type. In addition, Table 19.2 shows the modifiers available to create array, vector, and pointer types.

TABLE 19.1   COMMON COLUMN TYPES RETURNED FROM `GetColumnType`

Type	Description
DBTYPE_STR	`char[]`; a null-terminated ANSI string.
DBTYPE_WSTR	`wchar_t[]`; a null-terminated Unicode string.
DBTYPE_BSTR	BSTR; a null-terminated character string that includes its length.
DBTYPE_I1	Signed `char`; a one-byte, signed integer.

Type	Description
DBTYPE_UI1	Unsigned char; a one-byte, unsigned integer.
DBTYPE_I2	short; a two-byte, signed integer.
DBTYPE_UI2	Unsigned short; a two-byte, unsigned integer.
DBTYPE_I4	long; a four-byte, signed integer.
DBTYPE_UI4	Unsigned long; a four-byte, unsigned integer.
DBTYPE_I8	_int64; an eight-byte, signed integer.
DBTYPE_UI8	_int64; an eight-byte, unsigned integer.
DBTYPE_R4	float; a single-precision floating point.
DBTYPE_R8	double; a double-precision floating point.
DBTYPE_CY	LARGE_INTEGER; a currency value scaled by 10,000.
DBTYPE_DATE	DATE; a double-precision value. The whole part indicates the number of days from the first day of the year 1900, and the fractional part is the part of the day.
DBTYPE_DBDATE	DBDATE; year, month, and day.
DBTYPE_DBTIME	DBTIME; hour, minute, and second.
DBTYPE_DBTIMESTAMP	DBTIMESTAMP; year, month, day, hour, minute, second, and fraction of a second.
DBTYPE_ERROR	SCODE; a 32-bit error code.
DBTYPE_BOOL	VARIANT_BOOL; a Boolean value in which 0 is FALSE and -1 is TRUE.
DBTYPE_DECIMAL	DECIMAL; a value with fixed precision and scale.
DBTYPE_BYTES	BYTE[]; a binary array of byte values.

TABLE 19.2 COLUMN TYPE MODIFIERS RETURNED FROM GetColumnType

Flag	Description
DBTYPE_ARRAY	SAFEARRAY *; an array
DBTYPE_BYREF	void *; a pointer
DBTYPE_VECTOR	DBVECTOR; a pointer to an array with a size

19

ADVANCED
DATABASE
SUPPORT

GetValue, and SetValue

The GetValue and SetValue family of methods obtains or changes the value associated with a specified column in the current record in the associated rowset. These methods are declared as follows:

```
void* GetValue(ULONG nColumn) const;
void* GetValue(TCHAR* pColumnName) const;
template < class ctype >
```

```
bool GetValue(ULONG nColumn, ctype* pData) const;
template < class ctype >
bool GetValue(TCHAR *pColumnName, ctype* pData) const;
template < class ctype >
bool SetValue(TCHAR *pColumnName, const ctype& data);
template < class ctype >
bool SetValue(ULONG nColumn, const ctype& data);
```

Use the template versions of these methods to get or set the value of a column's data using a specific datatype.

GetStatus and SetStatus

The GetStatus and SetStatus methods allow you to modify a nondata value associated with the data that indicates the validity of the column's data. These methods are declared as follows:

```
bool GetStatus( ULONG nColumn, DBSTATUS* pStatus ) const;
bool GetStatus( TCHAR* pColumnName, DBSTATUS* pStatus ) const;
bool SetStatus( ULONG nColumn, DBSTATUS status );
bool SetStatus( TCHAR* pColumnName, DBSTATUS status );
```

Use these methods when you need to check whether a column's data is null or set a column's data as null. Table 19.3 lists the possible DBSTATUS values returned from GetStatus. Table 19.4 lists the possible DBSTATUS values passed to SetStatus.

TABLE 19.3 STATUS VALUES RETURNED FROM GetStatus

Type	Description
DBSTATUS_S_OK	The data is valid.
DBSTATUS_S_ISNULL	The data is a null value.
DBSTATUS_S_TRUNCATED	The data was truncated.
DBSTATUS_E_BADACCESSOR	The data binding was invalid for this column.
DBSTATUS_E_CANTCONVERTVALUE	The data conversion failed for this column's data.
DBSTATUS_E_CANTCREATE	A memory or COM object creation error has occurred.
DBSTATUS_E_DATAOVERFLOW	The data conversion failed because the data exceeded the bounds of the bound datatype.
DBSTATUS_SIGNMISMATCH	An unsigned value was bound to an signed value (or vice versa).
DBSTATUS_UNAVAILABLE	The data value was unavailable to the datasource.

TABLE 19.4 STATUS VALUES SET WITH SetStatus

Type	Description
DBSTATUS_S_OK	The data is valid.
DBSTATUS_S_ISNULL	The data is a null value.
DBSTATUS_S_DEFAULT	The datasource should use the default value for the column.
DBSTATUS_S_IGNORE	The datasource should skip this column's data.

CDynamicParameterAccessor

The CDynamicParameterAccessor class extends the CDynamicAccessor interface, allowing your program to get the metadata for the commands. Just as CDynamicAccessor provides information for output columns, the CDynamicParameterAccessor class provides information for parameters, including the number of parameters and each parameter's type, name, and value.

GetParamCount

The GetParamCount returns the number of parameters associated with the current command. This method is declared as follows:

```
ULONG GetParamCount() const;
```

Use GetParamCount to obtain the total number of parameters to iterate through each of the parameters for the command. Most of the other methods in this class (including GetParamName and GetParamType) allow you to specify a zero-based ordinal value to indicate which specific parameter to interact with.

GetParamName and GetParamType

The GetParamName and GetParamType methods return metadata about a specific parameter, specifically its name and type, respectively. These methods are declared as follows:

```
LPOLESTR GetParamName(ULONG ulParam) const;
bool GetParamType(ULONG ulParam, DBTYPE* pType) const;
```

The most common parameter types returned by GetParamType are shown in Table 19.1. Note that the return type includes one of the flags shown in Table 19.2 to indicate that the data is an array, vector, or pointer to the base column type.

GetParam and SetParam

The GetParam and SetParam family of methods obtains or changes the value associated with a specified parameter in the associated command. These methods are declared as follows:

19

ADVANCED
DATABASE
SUPPORT

```
void* GetValue(ULONG ulParam) const;
void* GetValue(TCHAR* pParamName) const;
template < class ctype >
bool GetValue(ULONG ulParam, ctype* pData) const;
template < class ctype >
bool GetValue(TCHAR * pParamName, ctype* pData) const;
template < class ctype >
bool SetValue(TCHAR * pParamName, const ctype& data);
template < class ctype >
bool SetValue(ULONG ulParam, const ctype& data);
```

Use the template versions of these methods to get or set the value of a parameter's data using a specific datatype.

CManualAccessor

The CManualAccessor class provides a mechanism for binding data buffers to your data-source at a low level. Intended for advanced use, the CManualAccessor class interface requires you to perform your own accessor buffer management.

You must call CreateAccessor or CreateParameterAccessor before calling the respective AddBindEntry or AddParameterEntry methods.

CreateAccessor and CreateParameterAccessor

The CreateAccessor and CreateParameterAccessor methods initialize the CManualAccessor object and prepare it for bind entries to be set in it via the AddBindEntry and AddParameterEntry method calls. The CreateAccessor and CreateParameterAccessor methods are declared as follows:

```
HRESULT CreateAccessor(int nBindEntries, void* pBuffer,
                       ULONG nBufferSize);
HRESULT CreateParameterAccessor(int nBindEntries,
                       void* pBuffer, ULONG nBufferSize);
```

Use these methods to specify the number of bind entries that are to be added and the buffer that contains all the bound memory locations.

AddBindEntry and AddParameterEntry

The AddBindEntry and AddParameterEntry methods specify the binding between the datasource column or parameter and the memory in a preallocated buffer. These methods are declared as follows:

```
void AddBindEntry(ULONG nOrdinal, DBTYPE wType,
                  ULONG nColumnSize,
                  void* pData, void* pLength = NULL,
                  void* pStatus = NULL);
void AddParameterEntry(ULONG nOrdinal, DBTYPE wType,
                  ULONG nColumnSize,
```

```
                        void* pData, void* pLength = NULL,
                        void* pStatus = NULL,
                        DBPARAMIO eParamIO = DBPARAMIO_INPUT);
```

The first parameter, *nOrdinal*, is equal to the bind entry ordinal to set. The type parameter, *wType*, can be one of the values shown in Table 19.1. The *nColumnSize* parameter indicates the number of bytes for the datasource column. The *pLength* parameter returns the number of bytes for the field in the buffer. The *pStatus* parameter points to a location in the buffer to be bound to the column's status values. Finally, the *eParamIO* parameter specifies whether the parameter is input (DBPARAMIO_INPUT), output (DBPARAMIO_OUTPUT), or both (DBPARAMIO_INPUT | DBPARAMIO_OUTPUT).

Rowsets

Programs send data to and retrieve data from a datasource using a rowset. Very similar to the MFC/ODBC CDBRecordset and DAO CDaoRecordset classes, the CRowset family of classes allows programs to move through a set of records from a datasource.

When using rowsets, you are most likely to use the CRowset class's interface, which provides basic, single-row retrieval and updating on the datasource. If you'd like to improve the performance of your application because it deals with large amounts of data at a time, use the CBulkRowset class, which is optimized for this situation. Finally, if you need to interact with a rowset as an array of elements (such as a C++ array), use the CArrayRowset class.

CRowset

The CRowset class is the base class for the CBulkRowset and CArrayRowset classes and provides the core rowset functionality for OLE DB. This functionality includes browsing, adding, updating, and deleting datasource rows.

MoveFirst, MoveLast, MoveNext, and MovePrev

The MoveFirst, MoveNext, MovePrev, and MoveLast methods are used to scan through a recordset from first record to last record (or vice versa). These methods are declared as follows:

```
HRESULT MoveFirst();
HRESULT MoveLast();
HRESULT MoveNext();
HRESULT MoveNext(LONG lSkip, bool bForward);
HRESULT MovePrev();
```

When a method call to each of these methods is successful, it returns an HRESULT equal to S_OK. Consequently, it is easy to iterate through a set of records by using a while loop as shown in Listing 19.3.

LISTING 19.3   DISPLAYING ROWS FROM THE BOOKS TABLE

```
static void getRecords()
{
   CBooks books;

   if (FAILED(books.Open())) {
      cerr << "Error in books.Open()" << endl;
      return;
   }

   while (books.MoveNext() == S_OK) {
      cout << (const TCHAR *) books.m_ISBN  << _T("\t")
           << (const TCHAR *) books.m_Title << endl;
   }

   books.Close();
}
```

Insert, Update, and Delete

The Insert, Update, and Delete methods provide a mechanism for doing the standard data operations for your datasource. Use the Insert method to create and initialize a new data row. Use the Update method to change the data in the current row. Use the Delete method to remove the current data row from the datasource. These methods are declared as follows:

```
HRESULT Insert(int nAccessor = 0, bool bGetHRow = false);
HRESULT Update(ULONG* pcRows = NULL, HROW* phRow = NULL,
               DBROWSTATUS* pStatus = NULL);
HRESULT Delete();
```

The Insert, Update, and Delete methods are demonstrated for the TechBooks sample database in Listings 19.4, 19.5, and 19.6, respectively.

> **NOTE**
>
> If you are using Update, make sure that your accessor does not include any key columns. Otherwise, the call to Update will fail.
>
> You can resolve this problem by creating an accessor that contains only the fields that you need to update and calling SetData to specify the accessor to use—before calling Update.

LISTING 19.4   INSERTING A NEW BOOK ENTRY USING OLE DB

```
static void addRecord()
{
    CBooks books;

    if (FAILED(books.Open())) {
        cerr << "Error in books.Open()" << endl;
        return;
    }

    books.ClearRecord();

    books.m_BookId = 123;
    _tcscpy(books.m_ISBN,  "1234567890");
    _tcscpy(books.m_Title, "MFC Unleashed");
    books.m_RetailPrice.int64 = (49.99) * 10000;

    if (FAILED(books.Insert())) {
        cerr << "Error in books.Insert()" << endl;
    }
    else {
        cout << _T("added record") << endl;
    }

    books.Close();
}
```

LISTING 19.5   UPDATING AN EXISTING BOOK ENTRY USING OLE DB

```
static void editRecord()
{
    CBooks books;

    if (FAILED(books.Open())) {
        cerr << "Error in books.Open()" << endl;
        return;
    }

    while (books.MoveNext() == S_OK) {
        if (_tcscmp(books.m_ISBN, _T("1234567890")) == 0) {
            _tcscpy(books.m_ISBN, _T("0987654321"));

            // set to use accessor #1, which only references
            // the ISBN column—since that's the only column
            // that we're updating...
            books.SetData(1);
```

continues

LISTING 19.5   CONTINUED

```
        books.Update();
        cout << _T("edited record") << endl;
    }
}

books.Close();
}
```

LISTING 19.6   DELETING A BOOK ENTRY USING OLE DB

```
static void deleteRecord()
{
    CBooks books;

    if (FAILED(books.Open())) {
        cerr << "Error in books.Open()" << endl;
        return;
    }

    while (books.MoveNext() == S_OK) {
        if ((_tcscmp(books.m_ISBN, _T("1234567890")) == 0)
            || (_tcscmp(books.m_ISBN, _T("0987654321")) == 0)) {

            if (FAILED(books.Delete())) {
                cerr << "Error in books.Delete()" << endl;
                return;
            }
            else {
                cout << _T("deleted record") << endl;
            }
        }
    }

    books.Close();
}
```

Close

The Close method releases all the allocated system resources associated with the open rowset. This method is declared as follows:

```
void Close();
```

CBulkRowset

The CBulkRowset class is a CRowset specialization that is optimized for accessing large amounts of data from a remote datasource. This class retrieves data from the datasource in blocks of multiple rows, thus reducing the amount of overall network traffic required to transmit and receive each row of data.

SetRows

Use the SetRows method to specify the number of rows that the CBulkRowset should manage at a time. If you do not call this method, OLE DB uses a default value of 10 rows. This method is declared as follows:

```
void SetRows(ULONG nRows);
```

If your application is processing a large amount of data, except for the times that you've retrieved a multiple of this row value, you should notice that calls to MoveNext are much faster.

CArrayRowset

The CArrayRowset class template allows your application to interact with a rowset in a random access manner. Consequently, although you can still use the MoveNext and MovePrev methods to move sequentially forward and backward through the rowset, you can use an ordinal value to reference the specific row that you need. This class template is declared as follows:

```
template < class T, class TRowset = CRowset >
class CArrayRowset : public CVirtualBuffer <T> , public TRowset
```

Use CArrayRowset when you need optimized random access to a rowset from a datasource.

Operator[]

The only method that CArrayRowset provides to extend the CRowset interface is operator[]. This method is declared as follows:

```
T& operator[](ULONG nRow);
```

Accessing Datasource Data

Although CRowset-derived classes allow you to interact with the data retrieved from a datasource, the association of your datasource session with that rowset has not been discussed yet. This section describes the use of CAccessorRowset-based template classes to make this connection.

19

ADVANCED
DATABASE
SUPPORT

CAccessorRowset

The `CAccessorRowset` class is an abstract base class from which the `CTable` and `CCommand` template classes derive. The class hierarchy based at this class represents an association between a `CAccessor` class and a `CRowset` class. Consequently, it provides a few methods of interest: `FreeRecordMemory` and `Close`.

FreeRecordMemory

The `FreeRecordMemory` method frees all the memory and removes any references associated with the pointer-based types and objects in the current record. It is declared as follows:

```
void FreeRecordMemory();
```

Use `FreeRecordMemory` before reading each record to release the memory associated with the objects in the previous record.

Close

The `Close` method closes the associated rowset and releases any system resources associated with that rowset. This method is declared as shown here:

```
void Close();
```

CCommand

The `CCommand` class template allows you to send a command to the datasource. Objects of this class associate an open `CSession` object with a mechanism for processing the rowset (`CRowset`) and a mechanism for binding the data to user variables (`CAccessor`). This class template is declared as shown here:

```
template <class TAccessor = CNoAccessor, class TRowset = CRowset,
          class TMultiple = CNoMultiple>
class CCommand : public CAccessorRowset<TAccessor, TRowset>
                , public CCommandBase
```

The `TMultiple` template parameter can be either `CNoMultipleResults` (if a single set of results is returned) or `CMultipleResults` (if multiple result sets are returned).

Open

The `Open` method executes a command, optionally binding the accessor to the command. The `Open` method is declared as shown:

```
HRESULT Open(DBPROPSET *pPropSet = NULL, LONG* pRowsAffected = NULL,
             bool bBind = true );
HRESULT Open(const CSession& session, LPCTSTR szCommand = NULL,
             DBPROPSET *pPropSet = NULL, LONG* pRowsAffected = NULL,
             REFGUID guidCommand = DBGUID_DEFAULT, bool bBind = true);
```

Create, CreateCommand, and ReleaseCommand

The Create and CreateCommand methods associate a new session with the current command. The CreateCommand method also releases the current command and sets a new command. If you need to release the command without creating a new one, call ReleaseCommand. These methods are declared as follows:

```
HRESULT Create(const CSession& session, LPCTSTR szCommand,
               REFGUID guidCommand = DBGUID_DEFAULT);
HRESULT CreateCommand(const CSession& session);
HRESULT ReleaseCommand();
```

Prepare and Unprepare

The Prepare method validates the current command and prepares an execution plan for it at the datasource. The Release method destroys that execution plan. These methods are declared as follows:

```
HRESULT Prepare(ULONG cExpectedRuns = 0);
HRESULT Unprepare();
```

GetParameterInfo and SetParameterInfo

Use the GetParameterInfo method to retrieve the parameters to be passed to the current command. Use SetParameterInfo to specify these parameters. These two methods are declared as follows:

```
HRESULT GetParameterInfo(ULONG* pParams, DBPARAMINFO** ppParamInfo,
                         OLECHAR** ppNamesBuffer );
HRESULT SetParameterInfo(ULONG ulParams, const ULONG* pOrdinals,
                         const DBPARAMBINDINFO* pParamInfo );
```

GetNextResult

The GetNextResult method processes and returns the next result set for commands that return multiple result sets. This method is declared as shown here:

```
HRESULT GetNextResult(LONG* pulRowsAffected, bool bBind = true);
```

CTable

The CTable class template, derived from CAccessorRowset, provides a simple interface for interacting with a datasource that returns a rowset without requiring any parameters. This class template is declared as follows:

```
template <class TAccessor = CNoAccessor, class TRowset = CRowset >
class Table : public CAccessorRowset <T, TRowset>
```

This class only provides a single method (excluding those from its base classes) to access a parameterless rowset: Open.

19

ADVANCED
DATABASE
SUPPORT

Open

The Open method opens a simple, parameterless rowset for a datasource. Its two forms are declared as shown here:

```
HRESULT Open(const CSession& session, LPCTSTR szTableName,
             DBPROPSET* pPropSet = NULL);
HRESULT Open( const CSession& session, DBID& dbid,
             DBPROPSET* pPropSet = NULL);
```

Using the ADO C++ Interfaces

The ADO interfaces are a set of COM components. Consequently, you can use them in a variety of ways from Visual C++. This chapter discusses the use of ADO interfaces using the C++ interfaces supplied by Microsoft with Visual C++.

To use ADO in Visual C++ can sometimes be a bit more of a challenge than using it with some of the scripting languages (such as VBScript and JavaScript). However, with the ADO 2 extensions supplied with Microsoft Visual Studio 6, much of the pain is taken out of the process. Using the TechBooks database example, this section steps you through the key issues that you'll encounter when using ADO in your application.

First, to use the ADO C++ interfaces, make sure that the following file inclusion lines are in your application (most likely in stdafx.h):

```
#include <adoid.h>    // class and interface identifiers
#include <adoint.h>   // ADO interface
#include <icrsint.h>  // ADO 2.0 data binding extensions
```

These files declare the ADO class and interface identifiers, the interface itself, and the extensions for data binding, respectively.

Next, you need to derive a class that contains your bound data members from the CADORecordBinding class. Within this class, add data members to which you'd like to bind the data returned from the datasource provider. In addition, for each bound data member, create a status field (of type ULONG) that will be used for reporting bind errors to your application. Finally, create an ADO binding section within your class that maps the ordinal column numbers in the database table to your class members. Listing 19.7 shows the CBooks class, which is associated with the Books table in the TechBooks sample database.

LISTING 19.7 THE CBooks CLASS USING ADO DATA BINDING

```
class CBooks : public CADORecordBinding {
public:
    LONG    m_BookId;
    LONG    m_CategoryId;
```

```
    TCHAR      m_ISBN[13];
    DATE       m_PublicationDate;
    LONG       m_PublisherId;
    CURRENCY   m_RetailPrice;
    TCHAR      m_Title[251];
    LONG       m_TopicId;

    ULONG      m_stsBookId;
    ULONG      m_stsCategoryId;
    ULONG      m_stsISBN;
    ULONG      m_stsPublicationDate;
    ULONG      m_stsPublisherId;
    ULONG      m_stsRetailPrice;
    ULONG      m_stsTitle;
    ULONG      m_stsTopicId;

BEGIN_ADO_BINDING(CBooks)
    ADO_NUMERIC_ENTRY(1, adInteger, m_BookId, 10, 0, m_stsBookId, false)
    ADO_VARIABLE_LENGTH_ENTRY2(2, adVarChar, m_Title, sizeof(m_Title),
    m_stsTitle, true)
    ADO_NUMERIC_ENTRY(3, adInteger, m_PublisherId, 10, 0, m_stsPublisherId,
    true)
    ADO_FIXED_LENGTH_ENTRY(4, adDate, m_PublicationDate,
    m_stsPublicationDate, true)
    ADO_VARIABLE_LENGTH_ENTRY2(5, adChar, m_ISBN, sizeof(m_ISBN),
    m_stsISBN, true)
    ADO_FIXED_LENGTH_ENTRY(6, adCurrency, m_RetailPrice, m_stsRetailPrice,
    true)
    ADO_NUMERIC_ENTRY(7, adInteger, m_CategoryId, 10, 0, m_stsCategoryId,
    true)
    ADO_NUMERIC_ENTRY(8, adInteger, m_TopicId, 10, 0, m_stsTopicId, true)
END_ADO_BINDING()

    // You may wish to call this function if you are inserting a record and
    //wish to initialize all the fields, if you are not going to
    //explicitly set all of them.
    void ClearRecord()
    {
        memset(this, 0, sizeof(*this));
    }
};
```

19

ADVANCED
DATABASE
SUPPORT

Within the CBooks example, note that various macros are used to specify how each data member needs to be bound to the column. When you have a class derived from CADORecordBinding, follow the steps after Listing 19.8 to create and use an ADORecordset object within your application. Listing 19.8 illustrates these steps.

LISTING 19.8   INITIALIZING AND USING ADO

```
int _tmain(int argc, TCHAR* argv[], TCHAR* envp[])
{
   int nRetCode = 0;

   // initialize COM (step 1)
   CoInitialize(NULL);

   HRESULT hr;
   ADORecordset *rstADO;

   // create an instance of the CADORecordset class (step 2)
   hr = CoCreateInstance(
                        //"{00000535-0000-0010-8000-00AA006D2EA4}",
                        CLSID_CADORecordset,
                        NULL,
                        CLSCTX_INPROC_SERVER,
                        IID_IADORecordset,
                        (LPVOID *) &rstADO);

   if (FAILED(hr)) {
      cerr << "Unable to create ADORecordset object." << endl;
      CoUninitialize();
      return 1;
   }

   // obtain the IADORecordBinding interface (step 3)
   IADORecordBinding *rstADOBind;

   hr = rstADO->QueryInterface(__uuidof(IADORecordBinding), (LPVOID *)
   &rstADOBind);

   if (FAILED(hr)) {
      cerr << "Unable to obtain IADORecordBinding interface." << endl;
      CoUninitialize();
      return 1;
   }

   // open the recordset (step 4)
   CString table("Books");
   CString connect;

   connect += "DRIVER={Microsoft Access Driver (*.mdb)};";
   connect += "UID=Admin;";
   connect += "DBQ=";
   connect += argv[1];

   hr = rstADO->Open(COleVariant(table),
                     COleVariant(connect),
                     adOpenKeyset, adLockOptimistic,
```

```
                    adCmdTable);

    if (FAILED(hr)) {
        cerr << "Unable to open ADORecordset object." << endl;
        CoUninitialize();
        return 1;
    }

    // bind your class to the recordset (step 5)
    CBooks books;

    rstADOBind->BindToRecordset(&books);

    // add code here to browse, insert, update, or delete (step 6)

    // close the recordset and release the record bind (step 7)
    rstADO->Close();
    rstADOBind->Release();

    // clean up COM (step 8)
    CoUninitialize();

    return nRetCode;
}
```

1. Call `CoInitialize` to initialize COM.

2. Create an instance of the `ADORecordset` class using `CoCreateInstance`.

3. Obtain a pointer to the `IADORecordBinding` interface from this recordset object. (Note: If this call fails, it is probably because either you do not have ADO 2 installed or the CLSID and IID that you are using refer to ADO 1 objects. Refer to the following sidebar for more information on how to resolve this problem.)

ERRORS OBTAINING `IADORecordBinding`

If you get an error when trying to get a pointer to the `IADORecordBinding` interface, it is likely that your application is using ADO 1, not ADO 2.

To determine whether this is the case, run your program in the debugger in Visual Studio. When the call to `CoCreateInstance` is made, the output window should indicate that msado15.dll is loaded. (For whatever reason, msado15.dll contains the ADO 2 interface.)

If the debugger reports that msado10.dll was loaded, your application is passing the incorrect CLSID to `CoCreateInstance` to construct its interface.

continues

19

ADVANCED
DATABASE
SUPPORT

To correct this situation, you need to build a source file that contains the correct, newer class and interface identifiers. Listing 19.13 shows such a file. Simply compile this file (outside your current project—perhaps even in its own project) and link its object file into your application.

You might note that Microsoft ships a library file named adoid.lib with Visual Studio 6. However—and unfortunately—it contains the class and interface identifiers for ADO 1.

4. Open the created recordset object using its Open method.

5. Bind your CADORecordBinding-derived class to the record binding interface using its Bind method.

6. To browse the recordset's records, see the code in Listing 19.9. To add a new record, see Listing 19.10. To change a record, see Listing 19.11. To delete a record, see Listing 19.12.

7. When finished, close the recordset (using its Close method) and release the record binding interface (using its Release method).

8. Call CoUninitialize to release the COM resources owned by the application.

LISTING 19.9   DOING A FORWARD SCAN OF A TABLE'S RECORDS USING ADO

```
static void getRecords(ADORecordset *rst, CBooks& books)
{
    VARIANT_BOOL isEOF;

    while (true) {
        rst->get_EOF(&isEOF);

        if (isEOF == VARIANT_TRUE) {
            break;
        }

        cout << (const TCHAR *) books.m_ISBN  << _T("\t")
             << (const TCHAR *) books.m_Title << endl;

        rst->MoveNext();
    }
}
```

LISTING 19.10   ADDING A NEW BOOK ENTRY USING ADO

```
static void addRecord(ADORecordset *rst,
                      IADORecordBinding *rstADOBind,
                      CBooks& books)
{
   books.ClearRecord();

   books.m_BookId = 123;
   books.m_CategoryId = 1;
   _tcscpy(books.m_ISBN, _T("1234567890"));
   books.m_PublicationDate = 39000.0;
   books.m_PublisherId = 1;
   books.m_RetailPrice.int64 = (49.99) * 10000;
   _tcscpy(books.m_Title, _T("MFC Unleashed"));
   books.m_TopicId = 1;

   rstADOBind->AddNew(&books);

   cout << _T("added record") << endl;
}
```

LISTING 19.11   UPDATING AN EXISTING BOOK ENTRY USING ADO

```
static void editRecord(ADORecordset *rst,
                       IADORecordBinding *rstADOBind,
                       CBooks& books)
{
   VARIANT_BOOL isEOF;

   while (true) {
      rst->get_EOF(&isEOF);

      if (isEOF == VARIANT_TRUE) {
         break;
      }

      if (_tcscmp(books.m_ISBN, _T("1234567890")) == 0) {
         _tcscpy(books.m_ISBN, _T("0987654321"));

         rstADOBind->Update(&books);

         cout << _T("edited record") << endl;
      }

      rst->MoveNext();
   }
}
```

19

ADVANCED
DATABASE
SUPPORT

LISTING 19.12 DELETING A BOOK ENTRY USING ADO

```
static void deleteRecord(ADORecordset *rst, CBooks& books)
{
    VARIANT_BOOL isEOF;

    while (true) {
        rst->get_EOF(&isEOF);

        if (isEOF == VARIANT_TRUE) {
            break;
        }

        if ((_tcscmp(books.m_ISBN, _T("1234567890")) == 0)
            || (_tcscmp(books.m_ISBN, _T("0987654321")) == 0)) {
            rst->Delete(adAffectCurrent);

            cout << _T("deleted record") << endl;
        }

        rst->MoveNext();
    }
}
```

LISTING 19.13 THE SOURCE FILE FOR CREATING THE MOST RECENT CLASS AND INTERFACE IDENTIFIERS FOR ADO

```
// Yes, you only need the three header file inclusions shown below.
// However, you cannot include adoid.h at any point before this set
// of file inclusion statements.
#include <objbase.h>
#include <initguid.h>
#include <adoid.h>
```

ADOConnection

The ADOConnection class manages information required for connecting to a datasource provider and allows you to open a live connection to it via the Open and Close methods. In addition, you can create and manage transactions: BeginTrans, CommitTrans, and RollbackTrans. Finally, you can execute commands against the datasource via the Execute method.

Open and Close

The Open and Close methods create and destroy a network connection to a datasource, respectively. These methods are declared as shown here:

```
HRESULT Open(BSTR ConnectionString, BSTR UserID, BSTR Password,
            long Options = 0);
HRESULT Close();
```

The connection string must be in OLE DB format, as described in the OLE DB `CDataSource::Open` method earlier in this chapter. The *Options* parameter allows you to indicate whether to perform the connection synchronously (`adConnectUnspecified`) or asynchronously (`adAsyncConnect`).

ConnectionString, Provider, DefaultDatabase, ConnectionTimeout, and Mode

The `ConnectionString`, `Provider`, `DefaultDatabase`, `ConnectionTimeout`, and `Mode` properties are used to indicate how to connect to the datasource provider and in what manner. The methods associated with these properties are declared as follows:

```
HRESULT get_ConnectionString(BSTR *pbstr);
HRESULT put_ConnectionString(BSTR bstr);
HRESULT get_Provider(BSTR *pbstr);
HRESULT put_Provider(BSTR bstr);
HRESULT get_DefaultDatabase(BSTR *pbstr);
HRESULT put_DefaultDatabase(BSTR bstr);
HRESULT get_ConnectionTimeout(LONG *plTimeout);
HRESULT put_ConnectionTimeout(LONG lTimeout);
HRESULT get_Mode(ConnectModeEnum *plMode);
HRESULT put_Mode(ConnectModeEnum lMode);
```

The timeout values for the `ConnectionTimeout` property are in seconds. The `Mode` property controls access to the database; its values are listed in Table 19.5.

TABLE 19.5 VALUES ALLOWED FOR THE `Mode` PROPERTY

Value	Description
adModeUnknown	No permissions (default).
adModeRead	Read-only permissions.
adModeWrite	Write-only permissions.
adModeReadWrite	Read and write permissions.
adModeShareDenyRead	Deny other readers.
adModeShareDenyWrite	Deny other writers.
adModeShareExclusive	Deny other readers and writers.
adModeShareDenyNone	Allow others to access as readers and/or writers.

19

ADVANCED
DATABASE
SUPPORT

BeginTrans, CommitTrans, RollbackTrans, and IsolationLevel

The BeginTrans, CommitTrans, and RollbackTrans methods manage the transaction state for the current open connection. The IsolationLevel property informs the datasource about the characteristics of the transaction. The methods for managing transactions are shown here:

```
HRESULT BeginTrans(long *TransactionLevel);
HRESULT CommitTrans();
HRESULT RollbackTrans();
HRESULT get_IsolationLevel(IsolationLevelEnum *Level);
HRESULT put_IsolationLevel(IsolationLevelEnum Level);
```

Call BeginTrans to start a transaction, which causes all changes to the database through this open connection to be managed as a single entity. Upon completion of the database changes, call CommitTrans to save the changes to the database. If you need to undo the changes belonging to this transaction, call RollbackTrans.

The IsolationLevel property can have one of the values specified in Table 19.6.

TABLE 19.6   VALUES ALLOWED FOR THE IsolationLevel PROPERTY

Value	Description
adXactUnspecified	Unknown.
adXactChaos	Overwrite of higher isolation-level transactions is not allowed (default).
adXactReadUncommitted	Transaction can view uncommitted changes in other transactions.
adXactBrowse	Same as adXactReadUncommitted.
adXactCursorStability	Transaction can view only committed changes in other transactions (default).
adXactReadCommitted	Same as adXactCursorStability.
adXactRepeatableRead	Requeries of the same data sets can return different results—but only for committed data.
adXactSerializable	Transaction is isolated from other transactions.
adXactIsolated	Same as adXactSerializable.

Execute and CommandTimeout

Use the Execute method to send datasource-specific text to a datasource provider. In cases where your application is interacting with a relational database, this is likely to be a SQL statement. The CommandTimeout property allows you to specify the amount of time (in seconds) to wait for your commands to be executed before giving up waiting on results. The methods used for executing commands are shown here:

```
HRESULT Execute(BSTR CommandText, VARIANT *RecordsAffected,
                long Options, ADORecordset **ppiRset);
HRESULT get_CommandTimeout(LONG *plTimeout);
HRESULT put_CommandTimeout(LONG lTimeout);
```

The options allowed by the `Execute` method are shown in Table 19.7. Use the `ADOCommand` object if you need to pass parameters to the command—to invoke a stored procedure on a SQL Server that requires parameters, for example.

TABLE 19.7   OPTION VALUES FOR THE Execute METHOD

Value	Description
adCmdText	The command is a text string (probably SQL).
adCmdTable	The command is the name of a table, for which ADO should create a SQL query to return all its rows.
adCmdTableDirect	The command is the name of a table, for which the data-source provider should return all its rows.
adCmdStoredProc	The command is the name of a stored procedure.
adCmdUnknown	The type of the command is unknown.
adAsyncExecute	The command should execute asynchronously.
adAsyncFetch	The rows beyond the number indicated by the recordset's `CacheSize` property should be retrieved asynchronously.
adAsyncFetchNoBlocking	The data retrieval request never blocks the calling thread.

Errors

The `Errors` collection contains a list of `ADOError` objects that are created when an error occurs. This collection is accessed using the following method:

```
HRESULT get_Errors(ADOErrors **ppvObject);
```

Sometimes when a datasource provider error occurs, it can cause a domino effect of errors through the nested ADO classes. The collection of errors allows you to trace back to the original locus of the error.

Properties

The `Properties` collection is a set of datasource provider–dependent keys and values that modify the way the datasource handles this `ADOConnection` object. Use the following method to gain access to this collection:

```
HRESULT get_Properties(ADOProperties **ppvObject);
```

ADORecordset

The ADORecordset class encapsulates the set of results returned from a datasource provider. Using this class, you can browse the returned records and, optionally, insert a new record or update or delete an existing record.

Open and Close

Use the Open method to create a recordset by sending a command to a datasource over a specific connection. Use the Close method to release all the resources associated with the open recordset. These methods are declared as follows:

```
HRESULT Open(VARIANT Source, VARIANT ActiveConnection,
             CursorTypeEnum CursorType, LockTypeEnum LockType,
             LONG Options);
HRESULT Close();
```

The *Source* variant parameter can contain either a pointer to an ADOCommand object or a command text string. The *ActiveConnection* variant parameter can contain either a pointer to an ADOConnection object or a connection string. The *CursorType* parameter can contain one of the values listed in Table 19.8. The *LockType* parameter can contain one of the values listed in Table 19.9. The *Options* parameter can contain one of the values listed in Table 19.10.

TABLE 19.8   CURSOR TYPES FOR THE Open METHOD

Value	Description
adOpenForwardOnly	The recordset supports forward browsing only (default).
adOpenKeyset	The recordset uses a keyset cursor.
adOpenDynamic	The recordset uses a dynamic cursor.
adOpenStatic	The recordset uses a static cursor.

TABLE 19.9   LOCK TYPES FOR THE Open METHOD

Value	Description
adLockReadOnly	The data in the recordset is read-only (default).
adLockPessimistic	Use pessimistic locking, which locks the record upon edit.
adLockOptimistic	Use optimistic locking, which locks the record only at update.
adLockBatchOptimistic	Use optimistic locking when BatchUpdate is called.

TABLE 19.10 OPTION VALUES FOR THE Open METHOD

Value	Description
adCmdText	The command is a text string (probably SQL).
adCmdTable	The command is the name of a table, for which ADO should create a SQL query to return all its rows.
adCmdTableDirect	The command is the name of a table, for which the data-source provider should return all its rows.
adCmdStoredProc	The command is the name of a stored procedure.
adCmdUnknown	The type of the command is unknown.
adCmdFile	The recordset should be restored from the file named by the command.
adAsyncExecute	The command should execute asynchronously.
adAsyncFetch	The rows beyond the number indicated by the recordset's CacheSize property should be retrieved asynchronously.
adAsyncFetchNoBlocking	The data retrieval request never blocks the calling thread.

Source

The Source property contains the value that was supplied to the Open method via its *Source* variant parameter. This variant could contain a pointer to an ADOCommand object or a text string containing the table name, stored procedure name, or SQL statement used to create the recordset. The methods to access this property are declared as follows:

```
HRESULT putref_Source(IDispatch *pcmd);
HRESULT put_Source(BSTR bstrConn);
HRESULT get_Source(VARIANT *pvSource);
```

MoveFirst, MoveLast, MoveNext, MovePrevious, BOF, and EOF

The MoveFirst, MoveLast, MoveNext, and MovePrevious methods are used to scan through a recordset from first record to last record (or vice versa). Additionally, use the BOF and EOF properties to determine whether the recordset is currently at the beginning or end. These methods are declared as follows:

```
HRESULT MoveFirst();
HRESULT MoveLast();
HRESULT MoveNext();
HRESULT MovePrevious();
HRESULT get_BOF(VARIANT_BOOL *pb);
HRESULT get_EOF(VARIANT_BOOL *pb);
```

To use these methods to scan and list a set of database records, call these methods as shown in Listing 19.9. This code simply creates a `while` loop that checks the `EOF` property and calls `MoveNext` to advance to the next record. The data class members contain the data associated with the current record.

> **NOTE**
>
> If you make changes to the recordset's data class members while scanning the table, your changes will be lost. Use the `Update` methods to change the record's data and reflect the data in the recordset.

AddNew, Update, and Delete

The `AddNew`, `Update`, and `Delete` methods provide a mechanism for doing the standard data operations for your datasource. Use the `AddNew` method to create and initialize a new data row. Use the `Update` method to change the data in the current row. Use the `Delete` method to remove the current data row from the datasource. These methods are declared as follows:

```
HRESULT AddNew(VARIANT FieldList, VARIANT Values);
HRESULT Update(VARIANT Fields, VARIANT Values);
HRESULT Delete(AffectEnum AffectRecords);
```

The `Delete` method's *AffectRecords* parameter accepts the values displayed in Table 19.11.

TABLE 19.11   VALUES FOR THE `Delete` METHOD

Value	Description
adAffectCurrent	Delete the current record (default).
adAffectGroup	Delete all records satisfying the `Filter` property.
adAffectAll	Delete all records.
adAffectAllChapters	Delete all chapter records.

CacheSize

Use the `CacheSize` property to specify the number of rows that the recordset should cache. You can get and set this property using the following methods:

```
HRESULT get_CacheSize(long *pl);
HRESULT put_CacheSize(long CacheSize);
```

By default, the `CacheSize` property is set to one. You can modify this property to improve overall network traffic and performance.

ActiveConnection

Use the `ActiveConnection` property to get or set the connection to which this `ADORecordset` object belongs. The methods to manipulate this property are declared as follows:

```
HRESULT get_ActiveConnection(_ADOConnection **ppvObject);
HRESULT putref_ActiveConnection(_ADOConnection *pCon);
HRESULT put_ActiveConnection(VARIANT vConn);
```

Fields

The `Fields` collection contains the set of data elements for a single record. You can retrieve the values returned from the datasource provider by iterating through this collection of `ADOField` objects. The method for obtaining access to this collection is declared as follows:

```
HRESULT get_Fields(ADOFields **ppvObject);
```

Properties

The `Properties` collection is a set of datasource provider–dependent keys and values that modify the way the datasource handles this `ADORecordset` object. Use the following method to gain access to this collection:

```
HRESULT get_Properties(ADOProperties **ppvObject);
```

ADOCommand

The `ADOCommand` class encapsulates a command string that is sent to the database. Typically a SQL statement, this command could be the name of a table, stored procedure, or a datasource-dependent string.

CommandType and CommandText

Use the `CommandType` and `CommandText` properties to specify datasource-specific text for a datasource provider. In cases where your application is interacting with a relational database, this is likely to be a SQL statement. The methods used for executing commands are shown here:

```
HRESULT put_CommandType(CommandTypeEnum lCmdType);
HRESULT get_CommandType(CommandTypeEnum *plCmdType);
HRESULT get_CommandText(BSTR *pbstr);
HRESULT put_CommandText(BSTR bstr);
HRESULT get_CommandTimeout(LONG *plTimeout);
HRESULT put_CommandTimeout(LONG lTimeout);
```

The types allowed by the `CommandType` property are shown in Table 19.7.

Execute and `CommandTimeout`

Use the `Execute` method to send datasource-specific text to a datasource provider. In cases where your application is interacting with a relational database, this is likely to be a SQL statement. The `CommandTimeout` property allows you to specify the amount of time (in seconds) to wait for your commands to be executed before giving up waiting on results. The methods used for executing commands are shown here:

```
HRESULT Execute(BSTR CommandText, VARIANT *RecordsAffected,
                VARIANT *Parameters,
                long Options, ADORecordset **ppiRset);
HRESULT get_CommandTimeout(LONG *plTimeout);
HRESULT put_CommandTimeout(LONG lTimeout);
```

The options allowed by the `Execute` method are shown in Table 19.7. Use the `ADOCommand` object if you need to pass parameters to the command—to invoke a stored procedure on a SQL Server that requires parameters, for example.

CreateParameter and `Parameters`

The `CreateParameter` method adds a new parameter to the `Parameters` collection for the current command. Use the following methods to interact with command parameters:

```
HRESULT CreateParameter(BSTR Name, DataTypeEnum Type,
                        ParameterDirectionEnum Direction,
                        long Size, VARIANT Value,
                        ADOParameter **ppiprm);
HRESULT get_Parameters(ADOParameters **ppvObject);
```

The values for the *Type* parameter are shown in Table 19.12. Flags that can modify the *Type* parameter (via a logical OR operation) are listed in Table 19.13. The *Direction* parameter designates whether the parameter is input or output (or both) and can have one of the values listed in Table 19.14.

TABLE 19.12   COMMON ADO DATATYPES

Type	Description
adChar	char[]; a null-terminated ANSI string.
adWChar	wchar_t[]; a null-terminated Unicode string.
adBSTR	BSTR; a null-terminated character string that includes its length.
adTinyInt	signed char; a one-byte, signed integer.
adUnsignedTinyInt	unsigned char; a one-byte, unsigned integer.
adSmallInt	short; a two-byte, signed integer.
adUnsignedSmallInt	unsigned short; a two-byte, unsigned integer.
adInteger	long; a four-byte, signed integer.

Type	Description
adUnsignedInt	unsigned `long`; a four-byte, unsigned integer.
adBigInt	`_int64`; an eight-byte, signed integer.
adUnsignedBigInt	`_int64`; an eight-byte, unsigned integer.
adSingle	`float`; a single-precision floating point.
adDouble	`double`; a double-precision floating point.
adCurrency	`LARGE_INTEGER`; a currency value scaled by 10,000.
adDate	`DATE`; a double-precision value. The whole part indicates the number of days from the first day of the year 1900, and the fractional part is the part of the day.
adDBDate	`DBDATE`; year, month, and day.
adDBTime	`DBTIME`; hour, minute, and second.
adDBTimeStamp	`DBTIMESTAMP`; year, month, day, hour, minute, second, and fraction of a second.
adError	`SCODE`; a 32-bit error code.
adBoolean	`VARIANT_BOOL`; a Boolean value in which `0` is `FALSE` and `-1` is `TRUE`.
adDecimal	`DECIMAL`; a value with fixed precision and scale.
adBinary	`BYTE[]`; a binary array of byte values.

TABLE 19.13 ADO DATATYPE MODIFIERS

Flag	Description
adArray	`SAFEARRAY *`; an array
adByRef	`void *`; a pointer
adVector	`DBVECTOR`; a pointer to an array with a size

TABLE 19.14 PARAMETER DIRECTION VALUES

Value	Description
adParamUnknown	Unknown direction.
adParamInput	Input parameter (default).
adParamOutput	Output parameter.
adParamInputOutput	Input and output parameter.
adParamReturnValue	Return value.

19

ADVANCED DATABASE SUPPORT

Prepared

Use the `Prepared` property to specify whether the datasource provider should precompile the command. If the datasource supports preparing commands, this can improve the performance of commonly executed queries. The methods to get and set this property are declared as follows:

```
HRESULT get_Prepared(VARIANT_BOOL *pfPrepared);
HRESULT put_Prepared(VARIANT_BOOL fPrepared);
```

ActiveConnection

Use the `ActiveConnection` property to get or set the connection to which this `ADOCommand` object belongs. The methods to manipulate this property are declared as follows:

```
HRESULT get_ActiveConnection(_ADOConnection **ppvObject);
HRESULT putref_ActiveConnection(_ADOConnection *pCon);
HRESULT put_ActiveConnection(VARIANT vConn);
```

Properties

The `Properties` collection is a set of datasource provider–dependent keys and values that modify the way the datasource handles this `ADOCommand` object. Use the following method to gain access to this collection:

```
HRESULT get_Properties(ADOProperties **ppvObject);
```

ADOField

The `ADOField` class represents an output datatype from the data provider. Because `ADOField` is a member of the `ADORecordset`'s `Fields` collection, you can retrieve the field's metadata and associated value from objects of this class.

Name, Type, DefinedSize, and ActualSize

The `Name`, `Type`, `DefinedSize`, and `ActualSize` properties contain information about the structure of the data itself. These properties can be get and set using the following methods:

```
HRESULT get_Name(BSTR *pbstr);
HRESULT get_Type(DataTypeEnum *pDataType);
HRESULT get_DefinedSize(long *pl);
HRESULT get_ActualSize(long *pl);
```

The values for the `Type` property are shown in Table 19.12. Flags that can modify the `Type` property (via a logical OR operation) are listed in Table 19.13.

Value and Attributes

Use the Value and Attributes properties to specify the data associated with the specific fields whose value is being set. The methods for manipulating the Value and Attributes properties are shown here:

```
HRESULT get_Value(VARIANT *pval);
HRESULT put_Value(VARIANT val);
HRESULT get_Attributes(long *plAttributes);
HRESULT put_Attributes(long lAttributes);
```

Properties

The Properties collection is a set of datasource provider–dependent keys and values that modify the way the datasource handles this ADOField object. Use the following method to gain access to this collection:

```
HRESULT get_Properties(ADOProperties **ppvObject);
```

ADOProperty

The ADOProperty class encapsulates a single data provider–dependent value that is passed to the data provider via many of the ADO objects. The whole list of parameters that are to be sent to and retrieved from the datasource is in the Fields collection of the ADOConnection, ADOCommand, ADORecordset, and ADOField classes. The ADOProperty class contains the metadata for the property (name and type), as well as its value.

Name and Type

The Name and Type properties contain information about the property itself. These properties can be manipulated using the following methods:

```
HRESULT get_Name(BSTR *pbstr);
HRESULT get_Type(DataTypeEnum *ptype);
```

The values for the Type property are shown in Table 19.12. Flags that can modify the Type property (via a logical OR operation) are listed in Table 19.13.

Value and Attributes

Use the Value and Attributes properties to specify the data associated with the specific properties whose value is being set. The datasource provider defines the values and attributes associated with each property. The methods for manipulating the Value and Attributes properties are shown here:

```
HRESULT get_Value(VARIANT *pval);
HRESULT put_Value(VARIANT val);
HRESULT get_Attributes(long *plAttributes);
HRESULT put_Attributes(long lAttributes);
```

ADOParameter

The `ADOParameter` class encapsulates a single parameter that is to be passed to a stored procedure or query via an `ADOCommand` object. The whole list of parameters that are to be sent to and retrieved from the datasource is in the `ADOCommand` class's `Parameters` collection. The `ADOParameter` class contains the metadata for the parameter (name, type, and size), as well as its value.

Name, Type, and Size

The `Name`, `Type`, and `Size` properties contain information about the parameter itself. These properties can be manipulated using the following methods:

```
HRESULT get_Name(BSTR *pbstr);
HRESULT put_Name(BSTR bstr);
HRESULT get_Type(DataTypeEnum *psDataType);
HRESULT put_Type(DataTypeEnum sDataType);
HRESULT put_Size(long l);
HRESULT get_Size(long *pl);
```

The values for the `Type` property are shown in Table 19.12. Flags that can modify the `Type` property (via a logical OR operation) are listed in Table 19.13.

Value

The `Value` property contains the parameter's value in the form specified by its `Type` property. This property can be accessed using the following methods:

```
HRESULT get_Value(VARIANT *pvar);
HRESULT put_Value(VARIANT val);
```

ADOError

The `ADOError` class contains detailed information about the ADO error that has occurred. You can access `ADOError` objects via the `Errors` collection in the `ADOConnection` object.

Description, Number, NativeError, and Source

The `Description`, `Number`, `NativeError`, and `Source` properties provide the detailed error information that your application can use to perform appropriate error handling—including the display of an error to the user. The methods to interact with these properties are shown here:

```
HRESULT get_Number(long *pl);
HRESULT get_Description(BSTR *pbstr);
HRESULT get_NativeError(long *pl);
HRESULT get_Source(BSTR *pbstr);
```

> **TIP**
>
> Although you can use the `NativeError` property to get an error code from the data provider, make sure that your connection is to the data provider that you expect before handling this error code.

Summary

This chapter discusses the next step in the evolution of Microsoft data access technologies. This step unites component-based software development and datasource-independent programming interfaces. The set of Microsoft technologies that achieves these goals is called Universal Data Access (UDA).

One of the key technologies within this set is called OLE DB, which defines standard COM components for the development of data providers and data consumers. A higher-level, language-independent interface called ActiveX Data Objects (ADO) is implemented using the OLE DB consumer interfaces.

MFC Utility Classes

PART

V

Strings and Collections

by K. David White

IN THIS CHAPTER

CHAPTER 20

Character manipulation and managing data in lists and sets have been among the staples of software development since the beginning of "computerdom." In fact, most of you have probably grown weary of the "Hello World" program in all its varied forms. It seems as if you can't pick up a beginner's programming book, in any language, without finding it.

I don't have the heart to do that to you, and because this is not a beginner's book, you've probably been through it. You might have even used CString in some fashion, or one of the templated list classes that MFC provides. In this chapter, you will take a closer look at what MFC gives you as far as managing strings, lists, sets, and maps.

Without going into much detail, I will also introduce you to the Standard Template Library (STL) functions that you might end up using in place of the MFC classes. Remember, you may be asked to develop COM objects without using the MFC DLLs. Understanding what MFC gives you, and then taking a look at other alternatives, only helps to expand your capabilities.

Strings and String Classes

In Fortran, you were introduced to the concept of a string in all its formatted glory. If you haven't programmed in Fortran, you haven't lived! In C, you were introduced to character strings. These were treated differently, even though they did the same thing. In fact, a big part of your learning experience with C was learning to deal with character pointers. I don't have a fond memory of those days, only the day that it finally sunk in and the world opened up! (Well, almost!)

C++, with the object-oriented approach, still makes use of character strings, but people started encapsulating string functions into string classes that could be used easily. Well, MFC does the same thing. The CString class encapsulates character string functionality to make string manipulation a breeze.

Inside the CString Class

The CString class is defined in the MFC header file AFX.H. If you look inside this file for the CString declaration, you will notice that it goes on for quite a few pages. The main element, though, is the buffer that CString encapsulates, as you see in Listing 20.1.

LISTING 20.1 THE CString PROTECTED DATA MEMBER (AFX.H)

```
protected:
    LPTSTR m_pchData;    // pointer to ref counted string data
```

Listing 20.1 shows the only data member of CString, m_pchData. It makes sense! CString encapsulates a single string, or character buffer. The LPTSTR is defined as a 32-bit pointer to a character string. Now that you know CString contains a string pointer, you probably have questions about memory allocation and reallocation and where that buffer is actually kept. Are you ready to look at some MFC code to solve this mystery?

Notice the comment in Listing 20.1, // pointer to ref counted string data. This is a pointer to a reference-counted string. What exactly does it mean to have reference counting on a string? To solve the problem of memory leaks, and having copies of strings floating around that are no longer used, MFC implements a form of reference counting to verify that no unnecessary copies of the buffer are hanging around. If you've read my COM chapter (Chapter 10), you understand the concept of reference counting. Notice in Listing 20.2, which is an expanded listing of the CString declaration, that you don't have anything to store the reference count.

LISTING 20.2   THE EXPANDED CString DECLARATION (AFX.H)

```
// Implementation
public:
    ~CString();
    int GetAllocLength() const;
    protected:
    LPTSTR m_pchData;    // pointer to ref counted string data
        // implementation helpers
    CStringData* GetData() const;
    void Init();
    void AllocCopy(CString& dest, int nCopyLen,
    ➥int nCopyIndex, int nExtraLen) const;
        void AllocBuffer(int nLen);
        void AssignCopy(int nSrcLen, LPCTSTR lpszSrcData);
        void ConcatCopy(int nSrc1Len, LPCTSTR lpszSrc1Data,
        ➥int nSrc2Len, LPCTSTR lpszSrc2Data);
        void ConcatInPlace(int nSrcLen, LPCTSTR lpszSrcData);
        void CopyBeforeWrite();
        void AllocBeforeWrite(int nLen);
        void Release();
        static void PASCAL Release(CStringData* pData);
        static int PASCAL SafeStrlen(LPCTSTR lpsz);
        static void FASTCALL FreeData(CStringData* pData);
```

You will notice that many functions are defined that appear to do the reference counting for the CString buffer, but it still doesn't have a reference count holder. Notice the line CStringData* GetData() const;. This declaration is a clue! Back to AFX.H. Listing 20.3 shows you that the CStringData structure contains the reference count and string information important to the other CString functions. You will also notice that MFC used to store the data buffer here as well.

LISTING 20.3   THE `CStringData` STRUCTURE (AFX.H)

```
struct CStringData
{
    long nRefs;              // reference count
    int nDataLength;         // length of data (including terminator)
        int nAllocLength;        // length of allocation
        // TCHAR data[nAllocLength]

        TCHAR* data()            // TCHAR* to managed data
            { return (TCHAR*)(this+1); }
    };
```

String Allocation

The `CString` class uses the `AllocBuffer` member helper function to allocate and manage the memory during the construction phase. Listing 20.4 is the source code for the buffer allocation logic. Notice the comment starting at the second line, `// always allocate one extra character for '\0' termination`. This allocation will automatically add the null terminator, so remember to send the actual length of the string that you need to create. If the length passed is zero, which is the case during a declaration without assignment, this routine will call the `Init()` routine to reserve some space. Okay, what are the following lines doing?

```
pData = (CStringData*)
    new BYTE[sizeof(CStringData) + (nLen+1)*sizeof(TCHAR)];
pData->nAllocLength = nLen;
```

It looks as if the allocation adds the length of the desired string to the length of a `CStringData` helper. At first glance, this might be confusing, but remember that `CStringData` maintains the reference count for the string buffer.

LISTING 20.4   THE `CStringData` STRUCTURE (AFX.H)

```
void CString::AllocBuffer(int nLen)
// always allocate one extra character for '\0' termination
// assumes [optimistically] that data length will equal
// allocation length
{
    ASSERT(nLen >= 0);
    ASSERT(nLen <= INT_MAX-1);   // max size (enough room
                                 // for 1 extra)

    if (nLen == 0)
        Init();
    else
    {
```

```
        CStringData* pData;
#ifndef _DEBUG
        if (nLen <= 64)
        {
            pData = (CStringData*)_afxAlloc64.Alloc();
            pData->nAllocLength = 64;
        }
        else if (nLen <= 128)
        {
            pData = (CStringData*)_afxAlloc128.Alloc();
            pData->nAllocLength = 128;
        }
        else if (nLen <= 256)
        {
            pData = (CStringData*)_afxAlloc256.Alloc();
            pData->nAllocLength = 256;
        }
        else if (nLen <= 512)
        {
            pData = (CStringData*)_afxAlloc512.Alloc();
            pData->nAllocLength = 512;
        }
        else
#endif
        {
            pData = (CStringData*)
                new BYTE[sizeof(CStringData) + (nLen+1)*sizeof(TCHAR)];
            pData->nAllocLength = nLen;
        }
        pData->nRefs = 1;
        pData->data()[nLen] = '\0';
        pData->nDataLength = nLen;
        m_pchData = pData->data();
    }
}
```

I think that reference counting for strings deserves a closer look because it is evident that each buffer carries with it a reference count. Suppose that the MFC CString class didn't maintain a pointer to a buffer, but contained the buffer itself. Each time a CString was created from another CString, it would get a copy of that buffer. With the MFC implementation, the new CString will be created to point at the same data buffer and will maintain its pointer to that buffer. Meanwhile, back in CStringData, the reference count gets bumped, indicating that another allocation of the buffer is active. That way, if the original CString gets "blown away" (a common occurrence), the buffer for the copied CString still has the buffer. When there are no more CStrings pointing to the same buffer, its reference count becomes 0, and it can go away peacefully—no more memory leaks!

I implore you to investigate the CString code to learn more about how it really works. You might someday thank me! Friends of mine, doing things not meant to be done with MFC, have had to roll their own string class and have paid some dues with reference counting and memory allocation.

> **Tip**
>
> Assigning a CString to be a single character, although supported, is not really a wise choice. The CString allocation and reference counting for a single character is decidedly an unnecessary thing to do.

Some CString Functions

Before you walk away from this discussion about what makes up the CString, I think you should come with me on a tour of some of the more interesting functions. By finding out how CString encapsulates its functionality, you might be better able to develop without it if the need ever arises.

Concatenation

It is common practice to concatenate one string with another. This is primarily done with the concatenate operator (+=), which is defined in AFX.INL. Listing 20.5 shows the concatenate operator.

LISTING 20.5   THE CString CONCATENATE OPERATOR (AFX.INL)

```
#ifdef _UNICODE
_AFX_INLINE const CString& CString::operator+=(char ch)
    { *this += (TCHAR)ch; return *this; }
_AFX_INLINE const CString& CString::operator=(char ch)
    { *this = (TCHAR)ch; return *this; }
_AFX_INLINE CString AFXAPI operator+(const CString& string, char ch)
    { return string + (TCHAR)ch; }
_AFX_INLINE CString AFXAPI operator+(char ch, const CString& string)
    { return (TCHAR)ch + string; }
 #endif
```

Notice in each of these overloaded operators the use of TCHAR. TCHAR is defined as an 8-bit ANSI character unless it is defined as a Unicode character. If it is a Unicode character, it is defined as a 16-bit Unicode character. Notice that there are many different forms of concatenation. You can add single characters or another CString.

Searching a `CString`

There are two primary functions when it comes to searching a `CString` for characters or smaller substrings. The `Find` function will find the search string in a forward direction in the buffer. The `ReverseFind` function will do the exact opposite. Listing 20.6 contains the code for the `Find` functions from STRCORE.CPP. Listing 20.7 contains the `ReverseFind` implementation, which resides in STREX.CPP. Notice from the comment in the second line of the STRCORE.CPP listing, `// Commonly used routines (rarely used routines in STREX.CPP)`, that the rarely used routines are implemented in STREX.CPP.

LISTING 20.6 THE `CString` FIND FUNCTIONS (STRCORE.CPP)

```
//////////////////////////////////////////////////////////////////////
// Commonly used routines (rarely used routines in STREX.CPP)

int CString::Find(TCHAR ch) const
{
    return Find(ch, 0);
}

int CString::Find(TCHAR ch, int nStart) const
{
    int nLength = GetData()->nDataLength;
    if (nStart >= nLength)
        return -1;

    // find first single character
    LPTSTR lpsz = _tcschr(m_pchData + nStart, (_TUCHAR)ch);

    // return -1 if not found and index otherwise
    return (lpsz == NULL) ? -1 : (int)(lpsz - m_pchData);
}

int CString::FindOneOf(LPCTSTR lpszCharSet) const
{
    ASSERT(AfxIsValidString(lpszCharSet));
    LPTSTR lpsz = _tcspbrk(m_pchData, lpszCharSet);
    return (lpsz == NULL) ? -1 : (int)(lpsz - m_pchData);
}
```

LISTING 20.7   THE CString ReverseFind FUNCTION (STREX.CPP)

```
/////////////////////////////////////////////////////////////////////
// Finding

int CString::ReverseFind(TCHAR ch) const
{
    // find last single character
    LPTSTR lpsz = _tcsrchr(m_pchData, (_TUCHAR) ch);

    // return -1 if not found, distance from beginning otherwise
    return (lpsz == NULL) ? -1 : (int)(lpsz - m_pchData);
}
```

In both listings, you should notice the use of _tcschr (or a related function, such as _tcspbrk). This is one of many string functions that is similar to the C runtime library functions for manipulating character strings. Okay, you've come full circle. I started off by explaining that MFC provides this really neat class that handles the character string stuff for you. Well, MFC encapsulates the exact functionality that you were using in C.

Comparing CStrings

The CString class provides two methods of comparing strings. These are the Compare() member function and the == operator. In fact, if you look at the MFC code, these functions are essentially identical. These functions also use the _t string manipulation functions for comparing strings.

Practical CString Usage

Your brain is probably buzzing from the MFC code that I've given you, but let's put some of this newfound knowledge to work. Listing 20.8 is from the UNL_MultiEd application (the SplitPartsString utility function found in cx_eventrecorder.cpp). This application is explained in better detail at the end of this chapter.

LISTING 20.8   THE UNL_MultiEd SplitPartsString UTILITY

```
//**********************************************************************
// This utility function takes a delimited string and splits
// parsed strings based on the delimiter.  Useful for parsing
// COMMA delimited strings...
//
// NOTE:    This is strictly the MFC version.
//
void
SplitPartsString( const CString&    cr_sLine,
                  CStringList&      r_lParts,
```

```
                const CString&    cr_sDelimiter)
{
    CString  sPart            = "";
    CString  sTemp;
    int      iLineLength = 0;
    int      iCurrentPos = 0;
    int      iTmpPos     = 0;
    r_lParts.RemoveAll();
    sTemp =  cr_sLine;
    iLineLength = sTemp.GetLength();
    /*******************************
    **      Main parsing loop..      **
    *******************************/
    while (0 != iLineLength)
    {
        /***************************************************
        **  You should have a delimiter in this string    **
        **  ...if not, then jump to else loop comment      **
        ***************************************************/
        if (-1 != (iTmpPos = sTemp.Find(cr_sDelimiter)))
        {
            iCurrentPos = iTmpPos;

            sPart = sTemp.Left(iCurrentPos);

            if (CString("\t") ==
            ➥sTemp.Right(iLineLength - iCurrentPos))
            {
                sTemp += " ";iLineLength++;
            }
            sTemp = sTemp.Right(iLineLength - iCurrentPos - 1);

            //  You have a clean partial string.. add it to
            //  the StringList to pass back.
            r_lParts.AddTail(sPart);
        }
        else
        {
            //
            // Okay... You are out of delimiters in the main
            // string.  Make the rest of the string the
            // last part
            //
            sPart = sTemp; // Set remaining part.

            sTemp = sEMPTY_STRING;

            if (sEMPTY_STRING != sPart)
            {
                // Strip the \255 character that
```

continues

LISTING 20.8 CONTINUED

```
                        // the MFC_CSTR_KLUDGE macro inserted
                        // (MFC StdioFile::ReadString buffer bug...)
                        if (-1 != (iTmpPos = sPart.Find('\255')))
                            sPart = sPart.Left(iTmpPos-1);
                        r_lParts.AddTail(sPart);
                    }
                }
            }
        }
```

This routine will take a string read in from a file and will split it into several strings. The main string contains a delimiter that will be used to separate the string. Later in this chapter, when I introduce you to collection classes, I'll explain the `CStringList` collection class. I've included the entire routine here because it will be referenced at that point.

I want to point out the general `CString` functions that every developer should become infinitely familiar with. First of all, look at the following lines:

```
CString  sPart          = "";
CString  sTemp;
```

Remember the allocation discussion. In the first of these lines, you did the allocation via an equate. It could be done as follows:

```
CString sPart("");
```

Either way is acceptable and is simply a matter of preference, but the allocation discussion still holds. Remember what I said about reserving an unknown amount that would later be allocated and reference counted when an assignment was performed? The string will get allocated later when the assignment is done.

The `GetLength()` function member will return the number of characters minus the null terminator character. The `Find()` function member is used to locate the delimiter being used to separate the substrings.

This routine also contains the substring functions, which will return substrings of the main string. When I first started using these functions, I had countless hours of frustration. The `Left()` function will return a subset of the string from the length passed into as an argument. The line `sPart = sTemp.Left(iCurrentPos);` will receive the subset of the string up to the position of the first delimiter—your first part! The line

```
sTemp = sTemp.Right(iLineLength - iCurrentPos - 1);
```

will return the remainder of the string for further parsing.

Although they don't exist in this routine, another popular `CString` feature set that is of interest is the `Trim()` functions. The `TrimRight()` function will remove whitespace characters from the end of the string. If a character is entered as the parameter, `TrimRight()` will remove everything to the right of that character, including that character. Be careful here! If another `CString` is entered as the parameter, it will remove everything to the right of that substring, including the substring. `TrimLeft()` will trim off leading whitespace characters from the string. The same parameter functionality applies in reverse here.

> **NOTE**
>
> A whitespace character can be defined as a space, newline, or tab character.

Although I haven't provided every possible example of what you can do via the `CString` class, I'm sure you'll agree that it's pretty flexible. Spend some time writing some code to use all the functions of the `CString` class, and you will soon appreciate its features.

`CString` Summary

You might be thinking that a tour of the MFC seems to simply cloud the mind with useless information. I disagree. I feel that if you understand how something works, implementing it becomes easier. I hope that you will search the MFC code archives for how the `CString` class is put together and spend some time understanding how it does its allocation. Understanding when and how to implement `CString` versus some other mechanism is an essential coding practice.

The example, although quite simple, is a very good representation of much of what goes on when implementing `CString` code. Other examples are available through the samples in this book and on many Web sites that contain information about MFC coding.

Now, on to collections.

Collections

What are collections? A *collection* can be defined as a set of like or unique items that are collectively rendered. Linked lists come to mind when discussing collections, and you will soon find out that MFC provides a very usable set of collection classes to deal with data collection problems. Before discussing the collections themselves, I should probably point out something that you are currently thinking about. A collection is defined by

20

STRINGS AND
COLLECTIONS

what it is storing. MFC gives you a set of data structures that store the application's data. For each of these shapes or structures, MFC provides non-templated classes to hold the data. BYTE, int, and WORD are just a few. MFC also provides templated versions of each of these structures that you can use to create collections.

Table 20.1 defines the list of MFC-provided template classes that allow you to work with application data.

TABLE 20.1   COLLECTION CLASSES

Name	Structure
CObList	List
CPtrList	List
CStringList	List
CByteArray	Array
CDWordArray	Array
CObArray	Array
CStringArray	Array
CWordArray	Array
CUIntArray	Array
CMapPtrToPtr	Map
CMapStringToPtr	Map
CMapWordToPtr	Map
CMapStringToString	Map
CmapStringToOb	Map
CMapWordToOb	Map

Inside Collection Classes

Time to look inside at what MFC is really doing, with a look at allocation issues. The non-templated arrays and list are defined in AFXCOLL.H. There is behavior that is similar between the different collection classes, but there are also unique implementation details that deserve some level of attention.

The Array Type Collections

Taking a look at Listing 20.9 provides some insight as to the functionality that is encapsulated in these classes. Although this is only one of the many types available, it will paint a picture for the remainder of the classes.

LISTING 20.9   THE CByteArray DEFINITION (AFXCOLL.H)

```
class CByteArray : public CObject
{

    DECLARE_SERIAL(CByteArray)
public:

// Construction
    CByteArray();

// Attributes
    int GetSize() const;
    int GetUpperBound() const;
    void SetSize(int nNewSize, int nGrowBy = -1);

// Operations
     // Clean up
    void FreeExtra();
    void RemoveAll();

    // Accessing elements
    BYTE GetAt(int nIndex) const;
    void SetAt(int nIndex, BYTE newElement);

    BYTE& ElementAt(int nIndex);

    // Direct Access to the element data (may return NULL)
    const BYTE* GetData() const;
    BYTE* GetData();

    // Potentially growing the array
    void SetAtGrow(int nIndex, BYTE newElement);

    int Add(BYTE newElement);

    int Append(const CByteArray& src);
    void Copy(const CByteArray& src);

    // overloaded operator helpers
    BYTE operator[](int nIndex) const;
    BYTE& operator[](int nIndex);

    // Operations that move elements around
    void InsertAt(int nIndex, BYTE newElement, int nCount = 1);

    void RemoveAt(int nIndex, int nCount = 1);
    void InsertAt(int nStartIndex, CByteArray* pNewArray);

// Implementation
```

continues

LISTING 20.9   CONTINUED

```
protected:
    BYTE* m_pData;    // the actual array of data
    int m_nSize;      // # of elements (upperBound - 1)
    int m_nMaxSize;   // max allocated
    int m_nGrowBy;    // grow amount


public:
    ~CByteArray();

    void Serialize(CArchive&);
#ifdef _DEBUG
    void Dump(CDumpContext&) const;
    void AssertValid() const;
#endif

protected:
    // local typedefs for class templates
    typedef BYTE BASE_TYPE;
    typedef BYTE BASE_ARG_TYPE;
};
```

At first glance, you notice functions in this class that you would expect for any array. Functions such as RemoveAll(), GetAt(), and SetAt() are self-explanatory. These functions manipulate the collection, in this case an array of BYTES. The data members are defined in the following lines:

```
BYTE* m_pData;    // the actual array of data
int m_nSize;      // # of elements (upperBound - 1)
int m_nMaxSize;   // max allocated
int m_nGrowBy;    // grow amount
```

Notice the last two lines. Do you think these play a part in memory allocation for the array? Absolutely!

There are two data members that refer to the size. The m_nSize data member refers to the actual size, and the m_nMaxSize is the reserved allocated space for the array. The m_nGrowBy data member indicates the number of elements to allocate in each allocation chunk. The array grows by chunks of elements, not necessarily by one element—unless, of course, the chunk is defined to be one element.

Listing 20.10 is a listing for the SetSize() function for the CByteArray. This is found in ARRAY_B.CPP. Notice in the line if (nNewSize == 0) that the first thing done is to see whether the array is to be deallocated. At this point, the users entered a new size of 0 instead of calling the destructor. If you are on your toes, you should catch this. The CByteArray class encapsulates the array, and by deallocating the array inside the class, it can be reallocated later without having to reconstruct the CByteArray class.

LISTING 20.10 THE CbyteArray::SetSize FUNCTION (ARRAY_B.CPP)

```cpp
void CByteArray::SetSize(int nNewSize, int nGrowBy)
{
    ASSERT_VALID(this);
    ASSERT(nNewSize >= 0);
        if (nGrowBy != -1)
        m_nGrowBy = nGrowBy;   // set new size
        if (nNewSize == 0)
    {
        // shrink to nothing
        delete[] (BYTE*)m_pData;
        m_pData = NULL;
        m_nSize = m_nMaxSize = 0;
    }
    else if (m_pData == NULL)
    {
        // create one with exact size
#ifdef SIZE_T_MAX
        ASSERT(nNewSize <= SIZE_T_MAX/sizeof(BYTE)); // no overflow
#endif
        m_pData = (BYTE*) new BYTE[nNewSize * sizeof(BYTE)];

        memset(m_pData, 0, nNewSize * sizeof(BYTE));   // zero fill

        m_nSize = m_nMaxSize = nNewSize;
    }
    else if (nNewSize <= m_nMaxSize)
    {
        // it fits
        if (nNewSize > m_nSize)
        {
            // initialize the new elements

            memset(&m_pData[m_nSize], 0,
            ➥(nNewSize-m_nSize) * sizeof(BYTE));

        }

        m_nSize = nNewSize;
    }
    else
    {
        // otherwise, grow array
        int nGrowBy = m_nGrowBy;
        if (nGrowBy == 0)
        {
            // heuristically determine growth when nGrowBy == 0
            //   (this avoids heap fragmentation in many cases)
            nGrowBy = min(1024, max(4, m_nSize / 8));
        }
```

continues

LISTING 20.10   CONTINUED

```
        int nNewMax;
        if (nNewSize < m_nMaxSize + nGrowBy)
            nNewMax = m_nMaxSize + nGrowBy;  // granularity
        else
            nNewMax = nNewSize;  // no slush

        ASSERT(nNewMax >= m_nMaxSize);  // no wrap around
#ifdef SIZE_T_MAX
        ASSERT(nNewMax <= SIZE_T_MAX/sizeof(BYTE)); // no overflow
#endif
        BYTE* pNewData = (BYTE*) new BYTE[nNewMax * sizeof(BYTE)];

        // copy new data from old
        memcpy(pNewData, m_pData, m_nSize * sizeof(BYTE));

        // construct remaining elements
        ASSERT(nNewSize > m_nSize);

        memset(&pNewData[m_nSize], 0,
    ➥(nNewSize-m_nSize) * sizeof(BYTE));


        // get rid of old stuff (note: no destructors called)
        delete[] (BYTE*)m_pData;
        m_pData = pNewData;
        m_nSize = nNewSize;
        m_nMaxSize = nNewMax;
    }
}
```

The line `else if (m_pData == NULL)` tests for the condition where the array data is empty, and the `SetSize` function has been called to allocate a chunk of memory. Notice the line `memset(m_pData, 0, nNewSize * sizeof(BYTE)); // zero fill`. The allocation is done via the `memset` function. After looking at this code, you should realize just how simple and elegant some MFC classes actually are.

The List Type Collections

An array defines a bounded collection of like items. A list is similar to a single bounded array. MFC encapsulates this functionality in much the same way. The primary difference here is that a list contains pointers to indicate position in the list, as opposed to indexes into an array. With MFC, you get both Head pointers and Tail pointers.

The `POSITION` pointer is an abstract datatype used to control iteration of a list. There are functions that will return the `POSITION` of the Head and Tail pointer that you can use to insert, remove, and copy list elements.

Because the memory allocation follows similar paths to that of the arrays, I won't bog you down with MFC source code. The following are list functions that are useful to controlling your list data:

- `GetHead()`—Returns the Head pointer `POSITION`.
- `GetTail()`—Returns the Tail pointer `POSITION`.
- `AddHead()`—Adds the data element to the front of the list.
- `AddTail()`—Adds the data element to the back of the list.
- `GetCount()`—Returns the number of elements in the list.
- `GetNext()`—Returns the `POSITION` of the next element in the list.
- `IsEmpty()`—Returns `TRUE` if the list is empty.
- `SetAt()`—Modifies element at `POSITION`.
- `GetAt()`—Returns the element at `POSITION`.
- `RemoveAll()`—Removes all elements from the list.
- `RemoveHead()`—Removes the element located at the Head pointer.
- `RemoveTail()`—Removes the element at the Tail pointer.
- `InsertAfter()`—Inserts an element after the element pointed to by the `POSITION` iterator.
- `InsertBefore()`—Inserts an element before the element pointed to by the `POSI-TION` iterator.

Map Type Collections

You can think of a map as a hash table, with key/element pairing. That key can take many forms, and its simplest form would represent an array bound. I said this to set the stage for a discussion of maps and hashing the map. In an array, the elements are stored in sequential fashion, with sequential indexes. This is not always true for a `Map`. The associated key for the mapped element might not be numerical, or there could be gaps if it is numerical.

Hashing refers to the practice of generating an index from a key. An algorithm, or simple function, referred to as a hashing function, is applied to the key to produce a unique lookup index to the element desired. When adding elements to a map, you generate the index by passing in the key for the element. When you need to retrieve the element, you pass the key into the same hash function and then use the returned index to find the data.

> **TIP**
>
> If the data collection is to be quite large, you should consider using the Map classes. Iterating a large list or array can be costly.

MFC associates items stored in the CMap classes using a simple yet effective hash key generation algorithm. Listing 20.11 shows you the CMapStringToString hashing implementation. (Note that it is inline to further increase its efficiency.) This is representative of all map hashing algorithms. You also can see how the hash table is initialized, which is also quite efficient.

LISTING 20.11   THE CMapStringToString ASSOCIATIVE HASHING FUNCTION AND HASH TABLE INITIALIZATION (MAP_SS.CPP)

```cpp
inline UINT CMapStringToString::HashKey(LPCTSTR key) const
{
    UINT nHash = 0;
    while (*key)
        nHash = (nHash<<5) + nHash + *key++;
    return nHash;
}
    void CMapStringToString::InitHashTable(
    UINT nHashSize, BOOL bAllocNow)
//
// Used to force allocation of a hash table or to override the default
//   hash table size of (which is fairly small)
{
    ASSERT_VALID(this);
    ASSERT(m_nCount == 0);
    ASSERT(nHashSize > 0);
        if (m_pHashTable != NULL)
    {
        // free hash table
        delete[] m_pHashTable;
        m_pHashTable = NULL;
    }
        if (bAllocNow)
    {
        m_pHashTable = new CAssoc* [nHashSize];
        memset(m_pHashTable, 0, sizeof(CAssoc*) * nHashSize);
    }
    m_nHashTableSize = nHashSize;
}
```

As I mentioned previously, the hashing function is indeed an inline function (see the first seven lines of Listing 20.11), which is decidedly quicker than accessing typical CMap class methods. In this case, the string is iterated to determine the hashing value, based on content. Regarding initialization—note that the InitHashTable routine allocates the memory for the hash table to store its indexes. If one already exists, it is deleted. It then uses memset to allocate the memory.

> **TIP**
>
> Defining your own hash table size can also greatly increase performance.

Templated Collections

MFC provides a way for you to define your own collections. Some data is not always easily defined by the generic set. You can have user-defined classes that need to be kept in a list or array. These are defined in the AFXTEMPL.H file. For the sake of getting to practical application, I won't list this for you.

The UNL_MultiEd Application

The UNL_MultiEd application, which is introduced in Chapter 7, "The Document/View Architecture," is a good example of collections and strings. This section briefly details this application and provides listings of most items that pertain to strings and collections.

Overview

The application is an event management tool that will allow the user to define an event with multiple contests. The goal is to provide a list of participants and a list of events and to determine the overall winner. The user has the ability to enter events and participants into an ASCII-delimited file that can be loaded into the application. The data is kept globally and is pointed to by the application object.

The CXEventRecorder object contains a list of participants, a list of events, and an array that keeps a sorted list based on total points. Each participant has a running total of his or her points. Participants can be added to an event and can be placed in that event based on the outcome of that event.

This application would be a good starting point for someone who has to maintain the records for a decathlon, or any other event that has multiple contests (see Listing 20.12).

20

STRINGS AND COLLECTIONS

LISTING 20.12 THE CXEvent, CXParticipant, AND CXEventRecorder DEFINITIONS

```
// xeventrecorder.h

#ifndef cxeventrecorder_h
#define cxeventrecorder_h

#include "stdafx.h"
#include <stdio.h>
#include <afxtempl.h>



//
// CXParticipant:
//
// This class stores information about the participants in the/
// Games. The constructors will insert the information.
// This class is added in the map for the EventRecorder class.
//

class CXParticipant
{
    public:

        CXParticipant();
        CXParticipant(CString sLastName);
        CXParticipant(CString sLastName, CString sFirstName);
        CXParticipant(CString sLastName, CString sFirstName,
        ➥CString sTeam);

        virtual ~CXParticipant();

        void SetFirstName(CString sFirstName);
        void SetLastName(CString sLastName);
        void SetTeam(CString sTeam);

        CString *GetFirstName();
        CString *GetLastName();
        CString *GetTeam();

        void AddPoints(int nPoints);
        void BumpEvent();

        int GetRunningTotal();
        int GetEventsEntered();

    private:

        CString     m_sLastName;
        CString     m_sFirstName;
        CString     m_sTeam;
```

```
            int         m_nEventsEntered;
            int         m_nRunningPoints;
};


//
// CXEvent:
//
// This class stores information about the event. However, it
// only stores whether participants competed.
//

class CXEvent
{
    public:

        CXEvent();
        virtual ~CXEvent();

    CXEvent&    operator = (const CXEvent& pOther);
    int         operator == (CXEvent *pOther);

        void SetEventName (CString sName);
        CString *GetEventName ();

        void SetEventRan (BOOL bEventRan);
        BOOL GetEventRan ();

        void AddParticipantToEvent(CXParticipant * eventParticipant);
        void RemoveParticipant(CXParticipant * eventParticipant);

        /*********************************************
        **   This method will place the participant  **
        **   in the event (First, Second, etc..)     **
        *********************************************/
        void PlaceParticipantInEvent (int nPos,
        ➥CXParticipant * ourParticipant);

    private:

        CString     m_sName;
        BOOL        m_bEventRan;

        CList <CXParticipant *, CXParticipant *> *m_slEventParticipants;
        CMap <int, int, CXParticipant *, CXParticipant *>
        ➥*m_mEventPlaces;
};


//
// CXEventRecorder Class.
//
```

continues

LISTING 20.12 CONTINUED

```
**       This class is a global store for the games...      **
// Maps are kept of events and participants and event totals
// It also contains information regarding the reporting
// of the events.
class CXEventRecorder
{
    public:

    CXEventRecorder();
        virtual ~CXEventRecorder();

        /**********************************************
        **   This will take an ASCII delimited file  **
        **   containing the events to take place     **
        **   and load them into the Event Map..      **
        **********************************************/
        void LoadEvents(CString sFileName);

        /**********************************************
        **   This is called from LoadEvents and will **
        **   create the participants                 **
        **********************************************/
        void LoadParticipants ( CString sLastName,
                                CString sFirstName,
                                CString sTeam);


        /**********************************************
        **   This method will set the Event number   **
        **   that is currently being recorded.       **
        **********************************************/
        void SelectEvent(int EventNum);

        CList <CXEvent *, CXEvent *> *GetEvents ();
        CList <CXParticipant *, CXParticipant *> *GetParticipants ();

        void AddParticipant (CXParticipant * ourParticipant);
        void AddEvent(CXEvent * ourEvent);

        void RemoveParticipant (CXParticipant *ourParticipant);
        void RemoveEvent (CXEvent *ourEvent);

        /**********************************************
        **   Using the Running Totals structure..    **
        **   this routine will clear and then recalc **
        **   the m_TotalPlaceMap map                 **
        **********************************************/
        void CalculatePoints ();

    private:
```

```
        //
        // You need to keep a list of Events and a list of
        // Participants.  The Event class will place the
        // Participants in that event.  The m_plParticipants
        // map will be used to calculate overall winning
        // participant.
        //
        CList <CXParticipant*, CXParticipant *m_plParticipants;
        CList <CXEvent *, CXEvent *> *m_elEvents;

        CArray <CXParticipant*, CXParticipant*> *m_paTotalPoints;

        int     m_nActiveEvent;
};

#endif // cxeventrecorder_h
```

Notice that the CXEvent maintains a list of participants for that particular event. The EventDefineView is used to assign participants to an event. The EventTallyView is used to place the participants after their competition. The CalculatePoints() method of the CXEventRecorder will iterate the Events list, pull out Participants placement, and tally running totals for each participant. After this is done, it will iterate the list and find the top three overall contestants. See Listing 20.13 for a routine to add a participant to an event.

LISTING 20.13   A ROUTINE TO ADD A PARTICIPANT TO AN EVENT

```
void
CXEvent::AddParticipantToEvent (CXParticipant * eventParticipant)
{
    POSITION pos = m_slEventParticipants->GetHeadPosition( );
    while( pos )
    {
        //Already in the list... Don't do anything...
        if (m_slEventParticipants->GetNext(pos) == eventParticipant)
            return;
    }
    // Ok... This isn't a duplicate... add to our list...
    m_slEventParticipants->AddTail(eventParticipant);
}
```

The line POSITION pos = m_slEventParticipants->GetHeadPosition( ); defines the POSITION iterator to point to the front of the list. You could simply add a participant here because your view deletes from the available list when a participant is added to the event. However, it is good practice to verify that your list doesn't have a duplicate. If there is no duplicate, you simply add the participant to the end of the list (see the next-to-last line of

20

Listing 20.13). If the list needed to be sorted, it would be wise to apply a sorting algorithm and use the `InsertAfter()` or `InsertBefore()` member functions to enter participants into the list.

Returning to Listing 20.8 for a minute, you will notice the use of `CStringList`, which is not a templated list. Notice again that you are simply adding the part strings to the end of your string list. In most cases, your element insertion into a list will be at the tail or the head. See Listing 20.14 for a routine to remove a participant from an event.

LISTING 20.14 A ROUTINE TO REMOVE A PARTICIPANT FROM AN EVENT

```
void
CXEvent::RemoveParticipant (CXParticipant * eventParticipant)
{
    POSITION pos = m_slEventParticipants->GetHeadPosition( );
    while( pos )
    {
        if (m_slEventParticipants->GetNext(pos) == eventParticipant)
            m_slEventParticipants->RemoveAt(pos);
    }
}
```

Here again, the code is quite simple. The list is iterated until the desired element is located and then removed via the `RemoveAt()` function. Notice that the `RemoveAt()` function takes the `POSITION` iterator.

An STL Approach

I would not want to leave this discussion without some mention of the Standard Template Library functions available for managing strings and lists. If you were tasked with the job of creating a lightweight ATL COM component that makes heavy use of strings and lists, would you know how?

To manage character string data, the STL provides the `<string>` templated class. In many respects, it is very similar to the `CString` class. I won't go into extensive detail here, primarily because this is an MFC book. This string has operators that allow you to assign it and allocate memory. The buffer maintained in this template is available through the `c_str()` function.

> **NOTE**
>
> The string buffer available via `c_str` is not directly assignable to a `CString` value.

The following code snippet is an example of how you might define and use the string template class:

```
LPCSTR szTempString;
szTempString = (*it_sList).c_str();
```

When you have `szTempString`, you can then create or assign it to an MFC `CString`. The `it_sList` is a list iterator. The list is a string list.

Many functions available through the MFC `CList` class are also available through the STL template class, `<list>`. Refer to the online documentation for information on the STL template classes.

Summary

My wish is that you take this chapter as a beginning point for looking inside the MFC utility classes and learning how to effectively model your application's data. The `CString` class, although powerful, can lead to many frustrating hours of memory allocation problems. Modeling your set data into a `CList` or a `CMap`, or some other collection class, can be a daunting task. The key to understanding these utility classes is first understanding your data.

I have presented a fairly robust, but purposely incomplete, sample application that is used not only in this chapter, but also in Chapter 7 and Chapter 21, "File I/O and MFC." I have left the total calculations method up to you. This is a simple test to see whether you picked up anything about collections! The other item that is missing here is primarily for Chapter 21. There is no reporting mechanism for this application. You might want to display a report in HTML to a Web browser component and write that out to a file. The choices are endless. When you have a fun application with the two missing parts put together, email me, and we will compare approaches. I have the completed version and will be able to email you with that.

File I/O and MFC

by K. David White

CHAPTER 21

File-based computing has been around for ages, or so it seems. Long before databases became the predominant data persistence mechanism, data was stored in files that resided on system disk. Although the database is currently persisted to a file system, the user is not concerned about how this file system is represented. There are many forms of data, and by the nature of the beast, it is apparent that binary representation of data in a file system presents a whole new set of problems.

Most applications use the file system in some fashion, and it is important for the MFC developer to understand what the file system represents as well as how to use it. In this chapter, you will discover that MFC provides a consistent interface, CFile, for handling data persistence to the file system. You'll also take a cursory look at serialization and what takes place under the covers there.

These classes are straightforward and online documentation is fairly adequate, but I want to take an in-depth look at how it fits together. When you understand how the file system is put together, you will better understand how to use it.

The **CFile** Class

The MFC library provides the CFile class to handle normal I/O processing to the file system. This class provides basic nonbuffered file access that essentially wraps the Windows file API calls. There are derived classes of CFile that are used specifically for doing the file-related work. These are CStdioFile and CMemFile. The CStdioFile handles general I/O processing for ASCII type data buffers. The CMemFile handles processing for memory data.

> **NOTE**
>
> Serialization is another method to write information from the application to a file. Although this is primarily a function of the document/view architecture, I will take a look at it in this chapter. The MFC CDocument object framework handles serialization for you. It uses the CFile object. To take advantage of this, implement code in the Serialize member function of your derived CDocument object to process input and output.

The CFile class provides an interface for general-purpose binary file operations. The CStdioFile and CMemFile classes derived from CFile and the CSharedFile class derived from CMemFile supply more specialized file services.

A `CStdioFile` class represents stream-based file processing as opened by `fopen`. Stream files can be either text files or binary files, but the `CStdioFile` class handles the input and output in stream mode. The last section of this chapter provides some insight into file stream operations.

> **NOTE**
>
> The `Duplicate`, `LockRange`, and `UnlockRange` methods of `CFile` are not supported in `CStdioFile`.

Text mode, as with ASCII files, handles the carriage return-linefeed pair as an end-of-line. The newline character (0x0A), when applied to a string to be sent to the text-mode `CStdioFile` object, is actually written out as the byte pair (0x0A, 0x0D)(CR/LF). When that pair is read in, it translates it back to the newline character.

Let's take a look inside `CFile`!

Processing Files with `CFile`

This section takes a general look at processing file data using the `CFile`-derived classes.

To use `CFile`, you first must create a `CFile` with a filename and indicate how the file is to be opened (that is, its access mode, including privilege settings). With the `CFile` class, you have the option of defining the privileges either in the constructor, or when the file is opened. Table 21.1 is a list of possible modes. Modes define the access privileges for handling the file operations.

TABLE 21.1   FILE MODES

Mode	Description/Notes
modeRead	Opens the file for reading only.
modeWrite	Opens the file for writing.
modeReadWrite	Opens the file for reading and writing.
modeCreate	Will create the file. If the file already exists, the size will be set to zero.
modeNoTruncate	Creates the file without truncating it.
modeNoInherit	Prevents the file from being inherited by a child process.
shareDenyRead	Denies Read access to the file from other applications/processes.
shareDenyWrite	Denies Write access to the file from other applications/processes.

continues

TABLE 21.1   CONTINUED

Mode	Description/Notes
shareDenyNone	Does not apply any sharing restrictions to the file.
shareExclusive	Denies Read and Write access to the file from other applications/processes.
shareCompat	Allows other processes to open the file any number of times.
typeBinary	Sets the binary mode for the file. This mode is exclusive to the CStdioFile class.
typeText	Sets the text mode for the file. This mode is exclusive to the CStdioFile class.

There are many member functions of CFile that let the developer perform a myriad of functions to a file. These are presented fairly well in the online documentation for Visual C++. However, let's take a quick tour of some of the more commonly used functions. Table 21.2 presents my list of the functions that you as a developer should become familiar with.

TABLE 21.2   CFile MEMBER FUNCTIONS (SHORT LIST)

Mode	Description/Notes
Open	Opens a file.
Close	Closes a file.
Read	Reads data from a file based on a position in the file.
Write	Writes data to a file based on a position in the file.
SeekToBegin	Positions the file pointer to the beginning of the file.
SeekToEnd	Positions to the end of a file.
GetLength	Returns the length of the file.
SetLength	Specifies the length of the file.
GetPosition	Returns the current file position pointer.
GetStatus	Returns the status of the file (more about this later).
GetFileName	Returns a string representing the filename for the file.
GetFileTitle	Returns the selected title of a file.
GetFilePath	Returns the path associated with a file.
Rename	Renames the file.
Remove	Removes the file (delete).
GetStatus	Returns the status of the file.

As most of us develop our skills as software developers, we become increasingly aware of the multitude of protection and access rights placed on files. You first look at file processing as simple input and output of text data. If you are like me, you have a tendency to overlook the necessary functions that prepare the file to do the work you need it to do. When processing files, it's important to understand how the file is represented and what state it may be in. If you look inside the GetStatus method, you see that it takes a structure called CFileStatus. This structure, shown in Listing 21.1, provides a mechanism to query the file for its status prior to using it.

LISTING 21.1   THE CFileStatus STRUCTURE REPRESENTED IN THE **MFC** HEADER FILE AFX.H

```
/////////////////////////////////////////////////////////////////
// File status

struct CFileStatus
{
   CTime m_ctime;      // creation date/time of file
   CTime m_mtime;      // last modification date/time of file
   CTime m_atime;      // last access date/time of file
   LONG m_size;        // logical size of file in bytes
   BYTE m_attribute;   // logical OR of CFile::Attribute enum values
   BYTE _m_padding;    // pad the structure to a WORD
   TCHAR m_szFullName[_MAX_PATH]; // absolute pathname

#ifdef _DEBUG
void Dump(CDumpContext& dc) const;
#endif
};
```

As you can see from Listing 21.1, the file status structure contains some useful information. It contains a creation time, modification time, and an access time variable. These time variables, along with the size and attributes, determine when and how the file was used.

Inside the CFile Class

The CFile declaration resides in the AFX.H file, as shown in Listing 21.2.

LISTING 21.2   THE CFile DECLARATION (AFX.H)

```
01:   /////////////////////////////////////////////////////////////////
02:   // File - raw unbuffered disk file I/O
03:
```

continues

LISTING 21.2   CONTINUED

```
04:     class CFile : public CObject
05:     {
06:         DECLARE_DYNAMIC(CFile)
07:
08:     public:
09:     // Flag values
10:         enum OpenFlags {
11:             modeRead =          0x0000,
12:             modeWrite =         0x0001,
13:             modeReadWrite =     0x0002,
14:             shareCompat =       0x0000,
15:             shareExclusive =    0x0010,
16:             shareDenyWrite =    0x0020,
17:             shareDenyRead =     0x0030,
18:             shareDenyNone =     0x0040,
19:             modeNoInherit =     0x0080,
20:             modeCreate =        0x1000,
21:             modeNoTruncate =    0x2000,
22:             typeText =          0x4000, // typeText and typeBinary
            ➥are used in
23:             typeBinary =   (int)0x8000 // derived classes
            ➥only
24:             };
25:
26:         enum Attribute {
27:             normal =    0x00,
28:             readOnly =  0x01,
29:             hidden =    0x02,
30:             system =    0x04,
31:             volume =    0x08,
32:             directory = 0x10,
33:             archive =   0x20
34:             };
35:
36:         enum SeekPosition { begin = 0x0, current = 0x1,
            ➥end = 0x2 };
37:
38:         enum { hFileNull = -1 };
39:
40:     // Constructors
41:         CFile();
42:         CFile(int hFile);
43:         CFile(LPCTSTR lpszFileName, UINT nOpenFlags);
44:
45:     // Attributes
46:         UINT m_hFile;
47:         operator HFILE() const;
48:
49:         virtual DWORD GetPosition() const;
```

```
50:          BOOL GetStatus(CFileStatus& rStatus) const;
51:          virtual CString GetFileName() const;
52:          virtual CString GetFileTitle() const;
53:          virtual CString GetFilePath() const;
54:          virtual void SetFilePath(LPCTSTR lpszNewName);
55:
56:     // Operations
57:          virtual BOOL Open(LPCTSTR lpszFileName, UINT nOpenFlags,
58:               CFileException* pError = NULL);
59:
60:          static void PASCAL Rename(LPCTSTR lpszOldName,
61:                        LPCTSTR lpszNewName);
62:          static void PASCAL Remove(LPCTSTR lpszFileName);
63:          static BOOL PASCAL GetStatus(LPCTSTR lpszFileName,
64:                        CFileStatus& rStatus);
65:          static void PASCAL SetStatus(LPCTSTR lpszFileName,
66:                        const CFileStatus& status);
67:
68:          DWORD SeekToEnd();
69:          void SeekToBegin();
70:
71:          // backward compatible ReadHuge and WriteHuge
72:          DWORD ReadHuge(void* lpBuffer, DWORD dwCount);
73:          void WriteHuge(const void* lpBuffer, DWORD dwCount);
74:
75:     // Overridables
76:          virtual CFile* Duplicate() const;
77:
78:          virtual LONG Seek(LONG lOff, UINT nFrom);
79:          virtual void SetLength(DWORD dwNewLen);
80:          virtual DWORD GetLength() const;
81:
82:          virtual UINT Read(void* lpBuf, UINT nCount);
83:          virtual void Write(const void* lpBuf, UINT nCount);
84:
85:          virtual void LockRange(DWORD dwPos, DWORD dwCount);
86:          virtual void UnlockRange(DWORD dwPos, DWORD dwCount);
87:
88:          virtual void Abort();
89:          virtual void Flush();
90:          virtual void Close();
91:
92:     // Implementation
93:     public:
94:          virtual ~CFile();
95:     #ifdef _DEBUG
96:          virtual void AssertValid() const;
97:          virtual void Dump(CDumpContext& dc) const;
98:     #endif
```

continues

LISTING 21.2   CONTINUED

```
99:         enum BufferCommand { bufferRead, bufferWrite,
        ➧bufferCommit, bufferCheck };
100:        virtual UINT GetBufferPtr(UINT nCommand, UINT nCount = 0,
101:            void** ppBufStart = NULL, void** ppBufMax = NULL);
102:
103:    protected:
104:        BOOL m_bCloseOnDelete;
105:        CString m_strFileName;
106:    };
```

Wow! What a declaration! Notice lines 9 through 34. These enum structures define not only the mode for the file, but also the attribute. You might be wondering what the primary difference is here. The attribute indicates the file's current status, where the modes are used to define how the file can be accessed or shared. Reference the comment that Microsoft provides for you in this listing. The modes are given the member name of OpenFlags.

Now jump to line 99. This line contains an enum declaration for defining access privileges for CFile's buffer. Confused yet? Specifically, CMemFile (and CArchive) use the buffer modes when processing shared memory buffers. If you are interested in looking at some code, the GetBufferPtr routine of CMemFile uses this enum structure when processing the buffer pointers (this is located in the Filemem.cpp file, which is supplied with MFC).

If you were to spend time looking at code for CFile functions, you would soon discover that it is nothing more than a wrapper for the Windows API functions. So to prevent a walkthrough of the MFC code, Table 21.3 can be of some value to you.

TABLE 21.3   CFile TO WINDOWS API FUNCTION MAP

MFC CFile *Function*	Windows API *Function*
Open()	::Createfile()
Close()	::CloseHandle()
Duplicate()	::DuplicateHandle()
Read()	::ReadFile()
Write()	::WriteFile()
Seek()	::SetFilePointer()
GetPosition()	::SetFilePointer()
SetLength()	::SetEndOfFile()
Rename()	::MoveFile()

MFC CFile *Function*	*Windows API Function*
Remove()	::DeleteFile()
GetStatus()	::GetFileTime(), GetFileSize()
LockRange()	::LockFile()
UnlockRange()	::UnlockFile()
Flush()	::FlushFileBuffers()

In addition, Microsoft sometimes provides undocumented helper functions you are free to use, if you accept the risk that the helper functions might be renamed or might even disappear altogether in future versions of MFC. That said, the following list shows file-name helper functions that are available through the CFile implementation in FILECORE.CPP.

- AfxResolveShortCut()—This helper function looks up a Windows 95/98/NT 4 or 5 formatted shortcut and converts it to a full filename.

- AfxFullPath()—Pretty straightforward function here. This function turns a file path into an absolute (network and all) file path.

- AfxGetRoot()—Not so straightforward! Takes the volume out of a Uniform Naming Convention (UNC) path and returns the root name of the file. The UNC is formatted like this: *server\share*

- AfxComparePath()—Compares two paths and determines if they are identical.

- AfxGetFileTitle()—Returns just the filename from a path declaration.

You now have a pretty good understanding of what CFile really is. However, most applications don't specifically use CFile, but one of the derived CFile classes, such as CStdioFile, or CMemFile.

The CStdioFile Class

Because CStdioFile derives from CFile, there is no need to look at functions that you might be already familiar with. CStdioFile provides a mechanism to process stream-based file data. It adds two new functions for processing this data: ReadString() and WriteString(). The ReadString() function, shown in Listing 21.3, will read in a string until it encounters one of the following conditions:

- Specific number of characters—If you pass in the number of characters to read (not including the string's NULL terminator), the ReadString function will continue reading until this number is read or one of the other conditions is met, whichever comes first.

- End-of-line (newline)—If the ReadString encounters a CR/LF pair, it will stop reading. This happens even if the specified number of characters has not been read in.

- End-of-file—If the ReadString encounters the end of the file, it will not be able to process the stream any further.

> **NOTE**
>
> Remember that stream processing essentially is processed in a sequential fashion until an end character is encountered. By specifying the number of characters to process, the stream is read a character at a time, and a character count is applied. If an ending character has not been reached, and the count has, the ReadString function will terminate the stream with an end-of-line character.

If you were to dive into the code for CStdioFile, you would notice quite a bit of processing above and beyond CFile specifically dealing with data buffering. Because CFile is generic and concerns itself primarily with nonbuffered data, CStdioFile must implement the buffering necessary to handle stream input and output.

Because CStdioFile processes stream data, it makes sense for it to wrap the C runtime library file-handling routines (fstream, fopen, and so on). The declaration for CStdioFile lives within AFX.H, whereas its implementation resides in FILETXT.CPP. The ReadString implementation is represented in Listing 21.3, which resides in FILETXT.CPP.

LISTING 21.3   THE CStdioFile::ReadString IMPLEMENTATIONS

```
LPTSTR CStdioFile::ReadString(LPTSTR lpsz, UINT nMax)
{
    ASSERT(lpsz != NULL);
    ASSERT(AfxIsValidAddress(lpsz, nMax));
    ASSERT(m_pStream != NULL);

    LPTSTR lpszResult = _fgetts(lpsz, nMax, m_pStream);
    if (lpszResult == NULL && !feof(m_pStream))
    {
        clearerr(m_pStream);
        AfxThrowFileException(CFileException::generic,
        ➡_doserrno, m_strFileName);
    }
    return lpszResult;
}
```

```
BOOL CStdioFile::ReadString(CString& rString)
{
    ASSERT_VALID(this);

    rString = &afxChNil;      // empty string without deallocating
    const int nMaxSize = 128;
    LPTSTR lpsz = rString.GetBuffer(nMaxSize);
    LPTSTR lpszResult;
    int nLen = 0;
    for (;;)
    {
        lpszResult = _fgetts(lpsz, nMaxSize+1, m_pStream);
        rString.ReleaseBuffer();

        // handle error/eof case
        if (lpszResult == NULL && !feof(m_pStream))
        {
            clearerr(m_pStream);
            AfxThrowFileException(CFileException::generic,
                doserrno, m_strFileName);
        }

        // if string is read completely or EOF
        if (lpszResult == NULL ||
            (nLen = lstrlen(lpsz)) < nMaxSize ||
            lpsz[nLen-1] == '\n')
            break;

        nLen = rString.GetLength();
        lpsz = rString.GetBuffer(nMaxSize + nLen) + nLen;
    }

    // remove '\n' from end of string if present
    lpsz = rString.GetBuffer(0);
    nLen = rString.GetLength();
    if (nLen != 0 && lpsz[nLen-1] == '\n')
        rString.GetBufferSetLength(nLen-1);

    return lpszResult != NULL;
}
```

Notice the use of standard C runtime library functions.

Some time ago, during a project where I had implemented a parsing function using
ReadString(), I ran across a particularly annoying problem. Listing 21.4 is a macro that
I wrote to get around that problem.

LISTING 21.4 THE MFC_CSTR_KLUDGE MACRO

```
// -STUMBLED on the fact that the MFC code for
// StdioFile::ReadString will fail when you have
// a newline character in a location that is a
// multiple of the MFC_BUFLENGTH.  (go figure — )
// This stuffs a character in that location and then
// adds a newline character... ** SuperKludge !!! **
//////////////////////////////////////////////////////
#define MFC_BUFLENGTH 128
#define MFC_CSTR_KLUDGE(s)                                    \
   {                                                          \
      if (s.GetLength() % MFC_BUFLENGTH == (MFC_BUFLENGTH - 1)) \
         { s = s + "\255\n"; }                                \
      else                                                    \
         { s = s + "\n"; }                                    \
   }
```

Notice the comment in the first six lines. It tells the story about this annoying little bug. If for some reason a newline is encountered in the location pointed to by the maximum buffer length defined in ReadString, ReadString loses the newline character. Go back to Listing 21.3 for a minute. The line const int nMaxSize = 128; defines a maximum buffer length of 128. At first glance, you might be wondering why. Because you are working in a buffered mode, you want to buffer in chunks, hence the value. The GetBuffer function called in the line LPTSTR lpsz = rString.GetBuffer(nMaxSize); requires this chunk size. You process the chunk and then check to see if your running count has been obtained, or whether you hit an end-of-line or an end-of-file. By looking at the line lpsz = rString.GetBuffer(nMaxSize + nLen) + nLen;, you see that the for loop continues if the total size is not met. The line (nLen = lstrlen(lpsz)) < nMaxSize ¦¦ contains the annoying problem. This is not really a bug, but if you are processing for the newline during a parse operation, you might encounter this. If the newline character happens to fall at location 128 of the buffer, it gets chopped off, and the ReadString finishes the loop without returning it to you (ouch!).

The CMemFile Class

Because I discussed CStdioFile in some detail, I think it only fair for those of you having to deal with shared memory processing to discuss the CMemFile class. However, you might be disappointed to find out that CMemFile doesn't deal directly with shared memory. That's up to you!

The primary reason that CMemFile is provided is so the user can write out, or serialize, a chunk of memory. Memory files are like disk files except that the file is stored in memory rather than on a disk. However, it's nice to take advantage of file processing techniques when handling memory chunks. This keeps the user from having to manage the memory allocation each time a buffer is written to the memory. These chunks of memory can later be processed out to a file, or to the Registry. It can also be useful in transferring memory chunks between processes.

> **NOTE**
>
> It's important to note here that dealing with memory is not exactly like dealing with disk files. The CMemFile member variable, m_hFile, is always null because of this fact. Because a file contains a handle for processing by the operating system, it must use this handle for opening and closing, and reading and writing. The same is not true for memory.
>
> CMemFile does support Read() and Write(), but not the Open() and Close() functions.

CMemFile memory processing is similar in some respects to the CArray processing discussed in Chapter 20, "Strings and Collections." The memory is *grown* when needed, and then *shrunk* when not needed. To grow the memory needed, all functions first check to see that they have enough memory for the operation. If not, they then call GrowFile() to add the needed memory.

The **CSharedFile** Class

This newly documented class is derived from CMemFile and provides wrappers for the global memory API functions. Shared memory files differ from process memory files in that the memory is allocated by the GlobalAlloc() Windows function. This global chunk can be shared using the Clipboard, or other OLE/COM uniform data transfer operations.

GlobalAlloc returns an HGLOBAL handle rather than a pointer to memory. HGLOBAL handle is used in certain applications, such as the Clipboard.

> **NOTE**
>
> CSharedFile does not use memory-mapped files as one might expect. The data cannot be shared between processes either. This might seem out of the ordinary, but it is done this way to allow growing of the memory area.

The implementation for `CSharedFile` is located in the FILESHRD.CPP file. If you have an opportunity to look at this file, notice that it contains global allocation function calls.

The `CFileDialog` Class

You've taken a quick tour of what MFC provides in the way of file processing, but getting your application to enable their usage is another subject. With every user interface application that stores data to a file, you must provide some mechanism to allow the user to select, open, or close the application's file. MFC provides the `CFileDialog` class for just this functionality. As you can probably tell from the name, it is derived from the `CDialog` class.

The `CFileDialog` class is referred to as a common dialog class. This simply means that the Windows common API functions are grouped and wrapped by these dialog classes, giving them a dialog interface.

The `CFileDialog` class contains a structure that describes the settings for the dialog wrapper. The `OPENFILENAME` structure is used to define the `CFileDialog` settings, and the class wraps the `GetOpenFileName()` API function.

The `CFileDialog` is implemented in DLGFILE.CPP. Listing 21.5 shows the `DoModal` function for `CFileDialog`.

LISTING 21.5 `CFileDialog::DoModal()` IMPLEMENTATION

```
int CFileDialog::DoModal()
{
    ASSERT_VALID(this);
    ASSERT(m_ofn.Flags & OFN_ENABLEHOOK);
    ASSERT(m_ofn.lpfnHook != NULL); // can still be a user hook

    // zero out the file buffer for consistent parsing later
    ASSERT(AfxIsValidAddress(m_ofn.lpstrFile, m_ofn.nMaxFile));
    DWORD nOffset = lstrlen(m_ofn.lpstrFile)+1;
    ASSERT(nOffset <= m_ofn.nMaxFile);
    memset(m_ofn.lpstrFile+nOffset, 0, (m_ofn.nMaxFile-nOffset)*
    ➥sizeof(TCHAR));

    // WINBUG: This is a special case for the file open/save dialog,
    //   which sometimes pumps while it is coming up but before it has
    //   disabled the main window.
    HWND hWndFocus = ::GetFocus();
```

```
    BOOL bEnableParent = FALSE;
    m_ofn.hwndOwner = PreModal();
    AfxUnhookWindowCreate();
    if (m_ofn.hwndOwner != NULL && ::IsWindowEnabled(m_ofn.hwndOwner))
    {
        bEnableParent = TRUE;
        ::EnableWindow(m_ofn.hwndOwner, FALSE);
    }

    _AFX_THREAD_STATE* pThreadState = AfxGetThreadState();
    ASSERT(pThreadState->m_pAlternateWndInit == NULL);

    if (m_ofn.Flags & OFN_EXPLORER)
        pThreadState->m_pAlternateWndInit = this;
    else
        AfxHookWindowCreate(this);

    int nResult;
    if (m_bOpenFileDialog)
        nResult = ::GetOpenFileName(&m_ofn);
    else
        nResult = ::GetSaveFileName(&m_ofn);

    if (nResult)
        ASSERT(pThreadState->m_pAlternateWndInit == NULL);
    pThreadState->m_pAlternateWndInit = NULL;

    // WINBUG: Second part of special case for file open/save dialog.
    if (bEnableParent)
        ::EnableWindow(m_ofn.hwndOwner, TRUE);
    if (::IsWindow(hWndFocus))
        ::SetFocus(hWndFocus);

    PostModal();
    return nResult ? nResult : IDCANCEL;
}
```

The lines

```
if (m_bOpenFileDialog)
    nResult = ::GetOpenFileName(&m_ofn);
else
    nResult = ::GetSaveFileName(&m_ofn);
```

are the important section to inspect here. The m_ofn member structure is the OPENFILE-NAME structure contained within the CFileDialog. The OPENFILENAME structure is a Windows API structure, and is defined as shown in Listing 21.6.

LISTING 21.6 THE tagOFN STRUCTURE

```
typedef struct tagOFN { // ofn
    DWORD           lStructSize;
    HWND            hwndOwner;
    HINSTANCE       hInstance;
    LPCTSTR         lpstrFilter;
    LPTSTR          lpstrCustomFilter;
    DWORD           nMaxCustFilter;
    DWORD           nFilterIndex;
    LPTSTR          lpstrFile;
    DWORD           nMaxFile;
    LPTSTR          lpstrFileTitle;
    DWORD           nMaxFileTitle;
    LPCTSTR         lpstrInitialDir;
    LPCTSTR         lpstrTitle;
    DWORD           Flags;
    WORD            nFileOffset;
    WORD            nFileExtension;
    LPCTSTR         lpstrDefExt;
    DWORD           lCustData;
    LPOFNHOOKPROC   lpfnHook;
    LPCTSTR         lpTemplateName;
} OPENFILENAME;
```

Because this structure is available, you can see that dialog items for CFileDialog are easily changed. Let's take a look at some things you need to do to "roll your own" CFileDialog class.

The User-Defined CFileDialog Class

Because m_ofn is readily accessible, you might think that you simply set the attributes that you are interested in and you are ready to go. However, there is more to it than that. The following list is a step-by-step guide to creating your own CFileDialog:

1. Copy the standard resource to your project's resource directory and add it to your project. This is a good place to start if you're not familiar with creating dialogs. You can choose to create a completely different look and feel instead of changing the standard.

2. Copy the DLGS.H header file to your project. To use the dialog that you are modifying, you will need this file.

3. Create code for any specific functionality. When you have a dialog, simply add the message handler functions to perform the specific steps that you need.

4. Adjust the m_ofn structure. Now you're ready to modify this structure and make it work for you. Do this by setting the hInstance member by calling AfxGetResourceHandle(). To set the template name (lpTemplateName member), call MAKEINTRESOURCE and pass it the IDD of the dialog. Next, set the Flags member of the structure to indicate the OFN_ initialization.

5. Override OnInitDialog. Because your new dialog is a dialog-derived class, you will need to put in any special initialization code. Don't forget to call CDialog::OnInitDialog()!

> **NOTE**
>
> You will notice that the m_ofn structure can be set to look like the Explorer dialogs by defining OFN_EXPLORER. This is a nice change, but if you are developing applications that use the old style (Windows 3.1 or NT 3.51), you probably would not want to use this.
>
> When you "roll your own" File dialog box, the OFN_EXPLORER bit actually uses the template that you supply to add to the existing dialog box. In other words, if you specify OFN_EXPLORER, you are adding to the supplied dialog and not creating new!

Practical Usage of `CFile` and `CFileDialog`

You've taken an in-depth "whirlwind" tour of CFile and CFileDialog and your head is swimming right now. You probably want to look at some practical examples to get a handle on all this information.

Opening a File

First, your application should allow the user to select the file. This is done with the CFileDialog.

Listing 21.7 is the CMainFrame::OnFileOpen() function for the UNL_MultiEd application. This function will display a CFileDialog to allow the user to select an EventRecorder document. If none exist, or he wants to create new, the user simply cancels and the EventTally CFormView is displayed. This application is detailed in Chapter 20.

LISTING 21.7   THE UNL_MultiEd CMainFrame::OnFileOpen() FUNCTION

```
01:    void CMainFrame::OnFileOpen()
02:    {
03:        CString sFileName;
04:
05:        CUNL_MultiEdApp* pApp = (CUNL_MultiEdApp*)AfxGetApp();
06:
07:        CXEventRecorder *ourEventRecorder = pApp->GetEventRecorder();
08:
09:        static TCHAR szFilter[] =
           _T("Event Recorder Files (*.erx)|*.erx|AllFiles(*.*)|*.*|") ;
10:
11:        ////////////////////////////////////////////////////////////
12:        //  Define the common dialog for opening the file..      //
13:        ////////////////////////////////////////////////////////////
14:        CFileDialog dlg( TRUE, _T("*.erx"), NULL,
15:                    OFN_HIDEREADONLY | OFN_PATHMUSTEXIST,
                       szFilter,NULL)   ;
16:
17:        dlg.m_ofn.lpstrTitle = "Event Recorder File";
18:        dlg.m_ofn.lpstrInitialDir =
           CString("C:\\EventRecorderFiles\\");
19:
20:        /***********************************************************
21:        ** Here you want to give them the chance to use an ASCII  **
22:        ** delimited file to load events and participants. Open   **
23:        ** Event Tally document to let them continue working with **
24:        ** events. If they cancel, start with participant's view. **
25:        ***********************************************************/
26:
27:        if (IDOK != dlg.DoModal())
28:        {
29:
30:        POSITION curTemplatePos = pApp->GetFirstDocTemplatePosition();
31:
32:            // Start with the Participants view..
33:        while(curTemplatePos != NULL)
34:            {
35:            CDocTemplate* curTemplate =
36:                pApp->GetNextDocTemplate(curTemplatePos);
37:            CString str;
38:            curTemplate->GetDocString(str, CDocTemplate::docName);
39:            if(str == _T("PartForm"))
40:            {
41:                    CPartDoc* pPartDoc;
42:            pPartDoc = (CPartDoc*)curTemplate->OpenDocumentFile(NULL);
43:            return;
44:            }
```

```
45:            }
46:        }
47:        else
48:        {
49:        sFileName = dlg.GetPathName();
50:
51:    //  Object not created yet, so create it now.
52:      if (ourEventRecorder == NULL)
53:          {
54:              ourEventRecorder = new CXEventRecorder();
55:               pApp->SetEventRecorder(ourEventRecorder);
56:           }
57:
58:          //Load in the Event information::
59:          ourEventRecorder->LoadEvents(sFileName);
60:
61:     POSITION curTemplatePos = pApp->GetFirstDocTemplatePosition();
62:
63:          // Start with the Participants view..
64:     while(curTemplatePos != NULL)
65:          {
66:          CDocTemplate* curTemplate =
67:              pApp->GetNextDocTemplate(curTemplatePos);
68:          CString str;
69:          curTemplate->GetDocString(str, CDocTemplate::docName);
70:          if(str == _T("EventTallyForm"))
71:          {
72:              CEventTallyDoc* pEVTallyDoc;
73:            pEVTallyDoc =
     ➥(CEventTallyDoc*)curTemplate->OpenDocumentFile(NULL);
74:          return;
75:          }
76:        }
77:      }
78:  }
```

Notice the setup for the CFileDialog. Line 9 contains what is known as a extension fil-ter. This extension filter is used to filter file types that contain only the supplied filter. For example, when you open a Microsoft Word document, you see only the files having .DOC as an extension. In this case, you want to see the files with an .ERX extension, which represents an ASCII delimited form file (explained in Chapter 20). You then create the CFileDialog (see lines 14 and 15) with the filter applied. At this point, you could go on your merry way, but it wouldn't be yours without modifying the m_ofn structure to your liking. Lines 17 and 18 will apply your own title and initial directory to the dialog box.

> **NOTE**
>
> At this point, you aren't really rolling your own `CFileDialog`. The `m_ofn` struc-
> ture is easily modified with standard items to obtain most of the functionality
> you will ever need for `CFileDialog`.

If the user selects Cancel from the dialog, you will pull up the Participant view for him
to enter participants, and essentially create a new `EventRecorder` file. However, if he
wants to load the events and participants from the file, you get the information from the
`CFileDialog` and pass that on to the `LoadEvents()` function of the `CXEventRecorder`
class.

Reading Data from a File

In the UNL_MultiEd application, you read in an Events file (.ERX) that contains event
and participant information. The Events are in the file in the manner shown in Listing
21.8. The code in Listing 21.8 is from an Events (.ERX) file supplied with the
UNL_MultiEd sample application.

LISTING 21.8   THE UNL_MULTIED EVENTS FILE (DUMMY.ERX)

```
EVENT:
Broad Jump
Pole Vault
Hot Shots
Distance Run
```

The participants for the events are also in the same file, and are delimited by the format
shown in Listing 21.9.

LISTING 21.9   THE UNL_MULTIED EVENTS FILE (CONTINUED)

```
PARTICIPANT:
Scribner III, Kenn, CC-2
White, Dave, CC-2
Heyman, Bill, CC-1
Jonstone, Nancy, ST-4
Marshall, Mary, ST-3
Jones, William, AB-1
Alson, Abraham, AB-1
```

Although this file structure is quite simplistic, it serves your purpose. The string manipulation is covered in Chapter 20, but let's take a look at what is taking place when the file contents are read into memory. Listing 21.10 contains the actual file parsing routine that you need to investigate. The filename is passed into this function.

LISTING 21.10 THE `CXEventRecorder::LoadEvents` FUNCTION

```
01:    void
02:    CXEventRecorder::LoadEvents(CString sFileName)
03:    {
04:        BOOL    bDO_EVENT           = FALSE;
05:        BOOL    bDO_PARTICIPANT     = FALSE;
06:
07:        CStdioFile file;
08:        CString line;
09:
10:        if (file.Open(sFileName,CFile::modeRead))
11:        {
12:        while (file.ReadString(line))
13:        {
14:                if (line == "EVENT:")
15:                {
16:                    bDO_EVENT       = TRUE;
17:                    bDO_PARTICIPANT = FALSE;
18:                }
19:                else if (line == "PARTICIPANT:")
20:                {
21:                    bDO_EVENT       = FALSE;
22:                    bDO_PARTICIPANT = TRUE;
23:                }
24:            else
25:                {
26:            if (bDO_EVENT)
27:                {
28:                    CXEvent *ourEvent = new CXEvent();
29:                    ourEvent->SetEventName(line);
30:
31:                    if (m_pEvents.IsEmpty())
32:                        m_pEvents.SetAt(0,ourEvent);
33:                 else
34:                m_pEvents.SetAt(m_pEvents.GetCount(),ourEvent);
35:            }
36:
37:            if (bDO_PARTICIPANT)
38:                {
39:                    CXParticipant *ourParticipant =
                       ➥new CXParticipant();
40:                    CString sLastName,sFirstName,sTeam;
41:
```

continues

LISTING **21.10**   CONTINUED

```
42:                              CStringList slParts;
43:                              SplitPartsString(line, slParts, ",");
44:
45:                              // The first token should be the last name
46:                              POSITION pPartPos = slParts.FindIndex(0);
47:                              sLastName = slParts.GetAt(pPartPos);
48:
49:                              // Next you have the first name..
50:                              pPartPos = slParts.FindIndex(1);
51:                              sFirstName = slParts.GetAt(pPartPos);
52:
53:                              //Next you have the Team name
54:                              pPartPos = slParts.FindIndex(1);
55:                              sTeam = slParts.GetAt(pPartPos);
56:
57:                              ourParticipant->SetLastName(sLastName);
58:                              ourParticipant->SetFirstName(sFirstName);
59:                              ourParticipant->SetTeam(sTeam);
60:
61:                              m_plParticipants.AddTail(ourParticipant);
62:                      }
63:                 }
64:           }
65:       file.Close();
66:       }
67:
68:
69:    }
```

Lines 10 through 12 are the lines that you are concerned about here. Because this is a file parsing routine, there is no need to open the file with write permissions. Instead, you simply open the file with read access (see line 10) and then inside the while loop, you read each line. This loop will end when the end-of-file is met. After the while loop exits, you close the file (see line 65). Very simple! Even though this is a simple example, the functionality encapsulated by the CFile class provides a very flexible interface to implement file functions.

A Classical Approach

Still available to the developer is another approach: use of streams to persist data to a file system. Although you learned that MFC provides a fairly robust class for handling your file request, it is important to understand the traditional stream approach. I don't give you any examples, but I will discuss the various aspects of using a non-MFC approach.

You might be asking yourself why a statement would be made to that effect in an MFC book. Quite frankly, MFC is not a "cure-all" for developing applications. If you are tasked with developing COM objects that require lightweight implementation, you can choose to use the ATL library. This approach gives you lightweight objects; however, you leave the convenient world of MFC. Knowing alternative approaches to MFC gives you the ability to perform the task without worry.

I leave it as an exercise to create a file-handling class using the `fstream` library functions. You might find that after you develop this class, you will begin to use it exclusively!

What Are Streams?

The `fstream` class is derived from `iostream`, which in turn is derived from `istream` and `ostream`, and is specialized for combined disk file input and output. The `fstream` constructors create and attach a buffer used specifically for handling file input and output. This buffer is the `filebuf` buffer object.

The `filebuf` class is derived from `streambuf`. It is specifically designed for buffered disk file I/O. The file stream classes, `ofstream`, `ifstream`, and `fstream`, use member functions of `filebuf` to fetch and store characters.

The `streambuf` class contains three specific areas for handling data streams; the reserve area, put area, and get area. The derived `filebuf` objects use the put area and the get area. In fact, their pointers are tied together, so whenever one is moved, the other automatically moves with it.

Although the `filebuf` object's get and put pointers are tied together, it doesn't mean that both areas are active at the same time. In fact, they are independent of one another. Now you are totally confused. What I am saying here is that the get area and the put area are not active at the same time. During the input mode, the get area is active and will contain data. The reverse is true during output. When the mode switches, the active buffer will clear its contents, and the other buffer will then be ready for handling the stream. Thus, either the get pointer or the put pointer is null at all times. If both are null, you have problems!

Okay, you're getting swamped with information. Streams are nothing more than a series of data bits. These buffers are designed to organize the streams of data into cohesive, workable units. Are you ready to dig a little deeper?

The `istream` and `ostream` classes define the characteristics for input and output data. Input data can come from files, input terminal, and or over the network. The data is streamed in serially, thus the term *stream*. These streams are usually defined by starting and ending points, and will also contain a check character(s) at the end to verify the integrity of the data. This stream-handling functionality is maintained at the ostream and istream level.

The fstream class is derived from the iostream object, which is multiply derived from istream and ostream. Therefore, the very low-level handling of the data is actually handled at the lowest level. The fstream class then becomes responsible for handling the file handle architecture (operating-system-specific) that will process the creation, opening, closing, and destruction of data files.

Although MFC encapsulates all this functionality in the CFile classes, it would be a good idea to understand the basics. In fact, if you are a brave soul, you might want to roll your own iostream classes to define specific file input and output. Remember, MFC doesn't have all the answers. It was designed to create generic usable classes in order to create workable solutions. It is not a "cure-all" for handling user interface solutions.

Summary

The CFile class and its internals were spelled out for you in this chapter. This powerful utility class provides the basis for managing many different types of file manipulations. In this chapter, you took a close look at CStdioFile, which will probably be a staple of your programming repertoire. You also learned the steps that it takes to "roll your own" CFileDialog. Armed with this knowledge, you should be ready to tackle your application's file I/O requirements with ease, or at least have a better understanding of the MFC (and C++) file I/O mechanisms.

Exceptions

by Keith McIntyre

In This Chapter

CHAPTER 22

Exceptions—What Are They Good For?

When writing programs, you must be concerned not only with the normal operation of the program but also the kind of events that happen in the real world: unexpected user inputs, low memory conditions, disk drive errors, unavailable network resources, unavailable databases, and so on. One way a programmer can handle such real-world eventualities is to use exceptions.

The concept of handling exceptions is not foreign to software development. The ubiquitous if-then-else construct is often used to handle detection and processing of special cases such as bad user input or the inability to open a disk file. The code snippet in Listing 22.1 shows an example of making such runtime decisions.

LISTING 22.1 EXAMPLE OF USING NESTED If-Then-Else STATEMENTS

```
void NestedIfExample()
{
    // open an input file, and output file, and a log file
    FILE * fpIn;
    FILE * fpOut;
    FILE * fpLog;
    fpIn = fopen( "c:\\temp\\in.txt", "r" ); if ( fpIn )
    {
        fpOut = fopen( "c:\\temp\\out.txt", "w+" );
        if ( fpOut )
        {
            fpLog = fopen( "c:\\temp\\log.out", "a+" );
            if ( fpOut )
            {
                // do some processing on fpIn producing fpOut
                // while logging to fpLog
                // close all the files
                fclose( fpIn );
                fclose( fpOut );
                fclose( fpLog );
            }
            else
            {
                // error opening log file - close in and out
                fclose( fpIn );
                fclose( fpOut );
                printf( "error opening log file\n");
            }
        }
        else
```

```
   {
       // error opening out file - close the in file
       fclose( fpIn );
       printf( "error opening output file\n");
   }
   }
   else
   {
       printf("error opening input file\n");
   }

}
```

The code in Listing 22.1 uses nested conditional statements to detect and handle several errors that might occur during the normal processing of a simple function. If the logic becomes complex, the number of possible if-then-else statements, and consequently the level of nesting, becomes excessive and unruly.

Another way programmers have traditionally addressed this issue is to use the goto statement. The goto statement has been accused of many things including the demise of structured programming. Some would tell you the use of the goto is *never* warranted and that another logic construct *must* be used.

Sometimes the goto statement can be an elegant solution to the alternative of using nested if-then-else statements. Listing 22.2 shows how the goto statement can be used to simplify the handling of exceptional conditions. As you can see, all the cleanup logic is collected in one place. The same logic is used to deallocate resources regardless of whether the function succeeds or fails. Logic is simplified due to easy detection of which resources have been successfully allocated and hence must be freed up.

LISTING 22.2   EXAMPLE OF USING goto LOGIC

```
void GotoExample()
{
   // open an input file, and output file, and a log file
   FILE * fpIn = NULL;
   FILE * fpOut = NULL;
   FILE * fpLog = NULL;
   fpIn = fopen( "c:\\temp\\in.txt", "r" ); if ( ! fpIn )
   {
       printf("error opening input file\n");
       goto done;
   }

   fpOut = fopen( "c:\\temp\\out.txt", "w+" );
```

continues

LISTING 22.2 CONTINUED

```
    if ( ! fpOut )
    {
       printf( "error opening output file\n");
       goto done;
    }

    fpLog = fopen( "c:\\temp\\log.out", "a+" );
    if ( ! fpOut )
    {
       printf( "error opening log file\n");
       goto done;
    }

    // do some processing on fpIn producing fpOut while
    // logging to fpLog

done:
    // close all the files
    if ( fpIn )
       fclose( fpIn );
    if ( fpOut )
       fclose( fpOut );
    if (fpOut )
       fclose( fpLog );
}
```

Exceptions are another way to handle the special processing that is required when logic strays from the straight and narrow. Exceptions allow a section of code to be executed under the umbrella of a `try` block. If things go wrong during the execution of the code, the processor can be vectored to a `catch` block. The `catch` block can perform orderly cleanup of resources and program state info as well as logging the cause of the exception such that the source of the problem can be quickly determined and remedied. Listing 22.3 is an example of using exceptions to handle errors. (In this example, resources are cleaned up outside the `catch` block.)

LISTING 22.3 EXAMPLE OF USING EXCEPTION PROCESSING

```
void ExceptionExample()
{
    // open an input file, and output file, and a log file
    FILE * fpIn = NULL;
    FILE * fpOut = NULL;
    FILE * fpLog = NULL;
    try
    {
```

```
        fpIn = fopen( "c:\\temp\\in.txt", "r" );
        if ( ! fpIn ) throw "Error opening c:\\temp\\in.txt";

        fpOut = fopen( "c:\\temp\\out.txt", "w+" );
        if ( ! fpOut ) throw "Error opening c:\\temp\\out.txt";
        fpLog = fopen( "c:\\temp\\log.out", "a+" );
        if ( ! fpOut ) throw "Error opening c:\\temp\\log.out";

        // do some processing on fpIn producing fpOut while
        // logging to fpLog

    }
    catch( char * pszCause )
    {
        printf("%s\n", pszCause);

    }

    // clean up
    if ( fpIn )
        fclose( fpIn );
    if ( fpOut )
        fclose( fpOut );
    if (fpOut )
        fclose( fpLog );
}
```

Types of Exceptions

When programming in the MFC/C++ environment, a programmer should be cognizant of two major sources of exceptions: structured exceptions and C++ exceptions generated by MFC. Both of these sources of exceptions come along as "part of the territory" and, although you may choose to close your eyes and ignore them, they will probably occur at some point during the lifetime of your application and hence should at least be considered.

In addition to structured exceptions and MFC-generated exceptions, you can choose to derive your own exception classes based on MFC's CException class. This can provide an elegant method of passing out-of-the-ordinary conditions up the call stack.

There is also a legacy form of exception handling based on macros included with MFC back in the days before Visual C++ supported standard exceptions. These macros act much the same as the current "blessed" exception-handling logic except for some details regarding the way exception objects are caught and deleted. The differences are examined in detail near the end of this chapter.

As you can see, there are a number of types of exception-handling methodologies to consider. The balance of this chapter starts by examining the features and benefits of structured exception handling. C++ exceptions come next, followed by a simple implementation of the CException class. Then the chapter covers how MFC handles exceptions and gives a brief look at all the standard MFC exception classes. Next, you will focus on creating a custom exception handler class based on CException. Finally, the chapter considers the legacy macros introduced with MFC 1 and discusses how to mix exception-processing methodologies.

Structured Exception Handlers

Win32 implements structured exception handlers as a means of enabling applications to detect low-level events such as divide-by-zero errors, memory access violations, exceeding array bounds, floating-point overflow and underflow conditions, and so on. These low-level errors are often caused by faulty application logic, but nonetheless will result in an application terminating in a blaze of flames. Without an exception handler, the user will see a dialog box indicating that the program generated an unhandled exception and the application will be terminated. Figure 22.1 shows a typical dialog box.

FIGURE 22.1

Divide-by-zero structured exception dialog.

When the application dies, it does so in a very uncooperative fashion. The application does not get an opportunity to save state, close open files and databases, serialize objects, release GDI resources, and so on. The results can lead to instabilities in the application the next time the application runs.

This can be remedied by providing a _try block and an associated _except block. (Don't confuse the _try/_except syntax used by structured exception handlers with the try and catch keywords used by C++ exceptions. As you'll see later, the two are completely different beasts.)

So how do you implement the _try/_except block? Let's take a look at a simple example and see how it works.

Listing 22.4 implements a simple exception handler to catch divide-by-zero errors.

LISTING 22.4   A SIMPLE STRUCTURED EXCEPTION EXAMPLE

```
try
{
    int i, zero;
    zero = 0;
    i = 1/zero;
    i = 1;
}
_except( EXCEPTION_EXECUTE_HANDLER )
{
    ::MessageBox( NULL, "Saw exception...", "", MB_OK );
}

int j = 100;
```

The code starts with a _try block that has an obvious and intentional error that generates a divide-by-zero error. When the exception occurs, the processor is vectored to the _except block. The EXCEPTION_EXECUTE_HANDLER keyword causes code within the _except block to be executed. In this case, a simple MessageBox() is raised and the program continues without a hitch. Note that the line I = 1; in the _try block is never reached. After the _except block executes, control returns to the first statement that follows the _except block, in this case j = 100.

Several things are going on in this simple example. The code in the _try block is very simple in this case but in real life could include a lot of intricate logic. In fact, the _try block could wrap the entire logic of your application. The _try block would then protect the entire application against divide-by-zero errors.

The _except block is optionally executed based on the outcome of what's called a filter. The *filter* is the expression that is contained within the parentheses of the _except statement. In the case of the sample code, it is the constant EXCEPTION_EXECUTE_HANDLER. The filter associated with an _except block should evaluate to one of three values:

- EXCEPTION_CONTINUE_EXECUTION (-1)
- EXCEPTION_CONTINUE_SEARCH (0)
- EXCEPTION_EXECUTE_HANDLER (1)

In the previous example, the exception handler would be executed for all types of structured exceptions. In practice, the filter would often conditionalize execution based on the results of GetExceptionCode() as in the following example:

```
except(GetExceptionCode() == EXCEPTION_INT_DIVIDE_BY_ZERO)
```

If the filter returns 0, the search for another _except block continues. A single _try block can be followed by multiple _except blocks, each with a different filter. The _except blocks are searched until a filter is found that requests the continuation of execution by evaluating to -1 or that requests the execution of the "handler" by evaluating to 1. What's more, nested _try blocks with associated _except blocks can be spread out over one or more functions or methods. The search for a handler will continue to look up the call stack until it finds a handler that directs otherwise. If the search for a handler is not fruitful, the default handler takes over and terminates the application in a way that is similar to the behavior you saw when there were no _try blocks or _except handlers.

If the filter evaluates to 1, the code within the block executes (as in this simple example). The rest of the code in the _try block is short-circuited, and execution continues at the statement after the _except block(s) contained in the method that handles the exception.

If a filter resolves to EXCEPTION_CONTINUE_EXECUTION (-1), execution returns to the same statement that caused the exception in the first place. Unless some external event occurs to resolve the reason for the exception, an endless loop will result.

Nesting of Structured Exception Handlers

One big advantage of structured exceptions is the ability to unwind a frame stack when an exception is raised. In traditional code, a series of nested functions (or methods) would have to unwind by each function returning in order. If each function passes on its subordinate's return code, eventually the error is bubbled to the top of the stack. If one of the subordinate functions fails to pass along the return code, the cause of the error might easily be lost.

With exception handlers, an error condition can be detected deep down in the call stack and can be bubbled to the top of the stack without any functions or methods returning. If the _except block that handles the exception is at the top of the stack, all call frames are automatically "popped" off the stack. All automatic (stack-based) variables drop out of scope. (Static variables remain accessible after an exception is handled.) This behavior can be similar to using the exit() statement in a controlled fashion or can be localized to a single function or set of functions.

Listing 22.5 demonstrates using exception handling in a nested function call environment.

LISTING 22.5   STRUCTURED EXCEPTIONS IN A NESTED ENVIRONMENT

```
int CTestSEHExceptions::TestNestedSEH( void )
{
    _try
    {
        SEHCaller();
    }
    _except(GetExceptionCode() == EXCEPTION_INT_DIVIDE_BY_ZERO)
    {
        ::MessageBox(NULL,"Saw nested SEH exception...","",MB_OK );
    }

    // execution continues here after the exception handler runs
    return 0;
}

int CTestSEHExceptions::SEHCaller( void )
{
    return SEHGenerator();
}

int CTestSEHExceptions::SEHGenerator( void )
{
    int i, zero;
    zero = 0;
    i = 1/zero;

    return i;
}
```

In this simple and somewhat contrived sample class, `CTestSEHExceptions` contains a member method called `TestNestedSEH()` that contains a simple _try and _catch block. Within the _try block a call is made to method `SEHCaller()`. `SEHCaller()` subsequently calls `SEHGenerator()`, which performs a divide-by-zero. When the exception occurs, the CPU is executing two call frames down the stack. The first _except block found will handle the exception. The code within that _except block is immediately invoked. After the exception is handled, processing continues in `TestNestedSEH()`, as the comment indicates.

Raising Structured Exceptions

Raising structured exceptions is not something an application developer typically would do. Several structures associated with structured exceptions contain low-level information regarding the cause of the exception. Without access to hardware-level registers, these structures cannot be filled in. Generating structured exceptions is typically the responsibility of device drivers or other kernel mode logic.

The CONTEXT structure associated with a structured exception contains processor-specific information such as register values and stack pointers. The information is required in order that processing can be continued from the exact point where the infraction was detected if the exception is successfully handled. The EXCEPTION_CONTEXT structure is also associated with a structured exception. It contains a machine-independent description of the exception. Applications can receive pointers to these two structures from within an exception handler by calling the Win32 ::GetExceptionInformation() function.

The best way to raise an exception (for testing purposes, for example) is to simply perform an operation that causes the kernel mode code within the operating system to do the dirty work for you. In the examples in this chapter, an integer divide-by-zero has been used. Other structured exceptions can be raised easily enough. Getting creative with the _asm statement can render all sorts of structured exceptions!

Cleaning Up After an Exception

The ability of structured exception handling to unwind the stack is a powerful feature that sets it apart from other techniques of handling errors such as nested if statements, goto statements, or calling an error routine. But the automatic unwinding of the stack can cause a complication. What happens to resources allocated by the methods and functions that are removed from the call stack when an exception occurs? If the resources are not released, many problems can crop up, including memory leaks, resource starvation, and deadlocks due to resources being owned forever.

Structured exception handling provides the _try/_finally keywords as a means to deal with these issues. The way _try/_finally blocks work is as follows:

1. The code in the _try block is executed.
2. Whenever the processor leaves the _try block for any reason, the code in the _finally block is executed.

The "for any reason" in item 2 is quite literal. Even if the _try block is exited through a goto statement or an exception being thrown, the code in the _finally block is executed.

A great way to handle resources allocated within a function or method is to include the cleanup code within a _finally block. This assures that you will get a chance to free up memory, file handles, semaphores, mutexes, and so on when an exception is thrown.

Listing 22.6 demonstrates using the _try/_finally mechanism of structured exception handling.

LISTING 22.6   STRUCTURED EXCEPTION _finally EXAMPLE

```
int CTestSEHExceptions::TestSEHTermHandler( void )
{
   int retval = 0;
   try
   {
      retval = SEHTermA();
   }
   _except(GetExceptionCode() == EXCEPTION_INT_DIVIDE_BY_ZERO)
   {
      ::MessageBox(NULL,"Saw SEH exception...","",MB_OK );
   }

   return 0;
}

int CTestSEHExceptions::SEHTermA( void )
{
   _try
   {
      return SEHTermB() + 1;
   }
   _finally
   {
      ::MessageBox(NULL,"At Termination Handler A...","",MB_OK );
   }

   return 0;
}

int CTestSEHExceptions::SEHTermB( void )
{
   _try
   {
      return SEHTermC() + 1;
   }
   _finally
   {
      ::MessageBox(NULL,"At Termination Handler B...","",MB_OK );
   }

   return 0;
}
```

continues

22

EXCEPTIONS

LISTING 22.6   CONTINUED

```
int CTestSEHExceptions::SEHTermC( void )
{
    _try
    {
        return SEHGenerator() + 1;
    }
    _finally
    {
        ::MessageBox(NULL,"At Termination Handler C...","",MB_OK );
    }

    return 0;
}

int CTestSEHExceptions::SEHGenerator( void )
{
    int i, zero;
    zero = 0;
    i = 1/zero;

    return i;
}
```

The `TestSEHTermHandler()` calls `SEHTermA()`, which calls `SEHTermB()`, which calls `SEHTermC()`. `SEHTermC` calls `SEHGenerator()`, which causes a divide-by-zero exception. The `_except` handler that catches the divide-by-zero exception is all the way at the top of the call stack. Normally `SEHTermA`, `SEHTermB`, and `SEHTermC` would be immediately exited without regard for any cleanup that might be required. Because `_finally` blocks were included, they are invoked beginning with `SEHTermC()` and ending with `SEHTermA()`. In a real-world application, the `MessageBox` would be replaced by code that released any resources owned by the method.

C++ Exceptions

C++ provides a rich exception-handling environment that differs a bit from the structured exception-handling environment you have just looked at. First, C++ exception handlers are intended to be invoked by logic created by the programmer and for the programmer. Whereas structured exception handlers are invoked when low-level hardware events take place, C++ exceptions occur when the programmer places a `throw` statement in the path of the processor. Where structured exception handling is more a rigid mechanism for the OS to notify your application of external events, C++ exceptions are a tool made available to the programmer in order to better handle anomalies as they arise in application logic.

The general BNF syntax for C++ exceptions is as follows:

```
try-block :
    try compound-statement handler-list
handler-list :
    handler handler-list_opt
handler :
    catch ( exception-declaration ) compound-statement
exception-declaration :
    type-specifier-list declarator

type-specifier-list abstract-declarator

    type-specifier-list
...

throw-expression :
    throw assignment-expression_opt
```

So what does all that mean? Well, a sample is worth a thousand words. Listing 22.7 shows how simple it is to incorporate exception handling into a C++ application.

LISTING 22.7   A SIMPLE C++ EXCEPTION EXAMPLE

```cpp
int main(int argc, char* argv[])
{
    try
    {
        // lots of logic ultimately causes the world to degrade
        // to the point that your code gives up...
        throw "I'm melting...";
        throw 1.234; //never executed but would work
        throw 9; // also never executed but also valid
    }
    catch( int i )
    {
        printf("Saw the int exception %d\n", i);
    }
    catch( char * szCause )
    {
        printf("Saw the string exception - %s\n", szCause );
    }
    catch(...)     //ellipsis handler must be last
    {
        printf("Saw some other kind of exception");
    }

    return 0;
}
```

After looking at the structured exception-handling examples presented previously in this chapter, this should all seem pretty clear. Once again you wrap a section of code within a try block. This block of code is also known as a "guarded" block. At some point during the execution of the guarded block, an exception might (or in this example will absolutely) be raised. One or more handlers denoted by the catch keyword follow the try block. The type of the parameter passed during the throw operation determines which handler is entered. A "catch-all" (excuse the pun), default handler identified by an ellipsis may be included provided it's the last handler in the list. The handlers are "searched" in the order they appear after the try block. The search can continue up the call stack into any try/catch blocks that may appear in the current execution context.

After the exception is handled, execution continues with the statement following the last catch block of the try block that finally caught the exception. If the try block that caught the error is not the one who raised the exception, but rather one implemented higher up the call stack, the exception will cause the stack to be popped of all call frames subordinate to the function (or method) that caught the exception. That is, multiple functions or methods can be terminated simultaneously by throwing an exception handled somewhere up the call stack.

What if no exception is thrown? Execution continues until all statements within the try block are executed. Execution then jumps over all the catch blocks and continues from there. (In the sample code shown previously, execution would continue at the return 0; statement.)

What if no handler is found that is willing to process the exception? C++ specifies that a function called terminate() will be invoked. The default terminate() function raises an application modal dialog that informs the user that an unhandled exception has occurred and then terminates the application. Figure 22.2 shows what the terminate() dialog looks like.

FIGURE 22.2
Unhandled C++ exception dialog box.

The code within a catch block can only be entered through a thrown exception. It is illegal to try to enter a handler any other way. Handlers and exceptions are clearly a parallel code path that the programmer can take as logic dictates.

When an exception causes the stack to unwind, automatic variables are deleted. (Automatic variables are those allocated on the stack.) So if you create an automatic instance of a class, as Listing 22.8 does, the destructor of the class will be invoked when the stack unwinds.

LISTING 22.8 THROWING EXCEPTIONS WITH AUTOMATIC VARIABLES

```
int myFunc( void )
{
    CSimple Simple1;
    throw "Cool Stuff";
    return 0; // never reached
}
```

If, on the other hand, you create the instance of a class through new (or malloc some memory, open a file handle, and so on), the destructor will not be called and a resource leak will occur. Listing 22.9 exemplifies this potential problem.

LISTING 22.9 THROWING EXCEPTIONS WITH HEAP VARIABLES

```
int myFunc( void )
{
    CSimple * pSimple1 = new CSimple; // will not be deleted
    throw "Not So Cool Stuff";
    return 0; // never reached
}
```

You must take care to allocate resources in a way that coexists with your use of exception handlers. One approach is to allocate and deallocate all resources outside the scope of a try block. The try block and related exceptions are then used simply for logic or runtime errors that might occur during the course of execution. Another approach is to allocate resources within a try block, but use pointers and handles that are declared at sufficient scope that the exception handler can test for non-null pointers and handles and free up the resources in the event of an exception.

Defining a C++ Exception Class

As you have seen, C++ exceptions provide the mechanism to catch and handle an exception based on the type of the variable referenced in the throw statement. The previous examples dealt only with intrinsic C++ variable types: integers, singles, doubles, characters, character pointers, and so on. But C++ enables you to create additional types of variables through the use of structures, unions, and classes. What if you create a class called CException that supported saving the cause of the exception in a string that could be displayed to the user at an appropriate point in time? Could you throw the

CException class and have it be detected and handled in similar fashion to integers and strings? The answer is yes. Listing 22.10 provides a simple example.

LISTING 22.10   A SIMPLE CException IMPLEMENTATION

```
#include "stdafx.h"
#include "string.h"

class CException
{
private:
   int   m_iError;
   char  m_szError[255];

public:
   CException() { m_iError = 0; m_szError[0] = '\0'; }
   int GetErrno( void ) { return m_iError; }
   void SetErrno( int error ) { m_iError = error; }
   int GetErrorMessage( char * lpszError, unsigned uMaxError )
   {
      if ( lpszError && (uMaxError > strlen( m_szError )) )
      {
         strncpy( lpszError, m_szError, uMaxError );
         return 1;
      }
      return 0;
   }

   void SetErrorMessage( char * lpszError )
   {
      strncpy(m_szError, lpszError, 255);
      m_szError[ 255 ] = '\0';
   }
};

int SomeFunc( void )
{
   CException e;
   e.SetErrno( 99 );
   e.SetErrorMessage( "Throwing CExceptions" );
   throw e;
   return 0; // never reached
}

int main(int argc, char* argv[])
{
   try
   {
      SomeFunc();
   }
```

```
    catch( CException e )
    {
        char szerr[ 255 ] = "/0";
        e.GetErrorMessage( szerr, 255 );
        printf("Saw CException %d - %s\n", e.GetErrno(), szerr );
    }

    return 0;
}
```

MFC Exceptions

Given the intensely hot exception-handling capabilities of C++ and the coolness of MFC in general, the developers at Microsoft figured they had to combine the two and came up with MFC exceptions.

MFC defines its own CException class that is derived from CObject. As such, all MFC exception classes inherit the base functions of CObject. These include Dump(), AssertValid(), IsSerializable(), Serialize(), GetRuntimeClass(), and IsKindOf().

The IsKindOf() method is very useful when dealing with exceptions. Using IsKindOf() allows a generic CException handler to ascertain what kind of exception it is dealing with. If you plan on deriving any of your own exception classes based on CException, you should make certain they contain runtime class information required by IsKindOf(). You can accomplish this by using the DECLARE_DYNAMIC and IMPLEMENT_DYNAMIC macros defined by MFC. (You'll see an example of using these macros a bit later in the chapter.)

The CException class adds a few additional functions to the CObject implementation. The added methods provide a base level of functionality that all CException-derived classes will want to utilize. These methods include the CException constructor, Delete(), GetErrorMessage(), and ReportError().

The CException constructor has the following signature:

CException(BOOL b_AutoDelete);

The default value for b_AutoDelete is TRUE. (There are actually two constructors. One takes zero parameters and sets m_bAutoDelete to TRUE. The second constructor requires a BOOL parameter that is used to set m_bAutoDelete to either TRUE or FALSE.)

The member method Delete() works in conjunction with the CException::m_bAutoDelete flag to better handle the differences between stack-based and heap-based exceptions. The implementation of Delete() is pretty simple. It checks to see if the m_bAutoDelete flag is set and if so it calls "delete this."

The reason MFC provides the m_bAutoDelete flag and the Delete() method is to make it easy for exception handlers to delete the exception object when they are finished with it. When exception handlers are passed an exception object, the handler doesn't know if the exception object was allocated on the stack, created on the heap through the new operator, or created as a global or static object. The exception handler is responsible for deleting the exception object when it is done with it. (After all, the code that created the exception object will not be returned to after the exception is thrown. Someone's got to delete the exception object!) The combination of properly setting the m_bAutoDelete flag, in conjunction with ensuring that the exception handler calls Delete() when it's through processing the exception, helps ensure that no memory leaks are caused by the exception process.

The GetErrorMessage() method of CException is intended to be overridden by your CException-derived class. The base class implementation does little other than set the return values to 0. The signature is slightly different from the GetErrorMessage() implemented in the example shown earlier. CException::GetErrorMessage() looks like this:

```
BOOL GetErrorMessage( LPTSTR lpszError,
                      UINT uMaxError, PUINT pnHelpContext = NULL );
```

The lpszError and uMaxError parameters work pretty much like the sample implementation. The lpszError parameter points to a buffer where the error message should be stored. The uMaxError parameter specifies the maximum number of bytes that can be returned, which probably corresponds with the size of the buffer pointed to by lpszError. The additional, and optional, parameter is a pointer to an unsigned int that is used to return a help context resource id. As previously mentioned, the base class returns a zero-length error string, a 0 for a help context id, and FALSE as its completion status. Derived classes will need to implement a specialization of this method providing valid error strings and help ids.

The ReportError() method completes the base class. The signature for this method looks like this:

```
CException::ReportError( UINT nType = MB_OK, UINT nError = 0 );
```

ReportError raises an application modal dialog box based on the string and help context id returned by GetErrorMessage(). If GetErrorMessage() returns FALSE (probably because the derived class didn't implement it), the nError parameter is used as a string table resource ID that will be used to display a modal dialog box.

That completes the CException base class. Let's look at how MFC extends the functionality of the base class by deriving several specializations.

MFC `CException`-Derived Classes

MFC uses exceptions to inform application logic when things go awry. The following sections provide an overview of the exception classes provided with MFC.

CMemoryException

`CMemoryException` is used by MFC to inform applications that an out-of-memory condition has occurred. No additional public member variables or methods are available.

Microsoft's implementation of the new handler throws the `CMemoryException`. If you choose to replace `new()` with your own rendition, you must remember to throw `CMemoryExceptions` too. Other parts of MFC count on `CMemoryException` to trap low-memory conditions. If you don't throw the exception, other parts of MFC will behave in an undefined fashion.

It is recommended that you use `AfxThrowMemoryException()` rather than creating a instance of `CMemoryException` and throwing it yourself.

CNotSupportedException

The `CNotSupportedException` is raised by MFC when an application requests an unsupported feature. There are no public members or methods beyond those provided by `CException` to qualify the exception.

There are about 30 instances in MFC that throw the `CNotSupportedException`. They can be found in the `CArchive`, `CMemFile`, `CDataExchange`, `CStdioFile`, `CInternetFile`, `CGopherFile`, and `CDataExchange` classes, among others.

If you want to raise a `CNotSupportedException`, you should use the `AfxThrowNotSupportedException()` function.

CArchiveException

The `CArchiveException` is raised by `CArchive` member functions if something goes wrong while serializing a class instance. `CArchiveException` has one public member that can be used to determine the cause of the exception. Surprisingly, it is called m_cause. There is an enumeration associated with m_cause that provides a portable (OS-independent) error code. Table 22.1 lists the possible values `CArchiveExeception`'s m_cause can take on.

TABLE 22.1   `CArchiveException::m_cause` VALUES

Constant	Description
`CArchiveException::none`	Encountered no errors
`CArchiveException::generic`	Encountered an unspecified error
`CArchiveException::readOnly`	Attempted to write to a read-only archive
`CArchiveException::endOfFile`	Encountered end of file during a read
`CArchiveException::writeOnly`	Attempted to read from a write-only archive
`CArchiveException::badIndex`	Encountered an invalid file format
`CArchiveException::badClass`	Attempted to read an object into an object of the wrong type
`CArchiveException::badSchema`	Attempted to read an object with a different version of the class

Note that `CFileException` also has an `m_cause` member variable that takes on a similar set of values. The two enumerations are distinct.

The `AfxThrowArchiveException()` function can be used to raise a `CArchiveException` if you ever need to. Using the AFX function to raise the exception is the recommended procedure.

CFileException

`CFileException` is used to inform applications of file system-related errors. `CFileException` extends the base functionality of `CException` by including several public data members and methods that help determine which file has run into a problem and hence caused the exception to be raised.

The public member `m_strFileName` contains the name of the file that is associated with the exception. This is valuable because without it the application would have to keep track of which file was being accessed when the exception occurs. Making the association at the point of failure is a much better solution.

The `m_cause` public member provides a "portable" (non-OS-specific) error code. It will take on a value based on an enumeration contained in `CFileException`. Table 22.2 provides a list of possible values.

TABLE 22.2   CfileException::m_cause VALUES

Constant	Description
CFileException::none	Encountered no errors
CFileException::generic	Encountered an unspecified error
CFileException::fileNotFound	Could not locate the file
CFileException::badPath	Encountered an invalid path
CFileException::tooManyOpenFiles	Exceeded the maximum number of open files
CFileException::accessDenied	Could not access the file
CFileException::invalidFile	Attempted to use an invalid file handle
CFileException::removeCurrentDir	Could not remove the current working directory
CFileException::directoryFull	Could not create any additional directory entries
CFileException::badSeek	Could not set the file pointer
CFileException::hardIO	Encountered a hardware error
CFileException::sharingViolation	Could not load SHARE.EXE, or a shared region was locked
CFileException::lockViolation	Attempted to lock a region that was already locked
CFileException::diskFull	Attempted to write to full disk
CFileException::endOfFile	Reached end of file

The m_IosEerror public data member is a LONG that contains the Input/Output System-specific error code associated with the exception. This member contains values from either error.h or errno.h. If MFC was ported to a new operating environment that had a pre-existing set of error codes for the disk subsystem, they would be reflected in this member variable.

The idea is that the exception carries along both a portable and an IOS-specific code. The application can use whichever it pleases depending on the level of detail required.

AfxThrowFileException() is the recommended method of creating and throwing a CFileException. AFXThrowFileException() takes the portable cause, the IosError, and the filename as inputs, creates a CException object on the heap using the new operator, and then throws the exception.

The CFileException constructor takes three parameters: the portable "cause," the IosError, and the lpszArchiveName. All will default to 0 if not specified.

> **NOTE**
>
> The documentation on the MSDN CD-ROM indicates that only two parameters are accepted by the constructor: the cause and the `IosError`. One nice thing about MFC is that you get the source. When in doubt, use the source (Luke)!

Two public conversion methods, `OsErrorToException()` and `ErrnoToException()`, are used by `CFileException` when implementing two other public methods: `ThrowOsError()` and `ThrowErrno()`. The conversion functions are used to convert the IOS-specific errors supplied as parameters to `ThrowOsError()` and `ThrowErrno()` into a portable format required by the `CFileException` constructor. (The gory details can be found in ..\MFC\SRC\Filex.cpp.)

The `OSErrorToException( LONG IosError )` method is used to convert an IOS error (as found in error.h) into a portable error equivalent. The IOS error space might be more extensive than the portable error space. Hence the method might return `CFileException::generic` if there is no exact mapping. `ErrnoToException( int Errno )` performs the similar conversion for DOS errors as found in errno.h.

`ThrowOsError()` takes the IOS error code (from error.h) and the filename and, after converting the IOS error code to a portable "cause," invokes `AfxThrowFileException()` in order to get the dirty work done.

`ThrowErrno()` takes the DOS errno (from errno.h) and the filename and, after converting the errno to a portable "cause," invokes `AfxThrowFileException()` as well.

In both cases the `m_IosError` member of `CFileException()` is set to the OS-specific error code. Maybe it comes from error.h. Maybe it comes from errno.h. The application will need to know what it's working with if it uses the `m_IosError` public member. You're probably better off using the portable version if at all possible.

CResourceException

MFC raises the `CResourceException` when Windows cannot find or allocate a requested resource. No additional public are members available by which to qualify the exception.

There are about 30 incidences in MFC where the `CResourceException` is raised. Examples of activities that cause MFC to raise this exception include creating brushes, bitmaps, mutexes, events, loading strings, accessing sockets, and so on.

The `AfxThrowResourceException()` function is the recommended way to raise a `CResourceException`.

COleException

MFC raises this exception whenever an OLE error occurs. A public member called m_sc contains the error code that caused the exception. The m_sc data member is of type SCODE, which is an OLE status code. OLE status codes contain bit-mapped fields for severity, context, facility, and code.

There are two versions of AfxThrowOleException(). One expects an SCODE as a parameter, whereas the other expects an HRESULT. If an HRESULT is passed, AfxThrowOleException() converts the HRESULT to an SCODE and then creates an instance of COleException on the heap prior to throwing the exception.

COleException has one static public method called Process(). You can pass COleException::Process() a pointer to any CException-derived object and in return you get an OLE SCODE back that describes the error associated with the passed exception. So if you pass a CMemoryException, you get back an E_OUTOFMEMORY SCODE. Or if you pass in a CNotSupportedException, you get back an E_NOTIMPL SCODE.

CDbException

MFC uses the CDbException to alert applications about errors raised by ODBC database accesses. (A separate exception class is available to return errors associated with DAO database accesses.)

CDbException has three public member variables that help clarify the cause of the exception. The m_nRetCode variable is of type RETCODE and essentially represents the error value returned by the ODBC API. Table 22.3 provides a list of the possible return codes.

TABLE 22.3   CDbException::m_RetCode VALUES

Constant	Description
AFX_SQL_ERROR_API_CONFORMANCE	The driver used when calling CDatabase::OpenEx or Cdatabase::Open does not conform to required ODBC level.
AFX_SQL_ERROR_CONNECT_FAIL	The connection to the data source failed.
AFX_SQL_ERROR_DATA_TRUNCATED	Insufficient storage was provided for the requested data.
AFX_SQL_ERROR_DYNASET_NOT_SUPPORTED	The driver does not support dynasets.
AFX_SQL_ERROR_EMPTY_COLUMN_LIST	No columns were identified in the record field exchange (RFX) function calls in your DoFieldExchange override.

continues

TABLE 22.3   CONTINUED

Constant	Description
AFX_SQL_ERROR_FIELD_SCHEMA_MISMATCH	The RFX function(s) specified in the DoFieldExchange override is not compatible with the column data types of the recordset.
AFX_SQL_ERROR_ILLEGAL_MODE	CRecordset::Update was called without previously calling CRecordset::AddNew or CRecordset::Edit.
AFX_SQL_ERROR_LOCK_MODE_NOT_SUPPORTED	The ODBC driver does not support locking.
AFX_SQL_ERROR_MULTIPLE_ROWS_AFFECTED	A call to CRecordset::Update or Delete was made for a table with no unique key, and changes were made to multiple records.
AFX_SQL_ERROR_NO_CURRENT_RECORD	An attempt was made to edit or delete a previously deleted record.
AFX_SQL_ERROR_NO_POSITIONED_UPDATES	A request for a dynaset failed because the ODBC driver does not support positioned updates.
AFX_SQL_ERROR_NO_ROWS_AFFECTED	A call to CRecordset::Update or Delete was made, but the record could no longer be found.
AFX_SQL_ERROR_ODBC_LOAD_FAILED	An attempt to load the ODBC.DLL failed; Windows could not find or could not load this DLL. This error is fatal.
AFX_SQL_ERROR_ODBC_V2_REQUIRED	A request for a dynaset failed because a Level 2-compliant ODBC driver was required.
AFX_SQL_ERROR_RECORDSET_FORWARD_ONLY	An attempt to scroll did not succeed because the data source did not support backward scrolling.
AFX_SQL_ERROR_SNAPSHOT_NOT_SUPPORTED	A call to CRecordset::Open failed because it isn't supported by the driver.
AFX_SQL_ERROR_SQL_CONFORMANCE	CDatabase::OpenEx or CDatabase::Open failed because the driver does not conform to the required ODBC SQL Conformance level of Minimum (SQL_OSC_MINIMUM).
AFX_SQL_ERROR_SQL_NO_TOTAL	The ODBC driver was unable to specify the total size of a CLongBinary data value.
AFX_SQL_ERROR_RECORDSET_READONLY	An attempt to update a read-only recordset failed, or the data source is read-only.

SQL_ERROR	A function failed because the error message returned by ::SQLError is stored in the m_strError data member.
SQL_INVALID_HANDLE	A function failed due to an invalid environment handle, connection handle, or statement handle.

CDbException also includes a public member that describes the error through a string. m_strError contains a zero-terminated string of TCHARs that is initialized at the same time as m_nRetCode.

One additional public member is provided in order to help the application determine the cause of the error. This is the m_strStateNativeOrigin string. It is built of three components, as the name implies. The information is basically a repackaged version of the information returned by ::SQLError(). The format of the string is "State:%s,Native:%ld,Origin:%s". An example of an m_strStateNativeOrigin string would be "State:S0022,Native:207,Origin:[Microsoft][ODBC SQL Server Driver][SQL Server]".

An AfxThrowDbException() function is available for those who would like to generate CDbExceptions.

COleDispatchException

MFC provides the COleDispatchException exception for use with errors associated with the OLE IDispatch interface. IDispatch is a key part of implementing OLE automation. This exception is very closely tied to the application that is being automated, namely the one you're writing. The error codes, error strings, help context ids, help files, and so on returned by the public members of COleDispathException are all related to the application being automated.

Several public methods can be used to qualify the exception. m_wCode is an application-specific error code describing the cause of the exception. The m_strDescription provides a textual representation of m_wCode. The m_dwHelpContext is a DWORD that identifies a help context associated with the exception. The m_strHelpFile identifies the help file for which m_dwHelpContext refers. The m_strSource identifies the application that generated the exception.

Two versions of AfxThrowOleDispatchException() are available to aid in throwing COleDispatchExceptions. Both accept parameters for specifying the m_wCode and w_dwHelpContext values. The difference between the two versions is that one accepts lpszDescription, whereas the other accepts nDescriptionID, which is used to reference a string table from which the error description is pulled.

AfxGetApp()->m_pszHelpFilePath is used to fill in m_strHelpFile. AfxGetAppName() is used to fill in the m_strSource member variable.

CUserException

The CUserException is provided by MFC as a means of handling abnormal events that might occur while executing some user-requested process. Let's say your application performs a statistical analysis of stock market data. Somewhere during the processing, say a dozen method calls down in the bowels of the logic, a critical error occurs. Rather than unwinding the stack by returning from each method call (which means making sure each method knows how to handle error responses returned by called methods), the application programmer might choose to throw a CUserException.

Use AfxThrowUserException() to raise CUserExceptions. AfxThrowUserException() takes no parameters.

CDaoException

MFC database classes based on DAO (Data Access Objects) raise the CDaoException when things go awry. Several public members and methods are available to help determine the cause of the exception.

The m_scode public member contains an OLE SCODE that describes the error. You probably won't use the member variable too often because numerous other variables are available to aid in diagnosing the exception.

The m_nAfxDaoError is a more useful source of information. It contains the extended DAO error code associated with the exception. For more information about DAO extended error codes, refer to the Chapter 18, "MFC Database Processing." Table 22.4 shows the list of possible values.

TABLE 22.4 CdaoException::m_nAfxDaoError VALUES

Constant	Description
NO_AFX_DAO_ERROR	The most recent operation could have produced an error from DAO or OLE. Check m_pErrorInfo and possibly m_scode for more information.
AFX_DAO_ERROR_ENGINE_INITIALIZATION	An error occurred while initializing the Microsoft Jet database engine.
AFX_DAO_ERROR_DFX_BIND	An address used in a DAO record field exchange (DFX) function does not exist or is invalid.

| AFX_DAO_ERROR_OBJECT_NOT_OPEN | An attempt to open a recordset based on a `querydef` or a `tabledef` object failed because the object was not in an open state. |

The `m_pErrorInfo` public data member contains a pointer to a `CDaoErrorInfo` object. This object allows access to an error code, a textual description of the error, the name of the application or data source that generated the error, a path to a help file, and a help context id. This is probably the most valuable member of the `CDaoException` class.

When a `CDaoException` is raised, `m_pErrorInfo` is initialized with information regarding the most recent error. But you can extend the benefit of `m_pErrorInfo` by using two other methods made available through `CdaoException`: `GetErrorCount()` and `GetErrorInfo()`.

`GetErrorCount()` returns a `short` that indicates the number of error objects in the database engine's Errors collection. You can loop through the available errors to gain more insight into the specific cause of an exception. The value returned by `GetErrorCount()` determines the range of valid index values you can pass to `GetErrorInfo()`. Calling `GetErrorInfo()` with an index within the range of `0 .. ( GetErrorCount() - 1 )` will load `m_pErrorInfo` with new information relating to the requested error instance.

`CDaoExceptions` are usually raised by the MFC framework. You probably won't find much reason to raise your own exceptions. An `AfxThrowDaoException()` function is available in the unlikely event you want to throw a `CDaoException`. `AfxThrowDaoException()` takes no parameters. Rather it relies on the DAO database engine to provide the information required to fill in the exception.

CInternetException

MFC contains a number of classes directly targeted at making Internet access easier. These classes include `CInternetSession`, `CInternetFile`, `CFtpConnection`, `CGopherConnection`, `CHttpConnection`, and `CHttpFile`, all of which throw `CInternetExceptions` when things go awry.

The `CInternetException` contains two public data members that can shed light on the cause of the exception. The `m_dwError` member contains an error code based on the system errors delineated in WINERROR.H or the Internet class-specific error values found in WININET.H.

The second member element of `CInternetException` is `m_dwContext`. The value contained in `m_dwContext` is the same value assigned to a `CInternetSession` through the constructor. The `dwContext` is important when using asynchronous Internet operations because it identifies the CInternetSession when callbacks occur as the processing of Internet requests proceeds.

An AfxThrowInternetException() function is available if you want to throw your own exception. AfxThrowInternetException() takes two parameters: the error code and the context identifier.

Deriving Your Own MFC-Compliant Exception Objects

As you have seen, MFC provides a CException base class from which several MFC-supplied derivations exist. You can use the member methods and data elements of the MFC derivations when you catch exceptions thrown by the framework. You can also throw your own exceptions using the AfxThrow... functions provided for all the MFC-supplied exception classes.

Taking this one step further, you can derive your own specializations based on CException. You can then throw and catch instances of these exceptions as appropriate and beneficial to your application. You can include any public data members or methods that make sense within the context of exception handling.

Deriving CException-based classes is similar to deriving any other C++ class except that you need to include the DECLARE_DYNAMIC macro in the header file and the IMPLEMENT_DYNAMIC macro in the implementation (cpp) file. These macros work together with MFC to provide runtime type information for the derived exception class. That is, this enables use of the IsKindOf() method, which is quite valuable if you want to write exception handlers that conditionalize their logic based on the type of CException they are dealing with.

Let's start by looking at the header file (see Listing 22.11) for a new exception class, CAppException.

LISTING 22.11   CAppException HEADER FILE

```
class CAppException : public CException
{
   DECLARE_DYNAMIC( CAppException );
public:
   unsigned long m_ulTheCause;
public:
   CAppException() { m_ulTheCause = 0; }
   CAppException( unsigned long cause ) { m_ulTheCause = cause; }
```

```
    BOOL GetErrorMessage( LPTSTR lpszError,
                          UINT nMaxError,
                          PUINT pnHelpContext = NULL );
};
```

Note that the class is derived from CException. I've included the DECLARE_DYNAMIC macro as the first line in the class definition. The DECLARE_DYNAMIC macro can be placed anywhere in the header file, but putting it in the class definition itself is totally appropriate. CAppException includes one public data member called m_ulTheCause. It can be initialized through the constructor. The class also implements its own version of GetErrorMessage(). This is important because the ReportError() implementation from the base class utilizes GetErrorMessage() when building a dialog box used to inform the user of the error.

Next let's look at the implementation (cpp) file shown in Listing 22.12.

LISTING 22.12   CAppException IMPLEMENTATION

```
#include "stdafx.h"
#include "TestExceptions.h"

IMPLEMENT_DYNAMIC( CAppException, CException )

BOOL CAppException::GetErrorMessage
(
   LPTSTR lpszError,
   UINT nMaxError,
   PUINT pnHelpContext
)
{
   TCHAR szErr[ 255 ];
   stprintf( szErr, "Fatal Error - %ld", m_ulTheCause );

   // check if the buffer is too small
   if ( nMaxError <= _tcslen( szErr ) )
      return FALSE;

   tcsncpy( lpszError, szErr, nMaxError );
   if (pnHelpContext ) *pnHelpContext = 0;
   return TRUE;
}
```

Pretty simple stuff. The IMPLEMENT_DYNAMIC macro is included after the header files. It tells MFC that CAppException is derived from CException. This is the second step required to enable runtime type checking within MFC.

Next, there is a simple implementation of `GetErrorMessage()`. The `m_ulTheCause` data member is converted into a string. No help contexts are associated with this simple example, so the value of zero is returned through the supplied pointer.

Now let's look at a simple usage of `CAppException` in Listing 22.13.

LISTING 22.13   USING `CAppException`

```
int CTestMFCExceptions::TestAppException( void )
{
   unsigned short szErrString[ 255 ];
   int i = -1;

   try
   {
      CAppException * pe = new CAppException( 99 );
      throw( pe );
   }
   catch( CAppException * e )
   {
      e->GetErrorMessage( (LPTSTR)&szErrString, 255 );
      e->ReportError();
      e->Delete();
      ::MessageBox(NULL,"Saw custom App exception...","",MB_OK );
   }

   return 0;
}
```

The `try` block does nothing more than create an instance of `CAppException` on the heap through the new operator. The constructor initializes `m_ulTheCause` to 99. The exception is then thrown.

The `catch` block (handler) looks exclusively for `CAppException` pointers. The handler calls `GetErrorMessage()` just to prove it works. (Use the debugger to verify it for yourself.) `ReportError()` is then called to raise a dialog box identifying the error. Finally, the `Delete()` method of the base class is called to ensure the exception object is removed from the heap. If you fail to call `Delete()`, a memory leak will be detected and reported by the debugger.

Deleting Exceptions

As pointed out several places within this chapter, memory and resource leaks can arise from using exceptions. One cause is the exception object itself. MFC typically creates an exception on the heap through the new operator. It then throws a pointer to the exception.

After the exception is handled, the processor never returns to the logic that threw the exception. But the exception must be removed from the heap somehow. The convention is for the handler to delete the exception object when it is through with it.

Another way to create an exception object is to allocate it on the stack, as is the case with all automatic variables. When the exception is thrown, the exception object remains valid until the exception is caught and handled. Because the object is not allocated on the heap, it would be wrong to call `delete` on the exception object. Rather, the exception object will automatically be removed from the stack when the exception processing causes the call stack to unwind.

Another source of exception objects is static variables. Static exception objects live for the duration of the application. The exception handler should not attempt to delete a static exception object because it did not come off the heap. The exception object will remain in memory after the exception-handling logic unwinds the stack. It can be reused at other times during execution of the application.

To reiterate, the exception handler may be called with exception objects that are stack-, heap-, or static-based. The exception handler has no way to differentiate how an exception object it catches was initially allocated. MFC places the responsibility of noting how an exception was allocated on the creator of the exception object. As you saw earlier in the section that describes the `CException` constructor, the `CException` object maintains a data member called `m_bAutoDelete`. This flag must be set properly by the creator of the exception object. If the flag is set to `TRUE`, the `delete` operator will be called when the `Delete()` method is called. The `m_bAutoDelete` flag is defaulted to `TRUE`. Hence, when allocating exception objects off the heap (as MFC typically does), there is no need to specify any parameter to the constructor. If, on the other hand, you allocate a stack or static exception object, you must remember to set `m_bAutoDelete` by passing a `FALSE` to the `CException()` constructor.

The exception handler must cooperate with MFC by calling the exception object's `Delete()` (not `delete`) operator when it is through processing the exception. The exception handler doesn't need to be concerned about how an exception object was allocated. The rule is to simply call the `Delete()` operator in all cases and let the base class logic resolve the issue. This sounds simple enough. But there is always the proverbial "exception to the rule."

One thing an exception handler can choose to do with an exception is to throw it (or partially process the exception and then throw it), so someone else in the exception handler stack can pick it up and continue the processing. (Kind of like a game of hot potato.) In this case, the handler should not `Delete()` the exception object. If `Delete()` was called, bad things would happen when the invalid object pointer was referenced. So remember not to Delete() an exception object unless you are really sure the application is done processing it.

Using MFC Exception Macros

When MFC first came out, C++ exceptions were still being kicked around by the standards committees. Concurrently, the general consensus (arguably) in the programming community was that Borland had a bit of a lead on MSVC 1 and MFC 1 with its IDE and OWL implementations, which at the time were quite impressive products.

For whatever reason, lack of industry direction or competitive pressure to get a product out in a timely fashion, the initial version of MFC offered exception handling only through nonstandard macros. The macros worked with CException-derived objects exclusively and were not portable. (Borland offered C++ exceptions that were very much in line with the emerging standards at that time.)

The MFC exception macros appeared similar to the emerging standards for C++ exceptions. The macros available included TRY, THROW, and CATCH. But there were differences between the C++ exceptions and the MFC macros. The CATCH macro required two parameters—one that identified the class of object the handler should process, whereas the second parameter was the pointer to the exception object to be processed. Also, multiple catch blocks were delineated by AND_CATCH and END_CATCH macros. Thus, you would get something of the form shown in Listing 22.14.

LISTING 22.14 USING MFC EXCEPTION MACROS

```
TRY
{
}
CATCH(CMemoryException, pe)
{
}
AND_CATCH(CFileException, pe)
{
}
AND_CATCH(CUserException, pe)
{
}
END_CATCH
```

Another difference was the THROW_LAST macro, which substituted for the C++ throw pe construct and allowed for rethrowing an exception from within a CATCH block.

MFC continued to offer the exception macros as the sole solution for exception processing until version 3. MFC version 3 provided exception handling based on C++ exceptions, which had subsequently been added to MSVC.

You could have a legacy application that uses the macro forms of exception handling. (MFC itself still uses the macro form internally.) If you find yourself dealing with the macro versions, you should seriously consider porting the logic to C++ exceptions. (You will still use the MFC CException-derived classes. You will simply do away with the MFC exception macros by replacing them with the C++ keywords.)

The steps to converting from MFC exception macros to C++ exception keywords are pretty straightforward:

1. Replace TRY macros with the try keyword.
2. Replace CATCH and AND_CATCH macros with the catch keyword.
3. Change the signature of the CATCH invocation from (CException, pe) to (CException * pe).
4. Delete the END_CATCH macros.
5. Add calls to the Delete() method to exception handlers as required by MFC.
6. Replace THROW_LAST macros with throw pe as appropriate.

That's all there is to it. You will be rewarded by a smaller executable and more flexible exception handling that can detect C++ intrinsic types such as int, float, char *, and so on in addition to CException-derived objects.

Mixing Exceptions

There are limitations when mixing the various forms of exceptions discussed in this chapter. In general it's best to avoid mixing exception mechanisms within a single method or function.

Structured exception handlers need to be isolated to separate functions. Do not mix C++ exceptions with structured exceptions in the same function. You can use both forms within the same program without a problem as long as each is segregated. There are differences in the way each exception mechanism implements stack frame processing that requires separate stack frames.

You can mix MFC macros and C++ exception syntax within an application, but as mentioned earlier, it is much better to convert the legacy MFC macro code to the newer C++-based exception syntax.

MFC exception classes can be freely mixed with intrinsic C++ variable types when using the C++ form of exception handling. This is the preferred and recommended method of handling all exceptions other than structured exceptions.

Summary

This chapter looked at three major implementations of exception handling: Win32 structured exception handling, C++ exception handling, and MFC exception handling. You have seen how exceptions can be used to trap system-level errors that would otherwise cause an application to terminate without saving state or freeing resources. You have learned how exceptions can be used to handle error conditions raised by the MFC framework. You have also looked at ways to use exceptions to simplify the handling of error conditions within application-specific logic.

All the code snippets seen in this chapter are available in their complete form as part of the CD-ROM distributed with this book. Use the examples to experiment with exceptions in order to further your knowledge.

MFC and the Web

PART
VI

MFC and DHTML

by Kenn Scribner

IN THIS CHAPTER

CHAPTER 23

DHTML, MSIE, and the Internet

Until the introduction of *dynamic HTML*, Web pages were static ones presented to the browser. HTML (Hypertext Markup Language) was introduced to describe the visual formatting of information sent to Web browsers. After the page was published on the Web, the HTML-formatted information was simply to be viewed. If anything was to be changed, a request would be issued to and response received from the Web server, resulting in new HTML information being shipped to the client system.

When Microsoft designed Internet Explorer (IE) 4, though, they changed the rules of the game. Along with the usual Web browser functionality, Microsoft designed an HTML object model it called *Dynamic HTML* (DHTML). The whole idea behind DHTML was to allow scripted elements embedded within the HTML document to access and modify the contents of the Web page without interaction with the Web server. This makes for more snappy Web page performance, especially when the user's Internet connection is over a modem.

It wasn't long after DHTML's introduction that programmers realized DHTML was easily accessible from Visual Basic. The core of the Internet Explorer Web browser is an ActiveX control, and because ActiveX controls were originally designed to replace the Visual Basic Extension (VBX) controls, the IE ActiveX control (I'll call it MSIE for short) was and is a natural fit within Visual Basic.

I say "just another" ActiveX control, but this particular control packs a wallop. The Internet Explorer Web browser you see when you run IE 4 is a thin application built around this ActiveX control. MSIE handles the entire Web browsing task for the application, which includes visual formatting and rendering, HTML parsing, and even such arcane tasks as the user's "favorites" storage and retrieval. It manages its own window, handles server downloads asynchronously (and is multithreaded), and deals with several protocols such as the popular *File Transfer Protocol* (FTP) and *Hypertext Transport Protocol* (HTTP).

In addition to the browsing aspects, it provides you with DHTML. What this really means is that you are now able to access the browser's HTML document, parse through the HTML, and do with the results as your application requires. The truly exciting part is that you aren't limited to read-only HTML access—you can also modify the HTML contents on-the-fly.

> **TIP**
>
> The sample programs in this chapter don't do DHTML justice from an artistic standpoint (that subject is a book in itself). They will show you how to access DHTML from Visual C++. I highly recommend that you visit the Microsoft Web site to see some of the amazing things you can do with DHTML. Many of Microsoft's pages use DHTML to enhance the page's impact or present information in a new and different way.

In this chapter you'll see some of the exciting things you can do with DHTML using MFC. But before I get into the details of DHTML, I need to explain how you use the MSIE ActiveX control, both in a document/view scenario and from a dialog box. After you have MSIE working in your application, you can invoke its DHTML COM interfaces.

Using the Internet Explorer Web ActiveX Control

When using MSIE with Visual C++ 6, you have two primary alternatives. First, if you're interested in using the standard MFC document/view architecture, you can use the new CHtmlView class in place of CView, or some other view class. And second, you can insert MSIE into a dialog box just as you would any other ActiveX control. Both methods are very easy to implement at least as far as activating the browser control is concerned. I'll begin with an overview of the basic capabilities of the control and then discuss its use in your applications.

Internet Explorer ActiveX Control Basics

The total functionality MSIE exposes comes from many files, but the primary file is named shdocvw.dll. This file *is* MSIE for all intents and purposes. The other files have more to do with Internet communication than the actual browsing process (see Chapter 25, "WinInet Programming"). In this section, I'll address the browsing aspect of MSIE. I'll defer the DHTML aspect until later in the chapter.

MSIE is an ActiveX control, and as such it also exposes several COM interfaces. The Web browser COM interface itself is called IWebBrowser2. Probably the easiest way to grasp what this interface provides you is to examine Listing 23.1, which is the code Developer Studio generates for you when you insert MSIE into your application. The length of Listing 23. 1 alone gives you some idea as to the power this control wields!

> **NOTE**
>
> The function names and parameters you see in Listing 23.1 are valid only when MSIE is inserted into your application by Developer Studio. As with all ActiveX controls you insert, Developer Studio queries the ActiveX control for the methods and properties it exposes and creates a C++ wrapper for you. This is what you see in Listing 23.1. The effect of this is that the method signatures differ if you call `IWebBrowser2` directly. There is a direct correlation, though, so reading about `IWebBrowser2` in the online help should help you understand the use of functions in Listing 23.1 that aren't readily apparent to you at first glance.

LISTING 23.1   WEBBROSWER2.H, THE GENERATED IWebBrowser2 DECLARATION FILE

```
#if !defined(AFX_WEBBROWSER2_H__A1582E0F_A1BC_11D2_8329
➥_B28A8D2EBF19__INCLUDED_)
#define AFX_WEBBROWSER2_H__A1582E0F_A1BC_11D2_8329
➥_B28A8D2EBF19__INCLUDED_

#if _MSC_VER > 1000
#pragma once
#endif // _MSC_VER > 1000
// Machine generated IDispatch wrapper class(es) created by Microsoft
// Visual C++

// NOTE: Do not modify the contents of this file.  If this class is
// regenerated by  Microsoft Visual C++, your modifications
// will be overwritten.

/////////////////////////////////////////////////////////////////////
// CWebBrowser2 wrapper class

class CWebBrowser2 : public CWnd
{
protected:
   DECLARE_DYNCREATE(CWebBrowser2)
public:
   CLSID const& GetClsid()
   {
      static CLSID const clsid
         = { 0x8856f961, 0x340a, 0x11d0,
            ➥{ 0xa9, 0x6b, 0x0, 0xc0, 0x4f, 0xd7, 0x5, 0xa2 } };
      return clsid;
```

```
      }
      virtual BOOL Create(LPCTSTR lpszClassName,
          LPCTSTR lpszWindowName, DWORD dwStyle,
          const RECT& rect,
          CWnd* pParentWnd, UINT nID,
          CCreateContext* pContext = NULL)
      { return CreateControl(GetClsid(), lpszWindowName, dwStyle,
      ➥rect, pParentWnd, nID); }

       BOOL Create(LPCTSTR lpszWindowName, DWORD dwStyle,
          const RECT& rect, CWnd* pParentWnd, UINT nID,
          CFile* pPersist = NULL, BOOL bStorage = FALSE,
          BSTR bstrLicKey = NULL)
      { return CreateControl(GetClsid(), lpszWindowName,
      ➥dwStyle, rect, pParentWnd, nID,
          pPersist, bStorage, bstrLicKey); }

// Attributes
public:

// Operations
public:
      void GoBack();
      void GoForward();
      void GoHome();
      void GoSearch();
      void Navigate(LPCTSTR URL, VARIANT* Flags, VARIANT*
      ➥TargetFrameName, VARIANT* PostData, VARIANT* Headers);
      void Refresh();
      void Refresh2(VARIANT* Level);
      void Stop();
      LPDISPATCH GetApplication();
      LPDISPATCH GetParent();
      LPDISPATCH GetContainer();
      LPDISPATCH GetDocument();
      BOOL GetTopLevelContainer();
      CString GetType();
      long GetLeft();
      void SetLeft(long nNewValue);
      long GetTop();
      void SetTop(long nNewValue);
      long GetWidth();
      void SetWidth(long nNewValue);
      long GetHeight();
      void SetHeight(long nNewValue);
      CString GetLocationName();
      CString GetLocationURL();
      BOOL GetBusy();
      void Quit();
      void ClientToWindow(long* pcx, long* pcy);
```

23

MFC AND
DHTML

continues

LISTING 23.1   CONTINUED

```
    void PutProperty(LPCTSTR Property_, const VARIANT& vtValue);
    VARIANT GetProperty_(LPCTSTR Property_);
    CString GetName();
    long GetHwnd();
    CString GetFullName();
    CString GetPath();
    BOOL GetVisible();
    void SetVisible(BOOL bNewValue);
    BOOL GetStatusBar();
    void SetStatusBar(BOOL bNewValue);
    CString GetStatusText();
    void SetStatusText(LPCTSTR lpszNewValue);
    long GetToolBar();
    void SetToolBar(long nNewValue);
    BOOL GetMenuBar();
    void SetMenuBar(BOOL bNewValue);
    BOOL GetFullScreen();
    void SetFullScreen(BOOL bNewValue);
    void Navigate2(VARIANT* URL, VARIANT* Flags, VARIANT*
    ➥TargetFrameName, VARIANT* PostData, VARIANT* Headers);
    long QueryStatusWB(long cmdID);
    void ExecWB(long cmdID, long cmdexecopt, VARIANT* pvaIn,
    ➥VARIANT* pvaOut);
    void ShowBrowserBar(VARIANT* pvaClsid, VARIANT* pvarShow,
    ➥VARIANT* pvarSize);
    long GetReadyState();
    BOOL GetOffline();
    void SetOffline(BOOL bNewValue);
    BOOL GetSilent();
    void SetSilent(BOOL bNewValue);
    BOOL GetRegisterAsBrowser();
    void SetRegisterAsBrowser(BOOL bNewValue);
    BOOL GetRegisterAsDropTarget();
    void SetRegisterAsDropTarget(BOOL bNewValue);
    BOOL GetTheaterMode();
    void SetTheaterMode(BOOL bNewValue);
    BOOL GetAddressBar();
    void SetAddressBar(BOOL bNewValue);
    BOOL GetResizable();
    void SetResizable(BOOL bNewValue);
};


//{{AFX_INSERT_LOCATION}}
// Microsoft Visual C++ will insert additional declarations
// immediately before the previous line.

#endif // !defined(AFX_WEBBROWSER2_H__A1582E0F_A1BC_11D2_8329
       // _B28A8D2EBF19__INCLUDED_)
```

As you see from Listing 23.1, you have quite a bit of control over the browser aspects of MSIE. Look especially at the operations section. Here you see you can tailor aspects such as whether the control displays one or all of several different menu bars (address, menu, and so on), whether the browser window is full screen or not, and when and to where you navigate (forward, back, general navigation, and cancellation). When you use the DHTML aspects of the MSIE control you'll see later in the chapter, you'll use the very important `GetDocument()` method, which gives you access to the HTML document the browser is currently displaying.

What Listing 23.1 doesn't show you is the large number of events the control exposes. Events, as you may remember, are notifications from the control, such as when a navigation command has completed, or when a download has begun. Table 23.1 shows you the events MSIE fires.

TABLE 23.1 MSIE EVENTS

Event	*Meaning*
BeforeNavigate2	Preparing to navigate.
NavigateComplete2	Navigation completed.
CommandStateChange	Command-enabled state changed.
DocumentComplete	READYSTATE_COMPLETE.
DownloadBegin	Navigation is beginning.
DownloadComplete	Navigation finished, halted, or failed.
NewWindow2	A new window was created.
OnMenuBar	The MenuBar property changed.
OnToolBar	The ToolBar property changed.
OnStatusBar	The StatusBar property changed.
OnFullScreen	The FullScreen property changed.
OnTheaterMode	The TheaterMode property changed.
OnVisible	Containing window should be shown/hidden.
OnQuit	MSIE is ready to quit.
ProgressChange	Download progress updated.
PropertyChange	PutProperty method changed a property.
StatusTextChange	Status bar text changed.
TitleChange	Document title is available or changed.

You'll use the methods shown in Listing 23.1 and the events indicated in Table 23.1 when you deal with `CHtmlView` and the ActiveX control directly (such as when using MSIE from within a dialog box). Because this control is so rich in functionality, it might be most informative if I describe it further by using it from within an application. I'll turn now to `CHtmlView`.

CHtmlView

`CHtmlView` is a thin wrapper around MSIE. In fact, most of the `CHtmlView`-specific members delegate their functionality directly to the MSIE control, which the `CFormView`-based view creates when it itself is created. For example, here is the source code from the MFC source file Viewhtml.cpp for the `CHtmlView::GetHtmlDocument()` method:

```
LPDISPATCH CHtmlView::GetHtmlDocument() const
{
    ASSERT(m_pBrowserApp != NULL);

    LPDISPATCH result;
    m_pBrowserApp->get_Document(&result);
    return result;
}
```

You determine whether your application will use `CHtmlView` when you create your project using the MFC AppWizard. When you reach the last AppWizard step, step 6 (see Figure 23.1), choose `CHtmlView` as your view's base class.

FIGURE 23.1
MFC AppWizard view selection dialog (step 6).

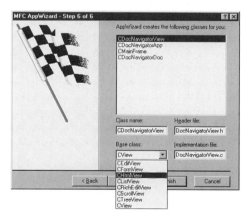

This chapter has two sample programs using `CHtmlView`. The first, WebApp, retrieves a few selected DHTML tags from the document and displays them in a tree control. The second, DocNavigator, pulls the bookmark anchors from an HTML document and allows you to navigate to the bookmarked position within the document (again using a tree control). You can see the WebApp application in action in Figure 23.2.

FIGURE 23.2

The WebApp sample program.

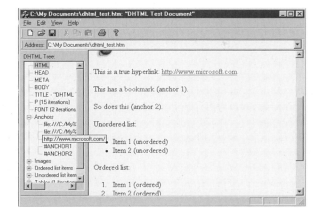

Although I'll discuss the DHTML aspects of these programs later in the chapter, now is a good time to examine how you know *when* to access the DHTML objects. When the application navigates to a new URL (using `CHtmlView::Navigate2()`), the URL's HTML document is loaded into the browser. When the browser completes this loading process, it fires the `DocumentComplete` event. For example, the WebApp sample program contains this code:

```
void CWebView::OnDocumentComplete(LPCSTSR lpszURL)
{
   CHtmlView::OnDocumentComplete(lpszURL);

   // Update the tree control
   CMainFrame* pFrame = (CMainFrame*)AfxGetMainWnd();
   pFrame->UpdateTree(GetHtmlDocument(),lpszURL);
}
```

When the HTML document has completely loaded, MSIE fires the `DocumentComplete` event, which is intercepted by the preceding code. In this case, the frame class notifies the tree control that the document has changed and allows it to query the HTML document for the information it requires to recreate itself (a tree view of the HTML document). Of course, at this time you can do anything you want to the HTML document—it is now stored within MSIE and available for your use.

`CHtmlView` and the Document/View Relationship

Notice that I said the HTML document is stored *within* MSIE. Put simply, `CHtmlView` doesn't require the `CDocument`-derived class for document management even though

MSIE clearly stores an (HTML) document. The control itself handles the HTML document management, leaving the `CDocument`-derived class to be used for other tasks, if you so choose.

At first glance, this in itself seems to be of little impact. After all, many MFC applications generated by the MFC AppWizard use the document/view architecture only to store all (or most) pertinent information within the view class. Many even *avoid* the document class (be honest). But this has (at least) one important ramification with respect to `CHtmlView`. The default document loading mechanism MFC employs *has no effect* upon MSIE. If you tried to load an HTML document into your `CHtmlView`-enabled application and expected the application to show your document by default, you would be disappointed. You would see nothing more than a blank view.

Knowing this, you must provide the document loading mechanism by overriding `CHtmlView::OnFileOpen()`. Listing 23.2 shows the code WebApp uses.

LISTING 23.2   C`WebView`'s HTML DOCUMENT FILE LOAD METHOD

```
void CWebView::OnFileOpen()
{
    // File filter
    static TCHAR BASED_CODE szHTMLFilter[] =
    ➥_T("HTM Files (*.htm)¦*.htm¦HTML Files (*.html)¦*.html¦
    ➥All Files (*.*)¦*.*¦¦");

    // Bring up a file dialog to browse for HTML files.
    CFileDialog dlgHTML(TRUE,
                _T("htm"),
                NULL,
                OFN_EXPLORER,
                szHTMLFilter,
                this);

    dlgHTML.m_ofn.lpstrTitle = _T("Open HTML file");

    if ( dlgHTML.DoModal() != IDOK ) {
        // User canceled...
        return;
    } // if

    // Pull file location
    CString strUrl(_T("file://"));
    strUrl += dlgHTML.GetPathName();

    // Open it
    Navigate2(strUrl,NULL,NULL);
}
```

In this case, I allow the user to browse locally for the HTML document he or she wants to load, and then when the document is located, I create the appropriate URL, using the file protocol, and have MSIE load the document using its navigate method. There is no requirement stipulating that the document must be a local HTML file—*any* URL would do. This is just how I implemented HTML file loading for the WebApp sample program. Feel free to load an HTML file as your requirements dictate, including even remote Internet documents.

> **NOTE**
>
> You do not necessarily need to format the URL to include the file protocol. I did so because it is the *formally correct* way to establish the URL to indicate a local HTML file. However, if you plan on loading remote documents through the Internet/intranet, you must format the URL to include either the HTTP or FTP protocol. In the remote case, your application will be communicating with a distant server and the transmission protocol must be specified.

`CHtmlView` and COM

One of the truly nice features about `CHtmlView` is the manner in which you interact with MSIE. The MSIE wrapper methods hide the COM nature of the MSIE control, enabling you to simply make method calls without regard to satisfying COM function call requirements. For many applications, this simplifies your code.

However, the underlying `CHtmlView` mechanism is MSIE, which *is* a COM object. Some of the `CHtmlView` method calls, such as `GetHtmlDocument()`, return to you a COM pointer (`IDispatch*`, in this case). All the rules of COM now apply in full force when using the `IDispatch` interface! Be sure to `AddRef()` the pointer when you first receive it and `Release()` it when you're through with it.

`CHtmlView` provides a wonderful view class with DHTML functionality. However, it is also possible to use MSIE from within a dialog box. That is the topic for the next section.

Using the Internet Explorer ActiveX Control in a Dialog Box

Dialog boxes and ActiveX controls are a natural fit, and it isn't much of a surprise to find that MSIE works well from within your application's dialog box(es). The only difference between using `CHtmlView` and MSIE directly from a dialog box is that the wrapper functions change slightly. Instead of using CHtmlView's wrappers, you use the wrapper functions Developer Studio creates for you when you insert the control. Although you saw the basic mechanics of loading an external ActiveX control into your dialog box in Chapter 15, "MFC ActiveX Control Containers," I'll recap the high points. These are the steps I took when I created this chapter's WebDlg sample program:

1. While Developer Studio is running with your project loaded, activate the Component Gallery dialog. You do this from the Developer Studio menu by clicking Project, Add to Project, Components and Controls.

2. Select the Registered ActiveX Controls folder in the list control.

3. Scroll the resulting list control horizontally until you see the Microsoft Web Browser ActiveX control. When the control is in view, either double-click it to insert it into your project or single-click the item and click the dialog's Insert button. Click OK when prompted to confirm the insertion.

4. You'll now be given the chance to change the control's C++ class name and source filenames. Modify them to suit your needs or accept the default values, and then click *OK*.

When you've completed the last step, Developer Studio will query the control for its type information and will generate for you the C++ wrapper(s) you need to use the control from your own source files. You will also see a new control button on the resource editor's control palette. Use this button to insert the control into your dialog box as you would any other control.

If you've completed all these steps successfully, you should have two new source files inserted into your project: webbrowser2.cpp and webbrowser2.h (it is webbrowser2.h you saw in Listing 23.1). At this point, you interact with MSIE in much the same manner you would if you were using CHtmlView. It really is that easy.

You can see this in action if you examine the WebDlg sample program I included with this chapter (shown in Figure 23.3). It has the same basic functionality as WebApp. The major difference is that WebDlg is a dialog-based MFC application that deals with MSIE through the Developer Studio wrappers rather than CHtmlView.

Now that you know how to load MSIE and use it as a browser, it's time to see how to deal with the DHTML aspects of MSIE. Fair warning, though! This involves a heavy dose of COM. I recommend you review the first half of Chapter 16, "Using MFC and ATL," because understanding ATL will simplify your code tremendously in this section.

Figure 23.3

The WebDlg sample program.

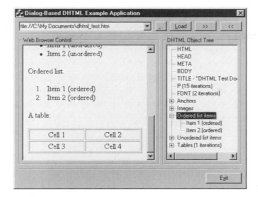

Using DHTML

It's important to realize that *dynamic* HTML is an object-oriented view of plain old HTML. Microsoft took HTML and built an object model around the HTML tagging structure. The result of this is that you now have a COM object for each and every HTML tag, and you are free to do many things with the HTML source document given a corresponding DHTML COM object. That COM object is what makes the HTML document dynamic. You can query the DHTML COM object for the text contained within a given set of tags. Or, you can ask the DHTML COM object for the HTML source contained within the tags. You're free to modify both the text and the HTML source.

The goal of DHTML is to reduce the dependency upon the server for document modifications. Of course, significant content changes generally require a server connection. But minor changes, and especially changes to a given HTML document's style or appearance, may not require server interaction. That's where DHTML steps in.

Browsers that implement the DHTML object model allow embedded scripts to manipulate the HTML document contents. You might consider the HTML document to be self-modifying. Even though the intent of DHTML is to allow the document to access its properties and make runtime modifications, it is possible to access the HTML document from Visual C++ (or Visual Basic or J++).

DHTML was designed for scripted access, so it's a natural fit for Visual Basic and J++. Those languages were designed with the scripting COM interfaces in mind. It is a bit more difficult to use DHTML from Visual C++, if only because you must access the DHTML COM objects directly instead of using the scripting features of each interface.

23

MFC AND DHTML

As an example, let's say you want to change the title of the document after it has been downloaded. From Visual Basic, you would execute code similar to this:

```
window.document.title = "New Title"
```

However, the same operation in Visual C++ would require the code you see in Listing 23.3.

LISTING 23.3   CHANGING THE TITLE OF AN HTML DOCUMENT

```
CComPtr<IDispatch> pDocDispatch = m_CMSIE.GetDocument();

// Check to see that you do have a document.  The
// HTML document pointer will be NULL if the
// browser was unable to load the HTML file.
if ( pDocDispatch.p != NULL ) {
    // You have a document, so now query for the
    // IHTMLDocument2 interface
    CComQIPtr<IHTMLDocument2,&IID_IHTMLDocument2>
    ➥pHTMLDocument2(pDocDispatch);
    if ( pHTMLDocument2.p != NULL ) {
        // You have an active document, so retrieve the
        // element collection.
        CComPtr<IHTMLElementCollection> pElements;
        HRESULT hr = pHTMLDocument2->get_all(&pElements);
        if ( SUCCEEDED(hr) ) {
            // Pull the elements and insert into the string
            // list.
            long iNumElements;
            hr = pElements->get_length(&iNumElements);
            if ( SUCCEEDED(hr) && iNumElements ) {

                // Loop through the number of items
                // and pull its IHTMLElement interface
                // pointer.
              for ( long i = 0; i < iNumElements; i++ ) {
                 // Retrieve item in collection
                 CComVariant varName(i);
                 varName.ChangeType(VT_UINT);
                 CComVariant varIndex;
                 CComPtr<IDispatch> pDisp;
                 hr = pElements->item(varName,varIndex,&pDisp);
                 if ( SUCCEEDED(hr) ) {
                   // You have the element, so retrieve its
                   // tag name.
                   CComQIPtr<IHTMLElement, &IID_IHTMLElement>
                   ➥pElement(pDisp);
                   if ( pElement.p != NULL ) {
                      // Pull the tag string
                      CString strTag(_T("???"));
```

```
                    CComBSTR bstrTag;
                    hr = pElement->get_tagName(&bstrTag);
                if ( bstrTag ) {
                    strTag = bstrTag.m_str;
                } // if

                // Determine the tag and pull
                // additional info depending...
                if ( !strTag.CompareNoCase("TITLE") ) {
                    // Title
                    CComBSTR bstrNewTitle(_T("New Title"));
                    CComQIPtr<IHTMLTitleElement,
                    ➥&IID_IHTMLTitleElement> pTitle(pDisp);
                    if ( pTitle.p ) {
                        hr = pTitle->put_text(bstrText);
                        if ( FAILED(hr) ) {
                            // Didn't work...
                            AfxMessageBox("Unable to set the
                            ➥document title",
                                        MB_OK | MB_ICONERROR);
                        } // if
                    } // if
                } // if
            } // if
        } // if
    } // for
} // if
} // if
} // if
else {
    // You couldn't retrieve the IHTMLDocument2
    // interface.
    AfxMessageBox("Unable to retrieve the active document",
                MB_OK | MB_ICONERROR);
} // else
} // else
```

Don't worry about understanding Listing 23.3 right now. That's what I'll concentrate on for the remainder of the chapter. Conceptually, though, the methodology used in the Basic code and the Visual C++ code is the same. The effect of the operation is identical—the document's title is changed. The difference is that you deal with COM in a different fashion when you program COM in C++ versus Visual Basic or J++. You have much more control over the operation in Visual C++, but the cost of this additional control is added COM support code. I'll revisit this code when I discuss the details of using the DHTML interfaces in an upcoming section. It's now time to examine the DHTML object model at a higher level than the COM interface.

The DHTML Object Model

DHTML starts with the document object, which represents the HTML text stored within MSIE. Perhaps a brief example will be informative. Here is a very simple HTML document:

```
<html>

<head>
<title>Simple HTML Document</title>
</head>

<body>

<p><strong>Hello, World!</strong></p>
</body>
</html>
```

The <html>...</html> tag pair denotes the document. Everything contained within these tags is considered part of the document. Most current browsers (generally) ignore anything outside the tag pair. The document has a header, as defined by the <head>...</head> tag pair. Within the header, there is a document title as indicated by the <title>...</title> tag pair. The document has a body (<body>...</body>), which is where you'll find the specific content of the document. This particular document contains a single paragraph, defined by the paragraph tags <p>...</p>, and the single line of text within the paragraph is to be rendered in bold font, which is indicated by the ... tag pair. Figure 23.4 provides a visual description of this structure.

FIGURE 23.4

Graphical depiction of the simple HTML document.

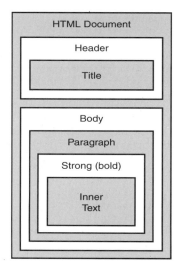

There are two ways to look at Figure 23.4. First, there is a hierarchical view. This view has the document as the top-level object, with the header and body as subobjects, and so on. The second way to look at Figure 23.4 is one of containment. The document *contains* a header and a body, and each of them contains *collections* of other *elements* (objects). As it happens, DHTML borrows from both of these views. Table 23.2 provides you with a complete listing of the current (Internet Explorer 4.01) DHTML objects.

TABLE 23.2   DHTML OBJECTS

Object	Interface	Collection
Style	IHTMLStyle	None
RuleStyle	IHTMLRuleStyle	None
FiltersCollection	IHTMLFiltersCollection	All
Element	IHTMLElement	All
Databinding	IHTMLDatabinding	None
StyleSheetRule	IHTMLStyleSheetRule	None
StyleSheetRulesCollection	IHTMLStyleSheetRulesCollection	All
StyleSheetsCollection	IHTMLStyleSheetsCollection	All
StyleSheet	IHTMLStyleSheet	Stylesheets
LinkElement	IHTMLLinkElement	Links
TxtRange	IHTMLTxtRange	None
TextRangeMetrics	IHTMLTextRangeMetrics	None
FormElement	IHTMLFormElement	Forms
ControlElement	IHTMLControlElement	All
TextElement	IHTMLTextElement	None
TextContainer	IHTMLTextContainer	None
ControlRange	IHTMLControlRange	None
ImgElement	IHTMLImgElement	Images
InputImage	IHTMLInputImage	None
ImageElementFactory	IHTMLImageElementFactory	None
BodyElement	IHTMLBodyElement	All
FontElement	IHTMLFontElement	All, Fonts
AnchorElement	IHTMLAnchorElement	All, Anchors
LabelElement	IHTMLLabelElement	All
ListElement	IHTMLListElement	All

continues

23

MFC AND DHTML

TABLE 23.2   CONTINUED

Object	Interface	Collection
UListElement	IHTMLUListElement	All
OListElement	IHTMLOListElement	All
LIElement	IHTMLLIElement	All
BlockElement	IHTMLBlockElement	All
DivElement	IHTMLDivElement	All
DDElement	IHTMLDDElement	All
DTElement	IHTMLDTElement	All
BRElement	IHTMLBRElement	All
DListElement	IHTMLDListElement	All
HRElement	IHTMLHRElement	All
ParaElement	IHTMLParaElement	All
ElementCollection	IHTMLElementCollection	All
HeaderElement	IHTMLHeaderElement	All
SelectElement	IHTMLSelectElement	All
SelectionObject	IHTMLSelectionObject	None
OptionElement	IHTMLOptionElement	All
OptionElementFactory	IHTMLOptionElementFactory	None
InputHiddenElement	IHTMLInputHiddenElement	All
InputTextElement	IHTMLInputTextElement	All
TextAreaElement	IHTMLTextAreaElement	All
InputButtonElement	IHTMLInputButtonElement	All
ButtonElement	IHTMLButtonElement	All
InputFileElement	IHTMLInputFileElement	All
MarqueeElement	IHTMLMarqueeElement	All
OptionButtonElement	IHTMLOptionButtonElement	All
TitleElement	IHTMLTitleElement	All
MetaElement	IHTMLMetaElement	All
BaseElement	IHTMLBaseElement	All
IsIndexElement	IHTMLIsIndexElement	All
NextIdElement	IHTMLNextIdElement	All
BaseFontElement	IHTMLBaseFontElement	All

Object	Interface	Collection
UnknownElement	IHTMLUnknownElement	All
MimeTypesCollection	IHTMLMimeTypesCollection	All
PluginsCollection	IHTMLPluginsCollection	All
OpsProfile	IHTMLOpsProfile	None
Location	IHTMLLocation	None
EventObj	IHTMLEventObj	None
FramesCollection2	IHTMLFramesCollection2	All
Screen	IHTMLScreen	None
Window2	IHTMLWindow2	None
DocumentEvents	HTMLDocumentEvents	None
Document	IHTMLDocument	None
Document2	IHTMLDocument2	None
EmbedElement	IHTMLEmbedElement	All
AreasCollection	IHTMLAreasCollection	All
MapElement	IHTMLMapElement	All
AreaElement	IHTMLAreaElement	All, Links
TableCaption	IHTMLTableCaption	None
CommentElement	IHTMLCommentElement	All
PhraseElement	IHTMLPhraseElement	All
SpanElement	IHTMLSpanElement	All
Table	IHTMLTable	None
TableCol	IHTMLTableCol	None
TableSection	IHTMLTableSection	None
TableRow	IHTMLTableRow	None
TableRowMetrics	IHTMLTableRowMetrics	None
TableCell	IHTMLTableCell	None
ScriptElement	IHTMLScriptElement	All, Scripts
NoShowElement	IHTMLNoShowElement	All
ObjectElement	IHTMLObjectElement	All, Objects
FrameBase	IHTMLFrameBase	None
FrameElement	IHTMLFrameElement	All, Frames
IFrameElement	IHTMLIFrameElement	All, Frames

continues

23

MFC AND
DHTML

TABLE 23.2 CONTINUED

Object	Interface	Collection
DivPosition	IHTMLDivPosition	None
LegendElement	IHTMLLegendElement	All
FrameSetElement	IHTMLFrameSetElement	All
BGsound	IHTMLBGsound	None
StyleElement	IHTMLStyleElement	All, Styles
StyleFontFace	IHTMLStyleFontFace	None

Clearly, from the sheer size of Table 23.2, you can see that there is a lot to DHTML, and it won't be possible to cover every aspect of each DHTML object. I will introduce the major objects, however, and several sample programs are included with this chapter to show you specifically how to use many of the objects you commonly encounter. I'll start with the granddaddy of all DHTML objects, the document object.

The Document Object

The DHTML document object is the most important and powerful DHTML object. After all, without a document, you have no Web page. You request access to the document object from the browser, and likewise you request access to other DHTML objects from the document object. Figure 23.5 shows you the document object and the element collections it contains as well as the corresponding HTML tags.

What Figure 23.5 says is: If you want to access all the anchors within the document, as the DocNavigator sample program included with this chapter shows you, you first get the document object, and then get the anchors collection from the document object.

Note the first collection, All. This collection is, in many cases, the only collection available to you for such things as the header and body objects, lists, tables, and many other HTML tagged structures. I'll refer back to this object when I discuss other important DHTML objects in the next section.

Aside from obtaining these collections, the document also provides mechanisms for determining and changing many aspects of the document. For example, you can easily change the foreground and background color. Or, you could change the colors of the links. You can even check on the security aspects of the document. The specific methods and properties are far too numerous to list here. I will show you how the document object is used and what methods are most commonly called later in the chapter when I discuss the COM aspects of the DHTML objects. The Visual C++ online documentation provides the other details. For now, let's examine some of the other DHTML objects you will commonly encounter.

FIGURE 23.5
*The DHTML doc-
ument object and
its collections.*

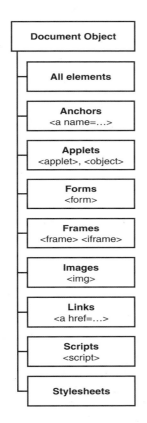

Other DHTML Objects

Oddly, there isn't a single DHTML object for the header, though there is one for the document body. The header information is instead broken down into the separate header parts, such as the title, metadata, and style information. Each of these has its own DHTML object.

The document body is further broken down into many objects, essentially an object for each HTML tag, to include objects for links, anchors, lists, and images, to name a few. Some of the body objects may be found in DHTML collection objects, whereas others simply exist in the document singly or in quantity. Table 23.2 lists the DHTML objects you will encounter and whether you will find them in a collection object or not.

Collection Objects

Some HTML tags are particularly interesting (at least according to the designers of DHTML), such as links and images, or stylesheets. These tag sets (the beginning and ending tags shown in Figure 23.5) are anointed with special object status. They are collected when the document is loaded and presented to you when you request their COM interfaces directly from the document object. There are other collections, however, and the complete list is shown in Table 23.2. There are some notable tags that do not have collections, such as paragraphs (<p>...</p>) and tables (<table>...</table>). If you are interested in these HTML document objects, you will have to access the All collection object to find them.

For each tag set, you have access to *all* the tag pairs within the document directly from the related collection object. For example, if you want to access all the document's images (by URL), you request the image collection from the document and iterate through the collection to access the individual image DHTML objects.

DHTML COM Interfaces

As you saw from Table 23.2, there are many DHTML objects and associated COM interfaces. Which interface you use and how you obtain it depends upon the interface. Several interfaces are actually polymorphic, in that the given interface could be used in several ways depending upon how you obtained the interface pointer. Luckily, the majority of the DHTML interfaces follow a pattern, which I'll discuss next.

> **NOTE**
>
> In order to compile C++ code accessing DHTML interface, you must include the MSHTML.H header file. This file declares all the DHTML interfaces and events.

Obtaining the Document DHTML Interface

You begin accessing the DHTML aspects of the document by requesting a document pointer from the browser using one of three methods depending upon how you loaded MSIE. If you've loaded MSIE as an ActiveX control (m_CMSIE in the following example), this code retrieves the document COM object's IDispatch interface using ATL and the webbrowser2.h code you saw in Listing 23.1:

```
// m_CMSIE is a CWnd object encapsulating the MSIE ActiveX control
CComPtr<IDispatch> pDocDispatch = m_CMSIE.GetDocument();
```

If you're using CHtmlView, you retrieve the document using the
CHtmlView ::GetHtmlDocument() method:

```
// The "this" pointer is CHtmlView*
CComPtr<IDispatch> pDocDispatch = GetHtmlDocument();
```

If you have a pointer to the browser COM object (IWebBrowser2), your code would look
like this:

```
// pMSIE is a (valid) IWebBrowser2 COM interface pointer
CComPtr<IDispatch> pDocDispatch;
HRESULT hr = pMSIE->get_document(&pDocDispatch);
```

When you have the IDispatch-based pointer, you need to cast it (in COM terms) to a
IHTMLDocument2 interface pointer, which you do using IUnknown::QueryInterface():

```
if ( pDocDispatch.p != NULL ) {
    // You have a document, so now query for the
    // IHTMLDocument2 interface
    CComQIPtr<IHTMLDocument2,&IID_IHTMLDocument2>
    ➥pHTMLDocument2(pDocDispatch);
    if ( pHTMLDocument2.p != NULL ) {
        // You have an active document
    } // if
} // if
else {
    // Handle the error condition...
} // else
```

When you have the IHTMLDocument2 interface pointer, you're free to begin your DHTML
work. Note that however you obtain the document object interface pointer, the pattern is
the same. You first run the browser, navigate to a URL (local or remote), and finally
request a document interface pointer from the browser (which you convert from
IDispatch to IHTMLDocument2).

> **CAUTION**
>
> If you have MSIE loaded but have not navigated to a URL (and loaded the
> resulting HTML document), you will get an error when you request the docu-
> ment interface pointer. There is no document, so no valid document interface
> pointer is available.

When you have a valid document interface pointer, you can call any of the
IHTMLDocument2 methods to begin accessing the other DHTML objects.

Obtaining the DHTML Collections Interfaces

The IHTMLDocument2 interface has several methods for obtaining collection object pointers, the foremost of which is the All collection (IHTMLElementCollection). This code, for example, obtains the All collection from the document:

```
// Retrieve the "all" element collection.
CComPtr<IHTMLElementCollection> pElements;
HRESULT hr = pHTMLDocument2->get_all(&pElements);
if ( SUCCEEDED(hr) ) {
    // Deal with the collection elements through pElements...
} // if
```

IHTMLElementCollection is a generic HTML collection object, which in this case (the All collection) is filled with all the DHTML objects the document contains.

You need not deal with all the document tags, however. As I mentioned previously, the document object exports several collection interface pointers. If, for example, you were interested in access to all the hyperlinks the document contained (for validation purposes, perhaps), you could directly access that collection using the IHTMLDocument2::get_links() method. This method returns to you an IHTMLElementCollection interface pointer you use for iteration. You'll see how this is done in the next section. Table 23.3 provides you with the IHTMLDocument2 methods used to retrieve the major element collections.

TABLE 23.3   IHTMLDocument2 COLLECTION EXPORT METHODS

Collection	IHTMLDocument2 *Method*
All	get_all()
Anchors	get_anchors()
Applets	get_applets()
Embeds	get_embeds()
Forms	get_forms()
Frames	get_frames()
Images	get_images()
Links	get_links()
Plug-Ins	get_plugins()
Scripts	get_scripts()
Style sheets	get_styleSheets()

You don't see the *embeds* and *plug-ins* collections in Figure 23.5 because they are not standard HTML objects. Rather, they have to do with embedded objects (a là OLE), so I omitted them from Figure 23.5. However, they are collections like any other, and if you are interested in them, you can access their collections as you would any other.

When you've obtained a DHTML collection object, it's time to retrieve the individual DHTML objects from the collection and actually do something with them. As it happens, that is a topic for the next section.

Using the DHTML Interface

Obtaining the collections objects isn't too difficult, if you obtained the document object in the first place (and assuming there are any elements within the document to merit the creation of the collection). If there are any elements contained in the collection, you'll need to iterate through the collection and withdraw each element. This is a bit more involved.

The basic recipe for iterating through a collection is this:

1. Loop through the elements in the collection.
2. Query each element for its tag name.
3. Compare the tag name to the tags you want to intercept.
4. If the tag names compare favorably, `QueryInterface()` the element interface pointer for the specific tag interface pointer.
5. Access the specific tag type's information.
6. Release all the interfaces.

Of course, you may skip steps 2 and 3 if you already know the collection contains a specific tag type, possibly because you requested a certain collection from the document. In any case, assuming you have a valid `IHTMLElementCollection` pointer, you can begin iterating through the collection using this code (step 1 in the preceding list):

```
// The pElements pointer is IHTMLElementCollection
long iNumElements;
HRESULT hr = pElements->get_length(&iNumElements);
    if ( SUCCEEDED(hr) && iNumElements ) {

        // Loop through the number of items
        // and pull its IHTMLElement interface
        // pointer.
        for ( long i = 0; i < iNumElements; i++ ) {
            // Retrieve item in collection
            CComVariant varName(i);
            varName.ChangeType(VT_UINT);
```

```
            CComVariant varIndex;
            CComPtr<IDispatch> pDisp;
            hr = pElements->item(varName,varIndex,&pDisp);
            if ( SUCCEEDED(hr) ) {
                // You have the element, so retrieve its
                // tag name.
                CComQIPtr<IHTMLElement, &IID_IHTMLElement>
                ➥pElement(pDisp);
                if ( pElement.p != NULL ) {
                    // You now have an individual element from
                    // the collection...
                } // if
            } // if
        } // for
} // if
```

For each iteration, you will be retrieving an `IHTMLElement` object from the collection. Like `IHTMLElementCollection`, `IHTMLElement` is also a generic DHTML interface. To get any really useful information from it, you must first determine what the element contains, if you don't already know, and then query the interface for the specific DHTML interface designed to deal with that tag. The following code snippet pulls the tag's text, which is contained in the `IHTMLElement` object. When you know the tag's text, you can easily compare that text to specific tags you want to handle and query the `IHTMLElement` interface accordingly. As an example, in this case I am looking specifically for the document title so that I can modify it. This code implements steps 2 through 6 in the preceding list.

```
if ( pElement.p != NULL ) {
    // Pull the tag string
    CString strTag(_T("???"));
    CComBSTR bstrTag;
    pElement->get_tagName(&bstrTag);
    if ( bstrTag ) {
        strTag = bstrTag.m_str;
    } // if

    // Determine the tag and pull
    // additional info depending...
    if ( !strTag.CompareNoCase("TITLE") ) {
        // Title
        CComBSTR bstrNewTitle(_T("New Title"));
        CComQIPtr<IHTMLTitleElement,
        ➥&IID_IHTMLTitleElement> pTitle(pDisp);
        if ( pTitle.p != NULL ) {
            hr = pTitle->put_text(bstrText);
            if ( FAILED(hr) ) {
                // Didn't work...
                AfxMessageBox("Unable to set the document title",
```

```
                              MB_OK ¦ MB_ICONERROR);
          } // if
        } // if
      } // if
    } // if
```

The methods any given DHTML object exposes depend upon the object itself, but there are several common methods you could use. In the preceding example, I replaced the text between the `<title>`...`</title>` tags using the `IHTMLTitleElement::put_Text()` method. I *could* have used a method from the element object, `IHTMLElement::put_innerText()`. The outcome will be the same—the text between the tags will be replaced with the text I provide. The element object is a key object when dealing with individual HTML tag sets because all HTML tags found in the document are given an element object. Because of this emphasis, I'll introduce some of the DHTML element object methods and describe their use in the next section.

The DHTML Element Interface Methods

You could think of the DHTML element object as the object common to all HTML tags within the document. A specialized DHTML object, such as the `IHTMLTitleElement` object you just saw in action, actually inherits behavior from `IHTMLElement`. All the DHTML objects found in a collection exhibit this inheritance relationship, and because all HTML tags wind up in some collection (if only the All collection), they all share these common methods. Specialization objects like `IHTMLTitleElement` simply add the methods related to the associated HTML tag, which in this case is the `<title>`...`</title>` tag pair. Table 23.4 shows you the more commonly used `IHTMLElement` methods.

TABLE 23.4   COMMONLY USED `IHTMLElement` METHODS

Method	Purpose
`get_tagName()`	Retrieve the HTML tag text
`get_parentElement()`	Retrieve parent element pointer
`get_document()`	Retrieve the document's `IDispatch` pointer
`get_innerHTML()`	Retrieve HTML between object's tags
`get_innerText()`	Retrieve text between object's tags
`get_outerHTML()`	Retrieve HTML including object's tags
`put_innerHTML()`	Replace the enclosed HTML
`get_innerText()`	Replace the enclosed text

continues

TABLE 23.4   CONTINUED

Method	Purpose
get_outerHTML()	Replace the object and enclosed HTML
get_children()	Retrieves the collection containing the object's immediate children
get_all()	Retrieves the collection containing the objects in the HTML document within the scope of this object
toString()	Returns a string representation of the object

Many of the IHTMLElement methods are self-explanatory, but the inner and outer functions may not be so obvious. *Inner* functions, such as IHTMLElement::get_innerText(), retrieve the text (or HTML) between the tags the object supports. As an example, assume you have this HTML within your document:

```
<body>
<p>
   This is paragraph 1.
</p>
<p>
   <font face="Arial">
      This is paragraph 2, with a different font.
   </font>
</p>
</body>
```

If you have an IHTMLElement object that represents the second paragraph, it contains this HTML:

```
<p>
   <font face="Arial">
      This is paragraph 2, with a different font.
   </font>
</p>
```

If you call the IHTMLElement::get_innerText() method, you will retrieve the text "This is paragraph 2, with a different font.", because this is the textual representation of what exists between the second <p>...</p> tag set. If you called IHTMLElement::put_innerText(), you would replace the text range with the text you provided. This code, for example, replaces the text with the string "This was replaced!":

```
CComBSTR bstrText(_T("This was replaced!"));
pPara2Element ->put_innerText(bstrText);
```

If you would rather deal with HTML instead of text, because the text methods filter the HTML tags from the text stream, you would use the inner and outer HTML methods. Using this same example, retrieving the inner text from the second paragraph DHTML object

```
<p>
   <font face="Arial">
      This is paragraph 2, with a different font.
   </font>
</p>
```

and the font object

```
<font face="Arial">
      This is paragraph 2, with a different font.
</font>
```

would result in the same string, `This is paragraph 2, with a different font.`. But if you requested the inner HTML of the paragraph object, you would receive the string `<font face="Arial">This is paragraph 2, with a different font.</font>`. Note that the HTML tags have *not* been filtered.

Using the `IHTMLElement::put_innerHTML()` method, you could replace the entire HTML stream within the given DHTML object. Using the same replacement example, you could change the HTML the second paragraph object contained to read "This was replaced!" in bold font:

```
<p>
   <strong>
      This was replaced!
   </string>
</p>
```

This code would do the trick:

```
CComBSTR bstrHTML(_T("<strong> This was replaced! </string>"));
pPara2Element ->put_innerHTML(bstrHTML);
```

The outer methods are similar in that they retrieve and replace text from the given object's tag set. The main difference is, however, that the *entire* object is referenced or modified. Using the `IHTMLElement::put_outerHTML()` method of the second paragraph's DHTML object, you could change the object from a paragraph object to an unordered list object in a single function call. The HTML

```
<p>
   <font face="Arial">
      This is paragraph 2, with a different font.
```

```
    </font>
</p>
```

would change to the HTML

```
<ul>
    <li>
        This is a list item.
    </li>
</ul>
```

using this code:

```
CComBSTR bstrHTML(_T("<ul><li> This is a list item.</li></ul>"));
pPara2Element->put_outerHTML(bstrHTML);
```

As you can see, the outer methods are quite powerful! You not only change the document, but you also possibly rearrange the collections of DHTML objects.

Document Navigation

As you saw earlier in Table 23.2, there are a tremendous number of DHTML objects and interfaces. Just describing them would fill an entire book and is beyond the scope of this chapter. However, I did want to share a real-world DHTML and Visual C++ application, that is, a C++ application that is capable of navigating through an HTML document.

The specifications of the application were such that HTML documents (search result reports) would be created on the server and transmitted to a client computer for viewing. The application's product manager envisioned a tree control in a left-hand pane of a split view with the HTML document visible in the right-hand pane. The idea was that the tree control would contain the HTML bookmarks (anchors) found in the document. As the reports could be quite large, the application's user would simply find the bookmark of interest to them in the tree view, select it, and have the HTML view automatically scroll to that location. DHTML seemed a natural fit to fill this requirement.

The DocNavigator sample program included with this chapter is a short sample application that does the same thing. When you open a file (or navigate to a URL), the anchor collection is extracted and its contents are displayed in a tree control. When you click a node in the tree control, the document automatically scrolls to the bookmark. Figure 23.6 shows DocNavigator in action.

The DHTML aspects of this application are very similar to those you have seen in this chapter. I load the document, obtain the document pointer, and retrieve the anchors collection using `IHTMLDocument2::get_anchors()`. When I actually access the anchor elements, I use the code found in Listing 23.4.

FIGURE 23.6

*The
DocNavigator
sample program.*

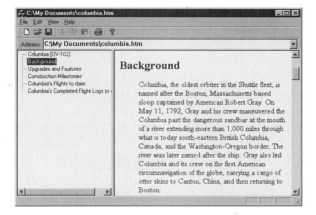

LISTING 23.4   DHTML DOCUMENT ANCHOR RETRIEVAL

```
CComQIPtr<IHTMLElement,
   &IID_IHTMLElement> pElement(pDisp);
if ( pElement != NULL ) {
   CComBSTR bstrAnchor;
   CComQIPtr<IHTMLAnchorElement,
      &IID_IHTMLAnchorElement> pAnchor(pDisp);
   if ( pAnchor ) {
   // Was a link...
   pAnchor->get_name(&bstrAnchor);
   if ( !bstrAnchor ) {
      // Not a bookmark...
      continue;
   } // if
   } // if

   // Retrieve anchor text
   CString strAnchor;
   strAnchor = bstrAnchor.m_str;
   CString* pstrBookmark = new CString(strAnchor);

   // Retrieve anchor text name
   pElement->get_innerText(&bstrAnchor);
   if ( !bstrAnchor ) {
      // No text...
      strAnchor = _T("???");
   } // if
   else {
      strAnchor = bstrAnchor.m_str;
   } // else

   // Add this anchor to the tree
```

continues

23

MFC AND
DHTML

LISTING 23.4   CONTINUED

```
    GetTreeCtrl().InsertItem(TVIF_TEXT | TVIF_PARAM,
        strAnchor,
        0,0,0,0,
        (LPARAM)pstrBookmark,
        reinterpret_cast<HTREEITEM>(TVI_ROOT),
        reinterpret_cast<HTREEITEM>(TVI_LAST));

    // Continue to next anchor
    continue;
    } // if
} // if
```

The interesting thing to note about the code in Listing 23.4 is that the IDispatch interface you receive from the IHTMLElementCollection is both an IHTMLElement interface *and* an IHTMLAnchorElement interface. How you use the interface depends upon what information you want to retrieve from the interface. In this case, you can use the IHTMLElement interface to retrieve the text associated with the anchor. After you have the IHTMLElement interface, then you can query for and use the IHTMLAnchorElement interface to retrieve the actual anchor text. The anchor's text is what the browser will require when it is instructed to navigate to the bookmark when a tree item is selected. You can see this in Listing 23.5.

LISTING 23.5   TREE VIEW ANCHOR SELECTION

```
void CSplitTreeView::OnSelchanged(NMHDR* pNMHDR, LRESULT* pResult)
{
    NM_TREEVIEW* pNMTreeView = (NM_TREEVIEW*)pNMHDR;

    // Examine notification structure to determine new
    // selection
    if ((pNMTreeView->itemNew.state & TVIS_SELECTED) &&
            (pNMTreeView->action)) {
        CString* pstrBookmark = reinterpret_cast<CString*>
        ➥(pNMTreeView->itemNew.lParam);
        ASSERT(!pstrBookmark->IsEmpty());
        if ( !pstrBookmark->IsEmpty() ) {
            CMainFrame* pFrame = (CMainFrame*)AfxGetMainWnd();
            pFrame->Navigate((LPCTSTR)pstrBookmark->GetBuffer(0));
        } // if
    } // if

    *pResult = 0;
}
```

Because I stored a CString containing the anchor text as the lParam of the tree node, I simply retrieve the node's lParam data and pass the text I find there to the frame window, which then passes the text to the browser view.

The browser's job is to navigate to the bookmark. This isn't as obvious as using the CHtmlView::Navigate2() method (or navigating directly using MSIE). If you truly *navigate*, in browser terms, you are attempting to load a new document. So CHtmlView::Navigate2() simply won't do. You don't want to load or reload a document—you really want to have the browser scroll to the given anchor.

The solution to this is, again, DHTML. The IHTMLLocation object has a method put_hash() designed just for anchor scrolling. A *hash* is the portion of the URL that specifies a bookmark, as in this URL:

http://www.somesite.com/index.html#*introduction*

The hash portion of this imaginary URL is italicized. The text following the # is the actual bookmark (anchor) the browser will use for navigation. In this case, I take advantage of this capability using DHTML. Listing 23.6 shows you how I do this.

LISTING 23.6 DHTML BROWSER ANCHOR SCROLLING

```
void CDocNavigatorView::NavigateAnchor(LPCTSTR strItem)
{
   // Navigate to an internal bookmark
   if ( strItem != NULL ) {
      // Retrieve the document's IDispatch pointer
      CComPtr<IDispatch> pDocDispatch = GetHtmlDocument();

      // QI for the IHTMLDocument2 pointer
      CComQIPtr<IHTMLDocument2,&IID_IHTMLDocument2>
      ➥pHTMLDocument2(pDocDispatch);
      if ( !pHTMLDocument2 ) {
         AfxMessageBox(_T("IHTMLDocument2 interface not supported."));
         // This version of Internet Explorer doesn't
         // support DHTML...
         ASSERT(FALSE);
         return;
      } // if

      // Retrieve the IHTMLLocation pointer
      CComPtr<IHTMLLocation> pHTMLLocation;
      HRESULT hr = pHTMLDocument2->get_location(&pHTMLLocation);
      if ( FAILED(hr) ) {
         AfxMessageBox(_T("Error retrieving IHTMLLocation
         ➥interface."));
         // Unknown internal Internet Explorer error...
```

continues

23

MFC AND
DHTML

LISTING 23.6   CONTINUED

```
        ASSERT(FALSE);
        return;
    } // if

    // Navigate to the bookmark (known as a "hash",
    // which is the address portion of the URL
    // following the pound, '#')
    CComBSTR bstrHash(strItem);
    pHTMLLocation->put_hash(bstrHash);
    // Note no check of the return code...it either
    // navigated or it didn't...if you wanted to check
    // the HRESULT for some error condition, feel free
    // to do so.
    } // if
}
```

The `IHTMLLocation::put_hash()` method does all the magic. Most of the remaining code in Listing 23.6 simply sets up the interface (as you've seen previously in this chapter).

Summary

Now you've seen the basics of using DHTML from Visual C++. It isn't as easy as using DHTML from Visual Basic or J++, but then, you have much more control, too. I've merely scratched the surface with respect to what the DHTML objects can do for you, so be sure to examine the online documentation for specific interface method help. DHTML is a rich and powerful object model and well worth your time to know and use if you routinely work with HTML-based documents and Visual C++!

CHAPTER 24

CSocket Programming

by Davis Chapman

IN THIS CHAPTER

Thanks in part to the explosion in popularity of the Internet, more applications have the capability of communicating with other applications over networks, including the Internet. With Microsoft building networking capabilities into its operating systems, starting with Windows NT and Windows 95, these capabilities are becoming common-place in all sorts of applications.

Some applications perform simple networking tasks, such as checking with a Web site to see whether there are any updates to the program and giving the user the option of updat-ing his or her copy of the program. Some word processing applications format docu-ments as Web pages, giving the user the option of loading the pages onto the Web server. Computer games enable the user to play against another person halfway around the world, instead of just competing against the game itself.

Applications can have any number of networking functions, and they all are built around the Winsock interface. If you know and understand how to program using the Winsock interface, and the MFC Winsock classes, this entire realm of application programming is open to you, expanding your programming options considerably.

How Do Network Communications Work?

Most applications that communicate over a network, whether it's the Internet or a small office network, use the same principles and functionality to perform their communica-tion. One application sits on a computer, waiting for another application to open a com-munication connection. This application is "listening" for this connection request, much as you listen for the phone to ring if you are expecting someone to call.

Meanwhile, another application, most likely on another computer (but not necessarily), tries to connect to the first application. This attempt to open a connection is similar to calling someone on the telephone. You dial the number and hope that the other person is listening for the phone on the other end. As the person making the call, you have to know the phone number of the person you are calling. If you don't know the phone num-ber, you can look it up using the person's name. Likewise, the application trying to con-nect to the first application has to know the network location, or address, of the first application.

When the connection is made between the two applications, messages can pass back and forth between the two applications, much as you can talk to the person on the other end of the phone. This connection is a two-way communications channel, with both sides sending information, as seen in Figure 24.1.

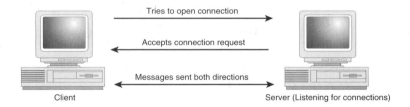

FIGURE 24.1
The basic socket connection process.

Finally, when one or both sides have finished their sides of the conversation, the connection is closed, much as you hang up the phone when you have finished talking to the person you called. When the connection is closed from either side, the other side can detect it and close its side, just as you can tell if the person on the other end of the phone call has hung up on you or if you've been disconnected by some other means. This is a basic explanation of how network communications work between two or more applications.

> **NOTE**
>
> This is a basic description of how network communications work with the TCP/IP network protocol, which is the primary network protocol over the Internet. Many other network protocols use a subtle variation on this description. Other protocols, such as the UDP protocol, are more like radio broadcasts, where there is no connection between the two applications; one sends messages, and the other is responsible for making sure that it receives all of the messages.

Sockets, Ports, and Addresses

The basic object used by applications to perform most network communications is called a *socket*. Sockets were first developed on UNIX at the University of California at Berkeley. Sockets were designed so that most network communications between applications could be performed in the same way that these same applications would read and write files. Sockets have progressed quite a bit since then, but the basics of how they work are still the same.

During the days of Windows 3.x, before networking was built into the Windows operating system, you could buy the network protocols required for network communications from numerous different companies. Each of these companies had a slightly different way that an application performed network communications. As a result, any applications that did perform network communications had a list of the different networking software that the application would work with. Many application developers were not happy with this situation. As a result, all the networking companies, including Microsoft, got together and developed the Winsock (Windows Sockets) API. This provided all application developers with a consistent API to perform all network communications, regardless of the networking software used.

When you want to read or write a file, you must use a file object to point to the file. A socket is similar; it is an object used to read and write messages that travel between applications.

Making a socket connection to another application does require a different set of information than opening a file. To open a file, you need to know the file's name and location. To open a socket connection, you need to know the computer on which the other application is running and the port on which it's listening. A port is like a phone extension, and the computer address is like the phone number. If you call someone at a large office building, you can dial the main office number, but then you need to specify the extension number, as shown in Figure 24.2. As with the phone number, you can look up the port number if you don't already know what it is, but this requires your computer to be configured with the information about which port the connecting application is listening on. If you specify the wrong computer address, or port number, you might get a connection to a different application; as with making the phone call, someone other than the person you called might answer the phone call. You also might not get an answer at all if there is no application listening at the other end.

FIGURE 24.2

Ports are used to route network communications to the correct application.

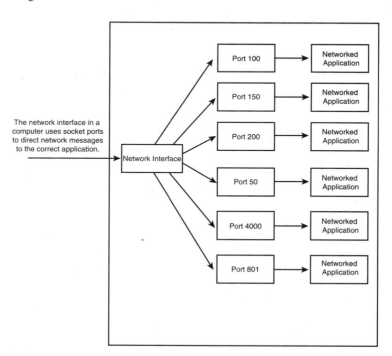

Only one application can be listening on any specific port on a single computer. Although numerous applications can listen for connection requests on a single computer at the same time, each of these applications must listen on a different port.

Winsock and MFC

When you build applications with MFC, you can use the MFC Winsock classes to add network communications capabilities with relative ease. The base class, CAsyncSocket, provides complete, event-driven socket communications. You can create your own descendant socket class that captures and responds to each of these events. The CSocket class is a descendant of the CAsyncSocket class, and encapsulates and simplifies some of the functionality of the base class.

Initializing the Winsock Environment

Before you can use any of the Winsock MFC classes, you have to initialize the Winsock environment for your application. This is done with a single function call in the application instance initialization, AfxSocketInit. This function can take a single WSADATA structure as an optional parameter. If you supply this structure to this function, it will be populated with information about the version of Winsock that is currently in use on the computer on which your application is running. Unless you really need to know some of the information that is returned in this structure, you don't need to pass it as a parameter, as in the following:

```
BOOL CSockApp::InitInstance()
{
    if (!AfxSocketInit())
    {
        AfxMessageBox(IDP_SOCKETS_INIT_FAILED);
        return FALSE;
    }
    .
    .
    .
}
```

If you include this function in the instance initialization function, the Winsock environment will be correctly initialized and shut down by your application.

24

CSocket
PROGRAMMING

Creating a Socket

To create a socket that you can use in your application, the first thing you need to do is declare a variable of `CAsyncSocket`, `CSocket`, or your descendant class, as a class member for one of the main application classes:

```
class CMyDlg : public CDialog
{
.
.
.
private:
    CAsyncSocket m_sMySocket;
};
```

Before you can begin using the socket object, you must call its `Create` method. This actually creates the socket and prepares it for use. How you call the `Create` method depends on how you will be using the socket. If you will be using the socket to connect to another application, as the one placing the call (the client), you do not need to pass any parameters to the `Create` method:

```
if (m_sMySocket.Create())
{
    // Continue on
}
else
    // Perform error handling here
```

However, if the socket is going to be listening for another application to connect to it, waiting for the call (the server), you need to pass at least the port number on which the socket should be listening:

```
if (m_sMySocket.Create(4000))
{
    // Continue on
}
else
    // Perform error handling here
```

You can include other parameters in the Create method call, such as the type of socket to create, the events that the socket should respond to (CAsyncSocket only), and the address that the socket should listen on (in case the computer has more than one network card).

> **NOTE**
>
> There are two types of sockets that you can create using the MFC Winsock classes. These are streaming, or TCP, sockets, and datagram, or UDP, sockets. The streaming sockets are connection-based, and have guaranteed delivery functionality built in. The datagram sockets are connectionless, and require you to write the code to make sure that the packets are received and, in the receiving application, placed in the order that they were sent. If a particular packet is not received, you also have to write the code to have the receiving application request that a particular packet be resent, and on the sending application, to resend the missing packet of data. To specify that a socket is to be a streaming socket, pass SOCK_STREAM as the second argument to the Create method. To specify that a socket should be a datagram socket, pass SOCK_DGRAM as the second argument.

> **NOTE**
>
> If you are building a server application that might be running on a computer with more than one network card installed, you might need to specify the network address that the socket will be listening on. This will tell the socket that it is only listening for incoming connection requests through a specific network card. To do this, you pass the network address to bind the socket to as the last argument to the Create method. This will be the fourth argument for the CAsyncSocket class, and the third argument for the CSocket class. The network address should be passed as a string, in the standard TCP/IP form 127.0.0.1.

Making a Connection

After you create a socket, you are ready to open a connection with it. Three steps go along with opening a single connection. Two of these steps take place on the server—the application listening for the connection—and the third step takes place on the client—the one making the call.

For the client, opening the connection is a simple matter of calling the `Connect` method. The client has to pass two parameters to the `Connect` method: the computer name, or network address, and the port of the application to connect to. The `Connect` method could be used in the following two ways:

```
if (m_sMySocket.Connect("thatcomputer.com", 4000))
{
    // Continue on
}
else
    // Perform error handling here
```

The second form is

```
if (m_sMySocket.Connect("127.0.0.1", 4000))
{
    // Continue on
}
else
    // Perform error handling here
```

After the connection is made, if you are using the `CAsyncSocket` class, or your own class that you derived from the `CAsyncSocket` class, an event is triggered to let your application know that it is connected or that there were problems and the connection couldn't be made. (How these events work is covered in "Socket Events," later in this chapter.) If you are using the `CSocket` class, the `Connect` function will not return until the connection has been made, or an error occurred that prevented the connection from being made.

For the server, or listening, side of the connection, the application first must tell the socket to listen for incoming connections by calling the `Listen` method. The `Listen` method takes only a single argument, which you do not need to supply. This parameter specifies the number of pending connections that can be queued, waiting for the connection to be completed. By default, this value is 5, which is the maximum. The `Listen` method can be called as follows:

```
if (m_sMySocket.Listen())
{
    // Continue on
}
else
    // Perform error handling here
```

Whenever another application is trying to connect to the listening application, an event is triggered in the `CAsyncSocket` class (and custom descendants) to let the application know that the connection request is there. The listening application must accept the connection request by calling the `Accept` method. This method requires the use of a second `CAsyncSocket` variable, which is connected to the other application. When a socket is placed into listen mode, it stays in listen mode. Whenever connection requests are received, the listening socket creates another socket, which is connected to the other application. This second socket should not have the Create method called for it because the Accept method creates the socket. You call the Accept method as follows:

```
if (m_sMySocket.Accept(m_sMySecondSocket))
{
    // Continue on
}
else
    // Perform error handling here
```

At this point, the connecting application is connected to the second socket on the listening application.

With the CSocket class, incoming connections are detected and accepted by calling the Accept function, as shown previously. When using the CSocket class, the Accept function will not return until a connection request has been received and accepted.

Sending and Receiving Messages

Sending and receiving messages through a socket connection gets slightly involved. Because you can use sockets to send any kind of data, and the sockets don't care what the data is, the functions to send and receive data expect to be passed a pointer to a generic buffer. For sending data, this buffer should contain the data to be sent. For receiving data, this buffer will have the received data copied into it. As long as you are sending and receiving strings and text, you can use fairly simple conversions to and from CString variables with these buffers.

To send a message through a socket connection, you use the Send method. This method requires two parameters and has a third, optional parameter that can be used to control how the message is sent. The first parameter is a pointer to the buffer that contains the data to be sent. If your message is in a CString variable, you can use the LPCTSTR operator to pass the CString variable as the buffer. The second parameter is the length of the buffer. The method returns the amount of data that was sent to the other application. If an error occurs, the Send function returns SOCKET_ERROR. You can use the Send method as follows:

```
CString strMyMessage;
int iLen;
int iAmtSent;
.
.
.
iLen = strMyMessage.GetLength();
iAmtSent = m_sMySocket.Send(LPCTSTR(strMyMessage), iLen);
```

```
if (iAmtSent == SOCKET_ERROR)
{
    // Do some error handling here
}
else
{
    // Everything's fine
}
```

When data is available to be received from the other application, an event is triggered on the receiving application for the CAsyncSocket and descendant classes. This lets your application know that it can receive and process the message. To get the message, the Receive method must be called. This method takes the same parameters as the Send method with a slight difference. The first parameter is a pointer to a buffer into which the message can be copied. The second parameter is the size of the buffer. This tells the socket how much data to copy (in case more is received than will fit into the buffer). Like the Send method, the Receive method will return the amount that was copied into the buffer. If an error occurs, the Receive method also returns SOCKET_ERROR. If the message your application is receiving is a text message, it can be copied directly into a CString variable. This allows you to use the Receive method as follows:

```
char *pBuf = new char[1025];
int iBufSize = 1024;
int iRcvd;
CString strRecvd;

iRcvd = m_sMySocket.Receive(pBuf, iBufSize);
if (iRcvd == SOCKET_ERROR)
{
    // Do some error handling here
}
else
{
    pBuf[iRcvd] = NULL;
    strRecvd = pBuf;
    // Continue processing the message
}
```

TIP

When you're receiving text messages, it's always a good idea to place a NULL in the buffer position just after the last character received, as in the preceding example. There might be garbage characters in the buffer that your application might interpret as part of the message if you don't add the NULL to truncate the string.

As with most CSocket versions of these functions, the Receive function will not return until data has been received from the connected application.

If you are using datagram sockets, there are alternative versions of these two methods that you will want to use. These methods are the SendTo and ReceiveFrom methods. These functions work the same as their streaming counterparts, only with the addition of the network address and port to send the data to (with the SendTo method), or variables to store the address of the application you are receiving from (for the ReceiveFrom method).

Closing the Connection

When your application has finished all of its communications with the other application, it can close the connection by calling the Close method. The Close method doesn't take any parameters, and you use it as follows:

```
m_sMySocket.Close();
```

> **NOTE**
>
> The Close function is one of the few CAsyncSocket and CSocket methods that does not return a status code. For all the previous member functions that this chapter has examined, you can capture the return value to determine if an error has occurred.

Sometimes you might want to shut down a socket before closing it. You can shut down a socket by using the ShutDown method. This method takes a single integer parameter, which specifies whether to shut down the sending or receiving of data over the socket. By default, the ShutDown method disables sending of data over a socket. You can specify which socket is disabled by passing the values shown in Table 24.1.

TABLE 24.1 SOCKET ShutDown PARAMETER VALUES

Value	Description
0	Prevents receiving of incoming data packets over the socket
1	Prevents the sending of data packets through the socket
2	Prevents both the sending and receiving of data packets through the socketm

> **NOTE**
>
> Calling the ShutDown method on a socket does not close the connection or release any of the resources being used by the socket. You will still need to close the socket using the Close method.

Socket Events

The primary reason that you create your own descendant class of CAsyncSocket or CSocket is that you want to capture the events that are triggered when messages are received, connections are completed, and so on. The CAsyncSocket class has a series of functions that are called for each of these various events. These functions all use the same definition—the function name is the only difference—and they are intended to be overridden in descendant classes. All of these functions are declared as protected members of the CAsyncSocket class and probably should be declared as protected in your descendant classes. The functions all have a single integer parameter, which is an error code that should be checked to make sure that no error has occurred. Table 24.2 lists these event functions and the events they signal.

TABLE 24.2 CAsyncSocket OVERRIDABLE EVENT-NOTIFICATION FUNCTIONS

Function	Event Description
OnAccept	This function is called on a listening socket to signal that a connection request from another application is waiting to be accepted.
OnClose	This function is called on a socket to signal that the application on the other end of the connection has closed its socket or that the connection has been lost. This should be followed by closing the socket that received this notification.
OnConnect	This function is called on a socket to signal that the connection with another application has been completed and that the application can now send and receive messages through the socket.
OnOutOfBandData	This function is called when out-of-band data has been received. Out-of-band data is sent over a logically independent channel, and is used to send urgent data that is not part of the regular communications between the two connected applications. The Send and Receive methods both have a third parameter, which can be passed a flag, MSG_OOB, to send and receive out-of-band data.

Function	Event Description
OnReceive	This function is called to signal that data has been received through the socket connection and that the data is ready to be retrieved by calling the Receive function.
OnSend	This function is called to signal that the socket is ready and available for sending data. This function is called right after the connection has been completed. Usually, the other time that this function is called is when your application has passed the Send function more data than can be sent in a single packet. In this case, this is a signal that all of the data has been sent, and the application can send the next bufferful of data.

In addition to these overridable event functions, the CSocket class provides one additional overridable function, OnMessagePending. This function is called when there are messages pending in the application event message queue. This enables you to look for particular Windows messages and respond to them in your CSocket class.

Controlling Event Triggering

By default, the CAsyncSocket class calls all of the overridable functions in Table 24.2, whereas the CSocket class doesn't call any of them. So what if you want to have your descendant class be somewhere in between, calling some of these functions, while ignoring the others? Well, you're in luck. There are two ways of controlling which of these event functions are triggered.

The first way to specify which of these event functions are called is available only with the CAsyncSocket class, and any custom classes directly descended from it. In the Create method, the third parameter that you can supply is a flag value that specifies which of these events to trigger. The CSocket class overrides this method, preventing you from providing this flag value. By default, the CAsyncSocket Create method combines all of the event flag values, specifying that all of the event functions be triggered.

The second method of specifying which events are triggered is available to the descendant classes of both CAsyncSocket and CSocket. This is the AsyncSelect method. This method takes only the combination flag to define which events to trigger. You can call the AsyncSelect method as follows:

```
iErr = m_sMySocket.AsyncSelect(FD_READ | FD_CONNECT | FD_CLOSE);
if (iErr == SOCKET_ERROR)
{
    // Do some error handling here
}
else
```

```
{
    // Continue processing
}
```

The default value for the parameter for the `AsyncSelect` method is to specify that all of the event functions be triggered. As a result, if you wanted to turn all event triggering off and then back on, you could first turn all events off by passing a zero as the flag value, as follows:

```
iErr = m_sMySocket.AsyncSelect(0);
```

And then to turn all event triggering back on, don't supply a value for the flag as follows:

```
iErr = m_sMySocket.AsyncSelect();
```

The flag values that you can supply for the `AsyncSelect` and `Create` (`CAsyncSocket` only) functions are listed in Table 24.3.

TABLE 24.3 SOCKET EVENT-NOTIFICATION FLAGS

Flag	*Description*
FD_READ	Triggers and calls the `OnReceive` function when data has arrived for reading.
FD_WRITE	Triggers and calls the `OnSend` function when the outbound Winsock buffers are available for sending data. This event function tells your application when it can send data.
FD_OOB	Triggers and calls the `OnOutOfBandData` function when out-of-band data has been received and needs to be read.
FD_ACCEPT	Triggers and calls the `OnAccept` function to inform your application that there is an inbound connection request on your listening socket. You should follow this with the `Accept` method to complete the connection.
FD_CONNECT	Triggers and calls the `OnConnect` function to inform your application that the connection request your application initiated with the `Connect` method has been completed. This event will be immediately followed by the `OnSend` event function to inform your application that it can now send data to the connected application.
FD_CLOSE	Triggers and calls the `OnClose` function to inform your application that the socket connection has been closed by the connected application.

Detecting Errors

Whenever any of the `CAsyncSocket` or `CSocket` member functions return an error, either `FALSE` for most functions or `SOCKET_ERROR` on the `Send` and `Receive` functions, you can call the `GetLastError` method to get the error code. This function returns only error codes, and you have to look up the translation yourself. All the Winsock error codes are defined with constants, so you can use the constants in your code to determine the error message to display for the user, if any. You can use the `GetLastError` function as follows:

```
int iErrCode;

iErrCode = m_sMySocket.GetLastError();
switch (iErrCode)
{
case WSANOTINITIALISED:
.
.
.
}
```

Getting Socket Information

At times you need to get information about the state of the sockets in your application, such as the address and port of the application on the other end of the connection, and whether the socket is waiting on a blocking function to complete. There are also several options that you can set or check on the sockets in your applications.

Getting the Connected Address

When you have a socket that is connected to another application, you can find out the network address of the other application. You can do this by calling the `GetPeerName` method, passing it a pointer to a `CString` and an unsigned integer. The address and port of the other application are returned in these two variables. You can call the `GetPeerName` method as follows:

```
CString sPeerAddress;
UINT iPeerPort;

iErr = m_sMySocket.GetPeerName(&sPeerAddress, &iPeerPort);
if (iErr == SOCKET_ERROR)
{
    // Do some error handling here
}
else
{
    cout << "Peer Network Address: " << sPeerAddress << "\n";
    cout << "Peer Port: " << iPeerPort << "\n";
    // Continue processing
}
```

Likewise, if you did not bind your socket to a specific port or network address, which you usually do not unless your socket is listening for incoming connections, you can get the same information about your application's socket by calling the `GetSockName` method, as follows:

```
CString sMyAddress;
UINT iMyPort;

iErr = m_sMySocket.GetSockName(&sMyAddress, &iMyPort);
if (iErr == SOCKET_ERROR)
{
    // Do some error handling here
}
else
{
    cout << "My Network Address: " << sMyAddress << "\n";
    cout << "My Port: " << iMyPort << "\n";
    // Continue processing
}
```

> **NOTE**
>
> With the `GetSockName` method, you are likely to get a network address of `0.0.0.0` as your application's network address. This is because your socket was never bound to a specific network address, and thus is using the default address (`0.0.0.0`) for its outbound connection requests. The Winsock interface translates this into the network address of your computer, so that even though your application sees your network address as all zeros, the application that you are connected to does see the actual computer network address.

Getting and Setting Options

Several options can be set on a socket that affect how the socket behaves. You can build most of your applications without needing to adjust any of these options. For those situations where you do need to adjust or check some of these settings, you can use the `GetSockOpt` and `SetSockOpt` methods.

The `GetSockOpt` method is used to check the current setting of various socket options. This method takes four parameters, of which the first three are required. The first parameter specifies which option you want the value of. The second is a pointer to a buffer into which the current value of the option is to be copied. The third parameter is an integer pointer to a variable containing the size of the buffer into which the setting value is to be copied. The fourth parameter specifies which level the option is defined for, the socket or protocol level. The default is the socket level, `SOL_SOCKET`, but there is one option that is defined at the protocol level, `IPPROTO_TCP`. The available socket options and their data types are listed in Table 24.4.

TABLE 24.4   SOCKET OPTIONS

Option	Data Type	Description
SO_ACCEPTCONN	BOOL	The socket is listening for an inbound connection request.
SO_BROADCAST	BOOL	The socket is configured for the transmission of broadcast messages.
SO_DEBUG	BOOL	Debugging is enabled on the socket.
SO_DONTLINGER	BOOL	If this option is set to TRUE, the SO_LINGER option is disabled.
SO_DONTROUTE	BOOL	Routing is disabled.
SO_ERROR	int	Retrieves the error status and clears the status.
SO_KEEPALIVE	BOOL	Keep-alives are being sent.
SO_LINGER	struct LINGER	Returns the current linger options.
SO_OOBINLINE	BOOL	Out-of-band data is being received in the normal data stream.
SO_RCVBUF	int	The buffer size used for receiving data.
SO_REUSEADDR	BOOL	The socket can be bound to an address (and port) that is already being used.
SO_SNDBUF	int	The buffer size used for sending data.
SO_TYPE	int	The type of socket (SOCK_STREAM or SOCK_DGRAM).
TCP_NODELAY	BOOL	Disables the Nagle algorithm for send coalescing.

To set or change any of these options, the SetSockOpt method takes the same four parameters with one small exception: The third parameter, the size of the buffer containing the value to set the option to, is passed as an integer, and not as a pointer to an integer. The other thing to keep in mind with the SetSockOpt method is that you can use it to set or change the value of any of the options in Table 24.4 except for the SO_ACCEPTCONN, SO_ERROR, and SO_TYPE options, which are read-only.

To check and set the value of a particular option, you can use these two methods as follows:

```
BOOL bStatus;
int iStatusSize;

iStatusSize = sizeof(BOOL);
iErr = m_sMySocket.GetSockOpt(SO_KEEPALIVE, &bStatus, &iStatusSize);
if (iErr == SOCKET_ERROR)
{
    // Do some error handling here
```

24

CSocket
PROGRAMMING

```
}
else
{
    // Are we sending keep-alives?
    if (!bStatus)
    {
        // if not, then start sending them
        bStatus = TRUE;
        iErr = m_sMySocket.SetSockOpt(SO_KEEPALIVE, &bStatus,
                                      sizeof(BOOL));
        if (iErr == SOCKET_ERROR)
        {
            // Do some error handling here
        }
    }
    // Continue processing
}
```

Determining If a Socket Is Blocking

When you are using the CSocket class, by default all socket communications functions block all thread processing until it has completed. If you have called the Connect function on a socket, the function will not return control of the thread until the connection has been completed, or the socket timeout has expired. The same thing is true for the Accept, Receive, and Send functions (along with the ReceiveFrom and SendTo functions). So what if you need to interrupt any of these functions before they return? There are two methods in the CSocket class that can be used for this purpose.

The first thing that you'll need to do is to check to see if the socket is blocking a thread. You can use the IsBlocking method to determine if a socket is in a blocking function. This method doesn't take any parameters, and returns a Boolean value that tells you if the socket is blocking or not.

After you have determined that a socket is blocking a thread, you can cancel the blocking method by calling the CancelBlockingCall method. This method will cause the socket to abort the function that is currently blocking, causing the blocking function to return with an error condition of WSAEINTR.

CAUTION

Using the CancelBlockingCall method to cancel any blocking function other than the Accept method can leave a socket in an unstable state. The only socket method that can be called with any predictability after a blocking function has been canceled is the Close method.

To determine if a socket is blocking, and if so, terminate it, you can do the following (in a second thread, of course):

```
if (m_sMySocket.IsBlocking())
    m_sMySocket.CancelBlockingCall();
```

Sockets and I/O Serialization

In those circumstances where the data that will be passed between the two applications communicating through a socket connection is of a known format, and can easily be serialized, there is a specialized MFC class specifically designed to enable you to serialize the communications. This class is the CSocketFile class. The CSocketFile class can be attached to an open CSocket class, and then treated just like a CFile class object.

When you have a connected CSocket, you can attach a CSocketFile class object to the CSocket object, specifying whether to make the CSocketFile archive compatible, as follows:

```
CSocketFile sMySocketFile(&m_sMySocket, TRUE);
```

The first parameter that you need to pass to the CSocketFile constructor is a pointer to the CSocket object that is to be serialized. The second parameter is a Boolean value specifying whether to make the CSocketFile object compatible with a CArchive object. By passing TRUE as the second parameter, you can now take the CSocketFile object and associate it with a CArchive object, as follows:

```
CArchive lArchive(&sMySocketFile, CArchive::load);
```

From here, you can pass the CArchive object to the standard MFC Serialize function to read and write data to the socket connection.

> **NOTE**
>
> Serializing socket communications requires both connected applications to be reading and writing the same data format to the socket. If one of the two connected applications is not using the same serialized data format as the other, you'll end up sending and receiving garbage data.

Building a Networked Application

To illustrate the basic Winsock functionality, you'll create a simple dialog application that can function as either the client or server in a Winsock connection. This will enable

24

**CSocket
PROGRAMMING**

you to run two copies of the sample application, one for each end of the connection, on the same computer or to copy the application to another computer so that you can run the two copies on separate computers and see how you can pass messages across a network. After the application has established a connection with another application, you will be able to enter text messages and send them to the other application. When the message has been sent, it will be added to a list of messages sent. Each message that is received will be copied into another list of all messages received. This will enable you to see the complete list of what is sent and received. It will also enable you to compare what one copy of the application has sent and what the other has received. (The two lists should be the same.)

Creating the Application Shell

For this application, just to keep things simple, you'll create a dialog-style application. Everything that you are doing in this application can be done in an SDI or MDI application just as easily as with a dialog-style application. By using a dialog-style application, you are getting everything that might distract from the basic socket functionality (such as questions about whether the socket variable belongs in the document or view class, how much of the application functionality belongs in which of these two classes, and so on) away from the sample application.

To start the application, create a new MFC AppWizard project, giving the project a suitable name, such as Sock. On the first step of the AppWizard, specify that the application will be a dialog-based application. On the second step of the AppWizard, specify that the application should include support for Windows Sockets, as in Figure 24.3. You can accept the default settings for the rest of the options in the AppWizard. This will cause the AppWizard to include the AfxSocketInit function call in the application instance initialization.

FIGURE 24.3

Including Windows Sockets support.

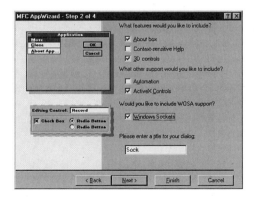

Window Layout and Startup Functionality

After you create your application shell, you can lay out the main dialog for your application. On this dialog, you'll need a set of radio buttons to specify whether the application is running as the client or server. You'll also need several edit boxes for the computer name and port that the server will be listening on. Next, you'll need a command button to start the application listening on the socket, or opening the connection to the server, and a button to close the connection. You'll also need an edit box for entering the message to be sent to the other application and a button to send the message. Finally, you'll need several list boxes into which you can add each of the messages sent and received. Place all these controls on the dialog, as shown in Figure 24.4, setting all of the control properties as specified in Table 24.5.

FIGURE 24.4

The main dialog layout.

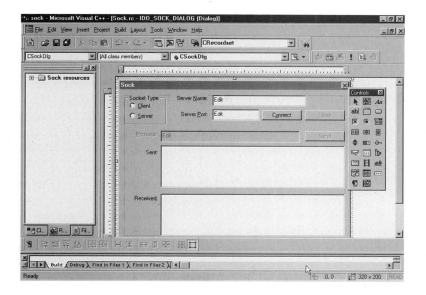

TABLE 24.5   CONTROL PROPERTY SETTINGS

Object	Property	Setting
Group box	ID	IDC_STATICTYPE
	Caption	Socket Type
Radio button	ID	IDC_RCLIENT
	Caption	&Client
	Group	Checked

continues

TABLE 24.5   CONTINUED

Object	Property	Setting
Radio button	ID	IDC_RSERVER
	Caption	&Server
Static text	ID	IDC_STATICNAME
	Caption	Server &Name:
Edit box	ID	IDC_ESERVNAME
Static text	ID	IDC_STATICPORT
	Caption	Server &Port:
Edit box	ID	IDC_ESERVPORT
Command button	ID	IDC_BCONNECT
	Caption	C&onnect
Command button	ID	IDC_BCLOSE
	Caption	C&lose
	Disabled	Checked
Static text	ID	IDC_STATICMSG
	Caption	&Message:
	Disabled	Checked
Edit box	ID	IDC_EMSG
	Disabled	Checked
Command button	ID	IDC_BSEND
	Caption	S&end
	Disabled	Checked
Static text	ID	IDC_STATIC
	Caption	Sent:
List box	ID	IDC_LSENT
	Tab Stop	Unchecked
	Sort	Unchecked
	Selection	None
Static text	ID	IDC_STATIC
	Caption	Received:
List box	ID	IDC_LRECVD
	Tab Stop	Unchecked
	Sort	Unchecked
	Selection	None

After you have the dialog designed, open the Class Wizard to attach variables to the controls on the dialog, as specified in Table 24.6.

TABLE 24.6 CONTROL VARIABLES

Object	Name	Category	Type
IDC_BCONNECT	m_ctlConnect	Control	CButton
IDC_EMSG	m_strMessage	Value	CString
IDC_ESERVNAME	m_strName	Value	CString
IDC_ESERVPORT	m_iPort	Value	int
IDC_LRECVD	m_ctlRecvd	Control	CListBox
IDC_LSENT	m_ctlSent	Control	CListBox
IDC_RCLIENT	m_iType	Value	int

So that you can reuse the Connect button to also place the server application into listen mode, you'll add a function to the clicked event message for both of the two radio buttons, changing the text on the command button depending on which of the two is currently selected. To add this functionality to your application, add a function to the BN_CLICKED event message for the IDC_RCLIENT control ID, naming the function OnRType. Add the same function to the BN_CLICKED event message for the IDC_RSERVER control ID. Edit this function, adding the code in Listing 24.1.

LISTING 24.1 THE CSockDlg OnRType FUNCTION

```
void CSockDlg::OnRType()
{
    // TODO: Add your control notification handler code here
    // Sync the controls with the variables
    UpdateData(TRUE);
    // Which mode are we in?
    if (m_iType == 0)    // Set the appropriate text on the button
        m_ctlConnect.SetWindowText("C&onnect");
    else
        m_ctlConnect.SetWindowText("&Listen");
}
```

Now, if you compile and run your application, you should be able to select one and then the other of these two radio buttons, and the text on the command button should change to reflect the part the application will play, as in Figure 24.5.

24

CSocket PROGRAMMING

FIGURE 24.5

Changing the button text.

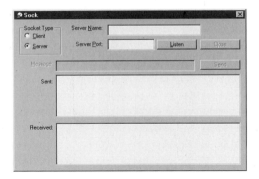

Inheriting from the `CAsyncSocket` Class

So that you will be able to capture and respond to the socket events, you'll create your own descendant class from `CAsyncSocket`. This class will need its own versions of the event functions, as well as a means of passing this event to the dialog that the object will be a member of. So that you can pass each of these events to the dialog-class level, you'll add a pointer to the parent dialog class as a member variable of your socket class. You'll use this pointer to call event functions for each of the socket events that are member functions of the dialog—after checking to make sure that no errors have occurred, of course.

To create this class in your application, select Insert, New Class from the menu. In the New Class dialog, leave the class type with the default value of MFC Class. Enter a name for your class, such as `CMySocket`, and select `CAsyncSocket` from the list of available base classes. This is all that you can specify on the New Class dialog, so click the OK button to add this new class to your application.

After you have created the socket class, add a member variable to the class to serve as a pointer to the parent dialog window. Specify the variable type as `CDialog*`, the variable name as `m_pWnd`, and the access as private. You also need to add a method to the class to set the pointer, so add a member function to your new socket class. Specify the function type as void, the declaration as `SetParent(CDialog* pWnd)`, and the access as public. Edit this new function, setting the pointer passed as a parameter to the member variable pointer, as in Listing 24.2.

LISTING 24.2   THE `CMySocket SetParent` FUNCTION

```
void CMySocket::SetParent(CDialog *pWnd)
{
    // Set the member pointer
    m_pWnd = pWnd;
}
```

The only other thing that you need to do to your socket class is add the event functions, which you'll use to call similarly named functions on the dialog class. To add a function for the OnAccept event function, add a member function to your socket class. Specify the function type as void, the function declaration as OnAccept(int nErrorCode), and the access as protected, and then check the virtual check box. Edit this function, adding the code in Listing 24.3.

LISTING 24.3   THE CMySocket OnAccept FUNCTION

```
void CMySocket::OnAccept(int nErrorCode)
{
    // Were there any errors?
    if (nErrorCode == 0)
        // No, call the dialog's OnAccept function
        ((CSockDlg*)m_pWnd)->OnAccept();
}
```

Add similar functions to your socket class for the OnConnect, OnClose, OnReceive, and OnSend functions, calling same-named functions in the dialog class, which you'll add later. After you've added all of these functions, you'll need to include the header file for your application dialog in your socket class, as in line 7 of Listing 24.4.

LISTING 24.4   THE CMySocket include STATEMENTS

```
// MySocket.cpp: implementation file
//

#include "stdafx.h"
#include "Sock.h"
#include "MySocket.h"
#include "SockDlg.h"
```

After you've added all the necessary event functions to your socket class, you'll add a variable of your socket class to the dialog class. For the server functionality, you'll need two variables in the dialog class, one to listen for connection requests and the other to be connected to the other application. Because you will need two socket objects, add two member variables to the dialog class (CSockDlg). Specify the type of both variables as your socket class (CMySocket) and the access for both as private. Name one variable m_sListenSocket, to be used for listening for connection requests, and the other m_sConnectSocket, to be used for sending messages back and forth.

After you've added the socket variables, you'll add the initialization code for all the variables. As a default, set the application type to client, the server name as loopback, and the port to 4000. Along with these variables, you'll set the parent dialog pointers in your two socket objects so that they point to the dialog class. You can do this by adding the code in Listing 24.5 to the `OnInitDialog` function in the dialog class.

> **NOTE**
>
> The computer name `loopback` is a special name used in the TCP/IP network protocol to indicate the computer you are working on. It's an internal computer name that is resolved to the network address `127.0.0.1`. This is a computer name and address that is commonly used by applications that need to connect to other applications running on the same computer.

LISTING 24.5   THE `CSockDlg` `OnInitDialog` FUNCTION

```
BOOL CSockDlg::OnInitDialog()
{
    CDialog::OnInitDialog();

    // Add "About..." menu item to system menu.

    .
    .
    .

    SetIcon(m_hIcon, FALSE);        // Set small icon

    // TODO: Add extra initialization here
    // Initialize the control variables
    m_iType = 0;
    m_strName = "loopback";
    m_iPort = 4000;
    // Update the controls
    UpdateData(FALSE);
    // Set the socket dialog pointers
    m_sConnectSocket.SetParent(this);
    m_sListenSocket.SetParent(this);

    return TRUE;  // return TRUE  unless you set the focus to a control
}
```

Connecting the Application

When the user clicks the Connect button, you'll disable all the top controls on the dialog. At this point, you don't want the user to think that she is able to change the settings of the computer that she's connecting to or change how the application is listening. You'll call the `Create` function on the appropriate socket variable, depending on whether the application is running as the client or server. Finally, you'll call either the `Connect` or `Listen` function to initiate the application's side of the connection. To add this functionality to your application, open the Class Wizard and add a function to the `BN_CLICKED` event message for the Connect button (ID `IDC_BCONNECT`). Edit this function, adding the code in Listing 24.6.

LISTING 24.6   THE `CSockDlg` `OnBconnect` FUNCTION

```
void CSockDlg::OnBconnect()
{
    // TODO: Add your control notification handler code here
    // Sync the variables with the controls
    UpdateData(TRUE);
    // Disable the connection and type controls
    GetDlgItem(IDC_BCONNECT)->EnableWindow(FALSE);
    GetDlgItem(IDC_ESERVNAME)->EnableWindow(FALSE);
    GetDlgItem(IDC_ESERVPORT)->EnableWindow(FALSE);
    GetDlgItem(IDC_STATICNAME)->EnableWindow(FALSE);
    GetDlgItem(IDC_STATICPORT)->EnableWindow(FALSE);
    GetDlgItem(IDC_RCLIENT)->EnableWindow(FALSE);
    GetDlgItem(IDC_RSERVER)->EnableWindow(FALSE);
    GetDlgItem(IDC_STATICTYPE)->EnableWindow(FALSE);
    // Are we running as client or server?
    if (m_iType == 0)
    {
        // Client, create a default socket
        m_sConnectSocket.Create();
        // Open the connection to the server
        m_sConnectSocket.Connect(m_strName, m_iPort);
    }
    else
    {
        // Server, create a socket bound to the port specified
        m_sListenSocket.Create(m_iPort);
        // Listen for connection requests
        m_sListenSocket.Listen();
    }
}
```

24

CSocket PROGRAMMING

Next, to complete the connection, you'll add the socket event function to the dialog class for the `OnAccept` and `OnConnect` event functions. These are the functions that your socket class is calling. They don't require any parameters, and they don't need to return any result code. For the `OnAccept` function, which is called for the listening socket when another application is trying to connect to it, you'll call the socket object's `Accept` function, passing in the connection socket variable. After you've accepted the connection, you can enable the prompt and edit box for entering and sending messages to the other application.

To add this function to your application, add a member function to the dialog class (CSockDlg). Specify the function type as void, the declaration as OnAccept, and the access as public. Edit the function, adding the code in Listing 24.7.

LISTING 24.7   THE CSockDlg OnAccept FUNCTION

```
void CSockDlg::OnAccept()
{
    // Accept the connection request
    m_sListenSocket.Accept(m_sConnectSocket);
    // Enable the text and message controls
    GetDlgItem(IDC_EMSG)->EnableWindow(TRUE);
    GetDlgItem(IDC_BSEND)->EnableWindow(TRUE);
    GetDlgItem(IDC_STATICMSG)->EnableWindow(TRUE);
}
```

For the client side, there's nothing to do after the connection has been completed except enable the controls for entering and sending messages. You'll also enable the Close button so that the connection can be closed from the client side (but not the server side). To add this functionality to your application, add another member function to the dialog class (CSockDlg). Specify the function type as void, the function declaration as OnConnect, and the access as public. Edit the function, adding the code in Listing 24.8.

LISTING 24.8   THE CSockDlg OnConnect FUNCTION

```
void CSockDlg::OnConnect()
{
    // Enable the text and message controls
    GetDlgItem(IDC_EMSG)->EnableWindow(TRUE);
    GetDlgItem(IDC_BSEND)->EnableWindow(TRUE);
    GetDlgItem(IDC_STATICMSG)->EnableWindow(TRUE);
    GetDlgItem(IDC_BCLOSE)->EnableWindow(TRUE);
}
```

If you could compile and run your application now, you could start two copies, put one into listen mode, and then connect to it with the other. Unfortunately, you probably can't even compile your application right now because your socket class is looking for several functions in your dialog class that you haven't added yet. Add three member functions to the dialog class (CSockDlg). Specify all of them as void functions with public access. Specify the first function's declaration as OnSend, the second as OnReceive, and the third as OnClose. You should now be able to compile your application.

After you've compiled your application, start two copies of the application, side by side. Specify that one of these two should be the server, and click the Listen button to put it into listen mode. Leave the other as the client and click the Connect button. You should see the connection controls disable and the message-sending controls enable as the connection is made, as in Figure 24.6.

FIGURE 24.6

Connecting the two applications.

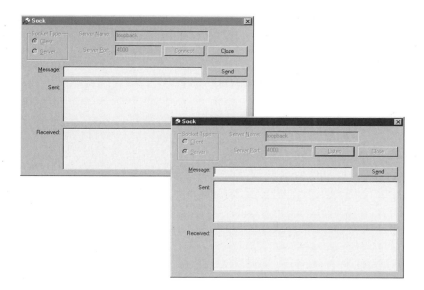

TIP

Be sure that you have the server application listening before you try to connect to it with the client application. If you try to connect with the client before the server is listening for the connection, the connection will be rejected. Your application will not detect that the connection was rejected because you haven't added any error handling to detect this event.

TIP

To run these applications and get them to connect, you'll need TCP/IP running on your computer. If you have a network card in your computer, you might already have TCP/IP running. If you do not have a network card, and you use a modem to connect to the Internet, you will probably need to be connected to

continues

the Internet when you run and test these applications. When you connect to the Internet through a modem, your computer usually starts running TCP/IP after the connection to the Internet is made. If you do not have a network card in your computer, and you do not have any means of connecting to the Internet, or any other outside network that would allow you to run networked applications, you might not be able to run and test these applications on your computer.

Sending and Receiving

Now that you are able to connect the two running applications, you'll need to add functionality to send and receive messages. After the connection is established between the two applications, the user will be able to enter text messages in the edit box in the middle of the dialog window and then click the Send button to send the message to the other application. After the message is sent, it will be added to the list box of sent messages. To provide this functionality, when the Send button is clicked, your application needs to check whether there is a message to be sent, get the length of the message, send the message, and then add the message to the list box. To add this functionality to your application, use the Class Wizard to add a function to the clicked event of the Send (IDC_BSEND) button. Edit this function, adding the code in Listing 24.9.

LISTING 24.9   THE CSockDlg OnBsend FUNCTION

```
void CSockDlg::OnBsend()
{
    // TODO: Add your control notification handler code here
    int iLen;
    int iSent;

    // Sync the controls with the variables
    UpdateData(TRUE);
    // Is there a message to be sent?
    if (m_strMessage != "")
    {
        // Get the length of the message
        iLen = m_strMessage.GetLength();
        // Send the message
        iSent = m_sConnectSocket.Send(LPCTSTR(m_strMessage), iLen);
        // Were we able to send it?
        if (iSent == SOCKET_ERROR)
        {
        }
        else
```

```
            {
                // Add the message to the list box.
                m_ctlSent.AddString(m_strMessage);
                // Sync the variables with the controls
                UpdateData(FALSE);
            }
        }
    }
```

When the OnReceive event function is triggered, indicating that a message has arrived, you'll retrieve the message from the socket using the Receive function. After you've retrieved the message, you'll convert it into a CString and add it to the message-received list box. You can add this functionality by editing the OnReceive function of the dialog class, adding the code in Listing 24.10.

LISTING 24.10 THE CSockDlg OnReceive FUNCTION

```
void CSockDlg::OnReceive()
{
    char *pBuf = new char[1025];
    int iBufSize = 1024;
    int iRcvd;
    CString strRecvd;

    // Receive the message
    iRcvd = m_sConnectSocket.Receive(pBuf, iBufSize);
    // Did we receive anything?
    if (iRcvd == SOCKET_ERROR)
    {
    }
    else
    {
        // Truncate the end of the message
        pBuf[iRcvd] = NULL;
        // Copy the message to a CString
        strRecvd = pBuf;
        // Add the message to the received list box
        m_ctlRecvd.AddString(strRecvd);
        // Sync the variables with the controls
        UpdateData(FALSE);
    }
}
```

At this point, you should be able to compile and run two copies of your application, connecting them as you did earlier. After you've got the connection established, you can enter a message in one application and send it to the other application, as shown in Figure 24.7.

FIGURE 24.7

Sending messages between the applications.

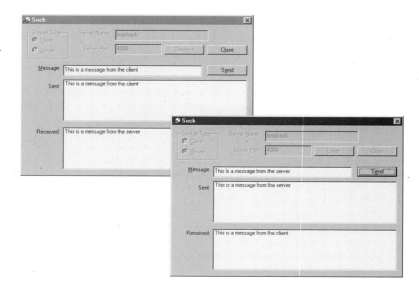

Ending the Connection

To close the connection between these two applications, the client application user can click the Close button to end the connection. The server application will then receive the OnClose socket event. The same thing needs to happen in both cases. The connected socket needs to be closed, and the message-sending controls need to be disabled. On the client, the connection controls can be enabled because the client could change some of this information and open a connection to another server application. Meanwhile, the server application continues to listen on the port that it was configured to listen to. To add all this functionality to your application, edit the OnClose function, adding the code in Listing 24.11.

LISTING 24.11   THE CSockDlg OnClose FUNCTION

```
void CSockDlg::OnClose()
{
    // Close the connected socket
    m_sConnectSocket.Close();
    // Disable the message sending controls
    GetDlgItem(IDC_EMSG)->EnableWindow(FALSE);
```

```
GetDlgItem(IDC_BSEND)->EnableWindow(FALSE);
GetDlgItem(IDC_STATICMSG)->EnableWindow(FALSE);
GetDlgItem(IDC_BCLOSE)->EnableWindow(FALSE);
// Are we running in Client mode?
if (m_iType == 0)
{
    // Yes, so enable the connection configuration controls
    GetDlgItem(IDC_BCONNECT)->EnableWindow(TRUE);
    GetDlgItem(IDC_ESERVNAME)->EnableWindow(TRUE);
    GetDlgItem(IDC_ESERVPORT)->EnableWindow(TRUE);
    GetDlgItem(IDC_STATICNAME)->EnableWindow(TRUE);
    GetDlgItem(IDC_STATICPORT)->EnableWindow(TRUE);
    GetDlgItem(IDC_RCLIENT)->EnableWindow(TRUE);
    GetDlgItem(IDC_RSERVER)->EnableWindow(TRUE);
    GetDlgItem(IDC_STATICTYPE)->EnableWindow(TRUE);
}
}
```

Finally, for the Close button, call the OnClose function. To add this functionality to your application, use the Class Wizard to add a function to the clicked event for the Close button (IDC_BCLOSE). Edit the function to call the OnClose function, as in Listing 24.12.

LISTING 24.12 THE CSockDlg OnBclose FUNCTION

```
void CSockDlg::OnBclose()
{
    // TODO: Add your control notification handler code here
    // Call the OnClose function
    OnClose();
}
```

If you compile and run your application, you can connect the client application to the server, send some messages back and forth, and then disconnect the client by clicking the Close button. You'll see the message-sending controls disable themselves in both applications, as in Figure 24.8. You can reconnect the client to the server by clicking the Connect button again and then pass some more messages between the two, as if they had never been connected in the first place. If you start a third copy of the application, change its port number, designate it as a server, and put it into listening mode, you can take your client back and forth between the two servers, connecting to one, closing the connection, changing the port number, and then connecting to the other.

24

CSocket
PROGRAMMING

FIGURE 24.8

Closing the connection between the applications.

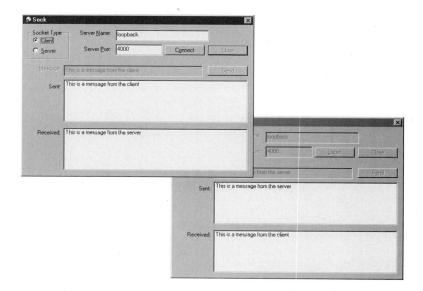

Summary

This chapter discussed how you can enable your applications to communicate with others across a network, or across the Internet, by using the MFC Winsock classes. You took a good look at the CAsyncSocket and CSocket classes and learned how to create your own descendant class from them that would provide your applications with event-driven network communications.

You also learned how to create a server application that can listen for and accept connections from other applications. You discovered how to build a client application that can connect to a server, and how to send and receive messages over a socket connection between two applications.

Finally, you learned how you can use the CSocketFile class to serialize your network communications, enabling you to perform your network communications much as you would read and write to a file on your local hard drive.

WinInet Programming

CHAPTER 25

by Davis Chapman

IN THIS CHAPTER

When you are building an application using Winsock functionality, you have to know and work with more than just the basic network communications. You also need to know and work with the appropriate protocol for the application that you are writing. An application protocol is the conversation that takes place between the client application and the server with which it is exchanging messages. This conversation is usually a series of commands issued by the client (and occasionally by the server) to which the server responds. These commands have to be formatted in a specific way, and often have to follow a specific order.

With the prevalence of the Web in computing now, Microsoft decided to ease the burden of incorporating Web functionality into any Windows applications. As a result of this decision, Microsoft introduced the Windows Internet (WinInet for short) extensions to the Windows API. By encapsulating the primary Web protocols as extensions to the Windows API, Microsoft has greatly simplified the process of Web- and Internet-enabling just about any application.

Web Application Protocols and WinInet

When the Web first began, few Web sites were actually running the Hypertext Transfer Protocol (HTTP) upon which the Web is based. Instead, what you had was a mixture of sites running mostly the File Transfer Protocol (FTP) and the Gopher protocols. Both of these application protocols were able to deliver the basic HTML Web pages to a browser, so all were in fairly equal use. It has only been through the passage of time, and the explosive growth of the Web, that the FTP and Gopher protocols have fallen out of use, as almost all sites are now running HTTP servers for their Web sites. Because of these origins, Web browsers started out having to support all three of these Internet application protocols. With the effort to Internet-enable other applications, it has been assumed that all three of these protocols would need to be supported.

Hypertext Transfer Protocol

The Hypertext Transfer Protocol started out as one of the simplest Internet application protocols. When the Web first started to become popular, the HTTP protocol consisted of three basic commands, GET, POST, and HEAD. These three commands performed the basic functions of the Web. The GET command would request a specific object from the Web server, such as an HTML page or image file, and the Web server would respond by sending the object through the same socket connection. The HEAD command would cause the Web server to respond with what was basically a description of the object that had been requested, like the type of file the object was (HTML, image, and so on), its size, and when it was last updated. The final command, POST, would be used to send data to the Web server, which would usually pass this information along to a separate application to process and generate some dynamic output to be returned to the Web browser.

Along with a small set of commands that could be issued to the Web server, the HTTP protocol was also a single-command-per-connection protocol. In other words, a Web browser would connect to a Web server, send one of these three commands, receive the response, and close the connection. If a Web page contained three images, the Web browser would make at least four connections to the Web server: one for the Web page and one for each of the three images.

Since those early beginnings, the HTTP protocol has undergone several changes. It now consists of several commands, including commands that can be used to place Web pages and other objects onto the Web server, and can keep the connection open for multiple commands. Along with all the changes in the way commands are sent and responded to, the HTTP protocol has also added requirements on how the commands and responses are formatted. All in all, there have been many changes in the HTTP protocol, and there will probably be more to come.

File Transfer Protocol

The File Transfer Protocol is a bit more involved and has been around for quite a while longer than the HTTP protocol. FTP is used for moving files between two or more computers, regardless of the type of computers involved. It provides the client application with the capability of moving around in the server's file system, getting files from and placing files onto the server wherever the client has permission to do so. If the user has appropriate permissions on the FTP server, the user can even delete files from the server using the FTP protocol.

Because of the more extensive requirements of the FTP protocol, it is quite a bit different from the HTTP protocol. First, the client application has to log in to the FTP server, providing a username and password before access is granted to the client application. Second, the FTP protocol has an extensive set of commands for navigating through the server's file system; getting directory listings; and moving, deleting, and renaming files, along with the basic file transfer commands to move files from the client computer to the server and vice versa.

A third aspect of the FTP protocol is that it uses more than one socket connection to perform its tasks. A single socket connection is opened by the client that remains open until the session is completed. This is known as the command connection. A second socket connection is opened either by the server or the client that is used to move any data between the two computers, as in Figure 25.1. This second connection is used to pass files between the two computers. It is also used to send directory listings from the server to the client. This connection is opened each time the client issues a command to the server that involves any data being passed between the two computers, and is closed when all of the data has been passed for that one command.

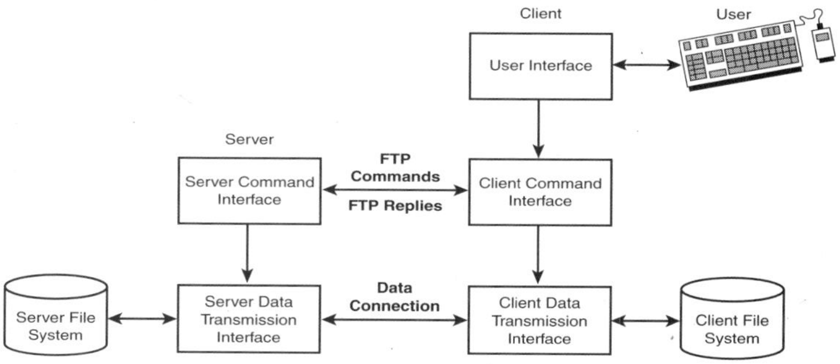

FIGURE 25.1
The FTP protocol uses two socket connections.

Gopher Protocol

The Gopher protocol is somewhere in between the FTP and HTTP protocols in terms of functionality and complexity. It can be used like the FTP protocol to browse server file systems, and to retrieve files from the server. It can also be used to search multiple servers for files on a particular subject. The Gopher protocol was originally developed as a document search and delivery mechanism, very much the same purpose for which the HTTP protocol was developed (and around the same time, too). The differences between the Gopher and HTTP protocols are that the Gopher protocol was originally more involved, containing much of the file system navigation functionality from the FTP protocol, and the HTTP protocol was tightly coupled with the Hypertext Markup Language (HTML) format for document presentation. It was because the HTTP/HTML combination lent itself to graphical displays—more than the Gopher protocol did—that the HTTP/HTML combination became the dominant protocol for the Web.

> **NOTE**
>
> The Gopher protocol is one of the few Internet application protocols whose name is not an acronym for a functional description of the protocol. The Gopher protocol was developed at the University of Minnesota, Minnesota being known as the "Gopher state." As a result, the Gopher protocol took its name from where it was developed, not from what it does.

WinInet API and MFC

Microsoft created the WinInet API to provide an easy-to-use interface for these three Internet application protocols. They provided a way of interacting with any of these protocols in much the same way that you would interact with a file on a local drive. If you want, you can issue any of the commands for any one of these protocols, or you can just pass a URL (Uniform Resource Locator) and read in the resulting object as you would read in any other file.

If you need to get more specific in your application functionality, and you need to use the specific protocol functionality of any of these three protocols, you can do this through the WinInet API just as easily as you can ignore these protocols. You don't need to declare or open a single socket connection: Just start an Internet session and then issue the appropriate protocol commands.

When you work with the MFC WinInet classes, you'll have a collection of classes that you can use in numerous combinations. One of the base classes that you'll always use is the `CInternetSession` class. This class will be used in all of your WinInet applications, regardless of what else you might use.

You'll use your `CInternetSession` class to open a connection class. This connection class can be a generic connection class, `CInternetConnection`, but it will more likely be a protocol-specific connection, `CHttpConnection`, `CFtpConnection`, or `CGopherConnection`. After you have a connection class open, you can issue protocol-specific commands to perform the various tasks that each of the protocols can do.

Through the connection object, you can open a file object, `CInternetFile`, `CGopherFile`, or `CHttpFile`, which understands the application protocol being used to retrieve the file. The `CInternetFile` class is used to read and write files using the FTP protocol. The other two classes, both descendants of the `CInternetFile` class, understand the differences between the FTP protocol and their respective protocols.

With the FTP and Gopher protocols, there are a group of classes that have file-finding and file-locating functionality. These classes are `CFileFind`, as the base class, and `CFtpFileFind` and `CGopherFileFind` as protocol-specific descendants. In addition, there is the `CGopherLocator`, which is used to get information about the Gopher server and what kind of files may be retrieved from the Gopher server.

The final WinInet MFC class is the `CInternetException` class, which is the exception class that is thrown on any WinInet exceptions. The `CInternetException` class can be used to handle any of the exceptions thrown by any of the other WinInet MFC classes.

Internet Session Basics

The starting point for any WinInet MFC application is with the base Internet classes, CInternetSession, CInternetFile, CInternetException, and CInternetConnection. With the exception of the CInternetConnection class, these are the classes that you have to use in any MFC WinInet application.

CInternetSession

In every WinInet application, you'll start with the CInternetSession class. This class is the base from which all other operations will be spawned. You'll start all of your WinInet functionality by creating an instance of the CInternetSession class, and then use it to create and open the various other WinInet classes.

Creating a CInternetSession Instance

Creating an instance of the CInternetSession class can be simple, or very involved, depending on the configuration with which your application needs to be able to work. The simple way of creating an instance is to simply declare an instance of the CInternetSession class, or of a descendant that you have created. This will create the instance using all of the default settings.

If your application needs to be able to work in a more complex environment, such as going through a proxy server, you may need to take more control of how you create the CInternetSession instance.

The first of the parameters that you can pass to the class constructor is the name of your application. This is used to identify your application to the server when you connect and download or upload files. You can pass in any name that you want to use, like "Davis' Internet Utility" or "World's Greatest FTP Client." If you do not supply this parameter, or pass in a null, the AfxGetAppName function will be called to get your application name.

The second parameter is the context ID in which your Internet session will be run. This context ID will be passed back to your application with any overridable functions to identify the CInternetSession instance that is passing an event to your code.

The third parameter specifies whether or not to use a proxy server to connect to the Internet. There are three possible settings for this parameter, listed in Table 25.1.

TABLE 25.1 ACCESS TYPE PARAMETER VALUES

Value	*Description*
INTERNET_OPEN_TYPE_PRECONFIG	The default value; this setting uses the access configuration in the registry.
INTERNET_OPEN_TYPE_DIRECT	Direct connection to the Internet.
INTERNET_OPEN_TYPE_PROXY	Connects to the Internet through a CERN proxy server.

The fourth parameter is the name of the proxy server to be used if the access type is specified as through a proxy server. If you also have a list of server addresses that need to bypass the proxy server, this list is to be passed as the fifth parameter.

The sixth and final parameter that can be passed to the CInternetSession constructor is a flag that can be used to specify a few options. These options are listed in Table 25.2.

TABLE 25.2 WININET SESSION OPTIONS

Value	*Description*
INTERNET_FLAG_DONT_CACHE	Specifies that all data requested not be cached, either locally or in any gateway server through which the data passes.
INTERNET_FLAG_ASYNC	Specifies that all WinInet operations be performed asynchronously. When an operation is completed, the status callback function is called with the status of INTERNET_STATUS_REQUEST_COMPLETE. This status callback function will be covered later in the section "Keeping Up with the Session Status."
INTERNET_FLAG_OFFLINE	All download requests are filled from the persistent cache only. If the requested file is not in the cache, the request fails.

After you have finished all Internet operations, you need to call the Close method to clean up the Internet session object before destroying the CInternetSession object.

Opening URLs and Connections

When you have a CInternetSession object, what can you do with it? You have several choices. You can open a URL to download a file, or you can open a connection to one of the three types of servers and interact with it. When you have a connection open, you can perform any of the standard actions that are available to a client of the particular application that you have connected to.

OpenURL

The most basic of the actions that you can perform is to open a URL. This is done with the OpenURL method, which returns a pointer to a CStdioFile object, which you can read in using the various methods of either that particular class, or the protocol-specific descendants.

The first parameter that you pass to the OpenURL function is the URL to be opened. This should be a complete URL, with the protocol, server, and object to be retrieved. The protocol determines the file type that is returned. The protocols listed in Table 25.3 are the only protocols available for use with the OpenURL function.

TABLE 25.3   OpenURL PROTOCOL FILE TYPES

URL Protocol	*File Type Returned*
file://	CStdioFile*
http://	CHttpFile*
gopher://	CGopherFile*
ftp://	CInternetFile*

> **NOTE**
>
> The file:// protocol retrieves files from local or networked drives.

The second parameter is the context flag that will be returned with any overridden event function. The third parameter is a flag that can be used to specify how the URL specified is retrieved. The possible values for this flag are listed in Table 25.4.

TABLE 25.4   OpenURL OPTIONS

Value	*Description*
INTERNET_FLAG_TRANSFER_ASCII	The default setting; transfers the file as ASCII text.
INTERNET_FLAG_TRANSFER_BINARY	Transfers the file as a binary file.
INTERNET_FLAG_RELOAD	Retrieves the file from the server, even if cached locally.

Value	Description
INTERNET_FLAG_DONT_CACHE	Don't cache the file, either locally or on any gateway or server.
INTERNET_FLAG_SECURE	Applicable for HTTP URLs only; this flag specifies to use Secure Sockets Layer or PCT for a secure transaction.
INTERNET_OPEN_FLAG_USE_EXISTING_CONNECT	If possible, reuse the connection to the server for new requests generated with the OpenURL function, instead of opening a new connection for each request.
INTERNET_FLAG_PASSIVE	Applicable for FTP URLs; uses passive FTP options.

The last two parameters are for use with HTTP servers. The fourth parameter is a string containing any additional headers to be sent to the HTTP server. The fifth parameter is the length of the additional headers passed in the fourth parameter. A typical use of the OpenURL function would look like the following:

```
CHttpFile* pURLFile;
CInternetSession isSession;
CString sURL;
CString sHeaders;

sURL = "http://www.myserver.com/file_to_get.html";
sHeaders = "X-Application=My Web Browser";
pURLFile = isSession.OpenURL(sURL, 1,
        INTERNET_FLAG_TRANSFER_ASCII ¦ INTERNET_FLAG_RELOAD,
        sHeaders, sHeaders.GetLength());
```

Another, more basic use of the OpenURL method would supply just the URL, as follows:

```
CHttpFile* pURLFile;
CInternetSession isSession;
CString sURL;

sURL = "http://www.myserver.com/file_to_get.html";
pURLFile = isSession.OpenURL(sURL);
```

GetHttpConnection

The GetHttpConnection method is used to create a CHttpConnection object. This method opens the connection to the specified HTTP server, but you have to call all of the appropriate CHttpConnection methods to perform the actions you need. The GetHttpConnection method returns a pointer to a CHttpConnection object.

25

WinInet PROGRAMMING

The first parameter is the server name to be connected to. This is the only required parameter for the `GetHttpConnection` method. The second parameter is the port to use to connect to the HTTP server. The third parameter is the username to connect as, if the HTTP server requires a login for access. The fourth parameter is the password for the login specified. A typical use of the `GetHttpConnection` method is as follows:

```
CHttpConnection* pConnect;
CInternetSession isSession;
CString sServer;

sServer = "www.myserver.com ";
pConnect = isSession.GetHttpConnection(sServer);
```

A more involved use for a server that required login access might look like this:

```
CHttpConnection* pConnect;
CInternetSession isSession;
CString sServer;
CString sUserName;
CString sPassword;

sServer = "www.myserver.com ";
sUserName = "MyName";
sPassword = "MyPassword";
pConnect = isSession.GetHttpConnection(sServer, 80,
        sUserName, sPassword);
```

GetFtpConnection

The `GetFtpConnection` method is very similar to the `GetHttpConnection` method. It requires all of the same information, with one addition, only in a slightly different order. The `GetFtpConnection` method returns a pointer to a `CFtpConnection` object.

As with the `GetHttpConnection`, the first parameter is the server name. This is the only required parameter for this method, although it's likely that the FTP server will require the second and third parameters also. The second parameter is the username to be used to log in to the FTP server. The third parameter is the password to be used. The fourth parameter is the port to use to connect to the FTP server. There is a fifth parameter, a Boolean value, which, if `TRUE`, specifies to use the FTP passive mode. A typical use of the `GetFtpConnection` method is as follows:

```
CFtpConnection* pConnect;
CInternetSession isSession;
CString sServer;
CString sUserName;
CString sPassword;

sServer = "ftp.myserver.com ";
sUserName = "MyName";
```

```
sPassword = "MyPassword";
pConnect = isSession.GetFtpConnection(sServer,
        sUserName, sPassword);
```

GetGopherConnection

The GetGopherConnection is just like the GetFtpConnection method, with several necessary differences. The first difference is that the GetGopherConnection returns a pointer to an instance of the CGopherConnection class, as you would expect it to. The second difference is that it does not take the fifth parameter available with the GetFtpConnection method because that parameter is an FTP-specific option.

In short order, the parameters for the GetGopherConnection start with the server name. The second and third parameters are the username and password to be used to log in to the Gopher server. The fourth parameter is the port to connect to on the Gopher server. A typical use of this method is as follows:

```
CGopherConnection* pConnect;
CInternetSession isSession;
CString sServer;
CString sUserName;
CString sPassword;

sServer = "gopher.myserver.com ";
sUserName = "MyName";
sPassword = "MyPassword";
pConnect = isSession.GetGopherConnection(sServer,
        sUserName, sPassword);
```

Working with Cookies

Cookies are a fact of life on the Web. They are small pieces of information that are placed on your computer by Web sites that are sent to specific Web addresses whenever you visit a specific site. Cookies have been regarded with suspicion by some, although they are considered an efficient solution to many Web programming problems by others. Regardless of which side you might be on in the argument over cookies, the WinInet MFC classes provide you with functionality to incorporate them into your applications.

The first of the cookie functions is the SetCookie function. This function will place a cookie on the computer your application is running on. The SetCookie function takes three parameters. The first parameter is the URL to which the cookie is to be sent. The second parameter is the name of the cookie, and the third parameter is the value of the cookie. A typical use of the SetCookie function is as follows:

```
CInternetSession isSession;
CString sURL;
```

25

WinInet
PROGRAMMING

```
CString sCookieName;
CString sCookieValue;

sURL = "www.myserver.com ";
sCookieName = "MyCookie";
sCookieValue = "MyValue";
if(isSession.SetCookie(sURL, sCookieName, sCookieValue)
{
    .
    .
    .
}
```

The next cookie function enables you to retrieve a cookie from your computer. This function, `GetCookie`, has two slightly different versions. Both versions have the URL as the first parameter, and the cookie name to retrieve as the second parameter. The first version requires a string pointer as the third argument, with the size of the buffer as the fourth parameter. The second version requires the address of a `CString` object as the third parameter.

If you are using the first version of the `GetCookie` function, you'll probably also want to use the third cookie function, `GetCookieLength`, to determine the size of the buffer needed. The `GetCookieLength` function takes the URL and cookie name as its only two parameters, and returns the cookie size. A typical usage of these two functions is as follows:

```
CInternetSession isSession;
CString sURL;
CString sCookieName;
char* sCookieValue;
DWORD dwCookieLength;

sURL = "www.myserver.com ";
sCookieName = "MyCookie";
dwCookieLength = GetCookieLength(sURL, sCookieName);
sCookieValue = new char[(dwCookieLength + 1)];
if(isSession.GetCookie(sURL, sCookieName, sCookieValue,
    (dwCookieLength + 1))
{
    .
    .
    .
}
```

If you want to use the second version of the `GetCookie` function, it might look like this:

```
CInternetSession isSession;
CString sURL;
CString sCookieName;
CString sCookieValue;
```

```
sURL = "www.myserver.com ";
sCookieName = "MyCookie";
if(isSession.GetCookie(sURL, sCookieName, &sCookieValue)
{
.
.
.
}
```

Keeping Up with the Session Status

Several functions are available for keeping track of the status of the Internet communications of your application. If you create your own descendant class from the CInternetSession class, there is a method that you can override called OnStatusCallback. This method is called whenever there is an operation pending, with information about the status of the operation. Before the OnStatusCallback callback function will be called, you have to enable it using the EnableStatusCallback function. The EnableStatusCallback function takes a single Boolean variable, enabling or disabling the OnStatusCallback callback function.

The OnStatusCallback function is defined as follows:

```
virtual void OnStatusCallback(DWORD dwContext,
        DWORD dwInternetStatus, LPVOID lpvStatusInformation,
        DWORD dwStatusInformationLength);
```

The first parameter passed to it is the context that was provided to the class constructor, or passed in with the OpenURL function. The second parameter is a status indicator, listed in Table 25.5. The third parameter is a pointer to a buffer containing additional information that is pertinent to the callback, with the fourth being the size of the buffer.

TABLE 25.5   INTERNET STATUS INDICATORS

Value	Description
INTERNET_STATUS_RESOLVING_NAME	Looking up the IP address for the server.
INTERNET_STATUS_NAME_RESOLVED	The IP address for the server has been found.
INTERNET_STATUS_CONNECTING_TO_SERVER	Connecting to the IP address indicated.
INTERNET_STATUS_CONNECTED_TO_SERVER	Successfully connected to the IP address.
INTERNET_STATUS_SENDING_REQUEST	Sending the information to the server. The lpvStatusInformation parameter is NULL.
INTERNET_STATUS_REQUEST_SENT	Successfully sent the information to the server. The lpvStatusInformation parameter is NULL.

continues

25

WinInet
PROGRAMMING

TABLE 25.5   CONTINUED

Value	Description
INTERNET_STATUS_RECEIVING_RESPONSE	Waiting for the server to respond. The lpvStatusInformation parameter is NULL.
INTERNET_STATUS_RESPONSE_RECEIVED	Successfully received the response from the server. The lpvStatusInformation parameter is NULL.
INTERNET_STATUS_CLOSING_CONNECTION	Closing the connection to the server. The lpvStatusInformation parameter is NULL.
INTERNET_STATUS_CONNECTION_CLOSED	The connection to the server has been closed. The lpvStatusInformation parameter is NULL.
INTERNET_STATUS_HANDLE_CREATED	Indicates that a new handle has been created for the Internet connection. This handle can be used to cancel a connection that is taking too long.
INTERNET_STATUS_HANDLE_CLOSED	Indicates that the connection to which the handle belongs has been closed.
INTERNET_STATUS_REQUEST_COMPLETE	Indicates that the asynchronous request is complete.

If you override the OnStatusCallback function, you need to call the AFX_MANAGE_STATE macro immediately upon entering the OnStatusCallback function. A typical use of the OnStatusCallback might look like the following:

```
// Enable the status callback function
m_misSession.EnableStatusCallback(TRUE);
.
.
.
void CMyInternetSession::OnStatusCallback(DWORD dwContext,
    DWORD dwInternetStatus, LPVOID lpvStatusInformation,
    DWORD dwStatusInformationLength)
{
    // Get the MFC module state (this is required)
    AFX_MANAGE_STATE(AfxGetAppModuleState());
    // What's the new status of the Internet Session?
    switch (dwInternetStatus)
    {
    // Resolving the server name
    case INTERNET_STATUS_RESOLVING_NAME:
    .
    .
    .
```

There are two more status and information functions that are members of the CInternetSession class. The first enables you to determine the type of server you are connected to, and the second enables you to get the context ID for a particular CInternetSession object.

The ServiceTypeFromHandle function takes the handle of a CInternetSession object, available from the HINTERNET operator, and returns a DWORD that indicates the service type of the current session. The possible return values are listed in Table 25.6.

TABLE 25.6 INTERNET SESSION SERVICE TYPES

Return Value	Service Type
INTERNET_SERVICE_FTP	FTP
INTERNET_SERVICE_HTTP	HTTP
INTERNET_SERVICE_GOPHER	Gopher
AFX_INET_SERVICE_FILE	File

The last of the status and informational functions is the GetContext function. This function takes no parameters and returns a DWORD value, which is the context ID that was either passed in through the CInternetSession constructor, or through the OpenURL function.

CInternetFile

The CInternetFile class is the base class from which all of the other WinInet file classes are descended. It is a descendant of the CStdioFile class, and is also the file class that is used for the FTP service type. It is a full file class, with all the functions you'd expect for reading, writing, and navigating through a file.

Opening and Closing

Opening a CInternetFile object is done through either the OpenURL method of the CInternetSession class, or through one of the connection classes, CHttpConnection, CFtpConnection, or CGopherConnection. These objects and functions will return a pointer to a CInternetFile object, or a CStdioFile object if you are using the OpenURL method to open a local file.

When you are ready or need to close the file, you have several options, depending on the circumstances. If you need to close the file in a clean fashion, you can use the Close method. This will close the file, cleaning up any outstanding data buffers. Also, if the file was opened for writing, it will call the Flush method, which makes sure that all contents of the write buffer have been sent to and received by the server, before closing the file. If you need to close the file and end all communications, ignoring any exception conditions or any unsent data, you can call the `Abort` method, which truncates all of the file data communications and closes the file for any additional reading or writing.

Reading and Writing

There are two methods for reading and writing data with a `CInternetFile` object. Which one you use depends partly on whether the file is an ASCII text file or a binary file.

The two basic read/write functions are `Read` and `Write`. Both of these functions take a pointer to a buffer as the first parameter, and a UINT containing the size of the buffer as the second parameter. For the `Read` function, the data read from the `CInternetFile` object will be placed into this buffer, and the function will return a UINT value specifying how much was read into the buffer. For the `Write` function, the data to be written to the `CInternetFile` should be in the buffer pointed to by the first parameter, with the second parameter specifying how much data to write.

Alternatives to the `Read` and `Write` functions are the `ReadString` and `WriteString` functions. The `ReadString` function can take a pointer to a `CString` object, into which it will read the input file. The `ReadString` function can also take a pointer to a buffer and the size of the buffer, just as with the `Read` function. The `ReadString` function will read in up to the total size of the input buffer, until it reaches a newline character. The `WriteString` function takes a pointer to a null-terminated string and writes the string to the output file on the server.

If you are reading an HTTP file, there is another function that you can use to control how you are maneuvering through the file. The `Seek` function enables you to provide random access for `CHttpFile` type files (it is not currently supported for other Internet file types). The `Seek` function takes two parameters. The first parameter specifies how far to move the file position, and in which direction (positive values move you forward through the file, whereas negative values move you backward), and the second parameter specifies the reference point in the file from which to move. The available values for the reference point parameters are listed in Table 25.7.

TABLE 25.7   INTERNET FILE SEEK STARTING POSITIONS

Return Value	Service Type
CFile::begin	Move the current position in the file the specified number of bytes from the start of the file.
CFile::current	Move the current position in the file the specified number of bytes from the current position in the file.

Return Value	Service Type
CFile::end	Move the current position in the file the specified number of bytes from the end of the file.

Controlling the Buffer

There are two more functions for the CInternetFile class that affect how the class performs communications over the Internet. These two functions control the size of the read and write communications buffers. The read and write communications buffers are used to hold data being sent to the server until it can all be sent over the Internet and received by the server, and to hold data being received from the server until your application can read it from the buffer. Both of these two functions, SetWriteBufferSize and SetReadBufferSize, take a single UINT parameter that specifies the new size of the buffer. These functions will return a Boolean value to specify whether or not they were successful at allocating the size buffer specified.

CInternetException

Whenever any of the WinInet classes throw an exception, you will need to use the CInternetException class to handle the exception. The CInternetException class has two member properties that you can use to determine what the error was, and what needs to be done to correct it. The first member, m_dwError, is the identifier of the error that occurred. This can be any base Windows error, defined in WINERROR.H, or an Internet-specific error, defined in WININET.H.

The second member of the CInternetException class is m_dwContext, which contains the context ID of the thread that the exception occurred in. This is the same context ID that was provided during the creation of the CInternetSession instance, or with the OpenURL function.

CInternetConnection

The CInternetConnection class is one of the classes that you'll rarely use directly. It is the base class for the CHttpConnection, CFtpConnection, and CGopherConnection classes. It's created by calling the GetHttpConnection, GetFtpConnection, or GetGopherConnection CInternetSession functions.

The CInternetConnection class contains only three functions. The GetContext function can be called to get the context ID of the connection. The GetSession function can be used to get a pointer to the CInternetSession instance that created the connection. And the `GetServerName` function can be called to get the name of the server to which the connection is open.

Building a Simple WinInet Application

You can use these basic WinInet classes to build a basic application. You can build a basic application around the `OpenURL` member function of the `CInternetSession` class. What this application will be able to do is to take a URL entered by the user, and retrieve the file specified. The file will be displayed for the user to see. The version that is included here is intended for working with text files only, but the same principles can be used for working with binary files also.

Creating the Application Shell

For this sample application, you can create a standard dialog-style application using the AppWizard. You don't need to include support for Windows Sockets, as the WinInet hides all of the socket programming from you, and you also don't need to include support for ActiveX controls. For the purpose of the sample code, name your project InetSession.

After you have the application shell created, lay out the main dialog window as shown in Figure 25.2. Configure the controls as specified in Table 25.8, attaching variables to the controls using the ClassWizard as specified in Table 25.9.

FIGURE 25.2

The main dialog layout for the InetSession project.

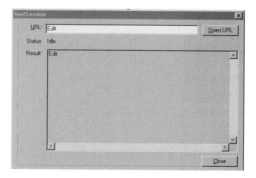

TABLE 25.8 CONTROL PROPERTY SETTINGS

Object	Property	Setting
Static text	ID	IDC_STATIC
	Caption	&URL
Edit box	ID	IDC_EURL

Object	Property	Setting
Command button	ID	IDC_BURL
	Caption	&Open URL
Static text	ID	IDC_STATIC
	Caption	Status:
Static text	ID	IDC_SSTATUS
	Caption	Idle
Static text	ID	IDC_STATIC
	Caption	Result:
Edit box	ID	IDC_ERESULT
	Multiline	Checked
	Horizontal scroll	Checked
	Vertical scroll	Checked
	Read-only	Checked
Command button	ID	IDCANCEL
	Caption	&Close

TABLE 25.9 CONTROL VARIABLES

Object	Name	Category	Type
IDC_ERESULT	m_sResult	Value	CString
IDC_EURL	m_sUrl	Value	CString
IDC_SSTATUS	m_sStatus	Value	CString

After you have finished adding the controls to the dialog window and have attached variables to all the controls, you are now ready to dig into the program code. You'll start by creating a descendant to the `CInternetSession` class and then move on to add the main application code that manipulates the Internet functionality.

Inheriting the `CInternetSession` Class

With this application, you'll use the `OnStatusCallback` function to display the status of the application communications. This requires that you create your own descendant of the `CInternetSession` class. For this sample application, name your descendant class `CMyInternetSession`. Declare the `CInetSessionDlg` class before the definition of your new class, as in Listing 25.1.

Listing 25.1 The CMyInternetSession Class Definition

```
class CInetSessionDlg;

class CMyInternetSession : public CInternetSession
{
public:
    CMyInternetSession();
    virtual ~CMyInternetSession();
};
```

Add a member variable to your new class, a pointer to the dialog class. Specify the type as CInetSessionDlg*, the name as m_pParentDialog, and the access as private. Next, add a function to initialize this pointer, named SetParentDialog (CInetSessionDlg* pParentDialog), and use this function to set the m_pParentDialog pointer, as in Listing 25.2.

Listing 25.2 The SetParentDialog Function

```
void CMyInternetSession::SetParentDialog(
        CInetSessionDlg *pParentDialog)
{
    // Set the parent dialog pointer
    m_pParentDialog = pParentDialog;
}
```

Finally, add the virtual override function OnStatusCallback, with the parameters specified earlier. Fill in this function to pass a description of the current status to the parent dialog as in Listing 25.3. You'll use a dialog function that you haven't defined yet to update the status display.

Listing 25.3 The OnStatusCallback Function

```
void CMyInternetSession::OnStatusCallback(DWORD dwContext,
    DWORD dwInternetStatus, LPVOID lpvStatusInformation,
    DWORD dwStatusInformationLength)
{
    // Get the MFC module state (this is required)
    AFX_MANAGE_STATE(AfxGetAppModuleState());

    CString sNewStatus;
    CString sStatusInfo((LPCSTR)lpvStatusInformation);

    // Do we have a valid pointer to the parent dialog?
    if (m_pParentDialog)
    {
        // What's the new status of the Internet Session?
```

```
switch (dwInternetStatus)
{
// Resolving the server name
case INTERNET_STATUS_RESOLVING_NAME:
    if (dwStatusInformationLength > 0)
        sNewStatus = "Resolving name - " + sStatusInfo;
    else
        sNewStatus = "Resolving name";
    break;

// Server name has been resolved
case INTERNET_STATUS_NAME_RESOLVED:
    if (dwStatusInformationLength > 0)
        sNewStatus = "Name resolved - " + sStatusInfo;
    else
        sNewStatus = "Name resolved";
    break;

// Connecting to the server
case INTERNET_STATUS_CONNECTING_TO_SERVER:
    sNewStatus = "Connecting to server";
    break;

// Connected to the server
case INTERNET_STATUS_CONNECTED_TO_SERVER:
    sNewStatus = "Connected to server";
    break;

// Sending the request
case INTERNET_STATUS_SENDING_REQUEST:
    sNewStatus = "Sending request";
    break;

// Request has been sent
case INTERNET_STATUS_REQUEST_SENT:
    sNewStatus = "Request sent";
    break;

// Receiving the response from the server
case INTERNET_STATUS_RECEIVING_RESPONSE:
    sNewStatus = "Receiving response";
    break;

// The response has been received
case INTERNET_STATUS_RESPONSE_RECEIVED:
    sNewStatus = "Response received";
    break;
```

continues

25

WinInet Programming

LISTING 25.3   CONTINUED

```
// Closing the connection
case INTERNET_STATUS_CLOSING_CONNECTION:
    sNewStatus = "Closing connection";
    break;

// The connection has been closed
case INTERNET_STATUS_CONNECTION_CLOSED:
    sNewStatus = "Connection closed";
    break;

// A handle to the Internet Status has been created
case INTERNET_STATUS_HANDLE_CREATED:
    sNewStatus = "Handle created";
    break;

// Closing the handle of the Status
case INTERNET_STATUS_HANDLE_CLOSING:
    sNewStatus = "Closing handle";
    break;

// Request has been completed
case INTERNET_STATUS_REQUEST_COMPLETE:
    sNewStatus = "Request complete";
    break;

// Unknown status code
default:
    sNewStatus = "Unknown Status";
    break;
}
// Update the dialog with the new status
m_pParentDialog->UpdateStatus(sNewStatus);
    }
}
```

Starting and Stopping the Internet Session

To initialize your Internet session, you need to create an instance of your Internet session class. This can be done very simply by declaring a variable of your class type in the dialog class of your application. Add this variable to the CInetSessionDlg class, specifying the variable type as CMyInternetSession, the variable name as m_misSession, and the access as private.

Starting the Internet session is a very simple matter that can be handled in your application initialization. In the OnInitDialog function, you can add the code in Listing 25.4.

LISTING 25.4   THE OnInitDialog FUNCTION

```
BOOL CInetSessionDlg::OnInitDialog()
{
    CDialog::OnInitDialog();
    .
    .
    .
    .

    // TODO: Add extra initialization here

    // Set the Session class's pointer to this dialog window
    m_misSession.SetParentDialog(this);

    // Enable the status callback function
    m_misSession.EnableStatusCallback(TRUE);

    // Initialize the screen variables
    m_sStatus = "Waiting";
    m_sUrl = "http://www.microsoft.com/";
    m_sResult = "";
    UpdateData(FALSE);

    return TRUE;   // return TRUE  unless you set the focus to a control
}
```

In this bit of code, you initialized the Internet session class pointer to the dialog with the SetParentDialog function. Next you enabled the use of the OnStatusCallback function with the EnableStatusCallback function. The remaining lines of the OnInitDialog function are used for initializing the variables that you defined and attached to screen controls earlier.

To close the Internet session, attach a function to your Close button. In this function, you'll call the CInternetSession Close function, and then call the ancestor OnCancel function to close the application, as in Listing 25.5.

LISTING 25.5   THE OnCancel FUNCTION

```
void CInetSessionDlg::OnCancel()
{
    // TODO: Add extra cleanup here

    // Close the Internet Session
    m_misSession.Close();

    // Close the dialog
    CDialog::OnCancel();
}
```

25

WININET
PROGRAMMING

To enable the status display to function properly, you need to add a function to the dialog class to receive the status description and update the display with it. To add this functionality, add a new member function to the `CInetSessionDlg` class, specify the function type as `void`, its name as `UpdateStatus(CString sNewStatus)`, and its access as `public`. This gives you the function definition as you used it back in Listing 25.3. Add the code in Listing 25.6 to this new function.

LISTING 25.6   THE `UpdateStatus` FUNCTION

```
void CInetSessionDlg::UpdateStatus(CString sNewStatus)
{
    // Update the screen with the current status
    m_sStatus = sNewStatus;
    UpdateData(FALSE);
}
```

Retrieving the URL Specified

The heart of your application is the retrieval of the URL file. This will be done using the `OpenURL` function. When you have a file pointer back from the `OpenURL` function, you can read lines of text from this file until the end of the file has been reached. To add this last bit of functionality to your application, add a function to the Open URL button using the ClassWizard. Add the code provided in Listing 25.7 to this function.

LISTING 25.7   THE `OnBurl` FUNCTION

```
void CInetSessionDlg::OnBurl()
{
    CStdioFile* fpUrlFile;
    CString sCurLine;
    // TODO: Add your control notification handler code here

    // Get the screen control variables
    UpdateData(TRUE);

    // Open the URL specified
    fpUrlFile = m_misSession.OpenURL(m_sUrl);

    // Did we receive a valid Internet file pointer?
    if (fpUrlFile)
    {
        // Read lines of text from the file until all has
        // been received
        while (fpUrlFile->ReadString(sCurLine))
        {
            // Add the new line to the text control
            // and sync with the dialog screen.
```

```
            m_sResult += sCurLine;
            UpdateData(FALSE);
        }
    }
}
```

Before compiling and running your application, make sure that your
CMyInternetSession code files include all the other class header files in your project.
The first part of your CMyInternetSession.CPP file should look like Listing 25.8. You'll
also want to make sure that the MyInternetSession.h file is included in the dialog code,
either in the source code file or the header file. (If you used the wizards throughout this
example, the header for your Internet session class might be included in the header file
for your dialog class.)

LISTING 25.8 THE CMyInternetSession.CPP include SECTION

```
#include "stdafx.h"
#include "InetSession.h"
#include "MyInternetSession.h"
#include "InetSessionDlg.h"
  .
  .
  .
```

At this point you should be ready to compile and run your application, downloading
HTML text files as shown in Figure 25.3.

FIGURE 25.3

*The running
Internet session
application.*

Application-Level Functionality

The WinInet classes that we've looked at so far are the base classes, from which the
application-level classes are descended. The application-level classes provide

application-specific functionality. The HTTP classes can only be used to connect to and interact with a Web HTTP server. The FTP classes can only be used with FTP servers. And the same with the Gopher classes. It is at this level that the WinInet classes gain a lot of flexibility and usefulness.

HTTP Classes

The HTTP classes enable you to incorporate HTTP-specific functionality into your applications with ease. Because of the simplicity of the HTTP protocol, the connection class is fairly simple, with only a single member function. The file class, however, has quite a number of functions dealing with the intricacies of the HTTP-specific use of the MIME message format.

CHttpConnection

The CHttpConnection class contains only a single member function, OpenRequest. This function does have two versions, with only a subtle difference between the two. The first parameter is the only difference between the two versions, and that parameter is the HTTP command being sent to the server in both versions.

In the first version of the OpenRequest function, the HTTP command is passed as a pointer to a string containing the HTTP command. If NULL is provided for this parameter, the GET command is assumed as a default. The second version of the OpenRequest function takes an integer constant that specifies the HTTP command to be sent to the server. The possible values of this parameter are listed in Table 25.10.

TABLE 25.10   HTTP COMMAND PARAMETER VALUES

HTTP Command	Integer Value
HTTP_VERB_POST	0
HTTP_VERB_GET	1
HTTP_VERB_HEAD	2
HTTP_VERB_PUT	3
HTTP_VERB_LINK	4
HTTP_VERB_DELETE	5
HTTP_VERB_UNLINK	6

Starting with the second parameter, the two versions of the OpenRequest function are identical. The second parameter is a string containing the target object, normally a file, of the specified HTTP command. The third parameter is a string containing the URL of the document where the current request originated. If you pass NULL for this parameter, no HTTP header is specified.

The fourth parameter is the context ID for this operation. This will be returned in the OnStatusCallback for identifying this particular transaction. The fifth parameter is a string containing the accept types for your application. This is a string containing a list of the MIME file types that your application can accept and understand. This won't prevent the Web server from sending you a file type that your application doesn't understand, but it may have some effect on CGI processes that are called using the PUT and POST commands.

The sixth parameter is a string specifying which version of the HTTP protocol your application supports. If you pass a NULL for this parameter, the supported version is assumed to be HTTP/1 and that is what is sent to the server. The seventh and final parameter is a flag value that can be used to set various options on how the command is processed. The possible values that can be used for this flag are listed in Table 25.11.

TABLE 25.11 OpenRequest OPTIONS

Value	*Description*
INTERNET_FLAG_RELOAD	Retrieve the file from the server, even if cached locally.
INTERNET_FLAG_DONT_CACHE	Don't cache the file, either locally or on any gateway or server.
INTERNET_FLAG_SECURE	Applicable for HTTP URLs only, this flag specifies to use Secure Sockets Layer or PCT for a secure transaction.
INTERNET_FLAG_MAKE_PERSISTENT	Adds the returned object to the local cache as a persistent entity that does not get removed when the cache is cleared.
INTERNET_FLAG_NO_AUTO_REDIRECT	Specifies that HTTP redirects should not be automatically handled.

If you need to extract the server and object from a URL for use with the OpenRequest function, you can use the global function AfxParseURL. The AfxParseURL function takes the entire URL as the first parameter, and parses it into its various parts. The protocol is returned in the second parameter, which is a pointer to a DWORD variable. The protocol is returned indicating the service type using the constants listed in Table 25.12.

TABLE 25.12   AfxParseURL PROTOCOL TYPES

Value	Protocol
AFX_INET_SERVICE_FTP	FTP
AFX_INET_SERVICE_HTTP	HTTP
AFX_INET_SERVICE_HTTPS	HTTPS (HTTP with Secure Sockets Layer)
AFX_INET_SERVICE_GOPHER	Gopher
AFX_INET_SERVICE_FILE	Local file
AFX_INET_SERVICE_MAILTO	SMTP email
AFX_INET_SERVICE_NEWS	Usenet News
AFX_INET_SERVICE_NNTP	NNTP (Usenet News)
AFX_INET_SERVICE_TELNET	Telnet (Network terminal session)
AFX_INET_SERVICE_WAIS	WAIS
AFX_INET_SERVICE_MID	MID
AFX_INET_SERVICE_CID	CID
AFX_INET_SERVICE_PROSPERO	PROSPERO
AFX_INET_SERVICE_AFS	AFS
AFX_INET_SERVICE_UNK	Unknown

The third parameter is a pointer to a string into which the server name will be placed. The fourth parameter is a pointer to a string into which the object to be retrieved will be placed. The fifth parameter is a pointer to a WORD variable (declared as an INTERNET_PORT type), into which the port number will be placed. A typical use of the AfxParseURL and OpenRequest functions is as follows:

```
CHttpConnection* pConnect;
CHttpFile* pFile;
CInternetSession isSession;
CString sServer;
CString sURL;
CString sObjectName;
INTERNET_PORT wPort;
DWORD dwProtocol;

sURL = "http://www.myserver.com/this_file.html";
if (AfxParseURL(sURL, &dwProtocol, &sServer, &sObjectName, &wPort);
{
   if (dwProtocol == AFX_INET_SERVICE_HTTP)
   {
      pConnect = isSession.GetHttpConnection(sServer, wPort);
      if (pConnect)
```

```
{
    pFile = pConnect->OpenRequest("GET", (LPCSTR)sObjectName);
    .
    .
    .
```

There is also the `AfxParseURLEx` function, which will also extract the username and password from the URL, assuming that they are included.

CHttpFile

The `CHttpFile` class is created whenever you use the `OpenRequest` method of the `CHttpConnection` class, or the `OpenURL` method of the `CInternetSession` class, requesting an HTTP resource. When you have a valid `CHttpFile` object, you can customize the request that is being sent to the Web server. The request hasn't actually been sent to the server yet; it's just been created and packaged in the form of a `CHttpFile` object. From here, you can add additional headers, attach data to the request for sending with a `POST` or `PUT` command, and so on.

Packaging and Sending a Request

When you have a valid `CHttpFile` object, you can add additional headers to the request before sending it by using the `AddRequestHeaders` function. There are two versions of this function, differing in how you supply the headers to the request. The first version takes a pointer to a string buffer containing the new headers as the first parameter, with the size of the buffer as the third parameter. The second version takes a pointer to a `CString` as the first parameter. If you are including multiple headers in this request, each header must be separated by a CR/LF (Carriage Return/Line Feed) combination. With both versions of this function, the second parameter is a flag that indicates what to do with the headers passed in. The available values for this flag are listed in Table 25.13.

TABLE 25.13 `AddRequestHeaders` OPTION VALUES

Value	Description
HTTP_ADDREQ_FLAG_COALESCE	Merges headers of the same name.
HTTP_ADDREQ_FLAG_REPLACE	Replaces headers of the same name. If the header value is found, and the new header value is empty, the header is removed. Can only supply a single header with this option.
HTTP_ADDREQ_FLAG_ADD_IF_NEW	Adds the header only if it does not already exist.
HTTP_ADDREQ_FLAG_ADD	Used with REPLACE; adds the header if it doesn't already exist.

25

WinInet Programming

When you have everything ready to send, you have two options for sending the actual request to the server, the SendRequest and SendRequestEx functions. The SendRequest function takes as the first argument a list of the names of the headers to send with the request. If you pass a pointer to this list, you need to pass the length of the string of header names as the second parameter. If you pass a CString as the list of headers to send, you don't need to specify the length of the string. The next parameter that you can supply is a pointer to a buffer containing any data to be sent with a POST or PUT command, followed by a DWORD indicating the size of the buffer to be sent.

The SendRequestEx function enables you to use the Write and WriteString member functions of the CInternetFile class to include the data to be sent using the POST or PUT command. The catch is that you need to specify with the SendRequestEx function the total length of the data to be sent. When you have sent all of the data, you need to close the request using the EndRequest function.

Retrieving Information About a Request

After you have sent your request to the Web server, you can retrieve information about the returned object. You can use several CHttpFile functions to get information from the response.

The QueryInfo function can be used to retrieve any of the headers that were included in the response received from the Web server. The QueryInfo function takes an indicator value as the first parameter that indicates the level of the header requested. The possible values for this indicator are listed in Table 25.14.

TABLE 25.14   QueryInfo HEADER LEVEL VALUES

Value	Description
HTTP_QUERY_CUSTOM	Finds the requested header and, if found, returns its value in the buffer pointed to by the second parameter.
HTTP_QUERY_FLAG_REQUEST_HEADERS	Queries the request headers sent by your application to the server.
HTTP_QUERY_FLAG_SYSTEMTIME	For those headers whose value is a date/time string, returns the value as a standard Win32 SYSTEMTIME structure.
HTTP_QUERY_FLAG_NUMBER	For those headers whose value is a number, returns the value as a 32-bit number.

The second parameter can vary depending on the type of header requested and the header level specified in the first parameter. The generic parameter is a pointer to a buffer to receive the value, followed by the size of the buffer. If the value requested is a date/time, and the HTTP_QUERY_FLAG_SYSTEMTIME level was requested, the second parameter needs to be a pointer to a SYSTEMTIME structure. If the value is a string value, you also have the option of passing a pointer to a CString object. The final parameter is a pointer to a DWORD, specifying the index of a header, for use with retrieving multiple headers with the same name.

If you want to get the HTTP status code of the request, you can use the QueryInfoStatusCode function. This function takes a pointer to a DWORD variable into which the request status code will be placed. Some common HTTP request status codes are listed in Table 25.15.

TABLE 25.15   COMMON HTTP STATUS CODE VALUES

Value	Description
200	URL located, transmission follows
400	Unintelligible request
404	Requested URL not found
405	Server does not support the requested method
500	Unknown server error
503	Server capacity reached

If you want to check to see what HTTP command is being sent with your request, you can use the GetVerb function, which returns a CString containing the command. Likewise, the GetObject function returns the object name being requested from the server, or you can use the GetFileURL function to return the entire URL requested. All three of these functions take no parameters and return a CString.

When you are finished with the HTTP request, call the Close function to close the request and free all resources allocated to it.

FTP Classes

The FTP classes provide you with FTP-specific functionality. The CFtpConnection class provides you with the server navigation functionality necessary to move around the FTP server. The CFileFind and CFtpFileFind classes provide you with the ability to get listings of the files in various directories on the FTP server.

CFtpConnection

The methods of the CFtpConnection class can be broken down into two basic areas of functionality: directories and files. The directory methods provide you with navigation and directory management functionality. The file methods enable you to move, rename, put, and get files—depending on your permissions on the FTP server.

Directories and Navigation

The directory functions for the CFtpConnection class can be used to navigate around the FTP server, or to create or delete directories. To start with, you probably will want to find out what directory you are currently in on the FTP server. This can be done with one of two functions. The GetCurrentDirectory or GetCurrentDirectoryAsURL functions both will take a pointer to a CString object as their only parameter. Both of these functions place the current directory into the CString object. The GetCurrentDirectoryAsURL function formats the directory name as a URL, where the GetCurrentDirectory only gives you the directory and path.

In order to navigate around the directories on the FTP server, you can use the SetCurrentDirectory function. This function takes a string pointer, specifying the directory to move to as the only parameter. It returns a Boolean value, indicating whether it was successful or not.

If you need to create or remove a directory from the current directory on the FTP server, you can use the CreateDirectory or RemoveDirectory functions respectively. Both of these functions return a Boolean value to indicate whether or not they were successful. The possibility of success or failure for these functions is primarily due to the security on the FTP server, and whether the user of your application is logged in to the server and has adequate permission to create, remove, or even navigate to a specific directory.

Working with Files

The functions for putting and getting files from the FTP server are all-inclusive. They eliminate any file manipulating on your application's part. You specify the filename on the FTP server, and the filename on your local computer, and the CFtpConnection object takes it from there.

For instance, if you want to copy a file that you have on your computer to an FTP server to which you are connected, you can use the PutFile function. The first parameter that you have to pass the PutFile function is the name of the local file to send to the FTP server. The second parameter is the name to be given to the file on the FTP server. The third parameter specifies which mode is to be used in the transfer, whether to send the

file as a binary file (FTP_TRANSFER_TYPE_BINARY), or as an ASCII text file
(FTP_TRANSFER_TYPE_ASCII). The fourth parameter is the context ID that can be used to
track the process using the CInternetSession object.

If you want to get a file from the FTP server, the GetFile function makes it almost as
easy. For the GetFile function, the first two parameters are reversed, the first being the
filename on the FTP server, and the second being the name to use on the local computer.
The third parameter is a Boolean value indicating whether the function should fail if the
local filename specified already exists. The fourth parameter is a flag used to indicate
any options to use for the local file to be created. The list of these options is provided in
Table 25.16. The fifth parameter specifies whether to send the file as binary or ASCII,
using the same two values as in the PutFile function. And finally, the sixth parameter is
the context ID to be used to identify the transaction with the CInternetSession status
monitoring functions.

TABLE 25.16   FTP GetFile OPTIONS

Value	Description
FILE_ATTRIBUTE_ARCHIVE	The file is to be marked as an archive file.
FILE_ATTRIBUTE_COMPRESSED	The file is to be compressed.
FILE_ATTRIBUTE_DIRECTORY	The file is a directory.
FILE_ATTRIBUTE_NORMAL	The file has no other attributes set. This is the default setting and must be used alone.
FILE_ATTRIBUTE_HIDDEN	The file is hidden.
FILE_ATTRIBUTE_READONLY	The file is to be marked as read-only.
FILE_ATTRIBUTE_SYSTEM	The file is to be used exclusively by the operating system.
FILE_ATTRIBUTE_TEMPORARY	The file is being used for temporary storage.

If you need to open a file on the FTP server for reading or writing, you can use the
OpenFile function. The OpenFile function takes the filename on the FTP server as the
first parameter. The second parameter indicates whether the file should be opened for
reading (GENERIC_READ) or writing (GENERIC_WRITE), but cannot be opened for both. The
third parameter indicates whether the file should be opened in binary or ASCII mode,
using the same indicators as with the GetFile and PutFile functions. Finally, the fourth
parameter is the context ID to be used for monitoring the status of the transaction. The
OpenFile function returns a pointer to a CInternetFile object, which you can use to
read or write to the file.

When you need to manage the files on an FTP server, you have two functions available
to use. If you need to rename a file on the FTP server, you can use the Rename function.

25

WinInet PROGRAMMING

The Rename function takes two parameters, the first being the current name of the file, and the second being the new name for the file. The function returns a Boolean value indicating whether it was able to rename the file. If you need to delete a file from the FTP server, you can use the Remove function, giving the filename as the only parameter. Like the Rename function, the Remove function returns a Boolean value to indicate its success or failure.

When you have finished your FTP session, you can close the connection using the Close method. It takes no parameters and doesn't return any indicators of success or failure.

CFileFind

The CFileFind class is the base class for both the CFtpFileFind and CGopherFileFind classes. It provides a lot of the basic functionality necessary for the two descendant classes for enumerating the files in a directory on an FTP or a Gopher server, and getting the various attributes of the files and directories. You do not create a CFileFind object directly, but instead create either a CFtpFileFind or CGopherFileFind object.

File Operations

To find the files in a specified directory, you have to start by calling the FindFile function. The first parameter to the FindFile function is the mask to use in searching for matching files. If you pass NULL for this parameter, the FindFile function does a wildcard search (assuming a mask of *.*). The second parameter is currently unused, and must be passed a value of 0. If you want to find all the files in the current directory on either the FTP or Gopher server, you can get away without providing any parameters for the FindFile function, allowing it to use the default values.

After you have called the FindFile function, you have to call the FindNextFile function to retrieve all of the files in the directory. You place your application into a loop, calling FindNextFile repeatedly, until it returns FALSE, indicating that all matching files in the directory have been found. The FindNextFile function does not take any parameters, and continues the search started with the FindFile function.

> **TIP**
>
> When you are using the FindFile and FindNextFile functions, you will use the CFileFind attribute functions to get the name and other attributes of the current file (these functions will be covered next). You won't have a current file to check the attributes of until you call the FindNextFile for the first time. The FindFile function starts the search, but doesn't position the search at the first file.

When you have finished finding all of the matching files in your search, you need to call the Close method to close the search before you can start another search using the CFileFind class.

File Attributes

The file attribute functions are called to get specific attributes of a file, such as the file-name or size. Most of these functions do not take any parameters, and return an appropriate data type for the type of attribute being requested. All of the attribute functions return the attribute specified in the function name. All of the attribute functions are listed in Table 25.17.

TABLE 25.17   FTP GetFile OPTIONS

Function	Return Type	Parameter	Description
GetLength	DWORD	None	Returns the size of the file, in bytes.
GetFileName	CString	None	Returns the name of the file, including the extension.
GetFilePath	CString	None	Returns the whole path of the file.
GetFileTitle	CString	None	Returns the name of the file without the extension.
GetFileURL	CString	None	Returns the URL of the file.
GetRoot	CString	None	Returns the directory in which the file was found.
GetCreationTime	BOOL	CTime&	Places the time that the file was created in the CTime object passed in as a parameter.
GetLastAccessTime	BOOL	CTime&	Places the time that the file was last accessed in the CTime object passed in as a parameter.
GetLastWriteTime	BOOL	CTime&	Places the time that the file was last written to in the CTime object passed in as a parameter.
IsDots	BOOL	None	Indicates if the filename is . or .., indicating that it is a directory.
IsReadOnly	BOOL	None	Indicates whether the file is read-only.

continues

TABLE 25.17 CONTINUED

Function	Return Type	Parameter	Description
IsDirectory	BOOL	None	Indicates whether the file is a directory.
IsCompressed	BOOL	None	Indicates whether the file is compressed.
IsSystem	BOOL	None	Indicates whether the file is a system file.
IsHidden	BOOL	None	Indicates whether the file is hidden.
IsTemporary	BOOL	None	Indicates whether the file is a temporary file.
IsNormal	BOOL	None	Indicates whether the file is normal with no other attributes.
IsArchived	BOOL	None	Indicates whether the file is archived.

CFtpFileFind

The CFtpFileFind is used to perform the FTP-specific file-finding functionality. It is created by passing a pointer to an open CFtpConnection object in the constructor. The other parameter that you can provide to the CFtpFileFind constructor is the context ID to be used for monitoring the status of its operations.

After you have created a valid CFtpFileFind object, you can call its variation on the FindFile function to start the file search. The CFtpFileFind version of the FindFile function takes two parameters. The first parameter is the mask to be used in the search. If you provide NULL for this parameter, a wildcard search is assumed. The second parameter is a flag that is used to control how the search is performed. The available values for this flag are listed in Table 25.18.

TABLE 25.18 CFtpFileFind.FindFile OPTIONS

Value	Description
INTERNET_FLAG_RELOAD	Retrieve the file from the server, even if cached locally.
INTERNET_FLAG_DONT_CACHE	Don't cache the file, either locally or on any gateway or server.

Value	Description
INTERNET_FLAG_EXISTING_CONNECT	If possible, reuse the connection to the server for new requests generated with the FindFile function, instead of opening a new connection for each request.
INTERNET_FLAG_RAW_DATA	Override the defaults to return the raw data.

A typical usage of the CFtpFileFind class and the underlying CFindFile functionality is as follows:

```
CFtpConnection* m_fcConnection;
.
.
.
CFtpFileFind fFiles(m_fcConnection);
CString sFileName;
BOOL bMoreFiles;

// Find the first file
bMoreFiles = fFiles.FindFile(NULL);
// Loop as long as there are additional files
while (bMoreFiles)
{
    // Find the next file
    bMoreFiles = fFiles.FindNextFile();
    // Get the file name
    sFileName = fFiles.GetFileName();
    // Is the file a directory?
    if (fFiles.IsDirectory())
        // Mark it as a directory
        sFileName += "      <DIR>";
    // Do whatever with the file
    .
    .
    .
    .
}
fFiles.Close();
```

Gopher Classes

When you are working with a Gopher server, it takes a slightly different approach than with either an FTP or HTTP server. Gopher servers require what's known as a *locator* for retrieving a file from the server. The locator is passed around the various classes and member functions of the Gopher classes as a token that is used to maintain the context of the session between the client and the server.

25

WinInet
Programming

CGopherConnection

After you have created a CGopherConnection object from the CInternetSession object, you can use it to create a Gopher locator and open a file, but you more likely will create a CGopherFileFind object and then use it to create the locator to use to open and download a file.

If you know the name of the file that you want to open on the Gopher server, you can use it to create a locator using the CreateLocator function. There are three versions of the CreateLocator function. The first version of the CreateLocator function requires a pointer to the name of the document or directory on the Gopher server to be retrieved. The second parameter is the selector string to be used. Either of these two parameters may be NULL, specifying that the default directory of the Gopher server be used. The third parameter specifies whether the object being requested is a directory or a document.

The second version of the CreateLocator function requires a single parameter, a pointer to a string indicating the file to open. The third version requires the server name as the first parameter, followed by the parameters (in order) of the first version of the CreateLocator function. The final parameter for the third version is the port to connect to on the Gopher server. All three versions of this function return a CGopherLocator object as the return value.

The next function of the CGopherConnection class is the OpenFile function, which is used to open a document on the Gopher server. It returns a pointer to a CGopherFile object, which can then be used to read the contents of the file. The first parameter the OpenFile function requires is a pointer to a CGopherLocator object. The second parameter is a flag controlling how the file is opened and downloaded. The available settings for this flag can be found earlier in the CInternetSession::OpenURL function. The third parameter is a pointer to a string indicating which view of the file to open. If NULL is provided, the default view is opened. The fourth parameter is the context ID that is used to monitor the status of the transaction.

The final member function of the CGopherConnection class is the GetAttribute function. This function can be used to retrieve attributes of a document on a Gopher server. The first parameter is a pointer to a GOPHER_ATTRIBUTE_TYPE structure, in which the attribute is returned. The second parameter is a CString containing the attributes to be returned. The third parameter is a pointer to a CGopherLocator object.

CGopherLocator

The CGopherLocator class is directly used during a Gopher session, but is passed from function to function as a token. There is one member function of the CGopherLocator class, GetLocatorType, which is passed a pointer to a DWORD variable. The type of the locator is placed into this DWORD variable. The possible locator types are specified in Table 25.19.

TABLE 25.19   CGopherLocator Types

Value	*Description*
GOPHER_TYPE_TEXT_FILE	Indicates that the object is an ASCII text file.
GOPHER_TYPE_DIRECTORY	Indicates that the object is a directory containing more Gopher items.
GOPHER_TYPE_CSO	The object is a CSO phone book server.
GOPHER_TYPE_ERROR	Indicates that an error condition has occurred.
GOPHER_TYPE_MAC_BINHEX	The object is a Macintosh file in BINHEX format.
GOPHER_TYPE_DOS_ARCHIVE	The object is a DOS archive file.
GOPHER_TYPE_UNIX_UUENCODED	The object is a UUENCODED file.
GOPHER_TYPE_INDEX_SERVER	The object is an index server.
GOPHER_TYPE_TELNET	The object is a Telnet server that can be connected to using a Telnet terminal session.
GOPHER_TYPE_BINARY	The object is a binary file (unknown file type).
GOPHER_TYPE_REDUNDANT	The object is a duplicated server.
GOPHER_TYPE_TN3270	The object is a TN3270 server, which can be connected to using a TN3270 terminal emulator.
GOPHER_TYPE_GIF	The object is a GIF graphics file.
GOPHER_TYPE_IMAGE	The object is a generic image file.
GOPHER_TYPE_BITMAP	The object is a bitmap file.
GOPHER_TYPE_MOVIE	The object is a movie file.
GOPHER_TYPE_SOUND	The object is a sound file.
GOPHER_TYPE_HTML	The object is an HTML document.
GOPHER_TYPE_PDF	The object is an Adobe PDF file.
GOPHER_TYPE_CALENDAR	The object is a calendar file.
GOPHER_TYPE_INLINE	The object is an inline file.
GOPHER_TYPE_UNKNOWN	The object is an unknown file type.
GOPHER_TYPE_ASK	The object is an Ask+ item.
GOPHER_TYPE_GOPHER_PLUS	The object is a Gopher+ item.

25

WinInet Programming

CGopherFileFind

The CGopherFileFind is used to perform the Gopher-specific file-finding functionality. It is created by passing a pointer to an open CGopherConnection object in the constructor. The other parameter that you can provide to the CGopherFileFind constructor is the context ID to be used to monitor the status of its operations.

After you have created a valid CGopherFileFind object, you can call its variation on the FindFile function to start the file search. There are two versions of the FindFile function in the CGopherFileFind class. The first version of the FindFile function is the same as with the CFtpFileFind class, using the same options. The second version requires a pointer to a CGopherLocator object as the first parameter, and is the same for the next two parameters.

After you have started a file find, you can traverse the list of files in the same way that you do with an FTP file find. When you have located a file, you can call the GetLocator function to create the CGopherLocator object that was used to find the file, and the GetScreenName function to get the screen name for the selected file.

CGopherFile

After you have opened a file on the Gopher server using the OpenFile function, you can read the file using the standard CInternetFile or CStdioFile functions. The CGopherFile class extends some of these functions to provide Gopher-specific functionality, but doesn't add any new functions, or alter how you need to use any of the underlying functions.

Building a Simple FTP Client

To see how the application-level classes work, you can build a sample FTP client application. This will be a very rudimentary FTP client, showing only the files on the server side, and only allowing you to retrieve files. It will also require you to type in directory names if you want to change directories, instead of selecting the directory name in the list of available files to automatically be taken to the selected directory. All of the necessary functionality to make the sample application a full-featured FTP client is not difficult, and doesn't take a lot of time or effort.

Creating the Application Shell

For this sample application, you can create a standard dialog-style application using the AppWizard. As with the previous sample application, you don't need to include support for Windows Sockets, as the WinInet hides all of the socket programming from you, and you also don't need to include support for ActiveX controls. For the purpose of the sample code, name your project InetFTP.

After you have the application shell created, lay out the main dialog window as shown in Figure 25.4. Configure the controls as specified in Table 25.20, attaching variables to the controls using the ClassWizard as specified in Table 25.21.

FIGURE 25.4

The main dialog layout for the InetFTP project.

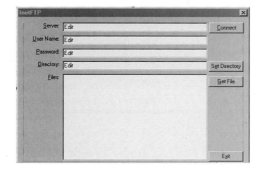

TABLE 25.20 CONTROL PROPERTY SETTINGS

Object	Property	Setting
Static text	ID	IDC_STATIC
	Caption	&Server
Edit box	ID	IDC_ESERVER
Command button	ID	IDC_BCONNECT
	Caption	&Connect
Static text	ID	IDC_STATIC
	Caption	&User Name:
Edit box	ID	IDC_EUSER
Static text	ID	IDC_STATIC
	Caption	&Password:
Edit box	ID	IDC_EPASSWORD
Static text	ID	IDC_STATIC
	Caption	&Directory:
Edit box	ID	IDC_EDIRECTORY
Command button	ID	IDC_BSETDIR
	Caption	S&et Directory

continues

TABLE 25.20 CONTINUED

Object	Property	Setting
Static text	ID	IDC_STATIC
	Caption	&Files:
List box	ID	IDC_LFILES
	Sort	Checked
	Vertical Scroll	Checked
Command button	ID	IDC_BGETFILE
	Caption	&Get File
Command button	ID	IDC_BCLOSE
	Caption	E&xit

TABLE 25.21 CONTROL VARIABLES

Object	Name	Category	Type
IDC_BCONNECT	m_cltConnect	Control	CButton
IDC_EDIRECTORY	m_sDirectory	Value	CString
IDC_EPASSWORD	m_sPassword	Value	CString
IDC_ESERVER	m_sServer	Value	CString
IDC_EUSER	m_sUser	Value	CString
IDC_LFILES	m_sFile	Value	CString
IDC_LFILES	m_lbFiles	Control	CListBox

Initializing the Application

In addition to the variables added through the ClassWizard, you'll need to add two additional variables to the dialog class. These two variables will be an instance of the CInternetSession class and a pointer to a CFtpConnection class. Both of these variables can be private in their scope. For this example, the CInternetSession variable will be named m_isSession, and the pointer to a CFtpConnection object will be named m_fcConnection.

After you have added these variables, you'll need to initialize all of the application variables. Set all of the control text variables to default values, and make sure the FTP connection pointer is NULL. To do this, add the code in Listing 25.9 to the OnInitDialog function.

LISTING 25.9   The OnInitDialog Function

```
BOOL CInetFTPDlg::OnInitDialog()
{
    CDialog::OnInitDialog();

    // Add "About..." menu item to system menu.
    .
    .
    .

    // Set the icon for this dialog.  The framework does this
    // automatically
    //  when the application's main window is not a dialog
    SetIcon(m_hIcon, TRUE);          // Set big icon
    SetIcon(m_hIcon, FALSE);         // Set small icon

    // TODO: Add extra initialization here

    // Initialize the form variables
    m_sServer = "ftp.brba.com";
    m_sDirectory = "";
    m_sUser = "anonymous";
    m_sPassword = "user@email.com";

    // And the FTP connection object
    m_fcConnection = NULL;

    // Update the screen
    UpdateData(FALSE);

    return TRUE;  // return TRUE  unless you set the focus
                  // to a control
}
```

To clean up the application, attach an event function to the Exit button and include the code in Listing 25.10. This code will close the Internet session, and then close the application.

LISTING 25.10   THE `OnBclose` FUNCTION

```
void CInetFTPDlg::OnBclose()
{
    // TODO: Add your control notification handler code here

    // End the Internet session
    m_isSession.Close();

    // Close the application
    OnOK();
}
```

Connecting to the FTP Server

For this sample application, you'll use the same button to open the connection to the FTP server and to close the connection. For opening the connection, you'll have to check to make sure you have a server name to connect to before opening the connection. When you have a connection open, you'll want to get the name of the current directory, and then get a listing of all of the files in the directory. To get a listing of the files in the directory, you'll call a function named `LoadListOfFiles`, which you'll write in just a minute. To add this functionality, attach an event function to the Connect button and add the code in Listing 25.11.

LISTING 25.11   THE `OnBconnect` FUNCTION

```
void CInetFTPDlg::OnBconnect()
{
    // TODO: Add your control notification handler code here

    // Get the data from the screen
    UpdateData(TRUE);

    // Do we have a current connection?
    if (!m_fcConnection)
    {
        // No, do we have a server name?
        if (m_sServer != "")
        {
            // Yes, open a connection
            m_fcConnection = m_isSession.GetFtpConnection(
                    m_sServer, m_sUser, m_sPassword);

            // Did we get a connection?
            if (m_fcConnection)
            {
                // Yes, get the current directory
                m_fcConnection->GetCurrentDirectory(m_sDirectory);
```

```
                    // Change the text on the button to close
                    // the connection
                    m_ctlConnect.SetWindowText("&Close");

                    // Load the list of files in the current directory
                    LoadListOfFiles();

                    // Update the screen
                    UpdateData(FALSE);
                }
            }
        }
        else     // We have a current connection
        {
            // Close the connection
            m_fcConnection->Close();

            // Delete the connection object
            delete m_fcConnection;

            // Reinitialize the connection object pointer
            m_fcConnection = NULL;

            // Reset the screen controls and variables
            m_ctlConnect.SetWindowText("&Connect");
            m_sDirectory = "";

            // Reset the contents of the directory list
            m_lbFiles.ResetContent();

            // Update the screen
            UpdateData(FALSE);
        }
    }
```

Getting a Listing of Files

For loading the list of files in the current directory, you'll need to first clear the list box of any files already listed in there. Next, you'll need to create a CFtpFileFind object from the current FTP connection object. When you have an FTP file find object, find the first file using the default wildcard, thus getting a listing of all files. Loop until you've found all of the files in the current directory, using the FindNextFile function to loop through each file, getting the filename and checking to see if it's a directory before adding it to the list box. When all files have been retrieved and added to the list box, close the FTP file finder and exit the function. To add this functionality to the sample application, add a member function to the dialog class named LoadListOfFile, and add the code in Listing 25.12.

25

WinInet
PROGRAMMING

LISTING 25.12   THE LoadListOfFiles FUNCTION

```cpp
void CInetFTPDlg::LoadListOfFiles()
{
    // Reset the contents of the list of files
    m_lbFiles.ResetContent();

    // Create a file find object
    CFtpFileFind fFiles(m_fcConnection);
    // And variables to keep track of the current file name
    // and if there are any more files
    CString sFileName;
    BOOL bMoreFiles;

    // Find the first file
    bMoreFiles = fFiles.FindFile(NULL);

    // Loop while there are more files to find
    while (bMoreFiles)
    {
        // Find the next file
        bMoreFiles = fFiles.FindNextFile();
        // Get the file name
        sFileName = fFiles.GetFileName();
        // Is the file a directory?
        if (fFiles.IsDirectory())
            // If so, then specify that it's a directory
            sFileName += "     <DIR>";
        // Add the file name to the list of files
        m_lbFiles.AddString((LPCTSTR)sFileName);
    }
    // Close the file find object
    fFiles.Close();
}
```

Changing Directories and Retrieving Files

For providing the functionality to enable the user to change directories, you'll want to perform the following actions. First, you'll want to check to make sure that there is a directory specified. Next, you'll set the current directory to the specified directory using the SetCurrentDirectory function. After you've changed directories, you'll want to get the current directory name so that the new current directory is displayed for the user in the form the FTP server understands. Finally, you'll want to call the LoadListOfFiles function to get a listing of the files in the new directory. To add this functionality to the sample application, attach an event function to the Set Directory button and add the code in Listing 25.13.

LISTING 25.13 THE OnBsetdir FUNCTION

```
void CInetFTPDlg::OnBsetdir()
{
    // TODO: Add your control notification handler code here

    // Get the data from the screen
    UpdateData(TRUE);

    // Do we have a directory name?
    if (m_sDirectory != "")
    {
        // Move to the specified directory
        m_fcConnection->SetCurrentDirectory((LPCTSTR)m_sDirectory);

        // Get the current directory name (if we were
        // successful, it should be the specified new
        // directory)
        m_fcConnection->GetCurrentDirectory(m_sDirectory);

        // Load the list of files in the new directory
        LoadListOfFiles();

        // Update the screen
        UpdateData(FALSE);
    }
}
```

The final bit of functionality that you'll add to the sample application is the capability to retrieve files from the FTP server. To perform this action, you'll want to get the name of the file currently selected in the list of files. After checking the name of the file to make sure it isn't a directory, you'll want to get the local location and name to copy the selected file to. You can use the standard File Save dialog class to perform this task. Finally, you'll call the FTP connection object's GetFile function to retrieve the file. To add this functionality to the sample application, attach an event function to the Get File button, and add the code in Listing 25.14.

LISTING 25.14 THE OnBgetfile FUNCTION

```
void CInetFTPDlg::OnBgetfile()
{
    // TODO: Add your control notification handler code here

    // Get the data from the screen
    UpdateData(TRUE);

    // Do we have a file name?
```

continues

25

WinInet PROGRAMMING

LISTING 25.14   CONTINUED

```
if (m_sFile != "")
{
    // Is it a directory?
    if (m_sFile.Right(5) == "<DIR>")
        // If so, warn the user
        MessageBox("Unable to download directory.");
    else
    {
        // Get the name of the destination file
        CFileDialog ldFile(FALSE, NULL, (LPCTSTR)m_sFile);
        if (ldFile.DoModal() == IDOK)
        {
            // Get the specified file
            if (!m_fcConnection->GetFile((LPCTSTR)m_sFile,
                    (LPCTSTR)ldFile.GetFileName()))
                // If unsuccessful, tell the user
                MessageBox("Error getting file");
        }
    }
}
}
```

At this point you should be ready to compile and run your application. When you have it running, you'll find that you have a fully functional, very basic FTP client, as seen in Figure 25.5.

FIGURE 25.5

The running FTP client application.

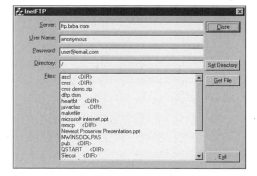

Summary

This chapter discusses how you can use the WinInet MFC classes to easily provide extensive Internet functionality using the HTTP (Web), FTP, and Gopher application protocols. It covers the basics of Internet application protocols and how extensive they can be. You also saw how using the MFC WinInet classes can hide a large amount of this complexity from you as an application programmer.

Among the first things covered in this chapter are the basics of WinInet programming using the MFC classes and how an extensive set of functionality is included in the base classes. You saw how you could build an entire Internet-enabled application using the base WinInet classes, without using any of the application-level classes. You saw how you could use the base classes to easily retrieve files from HTTP, FTP, or Gopher servers without delving into the higher classes.

Where the chapter covers the application-level classes, you saw how the application-specific classes could be used to easily provide a fully functional client application for each of the three protocols incorporated in the WinInet API. You saw how easy the WinInet MFC classes make it to build a fully functional FTP client, and how easy it would also be to build a HTTP or Gopher client using these classes.

ISAPI Extensions

by Stephen Genusa and Kevin Flick

CHAPTER

26

Version 4.1+ of the Microsoft Foundation Classes (MFC) comes with extensive support for Internet Server Application Programming Interface (ISAPI) extensions. The ISAPI Extension Wizard creates the MFC framework on which your Web server application is built.

Processing a form is the mainstay of Internet-based interactive applications and a key to unlocking the power of the Web. In this chapter, you learn how to use the framework supplied by the wizard to create an ISAPI extension that processes a Hypertext Markup Language (HTML) form.

The Foundation

You have some work to do before you build. In Microsoft Developer Studio, create a new project workspace. For the name, enter `My` and choose ISAPI Extension Wizard as the type. Click Create.

Leave the Extension Class Name as `CMyExtension`, click Finish, and click OK. Now open the FileView of your project. AppWizard, as you can see, has inserted seven files (see Table 26.1).

TABLE 26.1 MY PROJECT FILES

Filename	Description
MY.H	`CMyExtension`'s declaration
MY.CPP	`CMyExtension`'s implementation
MY.RC	My's resource file
MY.DEF	My's exports definition file
STDAFX.H	Application framework header
STDAFX.CPP	Includes STDAFX.H
MY.PCH	My's precompiled header

Open the MY.H file and you should see the code in Listing 26.1.

LISTING 26.1 MY.H—`CMyExtension`'S CLASS DECLARATION

```
// MY.H - Header file for your Internet Server
//    My Extension

#include "resource.h"

class CMyExtension : public CHttpServer
```

```
{
public:
    CMyExtension();
    ~CMyExtension();

// Overrides
    // ClassWizard generated virtual function overrides
        // NOTE - the ClassWizard will add and remove member
        // functions here.
        //    DO NOT EDIT what you see in these blocks of
        //    generated code !
    //{{AFX_VIRTUAL(CMyExtension)
    public:
    virtual BOOL GetExtensionVersion(HSE_VERSION_INFO* pVer);
    //}}AFX_VIRTUAL

    // TODO: Add handlers for your commands here.
    // For example:

    void Default(CHttpServerContext* pCtxt);

    DECLARE_PARSE_MAP()

    //{{AFX_MSG(CMyExtension)
    //}}AFX_MSG
};
```

As mentioned earlier, this file holds your CHttpServer-derived class declaration. If you've never used MFC before, this code probably looks like most other class declarations you've created.

A closer look reveals some lines that might seem strange. These are the ClassWizard's override declaration section shown in Listing 26.2.

LISTING 26.2   MY.H—CLASSWIZARD OVERRIDE DECLARATIONS

```
1    //{{AFX_VIRTUAL(CMyExtension)
2    public:
3    virtual BOOL GetExtensionVersion(HSE_VERSION_INFO* pVer);
4    //}}AFX_VIRTUAL
```

Lines 1 and 4 are the comment-delimited lines that help ClassWizard find the beginning and end of virtual function overrides. When AppWizard creates the extension's skeleton code, there is only one overridden function. As you override and remove CHttpServer virtual functions with ClassWizard, their declarations are automatically added and deleted from the AFX_VIRTUAL section in Listing 26.1.

Near the end of MY.H, you see the code in Listing 26.3.

LISTING 26.3 MY.H—CMy's PARSE MAP DECLARATION

```
DECLARE_PARSE_MAP()
```

Depending on when your extension links to MFC, the DECLARE_PARSE_MAP() macro adds one private member and up to four public members to your CHttpServer-derived class. The definition of DECLARE_PARSE_MAP() is in AFXISAPI.H.

> **TIP**
>
> When I first started Windows 3.x programming, I read somewhere that WINDOWS.H was the ultimate reference for Windows developers. By the same token, the ultimate encyclopedia for MFC developers is the MFC source code provided by Microsoft on your Visual C++ CD-ROM. Although it's substantially larger than WINDOWS.H, it's also where many questions can be answered.

Listing 26.4 shows the implementation file for your extension.

LISTING 26.4 MY.CPP—CMy's IMPLEMENTATION FILE

```
// MY.CPP - Implementation file for your Internet Server
//    My Extension

#include "stdafx.h"
#include "My.h"

/////////////////////////////////////////////////////////////////////
///
// The one and only CWinApp object
// NOTE: You can remove this object if you alter your project to no
// longer use MFC in a DLL.

CWinApp theApp;

/////////////////////////////////////////////////////////////////////
///
// command-parsing map

BEGIN_PARSE_MAP(CMyExtension, CHttpServer)
    // TODO: insert your ON_PARSE_COMMAND() and
    // ON_PARSE_COMMAND_PARAMS() here to hook up your commands.
    // For example:
```

```
    ON_PARSE_COMMAND(Default, CMyExtension, ITS_EMPTY)
    DEFAULT_PARSE_COMMAND(Default, CMyExtension)
END_PARSE_MAP(CMyExtension)


/////////////////////////////////////////////////////////////////
///
// The one and only CMyExtension object

CMyExtension theExtension;


/////////////////////////////////////////////////////////////////
///
// CMyExtension implementation

CMyExtension::CMyExtension()
{
}

CMyExtension::~CMyExtension()
{
}

BOOL CMyExtension::GetExtensionVersion(HSE_VERSION_INFO* pVer)
{
    // Call default implementation for initialization
    CHttpServer::GetExtensionVersion(pVer);

    // Load description string
    TCHAR sz[HSE_MAX_EXT_DLL_NAME_LEN+1];
    ISAPIVERIFY(::LoadString(AfxGetResourceHandle(),
                   IDS_SERVER, sz, HSE_MAX_EXT_DLL_NAME_LEN));
    _tcscpy(pVer->lpszExtensionDesc, sz);
    return TRUE;
}

/////////////////////////////////////////////////////////////////
///
// CMyExtension command handlers

void CMyExtension::Default(CHttpServerContext* pCtxt)
{
    StartContent(pCtxt);
    WriteTitle(pCtxt);

    *pCtxt << _T("This default message was produced by the
    ➥Internet");
    *pCtxt << _T(" Server DLL Wizard. Edit your
    ➥CMyExtension::Default()");
```

continues

LISTING 26.4   CONTINUED

```
    *pCtxt << _T(" implementation to change it.\r\n");

    EndContent(pCtxt);
}

// Do not edit the following lines, which are needed by ClassWizard.
#if 0
BEGIN_MESSAGE_MAP(CMyExtension, CHttpServer)
    //{{AFX_MSG_MAP(CMyExtension)
    //}}AFX_MSG_MAP
END_MESSAGE_MAP()
#endif        // 0


/////////////////////////////////////////////////////////////////////
///
// If your extension will not use MFC, you'll need this code to make
// sure that the extension objects can find the resource handle for
// the module.  If you convert your extension to not be dependent on
// MFC, remove the comments around the following AfxGetResourceHandle()
// and DllMain() functions, as well as the g_hInstance global.

/****

static HINSTANCE g_hInstance;

HINSTANCE AFXISAPI AfxGetResourceHandle()
{
    return g_hInstance;
}

BOOL WINAPI DllMain(HINSTANCE hInst, ULONG ulReason,
                                LPVOID lpReserved)
{
    if (ulReason == DLL_PROCESS_ATTACH)
    {
        g_hInstance = hInst;
    }

    return TRUE;
}

****/
```

Now that you've browsed MY.CPP, let's break it down piece by piece.

When you look at the code in Listing 26.5, you will probably do a double take. Don't worry, you're not seeing things. A `CWinApp` object is needed by all MFC programs. As long as your extension uses MFC, you'll need this object.

LISTING 26.5   MY.CPP—THE `CWinApp` DECLARATION

```
///////////////////////////////////////////////////////////////////
///
// The one and only CWinApp object
// NOTE: You can remove this object if you alter your project to no
// longer use MFC in a DLL.

CWinApp theApp;
```

Listing 26.6 shows `CMyExtension`'s parse map.

LISTING 26.6   MY.CPP—`CMyExtension`'S PARSE MAP

```
///////////////////////////////////////////////////////////////////
///
// command-parsing map

1   BEGIN_PARSE_MAP(CMyExtension, CHttpServer)
2     // TODO: insert your ON_PARSE_COMMAND() and
3     // ON_PARSE_COMMAND_PARAMS() here to hook up your commands.
4     // For example:

5     ON_PARSE_COMMAND(Default, CMyExtension, ITS_EMPTY)
6     DEFAULT_PARSE_COMMAND(Default, CMyExtension)
7   END_PARSE_MAP(CMyExtension)
```

By default, AppWizard creates a parse map for each MFC-based ISAPI extension. ISAPI parse maps are the way MFC ISAPI developers commonly chart requests from Web clients to specific functions in their extension DLL. Line 1,

```
BEGIN_PARSE_MAP(CMyExtension, CHttpServer)
```

is self-explanatory. This is where your parse map's definition begins. The first parameter, `CMyExtension`, specifies the owner of this parse map. The second must be `CHttpServer`, which is the base class. Now, move down to line 5.

```
ON_PARSE_COMMAND(Default, CMyExtension, ITS_EMPTY)
```

This is where the command-to-function mapping takes place. The first parameter, which in this case is `Default`, identifies the command name and member function it corresponds with. When using a parse map in ISAPI, each command must have a comparable handler function of the same name.

The second parameter, `CMyExtension`, represents the class the function is mapped to. The third parameter, `ITS_EMPTY`, specifies the number and types of arguments the function accepts, which in this case is none.

Line 6 is where you define the command to be used when one is not specified.

```
DEFAULT_PARSE_COMMAND(Default, CMyExtension)
```

The parameters this macro accepts are almost identical to `ON_PARSE_COMMAND`. In fact, the only difference is that you don't have to specify the number and type of the arguments.

The last line in Listing 26.6 is line 7:

```
END_PARSE_MAP(CMyExtension)
```

`BEGIN_PARSE_MAP` starts the definition of the parse map and `END_PARSE_MAP` ends the definition. The only parameter this macro takes is the name of the class that owns this parse map.

Although I've covered each of the entries in Listing 26.6, there's one parse map macro not represented: `ON_PARSE_COMMAND_PARAMS`. This macro is not part of the parse map created when a new ISAPI extension is started because the only command handler, `Default`, takes no parameters.

To illustrate this macro, you rewrite your parse map as follows:

```
  BEGIN_PARSE_MAP(CMyExtension, CHttpServer)
          // TODO: insert your ON_PARSE_COMMAND() and
          // ON_PARSE_COMMAND_PARAMS() here to hook up your commands.
          // For example:

5         ON_PARSE_COMMAND(Default, CMyExtension, ITS_PSTR)
6         ON_PARSE_COMMAND_PARAMS("Name")
          DEFAULT_PARSE_COMMAND(Default, CMyExtension)
  END_PARSE_MAP(CMyExtension)
```

The only lines you should be concerned with are 5 and 6. Notice how, when I add `ON_PARSE_COMMAND_PARAMS`, I also change `ON_PARSE_COMMAND`. Earlier, I said that `ON_PARSE_COMMAND`'s third parameter specifies the number and types of arguments the function accepts.

But because you added an argument to `ON_PARSE_COMMAND_PARAMS`, your command handler is no longer empty. The `ITS_PSTR` entry means the parameter is a pointer to a string. In MSVC 4.2, `ON_PARSE_COMMAND` recognizes six different constants as representing data types, as shown in Table 26.2.

TABLE 26.2   ON_PARSE_COMMAND DATA TYPES

Constant	Type
ITS_EMPTY	N/A
ITS_PSTR	String pointer
ITS_I2	Short
ITS_I4	Long
ITS_R4	Float
ITS_R8	Double

ON_PARSE_COMMAND_PARAMS is where the parameters accepted in ON_PARSE_COMMAND are specified by the name of the HTML form's input element. These two macros work hand-in-hand. In fact, the only time you shouldn't have the ON_PARSE_COMMAND_PARAMS macro after ON_PARSE_COMMAND is when the argument parameter of ON_PARSE_COMMAND has a value of ITS_EMPTY.

Here are some simple rules for using these two macros when ON_PARSE_COMMAND does not have an argument value of ITS_EMTPY:

- ON_PARSE_COMMAND_PARAMS must immediately follow the matching ON_PARSE_COMMAND macro.
- For each entry in ON_PARSE_COMMAND, you should have exactly one entry in ON_PARSE_COMMAND_PARAMS.
- Multiple entries in the argument parameter of ON_PARSE_COMMAND and ON_PARSE_COMMAND_PARAMS are separated with a single space, even if they span multiple lines.
- The order in which the data types are declared in ON_PARSE_COMMAND applies to the order in which the names are declared in ON_PARSE_COMMAND_PARAMS.

The last entry in the preceding list might be confusing, so let's look at some examples. For clarity, BEGIN_PARSE_MAP, END_PARSE_MAP, and DEFAULT_PARSE_COMMAND are not present.

```
ON_PARSE_COMMAND(WriteToFile, CSampleExtension, ITS_PSTR ITS_PSTR)
ON_PARSE_COMMAND_PARAMS("Name Country")
```

By now you should be able to recognize immediately what this code does. WriteToFile represents the function and CSampleExtension is the class. WriteToFile takes two string pointers: Name and Country.

This is simple. And because each parameter has the same data type, the order is irrelevant. Now, let's add another parameter:

```
ON_PARSE_COMMAND(WriteToFile, CSampleExtension, ITS_PSTR ITS_PSTR
➥ITS_I2)
ON_PARSE_COMMAND_PARAMS("Age Name Country")
```

A browser sends a command:

```
/scripts/sample.dll?WriteToFile&Age=21&Name=Joe&Country=US
```

Instead of assigning Age the integer 21, this example assigns it the string value of 21. Also, Country is not assigned the string value of US but the integer value of 0.

To fix this problem, you change the order of the variable names in ON_PARSE_COMMAND_PARAMS to match their respective data types declared in ON_PARSE_COMMAND:

```
ON_PARSE_COMMAND(WriteToFile, CSampleExtension, ITS_PSTR ITS_PSTR
➥ITS_I2)
ON_PARSE_COMMAND_PARAMS("Name Country Age")
```

Now the same command yields the anticipated results:

```
Name=Joe
Country=US
Age=21
```

This ends my overview of the parse map. You'll return to it when you reach the actual command handler. For now, let's keep inching down the source file.

Listing 26.7 is where your extension object comes to life. As in other object-oriented programs you might have written, before you can access the methods in a class, you must have an object created from that class.

LISTING 26.7   MY.CPP—THE CMyExtension DECLARATION

```
///////////////////////////////////////////////////////////////////
///
// The one and only CMyExtension object

CMyExtension theExtension;
```

Unless you're already familiar with programming in a multithreaded environment, you should understand what's involved before using constructors and destructors in an ISAPI DLL. For now, though, the classes you create don't use their constructors and destructors, as shown in Listing 26.8.

LISTING 26.8 MY.CPP—CMyExtension's STARTUP

```
/////////////////////////////////////////////////////////////////////
///
// CMyExtension implementation

1   CMyExtension::CMyExtension()
2   {
3   }

4   CMyExtension::~CMyExtension()
5   {
6   }

7   BOOL CMyExtension::GetExtensionVersion(HSE_VERSION_INFO* pVer)
8   {
9      // Call default implementation for initialization
10     CHttpServer::GetExtensionVersion(pVer);

11     // Load description string
12     TCHAR sz[HSE_MAX_EXT_DLL_NAME_LEN+1];
13     ISAPIVERIFY(::LoadString(AfxGetResourceHandle(),
                     IDS_SERVER, sz, HSE_MAX_EXT_DLL_NAME_LEN));
14     _tcscpy(pVer->lpszExtensionDesc, sz);
15     return TRUE;
16  }
```

Listing 26.8 begins simply enough. Lines 1 through 3 are the constructor for CMyExtension. Lines 4 through 6 are the destructor. As in other C++ programs, you can use these components to initialize and destroy any elements your class uses.

Lines 7 through 16 show the GetExtensionVersion()function. This is one of two functions that all ISAPI extensions, MFC and non-MFC, must export. The other, HttpExtensionProc(), is a virtual function that AppWizard does not automatically override.

GetExtensionVersion() is called by your server once when your extension is loaded and does two tasks. The first is to check the extension's ISAPI specification version number and compare it to the server's. The second is to give the server a short text description of the extension.

The default HttpExtensionProc() is shown in Listing 26.9.

LISTING 26.9   ISAPI.CPP—`HttpExtensionProc`

```
DWORD CHttpServer::HttpExtensionProc(EXTENSION_CONTROL_BLOCK *pECB)
{
        DWORD dwRet = HSE_STATUS_SUCCESS;
        BOOL bDefault = FALSE;
        LPTSTR pszPostBuffer = NULL;
        LPTSTR pszQuery;
        LPTSTR pszCommand = NULL;
        int nMethodRet;
        LPTSTR pstrLastChar;
        DWORD cbStream = 0;
        BYTE* pbStream = NULL;
        CHttpServerContext ctxtCall(pECB);

        pECB->dwHttpStatusCode = 0;

        ISAPIASSERT(NULL != pServer);
        if (pServer == NULL)
        {
                dwRet = HSE_STATUS_ERROR;
                goto CleanUp;
        }

        // get the query

        if (_tcsicmp(pECB->lpszMethod, szGet) == 0)
        {
                pszQuery = pECB->lpszQueryString;
        }
        else if (_tcsicmp(pECB->lpszMethod, szPost) == 0)
        {
                pszCommand = pECB->lpszQueryString;
                pszPostBuffer = new TCHAR[pECB->cbAvailable + 1];
                pszQuery = GetQuery(&ctxtCall, pszPostBuffer,
                ➥pECB->cbAvailable);
        }
        else
        {
                ISAPITRACE1("Error: Unrecognized method: %s\n",
                ➥pECB->lpszMethod);
                dwRet = HSE_STATUS_ERROR;
                goto CleanUp;
        }

        // trim junk that some browsers put at the very end

        pstrLastChar = pszQuery + _tcslen(pszQuery) -1;
        while ((*pstrLastChar == ' ' || *pstrLastChar == '\n' ||
                *pstrLastChar == '\r') && pstrLastChar > pszQuery)
        {
```

```
            *pstrLastChar—  = '\0';
}

// do something about it

if (!pServer->InitInstance(&ctxtCall))
        dwRet = HSE_STATUS_ERROR;
else
{
        pECB->dwHttpStatusCode = HTTP_STATUS_OK;
        try {
                nMethodRet = pServer->CallFunction(&ctxtCall,
                ➥pszQuery, pszCommand);
        }
        catch (...)
        {
                ISAPITRACE1("Error: command %s caused an unhandled
                ➥exception!\n",
                                pszQuery);
                nMethodRet = callNoStackSpace;
        }

        // was an error caused by trying to dispatch?

        if (nMethodRet != callOK && pECB->dwHttpStatusCode ==
        ➥HTTP_STATUS_OK)
        {
                dwRet = HSE_STATUS_ERROR;
                switch (nMethodRet)
                {
                case callNoStream:
                                pECB->dwHttpStatusCode =
                                ➥HTTP_STATUS_NO_CONTENT;
                                break;

                case callParamRequired:
                case callBadParamCount:
                case callBadParam:
                                pECB->dwHttpStatusCode =
                                ➥HTTP_STATUS_BAD_REQUEST;
                                break;

                case callBadCommand:
                                pECB->dwHttpStatusCode =
                                ➥HTTP_STATUS_NOT_IMPLEMENTED;
                                break;

                case callNoStackSpace:
                default:
                                pECB->dwHttpStatusCode =
```

continues

LISTING 26.9   CONTINUED

```
                                                ➥HTTP_STATUS_SERVER_ERROR;
                                    break;
                    }
                }

                // if there was no error or the user said they handled
                // the error, prepare to spit out the generated HTML

                if (nMethodRet == callOK ||
                        OnParseError(&ctxtCall, nMethodRet) == TRUE)
                {
                        cbStream = ctxtCall.m_pStream->GetStreamSize();
                        pbStream = ctxtCall.m_pStream->Detach();
                }
        }

CleanUp:
        // if there was an error, return an appropriate status
        TCHAR szResponse[64];
        BuildStatusCode(szResponse, pECB->dwHttpStatusCode);

        DWORD dwSize = cbStream - ctxtCall.m_dwEndOfHeaders;
        BYTE* pbContent = NULL;
        BYTE cSaved;

        if (pbStream != NULL)
        {
                cSaved = pbStream[ctxtCall.m_dwEndOfHeaders];
                pbStream[ctxtCall.m_dwEndOfHeaders] = '\0';
                pbContent = &pbStream[ctxtCall.m_dwEndOfHeaders];
        }

        if (!ctxtCall.ServerSupportFunction(
                HSE_REQ_SEND_RESPONSE_HEADER, szResponse, 0, (LPDWORD)
                ➥pbStream) &&
                ::GetLastError() != 10054)     // WSAECONNRESET
        {
                pECB->dwHttpStatusCode = HTTP_STATUS_SERVER_ERROR;
                dwRet = HSE_STATUS_ERROR;
#ifdef _DEBUG
                DWORD dwCause = ::GetLastError();
                ISAPITRACE1("Error: Unable to write headers: %8.8X!\n",
                ➥dwCause);
#endif
        }
        else
        {
                if (pbContent != NULL)
                {
```

```
                        // write a newline to separate content
                        // from headers

                        *pbContent = cSaved;
                        DWORD dwNewLineSize = 2;
                        if (!ctxtCall.WriteClient(_T("\r\n"),
                        ➥&dwNewLineSize, 0) ¦¦
                                        !ctxtCall.WriteClient(pbContent,
                                        ➥&dwSize, 0))
                        {
                                        dwRet = HSE_STATUS_ERROR;
                                        pECB->dwHttpStatusCode =
                                        ➥HTTP_STATUS_SERVER_ERROR;
                                        ISAPITRACE("Error: Unable to write
                                        ➥content body!\n");
                        }
                }
                else
                        ISAPITRACE("Error: No body content!\n");
        }

        if (pbStream != NULL)
                ctxtCall.m_pStream->Free(pbStream);

        if (dwRet == HSE_STATUS_SUCCESS)
                pECB->dwHttpStatusCode = HTTP_STATUS_OK;

        if (pszPostBuffer != NULL)
                delete [] pszPostBuffer;

        return dwRet;
}
```

HttpExtensionProc() is the second function that all ISAPI extensions export. Unlike
GetExtensionVersion(), which is called only once, HttpExtensionProc() is called by
the server each time a client makes a request to your DLL.

The server gives your DLL the necessary connection information through the EXTEN-
SION_CONTROL_BLOCK (ECB) structure. This structure is shown in Listing 26.10.

LISTING 26.10 HTTPEXT.H—THE ISAPI EXTENSION_CONTROL_BLOCK STRUCTURE

```
typedef struct _EXTENSION_CONTROL_BLOCK {

    DWORD       cbSize;                     // size of this struct.
    DWORD       dwVersion;                  // version info of this spec
    HCONN       ConnID;                     // Context number not to be
                                            // modified!
    DWORD       dwHttpStatusCode;           // HTTP Status code
```

continues

LISTING 26.10 CONTINUED

```
CHAR        lpszLogData[HSE_LOG_BUFFER_LEN];// null terminated
                                            // log info specific to
                                            // this Extension DLL

LPSTR       lpszMethod;              // REQUEST_METHOD
LPSTR       lpszQueryString;         // QUERY_STRING
LPSTR       lpszPathInfo;            // PATH_INFO
LPSTR       lpszPathTranslated;      // PATH_TRANSLATED

DWORD       cbTotalBytes;            // Total bytes indicated from
                                     // client
DWORD       cbAvailable;             // Available number of bytes
LPBYTE      lpbData;                 // pointer to cbAvailable
                                     // bytes

LPSTR       lpszContentType;         // Content type of client data

BOOL (WINAPI * GetServerVariable) ( HCONN       hConn,
                                    LPSTR
                                    ➥lpszVariableName,
                                    LPVOID      lpvBuffer,
                                    LPDWORD     lpdwSize );

BOOL (WINAPI * WriteClient) ( HCONN      ConnID,
                              LPVOID     Buffer,
                              LPDWORD    lpdwBytes,
                              DWORD      dwReserved );

BOOL (WINAPI * ReadClient) ( HCONN      ConnID,
                             LPVOID     lpvBuffer,
                             LPDWORD    lpdwSize );

BOOL (WINAPI * ServerSupportFunction)( HCONN       hConn,
                                       DWORD       dwHSERRequest,
                                       LPVOID      lpvBuffer,
                                       LPDWORD     lpdwSize,
                                       LPDWORD
                                       ➥pdwDataType );

} EXTENSION_CONTROL_BLOCK, *LPEXTENSION_CONTROL_BLOCK;
```

Just as all ISAPI extension DLLs must export `GetExtensionVersion()` and `HttpExtensionProc()`, the ECB is a common thread between MFC and non-MFC ISAPI extensions. The ECB is how the server and extension communicate—if your access to the ECB is the `CHttpServerContext` object created in `HttpExtensionProc()`:

```
CHttpServerContext ctxtCall(pECB);
```

Each command handler you create takes a pointer to the `CHttpServerContext` object created in `HttpExtensionProc()`. This pointer gives your functions easy access to the connection-specific information in the ECB and more.

Line 2 in Listing 26.11 shows the bond between your parse map and command handlers.

LISTING 26.11   ISAPI.CPP—THE DEFAULT HttpExtensionProc()

```
1       try {
2               nMethodRet = pServer->CallFunction(&ctxtCall,
                ➡pszQuery, pszCommand);
3       }
4       catch (...)
5       {
6               ISAPITRACE1("Error: command %s caused an unhandled
                ➡exception!\n",
7                               pszQuery);
8               nMethodRet = callNoStackSpace;
9       }
```

`CHttpServer::CallFunction()` is what the framework uses to find and execute command handlers. Because `CallFunction()` is a virtual function, you can override it and customize how the query string is parsed.

From There to Here

You now know how to use the parse map macros and how your parse map gets connected to your extension. Before you can act on the data sent by a client, however, you need to connect your parse map to your command-handling functions. You do this with the first parameter of `ON_PARSE_COMMAND`, the command handlers themselves.

Listing 26.12 shows `CMyExtension`'s default command handler.

LISTING 26.12   MY.CPP—CMyExtension's DEFAULT COMMAND HANDLER

```
/////////////////////////////////////////////////////////////////
///
// CMyExtension command handlers

1   void CMyExtension::Default(CHttpServerContext* pCtxt)
2   {
3       StartContent(pCtxt);
4       WriteTitle(pCtxt);

5       *pCtxt << _T("This default message was produced by the Internet");
```

continues

LISTING 26.12   CONTINUED

```
6     *pCtxt << _T(" Server DLL Wizard. Edit your
      ➥CMyExtension::Default()");
7     *pCtxt << _T(" implementation to change it.\r\n");

8     EndContent(pCtxt);
9   }
```

Recall that `Default`'s `ON_PARSE_COMMAND` macro had an argument value of `ITS_EMPTY` when AppWizard generated the ISAPI framework for you. If the macro says it was empty, why does the function show a single parameter?

For the handlers to have access to connection-specific information, each one must take a pointer to the `CHttpServerContext` object created in `HttpExtensionProc()`. This pointer is not shown in the parse map because when your command handler is called, the MFC framework automatically passes the `CHttpServerContext` pointer to your function.

This object is what allows the DLL to handle multiple connections with multiple threads instead of with multiple processes. If you were to edit your parse map's arguments parameter, you would also have to edit the declaration of the command handling function.

To illustrate, let's again look at the parse map you used earlier:

```
ON_PARSE_COMMAND(WriteToFile, CSampleExtension, ITS_PSTR ITS_PSTR
➥ITS_I2)
ON_PARSE_COMMAND_PARAMS("Name Country Age")
```

Given the preceding macros, your `WriteToFile()` handler would need to take four, not three, parameters:

```
void CSampleExtension::WriteToFile(CHttpServerContext* pCtxt,
➥LPTSTR pstrName, LPTSTR pstrCountry
                                    INT iAge)
```

If you change your parse map macros to reflect only two parameters, you would also need to change your function once again.

```
ON_PARSE_COMMAND(WriteToFile, CSampleExtension, ITS_PSTR ITS_PSTR)
ON_PARSE_COMMAND_PARAMS("Name Country")
void CSampleExtension::WriteToFile(CHttpServerContext* pCtxt,
➥LPTSTR pstrName, LPTSTR pstrCountry)
```

Notice how the arguments parameter types of `ON_PARSE_COMMAND` correspond with the types in your command handler. Just as you need to make sure that the names in `ON_PARSE_COMMAND_PARAMS` are in line with the arguments in `ON_PARSE_COMMAND`, you need to make sure that the declarations following the `CHttpServerContext` pointer in your command handlers match the types in the arguments section of `ON_PARSE_COMMAND`.

In addition, because you will be manipulating the data sent from a Web browser, the function declaration must also match the order in which you expect to get them. For example, in the previous command handler, you are expecting a name as the first parameter following the CHttpServerContext pointer. If you expected a Country instead, you would have to change not only the ON_PARSE_COMMAND_PARAMS macro but also the position of the variable you expect to hold the Country value.

```
ON_PARSE_COMMAND(WriteToFile, CSampleExtension, ITS_PSTR ITS_PSTR)
ON_PARSE_COMMAND_PARAMS("Country Name")
void CSampleExtension::WriteToFile(CHttpServerContext* pCtxt,
➥LPTSTR pstrCountry, LPTSTR pstrName)
```

Although this method is tedious and needs attention to detail, it keeps you from having to write your own parsing algorithm. MFC does not require you to use parse maps in your ISAPI extension. Instead, the parse maps are supplied as generic tools to speed the development cycle. For more information on parse maps, see Microsoft Visual C++ *Books Online*.

Now that you understand a little more about MFC's ISAPI implementation, you're ready to create your form processor. I'll point out common errors and solutions throughout.

The form you'll process is shown in Figure 26.1.

FIGURE 26.1

The target HTML form.

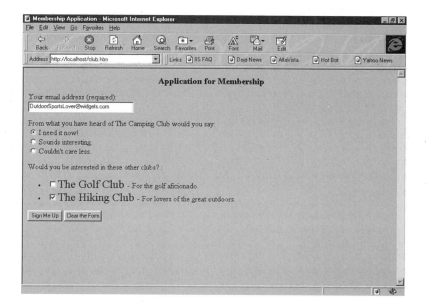

Once again, create a new project workspace in Developer Studio. From the New Project Workspace dialog box, select the ISAPI Extension Wizard type and enter MembrApp as the project name, as shown in Figure 26.2. Click Create.

FIGURE 26.2

The New Project Workspace dialog box.

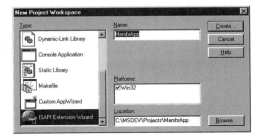

The one-step ISAPI Extension Wizard appears. The default settings are just right for your purposes.

You want an extension object and not a filter object, so the class name of CMembrAppExtension is fine. You'll use the MFC library as a shared DLL to make your extension compact (see Figure 26.3).

FIGURE 26.3

The one-step ISAPI Extension Wizard.

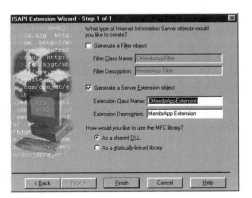

Click Finish. The wizard brings up a confirmation dialog box. Clicking OK allows the wizard to create the extension's skeleton code.

Just as you saw earlier in this chapter, the wizard takes care of many details. It creates a CWinApp object to cover the DllMain startup/shutdown processing. It also creates an exported `GetExtensionVersion()` and `HttpExtensionProc()`, which you are familiar with by now.

The wizard creates a derived `CHttpServer` object, in this example called `CMembrAppExtension`, shown in Listing 26.13. This object has a parse map, a `GetExtensionVersion` member function, and a `Default` function, which does very little at the moment.

LISTING 26.13   `CMembrAppExtension`—A `CHttpServer` OBJECT

```
void CMembrAppExtension::Default(CHttpServerContext* pCtxt)
{
        StartContent(pCtxt);
        WriteTitle(pCtxt);

        *pCtxt << _T("This default message was produced by the
        ➥Internet");
        *pCtxt << _T(" Server DLL Wizard. Edit your
        ➥CMembrAppExtension::Default()");
        *pCtxt << _T(" implementation to change it.\r\n");

        EndContent(pCtxt);
}
```

Now that you have constructed the framework using the wizard, you'll build the extension itself. Before you can do this, though, you need to iron out a couple of wrinkles.

First, a DLL needs a host application to run with. Second, because you're using Microsoft Internet Information Server (IIS), your host application is configured to run only as a service. If you are using a different ISAPI Web server, you might need to ask your vendor for instructions.

You need to set up your ISAPI extension to run with IIS and Visual C++ in debug mode in this sequence:

1. Make sure that you have set administrative privileges, including Act as Part of the Operating System and Log On as a Service for your account.

    To do this, go to the User Manager, Policies/User-Rights, and select the Show Advanced User Rights check box. Select each of the privileges and add your logon to the list of groups and users granted these rights.

2. Go to the Control Panel Services icon, scroll down to the World Wide Web Publishing Service, and stop the service. Only one copy of IIS can successfully run at one time, and you'll be running IIS from your debugger.

3. Back at the `CMembrAppExtension` extension, select Build/Settings and select the Link tab.

4. Type in the full pathname of the DLL in the Output File Name text box. Select and copy this pathname to the Clipboard.

5. Select the Debug tab and go to the Additional DLLs category. Under Modules, paste the full pathname into the first entry for Local Name. This ensures that the symbol table for the DLL is preloaded for debugging.

6. While in the Debug tab dialog box, go to the General category.

7. In the Executable for Debug Session text box, type in `c:\inetsrv\server\INetInfo.Exe` or the path for IIS if you installed it in a different directory.

8. In Program Arguments, type in `-e W3Svc`. This allows IIS to start as an application.

9. Save your work. Compile and run the `CMembrAppExtension`. Wait a few moments for IIS to initialize.

The next steps enable you to run your extension with IIS. If you are using a different ISAPI Web server, you might need to ask your vendor for instructions.

1. Go to the Internet Service Manager and notice that the State for your computer's WWW service says `Stopped`. Even though IIS is running under the debugger, this is what it says.

2. Double-click the Services computer name to see its properties. When you see the Directory Properties dialog box, you know that IIS is running in debug mode with your extension.

3. Add a virtual directory that points to your debug directory. Select an alias of `/MembrApp` and be sure to select the Execute check box in the Access group (see Figure 26.4). Turn Read permissions off by making sure that the Read check box is not on.

4. Now bring up your favorite browser and enter the URL of the directory you entered. For example, enter `http://127.0.0.1/MembrApp/MembrApp.Dll`.

FIGURE 26.4

Directory properties for the MembrApp *debug session.*

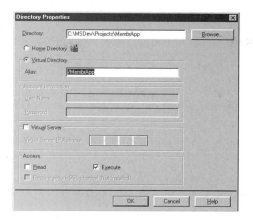

5. At last! You see the output of your extension DLL as follows:

```
This default message was produced by the
Internet Server DLL Wizard. Edit your
CMembrAppExtension::Default()implementation
to change it.
```

From GET to POST

In this section, you'll change the Default function to handle GET and POST requests separately. A GET request directs the user to an HTML file holding a basic form. A POST request acknowledges receipt.

You'll also create an HTML file holding the form. Creating a separate HTML file rather than coding HTML into the source code is often preferable. It is certainly more readable for your purposes.

So far, you have taken the supplied CHttpServer member functions StartContent, WriteTitle, and EndContent at face value. They are simple functions that hold the basic elements of an HTML page. To distinguish between a GET and a POST command, you must look at contents of CHttpServerContext, which I discussed earlier.

Change the preceding Default function as follows:

```cpp
void CMembrAppExtension::Default(CHttpServerContext* pCtxt)
{
    StartContent(pCtxt);
    WriteTitle(pCtxt);
    CString method = pCtxt->m_pECB->lpszMethod;
    if (0 == method.CompareNoCase("POST"))
```

```
            *pCtxt << _T("Thanks for the POST!\r\n");
    else
            *pCtxt << _T("<A HREF=\"/club.htm\">Click here to
            ➡continue.</A>\r\n");
    EndContent(pCtxt);
}
```

The `CHttpServer`-derived class, which in this case is `CMembrAppExtension`, is instantiated at DLL startup. Each time a request to the DLL is processed by the Web server, the
`CHttpServer` command handler is called with a request context as a parameter. Using
stack-based data this way is standard for passing data so that it is thread-safe.

The request context is an instance of the `CHttpServerContext` class, which holds useful
functions and data that are used when processing a request.

In the latest version of the `Default` function, you access the `lpszMethod` method string
of `CHttpServerContext`'s `EXTENSION_CONTROL_BLOCK`. You could have called the
`GetServerVariable` function with the `REQUEST_METHOD` argument.

Both requests yield the same result, whether the request was a `GET`, as when you typed in
`http://127.0.0.1/MembrApp/MembrApp.dll?URL`, or whether the request was a `POST`, as
when you submit the `club.htm` HTML form shown in Listing 26.14.

LISTING 26.14   CODE FOR THE HTML FORM

```
<HTML>
<HEAD>
    <TITLE>Membership Application</TITLE>
</HEAD>
<BODY>

<CENTER>
<H3>Application for Membership </H3>
</CENTER>

<FORM action="MembrApp.dll?" method="post">

<P><INPUT type=submit value="Access-Member-Area">
<INPUT type=reset value="Clear Form"></P>

</BODY>
</HTML>
```

You might have noticed that this form `POST`s precisely nothing. Now that you have come
this far, it is time to start processing some real data.

Adding Some Form Elements

In this section, you'll create a new function to handle the form's submission. To do this, you use the ON_PARSE_COMMAND family of macros covered earlier.

Recall that DEFAULT_PARSE_COMMAND sends a request without a command to the function in its first argument. Requests without a command have nothing following the question mark in their URL.

The wizard sets up a default DEFAULT_PARSE_COMMAND to pass control to the Default function you previously changed. The ON_PARSE_COMMAND and ON_PARSE_COMMAND_PARAMS work together to process non-Default commands.

Remember that ON_PARSE_COMMAND takes three parameters. The first is the name of the function to be called. The second is the CHttpServer class (here CMembrAppExtension). The third defines the number and type of the arguments to the function.

This third parameter can cause some confusion. It can have the ITS_EMPTY argument, or it can have a combination of the ITS_PSTR (a string) and ITS_I4 (a long integer) arguments, among others.

The confusion arises because this parameter must have at least one argument and can have several. But if this parameter has several arguments, these arguments *must not* be separated by commas, or compile errors will result. The ITS_EMPTY parameter shows that there are *no* arguments.

At runtime, this parameter provides crucial information for a special assembler function, _AfxParseCall, borrowed from the low-level OLE Idispatch implementation. This function pushes the right number of arguments onto the stack just before calling your handler function. It is coded differently for each NT-compatible processor type.

The ON_PARSE_COMMAND macros process both the URL query arguments (following the second question mark) and the posted contents of a form.

ON_PARSE_COMMAND_PARAMS gives the names and possible defaults for the arguments.

If you mismatch the number of parameters declared in ON_PARSE_COMMAND, you get either a stack leak from _AfxParseCall or the dreaded Document contains no data error message. So be careful to build your HTML forms, create the parameter maps, and declare the handler functions together so that all the parameters match up.

Change the Form

In your `club.htm` form, add the following lines right before the input-type-submit button directive:

```
Your email address (required):<BR>
<INPUT name="Email" size=40>
<P>
```

This permits the user to enter an email address of up to 40 characters.

Change the Parse Map

Add the following lines to the parse map:

```
ON_PARSE_COMMAND(HandleApp, CMembrAppExtension, ITS_PSTR)
ON_PARSE_COMMAND_PARAMS("Email=unknown")
```

This pair of commands shows that the `CMembrAppExtension::HandleApp` function handles one parameter of the string type, the parameter's HTML name is `Email`, and its default value is `Unknown`.

Note that although you declare a default value for `Email`, defaults generally apply only to URL queries. This is because `POST`ing a form with an empty `Email` text field overrides any default.

For example, if the user submits the preceding form without filling out any fields, the value for `Email` is an empty string and not `Unknown`.

Declare and Use the Handler Function

Add the function in Listing 26.15 to your `CMembrAppExtension` class.

LISTING 26.15   THE HANDLER FUNCTION

```
void CMembrAppExtension::HandleApp(CHttpServerContext* pCtxt,
➥LPCTSTR pstr)
{
    StartContent(pCtxt);
    WriteTitle(pCtxt);

    CString method = pCtxt->m_pECB->lpszMethod;
    if (0 == method.CompareNoCase("POST"))
            {
            *pCtxt << _T("Thanks for the POST, ");
            CString email = pstr;
            *pCtxt << _T(email);
            *pCtxt << _T("!\r\n");
            }
```

```
    else
            *pCtxt << _T("This forms processor expects to be Posted
            ➥to!\r\n");

    EndContent(pCtxt);
}
```

In Listing 26.15, you collect the form data into a convenient string and output a message to the user.

Now you are ready to compile and run the extension again. Be sure that the club.htm file resides in your /wwwroot (root HTML) directory. Start your browser, request the URL of http://localhost/club.htm, and fill in the form. If all goes well, when you enter your email address of email@net.com, the extension replies Thanks for the POST, email@net.com!

Congratulations!

Add a Radio Button

In this section, you add another input element, the radio button. You learn about error messages that commonly occur during development of an HTML file and its MFC ISAPI forms handler. This leads to the conclusion that HTML files and their MFC ISAPI forms handlers should be carefully designed and planned in advance.

Change the Form

In your club.htm form, add the following lines right before the input-type-submit button directive:

```
<P>
<INPUT type="radio" name="need" value="Need_now">I need it now! <BR>
<INPUT type="radio" name="need" value="sounds_interesting">Sounds
➥interesting. <BR>
<INPUT type="radio" name="need" value="dont_care">Couldn't care
➥less. <BR>
<P>
```

Save the changed form and reload the form in your browser.

Without making any changes to MembrApp (it should still be running), type in your email address again and select the Sounds Interesting radio button.

Submit the form and observe (if you are using Netscape) the Document contains no data browser error message. Other browsers, such as Microsoft Internet Explorer, might reply Unable to open file. Sometimes the browser just produces a blank screen.

Needless to say, this could cause some confusion on the part of the person visiting your Web site. It is not particularly helpful for the developer, either, when you are trying to track down the cause of an ISAPI problem.

For example, your production Webmaster might innocently decide to add a couple of fields to a form for which you have supplied an MFC forms handler. The Webmaster's problem report might be that nothing significant had been changed but that now "nothing works." Be aware that changing the elements of a form *is* a significant event in the life of an ISAPI MFC DLL.

What Went Wrong?

After `CHttpServer::HttpExtensionProc` is called and `CHttpServer::CallFunction` collects its data in `pszMethod` (HandleApp) and `pszParams` (Email=email@net.com& need=sounds_interesting), `CHttpServer::Lookup` finds the parse map entry you entered between `BEGIN_PARSE_MAP` and `END_PARSE_MAP`.

Then `CHttpServer::PushDefaultStackArgs` looks at the arguments supplied, pushing them onto the stack in preparation for the processor-dependent `_AfxParseCall`. But it finds that the number of arguments does not match the parse map definition. So `CallMemberFunc` (and `CallFunction`, in turn) returns `callBadParamCount`.

A 400 Bad Request response is generated. And because `CallMemberFunc` encountered an error, it creates no HTML content to be returned.

The difficulties are compounded because `CHttpServer::OnParseError` fails to load a string from the resource table and just outputs a `TRACE` debug message. So Listing 26.16 is a quick override of that function, which at least will give some indication of what is going on.

LISTING 26.16   MEMBRAPP.CPP—THE `OnParseError` OVERRIDE

```
BOOL CMembrAppExtension::OnParseError(CHttpServerContext* pCtxt,
➥int nMethodRet)
{
    UNUSED(nMethodRet);
    CString errString;

    if (pCtxt->m_pStream != NULL)
    {
        LPCTSTR pszObject = NULL;

        switch (pCtxt->m_pECB->dwHttpStatusCode)
        {
```

```
        case HTTP_STATUS_BAD_REQUEST:
            errString = "HTTP_BAD_REQUEST";
            if (pCtxt->m_pECB->lpszQueryString)
                pszObject = pCtxt->m_pECB->lpszQueryString;
            else
                pszObject = pCtxt->m_pECB->lpszPathInfo;
            break;

        case HTTP_STATUS_AUTH_REQUIRED:
            errString = "HTTP_AUTH_REQUIRED";     break;

        case HTTP_STATUS_FORBIDDEN:
            errString = "HTTP_FORBIDDEN";         break;

        case HTTP_STATUS_NOT_FOUND:
            errString = "HTTP_NOT_FOUND";         break;

        case HTTP_STATUS_SERVER_ERROR:
            errString = "HTTP_SERVER_ERROR";      break;

        case HTTP_STATUS_NOT_IMPLEMENTED:
            errString = "HTTP_NOT_IMPLEMENTED";
            pszObject = pCtxt->m_pECB->lpszQueryString;
            break;

        default:
            errString = "HTTP_NO_TEXT";
            pszObject = (LPCTSTR)
            ➥pCtxt->m_pECB->dwHttpStatusCode;
            break;
    }

    CHttpServer::StartContent(pCtxt);

    if (pszObject != NULL)
    {
        *pCtxt << pszObject;
        *pCtxt << "\r\n";
        *pCtxt << errString;
    }
    else
        *pCtxt << errString;
    CHttpServer::EndContent(pCtxt);
}

    return TRUE;
}
```

Change the Parse Map

Now that you have learned about keeping the form and the DLL synchronized, change the parse map again to handle the new radio button.

Add another ITS_PSTR to the ON_PARSE_COMMAND macro for HandleApp, remembering to leave just a space and no comma between the arguments. Compile and run the program, and resubmit the form (see Figure 26.5).

FIGURE 26.5

Assertion failed!

CHttpServer::ParseDefaultParams found a problem. Indeed, you forgot to match up ON_PARSE_COMMAND and ON_PARSE_COMMAND_PARAMS. If you continue beyond the assertion failure, your new OnParseError routine tells the browser

HandleApp HTTP_BAD_REQUEST

Bad request! Okay, let's fix ON_PARSE_COMMAND_PARAMS by adding radioButton. Now compile, run, and reload.

Uh-oh. This time a parameter has a bad format. Of course, you forgot to change the HandleApp function to accommodate the extra parameter you defined in ON_PARSE_COM-MAND_PARAMS, as shown in Listing 26.17.

LISTING 26.17 MEMBRAPP.CPP—THE HANDLE APPLICATION TO HANDLE radioButton

```
void CMembrAppExtension::HandleApp(CHttpServerContext* pCtxt,
➥LPCTSTR pstr, LPCTSTR radio)
{
    StartContent(pCtxt);
    WriteTitle(pCtxt);

    CString method = pCtxt->m_pECB->lpszMethod;
    if (0 == method.CompareNoCase("POST"))
        {
        *pCtxt << _T("Thanks for the POST, ");
        CString email = pstr;
        *pCtxt << _T(email);
        *pCtxt << _T("!\r\n");
        CString msg;
```

```
        msg = "You interest is ";
        msg += radio;
        msg += "\r\n";
        *pCtxt << _T(msg);
        }
    else
        *pCtxt << _T("This forms processor expects to be Posted
        ➥to!\r\n");

        EndContent(pCtxt);
}
```

Again, compile, run, reload.

```
HandleApp HTTP_BAD_REQUEST
```

Hmmm. What is it this time? Turns out that the name `radioButton` in `ON_PARSE_COM-MAND_PARAMS` does not match the name of the radio button in the form. Change the radio button's name to `radioButton` and reload. (Changing the form rather than changing `ON_PARSE_COMMAND_PARAMS` means that you don't have to recompile.)

Voilà!

The extension replies to the browser:

```
Thanks for the POST, email@net.com! Your interest level in the
club is sounds_interesting.
```

Granted, your usual development process doesn't include mistakes at every turn as it does here. But now you know what causes most errors and how to fix them.

I hope you agree that HTML files and their MFC ISAPI forms handlers should be carefully designed and planned in advance.

Other Form Input Elements

Now that you know the pitfalls to avoid, all that remains is to beef up your code and the HTML file so that you can handle the other elements in the example (refer to Figure 26.1). Because all input elements in a form are returned as strings, there is no difference in the handling of items such as check boxes and list boxes.

Change the Form

The final version of the form `club.htm` looks like the code in Listing 26.18.

LISTING 26.18   CLUB.HTM—FINAL HTML

```html
<HTML>
<HEAD>
    <TITLE>Member Application Form</TITLE>
</HEAD>
<BODY>
<CENTER>
<H3> Application for Membership</H3>
</CENTER>

<FORM action=" MembrApp.dll?HandleApp" method="post">

Your email address (required):<BR>
<INPUT name="Email" size=40>
<P>
From what you have heard of
The Camping Club
would you say:
<br>
<INPUT type="radio" name="radioButton" value="Need_now">I need it
➥now! <BR>
<INPUT type="radio" name="radioButton" value="sounds_interesting">
➥Sounds interesting. <BR>
<INPUT type="radio" name="radioButton" value="dont_care">Couldn't
➥care less. <BR>
<P>
Would you be interested in these other clubs? :
<UL>
<LI>
<INPUT NAME="TheGolfingClub"
    type=checkbox checked>
<font size = +2>
The Golf Club
</font> - For the golf aficionado.
</LI>
<LI>
<INPUT NAME="TheHikingClub"
    type=checkbox checked>
<font size = +2>
The Hiking Club
</font> - For lovers of the great outdoors.
</LI>
</UL>
<P><INPUT type=submit value="Sign Me Up">
<INPUT type=reset value="Clear the Form"></P>
</FORM>
</BODY>
</HTML>
```

Change the Parse Map

You need to add two more arguments to ON_PARSE_COMMAND and match up their names in ON_PARSE_COMMAND_PARAMS, as follows:

```
ON_PARSE_COMMAND(HandleApp, CMembrAppExtension, ITS_PSTR ITS_PSTR
➥ITS_PSTR ITS_PSTR)
ON_PARSE_COMMAND_PARAMS("Email radioButton=none_expressed
➥TheGolfClub=No TheHikingClub=No")
```

Now you have four string arguments, the last three of which have defaults.

Change the Handler Function

Along with adding the function parameters to handle the two new strings, let's clean up the code and make sure that the necessary email field is entered, as shown in Listing 26.19.

LISTING 26.19   MEMBRAPP.CPP—THE FINAL HANDLER

```cpp
void CMembrAppExtension::HandleApp(CHttpServerContext* pCtxt,
➥LPCTSTR emailIn, LPCTSTR radio, LPCTSTR TheGolfClub,
LPCTSTR TheHikingClub)
{
    StartContent(pCtxt);
    WriteTitle(pCtxt);

    CString method = pCtxt->m_pECB->lpszMethod;
    if (0 == method.CompareNoCase("POST"))
        {
        CString email = emailIn;
        if (email.IsEmpty())
            *pCtxt << _T("Email address is required!");
        else
            {
            CString msg;
            msg += "Your email is ";
            msg += emailIn;
            msg += "<P>Your interest level is ";
            msg += radio;
            msg += "<P>The Golf Club: ";
            msg += TheGolfClub;
            msg += "<P>The Hiking Club: ";
            msg += TheHikingClub;
            *pCtxt << _T(msg);
            }
        }
```

continues

LISTING 26.19 CONTINUED

```
else
    *pCtxt << _T("This forms processor expects to be Posted
    ➥to!\r\n");

EndContent(pCtxt);
}
```

Now your extension can process the form in Figure 26.1.

You now have a basis for developing fully functional, interactive applications on the Web.

Summary

In this chapter, you learned about the framework provided by the ISAPI Extension Wizard and how to build on it using MFC. You use these ISAPI classes to build an ISAPI extension that can process a form.

MAPI and MFC

by Peter Norton and Rob McGregor

CHAPTER 27

Microsoft's Messaging Application Programming Interface (MAPI—also called Mail API) is a messaging architecture that enables applications to interact with multiple messaging systems seamlessly across a variety of hardware platforms. MFC supports a subset of MAPI that allows the transmission of a document through electronic mail to mail-enabled machines. This chapter discusses MAPI, introduces the limited MAPI encapsulation provided by MFC, and presents a basic mail-enabled program.

The Messaging Application Programming Interface

The Microsoft Messaging API is a complex set of functions you can use to mail-enable your applications, giving them the ability to create, edit, transfer, and store mail messages. The MAPI architecture lets applications work with various messaging systems transparently. MAPI provides messaging services in a generic way because it's an open programming interface. This allows developers to customize functionality and provides for future expansion.

MAPI is built into the Windows 95 and Windows NT 4 operating systems. Because MAPI is an integrated part of Windows, application developers have access to a consistent interface. MAPI is split into two interfaces: one for front-end applications and another for the back-end service providers. This division provides true independence from specific messaging systems. This independence is what makes it possible for applications like the Microsoft Exchange's in-box to handle both fax messaging and Internet mail services, as well as LAN workgroup messaging. The MAPI programming interfaces provide the features developers need to mail-enable workgroup applications that deal with various messaging systems such as fax, voice mail, and online services like CompuServe and MCI MAIL.

MAPI for Win32 is found in the dynamic link library MAPI32.DLL. MAPI-compliant objects use the Component Object Model (COM) to define their behavior. Also, MAPI is the messaging component of the Microsoft Windows Open Services Architecture (WOSA). WOSA is an open architecture standard that is currently evolving for use with not only messaging, but database, security, and other technologies as well.

> **NOTE**
>
> The Microsoft Windows Open Services Architecture allows you to develop both front-end and back-end software using a standardized interface that fits easily into the distributed computing model.

Client Applications

MAPI client applications come in three general types:

- Applications that are *messaging aware.* Messaging-aware applications don't need the full services of the messaging system. They typically include a messaging option such as Send Mail in the File menu as an additional feature.

- Applications that are *messaging enabled.* Messaging-enabled applications require many of the services of the messaging system. These applications usually run on a network or on an online service.

- Workgroup applications that are *messaging based. M*essaging-based workgroup applications use the full services of the message system and are designed to execute and interact automatically across a network.

Two Higher-Level Alternatives: Simple MAPI and CMC

A couple of higher-level interface alternatives to the MAPI specification are available to Windows programmers on PC platforms. These abstractions are called *Simple MAPI* and *Common Messaging Calls (CMC).* This implementation supports existing messaging-enabled and messaging-aware Windows applications developed in any language that supports DLLs, including C, C++, Delphi, and Visual Basic. Simple MAPI gives you the tools to add basic messaging services to your applications.

When writing messaging-enabled and messaging-aware applications, either Simple MAPI or CMC is an appropriate MAPI interface choice. These interfaces are nearly identical; both provide a set of functions that lets clients create, send, receive, reply to, forward, edit, and delete messages.

Simple MAPI

The Simple MAPI specification uses the MAPI32.DLL library, just as the full MAPI specification does. There are 12 functions in Simple MAPI that give an application the power to send, address, receive, and reply to messages. Table 27.1 describes the functions provided by Simple MAPI.

27

MAPI AND MFC

TABLE 27.1 THE SIMPLE MAPI FUNCTION INTERFACE TO MAPI

Simple MAPI Function	Purpose
MAPIAddress()	Addresses a message.
MAPIDeleteMail()	Deletes a message.
MAPIDetails()	Displays a recipient-details dialog box.
MAPIFindNext()	Returns the identifier of the first or next message of a specified type.
MAPIFreeBuffer()	Frees memory allocated by the messaging system.
MAPILogoff()	Ends a session with the messaging system.
MAPILogon()	Establishes a messaging session.
MAPIReadMail()	Reads a message.
MAPIResolveName()	Displays a dialog box to resolve an ambiguous recipient name.
MAPISaveMail()	Saves a message.
MAPISendDocuments()	Sends a standard message using a dialog box.
MAPISendMail()	Sends a message, allowing greater flexibility in message generation than MAPISendDocuments() does.

Common Messaging Calls

If you think Simple MAPI sounds good, it is—for Windows-only applications written with Visual Basic or some similar development system. But when you are writing new applications with MFC, you shouldn't use Simple MAPI. Simple MAPI is mainly for backward compatibility with older applications that already use it. If you don't want the added complexity of the direct MAPI function calls, consider the Common Messaging Calls client interface, a set of 10 functions that provide simple messaging for your client applications. CMC is built on top of the core MAPI subsystem and, unlike Simple MAPI, is independent of the operating system and the hardware used by the underlying messaging system. This makes CMC a good MAPI choice if your application will run on multiple platforms and must provide messaging on each of these platforms. Table 27.2 describes the 10 CMC functions.

TABLE 27.2 THE CMC FUNCTIONS

Function	Description
cmc_send()	Sends a message.
cmc_send_documents()	Sends a message. This function is string based and is usually used in macro language calls.

Function	Description
cmc_act_on()	Performs an action on a specified message.
cmc_list()	Lists summary information about messages meeting specified criteria.
cmc_read()	Returns a specified message.
cmc_look_up()	Looks up addressing information.
cmc_free()	Frees memory allocated by the messaging system.
cmc_logoff()	Terminates a session with the messaging system.
cmc_logon()	Establishes a session with the messaging system.
cmc_query_configuration()	Determines information about the installed CMC service.

> **NOTE**
>
> Simple MAPI runs only on Windows-based platforms. CMC is designed to be independent of the operating system and runs on Windows, DOS, and UNIX.

The `MapiMessage` Structure

MAPI deals with messaging, and the MAPI `MapiMessage` structure, as defined in MAPI.H, contains information about a MAPI message. This structure is shown here:

```
typedef struct{
    ULONG           ulReserved;
    LPTSTR          lpszSubject;
    LPTSTR          lpszNoteText;
    LPTSTR          lpszMessageType;
    LPTSTR          lpszDateReceived;
    LPTSTR          lpszConversationID;
    FLAGS           flFlags;
    lpMapiRecipDesc lpOriginator;
    ULONG           nRecipCount;
    lpMapiRecipDesc lpRecips;
    ULONG           nFileCount;
    lpMapiFileDesc  lpFiles;
}MapiMessage, FAR *lpMapiMessage;
```

The members of this structure reveal the type of data a MAPI message uses; the members are described in Table 27.3.

TABLE 27.3 THE DATA MEMBERS OF THE MapiMessage STRUCTURE

Member	Description
ulReserved	Reserved; this must be zero.
lpszSubject	A pointer to the text string describing the message subject, typically limited to 256 characters or less.
lpszNoteText	A pointer to a string containing the message text.
lpszMessageType	A pointer to a string indicating the message type. Note that some messaging systems ignore this member.
lpszDateReceived	A pointer to a string containing the date that the message was received. The format of this string is YYYY/MM/DD HH:MM, with HH:MM referring to a 24-hour clock.
lpszConversationID	A pointer to a string that identifies the conversation thread to which a message belongs.
flFlags	A bitmask used to indicate message status flags.
lpOriginator	A pointer to a MapiRecipDesc structure containing information about the sender of the message.
nRecipCount	The number of MapiRecipDesc structures in the array pointed to by the lpRecips member.
lpRecips	A pointer to an array of MapiRecipDesc structures, each containing information about a message recipient.
nFileCount	The number of MapiFileDesc structures in the array pointed to by the lpFiles member.
lpFiles	A pointer to an array of MapiFileDesc structures, each containing information about a file attachment.

The MapiFileDesc Structure

The MapiMessage structure is supplemented by the MapiFileDesc structure, which contains information about a file attached to a message. This attachment can be either a simple data file or a compound OLE file. The MapiFileDesc structure is shown here:

```
typedef struct{
    ULONG    ulReserved;
    ULONG    flFlags;
    ULONG    nPosition;
    LPTSTR   lpszPathName;
    LPTSTR   lpszFileName;
    LPVOID   lpFileType;
}MapiFileDesc, FAR *lpMapiFileDesc;
```

Examination of the members of this structure shows information needed by MAPI to send a file attachment. These data members are described in Table 27.4.

TABLE 27.4   THE DATA MEMBERS OF THE MapiFileDesc STRUCTURE

Member	Description
ulReserved	Reserved; this must be zero.
flFlags	A bitmask of attachment flags. These can be MAPI_OLE and MAPI_OLE_STATIC. If no flag is set, the attachment is a standard file.
nPosition	An integer value used in the MapiMessage structure member lpszNoteText to indicate where an attachment should be placed in the body of a message.
lpszPathName	A pointer to the fully qualified path (including disk drive letter and directory name) of the attachment file.
lpszFileName	An optional pointer to the attachment filename as seen by the recipient.
lpFileType	An optional pointer to a descriptor that can be used to indicate the type of the attached file.

To determine the type of file being sent, MAPI looks at the file extension. Although this might seem like a crude method of figuring out the file type, it works well in most cases. For example, a file with a .TXT extension means that the file is a text file, an association provided by the registry.

Limited MAPI Functionality in MFC

The full MAPI specification is quite complex and comprehensive. Unfortunately, MFC implements only a small subsection of the entire MAPI. The only functionality implemented is in the form of sending messages and files. Other MAPI features such as retrieval and deletion of messages hasn't yet been implemented by the MFC developers.

The CDocument Connection

What minimal MAPI support MFC *does* provide is found buried deep within the CDocument class. In this class, you'll find the MFC MAPI wrapper method OnFileSendMail() and its corresponding user interface update handler OnUpdateFileSendMail(). The OnFileSendMail() method does a lot to provide messaging services for your MFC applications—with minimal effort on your part!

Doing MAPI the MFC Way

MFC provides a predefined command identifier associated with the `OnFileSendMail()` and `OnUpdateFileSendMail()` methods in message map entries. The command identifier `ID_FILE_SEND_MAIL` (defined in `AFXRES.H`) enables a Send Mail command in the case of `OnUpdateFileSendMail()` and sends a document to the user's mail service provider in the case of `OnFileSendMail()`. The `CDocument` class's message map entries for these methods look like this:

```
BEGIN_MESSAGE_MAP(CMyDoc, CDocument)
    ON_COMMAND(ID_FILE_SEND_MAIL, OnFileSendMail)
    ON_UPDATE_COMMAND_UI(ID_FILE_SEND_MAIL, OnUpdateFileSendMail)
END_MESSAGE_MAP()
```

No prototypes or implementations for these methods are required in the derived-document class, although they can be provided if you need them. If the user's system supports mail services, the methods are available through your `ID_FILE_SEND_MAIL` menu item. If mail support isn't available, MFC automatically removes the `ID_FILE_SEND_MAIL` menu item so that users don't see it.

The following section looks inside the `OnFileSendMail()` method to see how it interacts with MAPI. Using these methods as a model, you should be able to write MFC extension DLLs that encapsulate the entire Messaging API within MFC classes.

The `CDocument::OnFileSendMail(·)` Method

The `OnFileSendMail()` method is a real workhorse. There's a lot going on inside this `CDocument` MAPI wrapper—Listing 27.1 gives all the gory details. By studying this listing carefully, you can get a feel for how MAPI is *really* done, under the hood.

LISTING 27.1   THE CDocument::OnFileSendMail() METHOD

```
/////////////////////////////////////////////////////////////////
// CDocument MAPI support

void CDocument::OnFileSendMail()
{
    ASSERT_VALID(this);

    // update handler always gets called first
    ASSERT(_afxIsMailAvail);

    CWaitCursor wait;

    _AFX_MAIL_STATE* pMailState = _afxMailState;
    if (pMailState->m_hInstMail == NULL)
```

```
    pMailState->m_hInstMail = ::LoadLibraryA("MAPI32.DLL");

if (pMailState->m_hInstMail == NULL)
{
    AfxMessageBox(AFX_IDP_FAILED_MAPI_LOAD);
    return;
}
ASSERT(pMailState->m_hInstMail != NULL);

ULONG (PASCAL *lpfnSendMail)(ULONG, ULONG, MapiMessage*,
    FLAGS, ULONG);
(FARPROC&)lpfnSendMail = GetProcAddress(pMailState->m_hInstMail,
    "MAPISendMail");

if (lpfnSendMail == NULL)
{
    AfxMessageBox(AFX_IDP_INVALID_MAPI_DLL);
    return;
}
ASSERT(lpfnSendMail != NULL);

TCHAR szTempName[_MAX_PATH];
TCHAR szPath[_MAX_PATH];
BOOL bRemoveTemp = FALSE;
if (m_strPathName.IsEmpty() || IsModified())
{
    // save to temporary path
    VERIFY(GetTempPath(_countof(szPath), szPath) != 0);
    VERIFY(GetTempFileName(szPath, _T("afx"), 0, szTempName)!= 0);

    // save it, but remember original modified flag
    BOOL bModified = IsModified();
    BOOL bResult = DoSave(szTempName, FALSE);
    SetModifiedFlag(bModified);
    if (!bResult)
    {
      TRACE0("Warning: file save failed during File.Send Mail.\n");
      return;
    }
    bRemoveTemp = TRUE;
}
else
{
    // use actual file since it isn't modified
    lstrcpyn(szTempName, m_strPathName, _countof(szTempName));
}
#ifdef _UNICODE
    char szTempNameA[_MAX_PATH];
    _wcstombsz(szTempNameA, szTempName, _countof(szTempNameA));
#endif
```

continues

LISTING 27.1   CONTINUED

```
    // build an appropriate title for the attachment
    TCHAR szTitle[_MAX_PATH];
    if (!m_strPathName.IsEmpty())
        AfxGetFileName(m_strPathName, szTitle, _countof(szTitle));
    else
    {
        lstrcpyn(szTitle, m_strTitle, _countof(szTitle));
        if (m_strTitle.Find('.') == -1) // no extension
        {
            // append the default suffix if there is one
            CString strExt;
            CDocTemplate* pTemplate = GetDocTemplate();
            if (pTemplate != NULL &&
                pTemplate->GetDocString(strExt, CDocTemplate::filterExt))
            {
                lstrcat(szTitle, strExt);
            }
        }
    }

#ifdef _UNICODE
    char szTitleA[_MAX_PATH];
    _wcstombsz(szTitleA, szTitle, _countof(szTitleA));
#endif

    // prepare the file description (for the attachment)
    MapiFileDesc fileDesc;
    memset(&fileDesc, 0, sizeof(fileDesc));
    fileDesc.nPosition = (ULONG)-1;
#ifdef _UNICODE
    fileDesc.lpszPathName = szTempNameA;
    fileDesc.lpszFileName = szTitleA;
#else
    fileDesc.lpszPathName = szTempName;
    fileDesc.lpszFileName = szTitle;
#endif

    // prepare the message (empty with 1 attachment)
    MapiMessage message;
    memset(&message, 0, sizeof(message));
    message.nFileCount = 1;
    message.lpFiles = &fileDesc;

    // prepare for modal dialog box
    AfxGetApp()->EnableModeless(FALSE);
    HWND hWndTop;
    CWnd* pParentWnd = CWnd::GetSafeOwner(NULL, &hWndTop);
```

```
    // some extra precautions are required to use MAPISendMail as it
    // tends to enable the parent window in between dialogs (after
    // the login dialog, but before the send note dialog).
    pParentWnd->SetCapture();
    ::SetFocus(NULL);
    pParentWnd->m_nFlags |= WF_STAYDISABLED;

    int nError = lpfnSendMail(0, (ULONG)pParentWnd->GetSafeHwnd(),
        &message, MAPI_LOGON_UI|MAPI_DIALOG, 0);

    // after returning from the MAPISendMail call, the window must
    // be re-enabled and focus returned to the frame to undo the
    // workaround done before the MAPI call.
    ::ReleaseCapture();
    pParentWnd->m_nFlags &= ~WF_STAYDISABLED;

    pParentWnd->EnableWindow(TRUE);
    ::SetActiveWindow(NULL);
    pParentWnd->SetActiveWindow();
    pParentWnd->SetFocus();
    if (hWndTop != NULL)
        ::EnableWindow(hWndTop, TRUE);
    AfxGetApp()->EnableModeless(TRUE);

    if (nError != SUCCESS_SUCCESS &&
        nError != MAPI_USER_ABORT && nError != MAPI_E_LOGIN_FAILURE)
    {
        AfxMessageBox(AFX_IDP_FAILED_MAPI_SEND);
    }

    // remove temporary file, if temporary file was used
    if (bRemoveTemp)
        CFile::Remove(szTempName);
}
```

The `OnFileSendMail()` method is quite long and complex. Let's see if I can shed a little light on its internal workings.

The first thing the method does is check to see whether mail services are available on the user's machine. This is done by attempting to get an instance handle to the MAPI32.DLL:

```
pMailState->m_hInstMail = ::LoadLibraryA("MAPI32.DLL");
```

If this `LoadLibrary()` call fails, MAPI isn't available and the method returns. If the call to `LoadLibrary()` returns an instance handle, the `OnFileSendMail()` method checks to see whether this MAPI32.DLL contains the `MAPISendMail()` function. It does this by attempting to get a pointer to the `MAPISendMail()` function using the Win32 API function `GetProcAddress()`, like this:

```
ULONG (PASCAL *lpfnSendMail)(ULONG, ULONG, MapiMessage*, FLAGS,
    ULONG);
(FARPROC&)lpfnSendMail = GetProcAddress(pMailState->m_hInstMail,
    "MAPISendMail");
```

If the `lpfnSendMail` function pointer is `NULL` after this call to `GetProcAddress()`, the `MAPISendMail()` function doesn't exist in the DLL, and there's no point in continuing. If the pointer is not `NULL`, however, the method moves forward and checks to see whether the current document has been saved or modified since it was last saved. Regardless of whether or not it has been modified since the last save, the document is saved to a temporary file. The path and filename for this temporary file are determined by calling the `GetTempPath()` and `GetTempFileName()` Win32 API functions, like this:

```
VERIFY(GetTempPath(_countof(szPath), szPath) != 0);
VERIFY(GetTempFileName(szPath, _T("afx"), 0, szTempName)!= 0);
```

These statements store the path in the variable `szPath` and the filename in the variable `szTempName`. (Note that the `"afx"` string used in `GetTempFileName()` is a three-letter prefix for the new temporary file.)

The next order of business is to build an appropriate title for the file attachment. This is done by calling the undocumented MFC global function `AfxGetFileName()` if a temporary filename was generated; if the document was previously saved but not modified, you call the `CDocTemplate::GetDocString()` method. In either case, the attachment title is stored in the variable `szTitle`.

Next, a MAPI file description is prepared using the Simple MAPI `MapiFileDesc` structure (discussed in the section "The `MapiFileDesc` Structure," earlier in this chapter), and the `szTempName` and `szTitle` variables are used to fill in the `MapiFileDesc` `lpszPathName` and `lpszFileName` members:

```
MapiFileDesc fileDesc;
   memset(&fileDesc, 0, sizeof(fileDesc));
   fileDesc.nPosition = (ULONG)-1;
#ifdef _UNICODE
   fileDesc.lpszPathName = szTempNameA;
   fileDesc.lpszFileName = szTitleA;
#else
   fileDesc.lpszPathName = szTempName;
   fileDesc.lpszFileName = szTitle;
#endif
```

A `MapiMessage` structure is then prepared, with the message being empty except for the file attachment, like this:

```
// prepare the message (empty with 1 attachment)
MapiMessage message;
memset(&message, 0, sizeof(message));
message.nFileCount = 1;
message.lpFiles = &fileDesc;
```

`OnFileSendMail()` then takes some extra precautions to keep the parent window from getting the input focus until the mailing process is done, telling the parent window to stay disabled until further notice, like this:

```
pParentWnd->SetCapture();
::SetFocus(NULL);
pParentWnd->m_nFlags |= WF_STAYDISABLED;
```

At last, the mail message is sent, using the function pointer retrieved earlier to call the `MAPISendMail()` function:

```
int nError = lpfnSendMail(0, (ULONG)pParentWnd->GetSafeHwnd(),
    &message, MAPI_LOGON_UI|MAPI_DIALOG, 0);
```

As the final step, the parent window is reenabled:

```
::ReleaseCapture();
pParentWnd->m_nFlags &= ~WF_STAYDISABLED;
pParentWnd->EnableWindow(TRUE);
::SetActiveWindow(NULL);
pParentWnd->SetActiveWindow();
pParentWnd->SetFocus();
```

And that's all there is to it! What? You thought it was easier? Let's see how all this code, wrapped nicely into the `CDocument::OnFileSendMail()` function gets the job done in a sample application.

Sample Program: MAPI1.EXE

The sample program MAPI1 shows how easy it is to mail-enable your applications with the MFC MAPI wrapper methods in `CDocument`. Because the only MFC support is in `CDocument`, a document/view application model is used. This is the simplest way to go about adding the Send Mail command to your applications. The Visual C++ AppWizard allows you to choose the MAPI option when creating a skeleton application, as shown in Figure 27.1.

FIGURE 27.1

The Visual C++ AppWizard lets you add basic MAPI Send Mail functionality quickly and painlessly.

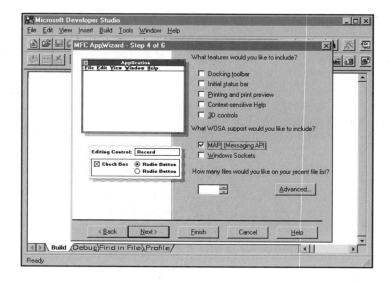

The sample program MAPI1 uses a CEditView-derived view class. To enable MAPI, the only steps you need to perform are as follows:

1. Add a Send Mail menu item and give it the corresponding command identifier ID_FILE_SEND_MAIL.

2. Add the two CDocument message map entries ON_COMMAND() and ON_UPDATE_COMMAND_UI() (both referring to the ID_FILE_SEND_MAIL identifier, of course) to provide the functionality directly from the CDocument class.

After these steps are complete and the program is built (assuming that mail is enabled on the system), you can open a document and choose the File, Send Mail menu command to see MAPI at work. When you activate the OnFileSendMail() method, it starts the mail service (see Figure 27.2).

NOTE

The document opened in the application for this example is MAPI1.REG, the AppWizard-generated file used by REGEDIT.

If you are sending an Internet mail message, the service must be properly configured using the Windows 95 Internet Mail information dialog box, shown in Figure 27.3.

FIGURE 27.2

The Choose Profile dialog box is the gateway to the Microsoft Exchange.

FIGURE 27.3

Setting up Internet mail information.

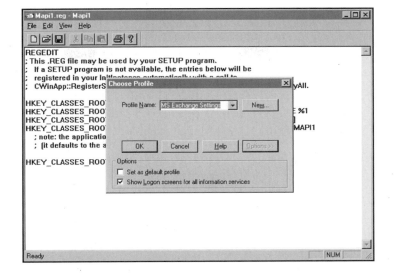

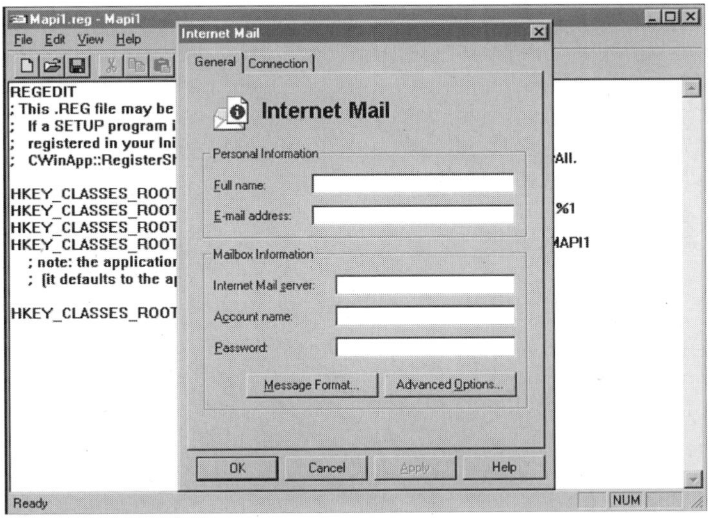

After the mail connection is ready, you must select an address book (see Figure 27.4) that contains information about where to send the mail message (and any attachments).

FIGURE 27.4

Selecting an address book.

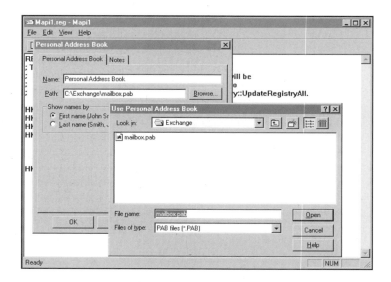

The final stop for the message before it's routed to the intended receiver is the mail service's out-box, where the message is made ready for delivery (see Figure 27.5).

FIGURE 27.5

At last, the MAPI1.REG message appears in Exchange, ready for delivery.

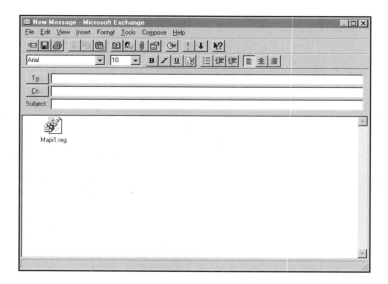

Summary

The Messaging Application Programming Interface allows applications to create, send, receive, edit, forward, and delete messages across a network. Two function-based interfaces to MAPI functionality are commonly used by Windows programmers: Simple MAPI (which provides a limited subset of MAPI) and Common Messaging Calls (which provides a similar interface).

The MFC library provides the `CDocument::OnFileSendMail()` method to handle the details of preparing a document as a mail attachment and sending it to the mail service. The use of this advanced feature is as simple as including the command identifier `ID_FILE_SEND_MAIL` and specifying the command in the document's message map.

TAPI and MFC

by Keith McIntyre

IN THIS CHAPTER

CHAPTER

28

TAPI is an abbreviation for Telephony Application Programming Interface. As the name implies, TAPI enables developers to write applications that take advantage of services provided by telephony vendors. The services can be good ol' Ma Bell services accessed over an analog modem or advanced telephony services provided by a proprietary Private Branch Exchange (PBX).

TAPI is one of the services defined by the Windows Open System Architecture (WOSA). It is a well-thought-out client interface and internal architecture that has proven to be powerful and extensible. As depicted in Figure 28.1, the TAPI architecture consists of TAPI-enabled applications and TAPI Service Providers. The TAPI-enabled applications talk to the Service Providers indirectly via the Telephony API. TAPI provides an abstraction that allows the applications to be written in a platform-independent fashion. The Service Providers are responsible for taking the platform-independent abstraction and implementing specializations (drivers) that control specific hardware devices.

Figure 28.1 provides a general description of the TAPI architecture. (Different versions of TAPI implement differing architectures underneath the covers. In particular, versions 1.4, 2, and 3 introduce drastic departures from previous versions.)

Figure 28.1

An abstraction of the TAPI architecture.

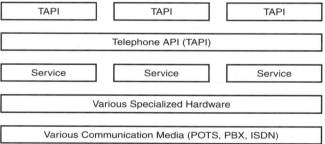

In this chapter, you'll start by looking at an overview of TAPI. Next you'll take a look at the history of TAPI and a peek at what the future of TAPI will offer. You'll then use both Assisted Telephony and Basic Telephony Services to write sample applications that allow an analog modem to dial an interactive voice call.

Overview

TAPI, the Telephony Application Programming Interface, enables a programmer to develop applications that interface with telephony systems ranging from a simple Plain Old Telephone Service (POTS) line to a modern Private Branch Exchange (PBX). TAPI can be incorporated into an application as an ancillary function. TAPI could, for example, enable an application to dial a phone number. Or an application can be written that is very TAPI-centric. Perhaps the application provides an interface to a PBX system whereby the user can store commonly dialed numbers, record greetings, page colleagues, and take dictation.

Four levels of service are provided by TAPI:

- Assisted Telephony
- Basic Telephony Service
- Supplemental Telephony Service
- Extended Telephony Service

Assisted Telephony

Assisted Telephony provides a short list of functions that allow non-telephony-centric applications to easily add the ability to dial outgoing calls to their feature set. Using Assisted Telephony in conjunction with VBA, one can add dialing capabilities into Microsoft Word documents or Excel spreadsheets. Assisted Telephony can also be used to add phone dialing to Visual C++/MFC applications you write with MSVC 6. Assisted Telephony only supports dialing numbers for interactive voice calls.

Currently, Assisted Telephony supports only two function calls:

- `TapiRequestMakeCall()`
- `TapiGetLocationInfo()`

`TapiRequestMakeCall()` works together with the Dialer.exe application provided with Windows 95 and Windows 98 to handle all the details of finding the right device on which to place the call, dialing the number, and providing a user interface from which the user can hang up the call.

`TapiGetLocationInfo()` provides a means of obtaining country and city code information that can be used when constructing the phone number given to `TapiRequestMakeCall()`.

Previous versions of Assisted Telephony supported two additional functions:

- `TapiRequestMediaCall()`
- `TapiDropRequest()`

These are no longer supported by Win32 applications and should not be used.

28

TAPI AND MFC

Basic Telephony Service

Basic Telephony Services is targeted at programmers who want to have increased control over the telephony operations their application provides but do not have to control advanced PBX functions.

The Basic Telephony Services are deliverable by all Service Providers regardless of the hardware employed. The abstraction provided by TAPI allows applications to be written that will run on different vendors' hardware platforms. In a similar fashion to the way GDI made platform independent graphics possible, TAPI makes hardware-independent telephony software possible. (And as you will see later, TAPI provides an API negotiation mechanism that allows applications to run against different versions of TAPI as well.)

The services made available through the Basic Telephony Services include the following:

- Address translation
- Making calls
- Answering calls
- Dropping calls
- Monitoring call states and events
- Call handle manipulation

Address translation is concerned with generating a locale-specific version of a canonical address. A *canonical address* contains all the information required to uniquely identify an endpoint. This includes country code, area code, and the phone number. Canonical addresses start with a + character. Hence, "+1 (619) 554-1400" would be a good representation of the telephone number for reaching Stellcom Incorporated located in San Diego, California (area code 619), USA (country code 1), with the phone number 554-1400.

The address translation process takes into account the current location the call is being placed from. The Modem applet contained in the Control Panel provides a Dialing Properties dialog. A tab in this dialog is titled My Locations. The associated user interface allows the user to establish a number of calling profiles each with independently specified settings for the current area code, country code, access number for dialing long distance or obtaining an outside line, and disabling call waiting. One can also specify a calling card number that should be used when placing long distance calls as well as specifying rules, based on area codes, as to when a call should be treated as long distance. Figure 28.2 shows the Dialing Properties dialog available with Windows 98.

FIGURE 28.2

The Dialing Properties dialog box.

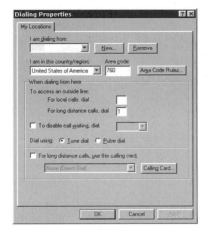

Address translation takes a canonical address as input, applies the rules specified through the current I Am Dialing From setting in the Dialing Properties dialog, and generates a locale-specific dial string. The locale-specific string includes all the information such as the digit required to get to an outside line, the calling card number to which the call should be called, the area code, and so on. So the canonical number presented earlier might translate to something like "T 9 5541400."

When you have a locale-specific dial string, you probably want to use it to place a call. Making calls is not a simple task when using Basic Telephony Service. As you will see later in the chapter, a significant amount of code is required to initialize TAPI, obtain a line handle that meets the required communications needs, negotiate a TAPI service level, and establish a call.

Alternatively, you might want to write an application to answer incoming calls. Basic Telephony Services provides for call establishment for either incoming or outgoing calls.

Dropping a call is a fairly obvious requirement of telephony. TAPI provides the `lineDrop()` function to facilitate dropping calls.

Calls move through an orderly set of states as the call is established, processed, and ultimately dropped. For outgoing calls, the states are as follows:

- Idle
- Dialtone
- Dialing
- Proceeding

- Ringback
- Connected
- Disconnected

For incoming calls, the states are as follows:

- Idle
- Offering
- Accepted
- Connected
- Disconnected

In the case of both incoming and outgoing calls, the call goes back to an idle state when disconnected. Figures 28.3 and 28.4 depict the states through which incoming and outgoing calls transition.

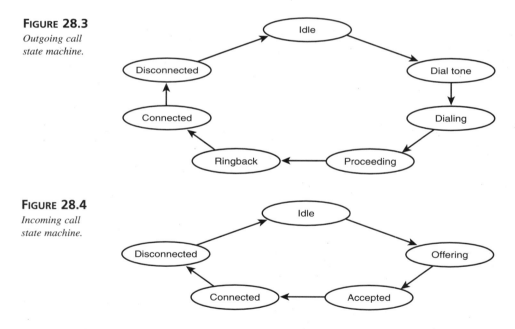

FIGURE 28.3
Outgoing call state machine.

FIGURE 28.4
Incoming call state machine.

TAPI provides a mechanism for monitoring and responding to the changes of state and events that are fired off by TAPI during the lifetime of a call. Your application must register a callback function through which commands and parameters are sent back to your application by means of TAPI. This model is similar to the way pre-MFC Windows applications received and handled messages. It is also similar to the way Winsock programs are notified about events associated with TCP/IP sockets.

Basic Telephony Services also provide the mechanism to retrieve and manipulate the call handle. This is important because TAPI itself provides no mechanism for transferring data over the call it establishes. You must resort to other classes and APIs to communicate (that is, transfer data) over the TAPI call. The method you use to transmit data depends on the type of data you are transferring. For message-based communications such as email or fax, the Messaging API (MAPI) would probably be most appropriate. For interactive, command-driven communication, the Win32 Communications API would be the right choice. You can use the WAVE API to send and receive audio data. For interactive voice, you would pick up the phone and converse. TAPI is used to establish and monitor calls, not transfer the data.

You will see an example of using TAPI to establish and monitor a call later in this chapter when you look at a Basic Telephony Services-based application.

Supplemental Telephony Service

The TAPI Supplemental Telephony Services are those services that are defined by the API but are not required by a particular TAPI Service Provider. The Supplemental Services go beyond basic call establishment, monitoring, and dropping. The Supplemental Services typically require additional hardware to implement. There is typically a PBX or a physical phone deskset on the other side of the Service Provider that handles the Supplemental Telephony Service request.

All TAPI Service Providers are required to support Basic Telephony Services. Implementing Supplemental Services is purely optional. For example, the Unimodem Service Provider provides a complete set of Basic Telephony Services but provides no additional Supplemental Telephony Services.

The additional functionality provided by Supplemental Telephony Services allows for implementing applications that interface to the advanced features of modern telephony systems. The services include the following:

- Call hold
- Transferring calls
- Conferencing calls
- Call forwarding
- Call parking
- Call pickup

- Call completion
- Call acceptance
- Generating and monitoring digits and tones
- Media mode monitoring
- Media stream routing and control
- Caller info
- Control over call parameters
- Phone terminal control

Several of these features are probably typical of those supplied by the PBX where you work. The call-related features are typical of user functions one might perform using a deskset. Using TAPI, an application can control the functions by using a computer application. The application might expose a GUI intended to replace or augment the deskset, providing a more user-friendly interface to the telephony system.

Additional Supplemental Telephony Services provide for monitoring calls, controlling media streams, responding to user inputs via DTMF tones, and so on. The TAPI application might implement a call desk that automates customer service requests. When a customer called, the application could prompt the caller to enter numbers to select help regarding a specific product or service. The TAPI application could control queues of calls and automate the forwarding for the calls to customer service representatives.

Additional Supplemental Telephony Services allow for control of the deskset. A modern deskset might contain an LCD display that can display alphanumeric data. A TAPI application could provide caller information via the deskset's LCD, allowing for call screening. Or perhaps the TAPI application would use the distinctive ringer capabilities of the deskset to alert the caller that an incoming call was from the boss.

Extended Telephony Service

TAPI was designed to provide an extensible framework through which vendors can offer access to features and functions specific to their hardware solutions.

Well-written applications that use only Basic Telephony Services should run in a hardware-independent fashion, that is, they should run on anyone's computer provided that they have a TAPI Service Provider to support the available hardware.

Well-written applications that use Supplemental Telephony Services are written in a vendor-neutral fashion. The Service Provider features they utilize are well documented by the TAPI interface. The software application should be able to run against multiple vendors' hardware and Service Providers without being rewritten if the Supplemental Telephony Services required by the application are provided by the Service Provider(s)— that is, the application is still written in a vendor- and hardware-neutral manner.

Extended Telephony Services allow a vendor to extend the Telephony API by adding device- and Service Provider-specific features and functions. Applications written to this level of service will typically be targeted at a specific vendor's product offering and hence will lack portability.

History of TAPI

A quick review of TAPI's past, as well as a peek at the next version of TAPI, will help round out the discussion of how TAPI can be used to enhance applications as well as to shed some light on the importance of TAPI within the overall Windows architecture.

TAPI 1.3

TAPI started out during the days of Windows 3.1 and Windows for Workgroups 3.11 as a means of negotiating for a modem attached to a serial port. Version 1.3 was the first released version of TAPI. (Earlier beta versions spanned the 1.0 to 1.3 version space.)

TAPI 1.3 was released as a standalone SDK. TAPI 1.3 was also known as version 1.03 because it was released as the TAPI 1 SDK, which was distributed through the MSDN Level II membership. It was not a part of any OS release or any of the developer tools of the time. It included the tapi.dll, tapi.lib, and tapi.h files required in order to build 16-bit applications and Service Providers.

TAPI 1.3 is the only 16-bit-compatible version of TAPI released. If for some reason you wanted to write a TAPI application that would run on all versions of Windows, TAPI 1.3 would be your only choice. Because backward compatibility has been maintained since 1993 when TAPI first was released, it should actually be possible to do such a foolish thing! I leave it as an exercise for the reader to implement a universal TAPI client using TAPI version 1.3.

TAPI 1.3 provided Basic Telephony Services and some of the Supplemental Telephony Services. Sending data over an established call was accomplished by using the now-defunct CommXXX calls. TAPI 1.3 was certainly not the tool for creating enterprise telephony server solutions. It was, however, a good tool for implementing client applications that could dial analog modems or interface with a PBX.

TAPI 1.4

TAPI 1.4 was released along with Windows 95. It was an integral part of the operating system and required no additional distribution files such as DLLs or EXEs. TAPI 1.4 provided a client API that was 32-bit-oriented. The Service Providers continued to be 16-bit drivers, but you could write 32-bit applications with C++, VB, or any other language that could call a function in a dynamic link library.

TAPI 1.4 also increased the feature set supported by TAPI. Some of the new features included

- Plug-and-Play support
- Common dialogs for setting dialing properties
- Access to country and area code info
- Get/Set operations for application priorities
- Provider-initiated conferences
- Other capability/status extensions
- Universal modem driver

TAPI 1.5

There was a version of TAPI labeled 1.5 that was released for WinCE only. It is mentioned here only for completeness.

TAPI 2

TAPI 2 was targeted at Windows NT Server and provided a new and improved 32-bit internal architecture that replaced the 16-bit Service Providers and support services. The 2.0 infrastructure was tailored to take advantage of all the benefits of NT Server including processor independence, pre-emptive tasking, multithreading, symmetric multiprocessing, and security.

TAPI 2 provided an infrastructure capable of hosting enterprise telephony server applications. Meanwhile the world was putting more and more demands on the networking infrastructure to deliver various and specific levels of data delivery services. File transfers, for instance, required 100% guaranteed accurate delivery but could be subject to delays imposed by packet retransmissions. Streaming audio and video required timely delivery of data packets. If a packet couldn't be delivered on time, the fact that it was accurately delivered became moot. Speech grade delivery required less than 4K bandwidth, whereas a full-bandwidth audio stream could require a 56K channel. A streaming video presentation might need to reserve 256K of bandwidth with a guaranteed latency not to exceed 500 milliseconds.

The capability of an application and/or Service Provider to specify and control the quality of service (QoS) was added to TAPI 2 as a means of allowing applications to negotiate (and renegotiate) the quality of service required by a specific TAPI call.

TAPI 2 added some additional features to make building call-center applications, such as automated help desk systems, easier to implement. These features included the addition of call queue management, call routing support, and message waiting support.

Although TAPI 2 was targeted at creating a robust TAPI infrastructure through which enterprise-class telephony server applications could be built, it was also available in the NT Workstation 4 environment. As a client platform, TAPI 2 provided backward compatibility for 16- and 32-bit TAPI applications written using TAPI 1.3 or 1.4.

Unicode support was also added to version 2. This made it easier for developers to write language-independent TAPI Service Providers and applications that could be localized by means of a resource file.

Previous versions of TAPI utilized a tapi.ini file to hold configuration information. TAPI 2 adopted use of the Registry.

TAPI 2.1

The biggest change between versions 2.0 and 2.1 was the addition of client/server functionality to the TAPI infrastructure. With version 2.1, telephony hardware could be distributed on multiple machines. Previous versions of TAPI required the hardware interface to reside on the same machine as the TAPI application that used the Service Provider. Under version 2.1, the TAPI infrastructure allowed a client application to be written that could establish calls utilizing remote resources. This was a powerful addition to the infrastructure.

The TAPI 2.1 API did not change significantly between version 2.0 and version 2.1. Indeed, the only difference in the tapi.h file associated with version 2.1 is the inclusion of a `LINEMEDIAMODE_VIDEO` constant that allowed for querying and opening line devices capable of processing video stream.

TAPI 2.2

Version 2.2 is the current version of TAPI. The tapi.h file provided with Visual C++ 6 defines `TAPI_CURRENT_VERSION` to 0x00020002 or 2.2. When you query TAPI for the version number, Windows 98 or newer installations of NT return version 2.2. But there

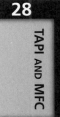

are no version 2.2 deltas to the tapi.h header file associated with version 2.2. For all intents and purposes, version 2.2 and version 2.1 are identical from an application programmer's vantage point.

I will review the 2.2 architecture in detail a bit later in this chapter.

TAPI 3

Let's take a peek at what TAPI 3 promises to offer.

Computers are used for many things these days. One of the largest uses of computers is communications. For those who have worked in the industry for several years, this is not news. We have been using email, BBSs, LANs, WANs, and the Internet for quite some time now.

The emergence of the Internet has, and will continue to, change the way both business and home users communicate. The Internet is a ubiquitous amalgamation of LAN and WAN technologies. It's cheap, reliable (arguably), and provides a wide selection of connection options in terms of price, performance, and connection options.

The Internet started as a highly reliable WAN technology that connected computers together. With time, the Internet became associated with WAIS, GOPHER, and FTP applications. Nowadays the Internet is almost synonymous with the World Wide Web and email. But the Internet is also used for Virtual Private Networks (VPNs), Electronic Data Interchange via XML, and streaming media.

The point is that the Internet has only started to change the way people use computers. The Internet is "forcing" many homes to buy computers, modem vendors to continually push the envelope on bandwidth, and cable and phone companies to deploy high-bandwidth connection options such as cable modems, ISDN, and xDSL. Satellite dishes are being employed to speed downloads over the net. Cell phone companies are working hard to build infrastructures to allow high-bandwidth digital communication over cellular modems. The future of the Internet promises much higher bandwidth connections at increasingly competitive prices. (Ain't free market economies great!)

So what does the Internet have to do with TAPI? Well, TAPI 3 is absolutely targeted at Voice-Over-IP (VoIP). TAPI promises to allow enterprising programmers to write powerful telephony systems that route voice and digital data throughout an enterprise using IP as the backbone, either in the form of a private, secure LAN or the Internet. It's not a giant leap to envision corporate or public phone systems that use VPNs in conjunction with TAPI and the streaming media CODECs provided by NetShow to build enterprise-wide "PBX" functionality that spans the nation or even the world.

And while you're at it, why not throw in a video stream or two so you can do audio/video telephony with all the bells and whistles of a PBX as well? Imagine never paying any long-distance charges beyond a basic ISP monthly service charge. How about being able to videoconference from a cabin in the woods using a cell phone? Cool?

TAPI 3 is aimed at Window 2000 (formerly known as Windows NT 5). It is specifically targeted at building enterprise-level applications such as call control, interactive voice response, voice mail, call centers, and IP conferencing. The Service Providers within TAPI 3 will not only support traditional telephony mediums but will also target IP Telephony. TAPI 3 will provide a convergence of public switch telephony networks with the Internet.

TAPI 3 will move from a C API to a COM-based interface that can be easily integrated into just about any programming environment. The new COM interface will provide for call control, media stream control, and NT 5 directory services. The TAPI COM implementation will communicate with the TAPI server by means of Remote Procedure Calls (RPCs), allowing the remoting of TAPI Services. The anticipated Service Providers will include H.323 and IP Multicast support. (H.323 is an International Telecommunications Union [ITU] standard for multimedia communications [voice, video, and data] over a connectionless networking backbone, as in IP). IP Multicast is used for video conferencing.

TAPI 3 will also interface through the Media Stream Provider Interface with Direct Show Media Streams. Direct Show takes advantage of the Real-Time Transport Protocol (RTP), which is an IETF standard designed to handle streaming audio and video delivery over the Internet.

TAPI will become the infrastructure that glues together traditional telephony infrastructure with Internet based streaming media including Voice-over-IP and video conferencing.

So much for the future of TAPI. It's time to look at how you can take advantage on TAPI when writing applications.

Using Assisted Telephony

As mentioned earlier, Assisted Telephony is an easy way to add phone dialer functionality to any application. Assisted Telephony requires only a single function call to be made to place an interactive phone call.

Listing 28.1 is an example of how to implement a phone dialer via Assisted Telephony.

LISTING 28.1   USING ASSISTED TELEPHONY

```
void CTapi::TestAssistedTelephony()
{
   CPhoneNum dlg;
   LONG lResult;

   lResult = dlg.DoModal();
   if ( lResult == IDOK )
   {
      lResult = tapiRequestMakeCall(
                   dlg.m_szPhoneNum,              // dest address
                   "TAPITest",                    // appname
                   "TAPITest",                    // caller
                   "Testing Assisted Telephony"); // comment
      if (lResult != 0L )
      {
         char szBuf[ 256 ];
         sprintf(szBuf, "tapiRequestMakeCall error - %ld", lResult);
         ::MessageBox(NULL,szBuf,"",MB_OK);
      }
   }
}
```

Pretty simple, isn't it?

The example starts by instantiating a CPhoneNum dialog. CPhoneNum is a simple class built with the ClassWizard. It prompts the user for a phone number, which is stored in a CString. DDX is used to update the public data member m_szPhoneNum. No input validation is performed. tapiRequestMakeCall() will let you know if a bad number has been entered.

The tapiRequestMakeCall() function expects four parameters. The first is the phone number that is to be called. Either a canonical address or a dialable address can be supplied. The canonical address, as you'll recall, takes the form "+<*countrycode*> (<*area code*>) <*phone number*>." A dialable address is a localized string, which might include characters required to access an outside line, a calling card number, long distance access code and area code, a pulse versus tone dial mode indicator, and so on.

The remaining three parameters are used when documenting the call in the dialer's log file. Parameter 2 contains a pointer to a null-terminated string that contains a user-friendly application name. Parameter 3 contains a pointer to a null-terminated string that represents the called party's name. The last parameter contains a pointer to a null-terminated string that contains a comment. You can pass NULL for any or all of the last three parameters.

`tapiRequestMakeCall()` returns 0 if successful. A negative number is returned if an error occurs. But success only means that the call-control application accepted the request. There is no notification that the call was successfully made.

The call-control application under Windows 95 and Windows 98 is the dialer.exe. The TAPISRV.EXE service performs the TAPI requests under NT. In response to the `tapiRequestMakeCall()` request, the dialer raises a dialog similar to the one shown in Figure 28.5.

FIGURE 28.5

The Dialing dialog box.

After the call is successfully placed, the dialog shown in Figure 28.6 is displayed for the user.

FIGURE 28.6

The Active Call dialog box.

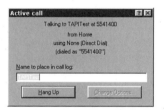

If an error occurs, the user will see a dialog similar to the one in Figure 28.7.

FIGURE 28.7

The Line in Use dialog box.

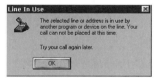

That's about all there is to using Assisted Telephony. It's pretty simple, but also pretty limiting in what can be accomplished. Only interactive voice calls can be placed, and there is no way to monitor the progression of the call as it transitions through the various states an outgoing call must transition through.

Now let's take a look at performing the same operation using Basic Telephony Services.

Using Basic Telephony

As you will recall, Basic Telephony Services provides an application with the ability to translate addresses, place calls, drop calls, monitor call state transitions, and manipulate call handles. The sample code you are going to look at next performs most of these functions.

MFC does not provide any wrapper classes for TAPI function calls. Coding TAPI is an exercise in calling C APIs. In the sample code, certain TAPI functions are wrapped in a C++ class called CTapi. CTapi is not intended to be production-quality code. Rather, it is simply a test environment used to demonstrate the steps required to make and drop a call using Basic Telephony Services. The code for the CTapi class, as well as the rest of the TAPITest application, is available on the CD-ROM distributed with the book. Feel free to enhance the CTapi class to meet your TAPI needs.

Before getting too far into looking at code, I need to define some terms that TAPI uses. Basic Telephony Services are concerned with lines, phones, addresses, and calls. A line is a logical entity that represents a physical phone line. When dealing with POTS circuits and Unimodem drivers, the physical line and logical line maintain a one-to-one relationship. Other physical infrastructures such as ISDN might provide multiple logical lines per physical line. When writing TAPI applications, you always deal with logical lines. Each logical line has characteristics that define the kinds of media it can support, the speeds it can be set to, and so on.

A line has one or more addresses associated with it. In the case of POTS circuits and Unimodem Service Providers, there is only one address associated with a specific line. But think of a typical PBX environment where a deskset has both an internal phone number and an outside direct-dial number. This is an example of two addresses being associated with the same logical line.

A logical phone represents a physical phone. The logical phone mirrors the features provided by the physical. At a minimum the logical phone has a switchhook and a transducer. A sophisticated phone might have buttons, lights, and an alphanumeric display that can be modeled by the logical phone.

The last construct is the call. A TAPI call mimics a real-world call. A call is initialized by a caller and can have many called parties associated with it. A call has a short life relative to lines, phones, and addresses. Many calls are typically placed using the same phone and line resources.

There are four basic stages that Basic Telephony sessions must be concerned with: configuration, connection, data transfer, and disconnection. Let's look at each of these stages in detail.

Configuring TAPI

Configuration of a TAPI session starts with the lineInitialize() function. Listing 28.2 demonstrates how to call lineInitialize().

LISTING 28.2 USING ::lineInitialize()

```
void CTapi::TestLineInitialize( void )
{
   LONG lResult;

   lResult = ::lineInitialize( &m_hTapi,
                               AfxGetInstanceHandle(),
                               TapiCallbackFunc,
                               "TAPITest",
                               &m_dwNumLines );
   if ( lResult )
      displayTapiError( lResult );
}
```

The first parameter to lineInitialize() is a LPHLINEAPP, a pointer to a line application handle. The handle returned in m_hTapi becomes the identifier for TAPITest's instance of TAPI. The handle is passed to TAPI as a parameter of most subsequent calls and consequently is stored in a public data member of the CTapi class.

The second parameter passed to lineInitialize() is an instance handle for your application. You use the AfxGetInstanceHandle() to retrieve the m_hInstance data member of the CWinApp class. TAPI requires an instance handle to identify and process events associated with your application.

The third parameter passed to lineInitialize() is a pointer to a callback function created by the application and used by TAPI to notify the application of changes in the state of the line(s) associated with the TAPI instance. The callback function needs to be declared as either FAR PASCAL or as a CALLBACK. Both evaluate the same. Win16 applications used to require that MakeProcInstance() was used to create callback pointers. Win32 applications do not require use of MakeProcInstance().

The fourth parameter to lineInitialize() is a pointer to a null-delimited string that identifies the application. Any user-friendly application name can be supplied. The name is used during logging operations. If NULL is passed, TAPI retrieves the application's filename and uses that instead.

The final parameter to lineInitialize() is a pointer to a DWORD into which lineInitialize() stores the number of "devices" available for use by your application.

28

TAPI AND MFC

As you will see, the available devices must be queried to find one that meets the application's specific requirements.

lineInitialize() returns a LONG that specifies the results of the function call. If lineInitialize() succeeds, it returns 0. Errors are returned as negative numbers that should be interpreted through the constants supplied in TAPI.H.

Note that lineInitialize() takes no parameters to identify a particular line or a particular type of line. The actual purpose for which you call lineInitialize() is to initialize "the application's use of Tapi.dll for subsequent use of the line abstraction." lineInitialize() is actually more a "tapiInitialize" than a line-device initialization function.

Now that lineInitialize() has been fully explained, I need to tell you that it is an obsolete function for use with TAPI 2 and higher applications. The newer lineInitalizeEx() version requires two additional parameters: a pointer to a DWORD specifying the highest version of API version that the application was designed for and a pointer to a LINEINITIALIZEEXPARAMS structure.

Listing 28.3 shows a simple use of lineInitializeEx().

LISTING 28.3   USING ::lineInitializeEx()

```
void CTapi::TestLineInitializeEx( void )
{
    DWORD dwVersion = 0x00020002;
    LINEINITIALIZEEXPARAMS LIP;
    LONG lResult;

    memset( &LIP, 0, sizeof( LIP ) );
    LIP.dwTotalSize = LIP.dwUsedSize = sizeof( LIP );
    LIP.dwOptions = LINEINITIALIZEEXOPTION_USEHIDDENWINDOW;

    lResult = ::lineInitializeEx( &m_hTapi,
                                  AfxGetInstanceHandle(),
                                  TapiCallbackFunc,
                                  "TAPITest",
                                  &m_dwNumLines,
                                  &dwVersion,
                                  &LIP );
    if ( lResult )
        displayTapiError( lResult );

    m_dwAPIVersion = dwVersion;
}
```

There are two advantages to using the new `lineInitializeEx()` call. The first is the ability to negotiate the API version, and the second is the ability to control how the application is notified of events. Version negotiation will be discussed a bit later when I talk about `lineNegotiateAPIVersion()`. For now, suffice it to say that a desired API version can be passed to `lineInitializeEx()`. `lineInitializeEx()` determines what API level is appropriate based on installed components and returns a negotiated API version number.

The big advantage of the new `lineInitializeEx()` function is the ability to control the means by which the application is informed of line events. There are now three ways to receive event notifications. The first, which is the one shown in the previous example, mimics the behavior of earlier versions of TAPI. Setting the `dw_Options` field of the `LINEINITIALIZEEXPARAMS` structure to `LINEINITIALIZEEXOPTION_USEHIDDENWINDOW` causes TAPI to create a hidden window within the context of the TAPI application. TAPI then subclasses the hidden window so that messages posted to the window are handled by TAPI itself. When TAPI wants to post a message to the application, it posts it to the hidden window. The application then retrieves the message when it calls `::GetMessage()`, which allows the TAPI `WNDPROC` to dispatch the message to the callback registered through the `lineInitialize()` function. The downside of using a hidden window is that the application must have a message loop.

TAPI 2 provides other mechanisms for event notification. If the `dwOptions` field is set to `LINEINITIALIZEEXOPTION_USEEVENT`, TAPI will create a Win32 event object that is used to signal state changes on TAPI devices. The application used the event object returned by `lineInitializeEx()` to call `WaitForSingleObject()`. When a TAPI message is available for processing, TAPI signals the event object and the blocked thread continues processing. The applications thread should call `lineGetMessage()` to retrieve the message. (An alternative to calling `WaitForSingleObject()` is to call `lineGetMessage()` directly. `lineGetMessage()` will block until TAPI has a new message available.)

The final mechanism available to TAPI applications for message notification is to create a completion port through the Win32 `CreateIoCompletionPort()` function. The handle to the completion port is passed to `lineInitializeEx()` along with the `LINEINITIALIZEEXOPTION_USECOMPLETION PORT` dwOptions flag. TAPI uses the Win32 `PostQueuedCompletiontStatus()` function to inform the application of pending messages. The application uses `GetQueuedCompletionStatus()` to retrieve a pointer to a `LINEMESSAGE` structure through which the application is informed of TAPI events.

Now that you have an initialized instance of TAPI, what comes next? The next step is to negotiate an API version that TAPI will use to communicate with the application. This is accomplished through the `lineNegotiateAPIVersion()` function. Listing 28.4 is an example of using `lineNegotiateAPIVersion()`.

28

TAPI AND MFC

LISTING 28.4   USING ::lineNegotiateAPIVersion()

```
void CTapi::TestLineNegotiateAPIVersion( void )
{
    LINEEXTENSIONID stExtensionID;
    DWORD dwAPIVersion;
    char buf[ 256 ];
    LONG lResult;

    if ( m_hTapi )
    {
        for ( DWORD line = 0; line < m_dwNumLines; line++ )
        {
            lResult = lineNegotiateAPIVersion( m_hTapi,
                                               line,
                                               0x00010003,
                                               0x00020002,
                                               &dwAPIVersion,
                                               &stExtensionID );

            if ( lResult )
            {
                displayTapiError( lResult );
                continue;   // try the next line...
            }

            // get info about the line
            LPLINEDEVCAPS lpLineDevCaps =
                GetDevCaps( line, dwAPIVersion );

            // generate a messagebox for info purposes
            if ((lpLineDevCaps) &&
                (lpLineDevCaps->dwLineNameSize) &&
                (lpLineDevCaps->dwLineNameOffset) &&
                (lpLineDevCaps->dwStringFormat == STRINGFORMAT_ASCII))
            {
                // This is the name of the device.
                char * lpszLineName = ((char *) lpLineDevCaps) +
                                      lpLineDevCaps->dwLineNameOffset;
                sprintf(buf,
                    "Device %d - name: %s - Negotiated API version 0x%lx",
                    line, lpszLineName, dwAPIVersion);
            }
            else
            {
                sprintf(buf,
                    "Device %d - no ASCII name - Negotiated API version 0x%lx",
```

```
                    line, dwAPIVersion);
                }
                ::MessageBox(NULL,buf,"",MB_OK);

                //check if the line supports voice communication
        if ((lpLineDevCaps) &&
            (lpLineDevCaps->dwBearerModes & LINEBEARERMODE_VOICE) &&
            (lpLineDevCaps->dwLineFeatures & LINEFEATURE_MAKECALL) &&
            (lpLineDevCaps->dwMediaModes & LINEMEDIAMODE_INTERACTIVEVOICE))
                {
                    // found a suitable line - keep it
                    m_dwLineToUse = line;
                    m_dwAPIVersion = dwAPIVersion;
                }

                free( lpLineDevCaps );
            }

        sprintf(buf,"Selected device %d - Negotiated API version 0x%lx",
            m_dwLineToUse, m_dwAPIVersion );
        ::MessageBox(NULL,buf,"",MB_OK);
    }
}
```

lineNegotiateAPIVersion() takes six parameters. The first is the handle to the TAPI instance that was returned by lineInitialize(). The second parameter is the id for the device you want to check. The id is actually a zero-indexed subscript. The maximum value for the device ID is one less than the dwMaxDevices value returned by lineInitialize(). The third parameter is the lowest version of the Telephony API with which the application is compliant. The fourth parameter is the highest version of the Telephony API with which the application is compliant. The fifth parameter is a pointer to a DWORD in which the negotiated API version number is returned. The final parameter is a pointer to a LINEEXTENSIONID struct. Each Service Provider can implement extensions. (Remember the Extended Telephony Services?) If an application wants to utilize device-specific extensions, it can use the information returned in the LINEEXTENSIONID to interface with the Service Provider. If the application doesn't want to use extensions, it can ignore the returned values.

When the specific API version number for a specific device id is known, it is possible to obtain additional information about the device, including what kind of media the device is capable of processing. In the previous example, a call is made to GetDevCaps(), which is a member of the CTapi class. Listing 28.5 shows the implementation of GetDevCaps().

LISTING 28.5   USING `::lineGetDevCaps()`

```cpp
// caller must free the returned LPLINEDEVCAPS pointer
LPLINEDEVCAPS CTapi::GetDevCaps( DWORD dwDevice, DWORD dwAPIVersion )
{
    LPLINEDEVCAPS lpLineDevCaps = NULL;
    size_t dwNeeded = sizeof(LINEDEVCAPS);
    LONG lResult = 0;

    // might take two callocs to get it right...
    for ( int i = 0; i < 2; i++ )
    {
        lpLineDevCaps = (LPLINEDEVCAPS)calloc( dwNeeded,1 );
        if ( !lpLineDevCaps )
            goto error;

        // always remember to set the size in the calloc'd struct
        // before trying to use it...
        lpLineDevCaps->dwTotalSize = dwNeeded;

        lResult = ::lineGetDevCaps( m_hTapi,
                                    dwDevice,
                                    dwAPIVersion,
                                    0,
                                    lpLineDevCaps );

        if ( lResult )
        {
            displayTapiError( lResult );
            goto error;
        }

        // do we have the whole structure?
        if ( lpLineDevCaps->dwNeededSize <= lpLineDevCaps->dwTotalSize )
            break;    // yes...

        // prepare to try a second time
        dwNeeded = lpLineDevCaps->dwNeededSize;
        free( lpLineDevCaps );
        lpLineDevCaps = NULL;
    }

    return lpLineDevCaps;    // SUCCESS!

error:
    if ( lpLineDevCaps )
        free( lpLineDevCaps );

    return NULL;
}
```

CTapi::GetLineCaps() uses the lineGetDevCaps() to fill in a LINEDEVCAPS structure. Unfortunately it's not as simple as allocating a LINEDEVCAPS structure on the stack and filling it. Many of TAPI's structures start off with three variables: dwTotalSize, dwNeededSize, and dwUsedSize. These variables allow for variable-length structures that allow vendor-specific data to be appended to the end of the "structure header." In order to retrieve a LINEDEVCAPS structure, two calls to lineGetDevCaps() are usually required. The first call retrieves the "structure header" from which the code determines the size of the full structure through the dwNeededSize member. Memory is then reallocated to allow loading of the entire structure via a second call to lineGetDevCaps().

An alternate approach would be to start off with a "worst-case" allocation and then hope that sufficient space was allocated. That might seem easier but is not the recommended technique.

You should look out for several things when accessing the LINEDEVCAPS structure (or any of Windows variable length structures). First, make sure the structure passed into Windows has the dwTotalSize parameter set. The minimum size dwTotalSize can be set to for lineGetDevCaps() to succeed is the size of the fixed portion (the "structure header"). Second, it is also a good idea to initialize the structure to zeros.

The LINEDEVCAPS structure defines the capabilities of the specific line device. Let's look at some of the fields contained in the LINEDEVCAPS structure to see what line devices might be capable of. If you want to get information about the Service Provider associated with the line device, use the dwProviderInfoSize and dwProviderInfoOffset members to index into the LINEDEVCAPS structure. The offset variable represents the number of bytes into the structure where the data starts. The size variable is the number of bytes of data that should be retrieved. The data is not null-delimited, so you typically need to copy the bytes with strncpy() and then delimit the string yourself.

Two other variables, dwSwitchInfoSize and dwSwitchInfoOffset, describe the telephone switch to which the line device is attached. The variables dwLineNameSize and dwLineNameOffset contain index info to the logical name for the line device. This name would represent a user-friendly name possibly assigned by an administrator or user when configuring the system.

The member variable dwStringFormat defines the character set used by the line device. TAPI supports ASCII, DBCS, and Unicode strings. The Service Provider specifies the mode it supplies information in.

The dwNumAddresses field returns the number of addresses associated with this line device. There can be many addresses (phone numbers) by which a line is known. The addresses can be accessed by using an "address identifier," which is really just an index ranging from zero to dwNumAddresses minus one.

28

TAPI AND MFC

The `dwBearerMode` field is particularly interesting. This variable indicates the generic type of data channel the line represents. Some of the options include `LINEBEARERMODE_VOICE`, `LINEBEARERMODE_SPEECH`, and `LINEBEARERMODE_DATA`.

`LINEBEARERMODE_SPEECH` mode represents a line capable of G.711 speech transmission. G.711 transmissions are typically subject to signal processing such as echo cancellation and compression/decompression. Such line devices are not suitable for analog modem use. Look for a `LINEBEARERMODE_VOICE` line instead. `MULTIUSE` and `ALTSPEECHDATA` bearer modes are usually associated with ISDN lines.

The `dwMaxRate` variable contains the maximum data rate at which transmissions can occur over the line as expressed in bits per second.

The `dwMediaMode` variable defines the media modes the line device can support. The bearer mode specifies the generic communication channel type, and the media mode specifies the types of data the communication channel can carry. Some of the values `dwMediaMode` can take on include `LINEMEDIAMODE_INTERACTIVEVOICE`, `LINEMEDIAMODE_AUTOMATEDVOICE`, `LINEMEDIAMODE_DATAMODEM`, `LINEMEDIAMODE_G3FAX`, `LINEMEDIAMODE_G4FAX`, `LINEMEDIAMODE_DIGITALDATA`, and `LINEMEDIAMODE_VIDEOTEX`.

The `dwLineFeatures` variable defines the capabilities of the line device to control calls. Some of the possible values are `LINEFEATURE_MAKECALL`, `LINEFEATURE_FORWARD`, and `LINEFEATURE_SETTERMINAL`.

There are many more variables in `LINEDEVCAPS`. Defining all possible values is beyond the scope of this chapter. (Entire books have been written about TAPI.) The online documentation supplied with MSVC should be referenced for a full treatment of the `LINEDEVCAPS` structure.

The goal of the Basic Telephony example is to dial an interactive voice call through TAPI. You have seen how to initialize a TAPI instance through `lineInitialize()`. The next step was to negotiate an API version through `lineNegotiateAPIVersion()`. After the API version was known, a call was made to `lineGetDevCaps()` to retrieve a `LINEDEVCAPS` structure so the characteristics of the line could be determined. The sample code you saw previously used the code in Listing 28.6 to ascertain if a line device was capable of making a interactive voice call.

LISTING 28.6 CHECKING A LINE'S CAPABILITIES

```
//check if the line supports voice communication
if ((lpLineDevCaps) &&
    (lpLineDevCaps->dwBearerModes & LINEBEARERMODE_VOICE) &&
    (lpLineDevCaps->dwLineFeatures & LINEFEATURE_MAKECALL) &&
```

```
            (lpLineDevCaps->dwMediaModes & LINEMEDIAMODE_INTERACTIVEVOICE))
{
    // found a suitable line - keep it
    m_dwLineToUse = line;
    m_dwAPIVersion = dwAPIVersion;
}
```

The code used three variables of the LINEDEVCAPS structure to make the determination. First a check was made to see if the bearer mode supported LINEBEARERMODE_VOICE. Next, the dwLineFeatures variable was checked to see if the line device could initiate a call. Lastly, the dwMediaModes variable was checked to see if the line device could handle interactive voice calls.

If the line device supported all these requirements, the associated id and API version was stored for future use.

Assuming an appropriate line device has been found, the next step is to open the line through lineOpen(). Listing 28.7 shows how to do this.

LISTING 28.7 USING ::lineOpen()

```
void CTapi::TestLineOpen( void )
{
    LONG lResult;

    lResult =
        ::lineOpen( m_hTapi,           // the app's TAPI instance handle
                    m_dwLineToUse,     // the line to open
                    &m_hLine,          // the returned hLine
                    m_dwAPIVersion,    // from lineNegotiateAPIVersion()
                    0,                 // extension version
                    (DWORD)this,       // app specific DWORD
                    LINECALLPRIVILEGE_NONE,  // outgoing calls only
                    LINEMEDIAMODE_INTERACTIVEVOICE, // dwMediaMode
                    0 ); // lpCallParams only used in LINEMAPPER mode


    if ( lResult )
        displayTapiError( lResult );
}
```

The first parameter to lineOpen() is the TAPI instance handle. The second parameter is the index of the line that was selected as having the right capabilities. The third parameter is a pointer to an HLINE parameter that is used to return the handle to the TAPI line instance. The fourth parameter is the API version negotiated through

28

TAPI AND MFC

lineNegotiateAPIVersion() for the line you selected. The fifth variable is a DWORD that specifies the extension number the application and Service Provider agreed to operate under. Use 0 if you do not plan on using Service Provider extensions.

The sixth parameter to lineOpen is a DWORD worth of opaque data that TAPI maintains and returns to the application when the callback function registered through lineInitialize() is called. In the sample code, the this pointer of the CTapi class is passed. This allows the callback function logic to access member variables and functions associated with the HLINE that caused the callback to be invoked. (In a C implementation, the DWORD would probably contain a LPVOID that pointed to a structure that contained associated variables.)

The seventh parameter to lineOpen() is the dwPrivileges to be associated with the line device instance. The possible values include LINECALLPRIVILEGE_NONE, LINECALLPRIVILEGE_MONITOR, and LINECALLPRIVILEGE_OWNER. (There are additional LINEOPENOPTION variables that are valid under TAPI 2.x, but these are aimed at more advanced server applications. For more information, refer to the online documentation supplied with MSVC++.)

The eighth parameter to lineOpen() is the dwMediaModes settings. This parameter applies only if the dwPrivileges parameter requests LINECALLPRIVILEGE_OWNER mode. The values assigned to this parameter are the LINEMEDIAMODE_ flags seen earlier in the description of the LINEDEVCAPS structure. These flags can be bit-OR'd together to build a complete set of modes of interest to the application. Setting the LINECALLPRIVILEGE_OWNER flag in conjunction with a specific media type flag indicates that the application is requesting the ability to own incoming calls of the specified media type. TAPI will check privileges and return LINEERR_INVALPRIVSELECT in the event that some other application already has ownership. Any application can place outgoing calls; there is no ownership of outgoing call resources.

If all goes well, a return code of 0, indicating SUCCESS, is returned and the handle to the line is returned.

Connecting with TAPI

It is now time to make a call on the line device. Listing 28.8 places a call.

LISTING 28.8   USING ::lineMakeCall()

```
void CTapi::TestLineMakeCall( CString csNumber )
{
    LPLINETRANSLATEOUTPUT lpLTO;
    char szDialStr[ 256 ];
```

```
    LONG lResult;

    lpLTO = (LPLINETRANSLATEOUTPUT)calloc( 512, 1 );
    if ( !lpLTO )
        return;

    lpLTO->dwTotalSize = 512;

    lResult = ::lineTranslateAddress( m_hTapi,
                                      m_dwLineToUse,
                                      m_dwAPIVersion,
                                      csNumber,
                                      0,      // card
                                      0,      // dwTranslateOptions
                                      lpLTO );

    if ( lpLTO->dwDialableStringSize >= 256 )
        return;

    strncpy( szDialStr,
        &((const char *)lpLTO)[ lpLTO->dwDialableStringOffset ],
        lpLTO->dwDialableStringSize );
    szDialStr[ lpLTO->dwDialableStringSize ] = '\0';
    free( lpLTO );

    LINECALLPARAMS lcp;
    memset( &lcp, 0, sizeof(LINECALLPARAMS) );
    lcp.dwTotalSize = sizeof( LINECALLPARAMS );
    lcp.dwBearerMode = LINEBEARERMODE_VOICE;
    lcp.dwMediaMode = LINEMEDIAMODE_INTERACTIVEVOICE;

    lResult = ::lineMakeCall( m_hLine,      // the line's handle
                              &m_hCall,      // returned call handle
                              szDialStr,     // the address to call
                              0,             // dwCountryCode
                              &lcp );        // call parameters

    // positive values indicate the async request was requested
    if ( lResult < 0 )
        displayTapiError( lResult );
    if ( lResult > 0 )
        m_lRequestID = lResult;
}
```

A dialing address must be generated before a call can be placed. This can be accomplished by calling `lineTranslateAddress()`, which will convert a canonical address into a localized dialing address. This was discussed earlier in the chapter.

The `lineTranslateAddress()` function takes several parameters. The first parameter is the TAPI instance handle you obtained from `lineInitialize()`. The second parameter is the device id (ordinal) for the line device you selected earlier. The third parameter is the API version you negotiated for the line device. The fourth parameter is a pointer to the canonical address (or arbitrary list of dialable digits) that is to be translated. The fifth parameter is the index for a calling card override. The sixth parameter is the `dwTranslateOptions` bit field that specifies any special instructions to be followed when converting the number. You can force a long distance or local address as the result of the translation. There is also a flag to request use of the calling card override specified by the fifth parameter. The final parameter is a pointer to the `LINETRANSLATEOUTPUT` structure the resultant address should be stored into. The application must allocate the structure and set the `dwTotalSize` field of the `LINETRANSLATEOUTPUT` structure prior to calling `lineTranslateAddress()`.

A return value of 0 indicates that `lineTranslateAddress()` succeeded. The values in the `LINETRANSLATEOUTPUT` structure contain size and offset pairs for dialable and displayable versions of the addresses. In addition there are fields for country codes for the originator and the called party, as well as a field that identifies how the translation proceeded.

The sample application uses the `dwDialableStringSize` and `dwDialableStringOffset` to retrieve the dial string. You are now almost ready to place a call. One remaining item needs to be accomplished, which is the initialization of a `LINECALLPARAMS` structure that tells `lineMakeCall()` precisely what bearer mode and media mode this call should use. Actually, the `LINECALLPARAMS` structure specifies a lot of information about the desired call parameters including min and max baud rates, handshake protocols, timeouts, and so on. The default values are fine for this example, and consequently you do not need to change many things. In fact, for interactive voice calls, there is no need to supply a `LINECALLPARAMS` structure at all. Passing a `NULL` pointer will work as effectively. For any other type of call, the `LINECALLPARAMS` structure is required and consequently is demonstrated in the sample application.

It's finally time to make the call. The `lineMakeCall()` takes six parameters. The first is the TAPI instance handle. The second is a pointer to an `HCALL` variable where the call handle is stored. The third parameter is the null-delimited dial string. The fourth parameter is the country code for the called party. This is essentially an override. If 0 is passed, the default country code is used. The fifth parameter is a pointer to the `LINECALLPARAMS` discussed previously. If `lineMakeCall()` fails immediately, it returns a negative number. If `lineMakeCall()` succeeds, it returns a positive number that represents the request id for the placed call as well as a handle for the newly placed call.

But you're not done yet! The call handle is valid only after the callback function registered in the `lineInitialize()` function receives a `LINE_REPLY` message with a 0 (SUCCESS) status in the `dwParam2` parameter. The `lineMakeCall()` function only requests TAPI to place a call. TAPI takes over and processes the call through each of the states required to establish the call. As the call is being set up, `LINE_CALLSTATE` messages are posted to the callback procedure. When the call is completed, the `LINE_REPLY` message is sent to the callback procedure. The `dwParam1` value will contain the request id previously returned by `lineMakeCall()`. The `dwParam2` value will contain the status of the request. A negative value in `dwParam2` indicates that the call could not be successfully established. Only if the call is successfully established can the call handle returned by `lineMakeCall()` be used successfully.

Listing 28.9 shows how the example implements the callback procedure.

LISTING 28.9   A TAPI CALLBACK FUNCTION

```
void CALLBACK CTapi::TapiCallbackFunc
(
    DWORD dwDevice, DWORD dwMsg, DWORD dwCallbackInstance,
    DWORD dwParam1, DWORD dwParam2, DWORD dwParam3
)
{
    CTapi * pctapi = (CTapi *)dwCallbackInstance;

    // Handle the line messages.
    switch(dwMsg)
    {
        case LINE_CALLSTATE:
            displayCallState( dwParam1, dwParam2 );
            break;

        case LINE_CLOSE:
            if ( pctapi )
            {
                pctapi->TestLineShutdown();
            }
            break;

        case LINE_REPLY:
            if ( pctapi && (dwParam1 == pctapi->m_lRequestID ) )
            {
                if ( dwParam2 )
                    displayTapiError( dwParam2 );
                else
```

continues

28

TAPI AND MFC

LISTING 28.9   CONTINUED

```
                pctapi->m_bhCallValid = TRUE;
        }
        break;

    case LINE_CREATE:
        ::MessageBox(NULL,"Saw LINE_CREATE","",MB_OK);
        break;

    default:
        OutputDebugString("TapiCallbackFunc message ignored\n");
        break;
    }
    return;
}
```

As mentioned earlier, the `dwCallbackInstance` parameter contains an opaque `DWORD`, which the sample application uses to pass the `this` pointer. This allows access to methods and data members of the `CTapi` instance that opened the line device. The logic that handles the `LINE_REPLY` sets the `m_bhCallValid` data member to `TRUE` if a `LINE_REPLY` message is received with a matching request id and a status of `SUCCESS`.

Transmitting Data with TAPI

Assuming that you receive the callback indicating that the requested call has been placed, you can start "transmitting data" over the line. In the case of the sample application, the data is interactive voice data. That is, someone can pick up the headset and start communicating by speaking and listening. If the call had been placed using different `LINECALLPARAMS` over a line that was indeed capable of a different media mode, say for instance `LINEMEDIAMODE_DATAMODEM`, transmitting data would entail calling Win32 function calls utilizing the modem handle retrieve through `lineGetID()`. The code in Listing 28.10 demonstrates how this might be accomplished.

LISTING 28.10   USING `::lineGetID()`

```
void CTapi::TestLineGetID( void )
{
    LPVARSTRING lpVarString = NULL;
    size_t dwNeeded = sizeof(VARSTRING);
    LONG lResult = 0;

    // it might take two callocs to get it right...
    for ( int i = 0; i < 2; i++ )
    {
        lpVarString = (LPVARSTRING)calloc( dwNeeded,1 );
```

```
        if ( !lpVarString )
           goto error;

        // always remember to set the size in the calloc'd struct
        // before trying to use it...
        lpVarString->dwTotalSize = dwNeeded;

        // get the modem's handle and name
        lResult = ::lineGetID( m_hLine, 0, NULL, LINECALLSELECT_LINE,
                               lpVarString, "comm/datamodem" );

        if ( lResult )
        {
           displayTapiError( lResult );
           goto error;
        }

        // do you have the whole structure?
        if ( lpVarString->dwNeededSize <= lpVarString->dwTotalSize )
           break;    // yes...

        // prepare to try a second time
        dwNeeded = lpVarString->dwNeededSize;
        free( lpVarString );
        lpVarString = NULL;
    }

    // now retrieve the modem handle from the VarString
    m_hModem = *(LPHANDLE)(lpVarString + lpVarString->dwStringOffset);

error:
    if ( lpVarString )
        free( lpVarString );

    return;
}
```

Once again, the logic must work with a variable-length structure called a VarString. Two calls to calloc will be made before you actually get the desired data. The first call to calloc allocated just enough memory for the static structure header. From the header you determine the exact number of bytes required to retrieve the desired information. Assuming the second call succeeds, ::lineGetID() will have filled in the VarString with the specific data that interests you. In this case, what you want is the modem handle, which you find at the very start of the memory located at lpVarString->dwStringOffset bytes into the VarString. (The modem name actually follows the modem handle in the VarString. You could retrieve it if you were interested.) When the handle is retrieved, the memory allocated for the VarString is freed up.

The modem handle can be used with Win32 functions such as ::ReadFile(), ::WriteFile(), ::GetCommConfig(), ::GetCommState(), ::SetCommTimeouts(), and ::TransmitCommChar(), to name a few. The same technique of using ::lineGetID() can be employed to retrieve an MCI handle through which you could play MIDI files over the phone line. In this case, the "comm/datamodem" designator would be replaced with "mci/midi." There are many device class strings that can be specified to lineGetID().

Disconnection with TAPI

After the data has been communicated across the phone line, (either by talking, using Win32 or MCI calls to transmit data, or using a proprietary protocol to transmit bytes), the next step is to hang up, or drop, the call. This is easy to accomplish with TAPI. Listing 28.11 drops an open call.

LISTING 28.11   USING ::lineDrop()

```
void CTapi::TestLineDrop( void )
{
    LONG    lResult = 0;

    if ( m_bhCallValid && m_hCall )
        lResult = ::lineDrop( m_hCall, NULL, 0 );

    if ( lResult < 0 )
        displayTapiError( lResult );
}
```

The ::lineDrop() function takes three parameters. The first parameter is the handle to the existing call. Note that in the example, you use the m_bhCallValid Boolean to validate that the call handle has been "authenticated" by the callback function as described earlier in the chapter. The second parameter to ::lineDrop() is a pointer to a string that contains user-to-user information that can be sent to the remote party as part of hanging up. The example sent no data and hence passed NULL. The final parameter is the size of the user-to-user data, which is 0 in the example.

::lineDrop() returns a positive request id in similar fashion to ::lineMakeCall().

Terminating a TAPI Session

When your application is finished using TAPI, it needs to let TAPI know that it is going away. As you've seen, TAPI can maintain a hidden window for the application that is used to post messages to the callback function. There are other internal structures and resources allocated by TAPI on behalf of the application. In addition, the line might have been opened with a privilege of LINECALLPRIVILEGE_OWNER, which would prevent other applications from answering calls on the specific line device. For all these reasons, plus the fact that the TAPI documentation says to, you should close down the TAPI session gracefully.

Listing 28.12 demonstrates how the sample application accomplishes this.

LISTING 28.12 USING ::lineShutdown()

```
void CTapi::TestLineShutdown( void )
{
   LONG    lResult = 0;

   TestLineDrop( );

   if ( m_hTapi )
      lResult = ::lineShutdown( m_hTapi );

   if ( lResult )
      displayTapiError( lResult );

   // initialize data members
   m_hTapi = NULL;
   m_dwNumLines = 0;
   m_dwAPIVersion = 0;
   m_dwLineToUse = 0;
   m_hLine = 0;
   m_hCall = 0;
   m_bhCallValid = FALSE;
}
```

The TAPI ::lineShutdown() function takes the handle first given to you by ::lineInitialize() as an input. This identifies your instance to TAPI and ensures that the right one gets closed down.

Summary

This concludes this chapter's treatment of the Telephony API. Much more could have been added and investigated. Indeed, whole books have been written about this subject. Be that as it may, you have learned about all the major topics and have seen examples of using all the high-level concepts made available through TAPI. The sample application

28

TAPI AND MFC

has shown how to initialize TAPI, configure a line device, place a call, transmit data, terminate a call, and shut down the TAPI session.

TAPI 3 promises to be a powerful blending of traditional telephony and Internet technologies such as NetMeeting. TAPI will continue to grow in power and complexity.

MFC and Graphics Programming

Part VII

IN THIS PART

MFC and OpenGL

by Kenn Scribner

IN THIS CHAPTER

CHAPTER 29

What Is OpenGL?

In a nutshell, OpenGL is a programmer's interface for developing interactive graphics-based applications. Although you can do simple two-dimensional (2D) work with OpenGL, it was really designed to work within the three-dimensional (3D) graphical display world. With relatively little effort on your part, you can *render* (draw) 3D objects and worlds, complete with lighting effects, aliasing, blending, and even fog. I'll be discussing these terms throughout this chapter, so don't be too concerned if you don't understand their meaning at this point. One thing to remember is that OpenGL itself provides you with the tools you require to easily build and display complex 3D scenes. It doesn't supply the models!

> **TIP**
>
> Though OpenGL itself doesn't come complete with ready-made models for you to use, there is an *auxiliary* OpenGL library that ships with practically every OpenGL implementation, including Microsoft's. You'll use this library to display some stunning shapes when you reach the first sample program.

Where did OpenGL originate, and why? To answer this, step back in time to the late 1980s. At that time, Silicon Graphics (SGI) dominated the high-end graphics processing market. Its true forte was custom innovative graphics processors, which accelerated the rendering speeds of its systems. But SGI knew hardware alone wasn't the answer. To sell systems, people needed to be able to program the processors easily. Therefore, SGI developed a graphics language, known as *GL*. GL was platform-specific, though, and it carried the additional burden of managing user interface elements. Although SGI wanted a language to express complex graphics, it ended up with a language that also managed mouse events and windows.

As GL grew, it became increasingly difficult to use. It wasn't that the graphical nature of the language was so difficult; the difficulty was with managing the user interface. Because SGI systems were UNIX-based, the systems also carried SGI's implementation of X Window (a popular open-system user interface standard still prevalent today in UNIX systems). SGI decided it was not wise to develop and maintain two parallel user interface implementations. Thus, OpenGL was born. SGI removed the user interface support from GL and forged a new graphical interface language that was lean and mean, at least when compared to its predecessor.

OpenGL is now an international standard that may be found on a wide range of systems. Windows NT and Windows 98 ship with OpenGL as a part of the basic operating system, and even Windows 95 Service Release 2 added OpenGL support as standard equipment.

NOTE

Those of you still using early releases of Windows 95 aren't out in the cold. Microsoft released OpenGL for Windows 95 and made it freely available in a self-extracting archive. You may download it from `ftp://ftp.microsoft.com/softlib/mslfiles/opengl95.exe`.

So you now know OpenGL is a programmer's interface for graphics programming, and you've read a bit of its history. Now I will turn to the core essence of OpenGL. If you've never studied the mathematics behind 3D computer graphics, you might not truly appreciate what OpenGL does for you (don't let that stop you from using it, however). The mathematics involves several successive transformations using *transformation matrices*, which naturally involve matrix algebra. You'll see a bit of this in a moment when you look at some of the most basic graphics concepts. OpenGL, however, manages much of the mathematics for you, allowing you to concentrate on the real problem at hand—your graphical scene. OpenGL, then, is really a mathematical *state machine* that captures the math behind graphics programming as well as some of the other basic fundamentals, such as *double buffering* (writing to separate graphics memory buffers for animation purposes). If you have one of the newer-generation 3D graphics accelerator video cards, its hardware probably supports OpenGL and the processing (and memory management) OpenGL must undertake to successfully render a scene even more quickly.

Graphics Boot Camp

This is a book about programming, but I'd be remiss if I didn't spend some time describing some core terms and key concepts you absolutely must understand before you attempt your first 3D masterpiece. You'll begin by exploring some fundamental graphics programming terms and then you'll move into some basic theory.

Core Terms and Key Concepts

To begin your look at OpenGL, you need to have a good understanding of the graphics programmer's language. Not their *programming language*, such as C++, but rather the way they speak. When they talk about their models and translations, you need to understand what they are talking about. So I will start with some core terms.

Model. When I talk about a model, I'm talking about an individual object within my (typically) 3D scene. Perhaps I have a model of a cube, or maybe a sphere. I could even have a model of a 3D *Tyrannosaurus rex*.

Polygons. A 3D surface appears to be solid, but it is really composed of several shapes (usually triangles for theoretical reasons). The triangles are arranged in a mesh, and the area within the polygon is left alone (*wireframe*), *shaded* (colored in, with or without lighting effects), or *texture-mapped* (external image applied). Wireframe is just that—the model is drawn using only lines. If you apply shading, or light properties, you fill in the area of the polygon with a color. If the polygons are numerous enough, and if your system has a large color palette, you can render terrific-looking, highly detailed models. The ultimate in polygon surface effects is texture-mapping, where you apply a *decal* (texture) to the polygon. The decal is typically a bitmapped image you create beforehand. You conform (distort) the decal to the polygon surface, thus making the polygon itself appear to be much more complex than it really is.

Normals. The polygons OpenGL accepts lie in a plane (the vertices are coplanar). The polygon's surface normal is a *vector* that resides in the third coordinate plane tangent to the surface of the polygon. Imagine that the top of your desk is a polygon. If you were to stand a sharpened pencil eraser down on the desk, the pencil would represent the desktop's polygonal (surface) normal. Normals, and their proper calculation, are critical for light calculations.

Translation. Translation means moving the model (intact) from one set of coordinates to another. Essentially, you're relocating your model to another location within the scene.

Scaling. When you scale a model, you're adjusting its size. That is not to say you must adjust all aspects of its size at the same time. You could, for example, scale in only one of the three *coordinate axes* (the *x-axis*, the *y-axis*, or the *z-axis*), thus stretching the model in one direction only to distort it from its original shape.

Rotation. Just as you can translate and scale, you can also rotate about a (arbitrary) coordinate axis. In effect, you spin the model about some given longitudinal axis.

Viewing frustrum. All your models (and the scene as a whole) will be contained in an imaginary area called the viewing frustrum (see Figure 29.1). The frustrum has six sides, each known as a *clipping plane*. If any part of your model is rendered outside this imaginary area, the part of the model outside will be summarily cut off (*clipped*) and not shown. The frustrum may be either an *orthographic* (parallel) or a *projection* frustrum. If the frustrum is parallel, objects will be rendered without regard to depth. You will have, effectively, a 2D scene. On the other hand, projected frustrums implement *perspective foreshortening* by using the depth information. Distant objects appear distant because they are scaled appropriately. The more distant they are, the smaller they appear.

FIGURE 29.1

The viewing frustrum.

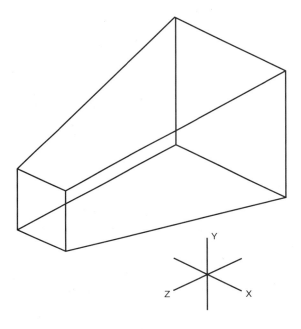

Light. Light in graphical terms is composed of many parts. First, there is *ambient* light, which is the natural light present in the 3D scene without any additional light source. Sunshine would be considered ambient lighting. Then there is the light reflected from the surface of the object, which is called *diffuse* light. The combination of ambient and diffuse light makes your scene appear brighter or dimmer depending upon the relative strength of each component. These light components typically provide the object with its color. *Specular* light, however, is light that reflects from the object's surface due to a focused light source. This light component is usually composed of the light source's color. If you imagine a red sphere, you see a red sphere because it reflects red light (it absorbs the rest of the color spectrum). If you were to shine a bright yellow light onto the surface of the sphere, you would see a red sphere with a bright yellow spot on the surface. This yellow spot is the specular light component.

Material properties. Each object, if it is rendered with light computations, will have material property assignments. These properties denote the object's color properties—

how much light it reflects, how it handles specular light, how shiny it is, and so on. By adjusting an object's material properties, you determine how the object will appear given certain light conditions. It could look shiny, like plastic or chrome, or it could appear dull, like mud.

You'll be seeing these terms and concepts throughout this (and the next) chapter. Now that you have a common foundation of terms and concepts, it is time for an introduction to the mathematics of graphics programming. Because OpenGL provides you with a rich mathematics library, I believe you must understand what's under the hood to properly use the tool.

The Basic Mathematics of Graphics Programming

My goal with this section is not to scare you away from 3D graphics. Rather, it's important for you to have some appreciation, if not a fundamental understanding, of what is happening within the bowels of OpenGL to use it effectively. I can't possibly go into enough detail here to derive the equations and matrices you'll see, but at least having seen them, you'll understand why OpenGL does some things the way it does and why you work with OpenGL the way you do.

To begin, you will be working in a 3D coordinate space where the three axes of the space are orthogonal. That is, they are all at right angles (90 degrees to each other). The fundamental meaning of this is that you didn't bend your 3D universe in some fashion. The result of this is that the math becomes very much simpler. Figure 29.2 gives you the basic idea.

FIGURE 29.2

3D coordinate axes.

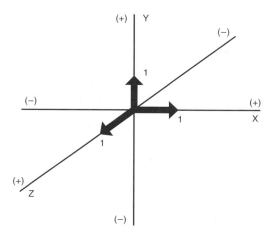

All your 3D models will be described using the three basic coordinates—x, y, and z. You also may see in Figure 29.2 the coordinate axes' unit vectors. A vector is a directed value. That is, it has a direction and a magnitude. When you drive a car, your speed is considered a *scalar* value. It is simply a number. But when you combine your speed with a given direction (say, northeast), you know your car's velocity, which is a vector quantity. It has magnitude (the speed component) and direction (northeast). It will be the same when you deal with 3D space. You may know a particular scalar value, such as the length of the side of a cube, but it isn't as informative if you don't know how the side of the cube is aligned because you lack the directional component.

The vectors shown in Figure 29.2 are known as unit vectors. That means nothing more than their magnitude (scalar) value is one (1). This also simplifies the mathematics in many cases. When you deal with light calculations in particular, you'll be interested in *normalizing* your vectors. You'll reduce their magnitude to the value one, again to simplify the mathematics. I'll refer back to this in a moment.

A single vector isn't particularly interesting. In essence, you have a line. It becomes far more interesting when you have *two* vectors that cross each other at a given point (called a *vertex*). Each vector has a magnitude and direction, so if you were to add them, in vector terms, you would find that you have a third vector (see Figure 29.3).

FIGURE 29.3

Vector addition and the resultant vector.

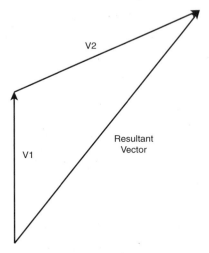

29

MFC AND
OPENGL

This vector, the result of the addition of the former two vectors, is the *resultant* vector. It essentially is a conglomerate of the magnitudes and directions of the first two vectors. I'll revisit these vectors shortly when I again talk about polygonal surfaces and surface normals.

Though some graphics students might argue this point, when you deal with vectors it sometimes simplifies life if you work the mathematics using matrices. The rows and columns of the matrices either represent the vectors you're interested in or they represent a *transformation* you want to apply to a coordinate system (all points within that system, as represented by the coordinate unit vectors). As an example, think about translation. Translation is the act of moving an object in 3D space from one location to another. If you consider your objects to be composed of vectors, that is, edges that connect the vertices of the polygons that compose the object, you run each edge vector through the translation matrix to calculate the new location for the vector (see Figure 29.4).

FIGURE 29.4

A translation matrix equation.

$$T(t_x, t_y, t_z) = \begin{bmatrix} 1 & 0 & 0 & t_x \\ 0 & 1 & 0 & t_y \\ 0 & 0 & 1 & t_z \\ 0 & 0 & 0 & 1 \end{bmatrix} \begin{bmatrix} x \\ y \\ z \\ 1 \end{bmatrix} = \begin{bmatrix} x' \\ y' \\ z' \\ h \end{bmatrix}$$

What the equation tells you is this: If you know a starting point and the amount you want to translate that point, you can use this matrix to relocate the given point. All the points in your model will be translated in the same manner. Other transformation matrices exist for scaling and rotation as well.

I mentioned previously the concept of normalization. Actually, when dealing with computer graphics, this term has two meanings. The first is to take a vector of some arbitrary size and make its scalar value (its length, so to speak) one. The other meaning is to determine the *surface normal* to a given coplanar polygon. If you have a polygon, and if the vertices of the polygon lie in a single plane (it isn't twisted), you have a coplanar polygon. But as you know, a plane is a 2D construction. What about the third dimension? In most cases, you ignore the third dimension when thinking about polygons, except when you have a vector that is perpendicular to the polygon (*perpendicular* means the vector rises 90 degrees from the surface of the polygon). This 90-degree vector is the polygon's surface normal, and it is critical for light calculations. You'll see why that is later in this chapter.

In many cases you will intuitively know what the surface normal vector should be for a given polygon. In terms of OpenGL, imagine you have this polygon:

```
glBegin(GL_POLYGON);
    glVertex3f(5.0f,5.0f,5.0f);
    glVertex3f(-5.0f,5.0f,5.0f);
    glVertex3f(-5.0f,-5.0f,5.0f);
    glVertex3f(5.0f,-5.0f,5.0f);
glEnd();
```

This forms a square you'll see as if you were directly on top of it (your eye would be looking down upon it). The polygon's plane is evident—see the z coordinate values?

They're all 5.0, which automatically tells you this polygon lies in the z plane. Therefore, the surface normal must be composed entirely of the z coordinate (it will have no x or y coordinate values). Again in terms of OpenGL code, the surface normal would be declared like this:

```
glBegin(GL_POLYGON);
    glVertex3f(5.0f,5.0f,5.0f);
    glVertex3f(-5.0f,5.0f,5.0f);
    glVertex3f(-5.0f,-5.0f,5.0f);
    glVertex3f(5.0f,-5.0f,5.0f);
    glNormal3f(0.0f,0.0f,1.0f);
glEnd();
```

There are two things you should note here. First, the surface normal is assigned within the same `glBegin()`/`glEnd()` pair as the polygon's vertices. This is how OpenGL associates this particular normal with this polygon. The second thing you should see is that the value of the z component of the normal vector is exactly one. The surface normal vector itself is *normalized*. This particular polygon is somewhat special in that it lies in the z plane. An infinite number of other polygons do not lie in the z plane, so don't be fooled into thinking that a surface normal vector will always have a couple of zeros and a one for vector components! It will always be true, however, that the length of the surface normal vector will be one.

Hard-coding the normal is fine if you are able to predetermine it. I'll now show you what to do if you have some arbitrary polygon in 3D space. Basically, you take two of the polygonal edges (represented as vectors) and take their *cross product*. The mathematics is such that when you take the cross product of two vectors, you get a normal vector as a result. In the case of graphical surface normals, you also must normalize the length of the resulting vector. Listing 29.1 gives you the code to take a cross product and normalize the result, which I took from this chapter's GLObject sample program. I'll leave it to you to trace through the code if you're unfamiliar with vector cross-product calculations. However, you should know that the input vectors were defined in a counterclockwise fashion. This is essential for the cross product to yield the proper result (the resulting vector will be in the wrong direction if you do it incorrectly!).

29

MFC AND
OPENGL

LISTING 29.1   VECTOR CROSS-PRODUCT CALCULATIONS

```
void CGLObjectView::Normal( GLfloat* pt1,
                            GLfloat* pt2,
                            GLfloat* pt3,
                            double* nml )
{
    // Form two vectors from the given input points
```

continues

LISTING 29.1   CONTINUED

```
    double v1[3], v2[3];
    v1[0] = pt2[0] - pt1[0];
    v1[1] = pt2[1] - pt1[1];
    v1[2] = pt2[2] - pt1[2];
    v2[0] = pt3[0] - pt1[0];
    v2[1] = pt3[1] - pt1[1];
    v2[2] = pt3[2] - pt1[2];

    // Take their cross product
    nml[0] = v1[1] * v2[2] - v1[2] * v2[1];
    nml[1] = v1[2] * v2[0] - v1[0] * v2[2];
    nml[2] = v1[0] * v2[1] - v1[1] * v2[0];

    // Normalize the resultant
    double dLen = sqrt(nml[0]*nml[0] +
                       nml[1]*nml[1] +
                       nml[2]*nml[2]);
    if ( dLen != 0.0 ) {
       nml[0] = nml[0] / dLen;
       nml[1] = nml[1] / dLen;
       nml[2] = nml[2] / dLen;
    } // if
}
```

To use this cross-product function, you pass in a number of double arrays. The first three are filled with the points that define the two vectors. The last is a result array that will contain the normal vector. You pass this to OpenGL when you specify the polygon's surface normal.

You've completed your tour of 3D computer graphics theory! I'm sure you'll be amazed by OpenGL's capability, especially knowing not only how complicated 3D graphics can be, but also knowing that the sheer number of calculations can be staggering for even trivial scenes.

OpenGL Boot Camp

Now it is time to turn to OpenGL to see how it mechanizes the 3D rendering process. In some fashion, OpenGL supports all the terms, concepts, and mathematics you've just examined. The beauty of OpenGL is you needn't concern yourself with the details. You need to understand the fundamentals to use this tool properly, but the details lie within the OpenGL implementation itself.

But just as OpenGL has tremendous beauty, I would be doing you a disservice if I didn't also mention OpenGL's warts. OpenGL was originally implemented in the UNIX environment, and if you've worked in both Windows and UNIX, you'll find that OpenGL still has a "UNIX-like" feeling to it. OpenGL simply wasn't developed within the Windows framework, so it doesn't have a natural feel within Windows. Why would I claim this? For one, OpenGL has its own breed of device context (the Windows version of which you looked at in Chapter 4, "Painting, Device Contexts, Bitmaps, and Fonts"). You still require a Windows-style device context, but you must also manage an OpenGL context as well. Further, there can be only one active OpenGL device context per thread. This isn't necessarily a problem, but you must be aware of this limitation and code accordingly.

OpenGL also attempts to be platform-independent, so there are OpenGL-specific definitions for things as basic as the floating-point datatype. In C++, you would declare a floating-point variable in this manner:

```
float fMyVar;
```

However, when using OpenGL, you would use a `GLfloat` variable:

```
GLfloat fMyGLVar;
```

For all intents and purposes, both variables are floating-point variables. They may, in fact, be the same. But your OpenGL code is now more portable, at the cost of ease of programming.

So, now that you understand OpenGL is a new programming interface with its own datatypes, I will introduce you to some OpenGL conventions you'll be using throughout this chapter. I'll start with the custom datatypes I just mentioned.

OpenGL Datatypes

As you've seen, 3D graphics programming is by nature mathematically intense, so it may not be too surprising to find that OpenGL has quite a number of custom datatypes geared towards mathematics and 3D graphics calculations. Table 29.1 lists the OpenGL datatypes and their equivalent C++ types.

TABLE 29.1 OPENGL DATATYPES WITH C++ EQUIVALENTS

OpenGL Datatype	C++ Datatype
GLbyte	signed char
GLubyte	unsigned char
GLboolean	unsigned char
GLshort	short

continues

29

MFC AND OpenGL

Table 29.1   CONTINUED

OpenGL Datatype	C++ Datatype
GLushort	unsigned short
GLint	long
GLuint	unsigned long
GLsizei	long
GLfloat	float
GLclampf	float
GLdouble	double
GLclampd	double
GLenum	unsigned long
GLbitfield	unsigned long
GLvoid	void
HGLRC	HGDIOBJ

By convention you'll use these datatypes when programming in OpenGL. Anyone reading your code who is familiar with OpenGL will expect this convention to be followed. But another good reason for using the datatype mappings is that the mappings could conceivably change given future microprocessors (say, for 64-bit machines). If you follow this convention, the burden of correcting the datatypes lies with the OpenGL vendor, not you. You simply recompile your code and continue selling your product.

OpenGL also follows its own convention when referring to such things as arrays. In OpenGL, you don't have an array of GLfloats. Rather, you have a *vector* of GLfloats. You will frequently need to pass an array of floats (or ints, or whatever) as a parameter to a given OpenGL function. In OpenGL terms, you are passing in a vector, even though the data may have nothing to do with an actual (mathematically based) vector. This distinction becomes important when I discuss the OpenGL function naming convention.

OpenGL Function Naming Conventions

When working with traditional Windows programs, many programmers prefer to embrace the *Hungarian* variable naming convention. For example, if a variable is an integer, its variable name will be prefaced with the letter *i*. OpenGL follows a similar vein, only not with variable types (it has its own), but rather with function names. Almost all OpenGL functions accept integer, float, and double variable datatypes, and many accept vectors of the same. To distinguish the function that accepts integers from the equivalent function that accepts doubles, the datatype is *concatenated* to the end of the function name. For example, consider this OpenGL function call (which establishes a vertex, or endpoint):

```
void glVertex2f(GLfloat x, GLfloat y);
```

You can see that it is an OpenGL function because it begins with the letters *gl*. You know its basic functionality is to assign vertex points. And you also know the function accepts *two* parameters, each being a `float` value. The equivalent function, using a vector, looks like this:

```
void glVertex2fv (const GLfloat *v);
```

Now the parameter indication is more interesting. You know the input parameter is a vector that contains two `float` values, which is something you don't normally know when passed a simple array of floating-point variables. The vector passed to the OpenGL function may include more members than the function will use, but it may not contain less or OpenGL will return with catastrophic results. Using OpenGL's vertex assignment function as an example, Table 29.2 shows you the function name with the corresponding expected datatypes. These datatypes are typical for almost all OpenGL functions (directly from gl.h).

TABLE 29.2　OPENGL VERTEX FUNCTION NAMES AND PARAMETER LISTS

Vertex Function Name	*Parameter List*
glVertex2d	GLdouble x, GLdouble y
glVertex2dv	const GLdouble *v
glVertex2f	GLfloat x, GLfloat y
glVertex2fv	const GLfloat *v
glVertex2i	GLint x, GLint y
glVertex2iv	const GLint *v
glVertex2s	GLshort x, GLshort y
glVertex2sv	const GLshort *v
glVertex3d	GLdouble x, GLdouble y, GLdouble z
glVertex3dv	const GLdouble *v
glVertex3f	GLfloat x, GLfloat y, GLfloat z
glVertex3fv	const GLfloat *v
glVertex3i	GLint x, GLint y, GLint z
glVertex3iv	const GLint *v

29

MFC AND
OpenGL

continues

TABLE 29.2   CONTINUED

Vertex Function Name	Parameter List
glVertex3s	(GLshort x, GLshort y, GLshort z
glVertex3sv	const GLshort *v
glVertex4d	GLdouble x, GLdouble y, GLdouble z, GLdouble w
glVertex4dv	const GLdouble *v
glVertex4f	GLfloat x, GLfloat y, GLfloat z, GLfloat w
glVertex4fv	const GLfloat *v
glVertex4i	GLint x, GLint y, GLint z, GLint w
glVertex4iv	const GLint *v
glVertex4s	GLshort x, GLshort y, GLshort z, GLshort w
glVertex4sv	const GLshort *v

OpenGL Render Function Scoping

Because OpenGL manages a graphical state, it must be told when a given set of operations is related. That is, just as you use the left and right brace in C++ to indicate a single C++ statement, you enclose many OpenGL function calls within glBegin() and glEnd(). For example, you could use this OpenGL code to draw a 2D square:

```
void DrawGLSquare() {
   glBegin(GL_LINES); // square in X-Y plane
      glVertex3f(-5.0f, 5.0f, 0.0f);
      glVertex3f(-5.0f, -5.0f, 0.0f);

      glVertex3f(-5.0f, -5.0f, 0.0f);
      glVertex3f(5.0f, -5.0f, 0.0f);

      glVertex3f(5.0f, -5.0f, 0.0f);
      glVertex3f(5.0f, 5.0f, 0.0f);

      glVertex3f(5.0f, 5.0f, 0.0f);
      glVertex3f(-5.0f, 5.0f, 0.0f);
   glEnd();
}
```

With this code you are telling OpenGL to draw lines (GL_LINES) from the first vector coordinate to the second (as indicated by their grouping). In Win32 GDI terms, the first glVertex3f() call performs the MoveToEx(), and the second performs the LineTo(). The first glVertex3f() pair then draws a line from (-5.0,5.0) (in *(X,Y)* format) to (-5.0,-5.0). The remaining groups draw the other three sides of the square. You'll revisit this code when you look at the GLMin sample program shortly. Note that some OpenGL commands are excluded from the `glBegin()`/`glEnd()` pair, so be sure to see the online help for more details.

> **NOTE**
>
> It is no accident that the vertices are drawn in counter-clockwise fashion. This is critical for cross-product calculations, which are used when rendering the square with light effects.

The OpenGL Matrix Stack

As you have seen, OpenGL uses matrices to manage the mathematical calculations required to render your 3D scene. To make the matrix manipulations much easier, OpenGL provides a *matrix stack*. The matrix stack operates like any other stack-based scheme. You first *push* a matrix onto the stack, which effectively saves the current matrix contents. You are then free to manipulate the matrix as required to render a given object or your entire scene. Finally, you *pop* the original matrix off the stack to make more manipulations.

This feature is most useful when rendering many 3D objects in a single scene. Typically, you'll prepare a matrix for initial use by making several OpenGL function calls. The stack-based approach allows you to establish your basic matrix a single time while reusing it as much as you require. For example, you could easily draw two squares in different locations using the same code I presented for drawing a single square:

```
void RenderView() {
   glPushMatrix();
DrawGLSquare();
glPopMatrix();

   glPushMatrix();
      glScalef(5.0f,5.0f,0.0f);
      glRotatef(45.0f,0.0f,0.0f,1.0f);
      DrawGLSquare();
   glPopMatrix();
}
```

In this case, the matrix was (presumably) initialized prior to the first `glPushMatrix()` call. Although in this example I didn't actually modify the matrix in any way for the first square, I could have. In fact, it's a good habit to get into, as matrix bugs are difficult to track down. Everything will seem to work correctly, yet your final scene is not rendered correctly. In any case, I save the matrix on the stack, render the first square, then pop the matrix off the stack to be used again.

The second square, however, *does* modify the matrix. As you've seen, whenever you translate, rotate, scale, or otherwise manipulate the model view, you mathematically change the model view matrix. Here, I first scale the model view matrix, and then rotate it. The resulting square is reduced to one-half of its original size, then rotated about the z-axis 45 degrees. The resulting scene is shown in Figure 29.5. The second square is the diamond-shaped object in the center of the first square. This also demonstrates a powerful feature OpenGL provides you. Notice that I manipulated the model view matrix, but I used the same model code (`DrawGLSquare()`). The objects in your model code are placed within your scene according to the resulting transformational matrix, so you may code your models as if they were centered at (0,0,0). This makes model development tremendously easier.

FIGURE 29.5

GLMin program output.

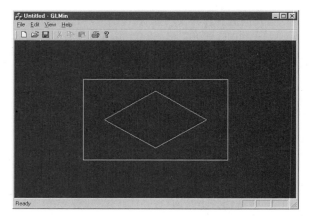

The OpenGL Rendering Context

As you saw in Chapter 4, Windows applications (MFC-based or otherwise) use a device context for graphical output. The Windows GDI manages device contexts and provides the functions you use to manipulate the images within those device contexts. OpenGL does not use the standard Windows device context, however. It uses a *rendering context*.

Like device contexts, rendering contexts maintain a graphical state. If you use the `SelectObject()` GDI function to select a new drawing pen into a device context, that pen remains active in that device context until you select in another. OpenGL's rendering context is similar. OpenGL uses the rendering context to maintain the information it requires to properly render a scene within a given window. In fact, this is the main purpose behind a rendering context. OpenGL must have a mechanism for associating its output with a Windows device context. By storing certain pieces of information within a rendering context, OpenGL is able to update (more or less portably) a window's graphical state in the Windows family of operating systems. This relationship is shown in Figure 29.6.

FIGURE 29.6

Device context/rendering context relationship.

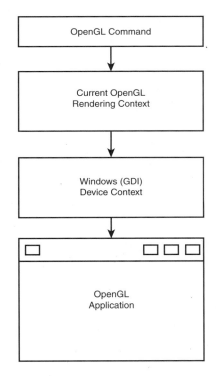

Rendering contexts are thread-safe, which means multiple threads can use a single rendering context. You may have several rendering contexts stored within your application, thus allowing you to easily select the context you require quickly. However, there cannot be more than one active rendering context per thread at any given time. Moreover, there *must* be a current, active rendering context per thread for you to successfully process OpenGL commands.

Unlike Windows GDI functions, OpenGL commands do not require a handle or pointer to a rendering context. Whichever rendering context is currently active will accept all processed OpenGL commands. The rendering context is implicit in the drawing command calls.

Rendering context management requires at a minimum the use of 3 of the 16 Windows-specific OpenGL function calls (the so-called "wiggle" functions). Table 29.3 outlines these. To use OpenGL, you first create a rendering context, initialize it, make it current, use it, make it not current, and then destroy it. This is not to say that you do this each and every time you draw your scene! Rather, you first create and initialize the rendering context, and then reuse it as long as your application is active (switching it for the current and noncurrent rendering context any number of times), and then destroy it when your application exits.

TABLE 29.3 PRIMARY WINDOWS-SPECIFIC OPENGL COMMANDS

Return Value	Command
HGLRC	wglCreateContext(HDC hDC)
BOOL	wglDeleteContext(HGLRC hRC)
BOOL	wglMakeCurrent(HDC hDC, HGLRC hRC)

You create a rendering context using wglCreateContext(), delete one using wglDeleteContext(), and make a particular rendering context the current context by using wglMakeCurrent(). The remaining Windows-specific OpenGL function calls are mainly convenience functions for retrieving information regarding the rendering context/device context mapping, or for setting specific (advanced) behaviors beyond the scope of this discussion.

At the heart of this context mapping is the format of a pixel. That is, OpenGL and Windows don't necessarily agree with Windows regarding pixel format, at least as a default condition. When you initialize OpenGL, what you will really be doing is moderating a negotiation process between what OpenGL desires and what the given Windows system can provide. The outcome of this negotiation process will be a rendering context that properly maps what OpenGL provides to what the Windows system is capable of displaying.

You will use several GDI functions to handle this negotiation process, which you'll examine in more detail later in this chapter. These functions, however, all require a PIXELFORMATDESCRIPTOR structure, the definition for which is shown in Listing 29.2 (taken from wingdi.h).

LISTING 29.2 PIXELFORMATDESCRIPTOR DEFINITION

```
/* Pixel format descriptor */
typedef struct tagPIXELFORMATDESCRIPTOR
{
```

```
    WORD  nSize;
    WORD  nVersion;
    DWORD dwFlags;
    BYTE  iPixelType;
    BYTE  cColorBits;
    BYTE  cRedBits;
    BYTE  cRedShift;
    BYTE  cGreenBits;
    BYTE  cGreenShift;
    BYTE  cBlueBits;
    BYTE  cBlueShift;
    BYTE  cAlphaBits;
    BYTE  cAlphaShift;
    BYTE  cAccumBits;
    BYTE  cAccumRedBits;
    BYTE  cAccumGreenBits;
    BYTE  cAccumBlueBits;
    BYTE  cAccumAlphaBits;
    BYTE  cDepthBits;
    BYTE  cStencilBits;
    BYTE  cAuxBuffers;
    BYTE  iLayerType;
    BYTE  bReserved;
    DWORD dwLayerMask;
    DWORD dwVisibleMask;
    DWORD dwDamageMask;
} PIXELFORMATDESCRIPTOR, *PPIXELFORMATDESCRIPTOR,
  FAR *LPPIXELFORMATDESCRIPTOR;
```

This large and admittedly complicated structure carries the specific system information between OpenGL and the particular Windows system device context on which your application is running. Between any two systems, the given capabilities of each, as expressed in device context terms (number of color planes, video memory, acceleration, and so on), are dependent upon the video hardware and drivers each of the systems is using. Some systems are capable of supporting OpenGL, and some are not, though it would be rare given the advanced features of contemporary hardware to lack support for OpenGL. In any case, you use the PIXELFORMATDESCRIPTOR structure to record the settings you require OpenGL to support, such as double buffering (using two video buffers to support flicker-free animation) and RGBA pixel types (*red*, *green*, *blue*, and *alpha*, which is used for blending effects like fog). You then pass the structure to a GDI function to assess the capabilities of your current system. Assuming your system is capable of supporting the needs of OpenGL, you advance to actually creating a rendering context using wglCreateContext(). You'll look at this process in the next section.

29

MFC AND OpenGL

Minimal OpenGL Program and a Custom View

You have now completed your introduction to OpenGL, as well as to computer graphics in general. It's now time to turn to integrating OpenGL into the MFC framework. This isn't difficult, but I will take an approach I find helpful to make it even easier. I will encapsulate the OpenGL functionality I require into a new view class. Then, when I require an OpenGL view, I'll derive my new view from the OpenGL base class that I will create in this section. Some editing will be required to integrate this OpenGL view class into the basic MFC AppWizard source code Developer Studio provides you, but that integration is minimal when compared to re-creating this base class each time you want to use OpenGL.

The steps required to run OpenGL from your MFC application are as follows:

- Create your basic MFC application using the MFC AppWizard.
- Add the custom view class you will create in this section to your project.
- Integrate the custom view class into your application.
- Build your 3D scene.
- Add the OpenGL libraries to your project's link list.

NOTE

This technique works for both single document (SDI) and multiple document interface (MDI) applications. I have included sample applications to demonstrate both situations (GLMin and GLMinMDI).

Creating Your Basic MFC Application

There is no special OpenGL requirement when creating your basic application framework. However, the GLView base class inherits directly from CView. If you use a view base class other than CView, you will need to create your own OpenGL-based class to act as the base class for the view you selected. That is, if you create an application that implements a CFormView view class, you will need to create a CGLFormView class to manage the OpenGL aspects of your application.

Adding the Custom OpenGL Base Class

Adding the OpenGL view class, `CGLView`, to your project is simple. Select Project, Add To Project, Files from the Developer Studio menu, then select GLView.cpp and GLView.h from the resulting file dialog and click OK. After the files have been added to your project, you can integrate them into your overall application.

This, however, presupposes that you have the `CGLView` class, so now is a good time to examine the mechanisms for running OpenGL from within a view. To begin, you must initialize OpenGL and its rendering context, modify your view's style bits, manage the lifetime of any custom palette you create, handle window sizing issues, and clean up when the view is destroyed. In effect, this means you must do something in each of these MFC methods:

```
CGLView::PreCreateWindow()
CGLView::OnCreate()
CGLView::DestroyWindow()
CGLView::OnSize()
CGLView::OnEraseBkGnd()
```

You will also need to include the OpenGL header files and libraries, and you may need to worry about palette management if your application is running on a system with a less capable video card. In any case, I will now describe each method individually.

View Precreation

OpenGL requires the style bits of the enclosing view to be modified to clip child and sibling windows. In effect, OpenGL requires your view to exclude the area occupied by child windows when drawing within the parent window (WM_CLIPCHILDREN) and clips all of the child windows relative to each other (WM_CLIPSIBLINGS). In this manner, OpenGL doesn't paint outside of its window. Listing 29.3 shows how I implemented this in `CGLView`.

LISTING 29.3 OPENGL WINDOW STYLE BITS AND WINDOW PRECREATION

```
BOOL CGLView::PreCreateWindow(CREATESTRUCT& cs)
{
    // Set up style to suit OpenGL
    cs.style |= WS_CLIPCHILDREN | WS_CLIPSIBLINGS;

    return CView::PreCreateWindow(cs);
}
```

Note that I logically *OR* the new style bits into the creation structure's style bits member. This modifies these particular bits without disturbing the existing bits. After I've adjusted the style bits, I need to handle the creation of the window.

View Creation

Creating an OpenGL view is one of those things that looks more difficult than it really is, primarily because you have to both initially tie a new rendering context to a device context and twiddle the PIXELFORMATDESCRIPTOR bits. As it happens, when you have code to do this, you'll probably find yourself using the same code over and over (in fact, I'll create a custom view class to do this for you in an upcoming section of this chapter).

Creating an OpenGL view-based application starts essentially the same as the creation of any other view. Windows, through MFC, will send a WM_CREATE message down through the message map chain. And as with any other Windows message, you elect to add a handler to process that specific message if you want to tailor your application's behavior from the normal (default) Windows behavior. In this case, you must add a handler for WM_CREATE, and when you intercept that message, you initialize OpenGL. Listing 29.4 shows you the code I use to do just this.

LISTING 29.4 OPENGL WM_CREATE HANDLER

```
int CGLView::OnCreate(LPCREATESTRUCT lpCreateStruct)
{
   if (CView::OnCreate(lpCreateStruct) == -1)
      return -1;

   // Initialize OpenGL parameters
   PIXELFORMATDESCRIPTOR pfd = {
      sizeof(PIXELFORMATDESCRIPTOR), // Structure size
      1,                             // Version number
      PFD_DRAW_TO_WINDOW |           // Property flags
         PFD_SUPPORT_OPENGL |
         PFD_DOUBLEBUFFER,           // (remove if no double buf)
      PFD_TYPE_RGBA,                 // PixelType
      24,                            // 24-bit color
      0, 0, 0, 0, 0, 0,             // Color bits and shift
      0, 0, 0, 0, 0, 0, 0,          // Alpha and accum buffer bits
      32,                            // 32-bit depth buffer
      0, 0,                          // No stencil or aux buffer
      PFD_MAIN_PLANE,                // Layer type
      0,                             // Reserved
      0, 0, 0                        // Unsupported
   };

   // Tell GDI to convert device context from Win32 to
   // OpenGL.
   CClientDC dcClient(this);
   int iPixelFormat = ChoosePixelFormat(dcClient.m_hDC,&pfd);
   if ( !iPixelFormat ) {
```

```
      // This system cannot run OpenGL
      TRACE("Error retrieving pixel format index...\n");
      ASSERT(FALSE);
      AfxMessageBox("Cannot initialize OpenGL...quitting.",
                    MB_OK | MB_ICONERROR);
      return -1; // will fail new document creation...
   } // if

   if ( !SetPixelFormat(dcClient.m_hDC,iPixelFormat,&pfd) ) {
      // This system cannot run OpenGL
      TRACE("Error setting new pixel format...\n");
      ASSERT(FALSE);
      AfxMessageBox("Cannot initialize OpenGL...quitting.",
                    MB_OK | MB_ICONERROR);
      return -1; // will fail new document creation...
   } // if

   // Update the PIXELFORMATDESCRIPTOR structure once
   // the device context has been modified.
   DescribePixelFormat(dcClient.m_hDC,iPixelFormat,
                       sizeof(pfd),&pfd);

   // The PIXELFORMATDESCRIPTOR has been updated, so you now
   // determine whether to create and manage a custom
   // palette.
   if ( pfd.dwFlags & PFD_NEED_PALETTE ) {
      // You do, so build a new palette...
      SetupPalette();
   } // if

   // Create the OpenGL rendering context
   m_hRC = wglCreateContext(dcClient.m_hDC);
   if ( m_hRC == NULL ) {
      // This system cannot run OpenGL
      TRACE("Error creating the rendering context...\n");
      ASSERT(FALSE);
      AfxMessageBox("Cannot initialize OpenGL...quitting.",
                    MB_OK | MB_ICONERROR);
      return -1; // will fail new document creation...
   } // if

   // You now make it the current rendering context so
   // you might set your clear color
   wglMakeCurrent(dcClient.m_hDC,m_hRC);
   glClearColor(0.0f,0.0f,0.0f,0.0f); // black
   wglMakeCurrent(dcClient.m_hDC,NULL);

   return 0;
}
```

29

MFC AND OPENGL

The very first thing I do is allow the base class to handle window creation in the normal fashion:

```
if (CView::OnCreate(lpCreateStruct) == -1)
    return -1;
```

If this code isn't successful, you won't need to initialize OpenGL because you'll have no window.

Then, I create a `PIXELFORMATDESCRIPTOR` structure and fill in its data members. You examined those members in the previous section. Here, I actually assign them values, with the overall goal being that OpenGL ultimately must provide its graphical output to a device context. But because device contexts are Windows-specific (not platform independent), OpenGL requires an intermediate initialization step to allow fast conversion from its rendering system to the particular platform (in this case, Windows). The `PIXELFOR-MATDESCRIPTOR` facilitates this initialization.

After I've established the `PIXELFORMATDESCRIPTOR` settings I want, I begin the process of building the OpenGL rendering context. First, I query the Windows device context for its pixel format information. `SetPixelFormat()` tries to match the closest system pixel format (as specified by the `PIXELFORMATDESCRIPTOR` structure), and if it finds a suitable match, returns a pixel format index that is the closest match. If I find no match, I terminate the application with a brief error dialog.

What I have now is the *closest match* pixel format index for this device context. What I want is a *precise match* (at least to a first approximation), so I use the `SetPixelFormat()` function to establish the pixel format I want. If this fails, I terminate the application with the same informative error dialog.

If I successfully established the new pixel format settings, I now need to retrieve the settings that actually took effect. With luck, they match those I requested. However, if the application initialized successfully to this point, OpenGL will work within my application's framework. I use the `DescribePixelFormat()` function to retrieve the now-current pixel format settings.

At this time, I elect to create a custom palette if one is required. I'll know if I require one by querying the `PIXELFORMATDESCRIPTOR` structure's `dwFlags` attribute. If the `PFD_NEED_PALETTE` flag is set, I know the system does not support full 24-bit color and will require a custom palette. If this is the case, I create a palette using a special function I provide for this purpose (the details of which are left to the reader to discern; they are not particularly interesting to OpenGL discussions).

Finally, I arrive at the really interesting part. I create the OpenGL rendering context using `wglCreateContext()`. `wglCreateContext()` accepts a device context handle as input and returns to you a handle to an OpenGL rendering context that matches the device context. Given this, you're now free to make other OpenGL command calls, which I do by setting the view clear color (the default background color).

When I mentioned previously that the OpenGL rendering context is directly mapped to a Windows device context, the `wglMakeCurrent()` function is the call that does this. Before I set the clear color, I make the rendering context I just created the current rendering context for this thread. When I do, I also provide a device context, which is the device context the rendering context will use to map OpenGL commands to the window in which the device context is assigned. After I set the clear color, using `glClearColor()`, I disassociate the rendering context from the device context by again calling `wglMakeCurrent()`. In this case, I set the rendering context to NULL. At this point, OpenGL cannot process drawing commands unless and until I make the rendering context current again.

View Destruction

Just as you had to create the OpenGL rendering context, you also must destroy it (or them, if you created multiples). You could destroy it in one of several places (such as after you're through using it), but I find it best to keep at least one in memory until my application either receives the `WM_DESTROY` message or `CWnd::DestroyWindow()` is called. In the case of a `CView`-derived class, I use the latter. Listing 29.5 shows the code I use to destroy the rendering context. Here, I first delete the context by calling `wglDestroyContext()` with the particular rendering context supplied as a parameter value. Then, if I happen to have created a custom palette, I use the GDI function `DeleteObject()` (through `CWnd`) to actually delete that too. Finally, I call my base class, which in this case is `CView`, to finalize the window's destruction.

LISTING 29.5 OPENGL VIEW DESTRUCTION

```
BOOL CGLView::DestroyWindow()
{
    // Shut down OpenGL by deleting the rendering context
    wglDeleteContext(m_hRC);

    // Delete your custom palette, if any was created
    if ( m_hPalette != NULL ) {
        DeleteObject(m_hPalette);
    } // if

    return CView::DestroyWindow();
}
```

29

MFC AND OPENGL

If you fail to delete the rendering context, you can potentially suffer the same fate as you would when you don't manage GDI objects correctly. That is, you will fill resource memory with useless data (memory leaks) and eventually possibly crash the operating system.

View Sizing

While your application is using an OpenGL rendering context, you'll find it important to manage sizing issues. If the user resizes the window, you must handle resizing the rendering context to match. While handling the WM_SIZE message, you may also want to reset your projection and model matrices, reset your viewport, and re-establish your viewing frustrum. You can see this is a fairly critical operation! Without managing these actions, OpenGL will not render anything at all. At best, you'll see a view painted with the current clear color. My view class uses the code you see in Listing 29.6.

LISTING 29.6   OPENGL VIEW WM_SIZE HANDLER

```
void CGLView::OnSize(UINT nType, int cx, int cy)
{
   CView::OnSize(nType, cx, cy);

   // Change OpenGL's rendering context size and
   // viewing frustrum.
   CClientDC dcClient(this);
   wglMakeCurrent(dcClient.m_hDC,m_hRC);
   glViewport(0,0,cx,cy);
   glMatrixMode(GL_PROJECTION);
   glLoadIdentity();
   glFrustum(-10.0,10.0,-10.0,10.0,18.0,70.0);
   glMatrixMode(GL_MODELVIEW);
   glLoadIdentity();
   glTranslatef(0.0f,0.0f,-35.0f);
   wglMakeCurrent(NULL,NULL);
}
```

There are two areas you might want to customize. The first area involves the viewing frustrum. My OpenGL code typically works with a frustrum size you see in Listing 29.6. This means my model coordinates generally range from -10.0 to +10.0. There is no reason, however, you could not scale the frustrum by another 10 to build your models using coordinates ranging from -100.0 to +100.0. OpenGL will work fine in either case.

Adjusting the frustrum is as simple as replacing the glFrustrum() code you see in Listing 29.6 with this:

```
glFrustrum(-100.0,100.0,-100.0,100.0,180.0,700.0);
```

As you can see, I simply multiplied the values I use by a factor of 10 to create a (seemingly) larger frustrum. Remember if you adjust the frustrum size from what I use here, you must either also adjust the model coordinates accordingly or scale them appropriately when you actually render them.

The second customization area involves setting the viewport. The code in Listing 29.6 simply sets the viewport coordinates from (0,0) to (cx,cy), the new size of the client area window. However, there is nothing in my code that says this area must be square. It could be rectangular, which would distort the models when their coordinates are converted from frustrum coordinates (OpenGL) to window coordinates (Windows device context). I added a feature to the GLMinMDI sample program to enable you to experiment with rendering context sizing, the output of which is shown in Figures 29.7 and 29.8. Figure 29.7 shows the MDI child windows with their viewports set to the height and width of the client area window. Figure 29.8, on the other hand, uses the minimum of either the height or width to specify the lower right-hand corner of the viewport using the code you see in Listing 29.7.

FIGURE 29.7

Viewport settings with distorted output.

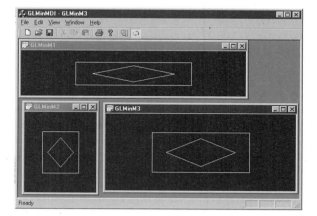

FIGURE 29.8

*Viewport settings
with proportional
output.*

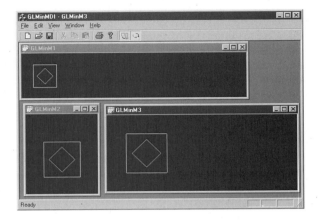

LISTING 29.7   OPENGL VIEW PROPORTIONAL VIEWPORT WM_SIZE HANDLER

```
void CGLMinMDIView::OnSize(UINT nType, int cx, int cy)
{
   CGLView::OnSize(nType, cx, cy);

   // Check for proportional rendering...
   if ( m_bRenderProportional ) {
      // Reset the viewport to render proportionally
      CClientDC dcClient(this);
      wglMakeCurrent(dcClient.m_hDC,m_hRC);
      glViewport(0,0,min(cx,cy), min(cx,cy));
      wglMakeCurrent(NULL,NULL);
   } // if
}
```

I've italicized the particular line of code that handles the viewport differently. Rather than modify my base class's code, I elected to add a WM_SIZE handler to my derived class. The base class's WM_SIZE handler executes the code you saw in Listing 29.6. However, the derived class then has the opportunity to change things, and in this case I make the rendering context current, adjust the viewport to be proportional (if set), and make the context not current. As you can see, I force the viewport to be square by using the same coordinate value for both the right and bottom values of the lower corner. To do this, I use the minimum of either the given cx or cy, which are the width and height of the client area window, respectively. Although this serves to reduce the size of the viewing area, it does provide a nondistorted view when rendering your models.

> **NOTE**
>
> This is but one method of adjusting the rendering context to device context coordinate space mapping. You can also just use `glOrtho()` or `gluPerspective()` to do the same thing.

View Background Erasure

The final view handler you should provide for is background erasure, `WM_ERASEBKGND`. When Windows sends this message to your application, it wants you to completely repaint your background (in some or all of your window's area). When using OpenGL, however, you want OpenGL to manage painting within its rendering context. If you simply accepted the default MFC behavior for `WM_ERASEBKGND`, the OpenGL view would flicker whenever you forced Windows to issue this message (such as when you resize the window). This is because Windows will first resize the window, erase the background using the windows default color (which is usually white), and then finally have OpenGL render its view. Your eyes will catch the brief moment when the screen turns to white, and then turns to the OpenGL clear color you defined when you created your rendering context (which is black for the sample programs in this chapter). To eliminate this flickering, you simply return `TRUE` from your `WM_ ERASEBKGND` handler, as I show in Listing 29.8.

LISTING 29.8 OpenGL `WM_ERASEBKGND` HANDLER

```
BOOL CGLView::OnEraseBkgnd(CDC* pDC)
{
    // Don't erase view...let OpenGL handle
    // that for you...
    return TRUE;
}
```

I added the capability to the GLMinMDI application to enable you to see and test this flickering effect. After you change the flicker handling status (turn it on or off), resize the child window to force Windows to send the `WM_ERASEBKGND` message. See if you see the flicker to which I refer.

View Palette Management

In some cases, such as when running on systems with 256-color video cards, you will need to manage your application's *color palette*. When I say 256-color video card, what I mean is that the video card can only display 256 colors at any one time. Although this may be fine for some applications, it spells disaster for OpenGL output, which is typically rich in color (especially given lighting effects). To help solve this, you must create a custom palette and manage its selection when requested to do so by Windows.

The code I use to create and manage the palette isn't terribly complicated, but I feel it isn't particularly interesting to discuss here. You'd have to wade through several pages of palette theory, when I imagine what you really want to do is create a 3D scene. So, I'll leave it to you to examine the code in any of the provided samples. I'm not trying to avoid a little extra work. I am trying to avoid clouding the true goal of this chapter, which is to introduce you to OpenGL and its capabilities. That you may (or may not) have to manage your application's palette is an implementation detail. Simply use the code you find in the sample programs and you should have no trouble.

Integrate the Custom View Class into Your Application

Now that I've covered the basic steps necessary to integrate OpenGL into a view class, it is time for you to use that view class in your own applications. To do that, you will need to take these measures:

- Add the CGLView class to your project.
- Modify your existing view class to inherit from CGLView.
- Make sure that you add the required libraries to your project's link list. (I'll cover this later.)

The first step is easy. Just copy the GLView.cpp and GLView.h files from any of this chapter's sample programs to your own application's directory. Then, using Developer Studio's menu, select Projects, Add To Project, Files to activate the Windows standard file dialog. After you've done this, navigate to the files' location, select them both in the list control, and click OK. The files will now be added to your compile and link list.

The slightly more difficult chore will be to modify your existing view class to accept the CGLView class as its parent, though this is also nearly trivial after you've done it for the first time. To integrate the GLView into your application, you must perform these two tasks:

- Add this line to your view's definition (.h) file:

  ```
  #include "GLView.h"
  ```

- Search for, and replace, every mention of your view class's original base class with GLView.

The first task is relatively straightforward. Because your view class will now be derived from a new base class, it makes sense that you would need to declare that base class before using it. By including CGLView's definition file within your own view's definition file, you not only declare your base class to the compiler, but you also provide the OpenGL header files to any other C++ class that includes your view's definition file. This can be handy, because you no longer need to constantly include the OpenGL header files. (Note that you will still have to include the OpenGL header files for classes that don't include your view's definition file.)

The second task is only slightly more difficult. I suggest using the Developer Studio's Replace function (menu option Edit, Replace) to reduce the potential number of errors this could introduce into your source code. If your current view class derives directly from CView, you will replace all occurrences of "CView" with "CGLView." If your current view doesn't derive directly from CView, you must follow the procedure I outlined previously to create a new OpenGL-enabled base class, and *then* perform the tasks I mention here. You would need to do this if your current view's base class was CFormView, for example.

After you've integrated CGLView into your current view's source files and compiled successfully, you can add your drawing code (CView::OnDraw()) to see the models you created rendered by OpenGL. This is precisely the topic I'll address in the next section.

Build Your 3D Scene

Now that you've successfully integrated OpenGL into your application, it's time for you to actually build your 3D (or 2D) scene. How you elect to render your models is completely up to you, but MFC and OpenGL will expect them to be provided when processing your OnDraw() function. The MFC AppWizard created the basic OnDraw() member for you; it simply obtained a pointer to the current document and left a *TODO* for you to add the appropriate drawing code. In this case, however, you must provide OpenGL with the appropriate palette (if one was created) and actually render your models. Listing 29.9 shows you one possible drawing alternative, which is the pattern I used for this chapter's sample programs (this listing was taken from GLMin).

LISTING 29.9   CGLView's DEFAULT OnDraw() HANDLER

```
void CGLMinView::OnDraw(CDC* pDC)
{
   CGLMinDoc* pDoc = GetDocument();
   ASSERT_VALID(pDoc);
```

continues

29

MFC AND
OPENGL

LISTING 29.9   CONTINUED

```
// Set your palette
if ( m_hPalette != NULL ) {
    SelectPalette(pDC->m_hDC, m_hPalette, FALSE);
    RealizePalette(pDC->m_hDC);
} // if

// Draw the OpenGL scene
wglMakeCurrent(pDC->m_hDC, m_hRC);
RenderView();
SwapBuffers(pDC->m_hDC);
wglMakeCurrent(pDC->m_hDC, NULL);
}
```

Here, I select and realize the palette my application created when the rendering context was created, if any. Then, I make my application's rendering context the current one, render my view, swap the back buffer for the front, and release my rendering context (make it not current). The nice feature with this approach is that I encapsulate my model rendering code within RenderView(), thus minimizing the effects of model changes to the basic mechanics of OpenGL rendering you see here. Note if you elected not to use double-buffering (by changing the PIXELFORMATDESCRIPTOR settings in CGLView::OnCreate()), you should remove the SwapBuffers() call.

Add the OpenGL Libraries to Your Project's Link List

Now that you have made all the previous changes to your source code, you still will find that the project will not compile and link properly. This is because you must add the OpenGL dynamic link libraries to your project's linker settings. To do this, either right-click on the project's name in the Workspace window and select Settings from the context menu, or select Project, Settings from the Developer Studio menu. In either case, be sure to select All Configurations in the Settings For drop list control.

> **CAUTION**
>
> If you forget to select All Configurations in the settings dialog, you will modify the settings for the current configuration only (which is typically set for a debug build). This will cause linker errors when you select another build type, such as for a release build.

When you have the settings dialog showing and have set the settings for all build configurations, select the Link tab. Under the General linker category, add the following to the Object/Library Modules edit control:

```
OpenGL32.lib GLAux.lib GLU32.lib
```

Now when you compile and link, the OpenGL libraries will automatically link with your project. You are ready to go!

2D and 3D Models

Up to this point, you've been reading the background necessary to use OpenGL. Now, it's time to actually use it to do something interesting. I'm specifically referring to developing your models and composing a 3D scene. A model might be a shaped object, such as a sphere, or it might be an algorithm you develop to create a colorful 3D chart or graph. The methodology many graphics programmers follow is to create the basic model, or models, centered about the origin (0,0,0), and then translate them into position (or rotate, or scale, and so on). If performance is a concern, the models are translated into one or several *display lists*.

Basic Model Development

I'll describe model creation by way of example. If you examine this chapter's GLObject sample program, you will find the code contained in Listing 29.10 buried in the CGLObjectView view class.

LISTING 29.10   OPENGL 3D CUBE MODEL

```
void CGLObjectView::RenderSolidCube()
{
    // Draw as a wireframe (use white always)
    glDisable(GL_LIGHTING);
    glDisable(GL_LIGHT0);
    glColor3f(0.8f, 0.8f, 0.8f);
    glPolygonMode(GL_FRONT_AND_BACK,GL_FILL);
    glEnable(GL_DEPTH_TEST);
    glEnable(GL_POLYGON_SMOOTH);

    // Draw your cube by hand...
    glBegin(GL_POLYGON); // front face of cube
        glVertex3f(-5.0f, 5.0f, 5.0f);
        glVertex3f(-5.0f, -5.0f, 5.0f);
        glVertex3f(5.0f, -5.0f, 5.0f);
```

continues

29

LISTING 29.10   CONTINUED

```
       glVertex3f(5.0f, 5.0f, 5.0f);
   glEnd();

   glBegin(GL_POLYGON); // "back"
       glVertex3f(5.0f, 5.0f, -5.0f);
       glVertex3f(5.0f, -5.0f, -5.0f);
       glVertex3f(-5.0f, -5.0f, -5.0f);
       glVertex3f(-5.0f, 5.0f, -5.0f);
   glEnd();

   glBegin(GL_POLYGON); // "right"
       glVertex3f(5.0f, 5.0f, 5.0f);
       glVertex3f(5.0f, -5.0f, 5.0f);
       glVertex3f(5.0f, -5.0f, -5.0f);
       glVertex3f(5.0f, 5.0f, -5.0f);
   glEnd();

   glBegin(GL_POLYGON); // "left"
       glVertex3f(-5.0f, 5.0f, -5.0f);
       glVertex3f(-5.0f, -5.0f, -5.0f);
       glVertex3f(-5.0f, -5.0f, 5.0f);
       glVertex3f(-5.0f, 5.0f, 5.0f);
   glEnd();

   glBegin(GL_POLYGON); // "bottom"
       glVertex3f(-5.0f, -5.0f, 5.0f);
       glVertex3f(-5.0f, -5.0f, -5.0f);
       glVertex3f(5.0f, -5.0f, -5.0f);
       glVertex3f(5.0f, -5.0f, 5.0f);
   glEnd();

   glBegin(GL_POLYGON); // "top"
       glVertex3f(-5.0f, 5.0f, -5.0f);
       glVertex3f(-5.0f, 5.0f, 5.0f);
       glVertex3f(5.0f, 5.0f, 5.0f);
       glVertex3f(5.0f, 5.0f, -5.0f);
   glEnd();

   // Because you're not using light, it's hard to distinguish
   // the sides, so you'll overlay the wireframe model to
   // make it easier to see...
   RenderWireCube();
}
```

In this case, I have drawn six polygons, one for each side of a cube. I could have drawn one polygon six times, translating and rotating it into place as appropriate, but this is a bit quicker because OpenGL doesn't perform so many floating-point calculations. I'll show you other improvements later when I discuss display lists. In any case, when you execute the GLObject program and select the solid cube object, this code will provide the OpenGL commands to render a solid cube. The cube initially is centered about the origin. If I required multiple cubes to be rendered, I would translate and rotate each into place individually using this same basic model code.

With this model, I begin by deactivating the lighting effects (I'll present these later in this chapter), establishing the basic polygonal color (gray), setting the polygon mode, enabling depth testing, and establishing the polygon shading mode. The `glEnable()` function is used to establish many OpenGL settings, and through it you communicate with the rendering context. These settings remain in effect until you specifically change them by enabling another related setting or disabling the setting entirely using `glDisable()`. Here, I disabled lighting entirely (`GL_LIGHTING`), as well as light number zero specifically (`GL_LIGHT0`).

The polygon mode, set using `glPolygonMode()`, tells OpenGL how to render polygons. Here I used `GL_FRONT_AND_BACK` and `GL_FILL`. This tells OpenGL to color both the front face and the rear face of the polygon (as defined by the order of the vertex definitions) using a color fill. I could have used just `GL_FRONT`, because the cube is closed. However, in many cases you will use `GL_FRONT_AND_BACK`. The reasoning is simple after you've seen how OpenGL handles polygonal rendering. If you rotate the 3D scene such that you are facing the front face of a polygon, the `GL_FRONT` setting will cause the polygon to be filled with color. However, rotate the same view 180 degrees so you are facing the rear of the front face, and you'll find OpenGL didn't render your polygon at all! This is done to save rendering time by reducing calculations. For complex polygonal structures, by all means use `GL_FRONT` if you are sure polygons won't disappear mysteriously from your scene. For general purpose rendering, though, the effects of the calculation overhead are typically not terribly draining, and `GL_FRONT_AND_BACK` mode is usually acceptable.

The polygon fill style I selected is `GL_FILL`. My other options are `GL_POINT` and `GL_LINE`. `GL_POINT` would render the polygonal vertices as points, whereas `GL_LINE` would render the polygon as a wireframe. Note for demonstration purposes the wireframe cube I render in the GLObject sample program is created by hand, not using polygons.

Now that you've created a basic model, it's time to shift it about within your scene. To do this, you'll have OpenGL make the many complex calculations you saw earlier in this chapter. However, you'll soon see the true power of OpenGL—making those calculations is as easy as a single line of code!

29

MFC AND
OPENGL

Model Transformations

When you transform a model, you're affecting the manner in which it is rendered by moving it, rotating it, or scaling it to meet your needs. The general recipe you'll follow is to create your model view matrix, push it, transform your model, render your model, and then pop the model view matrix from the stack to be used again. I'll now discuss each of the transformations individually.

Translation

When you translate, you move. Most models, for simplicity, are created at the origin. After all, it's much easier to describe a cube when the origin sits at its center than it is if the cube is located so many units up the x-axis and so many units down the y-axis. It's the same size cube; it's just been moved.

Models are translated using glTranslatef():

```
glPushMatrix();
   // Translate this sphere into place
   glTranslatef(5.0,5.0,-5.0f);

   // Draw a sphere
   auxSolidSphere(2.0);

// Restore your matrix
glPopMatrix ();
```

This code renders a sphere 5 units to the right (x-axis), 5 units up (y-axis), and 5 units further back (z-axis). As you see, I save my matrix, translate, render, and then restore my matrix.

Rotation

Rotation follows a similar vein, but there is a twist. When you translate, you specify a point of translation (actually, a *translation vector*, but you can think of it as a point in space). You specify the x, y, and z coordinates and the object gets translated there.

Rotation, however, is different in that you are specifying rotation vectors about which your object will be rotated. For example, this code rotates a dodecahedron first about the x-axis, and then about the y-axis:

```
// Save your model view matrix
glPushMatrix();
   // Spin the dodec for effect
   glRotatef(fXRotate, 1.0f, 0.0f, 0.0f);
   glRotatef(fYRotate, 0.0f, 1.0f, 0.0f);

   // Draw the dodec
```

```
   auxSolidDodecahedron(2.0);

// Restore your matrix
glPopMatrix();
```

The previous rotation is not the same as this:

```
// Save your model view matrix
glPushMatrix();
   // Spin the dodec for effect
   glRotatef(fXYRotate, 1.0f, 1.0f, 0.0f);

   // Draw the dodec
   auxSolidDodecahedron(2.0);

// Restore your matrix
glPopMatrix();
```

The first case spun the dodecahedron about the x-axis, then the y-axis. The second case spun the dodecahedron about a vector 45 degrees between the positive x- and y-axes. You can't mix rotations as you could translations!

In both cases, though, I used `glRotatef()` to perform the rotation. The first parameter is an angle of rotation, and the last three form the rotation vector about which the object will be rotated.

Scaling

When you scale an object, you're simply enlarging or shrinking it. It's common practice to build models to a standard size, say enclosed in a 1×1×1 cube. Then, when you need the model, you simply make it the size you want by using `glScalef()`. Here is an example that enlarges a cube 50%:

```
// Save your model view matrix
glPushMatrix();
   // Scale the cube to fit this scene size context.
   glScalef(1.50f,1.50f,1.50f);

   // Draw the cube
   auxSolidCube();

// Restore your matrix
glPopMatrix();
```

Note that there is no requirement to enlarge all sides equally. This code would make a cube a rectoid:

```
// Save your model view matrix
glPushMatrix();
   // Scale the cube to fit this scene size context.
```

```
    glScalef(5.00f,1.50f,1.50f);

    // Draw the cube
    auxSolidCube();

// Restore your matrix
glPopMatrix();
```

The object would be elongated (500%) on the x-axis, but it would be stretched only 50% down the y- and z-axes. If you're using light effects (and have calculated polygonal surface normals), you may want to also scale the normals. OpenGL will manage this for you if you enable automatic normalization:

```
glEnable(GL_NORMALIZE);
```

In this case, if any distortion would affect your surface normals, OpenGL will correct those normals for you (assuming you specified them to begin with!).

Now that you've seen how to build models, as well as how to move them into place within your 3D scene, it's time to think about packaging your models for ease of use and optimization. OpenGL provides a nice mechanism for doing just this—the OpenGL display list.

Display Lists

One optimization commonly used is to compile OpenGL commands into a *display list*. A display list is nothing more than a series of OpenGL commands rolled into the rendering context. Instead of executing your code to render a model, you tell the rendering context itself to retrieve and render one of its display lists. This is far more efficient, as the display list is stored in an OpenGL-friendly (easy to access and render) format within the rendering context.

> **TIP**
>
> It isn't precisely accurate to say the rendering context stores the display list. The list is compiled and stored in memory where the rendering context may access it later. This facilitates list sharing, whereby you share lists among rendering contexts (assuming you have more than one available). See `wglShareLists()` for details.

If you only realized performance improvements by using display lists, it would probably be enough reason to use them. As it happens, though, creating a display list is no more difficult than creating your model in the first place. Two OpenGL functions, glNewList() and glEndList(), mark the beginning and ending of the display list declaration. Listing 29.11, from the GLScene sample program, shows you the same type of basic code I used earlier in the chapter to render a solid cube. With the exception of hard-coding the normal vectors, I used the typical glBegin()/glEnd() pairings to create each of the six sides. All of the cube code is now encapsulated between the display list declaration pair glNewList() and glEndList().

glNewList() marks the beginning of the display list and requires two parameters. The first, a GLuint, is simply used as the display list *name* (even though it's an integer value). OpenGL will use the name to look up the list index so it might render the list when called upon to do so. In Listing 29.11, I defined the value SOLIDCUBE, the list's name, to be the value 32. The second parameter is the *mode*, and it can have two values, GL_COMPILE and GL_COMPILE_AND_EXECUTE. GL_COMPILE is used to preinitialize the display list without executing the commands it contains. GL_COMPILE_AND_EXECUTE, on the other hand, not only initializes the display list but also executes the contained commands.

LISTING 29.11 GLSCENE'S SOLID CUBE DISPLAY LIST

```
// Begin a display list for a solid cube
glNewList(SOLIDCUBE,GL_COMPILE);
    // You are free to place nearly any OpenGL command
    // in a display list.  You could, for example,
    // set the color here.  However, I elected to set
    // the color when I render, thus allowing me to
    // have the flexibility.
    glBegin(GL_POLYGON);
        // I could have calculated the normal vector, but
        // we know what it should be, so I simply set it
        // in this case.
        glNormal3f(0.0f,0.0f,1.0f);
        glVertex3f(1.0f,1.0f,1.0f);
        glVertex3f(-1.0f,1.0f,1.0f);
        glVertex3f(-1.0f,-1.0f,1.0f);
        glVertex3f(1.0f,-1.0f,1.0f);
    glEnd();

    glBegin(GL_POLYGON);
        glNormal3f(0.0f,0.0f,-1.0);
        glVertex3f(1.0f,1.0f,-1.0f);
        glVertex3f(1.0f,-1.0f,-1.0f);
        glVertex3f(-1.0f,-1.0f,-1.0f);
        glVertex3f(-1.0f,1.0f,-1.0f);
    glEnd();

    glBegin(GL_POLYGON);
```

29

MFC AND OPENGL

```
       glNormal3f(-1.0,0.0f,0.0f);
       glVertex3f(-1.0f,1.0f,1.0f);
       glVertex3f(-1.0f,1.0f,-1.0f);
       glVertex3f(-1.0f,-1.0f,-1.0f);
       glVertex3f(-1.0f,-1.0f,1.0f);
   glEnd();

   glBegin(GL_POLYGON);
       glNormal3f(1.0,0.0f,0.0f);
       glVertex3f(1.0f,1.0f,1.0f);
       glVertex3f(1.0f,-1.0f,1.0f);
       glVertex3f(1.0f,-1.0f,-1.0f);
       glVertex3f(1.0f,1.0f,-1.0f);
   glEnd();

   glBegin(GL_POLYGON);
       glNormal3f(0.0f,1.0,0.0f);
       glVertex3f(-1.0f,1.0f,-1.0f);
       glVertex3f(-1.0f,1.0f,1.0f);
       glVertex3f(1.0f,1.0f,1.0f);
       glVertex3f(1.0f,1.0f,-1.0f);
   glEnd();

   glBegin(GL_POLYGON);
       glNormal3f(0.0f,-1.0,0.0f);
       glVertex3f(-1.0f,-1.0f,-1.0f);
       glVertex3f(1.0f,-1.0f,-1.0f);
       glVertex3f(1.0f,-1.0f,1.0f);
       glVertex3f(-1.0f,-1.0f,1.0f);
   glEnd();
glEndList(); // SOLIDCUBE
```

After you've created your display list, you render it by using the `glCallList()` command:

```
glCallList(SOLIDCUBE);
```

When you execute the stored command list, the state of the OpenGL rendering context will be used (and applied) to the commands. Essentially, this means any matrix work, color, work, lighting work, and so on you perform prior to calling the display list will be in effect when the stored rendering commands are issued. This cube is created at the origin and is 1×1×1 units in size. But by using `glScale()`, though, I could make it any size I required. In fact, I do precisely this when I create the 3D scene in the GLScene sample program. I create nine cubes, each of which is scaled, translated, and rotated individually as it is placed within the scene (see Figure 29.9).

Figure 29.9

GLScene's program display.

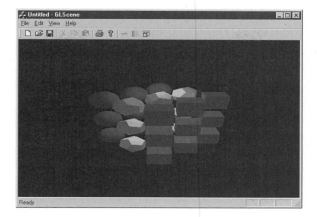

The code to render the cubes in the scene is shown in Listing 29.12. As you can see, I establish the cube's color (red), translate, rotate, *and* scale it before it gets rendered.

Listing 29.12   Rendering the Cube Display List

```
GLfloat glfMaterialColorCubes[] =
➥{ 1.0f, 0.0f, 0.0f, 1.0f };
glMaterialfv(GL_FRONT,GL_AMBIENT_AND_DIFFUSE,
➥glfMaterialColorCubes);

// Save your model view matrix
glPushMatrix();
   // Translate this cube into place
   glTranslatef((GLfloat)x,(GLfloat)y,5.0f);

   // Spin the cube for effect
   glRotatef (m_fYRotate, 0.0f, 1.0f, 0.0f);

   // Scale it (originates as a 1x1x1 cube, so
   // scale it to fit this scene size context).
   glScalef(1.50f,1.50f,1.50f);

   // Draw the cube
   glCallList(SOLIDCUBE);

// Restore your matrix
glPopMatrix();
```

29

MFC AND
OPENGL

> **NOTE**
>
> If you use the auxiliary OpenGL library to display shapes in your scene, be aware the auxiliary library will take the list names from 1 to the number of different auxiliary shapes you are using. These names, in that case, are not available for you to use. For example, GLScene uses the sphere and dodecahedron shapes, so list names 1 and 2 are not available to GLShape for locally defined display lists. If you forget and use an existing display list name, you won't receive an error, but neither will you render the correct model.

> **TIP**
>
> A handy OpenGL command to use with display lists is `glGetError()`. If you execute your program and don't see any output from the display list, it's likely there was an OpenGL error while creating the list. By calling `glGetError()`, you can at least look up the error code and have some idea where to start fixing the problem. The Visual C++ 6 online help file is helpful here because it lists the possible error codes and potential causes.

When you allocate memory, you must deallocate it. It is no different with OpenGL's display lists. You allocate display list memory using `glNewList()`. You must deallocate memory using `glDeleteLists()`. `glDeleteLists()` takes two parameters. The first specifies the list name to delete. The second tells OpenGL how many lists to destroy. You might destroy a single list, or you might destroy several depending upon your needs at the time.

Now that you've seen how to build, transform, and display your models, it's time to bring your scene to life. I believe nothing does more for a given 3D scene than to add lighting effects, and that's what I'll cover next.

Light

Few things in OpenGL are more complicated than light, but then, few things can be as spectacular when you get it right. In this section I'll explain how graphics programmers view light as a physical entity, and then I'll show you how light is modeled in OpenGL.

If you're a physicist, you might view light as both particle and wave. Theoretical physicists see light as a view into the universe's past. But graphics programmers see light as a calculation. A commonly used light model calculates the light intensity at any point on the surface of an object, as shown in Figure 29.10.

FIGURE 29.10

A light intensity equation.

$$I = I_aK_a + \sum_{j=0}^{m-1}[K_d(\mathbf{N}\bullet\mathbf{i}_j) + K_s(\mathbf{R}_j\bullet\mathbf{V})^n]$$

I don't show you this equation to scare you. (I'm not even going to try to explain it in detail!) It's here to give you an appreciation for the immense number of calculations required to render a properly shaded object given light sources. There is a lot under OpenGL's hood. I also presented it here to ease any concerns you might have about using lit 3D scenes. Don't worry—your first 3D scene attempt absolutely *will not* look right the first time. You'll probably have to try and try again to get things just as you want them to be. Such a complicated equation is the reason behind the difficult nature of light calculations.

However, it is possible to break this equation down and tackle the individual components separately. Dividing and conquering is a perfectly valid way to master OpenGL lighting.

The Basics of Light in OpenGL

Before I crack the light equation and begin flinging imaginary photons, you should know the mechanics of light and how things are described when using OpenGL. Using light sources in OpenGL is as easy as enabling certain settings in your rendering context. Which settings and how they are applied is the secret.

Before OpenGL will calculate lighting effects, you must enable the OpenGL lighting state. To do this, you use glEnable() with the GL_LIGHTING parameter. glDisable() with the same parameter deactivates the lighting state. This acts as a global circuit breaker for the light model. If GL_LIGHTING is disabled, none of your models will show the effects of light. In general, you'll also want to make sure GL_DEPTH_TEST is enabled. This causes OpenGL to make depth calculations when rendering polygons so objects closer to the eye point properly obscure more distant objects. Light serves to enhance that illusion.

OpenGL provides you with a total of eight light sources. These eight light sources, GL_LIGHT0 through GL_LIGHT7, may either be distant light sources, like the sun, or *point* light sources, such as lamps or spotlights. To "turn on" one of these light sources, you use glEnable() with the OpenGL enumeration (GL_LIGHT0, and so on) as the parameter. Similarly, you "turn off" the light source using glDisable(). Easy so far.

Each of the eight light sources has a position in 3D space. The position is recorded in the usual (x,y,z,w) form, but the w parameter is used to dictate the type of light source, positional (non-zero) or directional (0.0). Directional light is light from a far distant source that travels parallel to the vector formed by the given (x,y,z) values. Positional light, on the other hand, is more like a lamp. In that case, the (x,y,z) coordinate is the location of the lamp in 3D space.

If you are using a positional light, you have control over many of the light's properties. For example, you might specify the light source as a spotlight with a given cutoff angle or attenuation factor. See `glLightfv()` in the online help for more details, though I use a positional light in the GLObject sample program included with this chapter.

Types of Light

The light equation I presented earlier is composed of several terms. Each term in the equation represents a type of light. The sum intensity is the total of the terms in the equation; therefore, each type of light contributes some partial light intensity to the whole. By adding or removing the equation's terms, I modify a given object's appearance when OpenGL renders it. This, now, is the hard part. Getting this blend of light terms correct for your particular scene will usually be the challenge.

Ambient Light

The first term of the equation represents the ambient light present in your scene. The fact that it stands outside the summation tells you it is constant no matter how many additional light sources are present to illuminate your scene. Ambient light has this basic property: all of the light rays strike the object in parallel.

To see an example of ambient light, simply walk outside. If it's a sunny day, there is plenty of ambient light (from the sun). If it's a cloudy or rainy day, the ambient term is relatively smaller than it was on the sunny day, so there is less total light available to your eyes (even to the point you lose color perception). If it's night, there is probably very little ambient light available except on a clear night with a full moon.

Ambient light, and actually all of the other various types of light, is composed of red, green, and blue color intensities. If each of the three colors is present at roughly equal levels, the resulting light is white (or gray, if the overall intensity is low). If any one is greater than the others, that color will begin to dominate, and your scene will have additional color intensity in that color range. That is, if the ambient light is predominantly red, your objects will appear reddish, or at least have a reddish tint.

You establish the basic ambient color when you use the `glLightfv()` command:

```
GLfloat fLightAmbient0[4] { 1.0f, 1.0f, 1.0f, 1.0f };
glLightfv(GL_LIGHT0,GL_AMBIENT, fLightAmbient0);
```

Here, I specify which light I refer to (GL_LIGHT0), the type of light I want to adjust (GL_AMBIENT), and what the color intensities for the light are (fLightAmbient0).

Diffuse Light

Diffuse light forms the second term in the equation (the first term after the summation). This term is a vectored term, so the position of the light affects how the object appears. This is the first term where the *surface normal* is critical. If the light strikes the object parallel to the surface normal, you get the most intense reflection from the object. Light that strikes perpendicular (at 90 degrees) to the surface normal yields no additional light intensity at that point on the object's surface.

To see diffuse light in effect, take a dull object (a rubber basketball, for example) into a dark room and shine a flashlight upon its surface from a short distance. The surface of the basketball is illuminated most brightly at the point to which the flashlight is aimed. Surface points radiating away from there are not illuminated as brightly. The sides of the basketball aren't lit at all (a location about where your hand would be if you held the ball in one hand and the flashlight in the other). At this point, the light rays are coming in at 90 degrees to the basketball, so they contribute no light intensity there.

You can specify your light source have a diffuse component by using the glLightfv() command again:

```
GLfloat fLightDiffuse0[4] = { 0.5f, 0.5f, 0.5f, 1.0f };
glLightfv(GL_LIGHT0,GL_DIFFUSE,fLightDiffuse0);
```

These commands establish the diffuse term for light zero's intensity contribution to the overall diffuse tendencies of the objects it illuminates. Brighter lights use higher values for the components (the values in fLightDiffuse0). Again, there is no requirement that the individual color intensities be equal. You could have more blue, for example, shining on your objects if that's the effect you sought.

Specular Light

The final term in the light equation is the *specular* content. Specular light imprints a mirror image of the light source onto the surface of the object (or tries to; it depends on the object's material properties as well). Essentially, specular light makes objects appear shiny.

If you were to take a shiny metal ball into your dark room with your flashlight instead of a basketball, you would see the specular light component as a shiny spot on the surface of the metal ball directly parallel to the flashlight's beam. It's usually seen as a bright white spot on an otherwise colored object. The spot is intensely white at the point where the light strikes parallel to the surface normal, but it attenuates quickly as the surface normal's angle rolls off towards the perpendicular of the surface vector.

As with the other light components, you establish a specular content to your light using `glLightfv()`:

```
fLightSpecular0[0] = { 1.0f, 1.0f, 1.0f, 1.0f };
glLightfv(GL_LIGHT0,GL_SPECULAR,fLightSpecular0);
```

Specular light, and to a greater or lesser degree, diffuse light illuminate materials differently depend on the material they are striking. Some objects appear dull no matter how much light you shine upon them, whereas others reflect brilliantly with almost no light. This effect is controlled by the material properties of the object in question.

Object Material Properties

Just as light sources have different light intensity content, objects *reflect* different components of light differently depending upon their individual material properties. A chrome object will reflect far more light than dirt or grass. Further, chrome objects, and mirrors in general, reflect the incoming light perfectly, or nearly so. Grass and dirt, on the other hand, only reflect certain color intensities no matter what color of light is applied. The grass *is* greener than chrome because grass absorbs all incoming light spectra *but* green. Chrome reflects it all.

Therefore, it may not be surprising to find you have material properties similar to the light source properties you specified earlier. A given object *reflects* ambient, diffuse, and spectral light. It may also *emit* light as well.

> **TIP**
>
> It may be helpful to remember this when dealing with light in OpenGL that polygons don't have color. Rather, they reflect light of certain color intensities. If your object's material reflects mostly red ambient light, it will appear red when rendered in ambient light with some red light intensity.

Setting Object Material Properties

Setting an individual object's material properties is quite similar to setting a light source's light properties. However, instead of using `glLightfv()`, you would use `glMaterialfv()`. For example, to have an object appear blue (reflect blue ambient light), you might use code similar to this:

```
GLfloat fMaterialAmbient[4] = { 0.0f, 0.0f, 1.0f, 1.0f };
glMaterialfv(GL_FRONT,GL_AMBIENT_AND_DIFFUSE,fMaterialAmbient);
```

In this case, the object would reflect all blue light. If your light source contained some blue light, you would see this object. If not (you had a red light source), the object would appear black if you saw it at all.

Color Tracking

To ease things somewhat, OpenGL implements *color tracking*, which you can enable or not as your requirements dictate. You may set the individual material properties for a given object, as you saw in the last section, or you can elect to track the light source's color. To enable color tracking, use these OpenGL commands:

```
glEnable(GL_COLOR_MATERIAL);
glColorMaterial(GL_FRONT,GL_AMBIENT_AND_DIFFUSE);
```

Now, you may simply specify a color for your polygons using `glColor()`. OpenGL handles the calculations for you. Although you can get very precise results by not using color tracking, color tracking has the advantage OpenGL executes faster when color tracking is enabled. This becomes critical when you start dealing with objects with many, many polygons.

Both the GLObject and GLScene sample programs implement lighting effects. In the next section, I'll turn to another effect you can employ to give your objects the illusion of reality—texture mapping.

Texture Mapping

Texture mapping is a process where you apply a bitmap (the decal) to a polygon to make the polygon appear more realistic. In this manner you seemingly exceed the capabilities of OpenGL polygon rendering to create stunning scenes. Figure 29.11 shows you a texture-mapped cube from the GLTexCube sample program.

FIGURE 29.11

Texture-mapped (spinning) cube.

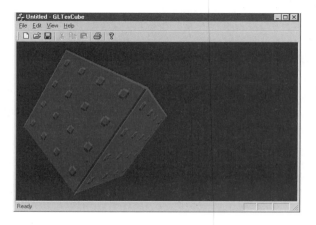

OpenGL Images and Windows Device-Independent Bitmaps

Unfortunately, not all computer systems store and display images in the same manner. As OpenGL strives to be portable, it had to implement its own form of image storage. Not too surprisingly, this storage format doesn't correspond with the Windows format, the Device Independent Bitmap or DIB.

When you use OpenGL texture mapping, you must perform three steps:

1. Load your Windows image into memory.
2. Map (copy) your Windows image into OpenGL's representation.
3. Apply the texture to a polygon.

I've encapsulated the first step in a class you can simply use. The details of Windows DIB storage are beyond the scope of this chapter; simply use the CDIBHolder class as I've shown in the GLTextCube sample program to contain your bitmap. The class has a member that takes a filename, and from there it loads the file, extracts what it requires, and saves the DIB in memory until you need it.

The more interesting step, at least for this section, is step two. You'll look at the final step, applying the texture, in the next section. Here, though, you need to map the DIB's storage format to OpenGL's image storage format. To do that, you will create a color table and use glPixelMapfv() to actually copy the colors from the DIB to your rendering context. Then when you actually apply the texture, the color map in the rendering context will handle the color associations for you. Listing 29.13 shows how to map colors.

LISTING 29.13 DIB TO OPENGL COLOR MAPPING

```
void CGLTexCubeView::InitColorTables()
{
   LPRGBQUAD pColorTable = m_CDIBHolder.GetDIBRGBTable();

   // Copy the colors used by the DIB to class local
   // storage.
   for( int i = 0; i <= 255; ++i ) {
      m_rgbRed[i]   = (GLfloat)pColorTable[i].rgbRed / 255;
      m_rgbGreen[i] = (GLfloat)pColorTable[i].rgbGreen / 255;
      m_rgbBlue[i]  = (GLfloat)pColorTable[i].rgbBlue / 255;
   } // for

   // Map the colors for OpenGL to use
   CClientDC dcClient(this);
   wglMakeCurrent(dcClient.m_hDC, m_hRC);
```

```
    glPixelMapfv(GL_PIXEL_MAP_I_TO_R,256,m_rgbRed);
    glPixelMapfv(GL_PIXEL_MAP_I_TO_G,256,m_rgbGreen);
    glPixelMapfv(GL_PIXEL_MAP_I_TO_B,256,m_rgbBlue);
    glPixelTransferi(GL_MAP_COLOR,TRUE);

    wglMakeCurrent(dcClient.m_hDC, m_hRC);
}
```

> **NOTE**
>
> OpenGL requires the texture image to have a width and height that is a power of 2. Also, because of the mapping mode I used, your images must be composed of 256 colors (no more, no less).

After you've loaded a bitmap file, you can extract the image's color information. This information is stored in the RGB table—which was retrieved using `CDIBHolder::GetDIBRGBTable()`. You then build red, green, and blue color arrays to store the individual colors used to display the bitmap. Then, after making the rendering context current, you actually map the DIB colors to OpenGL's color mapping table using `glPixelMapfv()`. After you've mapped the red, green, and blue colors, you call `glPixelTransferi()` to establish the pixel transfer mode you will use when you actually apply the texture to the polygon. When I say *pixel transfer*, I mean just that—pixels will be transferred from the DIB storage to the rendering context as determined by the pixel transfer mode. Here, you're doing a simple color mapping. Because you established the color map using the original DIB colors, the resulting texture should appear to be the same as the original DIB. There is no requirement to map the colors in this manner, but this is the most common use of color mapping in OpenGL. Now I'll apply the texture to a polygon.

Applying Texture

At this point, you have a bitmap loaded into memory and a color map established to marry the DIB's colors to your OpenGL rendering context. Now it is time to apply the texture. To do this, you locate the DIB's data in memory, as well as determine the width and height of the image, and then call OpenGL's `glTexImage2D()` command to create a OpenGL image (see Listing 29.14). The image is applied to your polygon when it is rendered (in this case I use a display list).

29

MFC AND
OPENGL

LISTING 29.14 RENDERING A TEXTURED POLYGON

```
void CGLTexCubeView::RenderView()
{
    GLvoid* pTextureBits = (GLvoid*) m_CDIBHolder.GetDIBBits();
    GLint iDIBWidth = m_CDIBHolder.Width();
    GLint iDIBHeight = m_CDIBHolder.Height();

    glTexImage2D(GL_TEXTURE_2D,0,3,iDIBWidth,iDIBHeight,
    0,GL_COLOR_INDEX,GL_UNSIGNED_BYTE,pTextureBits);

    glClear(GL_COLOR_BUFFER_BIT ¦ GL_DEPTH_BUFFER_BIT);

    glPushMatrix();
        // Scale it a bit
        glScalef(10.0f, 10.0f, 10.0f);

        // Rotate it
        glRotatef(m_yRotate,0.0f,1.0f,1.0f);

        // Render it
        glCallList(TEXCUBE);
    glPopMatrix();

    glFlush();
}
```

You tell OpenGL *how* to apply the texture *to* the polygon by specifying a texture coordinate with each of your polygon's coordinates:

```
glBegin(GL_POLYGON); // "front"
    glTexCoord2f(0.0f, 1.0f);
    glVertex3f(-1.0f, 1.0f, 1.0f);
    glTexCoord2f(0.0f, 0.0f);
    glVertex3f(-1.0f, -1.0f, 1.0f);
    glTexCoord2f(1.0f, 0.0f);
    glVertex3f(1.0f, -1.0f, 1.0f);
    glTexCoord2f(1.0f, 1.0f);
    glVertex3f(1.0f, 1.0f, 1.0f);
glEnd();
```

Here I create a cube face, and with each cube vertex, I assign a texture vertex. When OpenGL encounters the vertex mapping (when rendering the cube), it will transfer the pixels from the image it has (created using glTexImage2D()) to the rendering context, thus filling your polygon with the textured image. For the final OpenGL topic, I'll present a couple of special effects you can use to enhance your graphical scene—alpha blending and fog.

Special Effects

OpenGL is capable of rendering many interesting effects, and I'd like to briefly touch on two of them here. You can see both of these implemented in the GLScene sample program included with this chapter. The first, blending, is a mechanism to make objects transparent, or at least increase and decrease their relative transparency. The second cool effect is fog. Fog blends your objects into the specified fog color, thus making them disappear into the fog over some distance.

Blending

Blending, or specifically *alpha blending*, is used to render objects with some amount of transparency. You may have noticed on occasion in this chapter that I used color values with four components. The first three were the standard red, green, and blue. Nothing particularly noteworthy there. The fourth color value, however, was the alpha value. It ranges from 0 to 1, with 0 being invisible and 1 being totally visible. Values somewhere in between allow the object to be seen, but objects that would normally be culled (not seen because they would normally be hidden) will be seen through the alpha object. The "blending" comes into play because the colors of the background objects are blended into the colors of the foreground objects—how much blending will depend upon the alpha setting for each object.

You enable blending by using glEnable() with the GL_BLEND parameter and by specifying a blending function:

```
glEnable(GL_BLEND);
glBlendFunc(GL_SRC_ALPHA,GL_ONE_MINUS_SRC_ALPHA);
```

There are many settings for the OpenGL glBlendFunc() command, but what I've shown you here is usually the best combination, for theoretical reasons. (If you're interested, see glBlendFunc() in the online documentation). The resulting blending function is the most precise and one of the fastest true blending functions (there are trivial cases that would be faster).

In any case, after you've enabled blending, it's best to render your objects from rear to front. This will result in the best possible resulting color being transferred to your window. Any object rendered after blending is activated has blending applied, and blending remains in effect until you disable it. Figure 29.12 shows you the GLScene example with the alpha blended cube active.

FIGURE 29.12

GLScene with alpha blended cube activated.

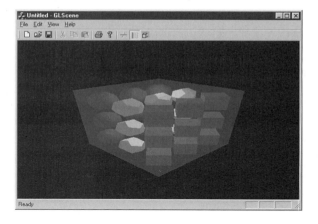

Fog

If you are interested in simulating a true 3D scene, such as an outdoor scene with weather, you can tell OpenGL to apply a *fog* effect that makes the scene appear as if it were really in a foggy weather pattern. It's also quite easy to use. You simply specify a fog color (typically white or light gray) and the type of fog you want to apply. Then, you let OpenGL do the hard work of remapping the individual object color to the fog color, as you see in Figure 29.13.

FIGURE 29.13

GLScene with fog activated.

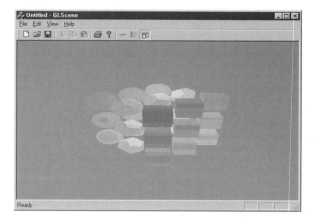

OpenGL offers three types of fog—linear, exponential rolloff, and exponential squared rolloff. That is, OpenGL will automatically change the colors of the objects it renders to take into account fog effects. You tell OpenGL what type of fog effect you want.

With linear fog, OpenGL applies the fog color evenly to all objects regardless of their distance from the eye point (the imaginary location from where you are viewing the scene). This would be fine for thick fog, but otherwise it isn't too realistic (it may be useful for simulating other effects, such as dimming the light available to the scene). It is less computationally intensive, however.

A more realistic fog effect, though, is *exponential rolloff*. In this case, distant objects blend into the fog (and eventually disappear), but closer objects retain some of their color. The closer they are to the eye point, the more of their color they retain. The difference between the exponential rolloff and the exponential squared rolloff is that the squared version shows a more pronounced effect. I elected to use the squared version to demonstrate fog effects in the GLScene sample program.

Using fog effects is very straightforward:

```
GLfloat m_fFogColor[4] = { 1.0f, 1.0f, 1.0f, 1.0f };
glEnable(GL_FOG);
glFogf(GL_FOG_DENSITY,0.03f);
glFogi(GL_FOG_MODE,GL_EXP2);
glFogfv(GL_FOG_COLOR,m_fFogColor);
glClearColor(0.6f,0.6f,0.6f,0.0f); // gray
```

Here I enable fog using `glEnable()`, set the fog density (how thick it is), set the mode (`GL_EXP2` for more pronounced effect) and set the fog color (white, in this case). OpenGL will blend the colors of the objects, near to far, with the fog color. Closer objects will have less of the fog color blended in than far objects, which will be rendered completely white if they're distant enough. Because fog has no effect on the background, I also set the background clear color to light gray. If I didn't do this, the background would remain black while the objects were rendered with fog, which doesn't look quite right.

Summary

With this, you have completed your look at OpenGL using MFC. Although the samples I've presented are quite simplified, the capabilities OpenGL offers are stunning in the extreme. Armed with some theoretical background and a few relatively modest function calls, OpenGL can become as simple as a tool to render 3D scenes or as complex as a 3D flight simulation. The possibilities are truly limitless, as many 3D games on the contemporary game market suggest. However, there is more to the 3D story. In the next chapter, you'll examine Microsoft's version of a high-performance graphics programmer's interface, DirectX.

MFC and DirectX

by Kenn Scribner

IN THIS CHAPTER

CHAPTER 30

Many aspects of application development set the truly professional job apart from the rest. One aspect that is surprisingly easy to exploit is the addition of colorful, fast graphics, sound, auxiliary input devices, and such. In this chapter, you'll explore the basics of Microsoft's multimedia extension library, DirectX, and you'll examine in particular DirectDraw, which targets graphics. Let's begin with a brief history lesson.

What Is DirectX?

Not so many years ago, Microsoft released the Game SDK in response to claims that Windows didn't offer game developers a viable platform for high-performance game execution. In fact, game developers had a point—Windows wasn't a good platform for high frame rate animation. Windows was (and is) a wonderful platform for software development because it provides you, the developer, with a platform-independent architecture. By and large, you are unconcerned with the specifics of any individual system. You program to the idealized Windows model, and Windows will handle the specific system details for you.

But platform independence always comes at a cost, and in this case (to the game developers, anyway), it was throttled animation frame rates. That is, the Windows GDI simply couldn't update the screen as fast as game developers required. Their games, therefore, were slow and sluggish, and Windows was pretty much abandoned as a game platform. Developers instead turned to DOS as their architecture of choice for the hottest games of the day (remember Doom?)

Of course, this was at a time in history when Microsoft was trying to wean the computer market off DOS. They had to invent some mechanism for high-performance animation (and later input and sound) if they wanted the game community to abandon DOS in favor of Windows. The Game SDK was Microsoft's initial answer. Today, the Game SDK has grown into the DirectX family of developer APIs. I won't be teaching game programming in this chapter. Instead, I'll concentrate on explaining DirectX technology. I'll specifically describe techniques to use DirectDraw (a major piece of DirectX) from within your own applications to enhance your application's capabilities and feature sets.

> **TIP**
>
> Don't believe for a moment that DirectX is only suited for game programming. Because of its performance-minded approach, it is an ideal technological choice for adding multimedia features to any application.

DirectX in a Nutshell

DirectX is a COM-based system that transcends both driver-level and application-level software layers. The main DirectX design goal was to be fast while still offering a measure of device independence. Microsoft achieved this by implementing the architecture you see in Figure 30.1. Here, you have the choice of using the full-flavored Windows API, or you can take the leaner and meaner DirectX path.

FIGURE 30.1

The DirectX architecture.

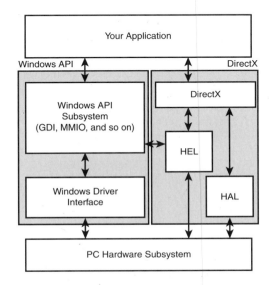

If you look specifically at the DirectX portion of Figure 30.1, you see two main components: the *HAL* and the *HEL*. HAL, or *Hardware Abstraction Layer* (a term no doubt borrowed from Windows NT) is responsible for determining the capabilities of the local hardware and offering them to you in a device-independent fashion. For those capabilities DirectX offers but that aren't supported by the local hardware configuration, the HEL, or *Hardware Emulation Layer*, takes over. On any given system, DirectX uses a blend of HAL and HEL functionality, though you do have the option of forcing DirectX to use only HEL functions. This would present your application with a worst-case performance scenario, which is well suited for development. If your application performs well with little to no special hardware support, it will perform well no matter what the configuration in the field.

30

MFC AND DIRECTX

DirectX Components

DirectX provides you with several components optimized to work with their respective subsystem. The first DirectX component, and probably the most well-known, is *DirectDraw*. DirectDraw provides you with the mechanisms you require to bypass the Windows GDI in favor of faster bitmap data transfers and the resulting higher animation frame rates. But drawing functions alone weren't enough for the gaming community, so Microsoft developed *DirectSound*, *DirectInput*, *DirectPlay*, and *DirectSetup*. There is also another component added more recently than the rest—*Direct3D*.

DirectSound enables you to transcend the Win32 `PlaySound()` API call by giving you access to hardware-based (or -emulated) sound mixing capability with the added feature of 3D sound emulation. Sound mixing enables you to generate a single sound stream from many simultaneous (stored) sound inputs. This clearly has benefit to the game development community, as games frequently require multiple sound tracks. The added benefit of directional sound is especially intriguing.

DirectInput is used to gather input device feedback, such as when using a keyboard, a joystick, or some other tracking device. And starting with DirectX Version 5, you not only receive inputs *from* a device, but you can also send outputs *to* the device to simulate force applied against the input device. This is known as *force feedback*. This would enable you to run a flight simulation on your computer and feel the yoke push back during simulated high-G maneuvers. Many game developers find this feature exciting, as it adds a tremendous amount of realism to their simulations and games.

DirectPlay adds the multiuser perspective to your application. If you've ever seen online games, you know the game participants all want to annihilate each other, and it's much more satisfying to them when they blow away a live player's character versus a computer-generated one. But gaming issues aside, imagine the possibilities for your application if you enable your users to connect to each other and collaborate. DirectPlay makes this quite easy to implement.

DirectSetup is the mechanism you use to install DirectX on systems that don't currently have DirectX capability. This currently includes Windows 95 installations only, however. Windows 98 is shipped with DirectX (upgrades may be possible when available, though) and Windows NT computers require DirectX to be installed through NT Service Packs only (security being a primary concern here).

Direct3D is built upon DirectDraw, so it uses many of the primitives DirectDraw provides you. It offers an alternative to other 3D programming APIs, including OpenGL. Inside Direct3D, you'll find the basic 3D programming support as well as some high-end 3D technology you don't commonly see in other PC-based APIs (high-end texture mapping, for example).

Given this high-level tour of DirectX, it's time to see how you add this compelling technology to your applications. I'll start with some basic concepts you need to begin working with DirectX. Then, I'll discuss DirectDraw in detail, which is the oldest and largest of the DirectX components.

DirectX Basics

The fundamental architecture that binds the DirectX family of components together is COM, and though you don't need to be a COM wizard to use DirectX from within your applications, you need to understand how COM works (if only at a high level) and be familiar with COM-specific coding practices. There are also some terms and concepts I should introduce. I'll start with the necessary COM information that varies from Chapter 10, "COM."

Differences in COM Programming Style and DirectX

When you program DirectX components, you will be dealing directly with COM components you (somehow) created and initialized. The first major difference you'll note when you program using DirectX is that you also combine traditional API library-based programming with your COM programming. Perhaps this is best illustrated by example.

Let's say you want to do some work with DirectDraw, as you'll do shortly. If you follow the traditional COM approach, you would expect to be given a CLSID and an IID, which, when used with CoCreateInstance() would a create new DirectDraw object. This method works just fine. As it happens, though, you can also call the DirectX function DirectDrawCreate(), which in turn calls CoCreateInstance() on your behalf and returns to you the DirectDraw COM object. Although this is not unheard of in COM programming circles, it is somewhat different. Don't be fooled into thinking you are *not* working with a COM object! You just obtained a new object using a different means. All the COM rules still apply.

> **NOTE**
>
> If you do create the DirectDraw object using the traditional CoCreateInstance() approach, you will need to call IDirectDraw::Initialize() before you actually use the object's capabilities. This is unnecessary when creating the object using DirectDrawCreate().

30

MFC AND DIRECTX

> ### CAUTION
>
> Do not be deceived. You are dealing with COM objects when you program using DirectX, so follow all the COM rules *no matter how* you obtained your objects initially. Any quality COM text should provide you with the information you need to follow the rules of COM if you are unsure.

The question most often asked at this point is where did `DirectDrawCreate()` come from? The answer is that the DirectX SDK ships with both debug and retail libraries you *must* link against to use DirectX. In the case of DirectDraw, you will link with ddraw.lib and possibly dxguid.lib. Other DirectX components require additional (or different) libraries. The DirectX component creation functions are certainly there, though there are other useful functions exported by the libraries as well. When in doubt, check with the online help files for both Developer Studio and the DirectX SDK.

> ### NOTE
>
> Visual C++ version 6 ships with the development tools you'll need to work with DirectX 6. You might still require the latest DirectX drivers, however. These can be obtained at the Microsoft DirectX Internet site free of charge. See `http://www.microsoft.com/directx` for download details.

Another minor variation is that the DirectX components all return custom function return and error codes. A good example of this involves the enumeration functions. I'll discuss this process further in a moment, but in most cases when using a DirectX component, you first (generally) enumerate the possible drivers, and then activate the component with the desired driver. The enumeration callback functions all return a Boolean value. The odd part is the enumeration functions return `DDENUMRET_OK` and `DDENUMRET_CANCEL` for `TRUE` and `FALSE` respectively.

DirectX Component Startup Sequence

Because I've mentioned driver enumerations, it's time to look more closely at the general sequence of events when creating a DirectX application. Here are the steps you normally follow to activate DirectX:

- Enumerate the supported drivers.
- Either ask the user or programmatically determine which driver you should use in this specific case.

- Create the component using the driver GUID you obtained from the enumeration process.

I use the term *drivers* loosely here. DirectPlay, for example, uses an enumeration of connection shortcuts to determine which connection is required for multiuser contacts. When you are creating a DirectDraw object, on the other hand, you literally enumerate through the installed display device drivers and select the one most appropriate for your application. I'll make this more concrete when I discuss DirectDraw in the next section.

By the way, much of what you see regarding DirectDraw applies to the other DirectX components, at least as far as general mechanics are concerned. You initialize them in a similar manner, check for errors, and in general integrate them into your application in very much the same way you will DirectDraw. When you see how DirectDraw is applied, you should find using the other DirectX technologies easily applied also.

DirectDraw Basics

The greatest benefit DirectDraw provides you is the means to access the given computer system's hardware in the leanest and meanest possible manner. You won't be coding video registers yourself, but the performance you realize using DirectDraw can be almost as stunning.

You can imagine DirectDraw as a replacement for certain parts of the standard Windows GDI (see Chapter 4, "Painting, Device Contexts, Bitmaps, and Fonts"). Although it won't algorithmically generate rectangles for you like the GDI, because DirectDraw doesn't actually *draw* anything in the GDI sense, it will put an image you provide onscreen very quickly. And unlike GDI, DirectDraw offers several special effects, such as enhanced stretching and transparency.

I'll start discussing DirectDraw by showing you how it's initialized, but I'll move on to other DirectDraw basic concepts later in the chapter and in this chapter's sample programs.

Initializing DirectDraw

In most cases, the very first thing you'll do when using DirectDraw is to determine what video output formats the given computer system supports. You'll see a notable exception to this later in the chapter when I discuss *windowed* DirectDraw. Normally, however, most DirectDraw applications will want to use the entire screen for rendering their output. This being the case, you will need to know what video modes the system offers so you might select the most optimum for your needs. If the optimum choice isn't available, you can gracefully downgrade to a secondary video mode you can still use effectively.

DirectDraw driver enumeration is done in much the same way you enumerate windows (using `EnumWindows()`). You call an API function, `DirectDrawEnumerate()`, in this situation and provide it a callback function. The callback function records the installed video drivers for later use. This code invokes `DirectDrawEnumerate()` for enumeration:

```
if ( FAILED(DirectDrawEnumerate((LPDDENUMCALLBACK)EnumDDrawDevices,
                                             (LPVOID)this))) {
    AfxMessageBox("Unable to enumerate DirectDraw devices.",
                  MB_OK|MB_ICONERROR);
    // Handle error...;
} // if
```

The parameters to `DirectDrawEnumerate()` are simply the address of the enumeration function and an arbitrary 32-bit parameter, which in the preceding case is a `this` pointer to the C++ class performing the enumeration.

The enumeration function itself has no requirement to do anything special, but you'll typically want to record the driver presented to the callback function each time the callback function is executed. If you build a selection list using the callback function, you'll know what is available to you when the enumeration has been completed. This chapter's first sample program, DXMode, uses the code you see in Listing 30.1 to build such a selection list.

LISTING 30.1   DXMODE DIRECTDRAW DRIVER ENUMERATION

```
BOOL WINAPI EnumDDrawDevices( GUID FAR *lpGUID,
                              LPSTR lpDriverDescription,
                              LPSTR lpDriverName,
                              LPVOID lpContext ) {
    // Cast your pointer
    CDXModeDlg* pDialog = reinterpret_cast<CDXModeDlg*>(lpContext);
    int iIndex = pDialog->m_CDevices.AddString(lpDriverDescription);

    // Add the device to the devices combo box
    if ( iIndex != LB_ERR ) {
        // You've added the string representing the device,
        // so you now create a GUID and store it with the
        // item.
        GUID* guidDevice = NULL;
        if ( lpGUID != NULL ) {
            // If you have a device GUID, create storage
            // for a copy, then copy.
            guidDevice = new GUID;
            *guidDevice = *lpGUID; // copy
        } // if
```

```
    // Set the item's data
    pDialog->m_CDevices.SetItemData(iIndex,
                reinterpret_cast<DWORD>(guidDevice));
} // if
else {
    // Return an error
    return DDENUMRET_CANCEL;
}

    return DDENUMRET_OK;
}
```

There are two interesting things to note regarding Listing 30.1. First, the this pointer passed as a parameter in DirectDrawEnumerate() is known as the *context* parameter in the enumeration function parameter list. Because DXMode is really a dialog box-based application, the this pointer I passed was the MFC CDialog-based class CDXModeDlg. After I recast it back to a CDXModeDlg pointer, I can add the driver's textual description, lpDriverDescription, to a combo box contained within the dialog box. This is how I save the driver descriptions for later presentation to the user.

The second interesting feature is that the drivers are really identified by GUID (a unique 128-bit COM object identifier). It's true you are given a textual description of the driver. But when you actually want to *do* anything with the driver, you have to provide its GUID identifier. I store this with the driver name in the combo box (I add the GUID as item data). When you select a driver and mode from the dialog's combo box, I retrieve the item data and cast it to a GUID pointer. From there, I access the driver itself.

At this time, you have a complete list of driver descriptions and GUID identifiers. This in itself is interesting, as you now know what drivers are currently loaded on the given computer. You could at this time load new or updated drivers, for example.

But what you will most likely do now is also enumerate the video modes the drivers support. For example, your application might have been designed to work with a 320×240 screen (a common gaming standard, but certainly *not* a standard Windows video mode). After you enumerate the supported video modes, you'll know whether you'll be able to use your application's native mode (320×240) or be forced into using another video mode (which will almost certainly introduce stretching artifacts when the screen is rendered).

But before you are able to determine the modes you can work with, you'll need to initialize DirectDraw with the driver GUID you obtained from the enumeration process. This code creates the DirectDraw object using the `DirectDrawCreate()` function I mentioned previously:

```
LPDIRECTDRAW pIDirectDraw = NULL;
if ( FAILED(DirectDrawCreate(lpGUID,&pIDirectDraw,NULL)) ) {
   AfxMessageBox("Error creating DirectDraw object",
                 MB_OK ¦ MB_ICONERROR);
   // Handle error...
} // if
```

Note that the first parameter to `DirectDrawCreate()` is a pointer to a GUID. The GUID you provide is the GUID associated with the driver you want to use (which, of course, is why I enumerated the driver list to begin with).

> **NOTE**
>
> You do not *need* to enumerate the drivers and modes, but it is common practice. If your application is not intended for the more esoteric video modes, you can skip the driver enumeration and pass NULL as the driver GUID to `DirectDrawCreate()`. This will create a DirectDraw object that uses the default system driver.

If `DirectDrawCreate()` was successful, it will return to you an `IDirectDraw` interface to the DirectDraw COM object. When you have this interface, you can set the *cooperative level* you plan to use. This is an application-wide setting that essentially tells DirectDraw how it should react to other Windows applications, and even to Windows itself. For example, you tell DirectDraw you want to use the full screen by using the DDSCL_EXCLUSIVE and DDSCL_FULLSCREEN cooperative level settings. With these particular settings, when your application has focus, the screen is yours to render as you require—other applications won't interfere.

> **NOTE**
>
> You must set the cooperative level before calling other DirectDraw methods. Many will fail outright if the cooperative level has not been set.

Table 30.1 lists the available cooperative level bits as well as their effect upon the system and other applications. Note that some are mutually exclusive, whereas others must be used in pairs.

TABLE 30.1 DIRECTDRAW COOPERATIVE LEVEL SETTINGS

Setting	*Meaning/Use*
DDSCL_FULLSCREEN	Application will use the full display screen (GDI can be ignored, must be used with DDSCL_EXCLUSIVE).
DDSCL_ALLOWREBOOT	Allow Ctrl+Alt+Delete while in full-screen exclusive mode.
DDSCL_NOWINDOWCHANGES	Prevents DirectDraw from modifying the application window state.
DDSCL_NORMAL	Application will work as a regular Windows application (cannot be used with DDSCL_EXCLUSIVE and DDSCL_FULLSCREEN).
DDSCL_EXCLUSIVE	Exclusive access (must be used with DDSCL_FULLSCREEN).
DDSCL_ALLOWMODEX	Application can handle displays using non-standard Windows display modes.
DDSCL_SETFOCUSWINDOW	Window will receive focus messages.
DDSCL_SETDEVICEWINDOW	Window is associated with the DirectDraw object and will cover the screen in full-screen mode (Windows 98/2000 only).
DDSCL_CREATEDEVICEWINDOW	Create a window to be associated with the DirectDraw object (Windows 98/2000 only).

You can set the cooperative level with IDirectDraw::SetCooperativeLevel(), using the following code:

```
if ( FAILED(m_pIDirectDraw->SetCooperativeLevel(m_hWnd,
                                    DDSCL_FULLSCREEN ¦
                                    DDSCL_EXCLUSIVE ¦
                                    DDSCL_NOWINDOWCHANGES)) ) {
    AfxMessageBox("Error setting cooperative level",
                MB_OK ¦ MB_ICONERROR);
    // Handle error
} // if
```

With the cooperative level set, you can now enumerate the video modes supported by the driver you've selected. You perform the enumeration using IDirectDraw::EnumDisplayModes(), as shown here:

```
if ( FAILED(pIDirectDraw->EnumDisplayModes(0,NULL,
                    reinterpret_cast<LPVOID>(this),
                    (LPDDENUMMODESCALLBACK)EnumDeviceModes)) ) {
    AfxMessageBox("Error enumerating modes",
                MB_OK ¦ MB_ICONERROR);
    // Handle error
} // if
```

30

MFC AND DIRECTX

Although the function signature for video mode enumeration is different than the API call used to enumerate the driver list, the same basic information is here. That is, you pass in a this pointer as a context value and a pointer to an enumeration function. Again using DXMode as an example, the device mode enumeration function is shown in Listing 30.2.

LISTING 30.2 DXMODE DEVICE VIDEO MODE ENUMERATION

```
BOOL WINAPI EnumDeviceModes( LPDDSURFACEDESC lpDDSurfaceDesc,
                             LPVOID lpContext )
{
   // Cast your pointer
   CDXModeDlg* pDialog = reinterpret_cast<CDXModeDlg*>(lpContext);

   // Add this mode to the listbox
   CString strMode;
   strMode.Format("%dx%dx%d, refresh %d",
                  lpDDSurfaceDesc->dwWidth,
                  lpDDSurfaceDesc->dwHeight,
                  lpDDSurfaceDesc->ddpfPixelFormat.dwRGBBitCount,
                  lpDDSurfaceDesc->dwRefreshRate);

   int iIndex = pDialog->m_CModes.AddString(strMode);
   if ( iIndex != LB_ERR ) {
      // Add the surface descriptor to the item's data
      LPDDSURFACEDESC lpDesc = new DDSURFACEDESC;
      memcpy(lpDesc,lpDDSurfaceDesc,sizeof(DDSURFACEDESC));
      pDialog->m_CModes.SetItemData(iIndex,
         reinterpret_cast<DWORD>(lpDesc));
   } // if
   else {
      // Return an error
      return DDENUMRET_CANCEL;
   } // else

   return DDENUMRET_OK;
}
```

Here, the interesting thing to note is that the enumeration is passed in not only a context value (as with driver enumeration), but it is also passed a surface description (more on this in the next section). You can access the surface description to extract the information you need to judge the video mode best suited for your application. In the case of DXMode, the video mode is stored in a list box. When you select the video mode from the list box, DXMode will enable that video mode for you.

At this point, you have selected a DirectDraw driver, created the DirectDraw object, and obtained the information you need to select an appropriate video mode. If your selected video mode requires a palette, you must create one now.

DirectDraw and Palettes

DirectDraw is capable of displaying many video modes, and many of them require *palettes*. A palette, distilled to its core functionality, is simply a table of color references. That is, a 256-color palette contains 256 table entries. The palettized bitmap is made up of entries into the table. When Windows displays a 256-color bitmap, it looks at the individual table entries in the bitmap and matches them to the color values stored in the palette table. The bitmap doesn't contain actual color information—it contains palette table indices.

The color information is actually stored in the palette. If you were to change one of the table color values while displaying the bitmap, you would change the appearance of the bitmap onscreen. Thus the secret to palettes is to make sure the palette you want (with the correct color values in its color table) is always used when your bitmap is displayed. If you fail to do this, your bitmap will have unpredictable colors and will almost certainly *not* appear onscreen as you would like.

Managing palettes, then, is critical to proper DirectDraw operation if you either plan to use a palettized display mode (256 colors, for instance) or you are working with DirectDraw in a window (versus full screen). There are three major steps to accomplish to manage the palette *you* want Windows to use when *your* application is active:

1. Create your palette.
2. Handle the situation where Windows tells you the system palette has changed (`WM_PALETTECHANGED`).
3. Handle the situation where Windows requests from you the palette you want to become the current system palette (`WM_QUERYNEWPALETTE`).

To create a new palette using DirectDraw, you simply create a table containing the color values you want, and then pass that to DirectDraw. How you create the color values is up to you. You could fill in each of the palette color entries by hand, thus selecting optimum color settings. You could generate the colors algorithmically. And, of course, you could peer inside a Windows device-independent bitmap (DIB) to see what color information is required by that bitmap and assign those colors to your palette. I'll leave the by-hand method as an exercise for the reader, but the algorithmic and DIB assignment methods require some explanation. You'll see these methods in action when I discuss this chapter's third sample program later in the chapter.

Windows will happily use whatever palette you provide, but there is an algorithm that generates a Windows default palette—a palette with the standard Windows color entries. This palette is called a *332 palette* for the entries created by the algorithm. I won't describe the algorithm in detail (that would require a lot of explanation), referring you instead to other Windows programming books (such as *Programming Windows 98/NT Unleashed*, from Sams Publishing). However, here is the code that executes the algorithm:

```
// Create a standard 332 palette
PALETTEENTRY ape[256];
for ( int i = 0; i < 256; i++ ) {
    ape[i].peRed   = (BYTE)(((i >> 5) & 0x07) * 255 / 7);
    ape[i].peGreen = (BYTE)(((i >> 2) & 0x07) * 255 / 7);
    ape[i].peBlue  = (BYTE)(((i >> 0) & 0x03) * 255 / 3);
    ape[i].peFlags = (BYTE)0;
} // for
```

As you can see, the loop assigns values to the red, green, and blue components of the palette color entry structure.

If your application doesn't use a standard 332 palette, or if you simply want to use whatever palette was stored with your DIB (which might or might not be a 332 palette), you need to dig into your DIB and retrieve the palette color information stored there. To do this, you look at the DIB's BITMAPINFOHEADER and retrieve the color information. Assuming your bitmap was stored as a resource (versus a disk-based DIB file), this code will retrieve the palette information for you:

```
// Locate the bitmap resource.  Note this assumes the
// bitmap is stored as a program resource (and not as
// a disk file).
HRSRC hBitmap = NULL;
if ( (hBitmap = ::FindResource(NULL,
                        MAKEINTRESOURCE(idBitmap),
                        RT_BITMAP))) {
   LPBITMAPINFOHEADER lpbi = (LPBITMAPINFOHEADER)::LockResource(
➥::LoadResource(NULL,hBitmap));
   if ( lpbi != NULL ) {
      // Locate the color information, which is stored past
      // the BITMAPINFOHEADER.
      RGBQUAD* prgb = (RGBQUAD*)((BYTE*)lpbi + lpbi->biSize);

      // Determine how many palettized colors you're
      // talking about.
      int iNumColors;
      if (lpbi == NULL || lpbi->biSize < sizeof(BITMAPINFOHEADER))
         iNumColors = 0;
      else if (lpbi->biBitCount > 8)
         iNumColors = 0;
```

```
        else if (lpbi->biClrUsed == 0)
            iNumColors = 1 << lpbi->biBitCount;
        else
            iNumColors = lpbi->biClrUsed;

        //  Pull the color information
        for( int i = 0; i < iNumColors; i++ ) {
            ape[i].peRed    = prgb[i].rgbRed;
            ape[i].peGreen  = prgb[i].rgbGreen;
            ape[i].peBlue   = prgb[i].rgbBlue;
            ape[i].peFlags  = 0;
        } // for
    } // if
} // if
```

In this case you find the bitmap resource, load it, and lock it in memory so you can access its information directly. Because the BITMAPINFOHEADER is the first part of the DIB in memory, after you lock it in place, you have a pointer to the DIB's information header. Given that, you then determine the type of bitmap by looking at the color information (stored as in-place RGBQUAD structures). If you find the bitmap indeed requires a palette, you assign to the palette entries the information stored in the RGBQUAD structures (which have nearly identical form to the PALETTEENTRY color information structures).

You now have a collection of 256 PALETTEENTRY values, each filled with color information. These will eventually compose the palette's color table. It's now time to actually create a palette. Naturally, you do this using DirectDraw:

```
// Create a new DirectDraw palette
// IDirectDraw* pIDirectDraw (declared previously)
IDirectDrawPalette* pIDDPalette = NULL;
HRESULT hr = pIDirectDraw->CreatePalette(DDPCAPS_8BIT,ape,
                                  &pIDDPalette,NULL);

if ( FAILED(hr) ) {
    // Some error
    AfxMessageBox("Error creating the DirectDraw palette",
                MB_OK | MB_ICONERROR);
    // Handle error
} // if
```

Windows, through DirectDraw, will now have a copy of the palette you want to use for your application and will assign it to the system palette. Note that this code creates a 256-color palette (established by the DDPCAPS_8BIT setting). There are other types of palettes—see the online help for more information. In any case, after the palette has been established, it's time to add palette management support.

The first thing to do is add a handler for the WM_PALETTECHANGED message. This message indicates that another application obtained focus and has changed the palette from

30

MFC AND
DIRECTX

underneath you. It's up to you to decide how you want to handle this situation. However, DirectDraw helps you here, too, as you'll see when I discuss the practical side to using DirectDraw later in the chapter. For now, I'll simply show you the basic handler code. I'll fill in some of the DirectDraw details later in the chapter when I discuss the RePalettize() helper method.

The basic WM_PALETTECHANGED handler code looks like this:

```
void CMyCWnd::OnPaletteChanged(CWnd* pFocusWnd)
{
    // Someone changed the palette...was it you?
    if ( pFocusWnd->GetSafeHwnd() == this->m_hWnd ) {
        // It was you, so let base class handle the
        // message
        CWnd::OnPaletteChanged(pFocusWnd);
    } // if
    else {
        // It wasn't you, so repalettize
        RePalettize(); // <-- a method you provide...
    } // if
}
```

It is critical to examine the CWnd pointer passed into OnPaletteChanged(). If you were responsible for changing the palette, you would enter an infinite loop trying to establish a new palette. In effect, you would call yourselves forever.

> **CAUTION**
>
> Always check to see if your window changed the palette before handling the WM_PALETTECHANGED message. You will enter an infinite loop if you don't.

Windows issues the WM_PALETTECHANGED message when an application, which could be the current application (yours), changes the system palette. Similarly, Windows will request from you a palette to use as the system palette when your application gains focus. This message, WM_QUERYNEWPALETTE, is Windows's way of asking you to re-establish your palette. The basic handler for WM_QUERYNEWPALETTE looks like this:

```
BOOL CTableView::OnQueryNewPalette()
{
    // You now control the palette, so repalettize
    return RePalettize();// <-- a method you provide...
}
```

If you change the palette in response to WM_QUERYNEWPALETTE, your handler returns TRUE. If not, it returns FALSE. Fortunately, you can use the same method to repalettize when using DirectDraw, as you'll see shortly.

Now that the palette management is in place, it's time to create a primary DirectDraw surface and possibly several secondary surfaces you might use as back buffers or for bitmap storage.

DirectDraw Surfaces

DirectDraw can do many things for you, as you've seen if you've tried DXMode. But the goal of DirectDraw is and always has been to provide you with the fastest, highest-performance bitmap data transfers possible. After all, when you display a bitmap on the computer's video screen, what you are really doing is copying bitmap color information from somewhere in the computer's main memory to the computer's video memory (advanced video hardware notwithstanding). When the information is there, the video hardware reads the video memory and actually displays the information.

The essence of this transaction is that data was copied from one memory location to another. The faster the data is copied from place to place, the faster your overall *frame rate* will be. The frame rate refers to the number of completed cycles your application can perform in one second. If your application is able to update the screen 30 times a second, you have a frame rate of 30 frames per second. Most PC applications run in the 10-15 frame per second range, with some of the better-performing games reaching into the 20-frame-per-second range.

Aside from calculations, which can take a significant amount of time to complete, the *bitmap block transfer* is typically the frame rate-limiting factor. Bitmap block transfers, or *blit* for short, are critical for smooth animation, simply because your eye can easily perceive breaks in the frames at somewhere around 10 frames per second. Frame rates in this range are usually considered poor for quality animation.

The DirectDraw *surface* is designed to minimize the blit *latency*, or in other words, move the data from here to there in the least amount of time possible. If you understand device contexts (see Chapter 4), you know that a device context contains bitmap information. Perhaps the bitmap will be rendered onscreen, or just as likely, a printer will render the bitmap. DirectDraw surfaces perform the same function (though not to printers). Unlike device contexts, DirectDraw surfaces *do not* access the Windows GDI directly. The means you can't draw ellipses, text, or polygons on a DirectDraw surface using GDI methods. For that, you request a device context from the DirectDraw surface using

IDirectDrawSurface::GetDC() and work with GDI using that device context, *not* via the surface itself (don't forget to release the device context afterwards!). But DirectDraw surfaces *are* like device contexts in that they manage blitting, or the transfer of bitmap data from one location to another. It's time now to see how surfaces are created.

Creating DirectDraw Surfaces

When you use DirectDraw, the first surface you will most likely create is your *primary* surface. This is akin to a Windows screen device context. Whatever bitmap you place on this surface will be rendered onscreen. When you have a primary surface, you then create secondary surfaces, of which there are two kinds. The first is a surface designated to simply contain a bitmap. You obtain a bitmap, from your resources or from a disk file, and load it into the surface. When the bitmap is there, it can be transferred quickly to the primary surface or another secondary surface. The other type of secondary surface is a *back buffer*. This is a surface used to assemble your frame, like a scratch pad. You use the back buffer as a staging area where you create the frame, and then blit the back buffer to the primary surface for viewing.

The first step is to create the primary surface. To do this, you use DirectDraw's IDirectDraw::CreateSurface() method, like this:

```
DDSURFACEDESC ddsd;
ZeroMemory(&ddsd,sizeof(ddsd));
ddsd.dwSize = sizeof(ddsd);
ddsd.dwFlags = DDSD_CAPS;
ddsd.ddsCaps.dwCaps = DDSCAPS_PRIMARYSURFACE;

// IDirectDraw* pIDirectDraw (declared previously)
IDirectDrawSurface* pDDSPrimary = NULL;
HRESULT hr = pIDirectDraw->CreateSurface(&ddsd,&pDDSPrimary,NULL);
if ( FAILED( hr ) ) {
   // Some error
   AfxMessageBox("Error creating primary surface",
                 MB_OK | MB_ICONERROR);
   // Handle error
} // if
```

Assuming CreateSurface() was successful, you now have the means to display bitmap information onscreen.

Creating secondary surfaces uses the same mechanism, but with the DDSURFACEDESC structure completed slightly differently:

```
DDSURFACEDESC ddsd;
ZeroMemory(&ddsd,sizeof(ddsd));
ddsd.dwSize = sizeof(ddsd);
ddsd.dwFlags = DDSD_CAPS | DDSD_HEIGHT | DDSD_WIDTH;
```

```
ddsd.ddsCaps.dwCaps = DDSCAPS_OFFSCREENPLAIN;
ddsd.dwWidth = cx;
ddsd.dwHeight = cy;

// IDirectDraw* pIDirectDraw (declared previously)
IDirectDrawSurface* pDDSSecondary = NULL;
HRESULT hr = pIDirectDraw->CreateSurface(&ddsd,&pDDSSecondary,NULL);
if ( FAILED(hr) ) {
   // Some error
   AfxMessageBox("Error creating primary surface",
                 MB_OK | MB_ICONERROR);
   // Handle error
} // if
```

DirectDraw creates a primary surface and associates it with the video display when you set the DDSCAPS_PRIMARYSURFACE bit in the DDSURFACEDESC ddsCaps field. Conversely, DirectDraw creates a secondary surface when you apply the DDSCAPS_OFFSCREENPLAIN bit in the dwCaps field. Another detail is that DirectDraw knows how big a primary surface needs to be—the size of your video output. For secondary surfaces, however, *you* must specify how large the surface is required to be, in pixels. You do this by setting the DDSD_HEIGHT and DDSD_HEIGHT bits in the dwFlags field, which tells DirectDraw the dwWidth and dwHeight fields in the DDSURFACEDESC structure are valid.

Transferring Bitmaps from Surface to Surface

Now that you have DirectDraw surfaces that you can work with, you load them with data and move the data around as required by your application. As I mentioned previously, many applications create a primary surface for display, a secondary surface for staging (the back buffer), and any number of secondary surfaces destined to contain bitmaps to be used as animated sprites (moving objects), backgrounds, and a myriad of other uses. A typical scenario would involve copying a sprite to the back buffer, then displaying the back buffer by copying the back buffer to the primary surface.

To reiterate, this bitmap transfer operation is termed a *blit*, for bitmap block transfer. Blitting data from one surface to another is a simple matter using DirectDraw, as you might expect. After all, it was designed for this purpose. You simply call the IDirectDrawSurface::Blt() method:

```
// IDirectDrawSurface* pDDSSecondary,
//                     pDDSSomeSurface (both declared previously)
CRect rcDest; // filled with valid destination location info
CRect rcSrc; // filled with valid source location info (may be NULL)
hr = pDDSSecondary->Blt(rcDest,pDDSSomeSurface,rcSrc,
                        DDBLT_WAIT,NULL);
if ( FAILED( hr ) ) {
   // Some error
```

30

MFC AND
DIRECTX

```
    AfxMessageBox("Error bltting to secondary surface",
                  MB_OK | MB_ICONERROR);
    // Handle error
} // if
```

In this example, the bitmap information contained in the pDDSSomeSurface surface will be copied to the pDDSSecondary surface. You first fill the destination rectangle with the location where you want to place the information in the target surface. The source rectangle may also be completed, or you can pass NULL to Blt() to copy the entire source surface contents to the target surface.

CAUTION

Unlike blitting to device contexts, DirectDraw is unforgiving when it comes to rectangles that extend outside the bounds of a surface. The rectangle locations you pass to Blt() must contain coordinates that exist within the surface's bounds. You will receive a DDERR_INVALIDRECT error if the rectangular region is out of a surface boundary.

NOTE

DirectDraw automatically stretches bitmaps to fit. If the source and destination rectangles differ in height and width, the resulting bitmap will be accordingly distorted.

Clearing DirectDraw Surfaces

Frequently, you will need to clear a secondary surface to some predetermined color as initialization prior to blitting bitmap data. This is easily accomplished using DirectDraw special effects combined with the IDirectDrawSurface::Blt() method you just saw:

```
DDBLTFX ddbltfx;
ddbltfx.dwSize = sizeof(ddbltfx);
ddbltfx.dwFillColor = 0; // black
// IDirectDrawSurface* pDDSSecondary (declared previously)
HRESULT hr = m_lpDDSSecondary->Blt(NULL,NULL,NULL,
                                   DDBLT_COLORFILL | DDBLT_WAIT,
                                   &ddbltfx);
if ( FAILED( hr ) ) {
    // Some error
```

```
    AfxMessageBox("Error clearing secondary surface",
                  MB_OK | MB_ICONERROR);
    // Handle error
} // if
```

Note the differences between this `Blt()` call and an actual bitmap transfer. Both the source and destination rectangles are NULL (though the destination rectangle need not be), the source surface is NULL, and I added the `DDBLT_COLORFILL` option along with a pointer to the completed `DDBLTFX` structure. If the destination rectangle is non-NULL and contains valid location information, only that area of the target surface will be filled with the fill color instead of the entire surface.

DirectDraw Page Flipping

A related concept to DirectDraw surfaces is *page flipping*. Until DirectDraw, many Windows animation-based applications (not just games) suffered from *tearing*. Tearing is a phenomenon you will see when the animation begins during one monitor refresh cycle but finishes during the next. That is, the images you see on a color display are created by electron guns shooting beams of electrons at the back surface of the monitor's glass face. (Of course, this assumes a cathode ray tube; you will see the same effects using a liquid crystal display even though the mechanics of the display are different.) The inside of the monitor's front glass surface is coated with phosphors that, when excited by the electron beam, glow red, green, or blue. The phosphors are actually separated (red, green, and blue), but because they are so small, your eye combines their respective color values. Your perception is of a single color, which is the blending of the red, green, and blue color values of the individual pixels.

The electron beam starts at the top of the screen, moves horizontally, then vertically, until it reaches the bottom of the screen. At that time, the electron beam must be deactivated and routed back to the top of the screen to scan the monitor's glass surface yet again. When the electron beam is deactivated, the monitor is said to be in *vertical retrace*, or *vertical blanking*. When the monitor is about to retrace, the video card issues a hardware interrupt called the *vertical blanking signal*.

As most professional game programmers know, the vertical retrace period is quite lengthy as compared to the processing speed of today's microprocessors. So, it makes sense to coordinate lengthy game calculations and bitmap data transfers with the monitor's vertical blanking signal. When the monitor is retracing, you can't display any new information anyway, so you might as well use the time to create the next image the video hardware will display.

Windows normally prevents you from intercepting the vertical blank signal, so you were faced with making these lengthy calculations and blits at random times. Because of this, the image being displayed on the screen might be updated at any time, including when the monitor is scanning the image. When this happens, the upper part of the image is scanned using information from one animation frame while the lower part of the screen is scanned using information from the next frame. If the frames were different, the image you would see would straddle the two frames and thus appear to be torn (the tearing phenomenon). If you've tried this chapter's second sample program, the tearing demo, you've seen this in action.

To allow developers the ability to manage the vertical blank signal, DirectDraw was introduced. This is a core DirectDraw feature, and Microsoft had to provide such a solution if game development (or any serious animation work) on a Windows platform was to be taken seriously. How DirectDraw manages the vertical blank signal is by page flipping. The *page* in page flipping refers to video hardware of yore that implemented noncontiguous (segmented) video memory banks. Each bank was called a page. The term has persisted even if the hardware has improved significantly.

When you use DirectDraw page flipping, you begin by creating a *complex* DirectDraw surface (this surface is very much analogous to the OpenGL double-buffered rendering context described in Chapter 29, "MFC and OpenGL"). The complex surface will appear to you to be two surfaces, though it is in reality considered a single surface. You simply copy whatever bitmap information you require to the back buffer surface, and DirectDraw will display it when *triggered*. When DirectDraw senses the vertical blank signal, it swaps the primary for the secondary. You tell DirectDraw when you are ready for this swap operation to take place by triggering DirectDraw.

Let's begin with creating the complex surface. To do this, you again use `IDirectDraw::CreateSurface()`, but you complete the `DDSURFACEDESC` structure slightly differently:

```
// Typically 1 unless there is hardware support
#define NUMBUFFERS   1

DDSURFACEDESC ddsd;
ZeroMemory(&ddsd,sizeof(ddsd));
ddsd.dwSize = sizeof(ddsd);
ddsd.dwFlags = DDSD_CAPS | DDSD_BACKBUFFERCOUNT;
ddsd.ddsCaps.dwCaps = DDSCAPS_PRIMARYSURFACE |
                      DDSCAPS_FLIP |
                      DDSCAPS_COMPLEX |
                      DDSCAPS_VIDEOMEMORY;
ddsd.dwBackBufferCount = NUMBUFFERS;
```

```
// IDirectDraw* pIDirectDraw (declared previously)
IDirectDrawSurface* pDDSprimary = NULL;
HRESULT hr = pIDirectDraw->CreateSurface(&ddsd,& pDDSPrimary,NULL);
if ( FAILED( hr ) ) {
    // Some error
    AfxMessageBox("Error creating primary surface",
                    MB_OK | MB_ICONERROR);
    // Handle error
} // if
```

In this case, when you request the primary surface, you ask for a number of back buffers
(DDSD_BACKBUFFERCOUNT), flipping capability (DDSCAPS_FLIP), a complex surface
(DDSCAPS_COMPLEX), and that the surface reside in video memory for higher performance
(DDSCAPS_VIDEOMEMORY).

If DirectDraw can support this (which it can for at least a single back buffer in emulation
mode), you then request access to the back buffer:

```
DDSCAPS ddscaps;
ddscaps.dwCaps = DDSCAPS_BACKBUFFER;
// IDirectDrawSurface* pDDSprimary (declared previously)
HRESULT hr = pDDSPrimary->GetAttachedSurface(&ddscaps,
                                             &m_lpDDSSecondary);
if ( FAILED( hr ) ) {
    // Some error
    AfxMessageBox("Error retrieving secondary back buffer".
                    MB_OK | MB_ICONERROR);
    // Handle error
} // if
```

As you can see, retrieving the secondary surface is very different from what you saw previously. This is an artifact of the complex surface. Without page flipping, you create both
surfaces, primary and secondary. With page flipping, you create a complex primary surface with *contains* a secondary surface. Therefore, the mechanics of obtaining the secondary surface are naturally a bit different.

> **TIP**
>
> Video memory is a limited resource, so create your primary surface and request
> your secondary surface *before* you create any other secondary surfaces to con-
> tain bitmaps. This should prevent resource contention errors when creating the
> primary surface.

30

MFC AND DIRECTX

> **CAUTION**
>
> Be sure to reverse the release order of the surface objects. With page flipping active, the secondary surface (back buffer) must be released *prior* to releasing the primary surface. This is the opposite of what is required when not using page flipping.

With the surfaces created, you work with the secondary back buffer as you normally would (clear it, copy bitmaps, and so on). When you have completed filling the back buffer, you trigger the page swap by using the `IDirectDrawSurface::Flip()` method:

```
// IDirectDrawSurface* pDDSprimary (declared previously)
HRESULT hr = pDDSPrimary->Flip(NULL,DDFLIP_WAIT);
if ( FAILED( hr ) ) {
   // Some error
   AfxMessageBox("Error flipping page",
               MB_OK | MB_ICONERROR);
   // Handle error
} // if
```

Here, the `DDFLIP_WAIT` setting tells DirectDraw to swap the primary and secondary surfaces when it receives the next vertical blanking interrupt.

DirectDraw from a Window

Many applications use DirectDraw using the `DDSCL_EXCLUSIVE` and `DDSCL_FULLSCREEN` styles. These styles are great for you, the developer, because you don't need to worry about interacting with other Windows applications. You own the screen when your application is active, so there is no need to worry about painting over another application's window.

This is definitely not true if you want to use DirectDraw from within a window. In fact, it becomes considerably more complicated because your window might have other windows overlapping it when displayed to the user. Part of your window might be obscured, and part might not be. A DirectDraw primary surface, however, has no compassion for other windows in the system. It only knows it is free to access the entire screen. When your application calls upon DirectDraw to update the screen, it will happily overwrite any other window that might happen to be onscreen.

> **NOTE**
>
> Page flipping is *not* available to you when using DirectDraw from within a window. Page flipping can only be used in full-screen, exclusive mode.

Of course, this type of behavior is discouraged in normal practice (to put it mildly). To solve this problem, the designers of DirectDraw provide a *clipping* object. In graphical programming terms, clipping refers to rendering your image only where you are supposed to render. Regions where you are not to render are *clipped*. Your image will not be rendered there, thus preventing your application from overpainting any other window.

Determining where your application may render and where it may not can get quite complicated, as there may be many overlapping windows. DirectDraw solves this problem by providing a special object designed just to handle this situation. The DirectDraw clipping object, called the *clipper*, dynamically manages all the relevant clip regions for you. You simply create the clipper, provide it with your window's handle, and assign the clipper to the primary surface. DirectDraw takes it from there.

Creating the clipper object is similar to creating other DirectDraw objects—you call an `IDirectDraw` method, which in this case is `CreateClipper()`:

```
// Since you're windowed, you need to create a clipper.
// IDirectDraw* pIDirectDraw (declared previously)
IDirectDrawClipper* pDDClipper;
HRESULT hr = pIDirectDraw->CreateClipper(0,&pDDClipper,NULL);
if ( FAILED( hr ) ) {
    // Some error
    AfxMessageBox("Error creating the clipper",
                MB_OK ¦ MB_ICONERROR);
    // Handle error
} // if
```

After the clipper object has been created, you must provide it with your window's handle (presumably so it can subclass your window). You do this using the `IDirectDrawClipper::SetHWnd()` method:

```
// You now associate the clipper with your frame
// so Windows will update the clipping region for
// you.
CMainFrame* pFrame = (CMainFrame*)AfxGetMainWnd();
ASSERT(pFrame);
HRESULT hr = pDDClipper->SetHWnd(0,pFrame->GetSafeHwnd());
if ( FAILED( hr ) ) {
    // Some error
    AfxMessageBox("Error setting the clipper\'s HWND",
```

```
                      MB_OK | MB_ICONERROR);
    // Handle error
} // if
```

When the clipper has your application window's handle, it is prepared to manage any clipping issues that might arise during your application's lifetime. However, you still must associate the clipper object with your application's primary surface:

```
// Associate your clipper with the primary surface
// IDirectDrawSurface* pDDSPrimary
HRESULT hr = pDDSPrimary->SetClipper(pDDClipper);
if ( FAILED( hr ) ) {
    // Some error
    AfxMessageBox("Error associating the clipper with the
➥primary surface",
                      MB_OK | MB_ICONERROR);
    // Handle error
} // if
```

When the primary surface has a copy of the clipper object's interface pointer, you're free to `Release()` your pointer (the primary surface will `AddRef()` it on its own):

```
// Release our copy of the clipper
pDDClipper->Release();
pDDClipper = NULL;
```

Now that you've seen how DirectDraw is initialized, how surfaces are created, how palettes are managed, and how to handle clipping issues in windowed applications, it's time to turn to the practical issues surrounding the use of DirectDraw.

Using DirectDraw in Practice

So far, you've seen the basic mechanics of using DirectDraw. But there is a practical side, too. For one thing, the surfaces you've created need to be initialized with bitmaps. For another, if your application uses DirectDraw from within a window, you must manage the drawing rectangle. And, of course, you must devise a cogent mechanism for dealing with DirectDraw errors, as any DirectDraw method could return a failed result code. And finally, you can't simply release your DirectDraw interface pointers in any order when your application quits. There is a certain order that must be followed to avoid access violations as parts of DirectDraw terminate. I'll begin with the relationship between surfaces and bitmaps.

Surfaces and Bitmaps

Like a device context, a DirectDraw surface contains a bitmap. Perhaps the bitmap will be rendered directly, or maybe the surface is simply holding the bitmap for later use.

In any case, you must have some method for loading the bitmap into a surface in the first place. And, if you remember from earlier in this chapter, I mentioned I'd revisit the topic of DirectDraw and Windows palettes. First, I'll explain how to load a bitmap, where I'll create some reusable code for palette management.

Loading Bitmaps into Surfaces

Loading bitmaps is actually a fairly simple process, when explained. Realize, though, that the method I present here assumes the bitmaps are loaded as resources. Loading bitmaps from disk follows nearly the same process when the bitmap is in memory.

Before you load a bitmap into a DirectDraw surface, you must have created a surface. Earlier in the chapter I provided some simplistic code to do just this, but as with any demonstration code, you must add more to provide for a more robust and practical method. If you examine this chapter's BlackJack sample program, you'll find the helper method shown in Listing 30.3 in TableViewDDraw.cpp.

LISTING 30.3   PRACTICAL DIRECTDRAW SECONDARY SURFACE CREATION

```
HRESULT CTableView::CreateSecondarySurface(int cx, int cy,
➥IDirectDrawSurface** ppDDS)
{
   // Check our pointer
   ASSERT(ppDDS != NULL);
   if ( ppDDS == NULL ) {
      // NULL input pointer...
      return E_POINTER;
   } // if

   // Complete the surface description structure
   DDSURFACEDESC ddsd;
   ZeroMemory(&ddsd,sizeof(ddsd));
   ddsd.dwSize = sizeof(ddsd);
   ddsd.dwFlags = DDSD_CAPS | DDSD_HEIGHT | DDSD_WIDTH;
   ddsd.ddsCaps.dwCaps = DDSCAPS_OFFSCREENPLAIN;
   ddsd.dwWidth = cx;
   ddsd.dwHeight = cy;

   // Create the surface
   CComPtr<IDirectDrawSurface> pIDDSTemp;
   HRESULT hr = m_pIDirectDraw->CreateSurface(&ddsd,&pIDDSTemp,NULL);
   if ( FAILED(hr) ) {
      // Some error
      *ppDDS = NULL;
      return hr;
   } // if
```

continues

LISTING 30.3   CONTINUED

```
// Return the surface
*ppDDS = pIDDSTemp;
(*ppDDS)->AddRef();

    return hr;
}
```

The first practical consideration you should note is that I encapsulated secondary surface creation within a single method. This makes sense because this code will be called over and over again as you load more and more bitmaps. The method is made to be general purpose by passing in the size of the surface to create. The second practical consideration is I that used ATL to manage my COM pointers. This also makes sense, as you will deal with many different COM pointers when working with DirectDraw. Using a smart pointer class such as CComPtr is only prudent, especially when you consider error conditions and handlers (did you release the pointer already or not when the error took place?).

> **CAUTION**
>
> Using the code in Listing 30.3, do not forget to AddRef() the outgoing interface pointer if you're using ATL to contain the interface pointer for the object (surface) you created. The smart pointer will dutifully release the interface pointer when it leaves the scope of the helper function, thus providing you with an invalid pointer if you don't tell the object to increment its interface count first.

Now that you have a helper function to create secondary surfaces, it's time to turn to using it in conjunction with bitmaps. I'll break bitmap loading into two steps. First, I'll create the surface I require, and then I'll copy the bitmap into the surface. I'll do things this in this fashion because, if it's done properly, I can reuse the copy function when realizing a new palette.

Loading the bitmap from the application's resources is a simple matter, and when you have it loaded, it's also easy to determine how large the bitmap is for surface creation. As you see in Listing 30.4, I use CBitmap::LoadBitmap() to retrieve the bitmap from the application's resource pool. I then use the CBitmap::GetBitmap() method to retrieve a BITMAP structure, from which I determine the overall size of the bitmap. Given that, I use the secondary surface creation method from Listing 30.3 to create the surface I'll associate with this bitmap. After the surface is created, I actually copy the bitmap to the surface using another helper function CopyDDBitmap(), which you see in Listing 30.5.

LISTING 30.4 LOADING A BITMAP FOR USE WITH DIRECTDRAW

```
HRESULT CTableView::LoadDDBitmap(UINT nID,
➥IDirectDrawSurface** ppDDS)
{
   // Check your pointer
   ASSERT(ppDDS != NULL);
   if ( ppDDS == NULL ) {
      // NULL input pointer...
      return E_POINTER;
   } // if

   // Pull the bitmap from resources
   CBitmap bmImage;
   VERIFY(bmImage.LoadBitmap(nID));

   // Determine its size
   BITMAP bm;
   bmImage.GetBitmap(&bm);

   // Create a surface to contain the bitmap
   CComPtr<IDirectDrawSurface> pIDDSTemp;
   HRESULT hr = CreateSecondarySurface(bm.bmWidth,bm.bmHeight,
                                    &pIDDSTemp);
   if ( FAILED(hr) ) {
      // Some error
      *ppDDS = NULL;
      return hr;
   } // if

   // Copy the bitmap to the surface
   hr = CopyDDBitmap(&bmImage,pIDDSTemp);
   if ( FAILED(hr) ) {
      // Some error
      *ppDDS = NULL;
      return hr;
   } // if

   // Return the surface
   *ppDDS = pIDDSTemp;
   (*ppDDS)->AddRef();

   return hr;
}
```

LISTING 30.5   COPYING A BITMAP INTO A DIRECTDRAW SURFACE

```
HRESULT CTableView::CopyDDBitmap(CBitmap* pbmImage,
➥IDirectDrawSurface* pDDS)
{
    // Restore the surface
    pDDS->Restore();

    // Create a memory DC to contain the bitmap
    CDC dcImage;
    dcImage.CreateCompatibleDC(NULL);
    CBitmap* pBitmapMono = (CBitmap*)dcImage.SelectObject(pbmImage);

    // Determine its size
    BITMAP bm;
    pbmImage->GetBitmap(&bm);

    // Complete the surface description
    DDSURFACEDESC ddsd;
    ddsd.dwSize = sizeof(ddsd);
    ddsd.dwFlags = DDSD_HEIGHT | DDSD_WIDTH;
    pDDS->GetSurfaceDesc(&ddsd);

    // Copy in the bitmap
    HDC hdc = NULL;
    HRESULT hr = pDDS->GetDC(&hdc);
    if ( SUCCEEDED(hr) ) {
        ::StretchBlt(hdc,0,0,ddsd.dwWidth,ddsd.dwHeight,
                     dcImage,0,0,bm.bmWidth,bm.bmHeight,SRCCOPY);
        pDDS->ReleaseDC(hdc);
    } // if

    // Clean up
    dcImage.SelectObject(pBitmapMono);

    return hr;
}
```

The bulk of the work loading bitmaps is done by CopyDDBitmap(). Here, I create a memory-based device context, into which I select the bitmap. Because DirectDraw surfaces must somehow marry their capabilities to Windows, it isn't surprising to find the DirectDraw surface object supports device contexts. You simply ask the surface for a device context and use the standard API function StretchBlt() to copy the image from your memory device context to that of the surface. After the image has been copied, you release the surface's device context (as you would normally do with device contexts), and then clean up the memory-based device context.

There is one detail I should also mention. Referring again to Listing 30.5, before I do anything with bitmaps, I call IDirectDrawSurface::Restore(). Surfaces, for a variety of reasons, could have their memory released yet still exist. This isn't a problem or error condition—perhaps Windows required display memory for another application. In any case, calling `Restore()` will reallocate the amount of memory you originally requested, though all previous information will have been unrecoverably lost. This call simply assures you that the memory for your bitmap will be available when you attempt to copy it into place.

Palette Issues

In this section, I'll revisit palette creation and look at the `RePalettize()` method I referred to previously in this chapter. Regarding palette creation, I'll put all the pieces I discussed previously together in one method. I'll then show you what it takes to re-establish a palette using DirectDraw.

Listing 30.6 shows you palette creation in a single method. The major difference between what you see in Listing 30.6 and the code snippets I provided when I discussed DirectDraw basics is the logic I use to return a valid palette no matter what I find in the bitmap. I also use ATL.

LISTING 30.6 CREATING A DIRECTDRAW PALETTE

```
HRESULT CTableView::LoadDDPalette(UINT idBitmap,
➥IDirectDrawPalette** ppDDP)
{
   // Create a standard 332 palette as the default
   PALETTEENTRY ape[256];
   for ( int i = 0; i < 256; i++ ) {
      ape[i].peRed   = (BYTE)(((i >> 5) & 0x07) * 255 / 7);
      ape[i].peGreen = (BYTE)(((i >> 2) & 0x07) * 255 / 7);
      ape[i].peBlue  = (BYTE)(((i >> 0) & 0x03) * 255 / 3);
      ape[i].peFlags = (BYTE)0;
   } // for

    // Locate the bitmap resource.  Note this assumes the
   // bitmap is stored as a program resource (and not as
   // a disk file).
   HRSRC hBitmap = NULL;
   if ( (hBitmap = ::FindResource(NULL,MAKEINTRESOURCE(idBitmap),
➥RT_BITMAP))) {
      LPBITMAPINFOHEADER lpbi = (LPBITMAPINFOHEADER)
➥::LockResource(::LoadResource(NULL,hBitmap));
      if ( lpbi != NULL ) {
         // Locate the color information, which is stored past
         // the BITMAPINFOHEADER.
         RGBQUAD* prgb = (RGBQUAD*)((BYTE*)lpbi + lpbi->biSize);
```

continues

LISTING 30.6   CONTINUED

```
            // Determine how many palettized colors you're
            // talking about.
            int iNumColors;
            if (lpbi == NULL || lpbi->biSize < sizeof(BITMAPINFOHEADER))
                iNumColors = 0;
            else if (lpbi->biBitCount > 8)
                iNumColors = 0;
            else if (lpbi->biClrUsed == 0)
                iNumColors = 1 << lpbi->biBitCount;
            else
                iNumColors = lpbi->biClrUsed;

            //  Pull the color information
            for( i = 0; i < iNumColors; i++ ) {
                ape[i].peRed   = prgb[i].rgbRed;
                ape[i].peGreen = prgb[i].rgbGreen;
                ape[i].peBlue  = prgb[i].rgbBlue;
                ape[i].peFlags = 0;
            } // for
        } // if
    } // if

    // Create a new DirectDraw palette
    CComPtr<IDirectDrawPalette> pIDDPTemp;
    HRESULT hr = m_pIDirectDraw->CreatePalette(DDPCAPS_8BIT,
➥ape,&pIDDPTemp,NULL);
    if ( FAILED(hr) ) {
        // Some error
        *ppDDP = NULL;
        return hr;
    } // if

    // Return the palette
    *ppDDP = pIDDPTemp;
    (*ppDDP)->AddRef();

    return hr;
}
```

The goal is to create a palette no matter what happens to be contained within the bitmap I choose to provide to LoadDDPalette(). So, I begin by creating a 332 palette. Then, if I find invalid data stored within the bitmap, I simply create a palette with 332 data. On the other hand, if there is valid palette information contained within the bitmap, I replace the 332 palette color information with the bitmap data I found. In this way, I always create a valid palette unless the CreatePalette() method fails. In that case I have deeper problems than invalid palette color information.

Re-establishing a palette is a very simple matter, at least when using DirectDraw. In fact, the primary surface will have already handled the actual palette work for you on your behalf. What really remains to be done is to reload all your bitmaps. When you do, their individual color information will either be converted to the new palette (WM_PALETTECHANGED) or restored (WM_QUERYNEWPALETTE).

I chose to encapsulate this functionality in two helper functions, RePalettize() and ReLoadDDBitmap(). RePalettize() simply calls ReLoadDDBitmap() repetitively, once for each bitmap I use in my application. In the case of the BlackJack sample program, RePalettize() appears as you see in Listing 30.7.

LISTING 30.7 BLACKJACK REPALETTIZATION

```
BOOL CTableView::RePalettize()
{
   // Reload our bitmaps...
   BOOL bReturn = TRUE;
   HRESULT hr = S_OK;
   try {
      hr = ReLoadDDBitmap(IDB_TABLE,m_lpDDSTable);
      if FAILED( hr ) {
         // Some error
         throw new CDDException(TRUE,"Error reloading table bitmap");
      } // if

      hr = ReLoadDDBitmap(IDB_CARDS1,m_lpDDSCards1);
      if FAILED( hr ) {
         // Some error
         throw new CDDException(TRUE,
                  "Error reloading first card bitmap");
      } // if

      hr = ReLoadDDBitmap(IDB_CARDS2,m_lpDDSCards2);
      if FAILED( hr ) {
         // Some error
         throw new CDDException(TRUE,
                  "Error reloading second card bitmap");
      } // if

      hr = ReLoadDDBitmap(IDB_CARDBACK,m_lpDDSCardBack);
      if FAILED( hr ) {
         // Some error
         throw new CDDException(TRUE,
                  "Error reloading card back bitmap");
      } // if
   } // try
   catch (CDDException* dde) {
```

continues

30

MFC AND DIRECTX

LISTING 30.7   CONTINUED

```
    // Intercept your special exception and
    // tell user of error
    dde->ReportError(MB_OK ¦ MB_ICONERROR,hr);

    // Delete the exception
    dde->Delete();

    // Return failure
    bReturn = FALSE;
  } // catch
  catch (...) {
    // Return failure
    bReturn = FALSE;
  } // catch

  return bReturn;
}
```

Here you see I call `ReLoadDDBitmap()` for each of the four bitmaps I use in the program. You also see how I handle DirectDraw errors, which I'll discuss in detail later in the chapter. For now, though, you can see I use C++ exception handling with a custom exception class.

The `ReLoadDDBitmap()` method is quite simplistic because the hard work is performed in `CopyDDBitmap()`, as you see in Listing 30.8. All that is required is to copy the bitmap associated with a given surface *back into* the surface. This is one major reason why `CopyDDBitmap()` calls the `IDirectDrawSurface::Restore()` method. In any case, merely copying the bitmap back into the surface causes DirectDraw to adjust the display of the bitmap appropriately no matter if the application is gaining or losing the focus (using its own palette or another application's). If you've never dealt with palettes before in your application development, you might believe that all this code to support the system palette is somewhat of a burden. However, those of you who have worked with palettes before will probably agree that this is a painless and simple way to be sure your application appears as it was intended. DirectDraw is certainly the major reason this is so simple to implement.

LISTING 30.8   RELOADING DIRECTDRAW BITMAPS

```
HRESULT CTableView::ReLoadDDBitmap(UINT nID, IDirectDrawSurface* pDDS)
{
    // Pull the bitmap from resources
    CBitmap bmImage;
    VERIFY(bmImage.LoadBitmap(nID));

    // Copy the bitmap back to the surface
```

```
     return CopyDDBitmap(&bmImage,pDDS);
}
```

Windowed Rendering

As I mentioned previously, those applications that want to use DirectDraw from within a window have the additional requirement of creating a clipper object and associating it with their primary surface. But it is also true that the window might be resized at any time, thus changing the rules of the game for the clipper. It has to re-establish any and all clipping regions, thus allowing your application to repaint itself properly when later obscured by other windows.

You might believe this would be done while handling the WM_SIZE message, and you certainly could handle matters there. However, I find it more useful to encapsulate resizing and repainting in a single method. After all, a WM_SIZE message will most certainly result in a WM_PAINT message, so you can handle both issues at the time you repaint. Therefore, I've added a WM_PAINT handler to the BlackJack sample program (see Listing 30.9), and in the handler I call another helper function, Blt(), which you see in Listing 30.10.

LISTING 30.9   BLACKJACK WM_PAINT HANDLER

```
void CTableView::OnPaint()
{
   CPaintDC dc(this); // device context for painting

   // Copy our secondary buffer to primary
   Blt();

   // Do not call CWnd::OnPaint() for painting messages
}
```

LISTING 30.10   DIRECTDRAW WINDOWED Blt() METHOD

```
HRESULT CTableView::Blt()
{
   CRect rcClient;
   GetClientRect(rcClient);
   ClientToScreen(rcClient);
   HRESULT hr = m_lpDDSPrimary->Blt(rcClient,m_lpDDSSecondary.p,NULL,
                     DDBLT_WAIT,NULL);
   if ( FAILED(hr) ) {
      AfxMessageBox("Error bltting primary surface",
                     MB_OK | MB_ICONERROR);
   } // if

   return hr;
}
```

All that is required is to simply supply the `IDirectDraw::Blt()` method with the current client area rectangle in screen coordinates. When the blit takes place, the `IDirectDraw::Blt()` makes sure to honor the rectangle you provided. Note that I elected not to use C++ exception handling in this case as I was making a single DirectDraw method call. In fact, this is a good time to discuss DirectDraw error handling in general.

Error Handling

The impetus for handling errors in the first place is to eliminate the problems associated with cascading return codes. By this I mean I want to avoid the following code situation:

```
HRESULT hr = pSomeObject->SomeFunction();
if ( SUCCEEDED(hr) ) {
   hr = pSomeObject->AnotherFunction();
   if ( SUCCEEDED(hr) ) {
      hr = pSomeObject->AThirdFunction();
      if ( SUCCEEDED(hr) ) {
         hr = pSomeObject->AUsefulFunction();
         if ( SUCCEEDED(hr) ) {
            // Do something interesting...
         } // if
      } // if
   } // if
} // if
```

As with many COM objects, such error checking can get nested many levels deep very quickly. Another way to look at this same issue is the multiple return-point situation:

```
HRESULT hr = pSomeObject->SomeFunction();
if ( FAILED(hr) ) {
   AfxMessageBox("I failed");
   return hr;
} // if

hr = pSomeObject->AnotherFunction();
if (FAILED (hr) ) {
   AfxMessageBox("I failed");
   return hr;
} // if

hr = pSomeObject->AThirdFunction();
if (FAILED (hr) ) {
   AfxMessageBox("I failed");
   return hr;
} // if

hr = pSomeObject->AUsefulFunction();
if (FAILED (hr) ) {
   AfxMessageBox("I failed");
   return hr;
```

```
} // if
```

```
// Do something interesting...
```

Multiple return points present a problem when deciding how to clean up after an error has occurred. You're faced with making a determination regarding what happened and what needs to be done to recover from the error. The tricky part is that you might not know precisely where the error happened, making it difficult to clean up and/or recover.

C++ exception handling is a clean and elegant way to avoid problems such as these, which crop up often when working with COM (which is why the topic is reiterated here with a COM flavor). If you're interested, be sure to read all about C++ exception handling in general in Chapter 22, "Exceptions." Handling exceptions makes error recovery much easier because the error can be managed within the scope of the erroneous condition. At this time, local variables are still within scope and may be queried or reset as required to recover. An added benefit is that there is no need to repeat the same or similar error code, as is the case with the multiple return point example. You put all the error-handling code into the exception handler (the `catch` block) and manage the error locally. If you want to pass the error condition on, you can do so, or you can retry the operation to see if the error condition has been cleared.

Using the same code snippets as an example, here is my contrived example using exception handling:

```
HRESULT hr = S_OK;
try {
   pSomeObject->SomeFunction();
   if ( FAILED(hr) ) {
      throw new CMyException();
   } // if

   hr = pSomeObject->AnotherFunction();
   if (FAILED (hr) ) {
      throw new CMyException();
   } // if

   hr = pSomeObject->AThirdFunction();
   if (FAILED (hr) ) {
      throw new CMyException();
   } // if

   hr = pSomeObject->AUsefulFunction();
   if (FAILED (hr) ) {
      throw new CMyException();
} // if

   // Do something interesting...
} // try
```

```
catch (CMyException* e) {
   e->Delete() // assuming CException-based
   AfxMessageBox("I failed");
   // Handle error
   hr = S_OK;
} // catch
catch (...) {
   AfxMessageBox("I failed");
   // Handle error
   hr = S_OK;
} // catch

return hr;
```

From a line count perspective, there is more code when using exceptions. However, program operation is enhanced because error handling is located in a single location, where you're better able to determine what should be done given the current error condition.

If you re-examine Listing 30.7, you'll see that this example and the code shown in the listing are very similar. This isn't coincidental. In the case of the BlackJack program, I merely give up, display an error message box, and punt. In general, though, more could be done if you were to examine the error code. Perhaps the error is recoverable.

Referring again to Listing 30.7, you see I created a CDDException object when I threw the exception. This exception object, as it happens, is particularly useful when working with DirectDraw (and DirectX in general). The reason for this is that DirectDraw (and DirectX) define custom return codes. When you're developing DirectDraw applications, you'll no doubt receive errors from the COM objects for one reason or another. When you do, you can't use the handy error lookup tool from Developer Studio to view a textual representation of the error. The tool won't find DirectDraw error codes. Therefore, I implemented a similar feature in CDDException. You will see the error message you pass in displayed in the first line of the error message box. However, the second line will contain a textual representation of the error from DirectDraw. Chapter 22 has the details regarding creating custom exception classes. In this case, CDDException is based upon CException and implements custom GetErrorMessage() and ReportError() methods. Be sure to look at DDError.cpp and DDError.h in the BlackJack project if you're interested.

DirectDraw Shutdown

The final topic for this chapter is to look at the proper way to shut down your application when using DirectDraw. If you use ATL, you might believe you don't need to worry about releasing the DirectDraw COM objects. And from a COM perspective, you would be correct. However, there is an order in which the objects must be released. If you fail to follow this order, you will most certainly receive access violations further on down the road as your application continues to close.

Listing 30.11 shows you BlackJack's WM_DESTROY message handler. The correct order to release the DirectDraw objects is

1. Release the primary surface.
2. Release any secondary surfaces.
3. Release the palette object.
4. Release the DirectDraw object itself.

As a side note, releasing the primary surface also releases any clipper object you might have previously associated with your application's window.

An interesting feature when using ATL to encapsulate your COM interface pointers is that you don't need to call Release() directly. All you need to do is simply set the CComPtr variable to NULL, and ATL will handle the Release() for you. You also see this in action in Listing 30.11.

LISTING 30.11 RELEASING BLACKJACK DIRECTDRAW OBJECTS

```
void CTableView::OnDestroy()
{
    // Release your surfaces first.  The order in which
    // DirectDraw objects are released is important.
    // Surfaces first, then the palette, then finally
    // the DirectDraw object.
    m_lpDDSPrimary = NULL;
    m_lpDDSSecondary = NULL;
    m_lpDDSCards1 = NULL;
    m_lpDDSCards2 = NULL;
    m_lpDDSCardBack = NULL;
    m_lpDDSTable = NULL;

    // Now the palette.  If you never created one,
    // this call will still succeed (thanks to
    // CComPtr).
    m_lpDDPalette = NULL;

    // Finally release your DirectDraw object
    m_pIDirectDraw = NULL;

    CWnd::OnDestroy();
}
```

30

MFC AND
DIRECTX

Remember to reverse the order of primary and secondary (back buffer) surface release calls when using page flipping. In this case, the secondary surface is released *before* the primary, as both the primary and secondary surfaces are, in fact, the *same* surface. If you fail to follow this order of release, you will most certainly face an access violation when your application attempts to release the DirectDraw objects. Listing 30.12 shows you how this is done in the tearing demo. Here, I keep track of what mode was used to initialize the program and take the proper steps to release the DirectDraw objects accordingly.

LISTING 30.12   RELEASING TEARING DEMO DIRECTDRAW OBJECTS

```
void CChildView::ReleaseDDObjects()
{
    // Release your surfaces first.  The order in which
    // DirectDraw objects are released is important.
    // Surfaces first, then the palette, then finally
    // the DirectDraw object.
    if ( !m_bFlip ) {
        // When you're not page flipping, we release the
        // DirectDraw objects in the normal order.
        m_lpDDSPrimary = NULL;
        m_lpDDSSecondary = NULL;
    } // if
    else {
        // When you're page flipping, you reverse the order
        // of release for the primary and secondary
        // surfaces.  This is because they really are
        // the SAME surface and must be released in an
        // order opposite to that which created them.
        m_lpDDSSecondary = NULL;
        m_lpDDSPrimary = NULL;
    } // else
    m_lpDDSCan = NULL;

    // Now the palette.  If you never created one,
    // this call will still succeed (thanks to
    // CComPtr).
    m_lpDDPalette = NULL;

    // Finally release your DirectDraw object
    m_pIDirectDraw = NULL;
}
```

Summary

In this chapter, you were introduced to DirectX and saw quite a bit of detail regarding DirectDraw. Armed with this information, you have what you require to add stunning graphics to your applications with surprising ease. Don't let the BlackJack sample fool you—you can use DirectDraw (and DirectX) in any application, not just games. On the other hand, if you have a game in mind…

CHAPTER 31

Multimedia and MFC

by Michael Morrison

IN THIS CHAPTER

Multimedia has become a critical part of many Windows applications. There was a time when multimedia applied only to games and special multimedia presentations. However, multimedia content is now used extensively in business applications such as TurboTax and Microsoft Money, not to mention the many uses of multimedia on the Web. As an MFC developer, you should be prepared to leverage some degree of multimedia content in applications that you develop.

This chapter explores multimedia and how it affects MFC application development. You learn about the DirectX `Media Player` control, as well as how to use DirectSound to add multimedia sound capabilities to applications.

Multimedia Fundamentals

Multimedia is probably one of the most overused terms in the history of computing. Interestingly enough, many users don't even understand exactly what the term means. *Multimedia* refers to the different types of content displayed and interacted with in an application. In a general sense, any application content that contains audio or video elements could be considered multimedia content. However, I'd like to make a clearer distinction between multimedia content and other application content.

In general, *multimedia content* can be defined as audio, video, or other content that is time based, which means that the content changes over time. This definition of multimedia eliminates static content such as still images. This isn't meant to lessen the importance of images in Windows applications. Rather, I'm trying to get the point across that multimedia content encompasses a specific type of data. Keep in mind that static images could still fit in to a multimedia presentation as components of an animation that is time based. However, this definition of multimedia requires that the images be changed or altered over time.

Practically all games are considered multimedia applications because of their heavy use of multimedia content. There are also multimedia applications that ship with Windows 95/98. The CD Player and Sound Recorder applications are multimedia applications used to play CDs and record audio clips. You could even think of Microsoft Word and some other productivity applications as multimedia applications because it's possible to embed audio and video clips within Word documents. Web browsers are also very good examples of multimedia applications because they can be used to view a wide range of media content.

Chapter 30, "MFC and DirectX," introduces you to DirectX, which is designed to allow applications to simultaneously display and manipulate 2D and 3D graphics, animation, video, and surround sound, as well as support advanced user input devices. DirectX figures heavily into Windows multimedia content. In fact, DirectX forms the basis of every Windows multimedia technology. This wasn't always the case—earlier versions of Windows supported different types of multimedia content with completely different technologies. DirectX serves as the integration of all the tools and programming interfaces for the playback and capture of multimedia content.

The DirectX `Media Player` Control

One particular facet of DirectX that is extremely valuable for working with media content is the DirectX `Media Player` control, which is an ActiveX control that is part of the DirectX Media layer. The `Media Player` control is based on the `DirectShow` component of the DirectX Media layer and is used solely for the playback of multimedia content. The `Media Player` control acts as a universal player for most standard multimedia formats, including both streaming and nonstreaming media content. This makes the `Media Player` control extremely versatile; you can use the control in both applications and Web pages.

Media Formats Supported by the `Media Player` Control

The `Media Player` control supports the following streaming media formats, which are typically used for playback over a network:

- Advanced Streaming Format (ASF)
- Video On Demand (VOD)
- Moving Picture Experts Group standard 1, 2, and 3 (MPEG-1, MPEG-2, and MPEG-3)
- RealAudio (RA) and RealVideo (RV)

> **NOTE**
>
> Advanced Streaming Format (ASF) is Microsoft's standard streaming media format recommended for use with the `Media Player` control. An ASF file is capable of storing both audio and video and is specially designed to be used over networks such as the Internet. ASF media content is delivered as a continuous flow of data with minimal wait time before playback begins.

The Media Player control also supports the following nonstreaming media formats, which are typically used for local playback:

- Audio-Video Interleaved (AVI)
- QuickTime (MOV)
- Musical Instrument Digital Interface (MIDI)
- Indeo 5
- Waveform Audio (WAV)
- Sound File (SND)
- UNIX audio (AU)
- Audio Interchange File Format (AIFF)

Inside the Media Player Control

As with all ActiveX controls, you interact with the Media Player control by setting properties and calling member functions on the control. You can also respond to events that are generated by the control. Because the control is implemented as an ActiveX control, you can interact with it from applications written in a variety of languages or from a scripting language in a Web page. Using the properties and member functions exposed by the control, you can

- Control playback with operations such as start, stop, pause, rewind, and fast-forward
- Adjust the volume level or mute the audio entirely
- Monitor the performance of the media stream
- Retrieve media content information such as the author and title

The Media Player control is used as the basis for the Windows Media Player application that ships with Windows 98. The Windows Media Player application uses the standard user interface provided by the Media Player control and enables you to open and play the different types of media supported by the control. This application is a good example of how the Media Player control can be used to play back media content. Figure 31.1 shows the Windows Media Player application in action.

Figure 31.1

The Windows Media Player application that uses the Media Player *control.*

NOTE

For more extensive information on the DirectX Media Player control, check out Microsoft's Windows Media Web site at
http://www.microsoft.com/windows/windowsmedia/.

The CMediaPlayer Class

Although you can certainly interact with the Media Player control directly from MFC using its COM interfaces, this can be messy. The DirectX Media SDK (Software Development Kit) includes an MFC class named CMediaPlayer that serves as a C++ wrapper around the Media Player control. The CMediaPlayer class doesn't really provide any functionality of its own; it simply hides the details of making function calls through the ActiveX control's COM interfaces. Even so, the CMediaPlayer class is very convenient and keeps you from having to hassle with the calling conventions required when interacting with ActiveX controls.

NOTE

Because the CMediaPlayer wrapper class isn't part of a formal class library, you have to include the header (MediaPlayer.h) and source code (MediaPlayer.cpp) files in any projects that utilize the class.

Following are a few of the most commonly used member functions defined in the `CMediaPlayer` class:

- `GetVolume()`—Gets the volume of the control
- `SetVolume()`—Sets the volume of the control
- `SetFileName()`—Sets the filename of the media clip to be played
- `Play()`—Plays the current media clip
- `Pause()`—Pauses the current media clip
- `Stop()`—Stops the current media clip
- `GetCurrentPosition()`—Gets the current playback position of the current media clip
- `SetCurrentPosition()`—Sets the current playback position of the current media clip

This is only a very small subset of the member functions available for use in the `CMediaPlayer` class. In fact, the `CMediaPlayer` class defines more than 150 member functions that are used to control a wide range of media playback parameters. To keep things simple, let's stick to the basic media player functions.

Assuming that you already have a pointer to a `CMediaPlayer` object in the variable `pMediaPlayer`, following is an example of setting the player to an AVI video clip named KingKong.avi:

```
pMediaPlayer->SetFileName("KingKong.avi");
```

To start playing the video clip, you simply call the `Play()` member function, like this:

```
pMediaPlayer->Play();
```

You can then pause or stop the playback of the video clip by calling the `Pause()` or `Stop()` member functions.

Using the `Media Player` Control

Although the Windows Media Player application is very powerful and serves as a great all-purpose media player, it doesn't reveal much about using the `Media Player` control. So, let's work through the development of an MFC media player application named Projector that uses the `Media Player` control. You'll use the `CMediaPlayer` wrapper class to access the functionality of the `Media Player` control.

The Projector application is intended to function somewhat like a film projector. You load a "film" (media clip) and then you can play it, pause it, or stop it; stopping a media clip automatically results in it being rewound. Because the Projector application uses the Media Player control, it supports all kinds of media types, including both streaming and nonstreaming audio and video.

The Projector application is structured as a dialog-based application, which means that the main frame window is created from a dialog resource. This makes it possible to construct the application's main frame window as a dialog box containing the Media Player control and a few buttons. This is a convenient approach because you can lay out the application user interface using the Visual C++ dialog editor.

Because the main frame window for the Projector application is based on a dialog box resource, resources play an extremely important role in the application. Listing 31.1 shows the Resource.h header file for Projector, which contains the application's resource identifiers.

LISTING 31.1 THE RESOURCE.H HEADER FILE FOR PROJECTOR

```
//-------------------------------------------------------
// Strings                    Range : 1000 - 1999
//-------------------------------------------------------
#define IDR_PROJECTOR         1000


//-------------------------------------------------------
// Commands                   Range : 2000 - 2999
//-------------------------------------------------------
#define ID_ABOUT              2000


//-------------------------------------------------------
// Dialog Boxes               Range : 3000 - 3999
//-------------------------------------------------------
#define IDD_ABOUTBOX          3000
#define IDD_PROJECTORBOX      3001


//-------------------------------------------------------
// Controls                   Range : 4000 - 4999
//-------------------------------------------------------
#define ID_PB_LOAD            4000
#define ID_PB_PLAY            4001
#define ID_PB_PAUSE           4002
#define ID_PB_STOP            4003
#define ID_MP_PLAYER          4004
```

The IDD_PROJECTORBOX identifier is used to identify the dialog box resource that the main frame window is based on. This dialog box resource contains a Media Player control and a series of buttons used to manipulate the control, as you'll soon see. The buttons and the Media Player control are identified by the control constants near the end of the header file.

The resources for the Projector application are defined in the Projector.rc resource script, which is shown in Listing 31.2.

LISTING 31.2 THE PROJECTOR.RC RESOURCE SCRIPT FOR PROJECTOR

```
//------------------------------------------------------------------
// Inclusions
//------------------------------------------------------------------
#include "AfxRes.h"
#include "Resource.h"


//------------------------------------------------------------------
// Icons
//------------------------------------------------------------------
IDR_PROJECTOR ICON "Projector.ico"


//------------------------------------------------------------------
// Dialog Boxes
//------------------------------------------------------------------
IDD_ABOUTBOX DIALOG 0, 0, 217, 55
CAPTION "About Projector"
STYLE DS_MODALFRAME ¦ WS_POPUP ¦ WS_CAPTION ¦ WS_SYSMENU
FONT 8, "MS Sans Serif"
BEGIN
  ICON          IDR_PROJECTOR, IDC_STATIC, 11, 17, 20, 20
  LTEXT         "Projector Version 1.0", IDC_STATIC, 40, 10,
                 119, 8, SS_NOPREFIX
  LTEXT         "Copyright (c)1998 Michael Morrison", IDC_STATIC,
                 40, 25, 119, 8
  DEFPUSHBUTTON "OK", IDOK, 178, 7, 32, 14, WS_GROUP
END


IDD_PROJECTORBOX DIALOGEX 0, 0, 311, 186
CAPTION "Projector"
STYLE DS_MODALFRAME ¦ WS_MINIMIZEBOX ¦ WS_POPUP ¦ WS_VISIBLE ¦
  WS_CAPTION ¦ WS_SYSMENU
EXSTYLE WS_EX_APPWINDOW
FONT 8, "MS Sans Serif"
BEGIN
  DEFPUSHBUTTON "&Load...", ID_PB_LOAD, 254, 7, 50, 14
  PUSHBUTTON    "&Play", ID_PB_PLAY, 254, 25, 50, 14
  PUSHBUTTON    "P&ause", ID_PB_PAUSE, 254, 43, 50, 14
  PUSHBUTTON    "&Stop", ID_PB_STOP, 254, 61, 50, 14
  PUSHBUTTON    "E&xit", IDCANCEL, 254, 79, 50, 14
  CONTROL       "", ID_MP_PLAYER,
    "{22D6F312-B0F6-11D0-94AB-0080C74C7E95}", WS_TABSTOP, 6, 7,
    242, 172
END

IDD_PROJECTORBOX DLGINIT
```

```
BEGIN
  ID_MP_PLAYER, 0x376, 344, 0
  0x0000, 0x0000, 0x0001, 0x0000, 0x2584, 0x0000, 0x1cf0, 0x0000,
    0x0003,
  0xffff, 0xffff, 0x000b, 0x0000, 0x000b, 0xffff, 0x000b, 0xffff,
    0x000b,
  0xffff, 0x000b, 0xffff, 0x0000, 0x0002, 0x0000, 0x0000, 0x000b,
    0x0000,
  0x0003, 0x0000, 0x0000, 0x0008, 0x0002, 0x0000, 0x0000, 0x0005,
    0x0000,
  0x0000, 0x0000, 0x4014, 0x0008, 0x0002, 0x0000, 0x0000, 0x000b,
    0xffff,
  0x0003, 0x0000, 0x0000, 0x0005, 0x0000, 0x0000, 0x0000, 0xbff0,
    0x0003,
  0x0000, 0x0000, 0x0008, 0x0002, 0x0000, 0x0000, 0x0013, 0x0000,
    0x0000,
  0x0013, 0xffff, 0x00ff, 0x0003, 0x0000, 0x0000, 0x0003, 0x0000,
    0x0000,
  0x000b, 0xffff, 0x000b, 0xffff, 0x000b, 0xffff, 0x000b, 0x0000,
    0x000b,
  0xffff, 0x0008, 0x0002, 0x0000, 0x0000, 0x000b, 0xffff, 0x0003,
    0xffff,
  0xffff, 0x000b, 0x0000, 0x0003, 0x0001, 0x0000, 0x000b, 0x0001,
    0x0005,
  0x0000, 0x0000, 0x0000, 0x3ff0, 0x0008, 0x0002, 0x0000, 0x0000,
    0x0008,
  0x0002, 0x0000, 0x0000, 0x0008, 0x0006, 0x0000, 0x002d, 0x0031,
    0x0000,
  0x0005, 0x0000, 0x0000, 0x0000, 0xbff0, 0x0005, 0x0000, 0x0000,
    0x0000,
  0xbff0, 0x000b, 0xffff, 0x000b, 0xffff, 0x000b, 0x0000, 0x000b,
    0x0000,
  0x000b, 0x0000, 0x000b, 0xffff, 0x000b, 0xffff, 0x000b, 0x0000,
    0x000b,
  0x0000, 0x000b, 0x0000, 0x000b, 0x0000, 0x000b, 0x0000, 0x000b,
    0x0000,
  0x000b, 0x0000, 0x000b, 0x0000, 0x000b, 0x0000, 0x0003, 0x0000,
    0x0000,
  0x0013, 0x0000, 0x0000, 0x000b, 0xffff, 0x0003, 0xfda8, 0xffff,
    0x000b,
  0x0000,
  0
END
```

The IDD_PROJECTOR dialog box resource defines the dialog box that will serve as the main application window. This dialog box contains a series of buttons used to manipulate the media player, along with the actual Media Player control. Unlike other types of controls, ActiveX controls require you to initialize them before they can be used. Because they often have lots of different attributes that need to be initialized, they require the use of a dialog initialization structure. This is the big structure consisting of hexadecimal numbers that you see toward the end of the Projector.rc resource script.

Fortunately, you don't have to worry about what the numbers mean in the dialog initialization structure—they are automatically generated by the Visual C++ dialog editor. The IDD_PROJECTOR dialog box was created using the Visual C++ dialog editor and is shown in Figure 31.2.

FIGURE 31.2

The IDD_PROJECTOR dialog box in the Visual C++ dialog editor.

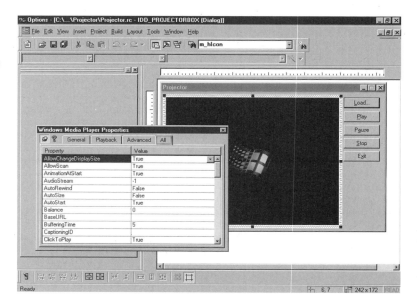

Notice in Figure 31.2 that the Media Player control is selected and the Properties window is displayed. The Properties window shows the different properties of the Media Player control, which are then written to the dialog initialization structure when the resource script is saved.

As you already know, the main frame window of the Projector application is implemented as a dialog box. Listing 31.3 contains the declaration of the CProjectorDlg class.

LISTING 31.3   THE PROJECTORDLG.H HEADER FILE FOR PROJECTOR

```
#ifndef __PROJECTORDLG_H__
#define __PROJECTORDLG_H__

//-----------------------------------------------------------------
// Inclusions
```

```
//------------------------------------------------------------
#include "Resource.h"
#include "MediaPlayer.h"

//------------------------------------------------------------
// CProjectorDlg Class - Projector Dialog Object
//------------------------------------------------------------
class CProjectorDlg : public CDialog {
  // Member Constants
  enum { IDD = IDD_PROJECTORBOX };

  // Member Data
protected:
  HICON        m_hIcon;
  CMediaPlayer* m_pMediaPlayer;

  // Public Constructor(s)/Destructor
public:
                  CProjectorDlg(CWnd* pParent = NULL);

  // Public Member Functions
public:
  virtual BOOL    OnInitDialog();

  // Message Handlers
public:
  afx_msg HCURSOR OnQueryDragIcon();
  afx_msg void    OnPaint();
  afx_msg void    OnSysCommand(UINT nID, LPARAM lParam);
  afx_msg void    OnPBLoad();
  afx_msg void    OnPBPlay();
  afx_msg void    OnPBPause();
  afx_msg void    OnPBStop();

  // Message Map & Runtime Support
protected:
  DECLARE_MESSAGE_MAP()
};

#endif
```

The CProjectorDlg class defines two member variables, m_hIcon and m_pMediaPlayer. The m_hIcon member stores the application's icon, which is necessary because dialog boxes don't typically have icons associated with them. Thus, you must manually support an icon in the application using the m_hIcon member variable. The m_pMediaPlayer member stores a pointer to the Media Player control in the dialog box window.

Four of the message handlers (PBLoad(), PBPlay(), PBPause(), and PBStop()) in CProjectorDlg are called in response to buttons on the dialog box. These buttons control the Media Player control through their corresponding message handlers. Listing 31.4 contains the complete source code for the CProjectorDlg class, which includes implementations of these button message handlers.

LISTING 31.4   THE PROJECTORDLG.CPP SOURCE CODE FILE FOR PROJECTOR

```
//-----------------------------------------------------------------
// Inclusions
//-----------------------------------------------------------------
#include "StdAfx.h"
//-----------------------------------------------------------------
#include <CommDlg.h>
#include "ProjectorDlg.h"
#include "AboutDlg.h"


//-----------------------------------------------------------------
// MFC Debugging Support
//-----------------------------------------------------------------
#ifdef _DEBUG
#undef THIS_FILE
static char BASED_CODE THIS_FILE[] = __FILE__;
#endif



//-----------------------------------------------------------------
// Message Map & Runtime Support
//-----------------------------------------------------------------
BEGIN_MESSAGE_MAP(CProjectorDlg, CDialog)
  ON_WM_QUERYDRAGICON()
  ON_WM_PAINT()
  ON_WM_SYSCOMMAND()
  ON_BN_CLICKED(ID_PB_LOAD, OnPBLoad)
  ON_BN_CLICKED(ID_PB_PLAY, OnPBPlay)
  ON_BN_CLICKED(ID_PB_PAUSE, OnPBPause)
  ON_BN_CLICKED(ID_PB_STOP, OnPBStop)
END_MESSAGE_MAP()


//-----------------------------------------------------------------
// Public Constructor(s)/Destructor
//-----------------------------------------------------------------
CProjectorDlg::CProjectorDlg(CWnd* pParent) :
  CDialog(CProjectorDlg::IDD, pParent) {
  // Load the application icon
  m_hIcon = AfxGetApp()->LoadIcon(IDR_PROJECTOR);
}


//-----------------------------------------------------------------
// Public Member Functions
//-----------------------------------------------------------------
```

```cpp
BOOL CProjectorDlg::OnInitDialog() {
  CDialog::OnInitDialog();

  // Add the About menu item to the system menu
  CMenu* pSysMenu = GetSystemMenu(FALSE);
  if (pSysMenu != NULL) {
    pSysMenu->AppendMenu(MF_SEPARATOR);
    pSysMenu->AppendMenu(MF_STRING, ID_ABOUT, "&About Projector...");
  }

  // Explicitly set the icon since the main window is a dialog
  SetIcon(m_hIcon, TRUE);

  // Get a pointer to the media player control
  m_pMediaPlayer = (CMediaPlayer *)GetDlgItem(ID_MP_PLAYER);

  return TRUE;
}

//------------------------------------------------------------------
// Message Handlers
//------------------------------------------------------------------
HCURSOR CProjectorDlg::OnQueryDragIcon() {
  // Return the cursor for the minimized application
  return (HCURSOR)m_hIcon;
}

void CProjectorDlg::OnPaint() {
  if (IsIconic()) {
    // Manually draw the application icon
    CPaintDC dc(this);
    SendMessage(WM_ICONERASEBKGND, (WPARAM)dc.GetSafeHdc(), 0);

    // Draw the icon centered in the client rectangle
    CRect rc;
    GetClientRect(&rc);
    int x = (rc.Width() - ::GetSystemMetrics(SM_CXICON) + 1) / 2;
    int y = (rc.Height() - ::GetSystemMetrics(SM_CYICON) + 1) / 2;
    dc.DrawIcon(x, y, m_hIcon);
  }
  else
    // Perform default painting
    CDialog::OnPaint();
}

void CProjectorDlg::OnSysCommand(UINT nID, LPARAM lParam) {
  if ((nID & 0xFFF0) == ID_ABOUT) {
    // Display the About dialog box
    CAboutDlg dlgAbout;
    dlgAbout.DoModal();
  }
```

continues

LISTING 31.4   CONTINUED

```
  else
    // Perform default processing of system menu command
    CDialog::OnSysCommand(nID, lParam);
}

void CProjectorDlg::OnPBLoad() {
  // Get the filename of the movie
  CFileDialog dlg(TRUE, "asf", "", OFN_FILEMUSTEXIST,
    "Active Streaming Format (*.asf)¦*.asf¦" \
    "Active Streaming Redirector (*.asx)¦*.asx¦" \
    "Audio Video Interleave Format (*.avi)¦*.avi¦" \
    "RealAudio/RealVideo (*.rm)¦*.rm¦" \
    "Wave Audio (*.wav)¦*.wav¦" \
    "All Files (*.*)¦*.*¦¦");

  // Set the movie filename in the media player
  if (dlg.DoModal() == IDOK)
    m_pMediaPlayer->SetFileName(dlg.GetPathName());
}

void CProjectorDlg::OnPBPlay() {
  // Play the movie
  m_pMediaPlayer->Play();
}

void CProjectorDlg::OnPBPause() {
  // Pause the movie
  m_pMediaPlayer->Pause();
}

void CProjectorDlg::OnPBStop() {
  // Stop playing the movie and rewind
  m_pMediaPlayer->Stop();
  m_pMediaPlayer->SetCurrentPosition(0);
}
```

The code that deals with the Media Player control is isolated in the last four message handlers in CProjectorDlg. The OnPBLoad() message handler first obtains a filename from the user by invoking the File Open common dialog box. It then calls the SetFileName() member function on the Media Player control to set the filename of the media content to be played.

The OnPBPlay() message handler calls the Play() member function on the Media Player control to play the media clip. Likewise, the OnPBPause() message handler calls the Pause() member function on the Media Player control to pause the playback of the clip. Finally, the OnPBStop() message handler calls the Stop() member function to stop the playback of the clip. The OnPBStop() message handler also calls SetCurrentPosition() and passes in 0 to rewind the Media Player to the beginning of the media clip.

Figures 31.3 and 31.4 show the Projector application playing several different types of media content.

FIGURE 31.3

The Projector application playing the Endorse.asf media file.

FIGURE 31.4

The Projector application playing the Drill.avi media file.

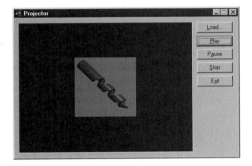

Playing Sound

Although the Media Player control is useful for playing media content within an application, it isn't as useful in applications that need to tightly control the playback of multiple sources of media content. More specifically, if you wanted to create a game that played multiple audio clips overlaid at once, the Media Player control wouldn't be your best option. In this case, you would be better off using DirectSound directly.

If you recall from Chapter 30, DirectSound is the audio portion of DirectX that supports low-latency audio mixing and playback. The latest version of DirectX, version 6.1, also allows you to generate and play interesting music using the DirectMusic API. The next few sections show you how to use DirectSound to play overlaid audio clips much as you would need to do in a game. You also learn how to control the volume of individual audio clips and control the panning between left and right speakers.

> **NOTE**
>
> In case the terminology is new to you, *low latency* refers to the speed at which an audio clip is played. *Latency* is the delay between when you initiate the playback of an audio clip programmatically and when the user actually hears the clip. DirectSound has a very low latency, which means that there is a very small delay between the initiation of the playback of a sound and the user hearing the sound.

Working with Waves

Before getting into the specifics of using DirectSound, it's important for you to understand how audio content is modeled in Windows. The most popular digital sound form at used in Windows is the wave format, which is denoted by the .WAV file extension. Windows .WAV files are actually RIFF files, which stands for Resource Interchange File Format. The RIFF format serves as the basis for many of the Windows media file formats.

From the perspective of a multimedia application, waves are just another type of resource, like bitmaps and icons. This means that you can include waves as resources in the resource script for an application.

You can create your own waves using the Sound Recorder application that ships with Windows. Although Sound Recorder is fairly primitive compared to some other commercial wave editors, it does get the job done. If you have a microphone connected to your sound card, you can record just about anything you want. You can also record audio directly from an audio CD in your CD-ROM drive.

Playing Waves

Regardless of how you create wave files, you can use the Win32 `PlaySound()` function to play them. You'll use the `PlaySound()` function in a moment when you create an MFC class that encapsulates a wave audio clip. Following is the prototype for the `PlaySound()` function:

```
BOOL PlaySound(LPCSTR pszSound, HMODULE hmod, DWORD fdwSound);
```

The first parameter to the `PlaySound()` function, `pszSound`, is the name of the wave audio clip, which can be the name of a wave file, the name of a wave resource, or a pointer to a wave image in memory. In the case of playing a wave resource, the second parameter, `hmod`, is the module instance handle where the resource is located. Otherwise, you can pass `NULL` as this parameter. The last parameter, `fdwSound`, specifies flags that determine how the sound is played. Table 31.1 describes the flags supported by the `PlaySound()` function.

TABLE 31.1   FLAGS SUPPORTED BY THE PlaySound() WIN32 API FUNCTION

Flag	Description
SND_FILENAME	Specifies that the pszSound parameter is a wave filename.
SND_RESOURCE	Specifies that the pszSound parameter is a wave resource identifier.
SND_MEMORY	Specifies that the pszSound parameter points to a wave image in memory.
SND_ASYNC	Plays the sound asynchronously, which means that the function returns immediately after starting the playing of the sound.
SND_SYNC	Plays the sound synchronously, which means that the function doesn't return until the sound finishes playing.
SND_LOOP	Plays the sound repeatedly until it is explicitly stopped; looped sounds must be asynchronous, which means that you must use the SND_ASYNC flag with SND_LOOP.
SND_NOSTOP	Specifies that the sound won't interrupt any other sound that is already playing; the sound won't be played if another sound is being played.
SND_NODEFAULT	Specifies that the default system sound won't be played if the wave sound isn't located.

This table alludes to a few interesting points regarding the PlaySound() function. First, the PlaySound() function can only be used to play one sound at a time. Secondly, the PlaySound() function will play the default system event sound if the specified wave sound cannot be located. The SND_NODEFAULT flag can be used to circumvent this default behavior.

> **NOTE**
>
> The PlaySound() function is part of the original Windows multimedia support and isn't technically part of DirectX. However, it is useful in situations where you don't need the extensive audio capabilities of DirectSound.

Following is an example of playing a looped wave file asynchronously using the PlaySound() function:

```
::PlaySound("Siren.wav", NULL, SND_NODEFAULT ¦ SND_ASYNC ¦ SND_LOOP);
```

The `CWave` Class

Although the `PlaySound()` function is useful in some situations, it can't compare to the rich audio features offered by DirectSound. The good news is that you still use waves when working with DirectSound. However, it is necessary to extract the wave data from a wave in order to play the wave using DirectSound. This involves digging into a wave and navigating through it to extract wave data.

To make using waves easier in MFC, it is helpful to create an MFC class, `CWave`, that encapsulates the functionality of a wave. This class could actually serve two purposes:

1. Provide a high-level means of playing wave audio via the `PlaySound()` Win32 API function

2. Provide a low-level means of mixing wave audio with advanced playback capabilities via DirectSound

Not surprisingly, supporting the `PlaySound()` Win32 API function in the `CWave` class is very straightforward. Supporting DirectSound, however, is not so easy. Listing 31.5 contains the declaration of the `CWave` class, which gives you an idea about the member functions that you can use to work with waves.

LISTING 31.5   THE WAVE.H HEADER FILE FOR THE `CWave` CLASS

```
#ifndef __WAVE_H__
#define __WAVE_H__

//-----------------------------------------------------------------
// Inclusions
//-----------------------------------------------------------------
#include <MMSystem.h>

//-----------------------------------------------------------------
// CWave Class - Wave Object
//-----------------------------------------------------------------
class CWave : public CObject {
  // Public Constructor(s)/Destructor
public:
        CWave();
        CWave(const CString& sFileName);
        CWave(UINT uiResID, HMODULE hmod =
          AfxGetInstanceHandle());
  virtual ~CWave();

  // Public Methods
public:
  BOOL    Create(const CString& sFileName);
  BOOL    Create(UINT uiResID, HMODULE hmod =
```

```
             AfxGetInstanceHandle());
  BOOL     IsValid() const { return (m_pImageData ? TRUE :
             FALSE); };
  BOOL     Play(BOOL bAsync = TRUE, BOOL bLooped = FALSE) const;
  BOOL     GetFormat(WAVEFORMATEX& wfFormat) const;
  DWORD    GetDataLen() const;
  DWORD    GetData(BYTE*& pWaveData, DWORD dwMaxToCopy) const;

  // Protected Methods
protected:
  BOOL     Free();

  // Private Data
private:
  BYTE* m_pImageData;
  DWORD m_dwImageLen;
  BOOL  m_bResource;
};

#endif
```

As you can see, the CWave class supports three constructors: a default constructor, a file constructor, and a resource constructor. The default constructor simply creates an empty CWave object with no actual wave data. The file constructor takes a wave filename as the only parameter and constructs a CWave object from the wave file. Finally, the resource constructor takes a module instance handle and a resource identifier as parameters and creates a CWave object from the resource image of the wave. The destructor for the CWave class is responsible for freeing the image data associated with the wave. This will make more sense in a moment.

The Create() member functions take on the task of reading a wave from a file or resource. Both Create() methods call the Free() method to free any previous wave data before loading a new wave. The IsValid() member function checks whether the object contains valid wave data.

The Play() member function is used to play a wave using the Win32 PlaySound() function. However, it doesn't enter the picture when using the CWave object with DirectSound. For that, you must use the GetFormat(), GetDataLen(), and GetData() member functions. These member functions enable you to retrieve information about the format of the wave, the length of the raw wave data, and the raw wave data itself.

Listing 31.6 contains the definition of the CWave class, which shows how each of the member functions is implemented.

LISTING 31.6   THE WAVE.CPP SOURCE CODE FILE FOR THE CWave CLASS

```cpp
//------------------------------------------------------------------
// Inclusions
//------------------------------------------------------------------
#include "StdAfx.h"
//------------------------------------------------------------------
#include "Wave.h"
#include "MMIO.h"


//------------------------------------------------------------------
// MFC Debugging Support
//------------------------------------------------------------------
#ifdef _DEBUG
#undef THIS_FILE
static char BASED_CODE THIS_FILE[] = __FILE__;
#endif


//------------------------------------------------------------------
// CWave Public Constructor(s)/Destructor
//------------------------------------------------------------------
CWave::CWave()
  : m_dwImageLen(0), m_bResource(FALSE), m_pImageData(NULL) {
}

CWave::CWave(const CString& sFileName)
  : m_dwImageLen(0), m_bResource(FALSE), m_pImageData(NULL) {
  Create(sFileName);
}

CWave::CWave(UINT uiResID, HMODULE hmod)
  : m_dwImageLen(0), m_bResource(TRUE), m_pImageData(NULL) {
  Create(uiResID, hmod);
}

CWave::~CWave() {
  // Free the wave image data
  Free();
}

//------------------------------------------------------------------
// CWave Public Methods
//------------------------------------------------------------------
BOOL CWave::Create(const CString& sFileName) {
  // Free any previous wave image data
  Free();

  // Flag as regular memory
  m_bResource = FALSE;
```

```
  // Open the wave file
  CFile fileWave;
  if (!fileWave.Open(sFileName, CFile::modeRead))
    return FALSE;

  // Get the file length
  m_dwImageLen = fileWave.GetLength();

  // Allocate and lock memory for the image data
  m_pImageData = (BYTE*)::GlobalLock(::GlobalAlloc(GMEM_MOVEABLE |
    GMEM_SHARE, m_dwImageLen));
  if (!m_pImageData)
    return FALSE;

  // Read the image data from the file
  fileWave.Read(m_pImageData, m_dwImageLen);

  return TRUE;
}

BOOL CWave::Create(UINT uiResID, HMODULE hmod) {
  // Free any previous wave image data
  Free();

  // Flag as resource memory
  m_bResource = TRUE;

  // Find the wave resource
  HRSRC hresInfo;
  hresInfo = ::FindResource(hmod, MAKEINTRESOURCE(uiResID),
    "WAVE");
  if (!hresInfo)
    return FALSE;

  // Load the wave resource
  HGLOBAL hgmemWave = ::LoadResource(hmod, hresInfo);

  if (hgmemWave) {
    // Get pointer to and length of the wave image data
    m_pImageData= (BYTE*)::LockResource(hgmemWave);
    m_dwImageLen = ::SizeofResource(hmod, hresInfo);
  }

  return (m_pImageData ? TRUE : FALSE);
}

BOOL CWave::Play(BOOL bAsync, BOOL bLooped) const {
  // Check validity
  if (!IsValid())
    return FALSE;
```

continues

LISTING 31.6   CONTINUED

```
   // Play the wave
   return ::PlaySound((LPCSTR)m_pImageData, NULL, SND_MEMORY ¦
     SND_NODEFAULT ¦ (bAsync ? SND_ASYNC : SND_SYNC) ¦ (bLooped ?
     (SND_LOOP ¦ SND_ASYNC) : 0));
}

BOOL CWave::GetFormat(WAVEFORMATEX& wfFormat) const {
   // Check validity
   if (!IsValid())
     return FALSE;

   // Set up and open the MMINFO structure
   CMMMemoryIOInfo mmioInfo((HPSTR)m_pImageData, m_dwImageLen);
   CMMIO           mmio(mmioInfo);

   // Find the WAVE chunk
   CMMTypeChunk mmckParent('W','A','V','E');
   mmio.Descend(mmckParent, MMIO_FINDRIFF);

   // Find and read the format subchunk
   CMMIdChunk mmckSubchunk('f','m','t',' ');
   mmio.Descend(mmckSubchunk, mmckParent, MMIO_FINDCHUNK);
   mmio.Read((HPSTR)&wfFormat, sizeof(WAVEFORMATEX));
   mmio.Ascend(mmckSubchunk);

   return TRUE;
}

DWORD CWave::GetDataLen() const {
   // Check validity
   if (!IsValid())
     return (DWORD)0;

   // Set up and open the MMINFO structure
   CMMMemoryIOInfo mmioInfo((HPSTR)m_pImageData, m_dwImageLen);
   CMMIO           mmio(mmioInfo);

   // Find the WAVE chunk
   CMMTypeChunk mmckParent('W','A','V','E');
   mmio.Descend(mmckParent, MMIO_FINDRIFF);

   // Find and get the size of the data subchunk
   CMMIdChunk mmckSubchunk('d','a','t','a');
   mmio.Descend(mmckSubchunk, mmckParent, MMIO_FINDCHUNK);
   return mmckSubchunk.cksize;
}

DWORD CWave::GetData(BYTE*& pWaveData, DWORD dwMaxLen) const {
   // Check validity
   if (!IsValid())
     return (DWORD)0;
```

```
        // Set up and open the MMINFO structure
        CMMMemoryIOInfo mmioInfo((HPSTR)m_pImageData, m_dwImageLen);
        CMMIO           mmio(mmioInfo);

        // Find the WAVE chunk
        CMMTypeChunk mmckParent('W','A','V','E');
        mmio.Descend(mmckParent, MMIO_FINDRIFF);

        // Find and get the size of the data subchunk
        CMMIdChunk mmckSubchunk('d','a','t','a');
        mmio.Descend(mmckSubchunk, mmckParent, MMIO_FINDCHUNK);
        DWORD dwLenToCopy = mmckSubchunk.cksize;

        // Allocate memory if the passed in pWaveData was NULL
        if (pWaveData == NULL)
          pWaveData = (BYTE*)::GlobalLock(::GlobalAlloc(GMEM_MOVEABLE,
            dwLenToCopy));
        else
          // If you didn't allocate your own memory, honor dwMaxLen
          if (dwMaxLen < dwLenToCopy)
            dwLenToCopy = dwMaxLen;
        if (pWaveData)
          // Read waveform data into the buffer
          mmio.Read((HPSTR)pWaveData, dwLenToCopy);

        return dwLenToCopy;
}

//-------------------------------------------------------------------
// CWave Protected Methods
//-------------------------------------------------------------------
BOOL CWave::Free() {
    // Free any previous wave data
    if (m_pImageData) {
      HGLOBAL   hgmemWave = ::GlobalHandle(m_pImageData);

      if (hgmemWave) {
        if (m_bResource)
          // Free resource (Win95 does NOT automatically do this)
          ::FreeResource(hgmemWave);
        else {
          // Unlock and free memory
          ::GlobalUnlock(hgmemWave);
          ::GlobalFree(hgmemWave);
        }

        m_pImageData = NULL;
        m_dwImageLen = 0;
        return TRUE;
      }
    }
    return FALSE;
}
```

The implementation of the CWave class reveals that the file- and resource-based constructors call the Create() member function to initialize the object. If you use the default constructor to create a CWave object, you must call Create() yourself in order to properly initialize the object. This is a common object initialization approach in MFC and is referred to as *two-phase construction*.

The implementation of the Play() member function shows how the PlaySound() Win32 API function is used to provide a high-level means of playing waves using the CWave class. You're probably more interested in using the CWave class to play waves using DirectSound, however. More important to DirectSound are the GetFormat(), GetDataLen(), and GetData() member functions. These member functions use two multimedia support classes, CMMMemoryIOInfo and CMMIO, to retrieve information about the format of a wave and the raw data associated with a wave. This is necessary because DirectSound utilizes waves at a low level and must have access to raw wave data.

You probably noticed that the GetFormat(), GetDataLen(), and GetData() member functions operate on chunks of data. Chunks form the basis of RIFF files, which represent the format wave files are stored in. It isn't terribly important that you understand the structure of RIFF files, but it is worth mentioning to help make the CWave code a little clearer. For more information on RIFF files and how to navigate through them, refer to the multimedia I/O data structures and functions in the Win32 API. On the other hand, you could just use the CWave class and not worry about the hassles of navigating RIFF files.

Now that you've seen how the CWave class is implemented, you're probably curious to see how it works. Following is an example of playing a wave using the high-level Play() member function in the CWave class:

```
CWave wavGong("Gong.wav");
wavGong.Play();
```

Although the high-level approach to playing waves is certainly simple and effective, it doesn't offer the power and flexibility of DirectSound. Let's continue onward and see how to use the CWave class with DirectSound.

Revisiting DirectSound

Before getting into the code for using the CWave class with DirectSound, let's take a moment to revisit DirectSound. If you recall from Chapter 30, DirectSound is implemented as a set of COM objects for representing both physical sound devices and sound data buffers. Following are the DirectSound objects involved in the playback of audio:

- DirectSound—Represents a physical hardware sound device
- DirectSoundBuffer—Represents an audio stream

- `DirectSound3DBuffer`—Represents an audio stream positioned in 3D space
- `DirectSound3Dlistener`—Represents an audio listener positioned in 3D space
- `DirectSoundNotify`—Provides a mechanism for notifying an application of DirectSound events

To keep things relatively simple, I'm going to stick with 2D audio and show how to mix 2D audio clips using DirectSound. To use 2D audio, you really only need to use the `DirectSound` and `DirectSoundBuffer` objects. So, let's focus on these two objects and learn more about their role in DirectSound.

The `DirectSound` Object

The `DirectSound` object is a software representation of a physical audio hardware device (a sound card). Because most computers have only one sound card, you will typically use only one `DirectSound` object. This means that multiple applications that use DirectSound will have to share the `DirectSound` object because they all use the same physical audio hardware. Fortunately, DirectSound automatically tracks the input focus of each application and produces sound only for the application with input focus. In other words, you don't have to worry about sharing the `DirectSound` object.

`DirectSound` objects are manipulated through the `IDirectSound` COM interface. You create a `DirectSound` object by calling the global `DirectSoundCreate()` function, which returns a pointer to an `IDirectSound` interface. The `IDirectSound` interface member functions are used to get and set `DirectSound` object attributes, as well as to create `DirectSoundBuffer` objects. Following are the member functions defined in the `IDirectSound` interface, some of which you'll use a little later in the chapter:

- `Initialize()`
- `SetCooperativeLevel()`
- `CreateSoundBuffer()`
- `DuplicateSoundBuffer()`
- `GetCaps()`
- `Compact()`
- `GetSpeakerConfig()`
- `SetSpeakerConfig()`
- `AddRef()`
- `QueryInterface()`
- `Release()`

The `DirectSoundBuffer` Object

The `DirectSoundBuffer` object represents a stream of wave audio and comes in two forms: the primary sound buffer and secondary sound buffers. The primary sound buffer represents the audio buffer being played on the physical audio device. Secondary sound buffers represent individual audio streams that are mixed into the primary buffer for output. Figure 31.5 shows the relationship between the primary and secondary buffers.

FIGURE 31.5

The relationship between the primary and secondary sound buffers.

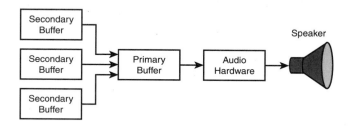

Figure 31.5 shows how the primary sound buffer represents the output of the `DirectSound` object and effectively serves as the result of mixing secondary buffers together. Secondary sound buffers are equivalent to the inputs on an audio mixer, except that in DirectSound there are no limits to the number of secondary sound buffers. Each secondary sound buffer is capable of being mixed with any other secondary buffer, with the resulting sound residing in the primary buffer for output.

Practically speaking, secondary sound buffers are used to represent each discrete sound in a multimedia application. You can create and mix as many secondary buffers as you need within a given application.

`DirectSoundBuffer` objects are manipulated through the `IDirectSoundBuffer` COM interface. You create `DirectSoundBuffer` objects by calling the `CreateSoundBuffer()` member function on the `DirectSound` object, which returns a pointer to an `IDirectSoundBuffer` interface. The `IDirectSoundBuffer` interface member functions are used to get and set `DirectSoundBuffer` object attributes, as well as to write audio data and play the sound buffers. Following are the member functions defined in the `IDirectSoundBuffer` interface, some of which you'll use a little later in the chapter:

- `GetCaps()`
- `GetFormat()`
- `SetFormat()`
- `GetStatus()`
- `Initialize()`

- `Restore()`
- `GetCurrentPosition()`
- `SetCurrentPosition()`
- `Lock()`
- `Unlock()`
- `Play()`
- `Stop()`
- `GetFrequency()`
- `SetFrequency()`
- `GetPan()`
- `SetPan()`
- `GetVolume()`
- `SetVolume()`
- `AddRef()`
- `QueryInterface()`
- `Release()`

Static and Streaming Sound Buffers

It's worth pointing out that the `DirectSoundBuffer` object supports both static and streaming sound buffers. A *static sound buffer* is a buffer that contains an entire sound, whereas a *streaming sound buffer* usually contains only part of a sound and requires the application to write new data to the sound buffer as the buffer is being played. Static buffers are more efficient because DirectSound will store them directly in the memory of a hardware audio device if possible. If a static buffer can be stored in the hardware audio device's memory, the sound hardware takes on the task of mixing the audio, which is much faster than leaving it up to the system CPU. It is also possible to utilize hardware mixing with streaming sound buffers, provided that the system data bus is fast enough to transfer the stream of data to the audio hardware as it is delivered.

Unless you are building an application that pulls audio off the Internet, you will more than likely want to use static sound buffers because they are more efficient. It is important to point out that audio hardware memory is limited, which means that there might not be enough room for it to hold all the static sound buffers you are using. Therefore, you should prioritize sound buffers so that the most commonly played buffers have the best chance of being stored directly in audio hardware memory. You do this by simply creating and initializing the most commonly played sound buffers first.

Using DirectSound to Play Sound Effects

Although I could continue on with a theoretical discussion of DirectSound, you're no doubt itching to see it in action. So, let's take a look at a practical application that demonstrates some of the main features of DirectSound. The remainder of the chapter focuses on the design and development of the War application, which uses DirectSound to create an audio simulation of a military battlefield. The War application mixes sound effects such as gunfire and explosions at random intervals and with random volume and panning values. By randomly altering the volume and panning of each sound, War gives the effect of the sounds occurring at different spatial locations.

> **NOTE**
>
> Because the War application simulates sounds occurring at different spatial locations, it would make an ideal application for using DirectSound's 3D audio features. However, I wanted to keep things relatively simple. Even so, you might be surprised at how effective it is to vary the volume and panning of sound effects to give the feel of a battlefield.

The first place to start with the War application is the application resources. Listing 31.7 contains the code for the Resource.h header file that defines resource identifiers for the application.

LISTING 31.7   THE RESOURCE.H HEADER FILE FOR WAR

```
//-------------------------------------------------------------------
// Icons                     Range : 1000 - 1999
//-------------------------------------------------------------------
#define IDR_WAR              1000


//-------------------------------------------------------------------
// Waves                     Range : 4000 - 4999
//-------------------------------------------------------------------
#define IDW_HELICOPTER       4000
#define IDW_RICOCHET1        4001
#define IDW_RICOCHET2        4002
#define IDW_GUNFIRE1         4003
#define IDW_GUNFIRE2         4004
#define IDW_GUNFIRE3         4005
#define IDW_GUNFIRE4         4006
#define IDW_GUNFIRE5         4007
#define IDW_EXPLODE1         4008
#define IDW_EXPLODE2         4009
#define IDW_EXPLODE3         4010
#define IDW_EXPLODE4         4011
```

```
#define IDW_SIREN          4012

//-----------------------------------------------------------------
// Timers                  Range : 5000 - 5999
//-----------------------------------------------------------------
#define IDT_SOUND          5000
```

Most of the resource identifiers are used to identify the wave resources, which you'll learn about in a moment. The other resource identifier of interest is IDT_SOUND, which identifies a timer used to play the different war sound effects. These resources are defined in the War.rc resource script, which is shown in Listing 31.8.

LISTING 31.8   THE WAR.RC RESOURCE SCRIPT FOR WAR

```
//-----------------------------------------------------------------
// Inclusions
//-----------------------------------------------------------------
#include "AfxRes.h"
#include "Resource.h"


//-----------------------------------------------------------------
// Icons
//-----------------------------------------------------------------
IDR_WAR           ICON       DISCARDABLE    "War.ico"


//-----------------------------------------------------------------
// Waves
//-----------------------------------------------------------------
IDW_HELICOPTER  WAVE       DISCARDABLE    "Helicopter.wav"
IDW_RICOCHET1   WAVE       DISCARDABLE    "Ricochet1.wav"
IDW_RICOCHET2   WAVE       DISCARDABLE    "Ricochet2.wav"
IDW_GUNFIRE1    WAVE       DISCARDABLE    "GunFire1.wav"
IDW_GUNFIRE2    WAVE       DISCARDABLE    "GunFire2.wav"
IDW_GUNFIRE3    WAVE       DISCARDABLE    "GunFire3.wav"
IDW_GUNFIRE4    WAVE       DISCARDABLE    "GunFire4.wav"
IDW_GUNFIRE5    WAVE       DISCARDABLE    "GunFire5.wav"
IDW_EXPLODE1    WAVE       DISCARDABLE    "Explode1.wav"
IDW_EXPLODE2    WAVE       DISCARDABLE    "Explode2.wav"
IDW_EXPLODE3    WAVE       DISCARDABLE    "Explode3.wav"
IDW_EXPLODE4    WAVE       DISCARDABLE    "Explode4.wav"
IDW_SIREN       WAVE       DISCARDABLE    "Siren.wav"


//-----------------------------------------------------------------
// Strings
//-----------------------------------------------------------------
STRINGTABLE PRELOAD DISCARDABLE
BEGIN
  AFX_IDS_APP_TITLE "War"
END
```

Beyond defining an icon and an application title string, the War.rc resource script defines resources for each of the wave sound effects used in the application. The WAVE resource type is used to define these wave resources.

The CMainFrame class in the War application represents the main application frame window and also takes on the responsibility of managing all DirectSound operations. Listing 31.9 contains the source code for the MainFrame.h header file, which declares the CMainFrame class.

LISTING 31.9   THE MAINFRAME.H HEADER FILE FOR WAR

```cpp
#ifndef __MAINFRAME_H__
#define __MAINFRAME_H__

//------------------------------------------------------------
// Inclusions
//------------------------------------------------------------
#include <MMSystem.h>
#include <DSound.h>

//------------------------------------------------------------
// Defines
//------------------------------------------------------------
#define NUMSOUNDS 13

//------------------------------------------------------------
// CMainFrame Class - Main Frame Window Object
//------------------------------------------------------------
class CMainFrame : public CFrameWnd {
  // Private Data
private:
  LPDIRECTSOUND       m_pDirectSound;
  LPDIRECTSOUNDBUFFER m_pDSBuffer[NUMSOUNDS];
  UINT                m_uiTimerID;
  LONG                m_lHeliPan;
  LONG                m_lHeliPanInc;

  // Public Constructor(s)/Destructor
public:
                      CMainFrame();
  virtual             ~CMainFrame();

  // Public Methods
public:
  BOOL                Create(const CString& sTitle);

  // Protected Methods
public:
  BOOL                InitDirectSound();
```

```
void               CleanupDirectSound();
BOOL               InitDSBuffers();
BOOL               RestoreDSBuffers();

// Message Handler Methods
protected:
  afx_msg int      OnCreate(LPCREATESTRUCT lpCreateStruct);
  afx_msg void     OnDestroy();
  afx_msg void     OnPaint();
  afx_msg void     OnTimer(UINT nIDEvent);

// Message Map & Runtime Support
protected:
  DECLARE_MESSAGE_MAP()
  DECLARE_DYNCREATE(CMainFrame)
};

#endif
```

The CMainFrame class declares some member variables for managing DirectSound objects and tasks. More specifically, the m_pDirectSound variable stores a pointer to the DirectSound object. The m_pDSBuffer array stores an array of pointers to the DirectSound buffers for each sound effect. The m_uiTimerID variable stores the identifier of the timer, which generates timing events that are used to play sounds. The m_lHeliPan and m_lHeliPanInc variables are used to control the panning of the helicopter sound effect, which is moved from right to left or left to right between speakers when played.

The protected member functions in the CMainFrame class are used to initialize, clean up, and manage DirectSound objects. The InitDirectSound() member function creates a DirectSound object and initializes DirectSound buffers, and the CleanupDirectSound() member function frees memory associated with the DirectSound object and sound buffers. The InitDSBuffers() member function is called by InitDirectSound() to create and initialize a sound buffer for each sound effect wave. It is possible for the memory associated with DirectSound buffers to be lost, in which case you must restore the buffers before attempting to play them. The RestoreDSBuffers() member function restores the memory for the sound effect buffers and reinitializes them with wave data.

The other notable member function in the CMainFrame class is OnTimer(), which is actually a message handler. The OnTimer() message handler is called in response to a timer event, which is set in the War application to occur once every half second. The OnTimer() message handler is responsible for playing random sounds with a random volume and panning.

To understand how the CMainFrame member functions are implemented, you must look to the CMainFrame class definition, which is shown in Listing 31.10.

LISTING 31.10   THE MAINFRAME.CPP SOURCE CODE FILE FOR WAR

```cpp
//-------------------------------------------------------------------
// Inclusions
//-------------------------------------------------------------------
#include "StdAfx.h"
//-------------------------------------------------------------------
#include "MainFrame.h"
#include "Wave.h"
#include "Resource.h"
#include <StdLib.h>


//-------------------------------------------------------------------
// MFC Debugging Support
//-------------------------------------------------------------------
#ifdef _DEBUG
#undef THIS_FILE
static char BASED_CODE THIS_FILE[] = __FILE__;
#endif



//-------------------------------------------------------------------
// CMainFrame Message Map & Runtime Support
//-------------------------------------------------------------------
BEGIN_MESSAGE_MAP(CMainFrame, CFrameWnd)
  ON_WM_CREATE()
  ON_WM_DESTROY()
  ON_WM_PAINT()
  ON_WM_TIMER()
END_MESSAGE_MAP()

IMPLEMENT_DYNCREATE(CMainFrame, CFrameWnd)

//-------------------------------------------------------------------
// CMainFrame Public Constructor(s)/Destructor
//-------------------------------------------------------------------
CMainFrame::CMainFrame()
  : m_pDirectSound(NULL), m_uiTimerID(0), m_lHeliPan(0),
    m_lHeliPanInc(0) {
  // Initialize member variables
  for (int i = 0; i < NUMSOUNDS; i++)
    m_pDSBuffer[i] = NULL;
}

CMainFrame::~CMainFrame() {
  CleanupDirectSound();
}

//-------------------------------------------------------------------
// Public Methods
//-------------------------------------------------------------------
```

```cpp
BOOL CMainFrame::Create(const CString& sTitle) {
  CString sClassName;

  sClassName = AfxRegisterWndClass(CS_HREDRAW | CS_VREDRAW,
    LoadCursor(NULL, IDC_ARROW),
    (HBRUSH)(COLOR_WINDOW + 1),
    LoadIcon(AfxGetInstanceHandle(),
    MAKEINTRESOURCE(IDR_WAR)));

  return CFrameWnd::Create(sClassName, sTitle);
}

//-------------------------------------------------------------
// Protected Methods
//-------------------------------------------------------------
BOOL CMainFrame::InitDirectSound() {
  // Create the DS object
  if (::DirectSoundCreate(NULL, &m_pDirectSound, NULL) != DS_OK) {
    MessageBox("Could not create DirectSound object!",
      "DirectSound Error");
    CleanupDirectSound();
    return FALSE;
  }

  // Set the cooperation level for the DS object
  if (m_pDirectSound->SetCooperativeLevel(GetSafeHwnd(),
    DSSCL_NORMAL) != DS_OK) {
    MessageBox("Could not set cooperative level!",
      "DirectSound Error");
    CleanupDirectSound();
    return FALSE;
  }

  // Initialize the DS buffers
  if (!InitDSBuffers()) {
    MessageBox("Could not initialize DirectSound buffers!",
      "DirectSound Error");
    CleanupDirectSound();
    return FALSE;
  }

  return TRUE;
}

void CMainFrame::CleanupDirectSound() {
  // Cleanup the DS object
  if (m_pDirectSound) {
    m_pDirectSound->Release();
    m_pDirectSound = NULL;
  }
```

continues

LISTING 31.10   CONTINUED

```
}

BOOL CMainFrame::InitDSBuffers() {
  // Initialize waves
  CWave waves[NUMSOUNDS];
  waves[0].Create(IDW_HELICOPTER);
  waves[1].Create(IDW_RICOCHET1);
  waves[2].Create(IDW_RICOCHET2);
  waves[3].Create(IDW_GUNFIRE1);
  waves[4].Create(IDW_GUNFIRE2);
  waves[5].Create(IDW_GUNFIRE3);
  waves[6].Create(IDW_GUNFIRE4);
  waves[7].Create(IDW_GUNFIRE5);
  waves[8].Create(IDW_EXPLODE1);
  waves[9].Create(IDW_EXPLODE2);
  waves[10].Create(IDW_EXPLODE3);
  waves[11].Create(IDW_EXPLODE4);
  waves[12].Create(IDW_SIREN);

  // Initialize DS buffers
  for (int i = 0; i < NUMSOUNDS; i++) {
    // Get the wave information
    DWORD         dwDataLen = waves[i].GetDataLen();
    WAVEFORMATEX  wfFormat;
    waves[i].GetFormat(wfFormat);

    // Set up the DS buffer description
    DSBUFFERDESC  dsbdDesc;
    ZeroMemory(&dsbdDesc, sizeof(DSBUFFERDESC));
    dsbdDesc.dwSize = sizeof(DSBUFFERDESC);
    dsbdDesc.dwFlags = DSBCAPS_CTRLDEFAULT | DSBCAPS_STATIC;
    dsbdDesc.dwBufferBytes = dwDataLen;
    dsbdDesc.lpwfxFormat = &wfFormat;

    // Create the DS buffer
    if (m_pDirectSound->CreateSoundBuffer(&dsbdDesc,
      &m_pDSBuffer[i], NULL) != DS_OK)
      return FALSE;

    // Lock the DS buffer
    BYTE* pDSBuffData;
    if (m_pDSBuffer[i]->Lock(0, dwDataLen, (LPLPVOID)&pDSBuffData,
      &dwDataLen, NULL, 0, 0) != DS_OK)
      return FALSE;

    // Write wave data to the DS buffer
    dwDataLen = waves[i].GetData(pDSBuffData, dwDataLen);

    // Unlock the DS buffer
```

```
      if (m_pDSBuffer[i]->Unlock(pDSBuffData, dwDataLen, NULL, 0) !=
        DS_OK)
        return FALSE;
  }

  return TRUE;
}

BOOL CMainFrame::RestoreDSBuffers() {
  // Restore the buffers
  for (int i = 0; i < NUMSOUNDS; i++)
    if (m_pDSBuffer[i]->Restore() != DS_OK)
      return FALSE;

  // Reinitialize the buffers
  return InitDSBuffers();
}

//-------------------------------------------------------------------
// CMainFrame Message Handler Methods
//-------------------------------------------------------------------
int CMainFrame::OnCreate(LPCREATESTRUCT lpCreateStruct) {
  // Initialize DirectSound
  if (!InitDirectSound())
    return -1;

  // Seed the random number generator
  ::srand((UINT)timeGetTime());

  // Set the timer
  m_uiTimerID = SetTimer(IDT_SOUND, 500, NULL);
  if (m_uiTimerID == 0)
    return -1;

  return 0;
}

void CMainFrame::OnDestroy() {
  // Kill the timer
  KillTimer(m_uiTimerID);
}

void CMainFrame::OnPaint() {
  // Get the DC
  CPaintDC dc(this);

  // Calculate where to draw the text
  CString sText("Close your eyes, crank the volume, "
    "and hunker down for war...");
  CRect   rcClient;
  CSize   sizText;
```

continues

LISTING 31.10 CONTINUED

```cpp
  CPoint  ptTextPos;
  GetClientRect(&rcClient);
  sizText = dc.GetTextExtent(sText, sText.GetLength());
  ptTextPos.x = (rcClient.Width() - sizText.cx) / 2;
  ptTextPos.y = (rcClient.Height() - sizText.cy) / 2;

  // Draw the text
  dc.TextOut(ptTextPos.x, ptTextPos.y, sText);
}

void CMainFrame::OnTimer(UINT nIDEvent) {
  if (nIDEvent == m_uiTimerID) {
    // See if you should play a sound (50-50 chance)
    if (::rand() % 2) {
      // Determine which sound to play
      int nIndex = ::rand() % NUMSOUNDS;
      if (m_pDSBuffer[nIndex] != NULL) {
        DWORD dwStatus;
        m_pDSBuffer[nIndex]->GetStatus(&dwStatus);

        // Check to make sure that the buffer hasn't been lost
        if (dwStatus & DSBSTATUS_BUFFERLOST)
          RestoreDSBuffers();

        // Check to make sure that the sound isn't already playing
        if (!(dwStatus & DSBSTATUS_PLAYING)) {
          if (nIndex > 0) {
            // Set the panning of the sound
            m_pDSBuffer[nIndex]->SetPan((::rand() % 2000) - 1000);

            // Set the volume of the sound
            m_pDSBuffer[nIndex]->SetVolume((::rand() % 3) * -250);

            // Play the sound
            m_pDSBuffer[nIndex]->Play(0, 0, 0);
          }
          else {
            // Set the panning of the helicopter
            LONG lStart = (::rand() % 2) ? -1 : 1;
            m_lHeliPan = lStart * 8000;
            m_lHeliPanInc = -(lStart * 400);
            m_pDSBuffer[nIndex]->SetPan(m_lHeliPan);

            // Play the helicopter sound
            m_pDSBuffer[nIndex]->Play(0, 0, DSBPLAY_LOOPING);
          }
        }
      }
    }
  }
```

```
    // If helicopter sound is playing, see if you should stop it
    DWORD dwStatus;
    m_pDSBuffer[0]->GetStatus(&dwStatus);
    if (dwStatus & DSBSTATUS_LOOPING) {
      if ((m_lHeliPan < -8000) || (m_lHeliPan > 8000))
        m_pDSBuffer[0]->Stop();
      else {
        m_lHeliPan += m_lHeliPanInc;
        m_pDSBuffer[0]->SetPan(m_lHeliPan);
        m_pDSBuffer[0]->SetVolume(-(::abs(m_lHeliPan) / 5));
      }
    }
  }
}
```

The implementation of the CMainFrame class reveals some interesting things about how DirectSound is used to mix audio clips. The InitDirectSound() member function first calls the DirectSoundCreate() function to create a DirectSound object. The cooperative level of the DirectSound object is then set with a call to SetCooperativeLevel(). Setting the cooperative level is a strict requirement before using a DirectSound object. In this case, the cooperative level is set to DSSCL_NORMAL, which provides the smoothest multitasking and resource-sharing behavior for the DirectSound object. The last step in the InitDirectSound() member function is initializing the DirectSound buffers with a call to InitDSBuffers(), which you'll learn about in a moment.

The CleanupDirectSound() member function is responsible for releasing the DirectSound object, which also releases the DirectSound buffers associated with the object.

The InitDSBuffers() member function creates and initializes the DirectSound sound effect buffers. This is where the CWave class enters the picture with DirectSound. The CWave class includes support member functions necessary to handle creating a sound buffer of the correct size and with the correct wave format, along with copying the wave data into the buffer. InitDSBuffers() creates an array of CWave objects as a means of initializing DirectSound buffers. The CWave objects are created from wave resources defined in the War application's resource script. The static DirectSound buffers are then created based on each of the CWave objects.

The RestoreDSBuffers() member function is used to restore DirectSound buffers in the event that their memory is lost. RestoreDSBuffers() simply calls the Restore() member function on each buffer and then reinitializes them with a call to InitDSBuffers().

With the DirectSound member functions in place, the other major part of the CMainFrame class to address is the timing mechanism used to play the sound effects. The OnCreate() message handler establishes the timing mechanism by setting up a timer that generates timer events at half-second (500-millisecond) intervals. The timer is destroyed in the OnDestroy() message handler.

The OnTimer() message handler is called every half second in response to timer events and is ultimately where the fun lies in the War application. The OnTimer() message handler first checks whether a sound effect should be played, which is given a 50-50 likelihood of happening. If a sound effect is to be played, OnTimer() then randomly selects one of the sound effects from the array of DirectSound buffers. The GetStatus() member function is then called on the selected sound buffer to make sure that the buffer hasn't been lost. If it has been lost, the RestoreDSBuffers() member function is called to restore all the sound buffers. OnTimer() also checks to make sure that the selected sound buffer isn't already playing.

The remainder of the code in OnTimer() sets the volume and panning of the sound buffer and then plays it. If the sound buffer isn't the helicopter sound effect, random panning and volume are set, and the sound buffer is started playing. However, if the buffer is the helicopter sound effect, the panning and volume are specially set so that the helicopter sounds like it is flying by. This also requires OnTimer() to update the settings of the helicopter sound effect buffer periodically, which is reflected by the last block of code in the OnTimer() message handler. The helicopter sound effect is the only one that is played looped, which means that it is played repeatedly until it cycles from one speaker to the other and fades out. This logic is entirely controlled by the OnTimer() message handler.

Figure 31.6 shows the completed War application, which admittedly isn't very revealing because this book isn't capable of playing the audio in the application.

FIGURE 31.6

The completed War application.

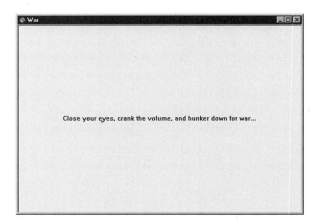

Close your eyes, crank the volume, and hunker down for war...

Summary

This chapter introduces you to MFC multimedia programming, which encompasses a lot of territory. As you learned, multimedia programming under Windows really translates into DirectX programming because DirectX forms the basis for all the latest Windows multimedia technologies. This chapter shows you how to use the DirectX `Media Player` control, which is an ActiveX control that supports the playback of a wide range of streaming and nonstreaming media content. You built an application that utilized the `Media Player` control to serve as a media viewer.

The chapter also focuses on DirectSound, the high-performance audio portion of DirectX. You learned how to use DirectSound to mix wave audio clips and tightly control certain aspects of their playback, such as volume and panning. You also created an all-purpose MFC wave class that encapsulates the functionality of a wave audio clip.

Advanced MFC

IN THIS PART

Inside the Registry

by K. David White

IN THIS CHAPTER

CHAPTER 32

If you are looking for information regarding wedding registries, you've come to the wrong place! This chapter discusses a commonly overlooked mechanism available in Windows that is very important to the commercial success of your application: the Windows Registry.

If you are somewhat familiar with the Registry, you might be asking what a chapter about the Windows Registry is doing in a book about MFC programming? Don't you want to get "under the covers" of MFC here?

Good question! Typically, you see this topic covered in topic-specific books. What I've noticed is that this topic is usually covered from a system administration viewpoint, with only passing mention of the API. I have seen some very good articles on the Registry in different magazines, but they only scratch the surface. Most authors and publishers simply feel that the Registry is a peripheral topic not directly related to programming. Most bookstores place a Registry book on the Operating System shelf!

Many moons ago, when I started developing Windows applications, I was a veteran "newbie" to the Windows world, not paying attention to the use of INI files and (later) the Registry. The primary reason for this was that I was reading and relying on programming books (such as this one) to provide me with the information that I needed. Coming from a different operating system (VMS) background (thus the veteran status), I didn't get to know the operating system components very well before jumping in and developing an application. It wasn't long before I came face to face with the installation "monster" that forced me to learn the Registry. When I realized how easy it was, I decided to investigate further.

In the not too distant past, Windows applications relied on ASCII-based files to store important information. These files came in the form of *.INI files and were usually stored in either the application's install directory or in the Windows system directory.

> **NOTE**
>
> Before the method of using INI files, Microsoft used the infamous CONFIG.SYS and AUTOEXEC.BAT (which are still in use). Applications had to maintain their own configuration files. Then along came the system-level INI files. These were PROGMAN.INI, SYSTEM.INI, WIN.INI, and CONTROL.INI.

This was fine as long as the application wasn't upgraded or moved. These files were easy to change, which gave system administrators a quick-fix method for correcting operating system and application problems. However, this flexibility would many times come back to haunt the administrator. "Easy to fix, easy to break."

Microsoft, with the release of Windows 3.1, created the Registry. Remarkably, this creation, although simple, has created much confusion and frustration among software developers. In this chapter, you will develop a better understanding of what the Registry is for and how to use it effectively.

What this chapter is not, however, is an in-depth guide to optimizing the Registry to make Windows NT or Windows 95/98 more efficient. This chapter looks at the Registry from the application's point of view.

Registry Usage

Imagine an application that requires no external direction as to where to run, where to display its interface, what to display on its interface, and so on. You are wondering how an application might "know" about these things without some sort of initialization/remembrance mechanism. One method to store important initialization and state data would be to put it into flat files that the application would read in at startup. These files, commonly called INI files, were widely used, but they are not without their problems:

- Files are sometimes deleted—In many cases, the INI files would accidentally be deleted. You can imagine the problems then!

- Files are sometimes moved—Files also have a tendency to get moved, thereby creating a situation in which the application can't find the file.

- File versioning problems—I have run into situations where an application's INI file would not be updated with an upgrade of the application. This happened much more frequently than most developers would like to admit, but it's something simple to overlook.

Although this list is not complete, you can readily see that the system of maintaining configuration in flat files can quickly run amuck.

Enter the Registry. Originally, the Registry was developed to assist the system administrator in controlling, configuring, and optimizing the Windows operating system. Although that is its primary purpose today, many applications also use it for a plethora of configuration and state information. Many developers believe that the Registry shouldn't really be used for GUI-related items, but what better way to save important interface information when the application is shut down?

> **NOTE**
>
> Of course, there are limitations to what can be stored in the Registry. The Registry is a file system, and the larger those files get, the longer the Windows operating system takes to boot. There is also a size boundary to the Registry that is operating system–dependent. With this in mind, you might want to limit the information stored. Stick with important configuration and state information, and store buffered data to a file.

I will define some terms here relating to the usage of the Registry.

Configuration

Configuration data is that data that defines not only the operating system runtime parameters, but also the runtime information for applications. The Registry is perfect for defining items such as background color, screen size and location, number of users, and COM property data. Sticking this information away in the Registry whenever an application exits makes it easy to restore at the next startup.

Services Information

You might be thinking that information about a service would fall under *configuration* or even *state,* but services are different from user applications. What sets the service apart from other applications is that the interface is normally handled through the Control Panel. Services generally don't have a user interface; therefore, certain information can only be maintained using flat files or the Registry.

State

State is commonly referred to in programming circles as the point in the programmatic flow that maintains a constant definition. In simpler terms, programmatic flow has steps involved in completion of the algorithm. A *state* is simply the condition of the data at a defined step. Many control applications are nothing more than state machines, where the application's state defines the step in the control flow. The Registry lends itself to managing state data for not only the operating system, but also any application.

User Preferences

I have yet to meet a computer user or developer who likes to use the computer exactly the same way as another does. Everyone is different; it's a fact of life! The Registry provides a placeholder to store user preferences. You might think that applies to operating system preferences, but if you expand your thinking, you can quickly see the benefit for multiuser applications.

The Registry Structure

You've learned a little about what the Registry is used for, but before you jump into it programmatically, take a quick look at the structure. Figure 32.1 shows a screen shot of the Registry on a Windows 95 system (my home system).

FIGURE 32.1

The Registry structure appears to be similar to a file structure.

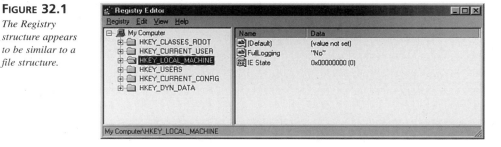

32

INSIDE THE
REGISTRY

The Registry is a file. However, through the Registry editor (RegEdt32 and RegEdit for Windows NT and RegEdit for Windows 95/98), it appears as a file system where the keys are displayed as directories and files, and the values are displayed as what is in the file. It is this key/value pair that provides the strength of the Registry. In this sense, it further appears that the Registry is an indexed database or a unique hash table. This, of course, is partially correct. To access data in the Registry, you look it up through its key. Provide the key, and you can set and get the associated value for that key.

Values stored in the Registry typically take the form of strings, compound strings, doubles, and binary data. A string value is made up of a C-style null-terminated string. Compound strings are several null-terminated strings appended together, with another terminator on the end. Doubles are self-explanatory, and binary data can be about anything. As you can see, this is a fairly open mechanism for storing configuration and state data.

Now that you know what kind of data is put into the Registry, the question that remains is where to store the data.

> **NOTE**
>
> A valuable source of information regarding the where question is the "Windows 95 Application Setup Guidelines for Independent Software Vendors" located on the MSDN CD-ROM or MSDN online (http://msdn.microsoft.com/developer/).

The first time I used RegEdit to modify a Registry, I was struck with confusion. The naming system appeared to be Greek. All the root folders started with HKEY, which I didn't realize was nothing more than a handle to a key. In this case, an HKEY is a handle to the "root" keys of the Registry structure.

Let's take a look at these keys:

- HKEY_CLASSES_ROOT—This key structure is taken from HKEY_LOCAL_MACHINE\SOFTWARE\Classes and primarily provides compatibility for 16-bit software. From the application's point of view, you will store file information in this area.

- HKEY_CURRENT_USER—This is where the user-specific data goes. Many applications are single-user, but many can use this key to store user preferences.

- HKEY_LOCAL_MACHINE—This is considered a major key. It stores information about the operating system and the hardware, as well as all the pertinent application data that the operating system needs.

- HKEY_USERS—This is also a major key and is officially the parent of the HKEY_CURRENT_USER key. However, you will notice that the Registry structure puts these two on the same level, and that is done simply for maintainability. This root key stores user profiles for all users on the system.

- HKEY_CURRENT_CONFIG—This is a subkey of HKEY_LOCAL_MACHINE and is used to store information about the current running configuration.

- HKEY_DYN_DATA—Dynamic data store. This is a scratch area for the operating system to store performance and other runtime data.

So what is it that you are looking at when you see the value portion of the key/value pair? The value portion itself is sometimes referred to as a name-value entity. There are essentially three parts to the value: a name for the value, the value associated with that name, and its datatype. Throughout this chapter, however, I will refer to it simply as the *value*.

Programmatic Control of the Registry

The preceding section discusses the structure, and some of you might already be somewhat familiar with the Registry from previous experience (and hopefully good guidance). Before looking at what MFC provides and how you can expand it, let's take a quick tour of the Registry API provided by Windows.

The Registry API

Table 32.1 lists a portion of the functions available for manipulating Registry data. More information is provided in the MSDN libraries, and in many other books, but I will pick a few important ones and expand them for my purposes.

TABLE 32.1 REGISTRY API FUNCTIONS

API Function	Description/Notes
RegOpenKey	Opens a key. Pass in the root HKEY and the name of the key to open, and the resultant HKEY is returned as the third parameter.
RegCreateKey	Same as RegOpenKey, except that it will create the key if the specified key doesn't exist.
RegCloseKey	Closes a key previously opened by RegOpenKey or RegCreateKey. Releases the handle to the key.
RegDeleteKey	Deletes the key from the Registry. (Will not delete the root key. On Windows 95/98, all child keys will also be deleted. On Windows NT, the key to be deleted must not have any children, or a failure is returned.)
RegDeleteValue	Deletes the value associated with a key and not the key itself.
RegEnumKey	Provides a way to enumerate children of a specified key (RegEnumKey is provided to support Windows 3.1 programming. Use RegEnumKeyEx).
RegEnumValue	Provides a way to enumerate all the values of a specified key.
RegFlushKey	Writes all the information about an open key back to the Registry.
RegLoadKey	Loads a key from a REG file to the Registry, writing all the information saved to the file.
RegSaveKey	Saves a key and its value data to a file (usually a REG file).
RegNotifyChangeKeyValue	Notifies the caller that value information has changed for the specified key.
RegQueryInfoKey	Provides a way to determine child key information, given a root key.

The application at the end of this chapter deals with setting and deleting keys within the application's configuration data, but first take a quick look at what MFC does for you.

32

INSIDE THE REGISTRY

Look inside `CWinApp` and you will find a member function called `SetRegistryKey()`. This function takes a single parameter, a string value that will be placed in `HKEY_CUR-RENT_USER\Software\(company name)\(application name)\`. In this example, the `(company name)` was defined as `"SAMS MFC Unleashed"`, and the application name is RegSamp. A `Settings` subkey will also be created by the MFC framework. You will use this in this chapter's example.

At this point, you might be wondering where in the application the `SetRegistryKey()` function is called. The framework also takes care of this when you use the `CWinApp` functions `GetProfileInt()`, `SetProfileInt()`, `GetProfileString()`, and `SetProfileString()`.

Let's take a closer look. Listing 32.1 is from the `InitInstance` routine. This is standard MFC boilerplate code.

LISTING 32.1   STANDARD BOILERPLATE CODE

```
// Change the Registry key under which your settings are stored.
   // TODO: You should modify this string to be something appropriate
   // such as the name of your company or organization.
   SetRegistryKey(_T("SAMS MFC Unleashed"));

   LoadStdProfileSettings();  // Load standard INI file options
                              // (including MRU)
```

From this, MFC will create the following Registry key:

```
HKEY_CURRENT_USER\Software\SAMS MFC Unleashed)\RegSamp
```

MFC will create a `Settings` child key by default. This enables you to use `Get/SetProfileInt()` and `Get/SetProfileString()` to manipulate the `Settings` child key. MFC makes Registry programming a snap by enabling you to use a single function call to define settings for the application. For example, you'll find this line of code in the RegSamp sample application:

```
// Change the Registry key under which your settings are stored.
// TODO: You should modify this string to be something appropriate
// such as the name of your company or organization.
SetRegistryKey(_T("SAMS MFC Unleashed"));

LoadStdProfileSettings();  // Load standard INI file options
                           // (including MRU)
```

In the sample application, you are saving the left coordinate of your window.

> **TIP**
>
> A common mistake is to use `CWnd::GetWindowRect()` to return the window coordinates, but this really doesn't return window state information. Use `CWnd::GetWindowPlacement()` instead. This function uses the `WINDOWPLACEMENT` structure and will return the window's current state, which you can then save to a key.

You are probably noticing that MFC provides a fairly easy mechanism for manipulating the Registry for your application, but you should also notice that this might be somewhat limiting. Your application might need to define child keys under different root keys than that of `HKEY_CURRENT_USER`.

MFC provides no clean way to do this, so you have to use the Registry API. One nice thing about MFC is that you are not restricted to a purely MFC framework when implementing an MFC application.

> **NOTE**
>
> If you are an MFC purist, you might decide to create an extension MFC class that "opens" up the remainder of the Registry root keys to your application. This is a good thing, but because you want to get to the lower level, this chapter will leave that exercise to your design prowess.

The best way to expand your knowledge of the Registry API is to jump in and do a sample application.

The Registry Sample Application

The RegSamp application is fairly simplistic in that it does nothing other than enable the user to create, modify, and delete keys. You will notice from the code in Listing 32.2 that it takes a lot of work to do something so simple. This is primarily because the API is designed to access the Registry at the lowest level.

The Registry Key Editor Dialog

Figure 32.2 is the Registry Key Editor dialog for the RegSamp sample application. RegSamp is an SDI application that contains only the Registry editing feature available from the File menu.

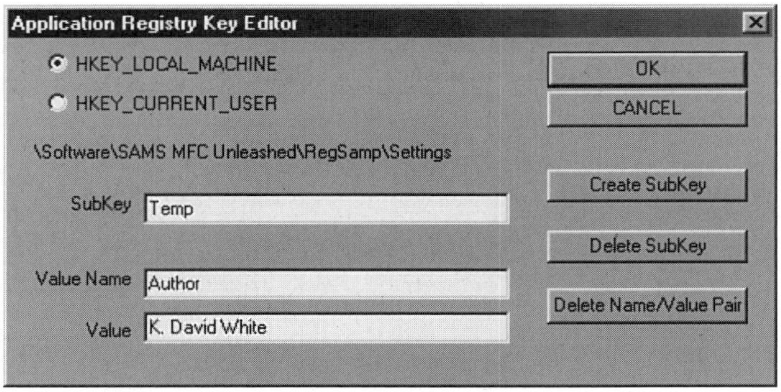

FIGURE 32.2

*The RegSamp
Registry Key
Editor dialog.*

The Registry structure for this application looks like this:

```
HKEY_LOCAL_MACHINE\Software\SAMS MFC Unleashed\RegSamp\Settings
HKEY_CURRENT_USER\Software\SAMS MFC Unleashed\RegSamp\Settings
```

Notice the radio button to select the parent path.

The first edit box control is for entering the path information for the child key (commonly referred to as the subkey definition).

The second edit box is for entering the value name to be created/deleted under the subkey.

The third edit box is for entering the value string associated with the value name.

> **NOTE**
>
> I've limited the editing to string values. The code could be easily modified/extended to test for datatypes. My aim is to show the process of managing the keys, not necessarily the information contained within the keys.
>
> In the interest of security and protecting the system, the code will limit the user to only the application-specific subkey of HKEY_LOCAL_MACHINE and HKEY_CURRENT_USER. You can quickly see where this functionality could destroy important information.

Creating a New Key

The user creates a new key by selecting the root key and entering the subkey. The user then selects the name of the value that he or she will be associating with the subkey, and then the value string itself. When this is done, the user will select the Create SubKey button.

Let's take a closer look at this code in Listing 32.2.

LISTING 32.2   THE OnCreateSubKey() FUNCTION

```
/*********************************************************************
 *      User has selected to create a subkey off of settings         *
 *      *NOTE*                                                        *
 *      This application dialog can easily be modified to create      *
 *      subkeys that are not a child of the SETTINGS subkey           *
 *      MFC defaults to this key, but notice the SOFTWARE_KEY_TEXT    *
 *      declaration at the beginning of this code...                  *
 *********************************************************************/
void CRegEditor::OnCreateSubkey()
{
    LONG    lnRes;
    HKEY    hMyKey;
    HKEY    hNewKey;

    DWORD dwDisp;

    UpdateData(TRUE);    //Get your Strings
    CString szTempString;

    switch(m_iRootSelected)
    {
        case 0:

            lnRes = RegOpenKeyEx(   HKEY_LOCAL_MACHINE,
                                    SOFTWARE_KEY_TEXT,
                                    0L,KEY_WRITE,&hMyKey    );
            if (ERROR_SUCCESS == lnRes)
            {
                lnRes = RegCreateKeyEx( hMyKey,
                                m_strSubKey,
                        0,
                        NULL,
                        REG_OPTION_NON_VOLATILE,
                        KEY_ALL_ACCESS,
                        NULL,
                        &hNewKey,
                        &dwDisp);

                if (ERROR_SUCCESS != lnRes)
                {
                    // Had an error creating the key.
                if (ERROR_ACCESS_DENIED == lnRes)
                    {
                        // Not an administrator on this machine...
                        AfxMessageBox("You must be an administrator",
                                MB_OK|MB_ICONEXCLAMATION,-1);
```

continues

32

INSIDE THE
REGISTRY

LISTING 32.2   CONTINUED

```
            }
        }
    }
    lnRes = RegCloseKey(hMyKey);
    break;

case 1:

    lnRes = RegOpenKeyEx(   HKEY_CURRENT_USER,
                            SOFTWARE_KEY_TEXT,
                            0L,KEY_WRITE,&hMyKey       );
    if (ERROR_SUCCESS == lnRes)
    {
        lnRes = RegCreateKeyEx( hMyKey,
                    m_strSubKey,
                0,
                NULL,
                REG_OPTION_NON_VOLATILE,
                KEY_ALL_ACCESS,
                NULL,
                &hNewKey,
                &dwDisp);

        if (ERROR_SUCCESS != lnRes)
        {
            // Had an error creating the key.
            if (ERROR_ACCESS_DENIED == lnRes)
            {
                // Not an administrator on this machine...
                AfxMessageBox("You must be an administrator",
                        MB_OK¦MB_ICONEXCLAMATION,-1);
            }
        }
    }

    lnRes = RegCloseKey(hMyKey);
    break;
}

unsigned char szKeyValue[MAX_KEY_VALUE];
lstrcpy((char *)szKeyValue,m_strValue);

lnRes = RegSetValueEx(hNewKey,
            m_strValueName,
            0,
            REG_SZ,
            szKeyValue,
            MAX_KEY_VALUE);
if (ERROR_SUCCESS != lnRes)
```

```
    {
        // Error writing to Registry, so close key and throw an exception
        RegCloseKey(hNewKey);
    }

}
```

It takes quite a bit of work just to create a new subkey. You were probably thinking that all you had to do was enter the parent key path, the new subkey name and any values, and presto! Unfortunately, it is not that easy. There are good reasons for going through the steps that you do. Think of the Registry as a type of database. For security purposes, you would want to open your parent key (reserve it). When you have the handle to your parent, you can create the new subkey. If you didn't reserve the parent key, and another application were to create a subkey for that same parent, your information wouldn't match or might invalidate the previous operation. Many installer scripts/applications create many keys directly off the root keys. The root key has to be reserved for this creation so that another application won't be able to change the substructure for the root key. This should never happen, but better safe than sorry.

Notice the `RegCreateKeyEx` function call. Important things to remember here are the `REG_OPTION_NON_VOLATILE` and the `KEY_ALL_ACCESS`. The `REG_OPTION_NON_VOLATILE` is the default options settings for key creation, but it's a good idea to include it here for readability. Following is a table of available options:

- `REG_OPTION_NON_VOLATILE` (default)—Indicates that the key is not volatile. The information is kept in a file. This allows it to be available when the system is restarted.
- `REG_OPTION_VOLATILE`—Indicates that the key *is* volatile. Is only loaded in memory.
- `REG_OPTION_BACKUP_RESTORE`—If this is defined, it will ignore the access mask and attempt to open the key for backup and restore functions.

The `KEY_ALL_ACCESS` parameter for the `CreateKey` function is basically an access privilege mask that is defined for the key. `KEY_ALL_ACCESS` basically opens up the entire world to your key.

Here is a simplified list of access masks:

- `KEY_ALL_ACCESS`—Provides global access to the key. Combination of `KEY_QUERY_VALUE`, `KEY_ENUMERATE_SUB_KEYS`, `KEY_NOTIFY`, `KEY_CREATE_LINK`, `KEY_SET_VALUE`, and `KEY_CREATE_SUB_KEY`.

- KEY_WRITE—Write access to the key.
- KEY_READ—Read access to the key.
- KEY_CREATE_LINK—Access to create a symbolic link for the key.
- KEY_CREATE_SUBKEY—Access to create a subkey to an open key.
- KEY_EXECUTE—Read access to the key.
- KEY_NOTIFY—Permission to change the notification information for a key.
- KEY_SET_VALUE—Access to set the value for an open key.
- KEY_QUERY_VALUE—Access to query a subkey for its value information. Valuable access to have if you have to enumerate keys.
- KEY_ENUMERATE_SUB_KEYS—Access to enumerate subkeys.

> **TIP**
>
> When opening keys for creating subkeys and other functions, it is better from a performance and security standpoint to limit this mask to KEY_WRITE, KEY_SET_VALUE, and KEY_READ privileges. If you are creating a new name/value pair for a key, open the key with KEY_WRITE. When changing the value of a name/value pair, use the Key_SET_VALUE.

> **NOTE**
>
> Notice that the parent key is predefined for this sample application to be SOFTWARE\SAMS MFC Unleashed\RegSamp\Settings. The dialog then enables the user to open a subkey off this parent. This dialog/code will enable the user to open subkeys that are several levels down from this parent, but the subpaths must be defined.
>
> For example, if the user wants to add an Authorize subkey and then a Priority subkey to the Authorize key, enter the path as Authorize\Priority. Don't forget to enter the name/value pair!
>
> The same can be done for deleting the keys.

Deleting a Key

In some instances, a key might no longer be needed. Using the dialog, the user can remove the key. The user enters the key that he or she wants to delete in the SubKey edit box. The user then selects the Delete SubKey button to activate the following code in Listing 32.3:

LISTING 32.3 THE OnDeleteSubKey() FUNCTION

```
/*********************************************************************
 *      Prior to deleting a key, you need to open its parent..      *
 *      This is done by going to the Settings dependent on what      *
 *      was selected on the dialog.                                  *
 *********************************************************************/
void CRegEditor::OnDeleteSubkey()
{
    LONG    lnRes;
    HKEY    hMyKey;

    UpdateData(TRUE);    //Get your Strings
    CString szTempString;

    switch(m_iRootSelected)
    {
        case 0:

            lnRes = RegOpenKeyEx(   HKEY_LOCAL_MACHINE,
                                    SOFTWARE_KEY_TEXT,
                                    0L,KEY_WRITE,&hMyKey    );
            if (ERROR_SUCCESS == lnRes)
            {
                lnRes = RegDeleteKey(hMyKey,m_strSubKey);

                if (ERROR_ACCESS_DENIED == lnRes)
                {
                    // Not an administrator on this machine...
                    AfxMessageBox("ACCESS
                    ➥DENIED",MB_OK¦MB_ICONEXCLAMATION,-1);
                }
                if (ERROR_FILE_NOT_FOUND == lnRes)
                {
                    // Not an administrator on this machine...
                    AfxMessageBox("KEY NOT
                    ➥FOUND",MB_OK¦MB_ICONEXCLAMATION,-1);
                }
            }
            lnRes = RegCloseKey(hMyKey);
            break;

        case 1:

            lnRes = RegOpenKeyEx(   HKEY_CURRENT_USER,
                                    SOFTWARE_KEY_TEXT,
                                    0L,KEY_WRITE,&hMyKey    );
            if (ERROR_SUCCESS == lnRes)
            {
                lnRes = RegDeleteKey(hMyKey,m_strSubKey);
```

32

INSIDE THE
REGISTRY

continues

LISTING 32.3   CONTINUED

```
                        if (ERROR_ACCESS_DENIED == lnRes)
                        {
                            // Not an administrator on this machine...
                            AfxMessageBox("ACCESS
                            ➥DENIED",MB_OK¦MB_ICONEXCLAMATION,-1);
                        }
                        if (ERROR_FILE_NOT_FOUND == lnRes)
                        {
                            // Not an administrator on this machine...
                            AfxMessageBox("KEY NOT
                            ➥FOUND",MB_OK¦MB_ICONEXCLAMATION,-1);
                        }
                    }

                    lnRes = RegCloseKey(hMyKey);
                    break;
            }

}
```

The `RegDeleteKey` API function is actually quite simple. After you open the parent key, you can then delete the subkey.

Deleting a Name/Value Pair

This function is quite different from deleting a key. Many times, the key might stick around, but the underlying name/value pairs might change. I personally wouldn't recommend this practice, but the following code will do just that.

The user selects the root key, enters the subkey, enters a name for the value to remove, and then clicks the Delete Name/Value Pair button to activate the code in Listing 32.4.

LISTING 32.4   THE `OnDeleteSubKey()` FUNCTION

```
/*********************************************************************
 *      This routine is a little different from the Delete Key       *
 *      routine.  You simply want to get rid of a value.             *
 *      You first have to Open your Settings Key and then the        *
 *      subkey that is contained within the EditBox on the dialog    *
 *      When you have that, you can use the DeleteKey value          *
 *********************************************************************/
void CRegEditor::OnNvDelete()
{
    LONG    lnRes;

    HKEY    hMyKey;
```

```
HKEY     hMySubKey;

UpdateData(TRUE);    //Get your Strings

CString szTempString;

switch(m_iRootSelected)
{
    case 0:
        lnRes = RegOpenKeyEx(    HKEY_LOCAL_MACHINE,
                                 SOFTWARE_KEY_TEXT,
                                 0L,KEY_WRITE,&hMyKey      );
        if (ERROR_SUCCESS == lnRes)
        {
            lnRes =
            ➡RegOpenKeyEx(hMyKey,m_strSubKey,0L,KEY_WRITE,&hMySubKey);
            if (ERROR_SUCCESS == lnRes)
            {
                lnRes = RegDeleteValue(hMySubKey,m_strValueName);

                if (ERROR_ACCESS_DENIED == lnRes)
                {
                    // Not an administrator on this machine...
                    AfxMessageBox("ACCESS
                    ➡DENIED",MB_OK¦MB_ICONEXCLAMATION,-1);
                }
                if (ERROR_FILE_NOT_FOUND == lnRes)
                {
                    // Not an administrator on this machine...
                    AfxMessageBox("KEY NOT
                    ➡FOUND",MB_OK¦MB_ICONEXCLAMATION,-1);
                }
            }
        }
        lnRes = RegCloseKey(hMySubKey);
        lnRes = RegCloseKey(hMyKey);
        break;

    case 1:

        lnRes = RegOpenKeyEx(    HKEY_CURRENT_USER,
                                 SOFTWARE_KEY_TEXT,
                                 0L,KEY_WRITE,&hMyKey      );
        if (ERROR_SUCCESS == lnRes)
        {
            lnRes =
            ➡RegOpenKeyEx(hMyKey,m_strSubKey,0L,KEY_WRITE,&hMySubKey);
            if (ERROR_SUCCESS == lnRes)
            {
                lnRes = RegDeleteValue(hMySubKey,m_strValueName);
```

continues

32

INSIDE THE
REGISTRY

LISTING 32.4   CONTINUED

```
                    if (ERROR_ACCESS_DENIED == lnRes)
                    {
                        // Not an administrator on this machine...
                        AfxMessageBox("ACCESS
                        ➥DENIED",MB_OK¦MB_ICONEXCLAMATION,-1);
                    }
                    if (ERROR_FILE_NOT_FOUND == lnRes)
                    {
                        // Not an administrator on this machine...
                        AfxMessageBox("KEY NOT
                        ➥FOUND",MB_OK¦MB_ICONEXCLAMATION,-1);
                    }
                }
            }
            lnRes = RegCloseKey(hMySubKey);
            lnRes = RegCloseKey(hMyKey);
            break;

    }

}
```

Notice the similarity to the `DeleteKey` function. However, there is a slight difference.
When you have the subkey, you have to open it to remove its value. It is a common mistake to forget this simple little step.

A Word About Wrapping the Registry Functions

I've talked a little bit about some important functions to give you access to the Registry.
However, you have a lot of code to do some pretty simple things. Making generic utility
functions to wrap the Registry API would make life easier for developers, but you are
working with MFC here! MFC, being C++, lends itself perfectly to creating a wrapper
class for the Registry.

As an added bonus, I have expanded the RegSamp application to use a simple `CRegKey`
class. This class is derived from `CObject`, primarily for serialization benefits in the
future. The RegSamp2 application is available on the CD-ROM.

A Word About Installation

Because this chapter's sample application is simple, installation requirements aren't discussed. There are several quality installation programs that will properly register an application during its installation. If an application is improperly installed, it might never get properly uninstalled. The operating system, through the Control Panel, provides a way for users/administrators to remove application programs. This is done by way of a shortcut to an uninstall program. Uninstall programs are usually synchronized with the installation program. If you choose to write your own install and uninstall program, follow the few simple rules shown in Table 32.2.

TABLE 32.2   INSTALLATION AND UNINSTALLATION RULES

Rule	Comment
Put Uninstall info in its place	Uninstall information is stored in the HKEY_LOCAL_MACHINE structure.
Keys Created = Keys Deleted	Be smart here. If an application creates a key at installation or during runtime, the uninstall must remove it.
Store directory information	An application normally resides in its own directory, or a subdirectory of a larger installation. Be sure that your install script/application removes the files and the directory. If the applications require unique DLL and INI files, store the directory path information for those files.

> **NOTE**
>
> Most commercial installers and uninstallers will perform all the steps shown in Table 32.2. If you are developing your own uninstall program, remember that the reference (usage) count for shared files (DLLs and so on) needs to be decremented when the application is removed. If the reference count for a system-wide shared file reaches zero, the uninstall program should prompt the user to remove it, giving him the option of leaving it on the system.
>
> I have noticed some applications leaving behind remnants in the Registry. This could be due to any number of problems. Most often, this is a case of not informing the deinstall program of every Registry element of an application. This is usually done through the install script by defining the elements that would need to be uninstalled. In a few cases, the developer might intentionally leave DLLs if more than one program can use them. Doing this should not affect the Registry cleanup, unless the DLL is in a direct execution path. In this case, when deinstalling, the user will be prompted to remove a DLL that can be shared by more than one application.

32

INSIDE THE REGISTRY

Summary

You've just taken a whirlwind tour of a fairly complex API. You were introduced to some of the important API functions and how to use them. Reading one chapter does not an expert make, and I wouldn't expect you to completely grasp the Registry until you've had the opportunity to explore it.

Although this chapter does not give in-depth coverage for the Registry API, you have learned some key points in dealing with the topic. Until more of the Registry API is encapsulated by MFC, you have no alternative but to "get down and dirty" with it. The Registry is a valuable source of state and configuration information for your applications, and as a developer, you should become familiar with it. I strongly recommend that you spend time with RegEdit and learn your Registry. Then take the sample code and expand it to fit your needs. Remember to back up your Registry files before editing the keys, or you might dread the experience!

CHAPTER 33

Writing and Using DLLs

by Ed Harris

IN THIS CHAPTER

Dynamic link libraries (DLLs) are executable modules that provide code, data, and resources to a process. Unlike static link libraries, which are used at build time, dynamic link libraries are distinct from the executables that invoke them; calls are resolved at load time. This makes it easy to fix bugs or make minor enhancements to the DLL without recompiling the executable modules that use them.

There are two basic types of MFC DLLs:

- Regular DLLs—These may contain MFC classes, but export functions that do not use MFC-derived classes. Older versions of MFC refer to these DLLs as *user DLLs*, after the preprocessor define (_USRDLL) used to create them. Regular DLLs can link with either the static or dynamic versions of the MFC and C runtime libraries. Because of restrictions in what can and cannot be done in regular DLLs, they are rarely used.

- MFC extension DLLs—DLLs that contain publicly accessible classes derived from MFC classes are known as *AFX extension DLLs*, or, more casually, AFX DLLs. AFX DLLs are the only DLLs that can publish MFC-derived classes for use by other DLLs or executable modules. Extension DLLs and the modules that use them are required to link with the DLL version of the MFC libraries, and, by implication, the DLL version of the C runtime libraries. By linking with the DLL version of the MFC libraries, extension DLLs can export window classes, message maps, and dynamic (serializable) objects.

This chapter concentrates on AFX DLLs.

Advantages of DLLs

When used properly, DLLs can provide many benefits. These benefits can more than offset the time and effort necessary to create the DLL.

Code Elimination

Moving shared classes into an AFX DLL eliminates duplicate code. Imagine a client/server application that uses a set of CObject-derived classes to store configuration information. If the shared classes are stored in an AFX DLL, the executable size of the modules that use them shrinks. This is also an effective mechanism to ensure that each module is using the most current version of the classes.

Of course, AFX DLLs require that your application link with and redistribute the MFC and C runtime DLLs. When you statically link with these libraries, only the necessary object modules are incorporated into your executable. But the DLL versions contain the entire class library and are quite large. Executable sizes can shrink by many thousands of bytes when linked with the DLL versions of the libraries. But when you add in the mammoth DLLs, the total application size can increase significantly.

When written properly, DLLs cut down on memory requirements. If a DLL is being used by multiple processes, the processes can often access the same copy of the DLL code.

Modularity and Packaging

As long as the exported functions are the same, an application can run with a different version of a DLL without recompiling or relinking. This lets software tool vendors ship updates or bug fixes to their products without requiring their users to make substantive changes.

Unlike static link libraries, DLLs contain not only code and data, but resources as well. This eliminates the need to "remember the resources" when linking with a library. It also allows DLLs to be truly self-contained.

The cardinal example of modularity is internationalization. Many applications, including MFC itself, use DLLs to contain Windows resources such as dialog boxes, menus, and string tables. Porting the application to another language merely requires the substitution of a DLL that contains the localized versions of the resources.

Extensibility

When designed correctly, DLLs provide applications with the capability to dynamically extend their functionality.

Inside an AFX DLL

Let's take a look at the process of creating an MFC extension DLL. Visual Studio provides an AppWizard to create MFC DLLs.

After you provide name and directory information, the AppWizard requires one key piece of information: the type of DLL to be created. Choices are regular DLL with MFC statically linked, regular DLL using shared MFC DLL, and MFC extension DLL (using shared MFC DLL).

The first AppWizard-generated module contains the DllMain function. The stock DllMain function integrates the extension DLL into the current process, and removes it upon shutdown. This process is done through two MFC constructs, AFX_EXTENSION_MODULE and CDynLinkLibrary.

33

WRITING AND
USING DLLs

AFX_EXTENSION_MODULE is a structure used by MFC to encapsulate key module-specific information. It contains the module handle of the DLL, the resource instance handle, the head of the dynamic class list, and the head of the OLE factory list. MFC uses these last two to create classes marked with the DYNCREATE macros and to instantiate the correct object factories for creating OLE objects. AFX_EXTENSION_MODULE objects are initialized and shut down through the AfxInitExtensionModule and AfxTermExtensionModule functions.

The CDynLinkLibrary class, which is constructed using an AFX_EXTENSION_MODULE reference, links this information into the MFC internals.

> ## CAUTION
>
> The AppWizard-generated DllMain allocates the CDynLinkLibrary class through the new operator, but fails to free it. This pointer is freed by the function AfxTermExtensionModule. This is a change from older (2.x) versions of MFC, where the user was responsible for unlinking and freeing the instance of CDynLinkLibrary.

The other AppWizard-generated modules include a skeleton resource file, an empty module-definition file, and the ubiquitous precompiled header files stdafx.h and stdafx.cpp.

Exporting Classes, Functions, and Data

Now that your AFX DLL has been generated, it's time to insert source and header files into the project. Now is the time to determine your export strategy.

In order for your classes and functions to be externally visible, and thus usable by other extension DLLs and executable modules, you must export them. This tells the compiler and linker that your functions should be externally entrant, and publishes an identifier used to reference them. These identifiers go into an *import library,* which is created by the linker. Modules that use your extension DLL are required to link with your import library.

The keyword to export an identifier is __declspec (dllexport), and, perhaps not surprisingly, the keyword to import an identifier is __declspec (dllimport). The declaration specification (declspec) tells the compiler and linker how to generate the entry and exit code for a function. It also tells the compiler how to call the function. There are several ways to use these identifiers, and many more caveats that restrict their usage.

The Big Deal About Exports

Export efficiency can be a very big deal to your DLL. When a module is loaded that references your DLL, the Win32 PE loader must adjust each symbol reference to point to the actual location of that symbol in memory. Although this fixup process might go unnoticed if your DLL exports few symbols, more complex DLLs will load more slowly, causing the user to wonder what's keeping your application from starting. MFC42.DLL, a fairly complex and mammoth MFC extension DLL, has more than 6500 exported functions. The MFC export strategy is complex and highly optimized.

There are two ways to export symbols: by name or by ordinal. Although name-based exports are far easier to manage than ordinal exports, name-based exports have some very significant performance drawbacks.

When you export by name, the entire function name must appear in the executable file. This causes the executable file to bloat with function names and further complicates the fixup process. On top of that, every executable that uses a DLL must include the name of each symbol being used. To give an example, the names exported from MFC42.DLL occupy 350KB. Their inclusion in the MFC42.DLL executable file would increase the file size by more than 25%! As if that weren't enough, resolving each symbol requires a character-by-character comparison to each exported name.

Fortunately, the linker enables you to export a symbol by assigning a numeric value (ordinal) to it. The ordinal value must be unique to the DLL. When ordinals are used, the import library for the DLL contains both the name and ordinal; however, the executable file and modules that reference the executable merely include the ordinal value. Unlike name-based exports, symbol resolution is a quick integer lookup.

Exporting by ordinal requires the use of a module definition (DEF) file. But, as you'll see, MFC extension DLLs must make some use of DEF files under the best of circumstances. Before discussing module definition files, let's visit the dark, evil secret of the compiler and linker: mangled names.

Mangled Names

You've probably seen them buried deep inside a map file: an identifier that kind of looks like one of your function names after being run through a blender.

If the following function appears in a C source file,

```
void StraightCFunction (int* pInput, const char* pszOutput)
```

the following symbol appears in the object and map files:

```
_StraightCFunction
```

This function is suitable for inclusion in the module definition file. Take the same function and insert it into a CPP source file, and you get the following:

```
?StraightCFunction@@YAXPAHPBD@Z
```

What's the stuff following the name? This is compiler-speak for the argument list and return types. In standard C, it is illegal to have two functions or variables with the same name (unless one or both are static scope). So the compiler merely refers to the symbol by its textual name, with an underscore prepended. C++, however, supports *function overloading*. Function overloading enables you to have two externally visible functions with the same name, provided their argument lists are different. Thus, in a C++ file, you could have the following:

```
int Addition (int nOperand1, int nOperand2);
long Addition (long lOperand1, long lOperand2);
```

To avoid name conflicts, and to ensure that the linker enforces strong typing, the compiler encodes (mangles) the parameter types, return type, and any qualifiers (such as const) into a single name.

This phenomenon is what leads to object and library incompatibilities between compiler vendors because each vendor uses a slightly different encoding scheme. And although compiler geeks try to put a positive spin on it (they call it *name decoration*), it complicates the DLL development process immensely. Listing 33.1 shows a sample module definition file that includes compiler-mangled names.

LISTING 33.1   SAMPLE MODULE DEFINITION FILE

```
;
; Sample Module Defintion File
;
LIBRARY       "afxsamp1"
DESCRIPTION   'Afx Sample Windows Dynamic Link Library'

EXPORTS
?StraightCPPFunction@@YAXPAHPBD@Z @1000 NONAME ; Exported by ordinal
StraightCFunction                @1001 NONAME  ; Exported by ordinal
?Addition@@YAHHH@Z                              ; Exported by name
?Addition@@YAJJJ@Z                              ; Exported by name
```

In this example, the StraightCFunction and StraightCPPFunction are exported by ordinal. The @*xxxx* assigns a unique numeric value to each identifier; the NONAME qualifier explicitly removes the textual name from the executable files. The two versions of Addition are exported by name; each identifier will be embedded in each executable file referencing it.

Where do you find the names to be inserted in the module-definition file? In the linker-generated map file.

Unfortunately, after doing a moderate amount of work with module definition files, you'll find yourself reading mangled names in their native form. It's a bittersweet day in any developer's life.

Exporting Classes

There is an alternative to mangled name madness. Microsoft provides a keyword to publish the contents of an entire class. However, it's the least efficient way to export your member functions, and it carries all of the performance hits discussed previously (bloated executables and longer load time).

Class exporting is done by embedding a declaration specification between the keyword `class` and the name of the class (see Listing 33.2). Using the export directive `__declspec (dllexport)` on the class declaration tells the compiler and linker that all member functions—public, protected, and private—should be published in the import file.

LISTING 33.2 EXPORTING CLASS BY CLASS

```
class __declspec (dllexport) CMyWindow: public CWnd
{
    CMyWindow();
    ~CMyWindow();
    // Generated message map functions
protected:
    //{{AFX_MSG(CMyWindow)
    afx_msg int OnCreate(LPCREATESTRUCT lpCreateStruct);
    //}}AFX_MSG
    DECLARE_MESSAGE_MAP()
};
```

It makes little sense, however, to publish *all* members—for example, private members can only be referenced by other members of your class and friend classes. Unless a friend class exists outside your DLL (a dubious design decision), this is a waste of an export, and a decrease in performance. Avoid class exporting in all but the simplest of cases.

What Goes Around, Comes Around

So far, I've only talked about exporting from DLLs. Consider the perspective of executables using your DLL. Rather than exporting identifiers, they will be importing them.

These executables should see your sample class as

```
class __declspec (dllimport) CMyWindow: public CWnd
```

As the DLL developer, you are left with one of two options: Maintain a duplicate copy of the class header file using __declspec (dllimport) (not a good long-term solution), or use the preprocessor to present the compiler with what it expects to see.

To use the preprocessor, define a special symbol in the project settings of your extension DLL: MY_DLL_INTERNALS. Then, in each header file, use the following construct:

```
#ifdef MY_DLL_INTERNALS
#undef EXPORTMODE
#define EXPORTMODE __declspec (dllexport)  // Export the identifiers
#else
#undef EXPORTMODE
#define EXPORTMODE __declspec (dllimport) // Import the identifiers
#endif
```

Then modify each class declaration to use the following form:

```
class EXPORTMODE CMyWindow: public CWnd
```

When the include file is read during the extension DLL compile, MY_DLL_INTERNALS will be defined, and the class will be exported. But when users of your DLL compile, MY_DLL_INTERNALS will be undefined and the class will be imported. This trick can also be used to export functions and data members.

Exporting Explicit Functions

You can cause a function to be exported by explicitly including the __declspec (dllexport) keyword on both its declaration and definition. This directs the compiler and linker to export the function in the import library. Unfortunately, the function is exported by name, not ordinal. You can override the export in the module definition file, but, if you're going to the trouble of looking up the mangled name anyway, why bother using the export keyword? Listing 33.3 contains an example of exporting member by member.

LISTING 33.3   EXPORTING MEMBER BY MEMBER

```
// Declaration of class
 class CMyClass : public CObject
{
    public:
        EXPORTMODE CMyClass();

    private:
        void DoSomething (int, void*);
};
```

```
// Implementation of members
EXPORTMODE CMyClass::CMyClass()
{
    ...
}

void CMyClass::DoSomething (int nValue, void* pData)
{

}
```

Should you forget to reset EXPORTMODE to __declspec (dllexport) in the implementation (CPP) files, the compiler will let you know in a hurry. __declspec (dllimport) tells the compiler that the actual function will be provided externally; when the compiler sees an actual definition, it knows something funky is going on.

Exporting Data

Most AFX DLLs only export functions and classes. But sometimes it is important to expose a data member to a caller. Much like functions, data members can be exported and imported using the __declspec (dllexport) and __declspec (dllimport) keywords.

```
EXPORTMODE CString g_strPublic;
```

Note that the compiler treats a __declspec (dllimport) as an implicit extern declaration. In other words, because dllimport tells the compiler the data member is defined in another executable, the compiler knows it has external scope and treats what would otherwise be a definition as an external declaration. However, it doesn't hurt to include an explicit extern if you're uncomfortable with that.

Exporting MFC Data

MFC dynamic objects (CObject) and message maps (CCmdTarget) depend on the export of certain data members you might not even know you had. In some cases, failure to export these members results in a link error. In other cases, executables will not work properly, possibly causing MFC internal ASSERTs or GPFs. These can be non-obvious and hard to track down.

When you include the keywords DECLARE_DYNAMIC, DECLARE_DYNCREATE, or DECLARE_SERIAL in your CObject-derived class, you declare a data member of type CRuntimeClass. CRuntimeClass is a struct containing the class name, schema number (for CArchive), a pointer to the base class information, and a function pointer to create a new object. Inclusion of the corresponding IMPLEMENT_ macro causes this data member to be defined. When MFC needs to create an object of that type (from serialization or dynamic creation), it uses the data in the struct to do the creation. If this structure isn't exported properly, modules using your DLL won't be able to use your classes.

When you include the keyword DECLARE_MESSAGE_MAP in your CCmdTarget-derived class, a similar process happens. In this case, two static members are added to your class: an AFX_MSGMAP struct and an array of AFX_MSGMAP_ENTRY structs. The BEGIN_MESSAGE_MAP macros cause these members to be defined. If the AFX_MSGMAP member isn't exported, your window class will fail to function properly when used by external modules.

On the surface, this poses a problem because the declaration and definition of these data members are embedded deep within the MFC macros. Microsoft's designers anticipated this problem, however, and have included a clever workaround.

Each data member created by an MFC macro (DECLARE_xxx or IMPLEMENT_xxx) contains the keyword AFX_DATA. By default, the AFX header files define AFX_DATA to be blank. If, however, you define AFX_DATA to be __declspec (dllexport) or __declspec (dllimport), the data members are correctly exported (or imported). Listing 33.4 contains an example of exporting MFC-generated data members.

LISTING 33.4   EXPORTING MFC-GENERATED DATA MEMBERS

```
// Top of header file
#ifdef MY_DLL_INTERNALS
#undef AFX_DATA
#define AFX_DATA    __declspec (dllexport)
#else
#undef AFX_DATA
#define AFX_DATA    __declspec (dllimport)
#endif

class CMyWindow : public CWnd
{
    public:
        CMyWindow();

    // Generated message map functions
    protected:
    //{{AFX_MSG(CMyWindow)
    afx_msg int OnCreate(LPCREATESTRUCT lpCreateStruct);
    //}}AFX_MSG
    DECLARE_MESSAGE_MAP()
};

#undef AFX_DATA
```

This technique will export the MFC-generated symbols by name. You can override this behavior by placing the mangled name in the module definition file and using an explicit ordinal value combined with the NONAME keyword.

Exporting the Destructor

Exporting destructors is a confusing proposition. Four different destructor functions are created by the compiler: the normal destructor, a vector destructor, a vector deleting destructor, and a static deleting destructor. Listing 33.5 gives examples of destructor usage.

LISTING 33.5 DESTRUCTOR USAGE

```
{
    CFoo* pFoo = new CFoo;
    CFoo* pFooArray = new CFoo[4];
    CFoo scalarFoo;
    CFoo aFoo[10];

    delete pFoo;          // Invokes the scalar deleting destructor
    delete [] pFooArray;  // Invokes the vector deleting destructor

    // scalarFoo goes out of scope and the normal
    // destructor is invoked.
    // aFoo goes out of scope and the normal vector
    // destructor is invoked.
}
```

The compiler invokes the deleting destructors when you call the delete operator on a pointer. The vector destructor is used to delete arrays, and scalar destructors are used on single objects. The normal destructor and normal vector destructors are invoked when a stack-based object or array of objects goes out of scope.

Do *not* export the deleting destructors. The deleting destructors free the memory associated with the object being deleted. Because the calling executable might be using a different memory manager than your DLL, exporting these destructors can cause hard-to-understand GPFs or ASSERTs. These GPFs are caused when memory allocated by one memory manager (the executable's) is freed by another memory manager (the DLLs). In the absence of a deleting destructor, the compiler and linker of the calling module will synthesize a deleting destructor to release the memory.

Visual Studio versions prior to 5 had a problem in which a normal vector destructor would not be created by the compiler and linker unless vector operations took place. This causes the wrong destructor to be invoked in calling executables when an array of objects is freed.

33

WRITING AND
USING DLLS

If you expect your DLL to be used with executables created with older versions of Visual Studio, you should consider the workaround given in Listing 33.6.

LISTING 33.6   DESTRUCTOR USAGE

```
static void _ForceVectorDelete()
{
#ifdef _DEBUG
    ASSERT(FALSE);   // never called
#endif

    new CFoo [2];
    new CBar [2];

}
void (*_ForceVectorDeleteInclusion)() = &ForceVectorDelete;
```

ForceVectorDelete is never invoked; however, the vector new syntax (new CFoo[2]) causes the compiler to synthesize a vector destructor for each class. The ForceVectorDeleteInclusion function pointer keeps the optimizing linker from eliminating ForceVectorDelete from the executable.

Export Toolkit `include` Files

The set of include files in Listings 33.7 through 33.10 automates dllimport/dllexport selection in source and include files.

LISTING 33.7   MAKESYMBOLSINTERNAL.H

```
#undef AFX_DATA
#define AFX_DATA __declspec (dllexport)
#undef EXPORTMODE
#define EXPORTMODE __declspec (dllexport)
```

LISTING 33.8   MAKESYMBOLSEXTERNAL.H

```
#undef AFX_DATA
#define AFX_DATA __declspec (dllimport)
#undef EXPORTMODE
#define EXPORTMODE __declspec (dllimport)
```

LISTING 33.9   RESETSYMBOLS.H

```
#undef AFX_DATA
#undef EXPORTMODE
```

LISTING 33.10 STARTOFCODE.H

```
#undef AFX_DATA
#define AFX_DATA __declspec (dllexport)
#undef EXPORTMODE
#define EXPORTMODE __declspec (dllexport)
```

Notice how these files don't prevent multiple inclusion. They are designed to be included multiply. At the top of your include files, use the following:

```
#ifdef MY_DLL_INTERNALS
#include "MakeSymbolsInternal.h"
#else
#include "MakeSymbolsExternal.h"
#endif

// Include exported classes, data, and other definitions here

#include "ResetSymbols.h"
```

Now, in your implementation files, include StartOfCode.h as the last include file. This causes symbols to be reset to dllexport so the proper executable code is generated.

What to Export

Now that you've learned about the techniques and rather baroque rules for exporting functions, let's take a look at guidelines for selecting functions to be exported. I'll assume that you've bowed to the inevitable and are exporting member by member, rather than class by class.

Of course, if you're developing your DLL for internal use only, you can always resort to the link-whoops method. The link-whoops method consists of compiling and linking a program that uses your DLL, and then adding any unresolved external functions to the DEF file. You run the risk, however, of missing exports that aren't used at the current time but might be needed at a later date.

Here's a checklist for determining what to export:

- Export any nonmember functions and/or static class members.
- Export any applicable constructors. If the class is dynamically creatable (DYNCREATE), be sure to export the default constructor.
- Export the destructor. If other executables can use your classes, they should be able to destroy them. Be careful not to export any deleting destructors and to abide by vector destruction rules.
- Export public methods. If you didn't want class users to call a method, why make it public?

33

WRITING AND
USING DLLs

- Export protected methods. Protected members can be invoked by derived classes and friends, and thus should be available from outside the DLL.
- Export virtual functions. If derived classes are expected or allowed to override a member function, the default method should be available to them.
- Do not export inline functions.
- Export static data members, such as message map entries (AFX_MSGMAP) or runtime class information (CRuntimeClass).

Other DLL Issues

Although exporting is certainly a large issue in using DLLs, other issues deserve consideration as well.

AfxLoadLibrary and AfxFreeLibrary

If your DLL gets dynamically loaded and unloaded (a very uncommon design), be sure to use the functions AfxLoadLibrary and AfxFreeLibrary to load and unload it (instead of LoadLibrary and FreeLibrary). The AFX versions of these functions lock the MFC internals so that the DLL can be linked into (or out of) the module list. Because most DLLs are loaded at runtime rather than dynamically linked, this is rarely an issue.

Designing for Extensibility and Reuse

There are some simple rules to obey if your DLL will be used by multiple projects. These rules help smooth bug fixes, feature enhancements, and versioning.

First, decide early whether your DLL file-naming scheme will include a version number. If you embed a version number within the name (such as MFC*42*.dll), major upgrades will be much easier. Because changing the DLL name requires a relink of any executables that use your DLL, you can safely make class changes at that time as well.

After your DLL has been shipped to customers, you are much more limited in the changes you can make without requiring a version change and/or a target recompile.

First, do *not* add functionality to your DLL. This is called blind-reving (blind revisioning), and causes uncounted headaches in the field. Blind-reving involves changing the behavior and/or exports of a module without changing the version number. Now, instead of simply checking a version number, installation utilities and technical support personnel must check the version number, file date and time, and file size. If you've ever received the message "Ordinal not found in DLL," you've been blind-reved.

Do not add or remove virtual functions from exported classes, or any base classes. Don't even reorder the virtual functions in a header file. Similarly, don't change the derivation chain of a class.

C++ uses a construct called a vtable to enable polymorphic behavior. Put simply, the vtable is a list of all virtual functions in a class and any base classes. If you write code to call a virtual function, the compiler looks up the address of the most derived implementation of that function in the vtable, and then invokes it. If you reorder the virtual functions in a class, the vtable changes. Normally, this is not a problem; however, if the vtable being used by your DLL is different from the vtable being used by an executable, chaos results. Executables compiled with the old header files will have the old vtable layout and will invoke the wrong function in classes created by your DLL.

If you need to add or remove virtual functions, change the version number and require your users to recompile.

A less obvious but similar problem area is inline functions. If a bug fix requires a change to an inline function, all class users must recompile to receive the fix. Again, the safest way to ensure that your customers recompile is to change the version number (and name) of the DLL.

Resource Location

One of the chief advantages of DLLs over static libraries is that they come packaged with their own resources. This can cause problems if executables linking with those DLLs expect to retrieve those resources.

All of the primary resource functions (`LoadString`, `LoadBitmap`, `LoadCursor`, `LoadIcon`, `DialogBox`, and so on) require an instance handle to identify the module that contains the resource. If the resource is stored in a DLL, you might have problems loading it.

There are several ways to solve this problem. One technique is to design your applications so that no module refers to the resources of another module. This can prove difficult, especially if you use the string table to store error message strings. If, however, you are a tool vendor, your DLL should be reasonably self-contained anyway.

A second strategy is to provide an exported function in each DLL that returns its instance handle. This pushes the problem onto the user of your DLL.

The best strategy, although the most problematic, is to use `AfxFindResourceHandle()` and `AfxLoadString()`. These functions properly traverse the list of registered AFX DLLs, searching for the first occurrence of a given resource type and ID. MFC uses these functions internally to find the correct dialog boxes, icons, and other resources to be used.

`AfxFindResourceHandle()` first checks the current executable for the resource. Failing that, it traverses all AFX DLLs in reverse load order (most recently loaded first). It then checks any MFC language DLL, and finally the MFC DLLs themselves.

`AfxLoadString` does the same thing, but loads the string contents into a provided buffer. Curiously, `CString::LoadString` *does not* take advantage of `AfxLoadString`. `CString::LoadString` merely checks the current executable, making string-table access through `CString` objects more tedious.

Although `AfxFindResourceHandle` and `AfxLoadString` make accessing resources easier, there is a sharp downside. Because each function stops as soon as it finds a resource matching the ID and type, resource identifiers in DLLs *cannot* collide. A resource collision would cause your program to display the wrong dialog box, icon, cursor, string, and so on.

Visual Studio makes this problematic because each resource file starts its identifiers at 100 and works upwards. A good solution is to create a spreadsheet or text file containing resource ranges assigned to each DLL. That way, different components can coexist.

> **TIP**
>
> String table entries are stored in groups of 16 strings, so be sure that your resource ranges don't overlap too closely. If one DLL has a range from 1-999 and another has the range 1000-1999, strings in the overlap range (992-1007) effectively collide. This is a quirk of the way strings are stored in resource and executable files.

Multiple Module Definition Files

Today's applications are expected to run in different modes and different locales. The Unicode standard provides double-byte character support for languages such as Kanji that cannot fit their character set into an eight-bit value. Under most circumstances, Visual Studio supports seamless movement between single-byte (ANSI) and double-byte (Unicode) builds. This is done through the header file tchar.h. TChar contains an alias to every runtime function that takes a character or string parameter. If the `UNICODE` preprocessor variable is defined, wide-character versions are invoked; otherwise, single-byte versions are invoked.

Unfortunately, character size affects compiler name-mangling. Functions that take a size-independent character pointer (`TCHAR*`, `LPCTSR`, and so on) have different mangled names when UNICODE is defined than when it isn't. Because the linker doesn't support conditional compilation in module definition files (that is, you can't embed an #ifdef UNICODE in the DEF file), you're stuck with maintaining multiple files.

This isn't too much of a problem at first blush. Only a small percentage of functions that generally take or return character pointers are arguments, and the linker points out when your export entries are incorrect.

However, if you attempt to add a second module definition file into your project, Visual Studio balks because it can't resolve which file to use. This requires you to enter the correct module-definition file directly into the linker Project Options edit window by using the /Def:<filename> linker directive. This has the unfortunate effect of removing the module definition file from the project dependencies. Put another way, a change to the module definition file will not cause Visual Studio to relink the project.

These same rules apply if your DLL requires different module definition files for debug and release builds. Each MFC DLL has four separate module definition files: Unicode release, Unicode Debug, ANSI Release, and ANSI Debug.

Load Addresses and the Linker

One of the oft-cited reasons for using DLLs is to save memory. After all, if two executables are running and use the same DLL, why would the operating system store two copies of the code?

This theory works as long as everybody plays by the rules. When the linker creates an executable module, it is required to "base" the executable at some starting point in virtual memory. The linker creates default values for fixup table entries relative to this point. By default, the starting point for executable files (EXEs) is hex 00400000. For DLLs, the starting point is 10000000.

When an executable is loaded, the Windows PE loader must find a place in virtual memory where each DLL can be loaded. If the load address specified is available, it is loaded at that point. If not, an arbitrary point in virtual memory is chosen, and all the fixup table entries in the executable are changed to conform to the new location. Two significant performance problems appear when this happens.

First, the load time of your executable increases dramatically. Every fixup address in the loaded DLL gets rewritten, and every module that uses that address rewrites its import table. This takes time.

33

WRITING AND
USING DLLs

More critically, the executable code of the DLL is no longer sharable. When a second or third process is started that references the DLL, the code will not be shared, but rather rewritten to memory. Here's why:

The loader takes advantage of a virtual-memory feature called copy-on-write. When the copy-on-write flag is set on a page of virtual memory, any attempt to write to that page causes the operating system to silently create a new copy of the page in physical memory. References to that page in Process A will no longer refer to the same page as Process B.

When an executable is loaded, the copy-on-write bit is set on all code pages. When a second copy of the executable is loaded, the loader receives the virtual address of the first copy of the page. If, however, the loader needs to change the base address because of a conflict, the process of writing new fixup offsets to the code causes the operating system to create a second (or third, or fourth) copy of each page. Thus, the code in the DLL is no longer shared between the processes.

The solution is to ensure that each DLL in your project loads at a unique address. If no address conflicts occur, the loader does not rewrite the executable, and a single copy of the code exists in memory. Be aware that system DLLs, network and hardware drivers, shell extensions, common control DLLs, and other modules are mapped into your process space at various times. Most vendors have changed to a unique load address. When you run your application in the debugger, check to ensure that no conflicts occur. If a conflict is detected, a message will be output to the debug console:

```
LDR: Dll COMCTL32.dll base 71030000 relocated due to collision with
E:\WINNT40\system32\SHLWAPI.dll
```

In this case, two Microsoft DLLs, the common control DLL and the Lightweight Shell API DLL, are conflicting. Other than complain to the tool vendor that the product should be more professional, there's not a lot you can do.

To change the load address of your DLL, use the linker /BASE directive. This directive is set through the Base Address window of the Output page of the linker options under Project Settings. The directive has two forms. First, you can insert a hard-coded address into the window (such as 0x10050000). A better way is to use a load-address text file. This form of the /BASE directive specifies a text filename and module name, using the following syntax: @<textfilename>,<modulename>. The linker reads the text file, looks for a line that starts with <modulename>, and uses the starting address and length found on that line to base the executable. Listing 33.11 contains a sample load address file.

LISTING 33.11 SAMPLE LOAD ADDRESS FILE

```
ControlDll    0x10300000 0x00100000
ConfigUtil    0x10400000 0x00200000
Server        0x10600000 0x00100000
```

So, for the server project, the /Base setting would be @LoadAddr.txt,Server. The control DLL would use @LoadAddr.txt,ControlDLL.

This form of the /Base directive gives you the ability to change the load addresses at a single location. It also helps you to form a mental map of what your process space looks like.

Summary

Writing an extension DLL can be a daunting task at first blush. It takes quite a bit of work to get the correct structure in place, and subsequent code changes take longer to complete.

The key to DLL development is planning, planning, and more planning. *Don't* rely on link errors to warn about unexported functions; have an export list ready prior to the completion of the code. The most common DLL development problem is the failure to export the correct functions. Unfortunately, this generally manifests itself during the *second* project that uses the DLL. This necessitates a new release of the DLL and eliminates some of the reusability benefits.

Create a strategy for resource ID ranges, module load addresses, and file naming schemes. Circulate these documents widely to the developers using your DLL. Finally, use the automation headers presented in this chapter (MakeSymbolsInternal, MakeSymbolsExternal, and StartOfCode): They will significantly reduce startup time by eliminating import/export convention problems.

33

WRITING AND
USING DLLs

CHAPTER 34

Creating Custom Wizards

by Rob McGregor

IN THIS CHAPTER

Modern Windows applications are chock full of gadgets and controls, including *wizards*. In an application context, as you know, a *wizard* walks the user through a series of simple steps to accomplish a complex task. This chapter explains the process of creating a basic wizard and the relationship of wizards to property sheets and property pages.

Property Sheets and Property Pages

Property sheets, also known as *tabbed dialog boxes*, are commonly used in modern Windows applications. A property sheet is a special type of dialog box usually used to modify the properties of some external object. A property sheet has three main parts:

- The main dialog box window containing OK, Cancel, and Apply buttons in the lower-right corner
- One or more property page dialog resources, shown one at a time within the main dialog box
- A tab at the top of each property page that the user can click to select that page

Property sheets are generally used when you have a number of related settings or options to change; they allow a large amount of information from multiple dialog boxes to be grouped within a single dialog box. For example, Windows uses a property sheet with various property pages to enable a user to change screen savers, wallpaper, video display modes, user interface attributes, colors, and so on.

MFC provides property sheets and property pages in the `CPropertySheet` and `CPropertyPage` classes. Let's take a quick look at these classes.

The `CPropertySheet` and `CPropertyPage` Classes

`CPropertySheet` objects represent property sheets, and even though `CPropertySheet` is derived directly from `CWnd` (and not from `CDialog`), managing a `CPropertySheet` object is similar to managing a `CDialog` object. The methods provided by the `CPropertySheet` class are listed in Table 34.1.

TABLE 34.1   `CPropertySheet` CLASS METHODS

Method	Description
AddPage()	Adds a page to the property sheet
Construct()	Constructs a `CPropertySheet` object
Create()	Displays a modeless property sheet

Method	Description
DoModal()	Displays a modal property sheet
EndDialog()	Terminates the property sheet
GetActiveIndex()	Gets the index of the active page of the property sheet
GetActivePage()	Returns the active page object
GetPage()	Gets a pointer to the specified page
GetPageCount()	Gets the number of pages in the property sheet
GetPageIndex()	Gets the index of the specified page of the property sheet
GetTabControl()	Gets a pointer to a tab control
PressButton()	Simulates the choice of the specified button in a property sheet
RemovePage()	Removes a page from the property sheet
SetActivePage()	Programmatically sets the active page object
SetFinishText()	Sets the text for the Finish button
SetTitle()	Sets the caption of the property sheet
SetWizardButtons()	Enables wizard buttons for a property sheet
SetWizardMode()	Enables wizard mode for a property sheet

Unlike CPropertySheet, the CPropertyPage class is derived from CDialog. CPropertyPage objects represent the individual pages within a property sheet. Just as you do for standard dialog boxes under MFC, you must derive a class from CPropertyPage for each property page in a property sheet. The methods provided by the CPropertyPage class are listed in Table 34.2.

TABLE 34.2 CPropertyPage CLASS METHODS

Method	Description
CancelToClose()	Changes the OK button to read Close and disables the Cancel button after an unrecoverable change in the page of a modal property sheet.
OnApply()	Called by MFC when the Apply Now button is selected.
OnCancel()	Called by MFC when the Cancel button is selected.
OnKillActive()	Called by MFC when the current page is no longer the active page. Data validation should be performed here.
OnOK()	Called by MFC when the OK, Apply Now, or Close button is selected.
OnQueryCancel()	Called by MFC when the Cancel button is selected and before the cancel operation has taken place.

continues

34

CREATING
CUSTOM WIZARDS

TABLE 34.2   CONTINUED

Method	Description
OnReset()	Called by MFC when the Cancel button is selected.
OnSetActive()	Called by MFC when the page is made the active page.
OnWizardBack()	Called by MFC when the Back button is selected while using a wizard-type property sheet.
OnWizardFinish()	Called by MFC when the Finish button is selected while using a wizard-type property sheet.
OnWizardNext()	Called by MFC when the Next button is selected while using a wizard-type property sheet.
QuerySiblings()	Forwards the message to each page of the property sheet.
SetModified()	Called to activate or deactivate the Apply Now button.

If this chapter is about Windows wizards, why all this chatter about property sheets and property pages? Did you notice the wizard-specific items in Tables 34.1 and 34.2? Let's try to make some sense of this. Read on!

The Wizard Walk and the Property Sheet Connection

A wizard is really just a property sheet dialog box with a series of application-defined modeless property page dialog boxes attached. Unlike standard property sheets, wizard-style property sheets don't have the familiar tabs. Instead, they use buttons to enable the user to move from one step to the next. These buttons are labeled Back and Next, although a Finish button replaces the Next button when the user has completed all the steps. There is also a Cancel button that the user can choose at any time during the wizard walk.

> **NOTE**
>
> Although I don't go into a great deal of class-specific detail about the CPropertySheet and CPropertyPage classes here, I will use these classes when creating the sample wizard for this chapter.

Wizards are best at breaking complex operations down into concise, easy steps. When a user has completed walking through these steps, the wizard typically performs the complex action for him.

Creating a Wizard

Creating a wizard with MFC isn't any more difficult than creating a property sheet. There are six general steps to follow when creating a wizard:

1. Create dialog template resources for each wizard page.
2. Create a dialog class for each dialog resource.
3. Allocate the property sheet and its property pages.
4. Add the pages to the property sheet.
5. Make the property sheet a wizard.
6. Add message handlers where appropriate.

Each of these steps is discussed in detail later in this chapter, using the sample application WIZARD1 as an example.

CAUTION

Because each of the wizard's pages is really just a property page, each must have the thin border style and the child window style. Dialog templates that use the extended styles are not supported by the property sheet API; if you attempt to use them, they will crash. I know—I've done it. It's a difficult bug to track down too, so be careful.

Setting the Wizard Mode

To make a property page think it's really a powerful wizard, you simply call the CPropertySheet::SetWizardMode() method to set the PSF_WIZARD flag. This method does, in fact, make a property page into a wizard, complete with Back, Next, and Cancel buttons all created automatically. The user walks through the wizard with these buttons, as opposed to using the standard property page tabs.

Enabling the Wizard Buttons

Although the standard Back, Next, and Cancel buttons appear by default, you can choose which buttons you want to be available at any given time by calling the SetWizardButtons() method. This method uses the following prototype:

```
void SetWizardButtons(DWORD dwFlags);
```

In this syntax, dwFlags is a set of bit flags used to set the wizard buttons. These flags are combined using the bitwise OR (|) operator and can be a combination of any of the values listed in Table 34.3.

34

CREATING
CUSTOM WIZARDS

TABLE 34.3 THE BIT FLAG VALUES USED FOR SETTING WIZARD BUTTONS

Bit Flag	Meaning
PSWIZB_BACK	Displays the Back button
PSWIZB_NEXT	Displays the Next button
PSWIZB_FINISH	Displays the Finish button
PSWIZB_DISABLEDFINISH	Displays Finish button disabled

The Finish and Next buttons are really one and the same, so both can be present at the same time. The caption used for the button changes depending on the flags used in SetWizardButtons(). You call this method only after the wizard is open for business—the CPropertyPage::OnSetActive() method is the perfect place to do this.

Displaying the Wizard

Before you can do anything in the wizard, you have to display it. A C++ property page object is created with a call to the constructor, but the actual Windows dialog box window is created by calling CWnd::DoModal(). This method creates a modal wizard. When used to create a wizard, the DoModal() method returns the value ID_WIZFINISH if the user finished the wizard successfully; it returns the value IDCANCEL if the user canceled the wizard.

Wizard Notification Messages

A wizard control sends notification messages for a page through the message map whenever the page gains or loses the input focus and when a user chooses any of the buttons. These notifications use the standard WM_NOTIFY messaging described in Chapter 3, "The Windows Common Controls." A wizard page gets the same messages as a standard property page, plus three extra because of its exalted wizard page status. These extra notifications are PSN_WIZBACK, PSN_WIZNEXT, and PSN_WIZFINISH (corresponding to the user choosing the Back, Next, or Finish buttons). The wizard property sheet is destroyed when a user chooses the Finish or Cancel button.

Moving Back

The current dialog page receives a PSN_WIZBACK notification when a user clicks the Back button. The OnWizardBack() notification handler is predefined by MFC to deal with this notification. By adding this method to your dialog class message map, your application can respond to the PSN_WIZBACK message.

Moving Next

The current dialog page receives a PSN_WIZNEXT notification when a user clicks the Next button. The OnWizardNext() notification handler is predefined by MFC to deal with this notification. By adding this method to your dialog class message map, your application can respond to the PSN_WIZNEXT message.

The Big Finish

The Finish button should be displayed or active only when the user has completed all the steps required by the wizard. When a user completes the wizard by choosing the Finish button, the dialog box receives a PSN_WIZFINISH notification. The OnWizardFinished() handler is predefined by MFC to deal with this notification. By adding this method to your dialog class message map, your application can respond to the PSN_WIZFINISH message. When you display the Finish button, you can also call the SetFinishText() method to set the text that appears on the button and to hide the Back and Next buttons.

> **NOTE**
>
> When a user chooses the Back or Next button, the wizard automatically moves to the previous or next page. To prevent this from occurring, return the value –1 from any of the three methods just described: OnWizardBack(), OnWizardNext(), or OnWizardFinished(). To cause a nonsequential jump to any page in the wizard, simply specify the desired page index.

Sample Program: Off to See the Wizard (WIZARD1.EXE)

Now turn your attention to the sample program WIZARD1.EXE. This application displays a sample wizard that does nothing useful at all except demonstrate how a wizard can be created using MFC. At its heart, the application consists of the typical simple application model you've used so often before. In this program, however, your old friends the application object and the frame window object team up with a new object: the CWizard object. The CWizard class is derived from CPropertySheet and is owned by the frame window class. In this program, the frame window also owns the five property page classes that are used by the CWizard class.

NOTE

WIZARD1.EXE, along with all its source files, can be found in the
CHAP34\SOURCE\WIZARD1 folder on this book's companion CD-ROM.

The following sections look at each of the steps needed to get the wizard off the ground.

Creating Wizard Page Dialog Template Resources

The first thing to do is create the wizard's dialog template resources that the five property pages use. Using a dialog editor, you'll create the five dialog pages required for this program. These five dialog pages are described in the next sections.

The Welcome Page

The Welcome page greets the user and tells him or her what to expect and what to do first. Figure 34.1 shows the IDD_INTRO dialog template under construction in the Visual C++ Developer Studio. The image on the left side of the dialog template is one of four bitmap resources used in this program.

FIGURE 34.1

IDD_INTRO: *The Welcome dialog box at design time.*

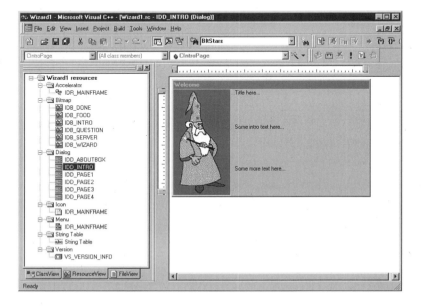

The About You Page

The second page in the sample wizard is IDD_PAGE1, the About You page. This page is used to gather the user's first and last names, company name, and email address. Figure 34.2 shows the IDD_PAGE1 dialog template under construction.

FIGURE 34.2

IDD_PAGE1: *The About You dialog box at design time.*

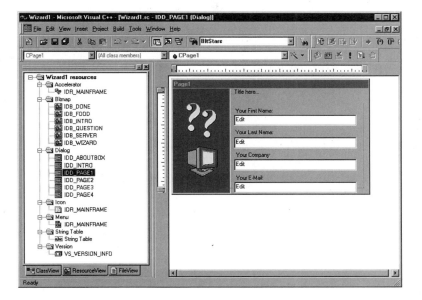

The Food for Thought and Compiler Preferences Pages

The next page used by the sample wizard is IDD_PAGE2. Because this page asks a question about food preferences, it's referred to as the Food for Thought page. Figure 34.3 shows the IDD_PAGE2 dialog template under construction.

Because the IDD_PAGE3 dialog template is used to ask a question about compilers, it's referred to as the Compiler Preferences page. Figure 34.4 shows IDD_PAGE3 under construction.

34

CREATING CUSTOM WIZARDS

FIGURE 34.3

IDD_PAGE2: *The Food for Thought dialog box at design time.*

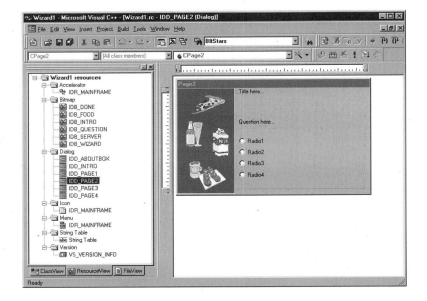

FIGURE 34.4

IDD_PAGE3: *The Compiler Preferences dialog box at design time.*

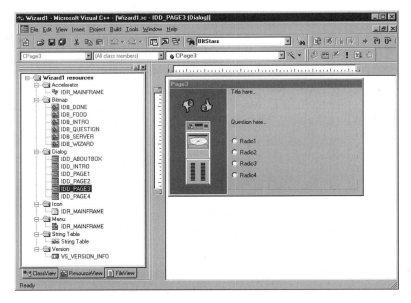

The Final Page

The final page used by the sample wizard is IDD_PAGE4. This page simply tells the user the wizard walk is over and displays the Finish button. Figure 34.5 shows the IDD_PAGE4 dialog template under construction.

FIGURE 34.5
The final wizard page.

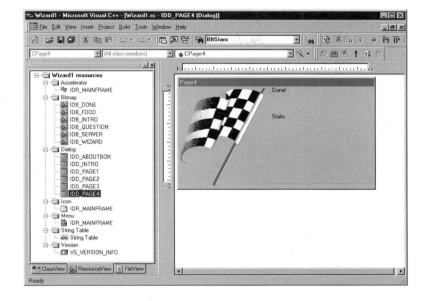

Create a Dialog Class for Each Dialog Resource

The next destination along the yellow brick road (yes, you really *will* see the wizard at the end of this journey) is the creation of MFC classes to wrap all those dialog templates. One class per template is needed. The classes are split into separate modules to keep things tidier; these modules are listed in Table 34.4.

TABLE 34.4 THE MFC CLASSES USED TO WRAP THE FIVE WIZARD DIALOG RESOURCES

Class	Dialog Resource
CIntroPage	IDD_INTRO
CPage1	IDD_PAGE1
CPage2	IDD_PAGE2
CPage3	IDD_PAGE3
CPage4	IDD_PAGE4

These five classes have the same general form. For the purposes of this sample wizard, I've kept things fairly minimal. The text on all the pages is read from a string table in the resource file, and the bitmaps displayed on each page are stored as resource data as well. To get a general idea how all these classes operate, the following sections look more closely at each.

Exploring the Welcome Page: Class `CIntroPage`

The `CIntroPage` class is very simple because nothing much happens on the Welcome page. The most interesting things about the class are the dialog box initialization in `CIntroPage::OnInitDialog()`, and the dialog box painting in `CIntroPage::OnPaint()`. The interface for the `CIntroPage` class is shown in Listing 34.1.

LISTING 34.1   THE INTERFACE FOR THE `CIntroPage` CLASS (INTROPG.H)

```
/////////////////////////////////////////////////////////////////////
// CIntroPage dialog

class CIntroPage : public CPropertyPage
{
    DECLARE_DYNCREATE(CIntroPage)

// Construction
public:
    CIntroPage();
    ~CIntroPage();

    // Dialog Data
    enum { IDD = IDD_INTRO };

protected:
    CFont m_fntTitle;   // font for the title of this page

    // DDX/DDV support
    virtual void DoDataExchange(CDataExchange* pDX);

    // Message map entries
    afx_msg void OnPaint();
    virtual BOOL OnInitDialog();

    DECLARE_MESSAGE_MAP()
};
```

Initializing the Welcome Page

Like any other MFC dialog box, the Welcome page uses the `OnInitDialog()` method to perform any dialog box-specific initialization of member variables and controls. The overridden method `CIntroPage::OnInitDialog()` is shown in Listing 34.2.

LISTING 34.2   THE `CIntroPage::OnInitDialog()` METHOD

```
/////////////////////////////////////////////////////////////////////
// CIntroPage::OnInitDialog()
```

```
BOOL CIntroPage::OnInitDialog()
{
   CPropertyPage::OnInitDialog();

   m_fntTitle.CreateFont(TITLE_SIZE, 0, 0, 0, FW_BOLD, FALSE, FALSE,
       0, ANSI_CHARSET, OUT_DEFAULT_PRECIS, CLIP_DEFAULT_PRECIS,
       DEFAULT_QUALITY, DEFAULT_PITCH ¦ FF_ROMAN, "Times New Roman");

   return TRUE;
}
```

This method calls the inherited method first and then uses the CFont::CreateFont()
method to create a custom Times New Roman font of size TITLE_SIZE (defined, in this
case, as 25). The new font is stored in the protected data member m_fntTitle to be used
throughout the life of the dialog box.

> **NOTE**
>
> All the other pages in the WIZARD1 program use the same type of initialization
> for a custom font. Each page stores its own custom font for later use in the pro-
> tected member m_fntTitle.

Using the New Font and Displaying Text Messages

The title for the Welcome page is displayed using the custom font created in
OnInitDialog(). Two static controls are supplied with text messages read from string
table resources defined in WIZARD1.RC. The CIntroPage::OnPaint() method shows how
all this is done (see Listing 34.3).

LISTING 34.3   THE CIntroPage::OnPaint() METHOD

```
/////////////////////////////////////////////////////////////////////
// CIntroPage::OnPaint()

void CIntroPage::OnPaint()
{
   CPaintDC dc(this); // device context for painting

   // Change the font
   CStatic* pTitle = (CStatic*)GetDlgItem(IDC_TITLE);
   ASSERT_VALID(pTitle);
   pTitle->SetFont(&m_fntTitle);
```

continues

34

CREATING
CUSTOM WIZARDS

LISTING 34.3   CONTINUED

```
// Draw the text
CString str;
str.LoadString(IDS_WELCOME);
SetDlgItemText(IDC_TITLE, (LPCTSTR)str);

str.LoadString(IDS_INTRO1);
SetDlgItemText(IDC_INTRO1, (LPCTSTR)str);

str.LoadString(IDS_INTRO2);
SetDlgItemText(IDC_INTRO2, (LPCTSTR)str);
}
```

To change the font for the Welcome title, this method first uses CWnd::GetDlgItem() to get a pointer to the control with the identifier IDC_TITLE. This pointer is cast as a CStatic* to the local variable pTitle. Then the pointer is used for a call to the CWnd::SetFont() method to set the custom m_fntTitle font as the default for the IDC_TITLE static control.

The messages displayed in the other static controls are read out of the application's resources using the CString::LoadString() method with the appropriate identifier. The result of all this manipulation can be seen in Figure 34.6.

FIGURE 34.6

The WIZARD1 *wizard's Welcome page at runtime.*

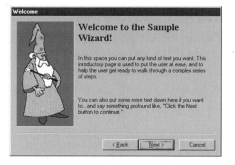

Exploring the About You Page: Class CPage1

The CPage1 class adds to the minimal functionality provided by CIntroPage. This dialog box expects you to fill in data in four edit controls, although only two are mandatory. The dialog box initialization and painting routines are much the same as for CIntroPage. The real fun comes in handling the edit controls. You use DDX and DDV as well as a custom data structure to store user selections. The interface for the CPage1 class is shown in Listing 34.4.

LISTING 34.4   THE INTERFACE FOR THE CPage1 CLASS (PAGE1.H)

```
/////////////////////////////////////////////////////////////////////////
// CPage1 dialog

class CPage1 : public CPropertyPage
{
    DECLARE_DYNCREATE(CPage1)

public:
    // Construction
    CPage1();
    ~CPage1();

    // Dialog Data
    enum { IDD = IDD_PAGE1 };

    CString    m_sCompany;
    CString    m_sEmail;
    CString    m_sFirstName;
    CString    m_sLastName;

public:
    // Overrides
    virtual LRESULT OnWizardNext();

protected:
    // DDX/DDV support
     virtual void DoDataExchange(CDataExchange* pDX);

protected:
    CFont m_fntTitle;

    // Control access methods
    inline CEdit& editFirst()
        { return *(CEdit*) GetDlgItem(IDC_FIRSTNAME); }

    inline CEdit& editLast()
        { return *(CEdit*) GetDlgItem(IDC_LASTNAME); }

protected:
    // Message map members
    afx_msg void OnPaint();
    virtual BOOL OnInitDialog();

    DECLARE_MESSAGE_MAP()
};
```

Note the usage of the `GetDlgItem()` function within the `editFirst()` control access method. This method returns a reference to a control and makes using the dialog controls very convenient; consider this example:

```
inline CEdit& editFirst()
    { return *(CEdit*) GetDlgItem(IDC_FIRSTNAME); }
```

DDX and DDV for `CPage1`

Like any other MFC dialog box, the About You page uses the `CPage1::DoDataExchange()` method to perform data exchange and validation on the edit controls and data members. The override method `CPage1::DoDataExchange()` is shown in Listing 34.5.

LISTING 34.5   THE `CPage1::DoDataExchange()` METHOD

```
//////////////////////////////////////////////////////////////////
//   CPage1::DoDataExchange()

void CPage1::DoDataExchange(CDataExchange* pDX)
{
    // Call the inherited method
    CPropertyPage::DoDataExchange(pDX);

    // Date map
    DDX_Text(pDX, IDC_COMPANY, m_sCompany);
    DDX_Text(pDX, IDC_EMAIL, m_sEmail);
    DDX_Text(pDX, IDC_FIRSTNAME, m_sFirstName);
    DDX_Text(pDX, IDC_LASTNAME, m_sLastName);
}
```

Ensuring that Required Data Is Entered

Of the four edit controls on the `CPage1` dialog box, only the first two (`IDC_FIRSTNAME` and `IDC_LASTNAME`) are required to have text in them. This requirement is enforced in the `CPage1::OnWizardNext()` method, which is called by MFC when a user clicks the Next button. If these two edit controls are empty, the wizard displays a dialog box explaining the problem and sets the focus on the control in question. The `CPage1` dialog box is shown in Figure 34.7 as it appears at runtime; the `CPage1::OnWizardNext()` method shows how all this is done (see Listing 34.6).

FIGURE 34.7

The WIZARD1 *wizard's About You page at runtime.*

LISTING 34.6   THE CPage1::OnWizardNext() METHOD

```
//////////////////////////////////////////////////////////////////
// CPage1::OnWizardNext()

LRESULT CPage1::OnWizardNext()
{
    // Updata and verify dialog data
    UpdateData(TRUE);

    // Check to see that text exists in Name edit controls
    if (m_sFirstName.GetLength() == 0)
    {
        MessageBeep(MB_ICONASTERISK);
        AfxMessageBox("You must enter your First Name...",
            MB_OK | MB_ICONINFORMATION);
        editFirst().SetFocus();

        // Prevent the page from turning
        return -1;
    }

    if (m_sLastName.GetLength() == 0)
    {
        MessageBeep(MB_ICONASTERISK);
        AfxMessageBox("You must enter your Last Name...",
            MB_OK | MB_ICONINFORMATION);
        editLast().SetFocus();

        // Prevent the page from turning
        return -1;
    }

    // Get the parent window
    CWizard* pWiz = (CWizard*) GetParent();
    ASSERT_VALID(pWiz);
```

continues

34

CREATING
CUSTOM
WIZARDS

LISTING 34.6 CONTINUED

```
    // Update the wizard data
    pWiz->m_swd.sFirstName = m_sFirstName;
    pWiz->m_swd.sLastName  = m_sLastName;
    pWiz->m_swd.sCompany   = m_sCompany;
    pWiz->m_swd.sEmail     = m_sEmail;

    // Call the inherited method
    return CPropertyPage::OnWizardNext();
}
}
```

By calling UpdateData(TRUE) and checking the lengths of the class member variable strings, you can determine whether the edit control is empty. If the string length is zero, a message box informs the user, as in this code snippet:

```
if (m_sLastName.GetLength() == 0)
{
    MessageBeep(MB_ICONASTERISK);
    AfxMessageBox("You must enter your Last Name...",
        MB_OK ¦ MB_ICONINFORMATION);
    editLast().SetFocus();

    // Prevent the page from turning
    return -1;
}
```

Note that by returning –1 as the LRESULT, you can prevent the page from turning. If the edit controls contain text, you get the parent wizard window (the property sheet) by using this code:

```
CWizard* pWiz = (CWizard*) GetParent();
```

And then you update the SAMPLEWIZDATA structure, like this:

```
// Update the wizard data
pWiz->m_swd.sFirstName = m_sFirstName;
pWiz->m_swd.sLastName  = m_sLastName;
pWiz->m_swd.sCompany   = m_sCompany;
pWiz->m_swd.sEmail     = m_sEmail;
```

Finally, you use the return value from the inherited method.

The SAMPLEWIZDATA Structure

The SAMPLEWIZDATA structure is an application-defined structure defined in the header file WIZDATA.H. The SAMPLEWIZDATA structure looks like this:

```
typedef struct tagSAMPLEWIZDATA
{
```

```
    CString   sFirstName;
    CString   sLastName;
    CString   sCompany;
    CString   sEmail;
    CString   sFood;
    CString   sCompiler;
}
SAMPLEWIZDATA;
```

This structure is used by the `CWizard` class to collect all the user's selections throughout the wizard walk.

Updating Wizard Information for `CPage2` and `CPage3`

The `CPage2` and `CPage3` classes each use a similar override of the `OnWizardNext()` method to update the data from radio button selections. Listing 34.7 shows how they do it. The `CPage2` dialog box is shown in Figure 34.8; the `CPage3` dialog box is shown in Figure 34.9.

FIGURE 34.8

The WIZARD1 *wizard's Food for Thought page at runtime.*

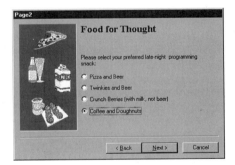

FIGURE 34.9

The WIZARD1 *wizard's Compiler Decisions page at runtime.*

34

CREATING CUSTOM WIZARDS

LISTING 34.7   THE CPage2::OnWizardNext() METHOD

```
///////////////////////////////////////////////////////////////////////
// CPage2::OnWizardNext()

LRESULT CPage2::OnWizardNext()
{
    // Get the parent window
    CWizard* pWiz = (CWizard*) GetParent();
    ASSERT_VALID(pWiz);

    // Update the wizard data
    CString str;

    if (btn1().GetCheck() == 1)
        str.LoadString(IDS_PAGE2_1);

    else if (btn2().GetCheck() == 1)
        str.LoadString(IDS_PAGE2_2);

    else if (btn3().GetCheck() == 1)
        str.LoadString(IDS_PAGE2_3);

    else if (btn4().GetCheck() == 1)
        str.LoadString(IDS_PAGE2_4);

    pWiz->m_swd.sFood = str;

    return CPropertyPage::OnWizardNext();
}
```

The Big Finish

A property page's OnSetActive() method is called by MFC when it becomes the active page. To display the Finish button on the last page of the wizard, the CPage4 dialog box calls the method CPropertyPage::SetWizardButtons() with the appropriate flags (see Listing 34.8). The end result is shown in Figure 34.10.

FIGURE 34.10

The Finished! page.

LISTING 34.8   THE `CPage4::OnSetActive()` METHOD

```
BOOL CPage4::OnSetActive()
{
    // Display the Finish button
    CPropertySheet* pParent = (CPropertySheet*)GetParent();
    pParent->SetWizardButtons(PSWIZB_BACK | PSWIZB_FINISH);

    // Call the inherited method
    return CPropertyPage::OnSetActive();
}
```

Figure 34.11 shows the results of data gathered by the wizard displayed in a simple message box.

FIGURE 34.11

Reviewing the results of data gathered by the wizard.

Creating and Displaying the Wizard

The work of creating and displaying the wizard is done in the `CMainWnd::OnFileRunWizard()` method. The `CMainWnd` data member `m_pwndWizard` is allocated with a call to the `CWizard` constructor `CWizard::CWizard()`. This constructor mirrors that of the `CPropertySheet` class because `CWizard` is directly derived from `CPropertySheet`. Each of the property pages follows suit, allocated using the new operator and initialized with the `CPropertySheet::Construct()` method. The `CMainWnd::OnFileRunWizard()` method is shown in Listing 34.9.

LISTING 34.9   THE `CMainWnd::OnFileRunWizard()` METHOD

```
//////////////////////////////////////////////////////////////////////
// CMainWnd::OnFileRunWizard()

void CMainWnd::OnFileRunWizard()
{
    // Create the wizard
    m_pwndWizard = new CWizard("Sample Wizard", this);
    ASSERT_VALID(m_pwndWizard);
```

continues

34

CREATING
CUSTOM WIZARDS

LISTING 34.9   CONTINUED

```
    // Construct the property pages
    m_pdlgIntro = new CIntroPage;
    ASSERT_VALID(m_pdlgIntro);
    m_pdlgIntro->Construct(IDD_INTRO, 0);

    m_pdlgPage1 = new CPage1;
    ASSERT_VALID(m_pdlgPage1);
    m_pdlgPage1->Construct(IDD_PAGE1, 0);

    m_pdlgPage2 = new CPage2;
    ASSERT_VALID(m_pdlgPage2);
    m_pdlgPage2->Construct(IDD_PAGE2, 0);

    m_pdlgPage3 = new CPage3;
    ASSERT_VALID(m_pdlgPage3);
    m_pdlgPage3->Construct(IDD_PAGE3, 0);

    m_pdlgPage4 = new CPage4;
    ASSERT_VALID(m_pdlgPage4);
    m_pdlgPage4->Construct(IDD_PAGE4, 0);

    // Add the property pages to the property sheet
    m_pwndWizard->AddPage(m_pdlgIntro);
    m_pwndWizard->AddPage(m_pdlgPage1);
    m_pwndWizard->AddPage(m_pdlgPage2);
    m_pwndWizard->AddPage(m_pdlgPage3);
    m_pwndWizard->AddPage(m_pdlgPage4);

    // Make the property sheet a Wizard
    m_pwndWizard->SetWizardMode();

    // Display the Wizard
    m_pwndWizard->DoModal();
}
```

The pages are added to the wizard by calling `CPropertySheet::AddPage()` and the property sheet is transformed into a wizard with a call to `CPropertySheet::SetWizardMode()`. To display the wizard, the `CWnd::DoModal()` method is called.

Summary

A wizard is simply a property sheet and some property pages. The property sheet has the style `PSH_WIZARD`. This chapter describes what a wizard is and goes step by step through the creation of a simple wizard. Although the sample wizard serves no useful purpose other than as a learning tool, it does reveal the secrets to performing true Windows wizardry!

INDEX

M

X-Y-Z

Other Related Titles

Building Enterprise Solutions with Visual Studio 6
G.A. Sullivan
ISBN: 0-672-31489-4
$49.99 USA/$74.95 CAN

Visual Basic 6 Unleashed
Rob Thayer
ISBN: 0-672-31309-X
$39.99 USA/$59.95 CAN

Oracle8 Server Unleashed
Joe Greene, et al.
ISBN: 0-672-31207-7
$49.99 USA/$74.95 CAN

Visual C++ 5 Unleashed, Second Edition
Viktor Toth
ISBN: 0-672-31013-9
$49.99 USA/$74.95 CAN

Sams Teach Yourself Visual C++ 6 in 21 Days
Davis Chapman
ISBN: 0-672-31240-9
$34.99 USA/$52.95 CAN

Sams Teach Yourself Visual InterDev 6 in 21 Days
Michael Van Hoozer, Jr.
ISBN: 0-672-31251-4
$34.99 USA/$52.95 CAN

Sams Teach Yourself Visual Basic 6 in 21 Days
Greg Perry
ISBN: 0-672-31310-3
$29.99 USA/$44.95 CAN

Sams Teach Yourself Database Programming with Visual Basic 6 in 21 Days
Curtis Smith and Mike Amundsen
ISBN: 0-672-31308-1
$45.00 USA/$67.95 CAN

Sams Teach Yourself Database Programming with Visual C++ 6 in 21 Days
Lyn Robison
ISBN: 0-672-31350-2
$34.99 USA/$52.95 CAN

Sams Teach Yourself SQL in 21 Days, Second Edition
Morgan, Stephens, Plew, and Perkins
ISBN: 0-672-31110-0
$39.99 USA/$59.95 CAN

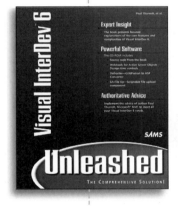

Visual InterDev 6 Unleashed
Paul Thurrott, et al.
ISBN: 0-672-31262-X
$49.99 USA/$74.95 CAN

Active Server Pages 2.0 Unleashed
Stephen Walther, et al.
ISBN: 0-672-31613-7
$39.99 USA/$59.95 CAN

SAMS

www.samspublishing.com

All prices are subject to change.